嗜古與體象

Recarving China's Past

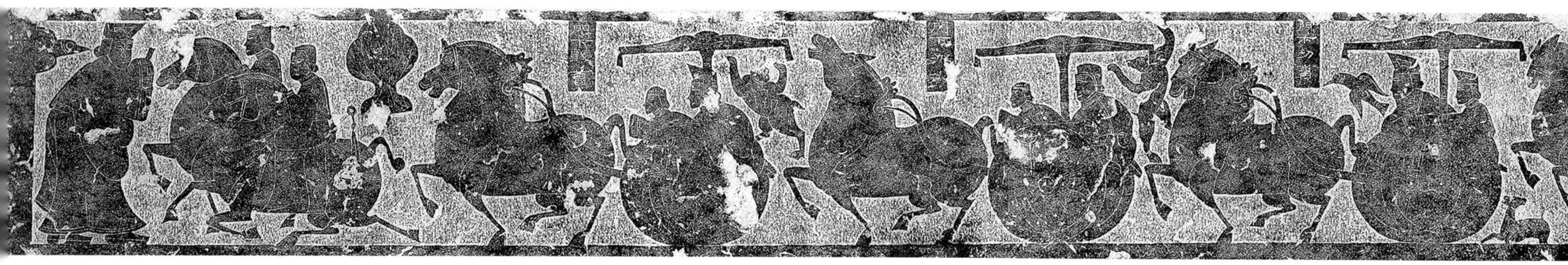

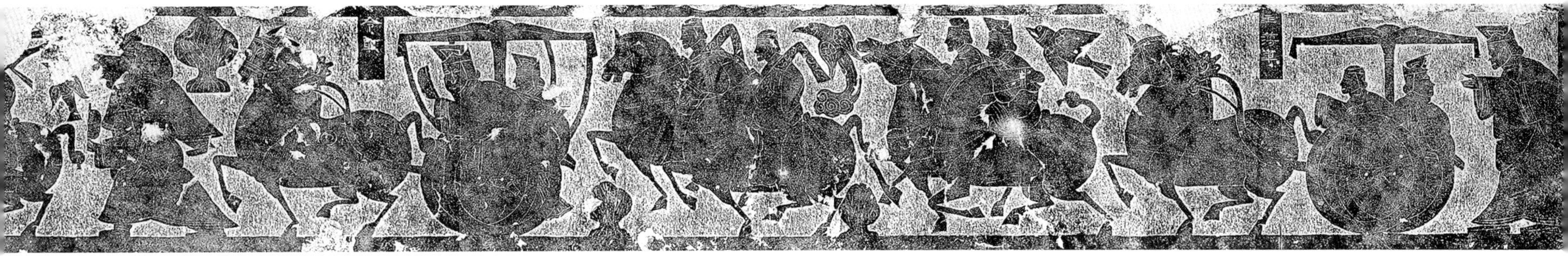

Recarving China's Past

Art, Archaeology, and Architecture of the "Wu Family Shrines"

Cary Y. Liu, Michael Nylan, Anthony Barbieri-Low

Edited by Naomi Noble Richard

With a keynote essay by Michael Loewe and contributions by Susan L. Beningson, Virginia Bower, Albert Dien, Susan N. Erickson, Ingrid Furniss, Eileen H. Hsu, Annette L. Juliano, Hiromi Kinoshita, Guolong Lai, David T. Liu, Sheri A. Lullo, Filippo Marsili, Elinor Pearlstein, Klaas Ruitenbeek, David A. Sensabaugh, Nancy S. Steinhardt, Lydia Thompson, and Haicheng Wang

Princeton University Art Museum
Yale University Press, New Haven and London

Table of Contents

Thematic Essays

Director's Foreword

In fall 1999 a seminar in Princeton University's Department of Art and Archaeology, led by visiting professor of history Michael Nylan, University of California at Berkeley, began an examination of a rare set of ink-on-paper rubbings taken from the so-called Wu family shrines in Shandong Province. Formerly located in the Department of Art and Archaeology's Far Eastern Seminar Study Collection, the rubbings had served as important teaching materials at the university since the mid-twentieth century. During the course of the seminar, these rubbings raised a number of questions about the archaeology, architecture, artistic illustration, history, intellectual life, and material culture of China's Han dynasty (206 BCE–220 CE)—questions that could not be adequately explored in a seminar format. Thus the work on a complex research project, exhibition, catalogue, and symposium was begun. The result is a remarkable international collaboration, led by Curator of Asian Art Cary Y. Liu, that has focused on the pictorial carvings and funerary structures from the "Wu family shrines," a pivotal monument in the arts of China. While this work was in progress, the rubbings, invaluable not only as teaching tools but also as works of art, formally entered the museum's collection. Their availability for direct study and close scrutiny not only inspired the project but has been instrumental to its accomplishment.

The exhibition brings a new focus to the complex relationship among funerary architecture, pictorial carvings, and mortuary objects through the concept of "brilliant artifacts" (*mingqi*)—a Chinese term frequently misused as a general reference to all burial objects placed in tombs. By presenting the Princeton rubbings as integral to the architectural forms that define and house the carvings, and by examining their conceptual relationship to funerary objects, beliefs, and practices, Cary Liu and the project team have been able to re-present these objects as a major art form in their own right. Included in the exhibition are no fewer than twenty works from the permanent collection and a number of loans from private and public collections in this country and abroad. The use of innovative architectural and interactive computer modeling in the exhibition further advances the premise embodied in the presentation, and allows us to present the results of their research in new ways. The university museum's role as a center for scholarly inquiry is fully realized in the scope and ambition of this project.

During the course of research the project team discovered and identified a pictorial stone column from the "Wu family shrines" that had long been thought missing, in the Ethnological Museum in Berlin. The Princeton University Art Museum supported the conservation of this column; it is reintroduced in the catalogue and exhibition after nearly a century of obscurity. The exhibition also marks the first occasion in which the museum has borrowed works of art from the People's Republic of China. Two pictorial stones carved in the same style and technique as the "Wu family shrine" stones are included in the exhibition, lent by the Shandong Provincial Museum and Shandong Stone Inscriptions Art Museum by arrangement with the China Institute in New York. We are grateful to our colleagues at the China Institute for their collaboration in presenting a companion exhibition, catalogue, and symposium. That project, entitled *Providing for the Afterlife: "Brilliant Artifacts" from Shandong*, was organized by cocurators Cary Liu and Susan L. Beningson.

Over forty scholars in the fields of archaeology, architecture, art history, history, literature, and religion participated in *Recarving China's Past*. Three Princeton University alumni served as the core members of the project team: Cary Liu, curator of Asian art and a specialist in Chinese architectural history; Michael Nylan, a specialist in Han history and culture;

and Anthony Barbieri-Low, assistant professor of history at the University of Pittsburgh and an authority on Chinese art and archaeology. My gratitude extends to each of the project organizers, with special thanks to Cary Liu. As the project director and exhibition curator, he shepherded this complex, multifaceted project through all of its phases with intellectual acuity, great sensitivity to the subject, and extraordinary diplomacy. Indeed, this project would not have materialized without him. A letter from the catalogue editor, Naomi Noble Richard, summarized the leadership of Cary Liu with the following: "Heartfelt thanks from the writers and the editor to the curator, for his idea, for his ability to articulate and realize the idea, and for his awesome ability to keep his cool and his courtesy, no matter what misadventure loomed." Whatever loomed was inevitably overcome by the remarkable efforts of each and every member of the project team.

I also thank the authors, researchers, and assistants on various aspects of this project, many of whom are current and former Princeton students. In addition, special thanks are owed to Susan Beningson, project coordinator; Eileen Hsu, research associate, and Virginia Bower, research coordinator. A special acknowledgment goes to Joseph Cho and Stefanie Lew, principals of the design firm Binocular, who worked closely with us to realize an exhibition design that not only reflects their thoughtful catalogue design but creates a striking opportunity to view the rubbings and related objects in context.

With each exhibition and publication, every member of the museum staff plays a critical role. Their commitment and exceptional efforts on behalf of this project are especially appreciated. In particular, I acknowledge the extraordinary work of Nicola Knipe, the museum's assistant editor, who worked in close coordination with the design firm Binocular to oversee every aspect of the production of this catalogue; Michael Jacobs, senior preparator, and Calvin Brown, preparator of prints and drawings; Alexia Hughes, associate registrar, Karen Richter, assistant registrar, photographic services; Frances Yuan, manager of community relations; Caroline Cassells, curator of education; and Michael Brew, business manager. I also acknowledge Lytisha Williams, associate director in Princeton University's Office of Corporate and Foundation Relations, and Becky Sender, the museum's associate director, who worked with Cary Liu to ensure that the project was fully funded.

Our gratitude extends to all lenders to the exhibition. Without their participation, this exhibition would not have been possible. I also acknowledge the Asian Studies Center at the University of Pittsburgh, the History Department and the East Asian Library at the University of California at Berkeley, and the P. Y. and Kinmay W. Tang Center for East Asian at Princeton University for their support of the project.

The exhibition and catalogue have received generous grants from the J. Paul Getty Trust's Collaborative Research Grant Program, E. Rhodes and Leona B. Carpenter Foundation, the Blakemore Foundation, The Andrew W. Mellon Foundation, the National Endowment for the Arts, Princeton University Art Museum Art and Apparatus Fund, the Friends and the Partners of the Princeton University Art Museum, and the Department of Art and Archaeology, Princeton University. The project also was supported by gifts from Lillian Schloss and several anonymous donors. The international symposium scheduled for April 30 and May 1, 2005, is funded in part by the Chiang Ching-kuo Foundation for International Scholarly Exchange, and the P. Y. and Kinmay W. Tang Center for East Asian Art.

To the many supporters of this project and to colleagues who have worked closely with us, I extend my sincerest thanks.

Susan M. Taylor, Director

Curator's Preface and Acknowledgments

Carved images of legendary rulers and paragons of filial piety and loyalty, historical and mythological stories, scenes of feasting, homage, processions, and omens, and other figural and decorative designs are the subjects of an assemblage of pictorial stones, steles, and inscriptions known as the "Wu family shrines." Since the Song dynasty these carvings, and the ink-on-paper rubbings made from them, have been recognized as some of the most valuable and authentic materials for the study of Chinese antiquity. For this reason the Wu family reliefs are fundamental to understanding historical approaches to and methods of studying Chinese art and history, and have also been central to the dating of archaeologically excavated Han tombs and artifacts. The nearly one thousand years of scholarship behind the monument known as the "Wu family shrines" is itself a kind of monument, and looking back over the past five years of research, dilemma, and toil, I must ask with trepidation, What have we done?

Our research and exhibition project was sparked by a 1999 seminar on Han-dynasty art and archaeology in the Department of Art and Archaeology, Princeton University, taught by Michael Nylan, professor of history at the University of California at Berkeley. During the seminar an uninventoried, rare set of early ink-on-paper rubbings of the "Wu family shrines" in the Far Eastern Seminar Study Collection, now in the Princeton University Art Museum, became a focus of great interest. At this time Anthony Barbieri-Low, assistant professor of early Chinese history at University of Pittsburgh, was completing his dissertation on Han-dynasty imperial workshops, and the museum was making significant acquisitions in the field of Han art. This set of circumstances prompted the project's core organizers—Michael, Anthony, and myself—to a concerted attempt to build on the wealth of past scholarship on the so-called Wu Liang Shrine (Stone Chamber 3), and to ponder the equally fascinating images on other pictorial stones found at the same site, which have now been reconstructed as the Front (Chamber 1) and Left (Chamber 2) Stone Chambers. Little did we expect what new direction our research would take.

Before we could begin to consider the style and iconography of the pictorial images carved in the stones, we had to address fundamental problems concerning the surviving stones themselves, and the long history of received textual and visual materials that has become associated with them. The assemblage known as the "Wu family shrines" was initially formulated during the Song dynasty, when it was dated to the mid-second century and held to comprise four inscribed steles, an inscribed gate-pillar, and a one-bay pictorial stone structure that has come to be known as the Wu Liang Shrine. These components have been known since the eleventh century through textual descriptions and transcriptions, and through recarved copies and rubbings of the stele and gate-pillar inscriptions, but only since the late eighteenth century through the actual pictorial stones. The received textual and visual records, however, show evidence of later interpolations and conflations that have colored the received story of the stones. It should also be noted that the history of the stones begins only with their so-called rediscovery in 1786, and that their subsequent preservation and documentation have materially affected how the assemblage of Wu shrine materials has been understood since the late eighteenth century.

Our preliminary research led us to reconsider some received opinions about the "Wu family shrines": do they date from the Han period? did they belong to a Wu family? were they originally intended as "shrines" (*ci* or *citang*)? what was their original arrangement at the site? Many of these questions are probed in my "Recarving the Past" and "Reconfiguring" essays in this catalogue. Michael Nylan, in her essay "Addicted to Antiquity," emphasizes the need to reassess both the textual and visual materials long understood as fundamental to the "Wu family shrines" assemblage. Anthony Barbieri-Low's essay, "Carving Out a

Living," considers the Wu cemetery structures in the context of stone-carving workshops and artisans, exploring how funerary structures were constructed in the Han period. Michael Loewe, professor emeritus at Cambridge University, presents a broad historical and intellectual context in his keynote essay, "Funerary Practice in Han Times," cautioning that such practices rested on diverse motives and beliefs rather than uniform standards or regulations.

It should also be noted that, because of the difficulty in gaining access to the stones, almost every past study has primarily relied on rubbings of the pictorial images rather than on the actual stone carvings. Although the research team has been able to view the surviving carvings in Shandong, we too have had to rely on rubbings and photographs of rubbings. Detailed study of the stones has yet to be conducted in any thorough or systematic fashion. The complexity and enormity of the problems we encountered in dealing with both the received textual and visual materials and the stones themselves are best expressed by the scholar He Zhuo (1661–1722), who, after carefully reviewing all the available materials for the site, commented that he could make no sense of them—the more materials he gathered, the more they scattered, "like leaves falling." (See Nylan's "Addicted to Antiquity.") In many ways we have been trying to retie the Gordian knot, in hopes that future scholars will ponder how to untie it properly. Our research is presented as preliminary studies—a prelude to connoisseurship and scholarship—intended to generate new directions for future research. Many Han stones besides those of the "Wu family shrines" may have been physically recarved or their cultural histories restoried, and that possibility has implications for how almost all Han-dynasty carvings and inscriptions are to be studied. The credibility of all such carvings and inscriptions must be reevaluated, and the results of such reevaluation may substantially alter our understanding of Han art, history, and culture.

At the beginning of the project, when I informed colleagues about our interest in reexamining the Wu shrines, I was usually met with polite disbelief and asked if the subject had not already been thoroughly covered. Indeed, many invaluable studies in the nineteenth and twentieth centuries have addressed the iconography of the pictorial scenes in the rubbings—particularly the scenes in the so-called Wu Liang Shrine. Much of this scholarship has accepted the consensus that the pictorial stones belonged to shrines from a Han-dynasty Wu family cemetery, an identification that may ultimately prove correct. But many basic questions concerning the stones themselves and the transmission of the received texts and visual materials remain uninvestigated. Let me review the course of the project and thereby acknowledge the assistance, encouragement, and support we have received.

In the spring of 1999 Michael Nylan and I formed a weekly study group. We were joined by Pricilla Chen, museum volunteer, and aided by Frank Chance, former curator of the Far Eastern Seminar Collection, Princeton University. For the past five years Pricilla has been a constant source of strength and cheer, and her keen observations have contributed greatly to our research. In the spring of 2000 Haitao Tang, lecturer emeritus in the Department of East Asian Languages, Princeton University, joined the study group and gave immeasurable assistance as we struggled through translations of inscriptions and documents. In 2002 Eileen Hsiang-ling Hsu joined the museum as research associate for this project; she also attended the weekly sessions and has been instrumental to our research (fig. 1).

Susan M. Taylor assumed the directorship of the Princeton University Art Museum in the summer of 2000 and immediately gave us her full support, encouraging us to "think big." With the leadership of Susan, along with that of Becky Sender, associate director, and the assistance of Lytisha Williams, associate director in Princeton University's Office of Corporate and Foundation Relations, successful applications were made

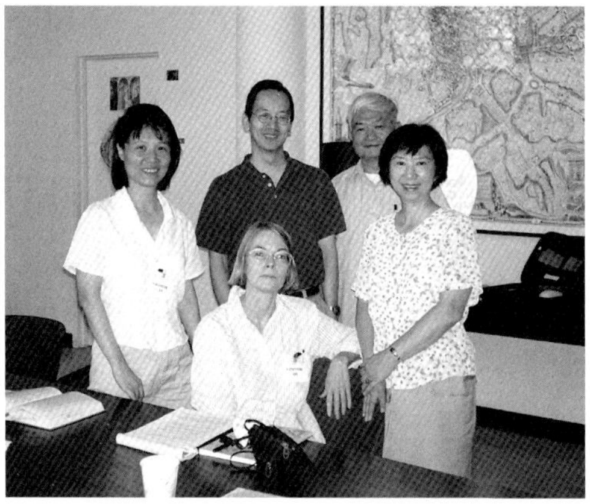

Fig. 1 *Weekly study group in McCormick Hall, Princeton University*. Michael Nylan, seated; from left to right, Eileen Hsu, Cary Liu, Haitao Tang, and Pricilla Chen. July 2002.

to the Collaborative Research Grant Program of the Getty Trust and to the Blakemore Foundation's Frances Blakemore Asian Art Grant Program. These initial research grants were critical to expanding the research team beyond the core organizers, ultimately involving more than forty scholars. Throughout the project, Lytisha and later Frances Yuan, manager of community relations at the museum, led the effort to ensure that the project was fully supported. I particularly thank Frances, whose commitment to the project and expertise in Asian art have been invaluable. It was also during this early stage that the "Wu family shrines" rubbing set (cat. no. 1) was saved from disposal and formally accessioned by the Princeton University Art Museum.

I cannot overemphasize the importance of the initial Getty and Blakemore grants to the research stage of the project. They allowed scholars to travel to Princeton to meet the core organizers, and allowed research team members to travel to China, Japan, Europe, Canada, and across the United States to view related materials and consult other scholars. The grants also allowed the museum's set of over sixty rubbings to be fully documented in film and digital photography. The grants also permitted Eileen Hsu, research associate, and Virginia Bower, research coordinator, to join the project in Princeton, and Mei-ling Williams, research assistant, to join in Berkeley. The contributions of these three researchers have been invaluable: they compiled biographies, chronologies, and bibliographies, translated documents and articles, chased down countless sources and loose ends, authored reports on various subjects of interest, and provided significant insights and suggestions for our research. Representing the project team, Eileen also traveled to Shandong and Taipei to meet with scholars and symposium participants, and visited the Field Museum in Chicago to view their sets of the Wu shrine rubbings. I thank Bennet Bronson, curator of Asian archaeology and ethnology at the Field Museum, for his cooperation.

Virginia Bower traveled with me on several scouting missions in search of loans for the exhibition. At the Los Angeles County Museum of Art, I am grateful for the support of my former classmate J. Keith Wilson, chief curator of Asian art. I am also grateful for the strong support we received from Amy Poster, curator and chair of the Asian Art Department at the Brooklyn Museum. For loans from the Metropolitan Museum of Art in New York, I am grateful to James Watt, Brooke Russell Astor Chairman of the Department of Asian Art; Zhixin Sun, associate curator, and Suzanne G. Valenstein, research fellow, for their support and assistance. At the Cleveland Museum of Art, I thank Ju-hsi Chou, curator emeritus of Chinese art, and Charles Venable, deputy director for collections and programs, for their support. I am especially grateful to Klaas Ruitenbeek, Louise Hawley Stone Chair of Far Eastern Art, Royal Ontario Museum, for his full support and active participation in the project. At the Art Institute of Chicago special thanks goes to Elinor Pearlstein, associate curator of Chinese art, for her dedicated participation in the project, and to Jay Xu, Pritzker Curator of Asian Art, for his support and friendship. At the Harvard University Art Museums, I thank Robert D. Mowry, Alan J. Dworsky Curator of Chinese Art and head of the Department of Asian Art, and Anne Rose Kitagawa, assistant curator of Japanese art, for their cooperation. I also thank Richard and Ruth Dickes, Howard and Mary Ann Rogers, Edward and Nancy Rosenthal, Anthony M. Solomon, and several collectors who wish to remain anonymous for their support and willingness to lend to the exhibition. At the American Numismatic Society in New York, I thank Michael L. Bates, curator of Islamic coins, and Elena Stolyarik, collection manager, for their backing and cooperation. It was a surprise to discover a collection of Chinese coins at Princeton University, and I offer our appreciation to Brooks E. Levy, curator emeritus of numismatics, Firestone Library, for allowing us to view the collection on several occasions.

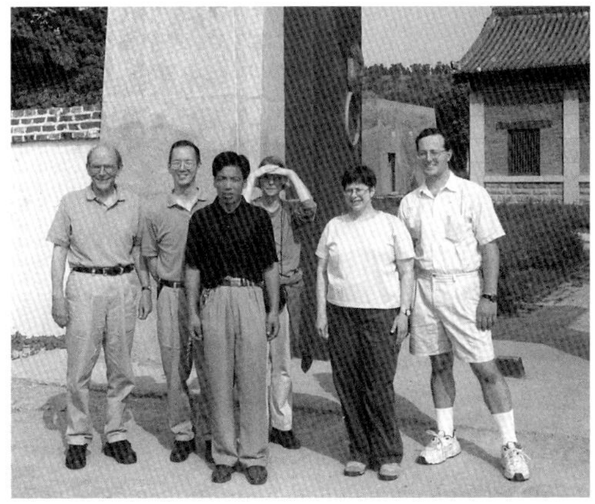

Fig. 2 *Research team at "Wu family shrines" site, Wuzhai Shan, Jiaxiang County, Shandong.* From left to right, David Sensabaugh, Cary Liu, Zhang Chaojie, Michael Nylan, Susan Beningson, and Anthony Barbieri-Low. June 2002.

In June 2001 Michael Nylan and I traveled to London to consult with our respected colleague Michael Loewe, who informed us about a set of Wu shrine rubbings donated by Dr. Lawrence Picken to the Needham Research Institute in Cambridge. Michael Nylan was able to examine the Picken rubbings and also to view several carved stones of unknown origin in the British Museum that had once been attributed to the Wu cemetery. For their assistance I thank Christopher Cullen, deputy director, and John P. C. Moffett, librarian, at the Needham Institute, and Jane Portal, assistant keeper in the Department of Oriental Antiquities at the British Museum.

In April 2002 Anthony Barbieri-Low organized the panel "Architectural Reconfiguration of the Wu Family Altars and Shrine," at the Association of Asian Studies National Conference in Washington, D.C. This provided an international forum to introduce our project and discuss ongoing research. The three core members delivered early versions of our research essays in this catalogue, and we were joined by Klaas Ruitenbeek, who presented a study of Han-dynasty money trees. Valuable comments were provided by our panel chair and discussant, Wu Hung, professor of Chinese art history at the University of Chicago, and by conference members.

Team members traveled to Beijing and Shandong Province in June 2002. Anthony Barbieri-Low, Michael Nylan, and I were accompanied by project members David A. Sensabaugh, curator of Asian art at the Yale University Art Gallery, Susan L. Beningson, project coordinator at the museum, Mei-ling Williams, and Bruce C. Williams, library assistant, East Asian Library, University of California, Berkeley. In Beijing a viewing was arranged at the Palace Museum to examine rubbings of Han artifacts, including an eighteenth-century handscroll of the Wu rubbing; for this I thank Yu Hui, department head, and Kong Chen and Yin Yimei of the Painting Department, Beijing Palace Museum. Special thanks to Alfreda and Christian Murck, whose friendship and planning on our behalf opened doors and made things happen. During our brief stay in the capital we were also fortunate to consult with Xin Lixiang, research associate in the Archaeology Division of the National Museum of China, An Jiayao, research professor at the Institute of Archaeology, Chinese Academy of Social Sciences, Yin Ji'nan, professor and head of the Department of Art History, Central Academy of Fine Arts, and He Xilin, associate professor at the Central Academy of Fine Arts.

In Shandong we were hosted by the Shandong Provincial Museum. I particularly thank Lu Wensheng, director, and Zheng Yan, former associate director, for arranging our viewing and travel itinerary, and Fan Zhengli, who accompanied us on a whirlwind tour of archaeological sites and museums throughout the province. In Ji'nan we met with distinguished archaeologists, curators, and scholars of Han pictorial carvings, including Jiang Yingju, honorary director emeritus, Jiao Desen, director, and Yang Aiguo, research associate, of the Shandong Stone Inscriptions Art Museum. That was our first meeting with Jiang Yingju, whose contributions to this project have been immeasurable. Our viewings at the Shandong Stone Inscriptions Art Museum and the Ji'nan Municipal Museum were extremely informative, and I thank the staffs of both museums. From Ji'nan, our primary visit was to the Wu cemetery site in Jiaxiang to examine the actual carved stones and cemetery site; there we benefited from the assistance of Zhang Chaojie, director of the Wu Family Shrines Cultural Management Bureau (fig. 2). On our Shandong tour I am grateful for the cooperation we received at the Confucius Temple in Qufu; Jining Municipal Museum, where two other Wu pictorial stones are stored; Zoucheng Prefectural Museum and Mencius Temple in Zoucheng; Tengzhou Han Pictorial Stones Museum in Tengzhou; Weishan Prefectural Museum in Weishan; Zhaozhuang City Museum in Zhaozhuang; Linyi Municipal Museum in Linyi; Yi'nan Han tombs at Beizhai Cun; Han tomb at Anqiu; and Qingzhou Museum in Qingzhou.

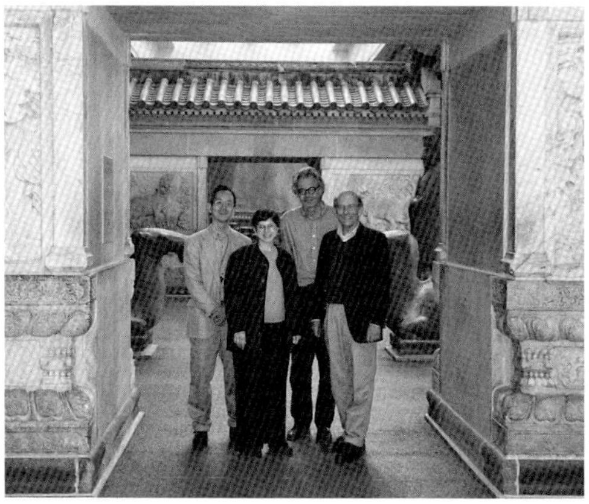

Fig. 3 *Research team at Royal Ontario Museum, Toronto.* From left to right, Cary Liu, Susan Beningson, Klaas Ruitenbeek, and David Sensabaugh. October 2002.

During this trip negotiations began with the Shandong Provincial Museum on borrowing two Han pictorial stones for the exhibition (cat. nos. 10, 11). The discussions became interlocked with plans for a companion exhibition and catalogue, *Providing for the Afterlife: "Brilliant Artifacts" from Shandong* (February 3–June 4, 2005), at the China Institute in New York. As cocurator of that exhibition with Susan Beningson, I thank Willow Chang, gallery director, for her leadership role in the negotiations and for organizing the exhibition and catalogue with contributions from Annette L. Juliano, professor of Asian art history at Rutgers University, Zhixin Sun, associate curator at the Metropolitan Museum of Art, and David A. Graff, professor at Kansas State University. The Princeton and China Institute exhibitions were planned around the concept of "brilliant artifacts" (*mingqi*) in the Han dynasty, focusing on the Shandong region. I thank John Curtis for his wise counsel and strong support for both exhibitions. At the China Institute I also thank Virginia A. Kamsky, chair, and Jack Maisano, president, for their support, and Jennifer Choiniere, gallery registrar, and France Pepper, associate director of public programs, for their efforts, with special thanks to May Lee Barrett for her editorial skills. The China Institute also helped negotiate, coordinate, and arrange the loans of the two pictorial stones to the Princeton exhibition.

On our return from China Susan Beningson and I traveled to Boston to view a set of Wu shrine rubbings that is related to the Princeton set. Both sets had formerly been in the collection assembled by Alan Priest in the early twentieth century. We are grateful to James F. Callahan, director of Asian works of art at Skinner, for taking a day to show us the rubbings.

In October 2002 Anthony Barbieri-Low, Susan Beningson, David Sensabaugh, and I spent several days at the Royal Ontario Museum in Toronto with Klaas Ruitenbeek, whose exhibition *Chinese Shadows: Stone Reliefs, Rubbings, and Related Works of Art from the Han Dynasty in the Royal Ontario Museum* (August 2–November 10, 2002) had special relevance to our project (fig. 3). In addition, Klaas arranged special viewings of Han materials in museum storage and in off-site storage; there among the wealth of riches we were able to select several works to borrow for our exhibition.

From 2001 through 2003 commitments of support for the research project and exhibition came in from the Asian Studies Center at the University of Pittsburgh, the History Department and the East Asian Library at the University of California at Berkeley, and the P. Y. and Kinmay W. Tang Center for East Asian Art at Princeton University. At Pittsburgh I thank Bell Yong, director of the Asian Studies Center, and professors Evelyn Rawski and Katheryn M. Linduff for supporting the project and supporting Anthony Barbieri-Low's participation. At Berkeley I acknowledge the support of Jon Gjerde, professor and chair of the Department of History, and Peter Zhou, director of the East Asian Library. At Princeton the project has benefited greatly from the support of the newly established P. Y. and Kinmay W. Tang Center for East Asian Art, for which I particularly thank Jerome Silbergeld, director, and Dora Ching, associate director.

In February 2003 Jiang Yingju and Xin Lixiang, two senior archaeologists whom we met on our China trip, came on a lecture tour principally organized by Anthony Barbieri-Low, with assistance from the Tang Center at Princeton. Jiang and Xin first lectured at "The Early China Symposium in Honor of Cho-Yun Hsu: Funerary Art and Architecture of the Han Dynasty" at the University of Pittsburgh (fig. 4). I was also honored to be asked to present a paper on the "Wu family shrines" on this occasion. Afterward, Jiang and Xin spoke at Princeton University, Yale University, Columbia University, and the University of Chicago, meeting and working with members of our project at each venue. At Princeton their public lecture was cosponsored by the Princeton University Art Museum with support from the Freeman Foundation, the P. Y. and Kinmay W. Tang Center for East Asian Art, and the East Asian Studies Program. Workshops with

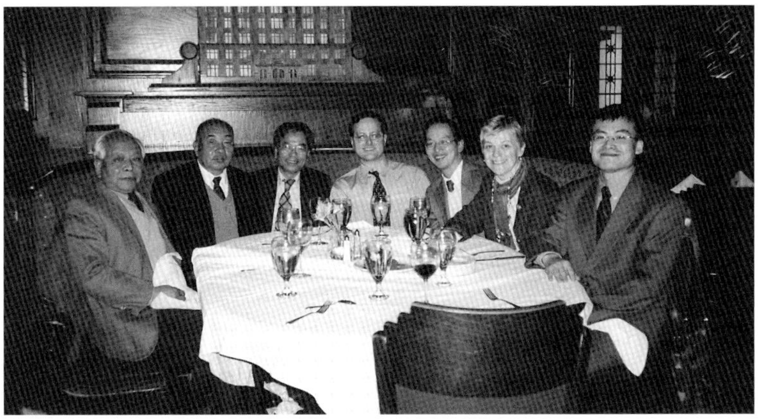

Fig. 4 *Dinner after "Early China Symposium" at the University of Pittsburgh.* From left to right, Jiang Yingju, Xin Lixiang, Bell Yong, Anthony Barbieri-Low, Cary Liu, Katheryn Linduff, and Wu Xiaolong. February 2003.

project members and graduate students were arranged, and a special viewing of the museum's set of Wu shrine rubbings was conducted; these productive events were made possible in part through the research grants we received from the Getty Trust and Blakemore Foundation.

While in Pittsburgh for the "Early China Symposium," we were able to examine Han artifacts in the collection of the Carnegie Museum of Art with Jiang Yingju and Xin Lixiang. Anthony and I were also able to meet with Sarah Nichols, curator of decorative arts at the Carnegie, to discuss plans to bring the exhibition *Recarving China's Past* to the Carnegie in the future. Likewise, discussions were well underway to bring the exhibition to the Art Museum of the University of California, Berkeley. Unfortunately, scheduling changes prevented the exhibition from traveling immediately after the Princeton venue, but I thank Sarah Nichols, and Lynne Kimura, academic liaison at the Berkeley Art Museum, for their strong support.

In Japan in April 2003 I was able to inspect a group of Han-dynasty pictorial stones carved in a style similar to the Wu shrine stones. These had been found at Xiaotang Shan, Changqing County, Shandong, and are now in the Tokyo National Museum. They had formerly been listed in the holdings of the Tokyo Imperial Household Museum, Imperial University of Tokyo, College of Engineering. I thank Masaaki Itakura, professor at the University of Tokyo, for helping me to locate these artifacts. Inspection of the stones prompted questions about their original architectural configuration. Surprisingly, several other Han pictorial stones from Shandong were also on display.

In spring 2003 Michael Nylan was awarded fellowships from the Institute for Advanced Study in Princeton and the American Council of Learned Societies, which allowed her to begin a year-long residency at Princeton to research and write her essay for this catalogue. The research team had planned to return to Shandong in the summer but were prevented by an outbreak of Severe Acute Respiratory Syndrome (SARS).

Michael Loewe visited Princeton in October 2003, thus providing team members with an opportunity to consult with one of the preeminent scholars of Han history about our research. In December a workshop was conducted in the Princeton University Art Museum to examine the Wu shrine rubbings, with David Sensabaugh and Robert E. Harrist, Jr., professor of Chinese art history at Columbia University. The workshop was an opportunity for the core organizers to discuss research problems with independent scholars who have been working on related topics.

In early June 2004 Anthony Barbieri-Low and I, along with Susan Beningson and catalogue author Annette Juliano returned to Shandong Province, where we revisited the Wu cemetery site, Shandong Provincial Museum, Shandong Stone Inscriptions Art Museum, and Ji'nan Municipal Museum of Art. We also visited the excavation site of the Western Han royal tomb at Shuangru Shan in Changqing County (fig. 5), along with the Changqing City Museum, where the excavated artifacts are displayed. Similarly, we visited the site of the newly excavated Han royal burial pits at Weishan and the Zhangqiu City Museum, where the recovered ceramic figures are stored in off-site facilities. Intensive discussions on archaeological and art-historical topics also took place between the Princeton research team and specialists in Shandong, including an afternoon with Jiang Yingju to continue discussions from our previous meetings. Director Lu Wensheng was once again chiefly responsible for helping us arrange access to archaeological sites and museum collections.

During the summer of 2004 I was able to trace the probable locations of two stones from the Wu cemetery that had long been considered missing. A column capital, given as a gift in the late eighteenth century, is now apparently in the collection of the Tianjin Municipal Museum of Art. I was also able to connect a cylindrical pictorial stone column, taken to Germany in 1907 by Adolf Fischer, to a square-format rubbing that has long been reproduced as part of the Wu cemetery materials. The rubbing

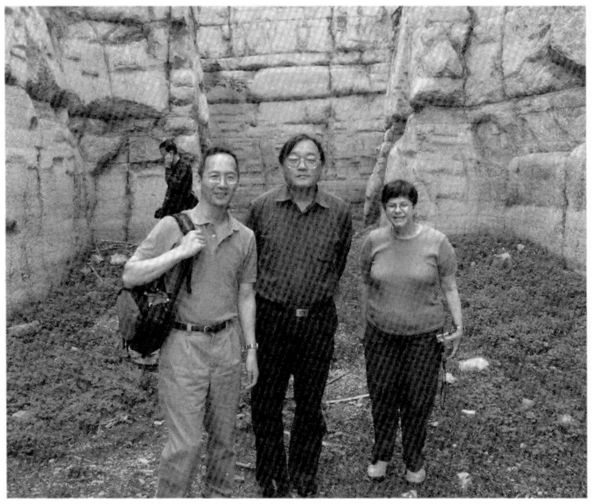

Fig. 5 *Cary Liu and Susan Beningson with Director Lu Wensheng (center).* Royal Han tomb at Shuangru Shan, Changqing County, Shandong. June 2004.

is evidently a wraparound image taken from the column, which is now in the collection of the Ethnological Museum in Berlin-Dahlem. I am grateful to Herbert Butz, curator at the Museum of East Asian Art in Berlin, and Adele Schlombs, director at the Museum of East Asian Art in Cologne, for directing me to the Ethnological Museum. At the Ethnological Museum I thank Siegmar Nahser, curator, Wu Shun-chi, curator, and Maria Gaida, collection department, for their cooperation in identifying the column and for working with us to conserve it so that it might be brought to Princeton for our exhibition. In October Bruce M. White, project photographer, traveled to Berlin to document the column prior to its conservation. (At the time of publication it is still uncertain whether the conservation will be completed in time for the exhibition. For this reason we have included the column as a supplement in the catalogue; see Part One: Pictorial Column.)

Acknowledgment should be made also to the professional staff at the East Asian Library (Gest Oriental Library), Princeton University, one of the world's outstanding collections of Chinese books and periodicals. Throughout the research and planning stages of the exhibition and the preparation of the catalogue we have received the support of the library staff. I am indebted to Martin Heijdra for his tolerance and for teaching us to use the online electronic libraries, including the *Siku quanshu* imperial library compendium, which allowed us to utilize unprecedented search capabilities for our research.

Project members exchanged preliminary drafts of their research and continued to consult with other scholars throughout 2003 and 2004 as priorities turned more toward exhibition and catalogue planning. The exhibition and catalogue are made possible in part by grants from the E. Rhodes and Leona B. Carpenter Foundation, the Blakemore Foundation, the Getty Trust, The Andrew W. Mellon Foundation, the National Endowment for the Arts, the Princeton University Art Museum Art and Apparatus Fund, the Friends and Partners of the Princeton University Art Museum, and the Department of Art and Archaeology, Princeton University, as well as through donations from Lillian Schloss and anonymous donors.

The nucleus of the exhibition *Recarving China's Past: Art, Archaeology, and Architecture of the "Wu Family Shrines"* is a set of rubbings of the "Wu shrines," which is presented in architectural relation to the walls, ceilings, and columns of three reconstructed stone chambers. Computer and architectural modeling are used to demonstrate the spatial relationships of the chambers and the possible organization of the site. More than sixty works of art related to images depicted in the rubbings are on view in the exhibition, the better to give visitors a vivid sense of the material culture and funerary practices of the Han dynasty. The close relationship between funerary architecture and burial objects, the latter conceptualized as "brilliant artifacts," is reflected in the exhibition and examined in the essay "Concept of 'Brilliant Artifacts' in Han-Dynasty Burial Objects and Funerary Architecture" in this catalogue. I am deeply grateful to my project teammates Michael Nylan and Anthony Barbieri-Low, who worked with me on the exhibition as curatorial consultants, and to Virginia Bower, whose expertise proved invaluable in finding and selecting works of art for the exhibition.

The exhibition design is the product of the imagination and remarkable efforts of Joseph Cho and Stefanie Lew of the design firm Binocular, who also are responsible for the catalogue design. From the outset, they were challenged to develop an integrated design for the exhibition and catalogue that would present the Wu shrine rubbings in a manner that makes discernible the architectural and positional relationships among rubbings. The featured rubbings also needed to be displayed as "brilliant artifacts" in relation with the other works of art in the exhibition.

Working with Binocular in the museum were Mike Jacobs, senior preparator, who supervised the exhibition installation with impressive calm and control; Calvin Brown, preparator of prints and drawings, who devised an extraordinary system to hang and display the rubbings; Craig Hoppock, museum superintendent, who coordinated building construction with his usual dependability; and Ed Murfit, assistant superintendent. For their dedication and hard work I thank the museum art preparators Gerrit Meaker and Mark Harris, assisted by John Franklin and Keith Crowley. This was a well-organized team effort and the entire crew deserves immense credit for carrying out such an ambitious and challenging design. Thanks, too, to David LaTouche of Benchmark, who created mounts for the exhibition, including the intricate framework he devised for the money tree (cat. no. 59). The exhibition installation also relied on the skill and professionalism of Vincent Scozzari Jr. of Scozzari Construction, Lawrenceville, NJ; Central Art Custom Plastic Fabrication, Cream Ridge, NJ; Anton Stayduhar and Tamara Block of Contour Woodworks, Warwick, NY; Mouse Design Studio, Roswell, GA; Charles Adams Exhibition Construction, Elkins Park, PA; Christopher Gorzelnik, Facilities Department, Princeton University; Theodore Harding Lewis III, Department of Physics, Princeton University, and Paul Didonato, Carpentry Shop, Princeton University.

Special thanks to Alexia Hughes, associate registrar at the museum, who served as project registrar. Alexia's experience was crucial in arranging for the loans, which entailed coordinating conservation, shipping, insurance, and loan agreements, as well as securing immunity from seizure authorization. I also thank Maureen McCormick, chief registrar, and Virginia Pifko and Karen Richter, assistant registrars, for their help and advice throughout the project. In charge of photo services, Karen had the seemingly impossible task of supervising the film and digital photography of the rubbings as well as catalogue photography. She was ably assisted by Nicole Gordon, photo services assistant. Nicole Fabricand-Person, former Asian art researcher at the museum (now assistant professor at Lafayette College), also helped to label and file the digital images of the overall rubbings and individual details. It was a pleasure to work again with Bruce M. White, project photographer. For an earlier Chinese calligraphy project, Bruce designed and built a vacuum table for large works on paper; this enabled us to photograph the Wu rubbings. Bruce also photographed many of the works of art, both here and abroad, for the exhibition catalogue. I also thank Trudy Jacoby, director, H. David Connelley, photographer, and Xia Wei, curator, Visual Resources Collection, Department of Art and Archaeology, Princeton University, for their help and support with book photography for the catalogue and with materials for public presentations. Digital scans were made for publication and for research purposes, and I thank Jeff Evans, the museum's digital imaging specialist, for his expertise.

An exciting component of the exhibition is the computer-generated architectural reconstruction of the Wu cemetery site, developed by Anthony Barbieri-Low. The video presentation in the exhibition is drawn from an interactive version that allows visitors to move through the site and to enter each reconstructed stone chamber. Anthony was sponsored in his efforts partly by the Collaborative Research Grant Program of the Getty Trust and by funding from the Central Research Development Fund Grant from the Office of Research and the Vice-Provost's Office at the University of Pittsburgh. The interactive version of the reconstruction will be incorporated into the museum's new Asian Art Resources web site, which is being developed by the museum and the Educational Technologies Center, Princeton University, with funds from the Freeman Foundation. At the museum, Caroline Cassells, curator of education, and Janet Strohl-Morgan, manager of information technology, have taken the lead in developing the web site. The Educational Technologies Center staff deserves praise for their hard work and patience. Special thanks to Janet Temos, director, Jill E. Moraca, multimedia specialist, Paula L. Hulick, projects manager, Kevin Perry, programming manager, and Kelly Cole, web developer. We also received authorial contributions from Elizabeth M.

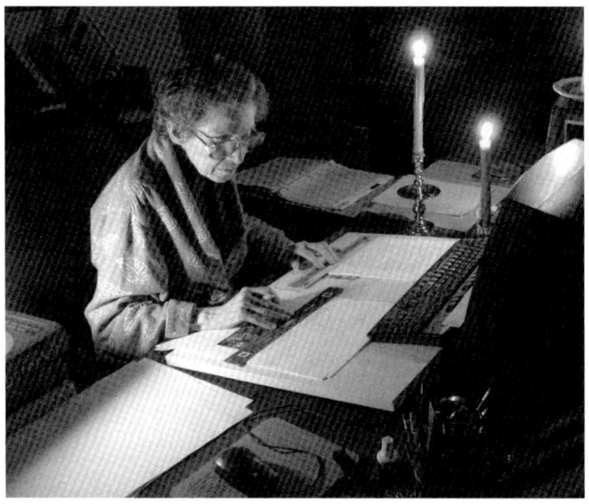

Fig. 6 *Naomi Richard editing by candlelight on Christmas Eve.* Photo by Joseph Richard, 2004.

Hammer, associate museum educator at the Metropolitan Museum of Art, and Nicole Fabicand-Person, as well as from Christine Tan and Sinead Kehoe, doctoral candidates in the Department of Art and Archaeology, Princeton University.

Academic and event programming for the exhibition was coordinated by Caroline Cassells. The international symposium with the same title as the exhibition and catalogue, held in conjunction with the exhibition at Princeton on April 30–May 1, 2005, was organized by the Princeton University Art Museum. Cosponsors for the symposium and accompanying publication include the Chiang Ching-kuo Foundation for International Scholarly Exchange and the P. Y. and Kinmay W. Tang Center for East Asian Art. Symposium speakers and chairs include Qianshen Bai, Boston University; Anthony Barbieri-Low; Miranda Brown, University of Michigan; Benjamin Elman, Princeton University; Susan N. Erickson, University of Michigan–Dearborn; Wen C. Fong, Princeton University; Hsing I-tien, Institute of History and Philology, Academia Sinica, Taiwan; Eileen Hsu; Jiang Yingju; Cary Liu; Michael Loewe; Huiwen Lu, National Tsing-hua University, Taiwan; Michael Nylan; Klaas Ruitenbeek; Lydia Thompson, independent scholar; Lillian Tseng, Yale University; Wu Hung, University of Chicago; and Zheng Yan, Central Academy of Fine Art, Beijing.

A special event scheduled in conjunction with the exhibition is a guided trip to China, with a focus on Shandong Province and a visit to the Wu cemetery. Entitled "Recarving the Past: Tombs, Temples, and Historical Sites in China" (October 16–31, 2005), the trip is sponsored jointly by the museum and the P. Y. and Kinmay W. Tang Center for East Asian Art. My thanks to Dora Ching and Frances Yuan, who have taken the lead in organizing this opportunity to extend the exhibition beyond the walls of the museum.

My deep gratitude to Susan L. Beningson, our extraordinary project coordinator for the Princeton exhibition, and my cocurator for *Providing for the Afterlife*. Susan assisted in all aspects of the Princeton exhibition, catalogue, and symposium, and spearheaded the China Institute exhibition and catalogue. She also coordinated the two research trips to Shandong for the project team, and was a constant positive force and committed scholar.

Press and publicity arrangements owe heavily to the efforts of Ruta Smithson, public information officer at the museum, who worked closely with the firm of Resnicow Schroeder Associates. Behind the scenes at the museum Mike Brew, business manager, kept track of the finances and made sure that everything proceeded smoothly.

The catalogue is the official record of the research project and the exhibition. The efforts of many individuals have made this publication a reality. In particular I thank all the authors for their scholarly contributions. A special feature of the catalogue is the attempt to establish a dialogue among scholars who approach selected objects in the exhibition from different points of view. Individual objects were selected as the focus of multiple essays to demonstrate how present-day scholars continue to recarve the past. For the entries and thematic essays they contributed to the catalogue, I thank Anthony Barbieri-Low, Susan Beningson, Virginia Bower, Albert Dien, professor emeritus at the University of California, Berkeley, Susan Erickson, Ingrid Furniss, doctoral candidate at Princeton University, Annette Juliano, Hiromi Kinoshita, doctoral candidate at the University of Oxford, David T. Liu, doctoral candidate at Princeton University, Guolong Lai, assistant professor at University of Florida, Sheri A. Lullo, doctoral candidate at University of Pittsburgh, Filippo Marsili, doctoral candidate at University of California, Berkeley, Michael Nylan, Elinor Pearlstein, Klaas Ruitenbeek, David Sensabaugh, Nancy S. Steinhardt, professor at University of Pennsylvania, Lydia Thompson, and Wang Haicheng, doctoral candidate at Princeton University.

Faced with a shortened production schedule, this catalogue relied heavily on the intense dedication of the editorial and design teams. My deepest appreciation to Naomi Richard, who brought her editorial brilliance to the publication. Without her total commitment, boundless energy, sharp wit, and the seemingly uncanny ability to transform even my writing into something intelligible, this catalogue could not have been satisfactorily completed. She improved every text and brought consistency to seeming chaos. Her analogy between our editorial scramble and the croquet scene in *Alice in Wonderland* was wonderfully apt: the manuscript was the Queen of Hearts and the rest of us were all hedgehogs and flamingos, tending to wander off on paths of our own. At the museum it fell to project editor Nicola Knipe, working closely with Naomi, to bring everything together with careful attention to detail and quality. I am indebted to Nicola for her devotion and unwavering sense of responsibility, her ability to keep track of papers and ride herd on their authors, and her willingness to work untold hours to bring the catalogue from start to finish. We were fortunate to have additional assistance. At the museum Mary Cason, editorial assistant, devoted many hours and lost many weekends to help us meet crucial deadlines, and Jill Guthrie, managing editor, kept an eye on our efforts. Susan Beningson, Nancy Greenspan, museum docent, Zoe Kwok, graduate student in the Department of Art and Archaeology, and Sinead Kehoe all helped review sections of the catalogue. Susan also coordinated the comparative photography in the catalogue and arranged for the photography of the loan objects. Zoe also compiled the Chinese glossary with the assistance of Haicheng Wang, and Eileen Hsu compiled the selected bibliography. Our thanks go also to Anandaroop Roy for the maps, to David W. Goodrich of Birdtrack Press for the Chinese character typesetting, and to Robert Palmer, who prepared the index.

The design of the catalogue rests with Joseph Cho and Stefanie Lew of the design firm Binocular. Overcoming all problems, they worked closely with the editorial team to arrive at a design that brings clarity to the complex combination of rubbings, works of art, entries, thematic essays, research essays, and other sections of the text. This same clarity is reflected in the exhibition design—their first. Their solutions to the architectural complexity presented by the Wu shrine rubbings and to the design challenge of the catalogue are perceptive and elegant, and I salute them for their accomplishments.

I cannot finish without revealing how utterly committed the editorial and design teams became to the catalogue. Possibly symptomatic of an "addiction to antiquity," the production schedule called for the teams to work through the year-end holidays. This dedication is best reflected in a memo that Naomi sent on Christmas Eve 2004 (fig. 6):

> *Dear Nicola and Cary,*
> *Home from hospital Wednesday 22d; began proofreading Thursday 23d, amid hard rain and high winds, 4:30 pm sun went down and power failed, finished proofreading by candlelight!*
> *Merry Christmas and Happy New Year — N.R.*

My heartfelt gratitude to the entire team, to Ho Chuan-hsing for his calligraphy, and to my family for their support and forbearance.

Cary Y. Liu
January 1, 2005

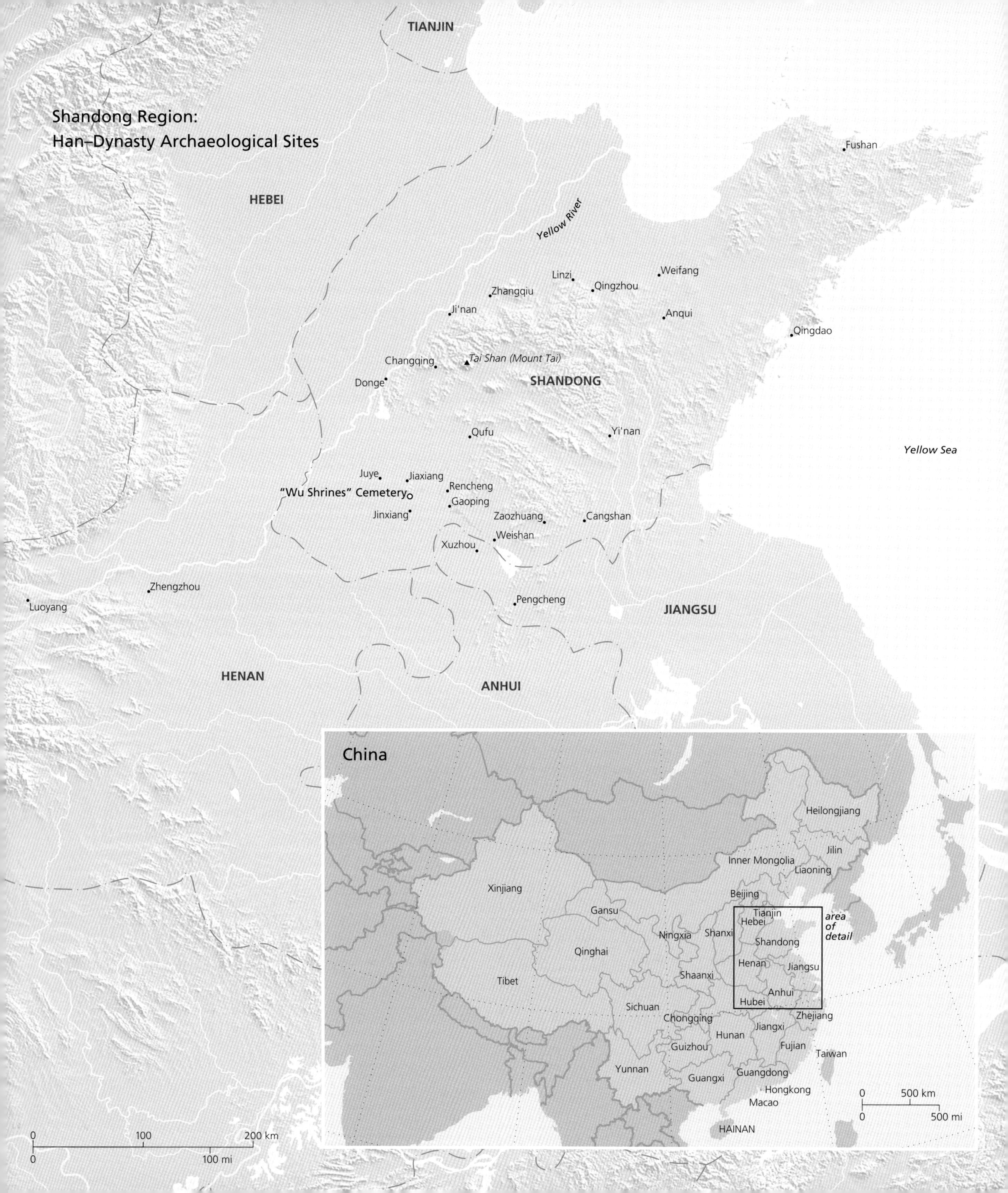

Shandong Region:
Han–Dynasty Archaeological Sites
TIANJIN
HEBEI
Yellow River
Fushan
Weifang
Linzi
Qingzhou
Zhangqiu
Ji'nan
Anqui
Qingdao
Changqing
Tai Shan (Mount Tai)
SHANDONG
Donge
Qufu
Yi'nan
Yellow Sea
Juye
Jiaxiang
"Wu Shrines" Cemetery
Rencheng
Gaoping
Jinxiang
Zaozhuang
Cangshan
Weishan
Xuzhou
Zhengzhou
Luoyang
Pengcheng
JIANGSU
HENAN
ANHUI
China
Heilongjiang
Jilin
Inner Mongolia
Liaoning
Xinjiang
Beijing
Gansu
Tianjin
Hebei
area of detail
Ningxia
Shanxi
Shandong
Qinghai
Henan
Jiangsu
Shaanxi
Tibet
Anhui
Hubei
Sichuan
Chongqing
Zhejiang
Jiangxi
Hunan
Guizhou
Fujian
Taiwan
Yunnan
Guangdong
Guangxi
Hongkong
Macao
HAINAN
0 500 km
0 500 mi
0 100 200 km
0 100 mi

Chronology

Neolithic period	**ca. 8000–ca. 2000 BCE**
Xia period (protohistoric)	**ca. 2100–ca. 1600 BCE**
Shang dynasty	**ca. 1600–ca. 1100 BCE**
Zhou dynasty	**ca. 1100–256 BCE**
Western Zhou	ca. 1100–770 BCE
Eastern Zhou	770–256 BCE
Spring and Autumn period	770–ca. 470 BCE
Warring States period	ca. 470–221 BCE
Qin dynasty	**221–206 BCE**
Han dynasty	**206 BCE–220 CE**
Western (Former) Han	206 BCE–9 CE
Xin dynasty	9–24 CE
Eastern (Latter) Han	25–220
Three Kingdoms period	**220–265**
Wei	220–265
Shu Han	220–265
Wu	222–280
Western Jin dynasty	**265–317**
Northern Dynasties	**386–581**
Sixteen Kingdoms	304–438
Former Liang	314–376
Later Liang	386–403
Southern Liang	397–414
Western Liang	400–422
Northern Liang	398–439
Cheng Han	304–347
Former Zhao	304–329
Later Zhao	319–351
Western Qin	365–431
Former Qin	349–394
Later Qin	384–417
Xia	407–431
Former Yan	333–370
Later Yan	384–409
Southern Yan	398–410
Northern Yan	409–436
Northern Wei	386–535
Eastern Wei	534–550
Western Wei	535–557
Northern Qi	550–577
Northern Zhou	557–581

Period of Disunity 220–589

Southern Dynasties	**317–589**
Eastern Jin	317–420
Liu Song	420–479
Southern Qi	479–502
Liang	502–557
Chen	557–589
Six Dynasties period	**222–589**
Wu	222–280
Eastern Jin	317–420
Liu Song	420–479
Southern Qi	479–502
Liang	502–557
Chen	557–589
Sui dynasty	**589–618**
Tang dynasty	**618–907**
Liao dynasty	**907–1125**
Five Dynasties period	**907–960**
Later Liang	907–923
Later Tang	923–936
Later Jin	936–946
Later Han	946–950
Later Zhou	951–960
Dali kingdom	**937–1253**
Song dynasty	**960–1279**
Northern Song	960–1127
Southern Song	1127–1279
Xi Xia	**1038–1227**
Jin dynasty	**1115–1234**
Yuan dynasty	**1260–1368**
Ming dynasty	**1368–1644**
Qing dynasty	**1644–1912**
Republic	**1912–1949**
People's Republic	**1949–**

Period of Disunity 220–589

Recarving China's Past

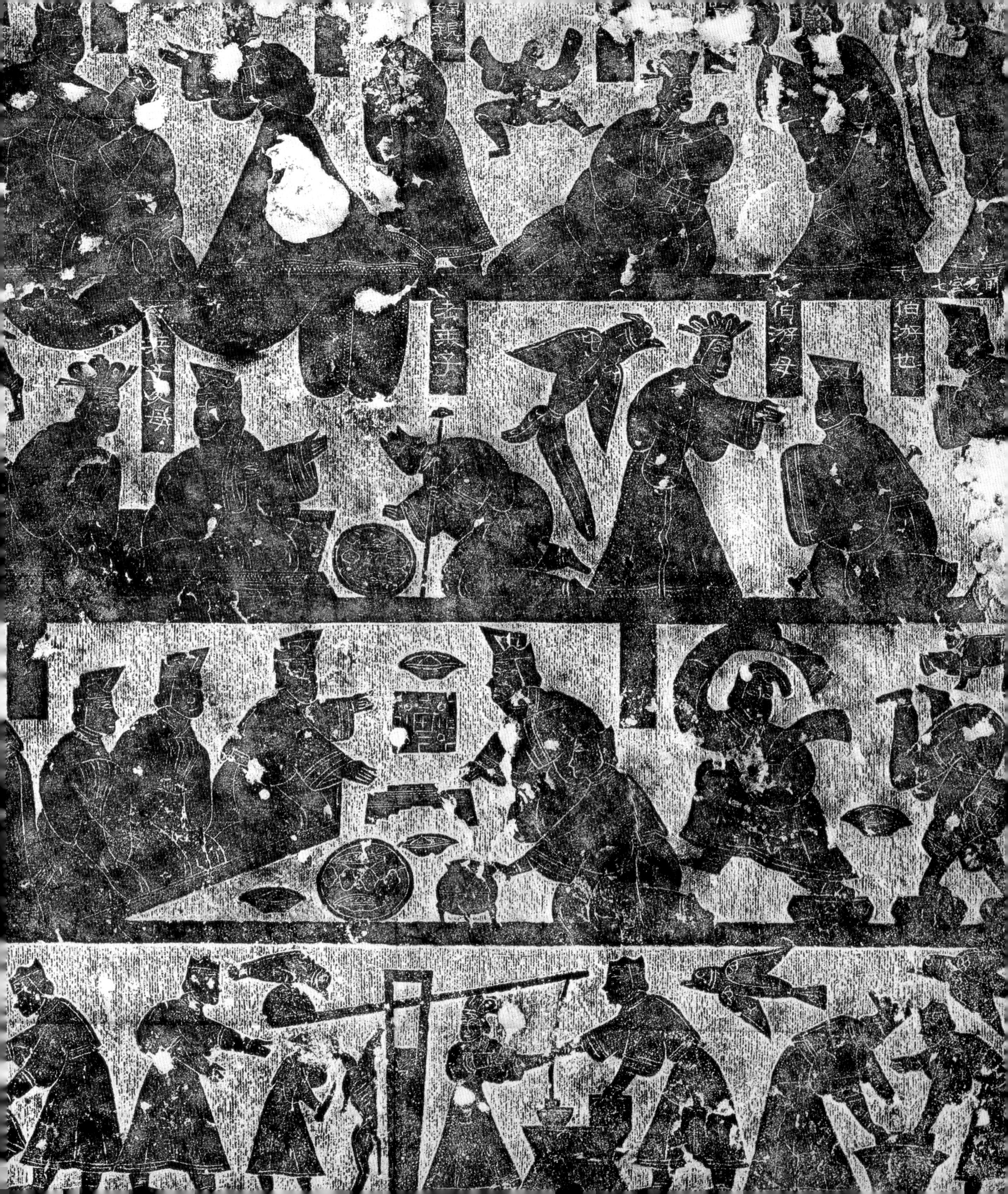

老萊子
伯游母
伯游也

Cary Y. Liu

The "Wu Family Shrines" as a Recarving of the Past

The desire to preserve the past for present and future encounters provides the impetus for recarving. In any recarving of history, literature, or the arts, a past model is reinterpreted, retold, reenvisioned (*zai xian*). More than preserving the past, recarving renders the past (*jiu*) new (*xin*) through repair and reconstruction. While the term "new" has the meaning of a "fresh start" or "beginning," it also has the connotation of "renovating" or "repairing the past" (*xiu jiu*). This is evidenced by wording in the "The Punitive Expedition to Yin" section of the *Book of Documents*, which relates that the chief criminals are to be punished, and their followers "who have long been stained by their filthy manners will be allowed to renovate [*xin*] themselves."[1] In this instance the repair of the past entails the recovery of exemplary conduct and correct behavior. It is in this sense that the recarving of China's past has often involved identifying what is proper or vital in the past as prerequisite to preserving exemplars for the present and future. It is this urge to recover and revitalize what is proper in the past (*fu gu*) that underlies much of antiquarian scholarship and artistic revival in China.[2]

Han-dynasty records attest a contemporary practice of depicting past exemplars of excellent conduct. Contemporary texts describe scenes of virtuous rulers, tyrants, loyal ministers, filial sons, just men, upright women, and supernatural phenomena painted in color on walls in imperial palaces, as well as in halls of temples, central and local government offices, and even in houses of affluent commoners.[3] As described in Wang Yanshou's (courtesy name [*zi*] Wenkao; act. 163) *Rhapsody on the Hall of Numinous Brilliance in Lu* (*Lingguang Dian fu*), in such scenes "the wicked are warnings to the world, /the good are examples for posterity."[4] The famed Hall of Numinous Brilliance was built in the Western Han period to the southeast of the Confucian Temple in the city of Qufu, in the southwest quadrant of present-day Shandong Province. Wang Yanshou's sentiment finds precedent in *The School Sayings of Confucius* (*Kongzi jia yu*), which relates that in the Spring and Autumn period the sage saw paintings that portrayed "the appearances of the good or bad, and warnings of the rise or fall."[5] Such pictorial scenes of exemplary figures are believed to have been imitated in the decoration of tombs and shrine structures.[6] They can be seen painted, carved and painted, and just carved in numerous archaeologically excavated examples (see cat. nos. 8, 10–12).[7] Figural scenes believed to embody exemplary conduct and correct behavior also adorn the "Wu family shrines" (cat. no. 1). Also located in southwestern Shandong, not far from the Hall of Numinous Brilliance, this was one of the earliest groups of pictorial stone carvings to be recovered, identified, and preserved as a Han-dynasty monument. Since the Song dynasty these carvings, and the ink rubbings made from them, have been identified as some of the most valuable and authentic materials for the study of Chinese antiquity. For these reasons, the Wu family reliefs are fundamental to understanding historical approaches to and methods of studying Chinese art and history, and have also been central to the dating of archaeologically excavated Han tombs and artifacts.

Scholars have too often accepted the conventional recarving of history surrounding the pictorial stones associated with the cemetery complex that has come to be known as the "Wu family shrines." In 1786, during

Opposite Detail of Stone Chamber 1, Stone 1-E.2 (cat. no. 1.12). "Wu family shrines" rubbings. Princeton University Art Museum, acc. no. 2002-307.2.

the Qing dynasty, the amateur archaeologist and official Huang Yi (1744–1802)[8] located the ruins of a cemetery complex in the northwest foothills of Ziyun Shan (Purple Cloud Hills) in present-day Jiaxiang County, Shandong Province. Numerous carved pictorial and architectural stones, two stone steles, one pair of gate-pillars (*men que*) and one of feline sculptures, two tombs excavated in 1980–1981, and one tomb opened in 2002 were recovered from the site and nearby areas. Traditionally dated to the mid-second century CE, during the Eastern Han dynasty, the pictorial stones were carved with exemplary images of legendary rulers, paragons of filial piety and loyalty, historical and mythological stories, and scenes of feasting, homage, processions, omens, and other figural and decorative subjects. These carved stones, even before they could be reconstructed into architectural structures, came to be recognized as among the most valuable materials for understanding and teaching Chinese pictorial art and the history and material culture of the Han dynasty. Because of their importance to China's artistic, archaeological, architectural, and cultural heritage, they were included in the initial roster of important historical monuments and cultural relics placed under national heritage protection by the State Council (Guowuyuan) in 1961.[9] Beyond China's borders rubbings of the "Wu family shrines" were among the earliest works of art from China to be examined internationally. In 1881 Stephen W. Bushell (1844–1908) presented a set of rubbings he had acquired in Beijing to the International Congress of Orientalists in Berlin.[10]

In the teaching of Chinese art history, the Wu cemetery rubbings have come to be viewed as a fundamental monument for the study of the pictorial arts. Portrayed as one of "the most direct expressions of Confucian ideas and ideals in early Chinese art," the "Wu family shrines" is one of the few Asian works to be highlighted in *A World History of Art* by Hugh Honour and John Fleming.[11] Similarly, among Chinese historians and art historians, the Wu shrine stones have received special attention. In his survey *Comprehensive History of Chinese Painting*, Wang Bomin recognized the significance of Han pictorial stone carvings for the understanding of Han architecture, history, painting, and sculpture. Wang selected pictorial stones of the Wu family stone chambers, the shrine or stone chamber at Xiaotang Shan (Hill of Filial Piety) (fig. 3A) in Changqing County, and Tomb 1 at Beizhai Zhuang Village in Yi'nan as noteworthy examples from Shandong Province.[12] The dating and identification of all three examples are still a matter of scholarly debate, and it is interesting to note that both the Wu cemetery and the nearby Xiaotang Shan stone chamber were both explored by Huang Yi.[13]

Since the 1786 recovery of the pictorial stones by Huang Yi, a broad consensus has accepted their identification as part of funerary shrines, as belonging to a Wu family, and as dating from the Han dynasty. It was generally assumed that the recovered stones corresponded to an assemblage comprising a single stone chamber or shrine with pictorial images and inscribed cartouches (*bangti*), four stele inscriptions, and a gate-pillar inscription. Before the discovery of the stones, this assemblage had been reconstructed from textual accounts and illustrations culled from later collated editions of Song-dynasty texts. These textual and visual records, however, were all based on ink-on-paper rubbings, not on examination of the actual stones. By the eighteenth century only the so-called Tang Rubbing (*Tang ben*), showing fourteen pictorial scenes, seems to have survived, but its provenance can be traced back no further than collectors in the Ming dynasty. After the Tang Rubbing was given to Huang Yi, sometime between 1775 and 1791, he traced the scenes by hand for woodblocks that were printed and included in later editions of his *Xiaopenglai Ge jinshi wenzi* (*Metal and stone writings from the Xiaopenglai Ge*).[14] From the identification of the stones recovered in 1786 with the "Wu family shrines" assemblage, for the next two hundred years the dating of the stones to the mid Eastern Han has primarily depended on the dates of the stele and gate-pillar inscriptions found in textual and visual records associated with the assemblage. Prior to the 1950s very few archaeologically excavated and firmly dated examples were available for study and comparison.[15] The carved pictorial images of the "Wu family shrines," consequently, came to be used as a stylistic benchmark for Han art and as a paradigm for Han pictorial art and material culture, against which the authenticity and dating of other works of art, archaeology, and architecture as well as historical records have been judged. As acclaimed in the *Ji'nian Wushi muqun shike faxian erbai zhounian zuotan huiyi ziyao* (*Summary of the symposium commemorating the 200th anniversary of the discovery of the Wu family cemetery carved stones*): "The Wu family cemetery stone carvings are the foremost representatives of Han-dynasty stone carvings" and the pictorial images bring to life, or reenvision (*zai xian*), the social conditions, tools, and Confucian ideology of the Eastern Han period.[16]

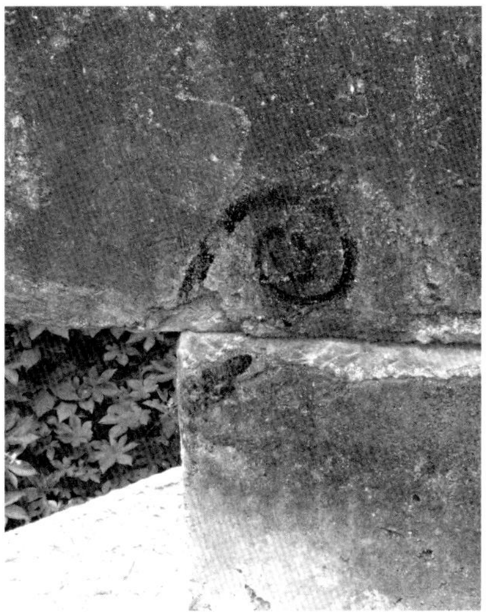

This identification of the recovered stone carvings as the Han-dynasty Wu family shrines may yet prove correct, but numerous Han-dynasty and Period of Disunity archaeological finds recently unearthed in the region encompassing Shandong, northern Jiangsu, northern Anhui, and eastern Henan, have made it possible, and therefore compelling, to reassess stone carvings in terms of their pictorial and calligraphic styles, architectural typology, and their regional context. This is underscored by three stone tombs opened at the cemetery site. The tombs, along with fragmentary burial artifacts found inside, have not adequately been integrated into any consideration of the other stone carvings at the cemetery. Tombs 1 and 2 were excavated in 1981 and a third tomb was discovered in 2002, which raises the likelihood that additional tombs may yet be located in the vicinity.[17] On-site examination of the tombs raises other interesting questions. The stone slab roofs of Tomb 2 have been removed, and the burial chambers are presently completely exposed to view. Visible on the plastered walls of Tomb 2 are traces of decorative lines in red pigment that were not mentioned in the earlier report (fig. 1).[18] The use of color in the tombs may have implications for reconstructing the original appearance of the "Wu family shrines" pictorial carvings. The architectural relationship between the tombs and other structures in the cemetery is also unclear: layout, dates, building practices, workshop organization, and burial ceremonies are still unknown. We even need to reconsider whether the recovered stone carvings and tombs all formed a single cemetery complex.

Similarly, characterizations and determinations concerning the pictorial and calligraphic styles, iconographic content and program, and architectural

Fig. 1 *Detail of traces of red paint wall decoration* (enhanced). Ca. second century CE. Tomb 2, Wuzhai Shan site, Jiaxiang County, Shandong. Photo by author, 2004.

reconstruction and function of the stone carvings found at the cemetery site have often proceeded from the hypothesis that the recovered stones match the "Wu family shrine" assemblage reconstructed from Song-dynasty texts. Pictorial stone carvings and calligraphic inscriptions associated with the assemblage were chiefly recorded in received versions of the *Jigu lu* (*Record of collected antiquities*) compiled by Ouyang Xiu (1007–1072), *Jigu lu mu* (*Catalogue of "Record of collected antiquities"*) by Ouyang Fei (1047–1113), the *Jinshi lu* (*Records of metal and stone*) by Zhao Mingcheng (1081–1129), and the *Li shi* (*Explications of clerical script*) and *Li xu* (*Supplement on clerical script*) by Hong Gua (1117–1184).[19] None of these Song texts, however, have been handed down in their original form. They all survive as reconstructed texts—compiled and collated recarvings of the past. Various recensions and editions of the same texts often include substantially different information about the so-called assemblage of Wu family pictorial carvings and inscriptions. Ouyang Xiu and Ouyang Fei only partly transcribed or listed two stele inscriptions and never related them to the same Wu family in Shandong, to shrines, or to each other. Zhao Mingcheng partly transcribed three stele inscriptions and was the first to record the existence of a Wu family gate-pillar inscription and pictorial carvings belonging to a "Wu family stone chamber" (*Wushi shishi*).[20] With Hong Gua the assemblage finally comprises four stele inscriptions, dedicated respectively to Wu Liang (courtesy name Suizong; 78–151), his brother Wu ? (courtesy name Kaiming; 92–148), and the latter's sons, Wu Ban (courtesy name Xuanzhang; d. 145) and Wu Rong (courtesy name Shehe [or Hanhe]; d. 167); a gate-pillar inscription dated to 147, and several pictorial stones including, for the first time, the "Confucius Meeting Laozi" slab.[21] It is also with Hong Gua that the architectural chamber first becomes known as the "Wu Liang Shrine" (Wu Liang Ci or Wu Liang Citang). The confused and complex collation history of each of the reconstructed texts will be examined in greater detail in Nylan's "Addicted to Antiquity" in this catalogue.

This means that any attempt to reconstitute the recovered cemetery stone carvings on the basis of a "Wu family shrines" assemblage relies on a series of nested anachronisms. The assemblage itself is a reconstruction based on reconstructed Song-dynasty texts. The fundamental identification of the recovered cemetery stones as dating to the Han dynasty, as belonging to a Wu family, and as designating funerary shrines, therefore, needs to be reexamined. This is all the more necessary when it is realized that the traditional acceptance of the recovered stones as dating from the mid Eastern Han has relied on dates found in the stele and pillar inscriptions. It is becoming increasingly clear, as will be discussed below, that the stele and pillar inscriptions may not be as dependable as once believed. The synthesis of a "Wu family shrine" assemblage, therefore, is really an interpretive reconstruction—a renovation or renewal (*xiu jiu*) that changes, reenvisions (*zai xian*), and recarves the past. For this reason, any reconstruction or restoration must be considered an anachronism and should not be used, without qualification, as basic evidence for further interpretations and reconstructions.[22]

Since the eleventh century antiquarians and scholars have found the assemblage of the "Wu family shrines" a fascinating puzzle. The components of the assemblage were identified, preserved, and transmitted at different times and in different ways. Their combination and transmission forms a complex cultural history, which since 1786 has become intertwined with the history of the physical stone carvings recovered at, or near, the Jiaxiang cemetery site where modern preservation halls and a compound now stand. The recarved history of the "Wu shrines," therefore, focuses on two different sets of evidence, the physical stones that have been recovered since 1786, and some one thousand years of visual and textual materials transmitted since the Song dynasty. Before these sets of evidence can be analyzed individually, it will be helpful to review some of the past scholarship and accounts that have conflated the history of the physical stones with that of the textual and visual assemblage, while calling attention to research problems and questions.[23]

The story of the "Wu family shrines" begins with a conspicuous absence. Before the Song dynasty there is no textual or visual record of any stone carving or cemetery structures belonging to a Wu family in Shandong. It is notable that there is no mention of the Wu shrines in Li Daoyuan's (d. 527) *Shuijing zhu* (*Commentary on the "Water classic"*). Li Daoyuan was a scholar and official during the Northern Wei dynasty, and sometime during the years 515–524 he compiled extensive commentary on the *Shuijing* (*Water classic*), which was probably written in the early third century. The later transmission and collated editions of the *Shuijing zhu* are not without controversy,[24] but the commentary attempted to explicate the course of ancient waterways while describing tombs, steles, and relics along the way. The *Shuijing zhu* follows the course of the several rivers near the Juye marshes in the area of modern Jiaxiang County in Shandong. It notes several Han tomb sites in the area, including those of the Regional Inspectors (*cishi*) of Jingzhou Li Gang (d. 172 CE) and Fan Shi, and the Colonel Director of Retainers (*sili xiaowei*) Lu Jun.[25] Surprisingly, it makes no mention of a Wu family cemetery or shrine, even though in Song-dynasty and later accounts these are described as prominently as many of the other monuments included by Li Daoyuan.

In the Song dynasty Ouyang Xiu's *Jigu lu*, Ouyang Fei's *Jigu lu mu*, Zhao Mingcheng's *Jinshi lu*, and Hong Gua's *Li shi* and *Li xu* each recorded different components of the assemblage. Each of these scholars apparently relied on rubbings as their primary evidence. They never traveled to identify a particular cemetery site, nor did they ever directly match any rubbing to an actual carved pictorial stone or stele.[26] The same ignorance of an original stone or site is also true of other Southern Song sources that mention components of the "Wu family shrines" assemblage. Sets of the Wu family pictorial rubbings, engraved illustrations, or copies were listed in the collections of official and private libraries. At about the time Hong Gua was completing his *Li shi* in 1166, Wei Bo (act. 1140–1167) in his *Colophon for the Pictorial Images of the Wu Family Stone Chamber* commented on a set of rubbings or illustrations that was shown to the Metropolitan Overseer (*yin*) of Jiankang (present-day Nanjing) in 1167. This set was identified as having come from the collection of Zhang Ruying (d. 1153), who had been Hong Gua's teacher, and it was "engraved and inserted in all the prefectural libraries, and in the walls of the Choushu Ge library hall [in Jiankang]."[27] Another Song-dynasty version of the pictorial images was made by Fang Wude (1102–1171).[28] In every case, the pictorial images discussed remain shadows of their material form, and it is also unclear if these sets and copies were ink rubbings, woodcut illustrations, or stone tablets.

Following the Southern Song period, the carved stones were virtually lost or forgotten. Standard accounts assume that sometime during the Yuan, Ming, and early Qing dynasties the stone carvings were buried by Yellow River or local flooding, but the exact circumstances require further investigation, as this area was also subject to serious earthquakes and not infrequent banditry and warfare.[29] Nevertheless, during this long period rubbings, illustrations, textual descriptions of the pictorial carvings, and especially calligraphic transcriptions of the inscriptions associated with the Wu shrine assemblage continued to be transmitted. In Zhang Xuan's (14th century) *Zhida Jinling xin zhi* (*New Jinling gazetteer of the Zhida reign*), there is listed the title "Slabs of the Wu Family Stone Chambers" ("Wushi shishi bei").[30] This probably refers to a set of rubbings in the Jinling area (present-day Nanjing) during the Yuan dynasty, and may possibly be the Southern Song version from the Choushu Ge library. The Tang Rubbing of fourteen pictorial scenes was examined by scholar and bibliophile Zhu Yizun (1629–1709) in 1704, and again in 1705 at the Ma family Kanzhai Shuwu library.[31] Rubbings of the Wu Ban and Wu Rong steles were catalogued by Qian Daxin (1728–1804) as being in the collection of the Ming dynasty Tianyi Ge private library.[32]

Research is only beginning on what materials survived and were transmitted during the Song to early Qing dynasties. During this period attention was focused on the rubbings of the inscriptions, which were written in clerical-script calligraphy (*lishu*),[33] but little attention was paid to the pictorial designs. Zhao Mingcheng is said to have written five chapters (*juan*) on the pictorial images, but they have not survived and he may have discussed only the clerical-script cartouche inscriptions on the stones. The first reproduction of the pictorial designs seems to have been Hong Gua's *Li xu*, but none of the illustrations in surviving editions may date from the Song dynasty. The focus on clerical-script calligraphy rested on the concept of "using clerical to explain the Classics" (*ligu*). Because the Confucian Classics were early on transmitted using forms of clerical script, the study of this script was deemed essential to their proper interpretation and to correcting later emendations. This emphasis on clerical script motivated the compilation of numerous clerical-script character epigraphic dictionaries, including Hong Gua's *Li shi* and *Li xu*, along with Liu Qiu's (twelfth century) *Li yun* (*Rhymes in clerical-script calligraphy*) and Lou Ji's (1133–1211) *Han lizi yuan* (*Sources of clerical-script characters*) in the Southern Song dynasty.[34] In the Qing dynasty the emphasis continued, with compilations of such works as Gu Aiji's *Li bian* (*Distinguishing clerical script*) and the recutting of Liu Qiu's *Li yun* with an 1810 preface and textual criticism by Weng Fanggang (1733–1818).[35] Weng Fanggang was a high official and well-known scholar of epigraphy and painting, an acquaintance of Huang Yi, who became closely connected with the study and preservation of the Wu cemetery carvings.

Further research is needed to investigate how the Wu cemetery inscriptions have shaped the understanding of clerical-script calligraphy and its use in the correcting and recarving of history and the Classics. Conversely, how has the recarving of history and the Classics in the Song to Qing dynasties shaped understanding of clerical-script calligraphy and the "Wu family shrines"? The resulting inseparability of these two questions is the Gordian knot intrinsic to any investigation of the "Wu shrines." The primacy usually given to the Wu cemetery inscriptions in past scholarship has created the following example of this Gordian knot. In a pictorial scene in the so-called Wu Liang Shrine, inscribed cartouches label the pictorial figures as Zhu Ming, his younger brother, son, and wife (cat. no. 1.36). Textual records indicate that Zhu Ming lived after the Han dynasty during the Eastern Jin.[36] Acceptance of the "Wu family shrines" as a Han-dynasty monument required that the texts should be corrected and history recarved.[37] On the other hand, if the textual records are presumed correct, then the carved inscriptions need to be explained. Perhaps the pictorial stones and cartouche inscriptions are in fact post-Han in date, or the pictorial carvings may date from Han but their inscriptions were carved at a later date. Alternatively, the original cartouche inscriptions may have worn away and been incorrectly recut or altered at a later date. In this latter scenario, modified rubbings and erroneous recorded transcriptions of the cartouches may have played a significant role. All these permutations and others plague the study of almost every aspect of the stones recovered at the Wu cemetery, and should be recognized at the outset.

The next significant development in the history of the "Wu shrines" occurred in 1786 during the Qing dynasty. While searching for remains of three offering halls (*xiang tang*) of a Han-dynasty prince, Huang Yi found three groups of pictorial carvings near a location designated by a local gazetteer.[38] Despite the gazetteer's identification of the structures as belonging to a Han prince, Huang Yi identified these groups of carvings as the "Wu family shrines" (Wushi citang). Before this time, the Wu family assemblage, reconstructed on the basis of textual collations, rubbings, and illustrations, consisted of a single stone chamber with its interior walls carved with pictorial designs, one slab depicting the scene of "Confucius Meeting Laozi," a gate-pillar inscription, and four commemorative funerary stele inscriptions traditionally ascribed to Wu Liang, Wu Kaiming, Wu Ban, and Wu Rong. None of the earlier reconstructions of a Wu family assemblage, however, had ever linked any of the transmitted textual and visual materials to a specific site or an actual group of carved stones. Consequently, Huang Yi became the first to link the assemblage to a particular site and to actual stones. In his 1787 *Xiu Wushi Citang ji lüe* (*Brief record on building the Wu Family Shrine* [*Preservation Hall*]) (hereafter, *Brief Record*; see Appendix),[39] Huang Yi expressed his excitement upon realizing that a few of the recovered stones corresponded to the Wu Liang Shrine and Wu Ban stele as recorded in the works of Zhao Mingcheng and Hong Gua. It is not certain, however, what editions of the Song texts he consulted, which may affect the validity of his identification. His identification also does not account for the majority of other recovered pictorial slabs found at, or in the vicinity of, the cemetery site.

Efforts to identify and make sense of the slabs recovered in 1786 plus additional stones discovered in 1789, resulted in their being arranged and numbered into four groups—the Wu Liang Shrine, Front, Rear, and Left

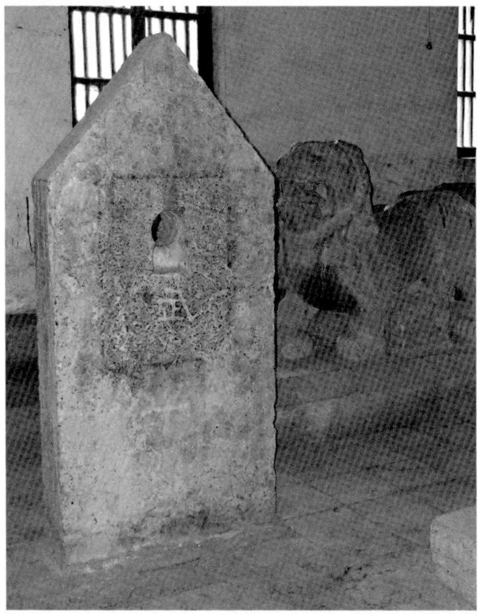

Groups—and miscellaneous stones. A group designation and number were carved onto each stone, and preservation facilities were built at the site between 1789 and 1792.[40] Stories were woven around the four groups and their supposed correspondence to the four stone steles from the assemblage said to commemorate four males of the Wu family: the extant Wu Ban and Wu Rong steles, and the Wu Liang and Wu Kaiming stones that may no longer survive. This assumed correspondence has led to attempts to match office titles and pictorial details carved on the four groups of recovered stones to the minimal biographies of each of the four men contained in the four stele inscriptions and the gate-pillar inscription.[41] At best, such attempts offer coincidental evidence that cannot be confirmed, but in some instances they also conflict with historical evidence.[42] This is especially true since we do not know if other steles may yet be discovered at the cemetery, or have already been lost. Strikingly, there is little evidence that the two surviving steles—those ascribed to Wu Ban and Wu Rong—originally came from the cemetery site. Huang Yi notes in his *Brief Record* that although the Wu Ban stele was recovered at the site, it had decades earlier been moved there.[43] As for the Wu Rong stele, at the time Huang Yi located the cemetery in 1786, the stone was already housed in the Minglun Tang hall in the Jining Prefectural Academy (Jining zhou xue; also known as the Confucius Temple or Wen Miao).[44] There seems to be no record of where or when this stele was originally found, or how it got to Jining. The transcriptions of this stele in Song-dynasty sources are fragmentary, and there are many questions about how and when it came to be associated with the "Wu family shrines."

Attention should also focus on a blank fifth stele that was reportedly found northwest of the cemetery's northeast gate-pillar and may have been original to the site (fig. 2).[45] Similar to the surviving Wu Ban and Wu Rong stones, this stele is shaped like a *gui*-tablet, with a tall oblong body and a triangular peak. Centered about one third from the top is a round hole through the stele with a square cutout at the bottom. Besides the pictorial and inscribed carved stones found at the site, there were many other architectural stones with little or no decoration or inscriptions. Being undecorated, these stones were of little interest to earlier scholars and were not documented or recorded. It is now unknown how many of these plain stones have been lost, but some still remain at the site. Only with relatively recent efforts at architectural reconstruction have these stones begun to receive attention. The blank fifth stele is among this group and is reported to have already been stored in the Wu Family Shrine (Wushi Citang) Preservation Hall during the Qing dynasty. When recovered, the stele no longer had, or never had, an engraved title or text, which accounts for its not having been documented earlier. A single clerical-script character, *Wu*, is now found carved on one side below the hole. Other stones bearing single characters, even if these were recognized to have been inscribed after the Han period, were meticulously recorded and transcribed by earlier scholars, so it is likely that this character on the otherwise blank stele was added after the site was located in 1786. The square cutout under the circular hole also indicates that the stone had been altered for later reuse, possibly as a well post.[46] Could this fifth stele have been the missing Wu Liang or Wu Kaiming stele? Even Huang Yi reasoned that the "steles of Wu

Fig. 2 *Blank stele (sometimes identified as the Wu Liang stele).* Ca. second century CE. Limestone; h. 210 cm, h. to shoulders 170 cm, w. 88 cm, d. 22 cm. Wuzhai Shan site, Jiaxiang County, Shandong. Photo by author, 2004.

Liang and Wu Kaiming are not yet found, so how do we know they are not still at this site?"[47] Could this stele have been dedicated to a fifth member of the Wu family or to someone else? Was it originally associated with the site? Although these questions may never be fully answered, nevertheless they make clear that there is no reason to assume that dedicatory steles were erected in one-to-one correspondence with funerary shrines or tombs at this cemetery. The traditional assumption that the four factitious groups of Wu family structures coincided with four steles dedicated to four males of the family, consequently, has become a serious methodological trap. It should also be remembered that Huang Yi was originally searching not for four but for three offering halls that were reported in a local gazetteer, and modern architectural reconstructions based on the four groups of stones found at the site have generally yielded three structures.[48]

Much of the rich corpus of scholarship and investigation of the "Wu family shrines" over the past two centuries was directed toward the study of the inscriptions and images on the stones, for the purpose of corroborating or correcting the Confucian Classics and historical texts, toward identifying the stories depicted by the pictorial scenes, and toward trying to recreate a Wu family lineage for the assembled shrines and cemetery complex. Important studies included Bi Yuan (1730–1797) and Ruan Yuan's (1764–1849) *Shanzuo jinshi zhi* (*Records of metal and stone carvings from the Shanzuo region*) (preface 1797), Wang Chang's (1725–1806) *Jinshi cuibian* (*Compilation of metal and stone inscriptions*) (preface 1805), the brothers Feng Yunpeng (act. nineteenth century) and Feng Yunyuan's (act. nineteenth century) *Jinshi suo* (*Index to metal and stone carvings*) (1821), and Rong Geng's (1894–1983) *Han Wu Liang Ci huaxiang lu* (*Record of the Han-dynasty Wu Liang Shrine pictorial images*) (1936). In some of these studies the pictorial scenes were recarved and rearranged to fit album, handscroll, and book formats, and damaged or unclear areas were sometimes repaired. In these and similar studies, scenes from the pictorial stones were commonly presented in isolation, giving no hint of the relationships between scenes across an entire stone or architectural structure.

Beginning in the late nineteenth century, the "Wu family shrines" were among the earliest works of Chinese art to be examined by Western and Japanese art historians. At this time photographic documentation of the rubbings and the site began to be published in the works of Berthold Laufer, Édouard Chavannes, Sekino Tadashi, Ōmura Seigai, and others.[49] Pictorial scenes were now accurately presented, but because the photographs mostly record compiled sets of disparate rubbings, there was no easy way to determine the sequential dates of the rubbings or to reconstruct the architectural context. Although rubbing sets of the "Wu family shrines" are not rare, the number of rubbings in each set has made it prohibitively expensive to reproduce them for detailed comparison and sequential dating. Comparing rubbings is all the more difficult because of wide variations in the techniques of cleaning the stone, in the materials and skill with which the rubbings were made, and in the selection of details or parts of the carving to be brought out in a given rubbing.[50] No two rubbings of the same stone are completely identical, and it is through the rubbing maker's care, skill, and judicious selection that the original carved stone comes to be embodied in a rubbing. Because carved stone

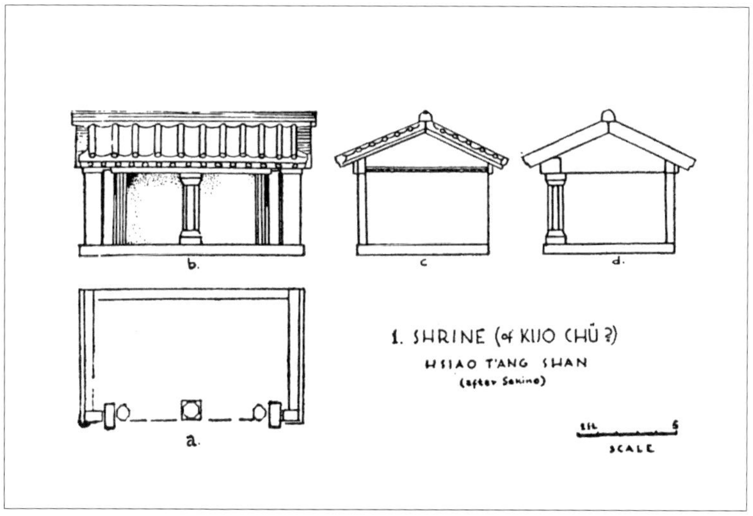

Fig. 3A Stone chamber at Xiaotang Shan. Reconstruction drawing by Wilma Fairbank, 1941. From Fairbank, *Adventures in Retrieval*, p. 61, fig. 3.

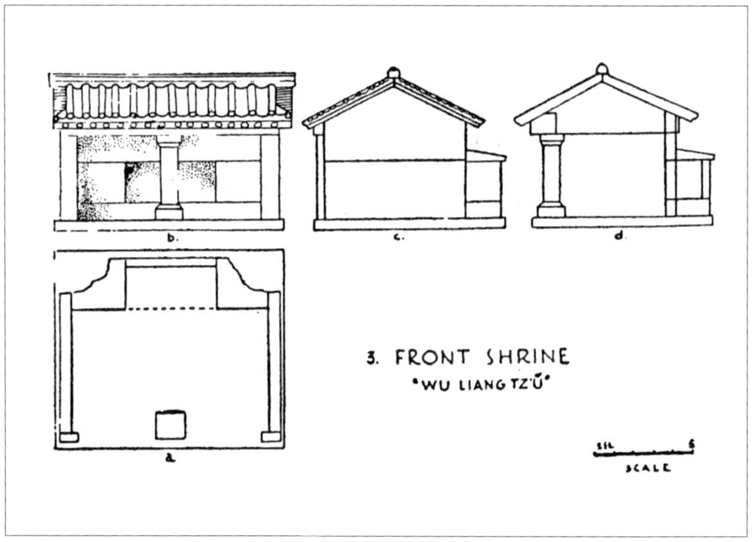

Stone Chamber 1

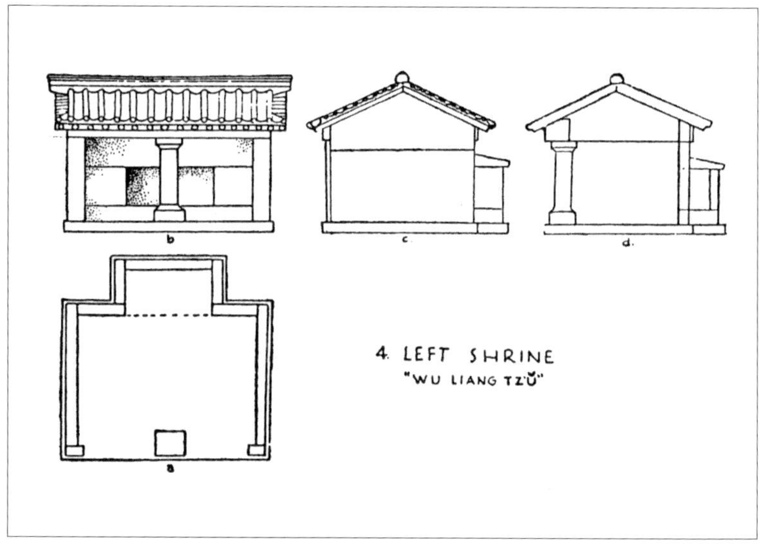

Stone Chamber 2

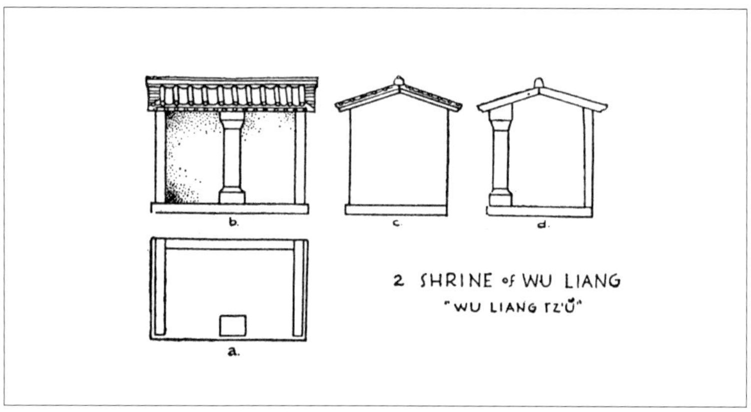

Stone Chamber 3

Fig. 3B Three stone chambers at the Wuzhai Shan site. Reconstruction drawings by Wilma Fairbank, 1941. From Fairbank, *Adventures in Retrieval*, p. 61, fig. 3.

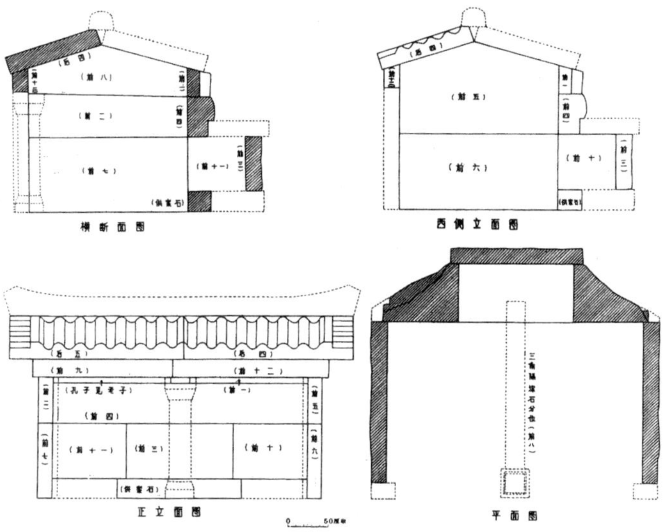

"Front Stone Chamber" (Stone Chamber 1)

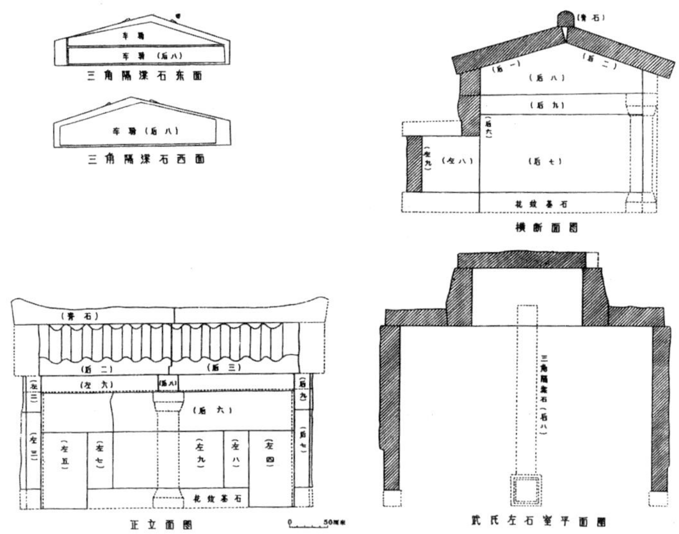

"Left Stone Chamber" (Stone Chamber 2)

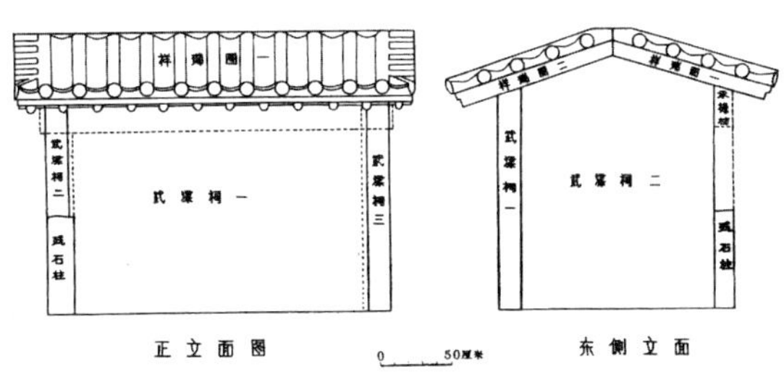

"Wu Liang Shrine" (Stone Chamber 3)

Fig. 4 *"Front Stone Chamber"* (*Stone Chamber 1*), *"Left Stone Chamber"* (*Stone Chamber 2*), and *"Wu Liang Shrine"* (*Stone Chamber 3*). Reconstruction drawings by Jiang and Wu, 1981, 1995. From Jiang and Wu, *Handai Wushi muqun shike yanjiu*, p. 39, fig. 10; p. 44, fig. 12; p. 36, fig. 9.

tends to become abraded or damaged with the passage of time, an early rubbing is often believed more authentic than the later aged stone that it was taken from. This skill and ability to embody an original validates rubbings as a form of art in China. The growing reliance on rubbings and photographs also led scholars to ignore the stones themselves. Thus scholars forgot that some stones had more than one pictorial surface. At least one stone, only recently rediscovered, was a cylindrical column. Moreover, it should also be recognized that commercial and scholarly rubbing makers were often quite selective in what they included. Some rubbing sets comprised only the calligraphic inscriptions, some highlighted pictorial scenes but omitted the architectural decoration, and almost no rubbing included the undecorated architectural joineries or the backs of the stones.

The next breakthrough in the scholarship on the "Wu family shrines" pictorial stones came in 1941, when Wilma Fairbank attempted the first architectural reconstruction of the pictorial slabs, in order to allow the "interrelationships and positional significance" of the individual scenes to be read as a coherent pictorial and architectural program.[51] When she visited the cemetery site in 1934, many of the stones were still embedded in the walls of the Preservation Hall, obscuring architectural features such as the backs, thicknesses, and joinery. On the basis of rubbings reproduced photographically to scale, Fairbank was able to reconstruct three stone chambers that she called the Front, Left, and Wu Liang Shrines (fig. 3B). These designations follow the relative locations where the groups of pictorial stones were reportedly found in 1786: the Wu Liang Shrine, Front, and Left/Rear Groups. Fairbank reconstructed the Wu Liang Shrine as a one-bay structure, and the Front and Left Shrines as two bays wide. In imitation of the Xiaotang Shan stone chamber (fig. 3A), Fairbank also installed a center column in the open front facade of each shrine.

In 1981 Jiang Yingju and Wu Wenqi refined Fairbank's reconstruction by making use of the actual stones, which now had been removed from the walls.[52] The way stones were originally joined together architecturally became visible, as it had not been in rubbings and photographs. The backs of stones were also exposed, revealing different levels of finish—crudely hewn, flat smooth finish, or carved with imitation roof tiles.[53] Jiang and Wu's findings basically confirmed (with some revisions and additions) Fairbank's earlier reconstruction of three halls, but removed the front column from the single-bay structure. They named the reconstructed structures the Front Stone Chamber (Qian Shishi), Left Stone Chamber (Zuo Shishi), and Wu Liang Shrine (Wu Liang Ci) (fig. 4). In earlier writings these titles had been applied to the scattered groups of pictorial stones found at the site. In applying these titles to the architectural reconstructions, Jiang and Wu seem to distinguish between the one- and two-bay structures, respectively, the so-called shrine and stone chambers. Whereas "stone chamber" (*shishi*) is a descriptive term without connotations of building rank or function, the term "shrine" (*ci* or *citang*) in the Han period seems to have designated funerary offering halls built for aristocratic families and high officials. Wu Liang, Wu Kaiming, Wu Ban, and Wu Rong, however, were all low-ranking local officials, which raises two questions: (1) were the original structures in fact shrines? and (2) did the cemetery originally belong to a Wu Family?[54]

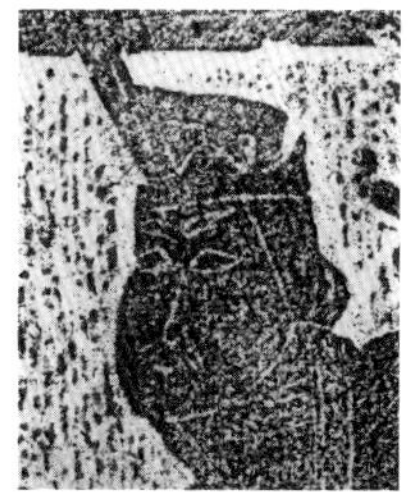
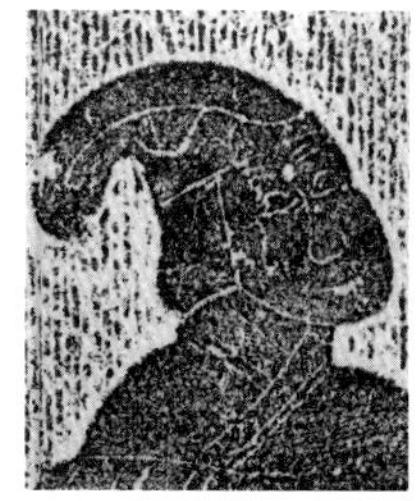
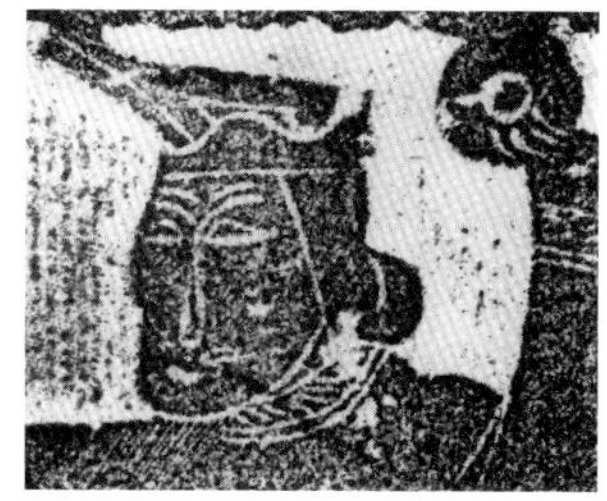

Carved stylistic details corroborate the architectural reconstructions made by Jiang and Wu. In human faces in three-quarters view, the noses are differently rendered in the three structures. In the pictorial stones forming the Wu Liang Ci, the nose is carved as a curved line in the shape of a half teardrop and pointed in the direction in which the head is turned (fig. 5A). In the stones of the Front Stone Chamber all the noses are likewise half-teardrop shaped, but all point opposite to the direction in which the head is turned (fig. 5B). In the stones of the Left Stone Chamber the faces in three-quarters view all have noses carved in the shape of a full teardrop but are flared at the top like the mouth of a vase (fig. 5C). This same open-teardrop nose is used for full frontal faces depicted in all three reconstructed structures. In general, the three-quarters–view noses within each of the three structures serve to corroborate that the stones in each of the reconstructed stone chambers indeed belong together.[55] This is especially helpful in placing the five roof slabs known as Rear Group Stones 1–5 (R.1–R.5) in the Front and Left Stone Chambers. These roof stones, bearing mythological scenes, had previously been treated as a separate group and sometimes posited as part of a fourth stone chamber.[56] From carved roof tiles on the back of these stones, dimensions, and mortise-and-tenon joint locations, Jiang and Wu matched Stones R.4 and R.5 to the Front Chamber, and R.1–R.3 to the Left Chamber. On Stones R.4 and R.5, the three-quarters–view noses are the same opposite-facing, half-teardrop shapes as on the other Front Chamber pictorial stones. On Stone R.3, the three-quarters–view noses match the open full-teardrop noses carved on the other stones of the Left Chamber. Unfortunately, unclarity in the rubbings or damage to the pictorial stones prevents us from seeing three-quarters–view noses in Stones R.1 and R.2. There are a few other stones in Jiang and Wu's reconstructed structures in which either the noses are not visible due to damage or there are no three-quarters–view faces. Many of the stones that were found away from the cemetery site but were integrated in the architectural reconstructions also fall into this "noseless" category. The exception is Rear Group Stone 9 (R.9), which both Fairbank and Jiang and Wu identified as the upper section of the west gable wall of the Left Stone Chamber. Although it was found away from the site, the carving style, including the carving of the noses, is consistent with the other stones in this chamber.

Building on the work of Fairbank as well as Jiang and Wu, in 1989 Wu Hung in his *Wu Liang Shrine: The Ideology of Early Chinese Pictorial Art* proposed a "Fourth Chamber." Recognizing similarities among four pictorial stones in the remaining group of miscellaneous slabs, he was able to partially reconstruct a fourth structure that may or may not have been originally connected with the cemetery site (discussed below).[57] Wu Hung also developed a detailed iconographical study focusing on the pictorial images in the structure traditionally believed to be dedicated to Wu Liang. He suggested that the carvings exhibit a coherent pictorial and architectural program in accord with Eastern Han cosmology.

Since the popularization of the pictorial stones and rubbings through photography, and following Fairbank's 1941 study, there have been numerous contributions to scholarship on the "Wu family shrines." Important studies include those by Patricia Berger, Doris Croissant, Hsing

Fig. 5A *Three-quarters pose with half-teardrop nose pointing in same direction as the face in "Wu Liang Shrine."* Detail of King of Qi, Stone Chamber 3, Stone 3-E.1 (cat. no. 1.37). "Wu family shrines" rubbings. Princeton University Art Museum, acc. no. 2002.307.34.

Fig. 5B *Three-quarters pose with half-teardrop nose pointing in direction opposite to that of face in "Front Stone Chamber."* Detail of Confucius' disciple, Stone Chamber 1, Stone 1-E.1 (cat. no. 1.11). "Wu family shrines" rubbings. Princeton University Art Museum, acc. no. 2002.307.1.

Fig. 5C *Three-quarters pose with full teardrop nose in "Left Stone Chamber."* Detail of First Emperor, Stone Chamber 2, Stone 2-S.4 (cat. no. 1.23). "Wu family shrines" rubbings. Princeton University Art Museum, acc. no. 2002.307.22.

I-tien, Jean James, Nagahiro Toshio, Zhu Xilu, and many others.[58] Many of these studies have focused on the iconography and stylistic development of particular pictorial scenes, basically accepting the consensus identification of the pictorial stones as belonging to shrines from a Wu family cemetery dating from the Han dynasty. This identification, reliant on past scholarship based on textual and visual materials, may ultimately prove correct. It is now possible, however, to take the stones themselves as primary evidence, thus shedding new light on their identification, preservation, and architectural reconstruction.

In summary, past scholarship has been mostly concerned with the epigraphy of the inscriptions and the iconography of the pictorial images, much less so with their pictorial and architectural programs. Since the location of the cemetery site in 1786 and Huang Yi's initial identification of the carved stones with the "Wu family shrine" assemblage, scholars have tended to conflate two different sets of evidence, the physical stones recovered at or near the cemetery, and some one thousand years of transmitted textual and visual materials. General acceptance of this conflation led scholars to take the Wu shrines as paradigms of Han carved pictorial stones—tableaux that allow a reenvisioning (*zai xian*) of Han art, history, ideology, and society. This identification, however, did not go completely unchallenged. In his *Mission archéologique dans la Chine septentrionale* of 1913–1915, Édouard Chavannes questioned the identification by consistently referring to the cemetery complex as the "pseudo-Wou Leang" shrines.[59]

We need now to reconceive the "Wu family shrines" by studying the physical stones—the set of recovered pictorial stones, steles, gate-pillars, feline sculptures, tombs—as distinct from the set of received textual transcriptions and descriptions as well as ink rubbings and illustrations. Below and in catalogue number 1, the author's "Reconfiguring," and Michael Nylan's "Addicted to Antiquity," these two sets of evidence will be examined to assess what is verifiable, what is interpretive, and what is fictitious or incorrect, in order to help clarify the complex cultural history that has been recarved around the "Wu family shrine" assemblage. For example, the "Wu Ban stele" exists as both a stone artifact and a transmitted text. Both must be examined, and the two compared. As noted earlier, the recovered stele stone was reportedly moved to the cemetery, therefore its place of origin cannot be confirmed. This opens various possibilities: that the stele comes from a Wu family cemetery at some other site, that in the Han dynasty funerary steles were not always erected at funerary sites, or that the stele is not dedicated to a member of the Wu family.[60] Furthermore, before the Wu Ban stele stone was identified in 1786, its carved text was said to be illegible, yet somehow Huang Yi was able to match it to received transcriptions of the Wu Ban stele inscription.[61] Personal inspection of the actual stele stone in 2002 and 2004 confirms that almost the entire carved inscription is heavily worn and quite illegible. In contrast, its opening nine characters are perfectly clear, carved with deeper, sharply outlined strokes (fig. 6). This is indisputable evidence of modern recarving. The recarved characters coincide with the only line of the text transcribed by Ouyang Xiu (discussed below), but also include one character that he had described as missing. Discussing the Wu Family Shrines Preservation Hall in the late nineteenth century, Chen Jin cautioned:

> I examined (*kao*)[62] Han stone inscriptions almost everywhere in Shandong. I fear [further] damage; half of them have had their characters smoothed off by the local people, while half have been recut by vulgar scholars (*shi*)[63] and have lost their authenticity.[64]

Textual transcriptions of the Wu Ban text are also not unproblematic. The earliest record of the Wu Ban stele is in Ouyang Xiu's *Jigu lu*. Working in exile at Rencheng (present-day Jining, Shandong), Ouyang Xiu noted in a 1064 entry that the family name and titles of office of the person named Ban were not legible and that eighty to ninety percent of the text was indecipherable.[65] Ouyang Xiu also did not record a courtesy name for the person who was only known as Ban. A 1069 supplementary entry in the *Jigu lu* adds that in a second rubbing of the stele, the surname "Wu" was visible, but notes no other differences. Only eight characters plus one missing character of the inscription's opening line were transcribed in the *Jigu lu*: "First year of the Jian[ ] reign-period when the Taisui[66] asterism was in the position of *dinghai*" (*Jian*[ ] *yuan nian taisui zai dinghai*).[67] Ouyang Xiu extrapolated the inscribed date to be the first year of the Jian[he] reign-period (147) of Eastern Han. It is this missing *he* character that can be seen in the recarved opening line on the present-day Wu Ban stele (fig. 6).

Zhao Mingcheng's *Jinshi lu* also transcribed very little of the stele inscription, although it described the stele as having a carved title head (*eti* or *ti'e*) reading, "Stele of the Former Dunhuang Chief Clerk the Lord Wu of the Han Dynasty" (*Han gu Dunhuang zhangshi Wu jun zhi bei*). This title clearly specifies a Dunhuang (in present-day Gansu Province) office title, which Ouyang Xiu had reported as absent.[68] The *Jinshi lu* also supplies Wu Ban's courtesy name as Xuanzhang, although in all received rubbings of the inscription and on the stele stone in its current condition the *zhang* character is illegible. It is likely that the courtesy name derives from the gate-pillar inscription that states that Wu Kaiming's son had the courtesy name of Xuanzhang. Zhao Mingcheng was also the first to record the gate-pillar inscription. The pillar inscription, however, does not identify Xuanzhang with Wu Ban, and the Wu Ban inscription does not say he was the son of Wu Kaiming. The identification was made via the office title of Dunhuang Chief Clerk, but again, according to Ouyang Xiu, there was no legible office title in the Wu Ban inscription.

Substantial new sections of the Wu Ban stele inscription appeared in later received editions of Hong Gua's *Li shi*, making the stele text now eighty to ninety percent comprehensible (contrast Ouyang Xiu). The stele text is relatively the same in many of the *Li shi* editions, but starting with Wang Rixiu's (eighteenth century) Lousong shuwu collated edition in 1777, Hong Gua's appended commentary was expanded to include part of his comments on the Wu Liang stele and the gate-pillar inscription, as well as other materials.[69]

Other problems of the Wu Ban inscription include internal discrepancies, anachronisms, and the possible reading of the character *wu* not as a family name, but as part of a military designation. Further beclouding matters, two different characters for "Ban" are used: in received versions of the *Jigu lu*, *Jigu mulu*, and *Jinshi lu*, the character for Ban is often

Fig. 6 *Wu Ban stele, detail of recarved characters "Jianhe yuan nian . . . ."* Ca. second century CE. Wuzhai Shan site, Jiaxiang County, Shandong. Photo by author, 2004.

written with a two-stroke knife component in the center, whereas in received versions of the *Li shi*, it mostly appears written with a four-stroke *wen* component in the center. In modern transcriptions of the inscription, the second character form is usually used to identify Wu Ban.[70] This only begins to touch on the complexity of the problems in identifying this transmitted stele inscription and the other "Wu family shrines" transmitted inscriptions.[71]

Whether as inscription on stone or as transmitted text, therefore, the identification of the Wu Ban stele recovered by Huang Yi cannot be verified. After 1786, when the two sets of evidence were declared a match, the stone transforms from near total indecipherability to almost full comprehensibility. The actual stone and the received texts, each unverifiable alone, intertwine to reinforce an appearance of mutual authenticity. The Wu Ban stele presents some of the most complicated and convoluted problems surrounding the identification of the "Wu family shrines." These problems, glossed above, will be examined again in the author's "Reconfiguring" and in Nylan's "Addicted to Antiquity," along with questions concerning the textual and visual transmission of the other inscriptions and pictorial images.

A reassessment of the Wu shrines both as physical stones and as transmitted textual and visual evidence is needed as a cautionary check, or corrective step, at a moment when the field of "Wu family shrine" studies has already produced a substantial body of modern scholarship on interpreting and understanding the calligraphic inscriptions and pictorial images. It is unlikely that the validity of this body of work will be much affected by the present analysis, which may help qualify certain aspects of the problem and which attempts to raise new questions for future research. Before proceeding, it will be necessary to set the stage by reviewing the story of the stones—their recorded history from discovery through identification, preservation, and reconstruction.

Story of the Stones—Problems of Identification

The craft of recarving, retelling, and reenvisioning the past entails both compilation and collation. Regarding the Wu cemetery pictorial stones, what is recarved are the stories on the stones as well as stories about the stones. Stone serves as an artistic, archaeological, architectural, historical, and literary medium upon which the stories are written and retold. Recarving cannot be separated from the artistic, technical, and cultural processes of recreating stories and duplicating embodied images (*ti xiang*) of the exemplary patterns of heaven-and-earth (*tian di*).[72] As past stories are interpreted, they are recarved as new embodied images, and creative choices must be made in style, composition, and technique. Each choice adds a layer of interpretation and recarving. Furthermore, at the moment of recarving, accommodations must also be made for external requirements, such as ritual program and architectural function, as well as workshop and building practices. Beyond the original carving of physical stone, the stones themselves also can be said to participate in the making of their story. They become central actors, both coloring and obscuring their own cultural history.

That history starts with the discovery of the stones in 1786. Before Huang Yi conflated the stones with the "Wu family shrines" assemblage, the latter had been unconnected with any specific site or actual stones. Ouyang Xiu and Ouyang Fei did not name any location for the stones. In *Jinshi lu* Zhao Mingcheng reported that many of the stones, not including the Wu Rong stele, were located in the Song-dynasty area of Rencheng in Jizhou Prefecture.[73] This fairly vague reference can mean that the stones were found either in the city of Rencheng (present-day Jining) or, more broadly, in the Rencheng area, which in the Song dynasty included present-day Jiaxiang and the nearby site where the 1786 stones were recovered. In Hong Gua's *Li shi* the site's location is equally vague.[74] It was these Song-dynasty scholars who brought the "Wu family shrines" assemblage together geographically, but curiously none of the writers seems ever to have visited an actual site or examined actual stones.

Two other accounts, one in the Southern Song period and the other in the Yuan dynasty, have sometimes been associated with the "Wu family shrines" and their possible location. In *Xuezhai zhanbi* (*Learning studio of careless study*), Shi Shengzu (act. 1190–1241) recorded that his grandfather Shi Zijian, a native of Sichuan Province, compiled the *Li ge* (*Clerical-script standards*) in one fascicle, in order to supplement lacunae in Hong Gua's writings on clerical-script inscriptions. He cites an entry from the *Li ge* describing how his grandfather in 1167 examined rubbings of three pictorial wall slabs of a stone chamber (*shishi*) found at a cemetery in Dongzhou (in present-day Shandong). The slabs were carved with fine clerical-script characters not larger than five to six *fen* inches and with crude designs of exemplary figures similar in subject to those found in the "Wu Liang Shrine." There are differences, however, between Shi Zijian's description and the "Wu Liang Shrine" stones, so it is unclear if he returned to Sichuan with rubbings of Wu cemetery stones or of some other Shandong stone chamber. Because of Shi Zijian's focus on clerical script, however, he likely made rubbings only of the calligraphic inscriptions, ignoring the pictorial figures. Writing some twenty years later, Shi Shengzu noted his own early frustration at having only rubbings and not being able to view the actual stones, not knowing where they were located. Subsequently, according to Shi Shengzu, the stones were found, badly eroded, in front of the Boya Tang hall of the provincial office at Zizhou in Sichuan. Shi Shengzu provided a copy of his grandfather's clerical-script rubbings so that they might be "filled in to be as clear as new" (*tian zhi ming xin*), but did not know if this was ever done.[75] Clearly this was not the same set of stones as those of the "Wu family shrines" in Shandong, but Shi Shengzu's record did not rule out the possibility that both were carved after a similar carved stone or calligraphy model, and during the Qing dynasty it evoked speculation as to the relationship between the Sichuan and Shandong sets of materials.[76]

In his *Qian Hou Shishi huaxiang ba* (*Colophon to the pictorial images of Front and Rear Stone Chambers*), Huang Yi quotes from a 1344 cliff inscription in the Hong Shan mountains.

> A Hong Shan mountain stone cliff has a Yuan inscription saying: "In the fourth year of the Zhizheng reign-period, [flooding] was extremely

> bewildering and devastating." At that time turbulent rushing muddy waters completely destroyed the [Wu shrine] stone chambers and silt piled up to one *zhang* rod in depth. Today all the stones each have to be sought underground.[77]

The story that the stones of the "Wu family shrines" assemblage were buried by flooding in the Song and Yuan dynasties has been commonly repeated.[78] Throughout history the Jiaxiang area has indeed been subject to river flooding and earthquakes. Earthquakes may have collapsed or damaged the structures; more significantly, they probably caused flooding of the Yellow River and Juye marshes, which submerged the site. Earthquakes and flooding also brought about famine and refugee conditions, giving rise to banditry and rebel movements in the region, a concatenation of calamities that would inevitably reduce the care of ancient relics.[79] The excerpt from the 1344 inscription cited by Huang Yi, however, records only devastating floods in the area of the Hong Shan mountains; the remainder of the inscription may well have said nothing about the "Wu family shrines" or even stone chambers. The following sentence, which gives the impression that the 1344 flooding was the direct cause of the destruction of the Wu shrines, is probably Huang Yi's comment, though later scholarship has often read it as part of the 1344 inscription.[80] Even if that sentence were part of the Yuan inscription, according to distances given in the gazetteer, the Hong Shan mountains and the Wu cemetery were at least 8 *li* miles apart.[81] Without the full cliff inscription, it is impossible to know if the "stone chambers" referred to by Huang Yi were local structures in the Hong Shan mountains, or all stone chambers in the flood zone, or the stone carvings recovered at Ziyun Shan, or (an intriguing possibility) a Wu family stone chamber located near the Hong Shan mountains.

Song, Yuan, Ming, and early Qing sources make no mention of actual stone carvings or of a specific site for the "Wu family shrines" assemblage. Only in 1786, when Huang Yi claimed to have located carved stone relics in the northwest foothills of the Ziyun Shan hills, does the story of the stones and their conflation with the assemblage begin. The earliest tale of their discovery, identification, and preservation is found in Huang Yi's *Brief Record* (see Appendix). The *Brief Record* was carved on one or more stone tablets and kept at the cemetery site until it disappeared sometime after 1907.[82] Although parts of the record text are vague and at times ambiguous, it presents an invaluable firsthand report of the initial recovery of the stone relics. For this reason the *Brief Record* should be analyzed in great detail in order to try to piece together what stones were actually found, and where, when, and how, before attempting any architectural reconstruction of the cemetery layout. In reading the *Brief Record* it is also important to note that Huang Yi describes the site as if he were approaching it from the south. In other words, indications of front correspond to south, rear to north, and left to west.

On the discovery of the stones, the *Brief Record* begins in the eighth month of 1786. In what was most likely a version of the *Jiaxiang Xian zhi* (*Jiaxiang County gazetteer*), Huang Yi noticed a report saying that "in the Ziyun Shan hills there is a Western Han tomb of a crown prince" (*Ziyun Shan Xihan taizi mu*), with three stone offering halls (*xiang tang*) whose walls still protrude aboveground.[83] Alternatively, this line has usually been read as "west of Ziyun Shan is a Han tomb of a crown prince" (*Ziyun Shan xi Han taizi mu*), which roughly accords with the location of Huang Yi's discovered cemetery to the northwest of the hills. The offering halls bore pictorial carvings of exemplary figures and omens on their stone walls, and there was also a Han stele whose inscription was no longer distinguishable. With this information, Huang Yi initiated a search for the supposed tomb of a Han crown prince, and obtained rubbings of pictorial stones and of a stele. He then identified the newly acquired rubbings with the "Wu family shrine" assemblage. In particular, Huang said that the rubbings of some pictorial carvings matched those of the Wu Liang Shrine, and that the rubbing of the illegible stele corresponded to the Wu Ban stele. Although it is not known what materials Huang Yi used as a point of comparison, his *Xiaopenglai Ge jinshi wenzi* of 1785 reproduced the so-called Tang Rubbing, which showed fourteen pictorial scenes from the Wu Liang Shrine. As mentioned in the *Brief Record*, he also had access to editions of Zhao Mingcheng's *Jinshi lu* and Hong Gua's *Li shi*.

If the gazetteer report was correct, the ruins of at least three stone chambers may still have been standing in 1786, along with partly buried gate-pillars with their tops exposed to a height of three *chi* feet. Flooding may have submerged the structures at times, but when the water receded, their tops stood exposed. They were not lost but had become unmarked and their original identity forgotten.[84] At this point in the story, though, Huang Yi only had rubbings, supposedly of the tomb of a Han crown prince, that had been brought to him; he had not yet seen the actual stone carvings. This either means that whomever he had sent to find the rubbings had actually pinpointed the site and uncovered stones in order to make rubbings, or that the rubbings had been purchased in the marketplace or from some private collection. The former alternative is more likely, because as soon as Huang Yi identified the rubbings with descriptions of the "Wu family shrines," in the very next month, he and his team were on site gathering the stones. When the site was located in 1786, parts of the structures probably survived in some architectural form. In harvesting his relics, Huang Yi and his associates proceeded to dismantle whatever existed without regard for its architectural arrangement.[85] The subsequent grouping of the recovered stones shows unawareness of the significance of the original architectural condition. Some stones were incorrectly grouped, and certain slabs, such as the "Confucius Meeting Laozi" stone, were singled out for their pictorial content and not grouped or stored with the others. Moreover, many architectural slabs were not recorded, and some stones were given away as gifts.

According to the *Brief Record*, the cemetery site was located some thirty *li* miles south of the Jiaxiang county seat near a hill commonly know in the Qing dynasty as Wuzhai Shan ("Wu Residence Hill") or Wu Zhai Shan ("Martial Zhai Hill").[86] This hill is is part of the Ziyun Shan range, and is sometimes called by that name. The range runs southwest to northeast and is shaped like a saddle, with two peaks at each end and a depression in the middle. The Wuzhai Shan hill is the southwest peak. On its north slope was a village called Wuzhai Cun or Wuzhaishan Cun, and the stone ruins were located in the northwest foothills. By calling the hill Wuzhai

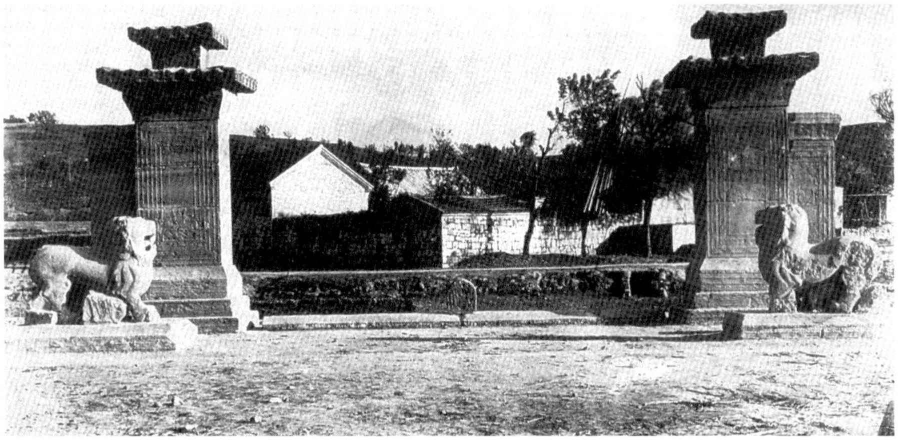

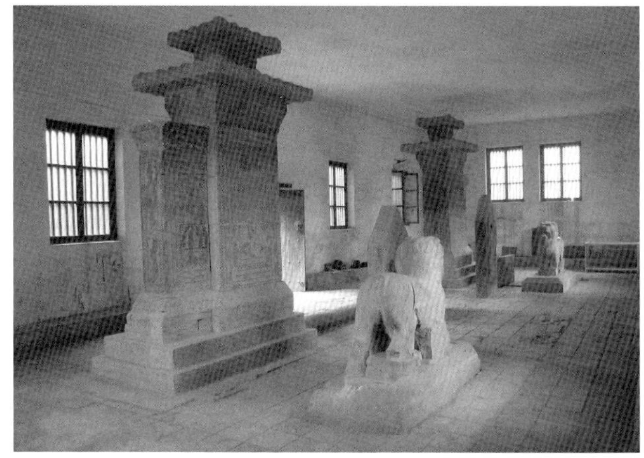

Shan ("Wu Residence Hill"), Huang Yi implied it was associated with the "Wu family shrines." But it is just as likely that the characters meaning Wu Residence can also be written as Martial Zhai, referring to a Zhai family.[87] How long before the Qing dynasty the names Wu Residence or Martial Zhai were applied to the hill or village we do not know, but a prominent Zhai family with military connections resided in this vicinity during the Song dynasty. This suggests that the hill may actually be named after the Zhai family, in which case the character *wu* likely signifies a military role.[88]

In contrast, there are few Han-dynasty records of people named Wu in the Jiaxiang area. There was a Wu family in Pei (present-day area of Xuzhou, Jiangsu) over one hundred kilometers south of Jiaxiang. This was apparently a consort family that included high military and civil officeholders during the Wei and Western Jin dynasties. Shortly after the Western Jin emperor Huidi assumed the throne in 290, three generations of the Wu family of Pei were executed on trumped-up charges of treason.[89] One possible indication of relationship between the "Wu family shrines" and the Pei area occurs in the Wu Ban stele inscription. Leading the donor list at the end of the inscription is the Attendant to the Secretariat (*shangshu cheng*) of Pei, Xiao Caozhi. But if the "Wu family shrines" had indeed been connected with this family centered in Pei, one would expect their shrines or tombs to have been destroyed or defaced in 290. Such a connection also may be the reason why there is no mention of the Wu shrines in Li Daoyuan's *Shuijing zhu*. In addition, in 165 orders had been issued to destroy shrines (*ci*) in the provinces, but it is not known how many shrines were actually demolished. Sima Guang (1019–1086) interpreted this order as aimed at unacceptable observances and abuses (*yinsi*).[90]

Huang Yi's *Brief Record* goes on to say that the cemetery ruins were buried by Yellow River flooding. It then lists the recovered stone carvings, dividing them into two main groups, those believed to match stones recorded in Zhao Mingcheng's *Jinshi lu* and Hong Gua's *Li shi*, and those previously unrecorded. The 1786 stones, along with additional stones found in 1789, were later assigned inventory numbers, which were carved on each stone. This numbering, usually attributed to Huang Yi, was based on the number of individual stones and their supposed relative positions when found. Revised numbering and inventory systems have since been devised by Wilma Fairbank, Jiang Yingju with Wu Wenqi, and others (see Tables and Foldouts).[91] Because confusion generated by these multiple systems has influenced the story of the stones, we must investigate anew when and where each stone was found.

Those stones that Huang Yi believed to have been previously recorded by Zhao Mingcheng and Hong Gua, he further subdivided into four groups: (1) three pictorial stones in five pieces forming the Wu Liang Shrine Group (cat. nos. 1.35–1.37), (2) the "Confucius Meeting Laozi" stone (cat. no. 1.4), (3) a pair of gate-pillars (figs. 7, 8, and cat. nos. 1.43–1.45), and (4) the Wu Ban stele (cat. nos. 1.46, 1.47). The three Wu Liang Shrine stones were assigned the Huang Yi (HY) numbers Wu Liang Ci 1 to 3 (WLC.1–.3), and in later architectural reconstructions correspond to the south, east, and west walls, respectively.[92] The Wu Liang Shrine Group formed the focal point around which Huang Yi postulated the

Fig. 7 *Early 1960s photograph of Wu cemetery stone felines, gate-pillars, and barrier with round-topped stone marker*. Wuzhai Shan site, Jiaxiang County, Shandong. From Zhu Xilu, ed., *Wushi Ci Han huaxiang shi*, p. 73, fig. 75.

Fig. 8 *Interior of front exhibition hall with stone felines, gate-pillars, and barrier*. Wuzhai Shan site, Jiaxiang County, Shandong. Photo by author, 2004.

relative positions of many of the other stones, yet its own location at the site is not specified in the *Brief Record*. This forms a major obstacle to reconstructing the cemetery layout.

The find-site of the "Confucius Meeting Laozi" stone was also never recorded, though it was said to have been found at the site. The *Brief Record* notes that, because of its revered subject, it was removed to the Minglun Tang hall in the Jining Prefectural Academy by Huang Yi with the assistance of the Jining Department Magistrate (*zhizhou*) Liu Yongquan.[93] An inscription was carved on the stone, noting that Zheng Wenzong and Li Dongqi (courtesy name Tieqiao) helped supervise its installation at the Academy.[94]

According to the *Brief Record*, the pair of stone gate-pillars stood opposite each other, but their position in relation to the Wu Liang Ci Group was not noted. When found, the pillars were buried, with only three *chi* feet exposed aboveground. Huang Yi's team dug down some eight to nine *chi* feet to reveal the top of the base stones, but no effort was made to raise or move the pillars at this time.

The *Brief Record* also records that the Wu Ban stele was found to the north of the gate-pillars, lying flat on the ground beside a road or path. This location outside the cemetery gate-pillars, if original, is odd. Most modern reconstructions of the cemetery layout place the steles inside the gate-pillars.[95] As Huang Yi noted, however, local lore indicated that this stele was recovered several decades earlier by villagers at some other location and moved to its find-site. The *Brief Record* also makes clear that at the time the cemetery was rediscovered, the Wu Rong stele was already housed at the Jining Prefectural Academy. The origins and history of this stele are also unclear.

Many of the previously unrecorded pictorial stones Huang Yi divided into three main groups: a Rear Stone Chamber Group, Front Stone Chamber Group, and Good Omen Picture Stones. According to the *Brief Record*, the Rear Group comprised seven pictorial stones found to the rear (*hou*), i.e., "to the northeast," of the Wu Liang Shrine Group. This stated equivalence between "rear" and "northeast" confirms that Huang Yi described the site as it appeared on approach from the south or southwest. In determining his initial approach to the site, Huang Yi may have been guided by the common notion that Chinese architecture generally faces south. In mountain settings, however, buildings and tombs were often oriented with their backs to the peak, regardless of the direction this required them to face. These seven pictorial stones were later assigned the Huang Yi numbers Rear Stone Chamber (Hou Shishi) 1 to 7 (R.1–R.7) (cat. nos. 1.17, 1.18, 1.20, 1.22, 1.32–1.34).

As reported in the *Brief Record*, two additional pictorial stones were found two *li* miles away from the site. Huang Yi listed them separately, yet by 1789 these two stones were integrated into the Rear Group as slabs R.8 and R.9 (cat. nos. 1.19, 1.30, 1.31).[96] Their carved pictorial surfaces are more worn and damaged than those of the other Rear Group stones.

The *Wu jia lin* ("Wu Family Grove") broken stone column is recorded in the *Brief Record* as found "alongside" the Rear Group stones, but it is not clear in which direction. Though often listed at the end of the Rear Group, it was not included in any group or assigned a number. It received

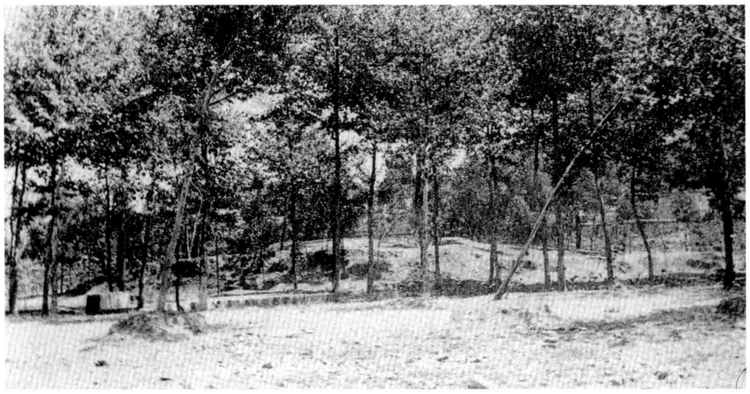

its name from the three characters *wu jia lin* carved in standard-script (*zhengshu*) calligraphy on one face (cat. no. 1.42). Because standard script is said to have developed in the Period of Disunity, Huang Yi believed the characters were probably added in the Wei or Qi dynasties. A photograph taken in about 1980 shows a burial mound above Tomb 1 that is located in a tree grove at the eastern sector of the site (fig. 9).[97] Since Huang Yi's identification of the site with the "Wu family shrine" assemblage, it has been commonly believed that *wu jia lin* refers to this wooded area and designates a Wu Family Grove. Alternatively, if the hill backing the site was actually named after a Zhai family, then *wu jia lin* can be understood as the Grove of the Martial [Zhai] Family. There are other possibilities. The site has also been known as the Grove of Sovereigns or Forest of Emperors (Huang Lin), which may refer to the legendary exemplary rulers—Three Sovereigns (San Huang) and Five Emperors (Wu Di)—who are depicted in the Wu Liang Shrine stones. Perhaps the stone carvings were originally part of some temple or offering complex dedicated to these exemplars, some of whom were local figures.[98] In particular, could the stones have been part of a nearby Yu Huang Ge ("Jade Emperor Pavilion") temple hall, which was charged with the upkeep of the recovered stones during parts of the Qing dynasty?[99]

Past records noted the *Wu jia lin* column chiefly for its three carved characters. It may not have been until 1981 that the column was fully described and reproduced. The actual column has a front side carved with a vertical band of joined-arc designs (*lian hu wen*) on the left and two plain bands to the right. The *wu jia lin* characters are carved on the otherwise plain left face. On the right face are two climbing figures above a scaly dragon. The back face was left rough, indicating that it abutted another stone. In their 1995 reconstruction of the Wu Liang Shrine structure, Jiang Yingju and Wu Wenqi speculated that this column may have supported the roof eaves at the front of the structure's east wall.[100] The column, however, was not found with the Wu Liang Shrine Group stones, and its 13.5 centimeter width is narrower than the thickness of any wall slab found at the site.

According to the *Brief Record*, fourteen pictorial stones constituted a Front Stone Chamber (Qian Shishi). Huang Yi noted that they were inscribed with at least 160 characters in *bafen* clerical-script calligraphy. In contrast, only traces of a few characters remained discernible on the Rear Group stones. The inventory numbers assigned in 1789, however, indicate only twelve stones, which were later designated as Front Stone Chamber 1 to 12 (F.1–F.12) (cat. nos. 1.1–1.3, 1.5–1.16). Like the Rear Group Stones R.8 and R.9, three stones among the Front Group have more than one pictorial face. Stones F.10 and F.11 are "turning-corner stones" (*zhuan jiao shi*), with pictorial carvings on perpendicular surfaces, and Stone F.8 is an interior triangular partition gable with designs on opposite faces. This means that the twelve surviving stones afford a total of fifteen pictorial surfaces. Although this agrees with Wilma Fairbank's numbering of the Front Group, it does not explain Huang Yi's initial count of fourteen stones. In describing the Rear Group, Huang Yi had been careful to count only the number of stones, not the number of pictorial faces. It is possible that in 1786 Huang Yi found fourteen stones in the Front Group, but only

Fig. 9 *Burial mound above Tomb 1*. Wuzhai Shan site, Jiaxiang County, Shandong. Photo ca. 1980. From Jiang and Wu, *Handai Wushi muqun shike yanjiu*, p. 143, pl. 10.

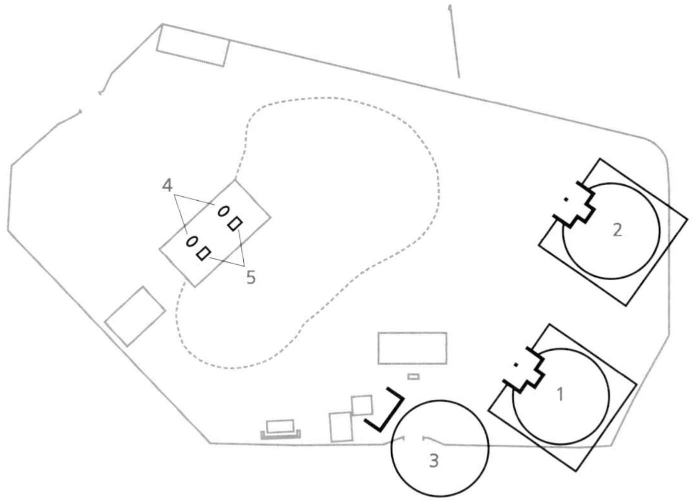

1 Front Group: Stone Chamber 1, Tomb 2
2 Rear/Left Group: Stone Chamber 2, Tomb 1
3 Wu Liang Group: Stone Chamber 3, possible tomb
4 Stone Felines
5 Gate-pillars

twelve stones were finally installed in the Wu Family Shrine (Wushi Citang) Preservation Hall that was built between about 1789 and 1792.[101] The two missing stones may be among the stones that Huang Yi gave as gifts to potential patrons and donors. These included a column capital with pictorial designs and inscribed characters that was given to Ruan Yuan, and a broken round stone column with pictorial carvings that will be discussed later. Other possibilities: the two missing stones may have been shifted from the Front Group to be included among the many stones that Huang Yi found at the site but did not record, or they may have been lost or destroyed.

From the *Brief Record*, it is not clear where at the site the Front Group stones were found.[102] Reading the text sequentially, if the Rear Group and the *Wu jia lin* stone column were "northeast" of the Wu Liang Shrine, then the Front Group was to the south. This would place the Front Group to the southeast or east of the Wu Liang Shrine Group (fig. 10). On the other hand, if the directional point of reference in the *Brief Record* is understood to center on the Wu Liang Shrine stones, then the Front Group is "to its front" in the south (possibly southeast). It is possible to tentatively reconstruct the architectural layout of the cemetery site by reading this account in relation to later descriptions of the site and the excavated locations of Tombs 1 and 2 (discussed in Liu's "Reconfiguring" in this catalogue).

The previously unrecorded pictorial stones in the third group were later assigned the titles Good Omen Picture (*xiangrui tu*) Stones 1 and 2 (Good Omen.1 and .2) (cat. nos. 1.38–1.41). Good Omen.1, "extremely worn" but unbroken when discovered in 1786, was said to have been "lying on the ground for a long time." Huang Yi recorded that the cartouche inscriptions were barely legible.[103] Unfortunately he did not indicate where this stone was found. Three fragments of Good Omen.2 were retrieved to the "north of the Wu Liang stone chamber." The pictorial carvings on these fragments survived in better condition, and Huang Yi noted at least 130 characters inscribed in their cartouches. Because these stones are similar in design, dimensions, and architectural construction, and in the roof tiles carved on their backs, and because of their proximity to the Wu Liang Shrine Group, these two Omen slabs were most probably roof slabs for that group.[104]

The *Brief Record* provides no clear picture of where at the site the stones were recovered. Huang Yi also painted several illustrations of his discovery of the "Wu family shrine" stones, entitled *Searching for Steles at Ziyun Shan* (*Ziyun Shan tanbei tu*). One version is included in the album *Illustrations of Obtaining Steles* (*Debei tu*), with several inscriptions including a colophon and preface dated to 1793 (fig. 11).[105] This album belonged to the Tianjin collector Xu Shizhang (d. 1954), who also owned a set of Wu shrine rubbings made by Huang Yi and a pictorial stone from the cemetery that Huang Yi had presented as a gift to Ruan Yuan. After Xu Shizhang died, these items entered the Tianjin Municipal Museum of Art.[106] Huang Yi also made handscroll paintings of the *Searching for Steles at Ziyun Shan* scene. There are records of one handscroll with a poem, dated to 1787, which may no longer survive, and of a second handscroll dated after 1791.[107] Huang Yi painted many such albums and handscrolls,

Fig. 10 *Site reconstruction map*. Drawing showing possible locations of Front, Left/Rear, and Wu Liang Groups as found by Huang Yi, and locations of Stone Chambers 1, 2, 3. Based on survey map of the Wu site in 1981; see Jiang and Wu, *Handai Wushi muqun shike yanjiu*, p. 2, fig. 2.

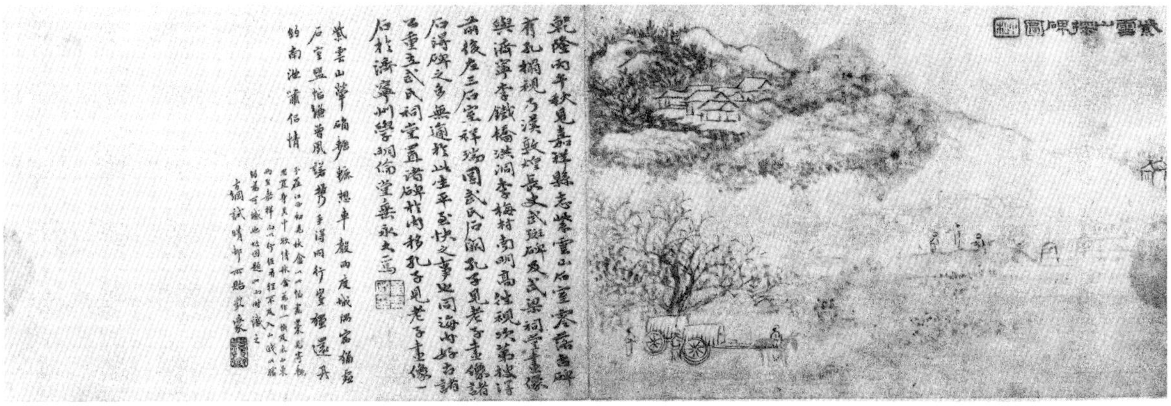

some in multiples, to document his searches for steles and relics. One such work is an album of preliminary sketches entitled *Seeking Steles on Mount Tai* (*Tai Dai fangbei tu*) in the collection of the Princeton University Art Museum (cat. no. 64).

The Tianjin Museum's *Searching for Steles at Ziyun Shan* album leaf has colophons by Huang Yi and Weng Fanggang (fig. 11). The tops of the gate-pillars protrude from the ground at the right side of the painting. Three figures stand to their left. Behind them to the left is a cluster of carved stones lying on, or protruding from, the ground. Left of the three figures, a *gui*-tablet stele with a hole, representing the Wu Ban stele, can be discerned lying flat on the ground.[108] The distant hill at far left must be Wuzhai Shan, and halfway up the slope is a cluster of buildings that indicates the village of Wuzhaishan Cun. The painting is very schematic, illustrating only the items that were important to Huang Yi: the gate-pillars, pictorial stones, and Wu Ban stele. The pictorial stones are not differentiated into groups, and the relative positions of the items are not distinguished. As expected, the pictorial stones are shown between the gate-pillars to the northwest and the southeast hill. The Wu Ban stele should have been depicted outside the gate-pillars (i.e., to their right), but Huang Yi took artistic liberties and moved it to their left.

Huang Yi's *Brief Record* and his paintings both document his discovery of the ruins found at the Wuzhai Shan site, thirty *li* miles south of the Jiaxiang county seat. Here for the first time text and visual records identifying a "Wu family shrines" assemblage are linked to actual stone carvings and a geographic site. But not without confusion. Various sources record the distance between Jiaxiang and Wuzhai Shan differently.[109] In addition, Huang Yi misleadingly stated that "Jiaxiang in the Han dynasty was the location of Rencheng," and in support he paraphrases Zhao Mingcheng as saying that "there are several tombs of the Wu family in Rencheng." As noted earlier, however, in the mid Eastern Han dynasty the present-day Jiaxiang area was under the jurisdiction of Shanyang Commandery, and not Rencheng Kingdom.[110] What Zhao Mingcheng actually said in the *Jinshi lu* was that many of the "Wu family shrine" stones were located in the Song-dynasty area of Rencheng in Jizhou Prefecture. This means that the stones were found either in the city of Rencheng (present-day Jining) or in its vicinity, which during the Northern Song probably included the area of present-day Jiaxiang. Huang Yi's reference to a Han-dynasty Jiaxiang, moreover, is anachronistic, because the city first received that name during the Jin dynasty.[111] If, on the other hand, Huang Yi was correct in locating the Wu cemetery within the Han-dynasty Rencheng Kingdom, then the recovered pictorial slabs and cemetery site found in the former Han-dynasty Shanyang Commandery area may not correspond to the recorded Wu shrines, or they may have been moved there from Rencheng. Giving Huang Yi the benefit of the doubt, he probably meant that the Han-dynasty cemetery and the place that would later be called Jiaxiang were close to the better-known city called Rencheng during the Qing dynasty. Regardless of the Jiaxiang-Rencheng muddle, Huang Yi's focus was unquestionably the stones he recovered at the Wuzhai Shan site.

Brief Record continues with a discussion of proposals for the care of the stones. Huang Yi would have liked to move all the stones to Jining, yet

Fig. 11 Huang Yi (1744–1802). *Searching for Steles at Ziyun Shan*. Leaf in the album *Illustrations of obtaining steles* (1793); ink on paper. Tianjin Municipal Museum of Art. From *Tianjin Shi yishu bowuguan cang hua ji*, vol. 2, p. 148.

the number of stones and their sizes made this unfeasible. It was decided to transport only the Wu Ban stele and "Confucius Meeting Laozi" stone to join the Wu Rong stele already housed in the Minglun Tang hall at the Jining Prefectural Academy. The Wu Ban stele proved too big to be moved, but "Confucius Meeting Laozi" was successfully relocated.[112] In order to protect the stones remaining at the site, plans were made to build a plain stone preservation hall under the supervision of Huang Yi's acquaintances Li Dongqi, Li Kezheng (style name [*hao*] Meicun), and Nan Zhengyan (style name[?] Minggao).[113] Donations were to be collected and the donors credited in a carved inscription to be composed by a "venerable master." It becomes clear that the *Brief Record*, written in the sixth month of 1787, was respectfully addressed as an entreaty to the venerable master Weng Fanggang, who four months later responded with *Chong li Wushi Ci shi ji* (*Record on rebuilding the Wu Family Shrine stones*) (cat. no. 1.51).[114] Weng Fanggang also became a major donor to the project, and his relationship with Huang Yi, their circle of mutual acquaintances, and their shared antiquarian interests and activities all deserve further investigation. Were Huang Yi's local activities as a procurer of antiquities officially or privately patronized by Weng Fanggang at court? Were there financial arrangements or promises of career advancement? As the most prominent figure among this circle, Weng Fanggang's connection to the recovery of the stones would sometimes be exaggerated in later stories.

In 1789, during construction of the Preservation Hall, several other stone carvings came to light. According to Huang Yi's *Zuo Shishi huaxiang ba* (*Colophon to the Left Stone Chamber pictorial images*), ten pictorial stones were recovered by Li Kezheng and Liu Zhaoyong (style name [?] Guixian).[115] Nine of the stones were found to the "left" (*zuo*) of the Wu Liang Ci Group, and they were assigned the inventory numbers Left Stone Chamber (Zuo Shishi) Stones 2 to 10 (L.2–L.10) (cat. nos. 1.21, 1.23–1.29). What direction corresponds to "left," however, is not specified. In this instance, by convention Huang Yi probably faced south, the direction the emperor faces, and left would be to the east. This would place the Left Group stones in close proximity with the Rear Group, which had been found to the northeast of the Wu Liang Shrine Group. A combination of Left Group slabs (found in 1789) and Rear Group slabs (found in 1786) were later brought together by Jiang Yingju and Wu Wenqi to form the reconstructed two-bay Left Stone Chamber, which tends to corroborate their original close proximity. Moreover, no Left Group stone fits into modern reconstructions of any of the other structures at the site.

Besides these nine Left Group stones (L.2–L.10), all found at the site, another pictorial stone, found elsewhere, was integrated into the Left Group as Stone 1 (L.1) (cat. no. 1.48). This rectangular slab had been reused as a component of a village bridge and had a construction hole drilled through its center.[116] Along with Stones R.8 and R.9, found two *li* miles away from the site, L.1 must also have been discovered by local villagers and brought to Huang Yi and his team at the cemetery site. Stylistic similarities probably caused this off-site stone to be counted among the Left Group, and it was so labeled, with an inscription by Li Dongqi added at the right end of the slab by 1789.[117] Modern architectural reconstructions of the three stone chambers at the site, however, do not support this attribution, and in 1880 this stone, along with another fragment, was identified as part of a longer stone.[118]

Among the Left Group, Stones L.2–L.9 are still preserved at the site, but Stones L.1 and L.10 were reported missing from the site in Feng Yunpeng's *Jinshi suo* (1821). Stone L.10 is said to be no longer extant, and L.1 was reportedly sold abroad in the early twentieth century and its present whereabouts is unknown.[119] Stone L.10 was described as a horizontal slab, three *cun* inches high and six *chi* feet wide, and was possibly placed under a front roof eaves. It was decorated with linked *wuzhu* coin designs and had pictorial images at both ends.[120]

Two additional pictorial stones were found away from the cemetery and brought to the site for storage by Li Dongqi and others in autumn 1789. One broken slab, found about three *li* miles south of the site by the side of the road, has become known as the South Road Stone.[121] Decorated with rows of armed equestrian figures, chariots, and a foot soldier chasing or following fleeing birds and animals at far right, and with imitation roof tiles carved on the back, this was a ceiling slab. The second stone was found in a tomb about a half *li* mile northeast of the site.[122] Known as the Northeast Stone, this was a turning-corner stone, with two pictorial faces.

Clearly, from 1786 on, stones found away from the cemetery were being brought to the site. It is not known if financial incentives or rewards were offered, but since the late eighteenth century pictorial stones found in the vicinity have continued to be brought to the cemetery.[123] Some of these stones, such as the South Road and Northeast Stones, were recorded with the Wu stone carvings by early scholars, while some others, such as Stones R.8, R.9, and L.1, were actually integrated into the groups of "Wu family shrines" stones found at the site. Many other stones were never recorded. In 1984 some sixty unrecorded pictorial slabs gathered from around the county were installed in a courtyard corridor at the present-day Preservation Hall compound.[124] Some of these stones may eventually prove to be missing components of the three reconstructed hall structures at the site, or parts of other structures that may have been part of the cemetery complex.

A simple total of the number of stones recovered by 1792, when the first Wu Family Shrine (Wushi Citang) Preservation Hall was completed, is difficult to provide. The criteria used for counting differ from source to source. Some sources count whole stones, others count the number of individual fragments, and some count the number of pictorial surfaces. In addition, the stele stones, gate-pillars, and *Wu jia lin* column are included by some but not by others. It is also likely that some stones were already lost or removed by 1792, and other unrecorded stones, such as the blank stele, may have entered the count at various times. A 1792 inscription by Qian Yong (1759–1844), probably carved to commemorate completion of the Preservation Hall (cat. no. 1.53), lists a total of forty-three stones.[125] In this brief inscription the Wu Ban stele and *Wu jia lin* column are counted, but not the gate-pillars or "Confucius Meeting Laozi" stone. In addition, the Good Omen stones were noted as four fragments (not two), and the Front Group was listed as comprising fourteen stones—actually twelve stones, two of which have two pictorial faces, for a total of fourteen. This explanation of the Front Group attempts to reconcile the fourteen stones recorded in Huang Yi's 1787 *Brief Record* with the twelve stones inventoried in 1789 and 1792. Qian Yong's explanation is not completely satisfactory because there are actually three double-faced stones, or fifteen pictorial faces, in the Front Group. As noted earlier, by 1789 the two missing stones may already have been given away as gifts by Huang Yi, shifted into the group of unrecorded stones, or lost.

Differing from Qian Yong's inventory, the Jiaxiang District Magistrate Liu Xiaoyou counted fifty-five stones in a stele inscription carved in 1907, Rong Geng counted forty-one stones, and Wu Hung in *The Wu Liang Shrine* (1989) notes that by 1789 there were thirty-nine pictorial stones, two gate-pillars, two steles (Wu Ban and Wu Rong), and the *Wu jia lin* column.[126] Wu Hung counted whole stones, not fragments. He counted twelve slabs in the Front Group and accepted Qian Yong's supposition that Huang Yi had actually counted fourteen pictorial surfaces. Unlike Qian Yong, however, Wu Hung included the "Confucius Meeting Laozi" stone, *Wu jia lin* column, and Good Omen stones. In his count the Good Omen stones included the two slabs (one found in three fragments) found in 1786 by Huang Yi, but he also seems to have added a third Omen stone, the *You niao ru he* ("There is a bird like a crane") ceiling stone (cat. no. 1.50), which was found about a century later.

The confusion surrounding this third Omen stone is typical of the recorded history of many of the stones and their preservation. Often this stone is associated with two others, the *He kui* ("Carrying provisions") (cat. no. 1.49) and *Wang Ling mu* ("Wang Ling's mother") pictorial stones. In Rong Geng's *Han Wu Liang Ci huaxiang lu*, written in 1936, the *You niao ru he* stone was said to have been found in 1871 along with the *He kui* slab, by Xuanyuan Hua of Nanwu.[127] But a near contemporary of Xuanyuan Hua, Chen Jin, in his *Chongxiu Wushi Citang ji* (*Record on the renovation of the Wu Family Shrine* [*Preservation Hall*]) composed in 1880, notes that Xuanyuan Hua and his elder brother Xuanyuan Dai had only owned the *He kui* stone. Chen Jin had obtained a rubbing of the *He kui* stone, which showed Confucius striking stone chimes and other pictorial scenes.[128] Because of this scene, Chen Jin wanted to put this stone beside the "Confucius Meeting Laozi" stone in Jining, but the Xuanyuan brothers would not part with it. Chen also noted that his son Chen Changyi obtained a rubbing of the *Wang Ling mu* stone, allowing him to determine that it was a fragment of Stone L.1 of the Left Group. He wanted to put this stone in the Wu Family Shrine Preservation Hall, but it was owned by a Zhang family in the district (*yi*). On the promise of the District Magistrate (*da ling*) Ding Rongjiang (given name Jingshu) to purchase both the *He kui* and *Wang Ling mu* stones, Chen Jin initiated plans to repair the old Preservation Hall. Local flooding in 1879–1880 delayed the work, but the repairs were completed in 1880.[129]

From Chen Jin's *Record on the Renovation*, it is assumed that the *He kui* and *Wang Ling mu* stones were installed in the Preservation Hall at this time, but the *Record* does not mention the *You niao ru he* stone.[130] No source mentions where any of these stones were originally found, and it is uncertain when the *You niao ru he* stone came to be stored at the

Preservation Hall. It may have been stored at the site from as early as 1871, when it was said to have been found. Although several early twentieth-century authors report the stone sold or lost, it is still at the site.[131] The current whereabouts of the *He kui* and *Wang Ling mu* stones, on the other hand, are not known, and both stones were reportedly sold abroad in the early twentieth century.[132]

The relationship among the *You niao ru he*, *He kui*, and *Wang Ling mu* stones, along with Left Group Stone L.1, should be further considered. Chen Jin in 1880 had already noted that the *Wang Ling mu* and L.1 fragments were adjoining pieces of a longer horizontal stone. Stone L.1 was recovered from a local bridge, but it may have originally come from the same unknown location where the *Wang Ling mu* stone was found. In pictorial carving style these two stones are similar to the stone carvings recovered at the Wuzhai Shan cemetery. In particular, the distinctive scrolling cloud pattern (*juan yun wen*) in the top decorative border of the *Wang Ling mu* stone seems to appear nowhere else in Shandong pictorial carvings, except in the top horizontal borders on the three wall stones of the Wu Liang Shrine Group (WLC.1–.3). This lends credence to Wu Hung's observation that the *Wang Ling mu* and L.1 stones may belong to a "Fourth Chamber" associated with the Wuzhai Shan cemetery. Alternatively, they may be from a nearby site but produced by the same stone workshop. Wu Hung also links the *You niao ru he* and *He kui* stones with this putative chamber on stylistic grounds.[133] The similarity in carving techniques, pictorial themes, decorative patterns, and artistic style among these stones and those found at the cemetery indicates that a local stone-carving workshop was likely responsible for the carvings. The 1978 and 1980 discoveries of several pictorial stones carved in a similar manner at nearby Songshan Village, Jiaxiang (cat. no. 11),[134] reinforces the need to examine the regional production of pictorial stones in a workshop system (see Barbieri-Low's "Carving Out a Living" in this catalogue).

It was also about 1880 that rubbings of the "Wu family shrines" assemblage began to attract the attention of Western and Japanese audiences. The set Stephen Bushell presented in Berlin in 1881 probably did not contain rubbings of the *You niao ru he*, *He kui*, and *Wang Ling mu* stones.[135] An 1886 article by R. K. Douglas on Han sculpture contains woodcut illustrations of the Wu carvings, reproduced from Feng Yunpeng's *Jinshi suo*.[136] Examining the pictorial images, Douglas proceeded to claim precedents for many of the Chinese figures in Egyptian, Babylonian, and Greek mythology. Also on December 5, 1886 Lieutenant Dudley A. Mills, traveling on leave, became the first European to visit the site.[137] He reported seeing the stone carvings housed in the Preservation Hall that had been repaired in 1880 by Chen Jin. By this time the *He kui* and *Wang Ling mu* stones were stored at the site, and the *You niao ru he* stone was likely there as well. Mills is said to have brought back a set of rubbings, which were donated to the British Museum.[138] A couple of years later, when writing about his travels, Mills had a chance to read Douglas's 1886 article, and with bravado characterized the Wu pictorial carvings as being "in the Assyrian style."[139]

Prior to Lieutenant Mills's visit, three additional pictorial stones were found in 1882 by the Jiaxiang official Cai Renqiu (Cai Shousheng) and donated to the Preservation Hall.[140] Known as the Cai Stones 1 to 3 (Cai.1–.3), these slabs were found away from the cemetery site. The Cai.1 stone, a ceiling slab with roof tiles carved on its back, is carved on its face with aquatic deities similar to those depicted on the Wu cemetery ceiling Stone R.1 (cat. no. 1.34). An inscription by Cai Renqiu carved on the stone records that it was found in spring 1882 at a location "east of the Wuzhai Shan hill."[141] The Cai.2 stone, also a ceiling slab, depicts what may be an apotheosis scene similar to the Wu cemetery ceiling Stone R.2 (cat. no. 1.33). This stone also has roof tiles carved on its back. A carved inscription by Cai Renqiu notes that he found this slab with Gong Zengfu of Changzhou on the ninth day of the second month of 1882 and moved it into the Preservation Hall. It is unclear, however, where this slab was found.[142] The Cai.3 stone is an interior triangular partition gable with designs on opposite faces. Cai Renqiu's inscription on this stone remarks on its similarity to the "two" partition gables (F.8, R.8) (cat. nos. 1.15, 1.16 and 1.30, 1.31) found by Huang Yi. The inscription, however, does not record when or where this stone was discovered.[143] All three Cai stones were probably found away from the Wu cemetery site.

Before the next series of stones was discovered at the Wuzhai Shan cemetery, Édouard Chavannes visited, on January 27, 1891, and published his observations in *Sculpture sur pierre en Chine* (1893). Included was the first relatively complete photographic documentation of the rubbings as well as interior elevation drawings of the Preservation Hall, showing the location of the stone carvings embedded in the four walls, and a plan showing other stones scattered across the floor (fig. 14).[144] Participating in the Jacob H. Schiff Chinese Expedition of the American Museum of Natural History from 1901–1904, Berthold Laufer visited the site in January 1903, and noted that he had collected rubbings of the stones in 1901 and 1904.[145] Comparing various versions of the rubbings, he judged the early nineteenth-century woodcuts in Feng Yunpeng's *Jinshi suo* to include more detail, attributing that to the better condition of the stones. He also noted, however, that the rubbing process tended to leave layers of ink, dirt, and paper fibers on the surface of stones, which obscured details in later rubbings.[146] The implication is that there is not necessarily a direct correspondence between the sharpness and clarity of details in a rubbing and the date of the stone carving from which it was taken. What appears to be a worn stone may only be the result of rubbing deposits, and simply washing the stone may restore it to its former clarity. This only begins to hint at the difficulty in reading the relationship between rubbings and the original stones.

In the year 1907 several major expeditions headed for the cemetery, as the fame of the pictorial rubbings became better known to an international audience through rubbings and photography. Chavannes returned to the site in early July with Vassili Michaelovich Alexéief (Vasilii Mikhailovich Alekseev; 1881–1951). Chavannes published his observations, along with what are probably the earliest photographs of the site, in *Mission archéologique dans la Chine septentrionale* (1913–1915). Included in this work were translations of the west gate-pillar and four stele inscriptions, and a more complete photographic record of the rubbings. Alexéief wrote a travelogue describing the deplorable conditions in which the

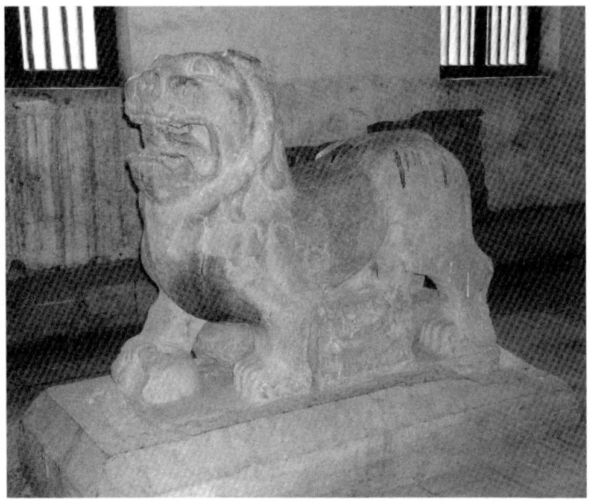

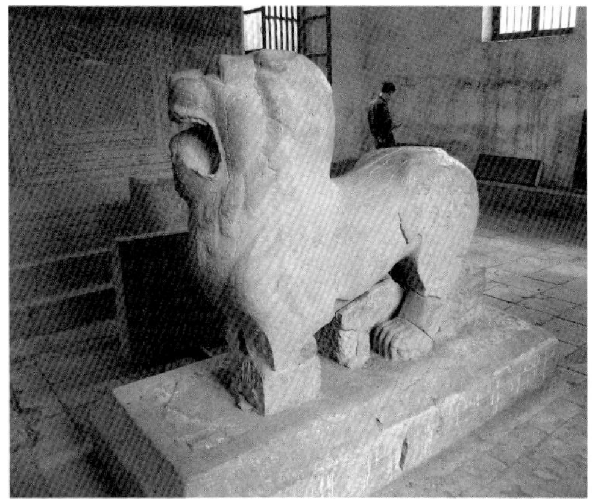

Preservation Hall was found and the poor care given to the stones by an opium addict who served as gatekeeper.[147] Working in the rain, Chavannes studied the stone carvings and was able to obtain rubbings of the gate-pillars (Chavannes, *Mission archéologique*, figs. 64–74), which had been difficult to acquire on the market except for one face (Chavannes, *Mission archéologique*, fig. 63).[148] According to Chavannes, in January 1891, while on his way from Beijing to Shanghai, he had bought rubbings of the other pictorial stones from merchants in Tainan. Having recognized the rubbings as identical to those Lieutenant Mills had acquired, he decided to make a detour to the cemetery site to verify his identification.[149] During his subsequent visit in 1907 Chavannes also made rubbings of an additional stone with three pictorial faces found in front of the southwest gate-pillar (Chavannes, *Mission archéologique*, figs. 144–46). This stone has since been identified as a capital on the southwest gate-pillar in modern reconstructions.[150] It becomes apparent that many of the rubbing sets acquired during this period, including the Princeton set (cat. no. 1), were compiled from several sources and contain different selections.

Several months after Chavannes and Alexéief were at the cemetery, on October 8, 1907, P. A. Volpert, accompanied by H. P. Mertens, came with a German expedition. Digging three paces north of the gate-pillars, Volpert is usually credited with the discovery of two stone sculptures of powerful feline creatures (figs. 12A–12B).[151] As reported in a 1931 article by Dong Jing, the sculptures were actually first discovered by Li Baoxun. Dispatched in about 1890 for service at Rencheng, Li had stopped at the site and discovered the heads of the feline sculptures in front of the gate-pillars, but did not have time to unearth them.[152] The statues were uncovered and recorded in 1907, when both Volpert and Sekino visited the site, but in about 1931 Dong Jing reported that the statues "remained deeply sunk in the muddy sediment." This suggests that, after being unearthed in 1907, the statues were reburied by renewed flooding. In a photograph of the site taken in the1940s or 1950s, flood waters surround the gate-pillars and the location of the statues (fig. 13).[153]

Each feline statue and its oblong base were originally carved as a unit from a single block; the feline stood on all four legs with its head turned slightly to the south. The male, on the east, stands with its right forepaw on top of a small curled animal, and in its open mouth its tongue curls up to touch the roof of its mouth.[154] The female feline, to the west, has mostly damaged legs, and it can no longer be determined if there was a small animal underfoot. Its tongue rests in its lower jaw. These felines with mane-like curls are usually identified as lions, because the west gate-pillar inscription records that "Sun Zong made [a pair of] lions. The cost was 40,000 [cash]" (see cat. no. 1.43). The primacy often given to texts has allowed this identification go unchallenged, yet both the early date of 147 CE contained in the inscription and the identification of the statues as lions should not go unquestioned.

Lions were not indigenous to China, and the earliest records of their introduction date to about the reign of the Eastern Han dynasty Zhang emperor (r. 74–88).[155] Because lion figures as Buddhist guardians only grew in popularity after the Han period, perhaps these early feline

Fig. 12A *Northeast stone feline*. Ca. second century CE. Wuzhai Shan site, Jiaxiang County, Shandong. Photo by author, 2004.

Fig. 12B *Southwest stone feline*. Ca. second century CE. Wuzhai Shan site, Jiaxiang County, Shandong. Photo by author, 2004.

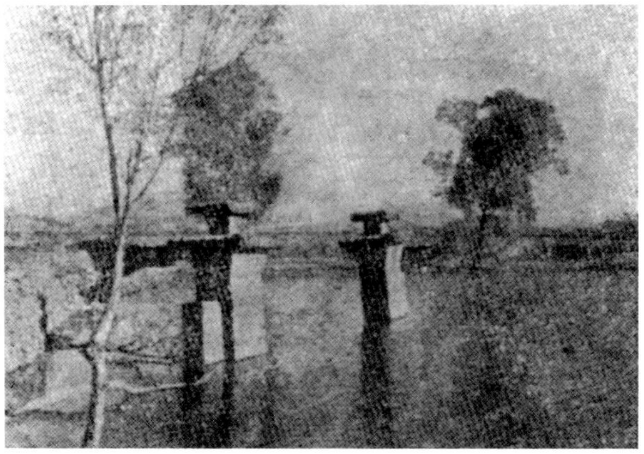

sculptures are not lions but instead represent tigers or some mythical beast with protective powers.[156] Such stylized lion-like carvings are probably not meant to represent actual lions, but were appropriated from Central or Western Asian leonine motifs.[157] The association of such exotic motifs with faraway lands "we may presume, signified something rare and precious, perhaps pertaining to the spirits, whose realms may have been thought to lie beyond the edges of the known world."[158] We must also reconsider when the southwest gate-pillar inscription at the cemetery may have been composed, carved, or recarved in part or in total (cat. no. 1.43). Note that the inscription uses the variant character *shi* (without the *quan* radical) instead of the later standard *shi* character for "lion." The variant form can refer to twin offspring of a dog or pig, and here the double or paired aspect may be what was emphasized.[159] This may also account for the feline statues' porcine snouts. The use of the variant character in the Eastern Han to designate such feline creatures is supported in another feline statue, in the collection of the Shandong Provincial Museum, that bears an inscription using the same variant character.[160]

Later in the fall of 1907, as part of a seventy-two day expedition through Shandong Province, the Japanese archaeologist Sekino Tadashi (1868–1935; also published under the romanized names Sekino Tei and Sekino Tadasu) visited the Wuzhai Shan cemetery to survey, inventory, and photograph the site. In 1909 Sekino published photographs along with map drawings of the site in a two-part preliminary report in *Kokka* art journal.[161] This report included the first published photographs of the Preservation Hall, gate-pillars, and the eastern feline statue. Also included were photographs of six rubbings as well as plan and elevation drawings of the interior of the Preservation Hall, showing the location of the stone carvings.[162] In 1916 Sekino issued a more in-depth study, with detailed observations, survey drawings, site photographs, and photographic reproductions of a compiled set of pictorial rubbings.[163]

Comparing Sekino's interior plan and elevation drawings of the Preservation Hall in 1907 with those made by Chavannes after his 1891 site visit, several differences can be noticed. The hall had a rectangular plan with a central door facing north. In the Chavannes elevation drawings (fig. 14), a total of twenty-six stones are embedded in the four walls, while in Sekino's (fig. 15) only twenty-five stones are drawn, excluding nine Qing-dynasty inscribed stone tablets. Because two stones were mistakenly drawn as if they were one, in actuality there are also twenty-six stones in the Sekino elevations, but a couple of stones differed from those recorded in Chavannes. Most of the stone carvings embedded in the four walls are in the same locations in both sets of drawings. Chavannes' drawings are more diagrammatic and do not show the nine Qing inscribed tablets and a title placard across the upper west portion of the south wall.[164] In the west section of the north wall, Stone 25 in Chavannes is absent in Sekino. In the Chavannes legend, this stone was labeled as Left Group Stone L.1. In the rubbings in *Sculpture sur pierre en Chine*, Stone L.1 was paired with its adjoining fragment, the *Wang Ling mu* stone, which may indicate that both stones were embedded at this location in 1891 and treated as a single stone. Additionally, in the east section of the north wall, Sekino's drawing shows two stones, a triangular peaked stone

Fig. 13 *Gate-pillars standing in flood waters.* Wuzhai Shan site, Jiaxiang County, Shandong. Photo 1940s or 1950s. From Chen Mingda, "Handai de shique," *Wenwu* 1961.12, p. 12, fig. 7.

on the left, and a single long rectangular slab on the right that was designated Left Chamber Stone 3 (L.3). At 13.96 *shaku* (4.23 m), this stone is about twice the length of the longest stones found at the site, and actually corresponds to two stones, L.3 and R.7, as correctly diagrammed by Chavannes.[165] The carved stones embedded in the short west and east side walls are about the same in both sets of drawings. The only exception is at the far left of the east wall, where Sekino's drawing adds a short column, 2.55 *shaku* (77.35 cm) high, with decorative bands of waves, double diamonds, and joined-arc designs. This stone probably corresponds to a slightly shorter stone fragment with similar patterns that presently survives in the Preservation Hall.[166]

The main differences between the 1891 and 1907 surveys are seen in the respective plan drawings. In Chavannes, thirteen stones—including the Wu Ban stele (plan drawing no. 15), a new inscribed stone marker (no. 16), two fragments of the second Good Omen slab counted as two individual stones (nos. 12, 13),[167] and two unidentified stones (nos. 21, 22)—are arranged in a rough concentric ring around the interior (fig. 14). In Sekino's plan the number of stones had grown to eighteen—including the Wu Ban stele, new inscribed marker, and several unidentified stones (fig. 15).[168] Besides the addition of new slabs, in 1907 the stones on the floor are scattered randomly across the interior. This rearrangement may coincide with unspecified repairs to the Preservation Hall in 1907 by the Jiaxiang District Magistrate Liu Xiaoyou.[169] In an inscription commemorating the repair work, Liu noted that there were fifty-five stones in the Preservation Hall, but did not itemize.[170] If the Qing inscribed tablets and title placard are counted, the total is close to the number of stones recorded that same year by Sekino. Any numerical discrepancy may result from how fragments of single stones were counted, or whether new stones such as the inscribed marker were included. Alternatively, the 1907 so-called repair work may very well have been the occasion when the embedded Stone L.1 and *Wang Ling mu* slab were removed from the Preservation Hall. These two stones, along with the *He kui* stone, were reported missing by Chavannes and Sekino when they visited the site in 1907.

A few of the rubbings reproduced by Sekino in 1916 were apparently acquired by the author during his 1907 travels in Shandong, but most were earlier rubbings in the collections of the Tokyo Imperial Household Museum, Imperial University of Tokyo, College of Engineering, and the family collection of Luo Zhenyu (1866–1940). In the instance of Front Group Stone 9 (F.9), an "old rubbing" (Sekino fig. 96) is juxtaposed beside a "modern rubbing" (Sekino fig. 97) of the same stone. The older version exhibits less damage, and more fine incised details can be seen on the flat raised surfaces of the figures. The newer version of about 1907 shows a new break through the first chariot from the left, as well as other areas of enlarged damage. The fine detail lines are less clear in the newer version, but this may be more indicative of rubbing skills and techniques than the condition of the stone. This point can be illustrated through another rubbing of the same stone in the Princeton University Art Museum collection (cat. no. 1.13). By visual comparison, the Princeton rubbing dates earlier than the 1907 Sekino rubbing. The crack through the left chariot is not

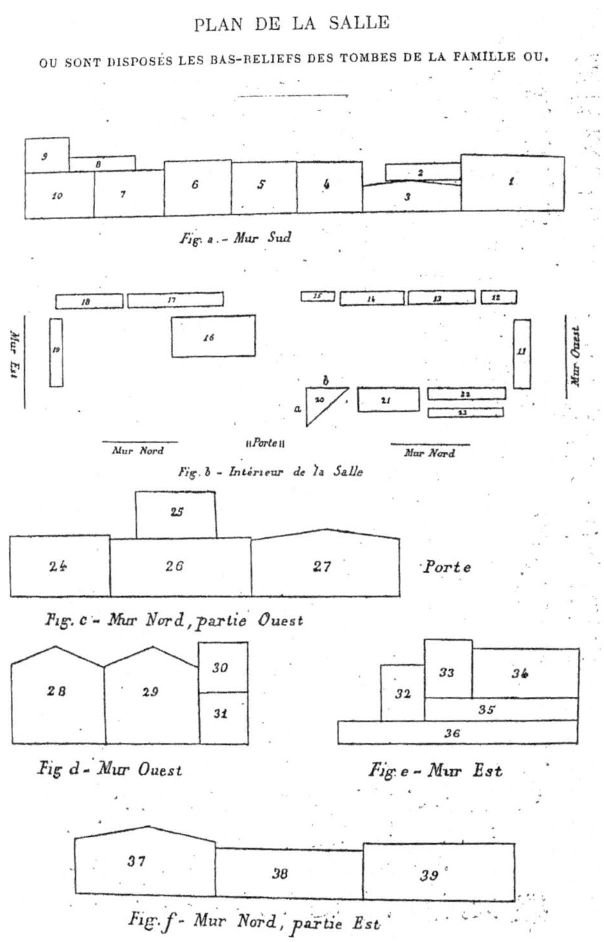

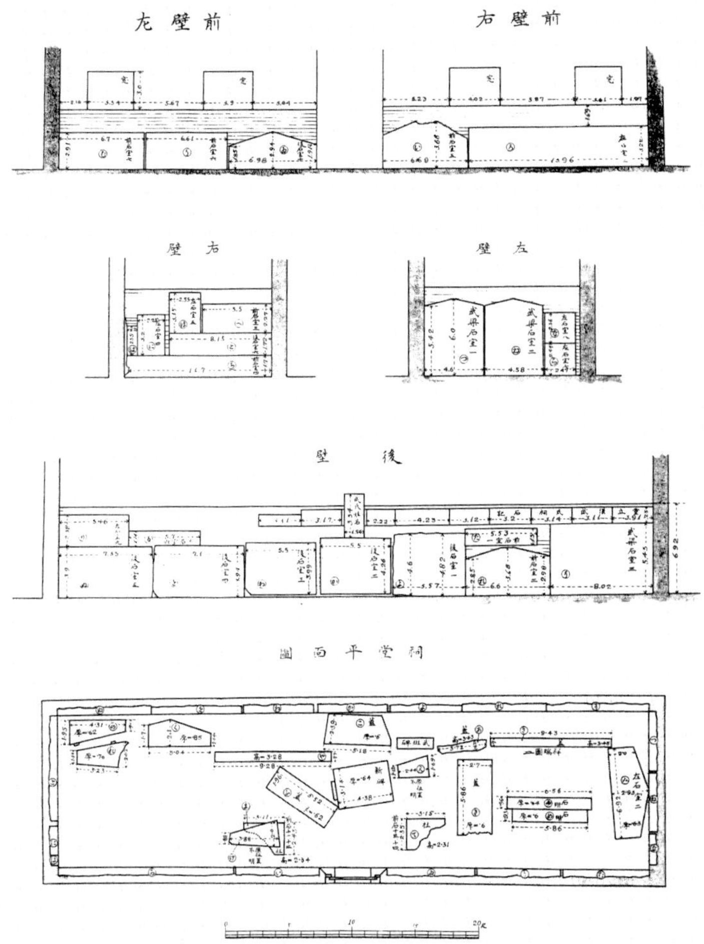

Fig. 14 *Interior plan and elevation diagrams locating the Wu pictorial stones in the Preservation Hall in 1891*. From Édouard Chavannes, *La Sculpture sur pierre en Chine aux temps des deux dynasties Han*, p. xxxviii.

Fig. 15 *Interior plan and elevation diagrams locating the Wu cemetery pictorial stones in the Preservation Hall in 1907*. From Sekino Tadashi, *Shina Santōshō ni okeru Kandai funbo no hyōshoku*, pl. 52.

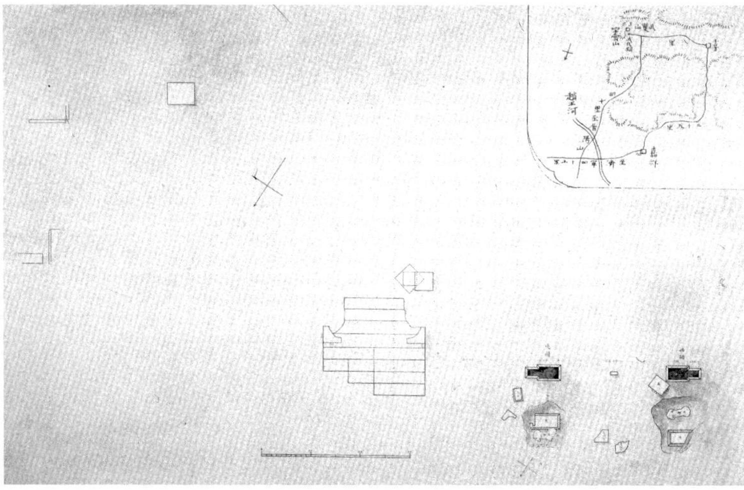

yet present in the Princeton version, but enlarged areas of damage can be seen when compared with the "old rubbing." Contrary to expectations, however, the finely incised details on the figures are less distinct on the Princeton rubbing than on the 1907 version. Probably this can be attributed to poor cleaning of the stone, careless rubbing skills, or crude materials. Sekino described this particular stone as a step-like stone (*kai seki*), and in modern architectural reconstructions it is the west half of a lintel stone across the front of a two-bay stone chamber.

It is evident from Sekino's description and survey maps of the cemetery that besides recorded or inventoried stones stored inside the Preservation Hall, the gate-pillars, and the pair of feline statues, numerous unrecorded stones were found scattered around the site. Sekino notes that to the right (northeast) of the gate-pillars were what appeared to be several "stones once used for pavement and steps" (*kaidan seki*) and stone columns, from which he concluded that there may have been other gate-pillars and stone chambers in this area.[171] His textual account corresponds to a large group of stones depicted to the northeast of the gate-pillars in his plan drawings of the site (fig. 16). Most of these pavement- and step-like stones appear to be long horizontal slabs. Two angled L-shaped stones are also seen, and it is reported that beyond this group, farther to the east, were more scattered pavement and step stones. Because many of these unrecorded stones may have been relatively undecorated architectural components, they were probably deemed of little historical or artistic significance.[172] One must bear in mind that before Wilma Fairbank's reconstruction in 1941, the recovered stone carvings were primarily treated as isolated stones or pictorial surfaces, and there was generally no interest in architectural reconstruction.

In any structure composed of stones of the size found at the cemetery site, the weight of the wall slabs would have required stone foundations, base stones, or flooring slabs. Ceiling slabs atop the triangular gable walls would have formed peaked roofs with a gap at the top center joint that required capping by ridge stones to prevent water seepage. Such architectural flooring or foundation slabs and ridge stones are likely to have been found among the many unrecorded stones at the site. It is probably from among these unrecorded stones that Jiang Yingju and Wu Wenqi identified three stones they integrated into their architectural reconstruction of three stone chambers in 1981 and 1995. Two of the stones, a broken roof ridge (*ji shi*) and a fragment of a decorative wall base (*huawen tiao shi*), were carved with ornamental patterns but had no pictorial figures or inscribed characters. The third stone had designs of swirling cloud scrolls inhabited with winged figures across the front. In Jiang and Wu's reconstructions of the Front Stone Chamber this stone was identified as a raised floor stone, inset across the front of a back-wall niche, that may have served as an altar stone (*gongan shi*).[173]

Besides these three stones, Jiang Yingju and Wu Wenqi also called attention to two other unrecorded pictorial stones. One is a damaged stone with three dancers and two figures brandishing weapons.[174] The other is an altar stone with carvings of fish in a pair of eared cups (*erbei*) flanking a sunken hemispherical bowl with a drain hole, and turtle- or chicken-like animals inside two round plates (fig. 17; see p. 357, fig. 3).[175]

Fig. 16 *Survey map of Wu site in 1907*. From Sekino Tadashi, *Shina Santōshō ni okeru Kandai funbo no hyōshoku*, pl. 28.

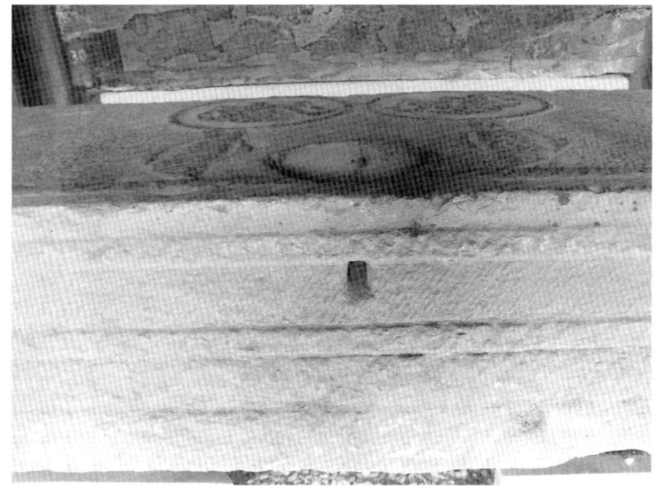

Fig. 17 *Detail of altar stone with carvings of fish in eared cups, plates, sunken bowl with a drain hole.* Wuzhai Shan site, Jiaxiang County, Shandong. Limestone; l. 132 cm, d. 49 cm, h. 23 cm. Photo by author, 2004.

The dates when, and locations where, all these stones were originally found is unknown. They raise the likelihood, however, that there are other unrecorded stones still preserved at the site that may yet be matched to architectural reconstructions of structures at the cemetery. Clearly, over time the site has served as a collection center for local pictorial carvings. Many of the assembled stones, including some of the recorded stones, such as Northeast, South Road, and Cai Stones, were found away from the site and are probably unrelated to the cemetery. In addition, in 1984 sixty unrecorded pictorial stones from around the county were brought for storage in a newly built seven-bay corridor at the Preservation Hall compound.[176]

The unrecorded stones may have also served as a stockpile from which later scholars selected stones as needed in order to reconcile the confusion surrounding the number of stones recorded by Huang Yi and other early inventories. Lost or missing stones may have been replaced from this stockpile, and it is also possible that a few recorded stones found their way into the ranks of the unrecorded or missing. As mentioned earlier, Huang Yi recorded fourteen stones in the Front Group in 1786, but only twelve stones (F.1–F.12) were inventoried in 1789. Many stories were later devised to explain this discrepancy. One scenario is that Huang Yi may indeed have found fourteen individual stones in 1786. Two of these stones may have been removed from the Front Group prior to the 1789 inventory. Some missing stones may have belonged to columns said to have been found at the site. In his 1796 *Colophon to the Pictorial Images of Front and Rear Stone Chambers*, Huang Yi remarked:

> Today in building the Wu Family Shrine [Preservation Hall], the various stones are all installed inside the Shrine [Preservation Hall]. There is only a broken stone column that could not be installed. At its top where there is a notch that receives the beam is carved a beast-shape [design]. To the side there is a column of calligraphy in *ba-fen* script that says: *ci* [ ] [ ] [ ] *jin* [ ] *wan* and other characters, whose meaning nobody understands. [I have had this stone] chiseled into a square block to preserve it.[177]

This passage has usually been interpreted as referring to a column capital with carved pictorial designs, traces of an inscription, and a notch on the top to support a beam. Rong Geng called this capital the "*Ci-Jin* Damaged Stone" (*Ci jin can shi*), and said:

> . . . only this [stone] has incised-line designs on a flat surface (*pingke*), [while all the other stones] have pictorial images and figures [carved] in relief (*longqi*). Huang Yi trimmed it into a square block and presented it to Ruan Yuan. [Ruan] Yuan further trimmed its top to become an inkslab. His cousin [Juan] Heng had it embedded into a wall in the Wenxuan Lou studio. I hear that today it has gone to the Pan family of Wu County.[178]

Despite never having seen the stone, Jiang Yingju and Wu Wenqi identified it as a bearing-block (*lu dou*) column capital, and reproduced a rubbing showing a horse-like animal in incised-line technique (*yinxian*)

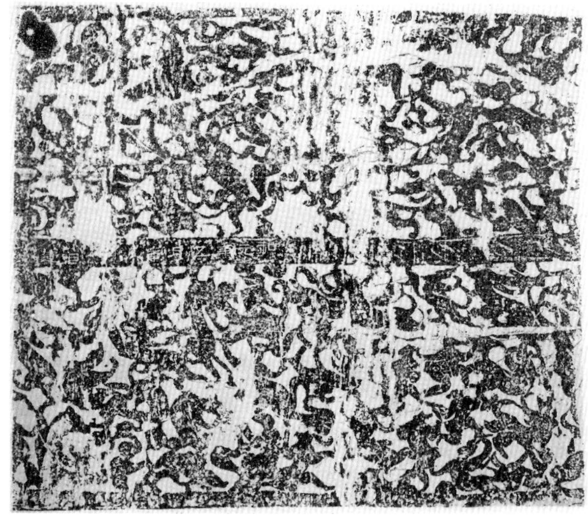

with the damaged inscription at right.[179] Although believed missing in recent times, this capital likely corresponds to a pictorial stone now in the Tianjin Municipal Museum of Art. As mentioned earlier, the Tianjin collector Xu Shizhang had owned a pictorial stone said to be from the Wu cemetery that Huang Yi had given Ruan Yuan. After Xu Shizhang's death in 1954 this stone entered the Tianjin Museum along with Huang Yi's *Illustrations of Obtaining Steles* (*Debei tu*) painting album, which was also from Xu's collection.[180]

The Tianjin Museum column capital may be one of the missing Front Group stones. Another missing stone is a column that Chavannes records as taken by Adolf Fischer to Germany in 1907 as part a of a group of perhaps the earliest Han stone carvings to enter a European collection.[181] Fischer brought most of the stones home to Cologne, where they later became the basis for the East Asian Art Museum in that city. Chavannes, however, reproduced a rubbing of the stone column in question and listed its location as Berlin (fig. 18A).[182] The square format of the rubbing is a partial wraparound of the column with two horizontal registers divided by a plain band carved with an inscription reading: "Made on the *gengchen* ... day in the fifth month of the first year (147) of the Jianhe reign period" (*Jianhe yuan nian wu yue gengchen* [ ] [ ] [ ] *ri zao*).[183] This is the same date found in the Wu Ban stele and southwest gate-pillar inscriptions. Carved around the column shaft are cavorting figures and animals, and Ōmura Seigai likened the style of the carving to the Wu cemetery Rear Group Stones R.1 and R.5. A photograph of the actual stone column was reproduced by Adolf Fischer (1857–1914) in 1908 (fig. 18B).[184] The column has a square capital on top and a round shaft with the pictorial carvings. Beneath the shaft is a round torus carved in the shape of intertwined animals, which sits on a square base. According to Fischer, the total height of this column is 157 centimeters. In Jiang Yingju and Wu Wenqi's reconstructions of both the Front Group stones into the Front Chamber, and a combination of Left and Rear Group Stones into the Left Chamber, this height is almost precisely the distance between the ground and the bottom of the front lintel and central-partition gable beam.[185] This long missing stone column has now been found in the collection of the Ethnological Museum in Berlin (Catalogue Part One: Supplement).[186]

The untold stories of the unrecorded and missing stones are only beginning to be written. It is likely that some unrecorded stones found at the site were abandoned or removed for reuse in local building projects. It is reported that many of the stone roof slabs of Tombs 1 and 2 at the cemetery were taken away for such purposes, and many of the pavement- and step-like stones recorded by Sekino may have met with similar treatment. Some stones that are now missing are documented, and rubbings of them survive. Examples include the *Wang Ling mu* stone, L.1, and the *He kui* slab. The *Wang Ling mu* stone left the Preservation Hall sometime during the Xuantong (1909–1911) reign-period and entered the collection of the Manchu official and collector Duanfang. In the early twentieth century this stone was reportedly sold abroad, as were Stone L.1 and the *He kui* stone. The whereabouts of all these stones is presently unknown.

Some stones that were believed missing are actually still preserved at the site. The *You niao ru he* stone had supposedly been sold overseas, but

Fig. 18A *Circular pictorial stone column taken from the Wu cemetery in 1907 by Adolph Fischer*. Wraparound rubbing; ink on paper. From Ōmura Seigai, *Shina bijutsushi: Chōso hen*, pl. 72, fig. 177.

as noted earlier, this stone is currently still housed in the Preservation Hall. Similarly, there are two pictorial stones with inverted trapezoidal profiles shown in a 1920s photograph by Osvald Sirén (fig. 19). These stones have been interpreted as missing column capitals in some modern studies, yet both stones still survive at the site. The two stones are actually rectangular in plan, but because the photograph only shows their narrow ends, they deceptively appear to be square capitals. In Jiang Yingju and Wu Wenqi's reconstruction, these two stones are placed on top of the smaller secondary columns attached to the gate-pillars.[187]

One surviving stone which is missing from the site but whose location has long been known is the "Confucius Meeting Laozi" slab. This stone was moved to Jining shortly after its recovery at the cemetery in 1786. Therefore in 1789 it was not assigned an inventory number or grouped with the other pictorial stones. An unrelated designation and inscription were carved into it, and it has frequently been treated as an isolated stone. Not uncommonly, a rubbing of this stone is absent from early rubbing sets of the "Wu family shrines" pictorial stones, as is the case with the Princeton rubbings (cat. no. 1).

Many of the pictorial stones of the gate-pillars should be included among the group of unrecorded stones found at the cemetery. Except for the carved inscription on the west gate-pillar, the pictorial carvings are rarely discussed. This may be because the gate-pillars either were treated as a separate architectural category or were considered of little interest until the early twentieth century. As noted by Huang Yi in his *Brief Record*, at the time when the cemetery site was discovered, the tops of the

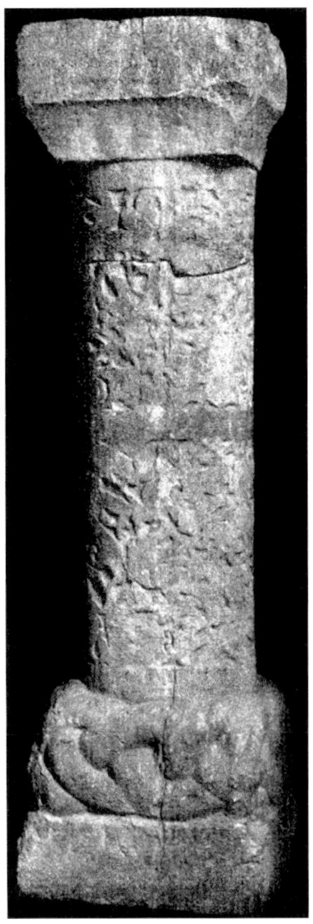

Fig. 18B *Circular pictorial stone column taken from the Wu cemetery in 1907 by Adolf Fischer*. Limestone; h. 157 cm. Ethnological Museum, Berlin. From *T'oung Pao*, ser. 2, vol. 9 (1908), p. 582, fig. 4.

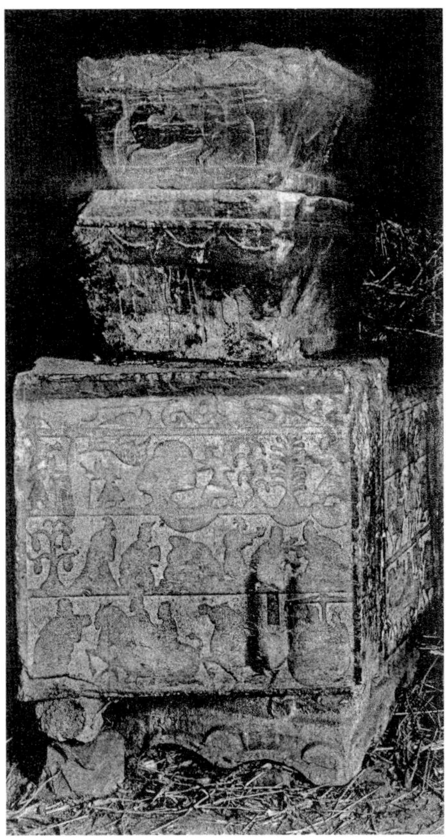

Fig. 19 *Two gate-pillar stones, a turning-corner stone, and a roof slab at the Wu site*. Photo 1920s, by Osvald Sirén. From his *Histoire des arts anciens de la Chine*, vol. 4, pl. 104-b.

gate-pillars protruded about three *chi* feet aboveground. Vulnerable to the elements, as expected, the exposed upper pictorial carvings are among the most eroded stones at the site. When inventory numbers were assigned in 1789, the gate-pillars were not included. Moreover, on the ground stretching between the gate-pillars was a long, low stone barrier with a rounded top (fig. 7). At the center of this barrier was set a round-topped stone marker (*shi jue*) with ringed beast masks (*pushou*) carved on each face. The stone marker can be seen in early twentieth-century photographs by Chavannes and Sekino, but only in 1995 were both the barrier and marker recorded by Jiang Yingju and Wu Wenqi.[188]

As prominent markers of the site, the gate-pillars also became a primary location for commemorative inscriptions and later graffiti. On the north side of both pillars, facing the Han-dynasty approach to the cemetery, is a stone panel without carved pictorial designs. On the northeast pillar the panel appears blank. Some rubbings of this panel, however, reveal traces of partially effaced pictorial images, suggesting the panel was originally decorated and later cleared for an inscription to be added.[189] On the southwest pillar the panel is carved with an eight-column inscription in ninety-three clerical-script characters dated to147 (translated in cat. no. 1.43). It is possible that this panel was also originally decorated with pictorial carvings and later cleared for the inscription. On both gate-pillars, on the narrow sides facing the central spirit path, the three characters "Wu Family Shrine" (*Wushi Ci*) were carved in large clerical-seal script over earlier pictorial designs. Curiously, this graffiti repeats what is already made clear in the inscription dated to 147. Perhaps the three characters were added because the dated inscription, being lower down on the gate-pillar, may have become buried.

On the other hand, it is not inconceivable that the three large characters "Wu Family Shrine" were carved prior to the ninety-three character gate-pillar inscription. As mentioned earlier, apart from the "Wu family shrine" assemblage of stele and gate-pillar inscriptions, there are no records of a Wu family in this area in the late Han. And any monument related to the Wu family of Pei Kingdom is likely to have been defaced in 290, when three generations of that family were executed for treason. The "Wu Family Shrine" characters many have been carved first, to claim or appropriate the cemetery for a local Wu family some time after the third century. The gate-pillar inscription self-dated to 147 may have been added later, to add historical authority to a claim of ownership or ancestry. The gate-pillar inscription was first recorded in Zhao Mingcheng's *Jinshi lu*, and it has already been noted that in some received editions of the *Li shi*, lines from the gate-pillar inscription appear in Hong Gua's commentary on the Wu Ban stele. This might have resulted from conflating the two inscriptions during editorial collation but, alternatively, these lines of the gate-pillar inscription may have been taken from the texts.

The possibility that the gate-pillar inscription may have been recarved, in part or in total, should be carefully considered.[190] The inscription plays a central part in the formation of the "Wu family shrines" assemblage. Ouyang Xiu and his son had recorded both the Wu Ban and Wu Rong steles, but apparently never recognized any relationship between them. Because the gate-pillar inscription records four male members of the Wu

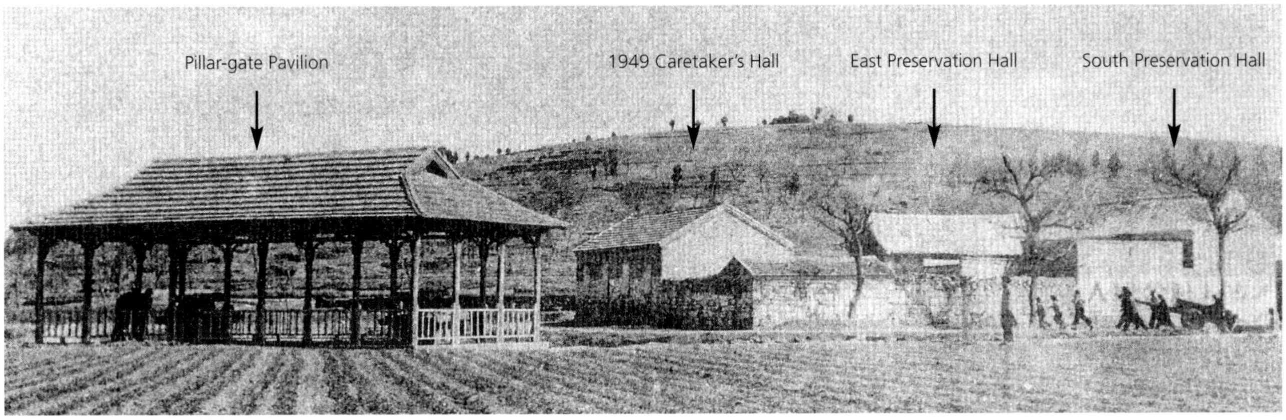

family, once Zhao Mingcheng's *Jinshi lu* appeared, it became possible to link specific stele inscriptions to each man. If the gate-pillar inscription proves authentic, the next step will be to examine the integrity of each of the four stele inscriptions dedicated to Wu Liang, Wu Kaiming, Wu Ban, and Wu Rong. If our brief examination of the complexities attending the Wu Ban stele is any indication, the other steles are equally challenging problems. A preliminary analysis suggests the possibility that each stele inscription may be based on a Han original, but that revisions and interpolations in the course of successive collations and compilations tailored the texts to form part of the "Wu family shrine" assemblage. In the case of the Wu Ban stele inscription, part of the interpolated text has actually been recarved onto to the actual stone (fig. 6).

Story of the Stones—Problems of Preservation

The preservation history of the gate-pillar stones differs somewhat from that of the other pictorial and inscribed stones found at the site, and a summary of their parallel histories may help clarify how the stones have come to be identified, presented, and preserved as the "Wu family shrines" assemblage. The building of several Preservation Halls at the site and their renovation and repair has also led to confusion in the story of the stones and needs clarification. When the site was first rediscovered, Huang Yi reported that only the tops of the gate-pillars were exposed and that he had to dig down 8 or 9 *chi* feet (approx. 3 m) to the top of the base stones. The other pictorial stones were found in groups, some lying partly exposed on the ground and others needing to be unearthed. In 1786 parts of the stone chambers probably survived in some architectural form, but preserving the architecture was not a priority. By 1792 most of the dismantled and collected pictorial stones were installed inside the newly built structure known as the Wu Family Shrine Preservation Hall. Many of the stones were embedded in the walls, but others were stored on the floor. Selected for inclusion inside the Preservation Hall were the inscribed and pictorial stones. Less decorated stones and architectural components were not included. Among the excluded stones were the round stone column brought to Germany in 1907 by Adolf Fischer and the column capital that was given to Ruan Yuan. In addition, Huang Yi also made plans to separate two of the most important stones from the other stones. It was planned to send both the Wu Ban stele and "Confucius Meeting Laozi" stone to the Jining Prefectural Academy, but only the latter stone was moved, and the stele was erected inside the Preservation Hall.

The 1792 Preservation Hall may have been a single large building erected along the south wall of the cemetery compound, southeast of the gate-pillars and south of the Caretaker's Hall built in 1949 (fig. 20).[191] The hall was designed to house the stone carvings initially recovered by Huang Yi. When ten stones of the Left Group were found in 1789, there was no longer room on the walls for all the stones, and many had to be placed on the interior floor. There are unsubstantiated reports that besides the main south hall, a three-bay east hall was also erected at this time to house the new stones.[192] Although both the number of halls and the exact interior arrangement of the stone carvings are now uncertain, the intended

Fig. 20 *Wu site: (left to right) Pillar-gate Pavilion, Caretaker's Hall, East Preservation Hall, and South Preservation Hall.* Photo 1963. From Jiang and Wu, *Handai Wushi muqun shike yanjiu*, pp. 5, 141, pl. 2.

program for the presentation of the stones can be garnered from an early description of the Preservation Hall and its title. In his *Jinshi cuibian*, with a preface dated to 1805, Wang Chang said that the shelter Huang Yi "built for the stone carvings (*bei*) was the Wu Family Shrine (Wushi Citang)," and described the hall's interior as having "all the stone carvings erected in four walls of the hall. In the center were presented four ancestral spirit tablets (*lizhu*) of the Wu family, and its [the hall's] doors were barred."[193] The Preservation Hall was apparently set up as a shrine, with altars holding spirit tablets of the four presumed males of the Wu family in the middle. The individual stone carvings collected in four groups at the site were embedded in the interior walls to constitute a single large composite shrine hall.[194] The pictorial images of exemplary figures, stories of the past, and scenes of banqueting, entertainment, food preparation, battles, official and supernatural processions, omens, and other subjects that had adorned the walls of the former stone chambers were consolidated to become the walls of the Wu Family Shrine Preservation Hall. The recovered pictorial stones were reused—in a sense recarved—to embellish the walls of a new shrine hall. Because this was an ancient cemetery, it may have been felt that an offering shrine needed to be built in order to sanction the desecration of funerary relics and appease the ancestral spirits. Probably because the gate-pillars would not have been appropriate for a shrine setting, they were not moved into the new Preservation Hall, but remained outside in partly excavated pits. Tampering with the tombs at the cemetery was probably also considered sacrilegious, so it is not unexpected that although one of the tombs was clearly marked by a mound surmounted by trees (fig. 9), there was no official attempt to excavate them until 1981.

When Feng Yunpeng visited the Preservation Hall in the twelfth month of 1820, he noted that the pictorial stones were embedded in the interior walls of a single large building that had been built by Huang Yi. The Wu Ban stele was said to be in the middle of the hall, and the two Good Omen stones were arranged on either side "like stone tables" (*ruo shi an zhuang*).[195] The Chinese characters for "stone tables" can also be read as "stone altars," which may indicate that offerings to the Wu family ancestors were still being presented. Feng Yunpeng recorded that the two gate-pillars stood half buried in sediment in front of the Wu Family Shrine Preservation Hall, and the local people identified them as stone candle towers (*latai*). He also noted that the southwest gate-pillar inscription was buried, and he had to dig it out in order to make a rubbing.[196]

The next major description of the Preservation Hall comes from a visit on the third day of the fifth month of what was probably 1841 by Xu Han (courtesy name Yinlin; 1797–1866) and friends.[197] In his diary, Xu Han records:

> . . . we visited the Wu Family Shrine (Wushi Citang) [Preservation Hall] . . . . Locals simply refer to this site as the Grove of Sovereigns (Huang Lin) . . . . The Shrine faces north, and opposite it is a large depression in which stand two gate-pillars. There are still quite a few stones jumbled in the hollow, and some have pictorial scenes. In the northeast corner [of the hollow] there are exposed stones below the

earth, apparently in the form of a tomb. How much effort must it have taken to raise its mound? The bricks and tiles of the Shrine [Preservation Hall] are falling apart; the doors and windows are completely missing. The pictorial slabs are inset around all four walls of the room. [The pictorial stones are skied] but not more than two slabs high, so the stones can be rubbed by raising one's arms. I had heard from the local instructor, Mr. Guo, that the Shrine was quite high and that rubbings could not be made of the slabs on top of the gable walls without a scaffold. What nonsense![198] The [remaining] slabs that could not fit into the walls were placed within the chamber, and each stone had to be paired east-west. Some stand in elevation; some lie flat—there is no uniformity. We could see that some slabs that were originally standing have now already collapsed. The local residents sit and lie down on them; kids play on them mixing mud, or worse, even urinate or defecate on them, so that they are unbearably filthy to the point of being disgusting. Shiqing[199] and I looked for water to clean the slabs. Searching for the places with characters, we made a set of rubbings by hand. Shiqing used *jian* paper and light ink, while I cut the paper according to the number and sizes of the cartouche panels in each of the stories [i.e., pictorial scenes on the stones]. The vertical [cartouches] were made vertically and the horizontal horizontally, and I kept a bit of the margins on all sides and used heavy ink [to rub them] . . . . Shiqing also made two sheets of rubbings of inscriptions on the gate-pillar. The gate-pillar inscription faces north on the lower part of the [south]west gate-pillar and was half buried in the earth. The rubbing maker had to dig a pit to begin to make the rubbing. The locals then presumed to defecate in this pit and collect manure there. Truly disgusting![200]

In this passage Xu Han describes the state of disrepair into which the Preservation Hall had fallen by 1841. Although the hall was still known as the Wu Family Shrine, it was no longer a protected shrine with altars. Quite the contrary, the doors were no longer barred, there is no mention of any caretaker, and the slabs had come to be abused by local people and children as chairs, beds, tables, and lavatories. The two gate-pillars stood outside the hall in a large hollow. The gate-pillars were again half buried, and a pit had to be dug in order to make rubbings of the southwest gate-pillar inscription.[201] In the northeast corner of the hollow, Xu Han noticed a group of stones that resembled a tomb which may once have been covered by a mound. The location of this group may coincide with one of the tombs or with the pavement- and step-like stones that Sekino found to the northeast of the gate-pillars in 1907, from which he concluded there may have originally been other gate-pillars and chambers in this area.

A few months after Xu Han's trip, in the fall of 1841, his friend Wang Xixun (1786–1847) also visited the site.[202] In a colophon on a version of Huang Yi's *Searching for Steles at Ziyun Shan* painting, he recorded that he had intended to visit the site a year earlier but had been prevented by flooding. He also mentions that following Xu Han's trip, the Magistrate (*ling*) of Jiaxiang soon ordered the installation of new protective doors and windows on the Preservation Hall.[203] This renewed concern for protecting the pictorial stones, however, did not last very long. When Chen Jin visited in the late nineteenth century, the hall exhibited serious structural damage. In his *Record on the Renovation of the Wu Family Shrine* of 1880, he wrote:

> ... I went several times to the Wu Shrine (Wu Ci) [Preservation Hall] and saw the cracked walls, fallen beams, and stones lying upside down. Thinking to repair the hall; this was not accomplished due to flooding of the Yellow River .... As it happened, the two Academy Heads (*guangzhang*),[204] the gentlemen Ma Qingyun and Li Weizun,[205] raised funds, getting 350 strings of capital currency (*jing qian*), then rebuilt the Shrine [Preservation] Hall [so that its] land and stones were as before .... I have also read Xiaosong's [i.e., Huang Yi's] "Record of the Wu Shrine" (*Wu Ci ji*), which says that for lack of funds the [precinct] walls of the shrine were not built, and only twelve *mu* acres of arable land were obtained to provide funds for the layman of Yu Huang Ge hall to care for the Shrine.[206] The Magistrate [Ding] Rongjiang repaired the Shrine walls, but the land was not identifiable. Examining distances in all four directions, he got 8 *mu* acres, 7 *fen* deci-acres, and 7 *li* centi-acres allotted to the head monk of the Yu Huang Ge hall ... who will take charge of keeping the archives, and who will supply the annual maintenance .... Construction began on the eighth day of the second month in the *gengchen* cyclical year (1880), and was completed after one month and eight days (*ba ri*).[207] A tablet was inscribed reading "Wu Family Stone Chamber" (Wushi Shishi) ....

In 1792 the Preservation Hall had been built as a shrine. Altars to the Wu family were installed inside, and the hall was called the Wu Family Shrine (Wushi Citang). The hall may have functioned as a shrine facility until as late as 1820, when Feng Yunpeng described stone tables or altars and mentioned use of the gate-pillars as candle towers (*latai*), possibly still associated with offering ceremonies. By the time of Xu Han's visit in 1841 and Chen Jin's visit in the late 1870s, however, the hall was no longer guarded and was in serious need of repair. Clearly it was no longer used as a shrine by the 1840s, but both Xu Han and Chen Jin continued to refer to it as the Wu Family Shrine (Wushi Citang). After the 1880 repairs, recorded by Chen Jin, the Preservation Hall was renamed the Wu Family Stone Chamber (Wushi Shishi).[208] The use of these two names for the Preservation Hall, and the use of the same two names in earlier and later texts to refer to the pictorial stones of the "Wu family shrines" assemblage, has spawned some of the confusion that envelops the story of how the recovered stone carvings have come to be identified, presented, and reconstructed.

It was the 1880 renovated Preservation Hall that Lieutenant Mills visited in 1886. In autumn of 1888 Wang Qizhe, Gao Wenhan, and Wang Qingyun visited the site together. They added a joint colophon to the inscription written by Li Dongqi in 1792, but unfortunately did not describe what they saw.[209] In 1890 Li Baoxun is reported to have discovered the heads of the feline stone statues but did not have time unearth them. The next recorded visitors to the site were Édouard Chavannes on January 27, 1891, followed by Berthold Laufer in 1903. Both must have seen the Preservation Hall with the stones embedded in the walls and arranged across the floor pretty much as they were since 1880, though disrepair was evident. Chavannes remarked on the small, unassuming appearance of the hall and noted the presence of a title placard in red and green colors over the door by Ding Jingshu (the District Magistrate Ding Rongjiang), which had been installed on the completion of the 1880 repairs.[210] Entering the hall, he found a dark chamber with carved slabs embedded in the walls and disposed across the floor in a large rectangular formation. Candles had to be lit in order to see the stones, which he found to be blackened from ink residue from numerous rubbings.[211] In 1893, after this visit, Chavannes published the earliest site photographs of the Preservation Hall and gate-pillars, as well as interior drawings of the hall showing the location of stone slabs (fig. 14).

Chavannes revisited the site with Vassili Michaelovich Alexéief in early July 1907, followed in October by Volpert. Alexéief recorded the deplorable conditions at the Preservation Hall and the poor care of the stones by an opium-addict caretaker. In late fall of 1907 Sekino arrived to survey and photograph the site. Sekino noted the remains of part of a stone wall with a gate structure attached to the front of the Preservation Hall. Hung in the gate was the title placard, reading "Wu Family Stone Chamber."[212] Nevertheless, in his writings Sekino continued to refer to the Preservation Hall as the Wu Family Shrine, while referring to the individual groups of pictorial stones as stone chambers. It is unclear if Sekino or Chavannes ever knew that the Preservation Hall had been built as a functioning shrine hall for the Wu family. Additionally, sometime before Sekino's 1907 visit unspecified repairs to the Preservation Hall were completed by Liu Xiaoyou. These repairs may have been the occasion of removing Stone L.1 and the *Wang Ling mu* slab, which could account for the differences between Chavannes's 1891 diagram of the carved stones and the one made by Sekino in 1907 (figs. 14, 15).

The 1907 surveys of the cemetery and Preservation Hall have largely shaped how the site has later been perceived. Almost immediately afterward, however, the site began to change. Wu Weinian (courtesy name Xiacun), Magistrate of Jiaxiang, recorded that additional repairs were made to the central bay of the hall built by Huang Yi.[213] He noted that of the fifty-five stone carvings inside the hall, twenty were scattered across the floor. For the scattered stones, he built a three-bay hall with assistance of the local officials Luo Zhengjun and Yao Pengtu. Funds were raised and construction was finished by summer 1910.[214] After 1910, consequently, there were two preservation halls: the old five-bay south hall with slabs embedded in the walls, and to its east a new three-bay hall housing the scattered slabs (fig. 20).

With Western and Japanese visitors now coming to the cemetery, the stone carvings began to be mentioned in popular travel guides from as early as 1912.[215] When Wilma Fairbank arrived at the site in May 1934, the gate-pillars stood ten feet high inside the western edge of a man-made depression 150 feet across, and their tops barely reached the surrounding ground level. Villagers were busy making bricks at the bottom of the depression, at whose south edge was a small walled courtyard with two low buildings. Inside the courtyard, opposite its north gate, was the old Preservation Hall with the stone slabs still set in the interior walls. According to Fairbank, this was the same five-bay hall Sekino had charted, but she described it as being only three bays wide.[216] During her visit this south hall was being used as a schoolroom. Fairbank also found the scattered stones sheltered in a three-bay building that coincided with the new hall erected by Wu Weinian in 1910. This smaller hall was located along the east side of the courtyard. At this time one of the feline statues was left exposed to the elements just inside the courtyard gate. Outside the walled courtyard, to the northeast opposite the gate-pillars on the other side of the depression, was a tree-covered mound that Fairbank presumed to cover an unexcavated tomb chamber (fig. 9).[217]

The cemetery site had changed significantly by the time of Fairbank's visit. The old and new Preservation Halls were now part of a walled schoolyard at the south side of the cemetery grounds. Fairbank noted that the title "Wu Liang Shrines" (Wu Liang Ci) was now generally associated with the entire cemetery complex, including the recovered stone carvings, gate-pillars, feline statues, and tombs.[218] Forgotten was any recognition that the old Preservation Hall had ever functioned as a shrine. It was during this period, from mid-nineteenth to early twentieth century, when Fairbank visited, that the identification of the "Wu family shrine" assemblage became entangled with the stories of the former shrine function and title of the old Preservation Hall. It was also during this time that perception of the site gradually changed: from merely a repository for ancient relics it was coming to achieve the status of a landmark. The site itself had become an object of study.

From the outbreak of war with Japan in 1937 until the formation of the People's Republic in 1949, conditions and activities at the cemetery are largely unreported. Flooding at the site seems to have been a recurrent problem, as indicated by Chen Mingda's 1940s or 1950s photograph of the site (fig. 13). Repeated descriptions of the gate-pillars as half buried, following accounts of their previous unearthing, are further evidence that flooding continued to be a problem. The site owed its continued importance during the war years in part to several scholarly publications. Rong Geng completed his major study *Han Wu Liang Ci huaxiang lu* in 1936, and Fairbank followed in 1941 with her article "The Offering Shrines of 'Wu Liang Tz'u'," in which she reconstructed three stone chambers. The importance of this latter study was recognized almost immediately. The article was praised by the French sinologist Paul Pelliot (1878–1945), and even during the war years it was translated into Chinese and published in 1945 in the *Bulletin of the Society for Research in Chinese Architecture*, with added line drawings of each slab showing outlines of the pictorial scenes.[219] Because of the continued cultural importance of the site, shortly after the establishment of the People's Republic in 1949, a Cultural Relics Preservation Office (*Wenwu baoguan suo*), which included the post of caretaker, was created for the site. At this time a five-bay Caretaker's Hall was built along the north side of the small walled courtyard containing the old and new Preservation Halls (fig. 20).[220]

In the 1950s the government funded repairs to the Preservation Halls. In addition, an open-air pavilion with a concrete balustrade was erected to shelter the gate-pillars and feline statues. According to a modern edition

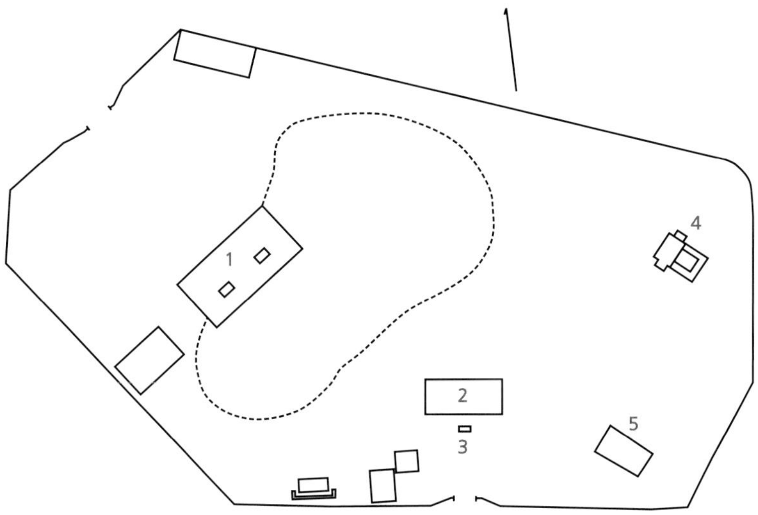

1 Exhibition Hall
2 Caretaker's Hall
3 1961 Stone Marker
4 Tomb 1
5 Tomb 2

of the *Jiaxiang Xian zhi*, the pavilion was built in 1959, at the same time that the gate-pillars and remaining feline statue were raised to the present-day ground level and set on concrete foundations.[221] The pavilion and the walled school courtyard, together with the Caretaker's Hall and two Preservation Halls that Fairbank visited, are visible in a 1963 photograph of the site (fig. 20).[222] In this photograph, however, the gate-pillars still appear to be below ground level. The 1959 date for raising the gate-pillars must be incorrect.

The landmark status of the site was officially acknowledged on November 17, 1960, but officially announced in 1961, when the cemetery was included in the first list of important national historical monuments and cultural relics placed under state protection.[223] In 1961 a commemorative granite marker was erected at the cemetery site. In 1964 the government allocated funds to elevate the gate-pillars to the present-day ground level and replaced the open-air pavilion with a five-bay hall around them and the feline statues.[224] The government again expended funds in 1972, to demolish the east and south Preservation Halls but leave the Caretaker's Hall. The stone carvings were moved into a five-bay Exhibition Hall (*chenlie shi*) measuring two hundred square meters, converted from the 1964 gate-pillar hall. The stones were arranged on platforms around all four sides of the gate-pillars. Additionally, a perimeter stone wall was built, encircling a precinct of over seven thousand square meters, and the 1961 commemorative marker was placed inside the south precinct gate, just south of the Caretaker's Hall. This new precinct layout with a main south entry is what is seen in a 1981 survey drawing of the site (fig. 21).[225]

Fig. 21 *Survey map of Wu site in 1981*. After Jiang and Wu, *Handai Wushi muqun shike yanjiu*, p. 2, fig. 2.

Today the marker stands outside the compound wall to the east of the new northwest main gate (fig. 25).

The changes carried out under the supervision of the Cultural Relics Preservation Office were probably all intended to ready the site for public presentation and tourism.[226] The 1792 Preservation Hall had been built as a guarded shrine, and after years of neglect punctuated by sporadic repairs, it was replaced by an Exhibition Hall and compound suitable for a national landmark. Similarly, while in the late eighteenth century the stone carvings had been viewed as relics for antiquarian scholarship and private collecting, by the late twentieth century they had transformed into national public treasures—historical and cultural relics from which exemplary lessons could again be drawn and taught. In effect, the relics from the past (*jiu*) were again reenvisioned (*zai xian*) and rendered new (*xin*) to "renovate" or "repair the past" (*xiu jiu*). The words from the past may have stayed the same, but the recarved stories identified, preserved, and reconstituted the stones to be encountered differently in the present and future.

After the Cultural Revolution, the late 1970s and 1980s saw renewed activities at the Exhibition Hall and compound. The Shandong Provincial Museum expressed concern about the care being provided by the local preservation office. Between 1979 and 1980 Jiang Yingju and Wu Wenqi, of the Shandong Provincial Cultural Relics and Archaeological Research Institute (*Shandong Sheng wenwu kaogu yanjiusuo*), were sent to survey and examine the stone carvings and cemetery site. From close assessment of the actual stones as architectural elements, they were able to refine

Fairbank's reconstruction of the cemetery structures.[227] In addition, during this period these two scholars supervised the location and excavation of Tombs 1 and 2 at the site (figs. 21–23).[228] Both tombs have a rear burial chamber with a gallery around three sides. Tomb 1 has a single front chamber with flanking small side rooms. The tomb is covered by a caisson roof over the rear chamber, two caissons over the front chamber, and flat roofs over the gallery and side rooms. Tomb 2 has front and middle chambers, the latter of which has flanking small side rooms.[229] A caisson roof covers the rear chamber, but the roof stones of the front and middle chambers had been removed, exposing them to the sky. Looking into the middle chamber in June 2002, the wall stones were found scored and covered with a white plaster. In certain locations in this chamber there were definite traces of red color applied in lines of simple architectural decoration. Over the lintel between the front and middle chambers a red-color spiral design was visible (fig. 1). On revisiting the tomb in June 2004, vegetation growth had caused the front lintel stone over the entrance to fall into the front chamber, the wall plaster had darkened, and of the color decoration little was visible besides the spiral.

In 1984 a seven-bay gallery was built; this is the present structure along the southwest wall of the precinct. Sixty stone carvings recovered from around Jiaxiang County were brought for storage into this gallery.[230] Many of these stones remain at the site, along with additional stones, but some stones are reportedly now in the collection of the Shandong Provincial Museum. Likely to be among the latter group is a pictorial stone showing another version of the scene of Confucius and his disciples

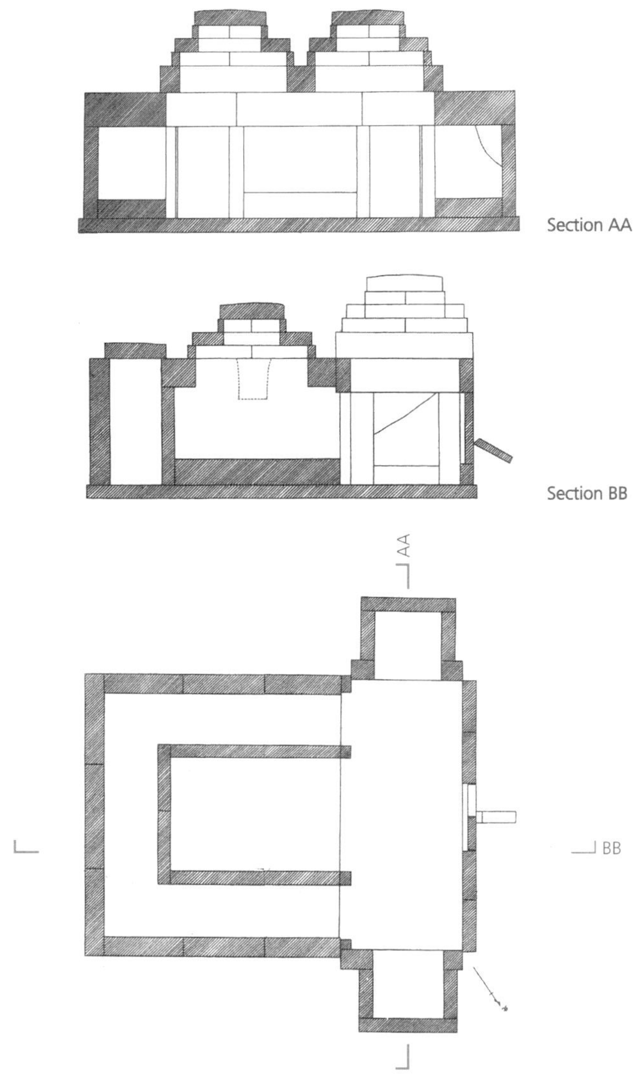

Fig. 22 *Tomb 1, plan and section drawings.* Ca. second century CE. Wuzhai Shan site, Jiaxiang County, Shandong. From Jiang and Wu, *Handai Wushi muqun shike yanjiu*, pp. 119–20.

meeting Laozi (cat. no. 10). In carving style and technique this stone is very similar to the Wu cemetery stones and may have originally come from the same workshop. The carving style may have distinguished this local workshop, but other stones presently housed in the 1984 gallery clearly indicate that there were other styles of carving in the Jiaxiang area.

In the years 1984 and 1985 several Chinese, Japanese, and American scholars, along with provincial officials, visited the precinct.[231] Events at the site peaked in 1986 with the 200th anniversary of Huang Yi's rediscovery of the cemetery. From July to October there were three visits by important central-government officials.[232] These activities led up to a symposium commemorating the anniversary, held on November 11–14, 1986.[233] On this occasion the site's association with Weng Fanggang and his connection to Huang Yi were highlighted to the point of exaggeration. At seventy-five years of age, Weng Kaiyun, a descendent of Weng Fanggang, sent the more than hundred symposium participants a poem composed following the prosody of a poem written by his ancestor for Huang Yi.[234] In the published symposium summary several points were made about the important role the "Wu family shrines" has played as a historical and cultural monument in furthering "the aims of the socialist spirit and cultural formation." The "Wu family shrine" stones were viewed as the foremost representative of Han-dynasty stone carving, and were accorded important historical and social value because they reenvisioned Han-dynasty art, Confucian thought and ideology, and social conditions. The summary also remarked on the worldwide fame of the stone carvings and recommended further restoration and reconstruction efforts along with

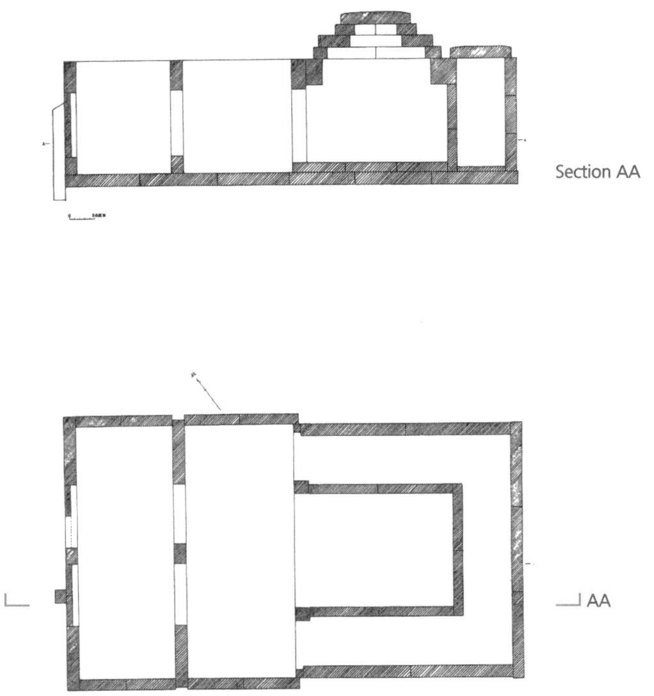

Fig. 23 *Tomb 2, plan and section drawings*. Ca. second century CE. Wuzhai Shan site, Jiaxiang County, Shandong. From Jiang and Wu, *Handai Wushi muqun shike yanjiu*, p. 125.

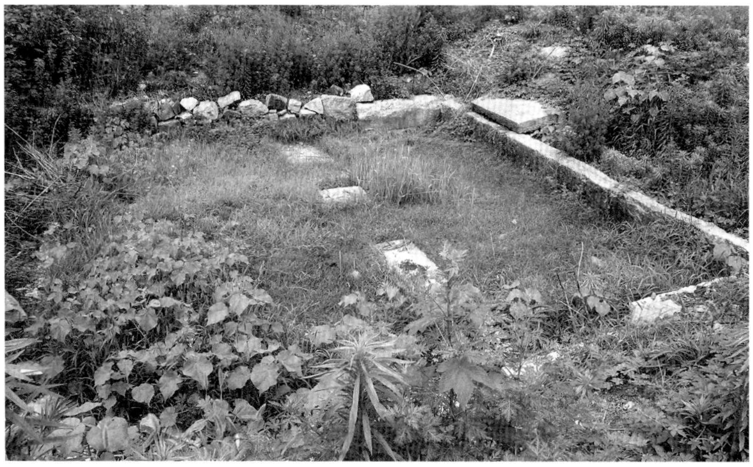

Fig. 24 *"Altar stones" at the Wu site*. Photo by author, 2004.

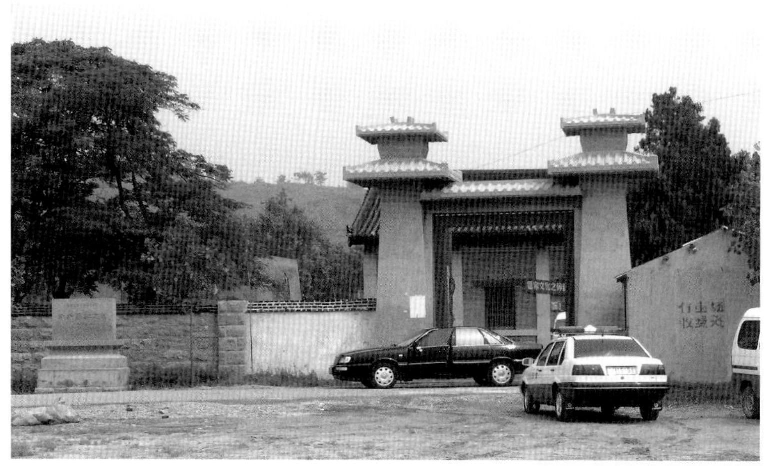

Fig. 25 *Present-day main entrance to Wu site, with 1961 commemorative marker at left*. Photo by author, 2004.

the establishment of a museum and research offices with dedicated funding. It also championed efforts to "strictly prohibit the production of artistic forged reproductions, which will detract from the reputation [of the national treasure]."[235]

In 1989 the Cultural Relics Bureau (*Wenwu ju*), at great expense, repaired the Exhibition Hall and erected flat-roofed red-stucco offices in four modules along the north wall of the precinct.[236] These offices, poorly constructed, are slated to be replaced, but during their construction in 1989, shaped stones (some possibly carved with pictorial decoration) were found just south of the easternmost office module (fig. 24). The tops of the stones are about four to five feet below the present ground level, and they are arranged in an incomplete rectangle with three slabs across the center. Many of the stones do not appear to be decorated with pictorial carvings, and it is not known how deep they extend into the ground. These stones are described as part of a sacrifice altar (*jitan*) by the office staff, but may actually be some of the "stones once used for pavement and steps" that Sekino had noticed in 1907.

As a national treasure, the site continued to receive visits from important government officials and international scholars and visitors. Despite the 1986 recommendations, however, the administrative status of the exhibition complex has yet to be raised to the level of a museum. In a 1993 listing of Shandong museums, the site was under the care of the Jiaxiang Wu Family Cemetery Stone Carvings and Cultural Relics Management Office (Jiaxiang Wushi muqun shike wenwu guanlisuo).[237] The present main entrance was apparently added along the northwest wall of the compound sometime after 1993. This gate was built in imitation of ancient gate-pillars (fig. 25), and the 1961 commemorative marker was relocated, probably at this time.

A large hall, five bays wide by three bays deep, was built in 1994 to the southwest behind the Exhibition Hall. In summer 2002 this hall served as a gift shop and meeting room. Also in 2002 a third tomb (fig. 26) was located between Tombs 1 and 2. In spring 2004 this hall was converted into a back Exhibition Hall, where the majority of pictorial stone carvings are currently displayed in modern glass cases with special lighting that illuminates only half the hall at a time (fig. 27). The gate-pillars, feline statues, Wu Ban and blank steles, and some Qing-dynasty inscribed tablets remain in the front Exhibition Hall (fig. 8).

Story of the Stones—Problems of Copying and Authenticity

The story of the stones found at the site and how they have come to be identified, presented, and preserved as the concrete actualities of the transmitted texts and rubbings that form the "Wu family shrines" assemblage, also needs to be examined with respect to copies and forgeries. For centuries the Jiaxiang area has been famous for its skilled stone carvers, and limestone similar to the "Wu family shrine" carvings is readily obtainable in nearby quarries. In the 1990s there were one thousand stone artisans in the county, and the Wu Family Shrine Stone Carvings Research Office (Wushi Ci shidiao yanjiusuo) manufactured over a hundred kinds of finely crafted stone carvings in traditional and modern styles.[238]

The potential for close copies of the Wu family stones, therefore, has always existed, and concern about this problem was openly recognized in the 1986 symposium summary's recommendation to "strictly prohibit the production of artistic forged reproductions."

Copies of the stones, and rubbings taken from them, are not rare. Many putative copies are carved with simplified designs or recombined motifs from different stones; these are easily recognizable as copies when compared with the actual stones or rubbings. Examples include several stones, sometimes attributed as Wu cemetery slabs, in the British Museum and the Walters Art Museum (fig. 28A).[239] Careful copies that closely matched textual descriptions were in some cases accepted as authentic. Unfortunately, in most instances we cannot know precisely what stones, rubbings, or copies past scholars relied upon as their sources in describing the stones. Because of the confused textual record, containing numerous contradictory accounts of the pictorial scenes and inscriptions, it is not implausible to suspect that some copies or forgeries have become the basis for description and have infiltrated the textual and visual record.

Before photography, ink-on-paper rubbings were the usual means for examining and studying pictorial carvings and inscriptions. Often viewed as mere copies, rubbings are one of the most complicated and subtle mediums among all the visual arts of China. In contrast to painting and calligraphy, where the hand of the artist is often directly visible, rubbings embody the original through multiple layers of reinterpretation and recarving. As Klaas Ruitenbeek has aptly characterized them, they are "shadows" of their originals.[240] In general, to make a rubbing, a thin sheet of moistened paper is laid over the stone and pressed into the incised depressions. The surface is then rubbed or tamped with an ink-soaked cloth-wrapped pad, after which the paper is peeled off the stone.[241] The common notion that the raised areas of a carved stone show black on the rubbing while the recessed areas appear white, however, is not always true. A skilled rubbing artisan can actually reverse this formula. No two rubbings are ever alike, given the individual skill, selection, and aesthetic taste that go into their creation. The choice of what to include or omit, the level of detail, the tools and techniques, and the care and attention given to the creation of a rubbing make this one of the most important forms of art in China.

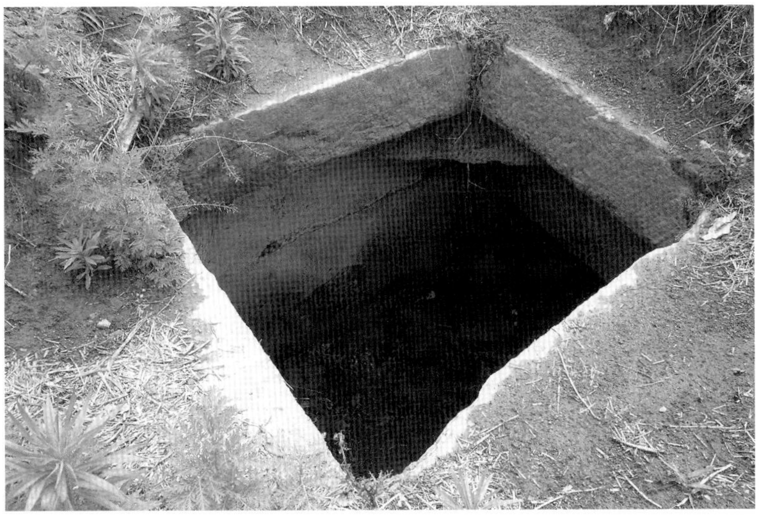

Fig. 26 *Tomb 3*. Ca. second century CE. Wuzhai Shan site, Jiaxiang County, Shandong. Photo by author, 2004.

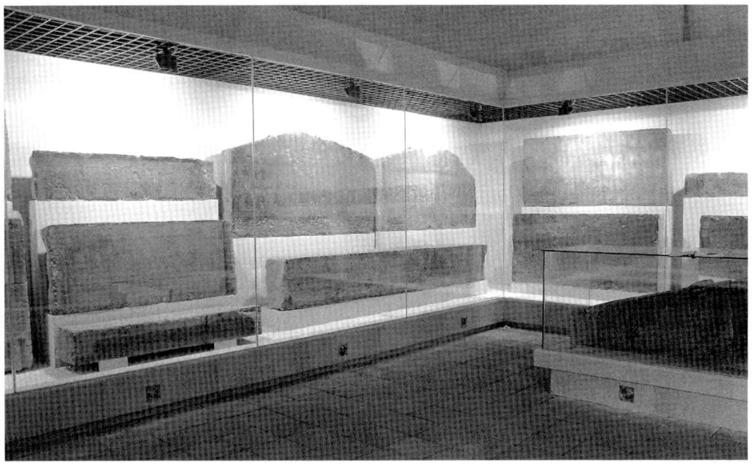

Fig. 27 *Back Exhibition Hall, interior gallery*. Wuzhai Shan site, Jiaxiang County, Shandong. Photo by author, 2004.

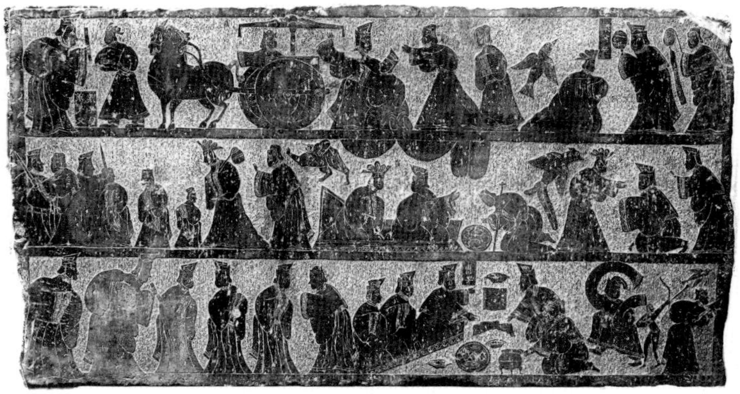

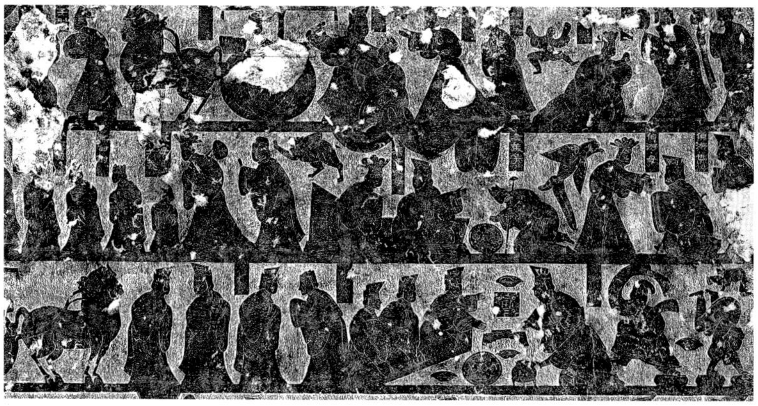

A "fine rubbing" (*jing ta*) depends in part on how the stone is cleaned. This may involve delicate removal of accumulated ink, adhesive, and paper fibers from incised areas with a brush, or even a light recutting of worn lines—a process commonly known as "cleaning" (*xi*) or "pointing" (*ti*). Careful tamping of the surface of the overlaid paper with special tools then produces a fine imprint with carefully selected details. A quicker and more economical process involves squeezing an inked pad against the surface in broad swaths. The resulting imprint is often fairly crude and lacks the fine detail produced by the more controlled tamping technique. Between the fine rubbing and squeezed imprints, there are many gradations, and in some cases the quality or technique varies across a single imprint, depending on what details the artisan chooses to emphasize. In addition, after the initial rubbing, the imprint can be manipulated in many ways. An imprint can be lifted, repositioned, and rubbed again, thereby changing the original composition. This is commonly done with rubbings of stele inscriptions and pictorial carvings that need to fit into certain physical formats, such as an album or handscroll. In other cases an entire rubbing is made, then cut into strips that are recombined to fit a desired format. After the initial rubbing, wax, ceramic, or wood filler blocks can also be used to supply missing content or restore damaged areas through targeted rubbing. All these various manipulations and others are well documented in rubbings of the "Wu family shrines" stones.[242]

In the early twentieth century photography began to rival rubbings as a means to document the Wu cemetery pictorial carvings. Photographic documentation of every pictorial scene, however, was not always readily available, or reproduced in large enough scale to reveal details. Photography has usually been limited to repeating the most popular scenes, and to date very few rubbing sets have been reproduced in their entirety.[243] Photography is also not a perfect medium to document the stones because it brings along its own set of problems. Photographs from a fixed angle showing the narrow ends of oblong stones have led viewers to identify them as square column capitals (fig. 19). Photographs have also made possible deceptively close copies and forgeries. Most significantly, almost all detailed photographs of the "Wu family shrine" pictorial stones are of rubbings. There are as yet relatively few published images of the actual stones, and photography may not be able to capture fully the variations in carving depth and technique that are essential to examining the stones. Except for the work of Jiang Yingju and Wu Wenqi, past scholarship, when it has turned its attention to visual concerns, has primarily relied on rubbings of the pictorial images and not on the actual stone carvings.

Although public access to the actual stones in the current exhibition halls is permitted, detailed study, photography, and technical testing have yet to be conducted in any thorough or systematic fashion. The stones themselves have much to add to their own story, but this remains an avenue for future research.[244] Ironically, when pictorial stone carvings are displayed in China, rubbings are often placed over the actual stones to enhance legibility. Even rubbings, however, despite the existence of numerous sets, have known very little systematic photography, hindering the development of criteria for dating the various sets. This catalogue

Fig. 28A *Copy of section of "Front Stone Chamber" (Stone Chamber 1, Stone 1-E.2)*. 19th–20th century. Stone with flat relief; h. 64.5 cm, w. 124.1 cm. Walters Art Museum, acc. no. 25.14.

Fig. 28B *Detail of "Front Stone Chamber."* Detail of Stone Chamber 1, Stone 1-E.2 (cat. no. 1.12). "Wu family shrines" rubbings. Princeton University Art Museum, acc. no. 2002.307.2.

supplies one additional set, in the collection of the Princeton University Art Museum (cat. no. 1), for consideration. It is hoped that digital photography will facilitate the documentation of additional sets in the future.

The stones, along with their rubbings and photographs, have long been one basis for a recarving of China's past to serve what was deemed proper or exemplary for a given moment's present and future. It is this process of "renovating" or "repairing the past" (*xiu jiu*) that needs to be more closely examined as it has affected the identifying, preserving, and reconstituting of the "Wu family shrines." A monument that has lost its identity in the form of a verbal or physical marker is no longer a monument.[245] For the Wuzhai Shan cemetery, the lack of a continuous cultural history from the Han to Song dynasties and from Yuan to Qing dynasties may be owing to the absence or loss of a recognizable marker. Surviving aboveground structures at the cemetery may have been in plain sight but without an identity. The "Wu family shrines" are not an isolated example. Numerous Han and later tombs, buildings, temples, and even cities became unmarked and consequently forgotten, misidentified, or mischaracterized. Quite possibly the Wuzhai Shan cemetery stone carvings were in certain periods not recognized because they lacked a clear marker.

Correct identification is another matter. The reconstitution of the stone carvings, rubbings, and textual materials comprising the "Wu family shrines" assemblage into a cemetery complex of a Wu family in the Han dynasty is the result of relatively modern efforts to identify and order the found relics in a comprehensible way—a reenvisioning and recarving of the past. The question is, how accurate is this reconstitution of an actual past, since "demands for intelligibility often justify altering ruins . . . ."[246] The desire to identify and protect past relics can lead to the alteration of what is to be preserved. Stone engravings have sometimes been recarved or reengineered to provide clarity or to satisfy cultural, historical, or political expectations. For example, as discussed earlier, in the Southern Song period Shi Shengzu allowed rubbings collected by his grandfather in Shandong to be used as models for the repair of badly eroded stones in Sichuan. The stones were to be recarved and "filled in to be as clear as new."[247]

The damage suffered by the "Wu family shrine" pictorial stones and stele inscriptions due to exposure to the elements, flooding, earthquakes, countless rubbings, and possibly warfare may have led to some stones, or parts of them, being altered for reasons of repair and preservation. Attempted preservation, therefore, "sets in train the extensive remodeling of the very past it aims to protect."[248] Signs that this may be the case with the "Wu family shrine" stone carvings include recarved calligraphy of different depths, sharpness, and sometimes style on the same stone, or instances when previously indecipherable characters in inscriptions are afterward supplied. The pictorial stones were executed using the technique of carving flat-relief figures with incised-line details on a lowered chiseled background (*zaowendi tumian xianke*).[249] Through repeated rubbing and cleaning of the stones, it is likely that the fine detail lines were worn down and occasionally needed to be reincised with a sharp tool, that is, "cleaned" (*xi*) or "pointed" (*ti*). Popular scenes that would have been continually rubbed were likely candidates for this treatment.[250]

Beyond repairing the stones, areas of damage or wear in the pictorial designs and particularly in the inscriptions were sometimes filled in on the rubbings in order to increase legibility.[251] Additionally, in the textual transmission of the stele, gate-pillar, and cartouche inscriptions, it was often scholarly practice to interpolate missing or ambiguous characters to supply intelligibility. This may expain why only ten to twenty percent of the Wu Ban stele was legible to Ouyang Xiu in the eleventh century, whereas in late eighteenth-century editions of Hong Gua's *Li shi*, some eighty to ninety percent could suddenly be read. Interpolation and collation of the various recorded texts has yielded multiple recensions of the transcribed inscriptions. Until the differences and relationships between earlier and later editions of commonly accepted texts, such as Ouyang Xiu's *Jigu lu*, Zhao Mingcheng's *Jinshi lu*, and Hong Gua's *Li shi* and *Li xu*, are fully understood, they should not be accepted as authoritative sources upon which to build a study of the "Wu family shrines" or of Han-dynasty art history and material culture.

The question of authenticity also applies to the reconstitution of architectural structures at the cemetery. Wilma Fairbank's process of reconstructing three structures from rubbings of the scattered stone pieces, which was refined by Jiang Yingju and Wu Wenqi, is akin to assembling a jigsaw puzzle. Although their reconstructions can be shown to be reasonably accurate, questions remain about the placement of some of the roof slabs, about areas of missing slabs, about the possibility of a fourth or additional structures, and about many miscellaneous stones that have yet to be included in any reconstruction. The original functions of the structures, their original locations at, or near, the cemetery, and the relationships among the structures also remain unresolved.

Reconstitution of the "Wu family shrines" assemblage presents an even greater problematic. The stone carvings, rubbings, and textual materials have been used to reenvision or recarve a Han world. The reconstructed stone structures are said to have been aboveground funerary shrines belonging to a Wu family cemetery, and are said to date from the Eastern Han. The pictorial carvings and inscriptions, consequently, have been used as the basis for reconstituting daily life, social rank, religious beliefs, Confucian ideology, artistic style, and pictorial iconography in the Eastern Han. It must be acknowledged, however, that all such reconstructions are essentially anachronisms that attempt to recarve a past as a memory for the present and model for the future. What has been recarved is an intellectual construct of a new (*xin*) world, recalling the fictional creation of the world of Tlön described by Jorge Luis Borges. A realm governed by fantastical idealism, with its own architecture, games, mythology, language, emperors, lands, creatures, math, logic, theology, and cosmology. In Tlön objects that are lost may be identical but not equal to what is later found, or may be sought and found in duplicate, or brought into being by hope. In Tlön, this "has been of enormous service to archaeologists. It has allowed them to question and even to modify the past, which nowadays is no less malleable or obedient than the future."[252] Has the assemblage of the "Wu family shrines" been just such a hopeful creation? What will detailed scrutiny of the actual carved stones eventually be able to tell us about the story of the stones?

Appendix

Huang Yi, *Xiu Wushi Citang ji lüe* (*Brief record on building the Wu Family Shrine* [*Preservation Hall*])

In autumn, the eighth lunar month of the *bingwu* cyclical year in the Qianlong reign-period [September 22 to October 21, 1786], on the way back east from the Yu region [present-day Henan area], I passed the Jiaxiang district offices and saw a gazetteer that recorded that thirty *li* miles south of the district [seat], in the Ziyun Shan hills, there is a Western Han tomb of a crown prince with three stone offering halls (*xiang tang*).[253] [These halls] have been buried in the ground for a long time, with only about three *chi* feet of them [still protruding]. Their stone walls were very finely carved with good omens from [the time of] Fuxi, as well as figures of ancient loyal and filial persons. There is a Han-dynasty stele, but all its characters are indistinguishable. [Huang] Yi searched for and obtained rubbings [from the offering halls], and the hall is that of Wu Liang, and the stele is that of Wu Ban. I consequently could not resist feeling wildly excited.

In the ninth lunar month I personally went to their location, and learned that the hill was named Wuzhai [literally, "Wu residence"], but also called "Wu Zhai" [meaning "martial Zhai"].[254] Through the ages the changing path of the Yellow River has covered the scattered ruins of the stone chambers with sediment. I recovered [the stones] in the following order:

— Three pictorial stones of the *citang* ("shrine hall") dedicated to Wu Liang, which were broken into five pieces long ago. [They have] more than 400 characters in *bafen* clerical-script calligraphy.

— One pictorial stone of "Confucius Meeting Laozi," which has eight characters in *bafen* calligraphy.

— Two gate-pillars stand erect facing each other to the north and south [i.e., northeast and southwest]. They protrude three *chi* feet aboveground, and on digging down eight or nine *chi* feet their bases begin to be seen. Each gate-pillar displays the three large characters "Wu Family Shrine" (*Wushi Ci*) in *bafen* calligraphy [on one side]. [The other] three sides [of each gate-pillar] have pictorial images of human figures, while the top layers are carved with birds and animals. The south[west] gate-pillar has the *Wushi shi que ming* ("Wu family stone gate-pillar inscription") of the first year of the Jianhe reign [147 CE in the Eastern Han[255]]. [The inscription] has ninety-three characters in *bafen* calligraphy.

— The Wu Ban stele was made in a *gui*-tablet shape with a pierced hole. It was found flat [on the ground] north of the gate-pillars to the side of the road. The local people say it was pulled out of a pit several decades ago.

These four [groups of items mentioned above] can be seen in records written by both Zhao [Mingcheng] and Hong [Gua].

— Behind the Wu Liang stone chamber, to the northeast, is a stone chamber with a total of seven stones. [Their] pictorial scenes are quite strange, and there are no inscribed characters. Only at the edges is there faint *bafen* calligraphy, such as the characters *zhong* ("center"), *ping* ("equal"), and others. Alongside [these seven stones] was a broken stone pillar with standard-script calligraphy (*zhengshu*) reading, *Wu jia lin* ("Wu Family Grove").

— To its front [i.e., to the south] was another stone chamber made of fourteen pictorial stones, which has more than 160 characters in *bafen* calligraphy resembling that on the Stele of Cao Quan.[256]

— One stone with good-omen designs had been lying on the ground for a long time, [and its pictorial carvings] are extremely worn and indecipherable. Again to the north of the Wu Liang Stone Chamber, three stone fragments with good-omen designs were retrieved. Together [they have] more than 130 characters in *bafen* calligraphy.

These three [foregoing groups] are not included in the recorded writings of earlier people; so I have named them the Wu family Front Stone Chamber and Rear Stone Chamber pictorial carvings, and the Good Omen Pictures.

In addition, about one or two *li* miles from this [cemetery location], there are two pictorial stones without any inscriptions [on them]. It is not possible to determine to which chamber they belong.

Not too many carved steles by people of the Han dynasty survive today, so it can be considered a miracle in this life to suddenly recover so many. Moreover, these pictorial images have a refined antiquity, and the *bafen* calligraphy is delicate and exquisite.

It can be noted that among the various Wu family steles of the Han dynasty, only the Wu Rong stele [had already been] erected at the Ji[ning Prefectural] Academy.[257] The Wu Ban stele, the pictorial carvings of the Wu Liang Shrine, and the Wu family stone [south] gate-pillar inscription, have now been unearthed. Only the two remaining steles of Wu Liang and Wu Kaiming are not yet found, so how do we know they are not still at this site?

Jiaxiang in the Han dynasty was the location of Rencheng. Zhao [Mingcheng] said that there are several tombs of the Wu family in Rencheng.[258] What he referred to is very clear, so how could the [Jiaxiang] district gazetteer mistake them for the tomb of a crown prince of the Han dynasty? Yet [it may be that] local people, seeing the skillful craftsmanship of the stone carvings, designated the tombs as imperial mausoleums. Consequently, [these tombs] have survived through successive ages without being destroyed. This may have been the benefit of having been misidentified.

Today there are various stones spread all through the wilderness. How do the herdsmen or woodcutters know to care for them? If we do not quickly collect and protect them, it will no longer be possible to inquire into antiquity. For this reason [Huang] Yi unearthed them [i.e., the stones of the Wu shrines]. Not to care for them would really be to let the ancients down, so it is [Huang] Yi's responsibility. The Wu Ban stele should appropriately be erected along with the Wu Rong stele at the Ji[ning Prefectural] Academy.[259] But the [Wu Ban] stone's large size makes it difficult to move a long distance. [Huang] Yi could only move the "Confucius Meeting Laozi" pictorial stone to Jining, and with the Department Magistrate Liu Yongquan carefully placed it in the Minglun Tang hall of the Academy (*xue gong*).[260] As for the other stones of the various [Wu cemetery] stone chambers, they are too large and numerous to be moved.

Li Tieqiao [i.e., Li Dongqi][261] of the [Jining] region came from a family with a reputation for an interest in antiquities. His success at collecting stele [rubbings] is very well known. Li Meicun [i.e., Li Kezheng][262] and Nan

Minggao [i.e., Nan Zhengyan][263] of Hongdong are skillful at calligraphy and have a passion for stele inscriptions, and have eagerly sought to complete this admirable endeavor (*cheng mei*).[264] [Huang Yi consulted] with all of them in planning, to appropriately erect the Shrine [Preservation Hall] at this location. The walls are made of stacked stones, and strength and stability are sought, not fancy decorations.

The pictorial stones are divided into four groups and arranged on the four walls. The Wu Ban stele is erected inside [the Preservation Hall]. Outside, an enclosing stone wall surrounds the pair of gate-pillars. Inside, a door placard is inscribed, "The Wu Family Shrine" (Wushi Citang). The empty area is planted with excellent trees, and the local people were given the duty of guarding this place for generations.

[Since] there are ancient steles [at this site], if the public [were free] to make rubbings, then this easily will result in damage. A price should be set [to make rubbings] for their benefit and to prevent their being worn away.

A stele is to be raised and a record kept for the long-term preservation of the stones. This project cannot be managed without several hundred gold taels. [Huang] Yi and several people from Jining have already contributed [funds for this project] according to their ability. Charitable donors in the country who hear about this project and agree willingly to donate funds can send them to [Li] Tieqiao, [Li] Meicun, or [Nan] Minggao, who are supervising this project.

After [Huang] Yi, together with these local officials and various gentlemen, brings this project to completion, they will seek a contemporary venerable master to compose a stele inscription to be handed down to posterity. The Han precedent for stele inscriptions will be imitated to read, "So-and-so, ten thousand cash; So-and-so, thousand cash," which will be inscribed carefully on the back of the stele to commemorate the generosity.

After the Han people built the stone gate-pillars, this area has been filled high [with silt]. On the start of construction, [the site] should be leveled [to a depth of] seven or eight *chi* feet to attain a solid building foundation. Moreover, the steles [and stones] that are presently buried should all be uncovered, so as not to leave any regrets [over unfound stones].

With a hall to provide shelter [for the stones], it will be convenient to make rubbings. The purplish-blue ink [rubbings] will then be transmitted more widely. From this, people will know to appreciate and care for them so that they can last forever. How can this [important task] be limited to two or three comrades enjoying themselves thoroughly for a particular moment?

Recorded in the summer, the sixth lunar month of the *dingwei* year in the Qianlong reign-period (July to August 1787), by Huang Yi of Qiantang.[265]

Acknowledgments

During research for this essay I have benefited greatly from work sessions held weekly at Princeton University with Pricilla Chen, Eileen Hsu, Michael Nylan, Haitao Tang, and others to exchange ideas and review translations. I want to thank my research associate Eileen Hsu for her ability to tackle whatever challenge was set before her, and special research assistant Mei-ling Williams for developing important position papers and compiling documentation that has been invaluable to the research team. I am also especially grateful to Lu Wensheng and the staff of the Shandong Provincial Museum for arranging viewings of the "Wu family shrines" stones and tombs, as well as related Han-dynasty archaeological sites and materials throughout Shandong. It was a special honor to have been able to discuss research problems with Jiang Yingju, whose expertise has shaped much of the debate over the "Wu family shrines" during the past three decades. Any errors, of course, are my own or the fault of some copy machine.

Notes

1. In *Shangshu zhengyi*, *Shisan jing zhushu* edition, 2 vols. (Beijing: Zhonghua shuju, 1980), "Yin zheng" sec., *juan* 7, p. 156. Translation follows James Legge, *The Chinese Classics* (reprint, Taipei: Southern Materials Center, 1985), vol. 3, p. 169. Zhongwen da cidian bianzuan weiyuanhui, ed., *Zhongwen da cidian* (Taipei: Zhongguo wenhua daxue chuban bu, 1973), no. 13888.4.

2. The term *fu gu* is often translated as "recovering the past." The term may be better translated as "recovering the legitimacy of what was orthodox and proper (*zheng*) in the past." For an analysis of *fu gu* and the arts, see F.W. Mote, "The Arts and the 'Theorizing Mode' of the Civilization," in *Artists and Tradition: Uses of the Past in Chinese Culture*, ed. Christian F. Murck (Princeton: Princeton University Press, 1976), pp. 3–8.

3. Lao Gan, "Lun Lu xi huaxiang san shi—Zhu Wei shishi, Xiaotang Shan, Wushi Ci," *Lishi yuyan yanjiusuo jikan*, vol. 8, no.1 (1939) (reprint, Beijing: Zhonghua shuju, 1987), pp. 94–96, 105; He Xilin, *Gu mu danqing: Handai mushi bihua di faxian yu yanjiu* (Xi'an: Shaanxi renmin meishu chubanshe, 2001), pp. 139–42.

4. In Xiao Tong (501–531), *Wen xuan: or Selections of Refined Literature*, trans. and annot. David R. Knechtges (Princeton: Princeton University Press, 1982–), vol. 2, p. 275. Similarly, in He Yan's (courtesy name Pingshu; d. 249) "Rhapsody on the Hall of Great Blessings" ("Jingfu Dian fu"), such paintings were "to serve as warnings and monition . . . . / These are examples, these are models." Trans. in ibid, p. 291.

5. D.C. Lau, ed., *Kongzi jia yu zhuzi suoyin* (Hong Kong: Shangwu yinshuguan, 1992), *juan* 3, "Guan Zhou" sec., p. 20, no. 11.2. The paintings were on the walls of a Brilliant Hall (Mingtang) in the state of Zhou. On the *Kongzi jia yu*, see Michael Loewe, ed., *Early Chinese Texts: A Bibliographical Guide* (Berkeley: Society for the Study of Early China, and Institute of East Asian Studies, University of California, Berkeley, 1993), pp. 258–62.

6. Lao Gan, "Lun Lu xi huaxiang san shi," p. 105; He Xilin, *Gu mu danqing*, p. 139.

7. On painted tombs, see Huang Minglan and Guo Yinqiang, eds., *Luoyang Han mu bihua* ([Beijing]: Wenwu chubanshe, 1996); He Xilin, *Gu mu danqing*. On carved-and-painted pictorial tombs, see Han Wei, gen. ed., *Shaanxi Shenmu Dabaodang Han caihui huaxiang shi* (Chongqing: Chongqing chubanshe, 2000); Klaas Ruitenbeek, *Chinese Shadows: Stone Reliefs, Rubbings, and Related Works of Art from the Han Dynasty (206 BC–AD 220) in the Royal Ontario Museum* (Toronto: Royal Ontario Museum, 2002), pp. 49–51. On various classification systems for pictorial stone carving techniques, see Jiang Yingju and Wu Wenqi, "Shilun Shandong Han huaxiang shi de fenbu, kefa yu fenqi," *Kaogu yu wenwu* 1980.4, pp. 108–14; Yang Boda, "Shilun Shandong huaxiang shi de kefa," *Gugong bowuyuan yuankan* 1987.4, pp. 4–24; Li Falin, *Hanhua kaoshi he yanjiu* (Beijing: Zhongguo wenlian chubanshe, 2000), pp. 79–93; Xin Lixiang, *Handai huaxiang shi zonghe yanjiu* (Beijing: Wenwu chubanshe, 2000), pp. 27–39. Many of these classifications attempt to establish a chronology of the development of pictorial carving techniques. These classification systems and many others, however, are speculative and often contradictory. I am indebted to Eileen Hsu for her assistance in compiling and cross-referencing the various systems. It is also likely that many of the pictorial carvings in funerary structures that now appear unpainted may originally have been painted. This possibility is further discussed in Liu's "Reconfiguring" and Barbieri-Low's "Carving Out a Living" in this catalogue.

8. For Huang Yi's biography, see *Qing shi gao*, comp. Zhao Erxun et al. (Beijing: Zhonghua shuju, 1976–1977), *juan* 486, p. 13420; Yu Jianhua, gen. ed., *Zhongguo meishu jia renming cidian* (Shanghai: Renmin meishu chubanshe, 1981), p. 1146.

9. See Wenwu bowuguan yanjiu ziliao shi, "Di yi pi quan guo zhongdian wenwu baohu danwei zhong de gu jianju," *Wenwu* 1961.4–5, p. 32. The *Shandong sishi nian jishi*, ed. Zhonggong Shandong Sheng wei yanjiu shi (Ji'nan: Shandong renmin chubanshe, 1989), p. 427, notes that national landmark status was actually decided on November 17, 1960.

10. Stephen W. Bushell, "Inscriptions from the Tombs of the Wu Family from the Tzu-yun-shan (Purple Cloud Hills), 28 *li* miles south of the city Chia-hsiang-hsien in the Province of Shantung," in *Abhandlungen und Vorträge des Fünften Internationalen Orientalisten-Congresses*, II, Ostasiatischen sec. (Berlin: A. Asher, 1882), pp. 79–80.

11. Hugh Honour and John Fleming, *A World History of Art*, 6th ed. (London: Laurence King Publishing, 2002), pp. 270–71.

12. Wang Bomin, *Zhongguo huihua tongshi*, 2 vols. (Taipei: Dongda faxing, 1997), pp. 118–25. In *Shandong fengwu daquan*, ed. Shandong Sheng difang shi zhi bianzuan weiyuanhui (Beijing: Shijie zhishi chubanshe, 1990), p. 128, the Wu cemetery stones are said to be "China's most important group of Han-dynasty pictorial stone materials."

13. Huang Yi probably made rubbings of the Xiaotang Shan stone chamber as early as about 1785. This may have been the set he sent Weng Fanggang (1733–1818) in 1786. See Huang Yi's painting of the Xiaotang Shan site reproduced and discussed in Cai Hongru, "Huang Yi *Debei shier tu*," *Wenwu* 1996.3, pp. 75, 76, fig. 4. He also made rubbings of this structure in 1797, which may be the set he sent to Ruan Yuan later that same year. See Huang Yi, *Dai yan fanggu riji* (1797), *Shike shiliao xinbian di san ji* edition, facsimile reproduction of 1921, *Dun'an jinshi congshu* edition (Taipei: Xinwenfeng chuban gongsi, 1986), p. 7b; Bi Yuan and Ruan Yuan, *Shanzuo jinshi zhi* (preface 1797), *Shike shiliao xinbian* edition (Taipei: Xinwenfeng chuban gongsi, 1977), *juan* 7, p. 12a–b. For discussion and summary of past studies on the Xiaotang Shan stone chamber, see Ruitenbeek, *Chinese Shadows*, pp. 11–14, 66–85. There are reports that some stones in this hall are Ming-dynasty recarvings or replacement stones. For the Yi'nan tomb, see Lydia duPont Thompson, "The Yi'nan Tomb: Narrative and Ritual in Pictorial Art of the Eastern Han (25–220 CE)" (PhD diss., Institute of Fine Arts, New York University, 1998). Early excavation reports dated this tomb to the Period of Disunity. In subsequent scholarship the tomb has generally been redated to the Eastern Han, but many questions remain unresolved.

14. On the so-called Tang Rubbing, see Ma Ziyun, "Tan Wu Liang Ci huaxiang de Song ta yu Huang Yi taben," *Gugong bowuyuan yuankan* 1960.2, pp. 170–77. In Huang Yi, *Xiaopenglai Ge jinshi wenzi* (first published in 1785), unpaginated *Shimo Xuan* edition, 8 fascicles (N.p.: 1834) (East Asian Library, Princeton University, coll. no. B347-1264), recut copies of the fourteen scenes of the Tang Rubbing were reproduced along with a record of the colophons. See Huang Yi's 1791 colophon in ibid., "Wu Liang Ci xiang taben" sec., pp. 23b–24a. The actual rubbing was severely damaged by fire, and photographs of a few surviving fragments are reproduced in *Shang Zhou zhi Qin Han shufa*, ed. Zhongguo meishu quanji bianji weiyuanhui, *Zhongguo meishu quanji, Shufa zhuanke bian* 1 (Beijing: Renmin meishu chubanshe, 1987), no. 72.

15. For a pre-1979 review of archaeologically excavated Han tombs, their precedents and development, see Robert Thorp, "Mortuary Art and Architecture of Early Imperial China" (PhD diss., University of Kansas, 1979). For a more recent review, see Jiang Yingju and Yang Aiguo, *Handai huaxiang shi yu huaxiang zhuan* (Beijing: Wenwu chubanshe, 2001).

16. The symposium was held on November 11–13, 1986. The *Summary* is recorded in *Jiaxiang Xian zhi* (Ji'nan: Shandong renmin chubanshe, 1997), pp. 806–7.

17. For Tombs 1 and 2, see Jiang Yingju and Wu Wenqi, *Handai Wushi muqun shike yanjiu* ([Ji'nan]: Shandong meishu chubanshe, 1995), pp. 119–27. In summer 2002, during a visit to the site, it was possible to look into Tomb 3, which had reportedly been only recently found. The capstone of the tomb roof had been removed to expose the interior.

18. There is no report of paint in Jiang and Wu, *Handai Wushi muqun shike yanjiu*, pp. 119–27. Jiang Yingju, in conversation in 2004, did not remember ever seeing traces of paint in the tombs.

19. On *Jigu lu*, *Jigu lu mu*, and *Jinshi lu*, see Etienne Balazs and Yves Hervouet, *A Sung Bibliography* (Hong Kong: Chinese University Press, 1978), pp. 199–202.

20. The Ouyangs had included two stele inscriptions that would later be known as the Wu Rong and Wu Ban steles. Zhao Mingcheng included the Wu Ban stele, added the Wu Liang and Wu Kaiming steles and the gate-pillar inscription, but did not include the Wu Rong stele. Five rubbings or sections entitled "Pictorial Images of the Wu Family Stone Chamber of the Han Dynasty" ("Han Wushi shishi huaxiang") are listed in the table of contents (*mulu*) but are missing in all received versions; Zhao Mingcheng, *Jinshi lu*, *Yingyin Wenyuange Siku quanshu* edition (Taipei: Taiwan shangwu yinshuguan, 1983–1986), *juan* 2, p. 3b, and *juan* 19, p. 2a. It is unknown if this work was just a written description or if illustrations or rubbings were originally included.

21. In Hong Gua's *Li shi* there were only entries for the Wu Liang, Wu Ban, and Wu Rong steles. Apparently he only had rubbings of these three. His knowledge of the Wu Kaiming and gate-pillar inscriptions is evidenced in his commentarial remarks and by citations of the *Jinshi lu*. The "Confucius Meeting Laozi" stone was first recorded in Hong Gua, *Li xu*, *Yingyin Wenyuange Siku quanshu* edition (Taipei: Taiwan shangwu yinshuguan, 1983–1986), *juan* 12, pp. 28b–29a. Curiously, this stone was not mentioned in Hong Gua's *Li shi*. Hong Gua's remarks on the pictorial carvings are included in *Li shi*, and although illustrations or possibly rubbings of the so-called Wu Liang Shrine were included in the *Li xu*, it is not clear how accurately the sets of illustrations in received editions reflect the originals.

22. David Lowenthal, *The Past is a Foreign County* (Cambridge: Cambridge University Press, 1985), pp. 278–82.

23. Helpful reviews of past scholarship on the Wu shrines are included in Édouard Chavannes, *Mission archéologique dans la Chine septentrionale*, 2 vols. of text, 4 vols. of plates (Paris: Imprimerie Nationale, 1913 and 1915), text vol. 1, pp. 109–17; Wu Hung, *The Wu Liang Shrine: The Ideology of Early Chinese Pictorial Art* (Stanford: Stanford University Press, 1989), pp. 3–70.

24. See Hu Shih, "A Note on Ch'üan Tsu-wang, Chao I-ching and Tai Chen: A Study of Independent Convergence in Research as Illustrated in Their Works on the *Shui-ching chu*" (1944), in *Eminent Chinese of the Ch'ing Period* (1943), ed. Arthur W. Hummel (reprint, Taipei: Chengwen chubanshe, 1975), pp. 970–82.

25. Wang Guowei, annot., *Shuijing zhu jiao* (Shanghai: Shanghai renmin chubanshe, 1984), pp. 290, 291, 292. For an excavated site that purports to be the Fan Shi tomb, see Jiaxiang Xian wenwu guan, "Jiaxiang faxian de Donghan Fan Shi mu," *Wenwu* 1972.5, pp. 63–64.

26. Zhao Mingcheng traveled to the Taishan area in Shandong, but did not specifically mention visiting the Wu shrines in Song-dynasty Rencheng. His interests, however, were primarily epigraphical, and he may therefore have considered his itinerary irrelevant. It is unlikely that Hong Gua ever had a chance to travel to Shandong which was then under Jin-dynasty control.

27. Wei Bo, *Ba Wushi shishi huaxiang*, in his *Ding'an lei gao*, *Yingyin Wenyuange Siku quanshu* edition, *juan* 4, pp. 19b–20a. Chen Si (act. 1200–after 1259), comp., *Baoke congbian*, *Yingyin Wenyuange Siku quanshu* edition, *juan* 15, p. 2a, cites the no longer extant *Zhu dao shike lu* in recording "Han-dynasty Wu family stone chamber pictorial images" (*Han Wushi shishi huaxiang*) in the Southern Song-dynasty Chouzhong Ge library hall in Jiankang. This same source is cited in Ni Tao (*jinshi* 1709), *Liuyi zhi yi lu*, *Yingyin Wenyuange Siku quanshu* edition, *juan* 54, p. 32a, where the library hall was identified as the Choushu Ge. On the Choushu Ge library, see Ye Mengde (1077–1148), "Choushu Ge ji," in his *Jiankang ji*, *Yingyin Wenyuange Siku quanshu* edition, *juan* 4, pp. 1a–2b.

28. In Ni Tao, *Liuyi zhi yi lu*, *juan* 116, p. 6b, 8a; Gu Aiji, *Li bian* (1718), *Yingyin Wenyuange Siku quanshu* edition, *juan* 8, p. 38b, it is noted that Fang Wude had a recut edition in Jining Prefecture. For criticism of this edition, see Hong Gua, *Li xu*, *Yingyin Wenyuange Siku quanshu* edition, *juan* 6, p. 15a.

29. Wu Hung, *Wu Liang Shrine*, p. 4. For a chronology of events that includes a list of serious flooding and earthquakes in the Jiaxiang area from the Jin dynasty to the modern period, see *Jiaxiang Xian zhi* (1997), pp. 9–45.

30. Zhang Xuan, *Zhida Jinling xin zhi*, *Yingyin Wenyuange quanshu* edition, *juan* 12b, pp. 37b–38a. Besides the listed title, Zhang Xuan, or a later compiler, added descriptions of the Wu cemetery stones drawn from Zhao Mingcheng and Hong Gua.

31. See Zhu Yizun's colophon on the Tang Rubbing recorded in Huang Yi, *Xiaopenglai Ge jinshi wenzi*, "Wu Liang Ci xiang taben" sec., pp. 20b–21a; and discussed in Ma Ziyun, "Tan Wu Liang Ci huaxiang de Song ta yu Huang Yi taben," p. 170.

32. Qian Daxin, comp., *Tianyi Ge bei mu*, preface dated to 1787; reprinted in Fan family, comp., *Tianyi Ge cangshu zongmu*, preface by Ruan Yuan dated to 1808 (Zhejiang: Wenxuanlou, n.d.), fascicle 10, pp. 1b, 2a, 2b. In this catalogue the Wu Ban stele has two entries (pp. 2a, 2b), indicating that there may have been two copies. These rubbings are not listed among the surviving works in the "Tianyi Ge xian cun beimu" supplement in Xue Fucheng (1838–1894), ed., *Tianyi Ge xiancun shumu* (1889) (reprint, Taipei: Jinxue shuju, 1970), *juan mo*, pp. 341–43.

33. For summaries on the development of clerical script in the Han dynasty, see Lai Fei, "Shandong Handai huaxiang shi bangti," *Meishu shi yanjiu* 1994.2, p. 28; Han Rende, *Zhongguo shufa shi: Liang Han juan* (Nanjing: Jiangsu jiaoyu chubanshe, 1999), pp. 136–60; Tseng Yuho, *A History of Chinese Calligraphy* (Hong Kong: Chinese University Press, 1993), pp. 117–24.

34. On these texts, see Balazs and Hervouet, *Sung Bibliography*, pp. 203–4, 206–7.

35. For Weng Fanggang's biography, see *Eminent Chinese of the Ch'ing Period*, pp. 856–58.

36. Xu Jian (713–742), *Chuxue ji* (Beijing: Zhonghua shuju, 1962), *juan* 17, p. 26a; Lu Guangwei (9th century), *Wudi ji*, *Yingyin Wenyuange Siku quanshu* edition, p.19a.

37. Rong Geng, *Han Wu Liang Ci huaxiang lu*, 2 fascicles (Beijing: Yanjing daxue kaogu xueshe, 1936), text vol., p. 22a; Jiang and Wu, *Handai Wushi muqun shike yanjiu*, p. 57, n. 40. The discrepancy between what is recorded in written texts and what is depicted in the pictorial carvings is noted in Wu Hung, *Wu Liang Shrines*, pp. 292–95.

38. See Huang Yi, *Xiu Wushi Citang ji lue*, in Jiang and Wu, *Handai Wushi muqun shike yanjiu*, p. 132; translated in Appendix.

39. Huang Yi, *Xiu Wushi Citang ji lue*, pp. 132–33. A distinction is made in this essay between the assemblage and carved stones known as the "Wu family shrines" (*Wushi citang*, *Wushi ci*, or *Wushi shishi*), and the reconstructed stone chambers (only one chamber before 1786) known as the Wu Family Stone Chambers (Wushi Shishi), but also called the Wu Family Shrines (Wushi Citang), or Wu Shrines (Wu Ci). In the Qing-dynasty and present-day contexts, care must also be taken not to confuse the reconstructed stone chambers with the Preservation Halls built at the cemetery site that were also called the Wu Family Shrines (Wushi Citang).

40. The four groups, however, did not include every stone that had been recovered. Because of their pictorial content, some stones were separately labeled as Omen slabs, and the "Confucius Meeting Laozi" slab was moved to Jining to be stored with the Wu Rong stele in the Jining Prefectural Academy. In addition, other stones were not grouped or numbered. Adding to later confusion, some of the slabs included in the four groups would later be shown to belong to a group other than the one to which they had been assigned—or to none of the four groups. The numbering of the stones in each group also differed from the number of actual carved surfaces. Some stones were carved on more than one face, and this gave rise to different numbering systems developed by scholars who worked solely with rubbings and illustrations but never saw the actual stones.

The group designations and numbering of stones in 1789 differs from the later numbering systems adopted by Wilma Fairbank and by Jiang Yingju and Wu Wenqi (see Tables and Foldouts). On the confusion between these systems, see Jiang Yingju and Wu Wenqi, "Wushi Ci huaxiang shi jianzhu peizhi kao," *Kaogu xuebao* (hereafter, *KGXB*) 1981.2 , pp. 165–84. Also see n. 91 below.

41. Aside from the Wu Liang Ci, the Front Group came to be associated with Wu Rong, the Left Group with Wu Ban, and the Rear Group with Wu Kaiming. For a historical summary of how these associations were made, see Wu Hung, *Wu Liang Shrine*, pp. 27–28.
42. Strong doubts about the historical accuracy of matching the inscribed office titles accompanying chariot processions and battle scenes on the pictorial slabs to the deeds of Wu Rong and Wu Ban as recorded in their stele inscriptions is discussed in Lao Gan, "Lun Lu xi huaxiang san shi," pp. 101–2.
43. Huang Yi, *Xiu Wushi Citang ji lue*, p. 132.
44. A gazetteer illustration showing the Minglun Tang hall in the Jining Prefectural Academy compound is included in *Jining zhilizhou zhi*, comp. Xu Zonggan, rev. Lu Chaoan, facsimile reproduction of 1859 edition (Taipei: Taipei xuesheng shuju, 1968), front matter illustrations, pp. 8b–9a [continuous pagination, pp. 64–65].
45. See Zhu Xilu, ed., *Wushi Ci Han huaxiang shi* (Ji'nan: Shandong meishu chubanshe, 1986), p. 133. For photographs of the stone, see ibid., p. 99, fig. 109; Gong Yanxing, ed., *Jining quan Han bei* (Ji'nan: Qi-Lu shushe, 1990), p. 239, pl. 105 (right), in which it is labeled as the Wu Liang stele. The stele is also described in Jiang and Wu, *Handai Wushi muqun shike yanjiu*, pp. 21–22. Elsewhere Qu Derun reports in 1909 that while he was supervising construction at the cemetery site he found the blank stele between the pillar-gate and the tombs. See *Jining zhilizhou zhi*, *juan* 19, p. 55a. The stele was then moved into the east building, which was probably the new three-bay hall erected in 1910 (see below).
46. Gong Yanxing, *Jining quan Han bei*, p. 104.
47. Huang Yi, *Xiu Wushi Citang ji lue*, p. 132. In Gong Yanxing, *Jining quan Han bei*, pp. 103–5, 239, the blank stele is identified as the Wu Liang stele.
48. The architectural reconstruction of three structures by Wilma Fairbank and refined by Jiang Yingju and Wu Wenqi will be discussed below. Wu Hung accepts their reconstructions but posits a fourth structure reconstructed from scattered pictorial slabs that were found away from the cemetery. See Wu Hung, *Wu Liang Shrine*, pp. 20–24.
49. Berthold Laufer, *Chinese Pottery of the Han Dynasty* (Leiden: E. J. Brill, 1909); Édouard Chavannes, *La Sculpture sur pierre en Chine aux temps des deux dynasties Han* (Paris: Ernest Leroux, 1893); Chavannes, *Mission archéologique*; Sekino Tei [Sekino Tadashi], "Stone Mortuary Shrines with Engraved Tablets of Ancient China under the Latter Han Dynasty," part I, *Kokka*, vol. 19, no. 225 (1909), pp. 229–41, and part II, *Kokka*, vol. 19, no. 227 (1909), pp. 299–315; Sekino Tadashi, *Shina Santōshō ni okeru Kandai funbo no hyōshoku* (Tokyo: Imperial University of Tokyo, 1916); and Ōmura Seigai, *Shina bijutsushi: Chōso hen*, 2 vols. (Tokyo: Bussho kankōkai zuzōbu, 1915).
50. On the art of making rubbings, see below. On complications in studying different rubbing versions and forgeries of some of the Wu cemetery stones, see Wu Huilin, comp., *Zengbu Jiaobei suibi* (Shanghai: Shanghai shuhua chubanshe, 1981), pp. 59–60, 84–85, 150–53.
51. Wilma Fairbank, "The Offering Shrines of 'Wu Liang Tz'u'," *Harvard Journal of Asiatic Studies*, vol. 6, no. 1 (1941), pp. 1–36; reprinted in her *Adventures in Retrieval: Han Murals and Shang Bronze Molds* (Cambridge: Harvard University Press, 1972), pp. 43–86.
52. Jiang and Wu, *KGXB* 1981.2, pp. 165–84; Jiang and Wu, *Handai Wushi muqun shike yanjiu*, pp. 23–51.
53. Personal observations made at the site with Anthony Barbieri-Low on June 21, 2002. There are few recorded descriptions of the exterior surfaces of the pictorial stones. The exterior of the Wu Liang Shrine is described as being polished and carved with decorative bands in Jiang and Wu, *Handai Wushi muqun shike yanjiu*, p. 35. Although Jiang and Wu do not describe the exterior walls of the Front and Left Stone Chambers, they are depicted as roughly hewn in their reconstruction drawings; see Jiang and Wu, *KGXB* 1981.2, pp. 173, 177, figs. 6, 8; Jiang and Wu, *Handai Wushi muqun shike yanjiu*, pp. 38–39, 43–44, figs. 10, 12. The significance of the exterior appearance of the structures will be discussed in Liu's "Reconfiguring."
54. For discussions about the development of shrines in the Han period, see Yang

Kuan, *Zhongguo gudai lingqin zhidu shi yanjiu* (Shanghai: Shanghai guji chubanshe, 1985), pp. 123–32; Xu Jianguo, "Xuzhou Han huaxiang shi shici jianzhu," *Zhongyuan wenwu* 1993.2, pp. 53–60; Xin Lixiang, *Handai huaxiang shi zonghe yanjiu*, pp. 66–83; Jiang and Yang, *Handai huaxiang shi yu huaxiang zhuan*, pp. 83–96.

55. This stylistic comparison of noses in the pictorial stones at the cemetery was developed in collaboration with Anthony Barbieri-Low, using the rubbing set in the Princeton University Art Museum (cat. no. 1).

56. Fairbank, *Adventures in Retrieval*, pp. 80–81.

57. Jiang and Wu were careful to note that their reconstruction of three structures did not rule out the possibility of a fourth structure. See Jiang and Wu, *Handai Wushi muqun shike yanjiu*, p. 49.

58. A succinct review of modern scholarship along with a convenient chronology and bibliography are found in Wu Hung, *Wu Liang Shrine*, pp. 3–70, 329–34, 371–92.

59. Already in 1893 Chavannes appears to have questioned the identification of the stones as belonging to sepulchers of the Wu family. See his *Sculpture sur pierre en Chine*, pp. xx, xxi. Also see Chavannes, *Mission archéologique*, text vol. 1, pp. 111–14 passim, 122.

60. Post-Han literature, such as Li Daoyuan's *Shuijing zhu* of the early sixth century, contains many records of funerary steles at Han-dynasty tomb sites, but to my knowledge archaeological excavation has produced no Han inscribed steles in front of a tomb. The nearest example is the Xianyu Huang stele, bearing the date equivalent to 165, which was reportedly found in a cemetery zone in 1973. See Tianjin Shi wenwu guanlichu and Wuqing Xian wenhua guan, "Wuqing Xian faxian Donghan Xianyu Huang mu bei," *Wenwu* 1974.8, p. 68–72. It is possible that steles were not commonly located at tomb sites during the Han, and that this practice only became popular afterward, as recorded in the *Shuijing zhu*. It is further possibile that many inscribed steles were carved by later generations for their Han ancestors and erected at family cemeteries. Finally, no known Han-dynasty pictorial stone carvings or paintings seem to depict steles in a funerary context.

61. In Zhang Yansheng, *Shanben bei tie lu* (Beijing: Zhonghua shuju, 1984), p. 17, it is reported that the Wu Ban inscription was relatively clear in a fine rubbing (*jing ta*) version by Li Dongqi, a close acquaintance of Huang Yi. Until a legible Qing-dynasty rubbing of the inscription is found, the accuracy of this report should be questioned.

62. In the "Chen Jin" entry in Matsumaru Michio, ed., *Shinpen kinsekigaku roku: fu jigō sakuin seisotsu nenpyō* (Tokyo: Kyūko shoin, 1976), p. 112, this character is written as "collected" (*shou*).

63. In the "Chen Jin" entry in Matsumaru Michio, ed., *Shinpen kinsekigaku roku*, p. 112, this character is written as "craftsmen" (*gong*).

64. Chen Jin, *Chongxiu Wushi Citang ji* (1880), cited in Jiang and Wu, *Handai Wushi muqun shike yanjiu*, p. 135.

65. Ouyang Xiu, *Jigu lu*, *Yingyin Wenyuange Siku quanshu* edition, *juan* 3, pp. 1b–2a, 24b.

66. *Taisui* can be translated as "Great Year" or "counter-Jupiter." It is an imaginary counter-orbital asterism called Taiyin or Taisui that tracks the motions of Jupiter. Explained in David Hawkes, *Ch'u Tz'u: The Songs of the South* (London: Oxford University Press, 1959), p. 211. The twelve positions of Taisui correlate to the twelve Earthly Branches (*dizhi*). In the Western Han they were joined in a cyclical pairing with the Suiyang order designated by the ten Heavenly Stems (*tiangan*). Also discussed in relation to cosmographs in John S. Major, *Heaven and Earth in Early Han Thought* (Albany: State University of New York Press, 1993), pp. 39–43. For a chart of the twelve Taisui positions and their *dizhi* correlations, see Wang Li, ed., *Gudai hanyu*, rev. ed. (Beijing: Zhonghua shuju, 1981), pp. 844–47.

67. Ouyang Xiu, *Jigu lu*, *Yingyin Wenyuange Siku quanshu* edition, *juan* 3, p. 1a.

68. The inclusion of the dynasty name in the title of this and many other Han steles may violate proper practice during the Han dynasty, in which case such titles are post-Han additions. This observation was already made in Shi She, comp., *Shuijing zhu bei lu* (Tianjin: Tianjin guji chubanshe, 1987), p. 42. Bi Yuan and Ruan Yuan, *Shanzuo jinshi zhi*, *juan* 7, p. 13a, note that Zhao Mingcheng "added" (*zeng*) the *Han* character to the Wu Ban stele. This is supported by Hong Gua's commentary at the end of his transcription of the stele text, which begins: "At right is the title head 'Stele of the Former Dunhuang Chief Clerk the Lord Wu' (*Gu Dunhuang zhangshi Wu jun zhi bei*), in clerical script." As recorded by Hong Gua, in the rubbings he was working with the title did not contain the *Han* character. If true, this suggests that the title head on the Wu Rong stele is also a later addition. As recorded in Ouyang Xiu's *Jigu lu*, without the title head, the Wu Rong stele also contains no mention of a Wu family name.

On the other hand, it may have been acceptable to refer to the dynasty by name in a title during the Han. One example is Wang Mang's (r. 9–23) title "Duke Who Gives Tranquility to the House of Han" (An Han Gong). Another example is an excavated inscribed stone dated to 170 with the line: "It was in the Jianning era of the Han" (*Wei Han Jianning*). See Nanyang Shi bowuguan, ed., "Nanyang faxian Donghan Xu Aqu muzhi huaxiang shi," *Wenwu* 1974.8, pp. 73–74. The circumstances surrounding this reused stone, found in a Three Kingdoms–period tomb, are vague, and the title and pictorial carvings at the top may be later additions.

69. Compare the Wu Ban stele entries in Hong Gua, *Li shi, Li xu*, collated by Wang Rixiu, facsimile edition (Beijing: Zhonghua shuju, 1985), *juan* 6, pp. 11a–13b, and Hong Gua, *Li shi*, *Yingyin Wenyuange Siku quanshu* edition, *juan* 6, pp. 12a–14a. The Wang Rixiu edition is now commonly cited as the authoritative version, but needs to be used with circumspection. It should be noted that Wang Rixiu was from Huang Yi's hometown. Later versions of his edition include an 1871 reprint by the Hong family of Hangzhou, known as the *Huimuzhai congshu* edition; see Hong Gua, *Li shi, Li xu*. The partial insertion of the gate-pillar inscription into the appended commentary is recorded in Bi Yuan and Ruan Yuan, *Shanzuo jinshi zhi*, *juan* 7, p. 17a.

70. See Wu Hung, *Wu Liang Shrines*, passim; and Jiang and Wu, *Handai Wushi muqun shike yanjiu*, pp. 18–20.

71. Many of these problems were first brought to my attention by Michael Nylan. We are grateful to Pricilla Chen, Eileen Hsu, Haitao Tang, and Mei-ling Williams for working closely with us to investigate numerous aspects of the textual transmission of the "Wu family shrines" inscriptions.

72. On the concept of "embodied image," see Cary Y. Liu, "Embodying Cosmic Patterns: Foundations of an Art of Calligraphy in China," *Oriental Art*, vol. 56, no. 5 (2000), pp. 2–9; Cary Liu, "Chinese Architectural Aesthetics: Patterns of Living and Being between Past and Present," in *House, Home, Family: Living and Being Chinese*, ed. Ronald G. Knapp (Honolulu: University of Hawai'i Press, forthcoming).

73. In Zhao Mingcheng's entry on the Wu family pictorial stone chamber, *Jinshi lu*, *juan* 19, p. 10a, the stones were said to be "in modern [Song-dynasty] Rencheng in Jizhou" (*zai jin Jizhou Rencheng*). For a map showing the territory of Jizhou Prefecture in the Song, see Tan Qixiang, gen. ed., *Zhongguo lishi ditu ji* (Shanghai: Ditu chubanshe, 1982), vol. 6, pls. 14–15. In entries for the Wu Liang stele and gate-pillar inscriptions in the *Jinshi lu*, and similarly in entries in Hong Gua's *Li shi*, however, the stones are located in Rencheng in Jizhou without specifying when this was so. This has led some later scholars to locate the cemetery in Rencheng during the Han dynasty. During Eastern Han the site was most likely under the jurisdiction of Shanyang Commandery; see Jiang and Wu, *Handai Wushi muqun shike yanjiu*, p. 3; Tan Qixiang, *Zhongguo lishi ditu ji*, vol. 2, map nos. 44–45. The jurisdictional borders of commanderies and kingdoms changed frequently during the Eastern Han, and boundaries can only be mapped for certain moments for which census records and documents survive.

74. See Hong Gua, *Li shi*, *Yingyin Wenyuange Siku quanshu* edition, *juan* 6, pp. 14a–b, and *juan* 12, p. 9a.

75. Shi Shengzu, *Xuezhai zhanbi*, *Yingyin Wenyuange Siku quanshu*, *juan* 3, 15b–16a.

76. In his 1705 colophon to the Tang Rubbing, Zhu Yizun identified the Shi rubbings with the Wu Liang shrine cartouche inscriptions; cited in Huang Yi, *Xiaopenglai Ge jinshi wenzi*, "Wu Liang Ci xiang Tang taben" sec., p. 21a. The inscriptions recorded by Shi Shengzu need to be carefully compared against the cartouche inscriptions of the Wu Liang group stones as recorded in different editions of Hong Gua's *Li shi*, to see if any conflation of the recorded texts occurred. The Shi Shengzu text is further discussed in Nylan's "Addicted to Antiquity" in this catalogue.

77. Huang Yi, *Qian hou shishi huaxiang ba* (1796), in Fang Shuo, *Zhenjingtang jinshi tiba* (1862), *Shike shiliao xinbian di er ji* edition, facsimile reproduction of 1864 edition (Taipei: Xinwenfeng chuban gongsi, 1979), *juan* 2, p. 34b. In Duan Songling, *Shanzuo beimu* (preface 1796), *Shike shiliao xinbian di er ji* edition, facsimile reproduction of 1908 edition, *juan* 2, p. 27b, and *Jining zhili zhouzhi*, "Suoshi Shan" entry, *juan* 3, p. 10a [p. 291], it is noted that there was a cliff carving of a "Hong Shui shi" ("Flood-waters Poem") in the Hong Shan mountains. It is unclear if this is the same cliff inscription cited by Huang Yi. According to *Jiaxiang Xian zhi* (1997), p. 10, in the fifth month of 1344 twenty days of rain caused the Yellow River to breach its banks, flooding Jiaxiang and surrounding areas to a depth of two *zhang* rods. The flood waters did not recede for seven years and there were reports of cannibalism in the area.

78. See Chen Jin, *Chongxiu Wushi Citang ji* (1880), cited in Jiang and Wu, *Handai Wushi muqun shike yanjiu*, pp. 134–35; Bushell, "Inscriptions from the Tombs of the Wu Family," p. 80; Wu Hung, *Wu Liang Shrine*, p. 4, esp. n. 11.

79. The following calendar of disasters occurred in the Eastern Han dynasty alone: famine in Rencheng in 151, leading to reports of cannibalism; see *Hou Hanshu*, comp. Fan Ye (Beijing: Zhonghua shuju, 1965), *juan* 7, p. 296. Rebellion in 154, affecting some 30,000 people before being defeated in 156; see *Hou Hanshu*, *juan* 7, pp. 300–302; *juan* 38, p. 1286; *juan* 62, p. 2063; *juan* 65, p. 2145. Taishan and Langye bandits rebelled in 160 but were quickly defeated; see *Hou Hanshu*, *juan* 7, p. 307. In 190 a million Yellow Turban rebels from Qingzhou entered Yanzhou and killed the Chancellor (*xiang*) of Rencheng before turning toward Dongping; see *Sanguo zhi*, comp. Chen Shou (Beijing: Zhonghua shuju, 1959), *juan* 1, p. 9.

80. Special thanks to Eileen Hsu for helping to distinguish Huang Yi's comments from the 1344 inscription. Because Huang Yi's comments have sometimes been taken as part of the 1344 inscription, this inscription has often become the basis for concluding that the Wu cemetery was buried by flooding in the Yuan dynasty. See Jiang and Wu, *Handai Wushi muqun shike yanjiu*, p. 6, n. 10; Wu Hung, *Wu Liang Shrine*, p. 329. In the latter, the inscription is translated as reading: "In the fourth year of the Zhizheng reign (1344), [the Yellow River] was in fierce floods . . . . All the stone chambers were destroyed; the mud deposited in the field was more than ten [Chinese] feet in depth." Only by finding the 1344 inscription can we verify the correct reading.

81. According to distances given in the *Jining zhili zhouzhi*, *juan* 3, p. 10a [p. 291], the Hong Shan mountains were located 22 *li* miles southwest of Jiaxiang. In Duan Songling, *Shanzuo beimu*, *juan* 2, p. 27, the Hong Shan mountains are said to be 22 *li* miles to the east of Jiaxiang.

82. Jiang and Wu, *Handai Wushi muqun shike yanjiu*, p. 131, and *Jiaxiang Xian zhi* (1997), *juan* 24, p. 653, both note that the engraved tablets no longer survive. Sekino, *Shina Santōshō*, text p. 23, records that the *Brief Record* tablets were embedded in the upper section of the back wall in the Preservation Hall in 1907. Transcriptions of the *Brief Record* are well recorded, but it is odd that no rubbings of it seem to have survived.

83. Jiang and Wu, *Handai Wushi muqun shike yanjiu*, p. 4, n. 10, note that there is a Shunzhi reign-period edition of the *Jiaxiang Xian zhi*. There is also a *Jiaxiang Xian zhi* compiled by Wo Shibu (1778) (not seen by author).

84. The relationship between markers and the identification of relics will be discussed below. On the importance of markers for identifying and preserving a relic, see Lowenthal, *The Past is a Foreign County*, pp. 265–71.

85. A similar conclusion was reached by Sekino Tadashi: "Huang-i, in conjunction with others of the same mind, unearthed one of these structures, but unfortunately instead of replacing the structure thus restored in its original form, they pulled it down and used the engraved slabs from it to decorate the inside walls of a brick shrine erected on its site." See Sekino, "Stone Mortuary Shrines," part II, p. 303.

86. In the place name "Wu Zhai Shan" the character *zhai* can also be pronounced *di*, which refers to a long-tailed pheasant or to the northern Di people.

87. After Huang Yi's identification of the "Wu family shrines" cemetery with the name of the hill, references to Martial Zhai Hill were replaced in the late nineteenth and early twentieth century by a general acceptance of the name Wu Residence Hill. This is a preliminary observation made in Mei-ling Williams, "A Sociological Study of Rubbing

Collecting in Qing Dynasty China: Two Case Studies," unpublished research paper prepared for this project (January 21, 2004).

88. For detailed discussion, see Nylan's "Addicted to Antiquity" in this catalogue.

89. For detailed discussion, see Nylan's "Addicted to Antiquity" in this catalogue.

90. See Sima Guang, comp., *Zizhi tongjian* (Beijing: Zhonghua shuju, 1956), *juan* 55, p. 1780; Denis Twitchett and Michael Loewe, eds., *The Ch'in and Han Empires, 221 B.C.–A.D. 220*, vol. 1 of *Cambridge History of China* (Cambridge: Cambridge University Press, 1986), p. 315. For *yinsi*, see Michael Loewe, *Chinese Ideas of Life and Death: Faith, Myth and Reason in the Han Period (202 BC–AD 220)* (London: George Allen & Unwin, 1982), p. 109.

91. See Fairbank, *Adventures in Retrieval*, p. 57, fig. 1; Jiang and Wu, *KGXB* 1981.2, pp. 181–84, and *Handai Wushi muqun shike yanjiu*, pp. 29–31, table 1. A convenient table is provided in Appendix C in Wu Hung, *Wu Liang Shrine*, pp. 335–38; note however, that the Huang Yi numbers given in this table actually follow the Fairbank numbering. The Huang Yi system counts the number of stones, some of which have two pictorial faces. In contrast, the Fairbank system counts the number of rubbings or pictorial faces. The stones and rubbings have also frequently been referenced to illustration numbers appearing in photographic publications, including Chavannes, *Mission archéologique*; Sekino, *Shina Santōshō*; Fu Xihua et al., comps., *Handai huaxiang quanji*, 2 portfolios (Beijing: Bali daxue Beijing Han xue yanjiusuo, 1950–1951), portfolio 2; *Zhongguo huaxiang shi quanji*, ed. Shandong huaxiang shi quanji bianji weiyuanhui, vols. 1–3: *Shandong Han huaxiang shi* (Ji'nan: Shandong meishu chubanshe, 2000).

92. The positions of Huang Yi's slabs WLC.1 and WLC.3 have been reversed by later writers, such as Fairbank and Wu Hung; see Jiang and Wu, *KGXB* 1981.2, p. 167. For the architectural reconstruction by Wilma Fairbank, see *Adventures in Retrieval*, pp. 43–86. For later refinement of the Fairbank reconstruction by Jiang Yingju and Wu Wenqi, see Jiang and Wu, *KGXB* 1981.2, pp. 165–84, and *Handai Wushi muqun shike yanjiu*, pp. 23–51.

93. In 1907 the "Confucius Meeting Laozi" stone was still in the Minglun Tang hall; see Chavannes, *Mission archéologique*, text vol. 1, p. 113. On the Minglun Tang, see n. 44, above. The slab is presently embedded in a wall inside the former stele pavilion of the Tieta Si, a former temple now located behind the Jining Municipal Museum. The Wu Rong stele is also presently stored in this pavilion.

94. The inscription is transcribed in Jiang and Wu, *Handai Wushi muqun shike yanjiu*, p. 65. For Li Dongqi's biography, see Yu Jianhua, *Zhongguo meishu jia renming cidian*, p. 367.

95. Jiang and Wu, *Handai Wushi muqun shike yanjiu*, p. 3; Wu Hung, *Wu Liang Shrine*, pp. 36–37.

96. Slab R.8 is a triangular stone with two pictorial surfaces. This single stone has often been counted as two separate carvings in later numbering systems. See Jiang and Wu, *Handai Wushi muqun shike yanjiu*, p. 25.

97. See Jiang and Wu, *Handai Wushi muqun shike yanjiu*, p. 143, pl. 10. Jiang Yingju, in personal conversation, dates this photograph to about 1980.

98. Among the Five Emperors, legend has it that Shun once farmed at Lishan. Today there are Lishan sites in Shandong and Shaanxi, and both areas claim the Shun legend. See Liu Xingzhen and Yue Fengxia, eds., *Han Dynasty Stone Reliefs—The Wu Family Shrines in Shandong Province* (Beijing: Foreign Languages Press, 1991), p. 21.

99. The name Huang Lin may refer the Yu Huang Ge. Huang Yi is said to have set aside twelve *mu* acres of arable land to be used by laymen from the nearby Yu Huang Ge hall for the care and upkeep of the Preservation Hall. This was reinstituted in 1880 after the renovation of the Preservation Hall; see Chen Jin, "Chongxiu Wushi Citang ji," p. 135 (partly translated below). Wang Chang records that more than ten *mu* were allotted for this purpose, and that the laymen also supervised access to the hall and the making of rubbings. See Wang Chang, *Jinshi cuibian* (preface 1805), *Shike shiliao xinbian* edition, facsimile reproduction of the *Jingxun Tang* edition, *juan* 20, p. 53a. Although the Yu Huang Ge temple hall was said to be near the site, it has yet to be identified. There were many Yu Huang Miao temples in Jiaxiang County. In a chart of current Daoist temples, one was located at Dashantou and another at Tang Shan; see

Jiaxiang Xian zhi (1997), *juan* 26, p. 716. There was also a Yu Huang Miao temple built as part of the Qingshan Si temple complex, 8.2 km south of the Jiaxiang county seat; see *Jiaxiang Xian zhi* (1997), *juan* 24, p. 658–59. In conversation, Jiang Yingju also raised this temple as a possible candidate. In addition, in Laufer, *Chinese Pottery of the Han Dynasty*, p. 69, n. 2, it is reported that the Xiaotang Shan stone chamber was part of a Yu Huang Dian temple.

100. A photograph of the stone and its full description was first published in Jiang and Wu, *KGXB* 1981.2, p. 168, fig. 1. The stone is first reconstructed as part of the Wu Liang Ci hall in Jiang and Wu, *Handai Wushi muqun shike yanjiu*, pp. 3, 35, 60–61, 152, pl. 22. A photograph of a rubbing of this stone is reproduced in *Zhongguo huaxiang shi quanji* (2000), vol. 1, nos. 52–54.

101. Planning for the Preservation Hall started in 1787, with requests for donations by Huang Yi and Weng Fanggang. During construction in 1789 additional pictorial stones were uncovered at the site, and the hall seems to have been completed in 1792, when Li Dongqi and Qian Yong (1759–1844) composed commemorative inscriptions (cat. nos. 1.52, 1.53). For transcriptions of Li Dongqi's *Wushi guanzhi minghao bei*, and for Qian Yong's inscribed record (*tiji*), see Jiang and Wu, *Handai Wushi muqun shike yanjiu*, pp. 133–34. I am grateful to Mei-ling Williams for developing this chronology.

102. One problem in deciphering locations in the *Brief Record* results from Huang Yi's inconsistent use of two different north-south coordinate systems. Besides true north-south, he also developed a coordinate system around the gate-pillars. Although the pillars are actually located to the northeast and southwest, for the sake of simplicity. Huang Yi called their positions north and south, respectively. This would imply that the site is oriented along an east-west axis.

103. Notwithstanding near illegibility in 1786, Good Omen.1 was "transcribed" in several later texts. See Bi Yuan and Ruan Yuan, *Shanzuo jinshi zhi*, *juan* 7, pp. 29b–30b; Feng Yunpeng and Feng Yunyuan, eds., *Jinshi suo* (N.p.: Ziyang Xian shu cang ban, 1821), vol. *Shi suo si*, "Han Wushi shishi xiangrui tu yi" sec.; Wang Chang, *Jinshi cuibian*, *juan* 21, pp. 19b–20b. The transcribed characters from these three sources were compiled with the characters on the surviving stone in Jiang and Wu, *Handai Wushi muqun shike yanjiu*, pp. 58–59. The characters may have been clearer in early rubbings, but this does not explain why Huang Yi could not read them. Possibly the later transcriptions extrapolated text from other sources that recorded omens. A detailed examination of the relationship between the Good Omen stone inscriptions and earlier texts on the subject of omens is required.

104. This agrees with the reconstruction of the Wu Liang Ci hall in Fairbank, *Adventures in Retrieval*, pp. 58–59; Jiang and Wu, *KGXB* 1981.2, pp. 170–72, and their *Handai Wushi muqun shike yanjiu*, pp. 34–37. The carved roof tiles on the back of the Good Omen stones were already noted in Feng Yunpeng and Feng Yunyuan, *Jinshi suo*, vol. *Shi suo si*, "Han Wushi shishi xiangrui tu yi" sec.

105. *Illustrations of Obtaining Steles* is an ink-on-paper album of twelve leaves plus one leaf with a preface by Weng Fanggang. Reproduced in Zhang Shulan, "Qing Huang Yi *Debei tu* ce," *Shoucang jia* gen. no. 17 (1996), p. 16; and in four leaves in *Tianjin Shi yishu bowuguan cang hua ji*, ed. Tianjin Shi yishu bowuguan (Beijing: Wenwu chubanshe, 1959–1963), vol. 2, pp. 148–49. Also reproduced under the title *Twelve Illustrations of Obtaining Steles* in Cai Hongru, "Huang Yi *Debei shier tu*," *Wenwu* 1996.3, pp. 74, 77–78, fig. 6; *Zhongguo gudai shuhua tumu*, ed. Zhongguo gudai shuhua jianding zu (Beijing: Wenwu chubanshe, 1993), vol. 10, pp. 215–16.

106. Cai Hongru, "Huang Yi *Debei shier tu*," p. 72.

107. The 1791 painting is reproduced in *Fine Classical Chinese Paintings and Calligraphy* (Hong Kong: Christie's, October 31, 2004), p. 130, lot 416; *Fine Chinese Paintings and Calligraphy* (New York: Christie, Manson, and Woods International, Inc., December 1, 1986), p. 128, lot 137. My appreciation to Eileen Hsu for bringing this painting to my attention, and to Cheng-ming Ma for his help in providing us with research photographs.

108. Because of Huang Yi's expressed excitement in finding the Wu Ban stele, one can say with confidence that this is the stele that is represented. It is important to recall, however, that a second, blank, stele may have also been at the site in 1786.

109. A distance of 15 km between Jiaxiang and Wuzhai Shan is cited in Jiang and Wu, *Handai Wushi muqun shike yanjiu*, p. 3. In the *Jiaxiang Xian zhi* (1997), *juan* 2, p. 76, the hill is said to be 13.1 km from Jiaxiang, covering 0.2 square km and with its main peak rising 86.1 m above sea level. There are several possible reasons for the discrepancy in distance. In many cases the actual distance was never scientifically measured, and may have been calculated by travel time. Additionally, many texts only repeat what was cited in earlier texts. It should also be remembered that flooding in this area caused the relocation of towns and villages at various times. In the Jin-dynasty Zhenglong reign-period (1156–1160) the Jiaxiang area was flooded, and the county seat was moved south to Heng Shan mountains. Another flood in 1175 forced the county seat to move to the foothills of the Meng Shan mountains, and a city wall was built at that time. See *Wanli Yanzhou fu zhi*, *Tianyi Ge cang Mingdai fangzhi xuankan xubian* edition (Shanghai: Shanghai shudian, 1990), *juan* 16, p. 30b.

110. See n. 73, above. Because the *Brief Record* is the only primary source describing the recovery of the stones, the misleading impression that the site was located in Rencheng in the Han dynasty has frequently been repeated in later writings.

111. The jurisdiction of Jiaxiang ("Auspicious Omen") was only established under that name during the Jin-dynasty Huangtong reign-period (1141–1148). The auspicious name derives from the legend of King Ai capturing a female unicorn (*lin*) in this location. See *Wanli Yanzhou fu zhi*, *juan* 16, p. 30b.

112. On the present location of the Wu Rong stele and "Confucius Meeting Laozi" stone, see n. 93, above.

113. Records differ on who actually built the Preservation Hall. A 1789 inscription on Stone L.1 records that Li Kezheng and Liu Zhaoyong built the hall. Because of Weng Fanggang's prominence, his role is exaggerated in the *Jiaxiang Xian zhi* (1997), *juan* 24, p. 650. The gazetteer claims that Weng Fanggang visited Jiaxiang, that he, along with Li Dongqi, Li Kezheng, and Nan Zhengyan, was responsible for moving the "Confucius Meeting Laozi" stone to Minglun Tang hall, and that he also funded the building of the Preservation Hall at the site.

114. The inscription was carved on seven rectangular stone tablets, each ca. 39 × ca. 95 cm. The first stone has the title written in large seal-script calligraphy. Carved on the second to fifth stones is the text of the inscription in clerical-script calligraphy, with six characters per column and sixteen columns on a stone. The sixth stone starts with part of Weng Fanggang's inscription, in four columns of six characters each. The following twenty-five columns on the sixth stone and thirty-four columns on the seventh stone list the donors and donations. Zheng Zhizong of Jizhou carved the stones. The donor list is in two groups, with two donors (Huang Yi and Li Meicun) appearing in both. Weng Fanggang was listed among the first three donors, along with Bi Yuan and Wang Chang. Huang Yi was the top donor, contributing twice for a total of 140,000 cash.

115. Also see the inscription by Li Dongqi on the right end of Stone L.1. Transcribed in Jiang and Wu, *Handai Wushi muqun shike yanjiu*, p. 50, n. 4.

116. See Huang Yi, *Zuo Shishi huaxiang ba*, *juan* 2, pp. 35a–b.

117. Cited in Jiang and Wu, *Handai Wushi muqun shike yanjiu*, p. 50, n. 4.

118. Stone L.1 is contiguous with the *Wang Ling mu* stone (discussed later) to its left. The two fragments form part of a longer horizontal stone that is now missing its left end. See Chen Jin, *Chongxiu Wushi Citang ji*, pp. 134–35; Wu Hung, *Wu Liang Shrine*, pp. 20–23.

119. Jiang and Wu, *KGXB* 1981.2, p. 167.

120. See Huang Yi, *Zuo shishi huaxiang ba*; Bi Yuan and Ruan Yuan, *Shanzuo jinshi zhi*, *juan* 7, pp. 53b–54a; Jiang and Wu, *Handai Wushi muqun shike yanjiu*, p. 26, n. 3.

121. See Bi Yuan and Ruan Yuan, *Shanzuo jinshi zhi*, *juan* 7, p. 54a–b; Duan Songling, *Shanzuo beimu*, *juan* 2, p. 26b. This stone is not included among the Princeton rubbings (cat. no. 1). Rubbings are reproduced in Sekino, *Shina Santōshō*, pl. 100; Ōmura Seigai, *Shina bijutsu shi: Chōso hen*, pl. 175; Jiang and Wu, *Handai Wushi muqun shike yanjiu*, p. 167, pl. 48; Zhu Xilu, *Wushi Ci Han huaxiang shi*, pp. 68, 127, fig. 68.

122. See Bi Yuan and Ruan Yuan, *Shanzuo jinshi zhi*, *juan* 7, p. 54b; Duan Songling, *Shanzuo beimu*, *juan* 2, p. 24a. This stone is not included in the Princeton rubbings (cat. no. 1). Rubbings are reproduced in Sekino, *Shina Santōshō*, pl. 101; Ōmura Seigai, *Shina bijutsu shi*, pl. 176; Zhu Xilu, *Wushi Ci Han huaxiang shi*, pp. 66, 126–27, fig. 65.

123. Huang Yi and his team could not have been randomly searching for relics throughout the area. With the cemetery site as their base, it is likely that some incentive was established to encourage local villagers to report ancient stone carvings.

124. *Jiaxiang Xian zhi* (1997), *juan* 24, p. 651.

125. Transcribed in Jiang and Wu, *Handai Wushi muqun shike yanjiu*, p. 134.

126. For Liu Xiaoyou's stele inscription, see Jiang and Wu, *Handai Wushi muqun shike yanjiu*, p. 136. Rong Geng, *Han Wu Liang Ci huaxiang lu*, text vol., p. 4b. Wu Hung, *Wu Liang Shrine*, pp. 6–7. In June 2004, the stone with this inscription was located in the front Exhibition Hall with the gate-pillars, steles, and feline sculptures.

127. Rong Geng, *Han Wu Liang Ci huaxiang kao lu*, text vol., p. 4b.

128. The *Analects* records that when Confucius was playing stone chimes in Wei, a passing recluse carrying a straw basket (*he kui* [note: different characters from those inscribed on the stone]) heard the music and from its character commented that Confucius sought office as opposed to reclusion. See *Lunyu zhushu*, *Shisan jing zhushu* edition, "Xian wen" sec., *juan* 14, p. 2513; trans. in James Legge, *The Chinese Classics* vol. 1, pp. 290–91.

129. Chen Jin, *Chongxiu Wushi Citang ji*, pp. 134–35; discussed below. Ding Rongjiang served as the District Magistrate of Jiaxiang from 1873 to 1875 or 1876; see *Jining zhilizhou xu zhi* (1911), rev. Pan Shoulian, comp. Yuan Shao'ang et al. (Taipei: Xuesheng shuju, 1968), *juan* 10, p. 28a.

130. A carved inscription by Chen Jin on the *He kui* stone says it was given by Ding Rongjiang in 1880. This is evidence that Ding eventually succeeded in buying the stone from the Xuanyuan brothers. Rong Geng, *Han Wu Liang Ci huaxiang lu*, text vol., p. 4b, noted that the *You niao ru he* stone was added to the Preservation Hall in 1880 with the other two stones, but his source was Chen Jin, whose *Record on the Renovation* does not mention it. Moreover, both the *He kui* and *Wang Ling mu* stones have carved inscriptions added by Chen Jin. There is no similar inscription on the *You niao ru he* stone, which suggests that it may have entered the Preservation Hall separately.

131. Sources saying the stone had been sold or lost include Chavannes, *Sculpture sur pierre en Chine*, pp. xxxviii–xxxix (labeled as the "third slab of marvelous objects," no. 14), and pl. 7; Rong Geng, *Han Wu Liang Ci huaxiang lu*, text vol., p. 4b; Fu Xihua et al., *Handai huaxiang quanji*, portfolio 2, fig. 192. The stone is noted as currently at the site in Jiang and Wu, *KGXB* 1981.2, p. 168; Jiang and Wu, *Handai Wushi muqun shike yanjiu*, p. 26. It is also possible the stone left the site and was returned later. When I visited in June 2004, the stone was there.

132. Rong Geng, *Han Wu Liang Ci huaxiang lu*, text vol., p. 4b. The *Shandong tong zhi*, comp. Sun Baotian (1840–1911), cited in *Jining zhilizhou xu zhi*, *juan* 19, p. 58a, records that in the early twentieth century the *Wang Ling mu* stone went into the collection of the Manchu official and collector Duan-fang (1861–1911) in Changbai, Shandong. For Duan-fang's biography, see *Eminent Chinese of the Ch'ing Period*, pp. 780–82. In 2002 a close copy of the *He kui* stone was offered for sale in Paris. The edges of this stone were trimmed, and it differed in many details from rubbings of the *He kui* stone.

133. Wu Hung, *Wu Liang Shrine*, pp. 20–24.

134. Songshan village is about 24 km southwest of the Wuzhai Shan cemetery site. The Songshan pictorial stones were reused building materials found in three post-Han tombs. The stones are currently in the collection of the Shandong Stone Inscriptions Art Museum (Shandong shike yishu bowuguan), and have been reconstructed as small offering halls. On their recovery and reconstruction, see Jiaxiang Xian Wushi Ci wenguansuo, "Shandong Jiaxiang Songshan faxian Han huaxiang shi," *Wenwu* 1979.9, pp. 1–6; Jining Shi diqu wenwuzu and Jiaxiang Xian wenguansuo, "Shandong Jiaxiang Songshan 1980 nian chutu de Han huaxiang shi," *Wenwu* 1982.5, pp. 60–70; Li Falin, "Jiaxiang Songshan chutu Yongshou sannian shike tiji jianshi," in his *Shandong Han huaxiang shi yanjiu* (Ji'nan: Qi-Lu shushe, 1982), pp. 101–8; Jiang Yingju, "Handai de xiao citang," *Kaogu* 1983.8, pp. 741–51; Zhu Xilu, ed., *Jiaxiang Handai huaxiang shi*

(Ji'nan: Shandong meishu chubanshe, 1992), nos. 43–77; Klaas Ruitenbeek, *Chinese Shadows*, pp. 40–46.

135. After presenting the rubbings to the Oriental Congress in Berlin, Bushell included several photographs of the rubbings in Stephen W. Bushell, *Chinese Art*, Victoria and Albert Museum Handbooks, 2 vols. (London: His Majesty's Stationery Office, 1910), vol. 1, pp. 3, 8, 26, 29–33, figs. 1–5, 15–17. Bushell also noted that "two were photographed at the South Kensington Museum, at the instance of Sir Philip Owen, who unsuccessfully urged the publication of the whole series." See ibid., p. 26. It is yet to be determined if the Bushell set is currently in the collection of the Victoria and Albert Museum.

136. R.K. Douglas, "Ancient Sculptures in China," *Journal Royal Asiatic Society* NS, vol. 18 (October 1886), pp. 469–76. It seems Douglas never saw actual rubbings, and had only heard that some rubbings of pictorial carvings might have been made. He also notes that Bushell had presented some "copy" (not necessarily rubbings) of the pictorial carvings at the 1881 Oriental Congress in Berlin, and that there was a "copy" in the British Museum. The latter may refer to a group of unprovenanced copied or forged stones in storage at the British Museum that were formerly thought to be Wu cemetery stones.

137. Lieutenant Mills, "A Tour in China, I–III," *The Chinese Times*, January 5, 1889, pp. 132–14; January 12, 1889, pp. 28–30; January 19, 1889, pp. 45–46; Bushell, *Chinese Art*, p. 26. Mills had been told about the site by Dr. Edkins of Beijing, who mentioned Mills's trip in *Chinese Recorder and Missionary Journal*, vol. XVIII (March 1887), pp. 117–118.

138. In 1886 R.K. Douglas had noted that there was already a "copy" of the Wu carvings in the British Museum. The Mills set must have been added after 1886. Because Mills was only passing through the district, the rubbings were likely not made during his visit, but acquired elsewhere. It will be important to compare the Bushell and Mills sets to determine if the *You niao ru he*, *He kui*, and *Wang Ling mu* rubbings were included.

139. Mills, "A Tour in China, II," p. 30. Mills reports that when some Chinese visitors were shown Assyrian antiquities in the British Museum, they exclaimed over their close stylistic resemblance to the Wu cemetery pictorial stones, saying that they "belong all same Wu-Leang-Sz [*sic*]."

140. For Cai Renqiu's work on water conservancy in Shandong, see *Jining zhilizhou xu zhi*, *juan* 10, pp. 49a–50b.

141. See Jiang and Wu, *KGXB* 1981.2, p. 168; Jiang and Wu, *Handai Wushi muqun shike yanjiu*, pp. 27, 31, 130. A photograph of the rubbing, reproduced in *Mission archéologique*, pl. 138, is incorrectly described as a floor stone. Also see Zhu Xilu, *Wushi Ci Han huaxiang shi*, pp. 62, 125–26, fig. 61.

142. See Zhu Xilu, *Wushi Ci Han huaxiang shi*, pp. 64, 126, fig. 63; Jiang and Wu, *Handai Wushi muqun shike yanjiu*, pp. 27, 31, 130, pl. 49.

143. Zhu Xilu, *Wushi Ci Han huaxiang shi*, pp. 67, 127, figs. 66–67; Jiang and Wu, *Handai Wushi muqun shike yanjiu*, pp. 27, 31, 130–31.

144. For a description of his travels and arrival at the site, see Chavannes, *Sculpture sur pierre en Chine*, pp. ii–iv, and for the interior plan and elevation drawings, see p. xxxviii. Most of the stones in the drawings are identified in the accompanying legend, but some were unidentified.

145. Laufer, *Chinese Pottery*, p. 70 n.2. Three sets of Wu shrine rubbings, collected by Laufer, are in the Field Museum, Chicago, but only one set is relatively complete. A set of loose folded sheets beginning with the series number F-244 was purchased in 1903 by Laufer for the American Museum of Natural History. A set with the series number F-116 is mounted as a handscroll and was purchased in Xi'an in 1908–1910 for the Field Museum. In Hartmut Walravens, ed., *Catalogue of Chinese Rubbings from Field Museum*, special edition of *FIELDIANA Anthropology* NS, no. 3 (November 30, 1981), pp. 51–64, it is noted that all three sets were acquired by Laufer in 1903.

146. See Laufer, *Chinese Pottery*, pp. 68–71, 86–87, 156–57, 267–69.

147. See Vasilii Mikhailovich Alekseev, *V starom Kitae: dnevniki puteshestviia 1907g.* (Moskow: Izd-vo Vostochnoi Literatury, 1958); translated into Chinese by Yan

Guodong as Miwa Aliekexienafu, *1907 nian Zhongguo jixing* (Kunming: Yunan renmin chubanshe, 2001), pp. 136–37. Also see Chavannes, *Mission archéologique*, text vol. 1, p. 116.

148. Miwa Aliekexienafu, *1907 nian Zhongguo jixing*, p. 137, notes that Chavannes "bought several fine rubbings from his [i.e., the gatekeeper's] hands."

149. Chavannes, *Sculpture sur pierre en Chine*, p. ii. Also see Laufer, *Chinese Pottery*, p. 70, n. 2.

150. Jiang and Wu, *Handai Wushi muqun shike yanjiu*, pls. 11, 12, 14. In Sekino, "Stone Mortuary Shrines," part II, p. 303, this stone was already identified as a gate-pillar capital and its location is plotted as no. 10 on the site map.

151. P. A. Volpert, "Die Ehrenpforten in China, II," *Orientalisches Archiv* 1 (1910/11), pp. 194–95; Chavannes, *Mission archéologique*, text vol. 1, pp. 21 n. 1, and 116. According to Volpert, ibid., p. 194: "On October 8,1907, in company of my brother, H. P. Mertens, I succeeded in excavating the lions mentioned on the inscription. They both lay three steps south [*sic*] of the stone columns. Together with the heavy base, each was hewn from a [single] block [of stone], but I found them broken off at the feet beside the base. The paws are still visible on the base." For the earliest published report and photographs of the east sculpture, see Sekino, "Stone Mortuary Shrines," part II, pp. 303, 305, 308–9. Also see Sekino, *Shina Santōshō*, pls. 32–33 (pl. 33 is incorrectly labeled as the west lion). A drawing of the east feline is reproduced in Volpert, "Die Ehrenpforten in China, II," p. 194, fig. 40. According to Chavannes, *Mission archéologique*, text vol. 1, p. 21, n. 1, the drawing suspiciously appears "to have been made after the photograph of Mr. Sekino." Early illustrations tend only to illustrate the east statue, which survived in better condition. For modern descriptions and photographs of both statues, see *Qin Han diaosu*, ed. Zhongguo meishu quanji bianji weiyuanhui, *Zhongguo meishu quanji, Diaosu bian* 2 (Beijing: Renmin meishu chubanshe, 1985), no. 91; Jiang and Wu, *Handai Wushi muqun shike yanjiu*, pp. 15–16, pls. 4–8; Wen Shaoming, ed., *Wushi Ci Han huaxiang shi* (N.p.: Shandong Sheng jiyou gongsi, n.d.), p. 22.

152. Dong Jing, "Shandong shengli tushuguan jinshi zhi chugao," *Shandong shengli tushuguan jikan*, vol. 1, no. 1 (1931), p. 63. Forty years after Li Baoxun's discovery of the felines, Dong Jing reports that the statues were "still deeply sunk in the mud." I am grateful to Anthony Barbieri-Low for bringing this reference to my attention.

153. Chen Mingda, "Handai de shique," *Wenwu* 1961.12, p. 12, fig. 7. I am grateful to Anthony Barbieri-Low for bringing this to my attention.

154. A pair of male and female feline stone statues dated to the Eastern Han were excavated in 1958 in the western outskirts of Xianyang, Shaanxi Province. The male also has a small animal under its forepaw; see *Qin Han diaosu*, no. 92. The felines in the Wu cemetery are anatomically correct, and in addition, the position of the tongue may indicate their sex. The male eastern statue with the raised tongue and small animal underfoot is similar to its Xianyang counterpart.

155. In the "Names of Wild and Legendary Animals" ("Shi shou") section of the *Erya* lexical compilation (ca. 3d century BCE), the *suanni* beast is described as a hairless tiger that eats tigers and leopards, and is identified in Guo Pu's (276–324) post-Han–dynasty commentary as a "lion" from the Western Regions brought to China during the reign of the Shundi emperor. See *Erya zhushu*, *Shisan jing zhushu* edition, *juan* 10, p. 2651. In the *Mu Tianzi zhuan* (3d or 2d century BCE), *Yingyin Wenyuange Siku quanshu* edition, *juan* 1, p. 4a, the *suanni* is just described as a creature capable of "traveling 500 *li* miles a day." *Houhan shu*, *juan* 3, p. 158.

156. On the development of the lion motif in China, see Laufer, *Chinese Pottery*, pp. 236–45; Jessica Rawson, *Chinese Ornament: The Lotus and the Dragon* (New York: Holmes and Meier Publishers, Inc., 1984), pp. 110–14; Jessica Rawson, "Strange Creatures," *Oriental Art*, vol. 44, no. 2 (1998), pp. 44–47. For examples of similar feline stone statues said to date from the Han period, see Ann Paludan, *The Chinese Spirit Road: The Classical Tradition of Stone Tomb Statuary* (New Haven: Yale University Press, 1991), pp. 39–44. The association of tigers as protectors of tombs is discussed in Sun Ji, *Handai wuzhi wenhua ziliao tushuo* (Beijing: Wenwu chubanshe, 1991), p. 418.

157. Rawson, "Strange Creatures," pp. 44–47. Berthold Laufer questioned whether the prototype of leonine figures in Han ceramics derived from lion motifs that had been earlier introduced "through the medium of Scythian and Old-Siberian art." See Laufer, *Chinese Pottery*, p. 245. Prior to the discovery of the two statues, both Bushell and Laufer had commented on the lion sculpture mentioned in the west gate-pillar inscription, and both said that the statues had been lost. See Bushell, *Chinese Art*, p. 29; Laufer, *Chinese Pottery*, p. 238.

158. Rawson, "Strange Creatures," p. 45. The association of "lions" (*shi*) with mythical protective beasts that devoured tigers and leopards seems to have developed after the Han period, when they became identified with legendary creatures known as *suanni*. See n. 155, above.

159. *Erya zhushu*, pp. 2650, 2653; *Zhongwen da cidian*, no. 9129/25.

160. See Shandong Sheng bowuguan, ed., *Shandong Sheng bowuguan cang pin xuan* (Guangdong: Shandong youyi shushe,1991), cat. no. 102.

161. Sekino, "Stone Mortuary Shrines," part I, pp. 229–41, and part II, pp. 299–315.

162. Each stone was assigned a number in the plan and elevation drawing, but no identifying legend was provided.

163. Sekino, *Shina Santōshō*, text pp. 23–49, 157–58, figs. 1, 6, 9, 12–16, 27, and pls. 27–101, 238, 242, 244.

164. Although not shown in his drawings, the nine inscribed tablets are reproduced in Chavannes, *Sculpture sur pierre en Chine*, pls. 44a–f, rubbing nos. 56–64, indicating that they were probably at the site when he visited in 1891.

165. One Japanese *shaku* unit = 30.3 cm. We can assume that both Chavannes and Sekino reconstructed their final drawings from notes taken at the site; therefore, some errors may be expected.

166. The stone is described in Sekino, *Shina Santōshō*, text p. 35. A similar stone but only 71.5 cm. long is described as a previously unrecorded stone in Jiang and Wu, *Handai Wushi muqun shike yanjiu*, p. 27 and p. 28, fig. 6 (center).

167. As noted earlier, the second Good Omen stone actually consists of three fragments.

168. In Sekino's drawings each of the stones is assigned a *hiragana* symbol, and many but not all are also identified by name. Unfortunately, the *hiragana* symbols do not seem to be keyed to the text or illustrations, making it difficult to identify several of the stones. Some of these may be identifiable by their dimensions.

169. Liu Xiaoyou was a native of Min County in Fujian Province, and served as Jiaxiang District Magistrate 1902–1904, and again 1906–1908 or 1909. See *Jining zhilizhou xu zhi*, *juan* 10, p. 29a. Research from Mei-ling Williams.

170. For Liu Xiaoyou's inscription, see Jiang and Wu, *Handai Wushi muqun shike yanjiu*, p. 136.

171. In Sekino, "Stone Mortuary Shrines," part II, p. 302, the English-language description as "stones once used for pavement and steps" corresponds to the term *kaidan seki* in Sekino, *Shina Santōshō*, text p. 26, and pl. 28.

172. This observation was already made in Fairbank, *Adventures in Retrieval*, p. 79, and Jiang and Wu, *Handai Wushi muqun shike yanjiu*, p. 32.

173. Jiang and Wu, KGXB 1981.2, pp. 168–69, figs. 2–4; Jiang and Wu, *Handai Wushi muqun shike yanjiu*, pp. 27, 28, fig. 6; *Zhongguo huaxiang shi quanji*, vol. 1, no. 67.

174. See Zhu Xilu, *Wushi Ci Han huaxiang shi*, pp. 69, 128, fig. 70; Jiang and Wu, *Handai Wushi muqun shike yanjiu*, pp. 27, 31, 131.

175. In Zhu Xilu, *Wushi Ci Han huaxiang shi*, pp. 63, 126, fig. 62, the animals in the plates are described as chickens and the sunken bowl between the two eared cups is said to be a joint hole for the bottom tenon of a column. In Jiang and Wu, *Handai Wushi muqun shike yanjiu*, pp. 27, 47, 131, and 167, pl. 50, the animals in the plates are described as turtles, and this slab is said to be an altar stone from one of the cemetery structures. On-site inspection of this stone in summer 2004 reveals carved decoration across the front face, with a small hole that connects to the bottom of the bowl. This channel possibly was used to help transfer sacrificial libations to a vessel, or it may have been a drain. According to "A Discussion of Rites" in *Xunzi*, raw fish were placed on the offering table during the triennial great sacrificial feast; see *Basic*

Writings of Mo Tzu, Hsün Tzu, and Han Fei Tzu, trans. Burton Watson (New York: Columbia University Press, 1963), p. 92.

176. *Jiaxiang Xian zhi* (1997), *juan* 24, p. 651.

177. Huang Yi, *Qian Hou Shishi huaxiang ba*, *juan* 2, p. 35a.

178. Rong Geng, *Han Wu Liang Ci huaxiang lu*, text vol., p. 37a. The Pan family is unidentified.

179. Jiang and Wu, *Handai Wushi muqun shike yanjiu*, pp. 27, 32 fig. 7. Also reproduced in Rong Geng, *Han Wu Liang Ci huaxiang lu*, plates vol., back matter, p. 13.

180. Cai Hongru, "Huang Yi *Debei shier tu*," p. 72. A viewing of the stone in the Tianjin Municipal Museum of Art is needed for confirmation.

181. Chavannes, *Mission archéologique*, text vol. 1, pp. 243–44.

182. Chavannes, *Mission archéologique*, pl. 92, fig. 172. A rubbing is also reproduced in Ōmura Seigai, *Shina bijutsushi: Chōso hen*, p. 63, and pl. 72, fig. 177.

183. The inscription is transcribed in Chavannes, *Mission archéologique*, text vol. 1, p. 243; Ōmura Seigai, *Shina bijutsushi: Chōso hen*, p. 63; and cited in Jiang and Wu, *Handai Wushi muqun shike yanjiu*, p. 32.

184. Adolf Fischer, "Vortag, Gehalten auf dem 15ten Internationalen Orientalistenkongress in Kopenhagen: Über Vorbuddhist Steinreliefs und Romanische Löwenköpfe aus China," *T'oung Pao*, ser. 2, vol. 9 (1908), pp. 582–83. In Ōmura Seigai, *Shina bijutsushi: Chōso hen*, p. 63, this column is said to be in the collection of "M. Adori [sic] Fischer."

185. Extrapolated from the scaled reconstruction drawings of the Front and Rear Chambers in Jiang and Wu, *Handai Wushi muqun shike yanjiu*, pp. 39, 44.

186. In correspondence with Wu Shun-chi, Maria Gaida, and Siegmar Nahser of the Ethnologisches Museum (formerly Museum für Völkerkunde), the stone column (Inv Nr ID 27099), with its inscription still visible, is reported in fragile and fragmentary condition. Special thanks to Herbert Butz, curator of the Museum für Ostasiatische Kunst, Berlin, and Adele Schlombs, director of Museum für Ostasiatische Kunst, Cologne, for their assistance in locating this stone.

187. Osvald Sirén, *Histoire des arts anciens de la Chine*, vol. 4: *L'architecture* (Paris and Brussels: G. Van Oest, 1930), pl. 104–b. This photo was taken by Sirén, who must have visited the site. The pictured stones were subsequently interpreted as column capitals in Fairbank, *Adventures in Retrieval*, pp. 77–78, fig. 9, and in Wu Hung, *Wu Liang Shrine*, pp. 18–19, 21, fig. 14. For reconstructions of the gate-pillars, see Jiang and Wu, *Handai Wushi muqun shike yanjiu*, pp. 7–15, 144–49, pls. 11–18 (note: in pl. 11 the rubbing of the body of the main pillar shaft is reversed left to right); see esp. p. 27, n. 6.

188. Chavannes, *Mission archéologique*, pl. 32, fig. 56; Sekino, "Stone Mortuary Shrines," part II, p. 303; Sekino, *Shina Santōshō*, pls. 19–21, figs. 28–30. Jiang and Wu, *Handai Wushi muqun shike yanjiu*, pp. 8–10 figs. 3–4, p. 142, pl. 4 (the same photo is reproduced in Zhu Xilu, *Wushi Ci Han huaxiang shi*, p. 73, fig. 75).

189. Anthony Barbieri-Low brought this to my attention using a rubbing of the northeast gate-pillar in the collection of Academia Sinica, Taipei.

190. Anthony Barbieri-Low has suggested to me that even if the pillar inscription was carved during the Han dynasty, it may have been done in two stages. The first-stage inscription may end with the description of the costs of the feline statues. The following lines about Wu Ban may have been appended (for translation, see cat. no. 1.43).

191. The Caretaker's Hall was located to the southeast of the gate-pillars, as seen in a 1981 map of the site in Jiang and Wu, *Handai Wushi muqun shike yanjiu*, p. 2, fig. 2. This building faced south on axis with the compound south gate where the 1792 Preservation Hall formerly stood.

192. Jiang and Wu, *KGXB* 1981.2, pp. 165–66, notes that the ten Left Group slabs were stored in an east hall built in 1789, while the original south hall housed the other pictorial stones. *Jiaxiang Xian zhi* (1997), *juan* 24, p. 650, states that a three-bay east hall was built and the new stones were embedded in the walls. Neither text cites any source, and both may refer to the three-bay east hall that was built in 1910 (discussed below).

193. Wang Chang, *Jinshi cuibian*, *juan* 20, p. 53a.

194. See n. 39, above.

195. Feng Yunpeng and Feng Yunyuan, *Jinshi suo*, vol. *Shi suo si*, "Han Wushi shishi xiangrui tu yi" sec.

196. Feng Yunpeng and Feng Yunyuan, *Jinshi suo*, vol. *Shi suo san*, "Han Wushi Ci shique" sec. In this section the gate-pillars are said to be 1 *zhang* rod plus 2 *chi* feet high, while in the previous "Han Wu Liang Ci shique tizi" section they are said to be 2 *zhang* 5 *chi*. The difference of 1 *zhang* 3 *chi* may be the length that remained buried. Chavannes also reported that as late as 1891 the local residents still described the gate-pillars as "chandeliers." See Chavannes, *Sculpture sur pierre en Chine*, p. ii.

197. As annotated in Xu Han, *Xu Han riji*, comp. and annot. Cui Wei (Shijiazhuang: Hebei jiaoyu chubanshe, 2001), p. 154, this section of the diary begins with an entry on the tenth day of the fourth month, but no year was specified. Cui Wei believes this section corresponds to 1841. For Xu Han's biography, see Yuan Xingyun, *Xu Han nian pu* (Ji'nan: Qi-Lu shushe, 1983).

198. The two gable walls of the Wu Liang Ci stone chamber (WLC.2–.3) are 1.84 meters tall, and the triangular pediment areas on top of these stones cannot be rubbed by a person standing on the ground. In fact, the pediments on these two stone are often missing in early rubbings, including the set in the Princeton University Art Museum (cat. no. 1) and the one reproduced in Chavannes, *Mission archéologique*. Xu Han was also not interested in making rubbings of the pictorial images but only of the calligraphic inscriptions, which were all within easy reach.

199. Yang Duo (courtesy name Shiqing), was a native of Shangcheng, Henan. According to annotations in Xu Han, *Xu Han riji*, pp. 158, 178, Yang Duo worked with Xu Han in Jining on an edition of the *Jining zhou zhi* gazetteer, a project in which Feng Yunyuan, one of the authors of the *Jinshi suo*, also participated. On the sixth day of the seventh month of the same year, Xu Han also received a copy of Huang Yi's *Xiaopenglai Ge jinshi wenzi* from Yang Duo; see Xu Han, *Xu Han riji*, p. 170.

200. Xu Han, *Xu Han riji*, pp. 159–60. Translation modifies drafts by Michael Nylan and Mei-ling Williams.

201. Huang Yi excavated down to the top of the base stones in 1786. Feng Yunpeng records the pillars were again half buried in 1820, and he had to excavate in order to make a rubbing of the inscription. Already located at the bottom of a large depression, the gate-pillar pits were probably easily refilled by sediment from rain and flooding.

202. Wang Xixun (courtesy name Mengci, original *ming* Xisun) was the son of the scholar, bibliographer, and collector of stone and bronze inscriptions Wang Zhong (1745–1795). See *Eminent Chinese of the Ch'ing Period*, pp. 814–15.

203. Wang Mengci, "Shu Huang Xiaosong Ziyun Shan tanbei tu" (1841) cited in Wang Xiantang, comp., *Gu huang shuliao za lu* (Ji'nan: Qi-Lu shushe, 1984), p. 92. This source was brought to my attention through the research of Mei-ling Williams. The original painting may no longer survive. According to Wang Xiantang, he saw the painting in 1932 and decided that it was a forgery but its colophons were authentic.

204. Unofficial reference to the head of a regional or local school. In the "Chen Jin" entry in Matsumaru Michio, *Shinpen kinsekigaku roku*, p. 112, the two men are referred to as "Litterateur" (*guangwen*), which refers to regional or local education officials (*xue guan*); also see Charles O. Hucker, *A Dictionary of Official Titles in Imperial China* (Stanford: Stanford University Press, 1985), no. 3351.

205. According to the *Jining zhilizhou xu zhi*, *juan* 10, p. 27b, Ma Qingyun was appointed as Instructor (*jiaoyu*) of Jiaxiang in 1870. For compositions by Li Weizun on the Wu cemetery stones, see ibid., *juan* 23, pp. 49a–50b. Research from Mei-ling Williams.

206. See n. 99, above.

207. In the "Chen Jin" entry in Matsumaru Michio, *Shinpen kinsekigaku roku*, p. 112, this line is read to mean that the period of construction was eight months (*ba yue*).

208. In summer 2004 the author saw a stone tablet with this title at the site. This is likely the stone carved for the 1880 renovation.

209. The colophon reads: "In mid-autumn of the *wuzi* cyclical year (1888) in the Guangxu reign-period, Wang Qizhe and Gao Wenhan of Weiyi, and Wang Qingyun of Xiayi viewed together." Transcribed in Jiang and Wu, *Handai Wushi muqun shike yanjiu*, p. 134. This line is not included in the Princeton rubbing (cat. no. 1.52).

210. This placard read, "The Wu Family Stone Chamber" (Wushi Shishi). For its description, see Jiang and Wu, *Handai Wushi muqun shike yanjiu*, p. 136.

211. Chavannes, *Sculpture sur pierre en Chine*, pp. ii–iii.

212. Sekino, *Shina Santōshō*, text p. 25.

213. Wu Weinian was a native of Anhui and was appointed the substitute District Magistrate of Jiaxiang in 1909. See *Jining zhilizhou xu zhi*, *juan* 10, p. 29b.

214. Recorded in Luo Zhengjun's 1910 inscription in the Ji'nan Fu Preservation Institute of Bronzes and Stone Carvings; cited in Sekino, *Shina Santōshō*, text pp. 104–5. In Wu Hung, *Wu Liang Shrine*, p. 8, the three officials are misidentified. Supervision of the construction seems to have been the responsibility of Qu Derun; see *Jining zhilizhou zhi*, *juan* 19, p. 55a.

215. One of the earliest examples may be Claudius Madrolle, *Northern China, the Valley of the Blue River, Korea* (Paris/London: Hachette and Company, 1912), p. 177. In this guide, the stones are hailed as the "celebrated bas-reliefs of the Wu family, studied and described by M. Chavannes." Madrolle had consulted Chavannes.

216. Exterior photos and Sekino's drawings of this hall show a masonry structure with a central door and two windows on either side. It is unclear, however, whether it was structurally five or three bays wide. It is unlikely Fairbank would have misidentified the hall, because she had access to both Chavannes's and Sekino's publications and photographs.

217. Fairbank, *Adventures in Retrieval*, pp. 48–49. In conversation of June 2004, Jiang Yingju noted that in the early 1960s, when he first visited the site, only the mound over Tomb 1 was visible. A photograph of the mound taken in about 1980 is included in Jiang and Wu, *Handai Wushi muqun shike yanjiu*, p. 143, pl. 10.

218. Fairbank, *Adventures in Retrieval*, p. 43.

219. Fei Weimei [Wilma Fairbank], "Han 'Wu Liang Ci' jianzhu yuan xing kao," trans. Wang Shixiang, *Zhongguo yingzao xueshe huikan*, vol. 7, no. 2 (1945), pp. 1–60 (non-continuous pagination). From a conversation with Jiang Yingju in April 2004, Eileen Hsu reports that in 1963 Jiang spent three days hand-copying the entire Chinese translation of Fairbank's work, and that the drawings were important to Jiang and Wu Wenqi's architectural reconstructions in 1981 and 1995.

220. In Jiang and Wu, *Handai Wushi muqun shike yanjiu*, p. 5. In conversation with Jiang Yingju in June 2004, it became clear that a five-bay hall was built to house the caretaker's office. This hall can be seen just to the right of the gate-pillar pavilion in a 1963 photograph of the site reproduced in ibid., p. 141, pl. 2.

221. Jiang and Wu, *Handai Wushi muqun shike yanjiu*, p. 5. *Jiaxiang Xian zhi* (1997), *juan* 24, p. 651.

222. Jiang and Wu, *Handai Wushi muqun shike yanjiu*, pp. 5, 141, pl. 2. Jiang Yingju first visited the site in 1963.

223. See n. 9, above. Also see *Jiaxiang Xian zhi* (1997), p. 651. A photograph of the stone marker is reproduced in Jiang and Wu, *Handai Wushi muqun shike yanjiu*, p. 141, pl. 3.

224. This is the Front Exhibition Hall now standing at the site. See Luo Chenglie and Zhu Xilu, "Jiaxiang Wushi muqun shike," *Wenwu* 1979.7, p. 91; Jiang and Wu, *Handai Wushi muqun shike yanjiu*, pp. 5, 143, pl. 9. In *Shandong fengwu daquan*, p. 129; and *Jiaxiang Xian zhi* (1997), *juan* 24, p. 651, these events are said to have occurred in 1962.

225. See Luo and Zhu, "Jiaxiang Wushi muqun shike," *Wenwu* 1979.7, p. 91, fig. 1. The photograph of the Exhibition Hall's interior with the stone carvings confirms that this is the same hall that I visited in summer 2002. Also see Jiang and Wu, *Handai Wushi muqun shike yanjiu*, p. 2, fig. 2 and p. 24, fig. 5. According to the *Jiaxiang Xian zhi* (1997), p. 651, the precinct walls and gates were constructed in 1964.

226. As a national treasure, the cemetery was included in popular travel guides and described as a site for tourism. See *Shandong fengwu zhi* (Ji'nan: Shandong meishu chubanshe, 1984), pp. 330–32; *Shandong fengwu daquan*, pp. 36, 128–29.

227. See n. 52, above.

228. The only description of the two tombs is included in Jiang and Wu, *Handai Wushi muqun shike yanjiu*, pp. 119–27.

229. The plan drawing of Tomb 2 in Jiang and Wu, *Handai Wushi muqun shike yanjiu*, p. 125, fig. 17.2, does not include the two side rooms off the middle chamber.

230. *Jiaxiang Xian zhi* (1997), *juan* 24, p. 651. Jiang Yingju believes many of these stone carvings are now in the Shandong Provincial Museum (conversation with Eileen Hsu in April 2004).

231. *Jiaxiang Xian zhi* (1997), pp. 37–38. Cui Chenggui (unidentified), from the Art History Department of the University of Pittsburgh, visited in October.

232. The State Council member Gu Mu visited the site on October 27 and wrote an inscription reading "Cherish national treasures" (*aihu guo bao*). See *Shandong sishi nian jishi*, p. 496. Also see *Jiaxiang Xian zhi* (1997), p. 39; the inscription and a group photo of the visit are included in the front matter.

233. See *Jiaxiang Xian zhi* (1997), pp. 39, 806. Also see *Shandong sishi nian jishi*, p. 496, which gives the dates of the symposium as November 11–13, and the number of participants as over eighty.

234. For Weng Fanggang's poem, see *Jiaxiang Xian zhi* (1997), *fu lu*, p. 794.

235. "Summary of the Symposium Commemorating the 200th Anniversary of the Discovery of the Wu Family Cemetery Carved Stones" (*Jinian Wushi muqun shike faxian erbai zhounian zuotan huiyi ziyao*), cited in *Jiaxiang Xian zhi* (1997), *fu lu*, pp. 806–7.

236. *Jiaxiang Xian zhi* (1997), *juan* 24, p. 651.

237. Jiang Yingju and Zhou Changfu, gen. eds., *Shandong bowuguan tonglan* (Beijing: Zhongguo guangbo dianshe chubanshe, 1993), pp. 342–43.

238. *Jiaxiang Xian zhi* (1997), *juan* 23, p. 642. This Research Office is probably connected to the Jiaxiang Wu Family Cemetery Stone Carvings and Cultural Relics Management Office.

239. Michael Nylan examined several stones formerly attributed as Wu cemetery stones in storage at the British Museum. She has generously shared digital images she took for research purposes. Unfortunately there is no documentation of when or how these stones entered the museum. The Walters Art Museum has three stones (acc. nos. 25.12–25.14) that Henry Walters acquired in 1919. These stones were sold as authentic by the Yamanaka gallery in Japan, and are reportedly from the former collection of Tan Fang (unidentified; possibly Duanfang), Governor-general of Shandong. I thank Lu Huiwen for alerting me to these stones. Alan Priest was responsible for compiling the Princeton set of rubbings (cat. no. 1). He also had an incomplete set of duplicate rubbings and loose copies that went into the collection of Robert Ellsworth. That set was offered at auction by Skinner, Boston, June 2002, sale 2149, lot 272.

240. Klaas Ruiteenbeek, *Chinese Shadows*, pp. 4–5.

241. On rubbings and the rubbing process, see Liu Shuoshi, *Tapian zhizuo yu xinshang* (Shanghai: Shanghai shudian chubanshe, 2002); Wu Hung, "On Rubbings: Their Materiality and Historicity," in *Writing and Materiality in China: Essays in Honor of Patrick Hanan*, ed. Judith T. Zeitlin and Lydia H. Liu (Cambridge, Mass., and London: Harvard University Asia Center for the Harvard-Yenching Institute, 2003), pp. 29–72. Also see cat. no. 1.

242. Wu Huilin comp., *Zengbu Jiaobei suibi*, pp. 59–60, 84–85, 150–53.

243. Very few rubbing sets are complete, and many, including the sets reproduced by Chavannes and Sekino, were compiled over time from different sets. Relatively complete modern sets are reproduced in *Zhongguo huaxiang shi quanji*, vol. 1 passim, and in small-size images in Jiang and Wu, *Handai Wushi muqun shike yanjiu*, p. 152, pls. 22–24. Digital images of a set at the Academia Sinica are posted on their current website.

244. During site visits in summers of 2002 and 2004, we were allowed to inspect the stones. For inspection to be meaningful, however, the stones need to be thoroughly washed to remove layered deposits of paper fibers, ink, and adhesives.

245. On identifying, marking, and preserving ancient relics, see Lowenthal, *The Past is a Foreign County*, pp. 265–71. In the Chinese conception of architecture, the imperishability of words marks the authenticity of a building. The physical structure may be rebuilt or moved, but the words that name and identify the building remain constant. See Cary Y. Liu, "Chinese Architectural Aesthetics: Patterns of Living and

Being between Past and Present"; and Eugene Y. Wang, "Tope and Topos: The Leifeng Pagoda and the Discourse of the Demonic," in *Writing and Materiality in China*, pp. 488–552.

246. Lowenthal, *The Past is a Foreign County*, p. 272.

247. See n. 75, above.

248. Lowenthal, *The Past is a Foreign County*, p. 278.

249. This category of carving technique in Xin Lixiang, *Handai huaxiang shi zonghe yanjiu*, pp. 31–33, corresponds to the shallow-relief flat-figure (*pingmian qian fudiao*) technique in Li Falin, *Hanhua kaoshi he yanjiu*, p. 81; the convex flat figures with line-cut (*pingtu ke*) technique in Yang Boda, "Shilun Shandong huaxiang shi de kefa," *Gugong bowuyuan yuankan* 1987.4, p. 9; and the lowered-ground flat relief with incised line (*jiandi pingmian xianke*) technique in Jiao Desen and Yang Aiguo, "Linyi, Weifang, Ji'nan dengdi Han huaxiang shi gailun," in *Zhongguo huaxiang shi quanji*, vol. 3, p. 7. I am indebted to Eileen Hsu for her assistance in compiling and comparing the various classification schemes developed for Han-dynasty stone-carving techniques by these and other authors.

250. In the collection of the Princeton University Art Museum is a rubbing of the 1299 carved map of the city of Suzhou (*Pingjiang tu*). The central section of this map showing the government offices was especially popular and was worn to almost indecipherability on the Princeton rubbing. On-site inspection of the carved stone in 1984 indicates that the central section of the stone has been repaired and is now fully legible in modern rubbings. Among the scenes in the "Wu family shrine" pictorial rubbings, the pavilion homage scene in each of the reconstructed stone chambers is a likely candidate for having been reincised. By developing a chronology of rubbings, it will be possible to determine if and when certain scenes, such as the homage scenes, were recut.

251. See n. 242, above.

252. Jorge Luis Borges, "Tlön, Uqbar, Orbis Tertius," in his *Ficciones* (New York: Grove Press, 1962), pp. 17–35.

253. Alternatively, this line can be read: "that 30 *li* miles south of the district [seat] to the west of Ziyun Shan was a Han tomb of a crown prince with three stone offering halls."

254. See n. 86, above.

255. The first year of the Jianhe reign-period of the Southern Liang corresponds to 400 CE.

256. The Stele of Cao Quan is dated to 185 and the stone is presently in Stele Forest (Bei lin) in Xi'an.

257. The Wu Rong stele had been recovered and installed in the Jining Academy before Huang Yi rediscovered the Wu family cemetery in 1786.

258. See n. 73, above.

259. See nn. 44, 93.

260. The "instructional complex" (*xue gong*) is the same as the Jining Prefectural Academy, or Confucius Temple.

261. See nn. 65, 113.

262. See n. 113.

263. See n. 113.

264. This refers to the line "The superior man seeks to perfect the admirable qualities of men" (*junzi cheng ren zhi mei*) in the *Analects*. See *Lunyu zhushu*, *Shisan jing zhushu* edition, "Yan Yuan" sec., *juan* 12, p. 2504; trans. in James Legge, *The Chinese Classics*, vol. 1, p. 258.

265. In Weng Fanggang, *Lianghan jinshi ji*, *Shike shiliao xinbian* edition, "Fulu Qiantang Huang Yi xiu Wushi Citang ji lue," *juan* 15, pp. 44a–47b; Jiang and Wu, *Handai Wushi muqun shike yanjiu*, pp. 131–33. Also partially translated in Wu Hung, *Wu Liang Shrine*, pp. 5–6.

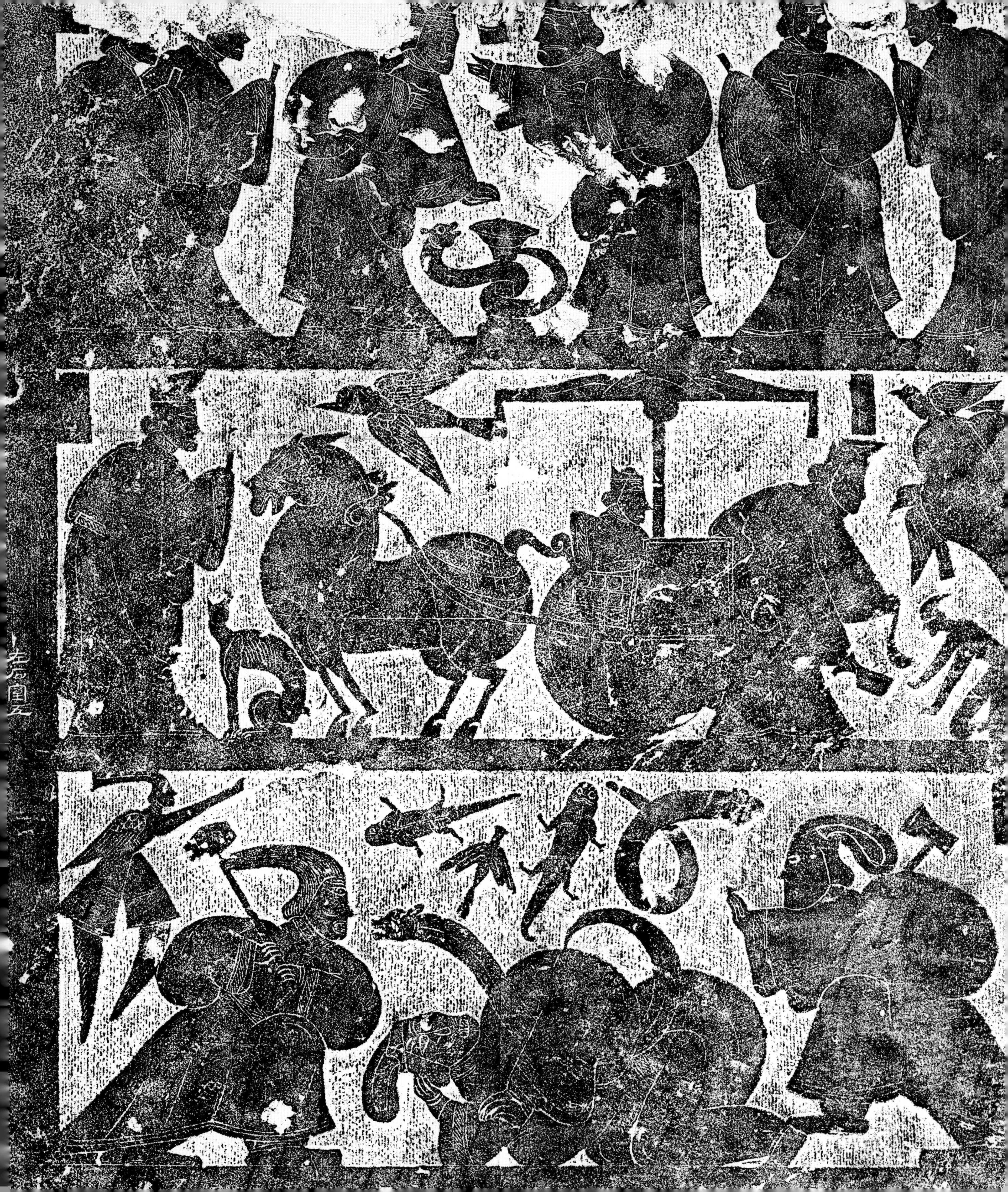
左石室五

Michael Loewe

Funerary Practice in Han Times

Funerary practice in Han times rested on a variety of beliefs in immortality and in different types of postmortem existence. Social conventions, a need to preserve the hierarchies of the political order, and the all-compelling force exerted by degrees of kinship affected the choice of type and the situation of the tombs. Mantic aspects of topographical and geographical conditions also affected the choice. The symbolism enshrined in the decorations and furnishings of a tomb drew from mythical accounts of a paradise that lay beyond the confines of this world and might well allude to human ancestors of long, long ago. A choice of objects interred with the corpse could be inspired by experiences known in this life; they might be intended to satisfy the needs of the corpse, still seen as mundane, to ease the ills that it might suffer, or to solve the problems that it might face. Formal prescriptions regulated the conduct of funerals from those of the emperor downward; little expense was spared in providing suitable obsequies for the highest in the land. At the lower reaches of the social scale some may have tried to emulate such luxuries; many would remain satisfied with tributes of a more humble nature; some may have used the occasion of a death to stage an ostentatious display of mourning that accorded ill with the degree of respect that they had shown their departed ones during their lives.

In very broad terms, two major influences or urges characterized Chinese social practice: officials attempted to regulate and organize society and to impose a sense of identity on each of its members; individuals called on their own initiative to practice a free way of life of their own choice—perhaps, in exceptional cases, as a hermit.[1] The great majority of our received literature derives from the first of these urges and may indicate the success achieved in molding practice to an approved style and in advertising the benefits that resulted therefrom. The work of artists and craftsmen that is preserved in tombs may savor of repetitiveness and reveal how far the accepted view of mundane and extra-mundane realities may have constrained an expression of personal intimations. In their own way mystics or poets might suggest reactions against an undue concentration on a conventional attitude to the major questions of life and death.

The four centuries of the Qin, Western Han, Xin, and Eastern Han dynasties witnessed the creation, operation, and decay of empires. Disillusion and lone protests followed attempts to gain acceptance for established norms of conduct and methods of official practice. A new, foreign faith with totally new concepts came to take root, and laid stress on a distinction between body and spirit that was not as yet generally acknowledged. If officials' influence on individual minds gathered strength, ties of loyalty to the central authorities may have weakened. The years saw the emergence of schemes and legal provisions to ensure a sufficiency of literate men to carry out the tasks of government; while learned scholars paid a marked attention to the interpretation of "scriptural writings," the masters of various occult arts consulted turtles' shells or created and examined hexagrams to determine truths and facts that were not self-evident. A few men, such as Wang Chong (27–?97 CE), concerned themselves with seeking a rational understanding of the workings of nature, as is seen in many chapters of his *Lunheng* (*Doctrines evaluated*); a few others, such as Zhang Heng (78–139 CE), could study

Opposite Stone Chamber 2, Stone 2-S.5 (cat. no. 1.24). "Wu family shrines" rubbings. Princeton University Art Museum, acc. no. 2002-307.23.

means and contrive instruments to prise such secrets from the heavens and the earth; as poets they could express their search for truths that lay beyond such researches.[2]

Throughout these years, and together with other religious and intellectual developments, attention to the normal and regular cycles of life held a position of paramount importance. Philosophers contrived to give reassurance and comfort at times of suffering and distress by describing the eternal rhythm of life, death, and rebirth as witnessed in all elements of the unitary world of Heaven, Earth, and Man. Some thinkers or writers proposed means of regulating human behavior so that it would accord with these inescapable cycles, and encouraged their followers to recognize how the lives of individuals ran in parallel with these sequences; there were also those who trusted to mantic practices that would persuade occult sources of wisdom to reveal the truths that they harbored.

Received literature shows how these ideas merged and developed, but it does not include statements of a personal belief in the nature of a life that survives the decay of the body. Some of these beliefs are adumbrated, as in the fear expressed by some that they would not be able to explain or excuse their conduct when they met their ancestors in the life hereafter; or in the foreboding of a man who was on the point of death that two of his adversaries, already dead, were lying in wait, ready to flog him to death.[3] But these hints are scarce and scant.

It is nonetheless possible to discern or infer some of the motives and beliefs that affected funerary practice, such as a need to dispose of the dead in a seemly and respectful manner, or to choose a style of burial, a type of tomb, and the symbols displayed on its furnishings that would be appropriate. The conduct of the funeral rites and maintenance of the regulations for the procedures of mourning required attention, devised as these were to safeguard the unity of a family line and the transmission of the ancestors' reputations throughout all generations to come. Such endeavors reflect a search for permanency that outlasts the individual, and they are matched by attempts to set up a permanent framework for other acts of human behavior in the form of *li*, those rules and conventions that molded social structure in a manner that satisfied family relationships and reflected the ideals of government.

Other motives derived from concepts of an afterlife, possibly of a religious nature, perhaps to be traced to mythology. Or they may have arisen from an intellectual search to relate mankind to the passage of time, to the more permanent structures and lives of other members or elements of the universe. Much about these motives remains uncertain, such as the times when certain ideas emerged, developed, or displaced others, and how they gained acceptance in the various classes of society. It was evidently quite possible for Chinese of this period to harbor contradictory ideas and beliefs and to observe certain mutually inconsistent practices. Until perhaps 200 CE the new ideas of Buddhism had yet to reach China's countryside in strength or to form a prominent feature of the land in stupa, lecture hall, or monastery;[4] by the sixth century they had gained sufficient ground to count an emperor, Wudi of Liang in the south (r. 502–549), as one of their most fervent devotees.

It may be surmised that from times that cannot be known or measured, as elsewhere, so in China there were men and women who nurtured the belief and hope that the life of the body could be prolonged to outlast the time span usually allotted; that there were herbs or drugs that brought the blessing of deathlessness, and that there were various ways of finding these elixirs, the *bu si zhi yao*.[5]

Other hopes followed from the belief that human beings include two nonmaterial elements that outlast the body and may require services.[6] One of these "souls," known as the *po*, probably remained earthbound; the other, known as the *hun*, might be able to ascend to exist in another realm. The living could render services that were intended to bring ease and comfort to the one of those souls, and they could also adopt means to guide the other soul to an appropriate and blissful destination. In both cases such measures were precautionary; they were partly devised and practiced so as to discourage the souls of the dead from inflicting harm on their surviving kinsfolk. Once arrived at the most highly prized destination, the *hun* soul would lead a blissful immortality, in company with some of the longest-lasting objects known to man, the sun and the moon, or perhaps in that of strange, elf-like creatures who lived beyond the realms of human ken. Following another way of thought that was more abstract than practical, the tomb would be located and the body set in place so that both it and *po* that survived with it would accord with the eternal rhythms of the universe and thus be in a position to enjoy a harmonious state of being.

These varying hopes and fears drew from mythology and gave rise to artistic expression, perhaps in symbols, perhaps in anthropomorphic guise. They commanded the activities and observances of the mourners, they affected the style of burial; and in their turn they were influenced by a basic Chinese addiction to hierarchies and a readiness to control all actions by reduction to convention.

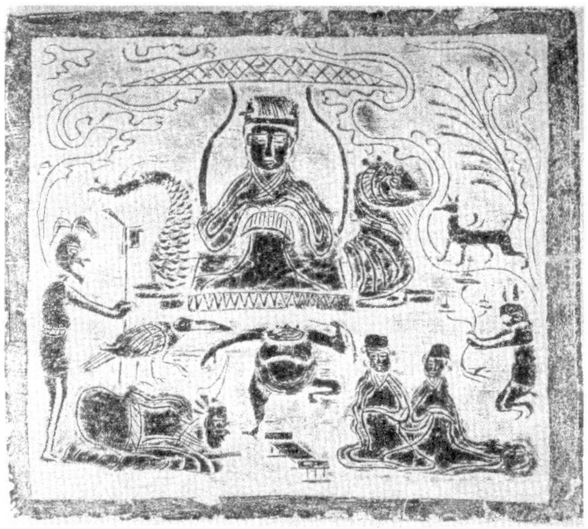

There was no easy means of finding that elixir of life, said to be in the possession of the Queen Mother of the West, mistress of the universe, who sat enthroned on a lofty and inaccessible mountain, served and guarded by her attendants (fig. 1).[7] One passage, perhaps to be dated in the fourth or third century BCE, describes her as follows:[8]

> On the summit of the mountains of the serpent shamans there is a man who stands facing east, holding a cup; one name for the place is the Mountain of the Turtles. The Queen Mother of the West wears her special crown, the *sheng*, leaning on a stool. To the south there are the three green birds, who collect food for the Queen Mother of the West, north of the wastes of Kunlun.

Her very existence, and her continued existence without interruption, were essential to the continuity of the rhythms whereby the world kept moving in harmony; for this purpose once a year she would meet and make contact with a partner, and from their union the cycle of universal being drew refreshment and renewal. The Queen herself lived beyond the powers of death; at her orders her birds would gather the rare herbs from which the elixir could be extracted; her hares would set to with pestle and bronze vase to compound therefrom the potion that gave its blessing to those who craved it and who had performed the necessary rites of obeisance before receiving their due measure of this sacrament. Whether this gift led to a permanent state of deathlessness in this world or to existence in another form in another world is not certain; but an incident dated to 3 BCE testifies to the hold that faith in the Queen's powers had come to

Fig. 1 *Queen Mother of the West*. Eastern Han dynasty. Chengdu, Sichuan. Molded brick; 46 × 41 cm. From Michael Loewe, *Ways to Paradise*, pl. I.

exercise over some minds.[9] Up and down the empire crowds were in a state of excitement, exchanging emblems of straw or hemp with one another, and their enthusiasm and abandon grew out of all proportion. They held meetings, tried their luck at the gaming boards, sang and danced in honor of the Queen. A message would run round the mob: "The Mother tells the people that those who wear this talisman will not die; and let those who do not believe Her words look below the pivots on their gates, and there will be white hairs there to show that this is true."

A different way to reach eternal bliss could be found in the east rather than the west. This led to eternal life in a body released from decay and transformed into a denizen of a different realm, in the company of the heavenly bodies who so affected human destinies and apparently existed from everlasting to everlasting. The path thither lay eastward, to the realm of Penglai, one of the three "Isles of the Blest" that lay out at sea.[10] As with the Queen Mother's mountain, these too were difficult of access, and they were likely to disappear from view at the approach of any alien vessel or visitor in human form. For they held a secret; it was there that there lived Immortal beings clothed in white, in a realm that the souls of the dead longed to join. Monarchs had sent messengers to find the way there, but none had reached their goal. Indeed, long, long ago the islands were drifting along the tide, and it was only by the direct intervention of the gods that they were secured fast against the winds and currents of the ocean.[11] It was by way of one of these islands, known sometimes as the Vases (Fanghu, Penghu, and Yinghu), that mortals could be led with their attendants, mortal or immortal, in train. Passing through different stages of a journey that was beset by dangers, they would eventually ascend to the highest of all stages, to become companions of the sun and moon, whose perpetual rhythms charged the universe with a dependable regularity. Here they would slough off their earthly bodies, to be transformed for the life that they would now lead.

Han Wudi (r. 141–87 BCE) had been persuaded that a visit to Penglai would enable him to achieve a state of deathlessness, and he heard tell of those who had all but made their way thither. Following the destruction of a terrace whose tower was intended to communicate with Heaven, in 104 BCE he sacrificed to the inhabitants of Penglai; and in setting out his plans for a new palace he simulated a journey to Paradise. He had a great lake made whose waters would lap round the shores of four man-made islands; these included the Holy Island of Penglai.[12]

Artists and craftsmen who created and decorated the furnishings of a tomb could choose, or be commissioned, to depict some of these ideas of the future life in the molded bricks, bronze vessels, or paintings on silk that were reverently buried with the dead, and on the murals painted within the tombs; these were intended to ensure the deceased a safe, smooth, and speedy passage to their destined ends. They could also turn to other themes of mythology that saw the life of the future in different terms. They might show the performance of a rite, the recitation of a prayer designed to bring about the desired end; or they might show a newly arrived soul reaching the company of those who had gone before. Sometimes these Immortal beings were portrayed as amusing themselves by taking a hand at *liubo*, the game of chance in which a lucky throw would reveal the future

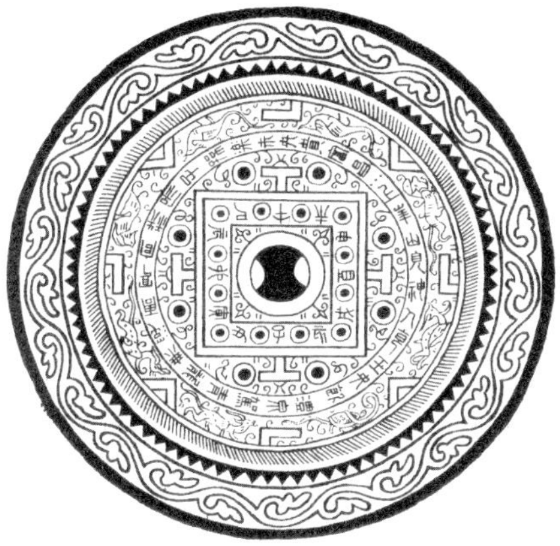

(see cat. no. 37). One possible destination for deceased persons does not appear to have formed the subject for an artist's skills, the region of the Yellow Springs (Huangquan).[13] It was there that souls and perhaps bodies would be relegated if they had been left uncherished, with no ceremonies performed to show that their survivors still respected them and no precautions taken to lead them to a happier place. As yet no scene of the Yellow Springs has been identified in the carved reliefs, molded bricks, mural paintings, or paintings on silk that adorned a tomb.

Other artists portrayed in symbolical manner how the dead could be guided to occupy the most fortunate situation in the cosmos, where they would enjoy complete harmony with the major forces whereby the universe operates. Buried alongside the deceased person, bronze mirrors bearing a special design, sometimes known as TLV, carried symbols that represented two schemes whereby the universal cycles of being ran (fig. 2; see cat. no. 38).[14] The series of twelve characters placed on the four sides of a square symbolized one of these schemes, which was based on the twelve divisions and sequences of time and space; in the other scheme four animals and a circular mound in the center represented the constant cyclical moves between five phases of activity. These, ranging from birth to decay and then to rebirth, could be seen in the changes from one season to another, or from one position in space to the next. An inscription declared how the four symbolic animals would preserve the occupant of the tomb from harm, in accordance with the eternal sequences of *yin* and *yang*. The inscription might also promise material blessings that all longed to enjoy on earth, such as an assured line of descendants and the gifts of wealth and glory. Some of these inscriptions would allude to the life of the Immortal beings, sustained by jade and manna; perhaps these beings were even depicted on other parts of the mirror as elf-like creatures thought to inhabit such a paradise. At the edge of the mirror circular banks of clouds formed a passage way by which the dead were to be brought to their appropriate positions within this comprehensive system. Examples of two such inscriptions follow:[15]

> The Shangfang[16] made this mirror to avert all harm. The fine copper which the Xin dynasty[17] possesses and which is drawn from Danyang has been refined and mixed with silver and tin, and the mirror is pure and bright. Skilled craftsmen have engraved it, forming its inscription and decoration. The dragon on the left and the tiger on the right forfend all evil; the scarlet bird and the black [warrior] accord with Yin and Yang. May children and grandchildren be provided for you in full number, and may you be present at the centre. Long may you preserve your two parents, and may you have joy, wealth and prosperity. Long life be yours, excelling that of metal and stone, as is fit for nobleman or king.

and:

> An excellent mirror from the *Shangfang*, truly very fine. Upon it [are] immortal beings, oblivious of old age. When they thirst they drink from the springs of jade, when they hunger they feed on jujubes. They roam at large throughout the world, wandering between the four oceans.

Fig. 2 *TLV* (guiju) *mirror*. Late Western Han dynasty. Provenance unknown. Bronze; diam. 22 cm. From Michael Loewe, *Ways to Paradise*, p. 81, fig. 13.

> The dragon on the left and the tiger on the right forfend [evil] and protect the Way. Long life be yours, like that of metal or stone, and may you be protector of the land.

These highly powerful talismans were made to perfection from perhaps 50 BCE and are to be found in some, but by no means all, of the 30,000 tombs and more that are identified as dating from the Qin, Han, and Xin periods.[18] The tombs are widespread, ranging from Liaoning in the northeast to Sichuan in the west or Guangdong in the southeast. They hold relics of burials of all classes of person, from almost the highest in the land to the lowest, from kings to convicts. Very considerable differences in the style of burial distinguished the social classes of those who were buried and mourned. Convicts were laid in serried ranks, crammed into small apertures in the ground; crudely written characters recorded their names and the sentences that they had suffered (fig. 3). An official, and sometimes an official and his wife, were buried within tombs whose stone slabs were decorated with symbolic devices that related to the beliefs and hopes described above. For some, a stone stele carried an elegantly phrased inscription executed in carefully embellished script, telling the onlooker details of the career of the man who lay buried within. Two or more ornamental towers, or pillar-gates (*que*), sometimes flanked the entrance to a tomb, thereby creating a landmark in the countryside (fig. 4). Fortunately, it is sometimes possible to identify the occupants of such tombs with persons whose contributions to public life had won recognition in the historical records of the dynasty. These included a very

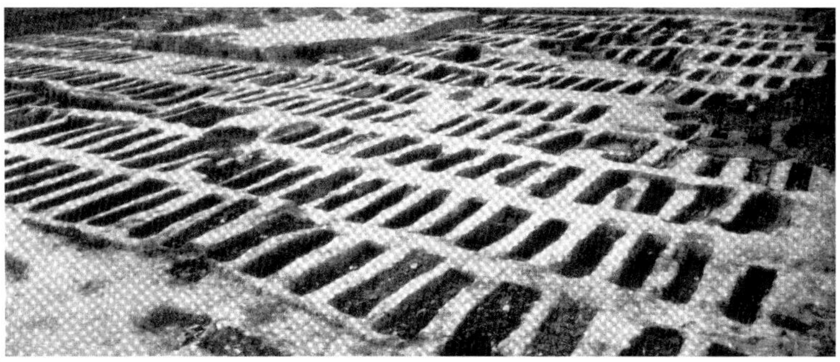

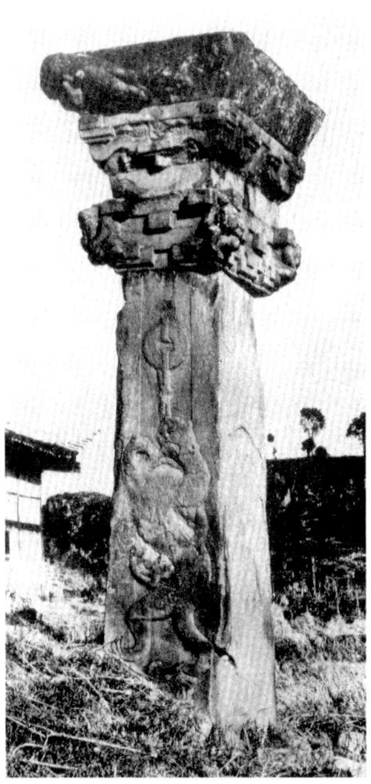

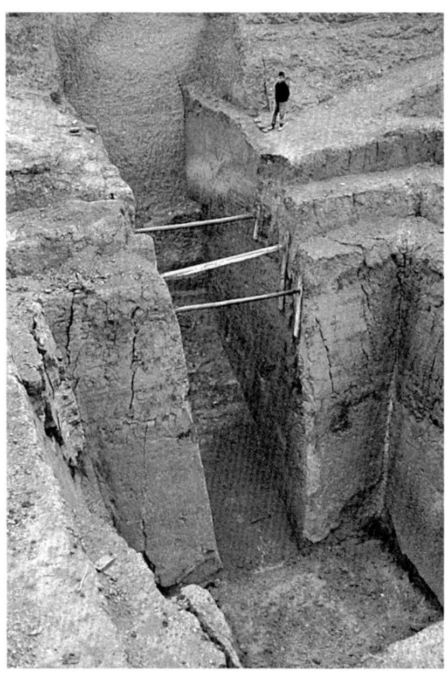

Fig. 3 *Convicts' cemetery*. Late Eastern Han dynasty. South of Luoyang. 250 × 200 m. From *Kaogu* 1972.4, pl. V.

Fig. 4 *Pillar-gate* (*que*). Late Eastern Han dynasty. Zhaojia Cun Village, Qu Xian County, Sichuan. Stone; h. 4.30 m. From Chongqing Shi wenhuaju et al., ed., *Sichuan Handai shique* (Beijing: Wenwu chubanshe, 1992), p. 144.

Fig. 5 *Pit tomb of the Countess of Dai*. 168 BCE. Tomb 1, Mawangdui, Changsha, Hunan. D. 20 m. From *Ōba Osamu, Shin Kan teikoku no iyō*, pl. 18 (published as *Chūgoku no rekishi* 2 [Tokyo: Kōdansha, 1977]).

1 Changling (Gaodi)
2 Anling (Huidi)
3 Baling (Wendi)
4 Yangling (Jingdi)
5 Maoling (Wudi)
6 Pingling (Zhaodi)
7 Duling (Xuandi)
8 Weiling (Yuandi)
9 Yanling (Chengdi)
10 Yiling (Aidi)
11 Kangling (Pingdi)

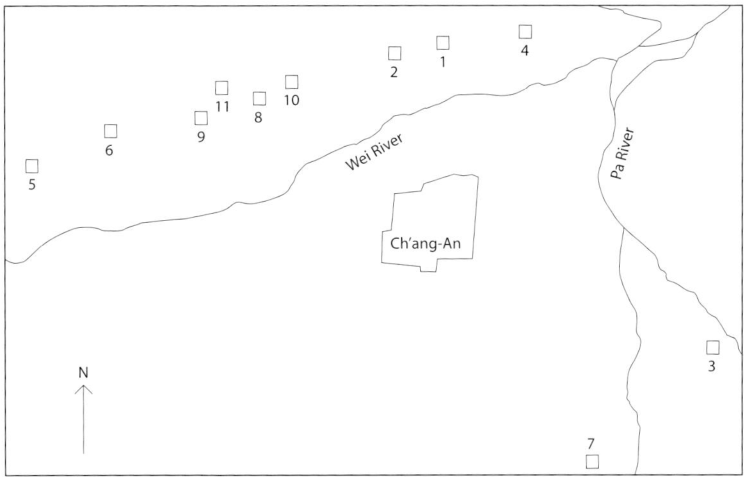

high-ranking and successful general, Huo Qubing, who died in or shortly after 117 BCE, and the Countess of Dai who died in 168 BCE; her husband had been chancellor (*xiang*) of the kingdom of Changsha, where her tomb lay (fig. 5).[19]

For the kings of the Han empire, who were near kinsmen of the emperor and whose social rank was inferior only to his, magnificent structures of brick or stone provided a luxurious residence with a regulated set of apartments, each with its own practical or religious significance, for holding court, banqueting, or perhaps performing rituals. No expense seems to have been spared in constructing these underground palaces, replete with the furnishings and equipment needed for a luxurious way of life. Beginning with the First of the Qin Emperors, who died in 210 BCE, and continuing with many of the Han emperors, sites of burial have long been identified; but as yet excavation has been limited to the outermost parts of no more than two, those of Jingdi (d. 141 BCE) and Xuandi (d. 48 BCE) (fig. 6). Literary sources, however, disclose that there were several component parts of these tombs. They were enclosed within a large park and included a shrine (*miao*) where descendants regularly paid their respects and presented offerings to the memorial tablets (*zhu*)[20] of their forebears; a chamber of rest (*qin*), where the emperor's robes, and perhaps other belongings, were stored; and the tomb itself. Further attention will be paid below to these integral parts of the tomb. We need harbor no doubts that these tombs were at least as spacious and imposing as those of their immediate inferiors, the kings, which did not comprise the same range of apartments. Provision of a staff to maintain these buildings was expensive.

The sites chosen for burial may have depended on local conditions. Some were hewn into the side of a mountain, as at Mancheng; others, in the lands close to the Yangzi River (e.g., Mawangdui), were deeply dug pits.[21] Some were designed and constructed as a residence, with several adjoining rooms. Some were built as a brick chamber, for one or perhaps two occupants, but in a number of cases burials were clustered together to form a cemetery. One such cemetery is seen at Shaogou, near Luoyang, where it has been possible to excavate no fewer than 225 tombs on the site, and to discriminate among six subperiods.[22] The reasons for choosing the site and maintaining it as a select place of burial for up to three centuries cannot be known; as yet no evidence has been seen of attempts to satisfy the demands of what was later termed *fengshui*.[23] Such cemeteries can be of very great value to investigators, as they may well provide the means of establishing chronological sequences for the style of tombs, the choice of furnishings to be buried, and the emergence of different types of decor.

Different considerations may be discerned in the choice of situations for the tombs of some of the Western Han emperors.[24] At first sight these seem to be situated at random to the north, south, and northwest of Chang'an city, but on closer inspection it seems that a pattern may have prevailed, in at least some cases. Possibly such a pattern governed the location of the tombs of the first three of these emperors; the tomb of Gaozu, the founder (r. as emperor 202–195 BCE) stands in a commanding position, centrally to the north of the city; Huidi, his immediate successor (r. 195–188 BCE), lies to his west, and Jingdi (r. 157–141 BCE) to the east.

Fig. 6 *Situation of Western Han imperial tombs.* 195 BCE–6 CE. North of Xi'an, Shaanxi. After Michael Loewe, *Divination, Mythology and Monarchy*, fig. 18.

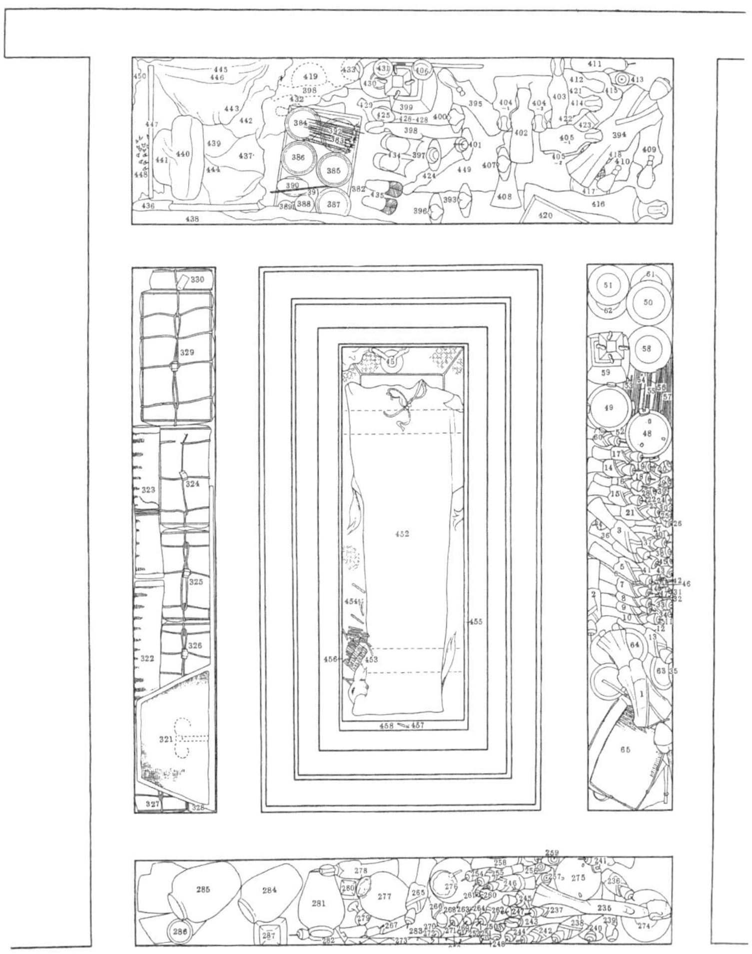

Fig. 7 *Funerary equipment and stores, buried with the Countess of Dai*. 168 BCE. Innermost coffin of lacquered wood; 202 × 69 × 63 cm. Mawangdui, Changsha, Hunan. From *Changsha Mawangdui yihao Han mu*, vol. 1, fig. 36.

The same pattern is noticeable in the burials of the last four emperors, Yuandi (r. 48–33 BCE), Chengdi (r. 33–7 BCE), Aidi (r. 7–1 BCE), and Pingdi (r. 1 BCE–6 CE). According to this pattern, tombs were situated alternately to the west and east of the tomb either of the founder, or of one of his successors who was accorded a comparable distinction.

Such a pattern follows a scheme traced back to two kings of Zhou, namely Zhao Wang (r. 977 or 975–957 BCE) and Mu Wang (r. 956–918 BCE), the scheme being named *Zhaomu*.[25] It provided a clear display of the permanency of the imperial family; the position of a tomb indicated the seniority of the occupant and his generation; and in view of that distinction mourners would regulate their mourning rites correctly, so as to display and accord with the precise degree of kinship. That such a pattern should be observed in the case of Yuandi and his successors is understandable enough, as it was precisely during their reigns that inspiration was being sought in the precedents of the kings of Zhou; it might be expected that the pattern would have persisted in Eastern Han times, when the example of those kings was exercising a stronger pull, and different as the situation of the imperial tombs at that time was, it may yet accord with the *Zhaomu* principle. If indeed this pattern was observed for the successors of Gaozu, the reasons for doing so are not so clear. Possibly this scheme was also operative in the establishment, maintenance, and final dismantling of the shrines which sheltered the memorial tablets of the kings or emperors. Reference to these matters follows below.

The great majority of our evidence derives from the tombs of those who occupied the highest ranks of society and whose families were able

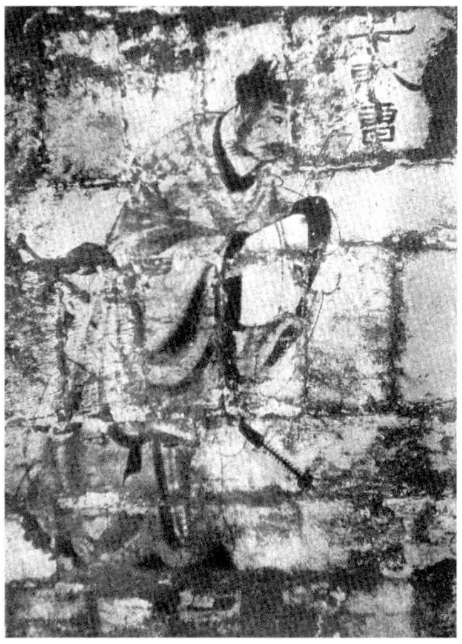

and willing to expend large sums on their funerals. For such was their duty, to serve their ancestors after their death with the same degree of respect that they had rendered previously, and as part of their devotions they paid for the burial of furnishings and artifacts to serve ritual, apotropaic, and practical purposes. In many instances their motive was a sincere wish to speed the deceased person to a blessed life of the future, as has been described. Or bereaved members of the family might wish to provide companions, material comforts, or amusements to while away the time; or they might think that bodily safeguards were necessary, in case one of the elements of the soul survived on earth, immured below the vault of a tomb and wishing to continue its existence there in the teeth of all dangers. Perhaps the family wished to display to all the status, rank, fame, and wealth of the deceased person, together with the treatment that he had merited during his lifetime, in the hope that he would receive comparable treatment from those authorities who managed the life of the world to come. Worldly ambition may have formed a further motive—a wish that the magnificence of a burial would add luster to the kin who had paid for it. It is even suggested that some families may have exploited the occasion of a death and a funeral as a means of enjoyment, setting up a feast accompanied by song and dance.[26]

These material comforts are seen in the profusion of implements and treasures buried in the tombs of the rich; in the food to be consumed, the clothing to be worn. Some of these supplies might be stored in bronze or lacquer containers; some of the goods might be stowed in sealed and corded packages. There would be a large supply of ready money, or if the mourners were mean-minded, of replica coins of clay in place of real cash. The figurines of an orchestra would be accompanied by their instruments; those of entertainers and jesters exhibit their skills. A simulacrum of a residence took the form of a towered building, a farm, or a wellhead (see cat. nos. 13–18). Sets of bronze vessels were at the ready, to be used perhaps for ablutions, perhaps for ritual purposes; sets of lacquer vessels lay in preparation for a banquet (fig. 7). Models of horse and carriage allowed a dead official to proceed on his journeys as duty demanded and to do so in lordly fashion. Their very presence indicated his importance and perhaps his rank, which he would certainly wish to show off in his future life. To call upon his subordinates, attendants, or servants he need only beckon to the paintings on the walls (fig. 8). Instruments used in divination and written manuals that went with them would help a deceased person to choose between different courses of action. Copies of the scriptural writings would recall the lessons with which he had been nurtured and drilled in the past; historical anecdotes could serve as fiction to while away the long hours of the future. Should the person buried find himself in danger, he could consult treatises on medicine or the military arts. Tables and diagrams would enable him to understand the movements of the heavenly bodies. Legal texts could advertise his professional specialities and assist him if he found himself in trouble with officials who were implementing the orders of their superiors in the next world.

Owing to the habits of those who kept records, the chance survival of certain documents, and the material evidences that have been unearthed, what we know of the rites and practices of burial for the highest in the

Fig. 8 *Mural painting of an official* (*Menxia zei cao*). 182 CE. Western Hebei. Painting on brick; dimensions unknown. From *Wangdu Han mu bihua*, pl. 12.

land is not matched by comparable information for that "great multitude that no man can number" of the men and women who lived, died, and were buried at the lower reaches of society. We can call on evidence that concerns the emperors themselves and their immediate inferiors, the kings; close kinsmen of the emperor, these men were at one time entrusted with the government of large areas of land. Fortunately we have a written account of the funeral arrangements ordered for a highly powerful and greatly praised statesman to whom Xuandi (r. 74–48 BCE) owed his throne. This was Huo Guang (d. 68 BCE), whose funeral was regulated by imperial commands that in some respects it should equal the arrangements for an emperor himself.[27] The rites of which we are aware included the services rendered to the dead, the obsequies that took place at an emperor's funeral, the treatment of the corpse, and the furnishings and the structure of tombs intended for those who had been highest in the land. Some of these practices called forth comments and protests that are not without interest.

Precedents of various sorts dated from preimperial times. From perhaps one century after the foundation of the empires, a large park was set aside as the resting place for an emperor, situated as has been seen in a carefully chosen locality and including three separate elements. The tomb held the bodily remains fast and secure; the chamber of rest perhaps replicated the living quarters of the emperor's former palace; the shrine perhaps replicated the court where he had received homage from officials and granted audience to his inferiors. At death a memorial tablet of mulberry or chestnut wood[28] was placed reverently within the shrine and did duty as a representative of the emperor's person; and just as in life he had received obeisances at the audiences that he granted, so after death his tablet received the gestures of respect of his descendants and the offerings that were designed to ensure his well-being. It is probably not correct to see these offerings as being presented to the gods; they were an integral part of the regular services rendered to living and dead as *xiao*, heavily rendered as "filial piety" and perhaps to be thought of as a feeling of respect and responsibility for one's parents. One particular ritual has yet to be completely explained. Once a month the robes and headdress of the dead emperor, which had been stored in the chamber of rest, were solemnly conveyed thence to the shrine. Sometimes this parade caused difficulties owing to the attendance of a large number of sight-seers and their carriages, disrupting the normal life of the city. Possibly this rite was a symbolical re-enactment of the emperor's last journey and an opportunity to present respects to his person.

Respects and services were first rendered to a deceased emperor immediately after his decease and the acknowledgement of his successor. Provided that the latter had reached the age of majority, his first act was to proceed to the shrine of his father, there to present himself as heir to his responsibilities, ready to carry out the duties that his position demanded. Two developments ensued as emperor succeeded emperor.

The regulations and conventions stipulated that no more than seven shrines should be maintained to honor the line of emperors; for persons of lesser ranks the number was limited to five, and for those of yet lower rank to three. It followed that at the death of an emperor who was eighth or later in succession to the founder of the line, although services must be paid to his memory, no special shrine could be erected for the purpose. To solve this problem, on such occasions the tablets of all preceding emperors (except that of the founder) were moved to the shrines of their immediate predecessors, thus leaving the seventh, or latest, shrine empty and free to receive the tablet of the last in the line, just deceased. In time, the shrine of the founding emperor might well become the depository for more than a few of these small but highly evocative memorial tablets. The purpose and function of this practice were clear; it demonstrated to all the continuity of the imperial line. By placing the successive tablets in shrines that lay alternately to the west and the east of that of the founder, successive generations followed the *Zhaomu* principle to which reference has been made above.

With the passage of the generations, the number and expense of the offerings that were presented to these shrines increased out of all proportion. In addition to the shrine situated at the place of burial, by imperial orders shrines were also erected in the provinces, and by the time of Yuandi's reign (48–33 BCE) the total had risen to no fewer than 176. Sharp questions were being raised over the value of maintaining them at so large a cost. A live political and dynastic controversy arose when it was proposed to dismantle some of these shrines and combine their services with those rendered elsewhere.[29] By a decision which had not passed without dispute, it was determined that, exceptionally, three shrines should be maintained in perpetuity, dedicated respectively to the memory of Gaozu (r. 206–195 BCE), Wendi (r. 180–157 BCE), and Wudi (r. 141–87 BCE). The provision of sacrifices was to continue without interruption at these shrines, and this special, privileged treatment would be marked by including the term *zu* or *zong* in the "temple" titles used posthumously to denote their ancestry; the two terms denoted "progenitor" and "ancestor"; their use indicated that the merits of emperors thus honored deserved exceptional recognition.[30] It was in this way that Wudi gained the reputation and praise lavished upon him ever since; the decision to include him along with the founder and Wendi had not passed without argument.[31]

According to the prescriptions or conventions, construction of an emperor's tomb started very shortly after his accession, and in a number of cases this duly took place. With no imperial tomb fully excavated, there is no direct evidence of the style of construction or the size of these tombs or the complexity of their design; but with a number of excavated tombs identified as the resting places of kings, it is safe to assume that those intended for emperors were no less luxurious or palatial. The best examples date from Eastern Han, and it is probable that these had developed in a number of respects from those built for the emperors of Western Han.

These edifices were planned as multichambered residences. A straight, sloping pathway (*shen dao*) led down to the entrance; different apartments served different purposes, as halls where visitors would pay court, where a banquet might be held, or perhaps where musicians or jesters could show off their skills. There might also be a chamber for the deceased king to purify himself and perform his religious obligations; if so, such an arrangement differs from that of the separate shrine and chamber of rest that were set up for the emperors, but we have no certain knowledge of what distinctions prevailed.

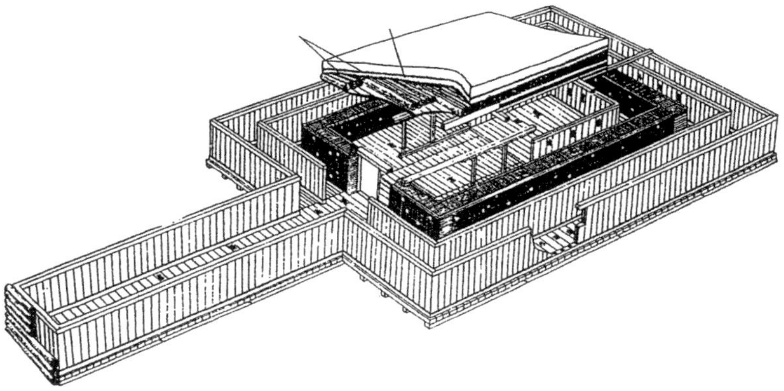

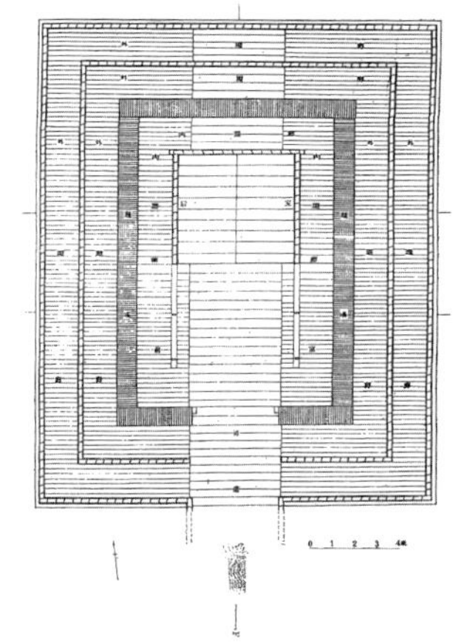

At the center of the royal tombs lay the closed chamber for the coffin, whose walls were sometimes painted in black and scarlet. Wooden walls separated the different apartments from one another and in some cases a stout barricade, formed of meter-long timbers, was laid laterally on four sides to protect the occupant from marauders. Sufficient material remains have permitted the reconstruction of one such example, dating from Western Han (fig. 9). One of two adjacent tombs at Dabaotai, in the outskirts of Beijing, this has been identified as that of Liu Jian (8),[32] king of Guangyang from 73 to 44 BCE (fig. 10). No fewer than fifteen thousand timbers, as estimated, were used in its construction, and examples of similar tombs were not much smaller. The freshly hewn cypress chosen for the purpose was still colored yellow on excavation, and the material is described in literary references as "Golden intestines" (*huang chang*). In some later examples, and in all probability in tombs constructed for some of the Eastern Han emperors, slabs of dressed stone had been carefully cut to measure for the purpose. Sometimes each stone was inscribed with a number indicating the position where it was to be laid, and a certification that it had been duly inspected and approved for use, e.g.:

> Shang Meng stone; width 3 feet; depth 1 foot five inches; length 2 feet ?seven inches; no. 14; Inspected, fourth month, Yongjian third year [128 CE].[33]

A coating of lime insulated the tomb against damp; a tumulus was raised overhead.

We may perhaps pause to place these tombs in context with others that were designed for royalty a little earlier. Thanks to the preservation of an architectural plan engraved on a bronze tablet (fig. 11), and traces of buildings that were found on the ground, it has been possible to reconstruct a series of tombs that were intended to house King Cuo of the small kingdom of Zhongshan and his consorts but were never completed (fig. 12).[34] King Cuo died in 313 BCE, and we may reflect that he was a near contemporary of King Mausolus of Lydia, whose magnificent tomb was built at Halicarnassus (present-day Bodrum). But reconstruction of King Cuo's tomb is less subject to controversy than is that of King Mausolus. Five separate tombs were planned, the central one for the king, those flanking it for his consorts; the central tomb rose to a higher point than did the others, as would befit the status of its occupant. But the structure of these five tombs varies drastically in one particular from that of the tombs for the kings of Han; the kings of Zhongshan were to be buried in a large chamber, lying in a crypt beneath the shrine. As yet there is no certainty regarding the structure or shape of the tomb of the First Qin Emperor; but it is possible that both his tomb and that of Jingdi, fourth of the Western Han emperors (r. 157–141 BCE) owed something to the type of tomb designed for King Cuo, while showing the way forward to those built eventually for the kings of Eastern Han.

Treatises in the histories and other passages reveal some of the steps taken to prepare a corpse for burial and for the ceremonies that characterized the interment of the highest in the land. Huo Guang died in 68 BCE, after ensuring that Liu Bingyi would be enthroned as emperor and

Fig. 9 *Reconstruction of Dabaotai Tomb 1.* 44 BCE. South of Beijing. From *Beijing Dabaotai Han mu*, fig. 13.

Fig. 10 *Plan of Dabaotai Tomb 1.* 44 BCE. South of Beijing. 23 × 18.3 m. From *Beijing Dabaotai Han mu*, fig. 9.8.

after seeing his own daughter established as empress. The funeral prescribed for this highly honored and most successful official was furnished with a wealth of jewelry and precious stones. Exceptionally, his body was to be encased in a suit made of small rectangles of jade; these were carefully sewn together, with thread passing through holes drilled neatly in the four corners of each piece.[35] Jade was thought to possess magical properties, including the ability to preserve the body for eternity. Jade suits were by no means available for general use, even by those who could afford to acquire them; they enclosed the bodies of emperors and their immediate kinsfolk, and it was only by special dispensation and privilege that the right to bury the dead within this highly valuable equipment was granted to others, such as an emperor's favorites. In addition, in ways that are not known the corpse of Huo Guang was to be fed with pearls that simulated grain; similar treasures sealed its mouth. Huo Guang's tomb was to include an inner structure guarded by a barricade of timbers; fifteen stout wooden cases were provided to store a whole variety of consumable and valuable goods, simulacra of such items, or requisites for the continuity and enjoyment of daily life. In addition, a lacquered wooden hood on which mirrors were suspended (*wen ming*) was drawn over the head of the corpse.[36] Finally, the coffin was conveyed on a specially furnished hearse, decorated with golden silk and feathered plumes in token of the honors that were being paid to the great man. So much we read from the histories; the site of Huo Guang's tomb has long been identified; it remains to be examined and excavated, in the hope that grave robbers have not already paid the site a visit.

Further details of these procedures appear in the prescriptions that we have for the long series of ceremonies with which the Eastern Han emperors and their immediate relatives were laid to rest.[37] A total of eleven stages was punctuated by vocal lamentation that took place at set intervals. Once it had been accepted that the emperor had died, officials donned white garments; the gates of the city were closed, and troops were put on alert. The corpse was laid out and perhaps embalmed, to be dressed in twelve layers of shrouds and then fitted with a jade suit whose pieces were linked with golden thread.[38] Supplies of ice delayed decomposition of the corpse before it was placed in the series of coffins; these were made of catalpa timber, chosen on account of its long-lasting properties and perhaps hauled over a long distance from the south.[39] Jade emblems and other types of insignia of officials were placed within the coffin before it was sealed, and the doweling was planed smooth. Officials presented the heir apparent with the text of the *Gu ming*, a document that takes its place in the *Shangshu*, those venerated texts of old that laid down the patterns and precedents that all good monarchs should emulate.[40] Solemnly he acceded to his august position; the gates of the palace and the city were reopened.

Divination decided the day chosen for interment; the cortege was prepared, the exorcist of the palace invoked his powers and performed his rituals to forfend all evil. A large banner proclaimed to all that the deceased Son of Heaven lay within the catafalque, and a senior official read aloud his valedictory rescript. At break of day the procession set out on its lengthy journey from the palace to the site of the tomb. Three hundred strong men who stood by with ropes for haulage were accompanied

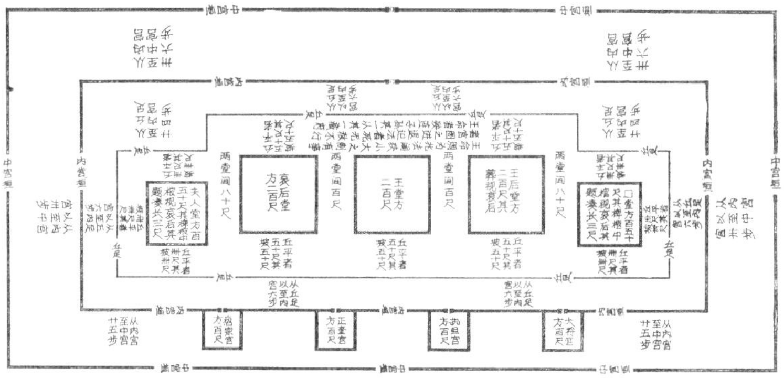

Fig. 11 *Plan of the tombs of King Cuo of Zhongshan and his consorts*. 313 BCE. Pingshan County, Hebei. Bronze inlaid with gold and silver; 94 × 48 cm. From *Kaogu xuebao* 1980.1, p. 125, fig. 5.

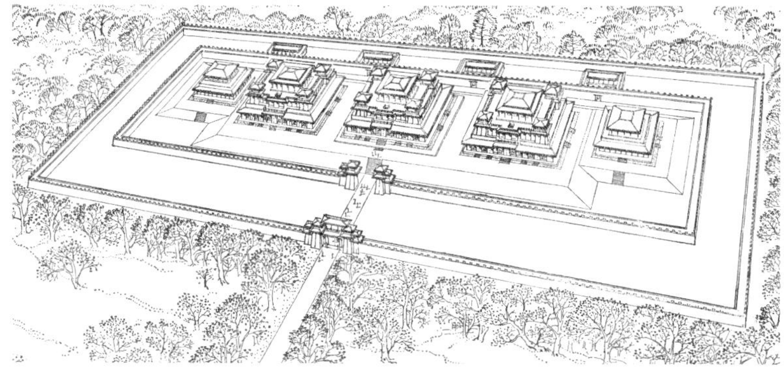

Fig. 12 *Reconstruction of the tombs of King Cuo and his consorts*. From *Kaogu xuebao* 1980.1, p. 110, fig. 10.

by three hundred officials, three hundred colonels, and sixty members of a choir and dancing troupe. Lowered through several stages, the coffin finally reached its last resting place, where the correct furnishings were duly brought together with those rendered by the newly acceded emperor. As the last act, the late emperor's clothing was conveyed to the chamber of rest, for reappearance according to the regular rite that has been described above.

Statements submitted by officials by way of protest testify to the great cost of these practices. The grandeur of some of the kings' tombs that have been excavated and the splendor of their contents show that such criticism was not misplaced, and some emperors responded by leaving instructions that their obsequies should be of the simplest kind, devoid of luxury. Thus in his valedictory rescript Wendi (r. 180–157 BCE) laid down that his own funeral should be a modest affair, with no public money used for the purpose.[41] Nearly one hundred years later (allegedly in 81 BCE) critics pointed out that the extravagance of these occasions signified a decline from the highly praiseworthy moderation of the past. Both Guangwudi (d. 57 CE) and Mingdi (d. 75 CE), first and second of the Eastern Han Emperors, reiterated the views expressed in Wendi's rescript,[42] and toward the end of Eastern Han, Wang Fu (ca. 76–157 CE) echoed the bitter protests voiced in 81 BCE. Meanwhile we are told that no less than 100 million cash was provided for the funeral expenses of Liu Yan, king of Zhongshan from 54 to 90 CE.[43] Elsewhere we read that persons who were of lower status than kings or nobles would, if possible, emulate their superiors, even ruining their households and their livelihoods in the process.[44]

From the foregoing remarks it is clear that funerary practice rested on diverse motives and beliefs rather than on a uniformity imposed by religious leaders or regulated by civil authorities. Throughout there are signs of an acknowledgement of status based on social distinctions and of a conformity with the conventions that officials and writers saw as essential to the preservation of an ordered way of life. Treatment of the dead may have derived from a sincere wish to render the reverence and services due to a deceased person in accordance with the degree of kinship between mourner and mourned. By this means it was possible to establish the fame of an ancestor and to enhance the reputation of a family. At the top of the social scale funerary practice served to strengthen political authority and to display the prestige of the highest in the land. Funerals may have afforded scope to the ambitious to aspire to a higher social status than was their lot; some families might attempt to stage an ostentatious show of their wealth so as to impress their neighbors. Critics could pour contempt on the motives and consequences of such activities.

> In ancient times when a man served his living parents he did so with his full love; when he followed their bodies after death he did so with complete grief. So the holy leaders drew up regulations and restrictions, regarding further extension of these rites as empty and void. But now, while parents are alive, sons cannot bring it upon themselves to render them their due love and obedience; but once they are dead they vie with one another to reach new heights of extravagance. They may harbour no feelings of grief, but by virtue of the luxurious funeral that

> they provide and the wealth of the gifts that they proffer, so do they win a reputation for fulfilling their duties; their name stands out in their generation and their call to glory shines out in public. So the people at large strive together to imitate these practices, even going so far as to bring ruin upon their households and to put their livelihoods up for sale.[45]

Not all obsequies evoked or deserved such contempt. As in other cultures, so in Han China it could well be that formalized procedures and rites enabled near kinsfolk to express their grief while at the same time setting bounds to prevent excess. The practices provided a chance to soothe sorrows and to indulge in hopes that were based on myth or intellectual concepts, and to do so without limitation to any one particular doctrine.

In the course of the last thirty years the fruits yielded by archaeology have enriched our knowledge of China's religious practices and social structure in a way that can only be called dramatic. Month by month further discoveries of material evidence and texts continue to call for research that may lead to confirmation, modification, or correction of our existing notions. In particular there is a call to see how funerary practices developed and changed in the centuries that followed the official close of the Han empire in 220 CE. These times saw the steady growth of Buddhism in country and town and the emergence of communities that centered around a leader who claimed religious sanction and possessed charismatic powers. With the coexistence of two or more political units, opportunities to exercise patronage changed; the abbots of monasteries taught a new approach to the Chinese ideas of life and death and new ways of symbolizing their beliefs. Tombs such as that at Yi'nan and bronze mirrors of the types found in tombs of the Tang period show immediately the development of new art forms and the appearance of new motifs to displace those that had become outworn and lost their power to inspire. Research and excavation may, it is hoped, lead to a fuller understanding of the stages of such developments.

Appendix: Principal sites and monographs

Preliminary reports of discoveries, sometimes well detailed, appear regularly in journals such as *Wenwu*, *Kaogu*, *Kaogu yu wenwu*, and *Kaogu xuebao*, and in regional journals such as *Zhongyuan wenwu* or *Jiang-Han kaogu*. For sequences and schemata of tomb types and artifacts, see *Luoyang Shaogou Han mu* (Beijing: Kexue chubanshe, 1959); for a study of the eleven tombs of Western Han emperors, see Liu Qingzhu and Li Yufang, *Xihan shiyi ling* (Xi'an: Shaanxi renmin chubanshe, 1987); for types of artifact, see Hayashi Minao, *Kandai no bunbutsu* (Kyoto: Kyōto Daigaku, Jinbun kagaku kenkyūjo, 1976); for a comprehensive catalogue of art motifs, see Käte Finsterbusch, *Verzeichnis und Motivindex der Han-Darstellungen*, 4 vols. (Wiesbaden: Otto Harrassowitz, 1966–2004); in her survey of Han civilization (*The Han Civilization of China*, copiously illustrated, trans. Janet Seligman [Oxford: Phaidon Press, 1982]), Michèle Pirazzoli-t'Serstevens draws on material evidence, including much that was found in tombs; for ornamental towers built at the entrances to tombs and their sculptures, see *Sichuan Handai shique* (Beijing: Wenwu chubanshe, 1992).

Examples of the larger tombs for which full-scale studies have been published, usually in monograph form and often with English abstracts, follow.

Pingshan, Hebei: set of five tombs designed for Cuo, king of Zhongshan (327–313 BCE); preservation of a bronze plaque engraved with the design and measurements enabled their reconstruction as originally planned. Contents included specially fine gold and silverware.—Hebei Sheng wenwu yanjiusuo, ed., *Cuo mu—Zhanguo Zhongshan guo guo wang zhi mu*, 2 vols. (Beijing: Wenwu chubanshe, 1995); *Zhongshan: tombes des rois oubliés; Exposition archéologique chinoise du Royaume de Zhongshan* (Paris: Galeries Nationales du Grand Palais, 1984).

Lishan, Xi'an: tomb of the First Qin Emperor (d. 210 BCE); as yet unexcavated; surmounted by a high tumulus; best known for excavated members of a large army of warriors in terra-cotta, stationed in columns leading from the tomb.—Lothar Ledderose and Adele Schlombs, *Jenseits der Grossen Mauer: der Erste Kaiser von China und seine Terrakotta Armee* (Gütersloh/Munich: Bertelsmann Lexicon Verlag GmbH, 1990).

Guangzhou: a total of 409 tombs (shaft, wooden chamber, and brick chamber) in the suburbs and city of Guangzhou include 182 of early Western Han, 64 of mid Western Han, 32 of late Western Han, 41 of early Eastern Han, and 90 of late Eastern Han.—Guangzhou Shi wenwu guanli weiyuanhui and Guangzhou Shi bowuguan, eds., *Guangzhou Han mu*, 2 vols. (Beijing: Wenwu chubanshe, 1981).

Mawangdui, Hunan: the Countess of Dai (wife of Li Cang or Li Zhu Cang), died 168 BCE; shaft tomb, tapered and stepped, with four inner and outer coffins, the corpse being preserved without corruption; funeral furnishings included a silken banner used in the funeral procession. The adjoining tomb (no. 3) included a large number of wooden and silken documents.—Hunan Sheng bowuguan and Zhongguo kexueyuan kaogu yanjiusuo, eds., *Changsha Mawangdui yihao Han mu*, 2 vols. (Beijing: Wenwu chubanshe, 1973); for photographs of artifacts and manuscripts, see Fu Juyou and Chen Songchang, *Mawangdui Han mu wenwu* (Changsha: Hunan chubanshe, preface 1991).

Mangdang, east of Shangqiu city, Henan: seven tombs of members of the family of the kings of Liang, including Liu Wu (2), king of Liang from 168 to 143, and his queen (Bao'an Tombs 1 and 2). These are cliff tombs with sloping entrance passageways (east to west) and with lateral branches and side chambers; both tombs are multichambered, no. 2 being more elaborate. Features include a tomb park and a colored wall painting.—Henan Sheng wenwu kaogu yanjiusuo, ed., *Yongcheng Xihan Liang guo wang ling yu qin yuan* (Zhengzhou: Zhongzhou guji chubanshe, 1996); Yan Genqi, ed., *Mangdang Shan Xihan Liang wang mu di* (Beijing: Wenwu chubanshe, 2001).

Yangling, Xi'an: Han Jingdi; external parts only excavated.—Jiao Nanfeng, ed., *Han Yangling* (Chongqing: Chongqing chubanshe, 2001).

Xianggang, north of Guangzhou city: Zhao Mo (also known as Zhao Hu), king of Nanyue 137 to 122 BCE; multichambered stone tomb; a long passageway leads (south to north) to a lateral branch with two side chambers, followed by the principal chamber and the coffin chamber; the king was dressed in a jade suit.—Guangzhou Shi wenwu guanli weiyuanhui, Zhongguo shehui kexueyuan kaogu yanjiusuo, and Guangzhou Sheng bowuguan, eds., *Xihan Nanyue wang mu*, 2 vols. (Beijing: Wenwu chubanshe, 1991); Margarete Prüch and Stephan von der Schulenburg, *Schätze für König Zhao Mo: das Grab von Nan Yue* (Heidelberg: Umschau/Braus Verlag, 1998).

Mancheng, Hebei: tomb of Liu Sheng (1), king of Zhongshan 154 to 112 BCE and his queen (d. shortly afterward); built in the cliff, two lateral arms (north to south) precede a central chamber which leads to the coffin chamber. Both bodies had been encased in jade suits.—Zhongguo shehui kexueyuan kaogu yanjiusuo and Hebei Sheng wenwu guanlichu, eds., *Mancheng Han mu fajue baogao*, 2 vols. (Beijing: Wenwu chubanshe, 1980).

Shizhaishan, Yunnan: over fifty tombs; one included a gold seal engraved for the king of Dian (ca. 109 BCE); there were fragments of a jade suit; artifacts included regular Chinese examples as well as those with

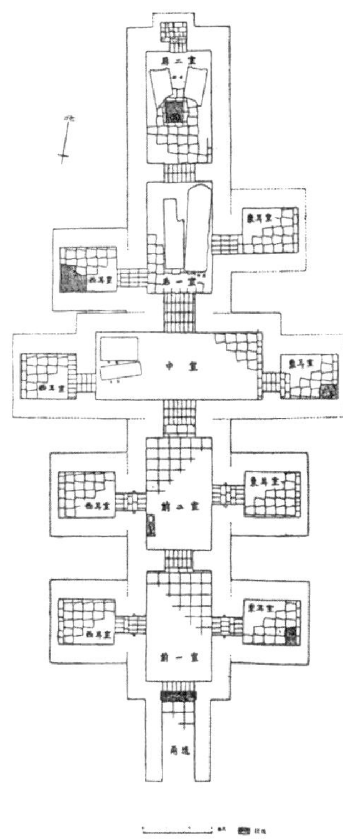

Fig. 13 *Wangdu Tomb 2, plan.* 182 CE. Western Hebei. From *Wangdu erhao Han mu*, p. 3.

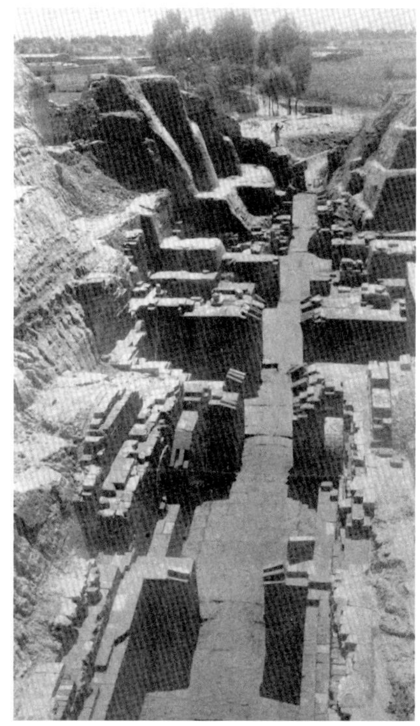

Fig. 14 *Wangdu Tomb 2, as excavated.* 182 CE. Western Hebei. Brick; 32.18 × 13.4 m. From *Wangdu erhao Han mu*, p.17.

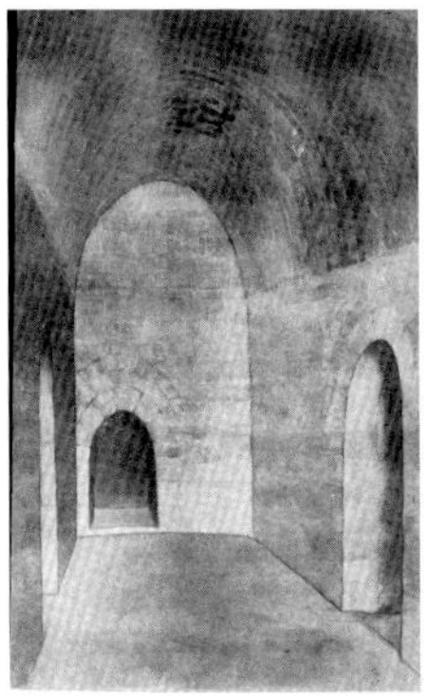

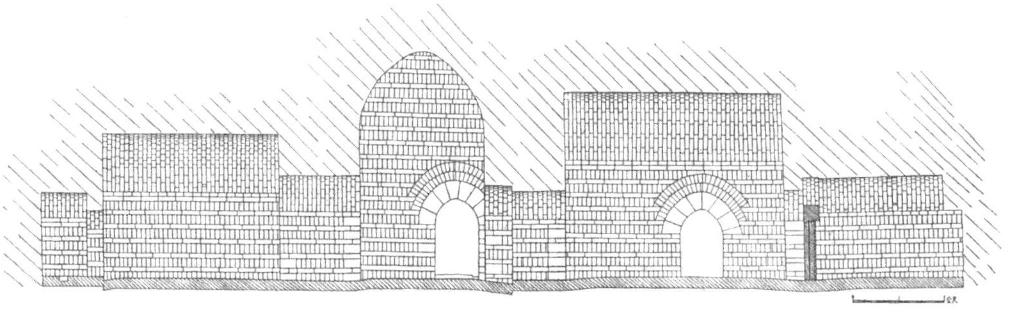

styles and decorative motifs characteristic of Scythian or Ordos culture, and of that of Dongson.—Yunnan Sheng bowuguan, ed., *Yunnan Jinning Shizhaishan gu mu qun fajue baogao* (Beijing: Wenwu chubanshe, 1959); and *The Chinese Bronzes of Yunnan*, preface by Jessica Rawson (London: Sidgwick and Jackson, and Beijing: Wenwu chubanshe, 1983).

Duling, southeast of Xi'an: Liu Bingyi (Xuandi: r. 74–48 BCE), his empress, and others; as yet not fully excavated.—Zhongguo shehui kexueyuan kaogu yanjiusuo, ed., *Han Duling ling yuan zhi* (Beijing: Kexue chubanshe, 1993).

Dabaotai, southern suburb of Beijing: Liu Jian (8), king of Guangyang 73–44 BCE; tomb surmounted by a mound; with horse and chariot burial in the *shen dao* (south to north); wooden walls separate the compartments of the tomb, which is protected by a barricade (*ti cou*) of timber; a second tomb was for his queen.—Dabaotai Han mu fajue zu and Zhongguo shehui kexueyuan kaogu yanjiusuo, eds., *Beijing Dabaotai Han mu* (Beijing: Wenwu chubanshe, 1989).

Beizhuang, Hebei: Liu Yan, king of Zhongshan 54–90; brick-built integrated chambers, surrounded by a stone wall; some of the 4,000 stones were inscribed with directions for their positions, and choice woods were used in other parts; 100 million cash was made available for expenses of the funeral.—*Kaogu xuebao* 1964.2, pp. 127–94; "State funerals," pp. 28, 42.

Helinge'er, Inner Mongolia: tomb of a provincial official of late Eastern Han; brick-built, multichambered, with the richest collection of wall paintings found in a Han tomb.—Nei Menggu zizhiqu bowuguan wenwu gongzuodui, ed., *Helinge'er Han mu bihua* (Beijing: Wenwu chubanshe, 1978).

Wangdu, Tomb 2, Hebei: unidentified occupant; tomb dated to 182 CE by an inscribed contract for sale. Brick built; five connected chambers along a spine (south to north) with two lateral branches, each with two chambers, decorated with many mural illustrations (figs. 13, 14, 15, 16).—Hebei Sheng wenhuaju wenwu gongzuodui, ed., *Wangdu erhao Han mu* (Beijing: Wenwu chubanshe, 1959); Beijing lishi bowuguan and Hebei Sheng wenwu guanli weiyuanhui, eds., *Wangdu Han mu bihua* (Beijing: Zhongguo gudian yishu chubanshe, 1955).

Yi'nan, Shandong: unidentified occupant. Probably to be dated no earlier than the middle or late third century. Stone built; a single, complex multichambered structure; richly sculptured columns, lintels, and other parts.—Zeng Zhaoyu and others, *Yi'nan gu huaxiang shi mu fajue baogao* (Beijing: Wenhua bu, 1956).

Fig. 15 *Central chamber of Wangdu Tomb 2.* 182 CE. Western Hebei. Brick; dimensions unknown. From *Wangdu Han mu bihua*, p. 4.

Fig. 16 *Wangdu Tomb 2, elevation (south-north).* 182 CE. Western Hebei. From *Wangdu Han mu bihua*, p. 5.

Notes

1. For the occurrence and practice of this type of escapism, see Aat Vervoorn, *Men of the Cliffs and Caves* (Hong Kong: Chinese University Press, 1990).

2. E.g., Zhang Heng, "Si xuan fu" ("Thoughts of the mysterious"), *Hou Hanshu* (hereafter, *HHS*) (Beijing: Zhonghua shuju, 1965) *juan* 59, p. 1914.

3. See *Shiji* (hereafter, *SJ*) *juan* 107, p. 2854; *Hanshu* (hereafter, *HS*) *juan* 52, p. 2393; Michael Loewe, *A Biographical Dictionary of the Qin, Former Han and Xin Periods (221 BC–AD 24)* (Leiden, Boston, and Cologne: Brill, 2000), p. 80, *s.v.* Dou Ying. There is possibly a reference to these beliefs in *HS*, *juan* 72, p. 3085.

4. See E. Zürcher, *The Buddhist Conquest of China* (Leiden: E. J. Brill, 1959), pp. 18–43.

5. For references to what would appear to be the least sophisticated of these beliefs, see, e.g., *Han Feizi* 22, "Shuo lin" (Liang Qixiong, *Han zi jian jie* [Beijing: Zhonghua shuju, 1960], p. 189).

6. For ideas regarding the tripartite constitution of human beings—body (*xing*), *hun* spirit, and *po* spirit, see Michael Loewe, *Ways to Paradise* (London: George Allen and Unwin, 1979), pp. 9–15.

7. For *Xiwangmu*, see Loewe, *Ways to Paradise*, pp. 86–96.

8. Yuan Ke, *Shanhaijing jiaozhu* (Shanghai: Guji chubanshe, 1980), *juan* 7 (12 "Hai nei bei jing"), p. 305.

9. *HS*, *juan* 27C(1), p. 1476.

10. See *SJ*, *juan* 28, pp. 1385, 1393; Loewe, *Ways to Paradise*, pp. 37–38.

11. See *Liezi* (*Sibu congkan* edition) 5.2a; A. C. Graham, *The Book of Lieh-tzu* (London: John Murray, 1960), p. 97.

12. *SJ*, *juan* 28, p. 1402.

13. Wang Chong (27–?97 CE) alludes perhaps rather skeptically to this belief; see Huang Hui, *Lunheng jiaoshi* (Changsha: Shangwu yinshuguan, 1938; reprint from a copy incorporating the handwritten notes of Hu Shi, published by Taipei: Taiwan Shangwu yinshuguan, 1969) *juan* 23 (67 "Bo zang"), p. 961; Alfred Forke, *Lun-heng: Part II: Miscellaneous Essays of Wang Ch'ung* (Shanghai: Kelly and Walsh; London: Luzac; Leipzig: Harrassowitz, 1911; reprint, New York: Paragon Book Gallery, 1962), vol. 2, p. 373; Joseph Needham et al., *Science and Civilisation in China*, vol. 5, part 2 (Cambridge: Cambridge University Press, 1974), pp. 84–85.

14. See Loewe, *Ways to Paradise*, pp. 66–75.

15. For Chinese text, see ibid., pp. 196, 198.

16. I.e., the workshops attached to the imperial palace.

17. It is fortunate that, owing to the brief life of Wang Mang's Xin dynasty (9–24 CE), the possible dates of this inscription lie within a narrow range.

18. For the figure of 30,000 tombs, probably including the years of Wang Mang, see *Kaogu* 1999.9, p. 807.

19. See Loewe, *Ways to Paradise*, pp. 27–30.

20. For the *zhu* as known in pre-imperial times, see Michael Loewe, "The Imperial Way of Death in Han China," in *State and Court Ritual in China*, ed. Joseph P. McDermott (Cambridge: Cambridge University Press, 1999), p. 89.

21. See Loewe, *Ways to Paradise*, pp. 21–23.

22. These range from mid Western Han to late Eastern Han; the evidence makes it possible to set up sequences and schemata which illustrate the development of tomb types and forms of a great variety of artifacts. See Luoyang qu kaogu fajue dui, ed., *Luoyang Shaogou Han mu* (Beijing: Kexue yuan, 1959).

23. Some of the principles of *kanyu* that were used to determine a suitable time for an action were later adapted for the selection of fortunate sites or directions, as was practiced under the general term *fengshui*; see Michael Loewe, *Divination, Mythology and Monarchy in Han China* (Cambridge: Cambridge University Press, 1994), chap. 5.

24. See ibid., pp. 274–79, esp. map on p. 275.

25. A study of the *Zhaomu* system has been published as a doctoral thesis by Li Hengmei, as *Lun Zhaomu zhidu* (Taipei: Wenjin chubanshe, 1992).

26. Wang Liqi, *Yan tie lun jiaozhu* (2d ed., Beijing: Zhonghua shuju, 1992), *juan* 6 (29 "San bu zu"), p. 353.

27. *HS*, *juan* 68, p. 2948; Michael Loewe, "State Funerals of the Han Empire," *Bulletin of the Museum of Far Eastern Antiquities*, vol. 71 (1999 [2001]), p. 9.

28. See Loewe, *Imperial Way of Death*, pp. 107, 108.

29. See Loewe, *Divination, Mythology and Monarchy*, pp. 286–97. Four offerings were made daily at the chamber of rest; two for each month (totaling 25) at the shrine; and one for each season at other separate apartments. Altogether it was estimated that 24,455 offerings were rendered annually, and that 45,129 servicemen were required to keep the shrines secure, in addition to over twelve thousand prayer reciters, musicians, and cooks.

30. For these titles, and others that were accorded under Wang Mang, and for the Eastern Han emperors, see Loewe, *Biographical Dictionary*, p. 823.

31. For questions raised in Eastern Han regarding the restoration of shrines and the maintenance of the *Zhaomu* principle, see Loewe, *Imperial way of death*, p. 94.

32. Numbers are used to distinguish holders of identical names, as given throughout in Loewe, *Biographical Dictionary* (see p. 317).

33. For these stones and the text of this inscription, see Loewe, "State Funerals," pp. 42–44.

34. See the preliminary report on this site in *Kaogu xuebao* 1980.1, pp. 97–138; for the bronze tablet, see Hebei Sheng wenwu yanjiusuo, ed., *Cuo mu—Zhanguo Zhongshan guo guo wang zhi mu*, 2 vols. (Beijing: Wenwu chubanshe, 1995) , vol. 1, pp. 104–10, and vol. 2, cpl. II.

35. For references to jade suits and archaeologists' reports of finds, see "State Funerals," pp. 14–34.

36. I am indebted to Ms. Pui Yin Marianne Wong, of Hong Kong, for a private communication drawing my attention to the following references: *Kaogu* 1982.3, pp. 238–39, fig. 6.1, pls. 4.1, 4.5; *Kaogu* 1986.11, pp. 990, 992, fig. 8.13; and *Wenwu* 1987.1, pp. 27–29, fig 6.1; and for informing me that a fine example of a *wen ming* is now preserved in the Yangzhou Museum, measuring l. 54.6 cm, w. 36.1 cm, and h. 38.7 cm.

37. *HHS*, (treatise) 6, pp. 3141–53; Loewe, *Imperial Way of Death*, pp. 91–99, 103–7.

38. For the prescribed use of gold, silver, or copper, depending on the rank of the deceased person, see *HHS* (treatise) 6, pp. 3141, 3152, and Loewe, "State Funerals," p. 18. Possibly the regulation was implemented by the use of a woven thread dutifully colored gold or silver.

39. Catalpa was specified for the coffins of Huo Guang (*HS*, *juan* 68, p. 2948). For the difficulties and labor involved in transporting these choice timbers from the south, as reported by Wang Fu, see Peng Duo, *Qianfu lun jian* (Beijing: Zhonghua shuju, 1979), 3 (12 "Fou chi"), p. 134.

40. *Shangshu* (*Shisan jing zhushu*), 18.13b. The text concerns the funeral arrangements for the king and the accession of his successor; for an English translation, see Bernhard Karlgren, *The Book of Documents* (Stockholm: Museum of Far Eastern Antiquities, 1950), pp. 70–74.

41. *HS*, *juan* 4, pp. 131–32.

42. *HHS*, *juan* 1B, pp. 77–78, and 2, pp. 123–24.

43. *HHS*, *juan* 42, p. 1450; the grandeur of the tomb that is identified as his (at Beizhuang) suggests that in fact no expense was spared; see Loewe, "State Funerals," p. 41, and p. 42 n. 72 for other examples of extravagant expenditure for this purpose.

44. See Wang Liqi, *Yan tie lun jiaozhu*, *juan* 6 (29 "San bu zu"), p. 353 for a criticism of those of medium wealth who were sparing little expense for their funerals and graves.

45. Ibid., p. 354; Peng Duo, *Qianfu lun jian* 1 (2 "Ben wu"), p. 20, and 3 (12 "Fou chi"), p. 137.

Catalogue

Part One: The "Wu Family Shrines"

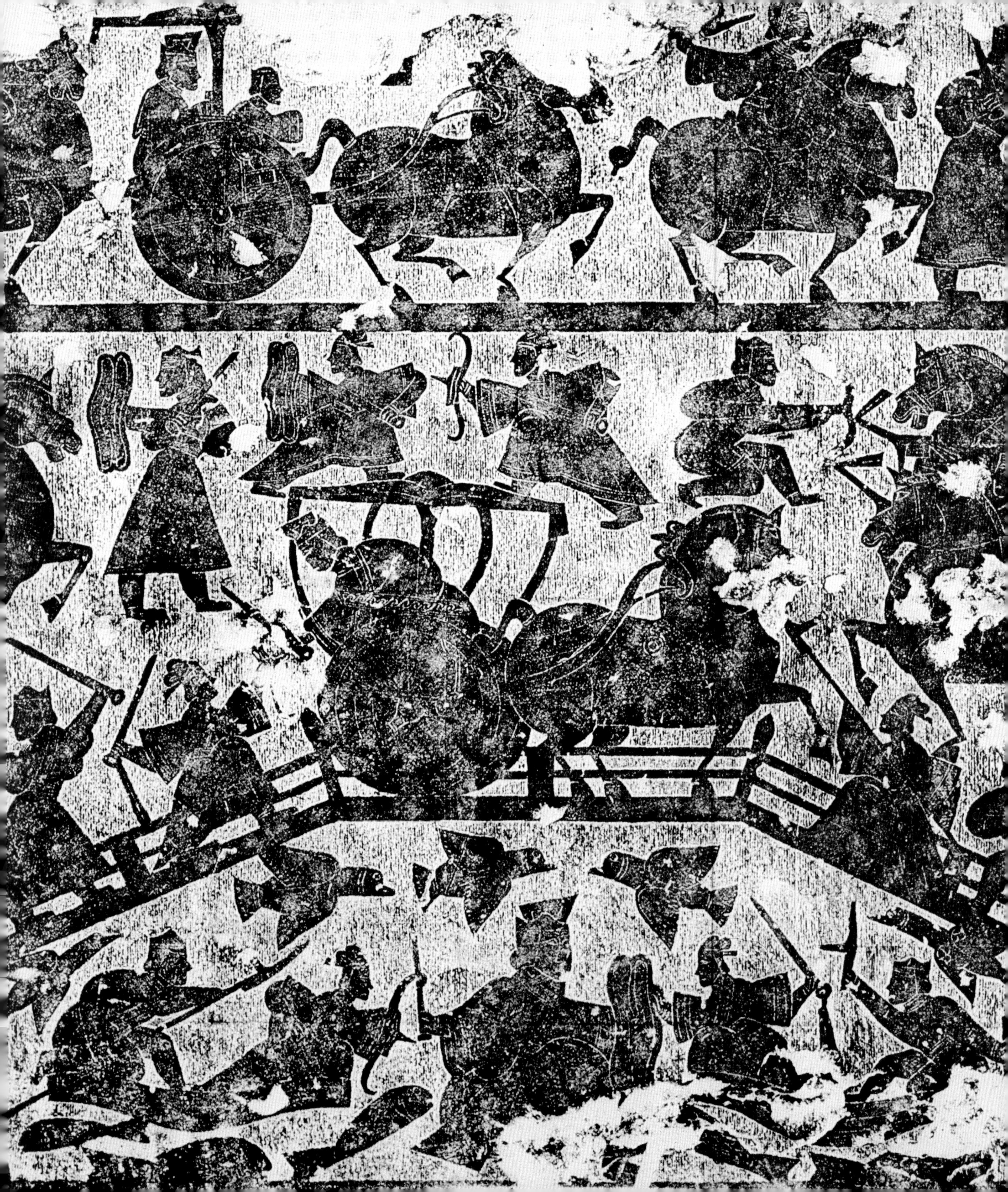

1 "Wu family shrines"

Eastern Han dynasty, mid-second century CE. Wuzhai Shan, Jiaxiang County, Shandong Province.
Ink-on-paper rubbings mounted on paper sheets. Late nineteenth–early twentieth century. Various sizes.
Princeton University Art Museum (PUAM), acc. no. 2002-307.1–.50. Far Eastern Seminar Collection.

Exemplary images of legendary rulers and paragons of filial piety and loyalty, historical and mythological stories, as well as scenes of feasting, homage, processions, omens, and other figural and decorative designs are the subjects of this set of ink-on-paper rubbings (*tapian*). The Wu rubbings are associated with an assemblage of pictorial stones, steles, and inscriptions known as the "Wu family shrines," and have been among the most valuable and authentic materials for the study of Chinese antiquity.

The assemblage known as the "Wu family shrines" was initially formulated during the Song dynasty, since when it has been dated to the mid-second century and held to comprise four inscribed steles, an inscribed gate-pillar (*que*),[1] and a one-bay pictorial stone structure that has come to be known as the Wu Liang Shrine (Wu Liang Ci). These have been known since the Song dynasty through textual descriptions and transcriptions, and through recarved copies and rubbings of the four stele inscriptions, the gate-pillar inscription, and the pictorial stones. But it is by no means certain that the four steles—said to be dedicated to four male progeny of the Wu family—originally belonged to this site. Confused textual transmission and the strong possibility that later scholars supplied interpolations and conflated different sources have cast doubt on the integrity of all the individual inscriptions and on the assemblage as such.

Moreover, from the Song through much of the Qing dynasty, scholars were primarily interested not in the pictorial scenes but in the clerical-script calligraphy (*lishu*) of the carved inscriptions. Because some early versions of the Confucian Classics had been written in forms of clerical script, and because explication of the Classics was considered fundamental to understanding and to ethics, establishing the correct form and definition of characters became surpassingly important. This method of inquiry was termed "using clerical script to explain the Classics" (*ligu*), and many of the Wu rubbing sets produced or transmitted during this period may have only included the stele and pillar-gate inscriptions, as well as the inscribed cartouches (*bangti*) accompanying the pictures in the Wu Liang Shrine. In smaller numbers, inscribed cartouches also occur on pictorial stones that have been reconstructed into two other structures at the cemetery site; prior to the eighteenth century, however, these stones and their cartouches were never recorded.

The Wu rubbings were only linked to actual carved stones in 1786, when the amateur archaeologist Huang Yi (1744–1802) claimed to have discovered matching stones at the cemetery ruins in present-day Jiaxiang, Shandong. Only after this date does the historical record begin for the majority of the pictorial stones, including wall slabs reported by Huang Yi as belonging to Front and Rear Groups at the cemetery, and the ceiling slabs decorated with good-omen designs. In 1789 another ten stones, said to belong to a Left Group, were added to the assemblage, and additional slabs have continued to be inserted until the present day. In addition, several architectural stones with little or no decoration remain at the site and have yet to be recorded, some stones have gone missing, while some formerly missing stones have recently been located in museums

Opposite Detail of Stone Chamber 1, Stone 1-W.2 (cat. no. 1.2). "Wu family shrines" rubbings. Princeton University Art Museum, acc. no. 2002-307.11.

in Tianjin and Berlin (see Liu's "Recarving the Past" in this catalogue).

Nineteenth- and twentieth-century sets of the "Wu family shrines" rubbings are not rare.[2] Comparison makes it apparent that the number of rubbings varies among sets and that there may be no set that can be definitively said to be complete. Most sets were compiled over time from several sources, and they contain different selections. In the Princeton set, for example, the "Confucius Meeting Laozi" slab (cat. no. 1.4) is an unbacked rubbing inserted from another set. This particular stone was found at the cemetery but moved to the nearby city of Jining for storage alongside the Wu Rong stele in the Minglun Tang hall of the Jining Prefectural Academy (Jining zhou xue).[3] Because these two stones were separated from the others, they were not assigned site inventory numbers and have frequently been treated as isolated stones. Not uncommonly, rubbings of these two stones are absent from early rubbing sets of the "Wu family shrines." Sets compiled in the late nineteenth and early twentieth centuries also tend to omit many of the pictorial scenes found on the gate-pillars, as well as those on the triangular gables atop the end walls. Such omissions and conflations are evident in the Princeton set.

The recovered pictorial stones have been studied almost exclusively through rubbings or photographs of rubbings. On-site studies have been done by Wilma Fairbank in 1941, and by Jiang Yingju with Wu Wenqi in the 1980s and 1990s. Fairbank was the first to consider the stones architecturally, but had to rely on rubbings and scale photographs of rubbings for her reconstruction of the stones into three stone chambers: Wu Liang, Front, and Left Shrines.[4] Working with the actual stones, Jiang and Wu essentially confirmed Fairbank's earlier architectural reconstructions, with some revisions and additions. Jiang and Wu reconstructed a single-bay structure, which they identified as the Wu Liang Shrine (Wu Liang Ci), and two double-bay structures, which they called the Front Stone Chamber (Qian Shishi) and Left Stone Chamber (Zuo Shishi) (see Liu's "Recarving the Past," fig. 4).[5] Wu Hung has partially reconstructed a possible "Fourth Chamber" from four stylistically similar pictorial stones that were found away from the cemetery site.[6] The exact relationship between this putative structure and the Wu cemetery is not yet known. Furthermore, the discovery in Jiaxiang County of other pictorial stones carved in similar styles (cat. nos. 10, 11) suggests that a local stone-carving workshop may have produced the stones for building numerous chambers in this area during the second and third centuries (see Barbieri-Low's "Carving Out a Living" in this catalogue). That possibility also raises questions about the exact relationship among the so-called Wu Liang Shrine and Front and Left Stone Chambers and about their respective dates.

The work of Fairbank and of Jiang and Wu at the cemetery site has rendered obsolete all the former numbering and inventory systems, including their own. A more precise—and hopefully more accurate—numbering system designates the three structures as Stone Chamber 1 (former Front and Rear Group stones), Stone Chamber 2 (former Left and Rear Groups), and Stone Chamber 3 (former Wu Liang Shrine and Good Omen stones). The new numbering system locates each stone in a given chamber according to wall, central gable crossbeam, and roof or ceiling slab (see Tables and Foldouts). It may also help to dispel the received story that there must have been four shrines corresponding to the four steles dedicated to four Wu family members during the Eastern Han.

The Princeton set of rubbings was reportedly a gift of Alan Priest (1898–1969), curator at the Metropolitan Museum of Art, to Princeton University to further Professor George Rowley's (1893–1962) work on a manuscript (never finished) on Chinese figure style.[7] The rubbings entered the Far Eastern Seminar Collection, formerly stored in Marquand Library, and served as an invaluable part of the teaching collection in the Department of Art and Archaeology. Threatened with disposal, the present Wu rubbing set along with remnants of the Far Eastern Seminar Collection, including another set and a half of Wu rubbings, entered the museum collection in 2002. Visually comparing Princeton's rubbing of Stone 1-N.2 (west side of the north wall lintel, labeled as Front Group Stone 9 by Huang Yi and as Front Shrine Stone 10 by Fairbank) with a 1907 rubbing of the same stone reproduced by Sekino Tadashi (1868–1935),[8] reveals that the Princeton rubbing was made earlier. The crack through the left chariot and other damage in the 1907 rubbing is not yet present in the Princeton version.

Often viewed as mere copies, rubbings are one of the most complicated and subtle visual mediums among all the arts of China. Whereas the hand of the artist is often directly evident in painting and calligraphy, rubbings embody the original through multiple layers of reinterpretation and recarving. Because time tends to abrade or otherwise damage carved stone, an early rubbing is considered more authentic than the now aged stone it was once taken from. One must keep in mind, however, that the practice of making ink rubbings (*ta*) did not begin until sometime in the Six Dynasties period. In other words, the making of rubbings only became popular centuries after the Eastern Han. If the Wu cemetery stone carvings were centuries old by the time rubbing became common practice, would the original designs not have been likely to need some recarving? For instance, if certain areas of the design had originally been rendered in paint, these would have had to be incised into the stone for the purposes of rubbing (see Liu's "Reconfiguring," and Barbieri-Low's "Carving Out a Living" in this catalogue).

In general, when making a rubbing of an inscribed or pictorial stone, the surface is first cleaned, by brushing from the fine incised lines any ink or paper fibers that might have accumulated during previous rubbings or by recutting worn lines—a process known as "cleaning" (*xi*) or "pointing" (*ti*). A thin sheet of paper is spread over the stone and wetted with a dilute adhesive fluid applied on the paper or directly onto the stone surface. The paper is smoothed and then pressed into the incised depressions or around the relief protrusions. Usually this is done by placing a second, protective, layer of paper over the rubbing paper, and then tamping the paper into or onto the design surface with brushes (*dashua* or *zashua*). Alternatively, felt (*nizhan*) is placed over the rubbing paper and beaten with a wooden mallet to press the paper into fine incised lines. The paper surface is then rubbed or tamped with ink-soaked cloth-wrapped pads (*tabao*) of various sizes, depending on the level of detail needed. When finished, the inked paper is peeled off the stone. No two rubbings of the same stone are ever completely alike, and it is in the artistic selection of details of the carved design included in the rubbing and in the level of skill by which the original carving is embodied that rubbings can be viewed as one of the most important forms of art in China.

Before the advent of photography, ink-on-paper rubbings were the way most pictorial carvings and inscriptions were reproduced and transmitted. Until recently, the large number of sheets in each set of Wu rubbings has made it prohibitively expensive to reproduce them photographically. This has made detailed comparison and sequential dating of various rubbing sets hard to accomplish. The tendency to rely on rubbings and photographs has also caused scholars to overlook the physical attributes of the stones: to forget that some stones have more than one pictorial surface, and that at least one stone, recently located in Berlin, which appears in the rubbing as a flat square, is actually a cylindrical column (see Supplement: Pictorial Column). Moreover, commercial and scholarly rubbing makers were often quite selective in what they included. Some rubbing sets only contain the calligraphic inscriptions, some highlight pictorial scenes but omit the architectural decoration, and almost no rubbing set shows the architectural joins, sides, or backs of the stones. The joins allowed Jiang and Wu to corroborate their architectural reconstructions. The history of the stones also has its own story to tell (see Liu's "Recarving the Past"), and close documentation and scientific analysis of the incised lines on the stones may yet reveal another layer of evidence to be considered.[9]

Little attention has focused on the back or exterior surfaces of the pictorial stones. The exteriors of both Stone Chambers 1 and 2 are roughly hewn stone, while Stone Chamber 3 has flat, finished walls with horizontal decorative bands continued from the interior and wrapping around the outside. The rough finish of Chambers 1 and 2 is typical of almost every Han pictorial stone found in Shandong said to come from a shrine hall (*citang*). In Shandong, to my knowledge, only Chamber 3 at the Wu cemetery and the first-century stone hall at Xiaotang Shan (Hill of Filial Piety) in Changqing County (traditionally said to be the Western Han shrine of Guo Ju), have flat exterior walls. In terms of architectural typology, this raises the dilemma that if the two-bay, rough-exterior Chambers 1 and 2 are shrines, then the one-bay, flat-exterior Chamber 3 is probably not, or vice versa. More to the point, however, the assertion that Chamber 3 is a shrine first occurs only late in the Song dynasty. Earlier it had been called a stone chamber (*shishi*). What such one-bay and two-bay stone structures may have actually been in the second and third centuries needs to be carefully reconsidered (see Liu's "Reconfiguring").

Many invaluable studies in the nineteenth and twentieth centuries have paid great attention to the iconography of the pictorial scenes in the Wu rubbings—particularly the scenes in Chamber 3, the so-called Wu Liang Shrine. Much of this scholarship has accepted the consensus view that the pictorial stones belonged to shrines from a Wu family cemetery dating from the Eastern Han dynasty. This identification may ultimately prove correct. But many basic questions remain concerning the stones themselves as primary evidence for their own history. Other essays in this catalogue may lay a firmer foundation for understanding the individual pictorial scenes, their iconography, and their "interrelationships and positional significance"[10] within an architectural and ceremonial context.

The pictorial carvings on each interior wall of the Stone Chambers 1–3 are generally divided into upper and lower sections by three or four horizontal bands that are left plain or decorated with geometric patterns or cloud-and-animal designs. Similar decorative bands frame the walls at top and bottom. Each section is further divided by thin borders into two or more horizontal registers that often line up with registers on adjoining walls. In the registers are carved scenes including images of historical figures, legendary kings and ancient sages, stories of filial piety and wise officials, tales of exemplary women and loyal assassins, and processions of horse-drawn chariots, riders, foot soldiers, and servants. Topping the east and west side walls are triangular gables with scenes of a central seated figure surrounded by mythological creatures. In the two-bay Chambers 1 and 2, a central, triangular-gable crossbeam with pictorial surfaces on the east and west sides extends from the center of the back wall to a column in the middle of the open front facade. Chamber 3 is roofed by two large rectangular slabs whose exteriors are carved to simulate roof tiles; Chambers 1 and 2 have two slabs on each side of the roof ridge. The undersides, or ceilings, are divided into horizontal registers and carved with images of good omens and supernatural scenes that are some of the most spectacular in the entire assemblage.

Among the three stone chambers, several types of scenes are repeated in the same relative positions on corresponding walls. The two-bay Chambers 1 and 2 share some scenes that are not found in the one-bay Chamber 3, including the well-known "battle at the bridge" scene in the west-wall bottom register. Scenes that are found in all three chambers include depictions of food preparation located in the east-wall bottom register, and frontal seated figures that are usually identified as the Queen Mother of the West (Xiwangmu) and King Father of the East (Dongwanggong) on the triangular gables on the side walls. It may be that these two figures played multiple roles, and in certain circumstances could also represent the patriarch and matriarch of the family, or the deceased husband and his wife. In a stone workshop system, if stock images were cut in advance, to be customized after purchase for each individual client, images that could serve multiple roles would have been especially advantageous (see Barbieri-Low's "Carving Out a Living"). If such a system indeed prevailed, many of the scenes, including the "battle at the bridge," whose identification has been much debated, may not represent any particular military event, but instead could be identified with martial prowess in general or with any historical battle.[11]

Several scenes in the Wu rubbings may well have been stock models, which clients could identify and inscribe as they saw fit. One such is the scene labeled as the story of the filial men from three islets (*san zhou xiao ren*) who banded together in a father-and-sons relationship (cat. no. 1.37). The carved scene shows three male figures and could easily be assigned to any story involving three men or two principals and an attendant. No trait or motif depicted in this scene specifically identifies it with the labeled story. In other scenes the inscribed labels are too long to fit the alloted cartouches, and in yet others no cartouche panels were provided, so the inscriptions had to be carved in the borders.[12] Some carved pictorial scenes do not match the story label in the inscribed cartouches. Many scenes are not labeled at all; their cartouche panels were left empty. Finally, different pictorial scenes in the three Stone Chambers are labeled as the same story, which affords further evidence for the use of stock models.[13]

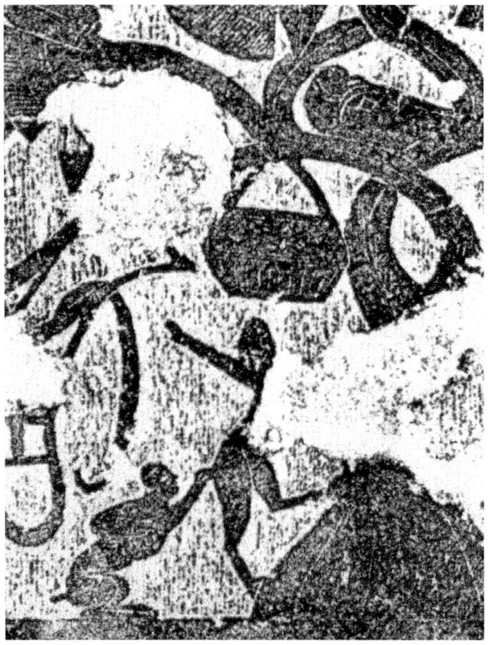

Fig. 1 *Bucket hanging in the tree in a central pavilion scene.* Detail of Stone Chamber 3, Stone 3-S.1 (cat. no. 1.36). "Wu family shrines" rubbings. Princeton University Art Museum, acc. no. 2002.307.35.

Rectilinear cartouche panels are interspersed among the pictorial scenes in all three chambers. In Chambers 1 and 2, respectively, the cartouches remain partly or mostly blank, but in Chamber 3 almost every cartouche is inscribed with clerical-script calligraphy identifying specific figures in the scene and sometimes describing the figure or the event depicted. Processions of horse-drawn chariots, riders, soldiers, and attendants are also found in all three stone chambers. In Chambers 1 and 2 long processions begin on the west wall, continue onto the south wall, and end on the east wall.

Probably the most famous and most debated scene common to all three chambers is the so-called homage, or central pavilion, scene, showing a two-story structure with flanking towers next to a tree whose intertwined branches hold birds and sometimes a monkey; an archer taking aim at the tree; and an unhitched horse next to a chariot.[14] This scene is located in the south-wall central niche of Chambers 1 and 2, and at the bottom center of the south wall in Chamber 3. It has been interpreted to represent homage, with male figures in the lower story and females above. The large seated male receiving obeisance is variously identified as a sovereign, the family patriarch, or the deceased, while the central lady in the upper level has been called the Queen Mother of the West, the family matriarch, or the wife of the male figure. The tree beside the pavilion has commonly been believed to represent the mythical *fusang* tree, but it could just as well be other mythological trees, known as *lianli* or *hehuan*, that symbolize intertwined harmony.[15] Sometimes the birds in the tree are said to represent the ten suns of which the divine archer Yi shot all but one. This explanation, however, does not agree with the number of birds in most scenes, nor does it explain the monkey in the tree or the unhitched horse and chariot. In a recent reevaluation of this picture, it has been proposed that the scene is actually composed of rebuses for attaining high office and rank. The archer aiming at a bird (*she que*) or monkey (*she hou*) are rebuses, respectively, for aiming for a gate-pillar (*que*), symbol of high office, and aiming for noble rank (*hou*). In addition, the unhitched horse and chariot may be a sign of retirement from office (*zhi zai xuan che*), and implies leaving office and success to one's children and grandchildren (*chuan yi zi sun*) (for a related phrase, see cat. no. 40).[16] In the central pavilion scene in Chamber 3 there is a bucket suspended in the tree (fig. 1; cat. no. 1.36). This same motif appears also in the pavilion scene on a pictorial stone found in nearby Songshan in Jiaxiang County, where the bucket is hung directly over the unhitched horse (fig. 2; cat. no. 11). This may be another rebus for leaving office, a substitute for the unhitched chariot that is not depicted in the Songshan stone.

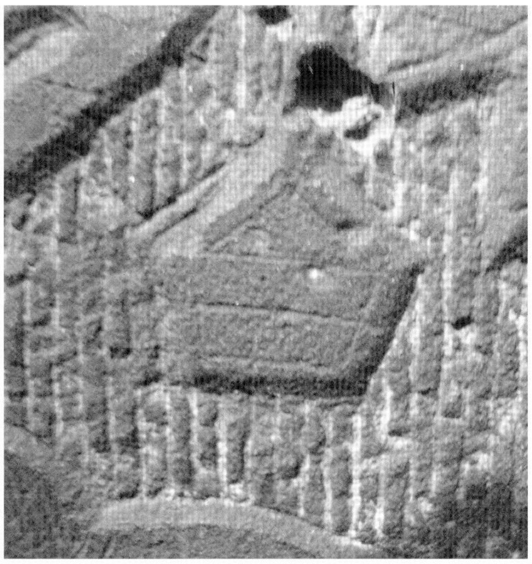

Fig. 2 *Bucket hanging in the tree in a central pavilion scene*. Detail of Songshan pictorial slab (cat. no. 11). Shandong Stone Inscriptions Art Museum.

For the rubbing set in the Princeton University Art Museum, the following descriptions of the pictorial scenes in each of the three Stone Chambers begin on the west wall, then move in order to the south, east, and other walls, followed by the roof slabs. Each wall is described from top to bottom, and some scenes that are missing from the Princeton rubbing set are also described and keyed to appended foldout plates in this catalogue. For Chambers 1 and 2, descriptions of the recessed niche at the bottom of the back (south) wall are inserted after the descriptions of the south walls. The few rubbings of the gate-pillars in the Princeton set are included at the end, along with rubbings of the Wu Ban stele, the possible "Fourth Chamber," and some Qing-dynasty inscriptions.
CARY Y. LIU

Stone Chamber 1

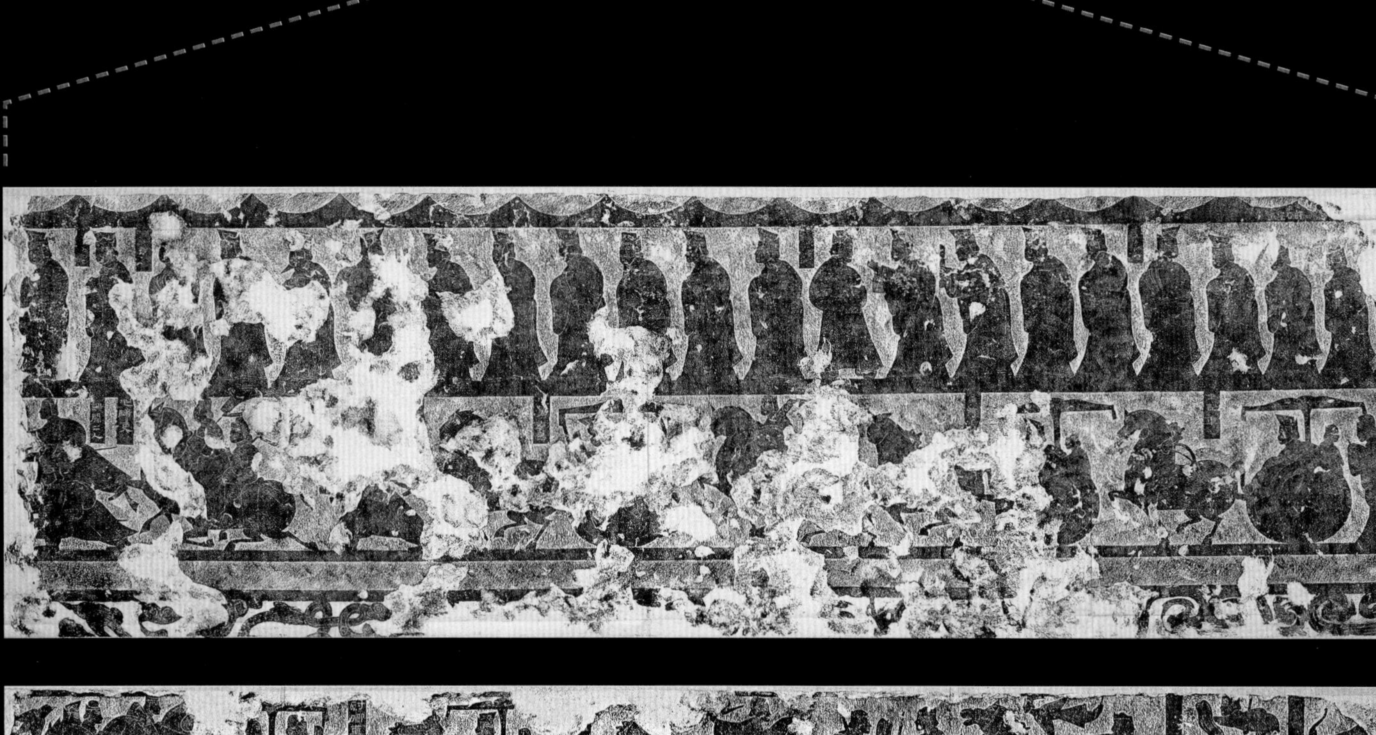

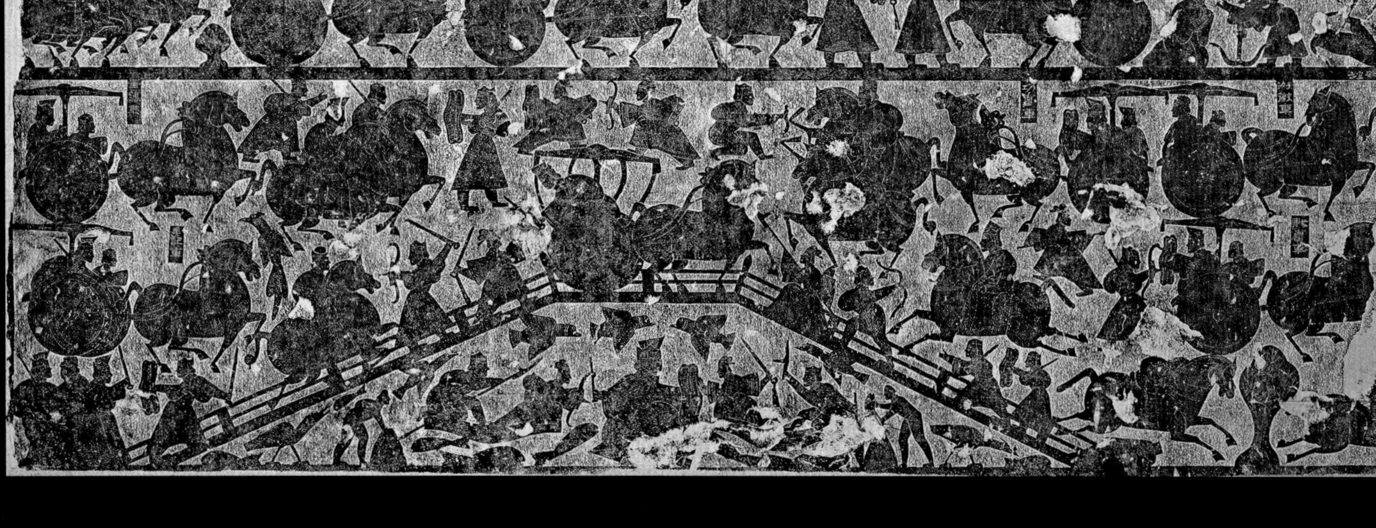

1.1
1.2

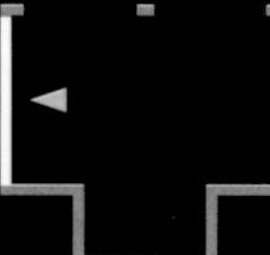

Stone Chamber 1 (former Front and Rear Group stones): West Wall

1.1 *West wall, Stone 1-W.1*. Rubbing; h. 63.5 cm, w. 199.4 cm. PUAM, acc. no. 2002.307.10.
1.2 *West wall, Stone 1-W.2*. Rubbing; h. 78.3 cm, w. 198.5 cm. PUAM, acc. no. 2002.307.11.

1.1

Triangular gable (missing from Princeton set; see foldout plate): the central winged figure in the west-wall gable is partially damaged, but most likely represents the Queen Mother of the West with possible dual roles as family matriarch or wife of the deceased. The figure sits on a throne supported by a pair of intertwined dragons. On the left are two hares pounding the elixir of immortality in a mortar held up by a toad, two figures among scrolling clouds, and at far left a winged Immortal, two birds, and a fish. On the right of the Queen Mother are two winged Immortals, dragons (partially damaged), and other fantastic creatures.

First register: twenty-two men move from right to left. All but three face left and most have their folded hands raised to their chests in a *gongshou* gesture of respect. Judging from the corresponding registers on the south and east walls, which continue the parade and contain inscribed cartouches identifying particular figures as Confucius, Laozi, and Zilu, these figures likely represent Confucius' disciples.

Second register: in the rubbing this area of the stone appears heavily damaged. Remaining traces show a procession beginning at the right with a figure who appears to be bidding farewell. Heading to the left are three horse-drawn chariots with occupants, mounted figures, and foot soldiers or attendants. The cavalcade continues in the corresponding registers on the south and east walls.

1.2

Third register: entering from the left are three horsemen and two *yaoche* canopied chariots[17] of officials whose titles are inscribed on rectangular cartouche panels. Leading the chariots are a horseman and a foot soldier, both with swords drawn. Toward them comes an uncanopied chariot whose rider is looking behind him. Before this chariot, its horse's reins in one hand and a large sword in the other, stands a foot soldier facing left. Above the chariot hovers a winged Immortal, and to its right is a woman kneeling in front of a man with a crossbow. Above them is another figure with a sword and shield, and to the right are traces of two figures loading crossbows. The accompanying cartouches are blank, and the story is not known.

Fourth register: this "battle at the bridge" scene can be divided into three zones: above, on, and below the bridge. Above the bridge chariots with officials' titles inscribed in cartouches, cavalry, and infantry come from both sides for battle. At the center of the bridge a prominent male figure in a canopied chariot engages with an armed female before and behind him. The left female wields a long sword in one hand and in the other she carries a double-sickle sword (*gouxiang*) that has become interlocked with the sword of the man in the chariot. All along the bridge are other combatants. At the foot of the bridge on the right side two horsemen gallop away from the bridge. Under the left horse lies a decapitated body whose head hangs in the stylized tree between the two horsemen. Under the bridge is a large figure who may be the same man seen in the chariot at the center of the bridge. Again, he is beset by two female warriors, one on each side, but here they stand in boats. Fishermen, fish, and cranes and other birds fill in the space around the action under the bridge.

CARY Y. LIU AND EILEEN HSIANG-LING HSU

Stone Chamber 1: South Wall

1.3 *South wall, Stone 1-S.1*. Rubbing; h. 26.0 cm, w. 149.9 cm. PUAM, acc. no. 2002.307.3.
1.4 *South wall, Stone 1-S.2*. Rubbing; h. 32.0 cm, w. 162.8 cm. PUAM collection.
1.5 *South wall, Stone 1-S.3*. Rubbing; h. 26.0 cm, w. 322.0 cm. PUAM, acc. no. 2002.307.4.
1.6 *South wall, Stone 1-S.4.a*. Rubbing; h. 69.0 cm, w. 92.2 cm. PUAM, acc. no. 2002.307.5.
1.7 *South wall, Stone 1-S.5.a*. Rubbing; h. 68.7 cm, w. 92.0 cm. PUAM, acc. no. 2002.307.7.

1.3

First register (west side): procession of fourteen men moving from right to left. Several of the figures carry book scrolls made of bundled strips of bamboo or wood. Judging by the corresponding registers on the west and east walls, which continue the parade of men, the figures on this stone likely represent Confucius' disciples.

1.4

First register (east side): this unmounted rubbing, added from a different rubbing set, depicts the popular theme of Confucius Meeting Laozi (see cat. no. 10). At right, three figures continue the procession from the west register (cat. no. 1.3). At left, the remainder of the stone shows the meeting of Confucius with Laozi, who leans on a crooked cane. Between the two sages is a bird flying over a small figure holding what looks like a stick with a wheel. This figure has often been identified as Xiang Tuo, a teacher of Confucius.[18] Chariots for the two sages flank the meeting.

1.5

Second register: a long procession with five canopied chariots moves from right to left; inscribed cartouches preceding each vehicle list an office title. Accompanying the chariots are four pairs of horsemen, some carrying halberds and others wrapped *bang* cudgels.[19] Leading the second chariot from the right are two men on foot, one of whom can be seen carrying a device that resembles a *bianmian* fan but is held reversed with the convex side facing the holder. The front rider in the second chariot holds a *bianmian* fan properly, shielding his face.[20] Stylized trees, birds (see cat. nos. 55, 56), bears (see cat. nos. 47–49), and a dog (see cat. no. 53) are interspersed along the procession, and large figures in official robes and peaked caps stand at the right and left ends, respectively, as if sending off and receiving the cavalcade.

1.6

This pictorial stone is located at the bottom of the south wall to the west side of the center niche.

First register: the story of the loyal assassin Jing Ke's attempt to kill the king of Qin (the future First Emperor) (cf. cat. nos. 1.23, 1.35). In the scene Jing Ke with disheveled hair is being tackled after having hurled his dagger at the king. The dagger is depicted piercing the bronze column. Left of the column the king is seen fleeing with a *bi* disc (see cat. nos. 20–22) in his right hand. In midair to the right of the column and just below the dagger is the king's sleeve, torn off during his escape, and below that a half-open box containing the head of General Fan Yuqi. Fan had slit his own throat so that Jing Ke could offer his head as a gift to gain admittance to the king. Cowering on all fours below Jing Ke is the figure of Qin Wuyang, who had been sent with Jing to act as his second but had fallen to the ground quaking with fear.[21]

Second register: a screened, canopied chariot with a figure peeking out the back at a following horseman. Bringing up the rear at right is a covered wagon.[22]

Third register: a covered wagon and canopied chariot proceed to the left. At far right a man holding a *hu* tablet gently bows, as if sending off the chariots. The procession continues in the corresponding register on the west wall of the niche.

1.7

This pictorial stone is located at the bottom of the south wall to the east side of the center niche. Scenes of banqueting are depicted in a three-story building on the right and scenes of food preparation and entertainment are seen in corresponding registers on the left. Four musicians play various instruments in the top left register. Below them, despite extensive damage, a figure holding a fish can be seen, along with female attendants who wait upon a party of four ladies in the third story of the building at right. In the damaged second left register from the bottom, a figure stoops over some large pans and a male attendant carries a bowl into the second story at right, where a prominent man is receiving a bowl from two respectful men. On the ground level on the left is a kitchen, with two servants attending a stove (see cat. no. 19). Fowl, fish, and meats hang from the ceiling. At right, attendants carry pans, bowls, and trays up a staircase to serve the banqueters.

CARY Y. LIU AND EILEEN HSIANG-LING HSU

1.4
1.5
1.7

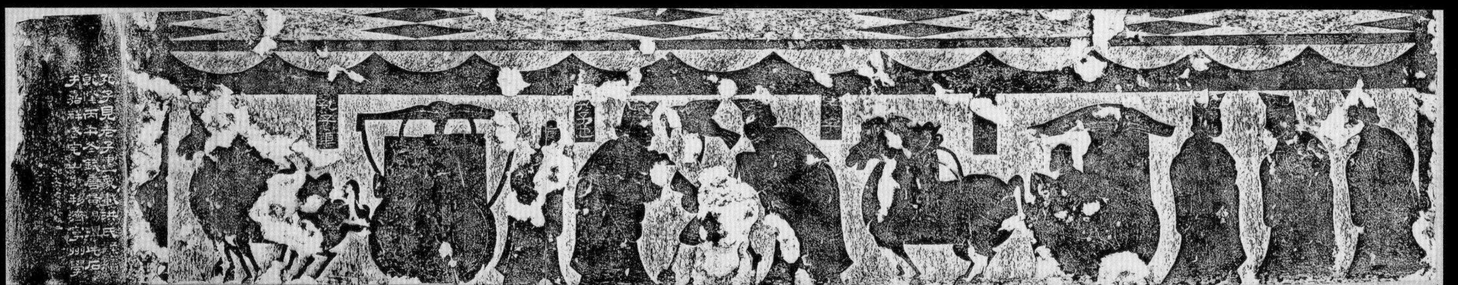

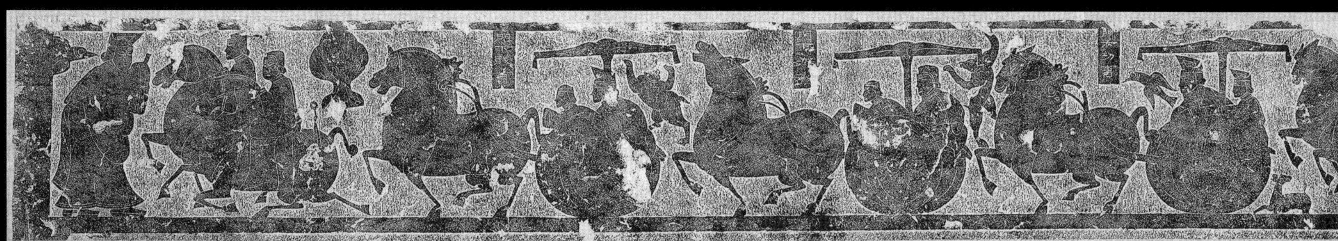

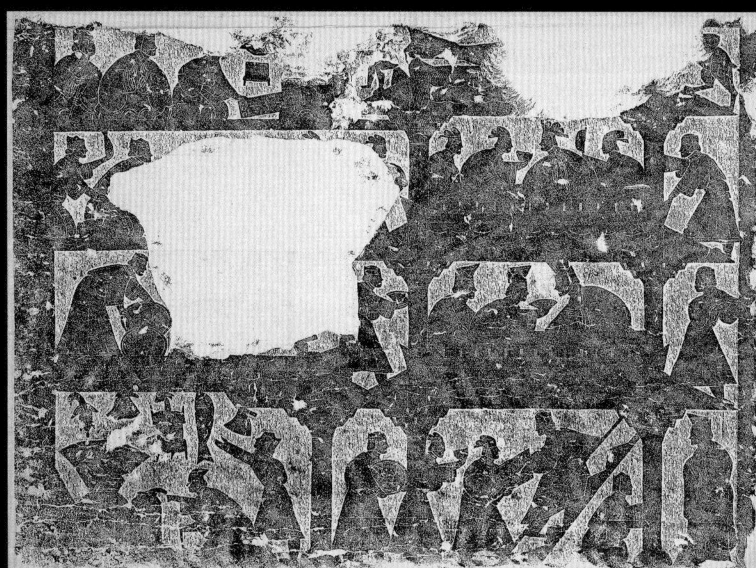

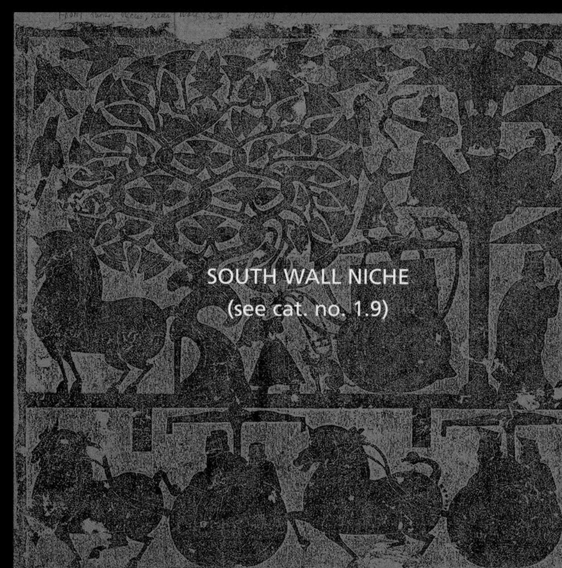

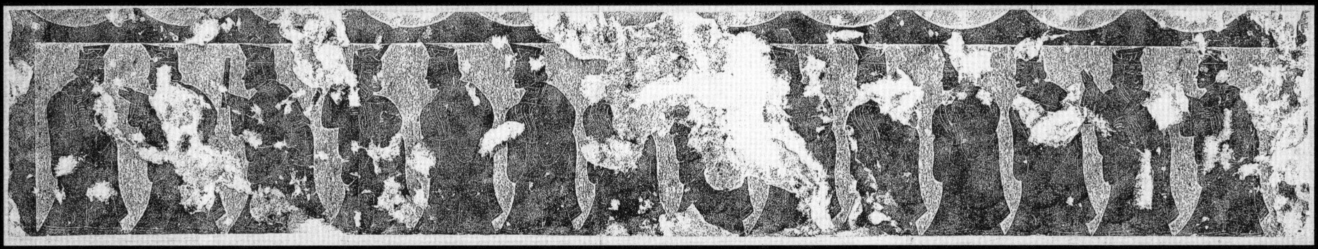

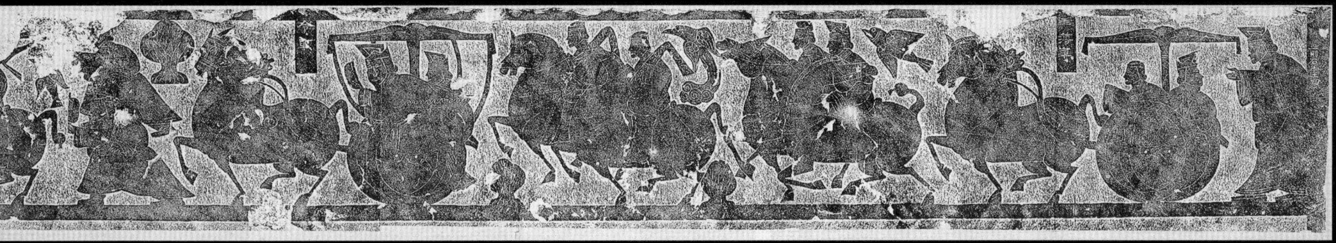

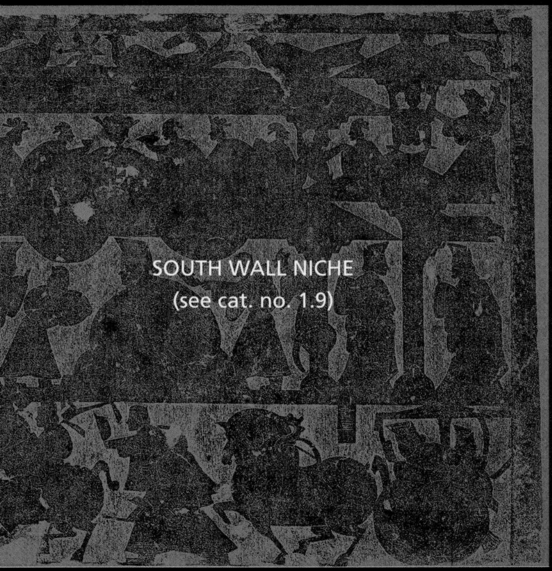

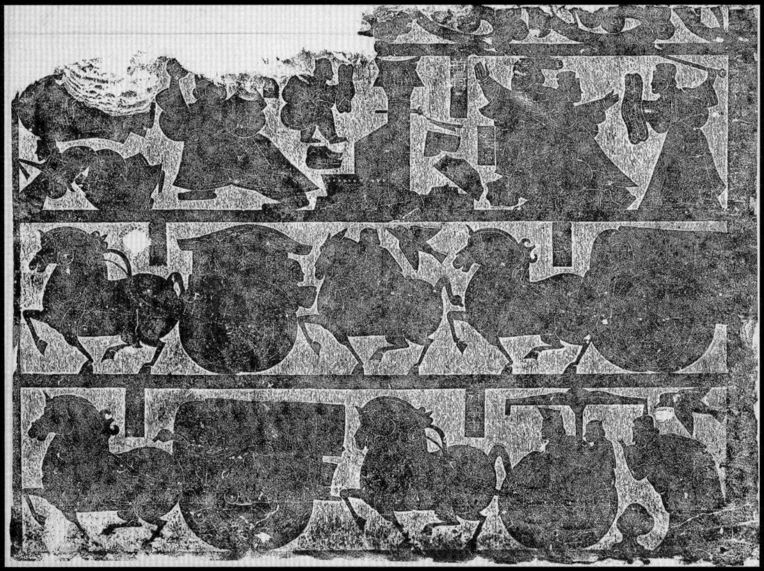

1.3
1.5
1.6

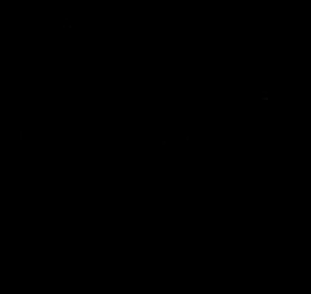

Stone Chamber 1: Niche Walls

1.8 *Niche, west wall, Stone 1-S.4.b.* Rubbing; h. 67.8 cm, w. 74.3 cm. PUAM, acc. no. 2002.307.6.
1.9 *Niche, south wall, Stone 1-S.6.* Rubbing; h. 68.5 cm, w. 143.3 cm. PUAM, acc. no. 2002.307.9.
1.10 *Niche, east wall, Stone 1-S.5.b.* Rubbing; h. 67.6 cm, w. 72.5 cm. PUAM, acc. no. 2002.307.8.

1.8

This face of a turning-corner stone (*zhuan jiao shi*) is divided into four horizontal registers.

First register: a decorative band of scrolling clouds with bird, animal, winged Immortal, and dragon heads. The same design is found in the corresponding register on the east wall of the niche.

Second register: four seated women on the left face four on the right. The lady at right center offers a tray to the prominent lady at left center, who is the only one wearing a three-lobed headdress. The lady at far right holds a mirror (see cat. nos. 38–41) with a tassel.

Third register: a horse-drawn chariot preceded by two horsemen. A cartouche next to the chariot lists an office title.

Fourth register: three horsemen, one carrying a *bang* cudgel and one wearing a peaked cap, precede a canopied chariot. A bear (see cat. nos. 47–49) fills the space between the horsemen and chariot. The cavalcade continues in the corresponding registers on the south and east walls of the niche.

1.9

First register: the homage, or central pavilion, scene (discussed earlier). In this version an attendant presents a round tray holding two eared cups (see cat. nos. 32–35) and a footed vessel to the large seated man in the ground story. Standing officials wearing peaked caps and holding *hu* tablets approach respectfully from both sides. On the left, or east, side stands the tree whose intertwined branches hold ten birds, and to its right the archer in the tower taking aim at the birds. Beneath the tree the unhitched horse and chariot are accompanied by an attendant and a dog (see cat. no. 53). The horse has a long free-hanging tail, unlike the bobbed or braided tails on most other horses depicted in the carvings.

Second register: a procession with three horse-drawn canopied chariots, two horsemen carrying halberds, and two footmen. Inscribed cartouches next to the chariots list office titles. The cartouche of the right chariot reads, "lord's vehicle" (*junche*), suggesting this may be the main chariot. Note that the free-hanging tail of this horse matches that of the unhitched horse in the central pavilion scene in the register above. The cavalcade continues in the corresponding registers on the west and east walls of the niche.

1.10

This face of a turning-corner stone (*zhuan jiao shi*) is divided into four horizontal registers.

First register: a decorative band of scrolling clouds ending in the heads of birds, animals, and a winged Immortal moves from right to left. This design echoes the corresponding register on the west wall of the niche.

Second register: at far left, two standing and two flying Immortals flank a square container enclosing what may be a tree or fountain.[23] To the right are a large, bulbous tree and another winged Immortal. Two more trees are depicted farther to the right, one with six drooping branches and the other an auspicious *mingjia* tree with fifteen leaves.[24] Another winged Immortal stands at far right.

Third register: at the left is a tree with six branches bearing four fruits. On the right are two stories of filial piety. Ding Lan lost his parents as an infant, so he made two wooden statues and served them as if they were his real parents. One day his drunken neighbor Zhang Shu rushed over, cursed the statues, and hit their heads. Later, upon seeing Ding Lan, the statues began to weep. Discovering the cause, Ding Lan killed Zhang Shu. The scene supposedly shows Ding Lan, with his wife standing behind him, kneeling before an amorphous wooden statue of a parent, saying good-bye before turning himself in to the authorities (cf. cat. nos. 1.25, 1.35).[25] Xing Qu was a filial son who cared for his aging toothless father by chewing the food for him (cf. cat. nos. 1.12, 1.25, 1.36).[26] The scene shows the son feeding his father, who is seated on a dais at far right.

Fourth register: a horse-drawn, canopied chariot proceeds from right to left, led by two horsemen. A figure standing at far left faces the approaching riders, offering a shield. An inscribed cartouche next to the chariot lists an office title. The cavalcade continues in the corresponding registers on the west and south walls of the niche.

CARY Y. LIU AND EILEEN HSIANG-LING HSU

1.10 1.9

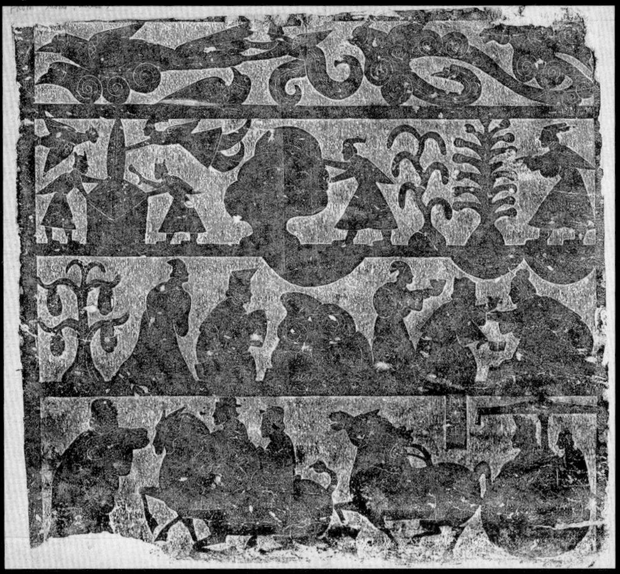

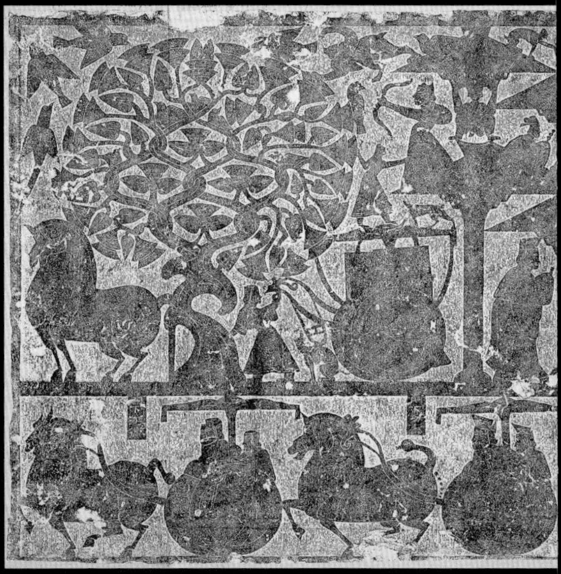

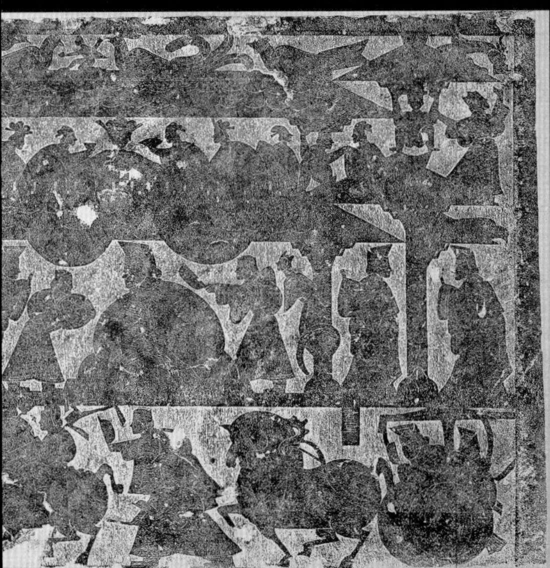

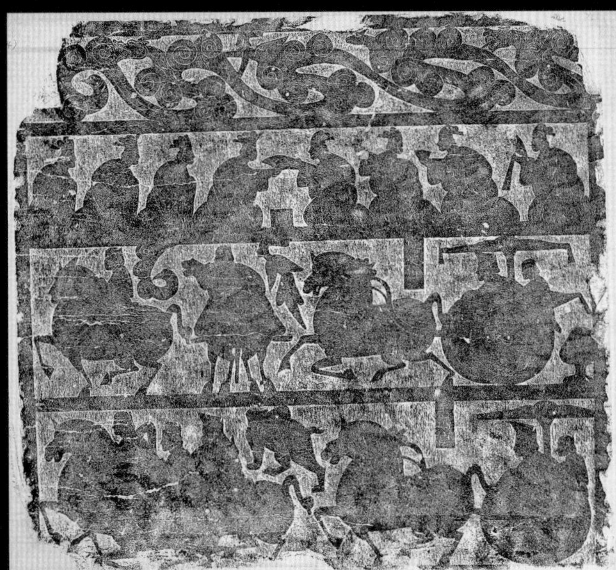

1.9 1.8

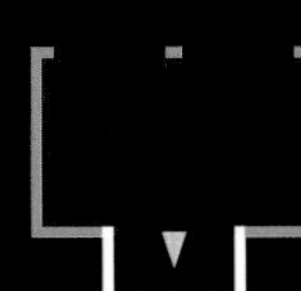

Stone Chamber 1: East Wall

1.11 *East wall, Stone 1-E.1.* Rubbing; h. 87.5 cm, w. 199.3 cm. PUAM, acc. no. 2002.307.1.
1.12 *East wall, Stone 1-E.2.* Rubbing; h. 80.2 cm, w. 201.0 cm. PUAM, acc. no. 2002.307.2.

1.11

Triangular gable: seated at the center is the King Father of the East, supported by a dragon and a winged Immortal. To his left is a kneeling winged Immortal making an offering. Other winged or cloud-body Immortals, including one with two heads, hover nearby. Above the Immortals is large bird, and at far left are a three-headed bird with cloud legs and a small bird. A similar host of creatures is seen to the King Father's right, including a standing winged Immortal, a pair of winged dragon-headed beasts, winged or cloud-body Immortals, and two toads.

First register: procession of nineteen men moving from right to left. The figures resemble those on the corresponding registers on the south and west walls. An inscribed cartouche identifies the ninth figure from the left as Zilu, a disciple of Confucius known for his courage and forthrightness, who is shown wearing a rooster cap (cf. cat. no. 10).

Second register: procession of three horse-drawn chariots with inscribed cartouches next to each vehicle listing an office title, four horsemen, and two footmen. Large bowing figures holding *hu* tablets and wearing official robes and peaked caps stand at the right and left ends, respectively, as if sending off and receiving the cavalcade. The procession continues the corresponding registers of the south and west walls.

1.12

Third register: four stories of filial piety and virtuous deeds. From the left to the right: Zhao Dun, Xing Qu, Min Ziqian, and the righteous aunt (*yi gujie*). Zhao Dun (also known as Zhao Xuanmeng) gave food to a starving man named Ling Zhe, who, when asked why he only ate half, replied that he wanted to save the other half to bring his mother. Later, when Duke Ling of Jin tried to kill Zhao Dun, Ling Zhe saved him. Xing Qu was a filial son who cared for his aging, toothless father by chewing food for him (cf. cat. nos. 1.10, 1.25, 1.36).[27] The next scene has been identified as that of Min Ziqian, who was ill-treated and poorly clothed by his stepmother. While driving a chariot in the winter cold, he lost the reins or whip. Comparing the clothes of his son with those of his stepson, the father realized why and wanted to send the stepmother away. Min Ziqian interceded on her behalf. In the rubbing the father is shown about to strike his kneeling son behind a chariot. This does not accord with the textual story and also does not resemble the Min Ziqian scene carved in Stone Chamber 3 (see cat. no. 1.35).[28] In the story of the righteous aunt, the lady chose to protect her nephew instead of her own son in time of grave danger (cf. cat. no. 1.36). Although parts of this register are quite damaged, many of the stories are identified by surviving inscribed cartouches. The three cartouches accompanying the Min Ziqian story, however, are blank.

Fourth register: the historical figures King Wen and his consort sit on a dais at left. Standing to their right are the king's ten sons, including the child Ran Jizai, who is cared for by his wet nurse. Female and male figures, respectively, stand at the left and right sides of this scene. Inscribed cartouches identify the king and the names of the sons, but only a few are still legible. Two filial stories are arranged

1.11
1.12

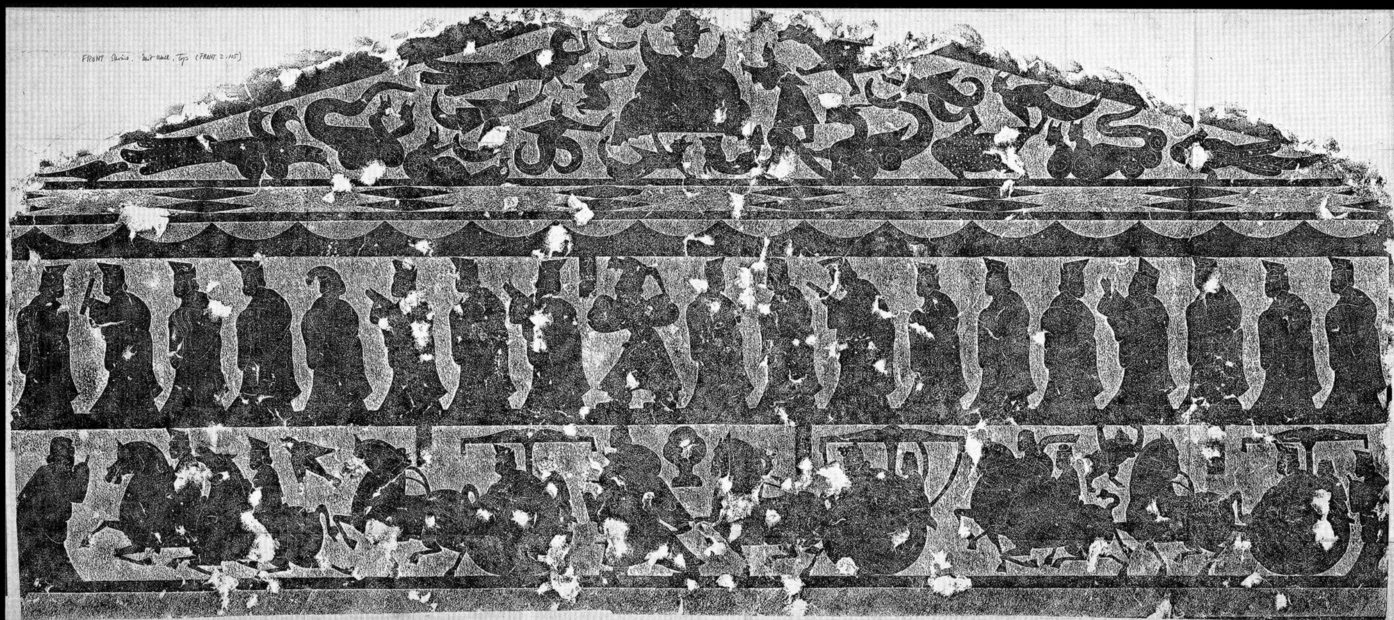

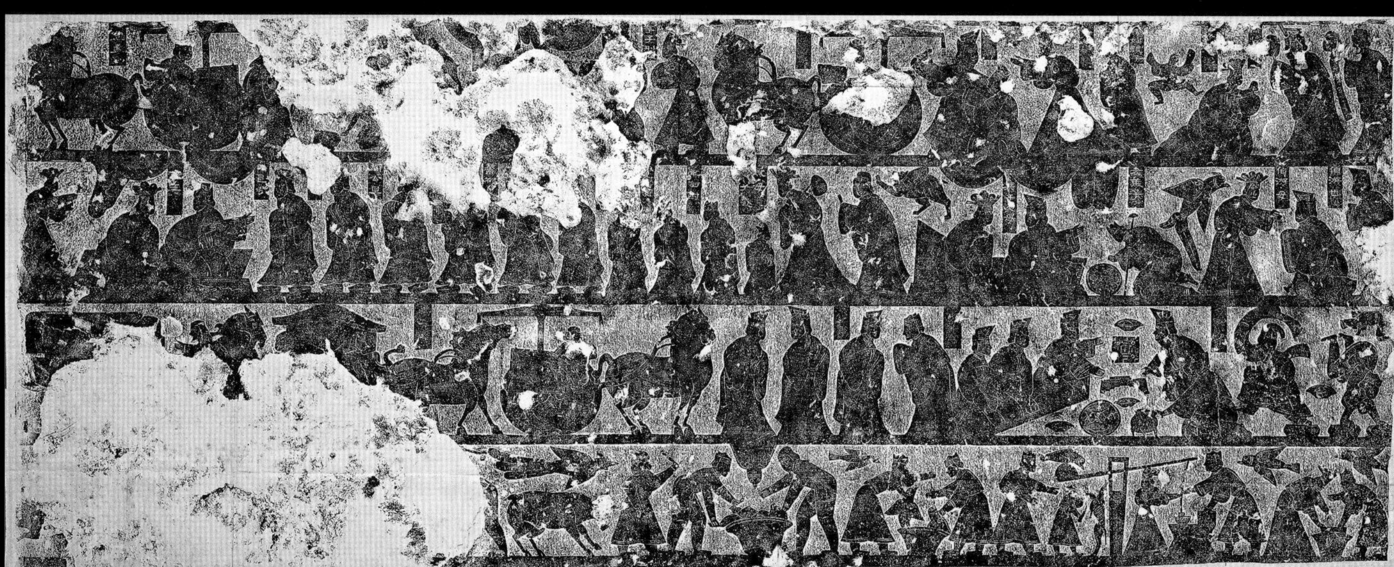

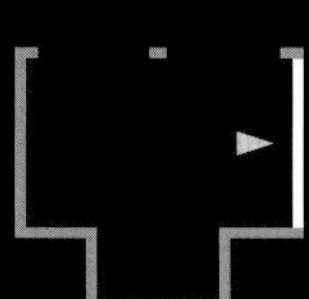

to the right. The first group depicts the story of Laizi, who in his seventies fed his parents while dressed in multicolored clothes and entertained them with childlike antics (cf. cat. no. 1.35).[29] In this scene Laizi carries a bird-finial staff, a royal gift to men in their seventies and eighties (see cat. no. 56). At far right is the story of Boyu, who wept after his mother flogged him. When asked why he had never wept after previous floggings, Boyu replied that before he had felt pain but now he felt none, at which he realized with sadness that his mother was growing older and weaker (cf. cat. no. 1.36).[30]

Fifth register: three horse-drawn chariots (partly damaged) enter from the left. Three officials wearing peaked caps stand in front and are greeted by another man. Farther to the right, the three officials are seated on the left and the host and an attendant face them on the right. In between are a *liubo* game board (see cat. no. 37), as well as a cauldron, three bowls, and a round tray holding four eared cups (see cat. nos. 32–35) and two bowls. At far right is a sleeve dancer (see cat. no. 6) and another entertainer performing an acrobatic drum dance. In the upper right corner is a small figure on his hands and knees. The cartouches in this register are blank.

Sixth register: a food preparation scene follows the damaged area at left. From left to right: a cow is being pulled by a man holding a knife or club, two men in pants prepare to cook a pig or bear, and two figures stuff birds or fowl into a pot. Farther to the right is a well-sweep, with a man and small figure holding a knife gutting a dog on its left, and a man and woman drawing water from the wellhead (cf. cat. nos. 17, 18) on its right. At far right two stooping figures appear to be preparing something in a pot.

CARY Y. LIU AND EILEEN HSIANG-LING HSU

Stone Chamber 1: North Wall

1.13 *North wall* (*west side*), *Stone 1-N.2*. Rubbing; h. 26.5 cm, w. 157.5 cm. PUAM, acc. no. 2002.307.13.
1.14 *North wall* (*east side*), *Stone 1-N.1*. Rubbing; h. 26.2 cm, w. 156.1 cm. PUAM, acc. no. 2002.307.12.

These two rubbings are from the interior face of two adjacent lintel stones that span from the east to west side walls. At the center the two stones are divided by the end of the central gable crossbeam, and all three are supported on a stone column (see Supplement: Pictorial Column; Liu's "Recarving the Past," figs. 18A, 18B). The two stones depict a single procession, with six horse-drawn canopied chariots accompanied by several horsemen and footmen. Oddly, the cartouche panels on the west stone are blank, whereas those on the east stone are inscribed. The exterior face of both stones is carved with decorative bands.[31]

CARY Y. LIU AND EILEEN HSIANG-LING HSU

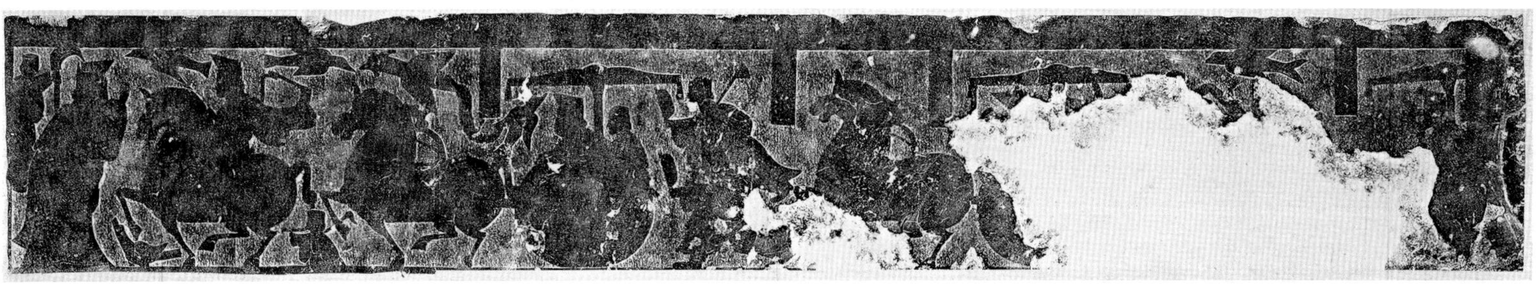

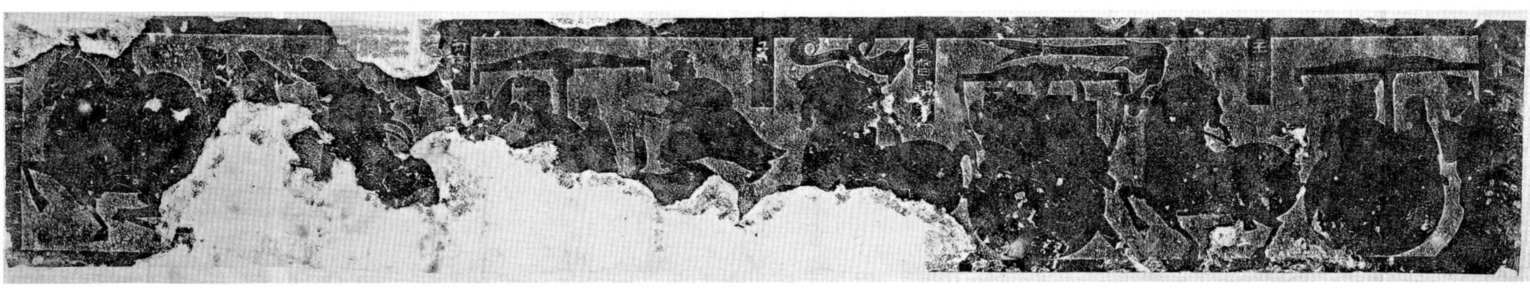

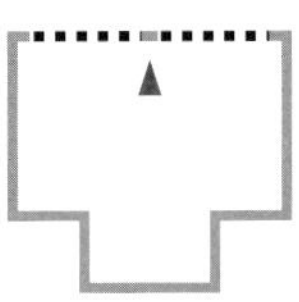

Stone Chamber 1: Central Gable Crossbeam

1.15 *Central gable* (*west face*), *Stone 1-CG.b*. Rubbing; h. 64.0 cm, w. 200.8 cm. PUAM, acc. no. 2002.307.15.
1.16 *Central gable* (*east face*), *Stone 1-CG.a*. Rubbing; h. 63.2 cm, w. 201.0 cm. PUAM, acc. no. 2002.307.14.

The two rubbings show the two faces of a triangular crossbeam that spans from the middle of the south wall to the middle of the north wall, where it is supported on a column. Both faces have three registers, and both are heavily damaged and worn. Immortals and dragons seem to have been depicted in the first registers; historical or exemplary figures may be depicted in the second registers, and chariot processions seem to occupy the third registers.

CARY Y. LIU AND EILEEN HSIANG-LING HSU

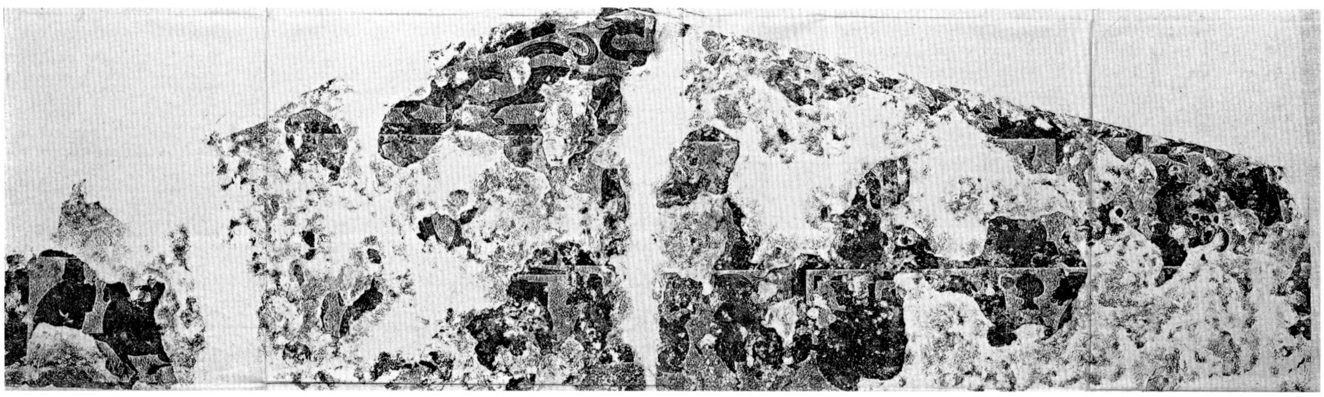

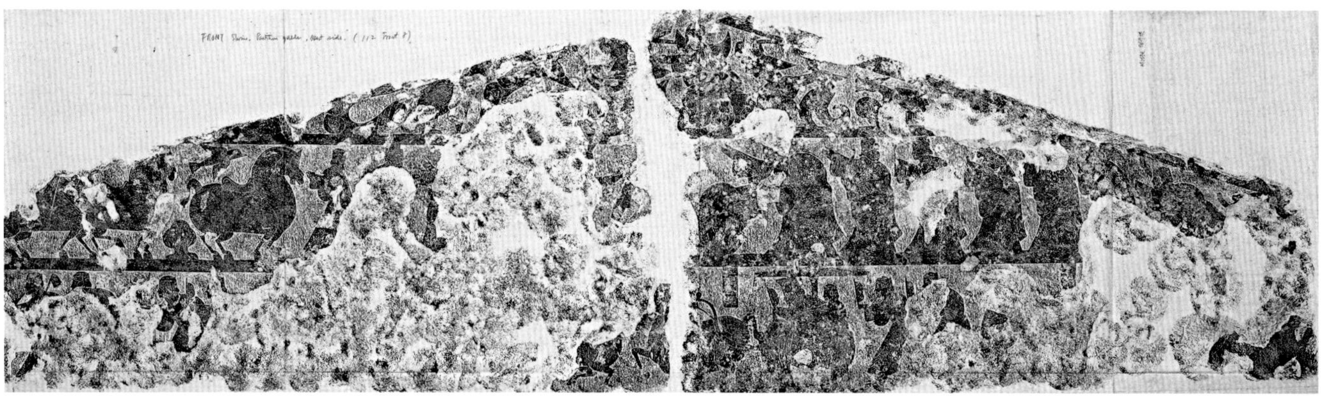

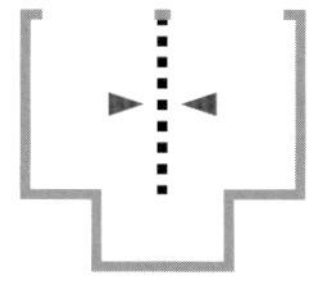

Stone Chamber 1: Roof Slabs

1.17 *Roof slab, north slope* (*west side*), *Stone 1-R.1*. Rubbing; h. 96.0 cm, w. 147.7 cm. PUAM, acc. no. 2002.307.16.
1.18 *Roof slab, north slope* (*east side*), *Stone 1-R.2*. Rubbing; h. 96.8 cm, w. 150.5 cm. PUAM, acc. no. 2002.307.17.

1.17

First register: a cloud chariot moves to the left accompanied by winged Immortals riding fabulous creatures. A large figure of an official stands at far left with his arm raised. At far right is a large demonic figure often identified as the Wind God (Fengbo). He stands in a half crouch and blows a bellows to produce a favorable wind. A fabulous creature emerges from his bellows. The entire procession may also have come out of the bellows.

Second register: the Thunder God (Lei Gong) rides in his drum chariot pulled by two rows of winged Immortals. Before them three female figures run to the right. Two hold long streamers or whips. The middle figure holds out a bowl in one hand and clutches a long-necked vessel (see cat. nos. 24–28) in the other. A continuous cloud band underlies the procession and ends in a dragon head. Two figures with hammers and chisels stand near the front of the cloud band, which curls over a figure on all fours. At far right is a large standing figure.

Third register: two cloud bands are depicted with the heads of animals and winged Immortals. At far right, standing in a half crouch, is a large demonic figure of the Wind God blowing his bellows (damaged).

Fourth register: the scene at left depicts Taiyi (The Great Unity) seated in his Northern Dipper (*Beidou*) chariot. Seven star discs form the body and handle of the dipper. Under the four-disc handle are four figures, and to the left of the chariot are three figures holding *hu* tablets. These seven figures may be personifications of the seven stars. Curiously, a small winged Immortal stands on the handle, holding a smaller orb. At right, a screened chariot accompanied by a horseman and footman approach. Positioned at the bottom right, they may represent the deceased soul at the beginning of its ascent into the afterlife.

1.18

First register: a cloud chariot drawn by three bird-headed beasts enters from the right and is led by three rows of fabulous creatures with bird, animal, and dragon heads galloping to the left over cloud scrolls and winged Immortals. At left stands a large figure with hands clasped respectfully before him to greet the oncoming procession.

Second register: three groups of intertwined figures among a host of immortal attendants and birds. Recognizable near the right side are the figures of the primeval rulers Fuxi holding a square and his female counterpart Nüwa holding a compass, facing each other with their scaly tails intertwined (cf. cat. nos. 1.23, 1.35).[32]

Third register: six Immortals carrying pennants and riding winged dragons accompany a cloud chariot drawn by three dragons. At right a large winged immortal holds a standard and faces the procession, while standing on bird-headed cloud whorls. Immediately to his left, a small kneeling Immortal extends his arms to push back the head of an onrushing dragon.

Fourth register: a bull is herded by cloud Immortals at far left. Fantastic cloud beings with dragon and bird heads follow behind. At right are four standing winged figures. The front leg and robes of the fourth figure from the right are beginning to transform into clouds swirls. These four figures in this position at the bottom right of the ceiling slab may represent the starting point for the soul on its afterlife journey.
CARY Y. LIU AND EILEEN HSIANG-LING HSU

1.17

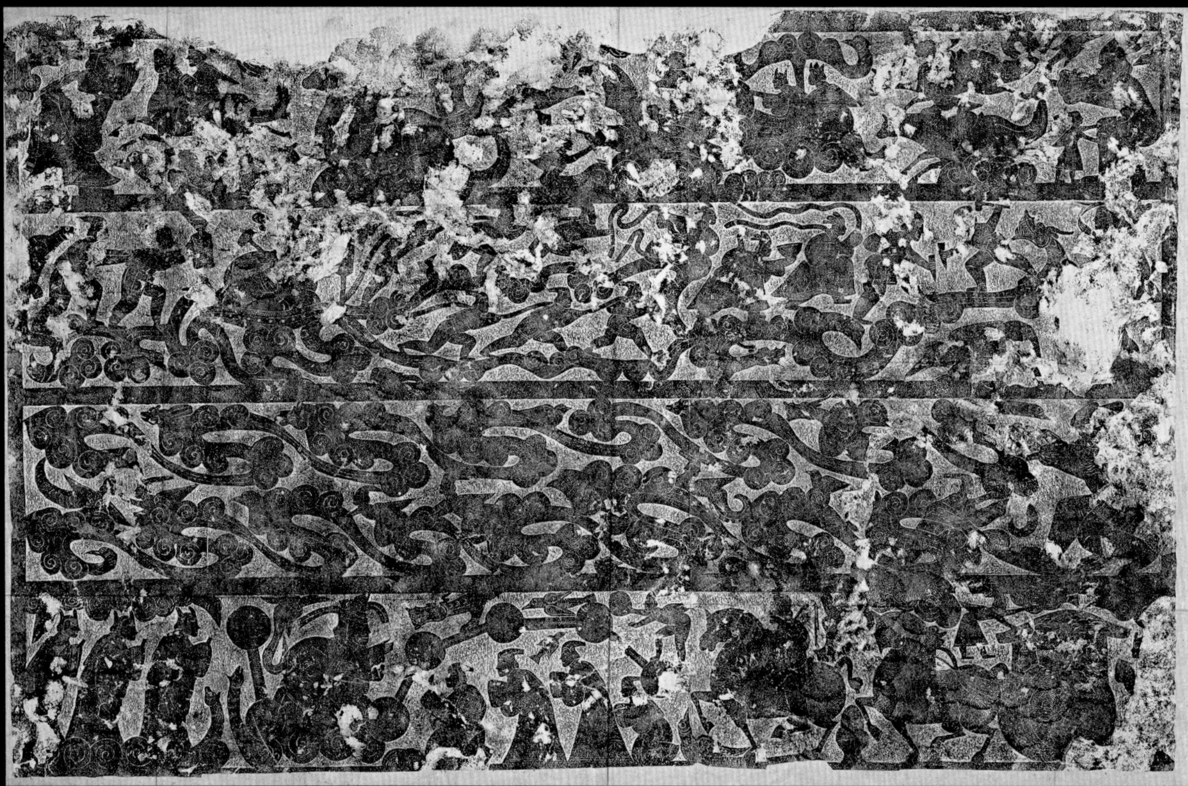

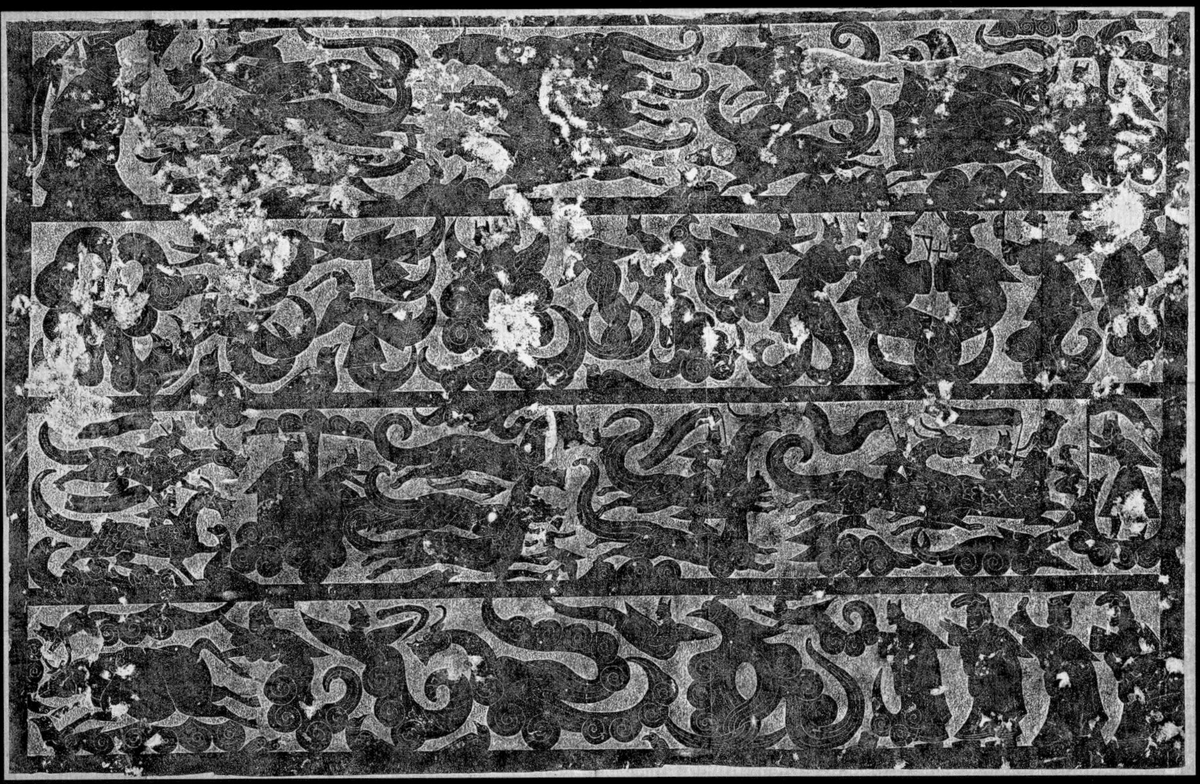

1.18

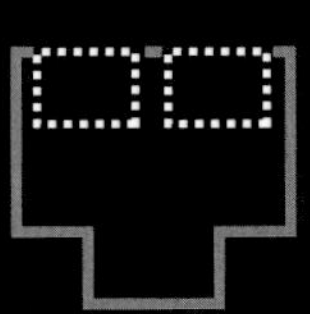

Stone Chamber 2

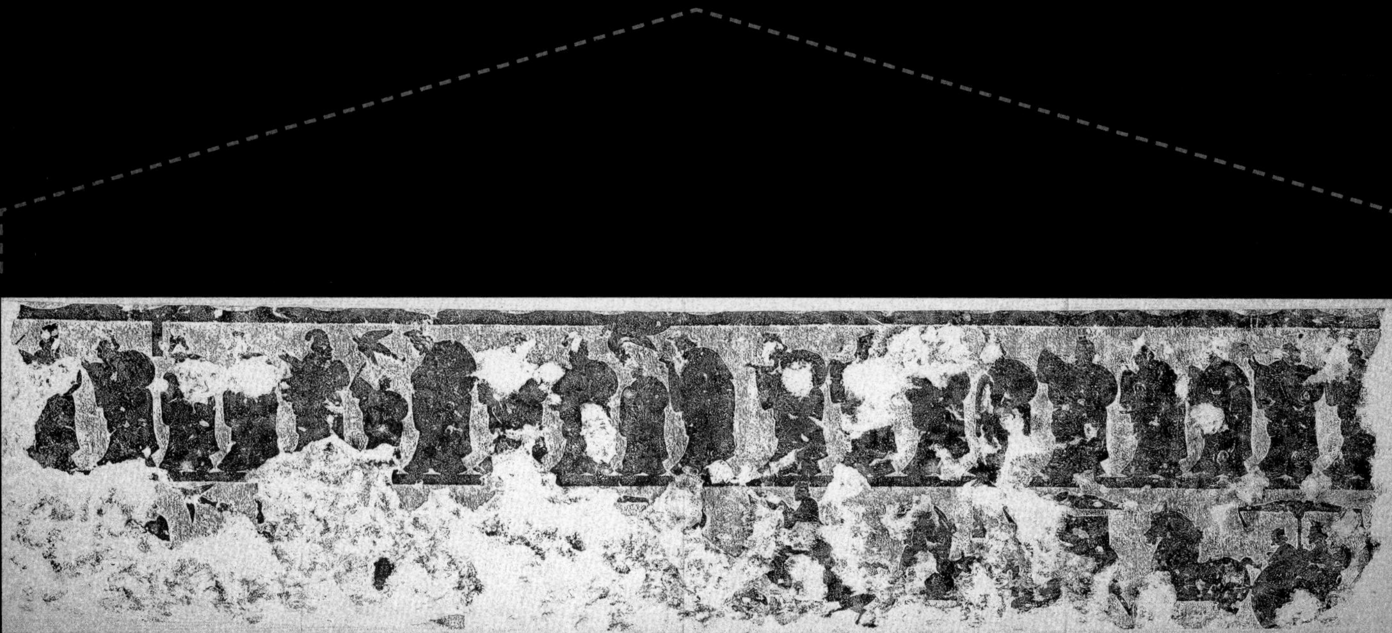

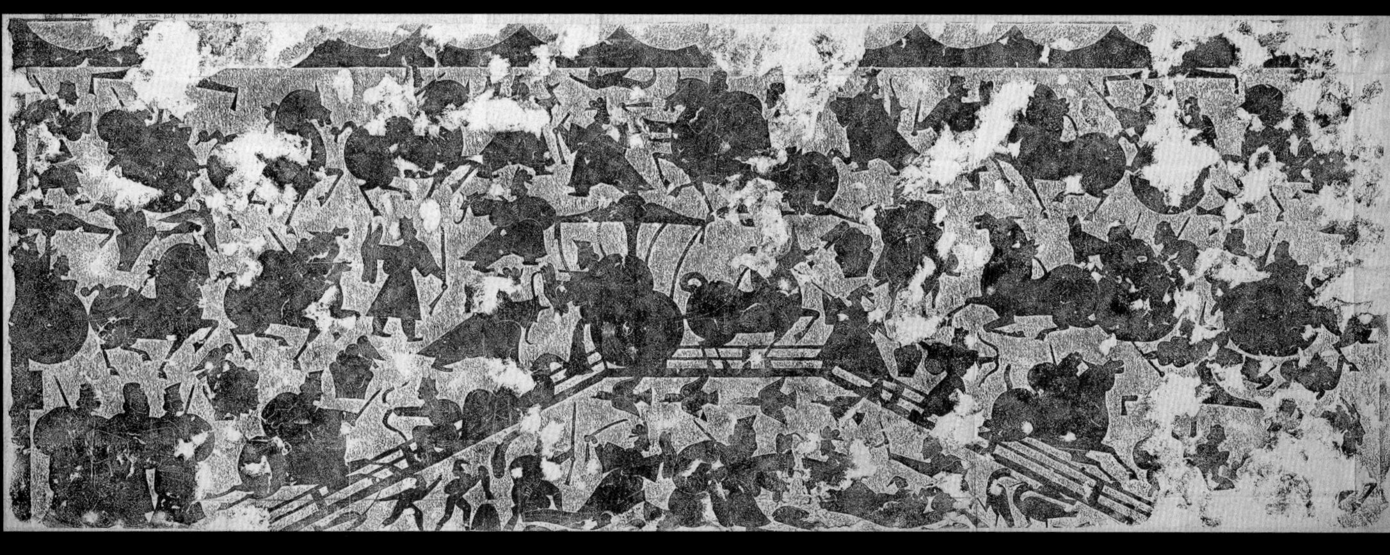

1.19
1.20

Stone Chamber 2 (former Left and Rear Group stones): West Wall

1.19 *West wall, Stone 2-W.1.* Rubbing; h. 48.1 cm, w. 207.9 cm. PUAM, acc. no. 2002.307.27.
1.20 *West wall, Stone 2-W.2.* Rubbing; h. 76.6 cm, w. 208.0 cm. PUAM, acc. no. 2002.307.28.

1.19

Triangular gable (missing from Princeton set; see foldout plate): the central figure seated in the gable most likely represents the Queen Mother of the West and possibly doubles as family matriarch or as wife of the deceased. She is accompanied by a host of Immortals and fantastic creatures. Two hares pounding the elixir of immortality can be seen on the right. To the left, two Immortals appear to be playing a *liubo* game (see cat. no. 37). Farther left is a human-headed bird that is probably Bian Que, a famed physician who is said to have invented acupunture and resided locally in Shandong.[33]

First register: twenty figures move from right to left in a fashion similar to the corresponding register in Stone Chamber 1 (cat. no. 1.1). Judging from the corresponding registers on the south and east walls that continue the parade, these figures likely represent Confucius' disciples.

Second register: although much of the stone is damaged, the surviving traces show a procession of chariots, horsemen, and footmen, which continues in the corresponding registers on the south and east walls.

1.20

Third register: the "battle at the bridge" scene occupies the entire stone. It is similar in composition to the same scene on the corresponding west wall in Stone Chamber 1 (cat. no. 1.2). Female warriors are again present, but the decapitated head and body are not at lower right; in the present rubbing a head hangs in a bush on the left side, just behind the horseman charging up the bridge with his sword drawn. In the bottom left corner two guards with swords support a figure between them. The adjoining cartouche, the only one in the entire composition, is blank.

CARY Y. LIU AND EILEEN HSIANG-LING HSU

Stone Chamber 2: South Wall

1.21 *South wall, Stone 2-S.2*. Rubbing; h. 25.5 cm, w. 142.7 cm. PUAM, acc. no. 2002.307.20.
1.22 *South wall, Stone 2-S.3*. Rubbing; h. 31.0 cm, w. 231.5 cm. PUAM, acc. no. 2002.307.21.
1.23 *South wall, Stone 2-S.4*. Rubbing; h. 74.0 cm, w. 64.0 cm. PUAM, acc. no. 2002.307.22.
1.24 *South wall, Stone 2-S.5*. Rubbing; h. 74.3 cm, w. 63.7 cm. PUAM, acc. no. 2002.307.23.

1.21

First register (east side): this stone is located at the top of the south wall to the east of the central gable crossbeam. The corresponding stone west of the crossbeam, Stone 2-S.1, has never been found. In this rubbing thirteen of Confucius' disciples walk from left to right. The fourth figure from the left is Zilu, renowned for his courage and forthrightness. He is depicted wearing a rooster cap and carrying a pig at his waist. The five cartouches on this stone are blank.

1.22

Second register: as reconstructed, the original stone would have spanned the entire length of the back wall. The surviving fragment is heavily damaged, broken at the left end, and missing about one-third of its length. The surviving traces reveal a procession with three chariots, accompanying horsemen, and footmen. The four cartouches in the register are blank.

1.23

This pictorial stone is located at the bottom of the south wall, to the west of the center niche.

First register: the story of Prince Xiaobai of the Qi kingdom being shot with an arrow by the archer Guan Zhong. A rival claimant to the throne had sent Guan Zhong to stop Xiaobai. Believing Xiaobai to be dead, the rival prince did not arrive until after Xiaobai, who had feigned death after the arrow struck his belt buckle (*daigou*), had already ascended the throne as Duke Huan (r. 685–643 BCE). Heeding the advice of Bao Shu, who had been his protector, the duke not only spared Guan Zhong but appointed him to high office in his government. The scene shows Xiaobai lying on the ground clutching an arrow. The figure shielding him with an umbrella is usually said to be Bao Shu. Guan Zhong is shown with his bow and two followers at right.[34]

Second register: this is an abbreviated illustration of the loyal assassin Jing Ke's attempt to kill the king of Qin (the future First Emperor) (cf. nos. 1.6, 1.35). A single cartouche in the upper left corner is blank.

Third register: the primeval rulers Fuxi (holding a square) and his female counterpart Nüwa (holding a compass) are shown with their snake-like tails intertwined (cf. cat. nos. 1.18, 1.35). Legend has it that Fuxi established kingly rule, social order, and marriage. He is also credited with inventing the Eight Trigrams (see cat. no. 54) and the calendar. Nüwa is known both as Fuxi's sister and as his wife. Other winged figures with cloud tails along with bird-headed clouds accompany the sovereigns. The cartouche panel at upper left is blank.

1.24

This pictorial stone is located at the bottom of the south wall, east of the center niche.

First register: at center two figures are conversing over a *dou* container enwound by a coiled snake. On either side stand two figures holding *hu* tablets. This scene is sometimes identified as the story of the Marquis of Sui saving a snake he found in the middle of the road while hunting. Later in the night the snake came bearing a great pearl as a gift.[35]

Second register: behind a canopied chariot, a dismounted figure stoops with a ladle and pan to feed a kneeling figure. The scene probably represents the story of Zhao Dun giving food to Ling Zhe (cf. cat. no. 1.12). In front of the chariot are a dog (see cat. no. 53) and a large figure holding a *hu* tablet.

Third register: a horrified man on his hands and knees is being attacked by a snake that coils around his body. To left and right, respectively, figures carrying a mallet and an ax rush toward him. Above the victim are four more creatures. This scene too has yet to be identified. It may be related to some story concerning the five poisonous creatures (*wu du*).

CARY Y. LIU AND EILEEN HSIANG-LING HSU

1.21
1.24

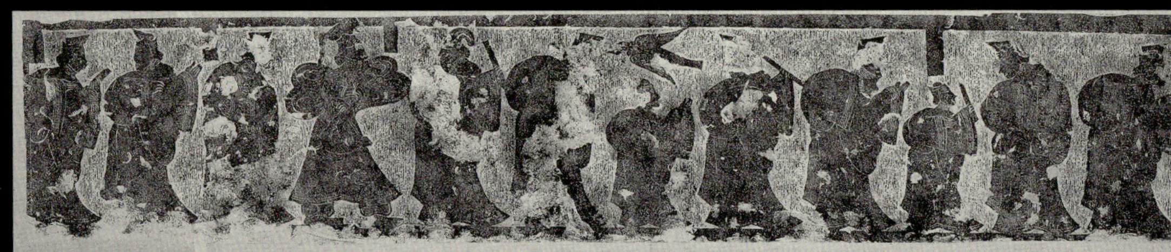

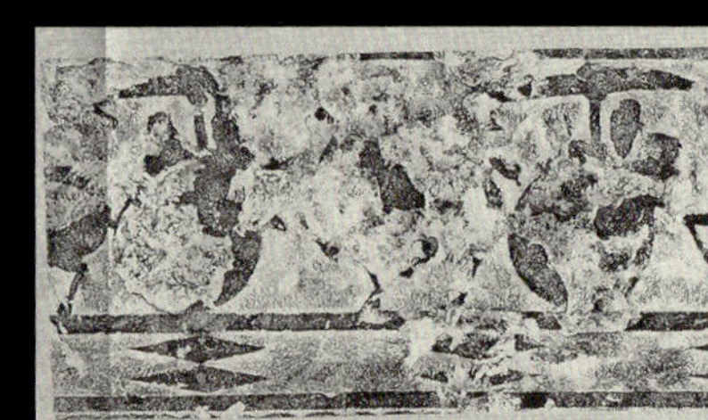

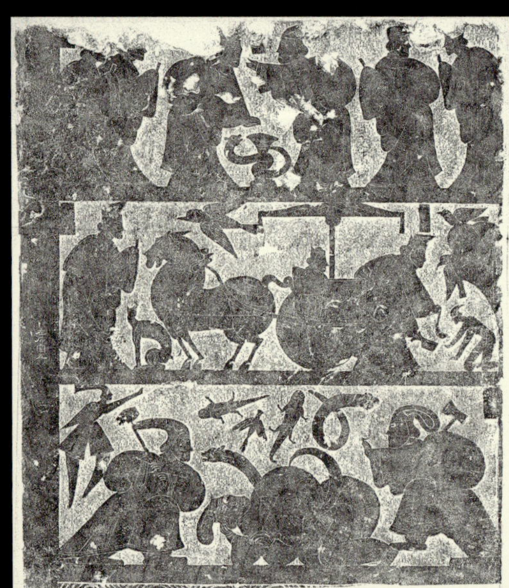

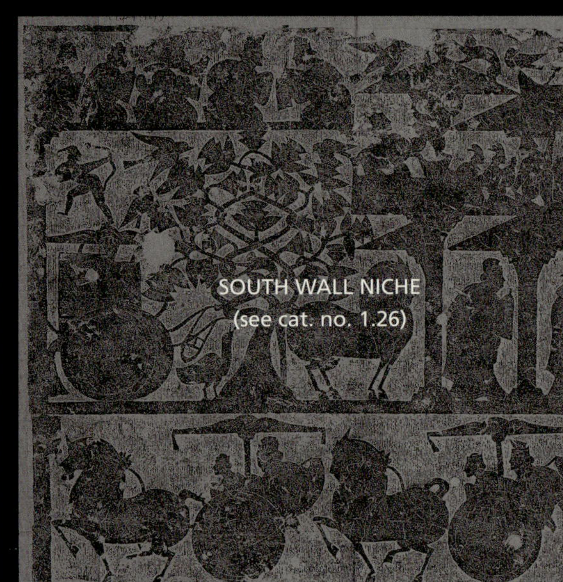

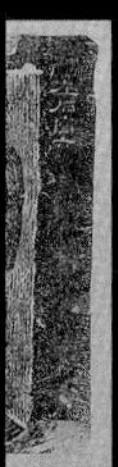

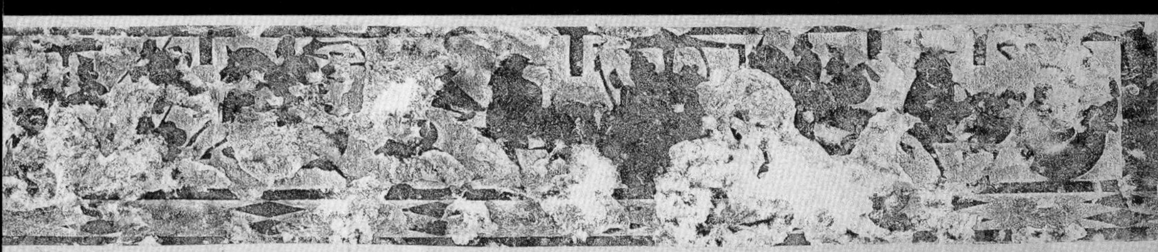

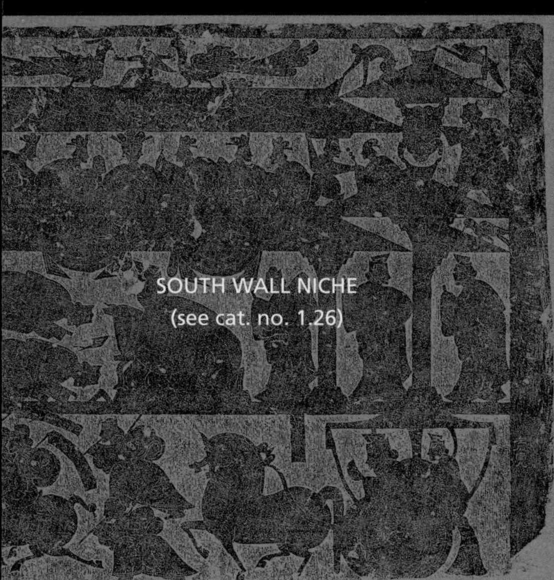

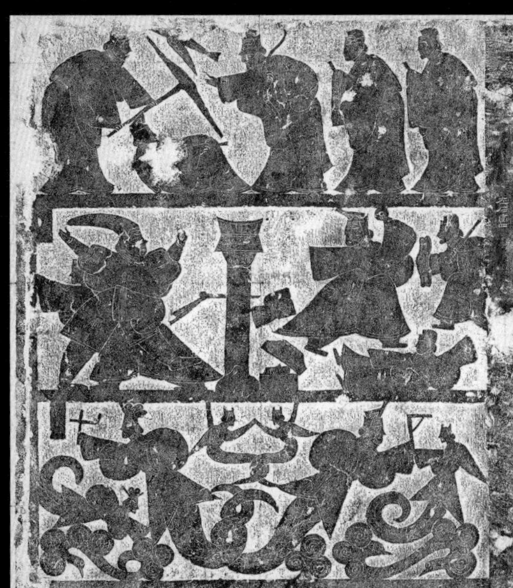

1.22
1.23

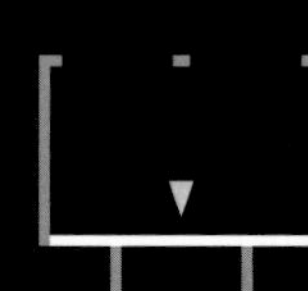

Stone Chamber 2: Niche Walls

1.25 *Niche, west wall, Stone 2-S.7.b.* Rubbing; h. 70.0 cm, w. 74.4 cm. PUAM, acc. no. 2002.307.25.
1.26 *Niche, south wall, Stone 2-S.6.* Rubbing; h. 70.3 cm, w. 145.3 cm. PUAM, acc. no. 2002.307.24.
1.27 *Niche, east wall, Stone 2-S.8.b.* Rubbing; h. 70.3 cm, w. 74.0 cm. PUAM, acc. no. 2002.307.26.

1.25

First register: at left is the story of Ji Zha (of the Eastern Zhou–dynasty state of Wu) hanging his sword on a tree over the lord of Xu's (Xu Jun) grave. The lord had admired Ji Zha's sword, so the latter vowed to himself to present it to him after he no longer had need of it. On his return he found that the lord had died, but Ji Zha remained faithful to his intention. The scene shows an owl (see cat. no. 57) perched on the tree with the sword. Ji Zha kowtows at the grave, while behind him an attendant carries an empty scabbard. A square tray or altar with offerings is set before the grave. The next two figures on the right are said to be Xing Qu feeding his aged father (cf. cat. nos. 1.10, 1.12, 1.36). At far right is a man kneeling in front of a seated cloud-swirl figure. This is identified with the story of Ding Lan (cf. cat. nos. 1.10, 1.35), and the cloud figure is said to be a wooden statue of a parent.

Second register: the three figures at left may represent the story of Liang Gaoxing, a beautiful widow who cut off her nose in order to repel wealthy and powerful suitors, including the king of Liang. Moved by her moral integrity, the king bestowed on her the honorary name Gaoxing ("lofty deed") (cf. cat. no. 1.36). In the rubbing a maid points to a kneeling emissary of the suitor-king. The scene to the right illustrates the story of the orphan of the Zhao family (*Zhaoshi gu'er*). The woman holding an infant and seated in front of a screen is the widow of Zhao Shuo, who had been murdered along with his brothers by the rebel Tu Angu. In order to save the orphan, Zhao's loyal retainer Cheng Ying lured Tu to a mountain hideout where the latter killed a substitute child. Cheng secretly raised the real orphan. In the carving the third figure from the right is said to be Cheng Ying. A maid and two other men are also present. The four cartouche panels in this register are blank.

Third register: the story of Duke of Zhou (Zhou Gong) assisting the young King Cheng (Cheng Wang) to govern. King Cheng is shown as a child wearing a crown, and Duke of Zhou kneels to his proper right. A standing figure holds a parasol over the child's head. Five officials holding *hu* tablets look on.

Fourth register: a procession with a canopied chariot led by three horsemen. At far right a small pony is seen entering into the picture frame and near the center a bear (see cat. nos. 47–49) hangs from the top border.

1.26

First register: the homage, or central pavilion, scene (discussed earlier). In this version, the top part of a peaked cap has fallen off in front of two men kowtowing to the large seated male in the ground story. Standing officials wearing peaked caps and holding *hu* tablets approach respectfully from both sides. On the left, or east, side, the tree with intertwined branches holds five birds and a monkey; the archer stands on the chariot canopy. Below the tree the unhitched horse and chariot are accompanied by a large bird. The horse has a long, free-hanging tail, not bobbed or braided like the tails of almost all the other horses depicted in the carvings. In the second story the main female figure, sitting frontally, is being presented with a round box on the left and a mirror (see cat. nos. 38–41) on the right. Unique to this scene is a partial register in the upper left corner, in which four kneeling figures face a fifth who holds a brush and writes on an unrolled scroll.

Second register: a procession with three horse-drawn canopied chariots, two horsemen carrying halberds, and two footmen. The chariot at right corresponds to the "lord's vehicle" (*junche*) labeled in Stone 1-S.6 (cat. no. 1.9), but here the accompanying cartouche is blank. The free-hanging tail on this chariot's horse matches that of the unhitched horse in the central pavilion scene in the above register. The cavalcade continues in the corresponding registers on the west and east walls of the niche.

1.27

First register: at left is part of a building in which sits a man facing a kneeling figure holding a *hu* tablet under the eaves. A man carrying a basket and a spade-like implement over his shoulder is depicted climbing a ladder. On the ground to his right are two children, then a female holding a bow. Two male figures stand at far right. The four cartouches in this register are all blank, but the scene is sometimes identified as the story of the legendary future sovereign Shun, whose ill-tempered father, jealous stepmother, and younger brother attempted to kill him. The scene is said to depict Shun complying with a request for him to fix the granary roof. Midway up the ladder, Shun looks back to see his stepmother with a bow in her hands. Shun's humility and tolerance won him the favor of the sovereign Yao, who selected him as his successor.

Second register: depicts the famous tale of using two peaches to kill three warriors. Yan Ying, a disciple of Confucius and minister of Duke Jing of Qi, had to eliminate the duke's three potential enemies who styled themselves the "Three Brave Heroes." Yan Ying presented the three with two peaches, then incited them to quarrel by suggesting that only the worthiest deserved to eat them. After boasting of their accomplishments, Gongsun Jie and Tian Kaijiang each grabbed a peach. Guye Zi then proclaimed his even greater merit and unsheathed his sword, whereupon the other two returned the peaches and killed themselves out of shame for their pettiness. Mortified by their deaths and his own boastfulness, Guye Zi then also committed suicide. In the rubbing the three warriors can be seen on the left with drawn swords, reaching for the two peaches. The short figure of Yan Ying and two other figures stand to the right. The four cartouches in this register are blank.

Third register: a procession with a canopied chariot and two horsemen approaching a large standing figure who presents a shield at far left. The three cartouches in this register are blank.

CARY Y. LIU AND EILEEN HSIANG-LING HSU

1.27 1.26

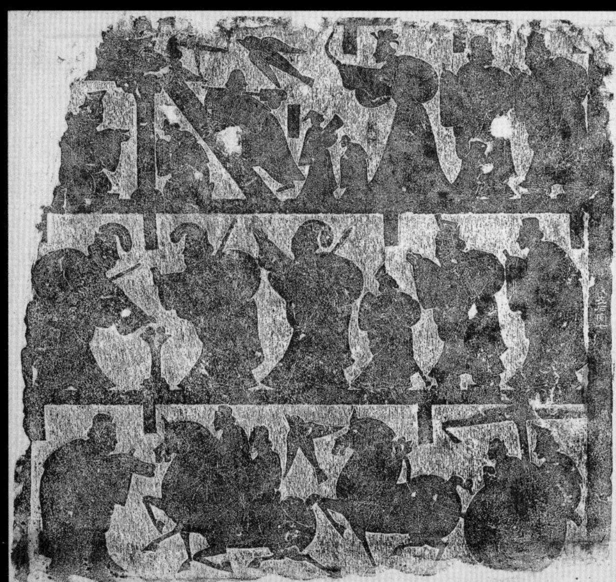

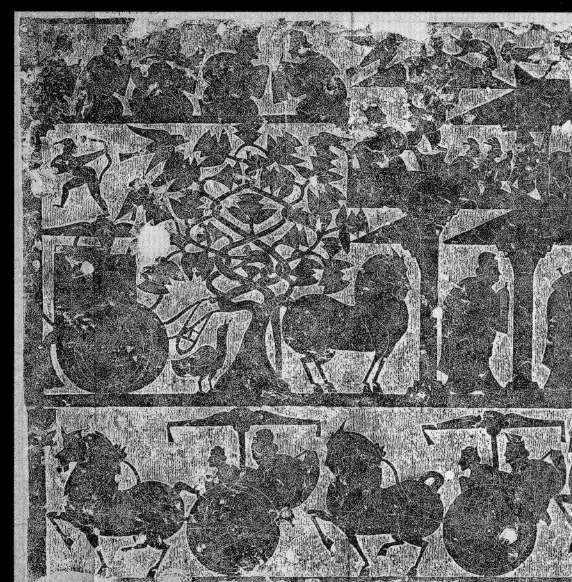

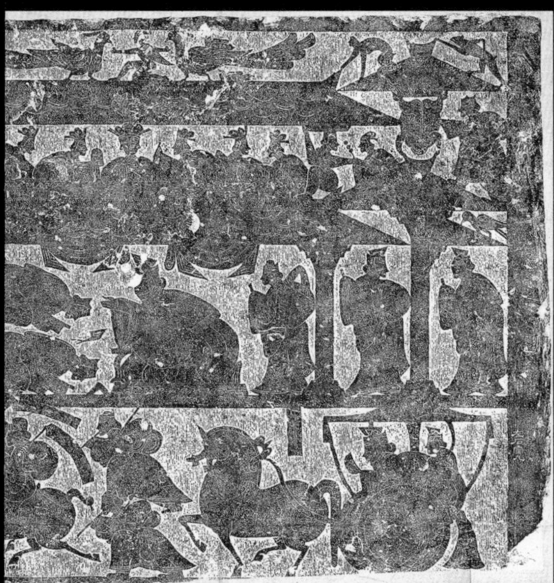
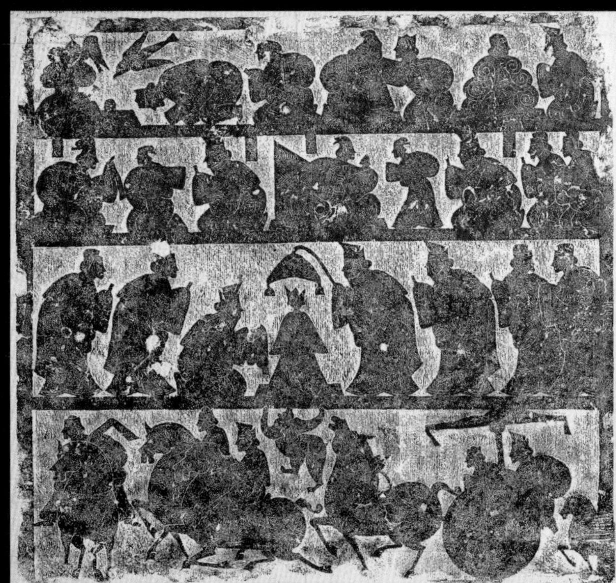

1.26 1.25

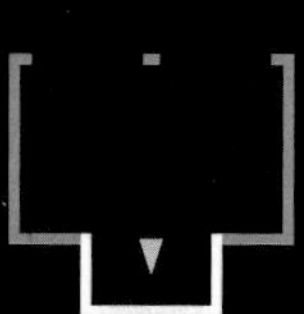

Stone Chamber 2: East Wall

1.28 *East wall, Stone 2-E.1.* Rubbing; h. 83.8 cm, w. 180.0 cm. PUAM, acc. no. 2002.307.18.
1.29 *East wall, Stone 2-E.2.* Rubbing; h. 71.7 cm, w. 207.7 cm. PUAM, acc. no. 2002.307.19.

1.28

The left edge of this rubbing has been trimmed.

Triangular gable: seated near the center is the King Father of the East with two toads and winged Immortals flying overhead. To his left stand two winged Immortals, beyond them two kneeling winged figures, one horse-headed and the other rooster-headed, and at far left the ancient physician Bian Que in the form of a long-tailed bird with a human head. Other fabulous creatures are seen to the King Father's right, including various Immortals and three creatures each with two human heads.

First register: the stone is carved with a line of eighteen men; this rubbing, which is trimmed at the left, only shows sixteen. All the figures move from left to right, save one kneeling figure who faces left (third from the left on the stone and only half-visible on the rubbing). The figures resemble those on the corresponding registers on the south and west walls and probably represent disciples of Confucius.

Second register: procession of three horse-drawn chariots with blank or damaged cartouches next to each. Accompanying the chariots are four horsemen and two footmen. A large bowing figure holding a *hu* tablet and wearing official robes and a peaked cap stands at the far right, as if sending off the cavalcade. The procession continues in the corresponding registers on the south and west walls.

1.29

This rubbing is divided into three horizontal registers on the left side and a single scene on the right.

Third register (left): entertainers are performing a drum dance on the left. Two facing groups of kneeling musicians occupy the remainder of the register—three males on the left and three females on the right. The third woman from the right plays a *qin*. A covered bowl and a rectangular tray holding eared cups (see cat. nos. 32–35) stand between the two groups.

Fourth register (left): procession of two canopied chariots with a horseman in front and back.

Fifth register (left): this register is largely damaged in the center. What remains depicts food preparation. At left various meats hang on a rack with two bears prancing across the top. Under the rack is a cooking stove (see cat. no. 19). A well-sweep is depicted at far right, together with a small figure holding a knife and gutting or skinning some animal, possibly a dog. In the middle of the scene are figures catching birds as if preparing to cook them.

Right side: the scene of raising the tripod (*sheng ding tu*) (see cat. no. 23) that is commonly, but not always, connected with the First Emperor's failed attempt to raise one of the legendary Nine Tripods (*jiu ding*) from the river Sishui. Cast in bronze collected from the nine provinces, the Nine Tripods symbolized the legitimacy of the state and had been transmitted from antiquity down to the Zhou dynasty. They were seized by a king of Qin, the father of the future First Emperor. While transporting the tripods to his capital, one of the bronzes fell into the river. During the Qin-dynasty reign of the First Emperor, the tripod resurfaced, and the emperor immediately tried to have it hoisted onto dry land. As the tripod was being raised, a dragon head emerged from the vessel and severed the rope. The tripod sank back into the river and was never again found. In the rubbing, men on the left and right banks pull on ropes to hoist the tripod. Below are two boatloads of men trying to help, and above stand two large figures looking down at the tripod just as the dragon has bitten through the ropes. One of these figures may be the First Emperor.

CARY Y. LIU AND EILEEN HSIANG-LING HSU

1.28
1.29

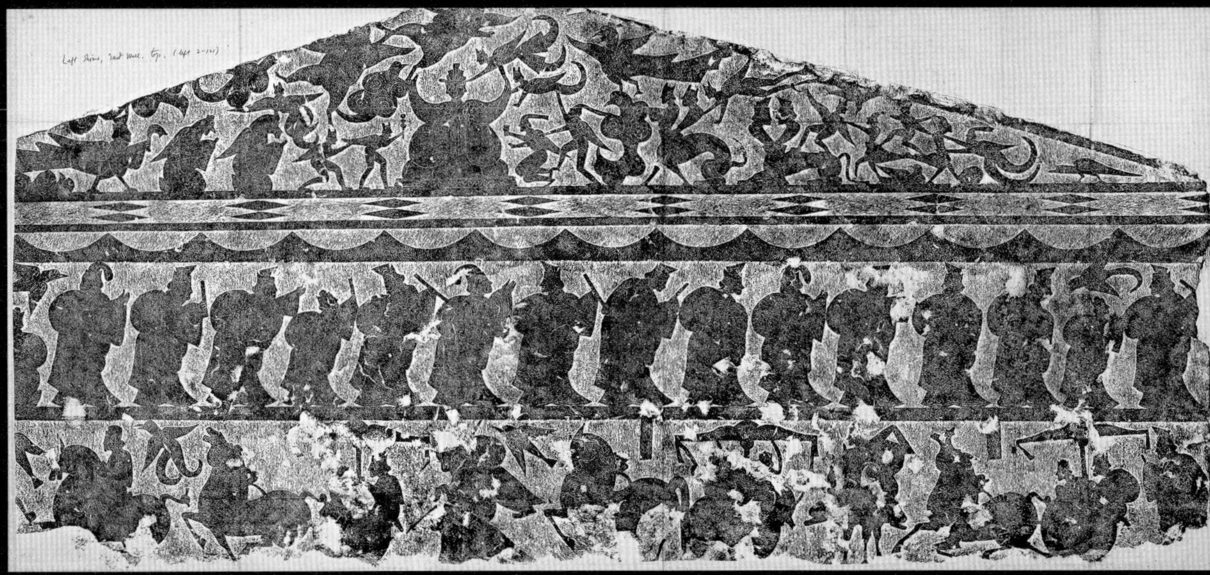

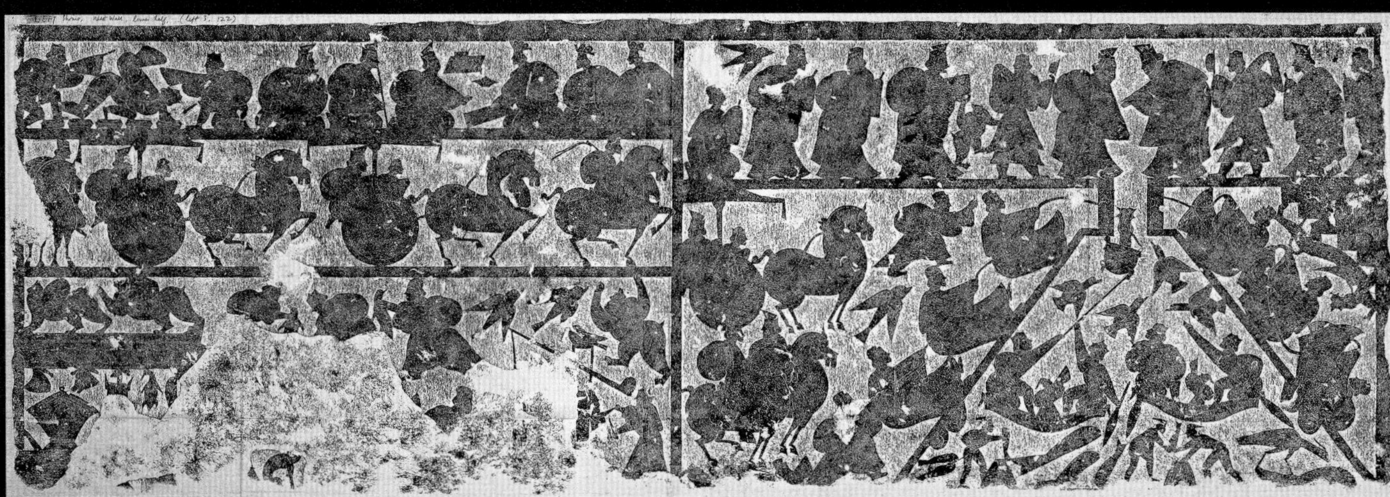

Stone Chamber 2: Central Gable Crossbeam

1.30 *Central gable* (*west face*), *Stone 2-CG.b*. Rubbing; h. 63.4 cm, w. 210.0 cm. PUAM, acc. no. 2002.307.30.
1.31 *Central gable* (*east face*), *Stone 2-CG.a*. Rubbing; h. 63.3 cm, w. 210.8 cm. PUAM, acc. no. 2002.307.29.

These two rubbings are from the two faces of a triangular crossbeam that spans from the middle of the south wall to the north wall, where it is supported by a central column. Both faces are heavily damaged and worn. The west face decor is a single register with a procession of chariots, horsemen, and foot soldiers crossing a bridge from right to left. At the center of the bridge is a large bird with outspread wings. Interspersed among the two columns that support the bridge are fishermen, birds, fish, and other creatures. At their center may be a *bi* disc or some coiled animal. The east face has two registers. The upper one appears to show a procession with two chariots and several figures on foot moving to the left, where they are received by three men carrying *hu* tablets. Flying above the scene are cloud Immortals and a cloud dragon (see cat. nos. 7, 24). In the lower register are traces of a chariot, figures on foot and on horseback, and Immortals.

CARY Y. LIU AND EILEEN HSIANG-LING HSU

1.30
1.31

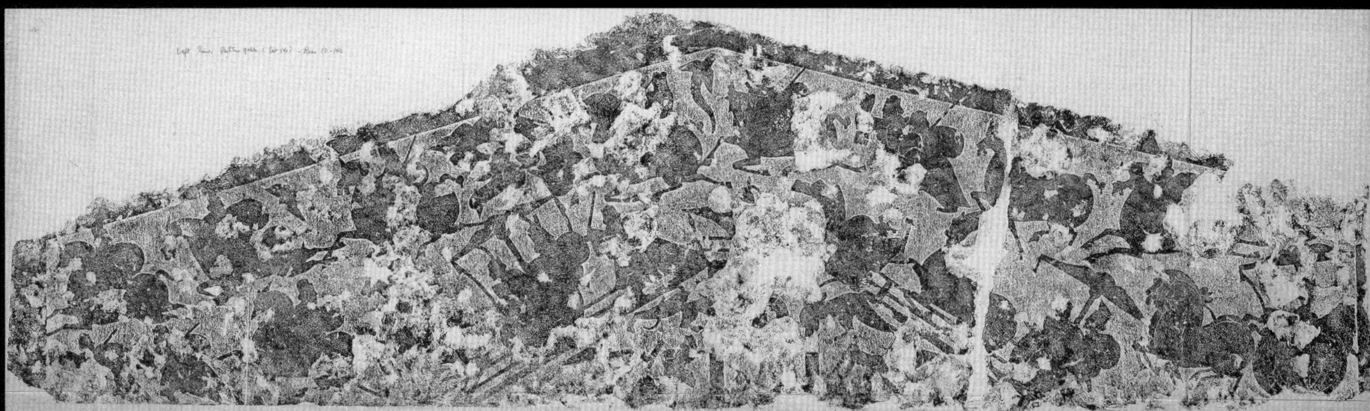

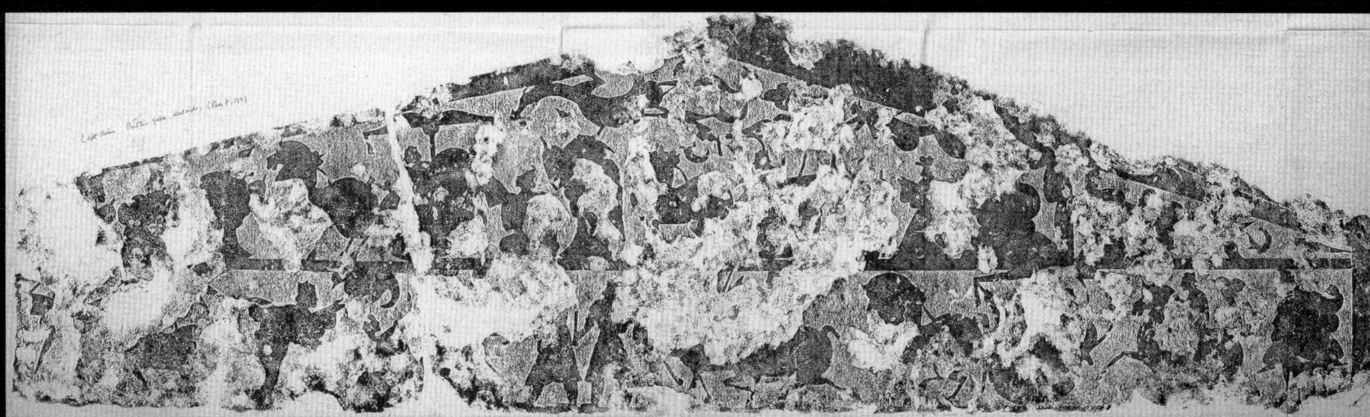

Stone Chamber 2: Roof Slabs

1.32 *Roof slab, north slope* (*west side*), *Stone 2-R.1*. Rubbing; h. 104.4 cm, w. 146.8 cm. PUAM, acc. no. 2002.307.31.
1.33 *Roof slab, north slope* (*east side*), *Stone 2-R.2*. Rubbing; h. 105.8 cm, w. 140.1 cm. PUAM, acc. no. 2002.307.32.
1.34 *Roof slab, south slope* (*east side*), *Stone 2-R.3*. Rubbing; h. 106.8 cm, w. 145.5 cm. PUAM, acc. no. 2002.307.33.

1.32

First register: a cloud chariot drawn by three dragons enters from the left, preceded by four winged Immortals riding dragons (cf. cat. no. 7). Amid the dragon riders are a single standing dragon and an Immortal riding what looks like a winged cloud seat. The entourage moves through a cloud landscape with dragon-head swirls and a fish. At right two figures hold *hu* tablets and kowtow to receive the procession. Behind them is a large standing figure also holding a *hu* tablet.

Second register: at far left the Wind God (Fengbo) blows his bellows. To his right, the Thunder God (Lei Gong) rides in his drum chariot, pulled by two files of winged Immortals. Running ahead on a cloud band are a female holding a long-necked vessel (see cat. nos. 24–28) and a large figure with an upturned mask-like face holding a jar; these may represent rain spirits. To the right, the cloud band transforms into a double-headed dragon-arch, with a female holding a streamer or whip atop the arch. Flanking the arch are two figures with hammers and chisels. At the base of the arch is a figure on all fours, with another figure holding a hammer and chisel standing on his back. The cloud band continues at far right. Below it are three small figures whose upraised arms suggest despair.

Third register: at left three men brandishing weapons chase three bears. To the right of the bears are two men who carry shovel-like implements; one of them carries a bowl and the other a scoop. A large figure holding a scoop and clutching a long-necked vessel (see cat. nos. 24–28) runs to the right. The next figure has a monster face or mask. Holding a sword and a double-sickle sword (*gouxiang*), he seems to lunge over a bear to aid, or to attack, a large bear-like figure to the right. This figure carries five different weapons and is usually identified as Chiyou. In legend, Chiyou invented weapons, rebelled, and was pursued and killed by the future Huangdi (Yellow Emperor; see cat. no. 1.35). At far right a large demonic figure faces left and is either eating a small figure or spitting him out.

Fourth register: a horseman is depicted at the bottom right, the possible starting point in the journey into the afterlife. To the left are figures that appear to be gathering food. Two men carry a tiger between them, and in addition, one carries a cow and the other a tiger over the shoulder. Below the suspended tiger are two dogs. Proceeding leftward, we come to a man uprooting a tree and figures reaching to grab a cow and a pig. Despite damage to the stone in the left end, two figures can be seen jumping over an animal below them.

1.33

First register: winged Immortals ride dragons, accompanying a cloud chariot pulled by three dragons through clouds. Facing the procession at far left is a large standing figure holding a *hu* tablet.

Second register: an apotheosis scene beginning at the bottom with two riderless horses standing at far left beside a screened and canopied chariot drawn by three horses. At far right is part of a building, and before it stands a pillar-gate. Under the house eaves a male and a female move leftward toward three mounds from which emerges a cloud band. To the left of the mounds stand three large figures, one pointing up. Incised in fine intaglio lines in the lower right mound is a female figure. In the top mound are traces of a second figure that may be a man or a winged Immortal. Two winged Immortals flank the base of the cloud band that swirls up to fill the sky above. In the clouds are two chariots, one encircled by a male contingent, the other by females. Near the top center of the scene is the large, seated frontal figure of a winged male who may be the King Father of the East or the family patriarch. The nearby kneeling male wearing a peaked cap and holding a *hu* tablet may be the deceased reaching the goal of his afterlife ascent. At upper right is the frontal figure of a seated female that may correspond to the Queen Mother of the West or the family matriarch. To her left, behind a kneeling attendant, is a female who wears a three-lobed cap and raises her arms in respect. The several cartouche panels in this scene are blank.

1.34

First register: occupies the top half of the stone and depicts a water world with fish emerging from wave whorls along the left border. The scene is filled with fantastic sea creatures, including a turtle (see cat. no. 54) holding a spear, armed toads, fish-body warriors, dragons, and armed figures riding fish. Among the water denizens is a wave chariot drawn by three fish. Behind the chariot stands a figure holding a *hu* tablet, and before it a kneeling figure also holding a *hu* tablet faces the approaching chariot. The cartouche panels in this scene are blank.

Second register: twelve figures are shown gathering or preparing food. Several of the figures seem to be placing items into containers. A pair at far right carry a waisted container between them. The fourth figure from the right holds a cudgel and may be ready to capture the chicken and bird to his left and put them into the basket below. The cartouches are blank. Curiously, a duck is depicted walking upside down on the top border near the left end.

Third register: despite heavy damage, the traces of thirteen figures can be seen. At the far right stands a man in a peaked cap, who may just be entering the afterlife realm. In front of him are several Immortals, each with two sets of wings. The cartouches in this register are blank.

CARY Y. LIU AND EILEEN HSIANG-LING HSU

1.32

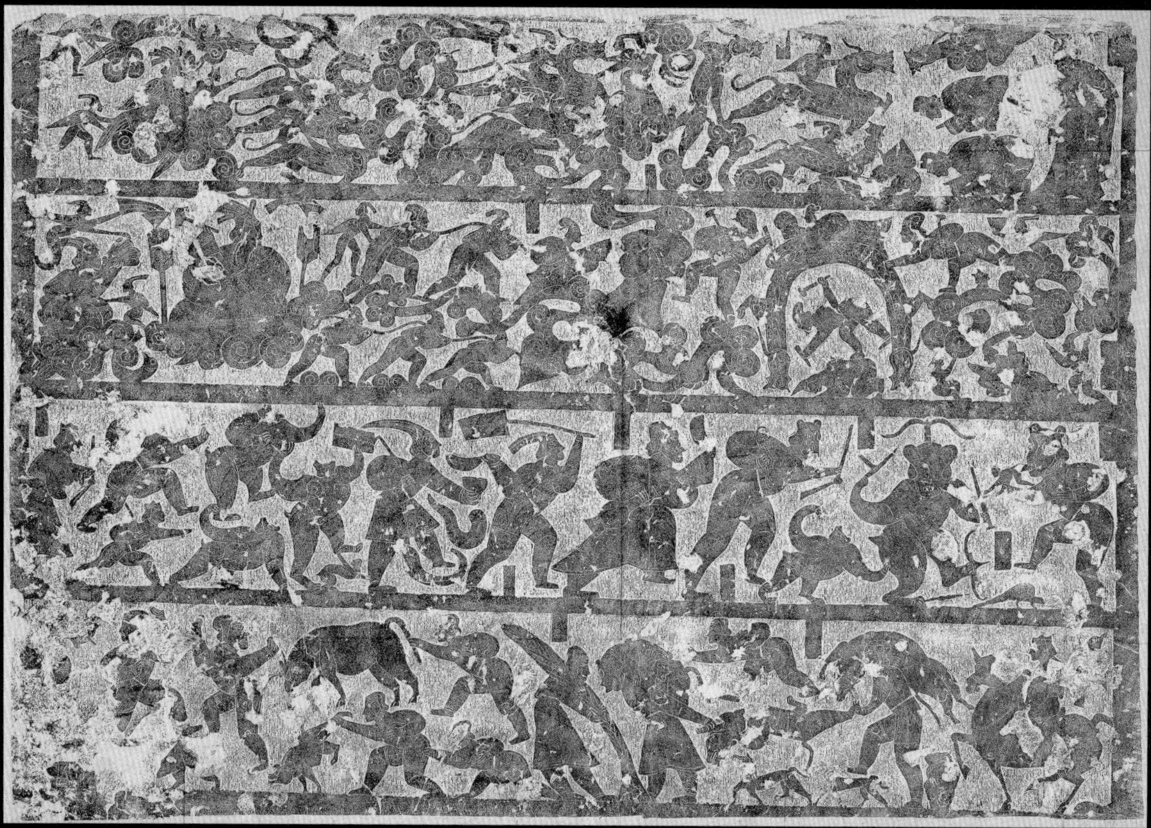

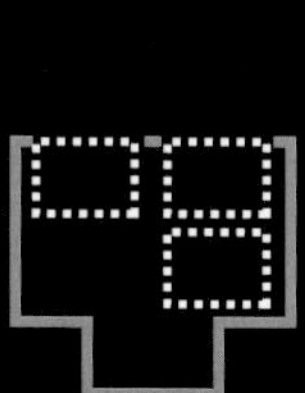

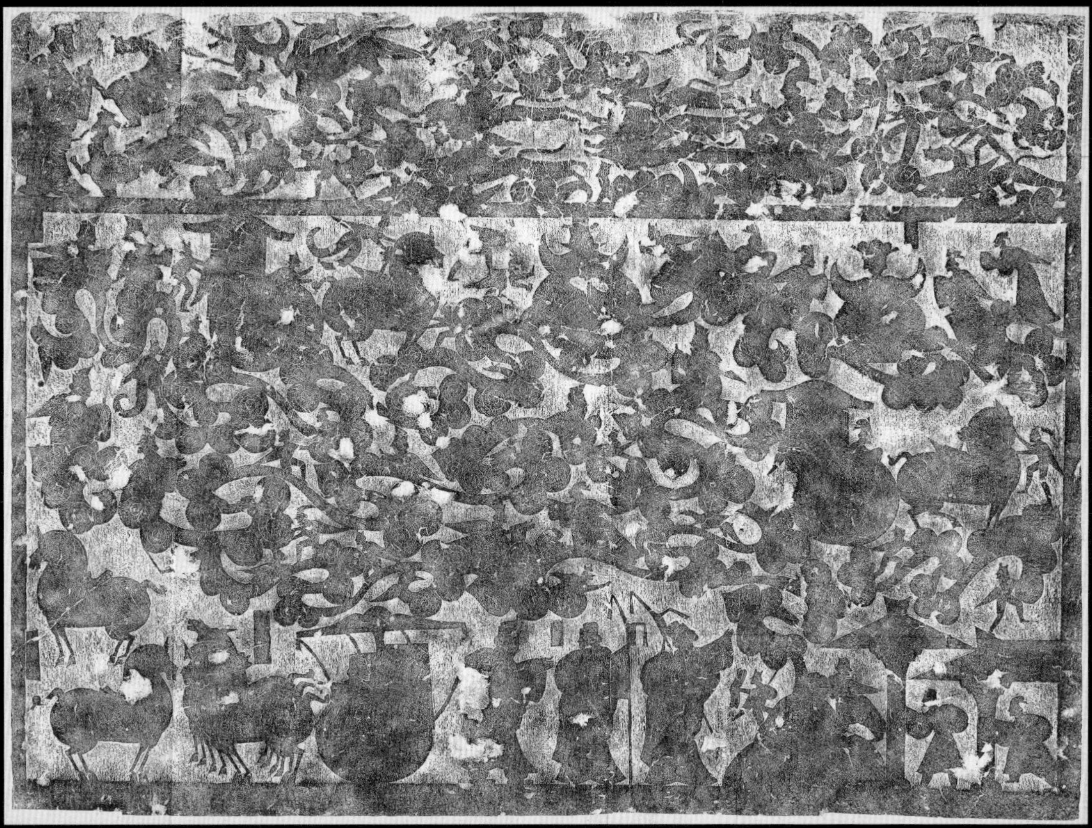

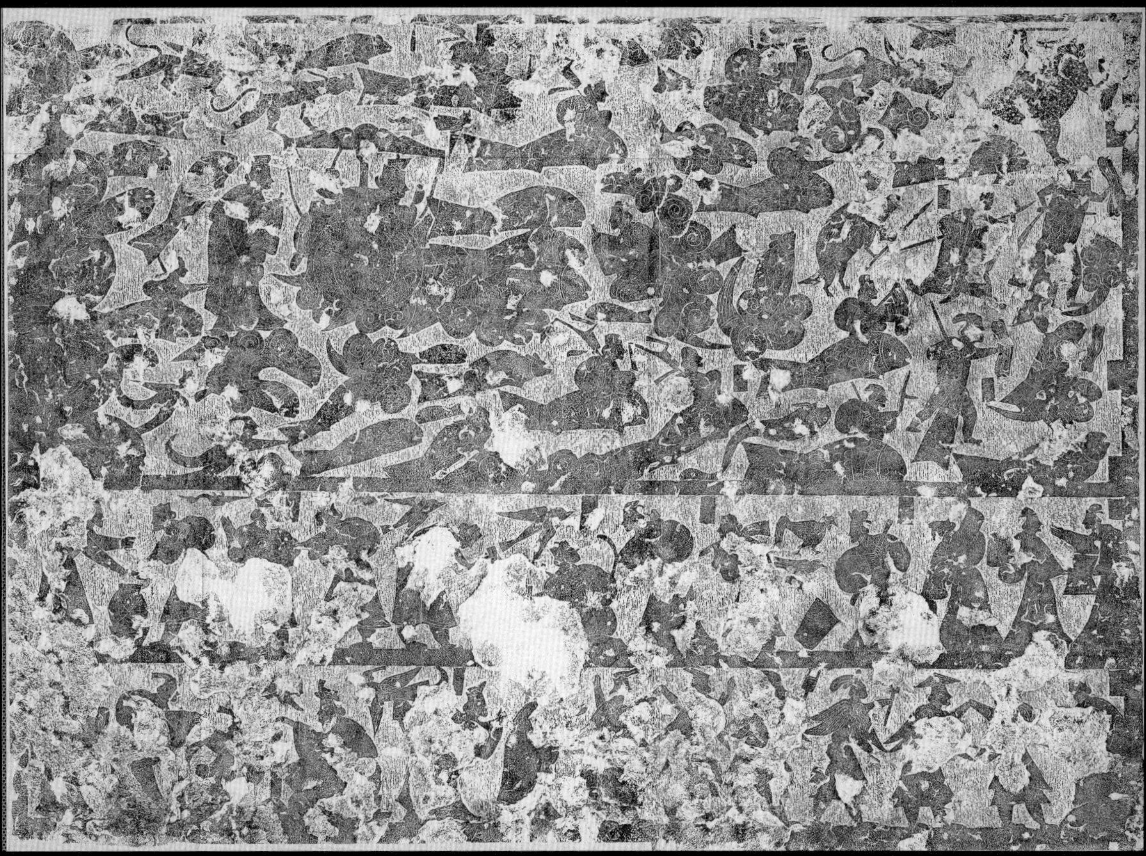

1.33
1.34

Stone Chamber 3

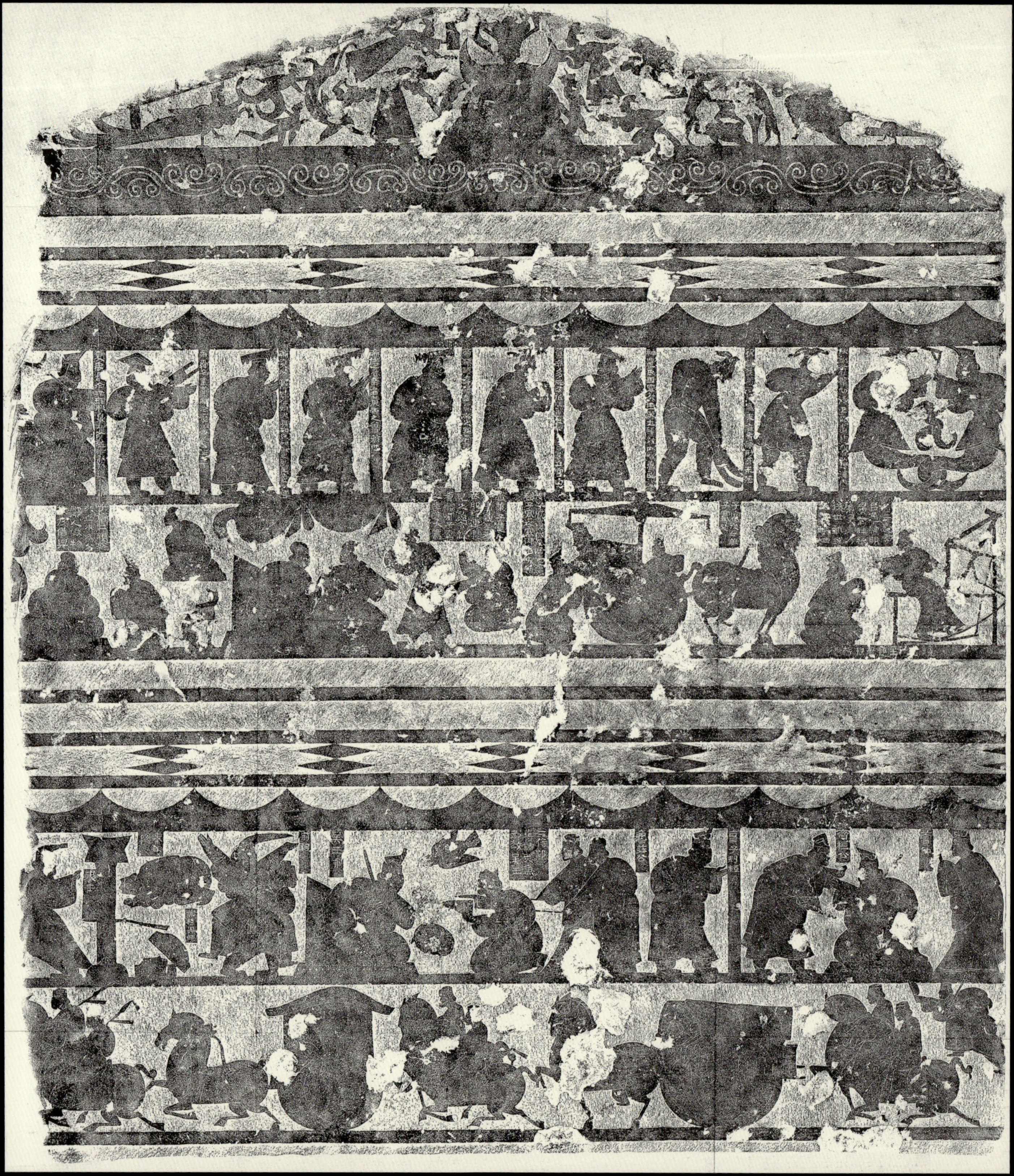

1.35

Stone Chamber 3 (former Wu Liang Ci Group stones)[36]: West Wall

1.35 *West wall, Stone 3-W.1.* Rubbing; h. 157.4 cm, w. 138.4 cm. PUAM, acc. no. 2002.307.36.

1.35

Triangular gable: the central figure in the gable most likely represents the Queen Mother of the West with possible dual roles as family matriarch or wife of the deceased. The figure sits on a throne with dragon heads on each side. On the right are female winged Immortals, two hares pounding the elixir of immortality in a mortar borne by a toad, a large toad, and a small bird. To the left of the Queen Mother are two female winged Immortals, a dragon, two small winged Immortals, and the figure of the ancient physician Bian Que in the form of a long-tailed bird with a human head.

First register: eleven figures forming the portraits of ten legendary sovereigns. Starting from the right are the Three Sovereigns (*Sanhuang*): Fuxi with his female counterpart Nüwa, who are counted as one sovereign (cf. cat. nos. 1.18, 1.23); Zhurong, who followed the path of non-action; and Shennong, the Divine Farmer, shown with a spade. Next are the Five Emperors (*Wudi*) who all wear crowns: Huangdi (Yellow Emperor), Zhuanxu, Ku, Yao, and Shun. At left are the portraits of Yu and Jie, respectively the virtuous founder and evil last ruler of the legendary Xia dynasty. Jie is shown holding a halberd and seated on two women. This side-by-side lineup of sovereigns in vertical oblong panels separated by vertical bands may be unique in Han pictorial representation. The band to the left of each figure serves as a cartouche on which the name and often the achievements of the sovereign are inscribed. Only Jie, because of his position against the far-left border, required a separate rectangular cartouche panel. The format itself is intriguing. Are the figures to be seen together in a synchronic procession, or are they meant to be seen isolated in both space and time? Are the vertical bands meant to represent architectural columns,[37] cartouche panels, or are they intended simply as visual dividers? What are the possible precedents for this visual format, and what influence did it have on later representations of rulers?

Second register: four scenes involving filial and loyal men. At right is a scene labeled in a large cartouche as the story of the filial son Zengzi. The carving shows a lady seated at a loom looking back at a kneeling man. Zengzi's mother was said to have dropped her weaving shuttle when she only began to doubt the rectitude of her son after three reports of calamity. As in many of the pictorial scenes, the depiction does not exactly match the received textual story. Possibily many workshop designs could more or less fit multiple stories, and the title carved in the cartouche identified the story selected by the client. The chariot scene to the left is labeled as the story of the filial Min Ziqian (cf. cat. no. 1.12). The scene of a standing man approaching two seated figures in front of a screen is labeled as the story of Laizi, who in his seventies entertained his parents with childlike antics (cf. cat. no. 1.12). The scene at left shows the filial son Ding Lan in front of a cloud-form wooden statue of his parent (cf. cat. nos. 1.10, 1.25). Scenes with similar themes are continued in the corresponding registers on the south and east walls.

Third register: three scenes of loyal assassins, beginning at the right with a scene involving four figures labeled as the story of Cao Mei seizing Duke Huan of Qi. In the middle is the scene of Zhuan Zhu assassinating the king of Wu with a dagger hidden in a cooked fish. At left is the story of Jing Ke's attempt on the life of the king of Qin (the future First Emperor) (cf. cat. nos. 1.6 and 1.23).

Fourth register: a procession with a covered wagon, screened chariot, six horsemen, and a single footman. The cavalcade moves from right to left and continues in the right section of the corresponding register on the south wall.

CARY Y. LIU AND EILEEN HSIANG-LING HSU

Stone Chamber 3: South Wall

1.36 *South wall, Stone 3-S.1.* Rubbing; h. 125.4 cm, w. 212.5 cm. PUAM, acc. no. 2002.307.35.

1.36

First register: three and a half scenes of stories about exemplary women. At right is a seated lady holding a mirror flanked by two female attendants. A man who has come by a chariot drawn by two horses approaches from the left. This is labeled as the story of the beautiful widow Liang Gaoxing, who cut off her nose to discourage would-be suitors (cf. cat. no. 1.25). The next scene shows a woman by a tree who looks over her shoulder at a man wearing a peaked cap and carrying over his shoulder a bundle tied to a stick. This is labeled as the story of the chaste wife of Qiu Hu. They were married for just a few days when her husband had to depart for official service. Years later, working by a mulberry tree, she did not recognize the man who tried to seduce her as her husband. Ashamed, she jumped into a river. Farther to the left is a woman reaching out to a child as a chariot and cavalryman charge at her. A figure partly damaged by a crack in the stone also seems to be falling toward her. This is labeled as the story of the righteous aunt (*yi gujie*) who, confronted with the enemy, sacrificed her own child to save her brother's son. This same story is illustrated very differently in Stone Chamber 1 (see cat. no. 1.12). The half scene at far left, which continues in the corresponding register on the east wall, shows a woman in a building with two female attendants behind her. She reaches out to the left toward two figures. She is labeled as the chaste Jiang, wife of king Zhao of Chu (*Chu Zhao zhen Jiang*). With a flood imminent, the king sent an official to fetch the queen to safety, but since he was not carrying the proper tally agreed upon by the royal couple, she chose to drown rather than leave the place where her husband had bid her stay.

Second register: six scenes of virtuous and filial men. From right to left, the first scene is labeled as the story of Boyu, depicted kneeling before his mother who leans on a cane (cf. cat. no. 1.12). The second scene shows a figure seated inside a building being fed with chopsticks by a kneeling man. This scene is labeled as the story of Xing Qu feeding his aged father (cf. cat. nos. 1.10, 1.12, 1.25). The third scene shows the filial son Dong Yong working in the field with a spade. He turns back to look at his aged father, holding a staff with a bird finial (see cat. no. 56), who is resting on a wheelbarrow. A large tree is being bent over as if to provide shelter. The fourth scene is a single female figure that has tentatively been identified with the story of the filial son Jiang Zhangxun and his stepmother.[38] The fifth scene is labeled as the story of Zhu Ming, whose affection for his younger brother caused disagreement with his wife. Zhu Ming is shown leaning on a cane. At left are his younger brother, his son (or a servant holding an infant), and his wife.[39] The two scenes at far left, badly damaged, are said to represent the loyal servant Li Shan kneeling next to an infant inside a basket, and Jin Midi, the son of the Xiongnu king Xiu Tu, worshiping a statue as his parent.[40]

Third and fourth registers: the bottom half of this wall is divided into three sections. In the middle is the homage, or central pavilion, scene (discussed earlier). In this version the ground level is partly damaged. In the second story a frontal lady near the center sits beside a second in three-quarters pose. Both ladies wear three-lobed hats and share the attention of the maids to either side. Having two principal ladies may argue against the identification with the Queen Mother of the West, and lends support to the idea that what is represented may be the family matriarchy or a particular wife and consort. In the tree with intertwined branches to the left, or east, of the pavilion, are nine birds, and at its base are two monkey-like creatures about to climb up. The archer who stands on the eaves of the adjacent tower, taking aim at birds or monkeys, may be a rebus for achieving high office. The unhitched horse and chariot under the tree also may be a rebus for retiring from office, and this meaning may be reinforced by the basket hanging from the lower branches.

Left and right of the pavilion the composition is divided into upper and lower registers. In the upper right register are two scenes of wise ministers. At far right a man raises his arms holding a *bi* disc (see cat. nos. 20–22) as two figures approach from the left. The scene is labeled as the story of Lin Xiangru, a minister of Zhao, negotiating with the king of Qin to exchange a precious jade *bi* disc for fifteen cities. The scene shows the minister threatening to smash the disc against a column after detecting that the Qin ruler intended a double-cross. In the left scene a standing man wearing a peaked cap seems to direct another man to approach a kneeling figure. This scene is labeled as the story of Fan Sui, the prime minister of Qin, sparing the life of Xu Jia, who had once falsely accused, beaten, and urinated on Fan Sui. Supposedly this scene illustrates a farewell banquet for Xu Jia, at which he is seized by tattooed criminals and forced to eat hay and beans like a horse. In the lower right register is a chariot with two horsemen preceding and a bear hanging from the top border.

Left of the pavilion scene, in the upper register, five standing men are moving from left to right. Two smaller figures kneel before them, holding *hu* tablets. In the lower register the unhitched chariot from the pavilion scene occupies the right side. To the left is a single canopied chariot. Standing behind this chariot is a man reaching out to grasp the central canopy shaft at the *bini* fitting (see cat. no. 29).

CARY Y. LIU AND EILEEN HSIANG-LING HSU

1.36

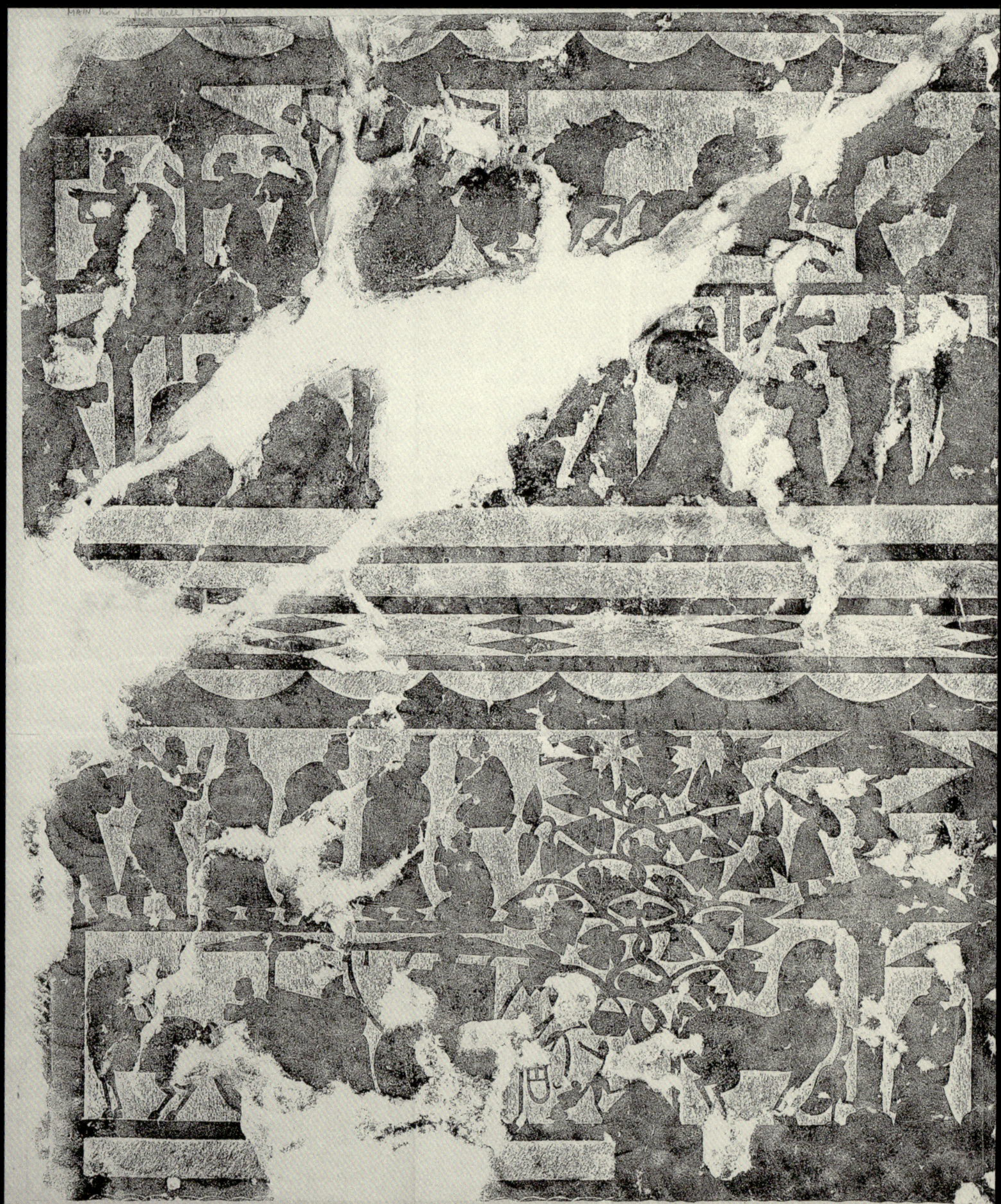

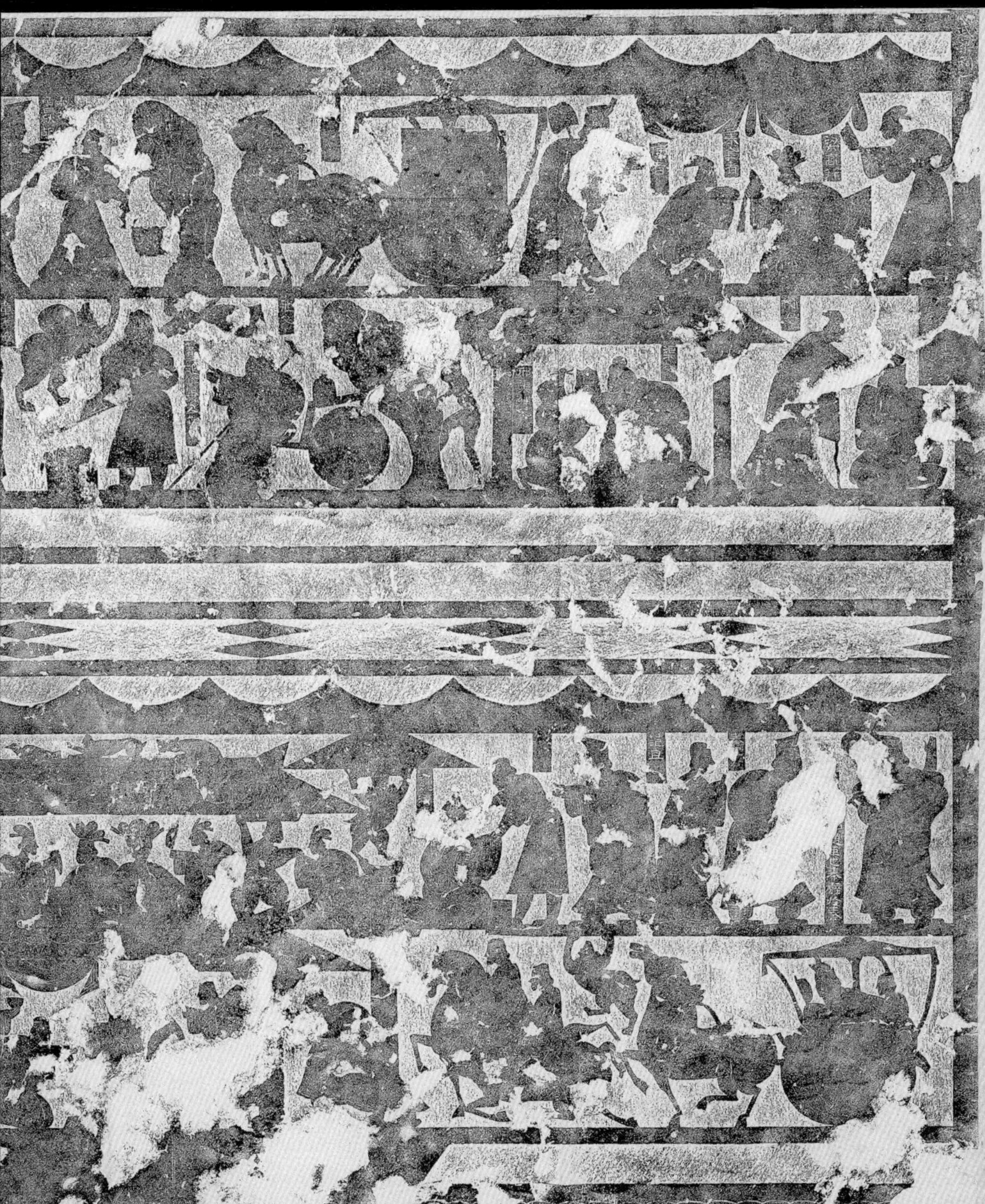

1.36

Stone Chamber 3: East Wall

1.37 *East wall, Stone 3-E.1.* Rubbing; h. 158.2 cm, w. 139.3 cm. PUAM, acc. no. 2002.307.34.

1.37

Triangular gable: seated frontally in the center is the King Father of the East, with two winged creatures flying overhead. To the left stand a winged attendant, a two-headed dragon, a creature with a human head at each end, and other winged figures. To the right of the King Father are a kneeling attendant, a creature with two human heads, a human-headed toad, and at farthest right a large bird.

First register: the half scene at far right continues the corresponding register on the south wall (cat. no. 1.36), completing the story of Lady Jiang who chose to perish in a flood rather than break a vow to her husband. The next three scenes to the left continue the theme of exemplary women. The virtuous aunt of Liang (*Liang jie gujie*) wanted to save her nephew from a fire but escaped with her own son by mistake. Fearful of appearing selfish and unrighteous, she rushed back into the deadly flames. The next scene shows a rider approaching a dead man on the ground and three other figures. This is labeled as the story of the righteous stepmother of Qi (*Qi jimu*). Given the opportunity to choose which son should be killed for murdering a man, rather than break her promise to her late husband to raise her stepson, she decided to sacrifice her own child. In tribute to her virtue, both sons were spared. In the final scene, an assassin approaches a figure lying in bed in a house. This is labeled as the story of the virtuous woman of the capital (*jingshi jie nü*). With her father held for ransom, she was blackmailed into helping to kill her own husband. She pretended to cooperate but took her husband's place in bed. The next morning the killers discovered that they had cut off the wrong head. Impressed by her righteousness, they abandoned their murderous plans.

Second register: possibly six scenes of virtuous and filial men. From right to left, the first scene shows three men and is labeled as the story of the filial men from three islets (*san zhou xiao ren*) who banded together and treated each other with mutual filial devotion. The second scene depicts an urn with a ladle on top between a seated and a standing figure. This is labeled as the story of the filial Elder Yang (Yanggong) who gave free water to travelers on the mountain where his parents were buried. Given magic pebbles by a stranger, he planted them in a field and grew jade *bi* discs (see cat. nos. 20–22). The third scene has a standing figure carrying a sword at right. Before him kneels a figure with his hands clasped before him in a beseeching manner. Above is a flying bird and behind him is a larger figure wearing a peaked cap who also kneels, seems to hold a *hu* tablet, and carries on his back a basket holding what may be a bird. This scene is labeled as the story of Wei Tang, a filial son who pleaded in vain with a young hooligan who beat his father and robbed him of a sword and halberd. After his father's death, Wei Tang killed the youth and offered his head to his father's tomb. There are several discrepancies between what is depicted and the received textual stories. Cartouches label the figure on the right as the bully, the small kneeling figure in the center as Wei Tang's father, and the larger figure behind him as Wei Tang. Why is the son depicted larger than the father, and why is he carrying a basket, with or

1.37

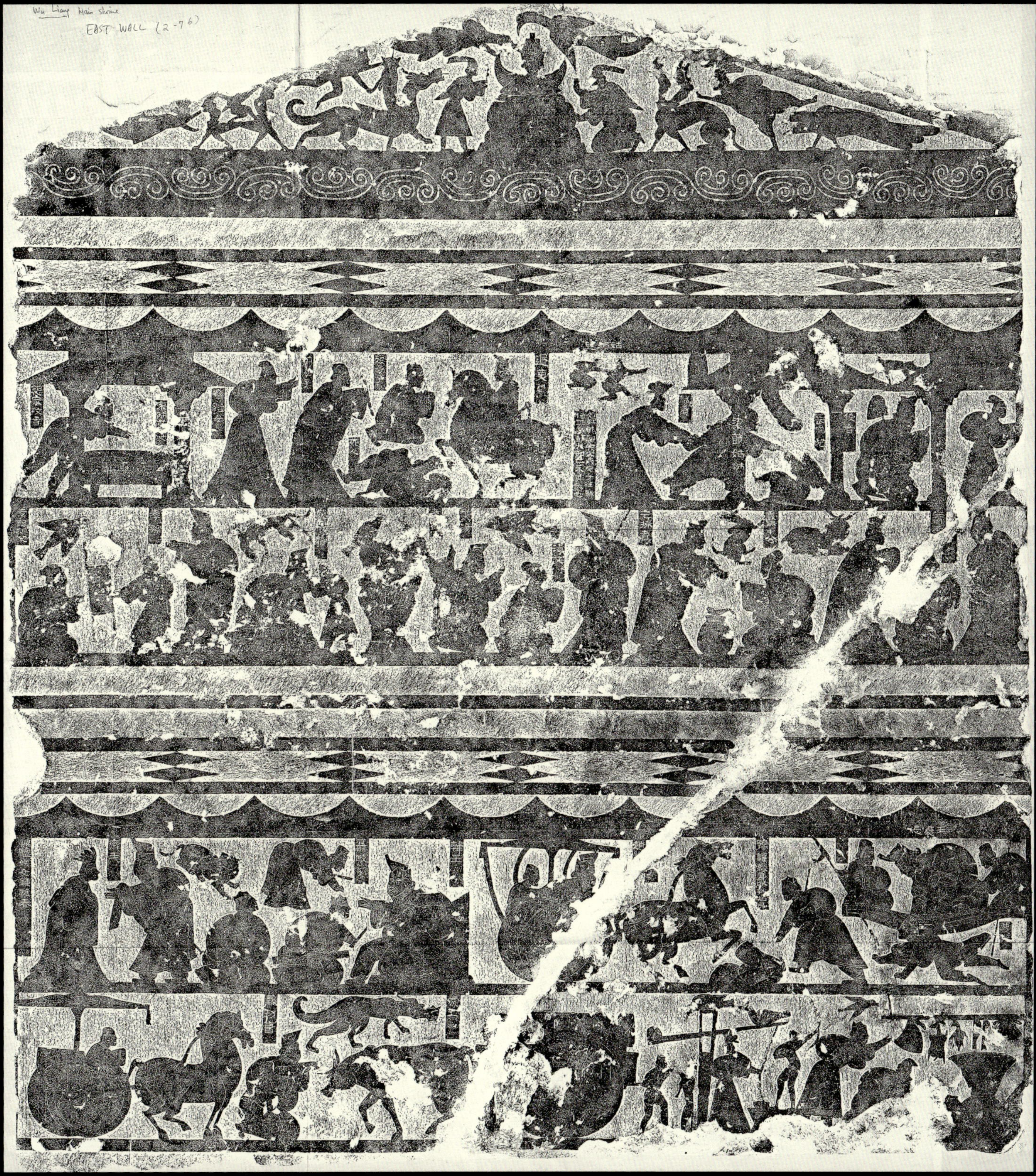

without what may be a bird? The fourth scene is sometimes conflated as part of the Wei Tang story. It shows a tree with a bird perched on top. The inscribed cartouche, which is damaged, is sometimes interpreted to label the scene as the story of the filial [crows] (*xiao* [*wu*]) that came to aide the filial son Yan Wu. Heaven, seeing Yan Wu carrying soil on his back to build his parents' burial mound, was moved, and sent a flock of crows to help him. The flying bird and bird in the basket, assigned above to the preceding scene, may originally have belonged to the Yan Wu story, later to be reassigned by the cartouche inscriptions to the story of Wei Tang. The fifth scene shows a small figure in front of a large seated man. The inscribed cartouche is damaged, and the story is usually not identified. Wu Hung has tentatively identified this as the story of the filial child Zhao Xun, who always offered his food to his father before eating it himself. This scene may show a child offering food to his father.[41] The sixth scene is labeled as the story of the filial grandson Yuan Gu, who remonstrated with his father for transporting his own aged father in a carriage or stretcher into the wilderness and abandoning him there. To make his point, Yuan Gu brought the conveyance home again, saying that he might need it when the time came for him to similarly abandon his own parents. His father was ashamed and brought Yuan Gu's grandfather home.

Third register: the first three scenes at right continue the theme of loyal assassins from the corresponding register on the south wall. At far right is the story of Yao Li's assassination of prince Qing Ji. In order to gain the prince's trust, Yao Li had false charges brought against himself. He fled, leaving his wife and children to be publically humiliated and burned. By thus establishing belief in his enmity to his own ruler, he won Qing Ji's trust. While crossing the Yangzi River, he fatally stabbed the prince. The dying prince grabbed the assassin and shoved him underwater three times. Then, recognizing Yao Li's bravery, he ordered him released unharmed. The assassin, unable to live with what he had done to his own family, cut off his hands and feet and then fell on his sword. The next scene shows Yu Rang's failed assassination of Zhao Xiangzi. After his master had been killed by Zhao, Yu Rang tried twice to assassinate Zhao. After the first attempt, Zhao spared him for his bravery, but he could not afford to spare him a second time. Yu Rang's last request was to be able to stab Zhao's empty robe in order to fulfill his vow of revenge and to die without regret. The scene shows Yu Rang with a sword pointing at the robe and Zhao riding in a chariot. The third scene from the right is labeled as the story of Nie Zheng's assassination of the king of Han with a dagger he had hidden in a *qin* instrument.[42] At far left is the scene of a man at right extending his arms toward a lady with a large mouth full of teeth. This scene is labeled as the story of Zhongli Chu, an ugly woman who gave sound advice to King Xuan of Qi, bringing stability to the state and becoming queen.

Fourth register: the scene at right shows food preparation with various meats hanging on a rack over a stove (see cat. no. 19) tended by two figures. A woman works a well-sweep to draw water. Under the sweep a man is skinning a dog. Standing on the wellhead (see cat. nos. 17, 18) is a small figure with a bow shooting a flying bird to the right. The scene at left shows an ox-drawn cart at right facing a horse-drawn canopied chariot at left. Between them is a kneeling figure wearing a peaked cap; a dragon saunters overhead. The inscribed cartouches label the kneeling figure as a county official who is paying respects to a retired gentleman (*chushi*). Many scholars have identified this retired gentleman as Wu Liang. Biographical details in the received Wu Liang stele inscription note that "province and commandery officials entreated him to serve," but on the pretext of illness he declined in order to live "at peace in the humility of his humble abode." But the received stele inscription text is problematic, and whether the actual stele stone comes from the "Wu family shrines" cemetery site is still a question.

CARY Y. LIU AND EILEEN HSIANG-LING HSU

Stone Chamber 3: Column Fragment

1.42 *North eaves column fragment* (*east wall*), *Stone 3-E.2*. Rubbing; h. 64.2 cm, w. 15.0 cm. PUAM, acc. no. 2002.307.47.

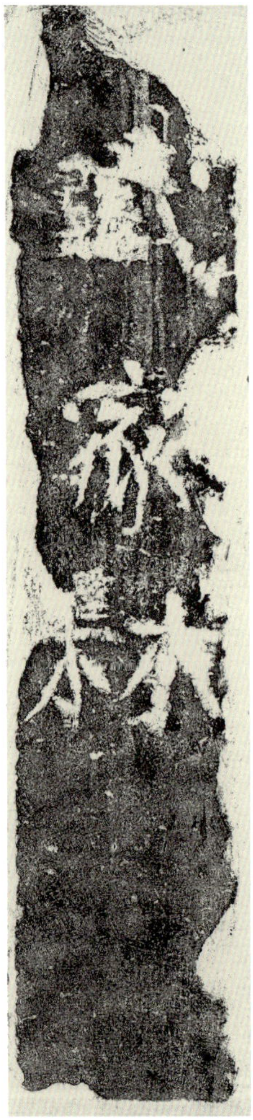

1.42

On one face of the column fragment are the three characters *wu jia lin* ("Wu Family Grove"), carved in standard-script calligraphy that was probably added after the Han dynasty. The front face of the actual column is carved with vertical bands of decorative designs. The *wu jia lin* characters are carved on the left face. The right face bears pictorial designs of two climbing figures above a scaly dragon, and the back side was unfinished, indicating a join abutting another stone. This column may have supported the roof eaves at the front of the structure's east wall; contradicting this possibility, the fragment was not found with the Chamber 3 stones, and it is less thick than the stones of the east wall (Stone 3-E.1). It is also possible that the east face of this column, with the three characters *wu jia lin*, may originally have been decorated with carved designs that were effaced for the inscribed characters.

CARY Y. LIU AND EILEEN HSIANG-LING HSU

Stone Chamber 3: Roof Slabs

1.38 *Roof slab, north slope, Stone 3-R.2.* Rubbing; h. 75.2 cm, w. 208.0 cm. PUAM, acc. no. 2002.307.38.
1.39 *Roof slab, south slope* (*west fragment*), *Stone 3-R.1.* Rubbing; h. 72.2 cm, w. 65.5 cm. PUAM, acc. no. 2002.307.37c.
1.40 *Roof slab, south slope* (*middle fragment*), *Stone 3-R.1.* Rubbing; h. 71.8 cm, w. 89.7 cm. PUAM, acc. no. 2002.307.37b.
1.41 *Roof slab, south slope* (*east fragment*), *Stone 3-R.1.* Rubbing h. 73.0 cm, w. 61.5 cm. PUAM, acc. no. 2002.307.37a.

1.38

The exterior, or roof surface, of this slab is carved with imitation roof tiles. The interior, or ceiling surface, is heavily damaged, but traces of good omen designs and inscribed cartouches are visible in three horizontal registers.

First register: six surviving omen images, from right to left: Surging well, which appears when the ruler is pure and at peace. Divine tripod, which can cook without fire and appears when a ruler has great virtue (see cat. no. 23). *Qilin* unicorn, which appears when animals and the young are well treated and the ruler is benevolent and righteous. Yellow dragon, which swims and flies when a ruler has provided his subjects with abundance (see cat. no. 24). *Mingjia*, an auspicious plant that grows a new leaf each day for fifteen days, then loses one a day for the next fifteen days. The *mingjia* grows when the virtue of the ruler is in harmony with heaven and earth.

Second register: Six-legged beast, which appears when the ruler cares for the people.

Third register: White tiger, which becomes benevolent when the ruler is not cruel or tyrannical.

1.39–1.41

The exterior, or roof surface, of these three fragments is carved with imitation roof tiles. The interior, or ceiling surface, is heavily damaged, but traces of good omen designs and inscribed cartouches are visible in three horizontal registers.

First register: eleven distinguishable omens, some only identified by inscribed cartouches. From right to left: Jade horse, which arrives when the ruler is pure and incorrupt. Jade flower, which arrives when the ruler cultivates benevolence, righteousness, propriety, knowledge, and sincerity. Red bear, which arrives when the ruler shuns flatterers and insincere advisers. Intertwining trees, which grow when the ruler's virtue is in harmony and all are united in a single family. Glass *bi* disc, which appears when a ruler is not given to extravagance and does not hide his own faults (see cat. no. 22). Dark *gui* tablet, which comes when the rivers come together and the seas join. Birds joined at the wing, which appear when the ruler's virtue reaches high and far. Beasts joined at the shoulder, which appear when a ruler's virtue extends to widows and widowers. White fish that once jumped into the barge of King Wu of Zhou. The fish had red characters under its eyes predicting victory over the Shang dynasty. Fish joined at the eye, which appear when a ruler's virtue extends to those who live in reclusion and retirement. Silver jar, which appears when punishments are just and people commit no crimes (see cat. no. 24).

Second register: Birth of Hou Ji, a descendant of the Taiyi (The Great Unity) and the purported ancestor of the Zhou-dynasty royal clan. *Juchang* millet wine that was given as tribute in the time of the Yellow Emperor. Qusou people presenting a fur coat as tribute in the time of the sovereign Yu. Red-maned white horse, which appears when a ruler employs virtuous officials. Lake horse, which arrives when a ruler works assiduously for the people. Jade *sheng* hair ornament, which appears when the country is at peace.

Third register: appears to show a chariot procession.

CARY Y. LIU AND EILEEN HSIANG-LING HSU

1.38
1.41 1.40

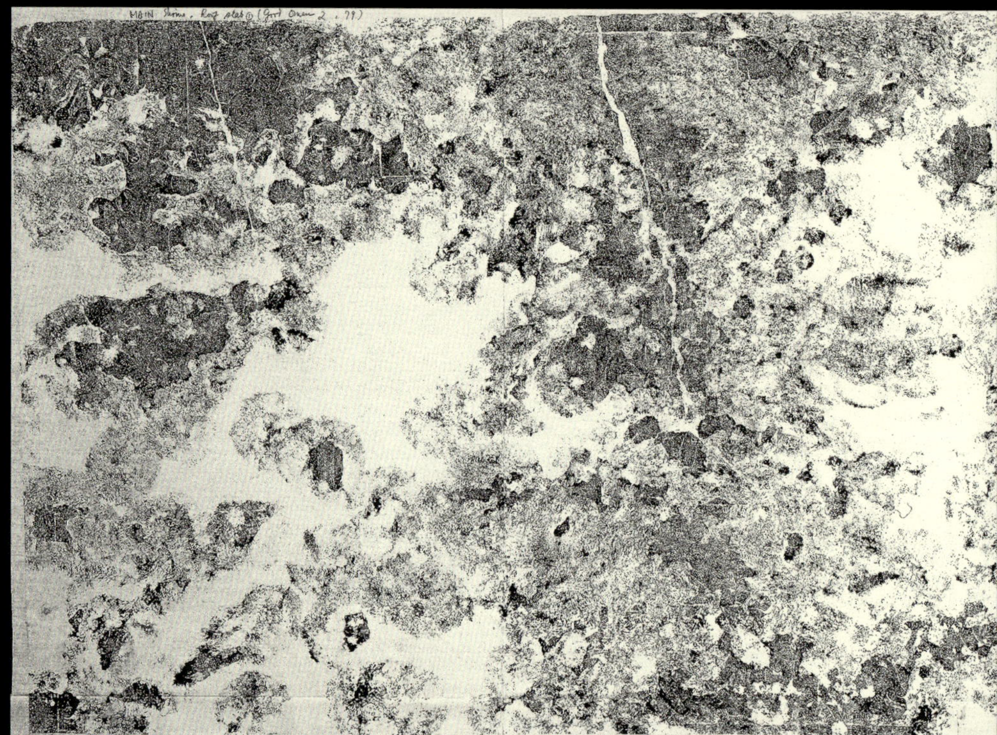

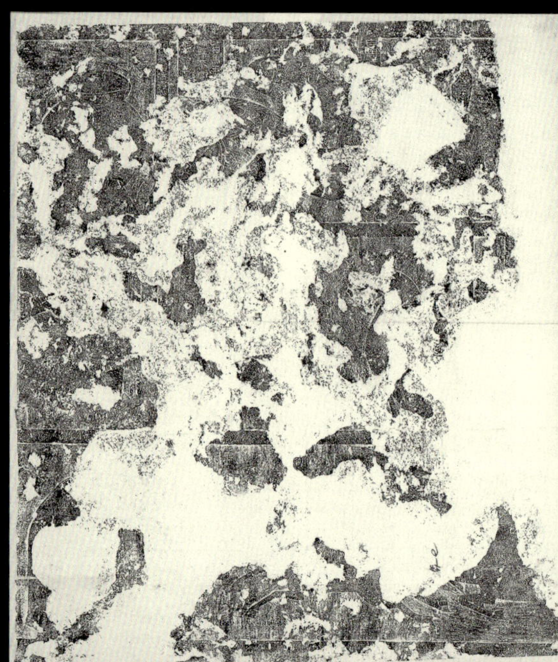

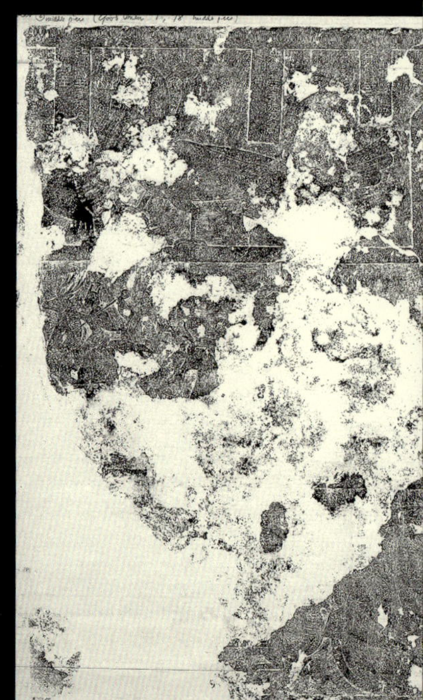

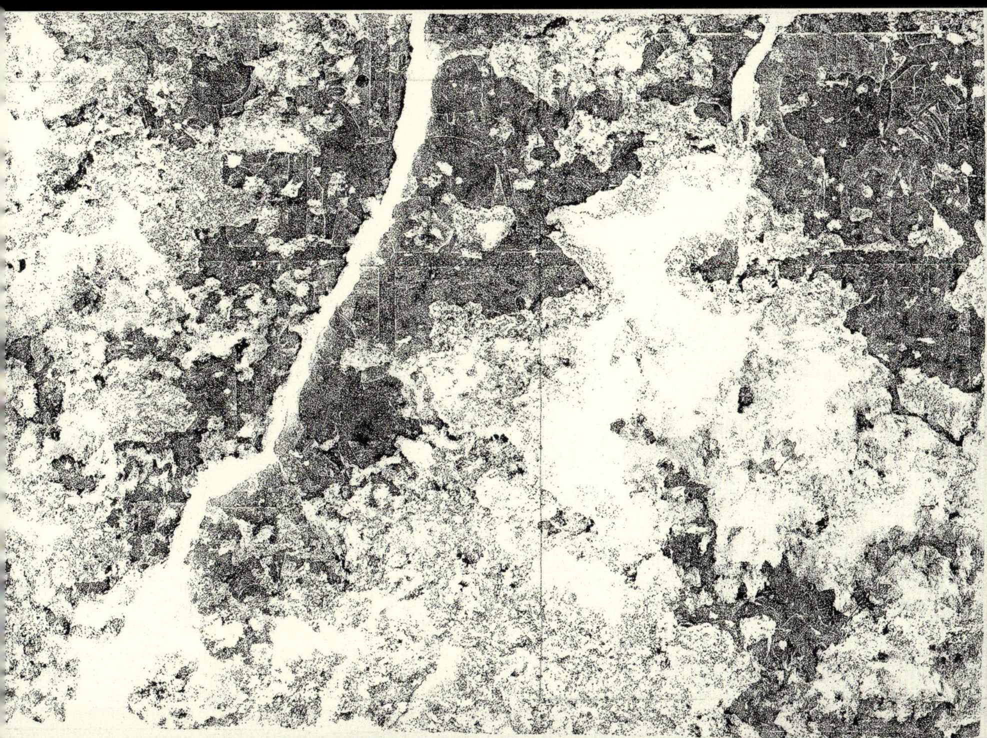

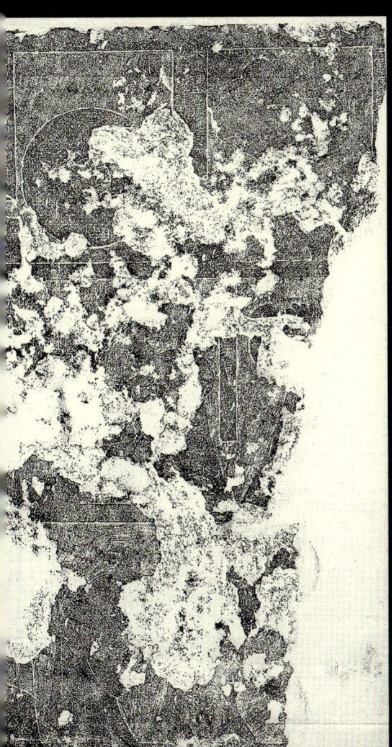

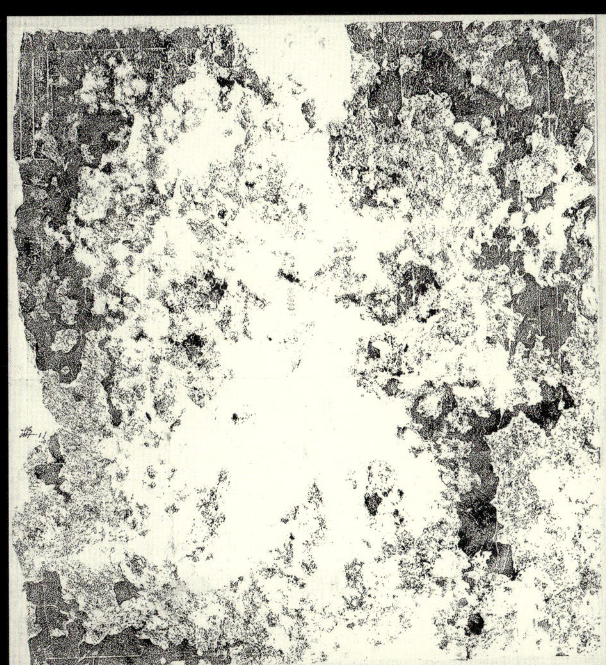

1.38
1.40 1.39

Gate-Pillars, Stele, "Fourth Chamber," and Qing-Dynasty Inscriptions

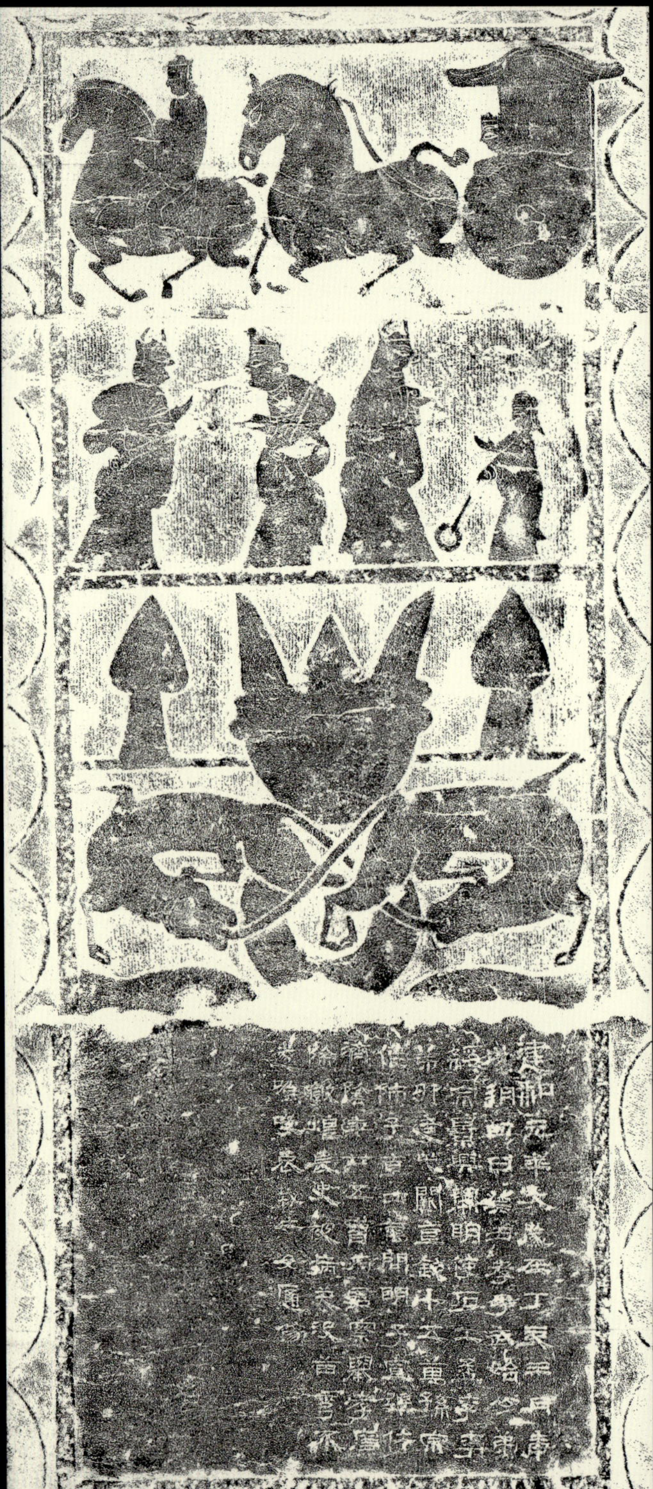

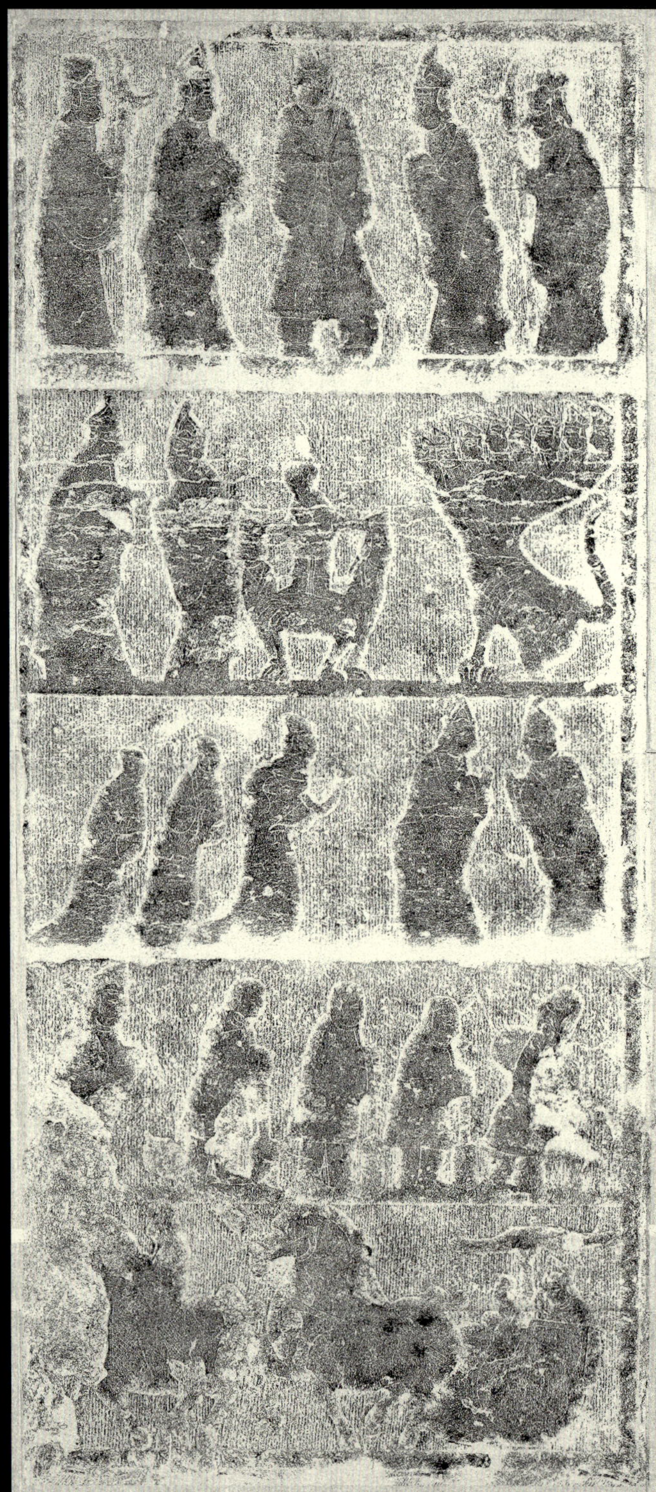

1.43
1.45

Gate-Pillars

1.43 *West gate-pillar, detail of north face.* Rubbing; h. 144.5 cm, w. 63.5 cm. PUAM, acc. no. 2002.307.39.
1.44 *West gate-pillar, detail of east face.* Rubbing; h. 64.0 cm, w. 24.0 cm. PUAM, acc. no. 2002.307.48.
1.45 *East gate-pillar, detail of south face.* Rubbing; h. 148.4 cm, w. 63.6 cm. PUAM, acc. no. 2002.307.40.

1.43

The full north face includes a top register that is omitted from this detail. This rubbing starts at the second register with four figures, including a man facing a small figure holding a push toy; these two may represent Confucius and Xiang Tuo (cf. cat. nos. 1.4 and 10). Occupying the third and fourth registers is a ringed beast mask (*pushou*) design, composed in part of two beasts each biting the other's tail. Below the beasts are two fish that face into the center. In the lower third of the rubbing is a panel containing a clerical-script inscription in eight columns, reading:

> On the first day of the moon on the fourth day of *guichou*, in the third month of *gengxu*, in the first year of the Jianhe era (147 CE) when the Taisui asterism was in the position of *dinghai*. The filial son Wu Shigong and his younger brothers, [Wu] Suizong,[43] [Wu] Jingxing, and [Wu] Kaiming, commissioned the stonemasons Meng Fu and Li Dimao to build these pillars.[44] The cost was 150,000 cash. Sun Zong[45] made [a pair of] lions. The cost was 40,000 cash.
>
> [Wu] Xuanzhang, a son of [Wu] Kaiming, was an official at Jiyin.[46] When he was twenty-five years old, the Prefect Cao having observed and recommended him as Filial and Incorrupt (*xiaolian*),[47] he was appointed to the post of senior scribe at Dunhuang. Because of illness, he died prematurely without realizing his great potential (*miao xiu bu sui*).[48] Alas, this is regrettable. The gentlemen and ladies were aggrieved.

The actual carved inscription became almost indecipherable after the Qing-dynasty Daoguang reign-period (1821–1850). The received texts of this inscription differ in transcription, indicating that special caution is needed to determine what parts of the text are reliable and what parts have been restored, interpolated, or recarved. The existence of at least two recarved recensions or copies of the inscription further complicates the story.[49]

1.44

Detail of the characters "Wu Family Shrine" (Wushi Ci) in large clerical–seal script calligraphy carved over the pictorial designs on the stone. The characters must postdate the Han dynasty.

1.45

This rubbing has five registers with five standing figures each in the first, third, and fourth registers. In the middle of the second register is a creature with a human head at each end and a small figure standing on its back, and to its right a beast with eight human heads. A chariot and horseman occupy the bottom register.

CARY Y. LIU

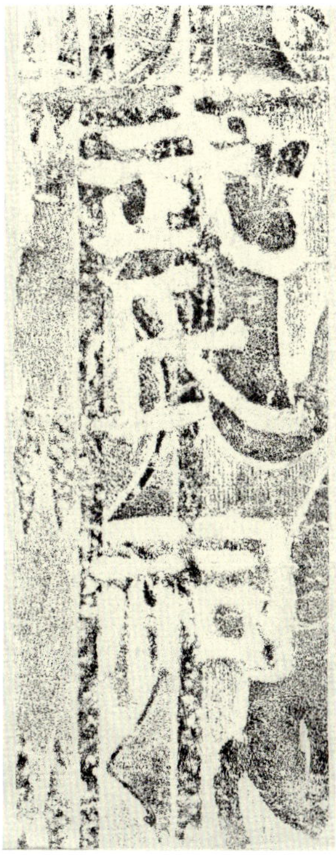

1.44

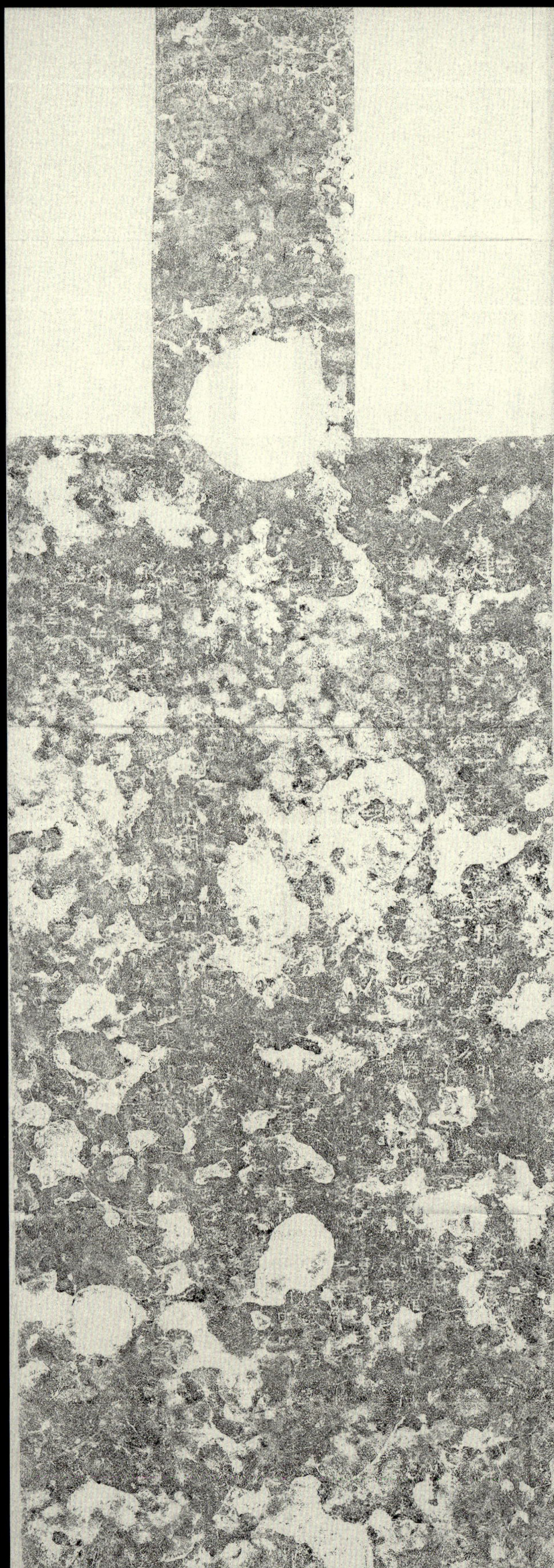

1.46
1.47

Stele

1.46 *"Wu Ban" stele, detail of front face.* Rubbing; h. 184.5 cm, w. 64.0 cm. PUAM, acc. no. 2002.307.41.
1.47 *"Wu Ban" stele, detail of back face.* Rubbing; h. 114.0 cm, w. 64.0 cm. PUAM, acc. no. 2002.307.46.

The surviving stele stone is shaped like a *gui* tablet, with a vertical oblong body and a triangular peak. Centered about one third of the way from the top is a round hole through the stele. On the front face are faint traces of a title in large characters above the hole. Below is a long inscription so worn that only scattered characters can be seen over the damaged surface. After discovering the cemetery site in 1786, Huang Yi noted the illegibility of this stele; yet he subsequently matched the inscription to received transcriptions of the Wu Ban stele as one piece of evidence that the site was the "Wu family shrines."

The received transcriptions and descriptions of the inscription, however, are not without their own set of problems. From being only ten to twenty percent legible in the earliest versions, they become eighty to ninety percent readable in later transcriptions. This argues that before any of these transcriptions can be used as a historical document, it must be carefully compared with the actual stone to determine what parts of the text are reliable and what parts have been restored, interpolated, or recarved. For example, in all recorded transcriptions the second character of the reign-period, "Jian[he]," is missing in the opening line and had to be interpolated. On the present stone, inspected in 2004, this line is now recarved to include the formerly missing *he* character (Liu's "Recarving the Past," fig. 6). Huang Yi also did not record any inscribed characters on the back face of the stele. The three large characters *Wu shi bei* ("Wu family stele"), therefore, must have been carved sometime after 1786 and before 1907, about when this rubbing set was made. We should also note that, according to Huang Yi, this stone, which has been so important to the story of the "Wu family shrines," may not be original to the cemetery site.

CARY Y. LIU

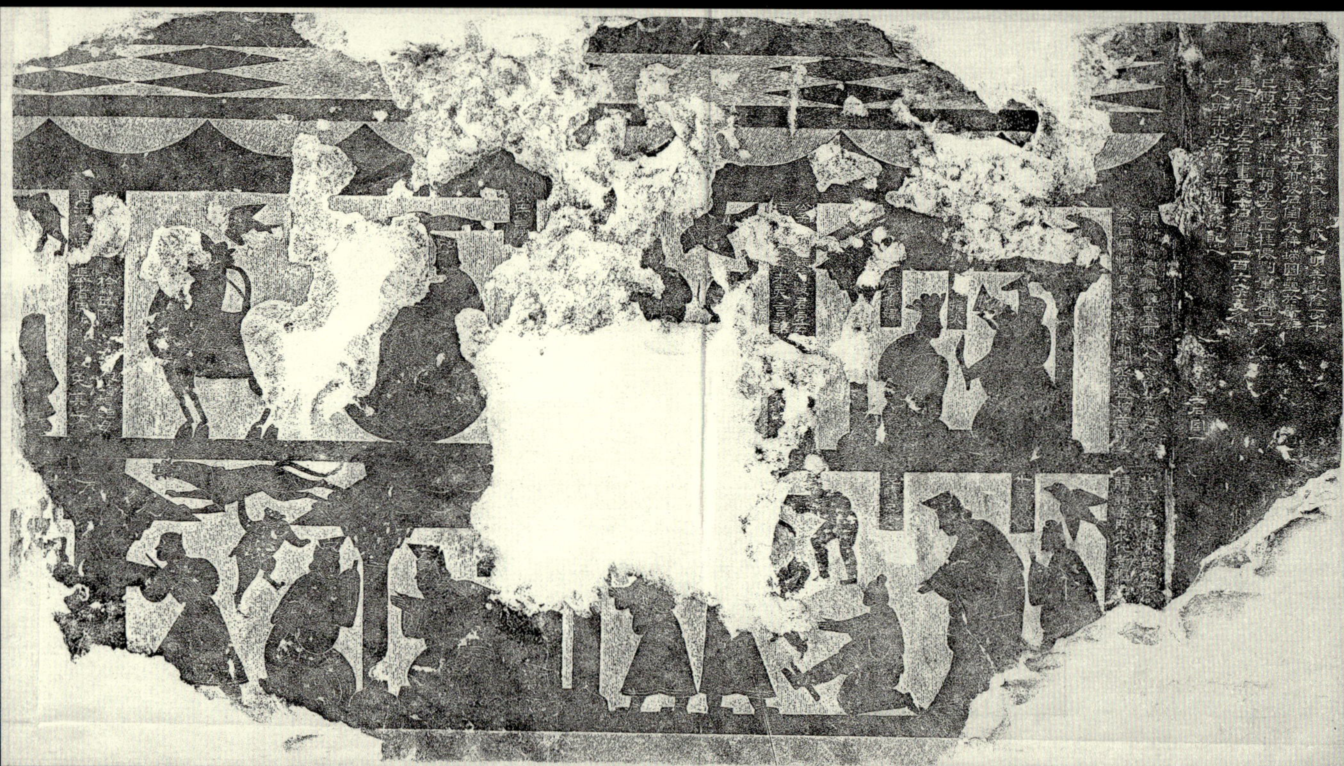

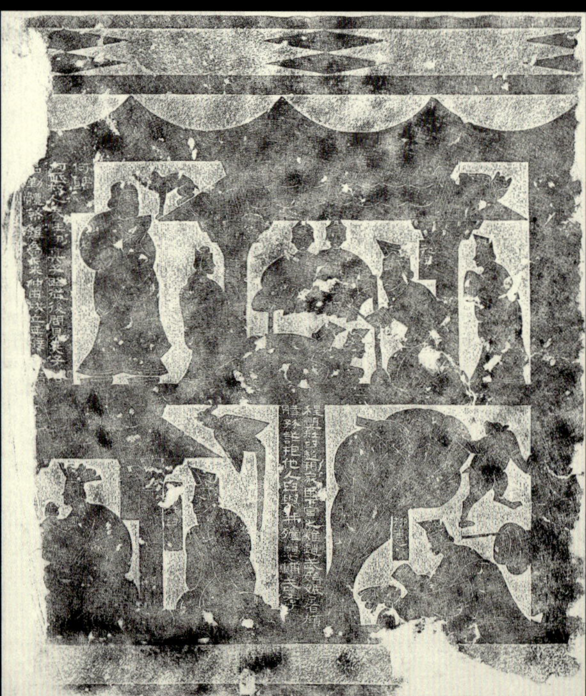

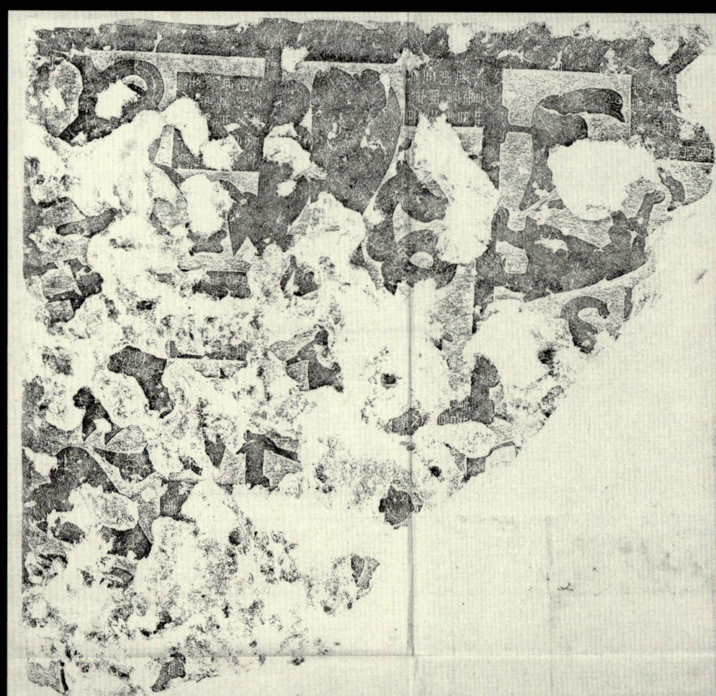

1.48
1.49
1.50

"Fourth Chamber"

1.48 *Left Group Stone 1*. Rubbing; h. 64.4 cm, w. 114.1 cm. PUAM, acc. no. 2002.307.42.
1.49 *He kui ("Carrying provisions") stone*. Rubbing; h. 64.3 cm, w. 58.0 cm. PUAM, acc. no. 2002.307.43.
1.50 *You niao ru he ("There is a bird like a crane") roof slab with omen designs*. Rubbing; h. 73.5 cm, w. 72.0 cm. PUAM, acc. no. 2002.307.44.

The Left Group Stone 1, *You niao ru he*, *He kui*, and *Wang Ling mu* (missing from the Princeton set) stones were all found at different times and brought to the Wu cemetery site for preservation. The stylistic similarity of the Left Group Stone 1 to the pictorial stones found at the cemetery caused it to be assigned its early designation as the first stone of the Wu cemetery Left Group, which was found in 1789. This early title had to be reassessed after the discovery of the other three stones. Already by 1880 Chen Jin had noted that the *Wang Ling mu* stone and Left Group Stone 1 were adjoining fragments of a longer horizontal stone. According to Wu Hung, these two stones may have been part of a "Fourth Chamber," along with the stylistically similar *He kui* and *You niao ru he* stones.[50] The stylistic similarity of these stones to the pictorial stones recovered at the Wu cemetery suggests that the "Fourth Chamber" may originally have been located at the site. It is more likely, however, that the "Fourth Chamber" belonged to a nearby site but was produced by the same stone workshop. Numerous pictorial stones with similar stylistic carving, pictorial themes, and decorative patterns have been found elsewhere in Jiaxiang County (cat. no. 10), including several stones recovered at Songshan village (cat. no. 11).

CARY Y. LIU

Qing-Dynasty Inscriptions

1.51 Weng Fanggang (1733–1818; author and calligrapher), Zheng Zhizong (act. ca. 1787; carver), *Record on Rebuilding the Wu Family Shrine Stones* (*Chong li Wushi Ci shi ji*), 1787. Rubbing; sheets vary in height from 31.0 to 31.5 cm and in width from 89.5 to 95.0 cm. PUAM, acc. no. 2002.307.45a-g.
1.52 Li Dongqi (Qing dynasty), *Inscription* dated to 1792. Rubbing; h. 64.0 cm, w. 40.1 cm. PUAM, acc. no. 2002.307.49.
1.53 Qian Yong (1759–1844), *Record of the Stones* dated to 1792. Rubbing; h. 31.0 cm, w. 85.8 cm. PUAM, acc. no. 2002.307.50.

1.51

Weng Fanggang, a high official and well-known scholar of epigraphy and painting, became closely associated with Huang Yi and his efforts to study, preserve, and promote the Wu cemetery carvings. Weng Fanggang's inscription is carved on seven rectangular stone tablets. On the first stone is the title, written in large-size seal-script calligraphy. On the second to fifth stones the text of the inscription is carved in clerical-script calligraphy with six characters per column and sixteen columns on a tablet. The sixth stone starts with four columns of Weng Fanggang's inscription. The following twenty-five columns on the sixth stone and thirty-four columns on the seventh stone list the donors and donated sums for the construction of a preservation hall at the site that would also serve as a shrine hall for the Wu family ancestors (i.e., the Wu Family Shrine).

1.52

Li Dongqi was closely associated with Huang Yi in his efforts to recover and preserve the Wu cemetery carvings. He helped supervise the building of the first Preservation Hall at the site. This inscription lists the four names and office titles of the four male progeny traditionally associated with the "Wu family shrines."

1.53

A twenty-column inscription written in clerical-script calligraphy with seven characters to a column.[51] Composed by Qian Yong in 1792, probably to commemorate the completion of the Preservation Hall, it records a total of forty-three stones. The Wu Ban stele and *Wu jia lin* column fragment are counted, but the gate-pillars and "Confucius Meeting Laozi" stone are not. In addition, the Good Omen stones are noted as four fragments, and the Front Group is listed as totaling fourteen stones, two of which have two pictorial faces.

CARY Y. LIU

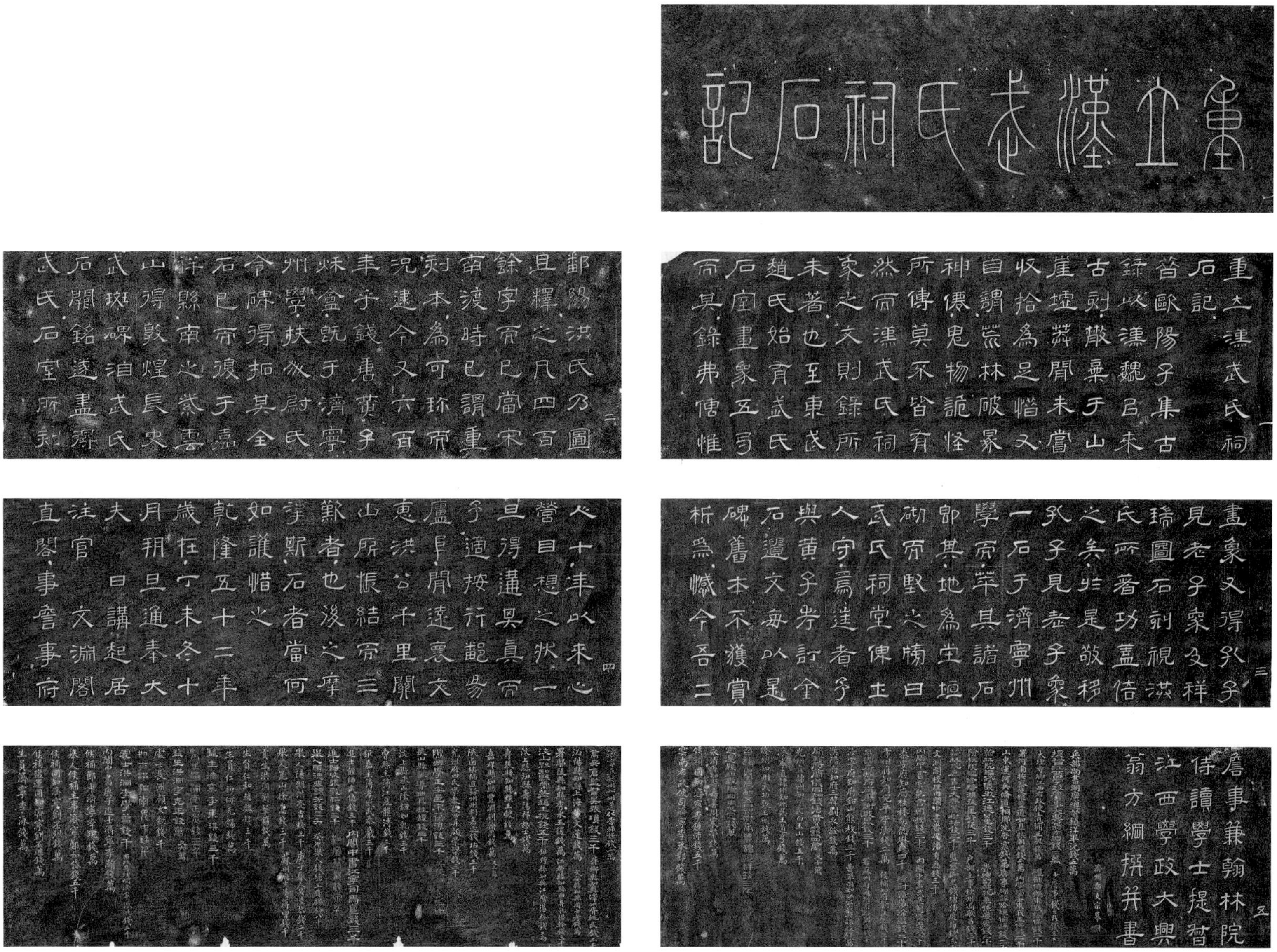

1.51

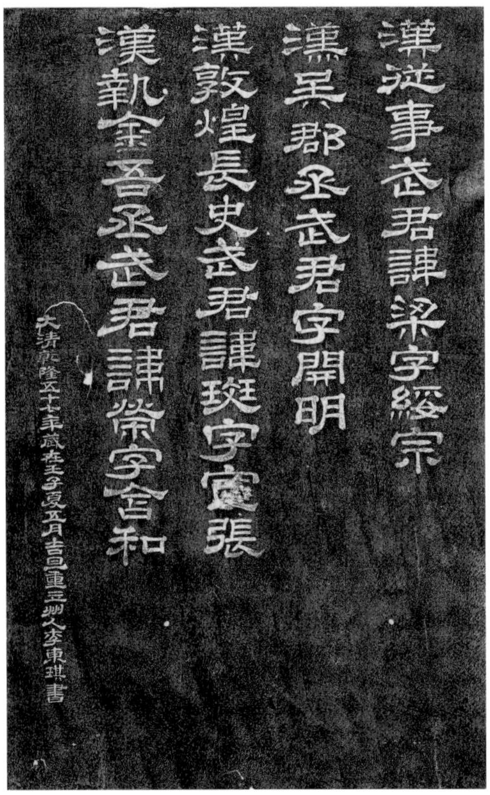
漢從事武君諱梁字綏宗
漢吳郡丞武君字開明
漢敦煌長史武君諱斑字宣張
漢執金吾丞武君諱榮字含和
大清乾隆五十七年歲在壬子夏五月吉日重立州人李東琪書

1.52

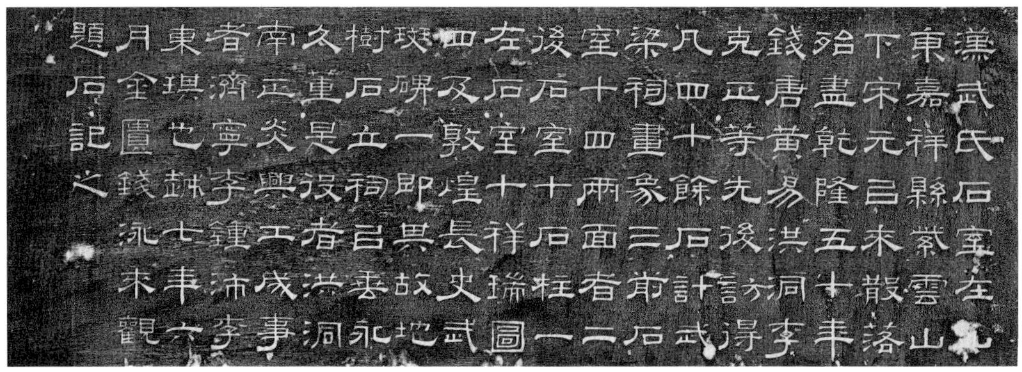

1.53

Notes

1. A distinction is made in this essay between a pillar-gate and the two gate-pillars of which it is composed. The character *que* includes both meanings.

2. Other Wu rubbing sets are found in institutional and private collections, including another set and a half in the Princeton University Art Museum; Academia Sinica, Taipei; three sets collected by Berthold Laufer in the Field Museum in Chicago; a set donated by Lawrence Picken at the Needham Research Institute in Cambridge, England; two sets in the Philadelphia Museum of Art, which entered the collection in 1924 and 1974, several sets in the Royal Ontario Museum; a set in the East Asian Library at the University of California, Los Angeles; a set in the Freer Gallery of Art, Washington, D.C.; and some pieces in the Fogg Art Museum at Harvard University. Other sets are found in institutions in Japan and Prague, and some of the earliest sets, including remaining fragments of the so-called Tang Rubbing, are in the collection of the Palace Museum, Beijing.

3. Both stones are currently in the former stele pavilion of the Tieta Si temple now located behind the Jining Municipal Museum, Shandong.

4. Wilma Fairbank, "The Offering Shrines of 'Wu Liang Tz'u,'" *Harvard Journal of Asiatic Studies*, vol. 6, no. 1 (1941), pp. 1–36; reprinted in Fairbank, *Adventures in Retrieval: Han Murals and Shang Bronze Molds* (Cambridge, Mass.: Harvard University Press, 1972), pp. 43–86.

5. Jiang Yingju and Wu Wenqi, "Wushi Ci huaxiang shi jianzhu peizhi kao" ("Architectural reconstruction of the Wu family shrines pictorial stones"), *Kaogu xuebao* 1981.2, pp. 165–84; and Jiang and Wu, *Handai Wushi muqun shike yanjiu* (*Studies on the Han-dynasty stone carvings at the Wu family cemetery*) ([Ji'nan]: Shandong meishu chubanshe, 1995), pp. 23–51.

6. Wu Hung, *The Wu Liang Shrine: The Ideology of Early Chinese Pictorial Art* (Stanford: Stanford University Press, 1989), pp. 20–24.

7. Alan Priest also compiled a partial set of Wu rubbings and copies that went into the collection of Robert Ellsworth. The set was offered at auction by Skinner, Boston, June 2002, sale 2149, lot 272.

8. Sekino Tadashi, *Shina Santōshō ni okeru Kandai funbo no hyōshoku* (Tokyo: Imperial University of Tokyo, 1916), fig. 97.

9. After the surface of each stone has been cleaned, microscopic inspection of the incised lines for tooling marks may be able to detect whether particular sections or details of the carvings have been retouched or recarved, and when such reworking may have taken place.

10. Fairbank, *Adventures in Retrieval*, p. 45.

11. For discussion about this scene, see Patricia Berger, "The Battle at the Bridge at Wu Liang Tz'u: A Problem in Method," *Early China*, vol. 2 (1976), pp. 3–8; Hsing I-tien, "Handai huaxiang hu han zhanzheng tu de goucheng, leixing yu yiyi," unpublished manuscript dated to June 4, 2003, pp. 1–50.

12. See the stories of Zengzi and Laizi on Stone 3-W.1 (cat. no. 1.35), and the story of Zhu Ming on Stone 3-S.1 (cat. no. 1.36), the stories of Yao Li assassinating Prince Qing Ji and of the virtuous aunt of Liang on Stone 3-E.1 (cat. no. 1.37).

13. Compare the stories of Laizi and Min Ziqian, both depicted in Stones 1-E.2 (cat. no. 1.12) and 3-W.1 (cat. no. 1.35).

14. For a study and overview of scholarly opinions about this scene, see Wu Hung, *Wu Liang Shrine*, pp. 193–213. Also see Nagahiro Toshio, "A Study on the Central Pavilion Scenes of the Wu Family Shrines," trans. M. Hickman, *Acta Asiatica*, vol. 2 (1961), pp. 40–58; Kenneth E. Brashier, "The Sweetpear Tree: Preserving the Historical Image of Historical Preservation," paper delivered at the Association of Asian Studies National Conference, San Diego, March 2004; and Jiang Yingju, "The Position of the Large Tree in the 'Pavilion Homage Scene' and Other Iconographies in Han Pictorial Carving," paper to be presented at the "Recarving China's Past" symposium at Princeton University, April 30–May 1, 2005.

15. When the center figure in the upper story of the pavilion at right is identified with Xiwangmu or some deity, the tree is usually said to be the *fusang* tree; eg., Nagahiro Toshio, "Study on the Central Pavilion Scenes," p. 42. When the main figures in the hall are identified as the husband and wife occupants of the tomb, or as the ancestral patriarch and matriarch, the intertwined tree is often viewed as a symbol of conjugal or family harmony and is designated *lianli* or *hehuan*. In a lecture presented at Princeton University on March 4, 2003, Jiang Yingju noted that in the Wu cemetery and Songshan pictorial stones (cat. no. 11), the tree is always placed to the east of the pavilion, regardless of whether the structure faces north or south.

16. Hsing I-tien, "Handai huaxiang neirong yu bangti de guanxi," *Gugong wenwu yuekan*, vol. 161 (1996), pp. 73–75; and in conversation with Jiang Yingju on June 9, 2004.

17. This open chariot with a canopy held by a central post is the most commonly seen type of chariot in the Wu carvings.

18. The iconography of this scene is discussed in Audrey Spiro, *Contemplating the Ancients: Aesthetic and Social Issues in Early Chinese Portraiture* (Berkeley: University of California Press, 1990), pp. 23–27.

19. For a study of the *bang* cudgel, see Jiang Yingju, "Han hua zhi bang xiaokao" ("Brief examination of *bang* in Han pictures"), *Wenwu* 1980.3, pp. 73–74. Others have suggested that the *bang* is a case for documents such as credentials for envoys.

20. According to some sources, the *bianmian* is a kind of fan held to cover the face in awkward situations; see Yan Shigu's (581–645) commentary to the biography of Zhang Jing in *Hanshu* (*History of the Former Han*), comp. Ban Gu (Beijing: Zhonghua shuju, 1962), *juan* 76, p. 3223 n. 3; and Luo Zhufeng, ed., *Hanyu da cidian* (*Extensive dictionary of Chinese*) (Shanghai: Hanyu da cidian chubanshe, 1990), vol. 1, p. 1364. Bamboo or reed strips woven into the shape of a hemisphere and attached to a stick have been archaeologically excavated. In silhouette these mask-like fans resemble flat bamboo fans that may be what the two footmen (one damaged) leading the chariot are carrying.

21. A full account of this episode is found in Jing Ke's biography in Sima Qian, *Records of the Grand Historian*, trans. Burton Watson (Hong Kong: Columbia University Press, 1993), pp. 171–78.

22. The two types of carriage are called *pianche* and *pengche*, respectively, in Jiang and Wu, *Handai Wushi muqun shike yanjiu*, p. 69.

23. In Jiang and Wu, *Handai Wushi muqun shike yanjiu*, p. 67, this surfboard-like object is identified as a tree, but in many descriptions it remains unidentified. The Immortal at right holds a ladle, which may suggest that it is a fountain.

24. The auspicious *mingjia* tree is said to have grown in the courtyard of the legendary Emperor Yao. It was said to produce one new leaf each day for fifteen days, and then to lose one each day for the next fifteen. The *mingjia* tree is also carved as a good omen design on a roof slab in Stone Chamber 3 (cat. no. 1.38).

25. Here the cloud figure does not have a human head, in contrast to other depictions of this scene (see cat. nos. 1.25, 1.35).

26. On the Xing Qu story, see Wu Hung, *Wu Liang Shrine*, p. 289.

27. On the Xing Qu story, see cat. no. 1.10. This scene, heavily damaged on the stone, is identified by inscribed cartouches. Oddly, this scene is repeated twice in the same stone chamber.

28. On the Min Ziqian story, see Wu Hung, *Wu Liang Shrine*, pp. 278–80. In *Handai Wushi muqun shike yanjiu*, p. 64, Jiang and Wu identify the scene based on its similarity to the Min Ziqian scene in Stone Chamber 3.

29. On the Laizi story, see Wu Hung, *Wu Liang Shrine*, pp. 280–82.

30. On the Boyu story, see Wu Hung, *Wu Liang Shrine*, pp. 286–87.

31. The exterior faces are reproduced in Jiang and Wu, *Handai Wushi muqun shike yanjiu*, pl. 23.

32. On Fuxi and Nüwa, see Wu Hung, *Wu Liang Shrine*, pp. 245–47.

33. According to Jiang and Wu, *Handai Wushi muqun shike yanjiu*, p. 72, this figure is holding an acupuncture needle.

34. Earlier records indicate that this scene may also have been carved on the second register of the east face of the center gable crossbeam in Stone Chamber 1 (cat. no. 1.16), where a cartouche was inscribed, "This is Duke Huan of Qi." The existing stone and the Princeton rubbing do not show any traces of this story, but a rubbing of the cartouche survives. See Jiang and Wu, *Handai Wushi muqun shike yanjiu*, p. 70, and p. 165, pl. 44.11.

35. See *Zhongguo huaxiang shi quanji*, ed. Zhongguo huaxiang shi quanji bianji weiyuanhui, vols. 1–3: *Shandong Han huaxiang shi* (Ji'nan: Shandong meishu chubanshe, 2000), vol. 1, no. 81.

36. For detailed discussion of the stories and textual references connected with each individual pictorial scene in Stone Chamber 3, see Wu Hung, *Wu Liang Shrine*, pp. 73–327.

37. A similar inscribed vertical band (top damaged) in the scene of Lin Xiangru on Stone 3-S.1 (cat. no. 1.36) is usually said to be a column.

38. Wu Hung, *Wu Liang Shrine*, pp. 291–92.

39. For discrepancies and agreement between the carved images and literary sources of this scene, see Wu Hung, *Wu Liang Shrine*, pp. 292–95. As discussed in Liu's "Recarving the Past" and Nylan's "Addicted to Antiquity," textual records indicate that Zhu Ming lived after the Han dynasty, during the Eastern Jin.

40. Both Wu Hung and Jiang Yingju identified and reconstructed the two scenes based on recorded descriptions in earlier works such as Hong Gua's *Li shi* (12th century) and Feng Yunpeng and Feng Yunyuan's *Jinshi suo* (1821); see Wu Hung, *Wu Liang Shrine*, pp. 295–98, and Jiang and Wu, *Handai Wushi muqun shike yanjiu*, p. 57. For Jin Midi, the textual stories record that the statue was of the mother. In the *Jinshi suo* the depicted statue is female; however, in the recorded cartouche inscription the statue is labeled as the father. As Wu Hung points out, the illustrations in the *Jinshi suo* may be reconstructed from textual sources and not from any surviving carving or rubbing. For Jin Midi's biography, see Michael Loewe, *A Biographical Dictionary of the Qin, Former Han and Xin Periods (221 B.C.–A.D. 24)* (Leiden: E. J. Brill, 2000), pp. 196–97.

41. The identifications of the fourth and fifth scenes are tentative, as the illustrations show only scanty details and some characters in the cartouche inscriptions are missing; see Wu Hung, *Wu Liang Shrine*, pp. 303–4. Jiang Yingju and Wu Wenqi do not identify the Yan Wu story, and for the fifth scene they cite Qu Zhongrong in reading the story as representing the orphan of the Zhao family (*Zhaoshi gu'er*), which was also depicted in Stone 2-S.7 (cat. no. 1.25); see Jiang and Wu, *Handai Wushi muqun shike yanjiu*, p. 55, n. 26 and p. 86.

42. On the possible conflation of this story with that of the assassin Gao Jianli, see Wu Hung, *Wu Liang Shrine*, pp. 325–27. Wu Hung notes that the latter story is illustrated in the Left Chamber (Stone Chamber 2), but does not specify in what scene. Very few of the scenes are labeled in Chamber 2, and it is difficult to connect many of them to particular stories.

43. Usually identified as Wu Liang.

44. In Rong Geng, *Han Wu Liang Ci huaxiang kao lu* (*Record of the Wu Liang Shrine pictorial carvings of the Han dynasty*), 2 fascicles (Beijing: Yanjing daxue kaogu xueshe, 1936), text vol., p. 6a, the character *fu* is transcribed as *li*; in which case the line could be read: ". . . stonemasons Meng Li and Li's younger brother Mao . . . ." In some transcriptions the repeated character *li* is written as *ji*; see Gong Yanxing, ed., *Jining quan Han bei* (*Complete Han steles*) (Ji'nan: Qi-Lu shushe, 1990), p. 43.

45. Some transcriptions write Sun Zong's name as Suizong (i.e., Wu Liang). See Gong Yanxing, *Jining quan Han bei*, p. 43.

46. Wu Xuanzhang is usually identified as Wu Ban. Jiyin was a Han commandery located northwest of present-day Dingtao County, Shandong.

47. See Charles O. Hucker, *A Dictionary of Official Titles in Imperial China* (Stanford: Stanford University Press, 1985), no. 2418.

48. The phrase refers to the line in the *Analects*: "There are cases in which the blade springs, but the plant does not go on to flower!" (*miao er bu xiu zhe*); see *Lunyu zhushu*, *Shisan jing zhushu* edition, 2 vols. (Beijing: Zhonghua shuju, 1980), "Zi Han" section, *juan* 9, p. 2491; trans. in James Legge, *The Chinese Classics* (reprint, Taipei: Southern Materials Center, Inc., 1985), vol. 1, p. 223.

49. See Gong Yanxing, *Jining quan Han bei*, p. 43.

50. Wu Hung, *Wu Liang Shrine*, pp. 20–24.

51. In Jiang and Wu, *Handai Wushi muqun shike yanjiu*, p. 134, this inscription is described as having sixteen columns with six characters per column.

Supplement: Pictorial Column from a "Wu Family Shrines" Two-Bay Stone Chamber

Eastern Han dynasty, dated to 147. Wuzhai Shan, Jiaxiang County, Shandong. Stone with relief and incised carving; h. approx. 122 cm. Ethnological Museum, Berlin, acc. no. ID27099.

Carved in two registers around the cylindrical shaft of the column are cavorting figures and animals. The registers are divided by a plain band around the middle, which bears the inscription "Made on the *gengchen* . . . day in the fifth month of the first year (147) of the Jianhe reign-period" (*Jianhe yuan nian wu yue gengchen* [ ] [ ] [ ] *ri zao*) (see detail). This same date occurs in the Wu Ban stele (cat. no. 1.46) and southwest gate-pillar (cat. no. 1.43) inscriptions. Wraparound rubbings of the column and transcriptions of the inscription were recorded in the early twentieth century by both Édouard Chavannes and Ōmura Seigai (see Liu's "Recarving the Past," fig. 18A), and Sekino Tadashi had reported the presence of stone columns at the Wu cemetery site.[1] By the late twentieth century, however, though the column was counted among the miscellaneous slabs associated with the site, its location was unknown.[2] The column was recently rediscovered in the collection of the Ethnological Museum in Berlin.[3] Fragile and in fragmentary condition, it has been conserved for this exhibition.[4]

A square capital bearing traces of fine-line intaglio designs surmounts the surviving column shaft. The column base was formed by a round torus carved in the shape of intertwined animals atop a square plinth; this is now missing but can be seen in a photograph published by Adolf Fischer (1857–1914) in 1908 (see Liu's "Recarving the Past," fig. 18B). Fischer, a specialist with the Imperial German legation in Beijing, purchased the column in Shandong in 1906, during a trip to acquire objects for the Museum für Völkerkunde (present-day Ethnological Museum) in Berlin. Chavannes records that Fischer brought the column to Germany in 1907.[5] Fischer presented the new acquisition in a lecture and published it in the journal *T'oung Pao* in 1908.[6] According to Fischer, the height of the intact column with its capital and base was 157 centimeters. In reconstructions of Stone Chambers 1 and 2 this height is almost precisely the distance between the ground and the bottom of the front lintel and the central gable beam.[7]

Among fourteen stones of the Front Group that Huang Yi reported finding at the site in 1786, only twelve were installed in the 1792

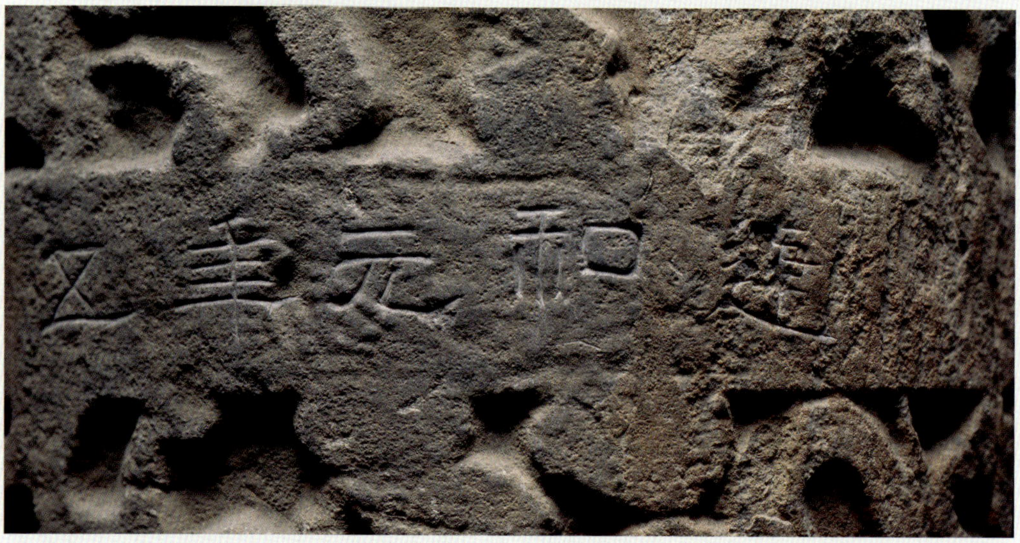

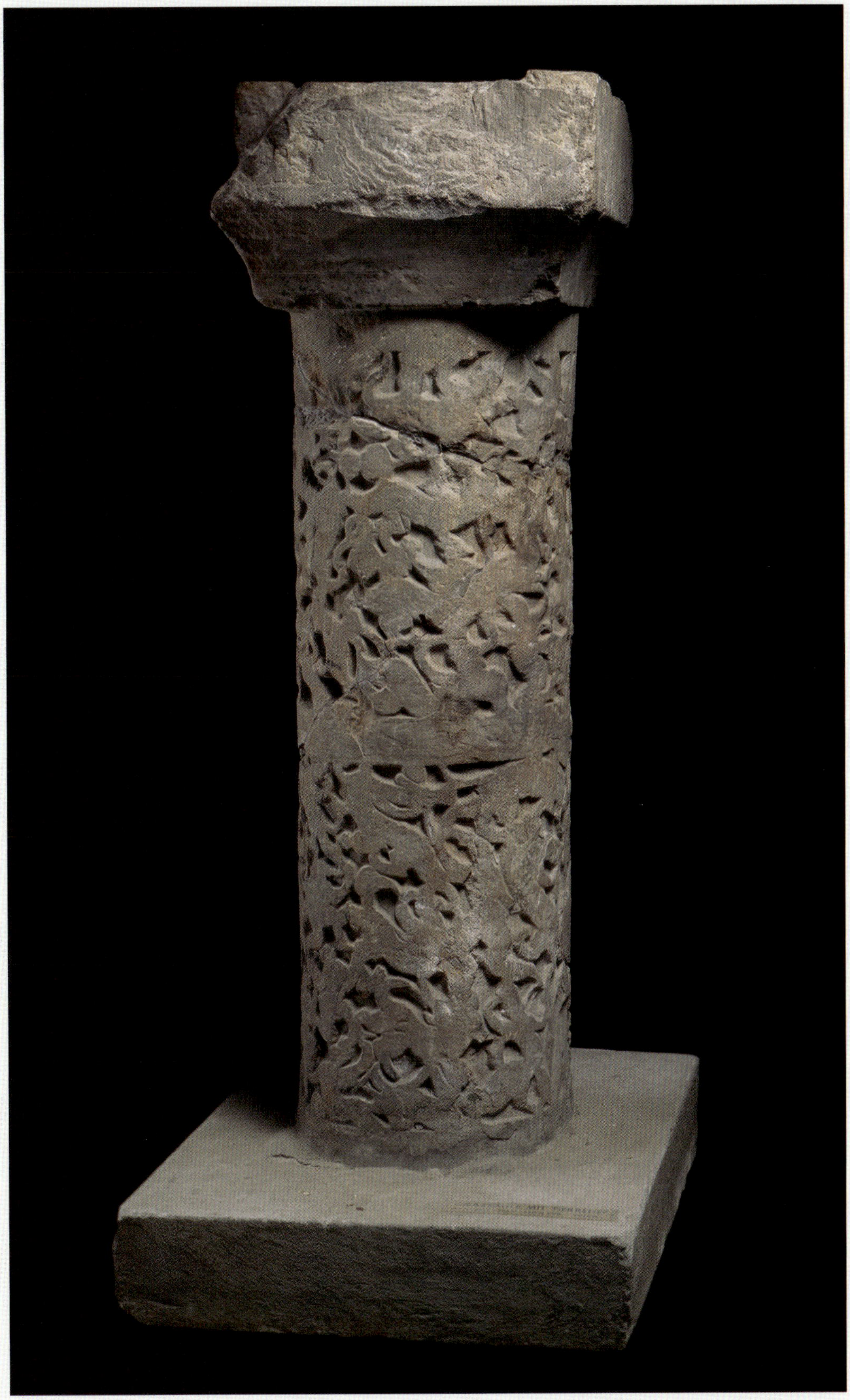

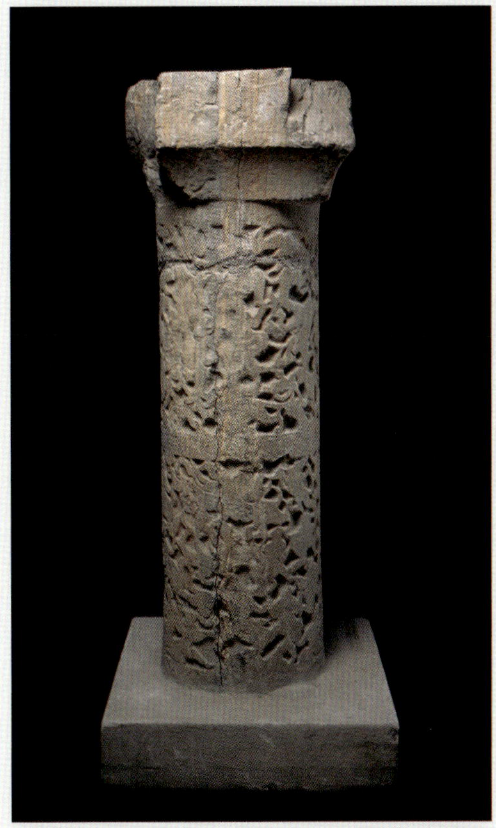

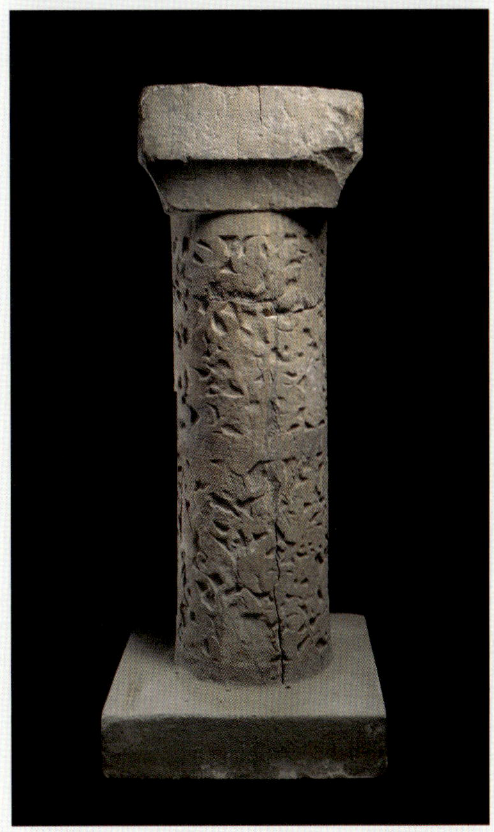

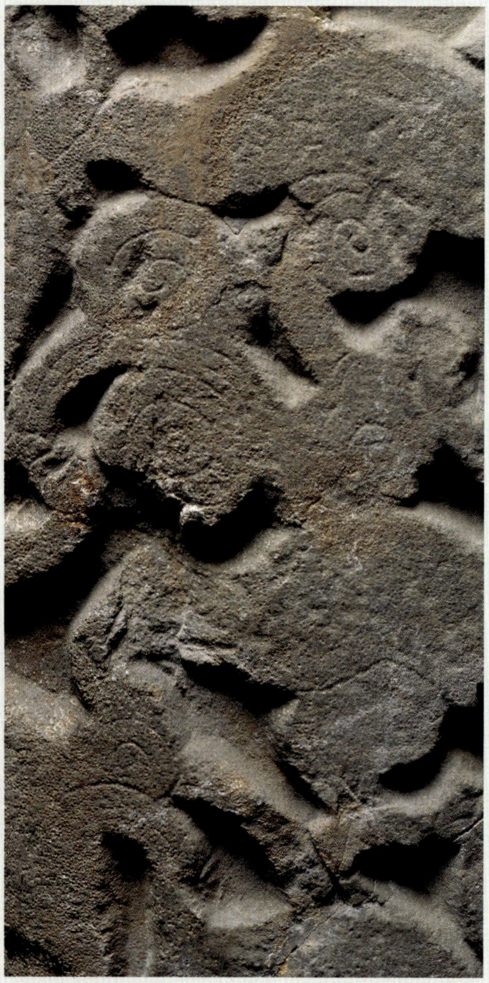

Wu Family Shrine Preservation Hall. The pictorial column may have been culled from the group because, like the gate-pillars, its shape perhaps made it inappropriate for the hall's early function as an actual ancestral shrine for the Wu family. Another stone column was also reported, and it too was excluded from the Preservation Hall. Huang Yi sent the capital of this column as a gift to Ruan Yuan. Known as the "*Ci-Jin* Damaged Stone" (*Ci jin can shi*), this capital likely corresponds to a pictorial stone now in the collection of the Tianjin Municipal Museum of Art.[8]

Stone columns were installed at the front of two-bay stone chambers, as evidenced by the octagonal column with capital and base at the offering hall at Xiaotang Shan (see Liu's "Recarving the Past," fig. 3A). Although few other columns belonging to aboveground stone chambers have been preserved or recorded, several carved pictorial stone columns have been unearthed in Eastern Han and later tombs in the Shandong region. Well-known examples have come from Tomb 1 at Yi'nan and the tomb at Anqiu.[9] Examples have also been found closer to the Wu cemetery site, in Tomb 1 at Zhangzhuang near Ji'nan, and in Tomb 1 near Mengzhuang, Pingyin County.[10] In carving style the Berlin column differs from the other pictorial stones at the Wu site; it is much closer in style and composition to the Mengzhuang columns. This may indicate the existence of a separate workshop, or group within a stone-carving workshop, that specialized in producing columns. The placement, decoration, and meaning of pictorial columns in the ritual and cosmological design of tombs and stone chambers are topics that merit further research.

CARY Y. LIU

Notes

1. The inscription and rubbing are recorded in Édouard Chavannes, *Mission archéologique dans la Chine septentrionale*, 2 vols. of text, 4 vols. of plates (Paris: Imprimerie Nationale, 1913 and 1915), text vol. 1, p. 243, and pl. 92, fig. 172; Ōmura Seigai, *Shina bijutsushi: Chōso hen*, 2 vols. (Tokyo: Bussho kankōkai zuzōbu, 1915), p. 63 and pl. 72, fig. 177; Sekino Tadashi, *Shina Santōshō ni okeru Kandai funbo no hyōshoku* (Tokyo: Imperial University of Tokyo, 1916), p. 26.

2. The column was reported missing in Jiang Yingju and Wu Wenqi, *Handai Wushi muqun shike yanjiu* (*Studies on the Han-dynasty stone carvings at the Wu family cemetery*) ([Ji'nan]: Shandong meishu chubanshe, 1995), p. 32.

3. The column was exhibited in the Ethnological Museum galleries in 1952–1968. For an installation photograph, see "Hundert-Jahre Museum für Völkerkunde Berlin," *Baessler-Archiv*, Neue Folge Band XXI (1973), p. 271. In 2004 the column stood in front of bookcases in the cellar as part of the study collection. I thank Maria Gaida, Siegmar Nahser, and Wu Shun-chi of the Ethnological Museum for their cooperation. I also thank Herbert Butz, at the Museum of East Asian Art in Berlin, and Adele Schlombs, at Museum of East Asian Art in Cologne, for pointing me to the Ethnological Museum.

4. In a 1908 photograph the column seems cracked and fragmented (see n. 6 below). In preparation for the present exhibition the column was conserved with funds, in part, from the Princeton University Art Museum.

5. Chavannes, *Mission archéologique*, text vol. 1, pp. 243–44.

6. Adolf Fischer, "Vortag, Gehalten auf dem 15ten Internationalen Orientalisten-kongress in Kopenhagen: Über Vorbuddhist Steinreliefs und Romanische Löwenköpfe aus China," *T'oung Pao*, ser. 2, vol. 9 (1908), pp. 582–83. In Ōmura Seigai, *Shina bijutsushi: Chōso hen*, p. 63, this column is said to be in the collection of "M. Adori [sic] Fischer."

7. Extrapolated from the scaled reconstruction drawings of the Front (Stone Chamber 1) and Rear (Stone Chamber 2) Chambers in Jiang and Wu, *Handai Wushi muqun shike yanjiu*, pp. 39, 44.

8. Discussed in Liu's "Recarving the Past" in this catalogue.

9. On the Yi'nan tomb, see Zeng Zhaoyu, Jiang Baogeng, and Li Zhongyi, *Yi'nan gu huaxiang shi mu fajue baogao* (*Excavation report of the ancient pictorial stone tomb at Yi'nan*) (Shanghai: Wenhuabu guanliju, 1956); Lydia duPont Thompson, "The Yi'nan Tomb: Narrative and Ritual in Pictorial Art of the Eastern Han (25–220 CE)" (PhD diss., Institute of Fine Arts, New York University, 1998). On the Anqiu tomb, see Anqiu Xian wenhuaju and Anqiu Xian bowuguan, *Anqiu Dongjiazhuang Han huaxiang shi mu* (*Stone relief tomb of the Han dynasty in Dongjiazhuang, Anqiu County*) (Ji'nan: Ji'nan chubanshe, 1992).

10. For the Zhangzhuang tomb, see Shandong Sheng wenwu kaogu yanjiusuo, "Shandong Ji'nan Zhangzhuang Handai mu de fajue jianbao" ("Brief excavation report on the Han-dynasty tomb grounds at Zhangzhuang, Ji'nan, Shandong"), in *Shandong gaosugonglu kaogu baogao ji (1997)* (*Collected Shandong highway construction archaeological reports of 1997*), ed. Shandong Sheng wenwu kaogu yanjiusuo (Beijing: Kexue chubanshe, 2000), pp. 297–313. For the Mengzhuang tomb, see Ji'nan Shi wenhuaju wenwuchu and Pingyin Xian bowuguan, "Shandong Pingyin Mengzhuang Donghan huaxiang shi mu" ("Eastern Han pictorial stone tomb at Mengzhuang, Pingyin, Shandong"), *Wenwu* 2002.2, pp. 38–52; *Zhongguo huaxiang shi quanji* (*Collected pictorial stones of China*), 8 vols. (Ji'nan: Shandong meishu chubanshe, 2000), vol. 3, nos. 191–202.

Catalogue

Part Two: Brilliant Artifacts

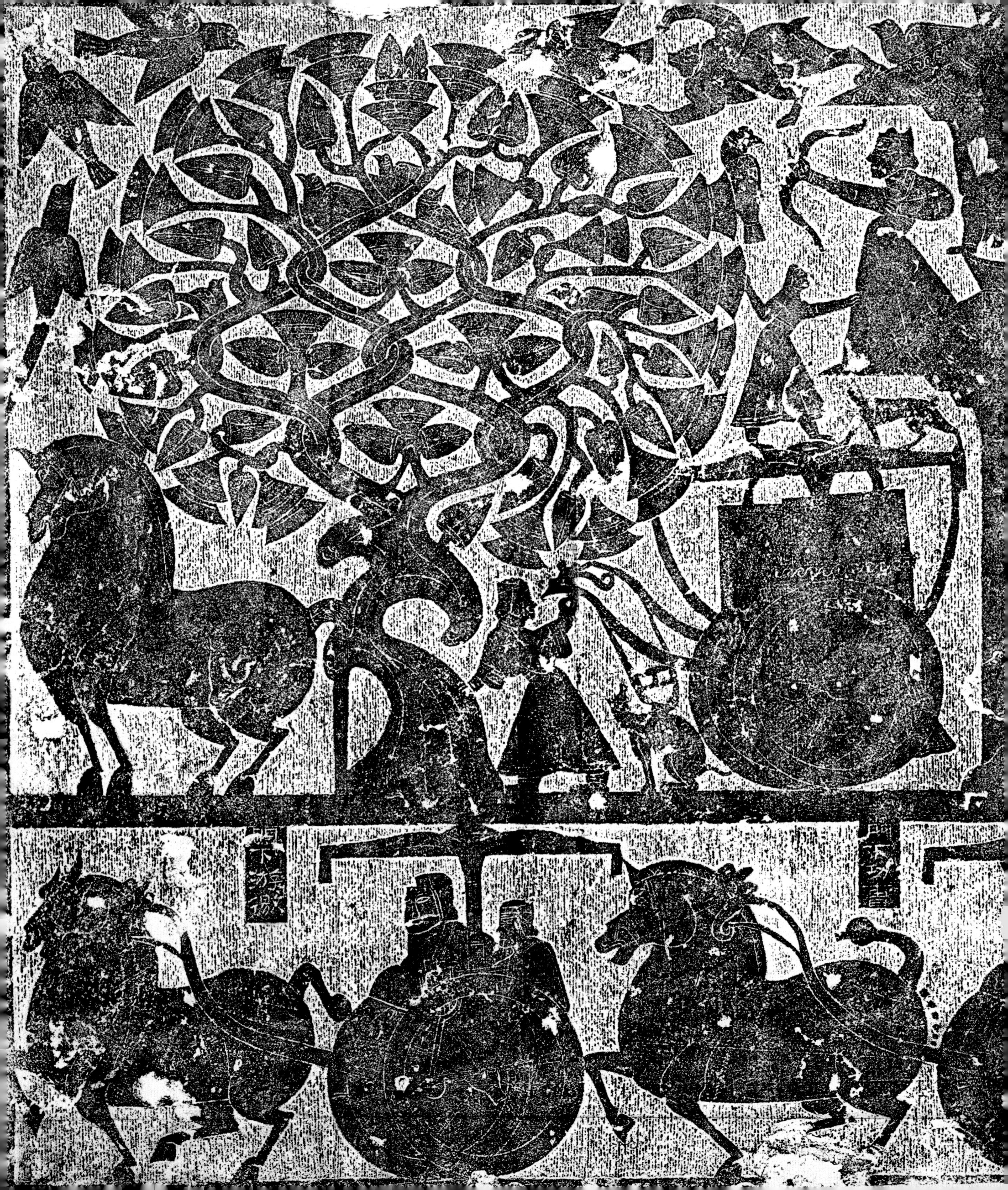

Cary Y. Liu

The Concept of "Brilliant Artifacts" in Han-Dynasty Burial Objects and Funerary Architecture: Embodying the Harmony of the Sun and the Moon

Han-dynasty funerary architecture and both the pictorial images and burial objects therein may sometimes have been conceived as an ensemble, that is, as sharing an artistic, ritual, and cosmological program. "Brilliant artifacts" (*mingqi*) are burial articles that were conceived as embodying a balance between the realms of the sun (*ri*) and moon (*yue*) (fig. 1; cat. no. 42). Preliminary exploration of these two concepts may reveal affinities between them, and the light each may shed on the other would better our understanding of both. Today the term *mingqi* is commonly applied generally to artifacts placed in tombs to provide for the dead in the afterlife, but this preliminary investigation will attempt to consider *mingqi* within the particular context of the Shandong region during the Han dynasty. Funerary architecture, in the form of tombs, tumuli and cemetery structures, and offering halls, spans the twilit boundary between the realm of life, lit by the sun, and the realm of afterlife, illumined by the moon. Mortuary architecture, often viewed simply as imitations of aboveground buildings for the living, should also be considered in relation to the concept of *mingqi*. There may be a close relationship between the pictorial images depicted in Han funerary monuments and the decoration on burial ceramics, bronzes, lacquers, and other items. Likewise, are the ordinary articles and daily activities pictured on the walls of Han mortuary structures—notably including the rubbings of the "Wu family shrines" (cat. no. 1)—merely representations, or do they also fulfill the same extraordinary role as brilliant artifacts? After a brief overview of modern interpretations of the term *mingqi*, this essay brings together some preliminary thoughts on the Han-dynasty concept of brilliant artifacts and the possible relationships between that concept and Han mortuary structures and their appurtenances.

In modern scholarship the term *mingqi* has been variously translated as "glorious vessels" or "spirit articles/vessels."[1] Each captures a partial meaning of *mingqi*, which Walter Perceval Yetts (1878–1957) in 1928 considered to be "objects made for burial with the dead." Yetts also noted: "The fact is surprising that until recently Chinese archaeologists have neglected to study the subject [of *mingqi*] . . . ."[2] Although the term *mingqi* was recorded in the ritual canons *Liji* (*Rites records*) and *Yili* (*Ceremonials*), reflecting Zhou-dynasty practices (discussed later), the earliest work to use it as an archaeological or art-historical category may be Luo Zhenyu's (1866–1940) *Gu mingqi tulu*, written in 1916 to record his own collection of ceramic tomb figures and models.[3] In that publication and others, such as *Zhongguo mingqi* (1933) by Zheng Dekun and Shen Weijun, the term *mingqi* is used to refer specifically to burial ceramics.[4] In later studies, however, the term is commonly used as a general designation for grave goods from pre-Han to the Qing dynasty. In each case, the modern application of the term *mingqi* was primarily adopted to help categorize groups of collected or excavated objects. We must ask, however, what constituted *mingqi* during the Han dynasty, and whether the objects so called differed over time, by region, or by funerary practice?

Starting in 1907, Luo Zhenyu put together what may have been the earliest collection of burial articles to be labeled *mingqi*.[5] Limited to burial ceramics that ranged widely in date, Luo divided the collection into four classes: human figures, models of everyday structures and objects, domestic

Opposite Detail of Stone Chamber 1, Stone 1-S.6 (cat. no. 1.9). "Wu family shrines" rubbings. Princeton University Art Museum, acc. no. 2002-307.9.

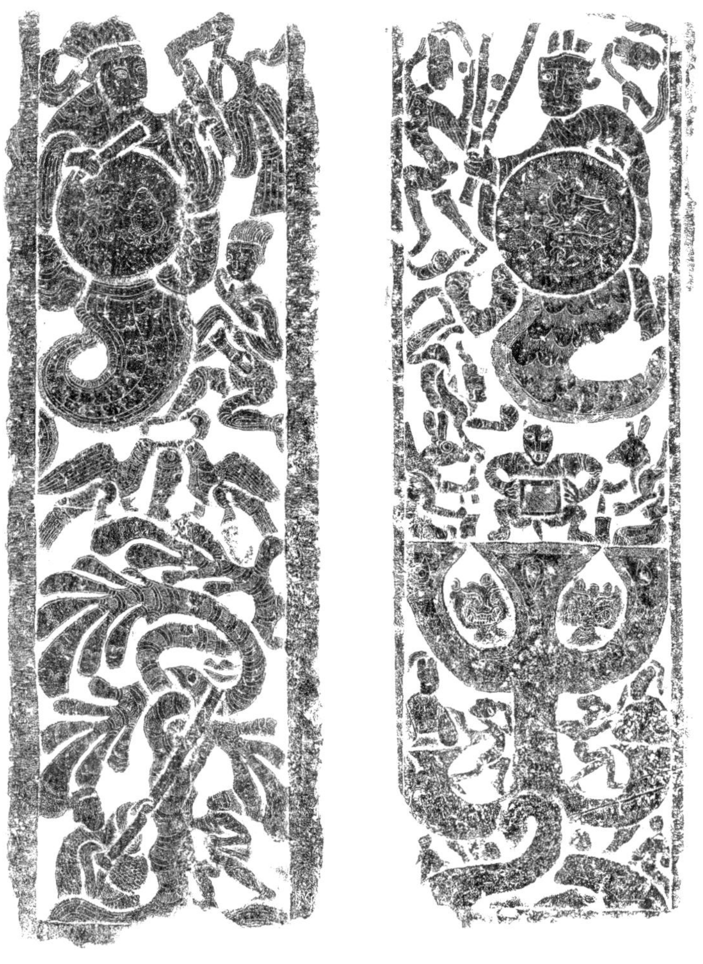

Fig. 1 *Fuxi with the sun* (*right*) *and Nüwa with the moon* (*left*). Eastern Han dynasty. Carved pictorial tomb stones from Baizhuang, Linyi County, Shandong. Ink-on-paper rubbings (modern); image height approx. 117 cm. From *Linyi Han huaxiang shi*, ed. Feng Yi et al. (Ji'nan: Shandong meishu chubanshe, 2002), p. 23, figs. 32–33.

animals, and, interestingly, architectural tomb tiles showing exemplary scenes of filial piety and loyalty. Those hortatory scenes are similar in subject to stories depicted in the Wu rubbings. The term *mingqi*, however, was never clearly defined. A similar lack of definition occurs in many attempts to classify large numbers of tomb artifacts that have been unearthed during modern archaeological excavations and salvage. In some cases, all objects buried in a tomb are considered to be *mingqi*, whereas in others the term is limited to artifacts believed to have been made specifically for the dead. The lack of any single definition is reflected in what scholars have variously identified as the earliest surviving examples of *mingqi*. In *Zhongguo mingqi*, Zheng Dekun and Shen Weijun characterized decorated pottery unearthed from Neolithic graves as *mingqi*. More recently, some scholars have designated late Shang-period tomb artifacts as the earliest examples.[6] In each case, a modern understanding of *mingqi* has been applied anachronistically to grave goods buried in periods when the term is unlikely to have existed. The modern application of the term *mingqi* grew from a need to categorize groups of burial artifacts that had suddenly become collectible (therefore marketable) and worthy of study in the early twentieth century.

In probing the meaning of *mingqi* in the Han dynasty, it may be best not to envision it as a physical category or group of objects. Instead, it may be more illuminating to investigate how *mingqi* might have differentiated the realms of life and afterlife, as reflected in grave articles and funerary architecture. A glimpse of Han conceptions of *mingqi* may be garnered from scattered discussions of funerary rites contained in Han and pre-Han texts (many compiled during and containing commentary from the Han). Such early texts distinguish between artifacts appropriate for life and those for afterlife. In discussing the official duties of the Palace Gatekeeper (*hunren*) in the Zhou dynasty, the *Zhouli* (*Rites of Zhou*) notes that "funerary garments and mourning artifacts (*xiongqi*) are not allowed to enter the palaces" of the living. In Han commentary by Zheng Xuan (127–200), mourning artifacts are equated with *mingqi*.[7] The term *xiongqi* is similarly glossed by Zheng Xuan in his commentary to the *Zhouli* discussion of the role of the Tomb Officer (*zongren*)

> who takes charge of the royal cemetery and sets the boundaries and makes drawings [for the tomb] . . . . For royal funerals (*dasang*), once the date is determined, the [Tomb Officer] requests [approval for] the dimensions [and permission] to begin building the tomb pit, and acts as a body double (*shi*) [for the deceased]. At the time the tomb pit [is dug], he follows the measurements for the mound and the ramp, and supplies the funeral equipment. At the time of the funeral, he speaks to the effigy (*xiangren*) [of the deceased] in the bell hearse (*luanche*). During the interment of the coffin, he holds an ax [to assist] and weeps. He then buries the mourning articles (*xiongqi*).[8]

The bell hearse in Zheng Xuan's commentary is a vehicle with cloth decoration as well as bells (*luanhe*) and pennants, which is used to transport the corpse to the grave.[9] According to later subcommentary by Jia Gongyan (act. 650), the hearse and effigy are forms of *mingqi*. If Jia accurately reflects Han practice, this suggests that some bronze, ceramic, and wood chariots and human figures (cat. nos. 2–6) recovered from Han tombs or depicted in the Wu cemetery rubbings (cat. no. 1) may, like the bell hearse and effigy, also have been *mingqi*. It is also important to note that as *mingqi*, the impersonator and effigy of the deceased mentioned in the above passage seem to have the ability to embody the spirit brilliance (*shenming*) of the dead. (The relationship between *mingqi* and *shenming* is discussed later). Controversy over the lifelikeness of figures, vessels, and even implements came to play a significant role in determining the characteristics of *mingqi*.

The early texts distinguish between objects for the living and those for the afterliving. The *Yili*, discussing the burial rituals for gentlemen or servicemen (*shi*),[10] divided burial objects into many types, including utilitarian artifacts (*yongqi*), banquet and musical objects (*yanyueqi*), sacrificial vessels (*jiqi*), warrior accoutrements (*yiqi*), and brilliant artifacts (*mingqi*).[11] Objects within each of these categories were generally subdivided into those made for the living, known as "objects for living people" (*renqi* or *shengqi*), and those made for burial, known as "fearsome artifacts" (*xiongqi*), "objects for the dead" (*guiqi*), or "brilliant artifacts" (*mingqi*).[12] Articles made for the dead were not to enter the palaces of the living except after being properly announced during certain indoor funerary ceremonies.[13] On the other hand, articles made for the living could reside in a tomb along with those made for the dead. Concerning burial rituals for gentlemen, in the *Yili* it is regulated that "there will be no sacrificial vessels." Commenting on this line during the Eastern Han, Zheng Xuan

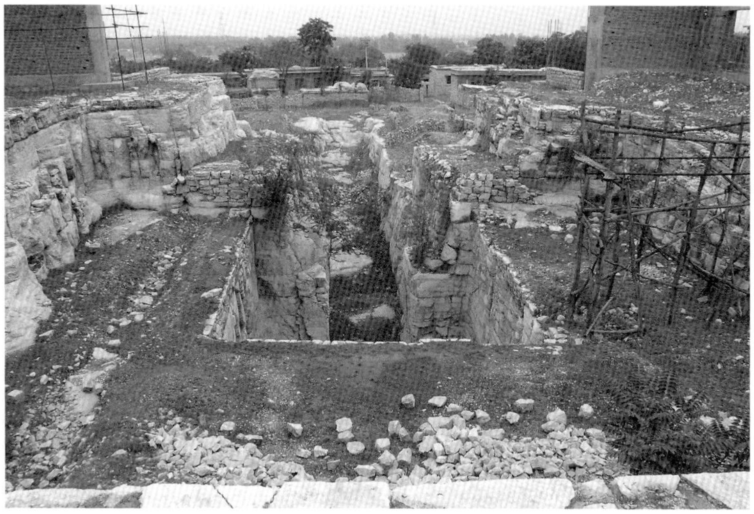

noted that "in burial ceremonies for gentlemen, [sacrificial vessels] are omitted. [For those with the official rank of] counselor (*dafu*) or above, however, both objects for the dead (*guiqi*) and objects for living people (*renqi*) are used."[14] Depending on rank, therefore, burials included objects for both the living and the dead, or were limited to those made only for the dead.

Objects made for the living and the dead have been found together in excavated Han royal tombs, such as Tomb 1 carved into the limestone cliffs of Shuangru Shan, a mountain in Changqing County (figs. 2, 3).[15] Excavated in 1995, Tomb 1 is the largest rock-cut Han royal tomb found to date. In square footage, each of the four Western Han rock-cut royal tombs excavated in 1970 at Jiulong Shan in Qufu County, Shandong, is less than one-third as large.[16] Tomb 1 was never robbed, and contained over two thousand burial artifacts, more than were found in the four tombs at Jiulong Shan combined. Tomb 1 is now believed to belong to Liu Kuan (r. 97–85 BCE), the last ruler of Jibei Kingdom (*Jibei guo*) during the Western Han. Liu was forced to commit suicide for his licentious behavior with his father's widow and for cursing the emperor during a sacrifice.[17] If the tomb's attribution is correct, Liu Kuan was granted royal burial privileges despite his disgrace. Ironically, the tomb's attribution is mostly based on his ignominy. The tomb is kingly in size, but that may be only because it was carved prior to Liu Kuan's disgrace. Instead of a complete jade suit (*yu yi* or *yu xia*),[18] only a jade mask, body-orifice plugs, and hand grips were found there. Furthermore, the rock-cut walls and ramp of the tomb were crudely finished, leaving a random patchwork of sunken rectangular panels that may reflect the stone-chiseling process.[19] Additionally, most of the two thousand burial items were small, and certain notable types of ritual objects were fewer than in other royal tombs.[20]

Burial articles found in Tomb 1 are of bronze, ceramic, jade, lacquer, iron, and gold. Bronzes are by far the most numerous, with over one thousand items, mainly articles of daily use plus horse and chariot fittings. Of ceramic, there are only six pots as well as figures of domestic animals, fish, and fowl, all in the side compartments around the coffin chamber. Skeletal remains of chicken and fish were found inside some of the burial vessels and containers in Tomb 1, as well as in the royal tombs at Jiulong Shan.[21] Jade artifacts include an eighteen-piece burial mask, one of the most elaborate examples found to date, a fourteen-part headrest, and a paltry number of jade *bi* discs. The lacquer items have deteriorated beyond recognition. A small button of gold was found at the waist of the corpse, and nineteen gold button-ingots (*jin bing*).[22] Bronze *wuzhu* coins were also unearthed. Similar ceramic vessels (cat. nos. 26, 27), animal figures (cat. nos. 15, 53), jade *bi* discs (cat. nos. 20, 21), lacquer items (cat. nos. 35, 36), and coins (cat. nos. 60–63) have been found in numerous other Han royal and common tombs.

Like royal burials, the tombs for officials and commoners were regulated by sumptuary codes that delimited their size, scale, and furnishings. At the Wu family cemetery three stone tombs have been discovered. Tombs 1 and 2 had been plundered before they were excavated in 1981, and a third tomb was only discovered in 2002 (see Liu's "Recarving the Past," figs. 1, 9, 21–23, 26). The fragmentary burial artifacts recovered from Tomb 1 included ceramic pieces of a basin, tray, *hu* jar, dishes, eared

Fig. 2 *Tomb 1 at Mount Shuangru Shan, Changqing County, Shandong*. Western Han dynasty. View from south overlooking coffin chamber and ramp. Photo by author, 2004.

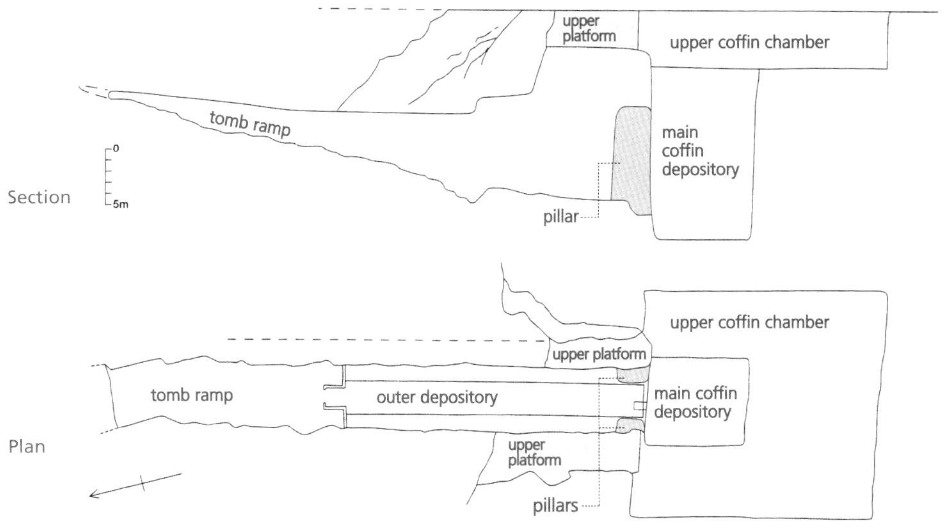

cups (cf. cat. nos. 32–35), and a model of a farm compound similar to the example in this exhibition (cat. no. 15). Also remaining was a single bronze *wuzhu* coin.[23]

Tomb 1 at Shuangru Shan also included life-size one-, two-, and four-horse chariots along with a half-size chariot; these were found in a front-to-back row in the outer depository (*waizang guo*).[24] In a row next to the chariots, but not attached to them, were buried seven horses as well as two deer. A second miniature chariot was found in the north side compartment of the main coffin depository (*zhengzang guo*). Among them, the four royal tombs at Jiulong Shan held some twelve chariots and fifty horses along with several miniature chariot models. At both sites some of the miniature chariots may have been equivalents of the *mingqi* hearse discussed above in the *Zhouli* passage about the duties of the Tomb Officer. In nonroyal tombs, where both size and propriety precluded life-size chariots, miniature replicas and carved or painted images of chariots may have sufficed for the occupant's afterlife needs. It has been posited that some of the chariot processions in the Wu rubbings depict official vehicles occupied by the deceased in life, but they are just as likely to represent vehicles for the afterlife.

In Han burials it is often difficult to distinguish objects made for the living from those made for the dead. Certain vessels, such as *ding* tripods (cat. no. 23) and *hu* jars (cat. nos. 24–27), may have been sacrificial vessels (*jiqi*) or storage articles originally made for the living and then placed in the tomb. They also could have been made specifically for burial. Many jade, wood, and metal items, such as belt hooks, weapons, musical instruments, books, and lamps (cat. nos. 2, 42) were used in daily life and are also commonly found in tombs. Some jade artifacts, such as burial masks, body-orifice plugs, and hand grips, were definitely made for burial. Jade and glass *bi* discs (cat. nos. 20–22) could have been made to serve the living as ritual symbols of power, as evidenced in two stories illustrated in the Wu rubbings. In illustrations of the loyal assassin Jing Ke's attempt to kill the king of Qin (the future First Emperor of the Qin dynasty [*Qin Shihuangdi*]), the king is shown grasping a *bi* disc (cat. nos. 1.6, 1.23, 1.35). In the story of the wise minister Lin Xiangru negotiating with the king of Qin, Lin is shown offering a precious jade *bi* disc in return for fifteen cities (cat. no. 1.36). Many *bi* discs, however, were made specifically for burial. In Tomb 1 at Shuangru Shan the corpse was found with large jade discs on its front and under its back, with smaller discs on its sides. Many other objects commonly recovered from tombs, such as mirrors (cat. nos. 38–41) and money (cat. nos. 60–63), might equally have been made for the living or for burial.[25] Among the Wu cemetery carvings, the Left Group Stone 10 (no longer extant) was described as having *wuzhu* coin designs. Coin designs are also found on various burial artifacts, including money boxes (cat. no. 58) and so-called money trees (cat. no. 59). These representations of coins may have functioned as surrogate money in the same way as imitation ceramic coins and ingots buried in tombs. There also are indications that objects originally made for daily use and rituals could be converted to burial purposes.

Objects included in burials are further differentiated according to source: burial gifts (*jiuqi*) from mourning guests, or objects belonging to

Fig. 3 *Tomb 1 at Mount Shuangru Shan, Changqing County, Shandong*. Western Han dynasty. Plan and section drawings.

the deceased. Moreover, in royal burials many of the burial items, including clothes, jade suits, and lacquer coffins, were made by the Artisans of the Eastern Garden (*Dong yuan jiang*), a department within the Superintendency of the Lesser Treasury (*Shaofu*), and were known as funerary, or hidden, equipment (*biqi*).[26] In the context of royal funeral equipage, terms such as *biqi* and *mingqi* may have distinguished between burial items supplied by different official departments.

Determining whether items placed in tombs were made originally for the living or for the dead is not only a problem for modern scholars. What to put in tombs was already controversial during the Han dynasty, as reflected in exegetical commentary to the three Confucian canons on rites and other ritual texts.[27] In the "Tan Gong" chapters of the *Liji* it is recorded that "at the burial of his wife, Duke Xiang of Song placed [in the grave] a hundred jars of vinegar and pickles. Zengzi exclaimed, 'They are called *mingqi*, and yet he filled them!'"[28] In this passage Zengzi, a disciple of Confucius (551–479 BCE), was remarking on the impropriety of filling *mingqi* with real food, that is, treating them as if they were vessels made for ordinary or daily use by the living.[29] In his commentary on this passage, Zheng Xuan of the Han dynasty noted that although the jars were for the dead and were called *mingqi*, Duke Xiang, by filling them with food, was using them just like sacrificial vessels (*jiqi*) for the living, and that this "confuses objects for the dead (*guiqi*) with objects for living people (*renqi*)."[30] Intimated in this passage was a key distinction between functional objects made for the living and their nonfunctional counterparts intended only for the afterlife—that is, respectively, between artifacts of ordinary use and those of extraordinary uselessness (from which an afterlife use emerges).[31]

The characteristics of *mingqi* are discussed in the "Tan Gong" chapters of the *Liji*, where Confucius is quoted as saying:

> In dealing with the dead, if we treat them as if they were entirely dead, that would show a want of affection, and should not be done; or if we treat them as if they were entirely alive, that would show a want of wisdom, and should not be done. On this account bamboo artifacts (used in connection with the burial of the dead) are not fit for actual use; those of earthenware cannot be used to wash in; those of wood are incapable of being carved; the lutes and harps are strung, but not evenly; the reed pipes are complete, but not in tune; the bells and musical stones are there, but they have not stands. They are called brilliant artifacts (*mingqi*); that is, [the dead] are thus treated as if they were spirit brilliances (*shenming*).[32]

According to this passage the spirit brilliance of the deceased is said to occupy a medial zone of an afterlife, between the entirely dead and the entirely living.[33] This parallels the belief that the soul of the departed lingers but gradually diminishes over time, which is "attested to by the ancient saying that 'the spirit of [one] newly dead is large and that of [one long dead] is small' (*xin gui da gu gui xiao*)."[34] In order to provide proper treatment and nourishment for spirit brilliances in this afterlife realm, therefore, *mingqi* are conceived as simulacra, extraordinary artifacts having the appearance and form of articles made for the living, but devoid of their use and function.[35] If this is the distinction between objects for the dead (*guiqi*) and objects for living people (*renqi*), then how are the life-size chariots, food-containing vessels, and real coins found in Han tombs to be accounted for? Is it possible that objects that were used during life could be simply converted for burial use by taking away their function? Could unhitched chariots or missing reins and harnesses negate a vehicle's ordinary use? Musical instruments could be untuned, or bells and stone chimes could be buried without stands to suspend them or hammers to play them. Simulacra could be made in miniature or in nonfunctional materials, imitating the forms of daily objects or activities but entirely inoperative. Wine vessels could be made of permeable earthenware that would leak, while miniature replicas of architecture (cat. nos. 13–16), wells (cat. nos. 17, 18), stoves (cat. no. 19), chariots and horses (cat. nos. 50, 51), domestic animals and birds (cat. nos. 53, 55–57), and human figures of attendants (cat. no. 5), entertainers (cat. no. 6), soldiers (cat. no. 2), and equestrians (cat. no. 52) all have "the appearance but not the substance or proper qualities"[36] of a living person or a mundane thing.

If *mingqi* are said to imitate the living and objects made for the living, but without their lively capabilities, was this consciously analogous to the notion that in China underground architecture for the dead was modeled after aboveground architecture for the living? The idea that mortuary architecture imitates that of the living had currency from as early as "A Discussion of Rites" ("Lilun") in the *Writings of Xunzi*, attributed to Xun Qing (late fourth–third century BCE), a man who served in office and lived in the Lanling region in southern Shandong.

> The grave and grave mound in form imitate a house; the inner and outer coffin in form imitate the sideboards, top, and front and back boards of a carriage; the coffin covers and decorations and the cover of the funeral carriage in form imitate the curtains and hangings of a door or a room; the wooden lining and framework of the grave pit in form imitate railings and roof. The funeral rites have no other purpose than this: to make clear the principle of life and death, to send the dead man away with grief and reverence, and to lay him at last in the ground.[37]

In this imitative relationship, the architecture for the dead is often presented as diametrically opposite to the architecture for the living.[38] The relationship should now be reevaluated in terms of the concept of *mingqi*. Funerary structures are not architecture for the entirely dead. Instead, they are architecture for spirit brilliances in the afterlife realm between the entirely living and the entirely dead. Tombs imitate the functional divisions of the palace, with front chamber and rear chambers, storage areas, lavatories, and horse and chariot stables; yet the living function and mundane use of the chambers are negated. The front doors of a tomb once closed do not open, the lavatories cannot be used, the ceilings of tomb chambers are often too low for a person to stand, and the stored items are often *mingqi* artifacts that cannot be used. Beyond this relationship, tomb architecture and *mingqi* artifacts share other similarities that need further scrutiny. Some tombs have brick wall tiles decorated with painted, stamped, or relief designs of pictorial figures and geometric patterns (cat. nos. 7–9). The same decorative techniques are used on ceramic *mingqi* vessels. Likewise, in stone tombs and funerary structures such as the Wu cemetery carvings, the walls are often decorated with pictorial carvings in fine incised lines, intaglio, relief, or openwork, sometimes enhanced with paint or other decorative techniques (cat. nos. 10–12). All of these techniques are comparably utilized in ceramic, bronze, jade, stone, and lacquer *mingqi* artifacts buried in tombs (cat. nos. 24 [incised lines]; 28, 29, 45 [relief carving]; 30 [openwork]; 26, 39 [painted]).

Beyond similarities in artistic techniques, many of the subjects and themes depicted in the Wu cemetery pictorial stone carvings (*huaxiang shi*) and in other Han pictorial tombs are also found in the decoration of *mingqi* placed in tombs. Shared images include horses and equestrians (cat. nos. 50–52), buildings (cat. nos. 13–16), food preparation and banqueting (cat. nos. 19, 32–35), animals (cat. nos. 47–49, 53–57), supernatural beasts (cat. nos. 18, 24, 30, 38), fabulous landscapes and cloudscapes (cat. nos. 26–29, 42–45), and fantastic concatenations (cat. no. 59). Additionally, the identification of tomb chambers by function—as reception halls, kitchens, stables, inner chambers, and other rooms—often depended on the types of *mingqi* artifacts placed inside.[39] And conversely, in some cases the placement of *mingqi* may have been determined by the location of pictorial images decorating the tomb walls. This allowed tomb chambers to simulate palace chambers, while negating the living functions of the latter in order properly to accommodate and serve spirit brilliances in the afterlife.

What then are the proper qualities of an afterlife person or thing? In Zheng Xuan's commentary to the aforementioned "Tan Gong" passage, he notes: "Those that are spirit brilliances (*shenming*) cannot be understood by living people, likewise their artifacts are also thus."[40] Examining the meaning of the individual characters *shen* and *ming* may provide some understanding. Passages that include the character *shen* are some of the most enigmatic in the *Book of Change* (*Yijing*). *Shen* can be translated as "numen" or "numinous," "divinities" or "divine," "spirits" or "spiritual." On this term, Willard Peterson notes: "The 'Commentary on the Attached Verbalizations' seeks to establish that the *Book of Change*, as a book and as a technique, effectively crosses the boundary of the square (which symbolically represents all-under-heaven, human society, the domain of sages, the man-made, what is known and knowable) into the realm of heaven-and-earth, the ten-thousand things, what is not man-made, what is not directly and never perfectly known, including what is numinous [*shen*]."[41] As something "not directly and never perfectly known," *shen* is described as a numinosity found in all things in heaven-and-earth, in life and afterlife.[42] The reason that the concept of brilliant artifacts has never been clearly defined may stem from this fundamental unknowability of spirit brilliances.

We should also examine the term *ming*, which can be translated as "brilliant," "bright," or "intelligent."[43] *Ming* is often associated with objects used in funerals and sacrifices. For example, vestments worn when performing sacrifices are called brilliant clothes (*mingyi*), and water used in sacrifices is called brilliant water (*mingshui*).[44] Why this term is so closely tied to burial and sacrificial ceremonies, however, is a matter of speculation. Possibly *ming* denotes (or connotes) a brilliance that makes evident the moral virtues (*mingde*) of a family through the body of a person, or a state through the body of the ruler. Burial objects and funerary architecture frequently include scenes of exemplary conduct and correct moral behavior, which may be meant not only as exhortations but also as manifestions of the virtues of the deceased, as well as of his ancestors and descendants. One aspect of brilliant artifacts, then, may be the embodiment of the virtue of a person's life and that of his family line. This aspect is the focus of a passage in the *Zuozhuan* (*Zuo traditions*) commentary to the *Chunqiu* (*Spring and autumn annals*), which chronicles events affecting the state of Lu (in present-day Shandong), the home state of Confucius. The passage in question concerns the significance of the size-to-weight ratio of tripod (*ding*) vessels.

> Long ago, when the Xia dynasty was still possessed of virtue, the distant regions sent pictures of various objects and tribute of metal was submitted from the governors of the nine provinces. This was used to cast tripods with various objects depicted on them .... Thus the superior and the inferior were brought into harmony and they enjoyed the providence of heaven .... When virtue is bright and comely, then the tripods, though small, are heavy. But when there is depravity and disorder, then although they are large, they are light.
>
> The bright virtue (*mingde*) bestowed by heaven has its limit and end ....[45]

In a royal context the Nine Tripods (*jiuding*) embody the virtues of the sovereign and the harmony of the state.[46] Similarly, it was popularly believed that if all was in harmony, tripods (cat. no. 23) could cook without fire, and could give forth food even if none had been put into them. This belief is found as early as the *Writings of Mozi* (*Mozi*) by Mo Di, who lived in the latter half of the fifth century BCE and is said by some to have been a native of the state of Lu in Shandong.[47] This belief continued into the Han dynasty, and was repeated in the *Doctrines Evaluated* (*Lunheng*) by Wang Chong (27–?97 CE).[48]

Besides tripods, other objects buried in tombs were probably credited with a similar brilliance that attested the exemplary virtues and moral rectitude of the deceased.[49] Like tripods, when all was in harmony, replicas of stoves cooked (cat. no. 19), replicas of wells supplied water (cat. nos. 17, 18), musical instruments played, storage vessels were always full (cat. nos. 24–27), and gaming sets brought success and winnings (cat. no. 37). Although the living function and mundane use of brilliant artifacts are negated, it is in their extraordinary uselessness that an afterlife use emerges.[50] The brilliance inherent in buried objects, however, apparently could only shine during conditions of harmonious balance, and by the Han dynasty, people may have seen this balance embodied in the character meaning brilliance (*ming*), which is composed of the characters for sun (*ri*) and moon (*yue*). This notion of cosmic equilibrium may have derived from the early conception of the human soul as *po*, meaning "lunar brightness." By the Han dynasty the soul was popularly conceived as dual—the *po* soul corresponding to the female, lunar *yin* element, and the *hun* soul to the male, solar *yang* element. As discussed by Ying-shih Yü and Mu-chou Poo, the idea of a *hun* soul is said to have derived from the earlier idea of the *po* soul.[51]

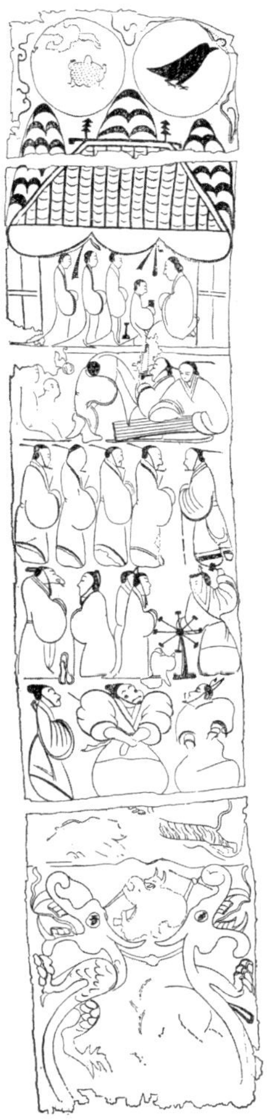

Fig. 4 *Mortuary banner with designs of the sun and moon.* Western Han dynasty. Unearthed from Tomb 9 at Jinque Shan, Linyi County, Shandong. Silk with pigments; h. 200 cm, w. 42 cm. Shandong Provincial Museum collection. Line drawing from *Wenwu* 1977.11, front inside cover.

It may be the harmony of spirit brilliances between cosmic *yang* and *yin* forces, respectively of the sun and moon, that is depicted in the pictorial stone carvings adorning funerary architecture of the Han dynasty (fig. 1).[52] The sun and moon are also paired on mortuary shrouds or mantles (*hu* or *feiyi*) that were draped over a newly dead body and then over the interred coffin (fig. 4).[53] Auspicious incantations pairing the sun and moon were also cast on Han-dynasty bronze mirrors (see cat. no. 41). This idea of harmonious balance may also underlie the royal ritual structure known as the Brilliant Hall (*mingtang*).[54]

It is the attainment of harmony through rites that is discussed in the *Writings of Xunzi*:

> Through rites heaven and earth join in harmony, the sun and moon are brilliant (*ri yue yi ming*), the four seasons proceed in order, the stars and constellations march, the rivers flow, and all things flourish . . . .[55]

This harmonious balance between the sun and moon, however, is upset if the burial artifacts are too lifelike. As discussed earlier, *mingqi* are conceived as items made for the afterlife, which lies between the realms of the entirely dead and entirely living. In order to maintain a balance, they are simulacra, having the appearance but not the capabilities of articles made for the living. Lifelike appearance connected these simulacra—vehicles, vessels, architectural replicas, musical instruments, and implements—to the realm of the living. From the beginning, however, human burial figures (cat. nos. 2–6) seem to have been problematic. Confucius worried that the burial of lifelike figures would lead eventually to a revival of human sacrifices as part of funeral rites. Recorded in the "Tan Gong" chapters of the *Liji*:

> Confucius said, "He who made the vessels which are so (only) in imagination, knew the principles underlying the mourning rites. They were complete (to all appearance), and yet could not be used. Alas! If for the dead they had used the vessels of the living, would there not have been a danger of this leading to the interment of living with the dead?"

It continues:

> They were called "vessels in imagination," (the dead) being thus treated as spirit brilliances. From of old there were the carriages of clay [*tuche*] and the figures of straw [*chuling*] . . . . Confucius said that the making of straw figures was good, and the making of the (wooden) automaton [*yongzhe*] was not benevolent. Was there not a danger of its leading to the use of (living) men?[56]

These "vessels in imagination," as translated by James Legge, are what I have termed "brilliant artifacts" (*mingqi*). Confucius approved of the practice of burying clay or painted carriage replicas (*tuche*) that did not function, and straw effigies (*chuling*) of human figures that were not realistic in appearance. In Zheng Xuan's commentary to the latter passage, he notes that straw was used to make effigies of people and horses. As for human burial figures (*yong* or *ou*), he notes that because they have faces and some are even mechanized, allowing them to move or jump (*yong* with a foot radical [*zu*]; hence "automaton"), they are too lifelike. For Confucius, burying lifelike human figures or functional objects was too dangerously reminiscent of the practice of burying the quick with the dead (*xun*).

It is commonly assumed that during Confucius' lifetime human burial figures were made of wood (cat. no. 3), but by the Eastern Zhou period and Han dynasty they were also being made of ceramic (cat. nos. 4–6). Crude painted earthenware human figures about ten centimeters in height were found in a tomb complex near Linzi in northern Shandong, dated to the fifth century BCE, roughly contemporary with Confucius and not far from where he lived.[57] The Linzi burial complex included several accompanying burials and skeletons of twenty-six human victims, some of whom may have been buried alive. The practice of live burials started as early as Neolithic times and was not uncommon during the Shang dynasty, but was growing less popular by the late Eastern Zhou period. Still, the practice endured into the time of Confucius, even as straw, wood, metal, and ceramic figures were coming into use—sometimes in combination with human victims and sometimes as substitutes—to serve the deceased soul in the afterlife.[58]

Prohibited in the Han dynasty, the practice of burying human victims became rare but not unknown.[59] Despite warnings by Confucius and his followers, however, the practice of burying lifelike human figures of wood and ceramic increased in popularity, as attested by the life-size terra-cotta army buried at the mausoleum of the First Emperor of the Qin dynasty, or the smaller figures found at Han-dynasty royal tomb sites (cat. no. 4), including those excavated in late 2002 at Weishan in Shandong.[60] Besides lifelike human figures, live horses, deer, and other animals continued to be buried alive or after ritual slaughter in Han tombs, as seen at Tomb 1 at Shuangru Shan.

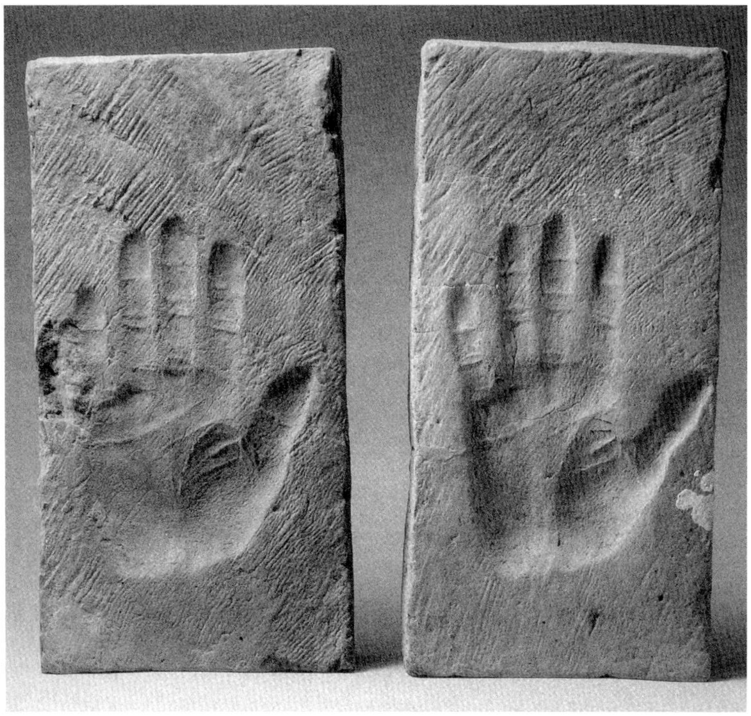

Fig. 5 *Hand-print tiles*. Late Han dynasty or post-Han, third century. Tomb excavated in 1988 at Jinque Shan near Linyi, Shandong. Ceramic; h. 33.5 cm, w. 16 cm, d. 6 cm. Linyi City Museum collection. From *Chūgokugo sennin no furusato: Santōshō bunbutsuten* (Osaka: Ōsaka furitsu yayoi bunka hakubutsukan, 1996), no. 72.

Finally, what are we to make of the prints of a left hand impressed into wall tiles found in a third-century tomb, late Han or post-Han, excavated in 1988 at Jinque Shan, a mountain near Linyi, Shandong (fig. 5)? The hand-print tiles, along with other tiles from this tomb bearing the designs of the Four Directional Spirits (*si shen*), all have the family name Zhang stamped in relief on their sides.[61] Who was this Zhang? Are the handprints his? Was he the workman responsible for building the tomb, as some speculate, or the tomb occupant? In either case, the imprint of an actual person was included in the tomb. Confucius might have considered this dangerously reminiscent of human sacrifice. But from a different perspective, the handprints can be considered the ultimate brilliant artifact. They are negative embodiments of a real person. They identify the individual and can be understood to make brilliant his or her exemplary virtues and moral rectitude.

Acknowledgments

This essay is written in conjunction with an essay included in Susan L. Beningson, Cary Y. Liu, et al., *Providing for the Afterlife: Brilliant Artifacts from Shandong* (New York: China Institute Gallery, 2005). I am indebted to Lu Wensheng, director of the Shandong Provincial Museum, for his assistance in visiting excavation sites and viewing objects. I want to thank Anthony Barbieri-Low, Annette Juliano, and Eugene Wang for their careful reading of early drafts of this manuscript. I am especially grateful to Eileen Hsu, who has made invaluable contributions to the research of this essay, and to Michael Loewe for calling my attention to an important source.

Notes

1. Carl Hentze, *Chinese Tomb Figures: A Study in the Beliefs and Folklore of Ancient China* (London: Edward Goldston, 1928); Robert Thorp, "Mortuary Art and Architecture of Early Imperial China" (PhD diss., University of Kansas, 1979); Eng-Lee Seok Chee, "Mingqi and Other Tomb Furnishings as Reflections of Han Culture and Society," in *Spirit of Han* (Singapore: Southeast Asian Ceramic Society, 1991), pp. 30–40.

2. W. Perceval Yetts, "Foreword," in Hentze, *Chinese Tomb Figures*, p. vii.

3. Luo Zhenyu, *Gu mingqi tulu* (*Illustrated catalogue of ancient* mingqi) (Shangyu: Luo shi, 1916).

4. Zheng Dekun and Shen Weijun, *Zhongguo mingqi* (*Chinese* mingqi) (Beijing: Harvard–Yenching Institute, 1933).

5. A brief history of the formation of his collection is included in the preface of Luo Zhenyu, *Gu mingqi tulu*. For an English summary, see Yetts, "Foreword," p. vii.

6. Zheng Dekun and Shen Weijun, *Zhongguo mingqi*, pp. 11–15. On Shang, see Thorp, "Mortuary Art and Architecture," p. 30. For the earliest *mingqi* human figure, see Cao Zhezhi, *Zhongguo gudai yong* (*Ancient burial figures of China*) (Shanghai: Shanghai wenhua chubanshe, 1996), pp. 2–3. The traditional belief that *mingqi* antedated the Zhou dynasty derives from a passage in the *Liji* (*Rites records*) that says *mingqi* were used to accompany the dead during the Xia dynasty, sacrificial artifacts (*jiqi*) were used during the Shang dynasty, and both were used during the Zhou dynasty. See *Liji ji jie* (*"Rites records" and collected explications*), comp. Sun Xidan (Beijing: Zhonghua shuju, 1989), p. 219. Solely on the basis of this passage, Rao Zongyi speculates that *mingqi* "originated before the Yin–Shang period"; see Jao Tsung-i (Rao Zongyi), *Chinese Tomb Pottery Figures* (Hong Kong: Hong Kong University Press, 1953), pp. 1, 5.

7. *Zhouli zhushu* (*"Rites of Zhou" and annotations*), *Shisan jing zhushu* edition (Beijing: Zhonghua shuju, 1980), p. 686. The term *xiongqi* is again equated to *mingqi* by Zheng Xuan in *Liji ji jie*, p. 115. Modern scholars sometimes translate *xiongqi* as "inauspicious vessels" (e.g., Thorp, "Mortuary Art and Architecture," p. 57). This is misleading, because it implies an opposition to "auspicious vessels" (*jiqi*), which to my knowledge is not a term used in a funerary context. More likely it is analogous to *xiongfu* mortuary dress, in contrast to *jifu* for daily dress for the living. In certain contexts *xiongqi* can also be translated as "fearsome articles," referring to military weapons.

8. *Zhouli zhushu*, p. 786.

9. Also see *Zhongwen da cidian* (*Grand dictionary of Chinese*), ed. Zhongwen da cidian bianzuan weiyuanhui (Taipei: Zhongguo wenhua daxue, 1973), nos. 39917.8, 48485.13.

10. In Denis Twitchett and Michael Loewe, eds., *The Ch'in and Han Empires, 221 B.C.–A.D. 220*, vol. 1 of *Cambridge History of China* (Cambridge: Cambridge University Press, 1986), p. 28, the *shi* (translated as "gentlemen") are described as being from "the lower fringe of the aristocracy...men of good birth without titles of nobility, who served as warriors, officials, and supervisors in the state governments and noble households, or who lived on the land..." Translated as "servicemen" in Charles O. Hucker, *A Dictionary of Official Titles in Imperial China* (Stanford: Stanford University Press, 1985), no. 5200.

11. See *Yili zhushu* (*"Ceremonials" and annotations*), *Shisan jing zhushu* edition (Beijing: Zhonghua shuju, 1980), pp. 1148, 1149.

12. For *renqi*, *shengqi*, and *guiqi*, see Zheng Xuan's commentary in *Yili zhushu*, pp. 1148–49. For *shengqi*, also see *Xunzi*, *Yingyin Wenyuange Siku quanshu* edition (Taipei: Taiwan shangwu yinshuguan, 1983–1986), *juan* 13, pp. 15b–16b.

13. For rare instances when burial objects (*xiongqi*) along with the burial register and funeral clothes were permitted inside the palace gates after being properly announced, see *Liji ji jie*, p. 115; and James Legge, *The Li Ki*, in *The Sacred Books of the East*, ed. F. Max Müller, vol. 28 (Oxford: Clarendon Press, 1885), p. 103.

14. *Yili zhushu*, p. 1149. Translation of *dafu* as "Counselor" follows Michael Loewe, *A Biographical Dictionary of the Qin, Former Han and Xin Periods* (*221 B.C.–A.D. 24*) (Leiden: E. J. Brill, 2000), pp. 757, 759.

15. For photos of Tomb 1, see the author's essay in Beningson and Liu, *Providing for*

the Afterlife. Although the tumulus and upper layers of this tomb were removed by mining and blasting before excavation work started, the untouched tomb interior provides valuable information about royal burial practices. See Shandong daxue kaogu xi, Shandong Sheng wenwu ju, and Changqing wenwu ju, "Shandong Changqing Xian Shuangru Shan yihao mu fajue jianbao" ("Brief excavation report on Tomb 1 at Shuangru Shan, Changqing County, Shandong") [hereafter, "Jianbao"], *Kaogu* 1997.3, pp. 1–9, 26; Ren Xianghong, "Shuangru Shan yihao mu muzhu kaolue" ("Research concerning the occupant of Tomb 1 at Shuangru Shan"), *Kaogu* 1997.3, pp. 10–15; Liu Shanyi, "Shuangru Shan Xihan Jibei wangling" ("Western Han Jibei Kingdom royal mausoleum at Shuangru Shan") in *Tokubetsuten Kandai "Ōsha" no kagayaki: Chūgoku Santōshō Sōnyūzan seihoku ōryō shutsudo bunbutsu* (Kyoto: Kyōto Fu Kyōto bunka hakubutsukan, Yamaguchi Ken Hagi bijutsukan, and Urakami kinenkan, 2001), pp. 18–23 (Japanese), 123–25 (Chinese); Ma Qianwei and Li Yong, "Changqing Jibei wang ling fajue ji" ("Excavation record of the Jibei Kingdom royal mausoleum"), in *Ji'nan zhongda kaogu fajue jishi* (Ji'nan: Huanghe chubanshe, 2003), pp. 170–80; Ren Xianghong, "Zao shi liangda de Han wang ling—Changqing Shuangru Shan Xihan Jibei wang ling" ("Largest rock-cut Han royal tomb—the Western Han Jibei royal tomb at Shuangru Shan, Changqing, Shandong"), in *Shandong zhongda kaogu xin faxian 1990–2003*, ed. Xie Zhixiu (Beijing: Shandong wenhua yinxiang chubanshe, 2003), pp. 113–31.

16. These royal tombs are believed to belong to kings of the Lu Kingdom (*Lu guo*). See Shandong Sheng bowuguan, "Qufu Jiulong Shan Han mu fajue jianbao" ("Brief excavation report on the Han tomb at Jiulong Shan, Qufu"), *Wenwu* 1972.5, pp. 39–44, 54.

17. *Hanshu* (*History of Western Han*), comp. Ban Gu (Beijing: Zhonghua shuju, 1962), *juan* 44, p. 2157.

18. On jade burial suits, see Michael Loewe, "State Funerals of the Han Empire," *Bulletin of the Museum of Far Eastern Antiquities*, vol. 71 (1999), pp. 14–34.

19. The rectangular panels of Tomb 1 at Shuangru Shan are described as niches (*kan*) in the 1997 excavation report and remain unexplained; see "Jianbao," p. 3. Apparently, the borders of each panel were chiseled first, and then the inner zone was removed to a depth of about 2 cm. These carved panels are only found in the lower level of the tomb, on the walls and floor of the ramp and coffin chamber. The walls of the upper platform level of the tomb are more roughly hewn, and no comparable panels are evident. This differentiation in carving techniques for the upper and lower sections of the tomb raises the possibility that the rectangular panels may have had some meaning. Perhaps different stone-carving techniques were stipulated for different parts of rock-cut tombs.

20. See Ren Xianghong, "Shuangru Shan yihao mu," pp. 14–15; and Liu Shanyi, "Shuangru Shan Xihan Jibei wangling," pp. 124–25.

21. "Jianbao," p. 7; and Shandong Sheng bowuguan, "Qufu Jiulong Shan," p. 40.

22. Large button-ingots were worth 10,000 cash in the Han dynasty; see Ren Xianghong, "Shuangru Shan yihao mu," p. 12.

23. Jiang Yingju and Wu Wenqi, *Handai Wushi muqun shike yanjiu* (*Studies on the Han-dynasty stone carvings at the Wu family cemetery*) (Ji'nan: Shandong meishu chubanshe, 1995), pp. 122–24.

24. The chariot remains have survived in a remarkable state of preservation, which has allowed their reconstruction. On the modern reconstruction of one chariot, see Cui Dayong, "Shuangru Shan yihao Han mu yihao mache de fuyuan yu yanjiu" ("Study and restoration of Chariot 1 in Han-dynasty Tomb 1 at Shuangru Shan"), *Kaogu* 1997.3, pp. 16–26. On the term "outer depository" (*waizang guo*), see Loewe, "State Funerals," pp. 44–45.

25. According to Anthony Barbieri-Low's "Coins and Coin Molds" in this catalogue, thousands of coins might be placed in tombs, but sometimes clay imitation coins were substituted. In some instances actual coins were embedded inside miniature roof-tile caps on ceramic architectural constructions made for burial. An example is a 1st–2d century, three-story tower model illustrated in *Kaikodo Journal*, vol. 9 (1998), cat. no. 48. In addition, coin designs were sometimes used as decoration on tomb carvings and bricks; see Linyi Shi bowuguan, "Shandong Linyi Jinque Shan huaxiang zhuan mu" ("Pictorial brick tomb at Jinque Shan, Linyi County, Shandong"), *Wenwu* 1995.6, p. 76, fig. 12.3.

26. See Loewe, "State Funerals," pp. 45–46, 47. On the Artisans of the Eastern Garden, see Anthony Barbieri-Low, "The Organization of Imperial Workshops during the Han Dynasty" (PhD diss., Princeton University, 2001), pp. 71–73.

27. On the *Yili* (*Ceremonials*), *Liji* (*Rites records*), and *Zhouli* (*Rites of Zhou*), see Michael Nylan, *The Five "Confucian" Classics* (New Haven: Yale University Press, 2001), pp. 168–201; Michael Loewe, ed., *Early Chinese Texts: A Bibliographical Guide* (Berkeley: Society for the Study of Early China and Institute of East Asian Studies, University of California, Berkeley, 1993), pp. 24–32, 234–43, 293–97.

28. *Liji ji jie*, p. 225. Translation modified from Legge, *Li Ki*, p. 154. Legge actually translates *mingqi* as "vessels to the eye of fancy."

29. This passage expressing Zengzi's concern about impropriety was appropriated in the "Miscellaneous Dissatisfactions" ("San buzu") section of the *Salt and Iron Debates* (*Yan tie lun*) by Huan Kuan (1st century BCE), to serve as an admonition against lavish burial furnishings and other wasteful expenditures. See *Yan tie lun jiaozhu* (*"Yan tie lun" with critical annotations*), annot. Wang Liqi (Tianjin: Tianjin guji chubanshe, 1983), p. 355.

30. Subcommentaries to the *Liji* by Kong Yingda and Jia Gongyan of the Tang dynasty tried to explain away this confusion by citing the *Yili*'s regulation (discussed above) that *mingqi* for the dead and sacrificial vessels for the living are both allowed in burials for those above the Counselor rank. They note that the tomb for a duke's wife, therefore, would have contained both. Kong and Jia are also of the opinion that because only *mingqi* vessels were allowed for tombs of gentlemen (*shi*) and those of lower rank, the vessels had to serve double duty and needed to be used, i.e., filled, during funerary ceremonies. See *Liji ji jie*, p. 225; *Yili zhushu*, p. 1149.

31. On the concept of uselessness in the arts of China, see Wai-yee Li, "The Collector, the Connoisseur, and Late-Ming Sensibility," *T'oung Pao*, no. 81 (1995), pp. 269–302; Cary Y. Liu, "*Admonitions Scroll* in the Context of Ming Aesthetics and Collecting: Material Artifact, Cultural Biography, and Cultural Imagining," in *Percival David Foundation Colloquies on Art & Archaeology in Asia*, no. 21 (2003), pp. 257–59.

32. *Liji ji jie*, p. 216. Translation modified from Legge, *Li Ki*, p. 148. Legge translates *mingqi* as "vessels to the eye of fancy" and *shenming* as "spiritual intelligences." My translation as "brilliant artifacts" and "spirit brilliances," respectively, is more in line with the French translation as *instruments brilliants* and *esprits brilliants* in Séraphin Couvreur, *Li Ki ou Mémoires sur les bienséances et les cérémonies*, 2 vols., 2d ed. (Ho Kien Fou: Imprimerie de la Mission Catholique, 1913), p. 164.

33. On early conceptions of the afterlife, see Ying-shih Yü, "'O Soul, Come Back!' A Study in the Changing Conceptions of the Soul and Afterlife in Pre-Buddhist China," *Harvard Journal of Asiatic Studies*, vol. 47, no. 2 (1987), pp. 363–95.

34. Yü, "O Soul, Come Back!" p. 380.

35. The ideas in this passage were appropriated in the *Discourses on Iron and Salt*. See n. 29.

36. *The New Shorter Oxford English Dictionary*, 2 vols. (Oxford: Clarendon Press, 1993), s.v. "simulacrum."

37. *Xunzi jinzhu jin yi* (*Modern annotation and explanation of "Xunzi"*), annot. Xiong Gongzhe, rev. ed. (Taipei: Taiwan shangwu yinshuguan, 1984), p. 396; Burton Watson, trans., *Basic Writings of Mo Tzu, Hsün Tzu, and Han Fei Tzu* (New York: Columbia University Press, 1963), p. 105. On the *Xunzi*, see Loewe, *Early Chinese Texts*, pp. 178–88.

38. See Thorp, "Mortuary Art and Architecture," pp. 52–53; Wu Zengde and Xiao Yuanda, "Jiu daxing Handai huaxiang shi mu de xingzhi lun 'Hanzhi'" ("On the 'Han system' tomb structure based on large-scale pictorial stone tombs"), *Zhongyuan wenwu* 1985.3, pp. 55–62. A modern, possibly 20th-century, elaboration asserts that underground architecture was built of imperishable stone and aboveground architecture was built of perishable wood. Before the Han, tomb chambers were predominantly built of wood, and this practice was still common in the Han. Moreover, the number of aboveground structures built of stone or masonry may have far outnumbered those built of wood.

39. Modern scholars have identified the function of chambers in tombs primarily based on the types of burial artifacts found within, and by comparison with the layout of a few Han tombs containing inscriptions naming various chambers. See Wu and Xiao, "Jiu daxing Handai huaxiang shi mu de xingzhi lun 'Hanzhi'," pp. 55–58.

40. *Liji ji jie*, p. 216.

41. Willard Peterson, "Making Connections: 'Commentary on the Attached Verbalizations' of the *Book of Change*," *Harvard Journal of Asiatic Studies*, vol. 42, no. 1 (1982), pp. 15–16.

42. Elsewhere I have discussed the concept of *shen* in the context of calligraphy as "embodied images" (*ti xiang*). See Cary Y. Liu, "Embodying Cosmic Patterns: Foundations of an Art of Calligraphy in China," *Oriental Art*, vol. 56, no. 5 (2000), pp. 2–9.

43. Henri Maspero, "Le mot *ming*," *Journal Asiatique*, vol. 223, no. 2 (1933), pp. 249–96. Maspero notes that while the character originally meant "brightness" or "light," it was later used also as a phonetic loan character (*jiajie*) meaning "sacred." The latter is the meaning associated with *mingqi*, which Maspero translates as *objets sacrés*: objects consecrated for the dead. See ibid., pp. 283–84. I want to thank Michael Loewe for bringing this article to my attention.

44. Wang Li et al., eds., *Wang Li gu hanyu zidian* (*Wang Li's dictionary of ancient Chinese*) (Beijing: Zhonghua shuju, 2000), s.v. "ming"; Henri Maspero, "Le mot *ming*," pp. 252–55, 283–84.

45. Translation slightly modified from *The Tso Chuan: Selections from China's Oldest Narrative History*, trans. Burton Watson (New York: Columbia University Press, 1989), p. 82. Also see translation by James Legge, *The Chinese Classics* (reprint, Taipei: Southern Materials Center, Inc., 1985), vol. 5, pp. 292–93. On the *Chunqiu* and *Zuozhuan*, see Nylan, *Five "Confucian" Classics*, pp. 253–306.

46. On the Nine Tripods or Vessels and their connection to the establishment of capital cities (*ding ding*), see Cary Y. Liu, "The Yüan Dynasty Capital, Ta-tu: Imperial Building Program and Bureaucracy," *T'oung Pao*, vol. 78 (1992), pp. 265–66.

47. *Mozi*, *Yingyin Wenyuange Siku quanshu* edition, "Gengzhu" sec., *juan* 11, p. 9b.

48. Wang Chong, *Lunheng suoyin* (*Concordance to the "Lunheng"*), ed. Zhang Xiangqing et al. (Beijing: Zhonghua shuju, 1994), "Ru zeng pian" sec., p. 1383. For an informed discussion of the symbolism and legends surrounding tripod vessels, see cat. no. 23.

49. This concept of *mingqi* may reflect changes in Han belief systems paralleling the changes in burial practices as discussed in Jessica Rawson, "The Eternal Palaces of the Western Han: A New View of the Universe," *Artibus Asiae*, vol. 59. no. 1/2 (1999), pp. 5–58. Rawson suggests there was a new preoccupation in the early Han to manifest "a microcosm of the universe within the confines of the tomb for the benefit of the tomb's occupant, as well as to assert the tomb occupant's claims to a prominent place in the afterlife hierarchy"; see ibid., p. 6.

50. See n. 31. The notion that usefulness can be found in what is useless finds parallels in the Daoist classic *Daodejing*: "We fire clay and make vessels;/ It is precisely where there's no substance, that we find the usefulness of clay pots./ We chisel out doors and windows;/ It is precisely in these empty spaces, that we find the usefulness of the room"; see Robert G. Henricks, trans., *Lao-tzu Te-tao Ching: A New Translation Based on the Recently Discovered Ma-wang-tui Texts* (New York: Ballantine Books, 1989), pp. 208–9.

51. See Yü, "O Soul, Come Back!" pp. 370, 372; Mu-chou Poo, *In Search of Personal Welfare: A View of Ancient Chinese Religion* (Albany: State University of New York Press, 1998), pp. 62–66.

52. Paired images of the sun and moon are also carved on a ceiling stone of Tomb 1 at Zhangzhuang in Shandong. See Shandong Sheng wenwu kaogu yanjiusuo, "Shandong Ji'nan Zhangzhuang Handai mu di fajue jianbao" ("Brief excavation report on the Han-dynasty tomb grounds at Zhangzhuang, Ji'nan, Shandong"), in *Shandong gaosugonglu kaogu baogao ji* (*1997*) (*Collected Shandong highway construction archaeological reports of 1997*), ed. Shandong Sheng wenwu kaogu yanjiusuo (Beijing: Kexue chubanshe, 2000), p. 309; p. 311, fig. 18. Another example dated to the early

Eastern Han was excavated in 1999 at Zaozhuang, Shandong, and is reproduced in *Zhongguo huaxiang shi quanji* (*Collected pictorial stones of China*), 8 vols. (Ji'nan: Shandong meishu chubanshe, 2000), vol. 2, no. 145.

53. A silk mortuary shroud with sun and moon designs was found on top of a coffin in Tomb 9, excavated in 1976 at Jinque Shan, Linyi County, Shandong. See Linyi Jinque Shan Han mu fajue zu, "Shandong Linyi Jinque Shan jiuhao Han mu fajue jianbao" ("Brief excavation report on the Han-dynasty Tomb 9 at Jinque Shan, Linyi County, Shandong"), *Wenwu* 1977.11, pp. 24–27; Liu Jiaji and Liu Bingsen, "Jinque Shan Xihan bo hua linmo hou gan" ("Further thoughts on and copy of the Western Han cloth painting at Jinque Shan"), *Wenwu* 1977.11, pp. 28–31, front inside cover, and pl. 1. Other well-known Han-dynasty mortuary banners (silk) with the sun and moon imagery were found in Tombs 1 and 3 at Mawangdui in Changsha, Hunan, and others (silk and hemp) in tombs at Mozuizi in Wuwei, Gansu. On burial mantles in the Han, see Yü, "O Soul, Come Back!" pp. 365–69 passim.

54. During the Western Han several ritual structures including a Brilliant Hall were built south of the city walls at the capital, Chang'an (present-day Xi'an). The designs of the ritual structures were meant to conform to Western Zhou models as recorded in ancient ritual texts such as the *Rites of Zhou*. On the archaeological remains of what is believed to be the hall and on its fanciful restoration, see Tang Jinyu, "Xi'an xi jiao Handai jianzhu yizhi fajue baogao" ("Excavation report on Han architectural relics in the western outskirts of Xi'an"), *Kaogu xuebao* 1959.2, pp. 45–55; Yang Hongxun, "Cong yizhi kan Xihan Chang'an mingtang (biyong) xingzhi" ("Configuration of the Mingtang [Biyong] as viewed from the remains at Western Han-dynasty Chang'an"), in Yang Hongxun, *Jianzhu kaogu xuelun wenji* (*Essays on archaeology and architecture in China*) (Beijing: Wenwu chubanshe, 1987), pp. 169–200; Nancy Shatzman Steinhardt, "The Han Ritual Hall," in *Chinese Traditional Architecture* (New York: China Institute in America, 1984), pp. 69–77. For general discussions on *mingtang*, see also William E. Soothill, *The Hall of Light* (London: Lutterworth Press, 1951); James Liu, "The Sung Emperors and the *ming-t'ang* or Hall of Enlightenment," in *Études Song in memoriam Étienne Balazs*, ed. Francoise Aubin, ser. 2, no. 1 (Paris: Mouton, 1973), pp. 45–58. On the early meaning of the term, also see Henri Maspero, "Le mot *ming*," pp. 268–69, 276–77, 284; Maspero, "Le Ming-Tang et la crise religieuse chinoise avant les Han," *Mélanges chinoises et bouddhiques*, vol. 9 (1948–1951), pp. 1–71.

55. *Xunzi jinzhu jin yi*, p. 380; translation modified from Watson, *Basic Writings of Mo Tzu*, p. 94. Conversely, an imbalance between sun and moon was deemed detrimental. For example, in Liu Xi (act. ca. 200), *Shiming* (*Explanation of names*), *Yingyin Wenyuange Siku quanshu* edition, *juan* 8, p. 7a, it is noted: "If the sun and moon are not complete [i.e., balanced] then the burial is called parched; that is to say, [if one] wants to rush, then the burial is without blessings."

56. *Liji ji jie*, p. 265. Translation slightly modified from Legge, *Li Ki*, p. 173.

57. Shandong Sheng bowuguan, "Linzi Langjiazhuang yihao Dongzhou xunren mu" ("Excavation of Eastern Zhou Tomb 1 with human sacrifices at Langjiazhuang, Shandong"), *Kaogu xuebao* 1977.1, p. 90, pl. 18.

58. On the belief in using figures and other burial articles to serve and provide for the deceased soul in the afterlife, see Poo, *In Search of Personal Welfare*, pp. 170–75 passim.

59. *Hanshu*, *juan* 53, pp. 2421–22. Wang Zhongshu, *Han Civilization* (New Haven: Yale University Press, 1982), p. 208.

60. Wang Shougong, "Ji'nan guowang de ling yi chu lingdi—Zhangqiu Weishan Handai muzang ji peizang keng" ("Another royal mausoleum at Ji'nan—Han-dynasty tomb and accompanying pit at Weishan, Zhangqiu County"), in *Shandong zhongda kaogu xin faxian 1990–2003*, pp. 151–58. Also see "Shandong Zhangqiu faxian bingma yong keng" ("Discovery of a pit with horse and warrior figures in Zhangqiu, Shandong"), *Shijie ribao*, December 4, 2002, sec. A, p. 9; John Noble Wilford, "Terra-Cotta Army from Early Han Dynasty is Unearthed," *New York Times*, February 18, 2003, sec. F, p. 3; Jarrett A. Lobell, "Warriors of Clay," *Archaeology*, vol. 56, no. 2 (2003), pp. 36–39.

61. Linyi Shi bowuguan, "Shandong Linyi Jinque Shan huaxiang zhuan mu," pp. 72–78. For these tiles, see Beningson and Liu, *Providing for the Afterlife*, cat. no. 51.

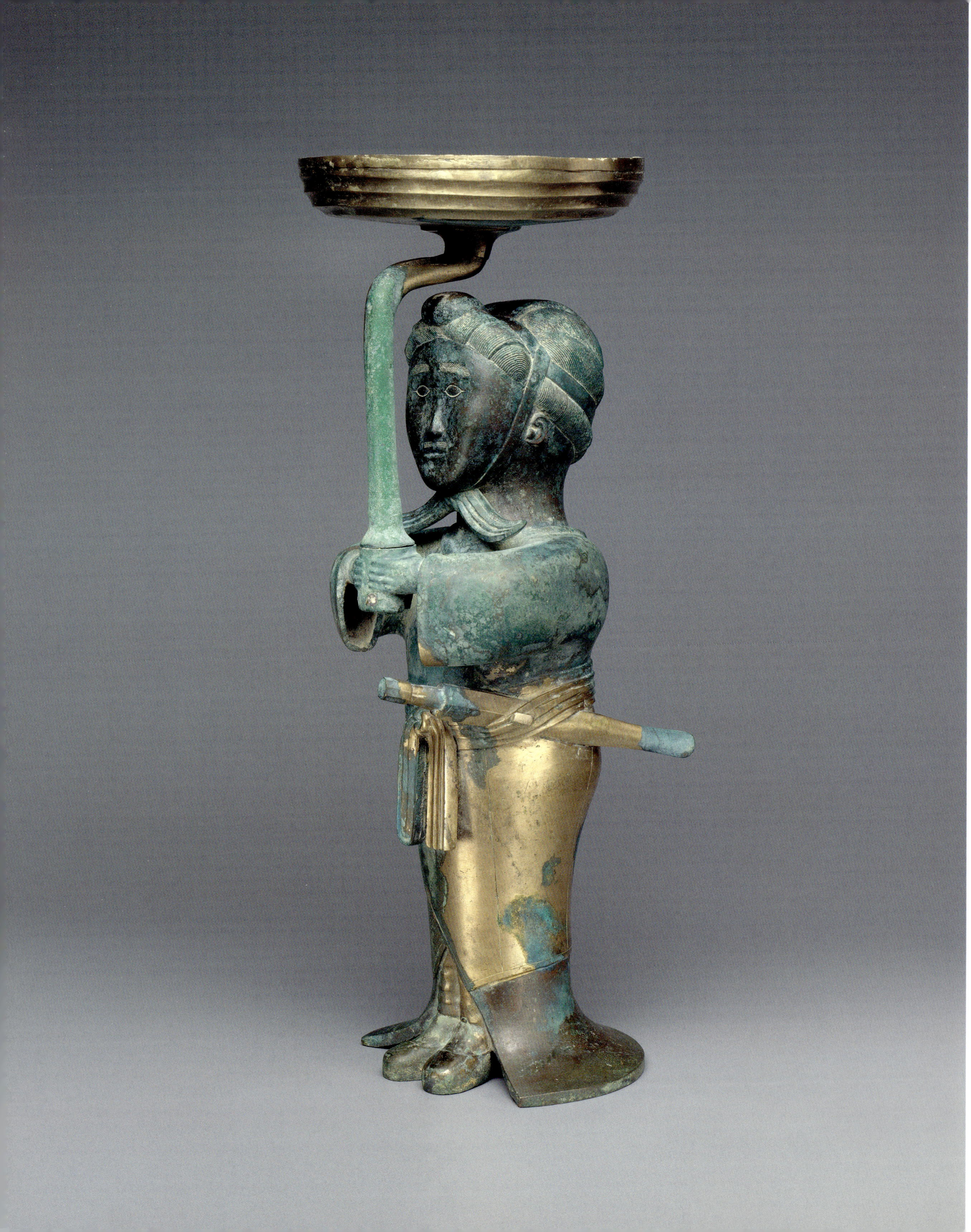

2

2 Sword-bearer lamp

Mid Warring States period to early Western Han dynasty, 4th–2d centuries BCE. Bronze with cast and engraved designs; h. 33.8 cm. Princeton University Art Museum, acc. no. 2003-29. Museum purchase, Fowler McCormick, Class of 1921, Fund.

Among the figural bronze lamps that were popular during the Warring States period, the present sword-bearer lamp is an exquisite specimen. Carrying a long sword at his left hip, this soldier holds his arms chest-high, his hands gripping a shaft that supports a large saucer decorated with horizontal concave fluting. This was the lamp itself, in which originally there must have been a wick soaked in a combustible material such as tallow; scientific analysis of the residues in the saucer confirms that the fuel was most likely derived from animal fat.[1] In the center of the saucer is a short spike on which the wick was fixed, so that the rate of burning could be controlled by adjusting the length of the wick above the level of the oil. The saucer and the spike are indeed the main features of early Chinese lamps.

The provenance of this lamp is uncertain. In recent years, however, similar lamps have been found in tombs of the Warring States and early Han period. According to the grave-goods inventories (*qiance*) written on bamboo strips, discovered in Tomb 2 (ca. 316 BCE) at Baoshan, Jingmen, Hubei Province, this type of lamp is called *zhuyong* ("lamp-figurine").[2] Scholars have been perplexed by the conspicuous absence of "lamp culture" in China before the fifth century BCE.[3] But the "sudden appearance" of lamps in the archaeological record does not mean that lamps as light-producing instruments were only invented in the Warring States period.[4] Rather, it means that only then were lamps included among grave goods and thus preserved underground. The present lamp is very well preserved, with the saucer, sword, and lower part of the robe still showing the original shining golden color, suggesting that it probably came from a mortuary context.

In addition to their obvious quotidian function of providing illumination, in mortuary contexts lamps also acquired religious significance. As I have argued elsewhere, in Warring States tombs lamps often counted as travel paraphernalia, to be used to illuminate the postmortem journey to the world beyond.[5] The inclusion of lamps among the grave goods corroborates the theory that a new conception of the afterlife emerged during the Warring States period. In this new conception, the soul of the deceased journeyed through a gloomy and malign underworld, starting from the tomb —a liminal point of departure—and eventually arriving at a final cosmic destination in the northwest of the universe.

Because the present lamp shares stylistic features with lamps datable to the middle or late Warring States period, it is similarly dated. Lamps in the basic format of a standing human figure holding a stemmed saucer often appear in sites of the southern state of Chu and adjacent areas. Two cases in point are a pair of identical bronze figural lamps discovered in Baoshan Tomb 2 in Hubei Province (see p. 228, fig. 2),[6] and a bronze lamp recently excavated from a Warring States–period Chu tomb at Jiuliandun, Zaoyang, Hubei.[7] Like the Baoshan figure, the present sword-bearer wears an elaborately modeled and detailed robe. Its golden color distinguishes the robe from the hem of the undergarment, which trails on the ground in a sort of short train. The sword is held against the left hip by a pleated sash, tied in front of the waist, whose ends hang down in an inverted U-shape.

In proportion to the overall size of the lamp, the present figure is large and stocky. The overall height of the lamp is 33.8 centimeters, and the diameter of the saucer is only about 12.6 centimeters, less than half of the overall height of the lamp. In contrast, the Baoshan figure extends his right arm to hold the support for an overwhelmingly large saucer, which is balanced by a square base. Furthermore, the present lamp is more compactly designed. Like the Jiuliandun lamp, its shaft rises vertically, bends to horizontal over the figure's head, then rises again to support the saucer. In contrast to the Jiuliandun lamp, on the present lamp the shaft makes its first bend just above the figure's head, and both bends are more nearly right angles than curves.

The present lamp also shares many features with Warring States figural lamps from northern China, especially with the one from Tomb 6 of the royal Zhongshan mausoleums, in present-day Pingshan, Hebei Province (see p. 227, fig. 1). Although the Zhongshan figure with its silvered funny face and gemstone pupils is more elaborately decorated, the two figures are quite similar in hair style, headpiece, and craftsmanship. In both, the heavy eyebrows, mustache, and winding strands of hair are all delineated with fine parallel striations. Their hair is combed back from the forehead and up from the nape and secured at the back under a sort of cloth cap. This headpiece is held in place with the aid of a device called *kui* in later Han terminology,[8] consisting of a horizontal rolled band around the lower edge of the cap and vertical cap strings knotted under the chin. The ends of the present figure's cap strings curl upward, which can be seen on some of Qin Shihuangdi's terra-cotta soldiers that wear the same cap-fixing device.[9] A small mortise under the chin of the Zhongshan figure suggests that it, too, might originally have boasted curled-up ends to its cap strings.[10]

Another feature common to the Zhongshan and the present figures is the U-shaped wedge inserted into the horizontal rolled band. As part of the device to fasten the headpiece, this wedge, judging from its shape, must have been used for tightening the rolled band. Later headdresses, such as those on the terra-cotta soldiers of the Qin dynasty, which have a more sophisticated way of fastening the rolled band and the cap strings, lack such a wedge; thus its presence here is further evidence that the lamp was made before the third century BCE.[11]

Finally, the distinctive plug ornaments in the ears of the present figure may point to a rhetorical function of figural lamps during the Warring States and Han periods.[12] Although scholars still differ about the meaning and function of these ear ornaments, they were apparently functional as well as decorative.[13] Though originally used to stop one's ears, the moral symbolism of ear ornaments is well substantiated in Han literature. These ornaments, which figured in the imperial regalia and in court ladies' adornments, were reminders to turn a deaf ear to slanderous talk or gossip.[14] Possibly the use of such earplugs as ear ornaments can be traced to the Warring States period.

In the recently published Warring States bamboo strips collected in the Shanghai Museum, one paragraph describes the "Golden Age" of remote antiquity, when rulers designated worthies other than their own sons as their successors. The prevailing political ideal in the utopian worlds that Warring States authors constructed was that people be employed according to their abilities: "Thus the dumb and the deaf are employed to hold lamps, the blind play the zithers, the lame guard doors, and the pygmies make arrows ...."[15] Certainly the idea of a lamp bearer turning a deaf ear to the conversations in his master's house is interesting in relation to the notion of privacy in early China. The figure's expressionless face and unfocused eyes may have been intended to depict real or discreetly assumed deafness. If the present lamp does reflect the prescription that lamp bearers be deaf and dumb, then it served also to embody a sociopolitical theory of its time, and perhaps a social reality as well. Images of crippled figures guarding doors, appearing on late Western Zhou bronze ritual vessels, have often been interpreted as penalized slaves.[16] The Shanghai bamboo strips may shed different light on our understanding of these images from the Warring States period.[17]

GUOLONG LAI

Notes

1. John Twilley, "Scientific Analysis of a Chinese Bronze Lamp" (January 7, 2003), Princeton University Art Museum curatorial archive.

2. Hubei Sheng Jingsha tielu kaogu dui, *Baoshan Chu mu* (*Chu tombs at Baoshan*) (Beijing: Wenwu chubanshe, 1991), vol. 1, p. 370, vol. 2, pl. 203, strip no. 262; the term *zhuyong* also appears on the inventories (strip no. 239) excavated from early Han Tomb 1 at Mawangdui, Changsha, Hunan Province, although no figural lamps as such have been identified at that site by modern archaeologists. See Hunan Sheng bowuguan and Zhongguo kexue yuan kaogu yanjiusuo, *Changsha Mawangdui yihao Han mu* (*Han Tomb No. 1 at Mawangdui in Changsha*) (Beijing: Wenwu chubanshe, 1973), vol. 1, p. 148, vol. 2, p. 238.

3. Emma C. Bunker, "A Late Eastern Zhou Lamp Stand: Questions of Gender and Identity," *Orientations,* October 1997, pp. 67–71, collected in *Chinese Bronzes: Selected Articles from Orientations 1983–2000* (Hong Kong: Orientations Magazine Ltd., 2001), pp. 283–87; David N. Keightley, *The Ancestral Landscape: Time, Space, and Community in Late Shang China* (*ca. 1200–1045 B.C.*) (Berkeley: Institute of East Asian Studies, University of California, Berkeley, and Center for Chinese Studies, 2000), pp. 24–25, n. 25.

4. Sun Ji has identified several specimens of bronze vessels of the Shang and Zhou periods as possible illumination devices, but these examples have not yet been confirmed through scientific analysis of the residue. See Sun Ji, "Zhongguo shenghuo" ("Chinese sacred fire"), in *Zhongguo shenghuo: Zhongguo guwenwu yu Dong Xi wenhua jiaoliu zhong de ruogan wenti* (*Chinese sacred fire: some questions concerning ancient Chinese material culture and East-West cultural exchange*) (Shenyang: Liaoning jiaoyu chubanshe, 1996), pp. 1–14.

5. Guolong Lai, "Lighting the Way in the Afterlife: Bronze Lamps in Warring States Tombs," *Orientations,* April 2002, pp. 20–28.

6. *Baoshan Chu mu*, vol. 1, pp. 189–94, vol. 2, cpl. 11.3, pl. 57.2.

7. For a picture of the Jiuliandun lamp, see the front cover of the recent issue of *Jiang Han kaogu* 2003.2; and a brief report in the same issue, pp. 29–30, "Hubei Zaoyang Jiuliandun Chu mu huo zhongda faxian" ("Important discoveries in the Chu tombs at Jiuliandun, Zaoyang, in Hubei Province").

8. *Hou Hanshu* (*History of the Eastern Han Dynasty*), Fan Ye, comp. (Beijing: Zhonghua shuju, 1965), p. 3670.

9. Wang Xueli, *Qin yong zhuanti yanjiu* (*Studies on specific topics about the Qin terra-cotta army*) (Xi'an: San Qin chubanshe, 1994), pp. 472–79.

10. Hayashi Minao, "Shunjū Sengoku jidai no kinjin to yokujin" ("The bronze and jade figurines of the Spring and Autumn and the Warring States periods"), in *Sengoku jidai shutsuto bunbutsu no kenkyū* (*Studies on excavated cultural relics of the Warring States period*),

ed. Hayashi Minao (Kyoto: Kyōto daigaku Jinbun kagaku kenkyūjo, 1985), p. 95.

11. Wang Xueli, *Qin yong zhuanti yanjiu*, pp. 472–79. The wedge appears on several human figures dated approximately to the 4th century BCE. See Hayashi Minao, "Shunjū Sengoku jidai no kinjin to yokujin," pp. 57–145; figs. 10, 11, 13.

12. Similar plug ornaments also appear on a bronze kneeling human figure in the Museum of Far Eastern Antiquities in Stockholm. See Hayashi Minao, "Shunjū Sengoku jidai no kinjin to yokujin," fig. 9, pp. 97–99.

13. Hayashi Minao insists that the ear ornaments are not functional earplugs (*zhen*) but decorative earrings (*er*), signifying social and cultural status, although other scholars, including many Han classicists, posit that the decorative and functional aspects of the ear ornaments are historically linked. See Hayashi Minao, *Chūgoku kogyokuki sōsetsu* (*Surveys on ancient Chinese jades*) (Tokyo: Yoshikawa Kōbunkan, 1999), pp. 113–19; and Gao Chunming, *Zhongguo fushi mingwu kao* (*Investigations in the terminologies of Chinese dress and personal adornments*) (Shanghai: Shanghai wenhua chubanshe, 2001), p. 413.

14. Gao Chunming, *Zhongguo fushi mingwu kao*, pp. 197, 410–13.

15. Ma Chengyuan, ed., *Shanghai bowuguan cang Zhanguo Chu zhushu* (*Chu bamboo books of the Warring States period collected in the Shanghai Museum*) (Shanghai: Shanghai guji chubanshe, 2002), vol. 2, pp. 10, 94–95, 251–52. Similar catalogues of occupations for those physically challenged individuals also appear in *Guoyu* (*Narratives of the states*) and *Liji* (*Rites records*). See *Guoyu* (Shanghai: Shanghai guji chubanshe, reprint, 1988), p. 387; *Liji zhushu*, *Shisanjing zhushu* edition (Taipei: Yiwen yinshuguan, reprint 1997), p. 267.

16. Guolong Lai, "Uses of the Human Figure in Early Chinese Art," *Orientations,* June 1999, fig. 4, pp. 50–51.

17. The lamps and associated figurines are a prominent cultural metaphor and rhetorical device in early Chinese art and literature. Another case in point is a figural lamp excavated from the tomb of Liu Sheng (d. ca. 113 BCE)—a member of the Han royal family—at Lingshan, Mancheng, Hebei Province. The title *danghu*, appearing in the inscription on the rim of the saucer, clearly identifies the figure as a Xiongnu official. Kneeling on his left leg with his right hand touching his right knee, the Xiongnu official raises his left arm to support the saucer. A lamp bearer in the image of a submissive Xiongnu official does make a political statement about the tension between the Han court and the Xiongnu during the middle of the Western Han dynasty. It was during the reign of Liu Sheng's brother, Emperor Wu, that the Han court changed its diplomatic policy and started waves of military campaigns against the Xiongnu. For the figural lamp, see Zhongguo shehui kexue yuan kaogu yanjiusuo and Hebei Sheng wenwu guanli chu, *Mancheng Han mu fajue baogao* (*Report on the excavations of the Han tombs at Mancheng*) (Beijing: Wenwu chubanshe, 1980), vol. 1, pp. 72–73; and for a brief discussion of the changes in the Han court's policy toward the Xiongnu, see Nicola Di Cosmo, *Ancient China and Its Enemies: The Rise of Nomadic Power in East Asian History* (Cambridge: Cambridge University Press, 2002), pp. 236–47.

Sword-Bearer Lamp (cat. no. 2): The Bronze Caster's Art

Ingeniously cast and remarkably well preserved, this bronze lamp (perhaps more accurately a candlestick) demonstrates the pinnacle of the bronze caster's art in ancient China. It takes the form of a standing armed guardian whose physical features, attire, and weaponry all suggest manufacture in southern China during the middle of the fourth century BCE.

The figure conveys an overall impression of solidity, with his thick and compact frame well balanced and supported by the flare of his inner robe. The columnar feel is somewhat interrupted, however, by the flying ends of his cap strings and the slanting projection of his scabbard. His broad, unnaturally flattened face, with its feather-form eyebrows, almond eyes, and gridded mustache, also contrasts with the rounded curves and realistic features of the rest of the figure, and may have been intentionally distorted to indicate an ethnic stereotype.

The guardian's hair has been upswept and secured with a *jin* ("head scarf"), which is fastened by an encircling band and tied down with *ying* ("cap strings") that extend into two pleated, flyaway ends. A curious flexible band has been doubly folded and tucked inside his headgear over the right ear, but does not appear to be part of the scarf-strapping system. A nearly identical head scarf, cap string, and folded band appear on the silver-faced lamp bearer found in Tomb 6 at the middle Warring States–era (ca. 330 BCE) Zhongshan royal cemetery at Pingshan, Hebei Province (fig. 1) and on another figural bronze candlestick from the Warring States–period site of Shangcunling, Henan Province.[1]

The guardian's arms are held chest-high and bent at the elbow, and his hands clasp the shaft topped by a pan for a tallow candle, the remains of which still clung to the pan when it was discovered. The pan assembly was cast separately from the rest of the figure, in a two-piece mold, and secured to the hands by means of two lead pins, seen just below the fingers. A similar attachment mechanism apparently secured the shafts of the lamps from Baoshan Tomb 2 (fig. 2) and from Shangcunling. The fluting on the pan is similar to that seen on the fifteen-branch tree-form lamp from King Cuo's tomb at Zhongshan (ca. 310 BCE) and on several other Warring States–era lamps.

The guardian wears a long inner robe, which parts in the front to reveal his ruffled leggings and rounded shoes, and trails in the back to form a generous train. Over this garment he wears a thick outer robe that ends above his ankles and is cinched at the waist

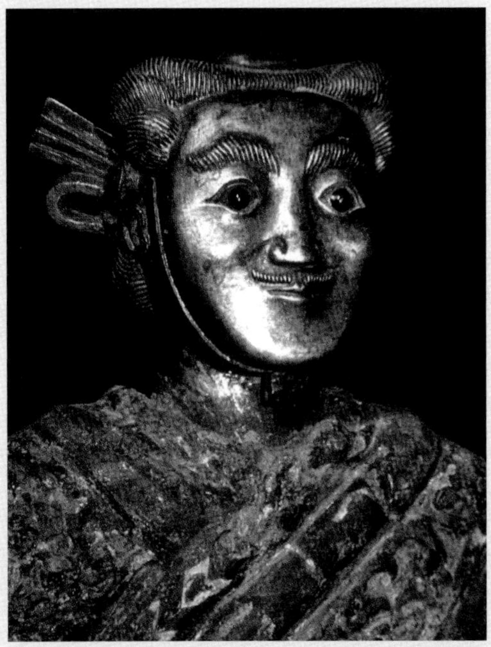

Fig. 1 *Figural lamp* (detail). Warring States period, ca. 330 BCE. Tomb 6, Pingshan, Hebei. Cast silver head, inlaid with stones, attached to lacquer-decorated bronze body; h. 66.4 cm. Hebei Provincial Museum. From *Treasures from the Tombs of the Zhongshan Guo Kings*, ed. Tokyo National Museum (Tokyo: Nihon Keizai Shinbunsha, 1981), pl. 41 (detail).

with a belt. Chased vertical lines on the outer robe suggest the seams of fabric panels. The bronze figural candlestick found in Baoshan Tomb 2 (fig. 2) wears nearly identical inner and outer robes, sporting the same semicircular train and fabric-panel chasing. A second, pleated belt secures the scabbard for a long, double-edged, bronze *jian* sword. The scabbard profile of this sword, with its distinctive flared "duckbill" tip, is very similar to that of the weapon carried by the figural supports of the bell rack from the Marquis Yi of Zeng's tomb (ca. 433 BCE) (fig. 3) and also resembles several other fifth- and fourth-century sword and scabbard sets found in the Changsha area (fig. 4).

Multiple-pour, piece-mold casting techniques, similar to those used for elaborate Anyang-period bronzes, were used to make the present lamp. The central torso appears to have been cast in one piece. Later, the feet and train of the robe were each cast separately onto the body. The head was also cast separately, probably in more than one pour, and joined to the body. It is unclear from the filed-down neck join whether the head was pre-cast and incorporated into the mold for the body pour or was cast onto the already completed body, though the former seems more likely. The arms were clearly cast separately and then joined to the shoulders by investing the joint in a temporary mold and then pouring molten metal over the junction to lock the arms in place. Projecting features like the cap strings, sword, and drooping ends of the scabbard belt were cast separately in molds and then either mechanically driven into slots in the figure or welded to it with an overlap of molten metal. Mold

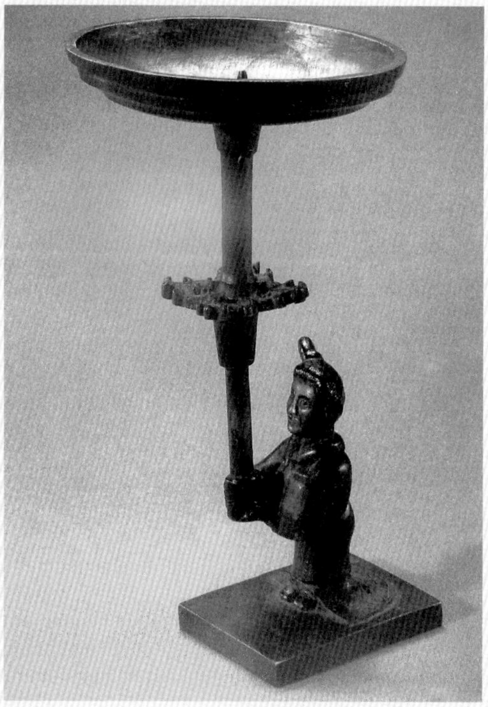

Fig. 2 *Figural candlestick.* Warring States period, ca. 316 BCE. Tomb 2, Baoshan, Jingmen, Hubei. Bronze with copper inlay; h. 16.3 cm, diam. of saucer 8.6 cm. Hubei Provincial Museum. From *Zhongguo qingtongqi quanji* (Beijing: Wenwu chubanshe, 1998), vol. 10, pl. 82.

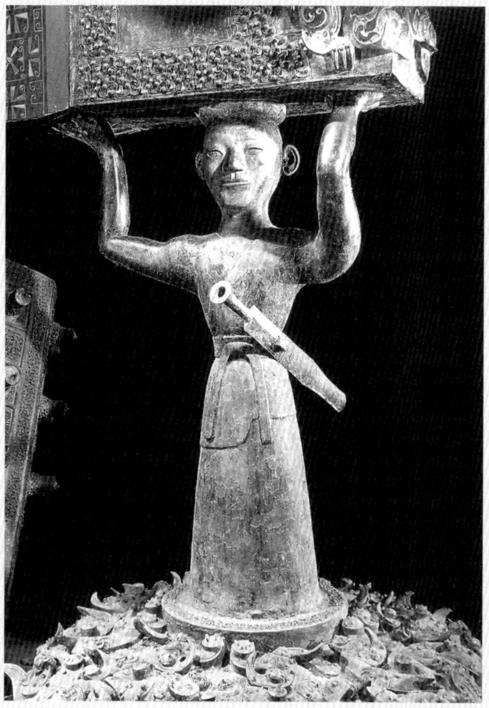

Fig. 3 *Figural support for bell rack.* Early Warring States period, ca. 433 BCE. Tomb 1, Leigudun, Suizhou, Hubei. Bronze with painted decoration; h. 96 cm. Hubei Provincial Museum. From *Zhanguo dixia yuegong*, ed. Hubei Sheng bowuguan (Beijing: Wenwu chubanshe, 1994), pl. 4.

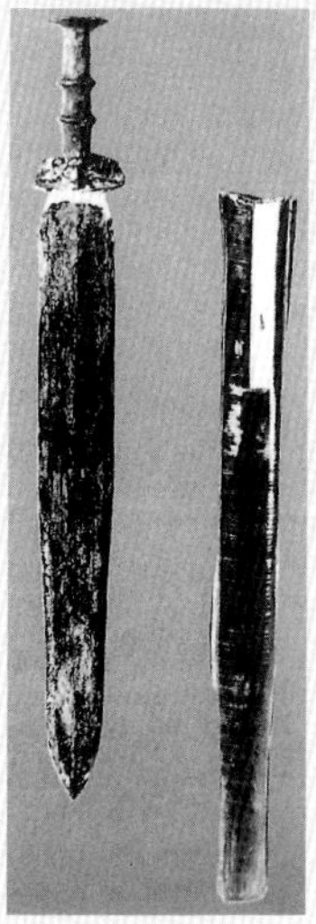

Fig. 4 *Sword and scabbard.* Late Spring and Autumn or Early Warring States period, ca. 550–450 BCE. Tomb 1, Liuchengqiao, Changsha, Hunan. Bronze sword, l. 44 cm; lacquered wood sheath, l. 39.8 cm. Hunan Provincial Museum. From *Kaogu xuebao* 1972.1, pl. 14.

lines and flashes of metal from these joining processes were meticulously filed away by the metalsmiths, making them very hard to detect.[2]

Central to the original appearance of the lamp was the use of at least two different alloys of bronze for different components, to achieve a polychromatic effect. For example, the face and the train of the inner robe were cast from a ruddy-colored alloy of bronze, proportionately higher in copper, while the lamp pan, outer robe, and sword were cast from a more golden-colored bronze alloy higher in tin (see detail). On the very similar candlestick from Baoshan Tomb 2 (fig. 2), the metalsmith achieved a slightly different polychromatic effect by pounding copper inlays into pre-cast trenches on the robe's train to simulate embroidered silk patterns.

The areas of bright metal on the pan and on the lower portion of the figure are not gilt, but rather represent the original, uncorroded surface of the higher-tin bronze. Through some accident of archaeological preservation, the metal in these areas has survived more than two thousand years untarnished by

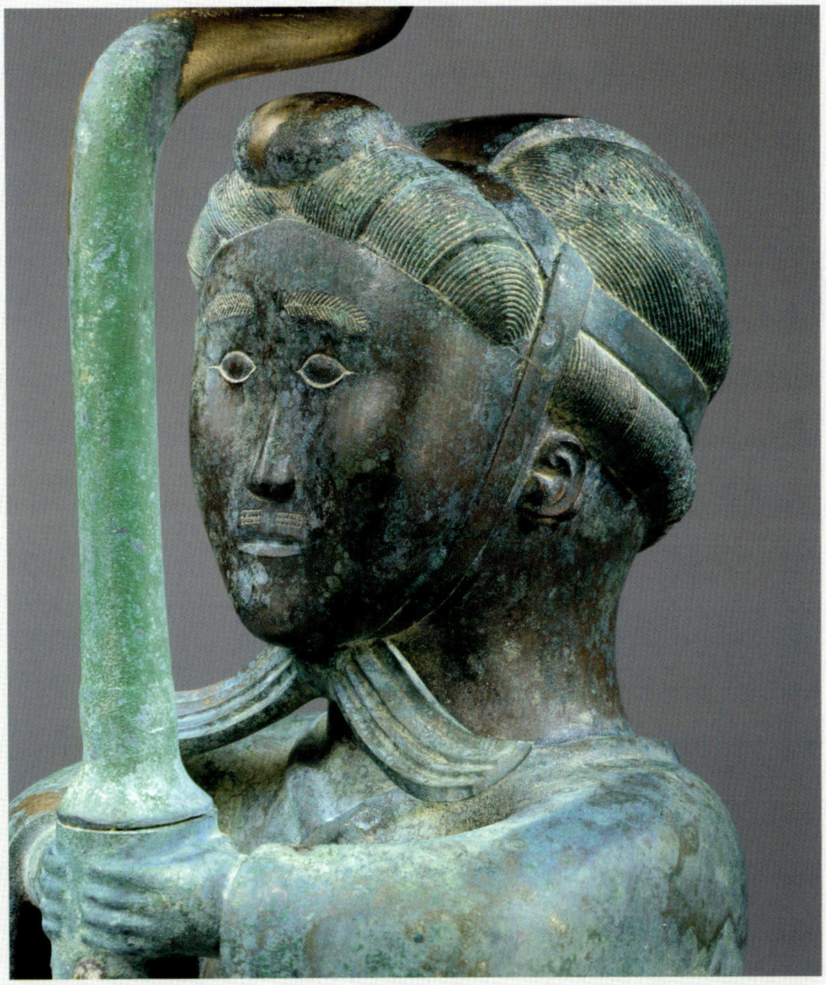

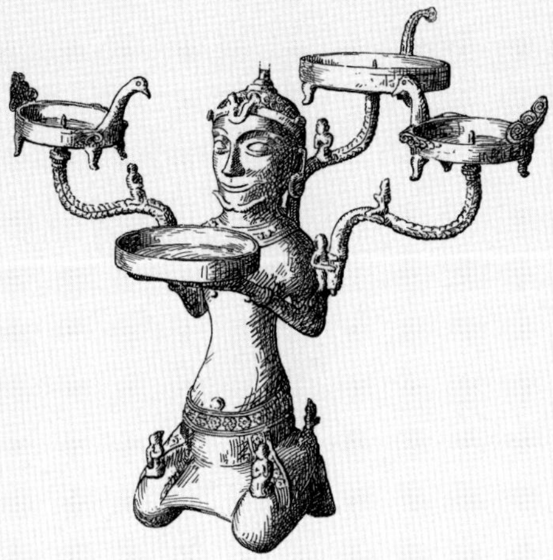

oxidation. The onset of corrosion may have been inhibited by the thorough polishing treatment the object received from its original maker or by the wrapping of silk it received prior to interment.

Another distinctive feature of this lamp is the cylindrical plug-like ornaments that pierce both ears of the guardian (see detail of head). All the flat-faced figural bronze bell-rank supports from the Marquis Yi of Zeng's tomb have ears pierced by large round holes (fig. 3), which probably once held plug ornaments similar to those seen on this lamp. The Chinese never practiced ear piercing in antiquity, so figures made in China with pierced ears probably represent individuals who were not ethnic Han.[3] Piercing does appear to have been widely practiced in far southern China and throughout Southeast Asia.[4] Figure 5 represents a bronze Dongson figural lamp with earrings, dating from the mid-first century BCE Tomb 3 at Lach Truong, Vietnam.[5] Later Cham and Khmer sculpture in Southeast Asia is certainly rife with ear spools, earplugs, and all variety of pierced-ear ornaments.

Fig. 5 *Figural lamp.* Dongson, ca. 150–50 BCE. Tomb 3, Lach Truong, Vietnam. Bronze; h. 33 cm. National Museum of Vietnam, Hanoi. From Olov R. T. Janse, *Archaeological Research in Indo-China*, vol. 1, pl. 9.

In ancient China figures representing non–ethnic Han persons were often used as caryatid-like supports for lamps, racks, basins, and screens.[6] One could speculate that the present guardian figure is a stereotypical representation of a man of southern Yue ethnicity, a broadly defined group whose members lived in the areas southeast of the Chu kingdom and into present-day Vietnam. The southern Yue group would have been considered barbarians by the Chu patrons who commissioned this lamp. In sum, given its obvious similarity to the Baoshan lamp and the Zeng bell-rack support, this lamp was probably made in the state of Chu, or in one of its satellite states, during the early to middle fourth century BCE. It likely depicts a male southern Yue soldier or guard wearing Chinese dress and military gear.

ANTHONY BARBIERI-LOW

Notes

1. See *Zhongguo meishu quanji: diaosu bian* (*Complete compilation of Chinese art: Sculpture*) (Beijing: Renmin meishu chubanshe, 1988), vol. 1, pl. 142.

2. These observations were guided by the extremely thorough analysis of art-conservation specialist John Twilley, in his "Scientific Analysis of a Chinese Bronze Lamp" (January 7, 2003), Princeton University Art Museum curatorial archive.

3. The bronze figural lamp reportedly found at Jin Cun, Henan, and now in the Museum of Fine Arts, Boston, represents a Mongolian who is wearing linked-hoop earrings through his ear lobes. See Emma C. Bunker, "A Late Eastern Zhou Lamp Stand: Questions of Gender and Identity," *Orientations,* October 1997, pp. 67–71.

4. I should like to thank Ms. Emma Bunker for her valuable suggestions concerning the identification of the plug-like ear ornaments.

5. For a description of the context of this find, see Olov R. T. Janse, *Archaeological Research in Indo-China* (Cambridge, Mass.: Harvard University Press, 1951), vol. 1, pp. 28–57, pl. 9, vol., 2, pl. 1.

6. A bronze figural lamp from the tomb of Prince Liu Sheng at Mancheng is inscribed with the title *danghu*, which was a noble title used by the northern nomads known as the Xiongnu. For other examples, see also Guolong Lai, "Uses of the Human Figure in Early Chinese Art," *Orientations*, June 1999, pp. 49–55; Guolong Lai, "Lighting the Way in the Afterlife: Bronze Lamps in Warring States Tombs." *Orientations*, April 2002, pp. 20–28.

Sword-Bearer Lamp (cat. no. 2): Warring States Lamps

This lamp in the form of a sword bearer is the product of the Chu cultural area of Henan-Hubei provinces in central China during the Warring States period, a time when the sword and the lamp, both illustrated by this figure, came prominently into use. The earliest evidences of artificial illumination in China are the scorch marks on Neolithic walls caused by torches inserted into holes. From the Shang and much of the Zhou dynasties there remain scant traces of the means of lighting, perhaps because the form of the lamp was the *dou*, a bowl set on a stem and base, resembling a chalice, which was also an important ritual offering vessel and so not easily differentiated as a lamp (fig. 1). It was only in the Warring States period that lamps came into their own. The *dou* shape persisted, along with a wide range of new shapes and styles. These included lamp trees, animals such as elephants bearing the lamp dish on their backs, birds supporting the lamp dish in their beaks, a bowl whose cover turns on a hinge to form the lamp dish, and a tripod with handles that lift up to support the reversed lid, which then becomes the lamp dish. In addition, a large number of the Warring States lamps are composed of human forms supporting the lamp dishes. In 1975, at Sanmenxia, Henan, a kneeling figure was found, wearing a formal belted robe and cap tied under the chin, and holding a Y-shaped support whose two arms fit into a ring-mold–shaped lamp dish that has three prickets, or spikes, to hold the candlewicks. Traces remain of the lacquer that once covered the figurine's bronze frame (fig. 2).[1] A number of similar lamps have been found at sites in Hubei, within the area of the Chu culture, that is, the mid-Yangzi River basin. The farthest north of these sites, at Zaoyang, disclosed a standing male figurine holding a bird in his left outstretched hand and in his right a curved stem that supports a lamp dish with only one pricket (fig. 3).[2] Another lamp has as its support a woman whose left hand is pressed to her chest while her right hand, outstretched, holds the straight stem of a shallow lamp dish with one pricket. The stem is composed of sections that fit together, with a square, ornamented collar at its midpoint. This lamp is one of a pair found in 1986 in a tomb at Baoshan, Jingmen, Hubei (fig. 4).[3] A lamp from Jiangling, also in Hubei, is made up of a shallow dish with a single pricket and a straight stem, held by a figure riding a camel. The modeling is notably realistic, even to the rider's legs clearly gripping the camel's sides in order to keep his seat (fig. 5).[4]

A number of such figurines, for the most part kneeling, were found at Jin Cun, Henan, in tombs that may be the burials of the kings of late Zhou and their ministers.[5] Since the objects held by these figurines have not survived, we do not know whether they were lamps. One figure of a woman, as now restored, appears to have represented an entertainer who balanced birds on the poles she is holding (fig. 6).[6]

Lamps from outside the Chu area incorporate figures in other ways. From Zhucheng, Shandong, far to the north, comes a more elaborate lamp, consisting of a figure in a short tunic standing on the back of a coiled dragon. His hands are held out on either side, the right a bit higher than the left. From a canister held in each hand rises a curved stem, with what appear to be leaves emerging at each curve of

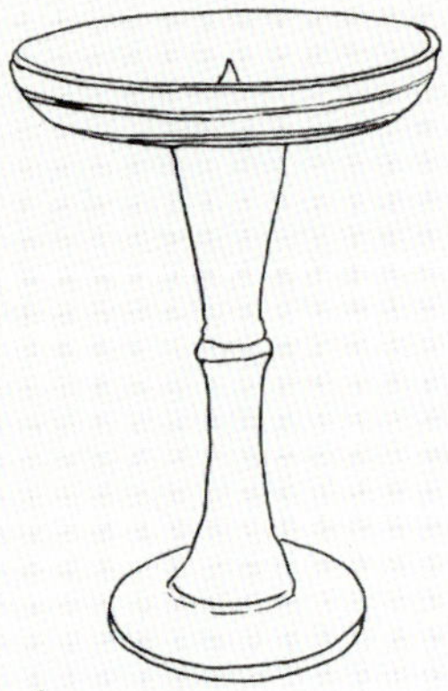

1

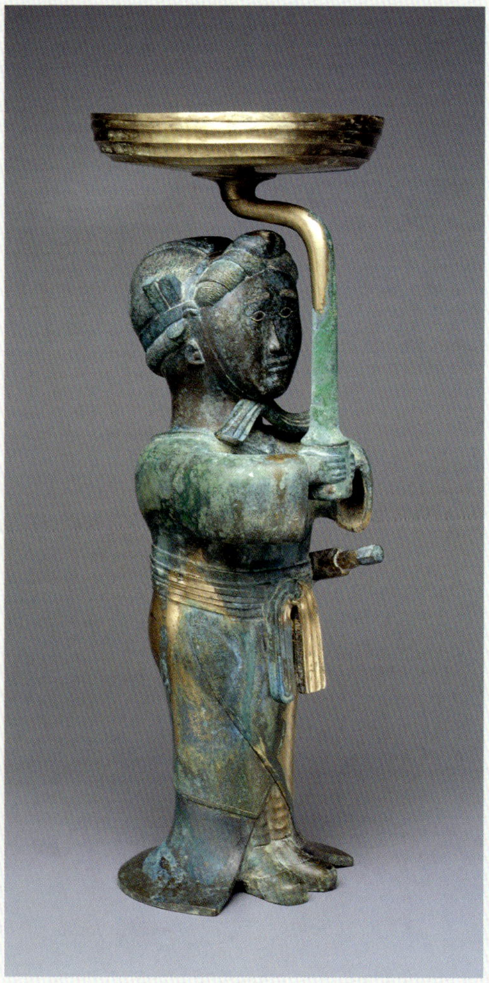

the stem, perhaps imitating curved bamboo stalks. Each stem supports a shallow lamp dish (fig. 7).[7]

Among the finest of these lamps are those found in the tombs of the rulers of the state of Zhongshan, at Sanjicun, Pingshan Xian, Hebei. One consists of a figure in a long-sleeved robe whose face is finely detailed in silver and whose right hand grasps the tail of a serpent. The serpent, rearing upward, holds in its mouth a shaft that in turn supports a ring-mold–shaped shallow pan. Inside the ring are three prickets that would have held candlewicks. A monkey perched on the shaft appears to be fleeing the serpent. A second serpent, held by the tail in the figure's left hand, bends in a U-shape to support another ring-mold, while a third serpent, coiled around a ring-mold on the ground, raises its head to the midriff of the second serpent, thus stabilizing the whole. These rings likewise have prickets (fig. 8).[8] Almost all the lamp dishes contain a pricket or spike to support the candlewick, which was made of slivers of bamboo or the piths of hemp stalks bound together and soaked in animal tallow. Oil lamps, that is, those that used liquid oil as fuel, did not become widespread until the third century CE.

The figure in this exhibition is thus typical of these human-figurine lamps of the Warring States period, and more narrowly, of the Chu cultural area. He is distinctive, however, in wearing a sword; none of the other figurines in this type of lamp carry such a weapon. But the figurines supporting the bronze bells in the tomb of the Marquis Yi of Zeng (dated to 433–400 BCE) at Sui Xian, Hubei, are equipped with swords of a similar sort (fig. 9).[9] Bronze swords became important in the late Spring and Autumn period, with the decline of chariot warfare that had emphasized archery and long-handled weapons. The best swords were originally produced in the states of Wu and Yue, in southeastern China, where the terrain was unsuited to chariots, and hand-to-hand combat was more common. Wu was annexed by Yue, which in turn was overrun by Chu in the fourth century BCE; the finest swords were taken as booty by the victors, who also appropriated the skill and technology of making them.[10] Thus

Fig. 1 *Dou-shaped lamp with pricket.* Warring States period. Unearthed at Chu Tomb 2, Wangshan, Jiangling, Hubei. Hubei Provincial Museum. After *Wenwu* 1966.5, p. 53, fig. 25.

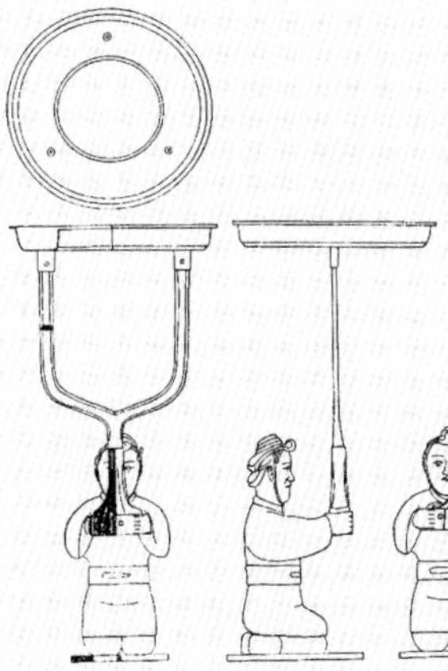

2

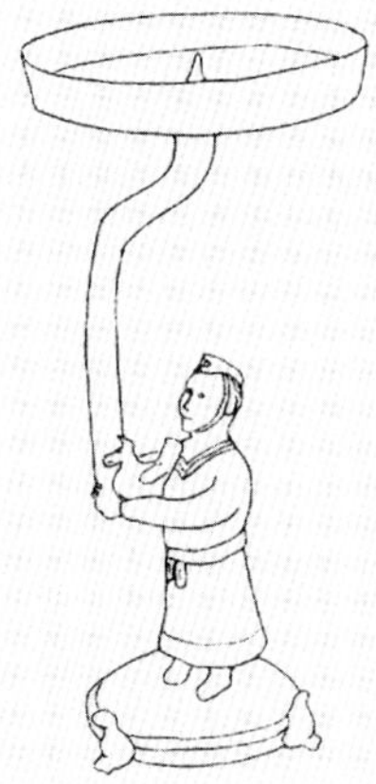

3

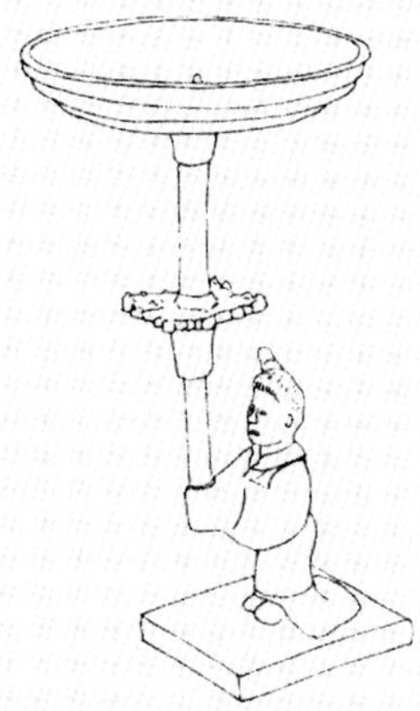

4

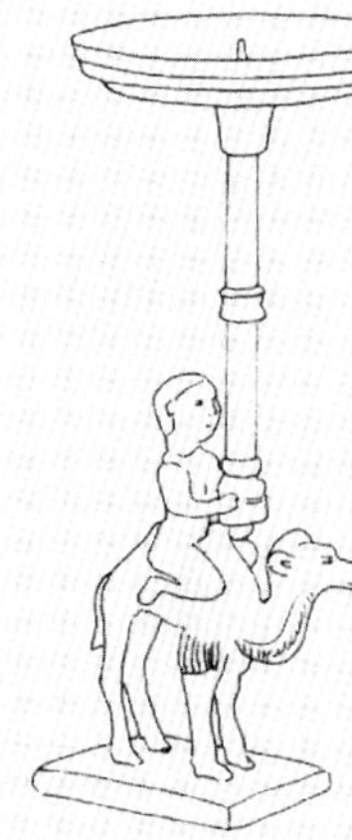

5

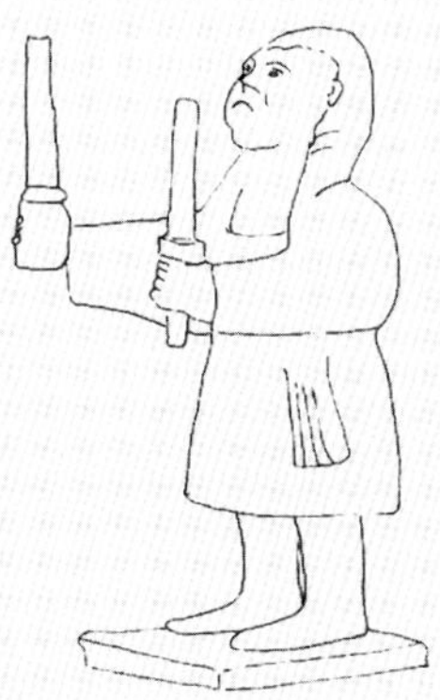

6

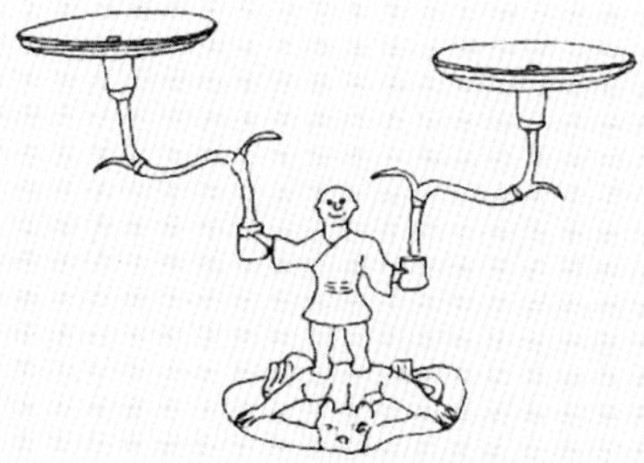

7

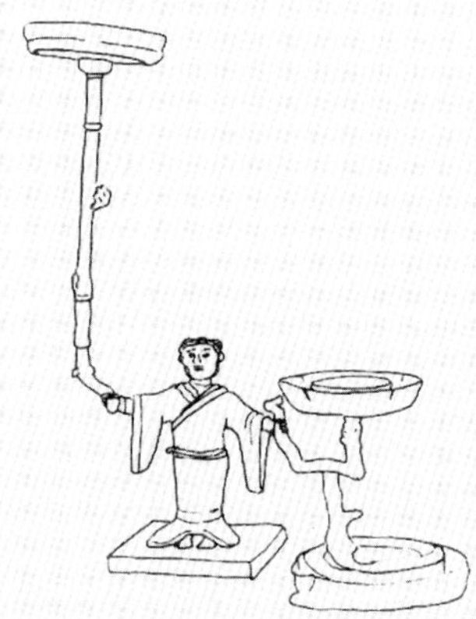

8

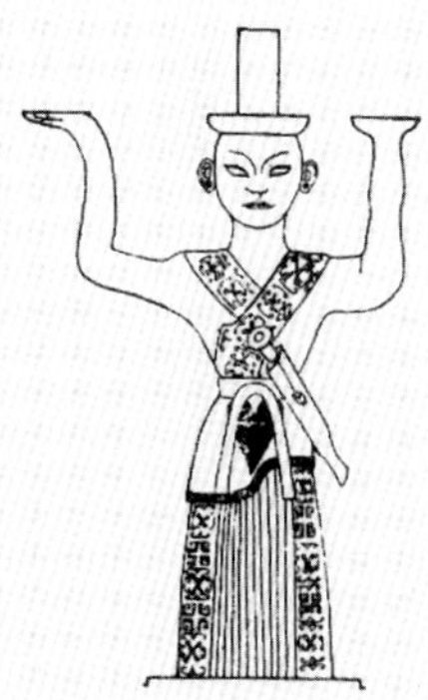

9

Fig. 2 *Lamp with kneeling figure.* Warring States period. Unearthed at Sanmenxia, Henan, 1975. Bronze, with flaking lacquer coating; h. 48.9 cm, diam. of lamp dish 32.7 cm. After *Wenwu* 1976.3, p. 54, fig. 4. **Fig. 3** *Lamp with figure holding a bird.* Warring States period. Unearthed at Jiuliandun, Zaoyang, Hubei, 2002. Bronze. After *Kaogu* 2003.7, cpl. 6.5. **Fig. 4** *Lamp with a standing woman.* Warring States period. Unearthed at Tomb 2, Baoshan, Jingmen, Hubei, 1986. Bronze; overall h. 16.3 cm, figurine h. 7.1 cm., diam. of lamp dish 8.8 cm. After Gao Canjiang, *Dengju*, p. 51. **Fig. 5** *Lamp with a camel rider.* Warring States period. Unearthed at Chu Tomb 2, Wangshan, Jiangling, Hubei, 1965. Bronze; h. 19.2 cm, diam. of lamp dish 8.9 cm. Hubei Provincial Museum. After *Wenwu* 1966.5, p. 53, fig. 25. **Fig. 6** *Figure of a woman with lamp support* (?). Warring States period. Unearthed at Jin Cun, Henan, ca. 1929. Bronze; h. 23 cm. After White, *Tombs of Old Lo-yang*, pl. 83, fig. 206. **Fig. 7** *Double lamp stand.* Warring States period. Unearthed at Gebukou, Zhucheng, Shandong, 1957. Bronze; h. 21.3 cm, diam. of lamp dish 11.5 cm. After *Wenwu* 1959.11, p. 31. **Fig. 8** *Triple lamp stand.* Warring States period. Unearthed from the Zhongshan royal tombs, Pingshan Xian, Hebei, 1977. Bronze with silver face and black stone eyes; h. 66.4 cm, w. 55.2 cm. After *Wenwu* 1979.1, pl. 1.2. **Fig. 9** *Support for a bell rack.* Warring States period. Unearthed from the tomb of the Marquis Yi of Zeng (d. between 433 and 400 BCE) at Leigudun, Sui Xian, Hubei, 1978. Bronze, overall h. 75 cm excluding tenon. After *Zeng Hou Yi*, vol. 1, p. 79, fig. 39.3.

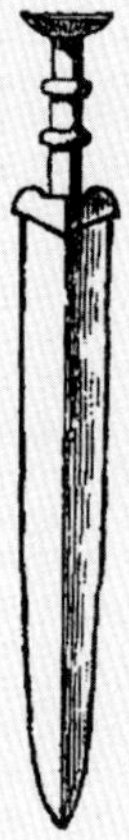

10

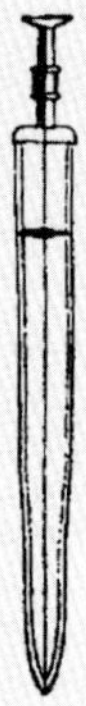

11

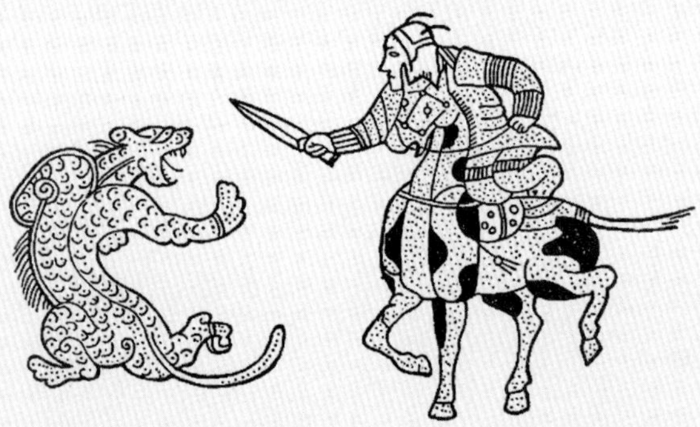

12

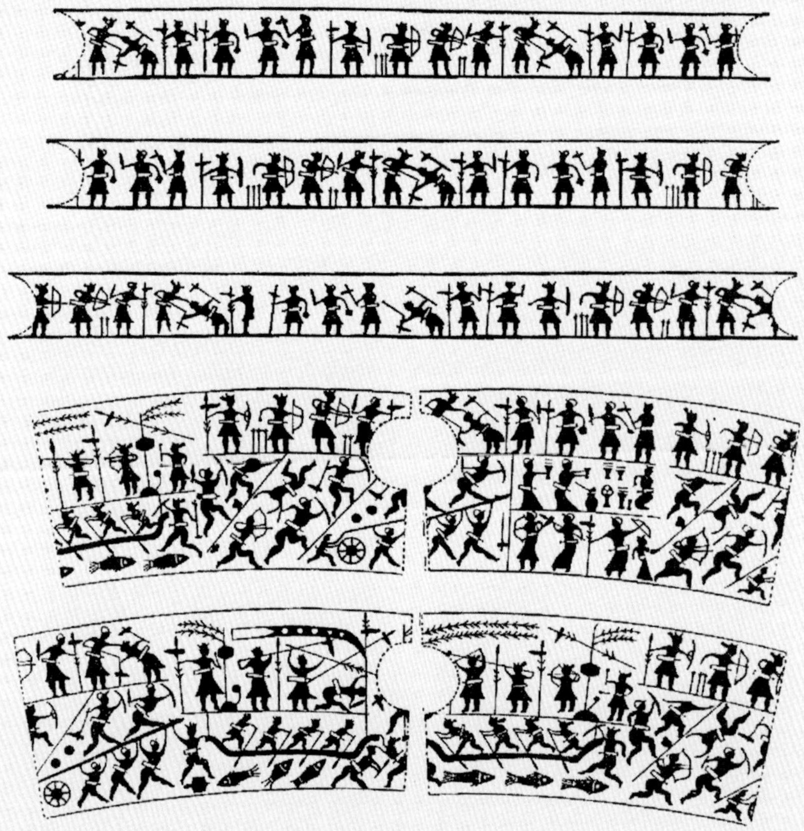

13

Fig. 10 *Zhou "classical" sword*. Warring States period. From Loehr, *Chinese Bronze Age Weapons*, p. 73, fig. 51:D.

Fig. 11 *Warring States sword*. From Liu Xu, *Zhongguo gudai bingqi tuce* (Beijing: Beijing tushuguan chubanshe, 1986), p. 52, no. 30.

Fig. 12 *Warrior fighting a feline*. Warring States period. Detail on a bronze mirror. From Yang Hong, *Zhongguo gubingqi luncong*, p. 95, fig. 75.

Fig. 13 *Battle scene*. Warring States period. Inlaid design on a bronze vessel. Unearthed from Tomb 1, Shanbiaozhen, Henan, 1935. After Li Xueqin, *Eastern Zhou and Qin*, p. 70, fig. 27.

it is that a sword inscribed as the possession of a king of Yue has been recovered from a Chu tomb at Tengdian, Jiangling, Hubei.[11]

The sword carried by the present figure seems to have a flat hexagonal pommel much longer than that of any archaeologically recovered example. Below the hilt or grip a square guard directly abuts the top of the scabbard. Judging from the shape of the scabbard, the sword has a pronounced median ridge and tapers to a point; swords of this period were thrusting rather than slashing weapons. The blade seems to begin to narrow past the bearer's hip, thus differing somewhat from the consistent, regular taper of what Max Loehr called the "classic" Zhou sword (fig. 10).[12] Loehr notwithstanding, many Warring States swords, like the present one, begin to narrow only toward the tip (fig. 11).

Assuming the height of the person represented by our bronze figurine to be 162 centimeters, the sword, including the scabbard, would have been 76 centimeters, or about 30 inches long, somewhat longer than usual for this period, but this extra length includes the unrealistically long pommel and the end, or chape, of the scabbard.[13] A Warring States mirror shows just such a short sword in use by a mounted warrior in combat with a feline (fig. 12).[14] Swords of this length could well have been carried by warriors who were also armed with the other weapons of the period, such as bows and arrows and dagger-axes (*ge*), as shown in scenes of battle inlaid on bronze vessels of the time (fig. 13).[15]

The rectangular shape on the scabbards of this figure and those in the tomb of the Marquis Yi of Zeng represents a scabbard slide, the device by which a sword was carried during the Warring States period and into the Han, when it was replaced by the double-locket or two-point suspension.[16] The scabbard slide, most commonly of jade, was mounted on the scabbard, usually some two-fifths down from the top, and a strap (not the garment belt) was passed through it so that the sword and scabbard swung at the bearer's left side and could be adjusted in position to suit his needs (fig. 14). The scabbard slide was used widely in Asia, but its place of origin is disputed.[17]

What is curious about the sword on the present figure is that the sword strap is made up of four strips, only one of which passes through the scabbard slide. This would, in effect, keep the sword in a fixed position, negating the advantage of flexibility afforded by the slide. On the figures from the tomb of the Marquis Yi of Zeng the swords are simply tacked onto the hips, with no indication of any belt passing through the scabbard slide. The end of the scabbard, or chape, would have been of a hard material, often jade, but the layer of patina obscures what kind of chape may have been indicated here.

One of the means used to improve the quality of bronze swords was to vary the amount of tin in the alloy: less tin in the rib portion reduced brittleness and more in the cutting edge made it harder.[18] Still, once it was learned how to convert iron to steel, longer and more effective swords came to be made of that metal. By the Qin dynasty, steel swords were eighty to ninety centimeters long, and the short bronze sword was being phased out.

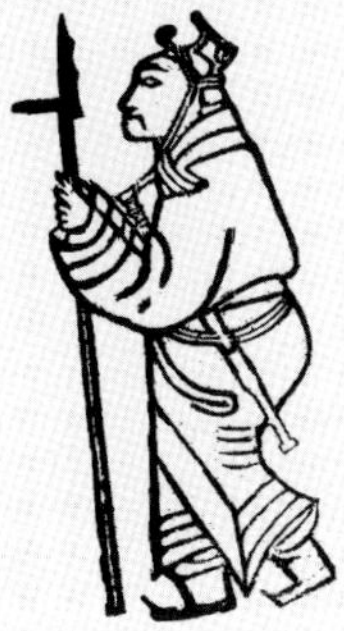

14

Fig. 14 *Rubbing of a tomb tile depicting a guard*. From Trousdale, *The Long Sword and Scabbard Slide in Asia*, p. 41, fig. 21.

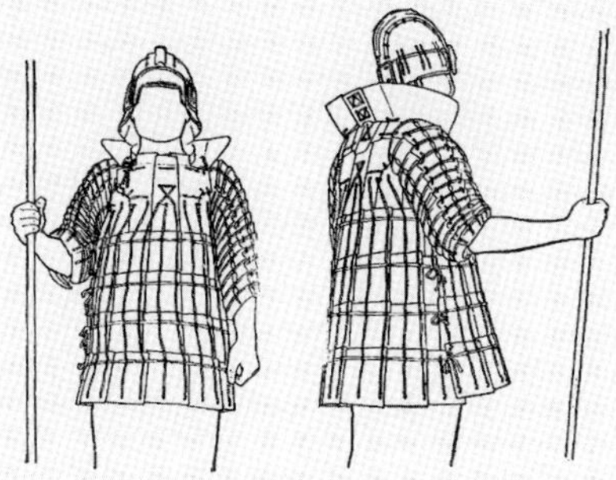

15

Fig. 15 *Lacquered leather lamellar armor*. Warring States period. Unearthed from the tomb of the Marquis Yi of Zeng (d. between 433 and 400 BCE) at Leigudun, Sui Xian, Hubei, 1978. From Yang Hong, *Zhongguo gubingqi luncong*, p. 6, fig. 4.

During the Warring States period soldiers wore lamellar armor made of lacquered leather. Suits of such armor were found in the tomb of the Marquis Yi (fig. 15), and figurines depicted in such armor have been found at Hui Xian, Henan.[19] But the present figure is dressed in formal robes, probably of exaggerated length so as to trail at the back and thereby provide added stability to the piece. It has been suggested that the lamp-holder figurines portray servants, and servile expressions have been read into their features. But surely one who wore a sword in the presence of his master was held in some higher regard.

ALBERT DIEN

Notes

1. Henan Sheng bowuguan, "Henan Sanmenxia Shi Shangcunling chutu de jijian Zhanguo tongqi" ("Some Warring States bronze utensils unearthed at Shangcunling City, Sanmenxia, Henan"), *Wenwu* 1976.3, p. 53, fig. 4 on p. 54, and pl. 3.3. The location of the find and its appearance suggest that it was produced in the Qin state. See also Guo Canjiang, *Dengju* (*Lamps*) (Taipei: Maotouying chuban, 2003), pp. 44–45. From the size of the lamp dishes, it has been conjectured that the wick was not made of tallow but was rather more like a torch (*ju*), which would have cast large amounts of cinders (*jin*); see Tang Xuanzhi and Liu Xinglin, "Zhongguo gudai deng, zhu yuanshi" ("The origins of the lamp and candle in China's antiquity"), *Zhongguo keji shiliao* (*Chinese historical materials of science and technology*), vol. 19, no. 2 (1998), p. 60.

2. Hubei Sheng wenwu kaogu yanjiusuo, "Hubei Zaoyang Shi Jiuliandun Chu mu" ("A Chu tomb at Jiuliandun, Zaoyang City, Hubei"), *Kaogu* 2003.7, p. 588 and pl. 6.5. That tomb was so rich in grave goods that although the lamp was mentioned, unfortunately no details were given. See also *Major Archaeological Discoveries in China in 2002* (Beijing: Wenwu chubanshe, 2003), p. 55.

3. Hubei Sheng Jing-Sha tielu kaogudui Baoshan mudi zhengli xiaozu, "Jingmen Shi Baoshan Chu mu fajue jianbao" ("Brief excavation report on a Chu tomb at Baoshan, Jingmen City"), *Wenwu* 1988.5, p. 8 and pl. 3.4.

4. Hubei Sheng wenhuaju wenwu gongzuodui, "Hubei Jiangling sanzuo Chu mu chutu dapi zhongyao wenwu" ("Many items of cultural importance unearthed from three Chu tombs at Jiangling, Hubei"), *Wenwu* 1966.5, p. 38 and fig. 25 on p. 53; Guo Canjiang, *Dengju*, pp. 48–49.

5. Li Xueqin, *Eastern Zhou and Qin Civilizations*, trans. K.C. Chang (New Haven: Yale University Press, 1985), p. 36.

6. William Charles White, *Tombs of Old Lo-yang: A Record of the Construction and Contents of a Group of Royal Tombs at Chin-ts'un, Honan, probably dating 550 B.C.* (Shanghai: Kelley and Walsh, 1934), pp. 106–8 and pls. 79–83. For these figures, see also Umehara Sueji, Rakuyō Kin-son kobō shūei (*Collected gems of the ancient tombs at Jin Village, Luoyang*) (Kyoto: Kobayashi Shushin Seihanjo Shuppanbu, 1943), pls. 45–51. For the woman, see Bradley Smith and Wan-go Weng, *China: A History in Art* (New York: Harper and Row, 1972), p. 56. I do not agree with the identification there and on p. 289 that this represents a Mongolian boy. The figure is now in the Museum of Fine Arts, Boston.

7. Ji Tao, "Shandong Sheng pucha wenwu zhanlan jianjie" ("Brief introduction to a survey exhibition of Shandong Province material culture"), *Wenwu* 1959.11, p. 30 and figure on p. 31; this source dates it to the

Table 1

	Overall length (in cm)	Length of handle	Length of blade
Princeton (estimate)	76.0	14.6	61.4
Qibeigu sword no. 1	64.0	9.6	54.8
Qibeigu sword no. 2	54.3	8.7	45.6
Goujian sword	55.7	8.4	47.3

Han dynasty, but Guo Canjiang, *Dengju*, pp. 52–53, dates it to the Warring States period.

8. Hebei Sheng wenwu guanlichu, "Hebei Sheng Pingshan Xian Zhanguo shiqi Zhongshanguo muzang fajue jianbao" ("Brief report on the excavation of Zhongshan State tombs of the Warring States period at Pingshan Xian, Hebei"), *Wenwu* 1979.1, p. 12 and pl. 1.3; Liu Jiansheng et al., eds. *Warring States Treasures—Cultural Relics from the State of Zhongshan, Hebei Province* (Hong Kong: Provisional Urban Council of Hong Kong, 1999), pp. 76–77. See also Ye Xiaoyan, "Zhanguo Qin Han de deng ji youguan wenti" ("Lamps of the Warring States, Qin, and Han, and related problems"), *Wenwu* 1983.7, p. 79; Tang and Liu, "Zhongguo gudai deng," p. 60. For an excellent photograph and discussion, see Jessica Rawson, ed., *Mysteries of Ancient China: New Discoveries from the Early Dynasties* (London: British Museum Press, 1996), pp. 156–58.

9. Hubei Sheng bowuguan, *Zeng Hou Yi mu* (*Tomb of Marquis Yi of Zeng*) (Beijing: Wenwu chubanshe, 1989), vol. 2, pls. 29–30.

10. Li Xueqin, *Eastern Zhou and Qin*, pp. 271–72; Yang Hong, *Zhongguo gubingqi luncong* (*Collected essays on ancient Chinese weaponry*) (Beijing: Wenwu chubanshe, 1980), p. 119.

11. Jingzhou diqu bowuguan, "Hubei Jiangling Tengdian yihao mu fajue jianbao" ("Brief report on the excavation of Tomb 1 at Tengdian, Jiangling, Hubei"), *Wenwu* 1973.9, p. 8, fig. 2 on p. 9, and pl. 2.1. This sword is 56.2 cm long.

12. Max Loehr, *Chinese Bronze Age Weapons: The Werner Jennings Collection in the Chinese National Palace Museum, Peking* (Ann Arbor: University of Michigan Press, 1956), pp. 72–82.

13. The Marquis Yi, whose skeleton survived, was estimated to have been about 162 cm in height (see *Zeng Hou Yi mu*, vol. 1, p. 601), and I use that figure for this calculation. The actual height of the figurine is 28.5 cm, and the sword including the scabbard is 13.4 centimeters.

See also Table 1 (above).

For the Qibeigu swords, also thought to be booty from the Chu conquest of Yue in 355 BCE, see Huang Guangxin, "Anqing Wangjiashan Zhanguo mu chutu Yuewang Qibeigu jian deng qiwu" ("The sword of Qibeigu, king of Yue, and other objects unearthed from a Warring States tomb at Wangjiashan, Anqing"), *Wenwu* 2000.8, pp. 84–88, and cpls. on inside of back cover. For the Goujian sword, see State Cultural Relics Bureau et al., *The Treasures of a Nation: China's Cultural Heritage, 1949–1999; Discovery, Preservation and Protection* (Beijing: Morning Glory Publishers, 1999), pp. 102–3.

14. White, *Tombs of Old Lo-yang*, p. 87, which states that the mirror on which the scene is depicted is now in the Marquis Hosokawa Collection, Japan. See the rendition in Yang Hong, *Zhongguo gubingqi luncong*, p. 95, fig. 75.

15. By the Han dynasty the *jian*, or double-edged sword tapering to a point, had lengthened and been replaced with single-edged swords, called *dao*. See David A. Graff, *Medieval Chinese Warfare, 300–900* (London: Routledge, 2000), p. 41.

16. William Trousdale, *The Long Sword and Scabbard Slide in Asia*, Smithsonian Contributions to Anthropology, no. 17 (1975), p. 46. This is the authoritative study on this subject. For the Chinese name of this slide, see pp. 270–71, n. 17. Sun Ji, *Zhongguo shenghuo: Zhongguo guwenwu yu Dong Xi wenhua jiaoliuzhong de ruogan wenti* (*Chinese sacred fire: some questions concerning ancient Chinese material culture and East-West cultural exchange*) (Shenyang: Liaoning jiaoyu chubanshe, 1996), pp. 17–19, comes to the same conclusion.

17. Trousdale, *Long Sword*, pp. 110–17, suggests that it was invented perhaps as early as the 8th or 7th centuries BCE by the Sauromatae in the Volga-Ural steppe zone to carry their long iron swords, and spread from there; Sun Ji, *Zhongguo shenghuo*, p. 41, n. 29, credits the invention to China.

18. Yang Hong, *Zhongguo gubingqi luncong*, p. 120.

19. Albert Dien, "A Study of Early Chinese Armor," *Artibus Asiae*, vol. 43, nos. 1–2 (1981–1982), pp. 6–7; Dien, "Armor in China before the Tang Dynasty," *Journal of East Asian Archaeology*, vol. 2, nos. 3–4 (2000), pp. 25–26.

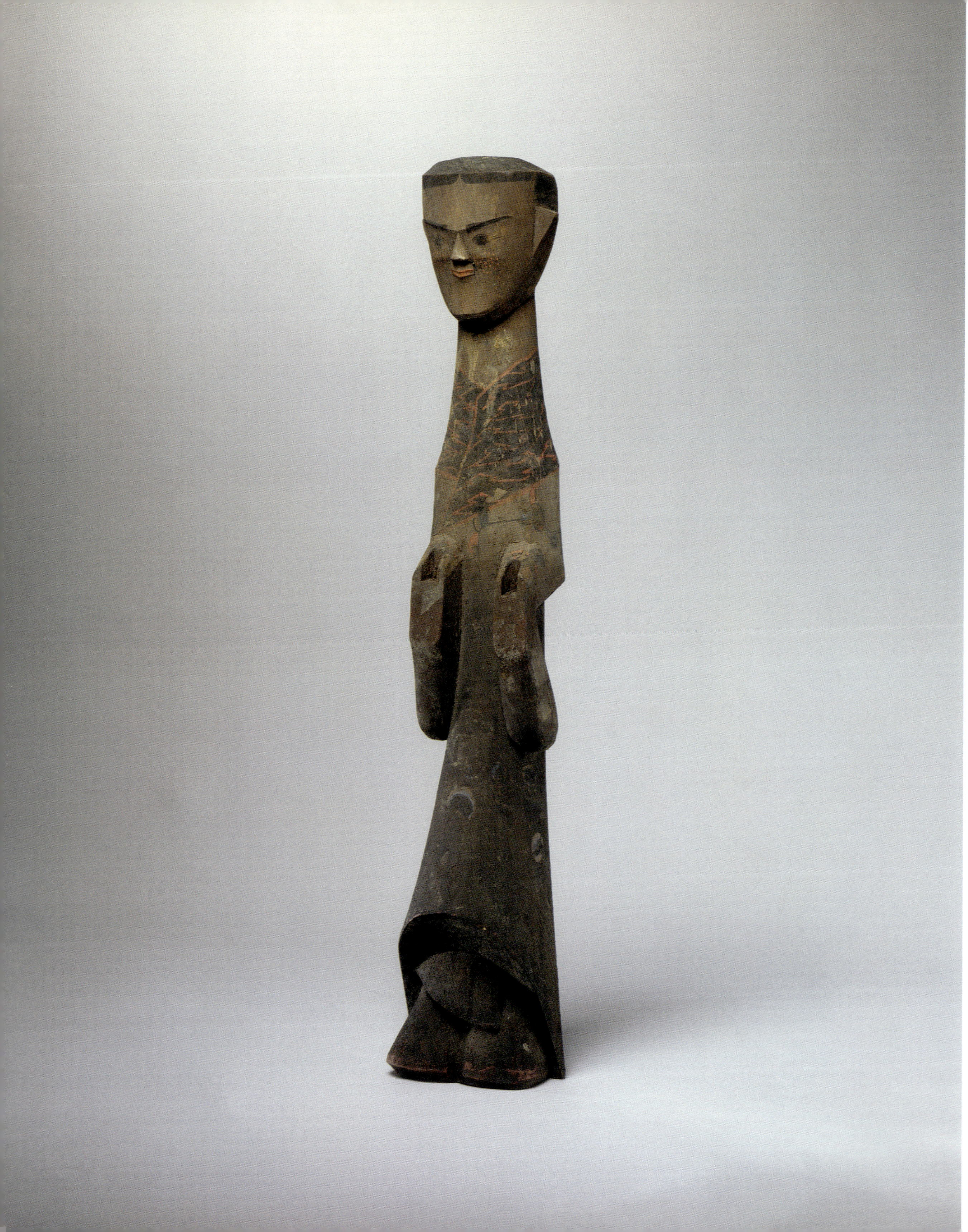

3

3 Human figure

Late Eastern Zhou period to early Western Han dynasty, ca. 3d century BCE. Wood with lacquer pigments; h. 56.5 cm. Princeton University Art Museum, acc. no. y1948-75. Museum purchase, Carl Otto von Kienbusch, Jr., Memorial Collection.

By the Eastern Han period mortuary figure sculptures were predominantly made of earthenware (see cat. nos. 4–6). Metal, stone, and wood figures are sometimes unearthed, but these are exceptional rather than expected. By contrast, during those centuries when tomb sculpture began to be commonly placed in burials, the largest, most lavish, and greatest variety of mortuary sculpture was made of wood, sometimes clothed in fabric, sometimes articulated and with movable limbs, and almost always painted in lacquer pigments. At the same time that these were being made, primarily in central and south China in regions under the influence of the Chu kingdom, "crude and rude" small ceramic figures were making their appearance in north China, including Shandong Province. How those small, crude figures were developed into the life-size naturalistic "terracotta" warrior figures placed in trenches outside of the necropolis of the First Emperor is still one of the great mysteries in art history.[1] The central/southern tradition of wooden mortuary sculpture did not die out immediately, and many examples have been unearthed from Western Han tombs in those areas.[2] But eventually in those areas too ceramic tomb sculpture became the norm.

In 1949 a large number of wooden figures, all simply and quite geometrically delineated, lacking their original forearms and hands, with traces of lacquer pigments, were reportedly dispersed among various private and museum collections in the United States. Three of them were brought together in 1973 as part of the pioneering exhibition *Unearthing China's Past*.[3] Judging from the date of its accession, the Princeton figure, which is very similar to the three then exhibited, may well be part of the same set or of similar provenance. Since the 1973 exhibition the number of wooden tomb figures found in many sites in China—even outside the heartland of the Chu kingdom in Hubei and Hunan provinces—has expanded to an astonishing degree. Still, certain figures unearthed from graves at Yangjiawan and Yangtianhu, sites in the Changsha area, remain the closest to this group of figures in proportion and appearance, as pointed out by Fontein and Wu.[4]

Although rarely, wooden figures have been found in some northern tombs, and bear some resemblance to their more common southern counterparts. Most northern wooden figures are larger than ceramic figures. They are usually posed not "doing" anything, standing quietly as if awaiting some order, though there are

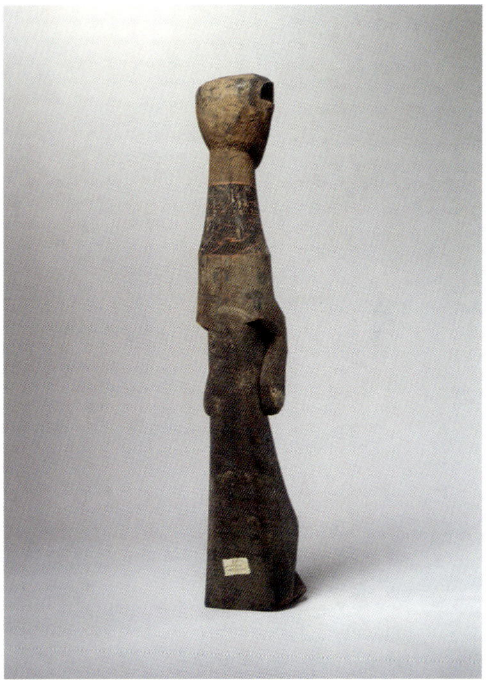

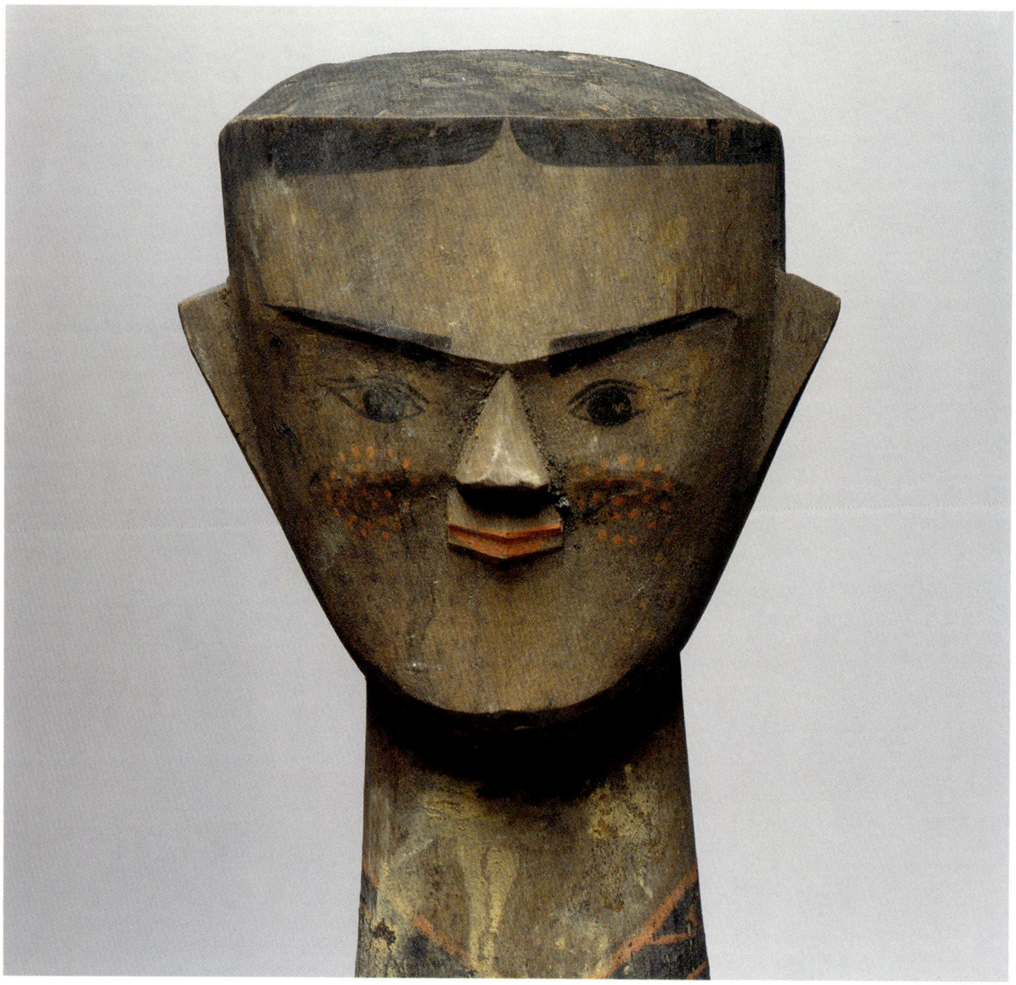

exceptions. Among the latter are four figures found in a tomb in Changzi County, Shanxi, which are attributed to the late Spring and Autumn period.[5] The relationship of these and other wooden figures in the north to those of the south, as well as the interactions between north and south generally, are subjects awaiting clarification through further excavation and research.

More information survives about wooden figures of Eastern Zhou date, particularly of the Warring States period, recovered from burials in areas under the influence of the Chu Kingdom in southern China.[6] These figures vary considerably in the number of parts of which they are made, whether their limbs are movable, the extent of their painted or carved decoration, and the presence or absence of textile clothing. The majority of these figures are judged to be household attendants or servants rather than entertainers, and many appear to be standing at attention rather than singing or dancing as is common among the early ceramic figurines unearthed in northern China. With their restrained, dignified expressions, and their hands sometimes drawn into their sleeves and held respectfully just below their waists, these may be viewed as the ancestors of the numerous ceramic attendant figures which became common beginning in the Qin and Western Han. Not all wooden figures are so static, however. Occasional figures have their arms extended in some sort of broad gesture, and the multipart figures could have been manipulated into various poses. Some of these southern standing wooden figures, like this one, are of considerable size, ranging from about 30 centimeters to more than 100 centimeters.[7]

VIRGINIA BOWER

Notes

1. See Virginia L. Bower, *From Court to Caravan: Chinese Tomb Sculptures from the Collection of Anthony M. Solomon*, ed. Robert D. Mowry (Cambridge, Mass.: Harvard University Art Museums, 2002), pp. 25–29.

2. Jessica Rawson, ed., *Mysteries of Ancient China: New Discoveries from the Early Dynasties* (London: British Museum Press, 1996), pp. 181–82, illustrates a group of wooden figures from an early Western Han tomb in Hubei. They are, typically for early Western Han, rather unisex in appearance, but graduated in size to indicate gradations of rank. These differ in important ways from the present figure, being quite naturalistically delineated, and in proportions and dress very much more like the two early Western Han ceramic figures included in this exhibition (cat. nos. 5, 6). Those pieces represent the taste prevalent in the Western Han capital at Chang'an (present-day Xi'an), Shaanxi Province. The present figure, with its triangular head and nose, is closer in appearance to wooden figures of the Chu Kingdom.

3. Jan Fontein and Tung Wu, *Unearthing China's Past* (Boston: Museum of Fine Arts, 1973), pp. 72–74.

4. Ibid., p. 74. Scholars disagree on the genders of these figures, a subject on which Fontein and Wu remain silent.

5. Shanxi Sheng kaogu yanjiusuo, "Shanxi Changzi Xian Dongzhou mu" ("Eastern Zhou tombs at Changzi County, Shanxi"), *Kaogu xuebao* 1984.4, pp. 503–29.

6. Jessica Rawson, "Thinking with Pictures: Tomb Figures in the Chinese View of the Afterlife," *Transactions of the Oriental Ceramic Society*, vol. 61 (1996–1997), pp. 25–27; Wu Hung, "The Art and Architecture of the Warring States Period," in *The Cambridge History of Ancient China: From the Origins of Civilization to 221 B.C.*, ed. Michael Loewe and Edward L. Shaughnessy (Cambridge: Cambridge University Press, 1999), pp. 732–40; and Patricia Berger, "Body Doubles: Sculpture for the Afterlife," *Orientations*, February 1998, pp. 46–53, contains illustrations of and references to the most important of these finds.

7. One of the best surveys of the wooden tomb sculptures associated with the Chu Kingdom is an essay by Gao Zhixi [spelled Chi-shi Kao], "Chu yong yanjiu," ("Study of Chu figures"), in *Taoyong lunwenji* (*Select research articles on ancient Chinese tomb figures*), ed. Guoli lishi bowuguan (Taipei: Guoli lishi bowuguan, 1998), pp. 8–34.

4 Standing man and woman

Western Han dynasty, ca. 141 BCE. Dark gray earthenware with traces of pigment; h. approx. 56 cm each.
Princeton University Art Museum, acc. no. 1998-282.1–2. Gift of Dr. Alvin E. Friedman-Kien in honor of Allen Rosenbaum.

These two armless nude earthenware figures with clearly delineated genitalia are of a type that originally had wooden or cloth arms attached by pegs through holes at the shoulders and were attired in fabric or other perishable materials. Mold-made with some handwork, these figures sometimes exhibit surprising individuality in facial type and variations in height. They are generally red or gray earthenware, and many were subsequently coated overall with a base coat of reddish brown pigment and then painted with facial features and hair. A second kiln firing may have been conducted to affix the pigments.[1] Painted details, such as the red headband visible here on the *Standing man*, can also sometimes be discerned.

Prior to the 1980s unprovenanced examples of nude sculpture of this type were generally dated to the Han dynasty, based on comparison with other Han sculpture. They were not much discussed in publications, however, perhaps because of doubts about their authenticity, or because of their discomfiting (in the context of the mainstream of Chinese art, whether pictorial or sculptural) nudity.[2]

Since the 1980s this type of mortuary sculpture, mostly males but also some females, began to be archaeologically recovered from burials associated with the Han imperial Liu family.[3] One of these burials is a large tomb thought to belong to a Liu family member, discovered in the vicinity of present-day Xi'an, Shaanxi Province.[4] Most commonly, however, these figures are found in pits or trenches associated with Western Han imperial necropolises. Finds have ranged in date from the tomb complex of the founding Han emperor Gaozu (r. 206–195 BCE) to the necropolis of emperor Xuandi (r. 74–49 BCE). Although examples may have continued to be made into the Eastern Han, other types and styles of ceramic mortuary sculpture, often glazed rather than painted, came to predominate.

Such nude figures were also found where they were manufactured, at government workshop and kiln sites in the area of the Western Han capital of Chang'an (present-day Xi'an).[5] In addition a few have been found at an imperial princely tomb complex at Mangdang Shan in Henan Province.[6] Filling ancillary pits, small-scale ceramic fully clothed "armies," exhibiting certain regional traits, have now been found in Jiangsu and Shandong provinces. It is not impossible that in the future nude figures might be uncovered at imperial burial sites in these areas. Archaeologists generally believe that this type of figure was restricted to burials of those of the highest rank.[7]

Excavated examples have not only firmly dated these sculptures in the Western Han dynasty, but also attest that they were originally dressed. Many reveal impressions of what is likely to have been fabric (hemp or perhaps silk) attire. More noticeable are the traces of sewn-together leather-plate armor that still cling to some warriors. As to the figures' missing arms, the consensus seems to be that these were made of wood, although some suggest that they may have been made of cloth.[8]

The best-published and most extensively excavated Western Han imperial necropolis (to date) is the Yangling mausoleum of emperor Jingdi (r. 157–141 BCE) and his consort empress Wang (d. 126 BCE). In numerous pits or trenches from this site, a wide range of ceramic funerary

4

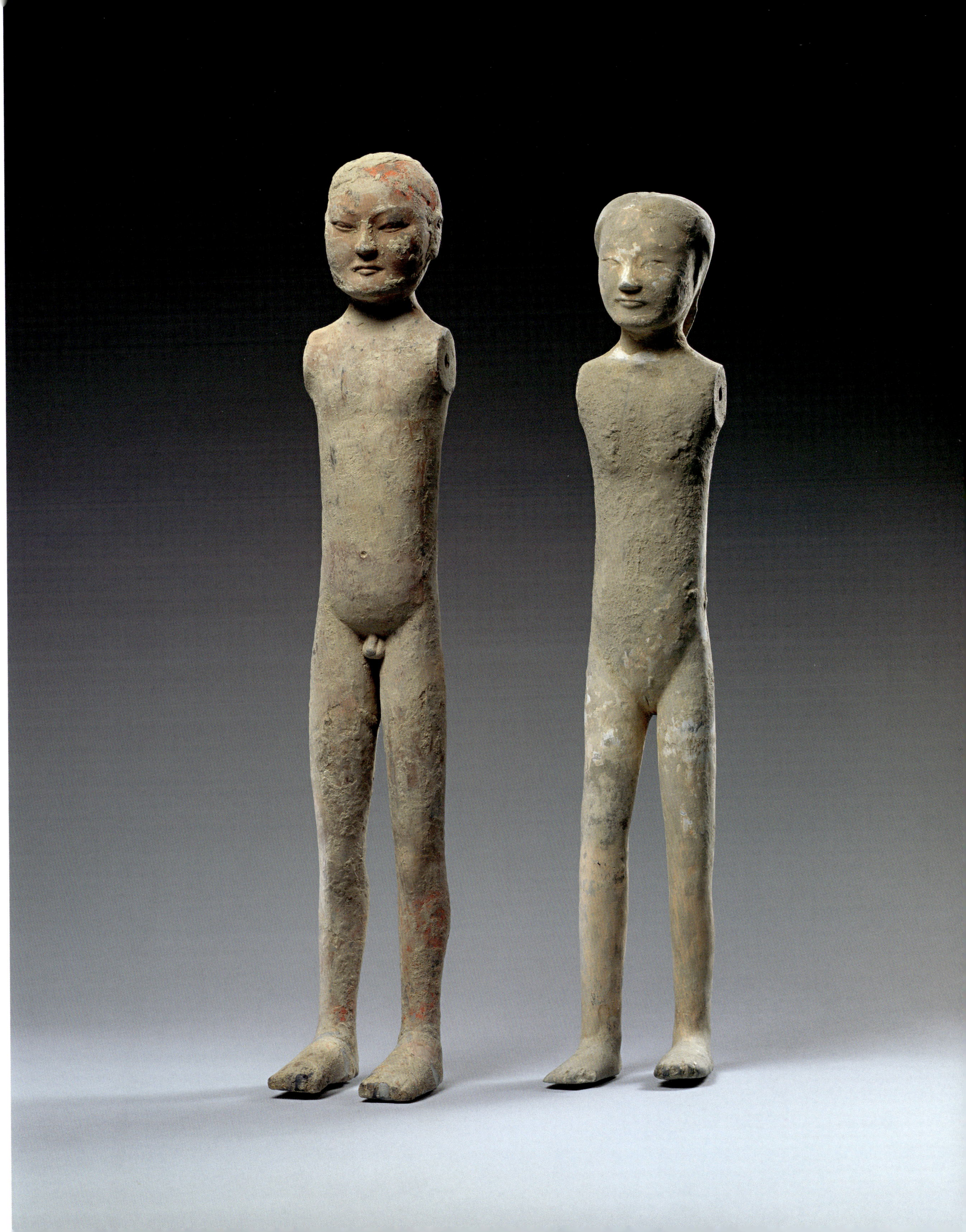

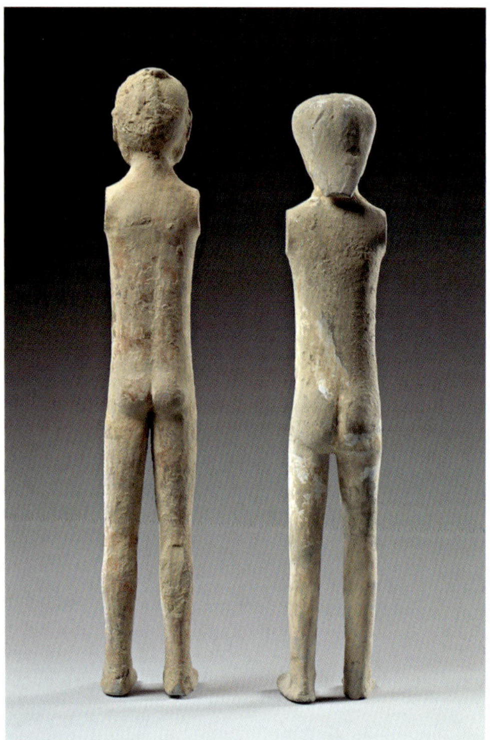

sculptures have been found. Many examples of standing unclothed males (some identified as eunuchs) and some females were recovered. Such figures recovered at Yangling and elsewhere are distinctive in having clearly defined genitalia. It should be emphasized that these unclothed figures were only part of a larger group of ceramic mortuary sculptures, which included various domestic animals as well as clothed men and women (ceramic figures whose attire is rendered in that medium). Noteworthy are some kneeling females, some with their arms held up concealed in large ribbed sleeves in a pose similar to that of *Kneeling female attendant* (cat. no. 5).[9]

Standing man and woman most likely originated in Shaanxi Province, as that is where the majority of such figures have been found, and likely date to the Western Han reigns of emperors Jingdi through Xuandi. Moreover, these two figures may not have come from the same pit or trench within a burial site, or even from the same site. Among excavated unclothed figures, males are more numerous, and these are predominantly soldiers though some may be civilian attendants. Fewer female figures have been unearthed, and less is known about them. They are generally smaller in stature, have longer torsos and slightly different buttocks, are sometimes found with oxcarts, and are often believed to be civilian attendants. Some scholars believe that some of these females may also be soldiers, which is not impossible since women played a more important role in combat in China than is sometimes known. Images of female warriors are depicted in the Wu rubbings (cat. nos. 1.2, 1.20).[10]

VIRGINIA BOWER

Notes

1. For detailed description of the manufacturing process for the unclothed tomb sculptures, see Shaanxi Sheng kaogu yanjiusuo, ed., *Han Yangling* (*Yangling Mausoleum of Emperor Jingdi of the Western Han Dynasty*) (Chongqing: Chongqing chubanshe, 2001), pp. 8–12. Also see Susan N. Erickson, "Catalogue Entries: Western Han Dynasty," in Li Jian et al., *Eternal China: Splendors from the First Dynasties* (Dayton: The Dayton Art Institute, 1998), p. 113.

2. Two male figures of this type dated to the Western Han were presented to the Tokyo National Museum between the years 1932–1941. See Tōkyō Kokuritsu Hakubutsukan, *Tōkyō Kokuritsu Hakubutsukan zuhan mokuroku: Chūgoku tōji hen* (*Illustrated catalogues of the Tokyo National Museum: Chinese ceramics*) (Tokyo: Tōkyō bijutsu, 1988), vol. 1, p. 11, p. 32, no. 118. Another unprovenanced example is in the Beijing National Museum, and included in Jessica Rawson, ed., *Mysteries of Ancient China: New Discoveries from the Early Dynasties* (London: British Museum Press, 1996), pp. 167–68, no. 79.

3. One of the earlier and still among the best-illustrated reports showing such figures is O. Louis Mazzatenta, "A Chinese Emperor's Army for Eternity," *National Geographic*, vol. 182 (August 1992), pp. 114–30. Also see Peter Hessler, "Treasures of Ancient China," *National Geographic*, vol. 200 (October 2001), pp. 48–67; and Shaanxi Sheng kaogu yanjiusuo, ed., *Han Yangling*, Chinese text p. 8 and p. 11, n. 32; in English p. 8 and p. 13, n. 30 (hereafter references will be to the English text).

4. Zheng Hongchun, "Shaanxi Xin'an jizhuanchang jitan Han chu mu fajue jianbao" ("Brief report on the excavation of the 'coal-protected' early Han dynasty tomb at the Xin'an brick factory in Shaanxi Province"), *Kaogu yu wenwu* 1994.4, pp. 31–56. The types of objects and a partial inscription found on a relic in this tomb led excavators to associate it with the Liu family.

5. Many of the archaeological reports describing the discovery of these figures are listed by Susan N. Erickson, "Catalogue Entries: Western Han Dynasty," pp. 112–14, 116–17, cat. nos. 34–35, and p. 186, nn. 8–10. Erickson's entries comprise one of the best overviews of the subject, and she notes the publication of male and female figures associated with emperor Gaozu's Changling mausoleum, in Patricia Berger and Jenifer Randolph Casler, *Tomb Treasures from China: The Buried Art of Xi'an* (San Francisco and Fort Worth: Asian Art Museum of San Francisco and Kimbell Art Museum, 1994), pls. 19, 20, thus pushing the date of the appearance of such pieces to the beginning of the Han dynasty.

6. Henan Sheng Shangqiu Shi wenwu guanli weiyuanhui et al., *Mangdang Shan Xihan Liangwang mudi* (*Mausoleums of the Liang princes of the Western Han at Mangdang Shan*) (Beijing: Wenwu chubanshe, 2001), pp. 171–89, cpl. 6.2, pls. 37–45.

7. According to Wang Xueli, "Zhaoyishi mubi taoyong de shidai yiyi" ("Significance of the date of clothed, wooden-armed ceramic tomb sculptures"), *Wenbo* 1997.6, pp. 71–75, this type of figure is closely associated with the imperial Liu family, and may have developed from Warring States–period wooden figures, often clothed, that were found in regions under the influence of the Chu Kingdom. Wang dates the appearance of the unclothed figures to the reign of the Emperor Jingdi. The find at Weishan, Shandong, of an "underground army" in a pit associated with a royal mausoleum was judged one of China's top ten archaeological discoveries of 2002; see Jarret A. Lobell, "Warriors of Clay," *Archaeology* vol. 56, no. 2 (2003), pp. 36–39.

8. Rawson, ed., *Mysteries of Ancient China*, p. 168.

9. Shaanxi Sheng kaogu yanjiusuo, ed., *Han Yangling*, pp. 47–48, nos. 71, 72; and for kneeling females with hands held out, see ibid., pp. 49–50, pls. 73–74. See also Peter Hessler, "Treasures of Ancient China," p. 67, for a group photograph of figures from this site: an unclothed male, a eunuch, and a female.

10. See Wang Zijin, *Zhongguo nüzi cong jun shi* (*History of women soldiers in China*) (Beijing: Junshi yiwen chubanshe, 1998).

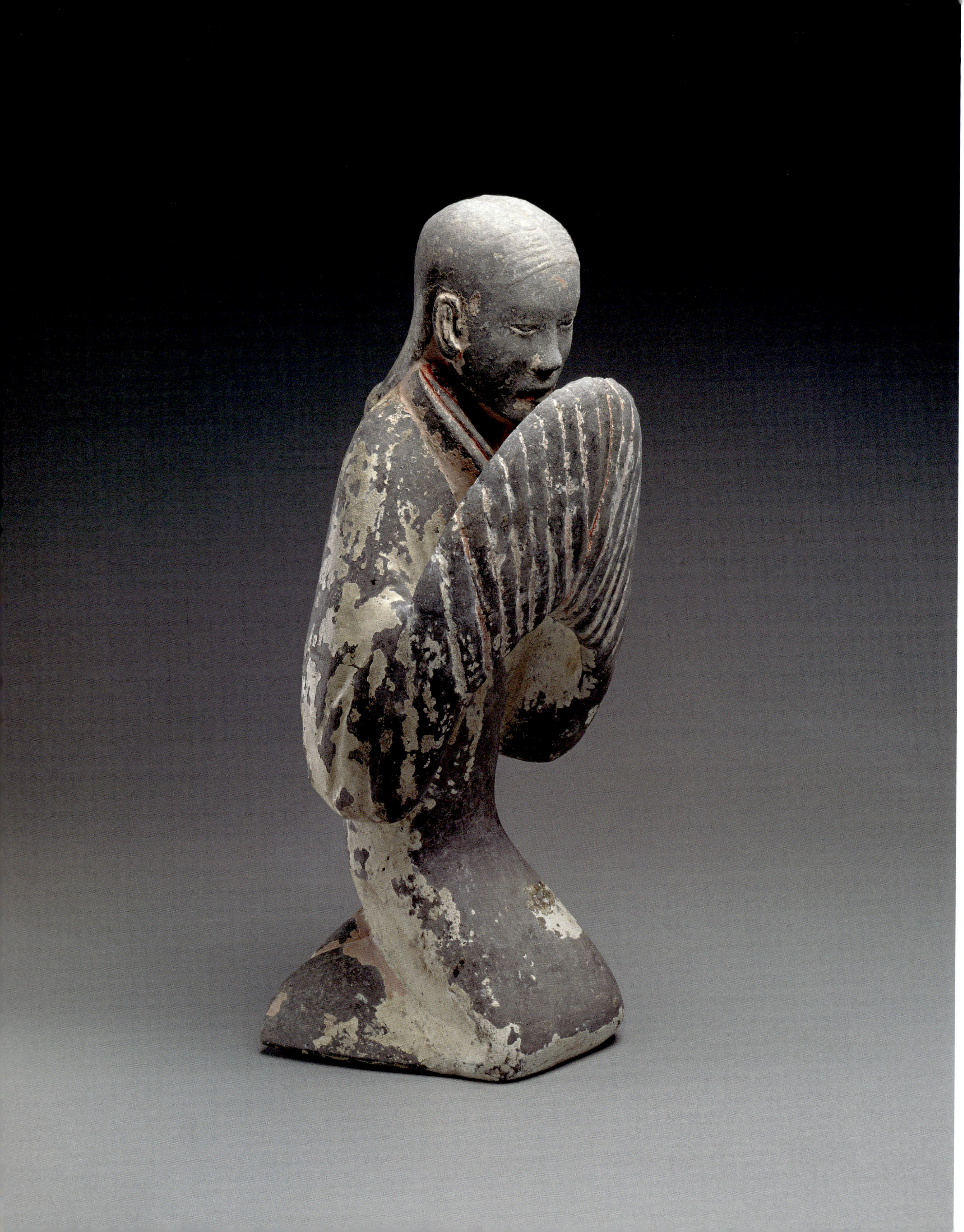

5

5 Kneeling female attendant

Western Han dynasty. Dark gray clay with pigments over white slip; h. 39.4 cm.
Princeton University Art Museum, acc. no. 1999-69. Museum purchase, Fowler McCormick, Class of 1921, Fund, in honor of Allen Rosenbaum.

A number of kneeling figures similar to the present one were excavated in 1966 from various pits at a site known as Renjiapo in the eastern suburb of Xi'an. This site is believed to be the necropolis of Empress Dou (d. 135 BCE), the wife of the early Western Han emperor Wendi (r. 180–157 BCE).[1] Its dark gray clay, once covered with white slip and pigments, as well as its serene oval face, make this is a very typical example of early Western Han mortuary sculpture, most likely created in the Xi'an area, where the Western Han capital Chang'an was located. As noted in *Sleeve dancer* (cat. no. 6), a large number of figures of women with oval faces and similar coiffures, made of gray earthenware and painted in white slip, have been recovered from the Xi'an area. These figures have generally been dated to the early Western Han period.

In its respectful kneeling posture this figure is comparable with the many kneeling male and female figures seen in the Wu rubbings (fig. 1). In the rubbings almost all the figures that can be identified as female wear elaborate lobed headdresses, whereas this figure, like many Western Han female figures, is shown with no headdress and hair hanging down in back and bound below the nape of the neck. The kneeling posture is generally interpreted as a show of respect, presumably for the deceased. Note, however, that in this era before the advent of the chair in China, even high-ranking persons knelt rather than sat, and that kneeling did not necessarily indicate low rank, let alone servility. The large male figures who kneel while receiving homage in the central pavilion scenes in the Wu rubbings (cat. nos. 1.9, 1.26, 1.36) are evidently of high status.

VIRGINIA BOWER

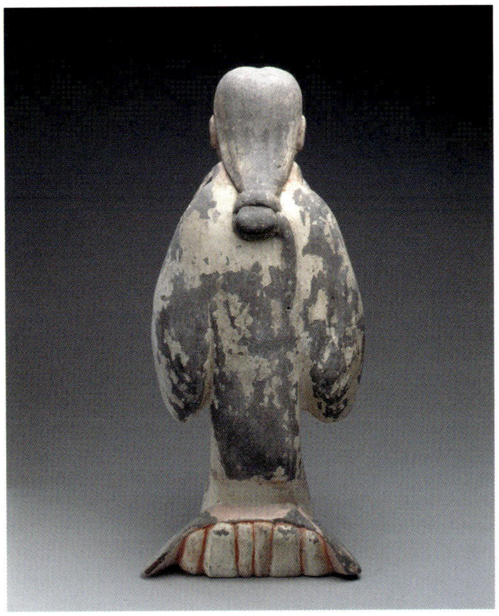

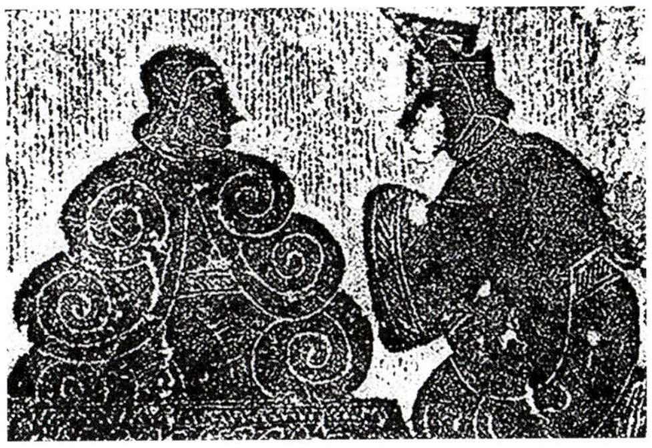

Fig. 1 *Ding Lan kneeling before a statue of a parent.* Detail of Stone Chamber 2, Stone 2-S.7.b (cat. no. 1.25). "Wu family shrines" rubbings. Princeton University Art Museum, acc. no. 2002-307.25.

Notes

1. Wang Xueli and Wu Zhenfeng, "Xi'an Renjiapo Han ling congzang keng de fajue" ("Ancillary burial pits at the Han mausoleum at Renjiapo, Xi'an"), *Kaogu* 1976.2, pp. 129–33, 75. Also see Los Angeles County Museum of Art et al., organizers, *The Quest for Eternity: chinese Ceramic Sculptures from the People's Republic of China* (Los Angeles: Los Angeles County Museum of Art and Chronicle Books, 1987), cpls. 16, 17, p. 107, nos. 16, 17.

6 Sleeve dancer

Western Han dynasty. Earthenware with pigments; h. approx. 40.6 cm.
Private collection.

Dances in which much of the effect was created by arm-controlled rippling of the dancer's sleeves—sometimes extremely long, sometimes extremely wide—are now generally referred to as "sleeve dances" (*xiuwu*). They were performed in China from as early as the Warring States period but in the popular imagination are most closely associated with the Han dynasty. Images of performers twirling their arms trailing lengthy sleeves may be found among Han tomb sculptures, jade plaques, paintings, decoration on bronze vessels, and pictorial stone carvings.[1] In a scene in the Wu rubbings (fig. 1), a male or female sleeve dancer and an acrobatic dancer doing a handstand perform atop a row of low drums. The object between the sleeve dancer and the acrobat-dancer is likely a plate or bowl used in the performance. Left of the dancers a group of figures are playing a game of *liubo* (cat. no. 1.12). Perhaps this entire scene can be viewed as entertainments enjoyed in the afterlife.

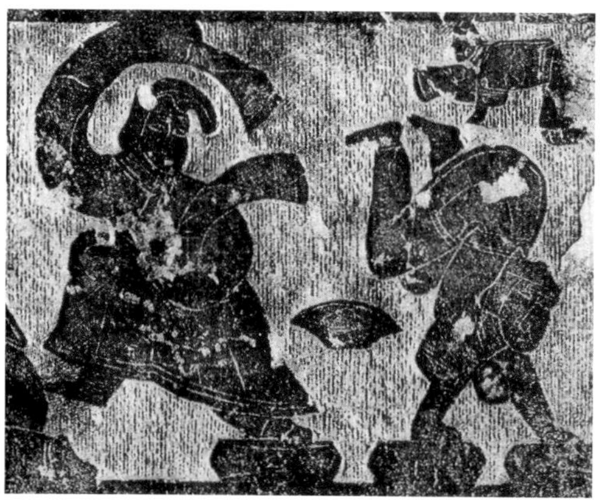

Fig. 1 *Sleeve dancer and acrobat on drums*. Detail of Stone Chamber 1, Stone 1-E.2 (cat. no. 1.12). "Wu family shrines" rubbings. Princeton University Art Museum, acc. no. 2002-307.2.

Images exist showing sleeve dancers performing with drums, with drums and bowls, and sometimes just with bowls; striking examples have been found in both Sichuan and Shandong.[2] In a scene of entertainments in an Eastern Han tomb at Zhucheng, Shandong,[3] people are shown beating on low circular objects upon which a dancer is performing, indicating these may really be drums. The general term used to describe this sort of sleeve dance is usually *guwu* ("drum dance") or *panguwu* ("bowl drum dance"); sometimes the latter term is thought to refer to the shape of the drums, but it may also indicate jumping over and around bowls as part of the dance.[4]

Sleeve dancing was done by males and females, alone, in pairs, or in groups, or as part of quasi-acrobatic performances utilizing low drums. Depictions of all these can be found in Han art. Most associated with sleeve dancing, however, are dances done by women wearing long robes. While male and female dancers could both wear this type of robe, sometimes they are distinguishable by their coiffures. Customarily during the Western Han women in this garb wore their hair long and self-looped at about shoulder level to hang down the back in a single neat tress, while men pinned their hair up and wore a cap. Nevertheless, though some surviving Eastern Han sleeve-dancer images wear an elaborate puffed hairstyle that is distinctly feminine, many others remain indeterminate of gender.[5]

Western Han-dynasty sleeve dancers are among the most beautiful of all Chinese ceramic tomb sculptures, and *Sleeve dancer* is an especially elegant example.[6] Originally this gray earthenware figure was coated with white slip and delicately colored. Traces survive of the original pigments of pink and brown. In form and stance, *Sleeve dancer* closely resembles a somewhat taller (49–50 cm) female dancer excavated along with several other earthenware

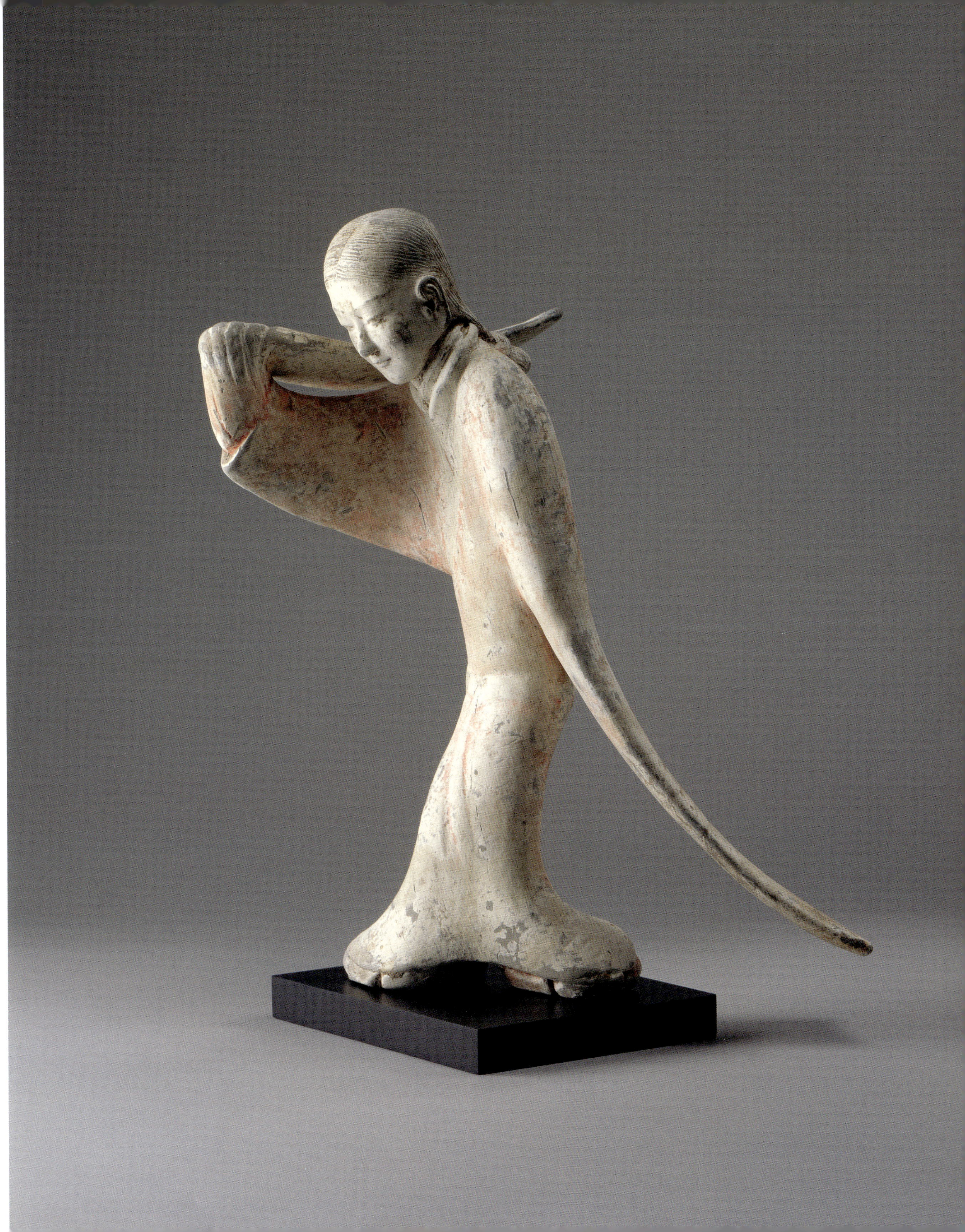

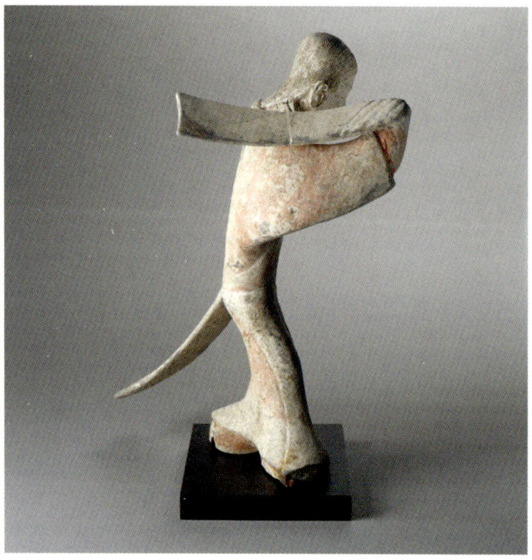

figures in 1954 from Tomb 24 at Baijiakou, northwest of present-day Xi'an.[7] Within the excavated group there was at least one kneeling figure, one figure standing in respectful pose, and one dancer. Importantly, this suggests that many sleeve-dancer mortuary figures may have originally been part of larger ensembles. This observation finds support in the original pairing of this *Sleeve dancer* with two other female figures presumably from the same tomb: a kneeling figure with hands held as if clapping, and a second dancer with both arms raised and long sleeves fluttering back over her shoulders.[8] Furthermore, given the close similarity in costume, coiffure, and manufacture of these figures to the Baijiakou and other excavated female figures, it is almost certain that this *Sleeve dancer* comes from the Xi'an area, where the capital of the Western Han was located.

Sleeve-dancer tomb figures have also been found away from the capital area. One of the most interesting representations of the sleeve dance is a Western Han ceramic tableau of musicians, acrobats, dancers, instruments, vessels, and figures, excavated in 1969 in Ji'nan, Shandong. Among the sleeve dancers is a male with a moustache accompanied by two probably female sleeve dancers.[9]

Han poetry contains descriptions of sleeve dancers, such as those by Zhang Heng (78–139) in his *Xijing fu* (*Western metropolis rhapsody*), that are especially apt for this *Sleeve dancer* and other Western Han examples from burials in the Xi'an area. An evocative description of sleeve dancing is included in Zhang Heng's *Nandu fu* (*Southern capital rhapsody*):

White cranes gliding by;
A cocoon unwinding its threads.
Their long sleeves, twirling and twisting, fill the hall;
Gauze-stockinged feet, taking mincing steps,
move with slow and easy gait.
They hover about long and continuously as if
stopped in mid-air . . . . [10]

Textual accounts of sleeve dancing are also recorded in pre-Western and early Western Han texts such as the *Han Feizi*, and even include one historical reference involving the founder of the Han dynasty. Su Yan correlated many of these textual references to all the various types of sleeve dancing with a variety of images from Sichuan, Henan, and Shandong.[11]

VIRGINIA BOWER

Notes

1. Susan N. Erickson, "'Twirling Their Long Sleeves, They Dance Again and Again . . . .' Jade Plaque Sleeve Dancers of the Western Han Dynasty," *Ars Orientalis*, vol. 24 (1994), pp. 39–63.

2. Wang Kefen, *Zhonghua wu dao tu shi* (*Illustrated history of Chinese dance*) (Taipei: Wenjin chubanshe, 2002), pp. 32–39.

3. Zhucheng Xian bowuguan and Ren Rixin, "Shandong Zhucheng Han mu huaxiang shi" ("Stone reliefs on a Han tomb in Zhucheng County, Shandong"), *Wenwu* 1981.10, p. 18, fig. 6.

4. Su Yan, "Changxiu posuo wu Han tian: cong kaogu chutu shiwu tan Handai changxiu wu" ("Long sleeves dancing gracefully under the Han sky: a discussion of the long-sleeve dances of the Han dynasty based on archaeologically recovered materials"), *Zhongyuan wenwu*, 2001.4, pp. 72–73.

5. Geng Baochang, ed., *Zhongguo wenwu jinghua daquan: Taoci juan* (*Great compendium of Chinese art treasures: Ceramics*) (Hong Kong: Shangwu yinshuguan, 1993), p. 104, no. 365.

6. Published in *Fine Chinese Ceramics and Works of Art*, auction catalogue, Sotheby's, New York, March 23, 2004, lot 594. For similar sleeve dancers in related

poses, see Julia K. Murray, "The Charlotte C. and John C. Weber Galleries for the Arts of Ancient China at the Metropolitan Museum," *Arts of Asia* (May–June 1988), p. 102, fig. 16; Qin Tingyu, *Zhongguo gudai taosu yishu* (*Ancient Chinese ceramic art*) (Beijing: Zhongguo gudian yishu chubanshe, 1957), pls. 1–4.

7. See Jessica Rawson, ed., *Mysteries of Ancient China: New Discoveries from the Early Dynasties* (London: British Museum Press, 1996), p. 206, no. 108; *Qin Han diaosu* (*Qin and Han sculpture*), ed. Zhongguo meishu quanji bianji weiyuanhui, *Zhongguo meishu quanji: Diaosu* (*Comprehensive collection of Chinese arts: Sculpture*), vol. 2 (Beijing: Renmin meishu chubanshe, 1985), no. 61; Kaogu yanjiusuo Shaanxi kaogu diaocha fajuedui, "Baoji he Xi'an fujin kaogu fajue jian bao" ("Brief report on the archaeological excavations in Baoji and the vicinity of Xi'an"), *Kaogu tongxun* 1955.2, pp. 33–40.

8. *Fine Chinese Ceramics and Works of Art*, lot 594.

9. *Qin Han diaosu*, no. 63. See also Geng Baochang, *Zhongguo wenwu jinghua daquan*, p. 85, no. 302.

10. Xiao Tong, *Wen xuan or Selections of Refined Literature*, trans. and annot. David R. Knechtges (Princeton: Princeton University Press, 1982), vol. 1, p. 327, as cited by Erickson, "Twirling Their Long Sleeves . . .," p. 61, n. 62.

11. Su Yan, "Changxiu posuo wu Han tian," pp. 68–74. According to Su, sleeve dancing may have sometimes been done for personal enjoyment, but was also performed to entertain others.

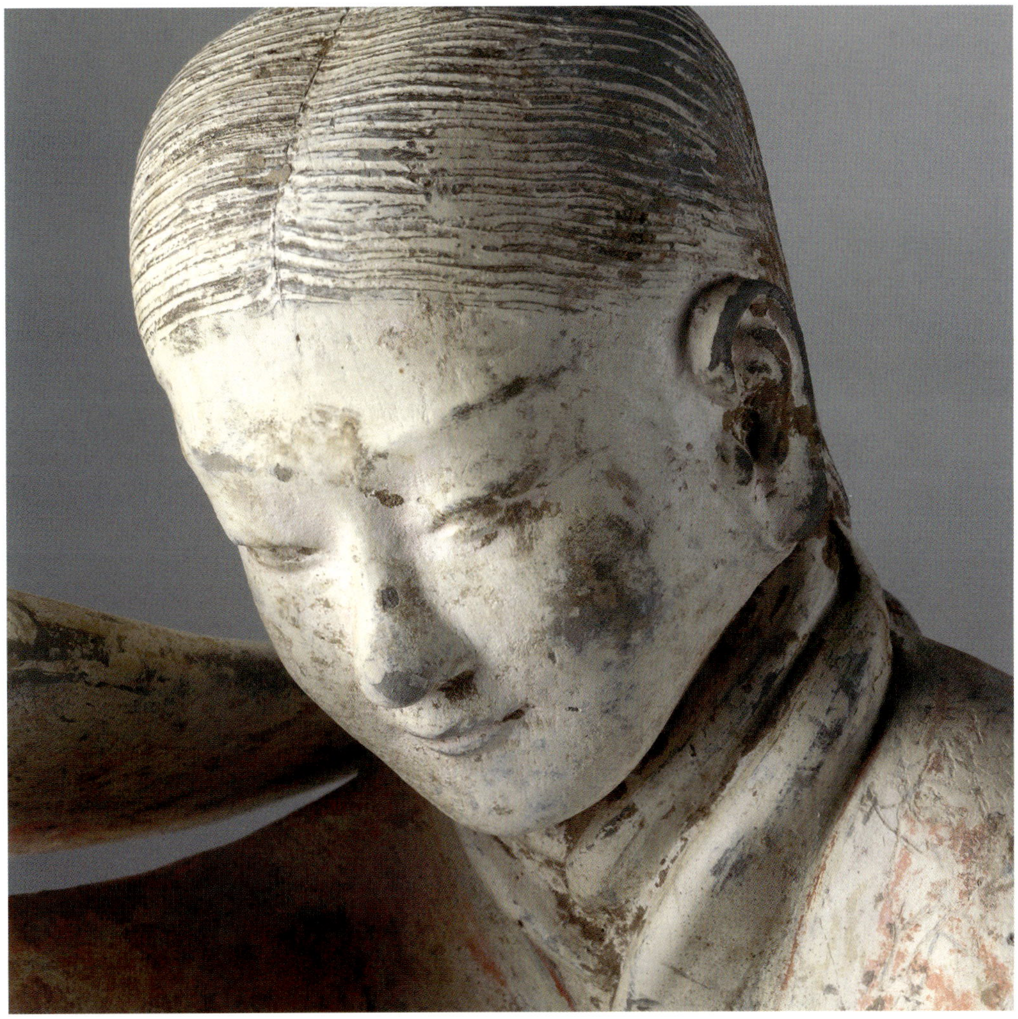

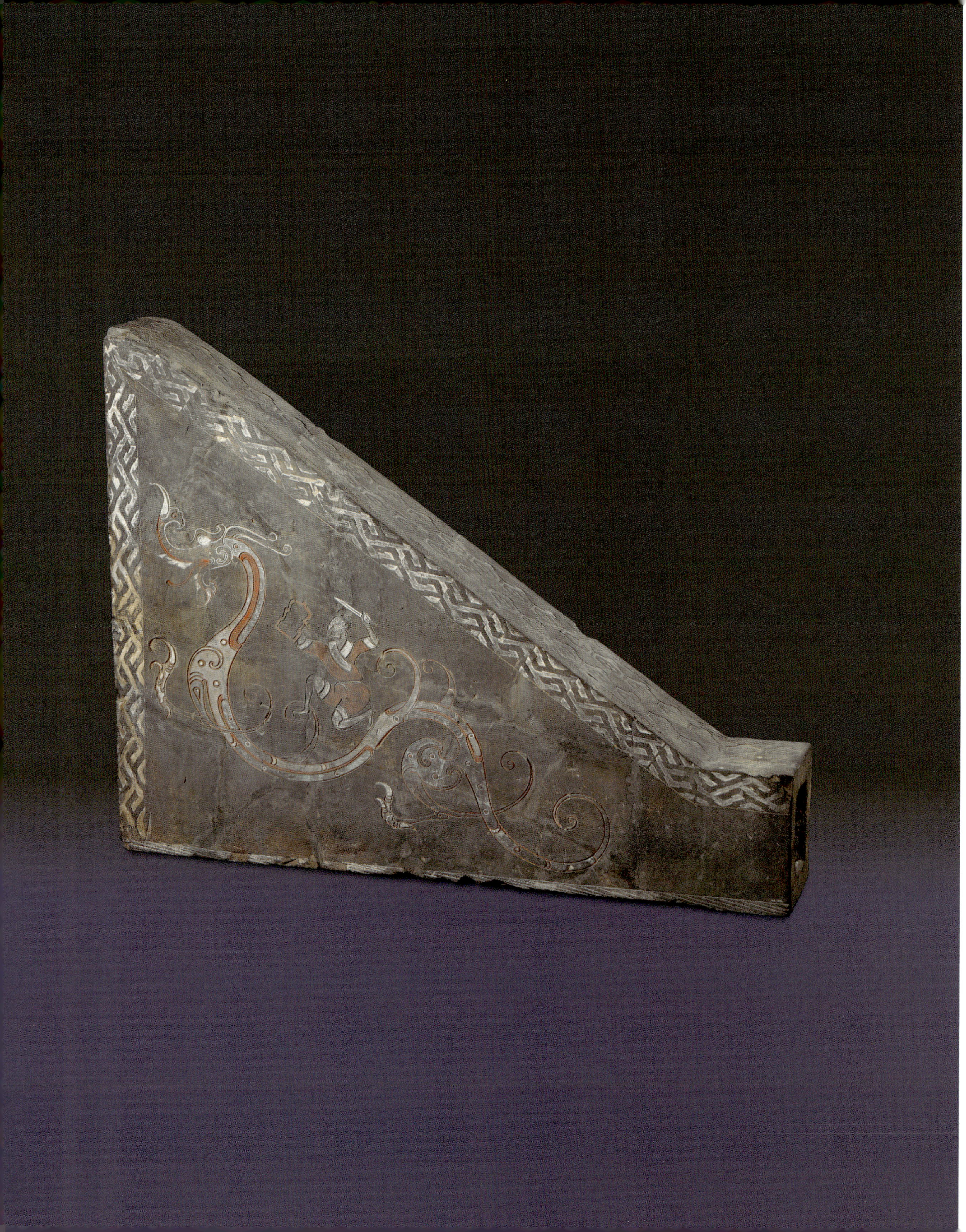

7

7 Triangular hollow tomb tile with dragon design

Western Han dynasty, 1st century BCE. Luoyang, Henan Province. Gray earthenware with red, white, green, and blue polychrome; h. 80 cm, w. 105 cm, d. 15 cm. Royal Ontario Museum, acc. no. 931.13.186. The Bishop William C. White Collection.

The period during which large hollow tiles were used for tomb construction coincides fairly precisely with the dates of the Qin and Western Han dynasties, with the majority dating from the first century BCE. The tiles are of two main types: the more common bear relief designs composed of many repeated impressions of different small stamps; less common are very large tiles with geometric borders framing large motifs executed in intaglio by a few large stamp impressions. Most of both types are rectangular; a few are triangular and were used in pairs to form the gables of house-shaped tomb chambers. All the intaglio tiles were found in Luoyang and vicinity; all share a naturalistically styled repertoire of large birds, human figures, horses, dogs, wild animals, dragons, and trees; and all seem to come from one workshop or a small number of closely related workshops. The Royal Ontario Museum owns about sixty intaglio tiles, purchased from the hundreds that were on the market in Luoyang in the 1920s and 1930s.[1] About sixty more have been published in China since the 1980s.[2] All are scattered finds; none have been properly excavated from a known site.

This gable tile is exceptional in that its decoration does not consist of a number of repeated motifs, but of one large stamped dragon on each face: one with a rider, one without (fig. 1). Both dragons measure about seventy centimeters from snout to tail, and thus are by far the largest single stamped design found on any tomb tile. They were not produced, however, by one giant stamp, but by carefully aligning a number of partial stamps. Five stamps were used for the dragon with a rider: head and breast, middle section with sword- and shield-brandishing rider; withers with hind leg; and the tail in two sections. We know that a single stamp rendered the dragon's midsection and the rider, because the rider's right foot covers a dragon tentacle without any crossing of lines. Exactly the same dragon with rider is found on another, rectangular, tile in the Royal Ontario Museum's collection; the riderless dragon is also stamped on a rectangular tile in the Carnegie Museum of Art in Pittsburgh.

Hollow tomb tiles were formed in a wooden trough of the same size and shape as the tile. It was lined with cloth to allow for easy removal of the formed clay. First a large slab of clay, cut with a string from a block, was pressed against the bottom of the form to fashion one face of the tile. At right angles to this slab were attached narrower strips of clay; these would form the narrow sides of the tile. A sandbag was then laid inside the clay-lined form and the top slab put in place over it; the sandbag prevented the top slab from sagging. After the assembled tile had dried to a leather-hard consistency, it was removed from the form. Almost all rectangular tomb tiles have one or two round holes cut into one of the two narrow sides, and an oblong aperture in the other. The aperture allowed for easy opening of the sandbag, pouring out the sand, and removing the bag. Some tiles, including this triangular one, have only the round holes, which means that the bag was sacrificed. According to W.C. White, the holes were used for connecting the tiles with rods or ropes. There is no evidence for this, and it seems much more likely that the holes were cut to permit good circulation of hot air during firing. After the tiles were wetted to soften the surface and carefully smoothed with

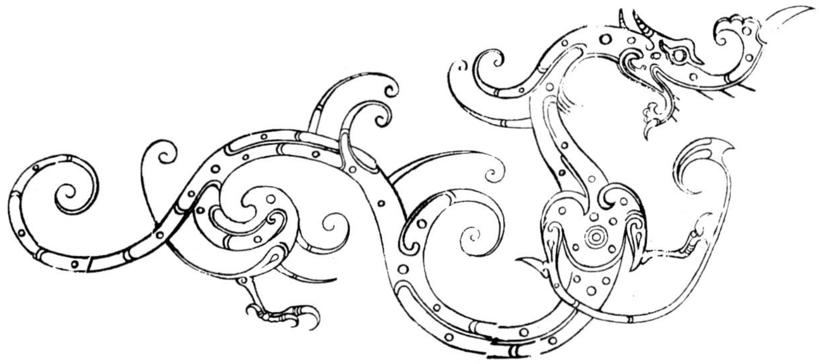

a spatula to remove the impression of the lining cloth, the stamped designs were impressed.[3]

On its longer vertical side this tile bears an inscription, scratched before firing, that reads *nan he xi* ("west of south gable"). *He* is the technical term for the head- and footboards of a wooden coffin,[4] and apparently was also used for the gables of tile tombs with a vault in the shape of an inverted V. The inscription provides linguistic evidence that tomb chambers of hollow tiles were originally conceived as ceramic versions of wooden outer coffins. Perhaps a further indication of this is the fact that all hollow tomb tiles of the type with intaglio lines are decorated on both sides. A hollow-tile tomb of the simpler type, with a flat ceiling, might be compared with an outer coffin of the Mawangdui type, with its richly decorated exterior (but undecorated interior). In Eastern Han tomb chambers such as Zuo Biao's tomb (cat. no. 12), the lining stones are carved on the interior only. This may indicate a chronological transition from outer coffins decorated primarily on the exterior (like the Mawangdui coffin), to tile chambers decorated on both sides (like the present one), and finally to stone burial chambers decorated only on their interior, visible, face.

Only one face of this triangular tomb tile is colored. Thanks to the inscription, we know that it was the interior face; evidently the tomb's interior was more important than its exterior. Hollow-tile tombs thus seem to be a transitional stage between the tombs of the Warring States and Western Han, constructed of heavy logs and containing nested coffins, and the brick and stone tomb chambers of the Eastern Han and later.

KLAAS RUITENBEEK

Fig. 1 *Stamped dragon on back face.* After William Charles White, *Tomb Tile Pictures of Ancient China*, pl. 81.

Notes

1. William Charles White, *Tomb Tile Pictures of Ancient China* (Toronto: University of Toronto Press, 1939), pp. 5, 20, 44; ill. 12, pls. 80, 81.
2. See Huang Minglan, *Luoyang Han huaxiang zhuan* (*Han-dynasty pictorial tiles from Luoyang*) (n.p.: Henan meishu chubanshe, 1986); Roger Goepper, ed., *Das alte China: Menschen und Götter im Reich der Mitte* (Munich: Hirmer, 1995), no. 101, pp. 399–401 (two intaglio tiles; entry by Peter Wiedehage); Zhang Xiang, "Luoyang xin faxian de Xihan kongxin huaxiang zhuan" ("Newly discovered Western Han hollow tomb tiles from Luoyang"), *Wenwu* 1990.2, pp. 61–66; Li Xianqi and Yang Haiqin, "Luoyang you faxian yipi Xihan kongxin huaxiang zhuan" ("Another group of Western Han hollow tomb tiles discovered in Luoyang"), *Wenwu* 1993.5, pp. 17–23; Shaanxi Provincial Institute of Archaeology, *Qin du Xianyang kaogu baogao* (*Archaeological report on the investigations and excavations at the ancient Qin capital Xianyang*) (Beijing: Science Press, 2004), pp. 311–15 and 383–97 (hollow tiles used in palace construction at Xianyang site).
3. Huang Minglan, *Luoyang Han huaxiang zhuan*, pp. 5–7.
4. Chen Qixian, *Lüshi chunqiu jiaoshi* (*Annotations to the "Annals of Lü Buwei"*) (Shanghai: Xinhua shudian, 1984), chap. "Kaichun," pp. 1426, 1434–35.

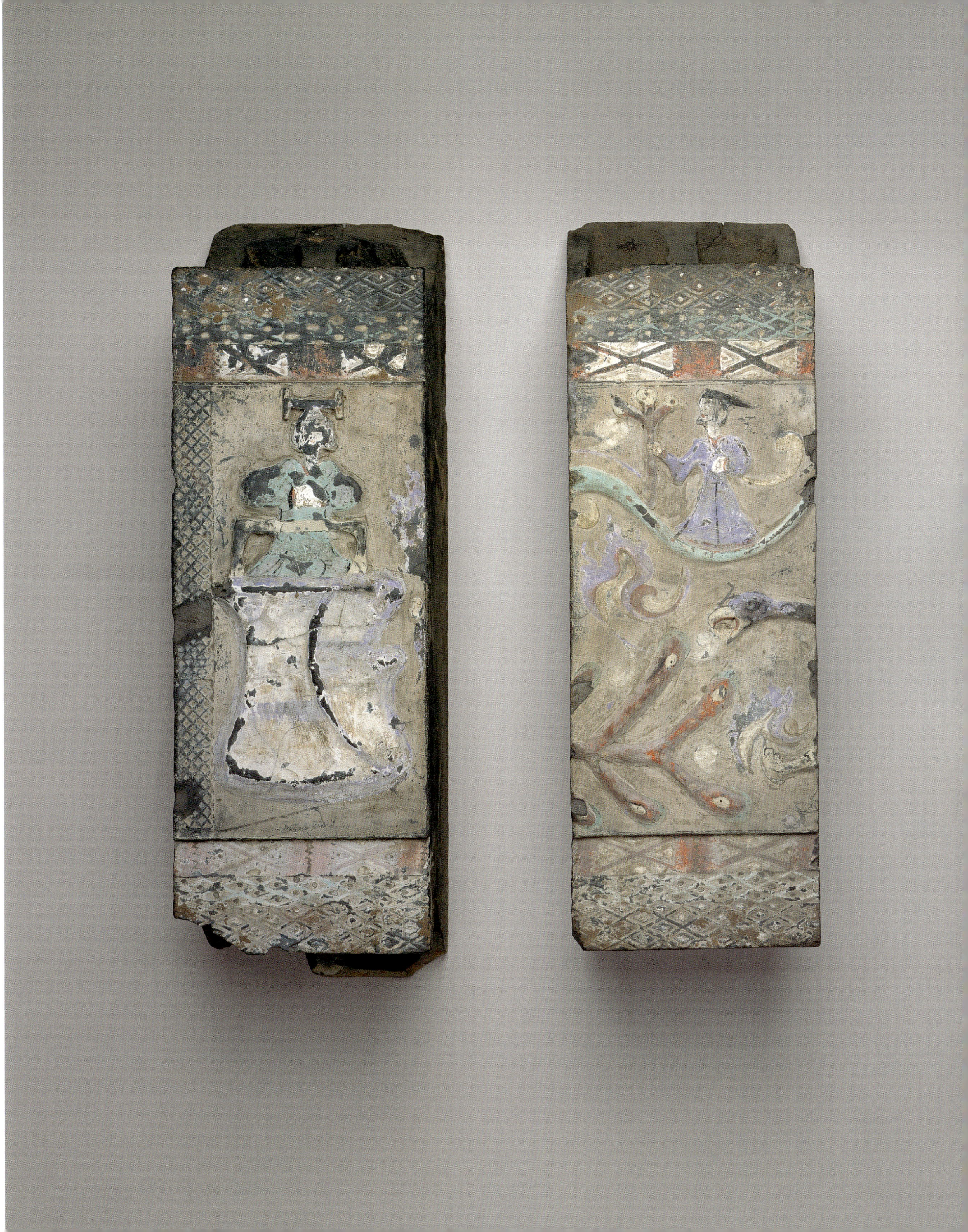

8 Queen Mother of the West and figure riding a snake

Western Han dynasty, 1st century BCE. Henan Province. Two hollow tomb ceiling tiles; gray earthenware with red, white, green, and blue polychrome; each tile h. approx. 77 cm, w. 23 cm, d. 22 cm (painted side 62.5 × 23 cm).
Royal Ontario Museum, acc. no. 922.20.625, 922.20.626. The George Crofts Collection.

These two hollow tiles come from the uppermost, horizontal part of the ceiling of a tomb with a false vault.[1] Into the mitered rabbets at both ends, large hollow tiles were fitted at an angle of 45 degrees; these rested on the vertical side walls of the tomb, likewise made of hollow tiles. The colored relief decoration of one tile shows the Queen Mother of the West (see Lullo's "Regional Iconographies" in this catalogue) with her identifying hair ornament shaped like two hourglasses connected by a shaft, sitting atop a biconcave column that represents Mount Kunlun and leaning on an armrest. The other shows a man holding a three-pronged branch and being borne along on a snake, and in the lower half the head and claw of a bird, and the tail of another large peacock-like bird. They must have been part of a larger composition that showed mythical animals, deities, and Immortals, as have been found on the ceilings of several hollow tile tombs of the first century BCE, most notably the Qianjingtou tomb (21 tiles), the Shaogou Tomb 61 (22 tiles), and the tomb of Bu Qianqiu (20 tiles) (fig. 1), all from Luoyang.[2] The two Royal Ontario Museum tiles are considerably larger than the ceiling tiles of these three tombs, which measure 56.0 × 27.0 × 18.0 centimeters, 55.0 × 23.0 × 16.0 centimeters, and 52.0 × 24.0 × 20.0 centimeters, respectively. They differ also in that the pictorial designs and geometric borders are not just painted, but executed in relief as well. A sun and a moon figure prominently in all three tombs (see Liu's "Concept of 'Brilliant Artifacts'" in this catalogue), but only in Bu Qianqiu's tomb does the ceiling have a larger narrative program, as it did in the tomb that disclosed the present tiles. On twenty tiles, numbered at the time they were made, and similar in shape to the Royal Ontario Museum tiles, are depicted a large snake; the sun; Fuxi; a man on a snake and a woman on a three-headed bird riding toward the Queen Mother of the West; the White Tiger; the Vermilion Bird; two winged leopard-like animals; the Blue (or Green) Dragon; a feathered man holding a staff; the moon; and Nüwa. The Royal Ontario Museum tile showing the Queen Mother of the West has a stamped geometrical border at the left, and thus most likely was placed at the left end of the original tableau.The Queen Mother occupies a similar position in a floor slab from Songshan, Jiaxiang County, Shandong, dated to about 158 CE. In Bu Qianqiu's tomb she is painted more toward the center of the composition, sitting on a cloud. The Royal Ontario Museum tile shows probably the earliest example of the Queen Mother of the West sitting on a columnnar Mount Kunlun, which in the Eastern Han became part of her standard iconography. A

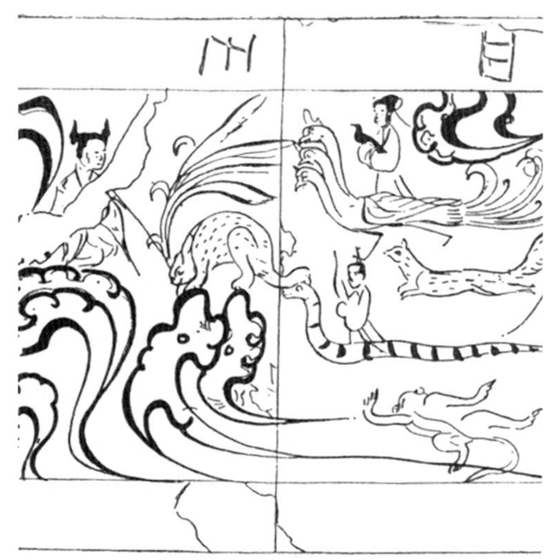

Fig. 1 *Detail of a mural from the tomb of Bu Qianqiu.* Western Han dynasty, first century BCE. Luoyang, Henan. From Luoyang Museum, "Luoyang Xihan Bu Qianqiu bihua mu fajue jianbao" ("A brief report on the painted Western Han tomb of Bin Qianqiu in Luoyang"), *Wenwu* 1977.6, p. 10, fig. 33.

very similar representation, which includes the armrest, is found on another of the Songshan stones.[3] In Bu Qianqiu's tomb the man riding on a snake toward the Queen Mother is generally interpreted as the tomb occupant ascending to paradise (the woman on the bird being his spouse) (fig. 1). It is likely that the man in the second Royal Ontario Museum tile, standing on what appears to be a snake's body, likewise is the tomb occupant. One of the two partially depicted birds under him may have carried his wife. The snake has been interpreted as the Flying Snake (*tengshe*), mentioned in third-century BCE works such as the *Xunzi*, *Erya*, and the *Shenzi*.[4] Although the two Royal Ontario Museum tiles represent only a small part of what most likely was a composition of at least twenty tiles, they are still important as remnants of a Western Han depiction of the land of the Immortals that was even larger and probably more detailed than the one found in the tomb of Bu Qianqiu, and include one of the earliest known images of the Queen Mother of the West.

KLAAS RUITENBEEK

Notes

1. Earlier published in Klaas Ruitenbeek, *Chinese Shadows: Stone Reliefs, Rubbings, and Related Works of Art from the Han Dynasty (206 BC–AD 220) in the Royal Ontario Museum* (Toronto: Royal Ontario Museum, 2002), pp. 38–39.

2. See, respectively, Luoyang Shi di'er wenwu gongzuodui, "Luoyang Qianjingtou Xihan bihua mu fajue jianbao" ("Preliminary report on the excavation of a Western Han tomb with murals at Qianjingtou, Luoyang"), *Wenwu* 1993.5, pp. 1–16; Henan Sheng wenhuaju wenwu gongzuodui, "Luoyang Xihan bihua mu fajue baogao" ("Report on the excavation of a Western Han tomb with mural paintings"), *Kaogu xuebao* 1964.2, pp.107–25; Luoyang Museum, "Luoyang Xihan Bu Qianqiu bihua mu fajue jianbao" ("Summary report of the excavation of a Western Han tomb with mural paintings, belonging to Bu Qianqiu"), *Wenwu* 1977.6, pp. 1–12.

3. For rubbings of the two Songshan stones, see Ruitenbeek, *Chinese Shadows*, p. 27, and Wu Hung, *The Wu Liang Shrine: The Ideology of Early Chinese Pictorial Art* (Stanford: Stanford University Press, 1989), p. 118.

4. See He Xilin, "Luoyang Bu Qianqiu mu mushi bihua de zai tantao" ("Reconsidering the tomb chamber murals of the tomb of Bu Qianqiu, Luoyang"), *Gugong bowuyuan yuankan* 2000.6, p. 73.

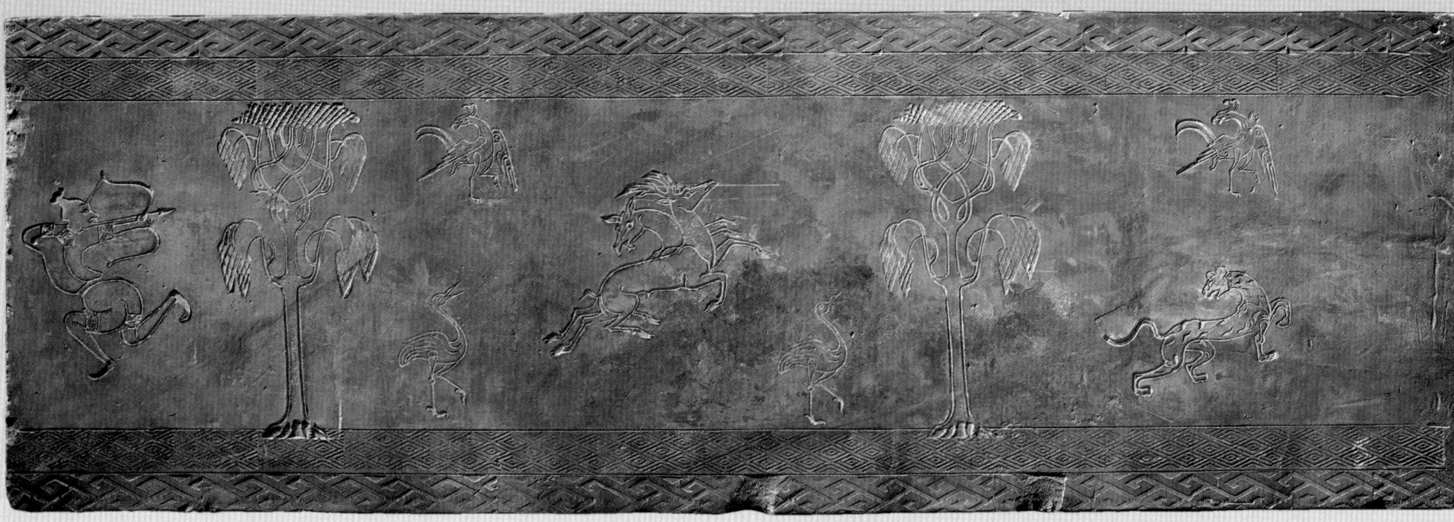

9 Tomb wall tile stamped with designs of an archer, trees, horses, and beasts

Eastern Han dynasty. Henan Province. Earthenware with traces of pigments; h. 50 cm, w. 153 cm.
Princeton University Art Museum, acc. no. 2002-287. Museum purchase with funds given by Lloyd E. Cotsen, Class of 1950.

Hollow bricks came into use in tomb construction during the late Warring States period.[1] During the Han dynasty they became an integral part of tomb architecture and imagery, particularly around modern-day Luoyang and Zhengzhou, Henan Province. Hundreds of bricks, many stamped with intaglio designs, were unearthed from 1925 to 1932, during the construction of the Longhai Railroad. The hollow pictorial brick in the Princeton collection first became known in 1936 as part of the C. T. Loo collection.[2]

Hollow bricks were made from gray clay that was made into thick slabs and formed in large draw molds. The two large faces of the brick were attached with narrower pieces of clay which formed the sides, to create the hollow box.[3] While still wet, the clay was impressed with molds or stamps, which created both the pictures and the geometric designs in intaglio lines. Unintentional overlapping of stamps was quite common, and can be seen in the inner border of the Princeton tile on the upper left side. Hollow bricks were lighter and less prone to fissuring during firing than solid bricks. They were used in conjunction with carved bricks, and were often left unstamped to accommodate painting, as in Bu Qianqiu's tomb.[4] They remained popular until the late Han dynasty, when tomb architecture became more complex, including long passageways or arches, which hollow-brick construction could not support. At that time they were replaced almost entirely by decorated solid bricks.

Hollow bricks were used for the doorframe on either side of the tomb door, for the top of the door lintel, and to seal the door (fig. 1). They were also included in the walls of the main tomb chamber, as well as for the ceiling ridge and the ceiling itself (cat. no. 8).[5] The hollow bricks for the ceiling supports were triangular sections that followed the ceiling slope and were often painted (cat. no. 7). Both these triangular slabs and the doorway lintel were supported on pillars. Usually the hollow bricks used for the tomb floor have plain surfaces and those for the ceiling have geometric designs. Typically bricks in other locations have pictures bordered by geometric designs. Hollow bricks were also used outside the main tomb structure in the construction of stairways and in other locations.[6]

The picture on the Princeton brick is divided into three sections that are demarcated by fruit-bearing trees whose roots extend beyond the lower border.[7] At far left a hunter sprints leftward while looking back over his shoulder to shoot an arrow from his bow. The upper arc of

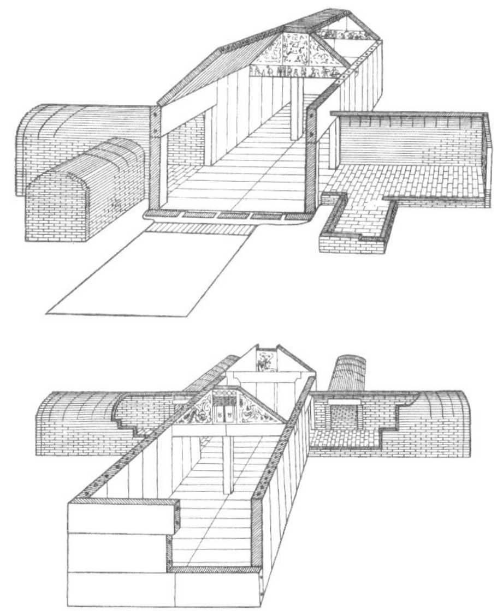

Fig. 1 *Diagram of layout of hollow-brick Tomb 61 at Luoyang.* View looking from east to west toward back of the burial chamber (top). View looking from west to east toward the tomb entrance (bottom). Western Han dynasty, second half of first century BCE. After *Kaogu xuebao* 1964.2, p. 110.

the bow mirrors the shape of his elongated and hooked nose, a feature perhaps intended to indicate a foreigner. To the upper right of each tree is a bird with two elongated tail feathers, facing left while flying to the right. Under the left-hand bird a crane both walks and faces right. In the center is a pair of deer, the male in front charging to the right, the doe also moving rightward but looking toward the left. To the right of the deer is a second, identical, crane. To the right of the second tree a tiger pounces to the right while looking back to the left, its neck arched in the same curve as that of the bird above it. Bordering and framing these images top and bottom are two bands of geometric designs, an inner band of lozenge and an outer band of wave patterns. The outermost borders are similar to the uppermost border on all four sides of the third layered coffin from Tomb 1 at Mawangdui, Changsha, Hunan Province.[8] The present hollow-brick tile may display auspicious imagery of the Han cosmological universe. The hunter, tiger, and deer all inhabit the celestial landscape on the bronze chariot fitting (cat. no. 29) in this exhibition, and archers, cranes, and birds can be found in the rubbings of the "Wu family shrines."

SUSAN L. BENINGSON

Notes

1. Zhengzhou Municipal Museum, "Zhengzhou Xintongqiao Handai huaxiang kongxin zhuanmu" ("Pictorial hollow brick tombs of the Han dynasty at Xintongqiao, Zhengzhou"), *Wenwu* 1972.10, pp. 41–48.

2. This brick was first published in the catalogue of the C. T. Loo collection. See C. T. Loo, *Briques et objets céramiques funéraires de l'époque des Han appartenant à C. T. Loo et Cie*, Les éditions d'art et d'histoire. (Paris: Olov Janse, 1936), p. 22, planche 15 1.

3. It has been argued that these hollow tiles were made around a sand core that could be poured out of the apertures at the ends of the tile (see cat. no. 7), and not around a wooden core which would have been removed before firing, as has been asserted elsewhere. My appreciation to Cary Liu for making me aware of this explanation.

4. Huang Minglan and Gao Yinqiang, eds., *Luoyang Han mu bihua* (*Wall paintings from Han tombs at Luoyang*) (Beijing: Wenwu chubanshe, 1996).

5. Cat. no. 8 in this exhibition is a pair of hollow tomb tiles used for the ceiling of the tomb. These were stamped and painted with the imagery of the Queen Mother of the West and a figure riding a snake. Common themes on painted tomb tiles include auspicious animals such as deer, bear, and birds, as well as chariots and references to Han cosmology.

6. Zhengzhou Municipal Museum, "Zhengzhou Xintongqiao," pp. 41–48.

7. This particular tree motif is the most common of all motifs found on Luoyang pictorial tomb tiles, and its roots often extend beyond the lower border. Other frequent images on these tomb tiles include horses, elderly scholars holding a staff in their arms, and a few other varieties of birds. Huang Minglan, *Luoyang Xihan huaxiang kongxin zhuan* (*Hollow-brick pictorial tiles of the Western Han at Luoyang*) (Beijing: Renmin meishu chubanshe, 1982).

8. See Xin Lixiang, *Handai huaxiang shi zonghe yanjiu* (*A comprehensive study of Han-period pictorial stones*) (Beijing: Wenwu chubanshe, 2000), p. 194, figs. 2–5.

10 "Confucius meeting Laozi" pictorial stone

Eastern Han dynasty. Jiaxiang County, Shandong Province. Stone with relief and incised carving; h. 48 cm, w. 111 cm, d. 20.5 cm. Shandong Provincial Museum, Ji'nan.

The "Confucius meeting Laozi" theme was extremely popular in Han literature and art. Stones featuring this theme appear in places as far distant as Shandong and Sichuan.[1] In literature, the *Zhuangzi* provides half-affectionate, half-sarcastic anecdotes about Confucius' consultations with Laozi (literally, "Old Master"), who far surpasses the Sage in two aspects: his ability to understand the changing phenomenal world, and his ability to maintain himself in perfect harmony with its transformations. Later, in the *Shiji*, the two masters have a more serious encounter: frustrated by his inability to convince the ruling families of his home state of Lu to undertake necessary political and ritual reforms, Confucius sets off in the company of Nangong Jingshu, a supporter, to visit the Zhou royal court, with the carriage, two horses, and a young manservant lent to them for the occasion by the duke. The *Shiji* reports, "They went to Zhou to inquire about rituals. People say that they probably had an audience there with the Old Master." When their inquiries were completed, and Confucius and Nangong Jingshu were on the point of saying goodbye, the Old Master saw them off, and counseled Confucius in the following words: "I have heard that those of wealth and rank send men off with gifts of money or objects. The truly humane person sends them off with parting words of advice .... Those who probe deeply with their ears and their eyes and risk death are those fond of debate. Those of broad discernment who yet endanger their persons are those who expose the other party's ugly faults. Take care not to harm yourself thereby as son or official."[2]

Explanations of the theme, somewhat anachronistically, have tended to portray the two masters as founders of two "schools" of thought, "Confucianism" and "Daoism," the first aiming to have public-officeholders perfect the social order through ritual observance and the second proposing that its followers "leave no traces" in the world. But when viewed from the increasingly sectarian stances of late imperial China, all Han thinking falls under the rubric of "eclectic." In consequence, many Han depictions work against such simple dichotomies, as here, inserting Xiang Tuo, a mere child pulling his toy, between the two supreme sages solemnly bowing, one middle-aged and the other old. If the child Xiang Tuo gains the respect of Kongzi and Laozi—as their mutual bowing low to him seems to indicate—are we to conclude that two men of legendary insight recognize innate genius when they see it? In other words, are we to interpret the illustration as didactic, or in any way reflecting important Han debates about the role of nature vs. nurture in human formation?[3] We simply do not know, in part because so few figures are given labels in Han art, and such labels as do exist tend to supply only names. For this reason, we do not even understand standard viewing conventions in Han. Did Han artists favor the synoptic convention, in which no figure is repeated more than once, or did they expect viewers to locate one or more repeated figures?[4]

The pictorial stone in this exhibition demands that we consider how the "Confucius meeting Laozi" episode might relate to the unlabeled and labeled scenes nearby. (As with all Chinese texts, one "reads" an image from right to left.) Confucius' brash disciple, Zilu, identified by his rooster cap, converses with an

unknown person (Confucius again or someone else?), followed by a finely robed and capped group surrounding Yanzi, wise minister of Qi, the powerful state bordering on Lu. By some traditions, this Yanzi deftly maneuvered to keep Confucius from attaining political influence, calculating that the strength of one state, embodied in its advisers, inevitably comes at its neighbor's expense. (Adopting this line of reasoning, Stephen Durrant casts Confucius and Yanzi as rival champions promoted in propaganda by Lu and Qi locals engaged in fierce interstate competition.)[5] In other traditions, however, including the canonical *Analects*, Confucius praises Yanzi as a model of mature propriety, though the pairing of Confucius, who was remarkably tall, with the extraordinarily short Yanzi, in some tales is meant to elicit a laugh.[6]

The register below is divided approximately at midpoint by a column. On the right, six mounted bowmen turn to aim Parthian shots at a pursuing seventh; on the left, six horsemen gallop furiously toward the column.[7] Given the several tales prompted by the stone's visual logic, I surmise that its images were not meant to convey a single interpretation; rather they were scenes intended to conjure up a host of anecdotes that entertain as well as enlighten.[8]

MICHAEL NYLAN

Notes

1. See Xin Lixiang, *Handai huaxiang shi zonghe* (*A comprehensive study of Han-period pictorial stones*) (Beijing: Wenwu chubanshe, 2000), pp. 217–18. The theme is discussed, in epigraphical classics, in conjunction with the Duke of Zhou's exemplary regency for King Cheng. See Gu Aiji, *Li bian* (*Distinguishing clerical script*), *Yingyin Wenyuange Siku quanshu* edition (Taipei: Taiwan shangu yinshuguan, 1983–1986), *juan* 8, pp. 40a–b.

2. Sima Qian, *Shiji* (Beijing: Zhonghua shuju, 1959; reprint 1997), *juan* 47, p. 1909.

3. On the didactic portrait, see Audrey Spiro, *Contemplating the Ancients: Aesthetic and Social Issues in Early Chinese Portraiture* (Berkeley: University of California Press, 1990), pp. 21–32; on Xiang Tuo as child genius, see Anne Behnke Kinney, *Representations of Childhood and Youth in Early China* (Stanford: Stanford University Press, 2004), pp. 39–41.

4. Wu Hung, *The Wu Liang Shrine: The Ideology of Early Chinese Pictorial Art* (Stanford: Stanford University Press, 1989), pp. 200–13, assumed the former when analyzing three pictorial stones.

5. This is taken from a lecture that Durrant [University of Oregon] gave at Reed College in October 2003.

6. *Analects* 5/16.

7. Cf. *Confucius: A l'aube de l'humanisme chinois* (Paris: Éditions de la Réunion des musée nationaux, 2003), pl. 26, p. 77. This illustrates another stone that shows in the top register Confucius meeting Laozi (with a smaller person in between, probably Xiang Tuo).

8. On this, see Anthony Snodgrass, *Homer and the Artists: Text and Picture in Early Greek Art* (Cambridge: Cambridge University Press, 1998).

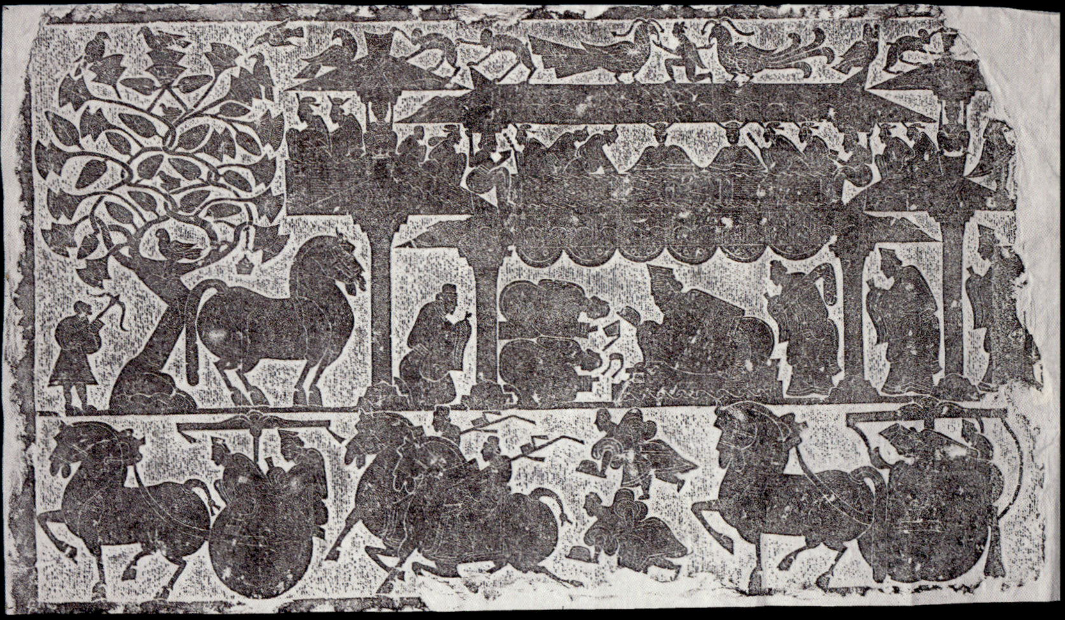

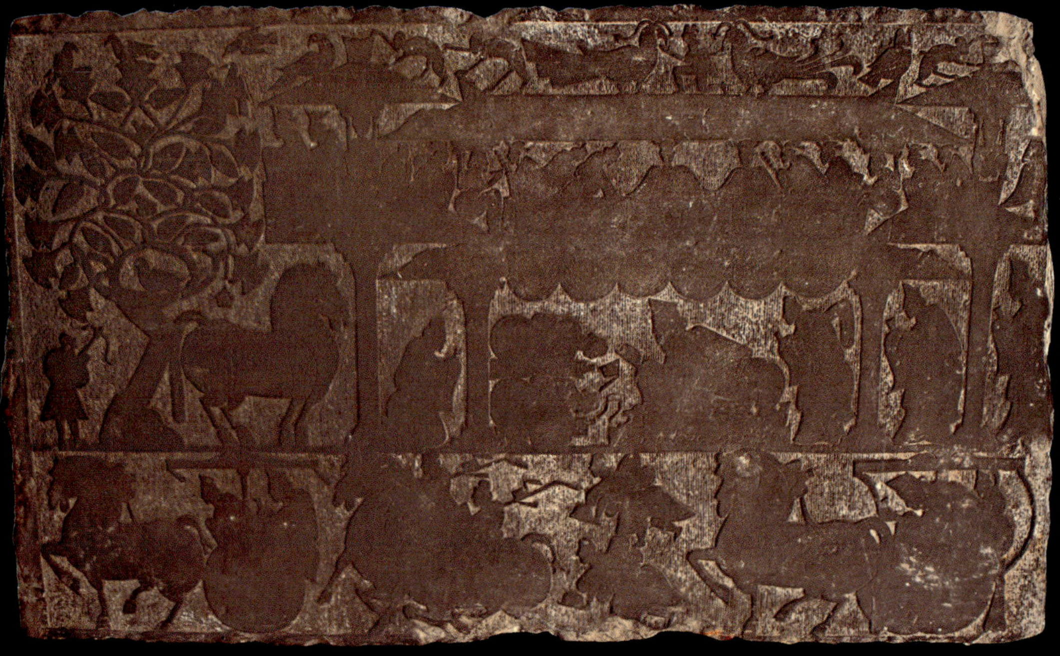

11 Central pavilion or homage scene pictorial stone with chariot procession, archer, and horse beneath a tree

Eastern Han dynasty. Songshan, Jiaxiang County, Shandong Province. Stone with relief and incised carving; h. 70.5 cm, w. 128 cm, d. 28 cm. Shandong Stone Inscriptions Art Museum, Ji'nan.

In 1978 and 1980 three intact tombs (M1, M2, and M3) were unearthed at Songshan, twenty-four kilometers south of the "Wu family" cemetery in Jiaxiang County.[1] Archaeologists discovered some forty stone reliefs, carved in a variety of styles typically seen in Han funerary monuments. Most importantly, a relief bearing an inscription dating to 157 CE was found in the front chamber of Tomb 3, stating that the relief was made for a shrine. The dated inscription, the fact that the imagery was obscured by a thick coating of lime, and the placement of the stones, which randomized the arrangement of the imagery, indicate that these stones were taken from dismantled Han funerary monuments and recycled to fashion tombs in a later period. The archaeologists' report proposes that the latest date of construction of these tombs is the Three Kingdoms–Western Jin period and the earliest is the late Eastern Han.[2] Of these forty-odd carvings, twenty closely resemble the carvings found at the "Wu family" cemetery.[3]

The Songshan homage scene found in Tomb 2 and presented in this exhibition is one of four almost identical homage scenes (each approx. 70 × 120 centimeters) found in Tombs 2 and 3. Each of the four carvings is divided into two registers; the upper register depicts a two-story pavilion with a large-scale male figure in the lower story receiving male visitors, and women receiving female visitors above; chariot processions fill the lower register. Flanking the pavilion in the exhibition slab is a pair of *que* gate-pillars, which were typically placed at the entrance to a cemetery. Monkeys, birds, and an owl perch on the roof of the building and its gate-pillars, and a winged *xian* Immortal feeds elixirs of immortality to two fantastic birds. Between the left gate-pillar and a tree growing out of a mound stands an untethered horse. Beneath and to the left of the tree an archer aims his crossbow at the six birds in the tree's branches. In the lowest register is a chariot procession, including robed and capped figures in the chariots as well as attendants on foot or horseback. This scene closely resembles homage scenes found at the "Wu family" cemetery, particularly Stone 2-S.6 (cat. no. 1.26) found in the area associated with the Left Chamber (Stone Chamber 2).

Additional finds at the Songshan site include eight slabs (each approx. 70 centimeters square), half of them depicting the Queen Mother of the West and the other half her consort, the King Father of the East; on each of these slabs, two or three registers below the deity present scenes such as worship at a tomb, preparation for a banquet, chariot processions, and well-known scenes from historical narratives. In his 1983 architectural reconstruction Jiang Yingju proposed that these twelve slabs originally constituted the side and back walls of four small shrines. Taken together, it is likely that these slabs comprised the walls and ceilings of four small shrines (approx. 150 centimeters high, 180 centimeters wide, and 90 centimeters deep; interior dimensions: approx. 120 × 70 × 65 centimeters), similar to but much smaller than those found at the "Wu family" cemetery.[4] As reconstructed by Jiang, the present homage scene occupied a prominent position as the back wall of a small shrine, while the slabs bearing the imagery of the Queen Mother of the West and King Father of the East were located on the west and east side of each shrine, respectively.

Also found in Tombs 2 and 3, though not included in Jiang's reconstruction, are nine slabs carved with eight-petaled flowers interspersed with images of fish, supernatural creatures, and constellations. These designs were probably positioned on the ceiling of a shrine or tomb.[5]

As mentioned above, one of the slabs found in the front chamber of Tomb 3 has a lengthy inscription, which records that a clerk named An Guo died in 157 CE, at the age of thirty-four, during an epidemic, and that his family established a tomb and shrine for him. The inscription also makes clear that this particular relief carving was once part of a shrine and states that Wang Shu, Wang Jian, and Jiang Hu, all artisans from Gaoping, were responsible for that shrine's construction and decor. The inscription also describes the types of designs that once embellished the shrine and states the cost of the project was 27,000 cash. There is also a sad addendum relating that An Guo's young sons Boxiao (age six) and Runde had died some time after.[6]

During the Eastern Han graveyards were socially important monuments, not only for aristocrats but also for commoners. Funerals for prominent members of local society were lavish affairs, attended by hundreds or even thousands of people. Tombs were often elaborately carved with imagery and/or furnished with grave goods, both intended to provide an ideal environment for the deceased. Aboveground shrines served as places where the souls of the deceased could lodge when the family gathered for ancestral worship.

The identity of the tree in the scene is subject to debate. It has been identified as the mythical *fusang* tree (a leaning mulberry), the sun tree located at the edge of the Eastern world. Associated with the sun tree is the myth of the archer Yi, who shoots down nine of ten suns (shown most often in Han imagery as sun-crows), leaving only one in the sky and thereby saving the world from a devastating drought.[7] Other authors consider it the *mulianli* (tree with intertwining branches), signifying political and familial harmony.[8] Most recently, Ken Brashier has proposed that it should be identified as the sweet-pear tree (*gantang*) mentioned in several pre-Han and Han texts and stele inscriptions. Brashier argues that the sweet-pear tree is associated particularly with the remembrance of the Earl of Shao, a cherished and respected official, and generally with the remembrance of one's forebears. He proposes that in the context of Han tombs and shrines, the sweet-pear tree and its fortuitous association with a revered official signifies commemoration of one's ancestors and preservation of ancestral shrines and grave steles.[9]

In the upper balcony of the pavilion two seated women face forward as other women approach them in attitudes of respectful greeting; the central position and hieratic scale of the two seated women indicate their relative importance. Other women stand on the balconies of the *que* gate-pillars, facing the tree, genuflecting and clasping their hands in respect. In the lower story a large-scale male figure in voluminous robes is receiving two smaller figures who bow deeply before him. Behind the host, more guests, holding *hu* tablets and gifts, arrive to pay their respects. In the lowest register visitors and their servants approach the pavilion in horse-drawn chariots.

The identity of the central male figure is a key element in interpreting the scene. Two theories have been proposed: (1) that the central figure is an ideal representation of the tomb occupant,[10] and (2) that it is a representation of the emperor. Wu Hung has proposed that a similar homage scene associated with the Wu Liang Shrine should be interpreted as a symbol of sovereignty. Wu's identification of the scene is based, in part, on his larger interpretation of the accompanying imagery as representing the personal ideology of Wu Liang. He offers the caveat that his interpretation does not necessarily apply to all homage scenes with large central figures; that one must consult identifying inscriptions or the pictorial context to discern individual meanings.[11]

In my view, the architectural elements in the Songshan scene can be read as a group of mortuary structures found in a typical Eastern Han cemetery. The *que* gate-pillars signify the entrance to the cemetery, and the two-story pavilion is an idealized version of the ancestral shrine. Omitted in previous discussions of this scene is the small mound beneath the tree, signifying the tomb. And what of the tree? In the Han period trees were planted on the tumulus to mark the tomb site and to ward off evil. In this case, the intertwined, flowering branches and the mound from which the tree grows suggest that it functions symbolically as a central axis or conduit for the soul in its heavenly journey. In Qin–Han cosmography sacred mountains such as Kunlun and mythic trees were conceived of as being located at the center of the world, serving as pathways between heaven and earth. The Songshan tree may allude to the *jian* tree, which in *Huainanzi* is described as being "used by gods and immortals to ascend (to and descend from heaven)" . . . and as forming a canopy over the center of the world.[12] A description of the *jian* tree in another passage of the *Huainanzi* recalls the blossoms and intertwined branches of the tree in the Songshan scene:

> There is a tree with green leaves, purple stems, black flowers, and yellow fruit. It is called the *jian* tree. The *jian* tree is more than 100 *zhang* tall and has nine branches which wend their way upward. Below are nine interwoven roots, which resemble hemp. The leaves resemble those of the pear tree.[13]

Here the leaves are said to resemble those of a pear tree, suggesting that the interpretation of the Songshan image as a *jian* tree, or central axis, does not preclude Brashier's interpretation of the tree as a sweet-pear.

Another passage in the *Huainanzi* describes the journey to heaven via Mount Kunlun. Ascending higher and higher, the would-be Immortal reaches Heaven. There he encounters both the *jian* tree and the *fusang* tree.

> *If one climbs to a height double that of the*
> *Kunlun Mountains,* (*that peak*) *is called*
> *Cool Wind Mountain.*
> *If one climbs it, one will not die.*
> *If one climbs to a height that is doubled again,*
> (*that peak*) *is called Hanging Garden.*
> *If one ascends it, one will gain supernatural*
> *power and be able to control the wind*
> *and rain.*
> *If one climbs to a height that is doubled yet*
> *again, it reaches up to Heaven itself.*

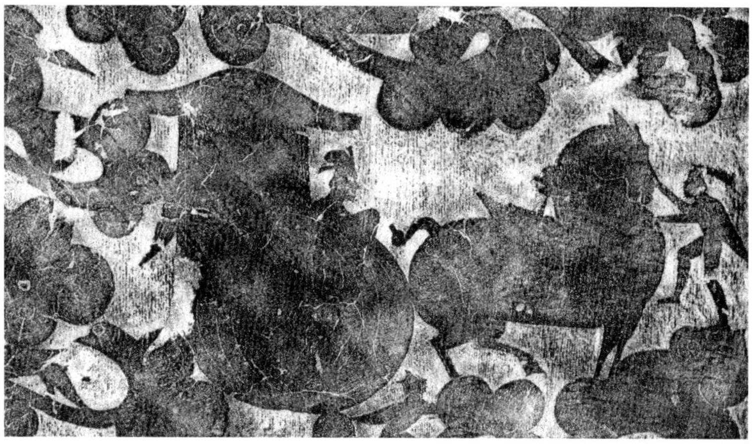

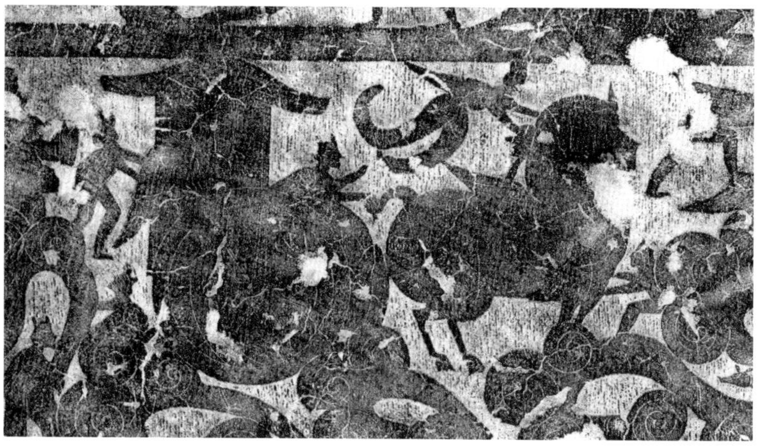

If one mounts to there, one will become a god.
It is called the Abode of the Supreme Thearch.

The Fu [= Fusang] *tree in Yang Province is baked*
by the sun's heat.
The Jian Tree on Mt. Duguang, by which
the gods ascend (*to and from heaven*) *and*
descend, casts no shadow at midday.
If one calls (*from that place*), *there is no echo.*
It forms a canopy over the center of the world.
The Ruo Tree is to the west of the Jian Tree.
On its branches are ten suns; its blossoms cast
light upon the earth.[14]

Here the *jian*, *fusang*, and *ruo* trees are all part of the heavenly landscape. Thus the tree in the Songshan scene is perhaps best understood as a composite image, incorporating allusions to several mythic trees. Any attempt precisely to identify the Songshan tree may be misleading, as the pictorial images selected to adorn the walls of shrines and tombs probably drew upon local oral traditions as much as on canonical textual sources.[15] Within the context of the accompanying imagery, it is perhaps best to keep the interpretation general and say that the tree in the Songshan scene signifies access to the heavenly domain. The women on the balcony of the *que* gate-pillars who bow toward the tree can be understood as paying homage to the deceased man and his two wives in their tomb dwelling, and the larger-scale figures in the pavilion can be identified as the deceased and his two wives receiving offerings in the shrine. Taken as a whole, the relief can be interpreted as a representation of the deceased's journey from death to the afterlife.

This becomes clearer when we look at the Songshan carving in relation to another relief carving, this one from the Left Stone Chamber (Stone Chamber 2) at the "Wu family" cemetery, depicting the ascension of the deceased from the tomb to the immortal domain (cat. no. 1.33).[16] This scene includes a number of motifs found in the Songshan homage scene, including a tumulus, a section of a pavilion, and a single *que* pillar, which function as metonymic referents to the cemetery's gate-pillars and shrine, and visitors arriving in horse-drawn chariots. A swirling cloud emerges from the mound, filling the upper two-thirds of the picture. Two horse-drawn chariots, presumably carrying the deceased, escorted by winged Immortals, wend their way upward through the cloud, one toward the Queen Mother of the West, the other toward the King Father of the East (figs. 1A, 1B). The undulating cloud form bears a resemblance to the intertwined branches of the tree in the Songshan relief, suggesting that the tree and the cloud may have a similar symbolic function as pathways to the heavenly domain. The only elements missing in the Songshan scene are the Queen Mother of the West and King Father of the East. As mentioned above, however, the slabs featuring the heavenly couple were probably located on the western and eastern walls of the shrine. Thus imagery found on the three walls of the shrine at Songshan can be viewed as an elaboration of the theme of the soul's journey after death as portrayed in the "Wu family shrines" relief carving.

LYDIA THOMPSON

Fig. 1A *Chariot-borne ascent toward Queen Mother of the West.* Detail of Stone Chamber 2, Stone 2-R.2 (cat. no. 1.33). "Wu family shrines" rubbings. Princeton University Art Museum, acc. no. 2002-307.32.

Fig. 1B *Chariot-borne ascent toward King Father of the East.* Detail of Stone Chamber 2, Stone 2-R.2 (cat. no. 1.33). "Wu family shrines" rubbings. Princeton University Art Museum, acc. no. 2002-307.32.

Notes

1. Jiaxiang Xian Wushi Ci wenguansuo, ed., "Shandong Jiaxiang Songshan faxiang Han huaxiang shi" ("Han pictorial stones discovered at Songshan, Jiaxiang, Shandong"), *Wenwu* 1979.9, pp. 1–6; Jining diqu wenwuzu and Jiaxiang Xian wenguansuo, eds., "Shandong Jiaxiang Songshan 1980 nian chutu de Han huaxiang shi" ("Han pictorial stones excavated in 1980 from Songshan, Jiaxiang, Shandong"), *Wenwu* 1982.5, pp. 60–70. For a summary and discussion of the Songshan carvings, see Klaas Ruitenbeek, *Chinese Shadows: Stone Reliefs, Rubbings, and Related Works of Art from the Han Dynasty (206 BC–220 AD) in the Royal Ontario Museum* (Toronto: The Royal Ontario Museum, 2002) pp. 15–18.

2. Jining diqu wenwuzu, "Shandong Jiaxiang Songshan," p. 70.

3. For good reproductions of rubbings of the relief carvings, see *Zhongguo huaxiang shi quanji: Shandong Han huaxiang shi* (*A complete collection of Chinese pictorial stones: Han pictorial stones from Shandong*) vol. 2, ed. Lai Fei (Ji'nan: Shandong meishu chubanshe, 2000), pls. 95–108.

4. Jiang Yingju, "Handai de xiao citang: Jiaxiang Songshan Han huaxiang shi de jianzhu fuyuan" ("Four small shrines of the Han dynasty: Architectural reconstruction of Han pictorial stones from Songshan in Jiaxiang"), *Kaogu* 1983.8, pp. 745–51.

5. A similar flower design is found on the recessed ceilings of the tombs at Anqiu and Yi'nan counties. The one on the ceiling of the Anqiu tomb is almost identical to the Songshan examples. *Zhongguo huaxiang shi quanji: Shandong Han huaxiang shi*, vol. 1, ed. Jiang Yingju and Wu Wenqi (Ji'nan: Shandong meishu chubanshe, 2000), pl. 170.

6. For a partial translation and discussion of the inscription, see Wu Hung, *Monumentality in Early Chinese Art and Architecture* (Stanford: Stanford University Press, 1995), pp. 193–94, and Ruitenbeek, *Chinese Shadows,* pp. 15–18. For a transcription of the inscription, see *Kandai Sekkoku shūsei* (*Compilation of stone inscriptions in the Han dynasty*), ed. Nagata Hidemasa (Tokyo: Dōhōsha, 1994) vol. 1, p. 128.

7. For a discussion of archer Yi and the ten suns, see Sarah Allan, *Myth, Art and the Cosmos in Early China* (Albany: State University of New York Press, 1991), pp. 36–37.

8. Ruitenbeek, *Chinese Shadows*, p. 44; Jean James, *A Guide to the Tomb and Shrine Art of the Han Dynasty (206 B.C.–A.D. 220)*, p. 120.

9. K. E. Brashier, "The Sweetpear Tree: Preserving the Historical Image of Historical Preservation," unpublished paper presented at the Association of Asian Studies National Conference, San Diego, March 4–7, 2004, pp. 1–8. I wish to thank Ken Brashier for providing me with a copy of his paper.

10. In Brashier's view the central figure can be thought of as the deceased represented by the figure of the Earl of Shao.

11. Wu Hung, *Monumentality,* p. 235.

12. John Major, trans., *Heaven and Earth in Early Han Thought, Chapters Three, Four and Five of the Huainanzi* (Albany: State University of New York Press, 1993) p. 158.

13. Yuan Ke, ed., *Shanhaijing jiaozhu* (*Annotated Classic of Mountain and Waterways*) (Shanghai: Shanghai guji chubanshe, 1980), p. 509.

14. Major, trans., *Heaven and Earth in Early Han Thought*, p. 158.

15. For a discussion of Confucian ideology vs. popular religion in Han carvings, see Lydia Thompson, "Confucian Paragon or Popular Deity? Legendary Heroes in a Late-Eastern Han Tomb," *Asia Major,* 3d ser., vol. 12, part 2 (1999), pp. 1–27.

16. For a discussion of this slab, see Wu Hung, "Where are they Going? Where did they Come From?—Hearse and 'Soul-Carriage' in Han Dynasty Tomb Art," *Orientations*, June 1998, pp. 29–30. See also Ruitenbeek, *Chinese Shadows*, pp. 9–11.

12 Carved and painted frieze from the tomb of Zuo Biao

Eastern Han dynasty, 150 CE. Mamaozhuang, Lishi, Shanxi Province. Sandstone, traces of black ink; combined h. 36.5 cm, w. 241 cm, d. 17 cm. Royal Ontario Museum, acc. no. 925.25.22.J, K. The George Crofts Collection.

The principal centers of Han-dynasty funerary stone reliefs, Shandong, Henan, and Sichuan, have long been well known: respectively since the Song dynasty, the early 1920s, and the late 1930s. Another major center of reliefs, the northeastern Shaanxi–northwestern Shanxi border area, has come to light more recently. Its principal sites are Suide, Mizhi, and Shenmu in Shaanxi, and on the other side of the Yellow River, Lishi in Shanxi. In the Han dynasty this was all part of Xihe Commandery, occupied by both Xiongnu and Han Chinese, who coexisted sometimes peacefully, sometimes in a state of war. The Suide stones were found first, in 1952; the Lishi and Shenmu stones were excavated only in the 1990s.[1] In general terms the Shaanxi-Shanxi style, also called the Northwestern style, is characterized by very free and painterly designs, rendered as perfectly flat, smoothly polished silhouettes slightly raised against a background of faint, shallow chisel marks. Typically there are no or very few incised lines in the raised designs to indicate details; instead, there is a generous use of black ink lines and red paint (fig. 1). Artistically, the Northwestern style is far removed from the more rigid, hieratic designs of the "Wu family shrines," and technically, far from the bold reliefs against an often rough, grooved background common to Henan and Sichuan. Certain iconographic themes, such as Xiwangmu-Dongwanggong imagery, and processions of carriages, are shared with the longer-known centers, but other features, such as the prominence of agricultural scenes and the style of rendering landscape and trees, are unique.

One isolated set of stones from the northwest has been known for much longer: the tomb of Zuo Biao, dated to 150 CE. Discovered in 1924, it can be called, with hindsight, the type-specimen of the Northwestern style. Immediately after the tomb's discovery some of the stones were removed to Beijing, whence they were shipped to the Royal Ontario Museum in Toronto. The remaining stones stayed in China and are now kept in Taiyuan and Lishi: eight large vertical slabs (135 × 90 centimeters), one frieze beam (l. 287 centimeters), and one doorpost (h. 36 centimeters, w. 33 centimeters). In the subsequent decades the stones in China and Canada were published and researched independently. Only in 2003 did the curators of all three museums where the stones are kept meet and exchange rubbings.[2]

The Royal Ontario Museum stones arrived in Toronto from Beijing in 1925: two stone columns with incised inscriptions (h. 136 centimeters) and fourteen fragments of a pictorial stone frieze in shallow relief (total length 16 meters, including two complete beams of 300 and 307 centimeters). They had been acquired by George Crofts, an Irish fur merchant and Chinese art wholesaler established in Tianjin, as part of his last shipment before his sudden death later that year. Crofts had sent more than four thousand Chinese antiquities and works of

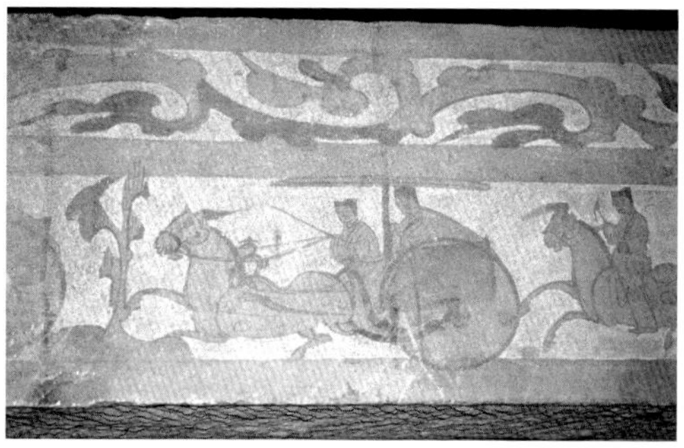

Fig. 1 *Part of the lintel frieze of the Shipan tomb.* Details are drawn in ink lines, the scroll pattern at the top is partially painted red. Approx. 35 × 50 cm. Photograph by author.

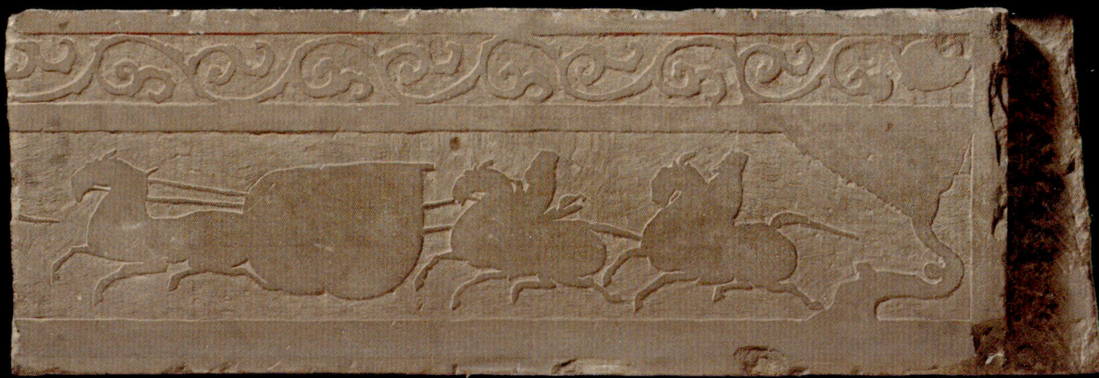

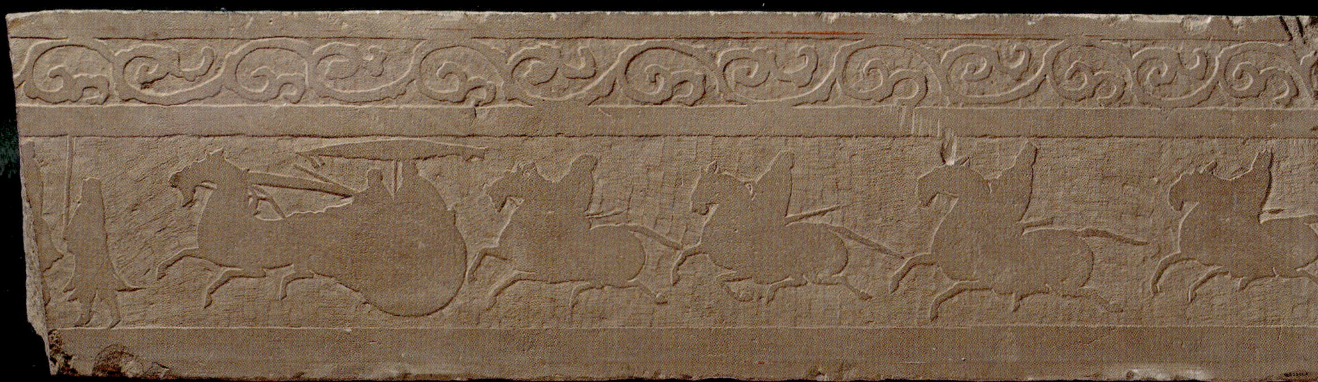

art to the Royal Ontario Museum between 1918 and 1925. His specification, dated February 25, 1925, gives a rough translation of the commemorative inscriptions for the tomb occupant (called General Zuo Yuanyi by Crofts), and states that the stones came "from a tomb at Yongning Zhou—Shanxi—(near the Jiuhe River) which still contains the memorial to the General's wife, and also the entrance gates to the tomb. . . . The tomb is about 35 feet long, 20 feet wide and high."[3] This is the earliest information available about Zuo Biao's tomb.

Before Crofts acquired the stones, rubbings had been made of the inscriptions on the two columns. Transcriptions were published in 1926 and reproductions in 1928.[4] A brief account of the discovery of the stones was published in 1939. It mentions that they were found in 1924 by shepherds, between the villages of Mamaozhuang and Wangjiapo near Lishi, after a flood of the nearby river. They were part of a square tomb chamber with brick walls, covered with a pointed dome. The walls were lined on the interior with carved stones. Some ceramic vessels and dishes and a shallow plate (*wapan*) containing human bones were found inside. Two carved stone columns and carved stones found next to the tomb chamber, and four or five carved stones from inside, were bought by the Beiping antiques dealer Li Zhongxian. After the local authorities learned of this, thirteen remaining carved stones were brought into Lishi and deposited in the Confucius temple there.[5]

Rubbings of some of the stones in China were published in 1958, and in 1962 Hsio-yen Shih published and discussed all the Royal Ontario Museum stones. She noted the relation with the stones from Suide, but the limited comparative material available at the time made it impossible to sketch a broader picture, let alone attempt a reconstruction of Zuo Biao's tomb. Shih's article was hardly noticed in China, and when Xie Guozhen in 1979 wrote an article about the inscriptions on the stone columns from the tomb, he mentioned only that Xia Nai had told him that the stones were then in a Canadian museum. The inscriptions can be translated as follows:

In the first year of the Heping reign-period (150 CE), Zuo Yuanyi of Guang Village in Zhongyang District, within Xihe Commandery, built this Dwelling of Ten Thousand Years.

The tomb of Zuo Biao from Xihe, courtesy name Yuanyi, scribe in the Memorials Section at the Military Headquarters of the Leader of Court Gentlemen and Envoy Commissioned with Special Powers.

As Xie demonstrates, from the latter it can be inferred that Zuo Biao worked at the Chinese mission in Xihe that oversaw the relations with the Southern Xiongnu, specifically the yearly dispatch of a son of the Xiongnu *shanyu* leader as a hostage to the Han court in Luoyang.[6]

In 1990, when a portion of the Sanchuanhe River at Mamaozhuang was canalized, excavations were conducted near the site where the Zuo Biao stones had been found in 1924. Three Eastern Han tombs were laid bare, numbered 2 to 4 in the excavation report. The archaeologists consider them part of a family graveyard to which Zuo Biao's tomb also belonged, and thus implicitly designate his tomb as Tomb 1.[7] The tombs all have a ramp leading to stone doors, from which a corridor with brick walls and a

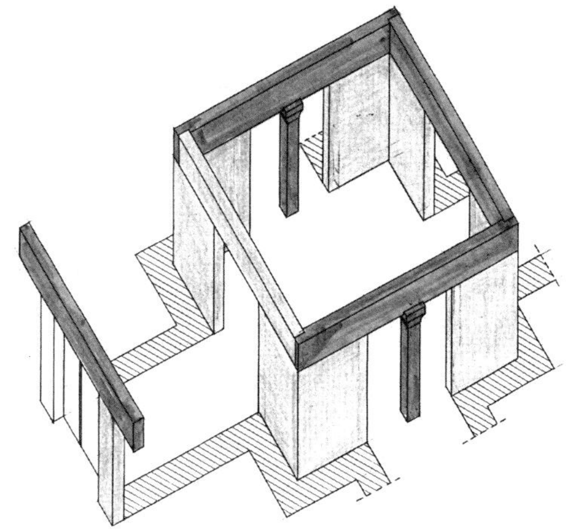

Fig. 2 The Shipan tomb in the Lüliang Museum used as a template for a reconstruction of Zuo Biao's tomb. The exact order of the eight vertical stone panels is not known. Illustration by author. (Dark gray = stones in Royal Ontario Museum; light gray = stones in China; white = stones presumably lost).

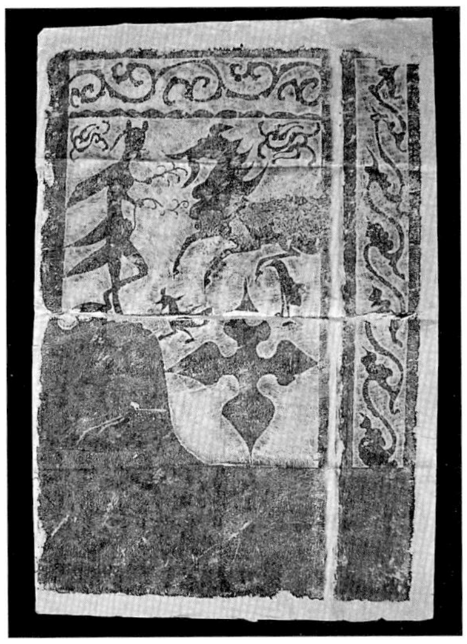

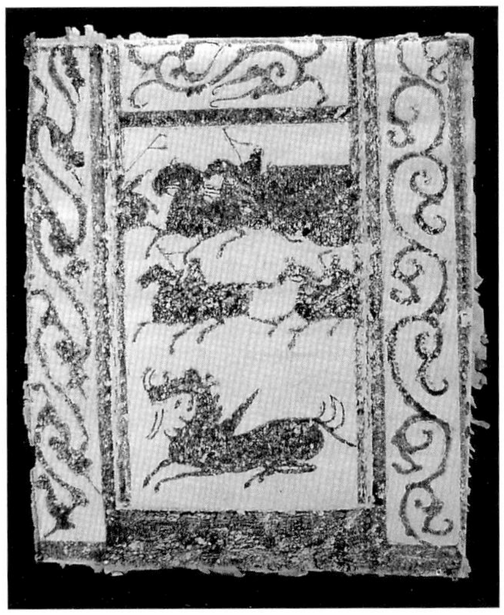

barrel-vault ceiling leads on to a square tomb chamber of brick, lined on the inside with vertical stone panels capped with a stone frieze, and with a brick dome as ceiling.

Tomb 2 is the largest, with openings in the side and back walls that give access to flanking chambers. Together with the entrance corridor, this gives the tomb the shape of a cross. In the rear opening, which is the widest, a column similar to the ones in the Royal Ontario Museum is positioned. On the doorposts Xiwangmu and Dongwanggong are depicted, and on the doors there are birds and *pushou* animal masks with rings. The tomb chamber's frieze shows a chariot procession and landscape elements similar to those on the Royal Ontario Museum frieze, and its eighteen vertical slabs are carved with mythical animals, Immortals, and ornamental scrolls.

In 1997 a tomb was found in Shipan, near Lishi, with a ground plan that fits the number and dimensions of the Zuo Biao stones even better than Tomb 2; in fact, the two tombs must have been almost identical (fig. 2).[8] Of the Zuo Biao stones, the eight vertical panels are the most remarkable. Scenes from the daily life of a landlord blend seamlessly with the world of Immortals: an ox at a trough and an oxcart are depicted above a tiger, two intertwined dragons, and a highly stylized phoenix; three long-eared Immortals ride in a conveyance pulled by four lions, with an enormous toad and a snake-tailed human being (Chang E?) below; a long-eared, winged Immortal stands on a cliff feeding herbs to a winged horse hovering in front of him (fig. 3); a similar winged horse is depicted under a horse cart and riders on horseback moving at great speed—the speed suggested by the fact that one of the horsemen and his mount are just emerging into the picture space (fig. 4).[9] The latter winged horse seems to have been tamed: it wears a pair of large, S-shaped cheek pieces as a bit. A pair of similarly shaped cheek pieces made of lead, 10.8 centimeters long, was among the few tomb gifts found in Tomb 2, which had been subject to robbery in the past.

If we look again at the Zuo Biao stones in China and in the Royal Ontario Museum, it is clear that the reliefs were originally partially painted in black and red, like the stones of the other tombs at Mamaozhuang, Shipan, and Shenmu. Traces of ink lines remain on most of the stones, and inside the engraved inscriptions are traces of red. The tomb had a gate and a three-meters-square tomb chamber with three side chambers (one gate post is in Taiyuan; the lintel is in the Royal Ontario Museum, identified as such by its scroll pattern, which alone differs from the scroll pattern common to all the other stones). All eight wall panels are preserved, as well as two columns and two complete frieze beams. Most of the other two frieze beams can be reconstructed from the remaining Royal Ontario Museum fragments. Three fragments (all right-end parts of beams) cannot be accommodated in the square tomb chamber. Either the side chambers of Zuo Biao's tomb had stone friezes, or these fragments came from a similar adjacent tomb. Apart from this uncertainty we are now, eighty years after the discovery and subsequent splitting up of the stones, able to reconstruct the original appearance of Zuo Biao's tomb.

KLAAS RUITENBEEK

Fig. 3 *Immortal feeding winged horse*. Rubbing of vertical panel from Zuo Biao's tomb. Lüliang Museum. Stone; approx. h. 134 cm, w. 96 cm, d. 18 cm. Rubbing; h. 133 cm, w. 90 cm. Royal Ontario Museum, Toronto.

Fig. 4 *Horse cart, riders, and winged horse*. Rubbing of vertical panel of Zuo Biao's tomb. Shanxi Provincial Museum. Stone; approx. h. 134 cm, w. 85 cm, d. 18 cm. Rubbing; h. 104 cm, w. 85 cm. Royal Ontario Museum, Toronto.

Notes

1. Tang Chi (ed.), *Zhongguo huaxiang shi quanji* 5: *Shaanxi, Shanxi Han huaxiang shi* (*Complete collection of pictorial stone engravings of China*, vol. 5: *The Han-dynasty pictorial stone engravings of Shaanxi and Shanxi*) (Ji'nan: Shandong meishu chubanshe, 2000); Li Guilong and Wang Jianqin, eds., *Suide Handai huaxiang shi* (*Han-dynasty pictorial stone engravings of Suide*) (Xi'an: Shaanxi renmin meishu chubanshe, 2001); Li Lin, Kang Lanying, and Zhao Liguang, eds., *Shaanbei Handai huaxiang shi* (*Han-dynasty pictorial stone engravings of northern Shaanxi*) (Xi'an: Shaanxi renmin chubanshe, 1995); Shaanxi Sheng kaogu yanjiusuo and Yulin Shi wenwu guanli weiyuanhui, eds., *Shenmu Dabaodang: Handai chengzhi yu muzang kaogu baogao* (*Shenmu Dabaodang: Archaeological report of a city site and burials of the Han dynasty*) (Beijing: Kexue chubanshe, 2001).

2. Except for two vertical slabs kept in the Museum of Han Pictorial Stones in Lüliang (Lishi), the stones are in the Shanxi Provincial Museum, Taiyuan. I wish to thank Zhang Shaokun, vice director of the Shanxi Provincial Museum, and Dong Louping, director of the museum in Lüliang, for providing the Royal Ontario Museum with rubbings of the stones in their institutions.

3. Yongning is present-day Lishi in western Shanxi; the Jiuhe flows into the Yellow River at Qikou, an ancient trading town and important ferry crossing 30 km northeast of Lishi.

4. *Xigulou jinshi cuibian* (*The best of bronzes and stone carvings from the Pavilion of Rare Antiquities*) (compiled by Luo Zhenyu on behalf of Liu Chenggan) (1926), *juan* 1. In his *Shijiao lu* (*Encounters with stones*) of 1939, Luo relates how he saw the stones at a dealer's in Beijing (and mentions that they were painted in colors; see Ruitenbeek, *Chinese Shadows: Stone Reliefs, Rubbings, and Related Works of Art from the Han Dynasty (206 BC–AD 220) in the Royal Ontario Museum* (Toronto: Royal Ontario Museum, 2002), p. 19. Illustrations of the rubbings were first published in *Yilin xunkan* (*Decadary of the arts*) (1928), *juan* 7, 8.

5. Wei Juxian, "Han Zuo Biao mu shihua shuoming shu" ("Explanatory note on the pictorial stones from the tomb of Zuo Biao of the Han") *Shuowen yuekan*, vol. 1, no. 1 (1939), p. 456. All People's Republic of China publications give 1919 as the discovery year of the Zuo Biao stones. They are based on Liang Zonghe, "Shanxi Lishi Xian de Handai huaxiang shi" ("Han-dynasty pictorial stone engravings from Lishi County"), *Wenwu cankao ziliao* 1958.4, pp. 40, 75, the first to publish reproductions of rubbings of the Zuo Biao stones still in Shanxi. Liang's information seems less reliable than Wei's, which is based on an investigation by a former schoolmate who was chief of police of Lishi at the time. Xie Guozhen (see next note) gives the name of the Beijing dealer involved as Huang Baichuan of the firm Zunguzhai—of course it is possible that the stones went through the hands of several dealers.

6. Hsio-yen Shih, "Some Fragments from a Han Tomb in the Northwestern Relief Style," *Artibus Asiae*, vol. 25 (1962), pp. 149–62; Xie Guozhen, "Ba Han Zuo Yuanyi mu shi tao pian tapian" ("A note on some rubbings of brick fragments and tomb stones of Zuo Yuanyi of the Han"), *Wenwu* 1979.11, pp. 43–45. Also see Ruitenbeek, *Chinese Shadows*, p. 88, n. 13). I wish to thank Anthony Barbieri-Low for correcting an error in my earlier translation of one of the inscriptions.

7. Archaeological Institute of Shanxi Province, Cultural Relics Station of Lüliang Region, and Cultural Relics Office of Lishi District, "Shanxi Lishi Mamaozhuang Donghan huaxiang shi mu" ("Eastern Han tombs witih pictorial stone engravings from Mamaozhuang, Lishi, Shanxi Province"), *Wenwu* 1992.4, pp. 14–40.

8. Unpublished; drawing in Lüliang Museum.

9. Descriptions and reproductions of rubbings of all Zuo Biao stones kept in Shanxi are given in Gao Weide, "Zuo Yuanyi mu Han huaxiang shi qianxi" ("A preliminary remark on the pictorial stone engravings from the tomb of Zuo Yuanyi of the Han"), in *Handai huaxiang shi yanjiu* (*Studies of pictorial stone engravings of the Han dynasty*) (Beijing: Wenwu chubanshe, 1987), pp. 270–79. Better-quality illustrations of most of the stones are in *Zhongguo huaxiang shi quanji* 5: *Shaanxi, Shanxi Han huaxiang shi*, pp. 208–15.

13 Pleasure tower model

Eastern Han dynasty. Earthenware with green glaze; h. 111.8 cm, w. 40.6 cm, d. 50.8 cm.
Collection of Edward and Nancy Rosenthal.

This four-story tower is a superb example of an art form primarily associated with the Han dynasty, as well as of the innovative and perhaps unique features that distinguish and characterize burial objects of this type. The tower also may provide information about architecture of the Han period.

Rising to a height of 111.8 centimeters, with base dimensions of 40.6 by 50.8 centimeters, the earthenware structure is assembled from five separate parts. The four stories diminish progressively from base to roof; the facade of each story is highly detailed while the other three sides are less so. A wall encloses the lowest level, and balustrades the upper three. The rectangular wall that surrounds the first story extends in front to form a courtyard, but is so close on the other three sides that it barely allows passage. Projecting outward from the front of this wall and shielding the space below is a roof fashioned to resemble parallel courses of tile, with decorative circular tiles concealing the ends of the rafters. Similar but larger eaves project on all four sides at the top of each of the interior structure's four levels, with inward-curving, pointed-leaf–shaped acroteria at the four corners. From the summit of each level's eaves rises the balcony- or porch-like structure that surrounds the next higher level. The prominence of the corner acroteria must have been intended, as each is longer from base to tip than its eaves are from inner to outer edge. The front of each of the balustrades has a distinctive center: diamond-patterned at the second story, a plain vertical oblong at the third, and uninterrupted parallel horizontal lines at the top and smallest balustrade. Offset above the rectangular entrance to the first story is a pair of symmetrically positioned windows with shutters that open upward and outward; a smaller pair, closer together, mark the second story; and single, central windows are positioned in the top two tower levels. Between the second-story windows incised lines form a square lozenge that suggests an X-pattern. A figure with outstretched arms appears at each window except those of the first story. The figures are echoed by the dog standing (presumably on hind legs) next to a crossbow and beneath a figure mounted on a dragon at proper left of the entry in the outer wall (cf. cat. no. 7). In front, the weight of the eaves is supported by a pair of two-arm brackets at every story but the top one. At the front corners of the second- and third-story eaves perch two figures, humans at proper right, animals at left; and a human, bare from the waist up, moves precariously across the tiles of the second-story roof. Apart from the ten humans and animals, seven birds—six perched on bracket sets and one on the top roof ridge—occupy the tower's front facade. In all, sixteen humans or beasts and eight birds look out from this tower, the most extraordinary being the dog adjacent to the crossbow and the figures mounted on dragons on both the front and the back. The entire tower was originally covered with green glaze; hints of blue, green, and red paint seem to remain.

Although ceramic towers have been found in both Western and Eastern Han tombs and occasionally in pre- and post-Han tombs in at least ten Chinese provinces (Hebei, Henan, Shanxi, Shaanxi, Jiangsu, Anhui, Hunan, Guangdong, Guangxi, and Sichuan), the majority are

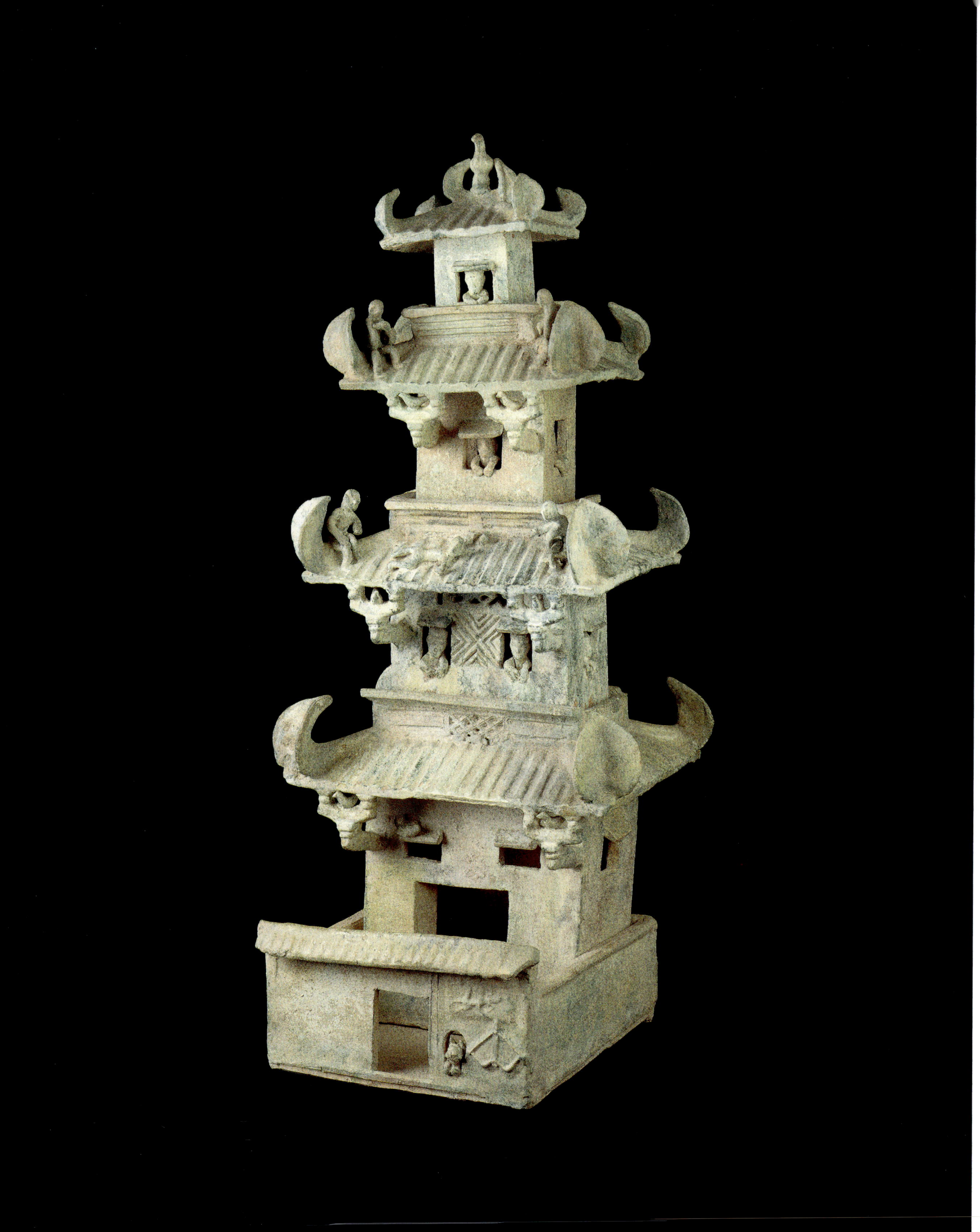

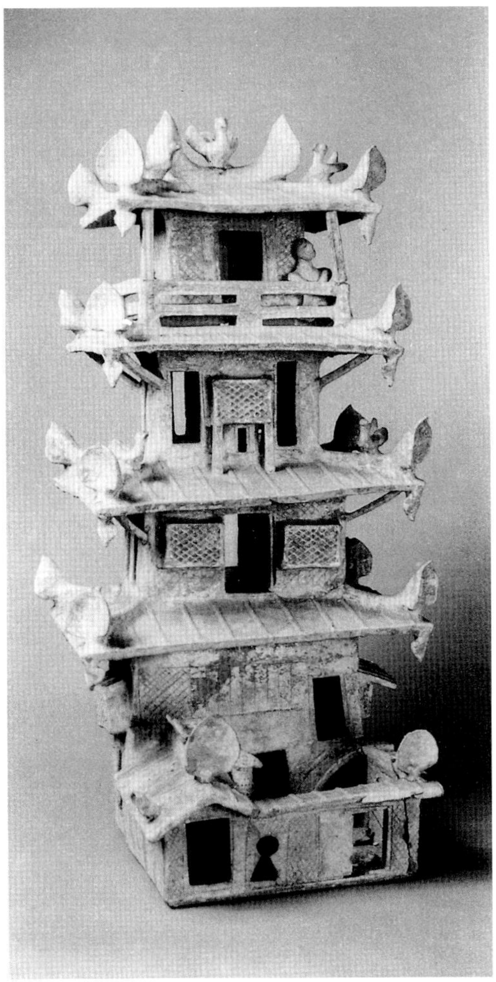

Fig. 1 *Tower*. Han dynasty. Excavated in Shan County, Henan. Glazed earthenware. From Zhang, *Henan chutu*, p. 52.

dated to the Eastern Han period, and most of the examples similar to this one are from tombs in the north central Chinese provinces Henan, Hebei, Shanxi, and Shaanxi.[1] Almost every feature of this tower can be found in others, but no identical one is known, nor, among the hundreds surviving, are there any exact duplicates. For example, another glazed earthenware tower (90 cm high and 28 by 31 cm at the base), dated to the late Eastern Han period and excavated in Shan County, Henan, exhibits the large, upturned-leaf decorations at the corners of ridge poles, a prominently displayed bird flanked by the same acroteria at the center of the top roof ridge, and clearly defined parallel roof rafters on every eaves (fig. 1). Yet the Shan County tower is smaller, only its top story has a porch, and it was molded in one piece. Originally it may have had more figures, attached or removable. It shares with the present tower a front courtyard and animals visible through an open window at proper left in the courtyard's front wall. A notable feature is the adjacent keyhole-shaped opening. Whether a variation of the more common quadrilateral apertures or possessing some still undetermined meaning, openings of this shape can be found on other Han towers, further evidence of the shared elements in a group of individual structures.

Miniature ceramic buildings have been considered an important component of Han burials since the initial studies of Chinese funerary objects. Already in the first half of the twentieth century, prior to widespread excavation in China, major museums, including the Museum of Fine Arts, Boston, the Nelson Gallery–Atkins Museum, and the Museum of the University of Pennsylvania, had acquired tall earthenware structures.[2] They were as well known as the rubbings from the "Wu family shrines," and usually were discussed together with the shrines in literature about Han art. The miniatures and rubbings figured in writings about both Chinese architecture and Chinese sculpture, for it was not determined if the *mingqi* and reliefs of buildings or the "Wu shrines" themselves were replicas of actual Han buildings, or idealizations made specifically for funerary contexts, or both, or neither.

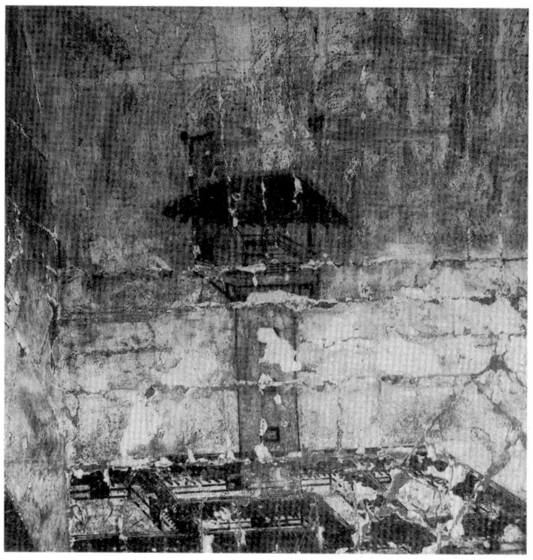

Five and one-half decades of excavation have yielded hundreds more towers. Over sixty Han tombs with extensive interior mural programs are now known, some including towers (fig. 2), in contrast to fewer than ten in the 1940s.[3] Regional types and subtypes of earthenware buildings have been suggested. Approximately one hundred earthenware structures from tombs in Henan Province, for example, have been classified into thirteen types: quadrilateral, multistory storehouses, including granaries; cylindrical storehouses; structures with courtyards; houses; towers; kiosks; multistory structures for performances; watchtowers; gate-towers; mills; places of manufacture, including ceramic workshops; animal pens, often joined with outhouses; and wells. The thirteen comprise forty subtypes, based on such characteristics as base shape and presence or absence of feet, among which are seventy-one categories, such as shape of windows and kinds of figures or animals, and well over one hundred subcategories, such as number of animals.[4] According to these criteria, figure 1 is a watchtower of the four- or five-story type, each of whose stories is individualized.[5] The present tower would fall into the same subcategory.

Yet fundamental questions about earthenware architecture, some of which also are prompted by representations of architecture on the "Wu family shrines," remain unresolved. The problem of what to call them is one that has plagued Chinese and Western scholars since the first modern writings about these earthenware buildings. Because the structures are funerary art, they are sometimes called *mingqi*. However, this widely used twentieth-century generic term for funerary objects (ceramic, wooden, or stone),[6] tells us nothing about the purpose or function of small buildings in burials. It has therefore been proposed that a pre-Han meaning for *mingqi*, a ritual funerary vessel, should be also applied to towers.[7] Yet there is no textual basis for equating a building with a ritual vessel. There is also the question of individuality. Mass production by workshops has been shown to dominate funerary art, and interchangeability of mass-produced parts is the basic tenet of Chinese architecture.[8] The bold silhouettes of men and horses on almost every surface of the "Wu family shrines," and figures from Chinese legend and lore that repeat on the same shrine and appear on more than one shrine, support ideas of mass production and interchangeability. Yet as noted above, a component such as a leaf-like eaves-end may be repeated on a tower, and identical or extremely similar figures or animals might appear on more than one tower, but each tower appears to have been integrally conceived and no two are the same overall. Finally, the most compelling question remains the most elusive: how much closer are we now than we were a hundred years ago, when Chavannes published the now universally recognizable silhouettes from the "Wu shrines,"[9] to being able to confidently reconstruct Han architecture? The earthenware forms are often referred to as models (*moxing*), but in fact we do not have buildings or documents that prove that the small buildings were based on actual structures or vice versa. Then as now, we turn to the earthenware structures in the absence of existing wooden architecture to inform us about the Han building tradition.

Fig. 2 *Painting of a tower*, 176 CE. Eastern Han dynasty. From north wall of central east-side chamber of tomb, Anping, Hebei. From Hebei Cultural Relics Research Institute, *Donghan Anping bihua mu* (*Eastern Han tomb with murals in Anping*) (Beijing: Wenwu chubanshe, 1990), pl. 51.

The most convincing associations between actual structure and "model" have been suggested through comparisons with *que*, another problematical Chinese term. Often translated "pillar-gate," *que* can form part of outer walls, sometimes at the wall corners and other times flanking an entry. *Que* also designates one of a pair of towers directly in front of an entry, sometimes along an approach lined with other pairs of monumental sculpture. A pair of *que*, for example, remained in front of the "Wu family shrines" when Chavannes studied the site (fig. 3).

In 1961 Chen Mingda published research on twenty-three Han *que*, most of them investigated by him in 1936, 1939, and 1941 in Henan and Sichuan, and a few additional ones studied by the Sichuan Cultural Relics Commission in 1956.[10] Thirty-one years later only six more Han *que* had been identified, for a total of twenty-nine. Of these, twenty were in Sichuan, four each in Henan and Shandong, and one in Beijing. No new hypothesis about their purpose or context had been offered.[11] It may not be coincidental that a majority of the earthenware towers have been uncovered in tombs in these three provinces and that the same provinces are also important sources of Han funerary relief sculpture (the regions of Chengdu in Sichuan, Nanyang in Henan, and the many sites in Shandong including the "Wu family," Zhu Wei, and Xiaotang Shan shrines). Still, the main point of similarity between any of the *que* and the earthenware towers is simply that they are tall in comparison with the actual or molded size, respectively, of the human figure. *Que* may be formed of four or five layers of brick or stone, but by the criteria that determine the stories of a "model"—roof eaves and/or porches—*que* are two stories, sometimes with an exterior balustrade suggesting a porch. *Que* were but one form of Han architecture, as earthenware towers are one type of funerary art, and it remains conjecture if equivalent forms in wood existed for either of them or if they shared purposes or symbolism.

Only a few features of the *que* or earthenware towers can probably be assumed to be facsimiles of Han timber architecture. Roof eaves of both *que* and earthenware towers are in all likelihood intended to replicate courses of ceramic tile over wooden roofs, occasionally with the circular decorated tiles that covered rafter ends. Cantilevered supports for the overhanging roof eaves are believed to follow the forms of bracket sets. Yet verification for these

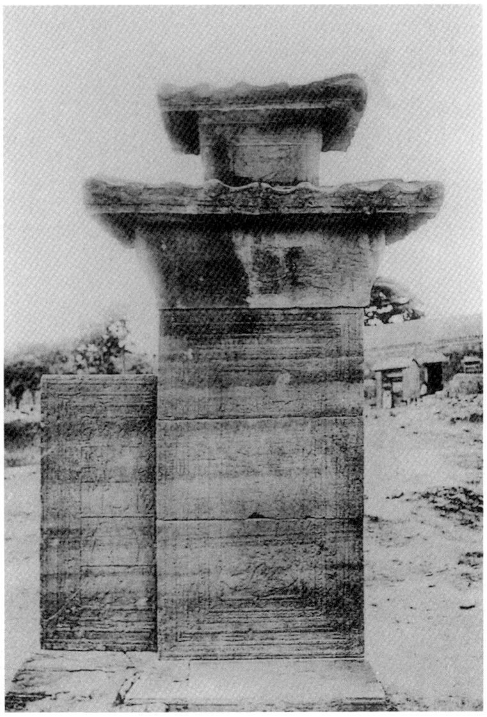

Fig. 3 *Que* that stood at the "Wu family shrines" cemetery site of at beginning of twentieth century. Published courtesy of Visual Resources Collection, University of Pennsylvania.

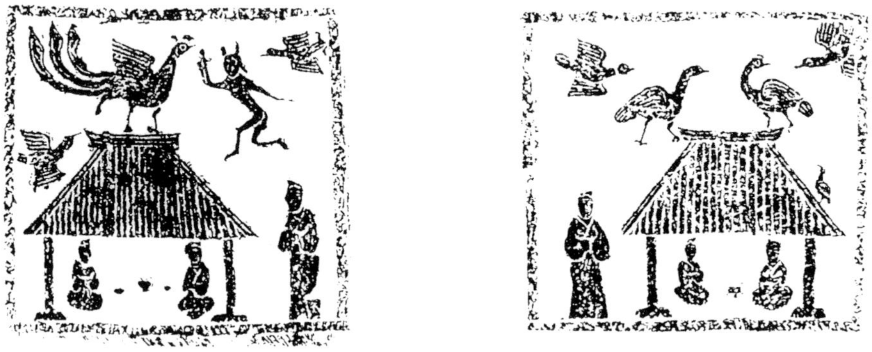

assumptions, today as a century ago, comes from the presence of these features in later architecture, from poetic descriptions of Han buildings, and through acceptance of the notion that a tomb sculpture replicates an aboveground timber or brick structure.

Separate from the form are those particular and perhaps individually commissioned features found on earthenware towers that only occasionally find equivalents in relief sculpture on a *que*. On the present tower they are the man clinging to the slippery roof slope, the terrier poking his face out of the courtyard window, the adjacent bow, and the figure borne by a dragon above them. Drawing on knowledge of the "Wu shrines" carvings, it is possible to speculate that the entire front presents interrelated units of narrative and that the tower might be understood as five registers, each narrating its own story or stories. So far, it has not been possible to associate these elements with heroes, legends, or literature of the Han, although the crossbow on the front and back courtyard walls seems to symbolize defense against intruders. Crossbow and dog together may be an image of "watch and ward."

Perhaps less specifically meaningful, but probably symbolic, are the birds perched on the bracket sets that support the eaves. Bracket sets on earthenware towers are often transformed into animals, much like the handles on bronze vessels of the Zhou period,[12] and birds are found on more Han roof ridges than not (fig. 4; cat. no. 16), including roofs pictured on the "Wu shrines."

One association for birds on a roof ridge is upward flight, in other words, toward the heavens, and another is the heavenly body brightest to the naked eye, the sun. One of the most common representations in Han funerary art, a black bird in the disk of the sun, symbolizes the positive energy of the cosmos, *yang*.[13] The *fenghuang*, a fantastic bird conventionally termed "phoenix," appears often in associations with the south, summer, vermilion, and cosmic harmony.[14] The linkage between bird and dragon, the latter appearing above the crossbow on the front and back of the earthenware tower, is especially intriguing, because it calls forth an image of the *feng*-bird or *fenghuang*, one of the guardians of the Immortal-inhabited Mount Kunlun, who in later times was paired with the *luan*-bird or dragon.[15] The frequency of birds on roof ridges in Han funerary art in all likelihood suggests an association between the bird and the heavens. Hence the omission of birds from roof ridges of *que* seems to indicate that the grave objects and the monumental freestanding towers did not carry the same symbolic freight.

The ceramic tower model appeared and largely disappeared with the Han. Its repeating motifs and their movement across horizontal planes attest its membership in the Han visual system. Although lacking the inscriptions, cavalcades, bridges, and labeled tales of heroes and paragons that cover the "Wu shrines" and so many other Han monuments, the ceramic tower is emblematic of Han funerary art.

NANCY S. STEINHARDT

Fig. 4 *Birds on roofs*. Han dynasty. Rubbings of relief sculptures from north wall of tomb in Weishan County, Shandong. From *Kaogu* 1998.3, p. 15.

Notes

1. For more on earthenware structures of the Han dynasty, see Candace J. Lewis, "Pottery Towers of Han Dynasty China," (PhD diss., Institute of Fine Arts, New York University, 1999), and Zhang Yong, *Henan chutu Handai jianzhu mingqi* (*Architectural burial objects of the Han dynasty excavated in Henan*) (Zhengzhou: Dajia chubanshe, 2002), each with an extensive bibliography. On this tower, see Candace J. Lewis, *Into the Afterlife: Han and Six Dynasties Chinese Tomb Sculpture from the Schloss Collection* (Poughkeepsie: Vassar College Art Gallery, 1990), pp. 68–69.

2. The Museum of Fine Arts, Boston, acquired two towers in 1950, the Kansas City tower was acquired in 1933, and the University of Pennsylvania acquired its tower in 1918.

3. The best-known Han tombs with murals are discussed in He Xilin, *Gu mu danqing: Handai mushi bihua de faxian yu yanjiu* (*Cream of ancient painting: discovery and research on Han tomb murals*) (Xi'an: Shaanxi renmin meishu chubanshe, 2001). Sixty-five tombs with interior murals known in 2004 are listed in the appendix of Hsin-mei (Agnes) Hsu, "Pictorial Eulogies in Three Eastern Han Tombs," (PhD diss., University of Pennsylvania, 2004).

4. Zhang Yong, *Henan chutu*, pp. 199–224.

5. Zhang Yong, *Henan chutu*, p. 210.

6. *Cihai* (*Sea of terms*) (Shanghai: Shanghai jishu chubanshe, 1979), vol. 2, p. 3178.

7. It is a premise of Lewis, "Pottery Towers," that the earthenware towers were ritual objects and further, that they had intrinsic sacred qualities (p. 1 and pp. 155–90).

8. This is the theme of Lothar Ledderose, *Ten Thousand Things: Module and Mass Production in Chinese Art* (Princeton: Princeton University Press, 2000).

9. As discussed in Liu's "Recarving the Past" in this catalogue, Édouard Chavannes published images from the "Wu shrines" in 1893, 1913/1915.

10. Chen Mingda, "Handai de shique" ("Stone *que* of the Han dynasty"), *Wenwu* 1961.12, pp. 9–23; reprinted and slightly edited in *Chen Mingda gu jianzhu yu diaosu shilun* (*Essays on ancient architecture and sculpture by Chen Mingda*) (Beijing: Wenwu chubanshe, 1998), pp. 142–55. It should be noted that although the structures are often referred to as *shi* (stone) *que*, they were built in both stone and brick.

11. Xu Wenpeng et al., *Sichuan Handai shique* (*Han* que *in Sichuan*) (Beijing: Wenwu chubanshe, 1992), preface (n.p.).

12. Exquisite examples of animal-form handles and feet on bronze vessels are among the objects excavated from the tomb of Marquis Yi of Zeng, dated to 433 BCE, in Leigudun, Sui County, Hubei. For illustrations, see Hubei Provincial Museum, *Zenghou Yi mu* (*Tomb of the Marquis Yi of Zeng*) (Beijing: Wenwu chubanshe, 1991), 2 vols.

13. In August 1995 Tanaka Tan presented a paper on the symbolic associations between birds and the heavens at an international conference on architecture at the Chinese University of Hong Kong. On associations between birds and the sun, see Michael Loewe, *Chinese Ideas of Life and Death* (London and Boston: Allen and Unwin, 1982), p. 66.

14. The ordered universe whose southern quadrant is described here was a central theme of Han scholars and theorists. Among the numerous writings on this subject are: William de Bary et al., *Sources of Chinese Tradition* (New York and London: Columbia University Press, 1964), vol. 1, pp. 191–210; John Henderson, *The Development and Decline of Chinese Cosmology* (New York: Columbia University Press, 1984); John Major, "The Five Phases, Magic Squares, and Schematic Cosmography," in *Explorations in Early Chinese Cosmology*, ed. Henry Rosemont, Jr. (Chico, Calif.: Scholar's Press, 1984), pp. 133–66; and Sarah Allan, *The Shape of the Turtle* (Albany: State University of New York Press, 1991).

15. The *feng*-bird and *fenghuang* feature prominently in *Shanhai jing* (*Classic of Mountains and Waterways*), written before and during the Western Han dynasty. For a recent study, see Richard Strassberg, *A Chinese Bestiary: Strange Creatures from the "Guideways through Mountains and Seas"* (Berkeley and Los Angeles: University of California Press, 2002). For one description of the bird, see pp. 193–94. For the sources of associations between the *fenghuang* and the dragon, see Jean-Pierre Diény, "Le Fenghuang et le Phénix," *Cahiers d'Extrême Asie*, vol. 5 (1989–90), pp. 1–13.

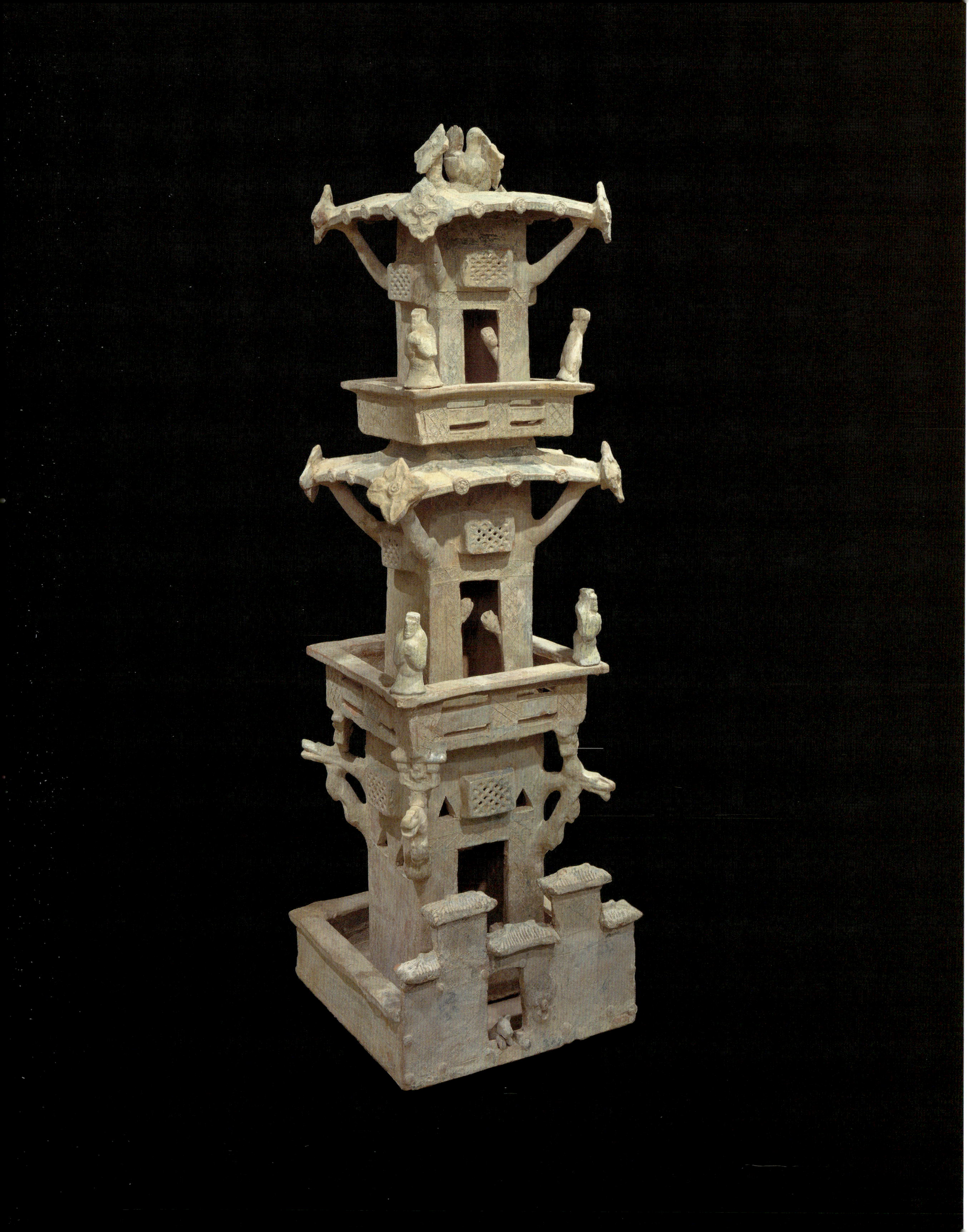

14 Tower model

Eastern Han dynasty. Earthenware with green glaze; h. 106.7 cm.
Brooklyn Museum, acc. no. 1997.142a–e. Purchased from the Schloss Collection with funds given by Dr. Richard and Ruth Dickes, Lucille and Martin E. Kantor, Dr. Robert and Bernice Dickes, Florence and Irving Kingdon, Dr. Bertram H. Schaffner, Dora Wong, and Diane Schafer; Frank Babbott Fund.

Standing 106.7 centimeters and with base dimensions of 34.5 by 38 centimeters, the three-story, green-glazed earthenware tower has much in common with catalogue number 13. Like that four-story tower, this tower has upper levels articulated by a porch and the base level enclosed by a wall. Similar, too, is the concentration of figures and decoration on the front, the bird capping the tower, the birds at the center of bracket arms (though here only on the lowest tier), the lozenge- and X-patterned decorations in relief above the door and the windows and along the exteriors of porches, the dog standing on hind legs to look out from the front courtyard, and the molding to the dog's right (in this case an animal-faced door knocker). Here, too, figures are included in the design: seven remain, posed either at balustrade corners or looking out front windows. Finally, the eaves are made to resemble ceramic tile and are ornamented at all four corners; the ornaments are identical diamond-shaped crockets. Two of these also flank the bird centered on the roof.

Other features are so specific that it is tempting to assign meaning or associate a place of origin or a patron to them. Most obvious is the shape and pattern of the crockets (or acroteria): they are eight-sided, with four points from which raised lines intersect at a prominent center marked by a double concentric circle. Similarly specific is the pattern on the decorative circular tiles edging all four sides of the roof eaves: four double-edged petals around a raised circular center. The imitation tiles are the only decorated features on the back and sides of the upper levels. Two other towers, also formerly in the Schloss collection, share the distinctive corner decoration of the eaves as well as the more common animal-faced bracket sets (fig. 1).[1] Persons leaning to peer out the windows, such as are found in the present tower, also appear in figure 1.

The rarest feature of this tower is the courtyard entry facade. The three low and two higher roofs and the very limited low-relief articulation have a presence more massive and much harder to penetrate than their height of fifteen or twenty centimeters would suggest. The facade of figure 1, by contrast, has only four imitation ceramic-tile roofs at the entry and a double-leaf closed door, decorated with animal-faced knockers not dissimilar to the one on the present tower. The door anticipates opening onto a residential courtyard, and figure 1 offers altogether a less severe image than that of the present tower. A tower excavated in Lingbao County, Henan (fig. 2) bears an even greater resemblance to the present one: it is only 88 centimeters high but nearly the same at the base, 37 by 42 centimeters; it has five roof sections, two of them doubled and capping *que* towers, the remaining three as copings, over the front wall and entry way. The acroteria that cover the eaves corners also are similar, eight-sided with four main segments, but the wide front opening suggests a less formidable passage. The decorative eaves-end tiles seem to be fairly common among green-glazed miniature towers excavated in Henan,[2] and animal-faced bracket sets also can be found in several towers in addition to those mentioned here,[3] and some towers were paired, making the very plain facade of the present tower all the more unusual by contrast.[4]

An explanation for the notably stark and thus severe facade may lie in the patterns on the depictions of circular tiles that edge the

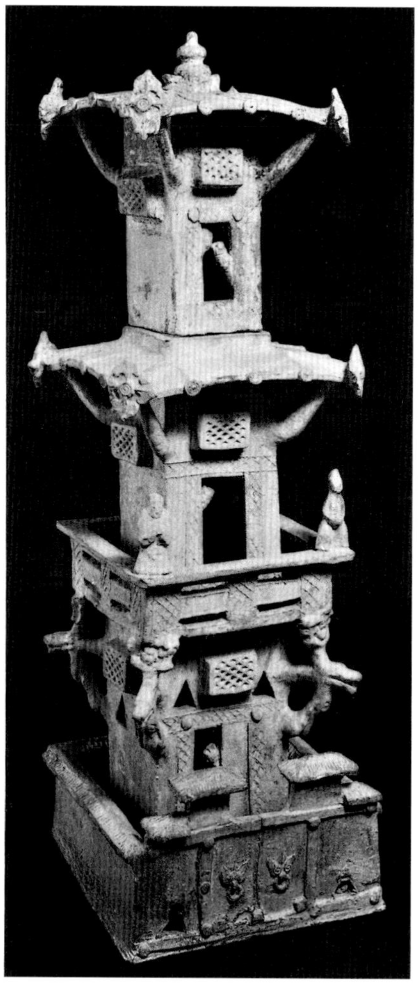

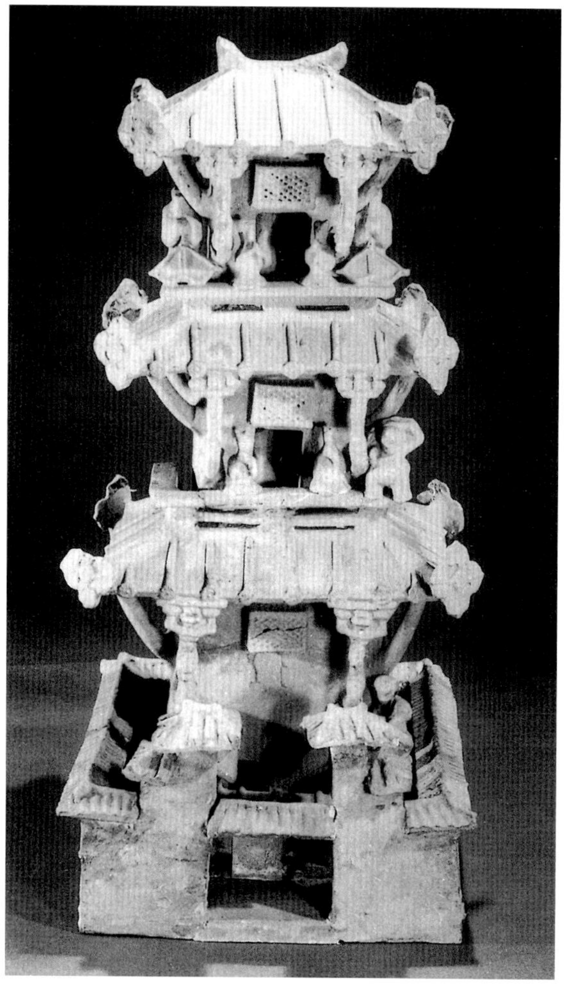

eaves-ends. Not only are they found on several green-glazed miniature towers that have the above-described corner acroteria,[5] but actual tiles with what appear to be the same pattern have been excavated at the ruins of both Han capitals, Chang'an of the Western Han and Luoyang of the Eastern Han. The tiles from Chang'an were uncovered at the ruins of the palace-complex Weiyang Gong (fig. 3), and those from Luoyang were found in a funerary precinct near White Horse Monastery (Baima Si), dated to the Eastern Han period (fig. 4).[6]

The similarities in roof-tile pattern among miniature towers and excavated objects of daily life seem to afford rare and highly indicative evidence that the earthenware miniatures might replicate real structures. Actual tiles bearing the patterns in question, discovered in urban architectural settings, inside the walls of Han emperors' own palaces and capital cities, may even indicate that the solid, formidable quality of the present tower's walls was intended to reflect the entryway to a Han capital.

NANCY S. STEINHARDT

Fig. 1 *Miniature tower*. Han dynasty. Earthenware with green glaze. From Candace Lewis, *Into the Afterlife: Han and Six Dynasties Chinese Tomb Sculpture from the Schloss Collection* (Poughkeepsie: Vassar College Art Gallery, 1990), p. 65.

Fig. 2 *Miniature tower*. Han dynasty. Earthenware with green glaze. Excavated from tomb in Lingbao County, Henan. From Zhang Yong, *Henan chutu*, pl. 50.

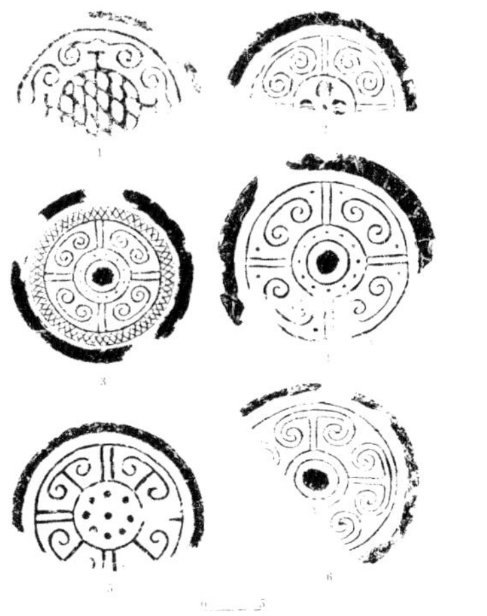

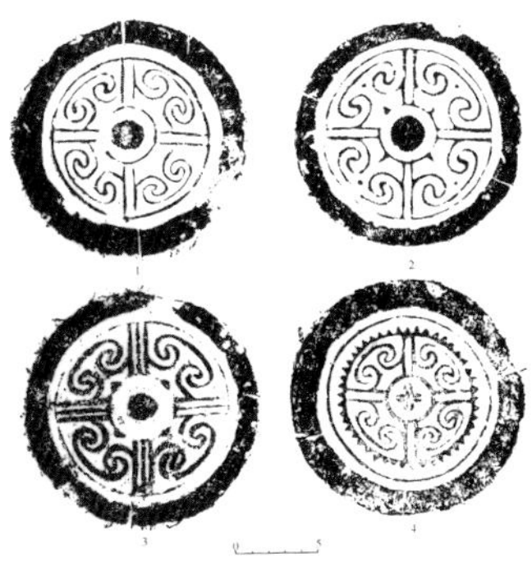

Notes

1. For an illustration of the other tower, see Candace Lewis, *Into the Afterlife* (Poughkeepsie: Vassar College Art Gallery, 1990), p. 65.

2. Another example was found in a tomb at Zhangwan, Lingbao County, in 1972, and yet another in Sanmenxia, in 1987, both in Henan. For illustrations, see Zhang Yong, *Henan chutu Handai jianzhu mingqi (Architectural burial objects of the Han dynasty excavated in Henan)* (Zhengzhou: Dajia chubanshe, 2002), pls. 38, 39. All towers known to date include more examples from Henan than from any other province. This does not necessarily mean that during the Han more towers were buried in tombs in Henan than in other provinces. Because the capital of the Eastern Han, Luoyang, was in Henan Province, it is logical not only that Henan holds many Han tombs, but also that in Henan excavation and publication of Han material has been a priority.

3. Including figure 1 and the second tower formerly in the Schloss collection, shown in Lewis, *Into the Afterlife*, p. 65.

4. It is not the pair of *que* that is striking, but the absence of decoration. Examples of the miniature towers boasting pairs of *que*, from Henan alone, can be seen in Zhang Yong, *Henan chutu*, cpls. 3, 6, 8, 9, 12, 13, 14, 15.

5. The two miniature towers mentioned in n. 2; Zhang Yong, *Henan chutu*, cpls. 38, 39.

6. The official excavation report of the most important Western Han palace complex, Weiyang Gong, is Zhongguo shehui kexueyuan kaogu yanjiusuo, *Han Chang'an cheng Weiyang Gong* (*Weiyang palace complex of Han Chang'an*), 2 vols. (Beijing: Zhongguo dabaike quanshu chubanshe, 1996). On the funerary precinct in the vicinity of White Horse Monastery, see Luoyang wenwuju and Luoyang Baima Si Han–Wei gucheng baoguansuo, *Han–Wei Luoyang gucheng yanjiu* (*Research on the ancient city of Han and Wei Luoyang*) (Beijing: Science Press, 2000), pp. 164–93.

Fig. 3 *Line drawings of patterns on circular ceramic eaves-end tiles.* Excavated from sector B of the front hall of Weiyang Palace in the Western Han capital, Chang'an. From Zhongguo shehui kexueyuan yanjiusuo, *Han Chang'an cheng Weiyang Gong*, vol. 1, p. 255.

Fig. 4 *Line drawings of patterns on circular ceramic eaves-end tiles.* Excavated from a funerary precinct of Han- or Wei-dynasty Luoyang. From Luoyang wenwuju et al., *Han–Wei Luoyang*, p. 183.

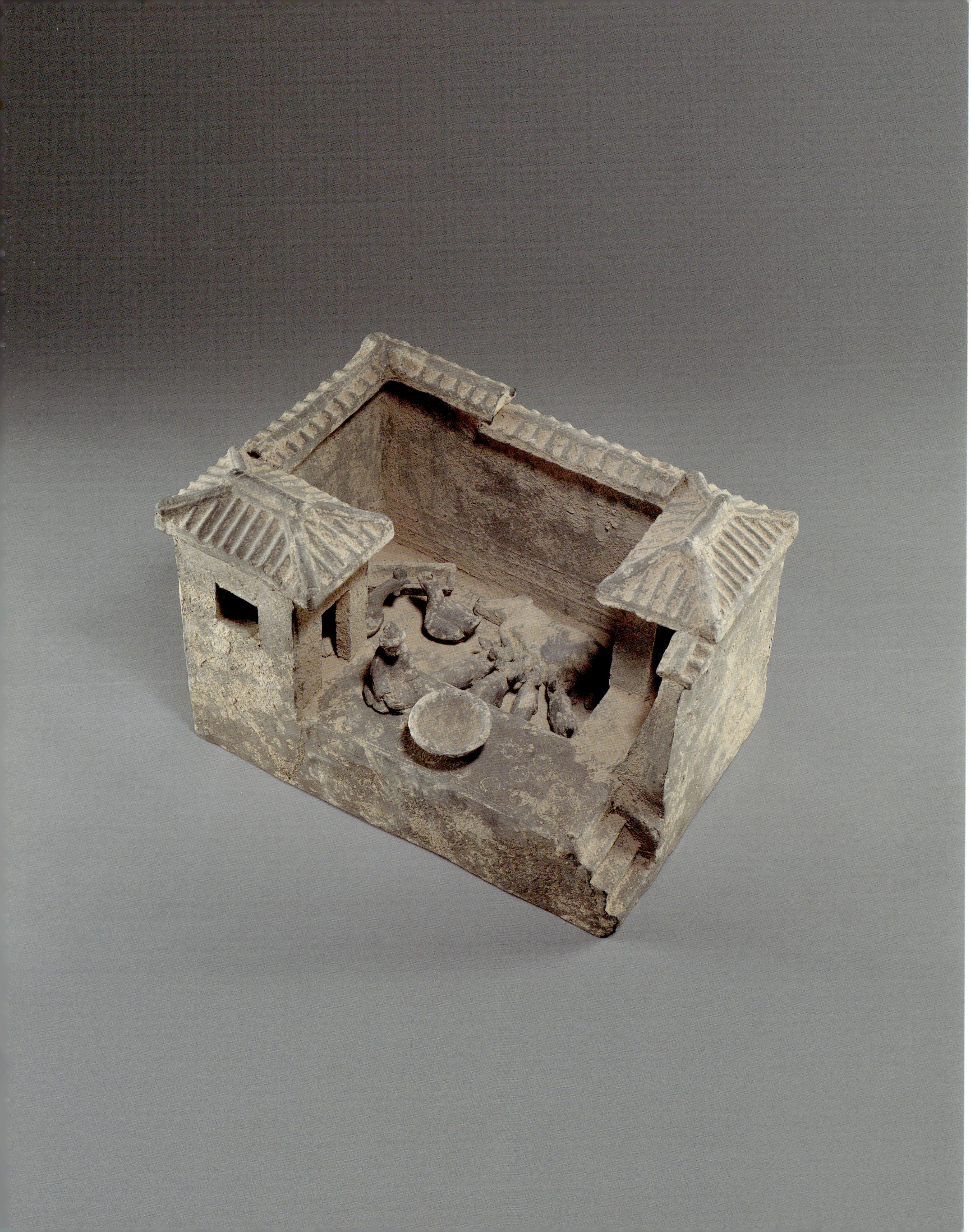

15 Model of farm compound with human figure, sow and suckling pigs, chickens, trough, and basin

Han dynasty. Dark gray earthenware; h. 23.2 cm, w. approx. 35.5, d. approx. 24.0 cm.
Princeton University Art Museum, acc. no. 2001-290 a–k. Gift of Dr. Alvin E. Friedman-Kien in honor of Allen Rosenbaum.

During the Han dynasty the quantity and variety of clay *mingqi* proliferated, so that the tomb furnishings record the prosperous lives of upper-class landowners. Tombs were fully equipped to sustain the deceased in the afterlife, and included models of servants, entertainers, musicians, and garden pavilions; oil lamps, guardians, and striking watch towers illuminated and protected the tomb. Included also were the more mundane necessities of life, such as stoves, wellheads, lamps, and storage jars. Often the *mingqi* paralleled pictorial images painted, carved in stone, or stamped on tiles to decorate the walls of tombs and shrines. Underlining the importance of agriculture in Han life and economy, the many types of architectural models that came into use then included farm buildings, ranging from modest single-story structures and granaries to large farm compounds with attached animal pens and yards.

This farmyard or compound, fashioned out of dark clay, has high walls topped with simulated tile roofs along the back, one side, and part of the other side and the front. On the unwalled front, steps lead up to a wide walkway, patterned with decorative circular tiles stamped into the clay; at the top of the steps are two rows of three circles followed by an arrangement of four circles forming the corners of a square with a fifth circle in the middle. This pattern of five is repeated three times. Within each circle is a smaller circle of six dots with a seventh filling the center space—almost reminiscent of a jade *bi*. The main walkway with its circles leads in one direction to a small roofed building with a door and two windows, perhaps a privy; in the other direction to a low parapet facing the courtyard. Along the bottom of the inside walls of this clay model, four parallel horizontal lines with periodic vertical scoring suggest a brick-like foundation that would have supported the stucco walls. Inside the enclosed farmyard is a sow suckling piglets, chickens, and a trough and basin for water and feed. Many very similar structures, containing pigs or a mix of animals, have been excavated from tombs across north China (fig. 1), and a fragment of one such example was recovered from Tomb 1 at the cemetery associated with the "Wu shrines" (fig. 2).[1]

Complementing clay models of stoves, wellheads, and farmyards with animals, lively kitchen scenes painted or carved on tomb walls, including those of the "Wu family shrines" (fig. 3), showed the preparation of food, from the butchering of the animals to the roasting. In these scenes, victuals hung on racks usually include fish, fowl, and meat.[2] Many Han tombs, especially those of Eastern Han, contained ceramic pigs, pigsty, and chickens. Meat, including chicken, pork, and beef, was certainly part of the diet of the rich but not readily available to the ordinary Chinese. Although beef was highly prized, oxen were so important as draft animals that the government occasionally prohibited their slaughter.[3] Chicken was probably the most accessible form of meat for average Chinese, though not for the very poor.

ANNETTE L. JULIANO

Notes

1. A very similar model but with somewhat fancier decorative windows cut into the walls was excavated in Ji County, Henan Province, and is now in the Henan Provincial Museum; see *Treasures from the Han*

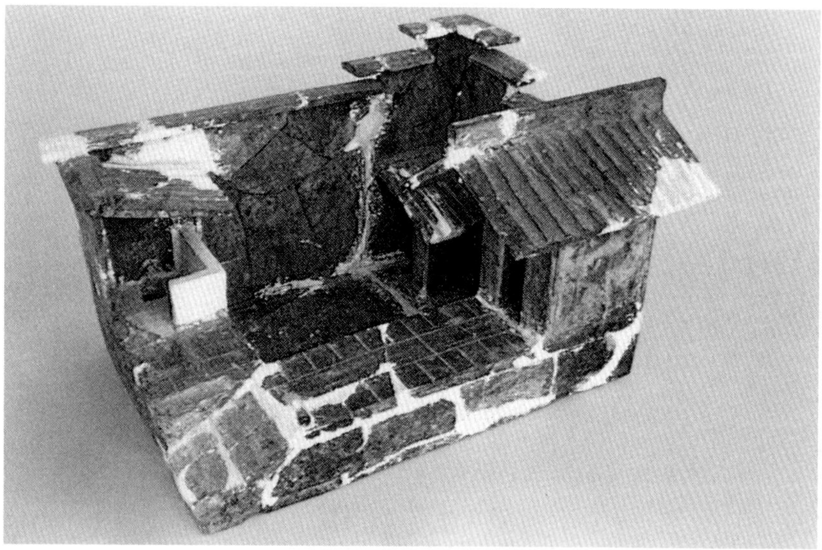

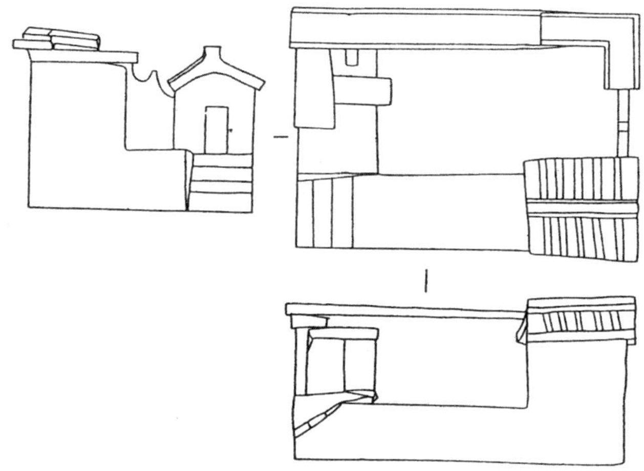

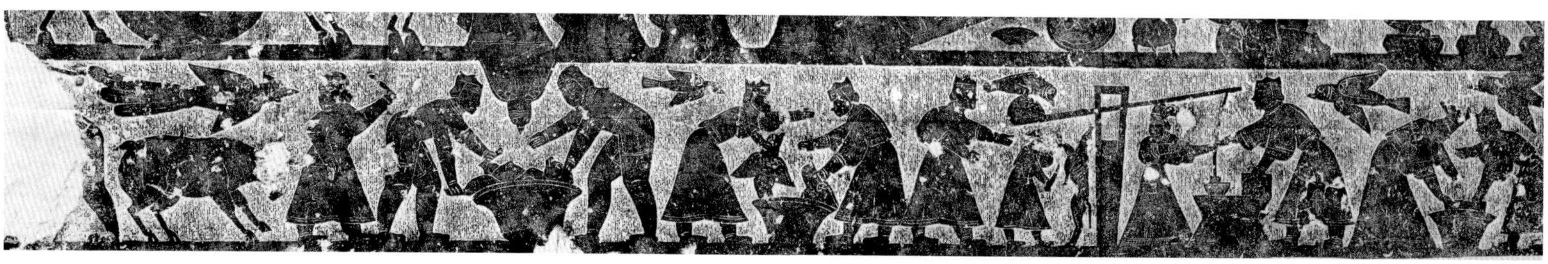

Fig. 1 *Farm compound.* Eastern Han dynasty. Excavated from Tomb 1, Jinlingzhen, near Linzi, Shandong. Gray earthenware. From *Kaogu xuebao* 1999.1, p. 109, fig. 12.2, pl. 11.2.

Fig. 2 *Farm compound.* Eastern Han dynasty. Reconstructed from a fragment excavated from Tomb 1, "Wu family shrines." Restoration drawing. From Jiang Yingju and Wu Wenqi, *Handai Wushi muqun shike yanjiu*, p. 123, fig. 16-10.

Fig. 3 *Kitchen scene.* Detail of Stone Chamber 1, Stone 1-E.2 (cat. no. 1.12). "Wu family shrines" rubbings. Princeton University Art Museum, acc. no. 2002-307.2.

(Singapore, Landmark Books, 1990), p. 47, top and right. The fragments recovered from Tomb 1 in the cemetery associated with the Wu shrines have been published as a line drawing by Jiang Yingju and Wu Wenqi, *Handai Wushi muqun shike yanjiu* (*Studies on the Han-dynasty stone carvings at the Wu family cemetery*) (Ji'nan: Shandong meishu chubanshe, 1995), p. 23. Other similar compounds from Eastern Han Tomb 1 at Jinlingzhen, near Linzi, Shandong, appear in *Kaogu xuebao*, 1999.1, p. 109, fig. 12.2, pl. 11.2. A very similar model is in the collections of The Brooklyn Museum and was published by Ezekiel Schloss, *Ming-Ch'i, Clay Figures Reflecting Life in Ancient China* (New York: Katonah Gallery, 1975), no. 8.

2. For a few examples of kitchen scenes, see Eastern Han tombs from Liaoyang in Liaoning, published in Ying-shih Yu, "Han China," in *Food in Chinese Culture, Anthropological and Historical Perspective*, ed. K. C. Chang (New Haven and London: Yale University Press, 1977), following p. 176, figs.10–12. A highly detailed kitchen scene can be found carved into stone slabs on the walls of the Eastern Han tomb at Tahuting, Mixian, Henan; see *Wenwu*, 1972.10, p. 61, fig.11, which shows the east wall of the eastern corner chamber of Tomb 1. Other examples appear on the lower left part of the east wall of the Xiaotang Shan shrine, Shandong; see rubbings published by Klaas Ruitenbeek, *Chinese Shadows: Stone Reliefs, Rubbings and Related Works of Art from the Han Dynasty (206 BC–AD 220) in the Royal Ontario Museum* (Toronto: Royal Ontario Museum, 2002), p.77; yet another kitchen scene was incised in stone in a Han tomb in Zhucheng County, Shandong, ibid, p. 19, fig. 9. Kitchen imagery continued into the post-Han era in the Wei–Jin tombs from Jiayuguan, Gansu; these have cooking scenes painted on tiles, see *Wenwu* 1972.12, p. 40, figs. 29–32.

3. Most of the information about food in China was drawn from K. C. Chang, ed., *Food in Chinese Culture*, 1997, chaps. 1 and 2, pp. 23–53; and from Wang Zhongshu, *Han Civilization*, trans. K. C. Chang and collaborators (New Haven and London: Yale University Press, 1982), chap. 3, "Han Dynasty Agriculture," pp. 52–80.

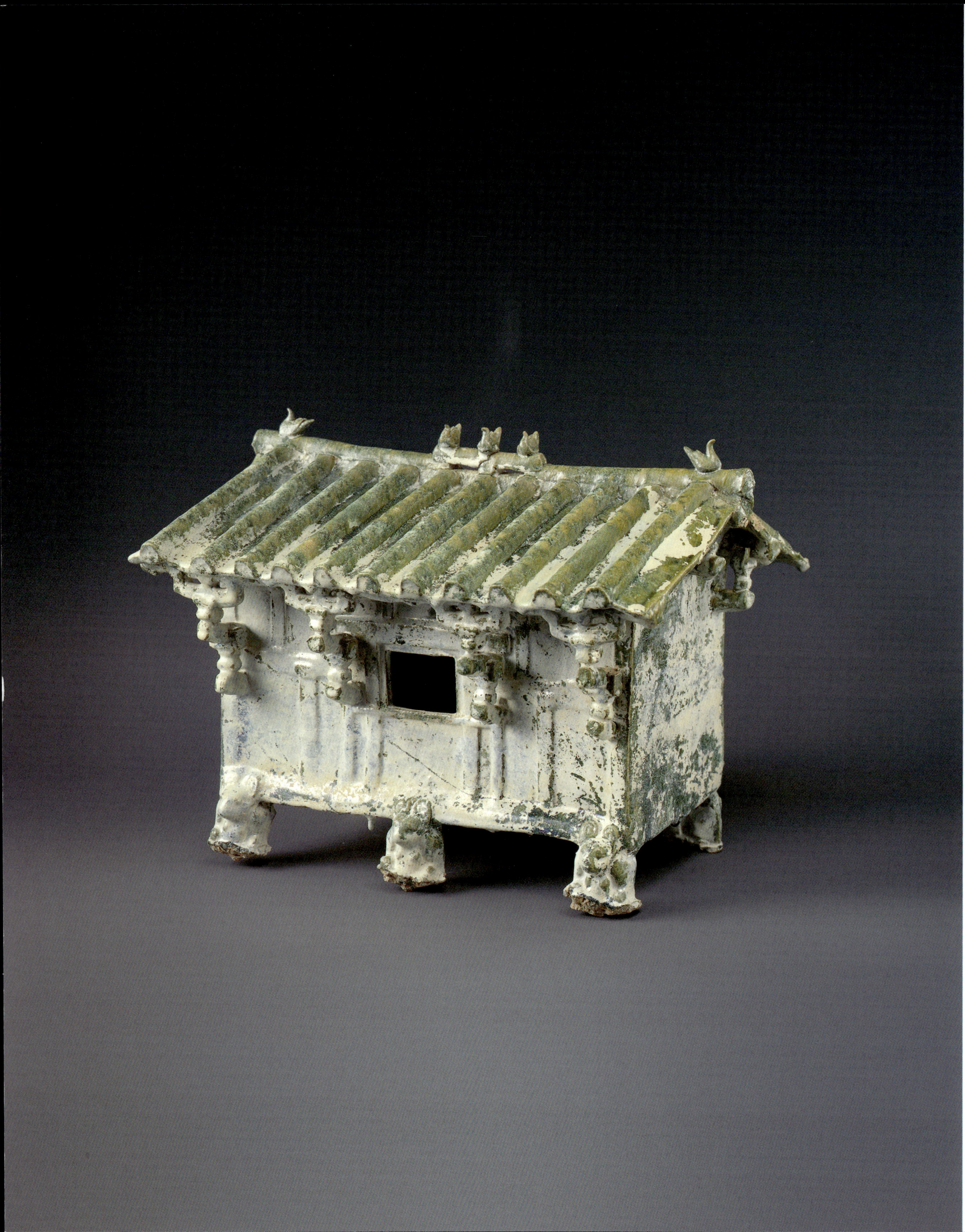

16 Storehouse model

Eastern Han dynasty. Earthenware with green glaze; h. 27.5 cm, w. approx. 35.5 cm.
Princeton University Art Museum, acc. no. 2000-347. Museum purchase, Fowler McCormick, Class of 1921, Fund.

This well-proportioned hollow rectangular structure clearly refers to a wooden prototype, even though the details are partly obscured by the green glaze, now a silvery iridescence from burial: the facade, pierced with a rectangular window in the center, is applied with clay strips in imitation of wooden slats, and the slanted tiled roof is supported by four *dougong* brackets. Five birds roost on the central roof ridge (detail). The entire structure is raised above the ground by six pot-bellied bears, depicted kneeling on their hind legs with front paws resting on their knees.

Glazed examples of architectural models, including watchtowers, granaries, and animal dwellings, likewise with bear-form supports, have frequently been excavated from Han tombs in northern China. Storehouses of related type appear especially in Henan Province.[1] Their prototype may have contained any number of things; the *Huainanzi*, a mid second-century BCE text, describes the royal storehouses as holding the raw materials of weapons and chariots used in hunting and warfare.[2]

HIROMI KINOSHITA

Notes

1. Unearthed from Han tombs at Zhangwan, Lingbao County, Henan, and at Shaan County, Henan. See *Wenwu* 1975.11, p. 87, figs. 13–17, and *Kaogu xuebao* 1965.1, p. 141, fig. 30.8–10 and pl. 7.1–3, respectively.

2. They included gold and iron, bamboo for arrowshafts and wood for bows, pelts and hides, sinew and horn, grease and glue, cinnabar and lac. See John Major, *Heaven and Earth in Early Han Thought: Chapters Three, Four, and Five of the Huainanzi* (Albany: State University of New York Press, 1993), pp. 231–32.

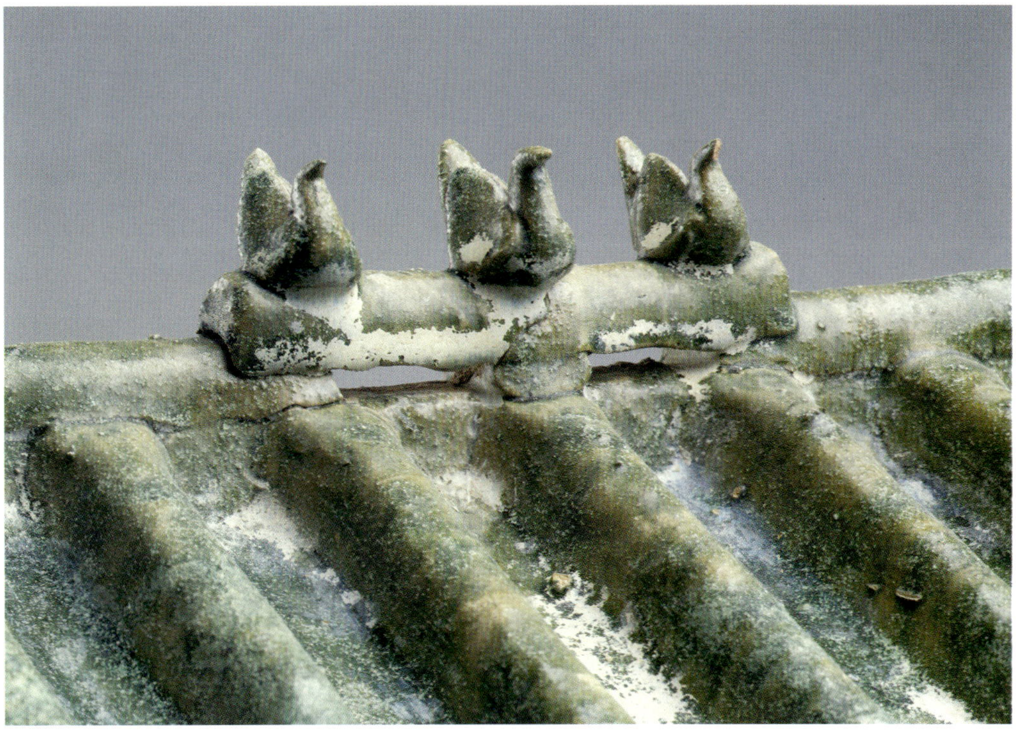

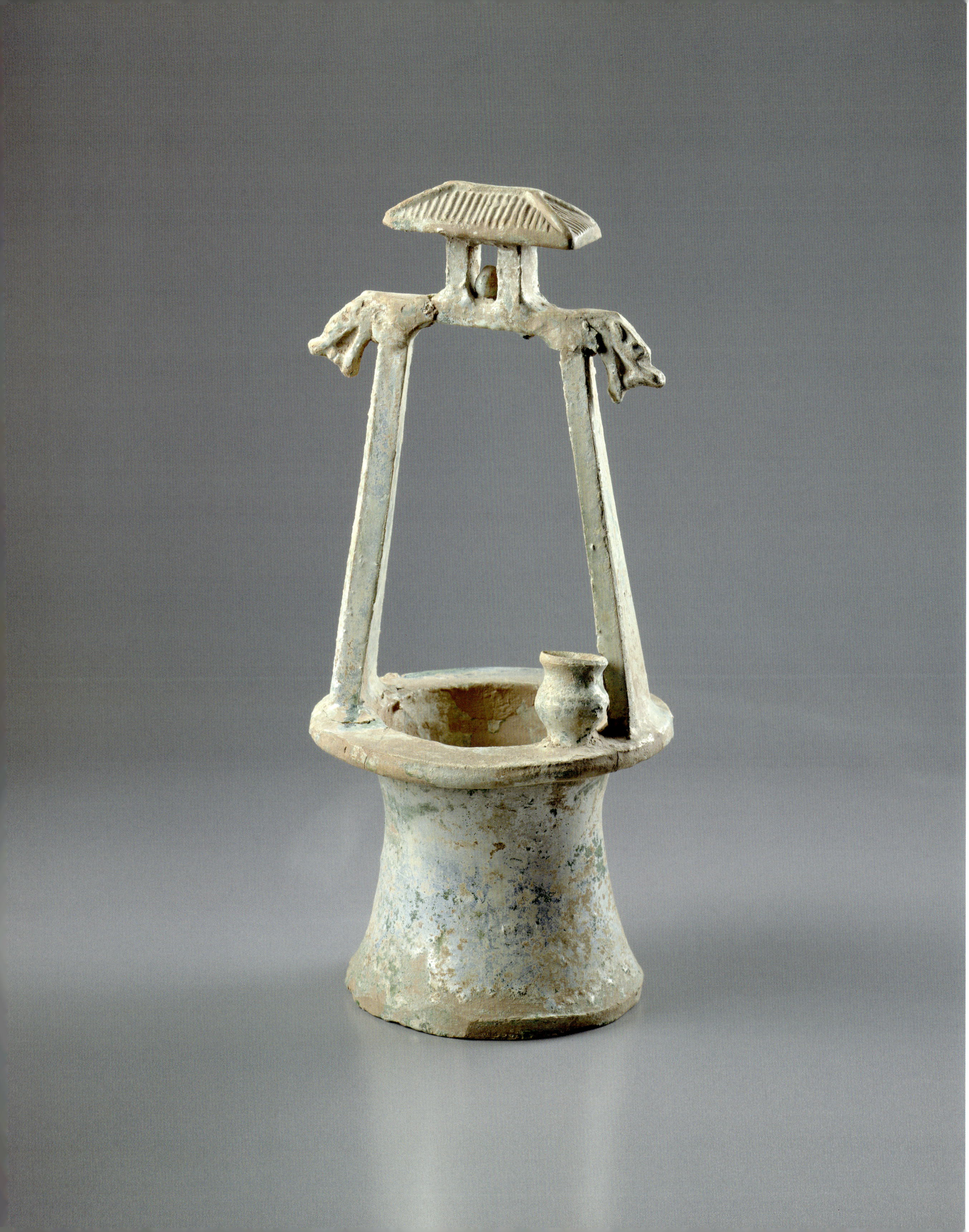

17 Green-glazed wellhead

Han dynasty. Earthenware with green glaze; h. 41.1 cm, rim diam. 18 cm.
Princeton University Art Museum, acc. no. 1997-76. Gift of an alumnus, Class of 1959.

This green-glazed ceramic model of the wellhead of a draw well takes the shape of a narrow-waisted cylinder rising to a broad, flat rim on which is set a small water bucket. Above the wellhead is an A-frame superstructure consisting of two inward-leaning struts that rise to support a crossbeam with projecting dragon-head finials at each end. At the center of the crossbeam two small posts carry a tiled hip roof. Housed under the roof is a pulley that would have been used for drawing water by means of a rope and bucket. The cylinder's interior is unglazed except for accidental drips from the rim, and the bottom is open to the ground. The latter suggests the possibility that in its burial setting the wellhead may have been placed over a hole in the tomb floor that imitated a well shaft. Similar wellhead models of varying heights are found in various collections.[1] Some of these models have closed bottoms, ruling out any shaft extension into the floor below. In certain wellhead models, however, the cylinder may actually represent the sunken well shaft.[2]

Since ancient times wells, as a source of life-giving water, came to be associated with water spirits and deities such as dragons. They were also believed to serve as a cosmic gate leading into the earth below, and were paired with heavenly gates (*tianmen*) and heavenly wells (*tianjing*) opening into the heavens above.[3]

A well was often the center of a village or house, and thus became a symbol of community and family order. The written character for well (*jing*) resembles a tic-tac-toe grid, and many Han-dynasty well models in ceramic and bronze are similarly rectilinear in plan (see cat. no. 18). This orderly configuration also became linked to the ancient, idealized well-field (*jingtian*) system of land-use division espoused by Mencius (fourth century BCE) and Dong Zhongshu (ca. 179–ca. 104 BCE), and unsuccessfully instituted by the usurper Wang Mang (r. 9–23 CE) as part of his reform efforts during the Han interregnum.[4] Wells are often depicted in food preparation scenes in Han pictorial carvings of home settings. In the "Wu family shrines" rubbings are several depictions of water being drawn for cooking from narrow-waisted wellheads with well-sweeps and buckets (fig. 1).

In agriculture, wells for field irrigation were used in northern China and along the Yellow

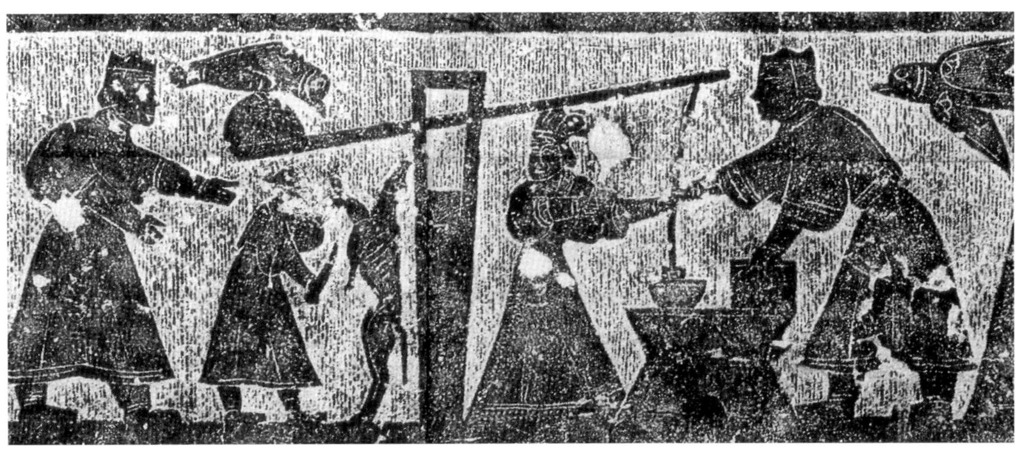

Fig. 1 *Well-sweep in food preparation scene*. Detail of Stone Chamber 1, Stone 1-E.2 (cat. no. 1.12). "Wu family shrines" rubbings. Princeton University Art Museum, acc. no. 2002-307.2.

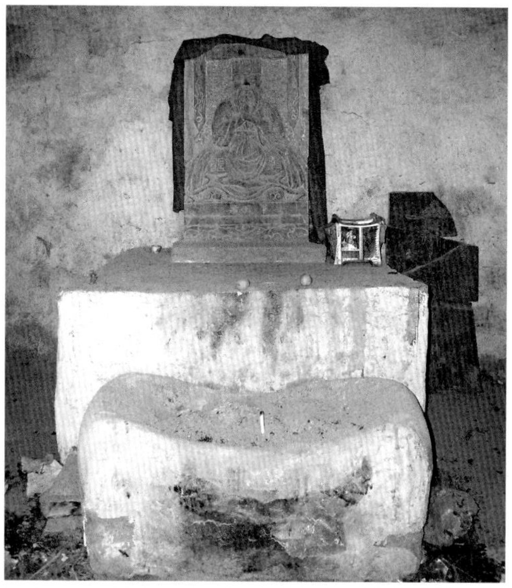

Fig. 2 *Dragon King (Long wang yeshen) altar*. Pictorial carved stone in offering shrine atop Wuzhai Shan, Jiaxiang County, Shandong. Photograph by author, 2004.

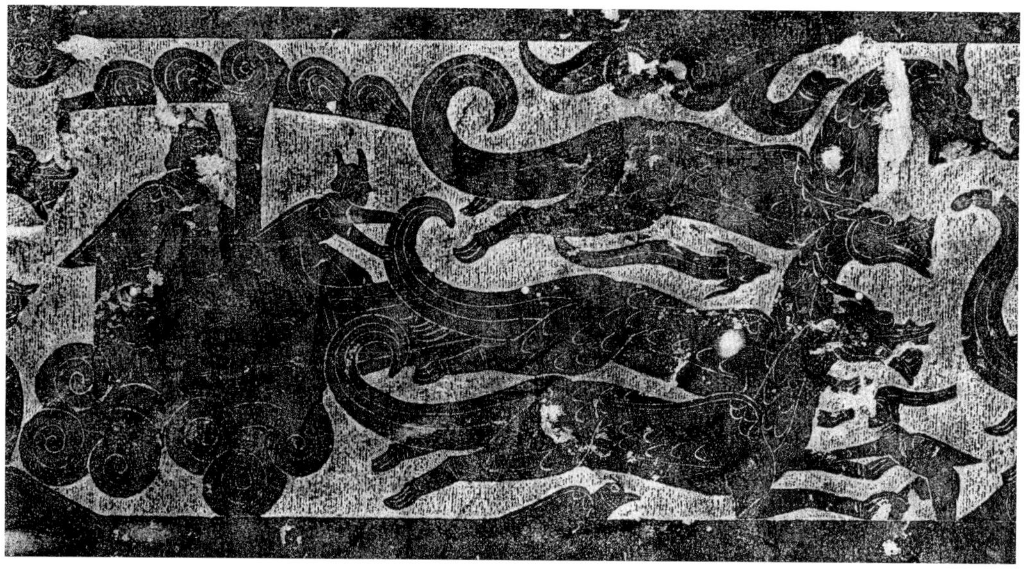

Fig. 3 *Dragons pulling a cloud chariot with winged Immortals*. Detail of Stone Chamber 1, Stone 1-R.2 (cat. no. 1.18). "Wu family shrines" rubbings. Princeton University Art Museum, acc. no. 2002-307.17.

River valley, including Shandong. Burial models and near life-size replicas of wells in tombs have been found throughout these regions.[5] Such models and replicas are believed to have been included in tombs—along with stoves, latrines, granaries, and sacrifice offerings—in order to provide for the tomb occupant in the afterlife. The special placement of wells in some tombs and the discovery of seeds and animal bones inside or near some wells, however, suggest that buried wells may also have played a role in mortuary ceremonies or have had special symbolic meaning.[6]

The dragon-head finials at the ends of the crossbeam fit the well's close association with water. Among the Four Deities (*sishen*) of the cardinal directions, the dragon correlates with the east and the color green. Green symbolized the verdant beginnings of spring and designated the eastern quadrant of the sky, the direction of the nascent sun and the Green Dragon deity (*qinglong*) asterism. As a supernatural creature dwelling in water and able to ascend into the sky to bring rain, the image of dragons evolved from composite zoomorphic forms in the Shang and Zhou periods.[7] By the Han dynasty the dragon motif had acquired auspicious meaning as a herald of spring rain and as a symbol of imperium. In funerary decoration dragon motifs were probably most often included as conjurations of ground- and rainwater to irrigate farm fields. For this reason, offering shrines to the Dragon King were often built in agricultural locales, such as the shrine altar currently found behind the Wu cemetery on top of the hill called Wuzhai Shan (fig. 2). During the Han dynasty designs of dragons in waves or clouds were carved on pictorial stones in funerary structures (fig. 3) and on burial artifacts (cat. no. 24). The dragon-head finials on this wellhead also resemble a dragon-head handle fragment from a ceramic *kui* vessel unearthed in Tomb 1 at the Wu cemetery (fig. 4).

CARY Y. LIU

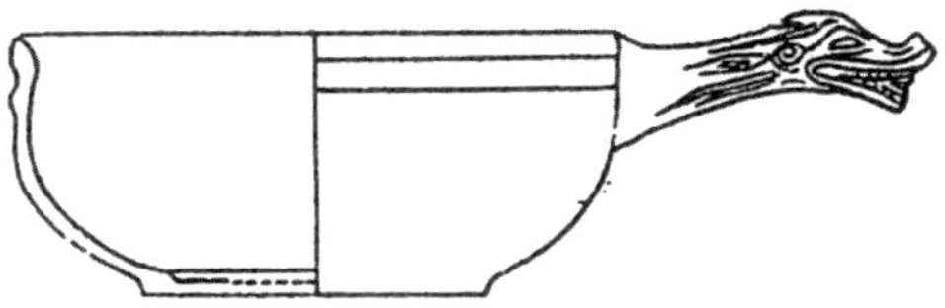

Fig. 4 *Dragon-head handle on* kui *vessel.* Found in Tomb 1, "Wu family shrines." Restoration drawing. From Jiang Yingju and Wu Wenqi, *Handai Wushi muqun shike yanjiu* (Ji'nan: Shandong meishu chubanshe, 1995), p. 123, fig. 16-4.

Notes

1. For similar wellheads, see Berthold Laufer, *Chinese Pottery of the Han Dynasty* (Leiden: E. J. Brill, 1909), pp. 62–64, pl. XIV; Aileen Lau, ed., *Spirit of the Han: Ceramics for the Afterlife* (Singapore: The Southeast Asian Ceramic Society, 1991), cat. nos. 190–91. Replicas of wells with shafts into the tomb floor were built in some Western Han royal tombs. See Huang Xiaofen, *Han mu de kaoguxue yanjiu* (*Archaeological research of Han tombs*) (Changsha: Yuelu shushe, 2003), pp. 218–19.

2. An example is a well model excavated in a Han tomb at Luoyang. See Wang Zhongshu, *Han Civilization*, trans. K. C. Chang et al. (New Haven: Yale University Press, 1982), p. 56, and fig. 73. Such models may have been set into a hole in the floor.

3. This vertical axis in the form of the legendary Mount Kunlun with its nine gates and nine wells linking heaven and earth is outlined in the *Shanhai jing* (*Classic of mountains and waterways*). See *Concordance to the Shanhaijing, Mutianzizhuan, Yandanzi*, ed. D. C. Lau (Hong Kong: Commercial Press, 1994), "Hai nei xijing" sec., p. 57; Huang Xiaofen, *Han mu de kaoguxue yanjiu*, p. 226. On heavenly wells, see Cary Y. Liu, "Heavenly Wells in Ming Dynasty Huizhou Architecture," *Orientations*, vol. 25, no. 1 (1994), pp. 28–36.

4. On the well-field system, see Kung-chuan Hsiao, *A History of Chinese Political Thought*, trans. F. W. Mote (Princeton: Princeton University Press, 1979), p. 30 n. 6, p. 151 n. 22, pp. 172, 502–3, 515.

5. On the development of wells and burial models of wells in the Han dynasty, see Sun Ji, *Handai wuzhi wenhua ziliao tushuo* (*Illustrated guide to Han-dynasty material culture*) (Beijing: Wenwu chubanshe, 1991), pp. 11–12. Near life-size replicas of wells were built in some Western Han royal tombs. Miniature wood, bronze, and stone models of wells also came into use during Western Han and became a standard burial object. See Huang Xiaofen, *Han mu de kaoguxue yanjiu*, pp. 217–27.

6. Huang Xiaofen, *Han mu de kaoguxue yanjiu*, pp. 225–26.

7. On the early development of the dragon motif, see Jessica Rawson, *Chinese Ornament: The Lotus and the Dragon* (New York: Holmes and Meier, 1984), pp. 93–95.

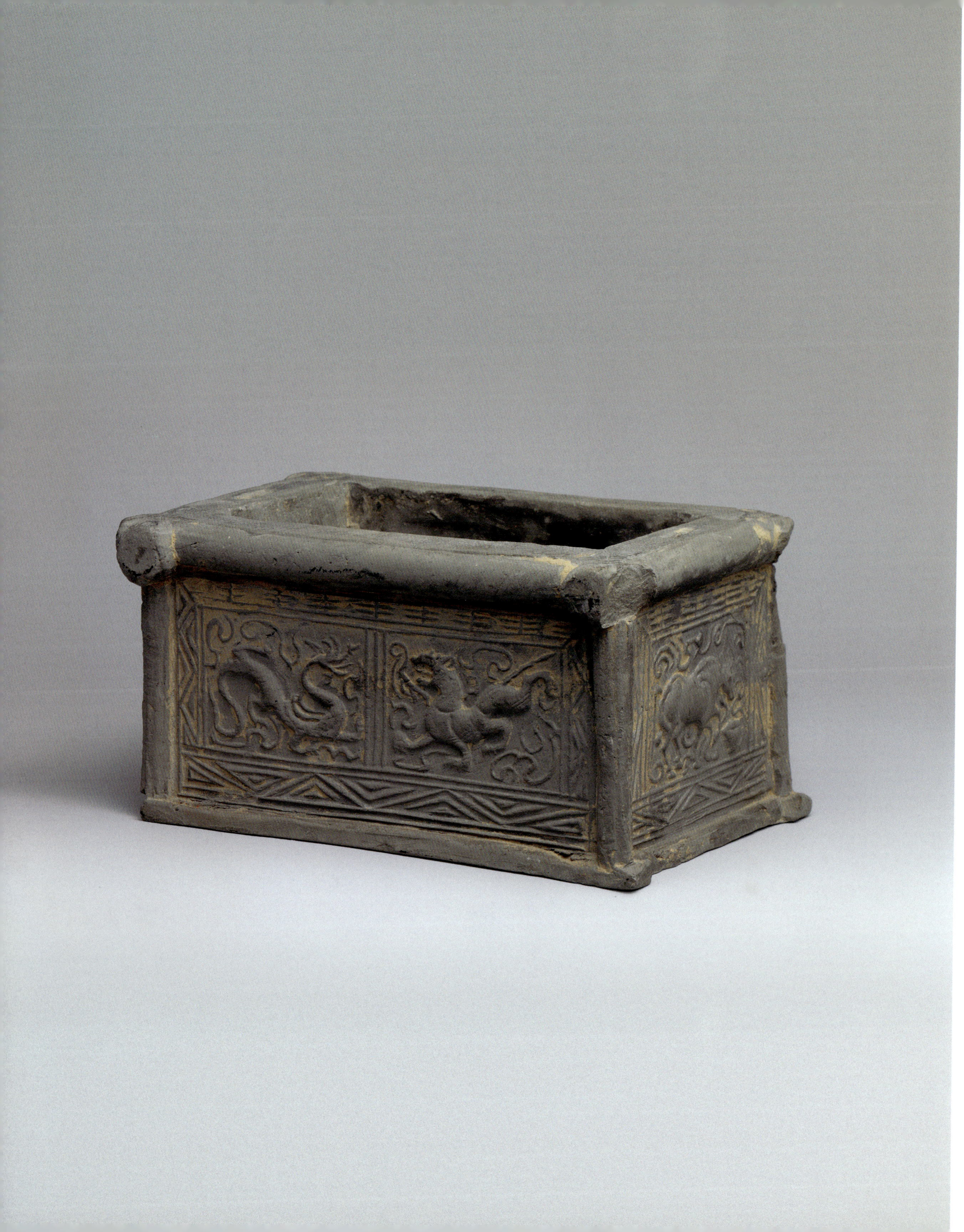

18

18 Wellhead with dragon, bird, and guardian designs

Han dynasty. Unglazed earthenware; h. 12.1 cm, w. 22.9 cm, d. 14.9 cm.
The Metropolitan Museum of Art, acc. no. 1911.7.1. Gift of Sadajiro Yamanaka.

Han-dynasty tombs were often furnished with ceramic grave goods intended to provide an ideal environment for the deceased. Model (in the sense of miniature) lamps, stoves, incense burners, granaries, courtyard dwellings, containers, servants, livestock, and wellheads are some of the items typically found in Han-period tombs. This use of model grave goods began in the Zhou dynasty, gradually replacing the practice of burying real objects and persons. It was hoped that the spirit of the deceased, which could be maleficent if neglected, would incline to remain contentedly in its tomb if accorded proper ritual observance and burial objects to sustain its existence in the afterlife.

Model wellheads, such as the present example, were intended to provide a water supply for the deceased after death, as their prototypes did in life. The sides were made in molds and then joined together. A wooden frame for holding a miniature bucket and winch probably originally fit into the two holes seen on the lip of the well.[1] Wells resembling this particular example have been excavated in the Henan region.[2]

The four sides of the wellhead are embellished with both farm animals and supernatural creatures molded in low relief. Represented on one short side of the wellhead is a goat, and on the other an ox. On one long side of the wellhead two of the four Directional Animals confront each other, the Dragon of the East and the Tiger of the West, standard imagery in mortuary art. On the other side are two battle-ready figures (see detail). On the left a human figure holding a battle standard and jar runs towards the anthropomorphic creature on the right, who holds a spear and a jar. Their fluid figural style most closely resembles that of imagery found on tomb bricks and relief carvings in Henan Province, particularly in the Nanyang area.[3]

In its splayed frontal posture and the flame-like emanations from its head and body, the anthropomorphic figure on the right resembles a creature appearing on several reliefs from Shandong-area tombs and shrines, including the late second-century tomb at Yi'nan and a slab associated with the Left Chamber (Stone Chamber 2) (fig. 1) excavated from the "Wu family" cemetery. Those figures can be identified as Chi You, the God of War and inventor of weapons, by the five weapons they hold,

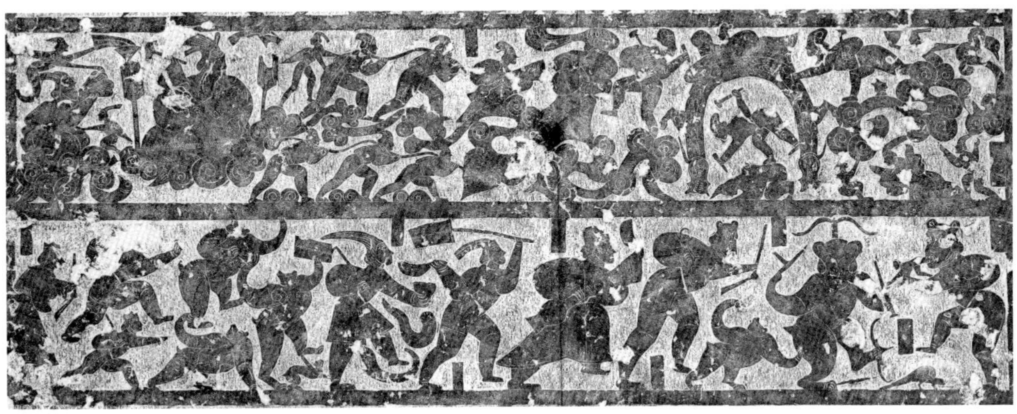

Fig. 1 *Battle Between Huangdi and Chi You*. Detail of Stone Chamber 2, Stone 2-R.1 (cat. no. 1.32). "Wu family shrines" rubbings. Princeton University Art Museum, acc. no. 2002-307.31.

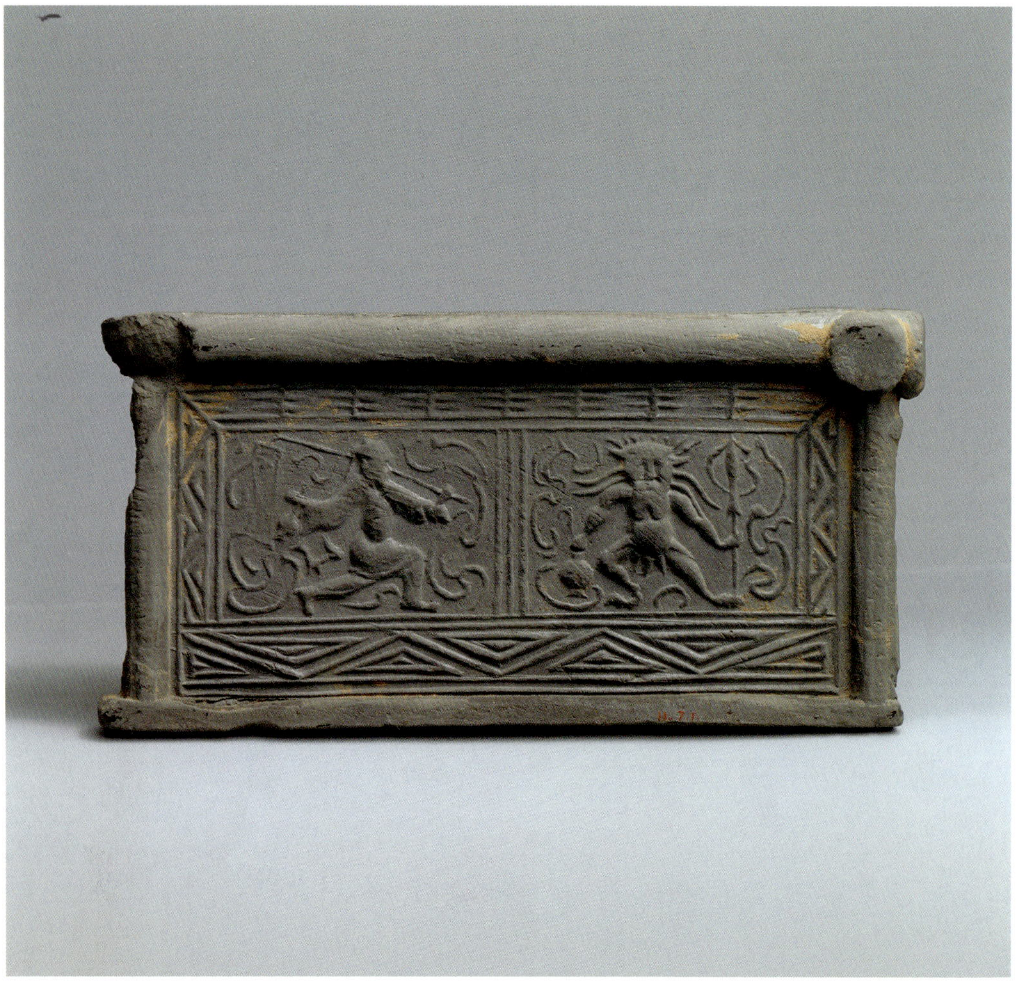

a spear, sword, crossbow, shield, and dagger. The creature represented on the present wellhead holds only one weapon, a spear. In the other hand he holds a water jar. These attributes, along with his presence on a wellhead, suggest that in this context Chi You is portrayed in his role as a Rain God. [4]

Chi You is perhaps best known for his epic battle with Huangdi to determine which of them would become the Son of Heaven.[5] In that narrative he plays the role of a would-be spoiler of order and statecraft, and the opponent of Huangdi, the civilizing sage. Alternative myths, however, better explain his presence on the wellhead in this exhibition. In the *Shanhai jing* version of the conflict between Chi You and Huangdi, their battle is a power struggle not just between two gods but also between the forces of nature. During their battle Huangdi dispatched Yinglong the Responding Dragon and Ba the Goddess of Drought to fight on his behalf. Chi You marshaled his own forces, the God of Wind and the Master of Rain. This legend became the basis of popular agricultural and rainmaking rituals such as the Zha festival, which marked the end of the agricultural year. Chi You was a tutelary deity during this time of ritual purification and renewal, invoked as both a purger of evil influences, a rainmaker, and by extension a god of agricultural and human fertility.[6]

This battle is represented in detail on the above-mentioned slab from the "Wu family" cemetery (fig. 1). Chi You is shown engaged in battle on the far right of the third register from the top. In the second register from the top he is assisted by the God of Thunder, seen being pulled in his cloud chariot, and by the God of Wind with a bag slung on his shoulder. Between these two deities the Master of Rain holds a water jar.[7] On the wellhead, Chi You's dual role as exorcist and rain/agricultural god is indicated by his attributes, the spear and the water jar. The accompanying figure, also holding a jar, probably represents his deputy, the Master of Rain.[8] The imagery of farm animals on the short sides of the wellhead reinforces the interpretation that Chi You is seen here in his role as an agricultural deity.

LYDIA THOMPSON

Notes

1. For an example of an intact ceramic well, see Jessica Rawson, *Mysteries of Ancient China: New Discoveries from the Early Dynasties* (London: British Museum, 1996) pl. 99.

2. See a rectangular well in Candace Lewis, *Into the Afterlife: Han and Six Dynasties Chinese Tomb Sculpture from the Schloss Collection* (Poughkeepsie: Vassar College Art Gallery, 1990), pl. 7. Lewis compares it with wells from the Shaogou cemetery in Luoyang, Henan. The ceramic wellhead cited above is also from the Henan region.

3. For examples of Nanyang-area relief carvings, see Wang Jianzhong, ed., *Nanyang Lianghan huaxiang shi* (*Pictorial stones of the two Hans from Nanyang*) (Beijing: Wenwu chubanshe, 1990).

4. For a discussion of Chi You in Han visual culture, see Lydia Thompson, "Demon Devourers and Hybrid Creatures: Traces of Chu Visual Culture in the Eastern Han Period," *Yishu shi yanjiu* 2001.3, pp. 261–93.

5. For a discussion of Huangdi–Chi You narratives in pre-Han and Han texts, see Michael Puett, "Sages, Ministers, and Rebels: Narratives from Early China Concerning the Initial Creation of the State," *Harvard Journal of Asiatic Studies,* vol. 58, no. 2 (1998), pp. 425–79.

6. Mark Edward Lewis, *Sanctioned Violence in Early China* (Albany: State University of New York Press, 1990), p. 184. For a discussion of Chi You as an agricultural deity as seen in Han relief carvings, see Thompson, "Demon Devourers and Hybrid Creatures," pp. 277–82.

7. The *Bibing tu* found at Mawangdui includes one of the earliest examples of the Rain Master (Yu Shi) and Thunder God (Lei Gong) represented together. They are located on either side of Taiyi and identified by inscription. They are also seen in the company of warrior disciples. See Li Ling's discussion, "An Archaeological Study of Taiyi Worship," *Early Medieval China*, vol. 2, (1995–1996), pp. 14–16.

8. A relief carving from Nanyang depicts four "Rain Masters" in the heavens, each holding an upended jar from which water flows. See Wang Jianzhong, ed., *Nanyang Lianghan huaxiang shi*, fig. 155.

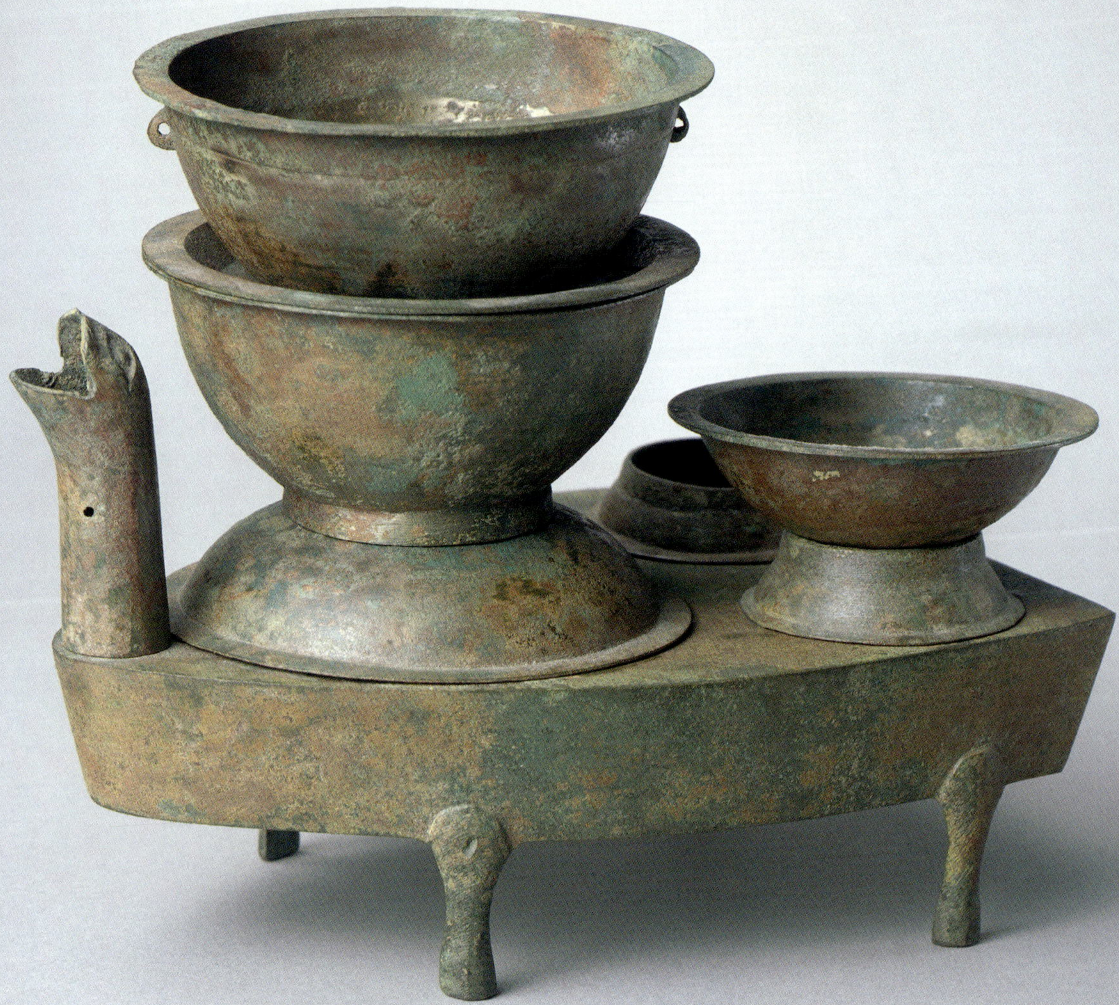

19 Stove model

Western Han dynasty. Bronze; h. 17.9 cm, l. 19 cm.
Private collection.

Model stoves made of bronze, and especially of earthenware, appear in tombs from the Western Han into the Six Dynasties. Their appearance in early Han tombs, along with other utilitarian objects such as braziers, lamps, incense burners, and mirrors, signals not merely the introduction of a new category of grave goods, but, more importantly, a change in conception of the afterlife. Beginning in the third century BCE, ritual vessels—containers for food and wine offerings to the ancestors of the deceased, which were of paramount importance in tombs of late Shang and early Zhou—appear to have decreased in importance. At this time new categories of objects were being made that were not necessarily used for ritual practice—that is, in offering food and wine for ancestor worship—but were part of secular banqueting.[1]

This animal-shaped stove illustrates the imagination and creativity of Han bronze makers. Raised on four slender horse-hoofed feet, the body of the animal functions as the firebox, into which fuel would have been placed through a rectangular opening at the back. The elongated neck of the tortoise-like creature would have vented the smoke from the firebox out through its open mouth. In the top surface of the stove body are three circular openings, one large, upon which two bronze flat-rimmed basins sit, and two smaller ones. A very similar example was excavated in 1983 from a late Western Han tomb in Shuo County, Shanxi.[2]

HIROMI KINOSHITA

Notes

1. See Jessica Rawson, "Ritual Vessel Changes in the Warring States, Qin and Han Periods," in *Di san jie guoji hanxue huiyi lunwen ji, lishi zu, zhongshiji yiqian de diyu wenhua zongjiao yu yishu* (*Papers from the third international conference on sinology, history section: Regional culture, religion, and arts before the seventh century*), ed. Hsing I-tien (Taipei: Institute of History and Philology, Academia Sinica, 2002), pp. 1–57.

2. See "Shanxi Shuo Xian Qin Han mu fajue jianbao" ("Brief excavation report on Qin and Han tombs at Shuo County, Shanxi"), *Wenwu* 1987.6: pl. 5:2. The piece is illustrated in color in *Zhongguo qingtongqi quanji* (*Complete works on Chinese bronzes*), vol. 12: *Qin, Han* (Beijing: Wenwu chubanshe, 1998), p. 85, no. 23.

Bi Discs of Jade and Glass

Jade *bi*

Excavations of China's Neolithic and Bronze Age tombs have unearthed an impressive number and variety of jade discs that are centrally perforated with large circular holes. These discs are termed *bi*, following descriptions in ritual texts and other accounts traditionally dated between the fourth century BCE and the second century CE. Archaeological finds during the past thirty years, however, confirm that the earliest known discs predate these texts by more than two millennia. The largest of these early jade discs, and the greatest number, have come from sites of the Neolithic Liangzhu culture (ca. 3200–2000 BCE), centered in the Yangzi Delta area of Lake Tai in southeastern coastal China (northern Zhejiang, southern Jiangsu, Shanghai). Many previously undisturbed Liangzhu tombs have been found to contain more than twenty discs, layered below and above remains of the deceased; in the most richly furnished, discs were interred together with blades, beads, plaques, bracelets, and tubular prisms (*cong*), all made of jade. Unlike either jade simulacra of weapons and tools, intended for use in rituals, or personal ornaments of jade, probably worn in life prior to burial with their owner, these discs and prisms were not, so far as we can tell, intended for use in this life. In the absence of contemporary textual sources, their precise significance in burials is not known.[1]

By contrast, aristocratic, jade-rich tombs of early dynastic China (Shang and early Western Zhou) have yielded relatively few discs; some of these resemble Neolithic finds and were likely of Neolithic make, unearthed and reburied as heirlooms. Mid- and late Western Zhou tombs reveal a sporadic revival of jade discs that appear to be of contemporaneous manufacture, but not until the politically fragmented Eastern Zhou do widespread burials of regional elites attest a resurgence of disc making and a florescence of new styles. In arrangements reminiscent of Liangzhu burials, major Warring States tombs in northeastern and south-central China have revealed large numbers of discs buried with the deceased, whose faces were also sometimes covered with veils of small jade plaques.[2]

Han-period aristocrats enlarged upon these jade-rich burials—most dramatically, by enclosing the corpses of imperial family members and high-ranking nobles and officials in full-body "suits" of small jade wafers that were pierced at all four corners and sewn together with fine metallic thread. Large jade discs were then placed under, over, and alongside the jade-enclosed body, over which jade pectorals or long pendant sets were laid. Some discs preserve impressions of silk cords or of silk or satin fabric, indicating that they had been attached to shrouds. Additional discs, especially those bearing traces of lacquer, appear to have been inlaid or placed on the lids of wood coffins. Still others have been found stacked in the corners of burial chambers. But the mortal or man-made supports of all these jades have disintegrated. Reconstructing the original arrangement of these discs, like that of all jades and other durable burial gifts excavated *in situ*, relies on careful analyses of their relative locations, their discoloration, and surface impressions of lost materials.[3]

Among *bi* discs recovered from scientifically excavated tombs, those finely carved with geometric and zoomorphic designs enable us progressively to revise and refine our understanding

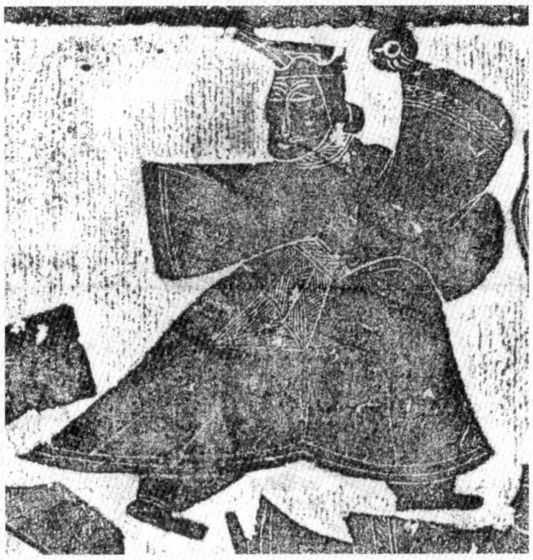

of their stylistic chronology. In broad sequence, late Eastern Zhou discs exhibit a variety of small-scale surface patterns—predominantly incised and low-relief scrolls and curls, some abstracted from animal-head silhouettes with rolled snouts that distinguished early Spring and Autumn period decor. Between the sixth and third centuries BCE, these patterns became increasingly uniform and tightly ordered, taking the form of relief spirals against a smoothly abraded ground. The refinement of bevel-edged grinding tools created rounded surfaces and sharp contours of remarkable precision. During the late Warring States and Western Han, some lapidaries contained these spirals within a diamond-shaped or hexagonal grid (cat. no. 21) and faceted their contours. By contrast, other Western Han craftsmen refined smooth rows of semispherical nipples.[4]

Warring States and Han craftsmen also revived zoomorphic decor, placing four *en face* animal masks in a band that symmetrically encircles the disc's circumference, and in rare examples, in a second band around the inner perforation. These masks, with slanted eyes and snub noses, feature ribbon-like horns that splay bilaterally, intertwining with other undulating ribbons that fill the spaces between the masks and terminate in limbs, wings, tails, or profile heads of felines, dragons, or birds (cat. no. 20).[5] Scholars debate the stylistic origin of this design, considered to resemble and perhaps derive from the venerable ogre mask (*taotie*) of Shang and Zhou design (see p. 322) that bronze casters in the northern state of Jin (sixth/fifth century BCE) had creatively revived and embellished into dense, fluently interlaced zoomorphs. But focusing on its affinity to intricate motifs found on bronze and gold artifacts of China's northern borderlands, Jessica Rawson has traced this animal-mask motif to West Asian prototypes of the sixth/fourth centuries BCE, including ivories from Achaemenid Iran and stone sculpture and wood plaques found in the frozen tumuli of Pazyryk in the Altai Mountains of Southern Siberia.[6]

Yet even scientifically excavated jades pose immediate questions of date and workshop origin. Discs with strikingly similar decor have been unearthed from both Eastern Zhou and Western Han sites in northeastern, south-central, and southern coastal China, leading scholars to speculate whether discs found in later sites represent inherited pieces or conservatively styled new creations. Moreover, discs and other jades from a single tomb often display diverse surface patterns and differing levels of technical and artistic finesse. Typically, the finest jades surround the principal occupant of the tomb. More crudely worked or reworked pieces were consigned to the burials of the accompanying attendants and/or concubines. Since jade is durable, portable, valuable, and recyclable, a single burial may combine up-to-date, conservative, and heirloom pieces.

Glass *bi*

Eastern Zhou and Han artisans also fashioned discs in materials less precious and more easily crafted than nephrite. These include talc, steatite and other common stones, wood, and, most notably, glass of milky white, pale green, or deeper green hue. For glass *bi*, a single mold created both form and surface decoration. Although the origins of China's glass industry

Fig. 1 *King of Qin (future First Emperor) holding a* bi *disc.* Detail of Stone Chamber 2, Stone 2-S.4 (cat. no. 1.23). "Wu family shrines" rubbings. Princeton University Art Museum, acc. no. 2002-307.22.

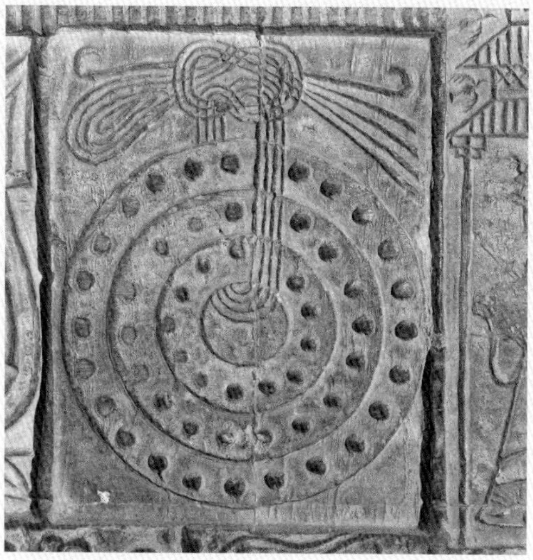

remain obscure, Chinese craftsmen had clearly mastered this technology by the Warring States and Han, when they created forms distinctly native and unmistakably mimicking jade discs, as well as shroud wafers and sword fittings. To date, the vast majority of glass discs have been unearthed from Chu-kingdom tombs in the southern province of Hunan. Hunan is rich in lead, barium, and silica—the first two being unique to ancient Chinese glass.[7]

Many of the finest glass discs are cast with patterns of curls or raised nipples that clearly simulate jade prototypes; others are simply patterned with a diagonal grid. Unlike jade discs, those of glass are often decorated only on one surface and crudely polished. Also unlike jade, after prolonged burial they may devitrify to form a chalky white surface "crust" (cat. no. 22). In these, the original translucency of glass is visible only in cross-section. But even pristine glass discs are opaque rather than transparent, most likely because the glass craftsmen were attempting to simulate jade.

Bi as numen, jade as metaphor

Prior to the discovery and publication of a substantial number of jade-rich burials, Chinese and Western scholars had few sources for dating jade and glass discs beyond literary descriptions ascribed to Warring States and Han authors. These, mostly ritual texts, identify jade *bi* as ceremonial paraphernalia for worshiping Heaven and paying homage to the king and also as sacrificial offerings to end drought.[8] But regardless of their age or their significance when written, these texts are not visually descriptive, nor do they distinguish *bi* discs initially made for secular or ritual use by the living from those made expressly for burial.

In more idealized literature, political theorists and philosophers evoked the luster and translucency of jade as metaphor for human virtue, and the laborious abrasion and polishing required to reveal the stone's "inner beauty" as allegory both of the inwardness of human virtue and of the moral labor of developing it. Perhaps most poignant is the tale of Bian He (third century BCE), a minister of the kingdom of Chu. Bian He presented a piece of raw jade to two successive kings, who rejected it as common stone. Twice punished by amputations for his presumed deception, Bian He wept "till his tears turned to blood." Hearing of his story, the next king, Wen, sent his jade expert to work on the stone and found the "gem within." King Wen had the jade made into a *bi* disc and designated it "Bian He's disc."[9]

Clearly indicative of their symbolic if not specifically ritual significance, jade discs are frequently depicted in the furnishings and interior decoration of Han-dynasty tombs and mortuary shrines (fig. 1). Pictorial images of discs are painted on silk funerary banners and lacquered wood coffins, and painted, carved, and impressed on tomb chamber walls. Some discs appear as isolated motifs (fig. 2); others are integrated within complex figural compositions that portray the deceased or mythical subjects. Many such images of *bi* bear simple geometric surface patterns—circles, dots, and concentric rings—and are shown with elaborately tied ribbons. Chinese and Western scholars describe virtually all of these images as representing discs of jade.[10]

Fig. 2 Bi *disc. Detail of tomb lintel.* Western Han dynasty, ca. first century BCE. Tomb lintel: horizontal rectangular hollow tile; earthenware with impressed decoration; lintel h. 121.9 cm, l. 20.3 cm, w. 20.3 cm. Art Institute of Chicago, acc. no. 1935.359. Gift of Miss Kate S. Buckingham as an addition to the Lucy Maud Buckingham Collection.

A notable exception is the disc with surface pattern of a dotted grid, depicted on a Wu Liang Shrine (Stone Chamber 3) ceiling slab (cat. no. 1.41). It is one of more than twenty clearly preserved images of auspicious omens (*xiangrui*) at the shrine. This disc is clearly identified in a cartouche: "Bi liuli wang zhe bu yin guo ze zhi" ("The *bi* disc of glass. It arrives when a ruler does not dissemble his faults.") In this token of imperial integrity, glass functions as a valid surrogate for jade—the most esteemed artistic medium in ancient China.[11]

ELINOR PEARLSTEIN

Notes

1. Most frequently quoted is the *Zhouli* (*Rites of Zhou*), traditionally dated to 4th/3d century BCE but now attributed to the Han. According to the *Zhouli*, members of the Zhou imperial court used *bi* discs in ceremonies of homage to Heaven. Other texts that mention *bi* discs include the *Liji* (*Rites records*), *Yili* (*Ceremonials*), and the *Erya*, a Han-dynasty thesaurus. The *Erya* distinguishes between *bi* and other discs (*huan* and *yuan*) by specific ratios of body-to-perforation widths—a classification invalidated by archaeological finds. See Hsia Nai, *Jade and Silk of Han China*, trans. and ed. Chu-tsing Li (Lawrence: University of Kansas, Spencer Museum of Art, 1983), pp. 23–26; and Hsia Nai, "The Classification, Nomenclature, and Usage of Shang Dynasty Jades," *Studies of Shang Archaeology* (New Haven and London: Yale University Press, 1986), pp. 210–16. For current dating of these texts, see entries in Michael Loewe, ed., *Early Chinese Texts: A Bibliographic Guide* (Berkeley: Society for the Study of Early China and The Institute of East Asian Studies, University of California, Berkeley, 1993).

Tombs of the Liangzhu culture were initially discovered near Hangzhou in 1936–1938, but archaeologists did not confirm their Neolithic date until the 1970s and early 1980s, following the excavation of lavishly furnished tombs surrounding Lake Tai. Thermoluminescence and radiocarbon tests of clay and organic artifacts buried with the jades established the age of these tombs. In some Liangzhu burials a few discs had been deliberately broken and their pieces widely distributed; other jades may have been burned, possibly during funerary rituals involving cremation. The significance of these practices is unknown. See Sun Zhixin, "Jades of the Liangzhu Culture" (PhD diss., Princeton University, 1996), and *Dongfang wenming zhi guang: Liangzhu wenhua yuqi; The dawn of civilization: Jades of the Liangzhu culture* (Chinese and English) (Hong Kong: Chinese University of Hong Kong, ca. 1998) and references cited therein. As noted by Wang Mingda (ibid., p. 19), discs range in diameter from under 10 to over 30 cm and in thickness from 0.5 to more than 3 cm. Most of these discs are identified as nephrite, although relatively few have been scientifically analyzed.

2. Plain jade discs have been found in Shang and Western Zhou tombs in the Yellow River valley—primarily at sites in Henan Province (notably Anyang, Sanmenxia Shancunling, Luoyang Zhongzhoulu, and Huixian Liulige)—but in small numbers. The tomb of Lady Fu Hao at Anyang, the only Shang royal tomb excavated intact, contained about 15 *bi* discs among 755 jades. Owing to inconsistent use of *bi* and other terms for discs (see n. 1), inventories of these pieces vary among writers. For discussions of these sites, see Jessica Rawson, *Chinese Jade from the Neolithic to the Qing* (London: British Museum, 1995), pp. 247–51.

Jade discs with geometric and zoomorphic patterns have been excavated from several Warring States cemeteries in Shandong. Tombs 52 and 58 of Lu Kingdom at Qufu contained 12 and 16 discs, respectively—most of these within the coffin remains; see Shandong Sheng wenwu kaogu yanjiusuo et al., *Qufu Luguo gu cheng* (*The Ancient City of Lu at Qufu*) (Ji'nan: Qi-Lu shushe, 1982), p. 129, fig. 80; p. 131, fig. 82; pp. 161–69. The tomb of Marquis Yi of Zeng at Sui Xian, Hubei (ca. 433 BCE), the most sumptuously furnished of China's Bronze Age, included about 65 jade and 45 stone discs among its burial gifts of bronze, gold, lacquer, and jade. Jade discs were placed in the marquis's inner coffin. In a Warring States tomb at Yanggong, Changfeng, Anhui, about 50 jade discs, variously decorated with spiral and animal-mask motifs discussed below, surrounded the body. See Anhui Sheng wenwu gongzuo dui, "Anhui Changfeng Yanggong fajue jiu zuo Zhanguo mu" ("Nine Warring States tombs excavated at Yanggong, in Changfeng, Anhui"), *Kaoguxue jikan* 1982.2, pp. 55–56, fig. 8:1, 2, pl. 7:6.

3. Han burials yielding elaborately decorated jade discs include the intact royal tombs of Prince Liu Sheng (d. 113 BCE) and his consort Dou Wan of the far northern kingdom of Zhongshan at Mancheng, Hebei, and the tomb of King Zhao Mo (d. 122 BCE) of the far southern kingdom of Nanyue in Guangzhou, Guangdong. See *Mancheng Han mu fajue baogao* (*Excavation report of the Western Han Tombs at Mancheng*) (Beijing: Wenwu chubanshe, 1980), and *Nanyue wang mu yuqi: Jades from the tomb of the king of Nanyue* (Guangzhou/Hong Kong: Guangzhou Xihan Nanyue wang mu bowuguan, Xianggang Zhongwen daxue wenwuguan, 1991). For specific plates, see citations in cat. nos. 20, 21.

4. Before an appreciable number of jades were scientifically excavated, major Western scholars attempted to draft chronological sequences of these patterns. Their precise descriptions remain valuable for visual analysis. See Max Loehr, "The Emergence and Decline of the Eastern Chou Decor of Plastic Curls," in Loehr, *Ancient Chinese Jades from the Grenville L. Winthrop Collection in the Fogg Art Museum, Harvard University* (Cambridge, Mass.: Harvard University Press, 1975), pp. 21–28, and Jessica Rawson, "The Surface Decoration on Jades of the Chou and Han Dynasties," *Oriental Art*, vol. 21, no.1 (Spring 1975), pp. 36–55.

5. This *en face* mask is variously termed *shoumian* ("bestial face"), *shuangtilong* ("double-bodied dragon"), *shuangweilong* ("double-tailed dragon") and *shuangshen shoumian* ("double-bodied bestial face") in Chinese; sometimes called *bucranium* in English after the classical Western motif of a horned ox skull.

Two horned masks that bisect the entire surface of a small jade disc excavated from a mid-Warring States tomb of the Chu kingdom in southern Hubei provide a magnified variation of this new motif. See Cui Renyi, "Hubei Sheng Jingmenshi Sizhongyu Chu mu" ("Chu Tomb 1 at Sizhong in Jingmen City, Hubei Province"), *Wenwu* 1999:4, pp. 29–31, fig. 7:4. This tomb was previously damaged and was sparsely furnished when discovered.

6. Jessica Rawson, "Jade and Gold: Some Sources of Ancient Chinese Jade Design," *Orientations*, June 1995, pp. 26–37; Rawson, "Transformed into Jade: Changes in Material in the Warring States, Qin and Han Periods," in *East Asian Jade: Symbol of Excellence*, ed. Tang Chung (Hong Kong: Chinese University of Hong Kong, 1998), pp. 125–36, esp. pp. 130–31. See also Rawson, "The Eternal Palaces of the Western Han: A New View of the Universe," *Artibus Asiae*, vol. 59, no. 1/2 (1999), esp. pp. 51–52.

The last and perhaps most dramatic achievement of accomplished Han lapidaries was to embellish fine discs with openwork borders of curvilinear creatures and scrollwork, transforming these purely circular silhouettes into magnificent tours de force of sculpture. Most stunning is the disc with openwork dragons excavated from the tomb of Liu Sheng at Mancheng. For this and other excavated examples, see *Zhongguo yuqi quanji* (*Complete survey of Chinese jade*), vol. 4: *Qin, Han, Nanbei Chao* (*Qin, Han, and Northern and Southern Dynasties*) (Hong Kong: Jin nian guo ji you xian gongsi, 1994), pls. 88, 125, 242, 256. A few Warring States tombs have yielded small, thick discs with openwork carvings bordering the circumference. See ibid., vol. 3: *Chunqiu Zhanguo* (Spring and Autumn and Warring States periods), pls. 175, 211.

7. The origin of glass making in China is generally dated to the transition between the Spring and Autumn and the Warring States period (5th century BCE) by discoveries of polychrome beads with stratified "eyes" in tombs of this period. These beads are chemically distinct from those of soda-lime glass imported from Western Asia. China's earliest monochrome glass is dated one century later. Examples discovered at earlier sites in China and initially identified by some scholars as native glass are now described as imports from the Mediterranean world and Western Asia, or scientifically determined to be faience. For extensive discussions and chemical analyses of early Chinese specimens, see Robert H. Brill and John H. Martin, eds., *Scientific Research in Early Chinese Glass: Proceedings of the Archaeometry of Glass Sessions of the 1984 International Symposium on Glass (Beijing, September 7, 1984) with Supplementary Papers* (Corning, N.Y.: Corning Museum of Glass, 1991). For more recent discoveries and their relevance to jade, see Cecilia Braghin, "Polychrome and Monochrome Glass of the Warring States and Han Periods," in *Chinese Glass: Archaeological Studies on the Uses and Social Context of Glass Artifacts from the Warring States to the Northern Song Period (fifth century B.C. to twelfth century A.D.)*, ed. Cecilia Braghin (Florence: Leo S. Olschki Editore, 2003), pp. 3–43, esp. pp. 19–34, devoted to *bi* discs. Braghin (p. 26) cites statistics on glass discs excavated to date and proposes that the few examples found outside Hunan may have been brought from that area when the Chu were conquered by the Qin in the 3d century BCE.

8. See references in n. 1.

9. Bian He's tale is recorded in the *Han Feizi*, a collection of essays attributed to the Legalist philosopher Han Fei (ca. 280–ca. 233 BCE). For English translation and commentary, see Stephen Owen, ed. and trans., *An Anthology of Chinese Literature: Beginnings to 1911* (New York and London: W. W. Norton & Co., 1996), pp. 83–84.

10. As illustrated in fig. 2, discs with dotted surface decor, often tied with ribbons, appear as individual, repetitive motifs stamped into hollow clay bricks that were mass-produced to construct small underground tomb chambers in Henan Province. These discs have been interpreted as auspicious symbols, denoting high rank, honor, and/or prosperity. See Sun Ji, "Ji zhong Handai di du an wenshi" ("Decorative patterns of the Han dynasty"), *Wenwu* 1982.3, p. 68; Zhang Zhihua and Wang Fuan, "Xihua Dongfuke Cun faxian Handai huaxiang zhuan gaishu" ("Han pictorial bricks discovered at Dongfuke, Xihua"), *Kaogu yu wenwu* 1987.2, p. 22.

Other discs are intertwined or juxtaposed with fantastic animals—notably dragons and phoenixes. Most striking are those depicted on the silk funerary banner and on the foot of the lacquered wood inner coffin of Lady Dai (d. ca. 168 BCE) in Tomb 1 at Mawangdui, Changsha, Hunan; see Hunan Sheng bowuguan and Zhongguo shehui kexueyuan kaogu yanjiusuo, eds., *Changsha Mawangdui yihao Han mu* (*The Han tombs at Mawangdui, Changsha*) (Beijing: Wenwu chubanshe, 1973), vol. 1, figs. 24, 38; vol. 2, cpls. 36, 77. Equally impressive are those on triangular components of an openwork doorway partition of Tomb 61, Luoyang, Henan (late 1st century BCE). Here, bears and wolf-like creatures grasp discs suspended by ribbons. Four additional discs are aligned across the central section on the opposite side of this partition. See description by Jonathan Chaves, "A Han Painted Tomb at Luoyang," *Artibus Asiae*, vol. 30 (1968), pp. 11–12, 19, figs. 5, 8, and details in Huang Minglan and Guo Yinqiang, eds., *Luoyang Han mu bihua* (*Murals from Han tombs in Luoyang*) (Beijing: Wenwu chubanshe, 1996), pp. 89, 95.

This imagery clearly predated the Han. For impressed bricks from the Qin palace complex at Xianyang, Shaanxi, showing discs with circular decor integrated with winding dragons and phoenixes, see Li Jian, ed., *Eternal China: Splendors from the First Dynasties* (Dayton: Dayton Art Institute, 1998), cat. 23.

11. See Édouard Chavannes, *Mission archéologique dans la Chine septentrionale* (Paris: Imprimerie Nationale, 1909–1915), tome 2, pl. 48: no. 92, and Wu Hung, *The Wu Liang Shrine: The Ideology of Early Pictorial Art* (Stanford: Stanford University Press, 1989), p. 240, fig. 98, which cites early textual references to this image.

Bi, the first character of the cartouche, which contains the *yu* ("jade") radical, identifies the image as a jade *bi* disc. But the compound *biliuli* (the same *bi* character), perhaps derived from the Sanskrit *vaidurya* ("lapis lazuli"), is also one of three early terms for glass, the others being *liuli* and *boli* (both *liu* and *bo* contain the jade radical). Some scholars believe that *biliuli* describes a material—jade-green glass made as a substitute for jade—rather than a specific type of object. The character *bi* may therefore carry double meaning. For these terms' origins and distinctions, see Joseph Needham and Wang Ling, *Science and Civilization in China*, vol. 4, pt. 1: *Physics* (London: Cambridge University Press, 1962), pp. 104–6; Robert H. Brill, "Some Thoughts on the Origin of the Chinese Word '*Boli*'," *Silk Road Art and Archaeology*, vol. 2 (Kamakura: Journal of the Institute of Silk Road Studies, 1991/2), pp. 129–36.

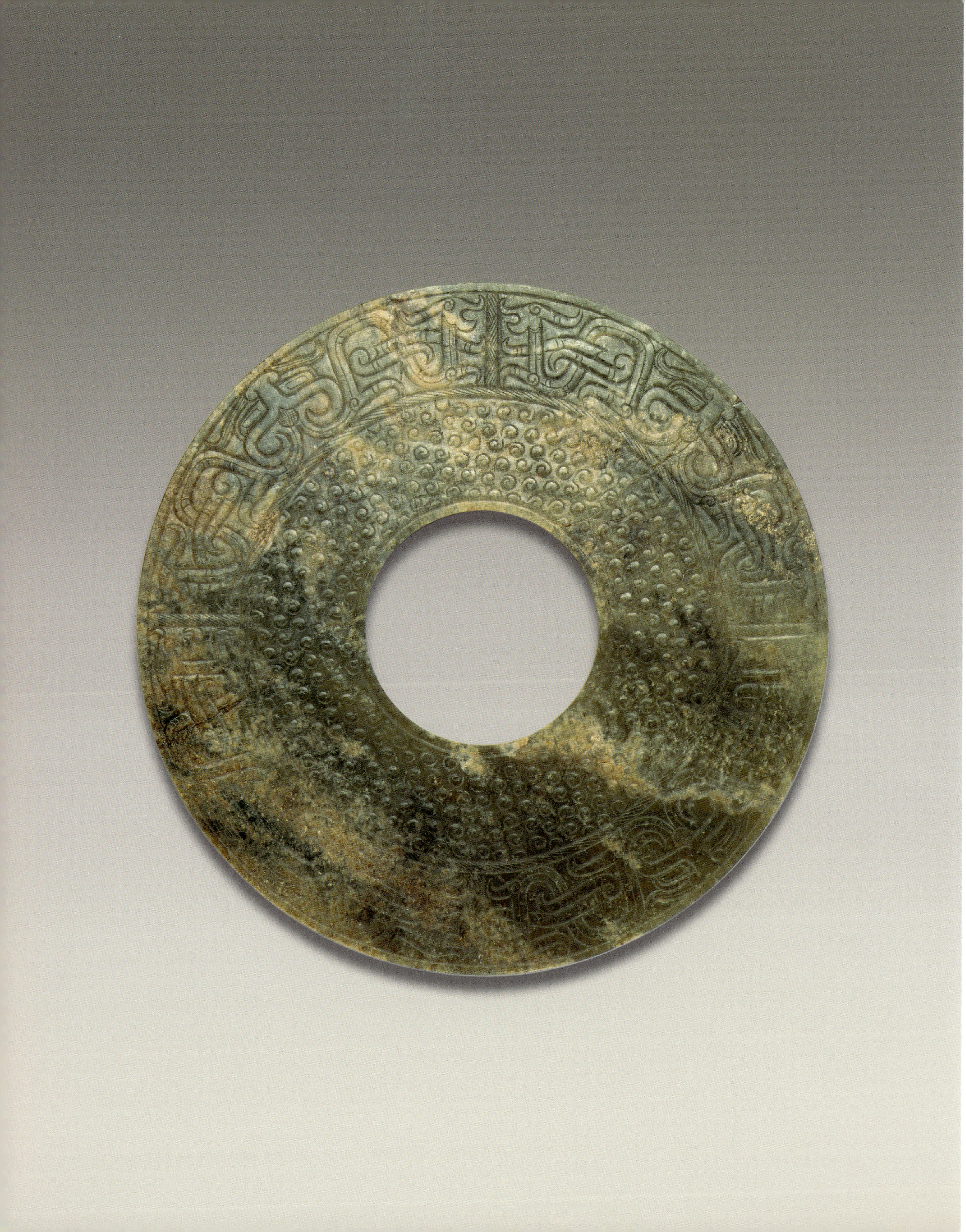

20 *Bi* disc

Late Eastern Zhou to Western Han dynasty, 4th–early 2d century BCE. Reported to come from Jin Cun, Henan. Mottled green jade; diam. 25.7 cm, d. 0.5 cm. Royal Ontario Museum, acc. no. 931.13.1. The Bishop William C. White Collection.

Each face of this disc contains two concentric zones—an inner zone of decorative pattern and an outer of zoomorphic pattern—divided by a finely striated band. On both faces the inner zone comprises low-relief, comma-like spirals, some of which interlink in S-shaped configurations. Traces of a slightly sunken diagonal grid separate these spirals, but less sharply than in the disc illustrated in catalogue number 21. By contrast, the outer zone is divided into four quadrants, with each quadrant containing a tightly compact and sharply executed interlacery centered on snub-nosed animal masks—a motif distinctive to many Eastern Zhou and Han jades (see p. 303). Each mask features a striated moustache and cross-hatched forehead knob, and undulant ribbons that spring from its forehead and terminate in profile dragon or feline heads with open mouths, upturned noses, and backswept crests. Each ribbon flows into the V-shaped forehead of the adjacent mask.

Bishop William Charles White (1873–1960) first published this disc in his *Tombs of Old Loyang*, which documented bronzes, jades, and other burial gifts that reportedly had been unearthed between 1928 and 1931 from the Eastern Zhou royal cemetery at Jin Cun, Henan, near the dynastic capital of Luoyang in China's central plain.[1] Although unresolved questions surround the coherence of those finds as well as the date and dynastic identity of the Jincun cemetery, subsequent excavations support the late Eastern Zhou dating of this disc. Jades of similar style have been unearthed from both late Eastern Zhou and Western Han tombs, but those discovered in the latter may have been heirlooms when buried.[2]

ELINOR PEARLSTEIN

Notes

1. William Charles White, *Tombs of Old Loyang: A Record of the Construction and Contents of a Group of Royal Tombs at Chin-ts'un, Honan, probably dating 550 B.C.* (Shanghai: Kelly & Walsh, 1934), no. 301, pp. 129–30 and pl. CXIX. White, later appointed Keeper of the Royal Ontario Museum's Far Eastern collection, served as Anglican Bishop of Henan Province when the Jincun tombs were pillaged. His book is carefully documented but based on secondary evidence. The opposite face of this disc is illustrated in *Homage to Heaven, Homage to Earth: Chinese Treasures of the Royal Ontario Museum* (Toronto: University of Toronto Press, 1992), cpl. 6.

2. See Shangdong Sheng wenwu kaogu yanjiusuo et al., *Qufu Luguo gu cheng* (*The ancient city of Lu at Qufu*) (Ji'nan: Qi-Lu shushe, 1982), figs. 109–16. These may be compared with discs buried with Prince Liu Sheng (d. 113 BCE) and his consort Dou Wan (d. 104 BCE). Discs in their tombs display three central patterns: plain curls, curls within a hexagonal grid, and hexagonal grid with faceted relief. See Zhongguo shehui kexueyuan kaogu yanjiusuo and Hebei Sheng wen guanlichu, eds., *Mancheng Han mu fajue baogao* (*Excavation of the Han tombs at Mancheng*) (Beijing: Wenwu chubanshe, 1980), vol. 1, figs. 199: 1–3 and vol. 2, pl. XCVI. For very clear illustrations, see *Nanyue wang mu yuqi: Jades from the tomb of the king of Nanyue* (Guangzhou/Hong Kong: Guangzhou Xihan Nanyue wang mu bowuguan and Xianggang Zhongwen daxue wenwuguan, 1991), esp. cpls. 31, 32, 44, 45, 48, 49, 96, 97, 99, 100, 120–25. Together, these discs display a wide variety of zoomorphic interlacery, none quite identical to the Royal Ontario Museum disc. This richly furnished Nanyue tomb is the burial of Zhao Mo (d. 122 BCE), ruler of the independent kingdom of Southern Yue, which maintained close relations with the Han court. His extraordinary jades likely included pieces brought from workshops in north-central or eastern China.

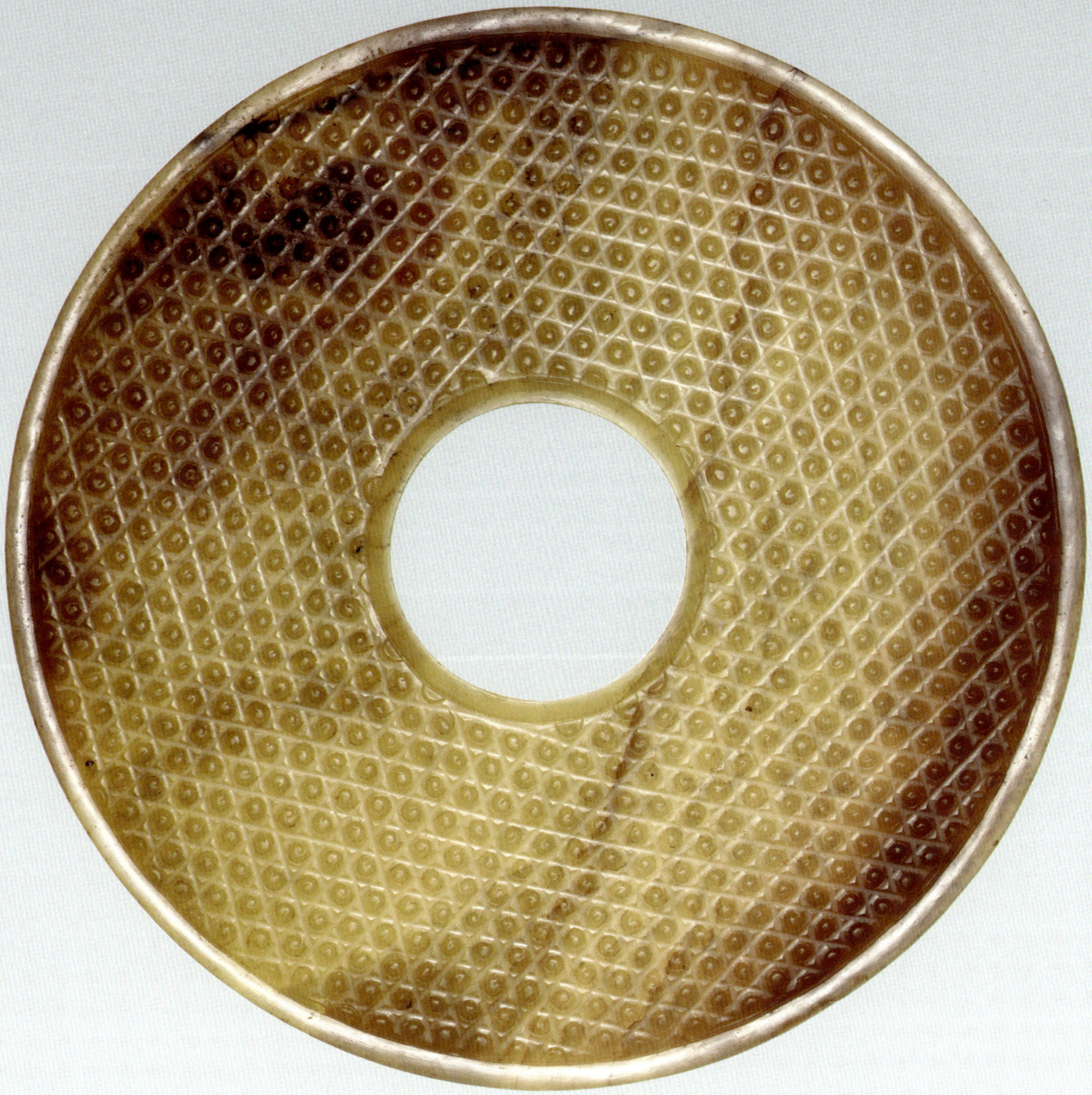

21 *Bi* disc

Late Eastern Zhou or Western Han dynasty, 3d–2d century BCE. Brownish green jade; diam. 14 cm, d. 0.4 cm. The Art Institute of Chicago, acc. no. 1950.592. Edward and Louise B. Sonnenschein Collection.

On both faces of this thin disc, the lapidary used two shafted rotary tools—one with a fine nail-like head, the second with a thicker, oblique head—to incise and model low relief, comma-like spirals within a net-like hexagonal grid formed by straight vertical lines crossed by parallel diagonal lines. A fine sandy paste applied to each tool head abraded the stone. Modern lighting illuminates the dual visual effect of this ancient design. Uniform rays from behind highlight the freely oriented but tightly contained pattern of spirals; raking beams from above accent the incised grid and slightly chiseled contours of the relief.[1]

Tomb finds indicate that jade discs with relief spirals against a smooth or lightly delineated ground (see cat. no. 20) were widespread by the fourth and third centuries BCE and probably antedated those discs with spirals within a clearly incised grid as seen here. Discs with this grid pattern—whether cherished heirlooms or newly made versions of venerable designs—remained prestigious burial furnishings through the early Western Han.[2] Compared with discs of similar diameter and style, this piece shows an unusually dense and small-scale pattern, its meticulous uniformity interrupted only by a few semicircles bordering the central perforation and outer perimeter.

ELINOR PEARLSTEIN

Notes

1. Among many premodern terms quoted by authors today, relief spirals are described as "grain pattern" (*guwen*) and the geometric grid as "rush mat pattern" (*puwen*).

2. For examples excavated from Western Han tombs, see Zhongguo shehui kexueyuan kaogu yanjiusuo and Hebei Sheng wenwu guanlichu, eds., *Mancheng Han mu fajue baogao* (*Excavation of the Han tombs at Mancheng*) (Beijing: Wenwu chubanshe, 1980), vol. 1, fig. 199:4; *Nanyue wang mu yuqi: Jades from the tomb of the king of Nanyue* (Guangzhou/Hong Kong: Guangzhou Xihan Nanyue wang mu bowuguan et al. and Xianggang Zhongwen daxue wenwuguan, 1991), pl. 47.

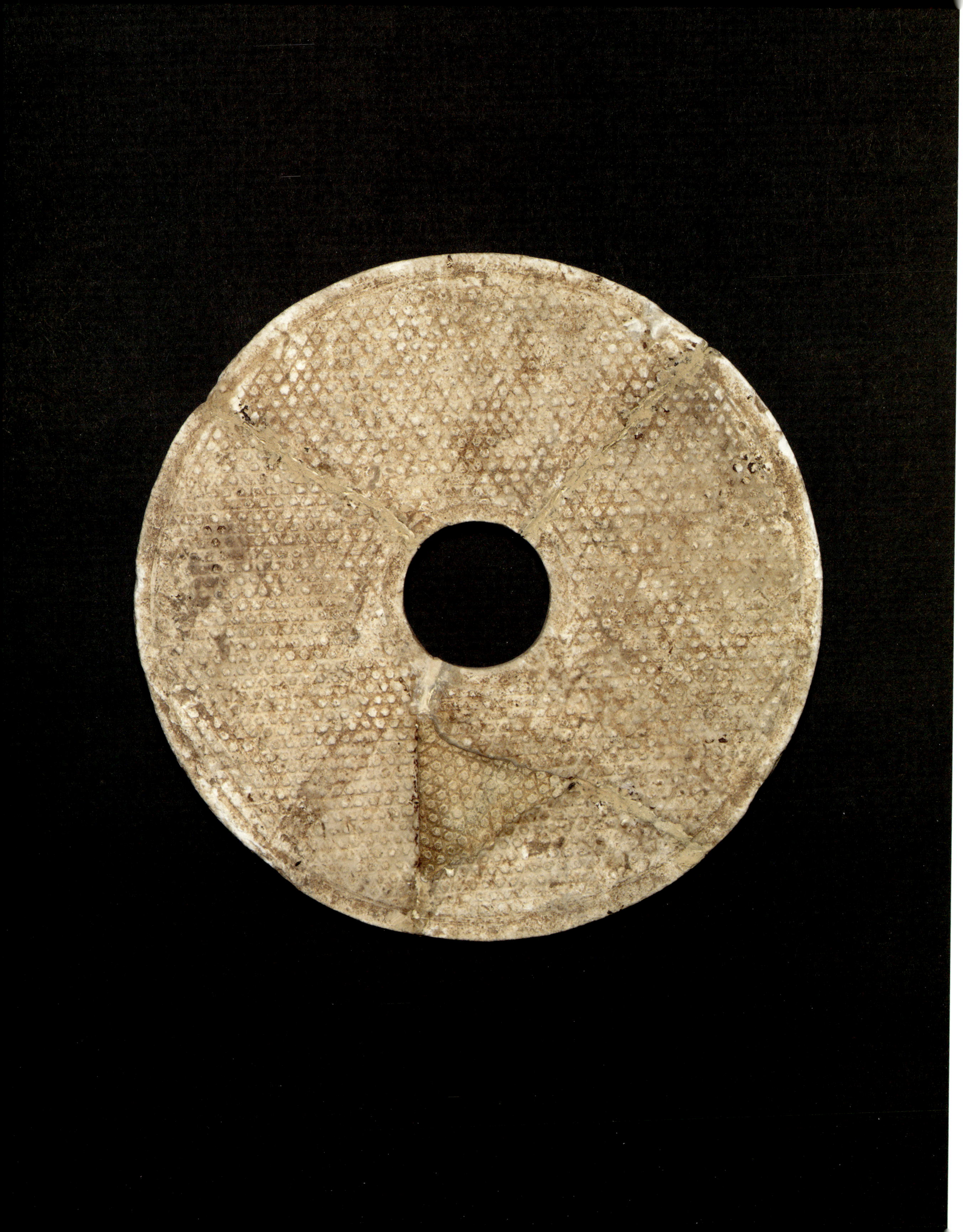

22

22 *Bi* disc

Han dynasty. Glass; diam. 16.0 cm, d. 0.8 cm.
The Art Institute of Chicago, acc. no. 2001.320. Gift of Muriel Kallis Newman.

One side of this glass *bi* disc is cast in an allover pattern of flat-topped knobs within a hexagonal grid; the reverse is plain. A replacement for a missing triangular section reproduces this sharp-edged relief pattern; devitrification and crizzling have softened the original edges. But the hexagonal relief, where sharply preserved, clearly simulates that of contemporary jades.[1] On glass *bi* discs, see Pearlstein's "*Bi* Discs of Jade and Glass" in this catalogue.

ELINOR PEARLSTEIN

Notes

1. In its heavily weathered surface, this disc is typical of many examples that have lain buried for centuries. It was broken in four pieces and has undergone poor restoration; the joins are out of plane and the join lines overpainted. For a clear drawing of this pattern in jade, see Zhongguo shehui kexueyuan kaogu yanjiusuo and Hebei Sheng wenwu guanlichu, eds., *Mancheng Han mu fajue baogao* (*Excavation of the Han tombs at Mancheng*) (Beijing: Wenwu chubanshe, 1980), vol. 1, fig. 199:5.

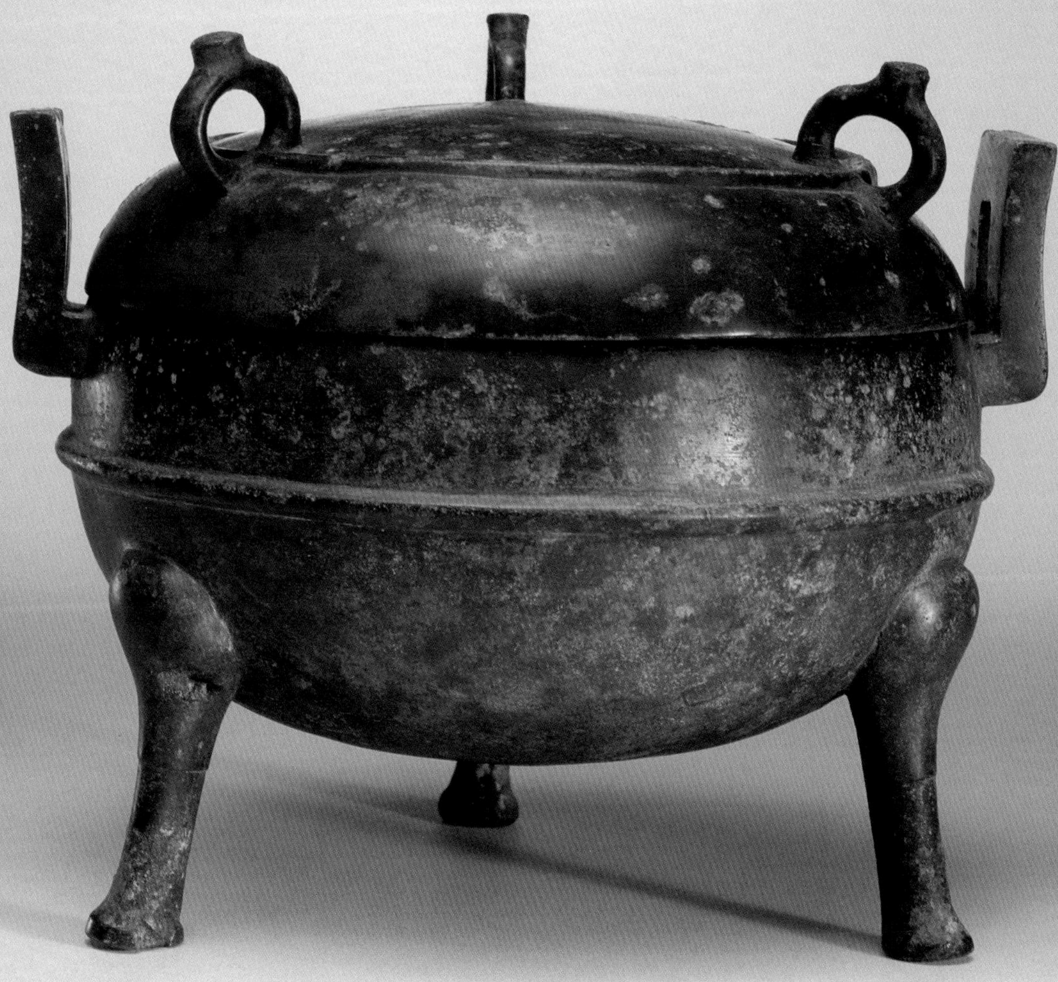

23 Tripod vessel (*ding*)

Western Han dynasty. Bronze; h. 17.3 cm, w. 20.0 cm.
Princeton University Art Museum, acc. no. y1965-73. Museum purchase, from the C. D. Carter Collection.

This tripod is consistent with the simplification of shape and decoration that characterized Chinese bronze vessels since the phase known in art history as the "ritual revolution" of the tenth and ninth centuries BCE.[1] Its unadorned surface is broken only by two thick welts, one around the widest part of the bowl, and one linking the rings of the cover. Three rings, each topped by a small stud, surmount the cover, which is less flat than standard *ding* covers of later Zhou. Also differing slightly from early *ding* are the three legs, which are rather thin and splayed; a style that began to replace thick, straight legs during late Western Zhou. A small ridge at about the midpoint of the legs may indicate that the lower part of each leg was cast on.[2]

The progressive disappearance of zoomorphic elements and standardization of models following the ritual revolution has been ascribed to the increasing mass production of ritual bronzes as the use of these spread to the lower ranks of the nobility, and also to the formation of a "shared system of political and religious values as well as homologies in the social organization of the elites."[3] Little is known about the ritual function of *ding* bronze tripods during the Han dynasties. The sources document a fierce debate on their symbolism—a debate that focused on the existence of a further realm beyond the visible, on the possibility and the necessity of communicating with it, and on the appropriate sphere of action of political power.

For the most important thinkers of Western and Eastern Han, determining the meaning of the *ding* was material—even critical—to answering such questions as: did imperial sovereignty need a superhuman legitimization? what sorts of contact with otherworldly forces might corrupt the conduct of the rulers? The *ding* itself was seen as the special locus of interaction among different realities: the five cosmic factors (*wu xing*: earth, wood, metal, fire, water),[4] the human and extra-human realms, and the hierarchically different components of society.

As presented by one of the most famous philosophical syntheses of the period, the *Tai xuan jing* (*Canon of supreme mystery*) of Yang Xiong (53 BCE–18 CE), it is in the *ding*—strictly associated with the *zao* (stove)—that the mixing of *yin* and *yang* occurs, that the "raw" becomes "cooked."[5] The *ding*, then, was a special implement that symbolized the process whereby cosmic principles informed social institutions and their moral foundations.[6] Cooking, in both the literal and the metaphysical sense, made it possible to sacrifice to the ancestors and to feast worthy officials at court. It can therefore be said that the *ding* was apt to embody and realize both "vertical and horizontal harmony." In other words, it was an eloquent metaphor of the "transformative" function of the political power and of its prerogatives and attributes, which at the time of the Han—since the process of establishing a canonical tradition was in its initial, crucial phases—could still be the object of passionate debate. In such debates, the symbol of the *ding* occupied a fundamental position: it was associated, in several competing myths widely disseminated at the time, with a series of archetypically good rulers and dynasties of the past.

The first and the most influential story about the *ding*'s significance is told in the *Zuozhuan* commentary to *Chunqiu*, the *Spring and Autumn Annals*, texts traditionally ascribed to Confucius (551–479 BCE) and his disciples or friends, and hence regarded by several

Western and Eastern Han authors as the ultimate model for a moral literary enterprise.[7] In the entry for 605 BCE (Duke Xuan, third year, spring), the ruler of Chu, after a victory over the Rong (probably a group of "less civilized," non-sedentary agriculturalists), nurtures imperial ambitions. In that connection, he then asks Wangsun Man about the weight and size of *ding*, since these are artifacts through which the spirits are believed to contact leaders of humanity. Wangsun Man, a diplomat sent by the Zhou, the relatively powerless but nominal rulers of "All under Heaven," to compliment the ruler of Chu on his military success, urges him to consider rather the weight of charismatic virtue in determining legitimacy. To bolster his argument, Wangsun offers the famous account of the Xia (ca. 2100–ca. 1600 BCE) receiving the metal for the Nine Tripods from the Nine Regions:

In the past, just when Xia possessed virtue, pictures of wondrous things (*wu*) were sent from afar, and the superintendents of the nine provinces submitted metal, so that tripod caldrons were cast with representations of wondrous things.[8] The hundred things were therewith completely set forth, and the people thus knew the spirits and the evil things. That was why when the people entered rivers, marshes, mountains, and forests, they would not meet what could harm them, nor would they encounter evil spirits. Thus they could harmonize with those above and below them, and received Heaven's blessings. The last Xia king, Jie, possessed dimmed virtue, and the tripods were moved to the house of Shang, to remain there for six hundred years. The last Shang king, Zhou, was tyrannical, and the tripod caldrons were moved to the house of Zhou. When virtue is bright and resplendent, the tripods, though small, grow weighty. When virtue is distorted, dimmed, and confused, the tripods, though big, are light. The bright virtue bestowed by Heaven has its basis and certainty. . . . Although Zhou virtue is in decline, the Heavenly Mandate has not yet changed. The question of whether the[ir?] tripods are weighty or not may not be asked yet."[9]

No commentator has ever fully understood the import of the passage. Apparently, the tripods visibly confirm the authority of the sovereign, insofar as both the realm under Xia and the more distant parts contributed to their casting. But to what degree does the remarkable power of the legendary tripods to avert evil derive from their completeness, or from the specific images that they bear, or from the charisma of the ruling house? And to what degree can the mere possession of such artifacts work in favor of their owner?

The question of the nature and function of the tripods, especially their weight in determining fate relative to the weight of virtue, agency, and material resources, is, in turn, a question about how the ruler may best secure Heaven's backing. The inability to answer these questions with any certainty occasioned debate in Han, as we can see from the later example of Wang Chong's (27–?97 CE) *Lunheng* (*Doctrines evaluated*). Wang Chong, in taking up the very question of the representation of "wondrous things" in connection with the *Zuozhuan* passage quoted above, interprets the tripods as symbols of legitimate authority, not as effective tools to realize legitimate authority. Nor does he conceive of them as a channel of communication between the divine and the human realms. In his secular view, sovereignty is not characterized by any magic or superhuman transformative power. Possession of sovereignty attests the moral superiority of the possessor. Since moral qualities have physical manifestations and physical phenomena have an intrinsic moral value, the appearance of the Nine Tripods is not a sign of divine favor but a physical manifestation of a state of surpassing virtue. Wang Chong asserts that the tripods attest possession of the Heavenly Mandate and attempts to define the proper field of action of sovereignty:

> The tribute metal from distant places was deemed to be very beautiful, and therefore it was cast into tripods, on which all sort of curious objects were depicted. How could this have had the effect that people in forests or by lakes did not meet with specters, and could ward off the evil influences of spirits? . . . Why should vessels, such as the tripods, have such power? . . . The appearance of the Nine Tripods was an auspicious sign of high virtue. Yet the wearing of a felicitous object does not attract happiness. . . . The same is maintained in regard to the Nine Tripods. They cannot ward off evil influences. . . . There is a popular tradition that the tripods of Zhou boiled of themselves without fire,[10] and that things could be taken out of them, which had not been put in. This is a popular exaggeration. According to the exaggerated statements preserved in the classical texts, the Nine Tripods, which were nothing special, must possess a divinely efficacious power for no reason. . . . If as a tribute from distant lands they were divine, why should things from distant countries be more divine? And if they were so because Yu cast them, well—Yu was a sage, I grant you, but he was not a god, so then could a vessel cast by him be divine?[11]

Wang Chong here seems engaged in a theoretical separation of what is *shen* (the "divine," the extraordinarily efficacious, the transformative) and not-*shen* (the human, the constrained). For Wang, these two dimensions clearly do not intermingle, nor can they be put in efficacious contact, either by the action of an enlightened ruler or by man's creations.

Whether or not it is legitimate to relate the *wu* that appeared on the *ding* to the decorative (often zoomorphic) motifs on the Shang bronzes and their possible meaning and function,[12] it seems clear that the reference to the archaic Xia, to which the development of Central States (*Zhongguo*) civilization was traced, had a precise import by the Warring States and Han periods. As for the nature of the *wu* (whether objects or animate things, relations or events)[13] and their connection with the *ding*, in the context of the *Zuozhuan* account they seem to have an apotropaic function. Though we cannot go beyond mere conjectures on the matter, we do know that in societies where "shamanism"[14] has historically played an important role, "totemic animals"[15] permitted communication between the human community and the mysterious forces of nature. They represented a link with the world of the ancestors, and provided indispensable assistance whenever the individual had to leave the boundaries of his social organization and face the wilderness and its fearsome inhabitants[16]—a concept also expressed in the *Zuozhuan* passage above. Was it the task of the empire's sovereign to make contact with and tame "the beyond," or had "the beyond" to be ignored or denied? And could such a beyond corrupt the actions of a wise ruler?

Wang Chong's insistence on the absolute divide between the human and the extra-human realm probably indicates his determination to oppose heterodox traditions advocating closer contact with the spirit realm, legacies of the Warring States period and still extremely popular in the northeast area occupied prior to unification by the states of Qi and Yan. Wang Chong's commitment had precedent in Sima Qian's (ca. 145–ca. 86 BCE) anxiety concerning *fangshi* ("necromancers"),[17] their esoteric doctrines, and their influence on the "superstitious" emperor Wu (141–87 BCE)[18] who clung to their versions of the myths of Huangdi, the Yellow Emperor (trad. 2697–2597 BCE), associated with immortality.[19] (Huangdi had become Wu's declared model in his search for immortality.) In these myths Huangdi used a *ding* to cross the divide between the mundane and extra-mundane worlds in order to achieve, through immortality, his own escape from society.[20]

> ... Sacrifice to *zao* [the stove, or the Stove God], then the *wu*[21] come; once the *wu* have arrived, then the powder of cinnabar can be transformed into yellow metal; with the yellow metal it is possible to make those tools to drink and eat which prolong life; once one has his life prolonged [he] can meet the Immortals who dwell in the Penglai islands in the middle of the sea; having met them it becomes possible to accomplish *feng* and *shan* and therefore not to die; Huangdi realized all this ....[22]

Given the emperor's fascination with alchemy and immortality, Sima Qian did not directly oppose such "esoteric" teachings. He voiced his skepticism, however, by describing in the first Basic Chronicle of his universal history (initially conceived as a celebration of the Han dynasty and the beginning of a new Golden Age)[23] a different kind of Yellow Emperor—one unconcerned with immortality, but specifically and entirely extolled for his political abilities and moral virtues. With these qualities rather than any superhuman powers, he was able to pacify the world and "delineate" its boundaries, both physically and culturally. That the Yellow Emperor honored *gui* and *shen* ("ghosts" and "spirits") Sima presented more as a consequence of his respectful and pious attitude than as a fundamental prerogative of his royal function. According to *Shiji*, the Yellow Emperor also received the precious *ding* and the yarrow stalks; but Sima Qian notes these only as attributes that follow an acknowledged and legitimate—and completely human—sovereignty. Although current belief might have connected them respectively with the possibility of getting in touch with the ancestors and of investigating the rules of the cosmos, Sima Qian focused in his portrait on the Yellow Emperor's political qualities, as if to suggest that transcending human boundaries was no longer a necessary royal attribute. Throughout the *Shiji*, by juxtaposing a variety of contradictory myths about the *ding*, Sima Qian the historian diminishes their sacred aura and directs our attention to the human authority—or lack of it—of the reigning emperor.

Following is one example of the views that Sima Qian, by his silence, spurned—views that posited the possession of *ding* as an important, autonomous factor in legitimacy. When in the summer of 113 BCE, a shamaness[24] unearthed a voluminous *ding* in Shui, discussion about the extraordinary find immediately turned to the legendary loss in the Si River (in present-day Shandong) of the Nine Tripods, purportedly cast by Yu, the culture hero, and last possessed by

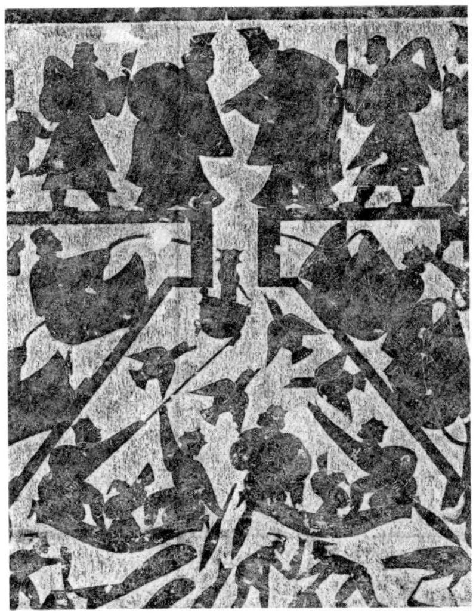

the Zhou dynasty. Since their disappearance was imputed to the Zhou's loss of power and the unworthiness of its successor, Qin (fig. 1),[25] the reemergence of even one tripod out of the original nine was touted by sycophantic courtiers as a sign that Heaven had reestablished the line of legitimate sovereigns with Han Wudi. Since Wudi was inclined, for once, to be skeptical about the likelihood of heaven sending auspicious portents (as the last harvest had been poor), the courtiers trotted out yet another myth in which the tripods played a central role:

> They say that under Taidi [Fuxi; trad. 2852–2737 BCE] there flourished (*xing*) just one *ding*, "one" meaning "the whole": the union of Heaven, Earth, and all creatures was perfect. Huangdi created (*zuo*) three *ding*, representing Heaven, Earth, and Man. Yu received (*shou*) the metal from the Nine Regional Pastors and cast the Nine Tripods. All used them to prepare the victims offered to the High Lord[s?],[26] *shen*, and *gui* [spirits and ghosts], down to the Xia and then to the Shang, but as the virtue of the Zhou became perverted and the Altar of the Soil of Song was lost, the Tripods fell in the water and disappeared.[27]

Fig. 1 *First Emperor's failed attempt to raise one of the legendary Nine Tripods*. Detail of Stone Chamber 2, Stone 2-E.2 (cat. no. 1.29). "Wu family shrines" rubbings. Princeton University Art Museum, acc. no. 2002-307.19.

This passage says, in essence, that in the remote age of Taidi (Fuxi), one of the three sovereigns of the "mythical" predynastic past, harmony reigned throughout the entire cosmos; all creatures had access to the gods and all existed in perfect equality and unity. Hence humans did not need to create the *ding*, the material channel between different existential realms; the *ding* flourished (*xing*) as a spontaneous, unprovoked phenomenon—it just "was."

In this version the Yellow Emperor, on the other hand, as the first emperor, had to produce or make (*zuo*) his "religious" tools in order to transcend the separation from the divine. The passage describes a transition from the natural to the cultural phase, from primeval unity to separation. Because of the intervention of a new factor (perhaps human agency itself), the unity and the harmony of the universe are no longer unquestioned; they must be guaranteed, and in a sense reestablished, through a sort of ritual, demiurgic, process—carried out through the tripods. Rightly, after this fall from primeval grace, the Yellow Emperor cast three *ding* standing for Heaven, Earth, and Man, to connect these three different components of reality. His sovereignty was justified by his ability to establish mediation among the three components, and the proper focus of his sovereignty was on the human rather than the cosmic sphere.

Unlike Huangdi, who, without any note of preparation, was able to cast three transformative *ding*, Yu, founder of the first Chinese dynasty and controller of the Flood, had first to acquire (*shou*) the metal for his *ding* from the Nine Regions of the empire. His supreme charismatic power and authority was derived, like Huangdi's, from his ability to connect the three realms, but he nevertheless depended upon the acquiescence and cooperation of his own officials and of the lords of the more distant regions—in other words, upon political sagacity.

In that passage the courtiers were clearly adducing the Yellow Emperor, who represented for both Sima Qian and Wudi the model of active sovereignty (even though the former was more interested in its human and the latter in its suprahuman attributes and prerogatives), as a worthy embodiment of a mystical conception of rulership. It is probable that the courtiers were metaphorically propounding a culturally and politically more constrained, less activist imperial authority.

It is clear that during the Han dynasties the tripods were still connected with the possibility of transcending the human condition; in association with the imperial power, they might define the realms in which the sovereign was believed or expected to develop his function. To a degree (either symbolically or actually) they were perceived as a channel toward the unknown and the invisible. It seems that a passionate debate flourished on whether or not such a medium, especially for the sake of a thriving and morally inspired government, had to be kept sealed.

FILIPPO MARSILI

Notes

1. See Jessica Rawson, "Western Zhou Archaeology," in *The Cambridge History of Ancient China: From the Origins to 221 BCE*, ed. Michael Loewe and Edward L. Shaughnessy (Cambridge: Cambridge University Press, 1999), p. 360.

2. The piece has already been described in Eleanor Von Erdberg [Consten], *Chinese Bronzes from the Collection of Chester Dale and Dolly Carter* (Ascona: Artibus Asiae Publishers, 1978), p. 58.

3. Lothar von Falkenhausen, "The Waning of the Bronze Age: Material Culture and Social Developments, 770–481" in *The Cambridge History of Ancient China*, p. 542.

4. See Michael Loewe, "Water, Earth, and Fire: The Symbols of the Han Dynasty," in his *Divination, Mythology, and Monarchy in Han China* (Cambridge: Cambridge University Press, 1994), pp. 55–60.

5. Claude Lévi-Strauss, *The Raw and the Cooked* (London: J. Cape, 1969).

6. Yang Hsiung, *The Canon of Supreme Mystery*, trans. Michael Nylan (Delhi: Sri Satguru Publications, 1995), pp. 280–86; on the centrality of food in Chinese culture and religion, see Jordan Paper, *The Spirits Are Drunk: Comparative Approaches to Chinese Religion* (Albany: State University of New York Press, 1995).

7. In Michael Loewe's opinion, it was Dong Zhongshu (179–104 BCE) who extrapolated from the *Chunqiu* a concept of unity that would inspire—especially beginning in Eastern Han—the acts of every conscientous and rightful sovereign: "The great united scheme of the *Chunqiu* is the everlasting warp that runs through heaven and earth and the principle that underlies all times, past and present." See Michael Loewe, "China's Sense of Unity," *T'oung Pao*, vol. 80 (1994), p. 15.

8. Wang Chong (*Lunheng* 26, 2), paraphrasing the same passage of the *Zuozhuan* in referring to the qualities accruing to *ding* made of gold, uses the term *wu* as well. In that context *wu* is clearly understandable as "thing capable by itself of transformation" (*Lunheng* 26, 28).

9. The translation of the passage, which I have slightly modified in order address the present topic, was very kindly provided by Li Waiyee.

10. This statement about the intrinsically extraordinary faculties of *ding* is found in the "Genzhu" chapter of *Mozi* (considered an Eastern Zhou text); see Sun Yirang, ed., *Mozi xian gu* (Beijing: Zhonghua shuju, 1986), p. 388.

11. Translation based on Alfred Forke, *Lun-Hêng*, Part 1: *Philosophical Essays of Wang Chung* (New York: Paragon Book Gallery, 1962), pp. 505–7.

12. For the debate on the meanings of motifs on Chinese bronzes, see Sarah Allan, "Art and Meaning," in *The Problem of Meaning in Early Chinese Ritual Bronzes*, ed. Roderick Whitfield, Colloquies on Art & Archaeology in Asia, no. 15 (London: School of Oriental Studies, 1993), pp. 9–34; see also in the same work Robert Bagley, "Meaning and Explanation," pp. 35–56.

13. See n. 8.

14. For a classic phenomenological analysis of shamanism, see Mircea Eliade, *Shamanism: Archaic Techniques of Ecstasy* (London: Arcana, 1989).

15. On the concept of totem in Chinese culture, see Sarah Allan, "Sons of Suns: Myth and Totemism in Early China," *Bulletin of the School of Oriental and African Studies*, vol. 44 (1981), pp. 290–326.

16. See Emanuela Monaco, *Manitu e Windigo: visione e antropofagia tra gli Algonchini* (Rome: Bulzoni, 1995).
17. On the debate between classicists and *fangshi* at Wudi's court, see Marianne Bujard, "Le 'Traité des sacrifices' du *Hanshu* et la mise en place de la religion d'état des Han," *Bulletin de l'Ecole Française de l'Extrême Orient*, vol. 84 (1997), pp. 111–27.
18. On Wudi and his legendary fascination with the extra-human realm, see Kristopher M. Schipper, *L'empereur Wou des Han dans la légende taoiste* (Paris: École Française d'Extrême-Orient, 1965).
19. On the myths of the Yellow Emperor, see Charles LeBlanc, "A Re-examination of the Myth of Huang ti," *Journal of Chinese Religions*, vols. 13–14, (1985–1986), pp. 45–63. The role of the Yellow Emperor in the Huang-Lao texts has not yet been the subject of a monographic study; the model of sovereignty he represented in such an unorthodox doctrine is summarized in Robin D. S. Yates, *Five Lost Classics: Tao, Huang-Lao, and Yin-Yang in Han China* (New York: Ballantine Books, 1997), pp. 104–11.
20. Throughout the "Fengshan shu" of *Shiji*, the concept of immortality seems also to be propounded in order to indirectly criticize the Confucian model of a hierarchically organized society based on familial ties; in *Shiji*, *juan* 28, p. 1394, Wudi regards immortality especially as a way to escape from his relatives. On the theme of immortality see Yü Ying-shih, "Life and Immortality in the Mind of Han China," *Harvard Journal of Asiatic Studies*, vol. 25 (1964–1965), pp. 80–120; Michael Loewe, *Ways to Paradise: The Chinese Quest for Immortality* (London: Allen & Unwin, 1979).
21. In this passage the translation of *wu* as the generic "things" is at least problematic; the passage clearly refers to a "something" with a strong transformative potential; see n. 8.
22. *Shiji*, *juan* 28, pp. 1385–86. This story was told at court in 132 BCE by Li Shaojun, a *fangshi* who tried to impress the emperor and to gain his favor by claiming to know the techniques necessary to reach the "Island of the Immortals." As is clearly stated at the beginning of "Fengshan shu," only "true emperors" could successfully accomplish the *feng* and *shan* sacrifices (Qin Shihuangdi had allegedly failed). Sima Qian toward the end of his life became pessimistic about the times in which he lived, but at the beginning of Wudi's reign he had hoped his emperor would be a new Yellow Emperor and inaugurate a new historical and cosmic cycle; see Michael Loewe, "The Great Beginning—104 BCE," in his *Crisis and Conflict in Han China* (London: George Allen & Unwin, 1974), pp. 17–36. Always in "Fengshan shu" Sima Qian reminds the reader that the association of the *feng* and *shan* sacrifices with immortality belongs exclusively to the mountebankery of *fangshi*, and that it is a fallacy he believes originated in Qi; see also *Shiji*, *juan* 28, p. 1397.
23. On the literary structure of the *Shiji* as metaphor of the unfolding of a coherent history, see Mark E. Lewis, "The Feng and Shan Sacrifices of the Emperor Wu of the Han," in *State and Court Ritual in China*, ed. Joseph McDermott (Cambridge and New York: Cambridge University Press, 1999), pp. 20–50.
24. Sima Qian tells us that this shamaness was originally from Fenyin (Shanxi Province), the same place where in 163 BCE the charlatan *fangshi* Xinyuan Ping had buried a *ding* in vain hope of exciting Wendi's (r. 179–156 BCE) fantasy; in *Shiji*, *juan* 28, p. 1383.
25. In *Shiji*, *juan* 28, p. 1365, Sima Qian states that in his time it was still debated whether the Nine Tripods were lost in the Si River or obtained by the Qin; in *Shiji*, *juan* 6, p. 248, Sima reports instead a version of the story in which the Qin lost just one of the Tripods, that which Qin Shihuangdi tried unsuccessfully to recover (as depicted on in the east wall of the Left Chamber in the "Wu family shrines" [fig. 1]). See Édouard Chavannes, *Mission archéologique dans la Chine septentrionale*, vol. 2 (Paris: Imprimerie Nationale, 1913), pl. 59, no. 121; Wu Hung, *The Wu Liang Shrine: The Ideology of Early Chinese Pictorial Art* (Stanford: Stanford University Press, 1989), pp. 92–96.
26. On the questions related to the term *shangdi* in early Chinese texts, see Robert Eno, "Was There a High God in Shang Religion?" *Early China*, vol. 15 (1990), pp. 1–25.
27. *Shiji*, *juan* 28, p. 1392.

Hu or *Zhong* Vessels

Among vessel forms that Western Han bronze casters inherited from the Eastern Zhou and Qin, most prominent are pear-shaped jars generally known as *hu*, whose rotund or ovoid bodies taper upward to slenderer necks and end in subtly flaring, trumpet-shaped mouth rims. Some *hu* preserve fitted lids; rare examples have chain handles. "Squared" (*fang*) styles are designed with four convex walls that intersect at sharp angles. Each vessel rises from a ring base whose profile may be straight, downward flaring, or crisply angled (see cat. nos. 24, 25).

Vessels ranging in quality and technical complexity were used by aristocratic and moderately well-to-do patrons throughout the expansive Western Han empire. Like their Warring States predecessors, Han craftsmen produced both the smoothly rounded and squared styles of bronze *hu* in costly, labor-intensive vessels of lacquered wood. Warring States potters had also created both forms in unglazed earthenware; Western Han potters greatly increased production in this medium and also introduced lead-glazed earthenware and the reduction-fired glazed stoneware known as celadon in the West.

Some Han-dynasty vessels were left austerely plain, others were decorated with images of great vitality. Elaborate bronzes were finely inlaid with gold or silver or painted with mercury amalgams of these precious metals (cat. no. 24).[1] Lacquers were painted, and unglazed earthenwares were often painted after firing (cat. no. 26). Lead-glazed earthenwares and celadon-glazed stonewares were relief-molded, carved, or incised before firing and glazing. This allowed the glaze to pool and thereby darken in the grooves, thus emphasizing the lines of the decoration (cat. no. 27).

Decorative motifs might be geometric or zoomorphic (the latter primarily dragons or other mythical creatures), or a mingling of the two in fluently dynamic patterns (cat. no. 24), or they might juxtapose creatures and human figures in realistic or imaginary hunting scenes (cat. no. 27). Lids of these vessels were often molded or painted with complementary motifs.

Further enlivening and firmly balancing the profiles of many bronze and ceramic *hu* are two ring-holder masks cast opposite one another on the shoulder, the rings free-swinging and functional in bronze (cat. nos. 24, 25), painted or molded onto the unglazed earthenware (cat. no. 26), molded onto the surface of glazed earthenwares (cat. no. 27) and stonewares. These rings typically loop through (functionally in bronze, emblematically in ceramic) a curved nose or beak that protrudes below the eyes of an ogre mask designed to fit the vessel's contour. This ring-handle mask or escutcheon, its facial features derived from the Shang and Zhou image later known as *taotie*, became elegantly decorative in Eastern Zhou bronzes and pervasive in many mediums and structural contexts throughout the Western and Eastern Han empires.[2]

Bronzes of this form have usually been regarded as wine vessels. Indeed, some Warring States and Han vessels have been unearthed from tombs with their lids tightly in place and grain wine or other liquids, presumably offered to the spirit of the deceased, preserved inside.[3] In the Western Han, however, some *hu*-shaped bronzes encircled by three bands of relief were

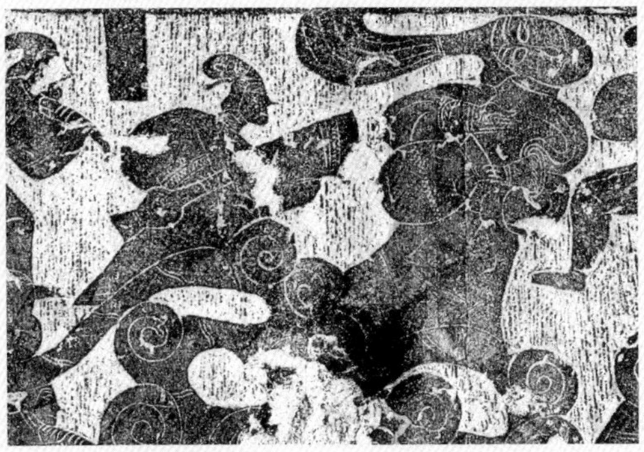

incised or cast with inscriptions that identify them as *zhong*. Yang Zhifeng of Beijing University has called these grain vessels and believes that their horizontal bands demarcated units of measure.[4]

Whereas many *hu* or *zhong* of bronze or lacquered wood were probably used in life before they were buried, most if not all of the earthenware versions and many stonewares seem to have been commissioned exclusively for the tomb. These ceramic simulacra reflect the widespread dissemination of burial rituals from royalty and nobility to a broader but less wealthy population of officials and landowners. Some Han aristocrats were buried with a combination of bronze and ceramic or lacquered wood and ceramic vessels, the ceramics often in greater quantity and of mixed quality.[5]

In Han mortuary art—stone reliefs (fig. 1), wall paintings, and funerary banners—jars of *hu* or *zhong* form are frequently depicted in formal tableaux, as well as in scenes depicting food preparation and banquets. Although these depictions rarely reveal the vessels' material or contents, they clearly indicate their pervasiveness in daily life as well as their burial function of holding sustenance for the dead.[6]

ELINOR PEARLSTEIN

Fig. 1 *Supernatural figures holding vessels and running on a dragon-headed cloud band.* Detail of Stone Chamber 2, Stone 2-R.1 (cat. no. 1.32). "Wu family shrines" rubbings. Princeton University Art Museum, acc. no. 2002-307.31.

Notes

1. For references to mercury amalgams, see catalogue number 24. Rarely, bronzes were gilt and inlaid or painted with lacquer. See, e.g., *Zhongguo qingtongqi quanji* (*Complete survey of Chinese bronzes*) (Beijing: Wenwu chubanshe, 1998), vol. 12: *Qin, Han*, pl. 54, for a finely gilt and lacquer-painted bronze jar, excavated in the southern coastal province of Guangxi. This may reflect a regional style.

2. Large bronze zoomorphic masks (*pushou*) with intersecting rings served as symbolically protective or apotropaic handles on wood coffins and as knockers or door pulls on wood and stone tomb doors. Such ring-holder masks were frequently simulated in stamped tomb tiles, wall paintings, and carved stone pillars and doors. For a carved depiction at the "Wu family" cemetery, see Édouard Chavannes, *Mission archéologique dans la Chine septentrionale* (Paris: Imprimerie Nationale, 1909–1915), tome 2, no. 70, east gate-pillar. Stone doors of Eastern Han Tombs 1 and 2 at Dahuting, in Mi County, Henan, more clearly depict large ring-holder masks in relief-carved images; see Henan Sheng wenwu yanjiusuo, ed., *Mixian Dahuting Han mu* (*Han tombs at Dahuting, Mi County, Henan*) (Beijing: Wenwu chubanshe, 1993), for numerous plates and accompanying line drawings. Large, beautifully crafted jade masks, their rings sometimes patterned to resemble jade *bi* discs (see Pearlstein's "*Bi* Discs" in this catalogue), have also been unearthed. For an extraordinary example in jade, see that excavated near Maoling, the tomb of Emperor Wu; Li Jian, ed., *Eternal China: Splendors from the First Dynasties* (Dayton: Dayton Art Institute, 1998), cat.no. 49 (this missing its ring), references cited therein; also one from the tomb of Zhao Mo, the second king of Nanyue (d. 122 BCE), whose ring is modeled with raised curls; *Nanyue wang mu yuqi: Jades from the tomb of the king of Nanyue* (Guangzhou/Hong Kong: Guangzhou Xihan Nanyue wang mu bowuguan et al., 1991), pl. 34. Upon excavation of this latter tomb, a large bronze ring-holder mask was found in place on each stone door of the front and main coffin chambers; six gilt and lacquered bronze masks that once adorned the wood coffin lay on the floor of the main coffin chamber. Many bronze and jade masks were likely attached to perishable materials, making it impossible to reconstruct their placement and function.

3. See, e.g., that from the tomb of King Cuo (d. ca. 310 BCE) of the state of Zhongshan at Pingshan, Hebei Province; *Chūgoku Sengoku jidai no yū: Chūzan Ōkoku bunbutsu ten* (*Treasures from the tombs of the Zhongshan kings*) (Tokyo: Tokyo National Museum, 1981), pl. 5. Another *hu* containing wine came from a Western Han tomb in Xi'an, Shaanxi; see Xi'an Shi wenwubao kaogusuo, "Xi'an beijiao Zhuyuan daxing Xihan mu fajue baogao" ("Report on the excavation of a Western Han tomb near the Zhu garden in northern Xi'an"), *Wenwu* 2003.12, pp. 32, 33, figs. 8–10.

4. Yang states that only bronzes showing three bands of relief around the body—one encircling the neck and two encircling the belly—should be designated *zhong*. He argues that *zhong* had become a standard measure for grain by Western Han. For his inventory of inscribed bronze vessels and list of contemporary textual references, see Yang Zhifeng, "Handai tong zhong yu liang zhi yan bian zhi guang xi xin tan" ("New inquiries into the relation between Han-dynasty bronze *zhong* and the development of units of capacity"), in *Su Bai xiansheng ba zhi hua dan jinian wenji* (*Essays in honor of the eightieth birthday of Su Bai*) (Beijing: Wenwu chubanshe, 2002), pp. 109–19. Yang does not discuss ceramic vessels.

Note, however, that *zhong* (the same character) is also defined as a Han-dynasty measure for liquid. See Michèle Pirazzoli-t'Serstevens, *The Han Dynasty* (New York: Rizzoli, 1982), p. 226, and references cited.

5. The richly furnished tomb of Liu Sheng (d. 133 BCE) at Mancheng, Hebei Province, contained six fine bronze *hu* (including three *fanghu*) and seventy-eight earthenware *hu*. See *Mancheng Han mu fajue baogao* (*Excavation report of the Han tombs at Mancheng*) (Beijing: Wenwu chubanshe, 1980), vol. 1, pp. 38–49, 120–26; vol. 2, pls. 4–7, 17–22. For discussion of these vessels, their placement in the tomb, and the role of such vessels in Han burial practices, see Jessica Rawson, "Chu Influences on the Development of Han Bronze Vessels," *Arts Asiatiques*, vol. 42 (1987), pp. 84–99. (Other Han bronzes, also called *hu*, include tall-necked, garlic-headed vessels and ovoid vessels with chain handles, not discussed here.)

Lacquered wood examples excavated from the Western Han Tomb 1 at Mawangdui, Changsha, Hunan (ca. 163 BCE), uninscribed but designated *zhong* by archaeologists, were found to contain traces of wine or broth. Painted ceramic vessels found in the same tomb, reported to contain "remains of a liquid material," are variously designated *zhong* or *hu*; the former are wider-bodied. See Hunan Sheng bowuguan and Zhongguo shehui kexueyuan kaogu yanjiusuo, eds., *Changsha Mawangdui yihao Han mu* (*Han Tomb 1 at Mawangdui, Changsha*) (Beijing: Wenwu chubanshe, 1973), vol. 1, pp. 80, 122–23, vol. 2, pls. 157, 240, 245. As the tomb was partially submerged upon discovery, contents of these vessels may be difficult to determine.

6. These vessels appear in stone engravings and reliefs of Eastern Han tombs in Shandong. See, e.g., Zucheng Xian bowuguan and Ren Rixin, "Shandong Zhucheng Han mu huaxiang shi" ("A Han carved stone tomb at Zhucheng, Shandong"), *Wenwu* 1981.10, fig. 7; and more clearly, Zeng Zhaoyu et al., *Yi'nan gu huaxiang shi mu fajue baogao* (*Excavation report on an ancient carved stone tomb at Yi'nan*) (Beijing: Wenhuabu wenwu guanliju, 1956), pls. 28 (no. 6), 48 (no. 35). As illustrated at Yi'nan and in excavated vessels, Eastern Han jars often have taller, faceted bases, by contrast with Western Han examples.

24 Ritual vessel (*hu* or *zhong*) with dragon and cloud designs

Western Han dynasty, 2d–1st century BCE. Bronze with incised decoration and gold and silver amalgams; h. 46.0 cm, diam. 36.0 cm. The Art Institute of Chicago, acc. no. 1927.315. Lucy Maud Buckingham Collection.

Encircling the shoulder and belly of this majestic vessel are two broad registers of dynamically intertwined dragons. Their profile heads with backswept horns, wide eyes, gaping, buck-toothed mouths, and their trunks with clawed forelegs flow into scrolling bands accented by decorative "cloud patterns" (*yunqi*). Double concave bands with cloud designs divide and border these registers; the same cloud designs encircle the sharply articulated mouth and ring-foot. Rising blades enclosing spade-like motifs climb the gently curving neck.

This fluent decor was incised into the bronze after casting. Filings of gold and silver were then liquefied in separate baths of hot mercury and these butter-like solutions brushed onto the bronze; the vessel was reheated to vaporize the mercury and then burnished, leaving a thin but brilliant two-toned surface. This technique, variously known as amalgam-, mercury-, or fire-gilding, created a splendid object with economical expenditure of precious metals.[1]

Accompanying this vessel to the Art Institute in 1927 was a dealer's report alleging its discovery three years earlier in Xianyang, Shaanxi.[2] But the widespread appearance of similar dragon arabesque and stylized cloud designs in Han bronzes and other mediums makes it difficult to identify its style as distinctive to a specific region.[3] Many scholars trace the origins of these designs to lacquer painting and other luxury arts perfected in the kingdom of Chu, which had dominated south-central China before the Qin conquest. These arts were perpetuated and disseminated throughout the Western Han empire.[4] Scholars also interpret both dragons and clouds—both being phenomena of flux and transformation—as graphic representations of the cosmic energy that Han-dynasty political theorists envisioned as animating the universe and portending good fortune (fig. 1).[5]

ELINOR PEARLSTEIN

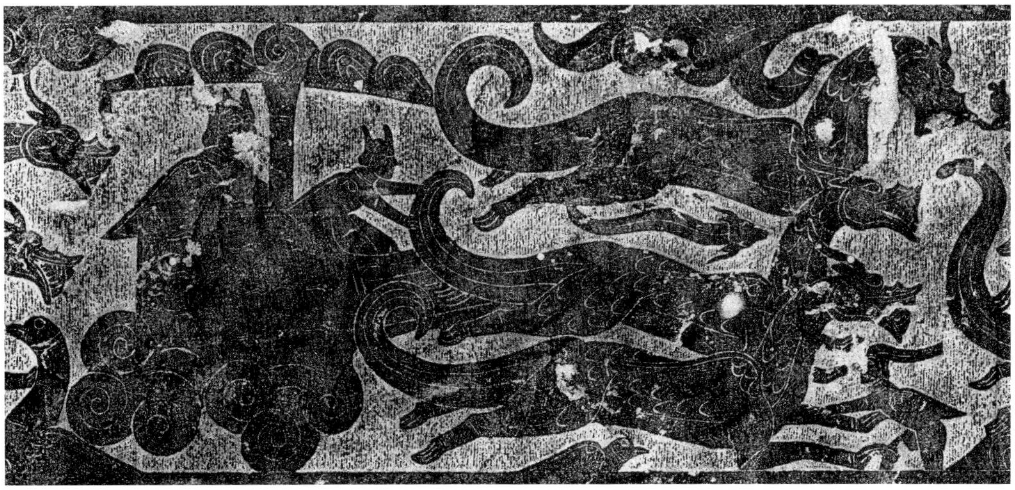

Fig. 1 *Dragons pulling a cloud chariot with winged Immortals*. Detail of Stone Chamber 1, Stone 1-R.2 (cat. no. 1.18). "Wu family shrines" rubbings. Princeton University Art Museum, acc. no. 2002-307.17.

Notes

1. For amalgam-gilding and silvering, see Robert Dale Jacobsen, *Inlaid Bronzes of Pre-Imperial China: A Classical Tradition and Its Later Revivals* (PhD diss., University of Minnesota, 1984), pp. 98–192; Joseph

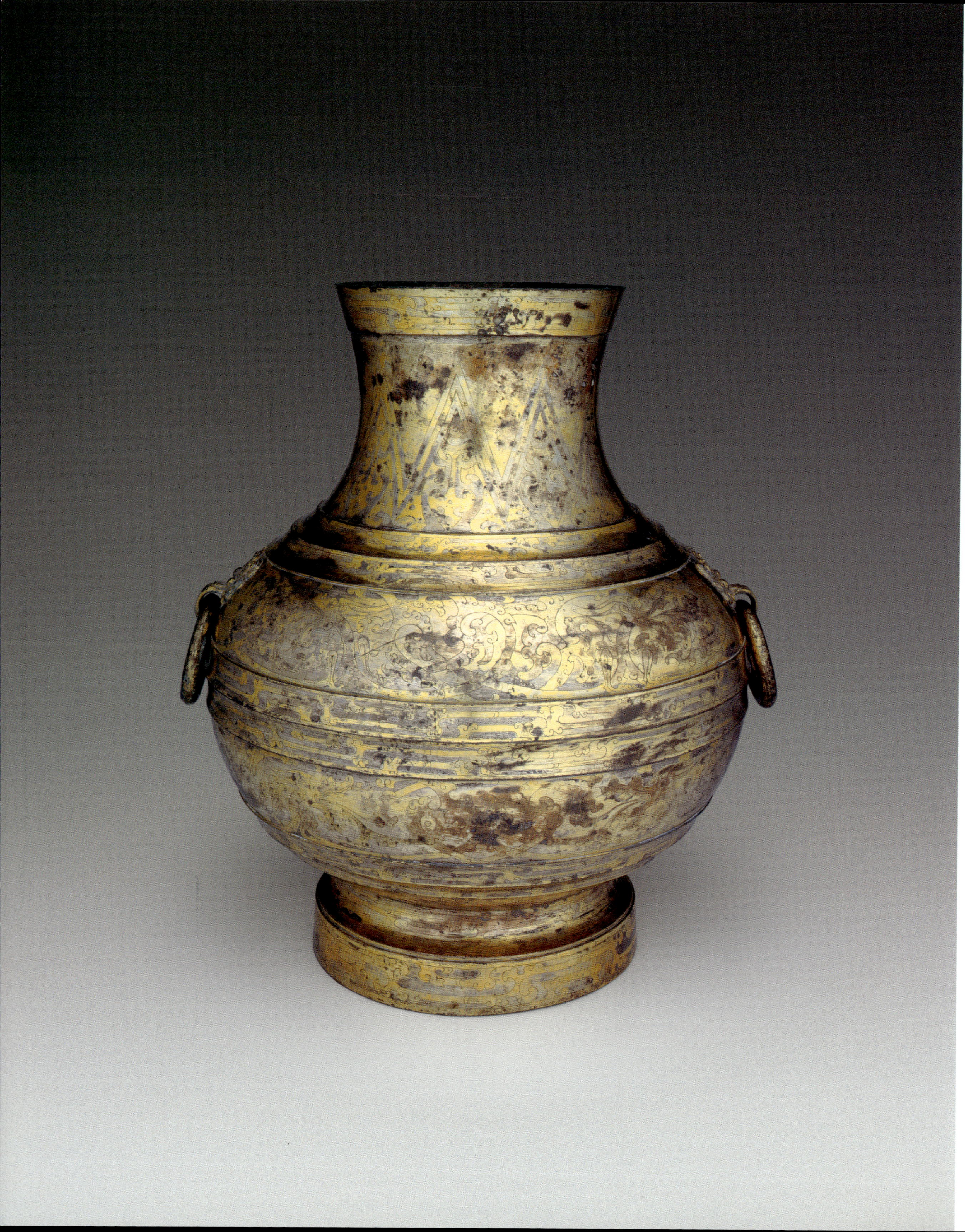

Needham with Lu Gwei-djen, *Science and Civilization in China*, vol. 5: *Chemical and Chemical Technology*, Part 2, *Spagyrical Discovery and Invention: Magisteries of Gold and Immortality* (Cambridge: Cambridge University Press, 1974), pp. 247–48; Paul Jett and W. T. Chase, "The Gilding of Metals in China," in *Gilded Metals: History, Technology, and Conservation*, ed. Terry Drayman-Weisser (London: Archetype Publications, 2000), pp. 149–51 and references cited.

2. Undated note, enclosed with invoice from Tonying & Co., New York. Early publications include Charles F. Kelley, "Two Gilt Bronze Jars of the Han Dynasty," *Bulletin of The Art Institute of Chicago*, vol. 21, no. 6 (September 1927), pp. 70–72; Umehara Sueji, comp., *Shina-kodo seikwa: Selected Relics of Early Chinese Bronzes from Collections in Europe and America* (Osaka: Yamanaka & Co., 1933), vol. 3, pt. I: pl. 223; Charles F. Kelley and Ch'en Meng-chia, *Chinese Bronzes from the Buckingham Collection* (Chicago: Art Institute of Chicago, 1946), pls. 72–74.

3. A smaller but similarly proportioned amalgam-gilt and silvered vessel in the Hakutsuru Museum, Kobe, Japan, features purely decorative cloud-scroll bands. Museum records attribute its provenance to Fengzhou, Shaanxi, about one hundred miles west of Xianyang (*Hakutsuru Bijutsukan meihensen* [*Kobe: Hakutsuru Bijutsukan*, 1989], pl. 66, p. 100). Recent excavations have unearthed bronzes with comparable designs in widely separated sites. An incense burner (*dou*) with domed lid of openwork dragons, displaying similar incised cloud-scroll bands and an amalgam-gilded surface, was excavated from a cave-tomb at Guishan, Xuzhou, Jiangsu, in 1972. Inscribed bronzes and coins found in this tomb suggest that its occupant was a descendant of the Han imperial house, who ruled as king of the Western Han fiefdom of Chu. The end of the state of Chu in 69 BCE provides a terminal date for this tomb. See Nanjing Sheng bowuguan, "Tongshan Xiaoguishan Xihan yatongmu" ("A Western Han cliff tomb in Xiaoguishan, Tongshan"), *Wenwu* 1973.4, pp. 21–34, illus. p. 23, fig. 5, p. 34, fig. 41; You Zhenyao, "An Everlasting Record of Craftsmanship: Treasures from Han Period Royal Tombs," *Orientations*, May 1989, pp. 56–57.

Intertwined dragons stylistically similar to those on catalogue number 24, but with coherent hind legs and tail, are cast in low relief on an extraordinarily large bronze rectangular plaque (115.1 × 57.7 cm) excavated from a Western Han tomb in north-central Shandong and preserved in the Zibo Provincial Museum. Scholars have identified this object, designed with suspension loops on its decorated face, as a mirror. See Shandong Sheng Zibo Shi bowuguan, "Xi'an Shi Qi wang mu Suiwangqi wu hang" ("The funerary pits round the princely tomb of the Qi Kingdom of the Western Han dynasty"), *Kaogu xuebao* 1995.2, p. 242 and pl. 13:1. This piece is not gilded.

4. This was first articulated by Jessica Rawson, "Chu Influences on the Development of Han Bronze Vessels," *Arts Asiatiques*, vol. 42 (1987), pp. 84–99. See also Chu origins of the incense burner cited in n. 3.

5. Wu Hung, "A Sanpan Shan Chariot Ornament and the Xiangrui Design in Western Han Art," *Archives of Asian Art*, vol. 37 (1984), pp. 38–59. For a different interpretation of these spiraling cloud patterns, some merged with zoomorphic images, see Martin J. Powers, "The Many Meanderings of the Meander in Early China," in *World Art: Themes of Unity and Diversity: Acts of the XXVIth International Congress of the History of Art*, ed. Irving Lavin (University Park: Pennsylvania State University Press, 1989), vol. 1, pp. 171–80.

25 Ritual vessel (*hu*)

Western Han dynasty. Bronze; h. 31.7 cm, w. 23.3 cm.
Princeton University Art Museum, acc. no. y1953-16. Gift of J. Lionberger Davis, Class of 1900.

Emphasizing the elegant proportions of this pear-shaped *hu* are single subtly concave relief bands of slightly different widths, one encircling its slightly flared mouth, and others at the shoulder, midriff, hip, and crisply angled foot. Two ring-holder masks between the shoulder and midriff bisect the body. The eyes of the masks are accented by upcurved lids and brows and their facial contours by raised S- and C-shaped curls. Thin parallel facets trace the circumference of the rings. Surface corrosion and incrustation obscure the once sharp edges of most of these features.

ELINOR PEARLSTEIN

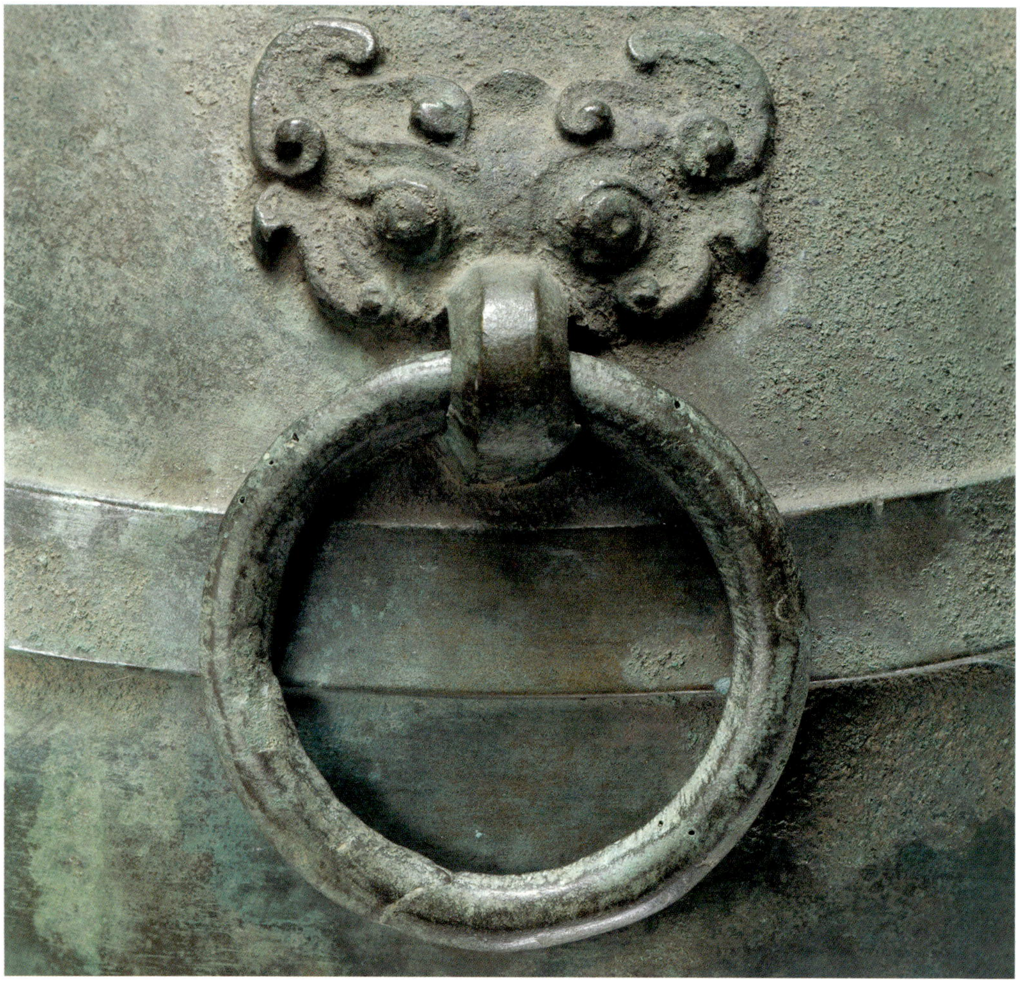

26 *Hu* storage jar with cover

Han dynasty. Gray earthenware with black, white, bluish lavender, and red pigments; h. with lid 55.0 cm, h. without lid 50.5 cm. Princeton University Art Museum, acc. no. y1986-111a–b. Museum purchase, Fowler McCormick, Class of 1921, Fund.

During the Han dynasty two categories of ceramic objects were produced to accompany the deceased in the tomb. The first consists of miniature clay replicas that create a microcosm of human activities, including servants, entertainers, houses, pavilions, stoves, wells, horses, barnyards, and farm animals. These models were meant to reflect the status and worldly pleasures of the deceased in life, and at the same time to provide for existence in the other world. The second category comprises life-size earthenware vessels and utensils, often painted or glazed, which were used for ritual offerings of food. This is a typical painted earthenware Han storage jar, or *hu* vessel, with its original cover. It has a handsome and elegant form, with a robust S-shaped profile. Two animal masks stamped from clay are attached opposite one another at the shoulder—a form adapted directly from bronze *hu*. Mostly articulated in low relief, each *taotie*-like animal mask has two prominent raised bosses for eyes flanked by a double spiral on each side, pointed horns, and a crest. Just below the eyes, a large loop of clay with the vestiges of a hole protrudes outward, referring to the bronze version of this animal mask, in which a bronze ring would have hung freely from this hole, forming a "ring-handle" mask (detail).[1]

The painted decoration balances, accentuates, and enlivens the form of the vessel. Black pigment was first applied to the entire surface of the *hu*, and then the white, red, and bluish lavender designs were painted on top of this black background. Wider white bands edged with thinner red lines divide the surface of the vessel horizontally into sections. In the upper section large isosceles triangles outlined in red hang point-down from the neck to the shoulder; in the middle of each triangle is a flower-like motif—a red circle with a white dot in the center and seven dots around the outer edge. Red and white cloud patterns swirl around the shoulder and belly of the vessel, creating a sense of vibrant energy and lively movement. Three large cloud spirals decorate the convex lid. Such swirling cloud scrolls embellished with additional curlicues are a ubiquitous motif in the Han pictorial and decorative vocabulary.

Comparable examples with similar decorative motifs and programs but in slightly different combinations have been unearthed in Shaanxi (fig. 1) and in Henan; the Henan vessel, unearthed at Luoyang City, is more closely similar to the present *hu*.[2] On all three *hu*, cloud patterns not only form the central decorative motif but also reveal the spontaneity of the brushwork—the deftness of the artist

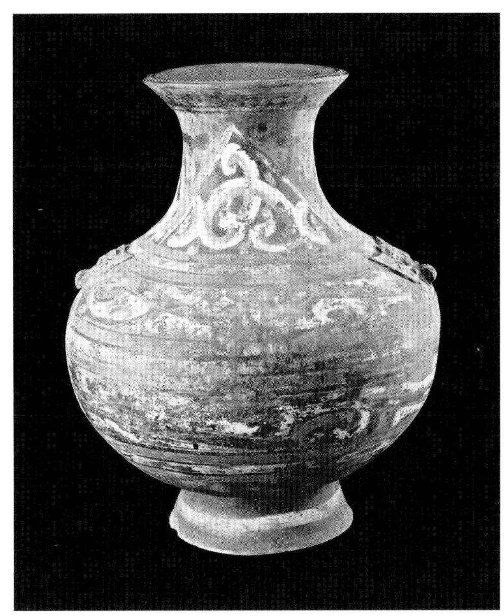

Fig. 1 Hu (*storage jar*). Han dynasty. Painted earthenware, lid missing; h. 32 cm. Shaanxi History Museum, Xi'an. From *Sanqin guibao, Shaanxi xin faxian wenwu jinghua*, p. 62.

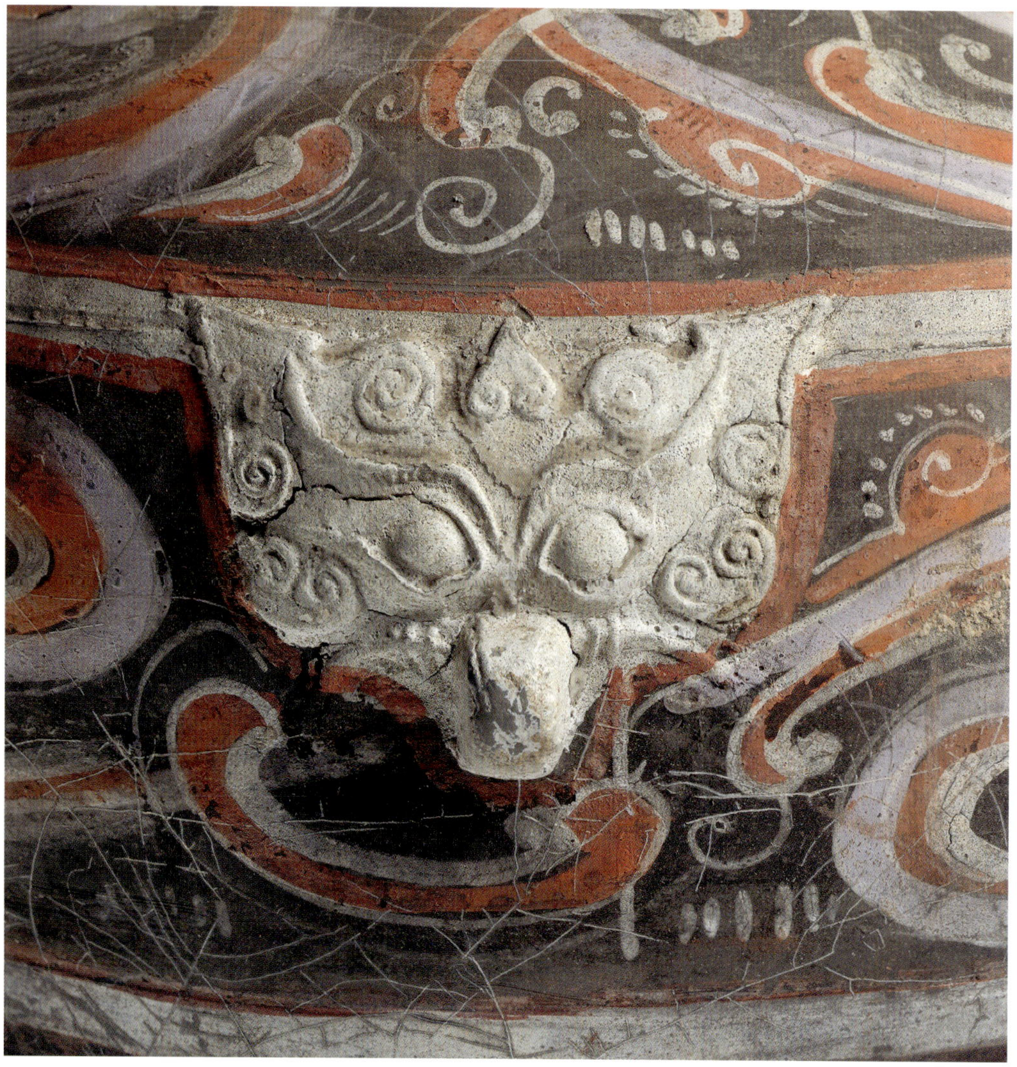

capitalizing on the flexibility and responsiveness of the brush.

The Chinese often identify such bronze and ceramic *hu* vessels as *zhong*, a reference to the ancient bronze measure used for grain. A lidded clay *hu* vessel unearthed from a Han Luoyang burial was filled with the remains of Job's tears, a grass with white pearly seeds that was occasionally substituted for standard cultivated cereals such as rice and barley.[3]

ANNETTE L. JULIANO

Notes

1. For an example of a Western Han bronze *hu* with *taotie* ring-handle masks, see *Shanxi wenwu guanzang zhenpin, qingtongqi* (*Selected cultural relics from local museums in Shanxi: Bronzes*), (Shanxi: Shanxi renmin chubanshe, n.d.), no. 177.

2. See *Sanjin guibao, Shaanxi xin faxian wenwu jinghua* (*Rare gems of the new archaeological discoveries in Shaanxi Province*) (Xi'an: Shaanxi renmin chubanshe, 2001), p. 62. The Henan vessel is currently in the Henan Provincial Museum and was published in *Treasures from the Han* (Singapore: Landmark Books, 1990), p. 98.

3. See Wang Zhongshu, *Han Civilization*, trans. K.C. Chang et al. (New Haven and London: Yale University Press, 1982), no. 58.

27 Storage vessel (*hu*)

Late Western Han dynasty. Earthenware with greenish glaze; h. ca. 48.5 cm, diam. at mouth 17.8 cm. Collection of Richard and Ruth Dickes.

The *hu* is a popular kind of container produced during the Han dynasty. Many undecorated bronze versions, of the type that was used in daily life, have been excavated from tombs. *Hu* made specifically for the tomb were of clay and covered with glazes that imitate the sheen of the more expensive metal containers. They often have a band of decor lacking on the utilitarian metal vessels. As an alternative to glazing, some *hu* bear painted designs that simulate much more expensive lacquer wares of this type (see cat. no. 26). Some of these unearthed ceramic urns still contain food products included as part of the tomb furnishings. For example, earthenware *hu* vessels excavated from Tomb 1 at Mancheng in Hebei Province contained animal and fish bones, as well as plant remains.[1]

The placement and selection of decor on catalogue number 27 is typical. A wide register of relief decor wraps around the shoulder of the vessel. Simulated handles, consisting of an animal mask (*pushou*) from which a flat circular ring is suspended, are placed opposite each other at the shoulder. Three raised bow-strings encircle the *hu* at the top of the register, and a single bow-string demarcates the bottom. Along the lower edge of the register, parallel lines periodically ascend to suggest a knoll, or rise dramatically and gather to become a hill. Striations on these hills suggest foliage. These rudimentary mountain forms create a landscape setting, but they also frame cells of space for the creatures inhabiting the intervals between the hills. Most of these creatures are depicted as silhouettes in profile view; some of the large felines, however, turn their heads to a frontal position. The decor within this register is comparable to that of *hu* vessels unearthed in Shaanxi Province in the environs of the capital of the Western Han dynasty. For example, a *hu* covered with a yellow glaze (h. 33.4 centimeters) was unearthed from a Western Han tomb at Xianyang in Xingping County.[2] The shoulder registers on both vessels contain the same kinds of motifs: hilly terrain, real and fantastic animals, and a backward-turning mounted hunter who prepares to loose an arrow at an animal running toward him. All of the beasts and figures are depicted in active poses, creating a dynamic scene.

Animals fill the register on the present *hu* more densely than on the Xianyang vessel. Without regard to their size in nature, animals are depicted relatively small in the lower part of the register, and larger in the upper part. Most of the creatures move in the same direction, from right to left, with the exception of the small boars and a figure confronting a leaping tiger. Within the face of each hill, silhouettes of a bird, a horned deer, a dragon, and a bear appear. Most of the animals are from the natural world, but fantastic dragons also are included in the terrain. In one instance a dragon flanks the left side of a handle and a tiger the right, perhaps taking on their roles as guardians of the cardinal directions east and west, respectively. A sole mounted hunter who turns to release an arrow at a tiger establishes the presence of humans in this landscape.

SUSAN N. ERICKSON

Notes

1. Zhongguo shehui kexueyuan kaogu yanjiusuo, and Hebei Sheng wenwu guanlichu, *Mancheng Han mu fajue baogao* (*Excavation report about the Han tombs at Mancheng*) (Beijing: Wenwu chubanshe, 1980), *shang*, p. 121.

2. Xianyang Shi wenwu kaogu yanjiusuo, Sun Derun, and He Ya'ni, "Xianyang zhibuchang Han mu qingli jianbao" ("Report on the Han-dynasty tombs at the textile mill at Xianyang"), *Kaogu yu wenwu* 1995.4, pp. 10–28, 87, fig. 22.2.

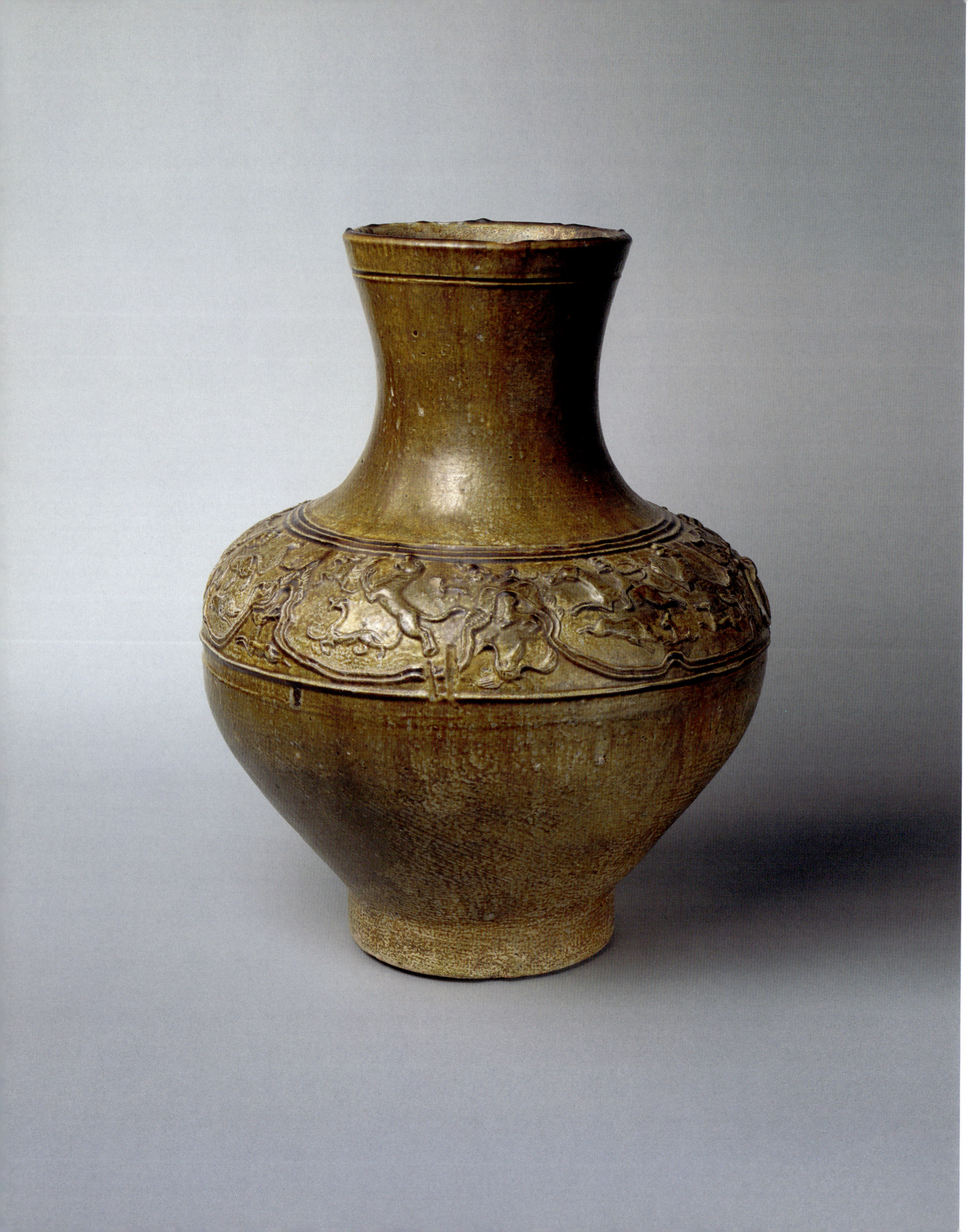

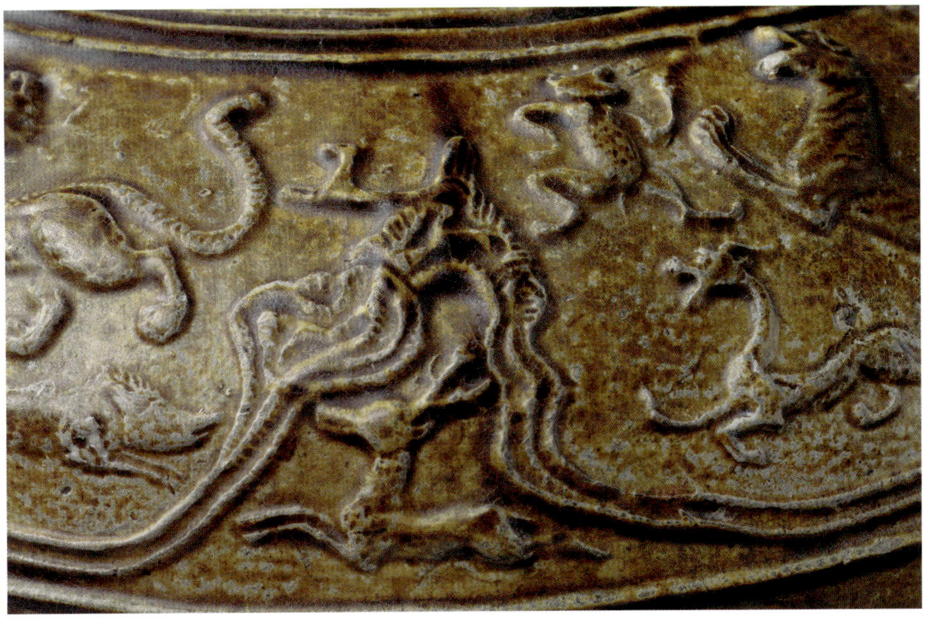

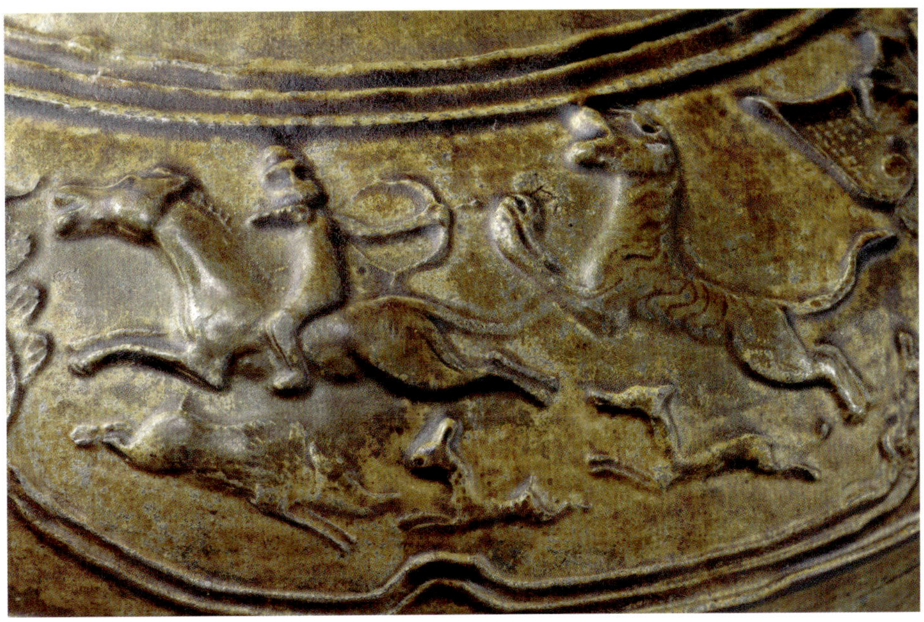

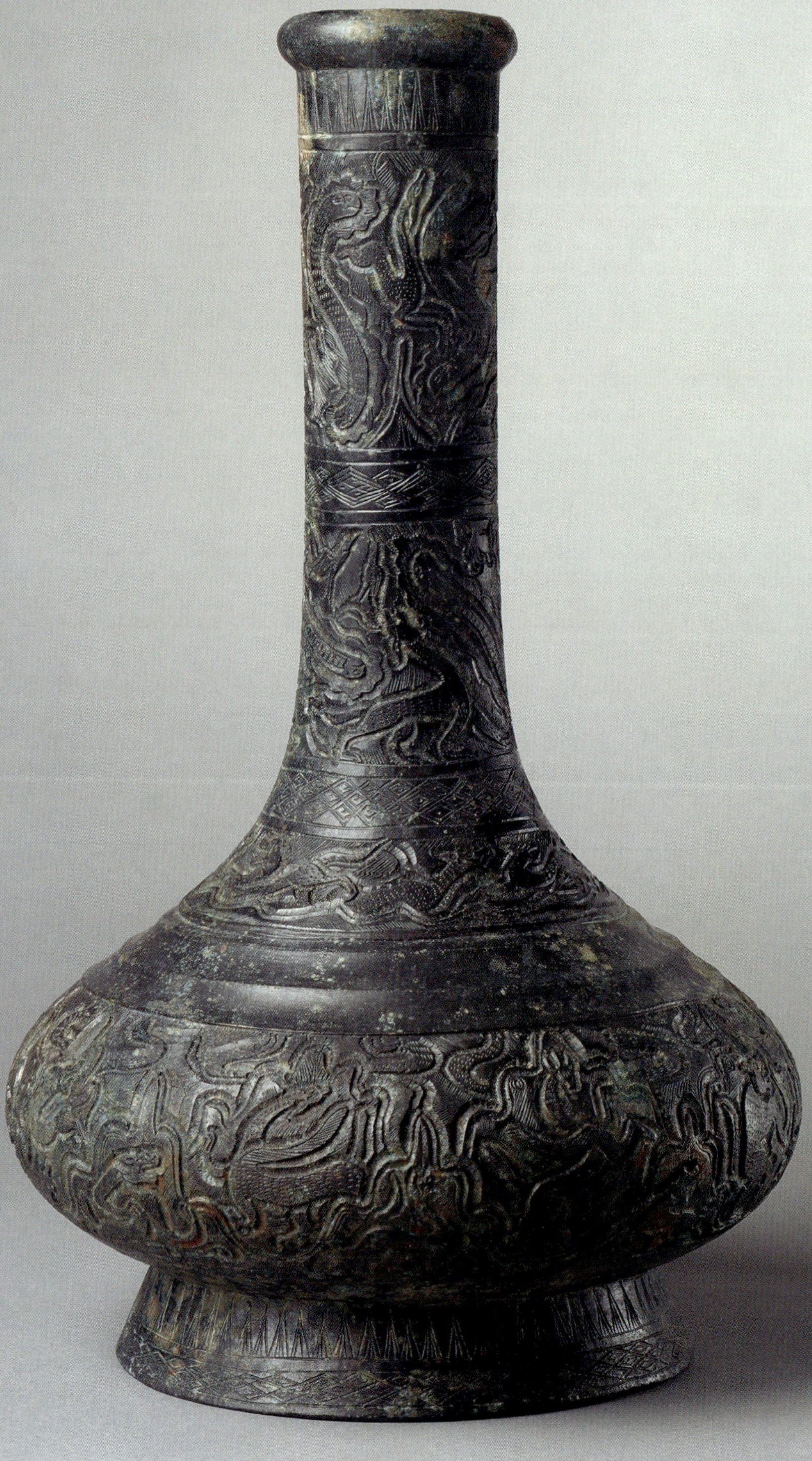

28

28 Vase with engraved decoration

Han dynasty, 1st century BCE–1st century CE. Bronze; h. 29.2 cm.
Private collection.

This handsome Han vase stands on a flared ring foot that supports a low-slung rounded belly, steeply sloping shoulders, and a tall, narrow, cylindrical neck ending in a smooth, thickly rolled lip.[1] Deeply carved outlines of energetic fantastic animals, wild beasts, birds, and landscape elements are densely packed into four registers decorating the surface of the vessel. Two of the registers wrap around the tall neck, the third around the top of the sloping shoulder; these registers alternate with narrower bands filled with repeated diamond or sawtooth patterns. The fourth register, the longest and widest, nearly covers the rounded belly. Two smooth concave bands, in sharp contrast to the decorated surfaces, separate the rounded belly from the tapered shoulder and narrow neck.

Two features of this rare and extraordinary vase make it distinctive, setting it apart from the majority of bronze vessels cast during the Han. The first is the use of engraving, or cutting of the metal, to define and embellish the decor. Incised channels undulate across the surface, outlining and separating a crowded array of real and fantastic animals, birds, snakes, and landscape elements; tool marks create not only these channels but also textures of repetitive triangles and parallel lines of varying lengths and directions (details).[2] The use of incised lines represents a significant departure from the traditional Chinese technique of casting decoration. In the first half of the twentieth century only a small number of comparable engraved bronzes were known to exist in museum and private collections outside of China. "Word of mouth" information supplied by dealers and collectors assigned these pieces a southern origin, mostly likely in Changsha, Hunan,[3] and suggested that they were a local tradition.

Subsequent archaeological evidence from China has confirmed an even more southerly origin, in Guizhou and Guangxi. One group of bronzes showing incised decoration was excavated from a large intact tomb in Hefu County, Guangxi, dating from the Western Han; the group includes a similar bronze vase of slightly smaller size and simpler decor, its bands filled with geometric patterns rather than animals (fig. 1).[4] An even closer parallel, although still with less elaborate decoration, comes from Han

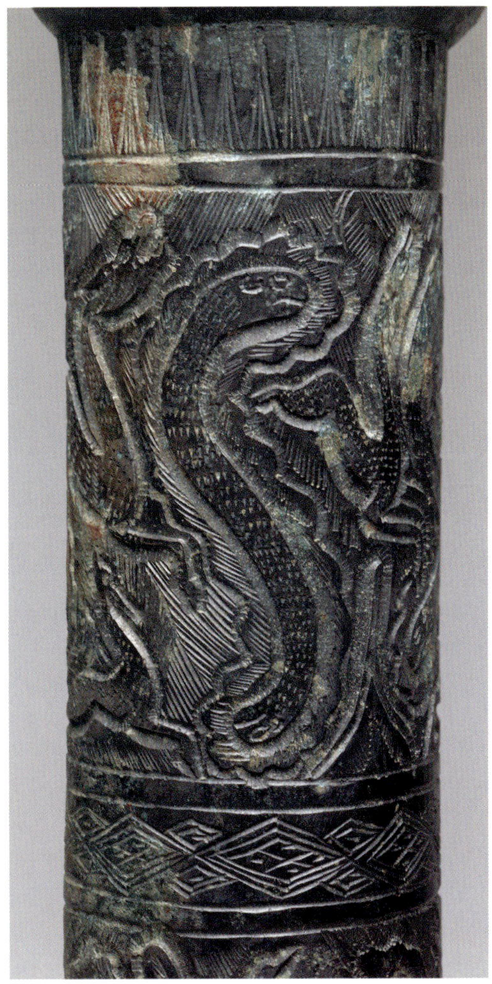

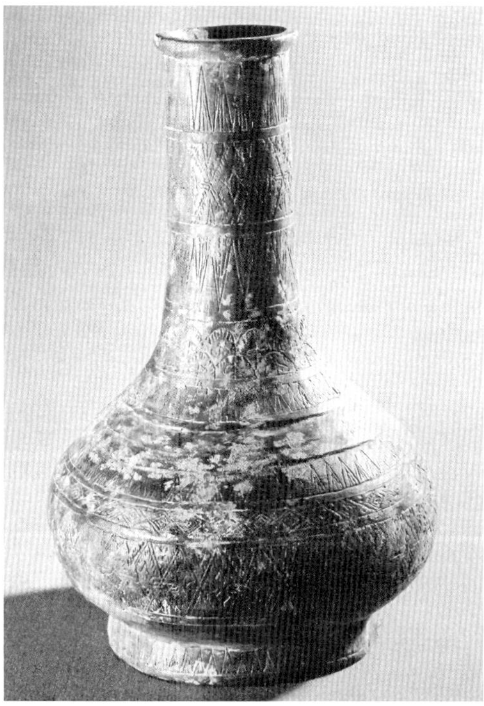

Fig. 1 *Vase*. Western Han dynasty. Excavated from Hefu County, Guangxi. Bronze with incised geometric patterns; h. 23.5 cm. From *Guangxi chutu wenwu*, no. 98 and p. 11.

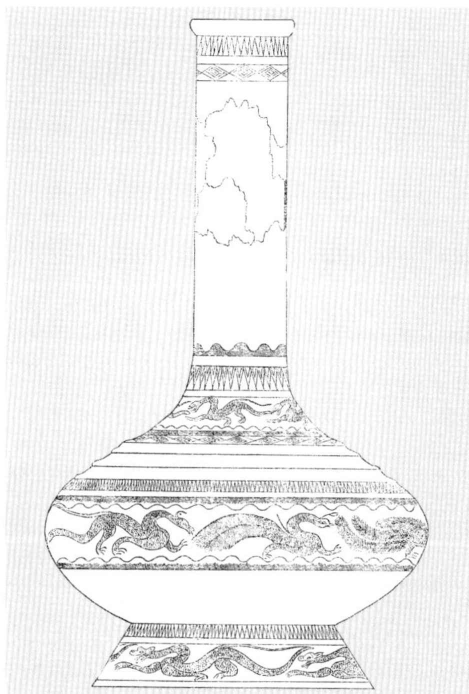

Fig. 2 *Vase*. Han dynasty. Excavated from Tomb 15, Pingba, Qingzhen County, Guizhou. Bronze with incised animals; h. 26.8 cm. From *Kaogu xuebao* 1959.1, p. 95, fig. 10:2.

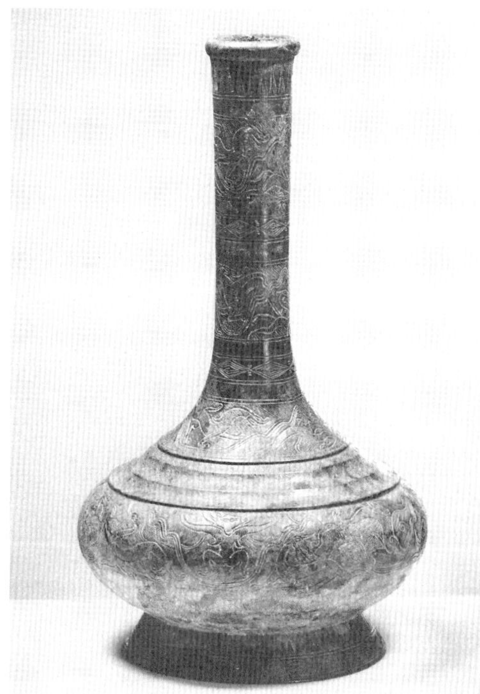

Fig. 3 *Vase*. Western Han dynasty. Bronze with incised animals, geometric patterns, and landscape elements; h. 23.3 cm. Collection of the late Dr. Paul Singer. From Jan Fontein and Tung Wu, *Unearthing China's Past*, p. 119, no. 52.

Tomb 15 in the village of Pingba, Qingzhen County, Guizhou (fig. 2).[5] Several comparable incised vessels are in the collection of the late Dr. Paul Singer. One bronze vase from the Singer collection shares the present vase's shape and organization of decor, with some related iconography as well as analogous execution (fig. 3).[6] A miniature covered tripod bowl from the Singer collection differs in size and shape but displays the diamond pattern, some of the landscape and animal elements, and in particular the same bold incising.[7]

The second distinctive feature of the present vase is its iconography. Both registers girdling the neck, one above the other and separated by a narrow band of diamond lozenges, include snakes with worm-like bodies, placed vertically or diagonally and dominating the narrow space. Each snake seems to have a head at each end of its body, and is enclosed in or radiating a scalloped, striated aura.[8] This scalloped edging that envelops the snake evokes a feeling that the snake may be underground or burrowing into the earth (detail, above). Interspersed between these snakes are animals; some resemble antlered deer, others are more fantastic. In the third register, encircling the upper shoulder, a bird-headed creature with a long, sharp beak and leonine and deer-like animals seem to dash around the vessel over a landscape of low hills suggested by an undulating textured band.

Nearly covering the rounded belly, the fourth and largest band unfolds a complex landscape composition teeming with creatures and activity. Overlapping scalloped lappets, each with a tall central peak, form hills or low mountains that structure the basic landscape (detail, below); often embellished with spirals, each hill form contains a fantastic creature or an animal, such as a dragon, deer, or feline. At every other hill, two snakes emerge from opposite sides of the hill and loop upward to face the peak. This compartmentalized style of early landscape composition appeared during the Han in many contexts, on hill jars, censers, *lian* boxes, stamped bricks, and other objects.[9] Overlapping compartments creating landscape spaces for animals and a hunt have been carved into the front chamber of the Eastern Han stone

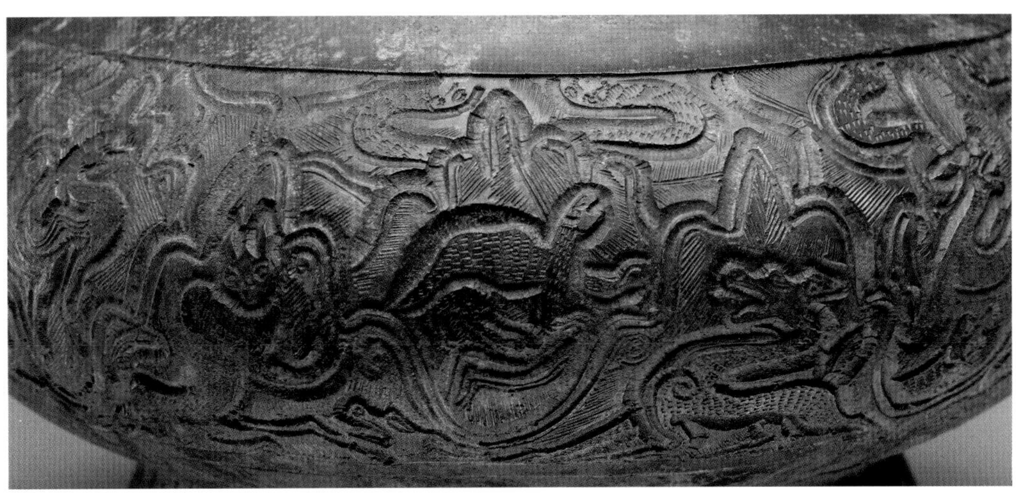

tomb of Minister Miao Yu at Pengcheng, Jiangsu.[10] A bronze wine warmer in the Freer Gallery of Art in Washington, D.C., parallels some of the motifs in the landscape on this vase, such as the mountain form with a central peak and spiral elements, but it is the combination of motifs, incising, and certain unusual iconographic features such as the snakes that gives this vase its distinction.

A much earlier pictograph of the snake appears in Shang-dynasty divination inscriptions on bone and tortoiseshell fragments, and the snake element is incorporated into the pictographs associated with sacrifice and death. Snakes appear on ritual bronze vessels as well. Whether or not this engraved bronze vase was made as part of a sacrificial ritual and then buried, the presence of the snake and the deer on the vase could refer to their natural association with death, transformation, and renewal. Snakes hibernate during the winter and emerge to slough off their skins in the spring, and male deer continually shed and re-grow their antlers.[11]

ANNETTE L. JULIANO

Notes

1. This vase was published in J. J. Lally & Co., *Bronze and Gold in Ancient China* (New York, 2003), no. 9.

2. Many of the textures incised on the vase were clearly drawn from other Han contexts; for example, the parallel lines or grooves used to embellish parts of the landscape as well as the animals can be found used in similar ways on stamped clay tomb bricks; see Michael Sullivan, *The Birth of Landscape Painting in China* (Berkeley and Los Angeles: University of California Press, 1962), figs. 36–37.

3. See the discussion of incised bronzes by Jan Fontein and Tung Wu, *Unearthing China's Past* (Boston: Museum of Fine Arts, 1973), pp. 118–27.

4. For the Western Han bronzes from Hefu County, Guangxi, see *Kaogu* 1972.5, pp. 20–30, and p. 24, fig. 4:1. See also *Guangxi chutu wenwu* (*Cultural relics unearthed from Guangxi*) (Beijing: Wenwu chubanshe, 1978), no. 98 and p. 11.

5. Tomb 15, Pingba Village, can be dated to 3 CE by an inscription on a lacquer cup from Sichuan found in the tomb; see *Kaogu xuebao* 1959.1, pp. 85–102, p. 95, fig. 10:2. See also Fontein and Wu, *Unearthing China's Past*, p. 121, fig. 55.

6. Fontein and Wu, *Unearthing China's Past*, p. 119, no. 52.

7. Ibid., p. 120, no. 54.

8. Apparently, strange "two-headed" snakes were residents of the bamboo thickets of Vietnam. This type of snake had markings on its tail that mimic the appearance of its head. Given the probable southern origin of these engraved bronzes, perhaps the presence of these snakes reflects the proximity of Guizhou and Guangxi to Vietnam and other Southeast Asian cultures. See Edward H. Schafer, *The Vermilion Bird* (Berkeley and Los Angeles: University of California Press, 1967), p. 216.

9. Michael Sullivan discusses the compartmentalized landscape device, its origin in ancient Assyrian art, and its modification in China and later in Central Asia; see Sullivan, *Landscape Painting*, pp. 132–38. Esther Jacobson, "Mountains and Nomads: A Reconsideration of the Origins of Chinese Landscape Representation," in *Bulletin of the Museum of Far Eastern Antiquities*, vol. 57 (1985), p. 147, argues that "the integrated development of a pictorial Chinese landscape representation must be sought in the nomad world and not in the Near East."

10. See *Wenwu* 1984.8, p. 25, fig. 8.

11. See various discussions of snakes by Sarah Allen, *The Shape of the Turtle: Myth, Art and Cosmos in Early China* (New York: State University of New York Press, 1991), pp. 71, 130–31, 163–64; Schafer, *The Vermillion Bird*, p. 139; Arthur de Carle Sowerby, *Nature in Chinese Art* (New York: John Day Co., 1940), pp. 105–7.

29 Chariot canopy shaft fitting (*bini*)

Western Han dynasty. Bronze; h. 25.0 cm, diam. 2.6 cm.
Princeton University Art Museum, acc. no. 2002-384. Museum purchase, Fowler McCormick, Class of 1921, Fund.

Raised bands divide this hollow tubular fitting into four horizontal registers. Each register is cast with intricate relief decoration; the raised designs have striated and stippled detailing, the background is finely striated. In carving the model for each register, one or two serpentine dragons were executed first; the enclosed spaces formed by the entwined dragon bodies were then set with major figures and delicate plant-like scrolls. Smaller animals and scrolls filled the remaining spaces. In one enclosure in the topmost register, two celestial hunters carry a boar slung upside down from a carrying pole, and below them a wild boar runs toward a slender, alert tiger. In the other enclosure in this register, an antlered deer lowers its head to graze, while below a hound chases a rabbit. In the second register a mounted archer riding at a gallop turns in the saddle to loose a Parthian shot at a charging tiger; below are two running hounds. The second enclosure holds a unicorn with a hound above and a tiger below. The third register is dominated by a peacock with a small disk in its beak and long tail feathers that sweep around the circumference; smaller animals include a hound chasing a rabbit and an antlered deer. In the fourth register the actors are a running camel, three monkeys, and two flying birds. The raised band that separates the second and third registers is wider than the other two and has three median ridges rather than one. Traces of wood and fabric remain on the interior of the shaft. The surface is lightly patinated with reddish brown and malachite green.

Fittings of this kind, called *bini* in Han texts, were used to reinforce the two joints of a chariot's canopy shaft. Hence they are often found in pairs in high-ranking tombs dating from the Spring and Autumn period through the Western Han dynasty. The earliest known chariot with canopy comes from an early Western Zhou chariot burial at Liulihe, Beijing, but to date neither Western Zhou or Eastern Han *bini* have been excavated.[1] Early Western Han tombs have disclosed several such fittings, however, with sections of the wooden pole meeting at a mortise and tenon join preserved inside them. Often the join was reinforced by a textile wrapping before it was inserted into the

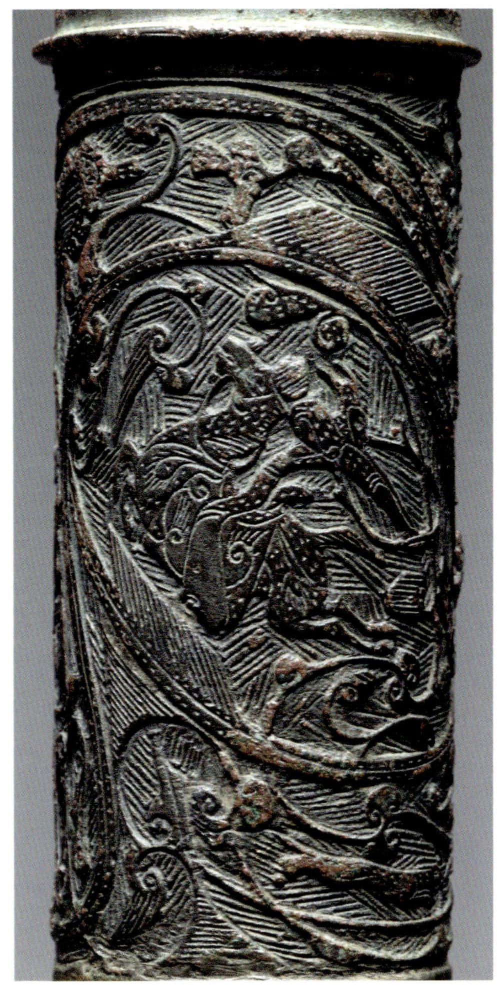

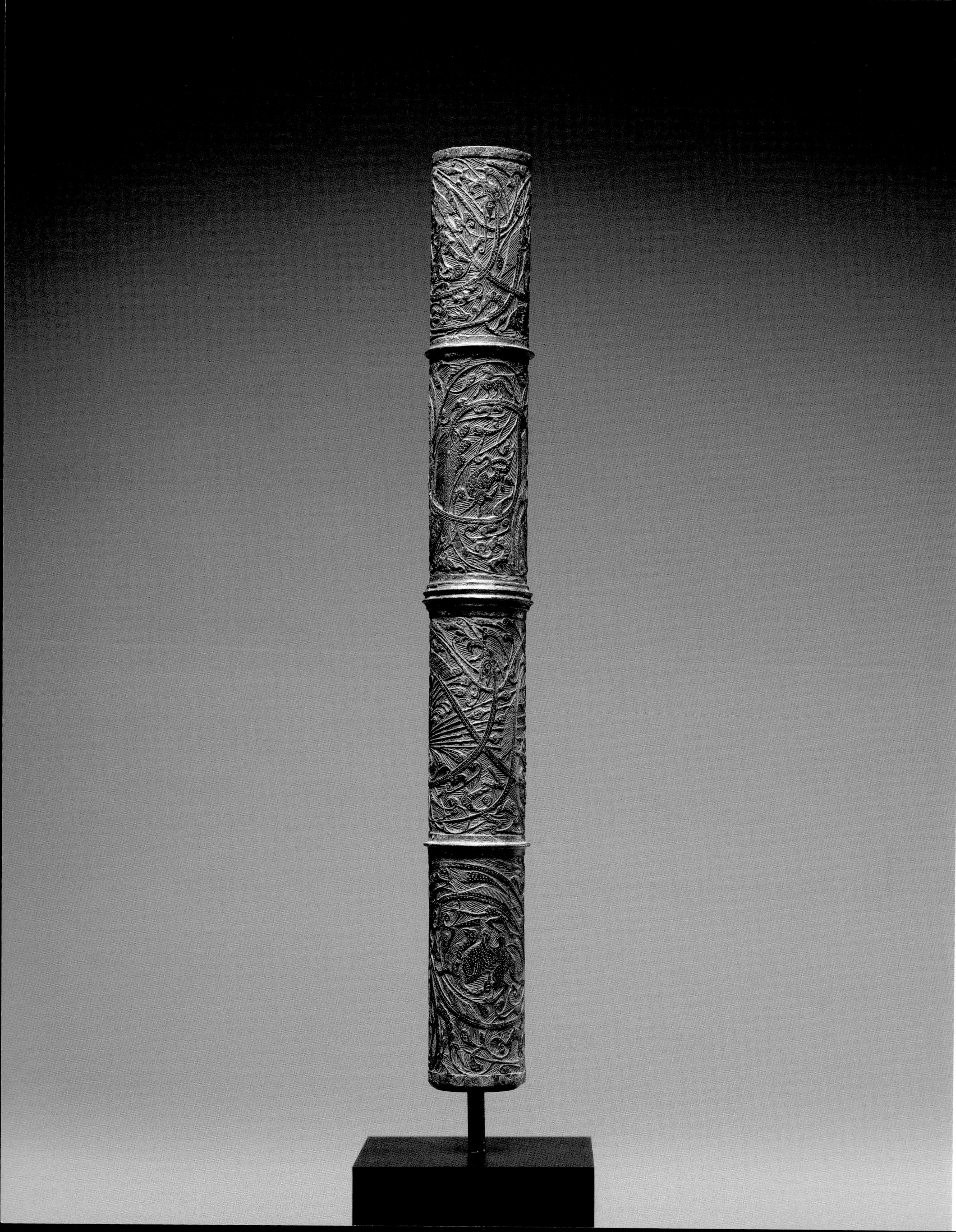

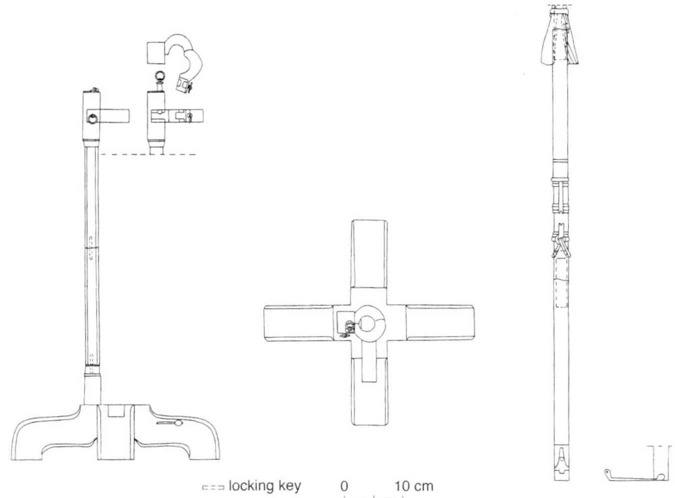

tube; sometimes wooden chocks or wedges were inserted. Some of the fittings have holes for attachment to the shaft.[2]

Sun Ji has theorized that the canopy with the upper part of the shaft could conveniently be detached at the upper *bini* and converted into a parasol to shield the nobleman when he had descended from his chariot; this practice is recorded in texts. He has further suggested that in battle or in a high wind or whenever the canopy was unwanted, it must have been similarly detached.[3] Yet the rabbet joints and the textile and wooden-chock reinforcement would have made such disassembly awkward, and frequent dismantling would also have loosened the joint and abraded the textile. Moreover, the rivets implied by the holes on *bini* would have made such disassembly virtually impossible. Finally, the uppermost section of the canopy shaft would have been too short to serve as a parasol stock. Archaeological evidence, in the form of the bronze model of a canopied chariot found in a pit at the foot of the tumulus at the First Emperor of Qin's mausoleum, shows that the lower end of the shaft enclosed by a *bini* was not directly attached to the chariot box as Sun suggested. Rather, it was connected by a mechanical lock to a canopy stand that stood on the chariot box. The locking device consisted mainly of two semicircular rings, one cast onto the stand and the other, movable, hinged to it. The end of the canopy pole enclosed by a *bini* was placed inside the fixed half-ring, and the movable half-ring was then locked to the fixed one (fig. 1).[4] It seems clear, therefore, that *bini* functioned simply to reinforce permanent joins.[5] The *bini* on the lower part of the pole might also have been used as a handle when the attendant dismounted the canopy from the chariot for use as a parasol.

The location of *bini* on the chariot and their rather large surfaces (compared with other chariot fittings) rendered them very suitable for complex decorations, in accord with the largely ceremonial function of chariots. One of the two *bini* would have been clearly visible to the aristocrat on board, whether he was standing or sitting on the chariot box. Nevertheless, decoration as complex and rich as that seen on the present fitting, with its abundance of animals in dynamic poses, is found in only five examples, and of those five only one has a provenance.[6] The present fitting stands out among the five in several aspects: instead of the inlay seen on the other four, it has patterns executed in relief; the ground to the patterns is striated, whereas on the other four it is plain; and the main design in the top register, along with the order of the motifs in the other registers, is distinctly different. The relief decoration and striated ground link it to a group of southern bronzes of the Western Han dynasty.[7] Yet the sweeping arcs on the present fitting can still be read as dragon bodies, and the dragons' heads are unmistakably indicated. In this respect the present *bini* is similar to one in the Tōkyō Geijutsu Daigaku, which resembles it also in the stippled detailing of the dragon bodies. The camel in the fourth register assumes exactly the same posture as the camel on a *bini* in the Miho Museum. It seems, therefore, that the present fitting was a hybrid of two traditions in bronze decor. The dragons derived ultimately from the lacquer designs popular in both south and north since late Eastern Zhou times. The relief and the striated background, which are southern features, might possibly have been inspired by embroidered silks. As Colin Mackenzie has pointed

Fig. 1 Diagram showing the structure of the canopy stand and canopy shaft from a bronze chariot model excavated from a pit west of the tumulus at the First Emperor of Qin's mausoleum complex, Lintong, Shaanxi, 221–206 BCE. From Qin Shihuang bingmayong bowuguan, *Qin Shihuang ling tong chema xiufu baogao*, p. 79, fig. 38.

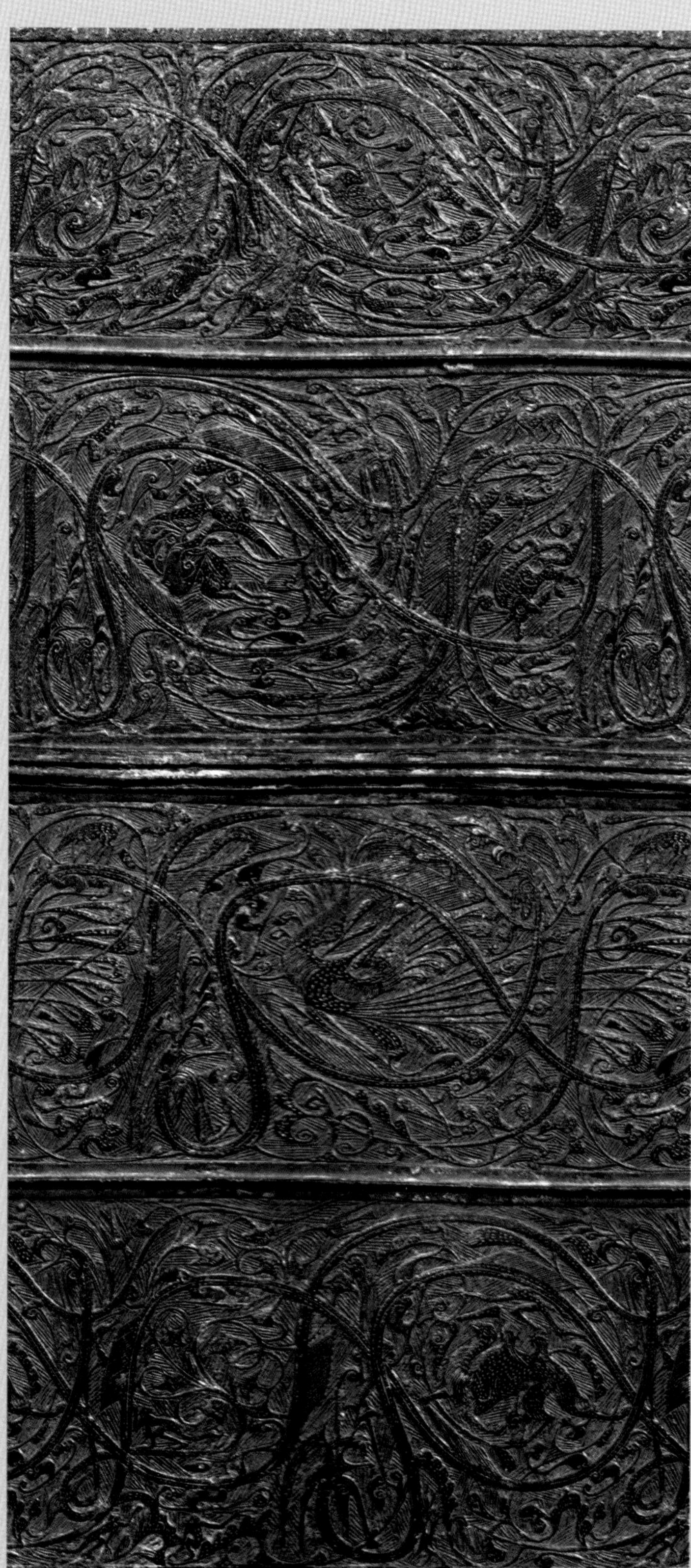

out, late Eastern Zhou and Han bronzes bearing relief designs of all sorts of animals may have been inspired by embroidery.[8] The striated background might imitate the weave of the silk, and the stippling very much resembles the pattern of stitches on embroidered animals. Furthermore, the plant-like scrolls, rare in other mediums, started to appear in Chu embroidered silks of the late Warring States period.

These myriad animals and celestial creatures have been interpreted in two ways. Wu Hung believes that the figures were images of auspicious omens (*xiangrui*), the creatures of good omen recorded in the hymns of the Han court.[9] Jessica Rawson rejects this interpretation, arguing that Wu overlooks both the overall setting and the fact that texts usually describe *xiangrui* as appearing singly or in small numbers, never the multitude of beasts represented in the chariot fittings. In her view the mountains, creatures, and plants might well represent the hunting parks mentioned in Chu literature and Han poetry. On the other four *bini* (see n. 6) the inlays of precious metals and semiprecious stones associate the bronze with the jewels in the poems, while the gilded scrolling that suggests mountains can be interpreted as *qi*, the "vital force" of the universe.[10]

Both interpretations may be credible in part. Yet the present fitting casts some doubt on their premises. First, are the scenes in fact visual realizations of a verbal conception, as both Rawson and Wu assume? Second, when the "mountains" were still recognizably dragons, as on the present fitting and the one in Tokyo, would Han viewers have understood the scene as a hunting park? Would they have considered the dragons to be "yellow dragons," which were *xiangrui*? How do the present dragons differ from the dragon in the top register of the Dingxian chariot fitting, which Wu interprets as a "yellow dragon"? Notice that the dragons on our present fitting have no color! If the major motifs on *bini* were intended to represent auspicious beasts, why does the motif of a mounted archer shooting a tiger appear on four of the five known examples? Third, can the scrolls be interpreted simultaneously as both mountains and *qi*, especially when some of them are unmistakably dragons? Fourth, since there is no metal or stone inlay on the present object, where shall we find the jewels mentioned in the texts? Is the present fitting a partial representation of a text? Fifth, though it is true that the theme of strange and miraculous creatures in certain kinds of settings was persistent in Han time, designs that originated as dragons had to undergo a lengthy development before they could serve as mountain settings or represent *qi*, as Max Loehr demonstrated long ago.[11] Meanings change over time. Should we agree with Loehr that these Han designs had not yet evolved to become a picture? Is the present decoration perhaps comparable instead with the Roman "inhabited scroll," which was sometimes overloaded with symbolism but also admired for its decorative richness? As in the Roman scroll, the multitude of plants and animals that figure on the Chinese shaft fittings could have been placed there for wholly or partly aesthetic reasons.[12]

HAICHENG WANG

Notes

1. Sun Ji, *Handai wuzhi wenhua ziliao tushuo* (*Illustrated history of Han antiquities*) (Beijing: Wenwu chubanshe, 1991), p. 107; Sun Ji, *Zhongguo gu yufu luncong* (*Essays on ancient Chinese vehicles and garments*), 2nd ed. (Beijing: Wenwu chubanshe, 2001), pp. 32–34.

2. Guangzhou Shi wenwu guanli weiyuanhui et al., *Xihan Nanyue wang mu* (*Tomb of the Western Han king of Nanyue in Guangzhou*), 2 vols. (Beijing: Wenwu chubanshe, 1991), vol. 1, p. 94; vol. 2, pls. 51.1–2; Henan Sheng shangqiushi wenwu guanli weiyuanhui et al., *Mangdang Shan Xihan Liang wang mudi* (*Cemetery of the Western Han king of Liang at Mangdang Shan*) (Beijing: Wenwu chubanshe, 2001), pp. 44–46, figs. 20.5, 20.7, pl. 10; Zhongguo shehui kexueyuan kaogu yanjiusuo et al., eds., *Mancheng Han mu fajue baogao* (*Excavation report of the Western Han tombs at Mancheng*), 2 vols. (Beijing: Wenwu chubanshe, 1980), vol. 1, pp. 191–92, 195, fig. 132.12, pp. 322–24, fig. 219.7; vol. 2, pls. 130.3, 224.3. Scholars have tried in vain to relate different types of chariots buried in tombs to those recorded in transmitted texts; see Gao Chongwen, "Xihan zhuhouwang mu chema xunzang zhidu tantao" ("On the chariot burial system in the kings' tombs of the Western Han dynasty"), *Wenwu* 1992.2, pp. 37–43; Zheng Luanming, "Xihan zhuhouwang mu suojian de chema xunzang zhidu" ("Chariot burial system seen from the kings' tombs of Western Han"), *Kaogu* 2002.1, pp. 68–75.

3. See n. 1 above.

4. Qin Shihuang bingmayong bowuguan, *Qin Shihuang Ling tong chema xiufu baogao* (*Restoration report of bronze chariots and horses unearthed from the Qin Shihuang Mausoleum*) (Beijing: Wenwu chubanshe, 1998), pp. 21, 79, fig. 38, pls. 15–17.

5. Jenny So rightly pointed out this function but without explanation. See Miho Museum, *Miho Museum, South Wing* (Shigaraki: Miho Museum, 1997), p. 212.

6. One from Lelang, Korea, now in the Tōkyō Geijutsu Daigaku collection, see Tōkyō Geijutsu Daigaku, ed., *Zōhin zuroku* (*Catalogue of the Tōkyō Geijutsu Daigaku collection*) (Tokyo: Tōkyō Geijutsu Daigaku, 1976), vol. 5: *Kōgei* (*Crafts*), no. 7; reproduced in *Tōkyō Geijutsu Daigaku Shozō meihinten* (*Catalogue of an exhibition of the Tōkyō Geijutsu Daigaku Collection held at Tokyo National Museum, September–October, 1977*) (Tokyo: Tōkyō Kokuritsu Hakubutsukan, 1977), no. 67. One in the collection of Marquis Hosokawa; see M. I. Rostovtzeff, *Inlaid Bronzes of the Han Dynasty in the Collection of C. T. Loo* (Paris and Brussels: G. Vanoest, 1927), pls. 2–3; reproduced in Max Loehr, "The Fate of the Ornament in Chinese Art," *Archives of Asian Art,* vol. 21 (1967–68), p. 14, fig. 14. One in the Miho Museum; see Miho Museum, *Miho Museum, South Wing*, no. 108; reproduced in Eskenazi, 1991 sales catalogue, no. 16, and Li Xueqin and Sarah Allan, *Ouzhou suo cang Zhongguo qingtongqi yizhu* (*Chinese bronzes: a selection from European collections*) (Beijing: Wenwu chubanshe, 1995), no. 207. For one excavated example from Dingxian, Hebei, see Zhongguo qingtongqi quanji bianji weiyuanhui, ed., *Zhongguo qingtongqi quanji* (*Complete catalogue of Chinese bronzes*), 15 vols. (Beijing: Wenwu chubanshe, 1993–1998), vol. 12, no. 151; reproduced in Wu Hung, "A Sanpan Shan Chariot Ornament and the Xiangrui Design in Western Han Art," *Archives of Asian Art*, vol. 37 (1984), pp. 40–41, figs. 1a–g.

7. Cf. Li Xueqin and Sarah Allan, *Ouzhou suo cang Zhongguo qingtongqi yizhu*, nos. 186, 192–93; see also Sarah Allan, "Yi zu Handai zhenke tongqi" ("A group of incised bronzes of the Western Han dynasty"), in ibid., pp. 423–28.

8. Colin Mackenzie, "The Influence of Textile Designs on Bronze, Lacquer and Ceramic Decorative Styles during the Warring States Period," *Orientations*, September 1999, pp. 88–91; reprinted in *Chinese Bronzes: Selected Articles from* Orientations *1983–2000* (Hong Kong: Orientations Magazine, 2001), pp. 337–46.

9. Wu Hung, "Sanpan Shan Chariot Ornament," pp. 38–59.

10. Jessica Rawson, "Commanding the Sprits: Control Through Bronze and Jade," *Orientations*, February 1998, pp. 40–43; reprinted in *Chinese Bronzes: Selected Articles from* Orientations *1983–2000*, pp. 288–300. Before Rawson, Shi Shuqing pointed out the relation with Han literature. See Shi Shuqing, "Woguo gudai de jincuo gongyi" ("The Inlay technique of China"), *Wenwu* 1973.6, p. 70.

11. Max Loehr, "The Fate of the Ornament in Chinese Art," pp. 11–15.

12. Michèle Blanchard-Lemée et al., *Mosaics of Roman Africa* (New York: George Braziller, 1995), pp. 249–79; James Trilling, *The Language of Ornament* (New York: Thames & Hudson, 2001), fig. 120.

Chariot Canopy Shaft Fitting: Potent Images and Spatial Configurations from Han Tombs to Buddhist Caves

Images of fantastical beasts and auspicious creatures adorn this cast bronze chariot fitting, creating a teeming forest landscape that is part real, part imaginary. In the topmost of four registers celestial hunters carry a captured boar slung upside down from a shoulder pole, deer graze, and a hound chases a hare. In the second register are an auspicious unicorn and a peacock preening its majestic feathers, as well as monkeys and birds.[1] In the same register a mounted archer at full gallop turns in his saddle to loose a Parthian shot at a feline.

The influence of the Silk Road upon the world of the Western Han dynasty is apparent in this object. Not only the Parthian shot but the camel in the lowest register alludes to western Asia, scene of Han Wudi's (r. 140–87 BCE) military expansion, of trading caravans, and of exploration.[2] Wudi launched missions both diplomatic and military into present-day Central Asia, seeking the renowned "blood-sweating" horses of Ferghana as cavalry chargers, and exotic creatures such as camels and peacocks as prestige-enhancing tribute from foreign kingdoms.[3] He also sent forth expeditions to search for the elixir of immortality and for the haven of deathlessness at Mount Kunlun, where the Immortals reside, thought to be in the far western regions.

The four registers of the present bronze fitting are separated by a raised triple-ridged band at the center and by narrower bands dividing register one from two, and three from four. Indentations in the center band may originally have held inlays. Within each register, rhythmic undulations of dragons unify the landscape, their serpentine bodies metamorphosizing into stylized cloud breath, or cloud pattern (*yunqi*).[4] The dragons' bodies as well as the cloud pattern are in higher relief than the other animals, and interlace not only with themselves but also with the animals' bodies.[5] In combination with the striated ground they serve to frame and highlight the placement of the animals inhabiting the dense landscape. These bronze chariot fittings[6] are among the earliest depictions of landscape in Chinese art.

Not only the imagery on the bronze but the shape of the bronze itself, as well as its placement in the chariot, are significant. Perhaps the four registers on this tubular bronze fitting, which formed part of the shaft connecting the carriage box below with the parasol above, functioned like a stupa pillar in later Buddhist

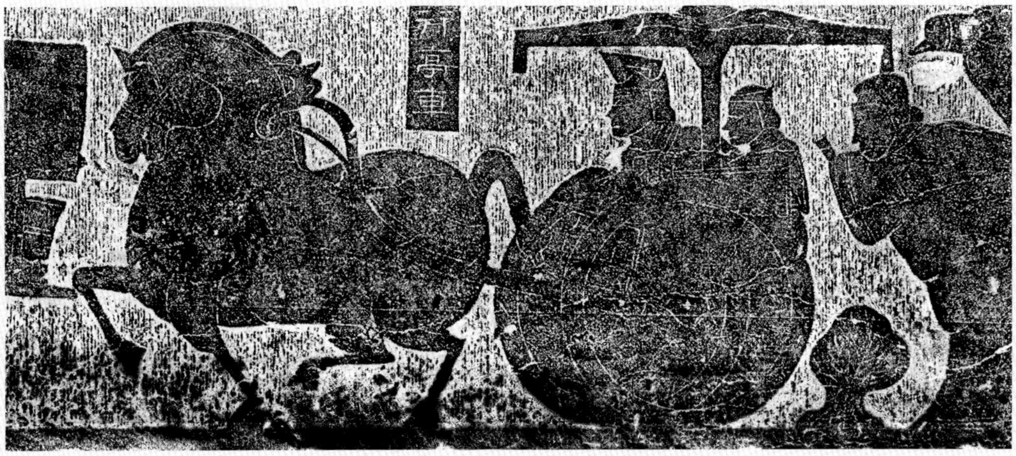

Fig. 1 *Canopied chariot.* Detail of Stone Chamber 1, Stone 1-S.4.a (cat. no. 1.6). "Wu family shrines" rubbings. Princeton University Art Museum, acc. no. 2002-307.5.

caves. In central-pillar caves at Dunhuang the central pillars typically have three registers with flying *apsarases* (*feitian*) at the highest level and donor figures at the base. As the viewer's gaze moved from bottom to top, the stupa pillar created a visual link between the mundane and spiritual worlds, allowing the devotee to begin his journey of spiritual enlightenment. The pillar was activated by the worshiper's circumambulation, just as rituals in the tomb might have activated the journey of the deceased from this world to the afterlife.

For much the same purpose, the architecture within Han-dynasty tombs often served as cosmic representation. Tomb pillars might function as axes mundi, cosmic structures like Mount Kunlun, connecting heaven and earth. The Western Han text *Huainanzi* describes the potency of this mountain as a cosmic pillar of the liminal realm between the mundane and spiritual worlds:

If one climbs to a height double that of the
Kunlun Mountains (that peak) is called
Cool Wind Mountain.
If one climbs it, one will not die.
If one climbs to a height that is doubled again,
(that peak) is called Hanging Garden.
If one ascends it, one will gain supernatural power
and be able to control the wind and the rain.
If one climbs to a height that is doubled yet again,
it reaches up to Heaven itself.
If one mounts to there, one will become a god.
It is called the Abode of the Supreme Thearch.[7]

The ascension to each succeeding higher peak of the mountain not only imparted greater supernatural power but brought the climber closer to the land of the Immortals. In the late Eastern Han tomb at Yi'nan, a stone pillar connecting the floor with the ceiling of the tomb depicts the mountains of Kunlun. The mountains rest on the back of a dragon; the Queen Mother of the West resides at the pillar's apex.[8] Thus the tomb pillar, like the mountain, might act as a conduit to immortal realms.

In addition to the vertical ascent enabled by a single pillar, the arrangement of multiple pillars in a tomb might provide a horizontal path to guide the soul on its afterlife journey. The horizontal path may be implied in the Eastern Han tomb at Anqiu in Shandong, where we find three pictorially carved pillars on axis down the center of the tomb from the door to the rear wall.[9] In tandem these pillars along with their pictorial decor may have outlined a path toward the afterlife for the soul of the deceased. This architectural pattern of multiple pillars with pictorial decor down the center of the tomb also occurs in Eastern Han tombs at Cangshan[10] and Yi'nan. Between this sort of horizontal progression and the vertical imagery seen in multiple registers on tomb pillars and on the present chariot fitting, there may well have been a relationship. The pictorial images and configurations of the tomb and its pillars, and of the chariot and its shaft fitting, all functioned as "embodied images" (*ti xiang*) that helped transport the soul in its journey from this world to the afterlife.[11]

Yet another spatial configuration may be embodied by the *bini* chariot fitting, which connected a square chariot box below with a round canopy above, as seen in the "Wu family shrines" (fig. 1).[12] We can extrapolate that the

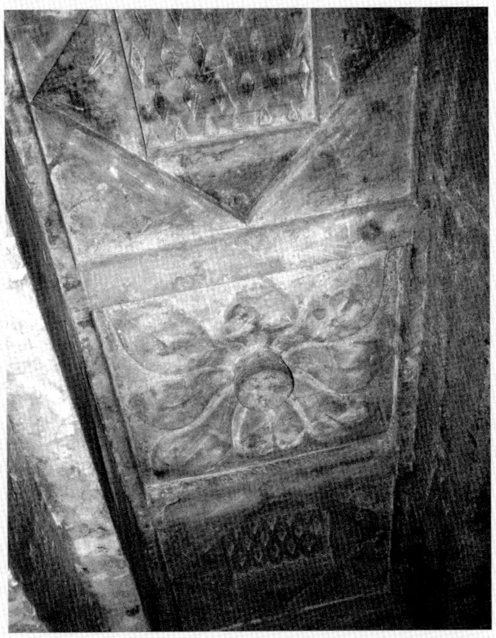

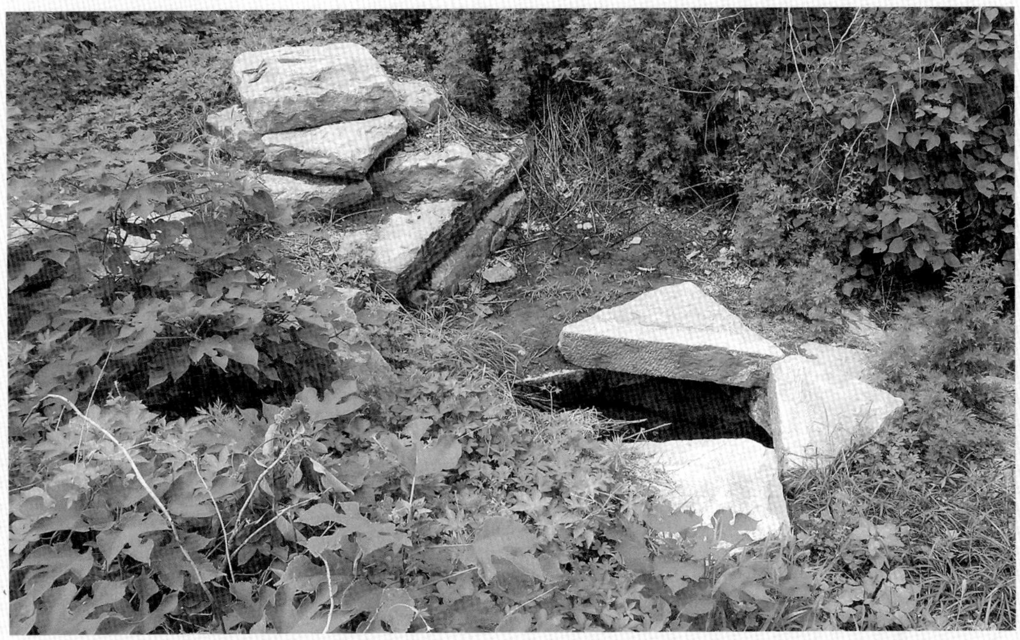

tubular shaft fitting might have functioned as an axis mundi connecting round heaven with square earth.[13] We see this juxtaposition of a circle in a square in the ceiling pattern of many Han tombs, including the Western Han tomb at Sanpan Shan[14] in Henan Province, as well as in the Eastern Han tombs at Cangshan and Yi'nan[15] (fig. 2) and in Tombs 1 and 2 at the Wu family cemetery in Jiaxiang County (fig. 3). The ceiling pattern called the "celestial well" or "well of heaven" (*tianjing*) is a *laternendecke* ceiling, typically composed of a square containing a rotated square that in turn sometimes contains a central painted circle. The "celestial well" functioned much like a cosmic mountain, allowing the deceased to achieve heavenly access. One of the earlier textual references—by Xue Zong (d. 243 CE)—describes this architectural form: "Right in the middle of the ridgepoles they intersected timbers, making a square like the well curb."[16]

At Dunhuang the *tianjing* ceiling motif was quite commonly used to exemplify Buddhist ritual space, drawing upon earlier Chinese

Fig. 2 Tianjing *ceiling as seen from inside*. Tomb 1, Yi'nan, Shandong. Photo by author, 2002.

Fig. 3 Tianjing *ceiling as seen from outside*. Tomb 1, Wu family cemetery, Jiaxiang County, Shandong. Photo by Cary Y. Liu, 2004.

cosmology and architectural forms to sinicize a foreign religion. At Dunhuang, too, it is often found in central-pillar caves.[17] But did the *tianjing* have the same meaning when transferred from a tomb to a Buddhist cave-chapel? There is compelling evidence that indeed it did. In Cave 248, a Northern Wei[18] cave-chapel at Dunhuang, there is a central pillar for the worshiper to circumambulate. On three sides of the central pillar, but not in the front, which faces the entrance of the cave-chapel, there are single rows of *tianjing* squares.[19] A ceiling with a trapezoidal cross section runs across the front between the central pillar and the front entrance. The sloped sides of the ceiling are decorated with rafters, and across the top is a row of *tianjing*. Directly under the *tianjing* on both side walls (north and south) are painted windows depicted as partly open.[20] There have also been reports of an inscription under a *tianjing* motif in Cave 249, describing it as a *tianchuang,* or "window to heaven," but this cannot be verified.[21]

Sima Qian in the *Hanshu*, writing about Han Wudi, reveals how imagery on chariot fittings was perceived during his time. The Emperor's exorcist (*fangshi*) Shaoweng says to him:

> "I perceive that Your Majesty wishes to commune with the spirits. But unless your palaces and robes are patterned after the shapes of the spirits, they will not consent to come to you." He fashioned five chariots, symbolizing the five elements and painted with cloud designs, and on the days when each of the five elements was in ascendancy, he would mount the appropriate chariot and ride about, driving away the evil demons. He also directed the emperor to build the Palace of Sweet Springs, in which was a terrace chamber painted with pictures of Heaven, Earth, the Great Unity, and all the other gods and spirits. Here Shaoweng set forth sacrificial vessels in an effort to summon the spirits of Heaven.[22]

Munakata translates the "five chariots" as *yunqi* chariots (*yunqi che*), that is, chariots whose ritual efficacy derived from images of "cloud breath" represented on tubular shaft fittings like the present one.[23] He posits that what he calls the *yunqi*-mountain design on the chariot parts was intended to enhance the power of exorcism to "drive away evil demons."[24] *Yunqi* also played a similarly protective role in the imagery on Lady Dai's famous lacquer-painted coffin from the early Western Han Tomb 1 at Mawangdui, where its swirls intermingle with various creatures, including human-animal chimeras.[25]

Much of the imagery in Han-dynasty tombs was reduplicated, thereby augmenting its spiritual efficacy in furthering the journey to the afterlife. Potent imagery on the present bronze fitting activated its dual role: as part of a vehicle for the immortal journey and as embodied images representing the patterns of the cosmos. In elite Western Han tombs such chariot fittings were interred as part of actual or miniature chariots; the practice changed in the Eastern Han, when chariots were increasingly depicted on pictorial stones of funerary structures, as on the "Wu family shrines." Chariots not only facilitated the journey of the soul from the tomb to the afterlife (see cat. no. 1.33); they also served as indicators of the high social and bureaucratic rank of the deceased. The architecture of the tomb as well as the objects placed within it served to activate the journey of the deceased to the afterlife. Single pillars within the tomb might function like Mount Kunlun, creating a personalized cosmic pillar for the soul to ascend to heaven. Multiple pillars in tandem might give visual form to help the deceased navigate his journey. Just as the deceased might reach heaven by climbing a mountain, heavenly access could also be achieved through the "celestial well" on the ceiling of the tomb. The apotropaic and cosmological benefits of such imagery explains in part why these architectural forms endured to influence post-Han Buddhist caves in the far west of China. Central pillars in Buddhist cave-chapels at Dunhuang and Jintasi in Gansu Province are not rounded, as in many Indian and Central Asian cave-chapels, but squared like those in earlier Han-dynasty tombs. Clearly, influences flowed in both directions: in the present chariot fitting we see the influence of the Silk Road on Western Han China, and in the later cave-temples of Gansu we see the continuation of Han-dynasty tomb architecture and imagery in the far western regions.

SUSAN L. BENINGSON

Notes

1. Wu Hung reads the representation of these animals on these chariot fittings as a way of actuating auspicious omens (*xiangrui*) by depicting them. See Wu Hung, "A Sanpan Shan Chariot Ornament and the *Xiangrui* Design in Western Han Art," *Archives of Asian Art*, vol. 37 (1984), pp. 38–59.

2. Camels were used by the thousands for commercial and military caravans in the far western regions of China during the Han dynasty. The supply of camels was procured from the Xiongnu for transport across the Gobi Desert and Tarim Basin in present-day Gansu and Xinjiang provinces. During the Tang dynasty camels were acquired as tribute, as commodities, and as war booty. See Edward H. Schafer, *The Golden Peaches of Samarkand* (Berkeley: University of California Press, 1963), p. 70.

3. Some of the related chariot fittings (see n. 6) show elephants. There are records of elephants being given as tribute from Vietnam to Han Wudi, and of tame elephants in the imperial hunting parks, which also symbolized cosmic wilderness. Elephants were also involved in imperial ritual activity. The *Hanshu* records that in 110 BCE, when Han Wudi performed sacrifices on Mount Tai in Shandong, "animals such as rhinoceroses and elephants were not set free, but were brought to Mount Tai and taken away again (after the sacrifices)." Sterckx argues that the idea that the "radiance of the emperor's virtue causes the arrival of exotic animals from all quarters of the empire to flock spontaneously around the sacrificial locus" of Mount Tai created an auspicious omen which resulted in good fortune for the emperor. See Roel Sterckx, *The Animal and the Daemon in Early China* (Albany: State University of New York Press, 2002), p. 116.

4. *Qi* is the cosmic vapor, or life breath, that animates the universe. The importance of the concept of *qi* in Han-dynasty art has been well explained in many publications, and is rooted in the *Yin-Yang* and Five Phases theories at the basis of Han cosmology.

5. A tomb pillar at Yi'nan, Shandong, shows the mountains of Kunlun resting on the back of a dragon with the Queen Mother of the West seated at the summit. Perhaps the dragons on the chariot fitting, which together with the *yunqi* cloud essence serve to define the contours of the landscape, are another reference to Kunlun and immortality. See Zeng Zhaoyu, Jiang Baogeng, and Li Zhongyi, eds., *Yi'nan gu huaxiang shi mu fajue baogao* (*Excavation report of the carved pictorial stones at Yi'nan tomb*) (Shanghai: Wenhuabu wenwu guanliju, 1956), pl. 66. Also see Beningson, cat. nos. 43, 44, in Susan L. Beningson and Cary Y. Liu, *Providing for the Afterlife: "Brilliant Artifacts" from Shandong* (New York: China Institute, 2005). The clouds could allude to the importance of rain in an agricultural society. In the Cangshan tomb, located in southern Shandong, the designer of the tomb described the imagery of heavenly beasts and undulating dragons on the pictorial stone carvings: "Here (on the central column in front of the rear section of the tomb) a pair of intertwining dragons guard the tomb's heart and ward off evil." Translation from Wu Hung, "Beyond the 'Great Boundary': Funerary Narrative in the Cangshan Tomb," in *Boundaries in China*, ed. John Hay (London: Reaktion Books, 1994), pp. 93, 96, 98.

6. A number of *bini* chariot fittings similar to the present bronze have been found, all quite similar in design and imagery. Most were probably originally inlaid with gold and silver, and some with precious stones. In catalogue number 29 Wang Haicheng discusses the differences in imagery among known *bini* chariot fittings. Published examples of *bini* include: (1) Miho Museum fitting, reproduced in *Miho Museum, South Wing Catalogue* (Shigaraki: Miho Museum, 1997), no. 108; (2) fitting unearthed at Dingxian, Hebei Province, in Shi Shuqing, "Wo guo gudai de jincuo gongyi" ("China's ancient metal-inlay technology"), *Wenwu* 1973.6, p. 70, pl. 6, and in Wu Hung, "A Sanpan Shan Chariot Ornament and the *Xiangrui* Design in Western Han Art"; (3) fitting unearthed at Mancheng, in Zhongguo shehui kexueyuan kaogu yanjiusuo et al., *Mancheng Han mu fajue baogao* (*Excavation report of the Han tombs at Mancheng*) (Beijing: Wenwu chubanshe,1980); (4) Tokyo Art Institute fitting, in Kiyohiko Munakata, *Sacred Mountains in Chinese Art* (Urbana and Chicago: University of Illinois Press, 1991), p. 23, fig. 10; (5) fitting in Eisei Bunko Collection, Tokyo, in Munakata, *Sacred Mountains*, p. 21, fig. 8; (6) fitting in a private collection, in Gisele Croès, *Treasures of Ancient China/Splendor of Yongle Painting* (2002), pp. 52–53; (7) miniature fitting, in Jessica Rawson and Emma Bunker, *Ancient Chinese and Ordos Bronzes* (Hong Kong: Oriental Ceramic Society of Hong Kong, 1990), no. 100.

7. John Major, *Heaven and Earth in Early Han Thought: Chapters Three, Four, and Five of the "Huainanzi"* (Albany: State University of New York Press, 1993), p. 158.

8. See n. 5. Also see Major, *Heaven and Earth in Early Han Thought*, p. 153, fig. 4.1.

9. Anqiu Xian wenhuaju and Anqiu Xian bowuguan, *Anqiu Dongjiazhuang Han huaxiang shi mu* (*Han-dynasty pictorial stones from the tomb at Dongjiazhuang Village, Anqiu County*) (Ji'nan: Ji'nan chubanshe, 1992).

10. See "Shandong Cangshan yuanjia yuan nian huaxiang shi mu" ("Excavation report of the pictorial stone carvings in the Cangshan tomb, Shangdong, dated to the first year of the Yuanjia reign-period"), *Kaogu* 1975.2, pp. 124–34. This tomb was originally dated to the year 424 CE, but that date was later revised to 151 CE. See Fang Pengjun and Zhang Xunliao, "Shandong Cangshan yuanjia yuan nian huaxiang shi wenji de shidai he you guan wenti de taolun" ("Discussion of the problems concerning the dating of the pictorial stone carvings at the Cangshan tomb in Shandong to the yuanjia yuan year (424 CE)," *Kaogu* 1980.3, pp. 271–78.

11. See Cary Y. Liu, "Embodying Cosmic Patterns: Foundations of an Art of Calligraphy in China," *Oriental Art*, vol. 56, no. 5 (2000), pp. 2–9.

12. There are indications that the chariot fitting and the bottom box might have been differently juxtaposed during the Qin dynasty. See *Qin Shihuang Ling tong che ma xiufu baogao* (*Restoration report of bronze chariots and horses unearthed from Qin Shihuang Mausoleum*) (Beijing: Wenwu chubanshe, 1998), p. 79, fig. 38. During the Eastern Han, however, they were placed as shown in the Wu shrines. For an example of a chariot and canopy in bronze from a tomb in Gansu, see "Gansu Wuwei Leitai Donghan mu qingli jianbao" ("Brief discussion of the Eastern Han tomb at Leitai, near Wuwei, Gansu"), *Wenwu* 1972.2, pl. 2.

13. For a discussion of mountains as cosmic pillars, particularly Mount Kunlun, see Major, *Heaven and Earth in Early Han Thought*, pp. 154-60. For more on the cosmological allusion of ascending to a "round" heaven from the "square" earth, see Klaas Ruitenbeek, *Chinese Shadows: Stone Reliefs, Rubbings, and Related Works of Art from the Han Dynasty (206 BC–AD 220) in the Royal Ontario Museum* (Toronto: Royal Ontario Museum, 2002), pp. 22–23. For a discussion of *wuzhu* coins in this same context, see Anthony Barbieri-Low's "Coins and Coin Molds" in this catalogue.

14. A bronze chariot fitting, similar to the present example, was found in the tomb at Sanpan Shan.

15. Yi'nan Tomb 1 offers a rare example of a circle-inside-square ceiling pattern in high relief with a central painted lotus. A variation of the central lotus design is also found carved in the stone ceiling of Tomb 1 on the Qi River at Santai, Sichuan Province. This cliff tomb is dated between the late Eastern Han and Shu of the Three Kingdoms period.

16. A variation of the *tianjing*, called the *zaojing* (see Dieter Kuhn, "Liao Architecture: Qidan Innovations and Han-Chinese Traditions?" *T'oung Pao*, vol. 86 [2000], p. 342), usually has floral motifs in the central well. It can be found in the tomb at Cangshan. An early reference to *zaojing* is found in the *Xijing fu* (*Western metropolis rhapsody*) by Zhang Pingzi (78–139 CE) (see Xiao Tong, *Wen xuan, or Selections of Refined Literature*, trans. David R. Knechtges [Princeton: Princeton University Press, 1982], vol. 1, 187, 189, and p. 186, note to line 102). On *tianjing* in Chinese architecture, see Cary Y. Liu, "Heavenly Wells in Ming Dynasty Huizhou Architecture," *Orientations*, January 1994, pp. 28–36.

17. The *tianjing* with a central lotus, painted in the center of the ceiling, is also found in the Foyemiaowan tomb group located near Dunhuang, dating from the Western Jin dynasty. The relationship between architecture and imagery from earlier tombs, as this relationship bore upon Northern Liang Buddhist cave-chapels at Dunhuang, is explored in my "Shaping Sacred Space: The Interaction of Ritual Architecture and Artistic Programs in Early Buddhist Caves and Tombs in Fifth Century China" (PhD diss., Columbia University, forthcoming).

18. Cave 248 is dated as Northern Wei in Dunhuang wenwu yanjiusuo, ed., *Zhongguo shiku: Dunhuang Mogaoku* (*China's cave series: Dunhuang Mogao caves*), 5 vols. (Beijing: Wenwu chubanshe, 1982–1987), vol. 1. It is dated as Western Wei in Dunhuang yanjiuyuan, ed., *Dunhuang shiku neirong zonglu* (*Compendium of content of the Dunhuang caves*) ([Beijing]: Wenwu chubanshe, 1996). The description follows my observations at the site.

19. This is common at Dunhuang, where in many caves a row of *tianjing* squares is located directly around the top of the central stupa pillar.

20. Directly below the window (or door?) is a balcony on which the *apsarases* stand. Moreover, in direct line with the opening in the window are the top of the Buddha's canopy and the head of the Buddha. This seems to be a merging of Chinese architecture and cosmology with those of Buddhism. In many of the caves at Dunhuang there are Chinese cosmological themes in the ceiling designs, including Xiwangmu and Dongwanggong as well as Fuxi with Nüwa, while Buddhist themes and *jataka* tales adorn the walls.

21. This commonly quoted inscription in Western Wei Cave 249 was first cited in Alexander Soper, "The 'Dome of Heaven' in Asia," *The Art Bulletin*, December 1947, pp. 225–48. But in June 2004 members of the Dunhuang Research Academy, responding to my questions, denied its existence. Soper also argues for a western source (not eastern, as I am suggesting) for the *laternendecke* ceiling, tracing its route from Ajanta to Bamiyan to Kizil and from there to Dunhuang. There is, however, an earlier Han-dynasty source for the *tianjing* ceilings. Flying *apsarases* in the corners of the *tianjing*, are common at Dunhuang.

22. Sima Qian, *Records of the Grand Historian: Han Dynasty II*, trans. Burton Watson, rev. ed. (New York: Renditions/Columbia University Press, 1993), p. 28.

23. Munakata, *Sacred Mountains*, p. 23. See also the *yunqi* design inlaid in gold and silver on bronze chariot parts excavated from the Western Han royal tomb at Shuangru Shan near Changqing County, Shandong. Both full-size and miniature chariots were found in Tomb 1, suggesting that for the efficacy of the chariot and its imagery, size was less important than completeness. See Beningson and Liu, *Providing for the Afterlife: "Brilliant Artifacts" from Shandong.*

24. Munakata, *Sacred Mountains*, p. 23.

25. For a discussion on how designs originally painted in lacquer became the source for inlaid bronze designs, including the cloud scroll motif, see Jessica Rawson, "Chu Influences on the Development of Han Bronze Vessels," *Arts Asiatiques*, vol. 44 (1989), pp. 84–99.

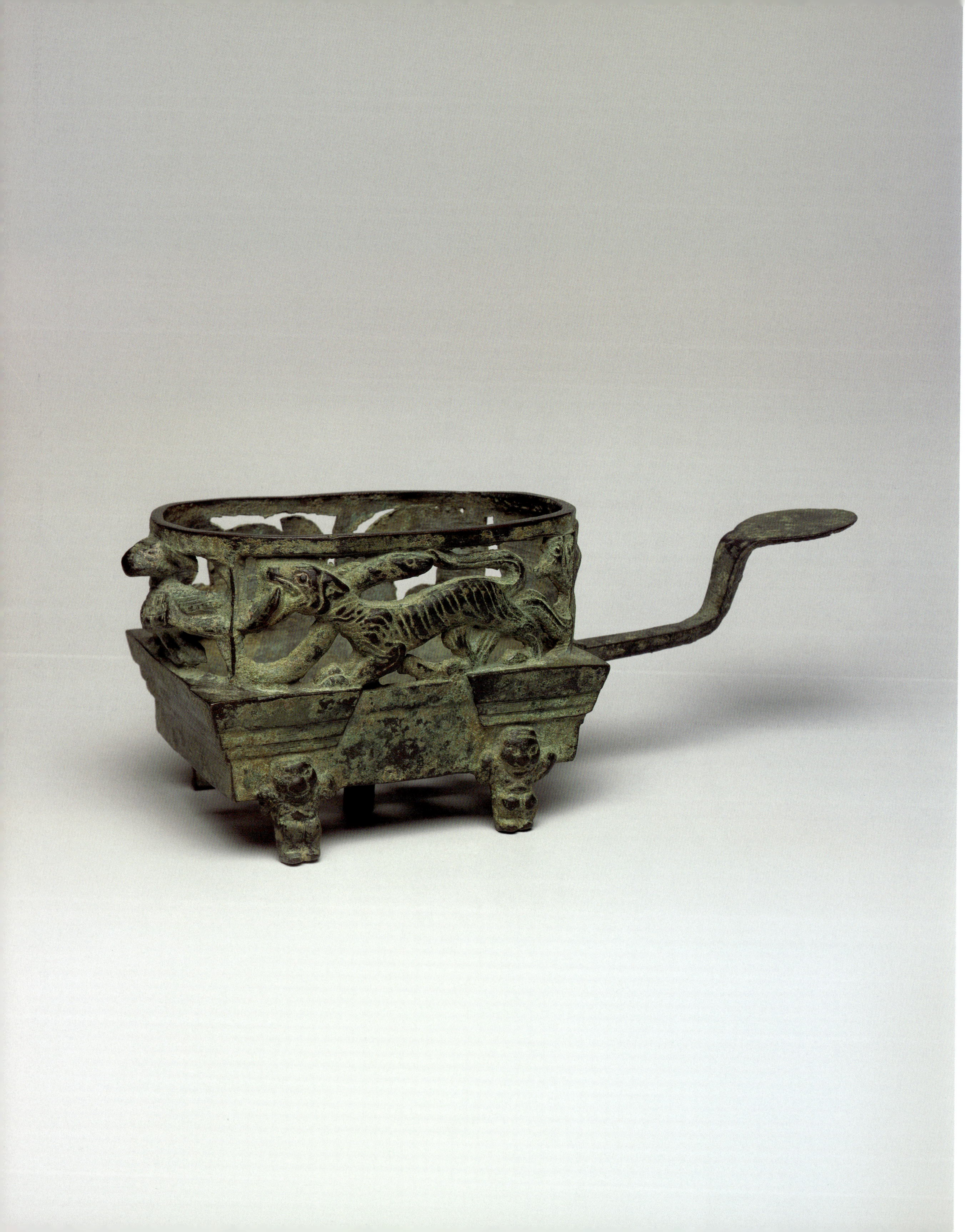

30

30 Brazier with animals of the Four Directions

Late Western Han–early Eastern Han, 1st century BCE–1st century CE. Bronze; h. 17.8 cm, l. 23.8 cm, w. 8.9 cm. Brooklyn Museum, acc. no. 73.125.1. Gift of John J. Waterman in memory of Edwin Mathews Blumenthal.

Braziers, along with shovels, ladles, and incense burners, may have come originally from the north or northwest, possibly imported from non-Han Chinese peoples. This new category of bronzes, which also includes lamps and other non-ritual paraphernalia, appears in tombs beginning in the third century BCE, and indicates a change in burial customs and beliefs.[1]

Four caryatids support the oblong container, which is surmounted by a tall collar decorated in openwork with animals symbolizing the four cardinal directions: the Dark Warrior of the North (*xuanwu*), comprising an entwined tortoise and snake, decorates the short side with the projecting angular handle; the Vermilion Bird of the South (*zhuque*) stands opposite; the Azure Dragon (*qinglong*) and the White Tiger (*baihu*), corresponding to the east and west directions, range the long sides. The base was cast with holes to allow air to reach the burning fuel.

As braziers of this type[2] have been excavated with an eared cup resting on top of the collar, and a shallow pan, which served to catch the falling ashes, below, we can infer that they were used to heat the contents of the cup. Removal of the heated eared cup from the brazier may have been facilitated by using a handled oval container placed between the eared cup and the brazier, similar to the one excavated from a Han tomb in the eastern suburbs of Xi'an, Shaanxi (fig. 1).[3]

The imagery of the four animals, also known as the Four Directional Spirits (*si shen*), representing the four cardinal directions, became widespread in the Han dynasty, and was directly related to cosmological beliefs of that time.[4] The canonical number of directions was in fact five, including the center, which was not symbolized by any animal.[5] Mirrors, themselves cosmic diagrams and talismans, were frequently cast with the Four Directional Spirits (cat. no. 38), as were earthenware roof tiles.

HIROMI KINOSHITA

Notes

1. See Jessica Rawson, "The Eternal Palaces of the Western Han: A New View of the Universe," *Artibus Asiae*, vol. 59 (1999), pp. 5–58.
2. Two have been found in Shanxi, one in a Western Han tomb in Shuo County. See *Wenwu* 1987.6, pl. 3:3; also in color in *Zhongguo qingtonqi quanji* (*Complete works of Chinese bronzes*) (Beijing: Wenwu chubanshe, 1998), vol. 12, p. 79, no. 77. Another, excavated from Taiyuan, is illustrated in *Kaogu* 1985.6, pl. 6:1, and p. 528, fig. 3.1. Both were found with an eared cup and a shallow pan, presumably used to catch falling ash. One, without the pan, was excavated from a Western Han tomb in Xianyang, Shaanxi Province (*Kaogu* 1979.2, pl. 10:1, and p. 129, fig. 5.7).
3. Now in the collection of the Shaanxi Institute of Archaeology. See *Kaogu yu wenwu* 1997.6, front cover, and p. 1 for a brief description.
4. See John Major, *Heaven and Earth in Early Han Thought: Chapters Three, Four, and Five of the Huainanzi* (Albany: State University of New York Press, 1993), pp. 23–53, for a discussion of Han cosmology.
5. The five directions directly correlated to the Five Elements and to their corresponding animal symbols, already mentioned. Thus the east was represented by the wood element, the south by fire, the west by metal, the north by water, and the center by earth.

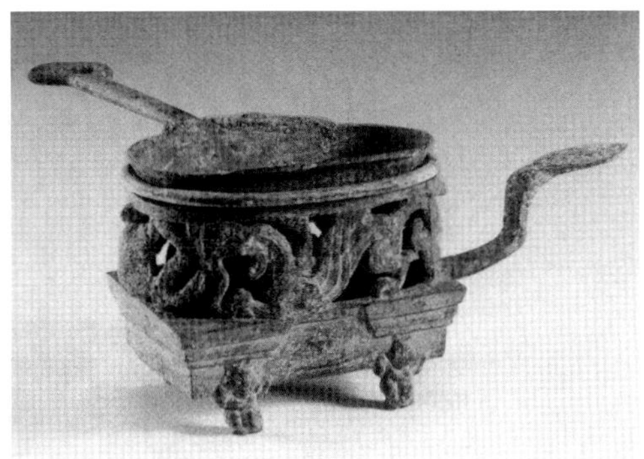

Fig. 1 *Brazier with eared cup resting on a handled oval contraption*. Excavated from a Han-dynasty tomb in the eastern suburbs of Xi'an, Shaanxi. Bronze. From *Kaogu yu wenwu* 1997.6, cover.

Eared Cups: "Suitable for Wine and Food"

Eared cups (*erbei*) are so called by Chinese archaeologists because of the flat handles resembling ears, one on either long side of the oval cup. The form appears to have originated in the ancient state of Chu (eighth century–221 BCE), roughly coextensive with present-day Hubei and Hunan provinces. Early examples have been found, made of lacquer over a thin, lightweight body material such as cloth or wood.[1] Lacquer is an exceptionally resilient substance. Organic materials such as wood painted with lacquer often survive burial due to the durability, imperviousness, and protective qualities of this natural resin. A wood-base eared cup in the exhibition (cat. no. 35) is painted in red and black lacquer. In the well, inscribed in red lacquer on black, are the three characters *yi jiu shi* ("suitable for wine and food" or "may there be wine and food"), suggesting that it could have been used for both eating and drinking. Lacquer eared cups of the third century BCE excavated from Tomb 1 at Mashan, Jianling, Hubei, were found in a set along with other eating and drinking accoutrements, confirming that these cups were banqueting utensils.[2]

Eared cups were made in a variety of materials beginning in the third century BCE, when the lacquer form was copied in bronze. From the Western Han onward, the form was executed in a range of mediums, especially in gilt bronze (cat. no. 32.1) and ceramic. Eared cups continued to be made in lacquer as well as in other "luxury" materials such as silver, jade, rock crystal (cat. no. 34), carnelian agate (cat. no. 33), and glass (figs. 2A, B),[3] but these were available only to the wealthy elite.

From the third century BCE, eared cups appear to have been associated with other accoutrements, indicating a change in how they were used. In Qin and Han tombs they are often found together with bronze braziers (cat. no. 30) or, in one case, fitted with legs attached to a tray (fig. 1) that could easily contain embers, suggesting that the contents of the cups were intended to be warmed.[4] Furthermore, archaeological artifacts and Han-dynasty stone carvings illustrate the various ways in which eared cups were "presented": several together on a large tray (see cat. no. 46, fig. 2) or a single cup on a smaller tray or saucer (figs. 2A, B).[5] For a more ostentatious presentation, the cup was elevated on a stand (cat. no. 31).

Traditionally, eared cups have been identified as wine cups—they are pictured along with *zun* wine-warming vessels (see cat. no. 46, fig. 1) at banqueting scenes in Han tombs.[6] They could have held other liquids as well, or even stews (*geng*),[7] as they are also frequently found along with ladles.[8] During the Han, however, their function may have been extended to other uses, such as containers of food offerings to the deceased. In the "Wu family shrines" carvings

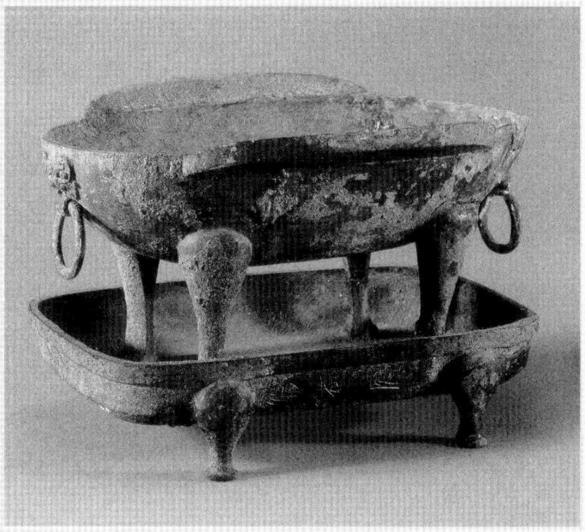

Fig. 1 *Eared cup with brazier*. Qin dynasty. Excavated from Xianyang, Shaanxi. Bronze. From *Zhongguo qingtongqi quanji*, vol. 12: *Qin, Han*, p. 14, no. 14.

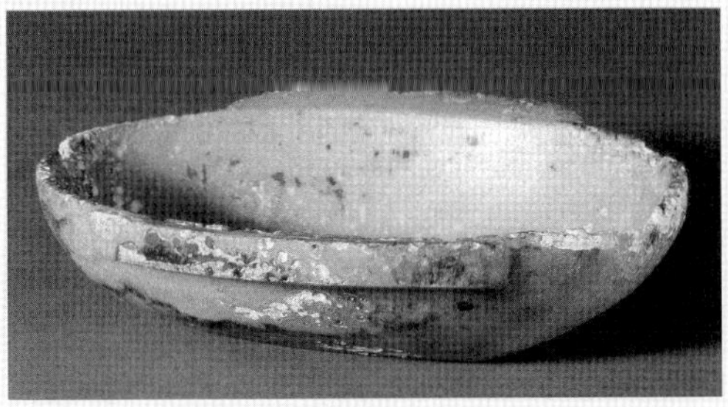

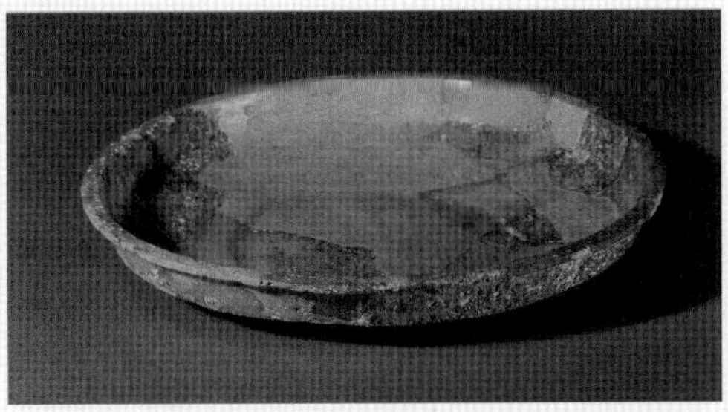

Figs. 2A, B *Eared cup and round plate.* Western Han dynasty, second century BCE. Excavated from the tomb of Liu Sheng at Lingshan, Mancheng, Hebei. Glass. From *Zhongguo meishu quanji*, Works of art series, vol. 10, *Gold, silver, glass, enamels*, p. 111, nos. 211, 212.

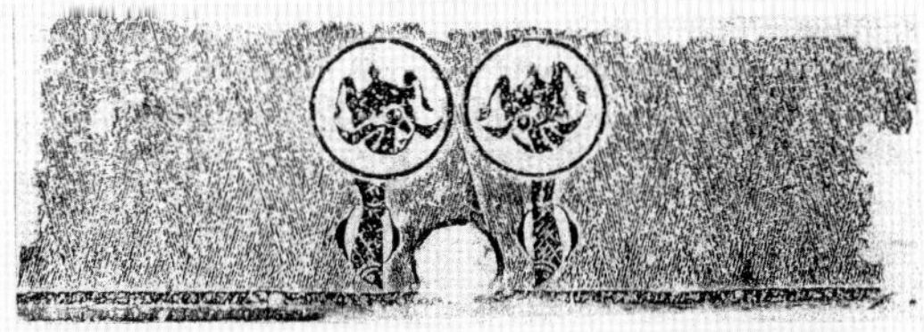

Fig. 3 *Fish in eared cups.* Rubbing of incised stone found near the "Wu family shrines." From Jiang Yingju and Wu Wenqi, *Handai Wushi muqun shike yanjiu*, p. 167, fig. 50.

four eared cups are depicted on a tray with two dishes of what appears to be food (cat. no. 37, fig. 1). Fish especially appear to be associated with eared cups. Two eared cups, seen from above, each containing a whole fish (fig. 3; p. 57, fig. 17), are pictured on a Han stone carving, found near the Wu site, that is now stored at the Exhibition Hall.[9] The two circular dishes on this same stone appear each to contain an animal, described by archaeologists as a turtle or a chicken.[10] Perhaps these stone images of food presented in luxury vessels were intended as an everlasting offering to the ancestors.[11] A whole fish is also modeled in the well of an eared cup found in a Han tomb at Shan Xian, Henan.[12]

HIROMI KINOSHITA

Notes

1. For a discussion of the impact of Chu culture on Qin and Han tomb structures and their contents, see Jessica Rawson, "The Eternal Palaces of the Western Han: A New View of the Universe," *Artibus Asiae*, vol. 59 1/2 (1999), p. 20; *Wenwu* 1982.12, pp. 51, 57.

2. See *Jiangling Mashan yihao chumu* (Beijing: Wenwu chubanshe, 1985), p. 87, fig. 74. A lacquer wine set containing a nesting set of eared cups was also excavated from a Chu tomb at Baoshan, Jingmen, Hubei; illustrated in *Wenwu* 1988.5, pls. 1:3, 1:4, with a description on p. 7.

3. A glass eared cup along with a round dish was excavated from the tomb of Liu Sheng at Lingshan, Mancheng, Hebei. See *Mancheng Han mu fajue baogao* (Beijing: Wenwu chubanshe, 1980), vol. 2, pl. 152, with a line drawing in vol. 1, p. 214, figs. 142.1, 142.2.

4. Found in Xianyang, Shaanxi, the bronze warming set is undecorated except for a pair of *taotie* masks with ring handles and a three-character inscription, *xiuwu fu*, on the exterior of the stand. Xiuwu was part of the Wei kingdom during the Warring States period and was eventually integrated into the Qin empire. See *Zhongguo qingtongqi quanji* (*Complete Works of Chinese bronzes*), vol. 12: *Qin, Han* (Beijing: Wenwu chubanshe, 1998), p. 14, no. 14.

5. The glass cup and plate found in the Western Han tomb of Liu Sheng in Mancheng, Hebei, is one such set. See *Zhongguo meishu quanji* (*Complete works of Chinese art*), Works of art series, vol. 10: *Gold, silver, glass, enamels* (Beijing: Wenwu chubanshe, 1987), p. 111, nos. 211, 212. Green-glazed porcelaneous stoneware sets have been excavated from Jin tombs of the 4th century in Zhejiang. See *Zhongguo taoci—yueyao* (*Chinese ceramics—Yue ware*) (Shanghai: Shanghai renmin meishu chubanshe, 1983), no. 88.

6. From a tomb at Zhucheng, Shandong; illustrated in *Wenwu* 1981.10, pp. 14–21, figs. 6, 8.

7. Or condiments, see Michele Pirazzoli-t'Serstevens, "From the Ear-Cup to the Round Cup: Changes in Chinese Drinking Vessels (2d to 6th century AD)," *Oriental Art*, vol. 48, no. 3 (2002).

8. *Kaogu xuebao* 1965.1, pls. XII:7, XIV:5, XVII:8.

9. Jiang Yingju and Wu Wenqi, *Handai Wushi muqun shike yanjiu* (*Studies on the Han-dynasty stone carvings at the Wu family cemetery*) (Ji'nan: Shandong meishu chubanshe, 1995), p. 167, fig. 50.

10. Jiang and Wu call the animals turtles (p. 131); Zhu Xilu calls them chickens in *Wushi ci Han huaxiang shi* (*Han pictorial stone carvings from the Wu family shrine*) (Ji'nan: Shandong meishu chubanshe, 1986), p. 63, fig. 62, p. 126.

11. See Jessica Rawson, "Ritual Vessel Changes in the Warring States, Qin and Han Periods," *Regional Culture, Religion, and Arts before the Seventh Century*, Papers from the Third International Conference on Sinology, History section (Taipei: Institute of History and Philology, Academica Sinica, 2002), pp. 1–57.

12. *Kaogu xuebao* 1965.1, pl. VIII.6. Fish are also painted in the well of lacquer eared cups found at a Han tomb in Gaotai, Jingzhou, Hubei. See *Jingzhou Gaotai Qin Han mu* (*Qin and Han tombs at Jingzhou Gaotai*) (Beijing: Kexue chubanshe, 2000), cpl. 5:4; p. 135, fig. 107.2 and cpl. 6:2; p. 137, fig. 109.3. We cannot tell, however, whether the paintings were meant as simulacra of offerings or were merely decorative.

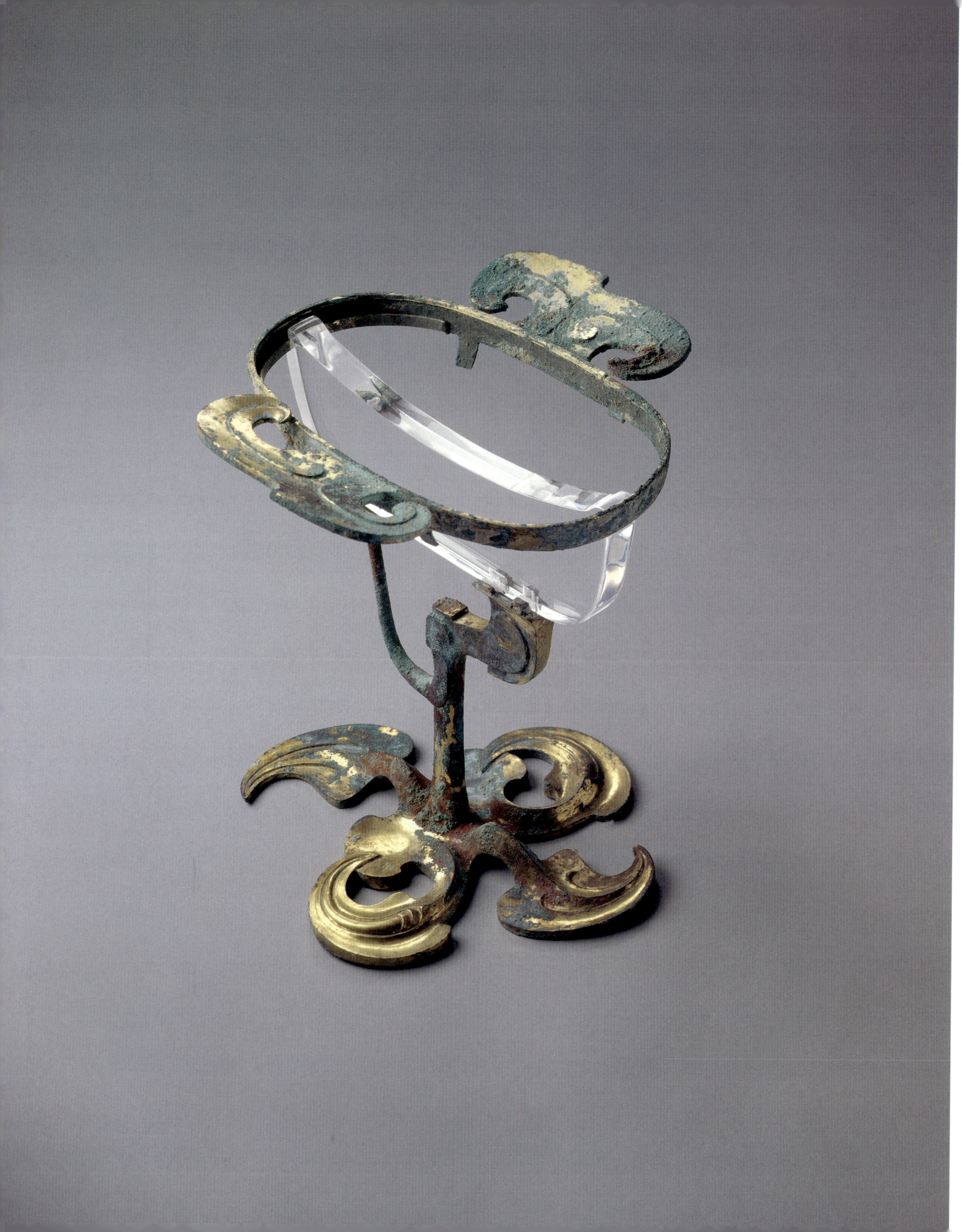

31 Stand for eared cup

Western Han dynasty, 2d–1st century BCE. Gilt bronze; h. 9.8 cm, l. 23.6 cm.
Collection of Howard and Mary Ann Rogers.

The sturdily cast stand used for presentation of an eared cup is pleasing as well as functional in form. Four talons or flail-like projections form the hollow quatrefoil base. From this base a central column tapers gradually upward to two arms branching in opposite directions; the more slender arm curves elegantly up and out and ends in a ledge supporting a metal peg, while the thicker arm, of rectangular section, is bent at right angles to support the base of an oval cup. The separately cast oval collar once bound the rim of an oval cup, held in place by the four pendent flat tabs evenly spaced along the bottom edge of the collar. Two flanges engraved with flowing volutes and with inward-curving ends tapering to a point are set opposite each other, one on each of the long sides of the collar.

Bronze stands for eared cups did not appear in the repertoire of tomb furnishings until the third century BCE.[1] The oval cup once supported on this stand was presumably made of a friable material such as lacquer or wood. That the gilt-bronze oval collar functioned together with the stand is confirmed by the discovery of six similar sets, which were excavated from a rich tomb located near Maoling, the tomb of the Han emperor Wudi (r. 140–87 BCE), in Xianyang County, Shaanxi.[2] These gilt-bronze stands each have a circular base decorated with a quatrefoil motif and four elegantly upward-curving arms which once cradled a lacquer eared cup. The eared cups have since disappeared, leaving only four sets of gilt-bronze ear-shaped flanges (fig. 1). Two oval collars (fig. 2) similar to the present one and made of gilt silver were also found.

HIROMI KINOSHITA

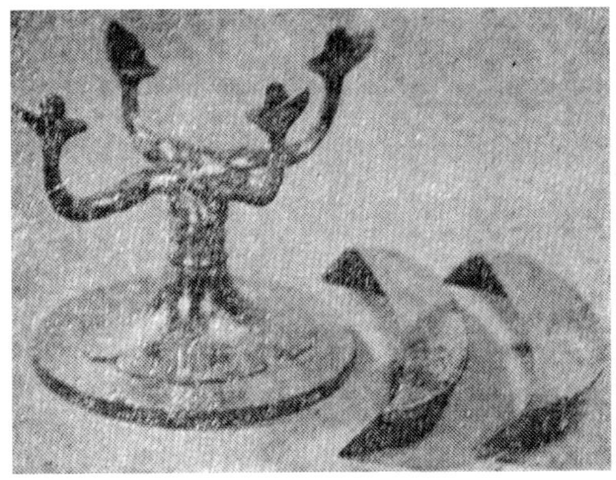

Fig. 1 *Stand for eared cups and pair of flanges*. Excavated from a Western Han tomb, Xianyang, Shaanxi. Gilt bronze. From *Wenwu* 1982.9, p. 11, fig. 24.

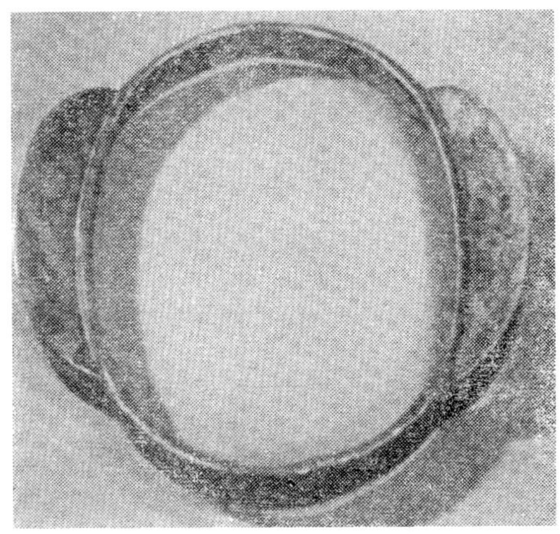

Fig. 2 *Collar for a lacquer cup*. Excavated from a Western Han tomb, Xianyang, Shaanxi. From *Wenwu* 1982.9, p. 10, fig. 22.

Notes

1. As Jessica Rawson has argued, this new category of bronze utensils, including lamps, braziers, and incense burners, does not appear to be connected with ritual offerings as were the bronzes of the previous Zhou and Shang dynasties, signalling a break from past burial practices. See Jessica Rawson, "The Eternal Palaces of the Western Han: A New View of the Universe," *Artibus Asiae*, vol. 59 1/2 (1999), and Jessica Rawson, "Ritual Vessel Changes in the Warring States, Qin and Han Periods," in *Regional Culture, Religion, and Arts before the Seventh Century*, Papers from the Third International Conference on Sinology, History section (Taipei: Institute of History and Philology, Academica Sinica, 2002), p. 21.
2. *Wenwu* 1982.9, p. 6; illustrated on p. 10, fig. 22; p. 11, figs. 24–26; and by line drawing on p. 15, fig. 51.

32 Three eared cups (*erbei*)

Han dynasty. Bronze; .1) gilt; l. 10.5 cm, w. 8.2 cm; .2) l. 8.8 cm, w. 7.2 cm; .3) l. 15.6 cm, w. 11.5 cm.
Princeton University Art Museum, acc. nos. 2001-291.1, 2001-291.2, 1998-245. Gift of Dr. Alvin E. Friedman-Kien in honor of Allen Rosenbaum.

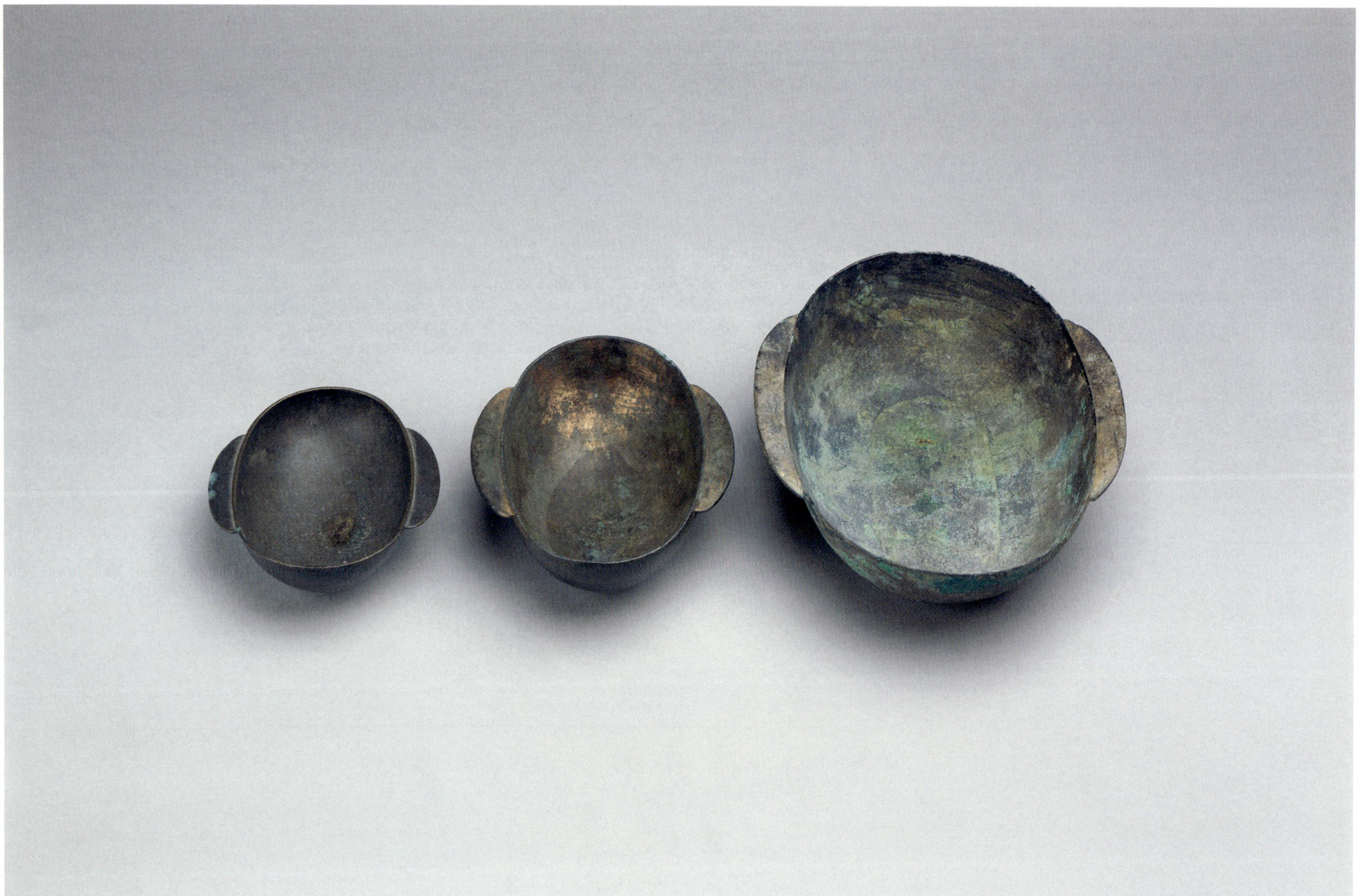

33 Eared cup (*erbei*)

Western Han dynasty. Carnelian agate; l. 9.0 cm.
Private collection.

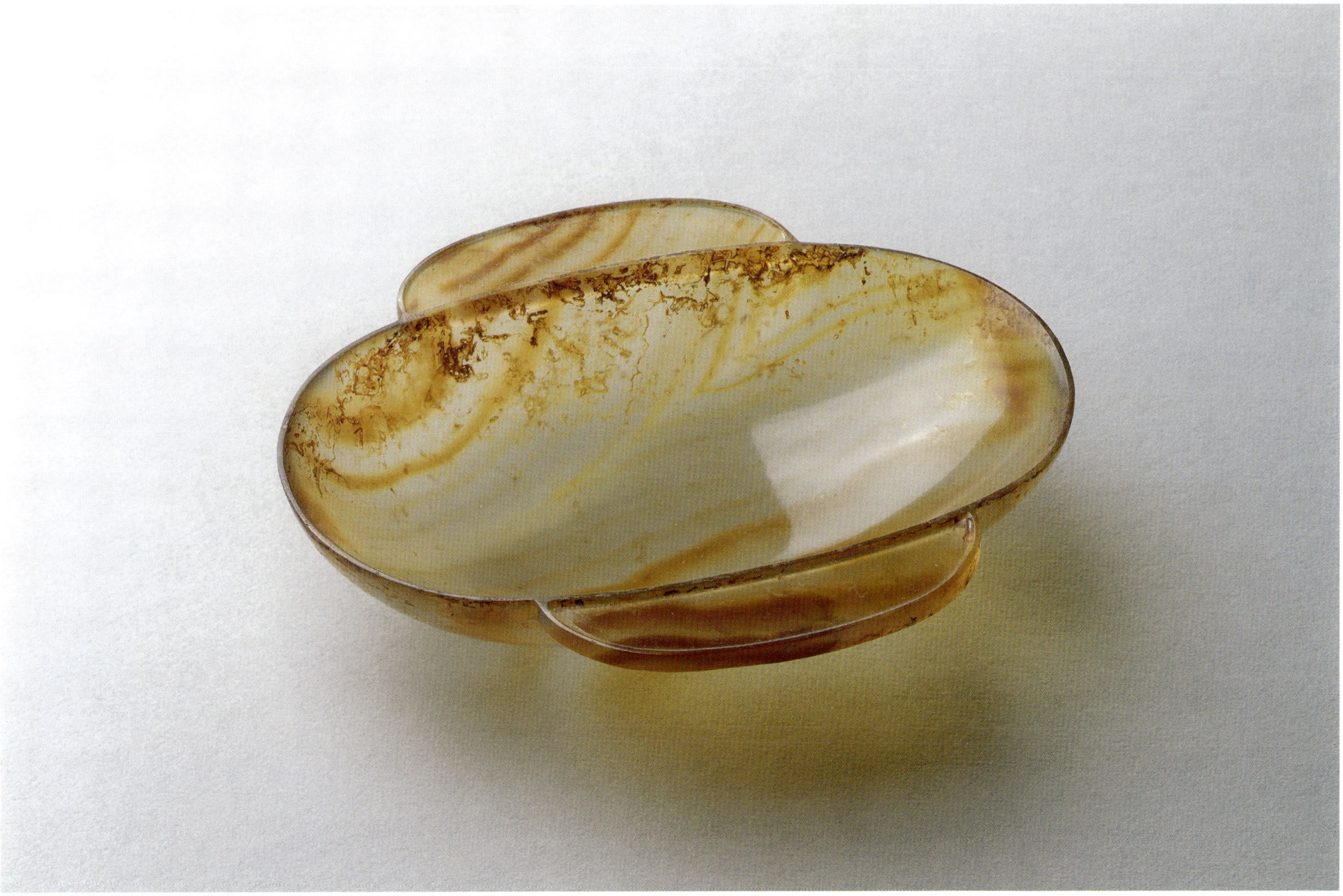

34 Eared cup (*erbei*)

Eastern Zhou, Warring States period–Western Han dynasty, 3d–1st century BCE. Rock crystal (crystalline quartz); h. 2.3 cm, l. 8.8 cm, w. 7.0 cm.
The Art Institute of Chicago, acc. no. 1995.270. Samuel M. Nickerson Endowment.

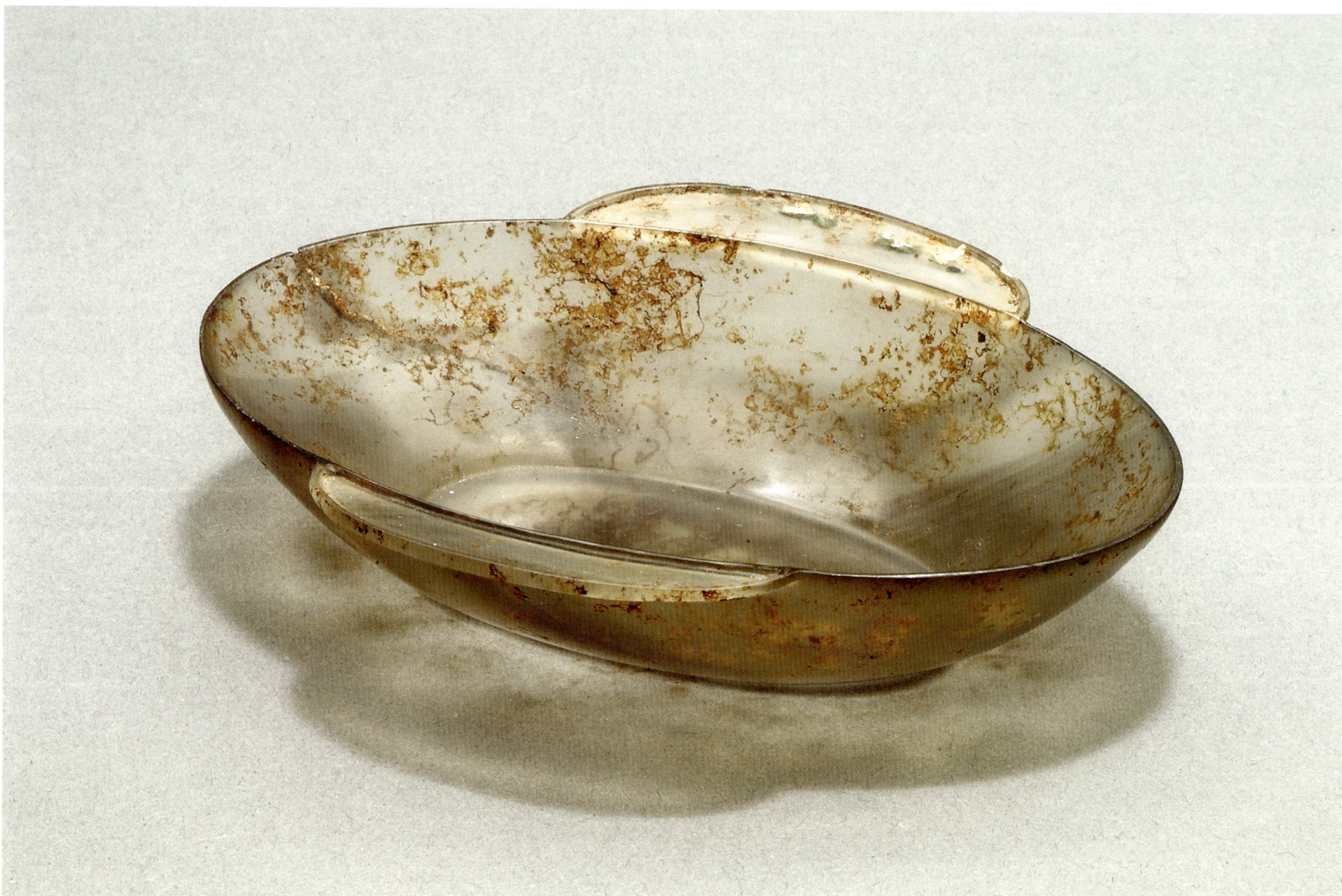

35 Eared cup (*erbei*)

Western Han dynasty. Black and red lacquer on wood; inscribed "Suitable for wine and food" (*yi jiu shi*); h. 4.45 cm, l. 14.29 cm, w. 9.53 cm. Los Angeles County Museum of Art, acc. no. AC1992.258.1. Gift of Howard K. Lee in memory of his friend Jack Nessley.

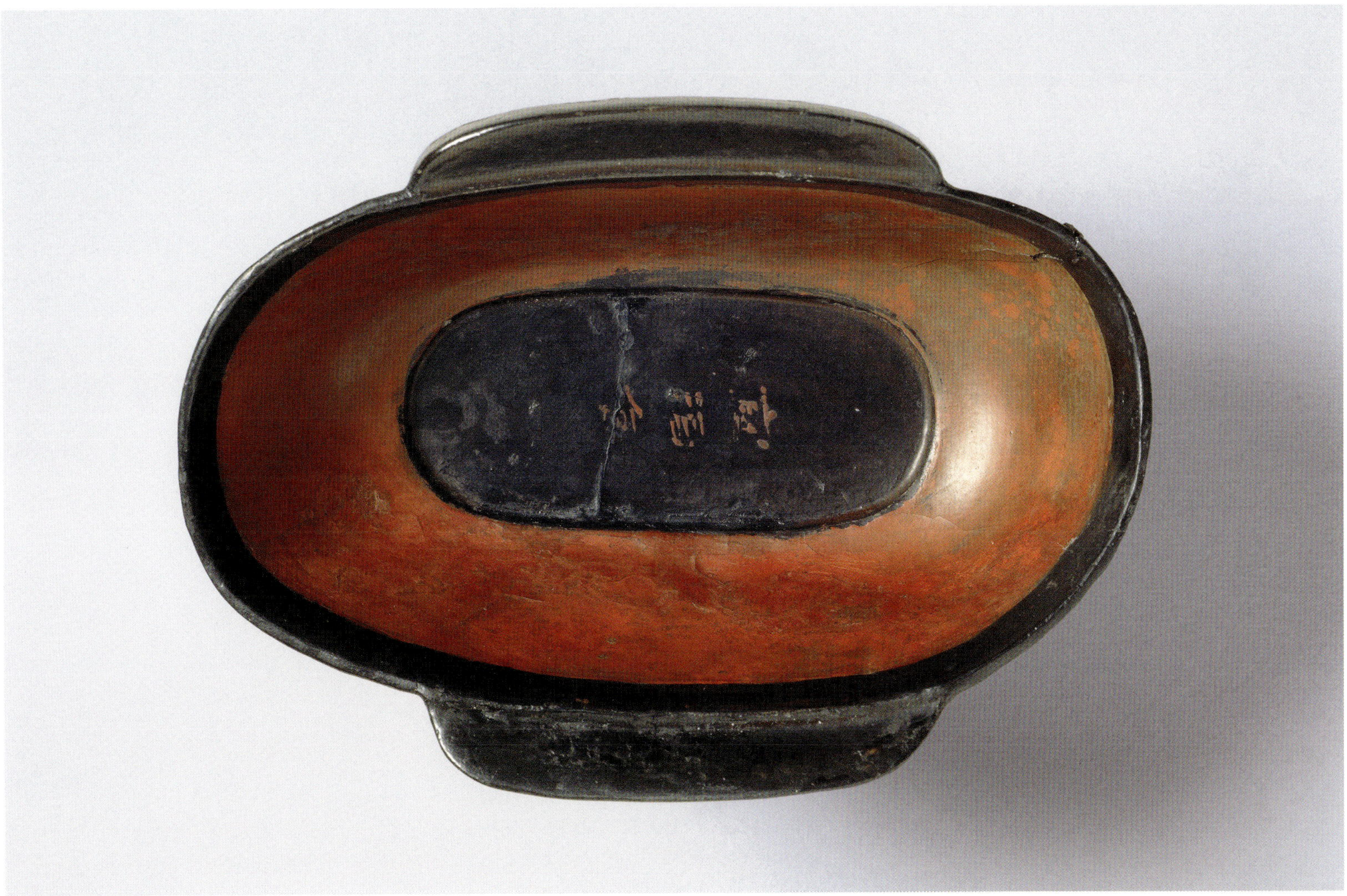

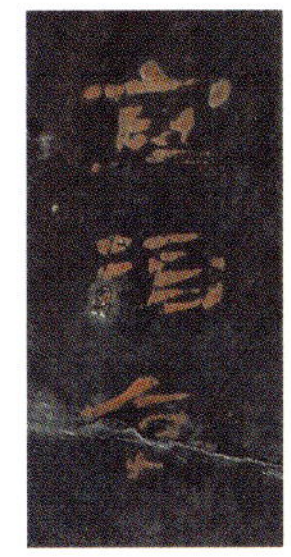

Detail of inscription "Suitable for wine and food" (*yi jiu shi*)

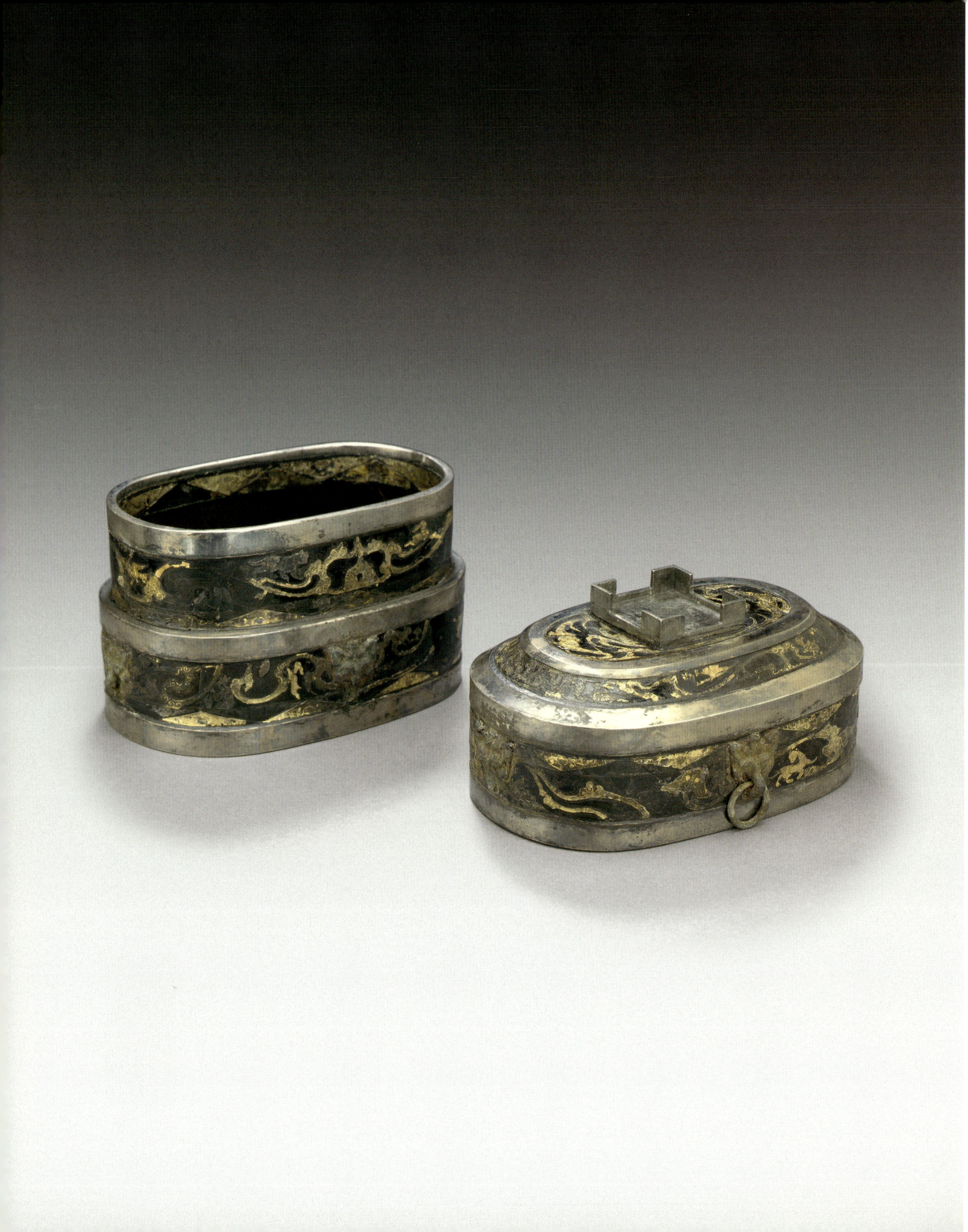

36

36 Three lidded cosmetic boxes (*lian*)

Late Western Han dynasty, ca. 60 BCE–25 CE. Black and red lacquer on fabric and clay core with red and yellow painted decoration, silver mounts, and gold and silver foil inlays: .1) Oval lidded cosmetic box; (box) 6.51 × 11.43 × 7.15 cm, (lid) 5.40 × 11.59 × 7.31 cm. .2) Half-oval lidded cosmetic box; (box) 6.04 × 5.72 × 8.26 cm, (lid) 6.04 × 6.67 × 9.51 cm. .3) Small cylindrical lidded cosmetic box; (box) 6.20 × 4.13 cm, (lid) 5.72 × 4.77 cm. Los Angeles County Museum of Art, acc. no. M.2001.32.1–3. Purchased with funds provided by an anonymous donor, Elly Nordskog, the Sammy Yukuan Lee Foundation, and Simon K. C. Li.

Originally these three lidded boxes (*lian*) were part of a woman's makeup kit. They probably fitted into a larger, circular, lidded makeup box, accompanied by a bronze mirror (cat. nos. 38–41). Based on archaeologically recovered examples, we know that each shape of subsidiary box held a different cosmetic preparation or toilet accessory. The half-oval piece was used to store hair combs. Often these were made in kits of two or three combs of differing tooth fineness, usually called *shu* for the coarsest and *bi* for the finer. The oval type of box usually stored white face powders or creams, made from powdered grain or ceruse (white lead). Small cylindrical boxes of the type seen here were used to store more sparsely applied products, like grease-based cheek, eye, or lip pigments. This subset of boxes is incomplete, however, and its members may have been brought together from at least two original sets. Box types missing from this partial set include those used to store items such as hairpins, false hair, eyebrow tweezers, makeup brushes, and sewing kits.

The body of the boxes was made by placing ramie or hemp fabric in molds and then impregnating the fabric with a mixture of ash and the processed sap from the lacquer tree. Repeated coatings of unpigmented lacquer fluid followed until the surface was black and lustrous. Black lacquer for the final ornamental layers was usually created by adding lampblack (carbon) or ferrous oxide (FeO) to the lacquer fluid, red by adding cinnabar (alpha-HgS), and yellow by orpiment (arsenic sulfide, or As_2S_3). The foil underlays were accomplished using a technique called *jinbo* during the Han, or, in later centuries and up to the present, *pingtuo* (J: *heidatsu*). The gold or silver foil (9–17 microns thick) was laid onto one of the lower coats of lacquer and then covered entirely by additional layers of lacquer. Once the piece was cured, the outer layers were polished away just to the level at which the design emerged. The foil was held in place by the adhesive power of the lacquer and by a small remaining lip of lacquer around the border of the design.

The foil designs on all these boxes represent fantastic landscapes of animals and Immortals. Though the present boxes have been moderately damaged and partially restored, comparable excavated pieces, mostly from Jiangsu Province, can help us understand their decoration.[1] Tigers and winged Immortals frolic in a landscape

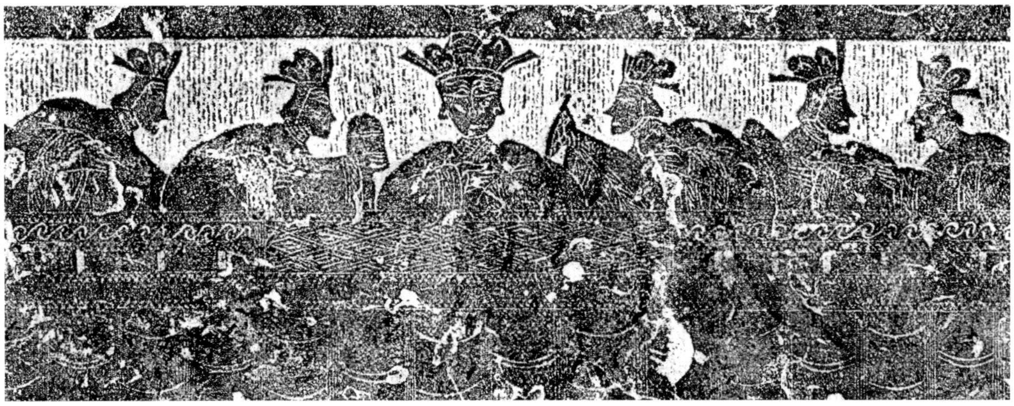

Fig. 1 *Lady with attendants (attendant on proper right holding a cosmetic box)*. Detail of Stone Chamber 2, Stone 2-S.6 (cat. no. 1.26). "Wu family shrines" rubbings. Princeton University Art Museum, acc. no. 2002-307.24.

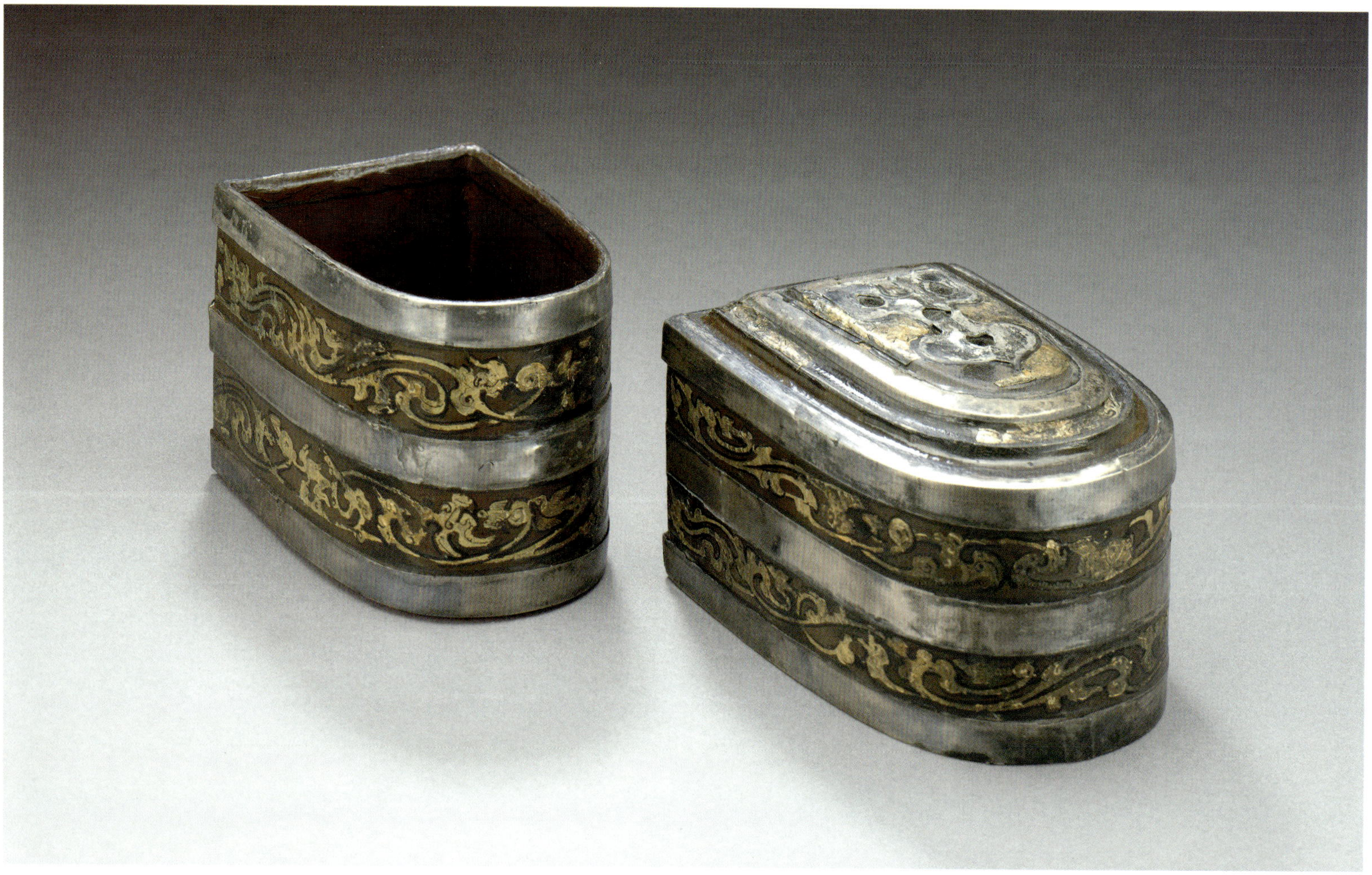

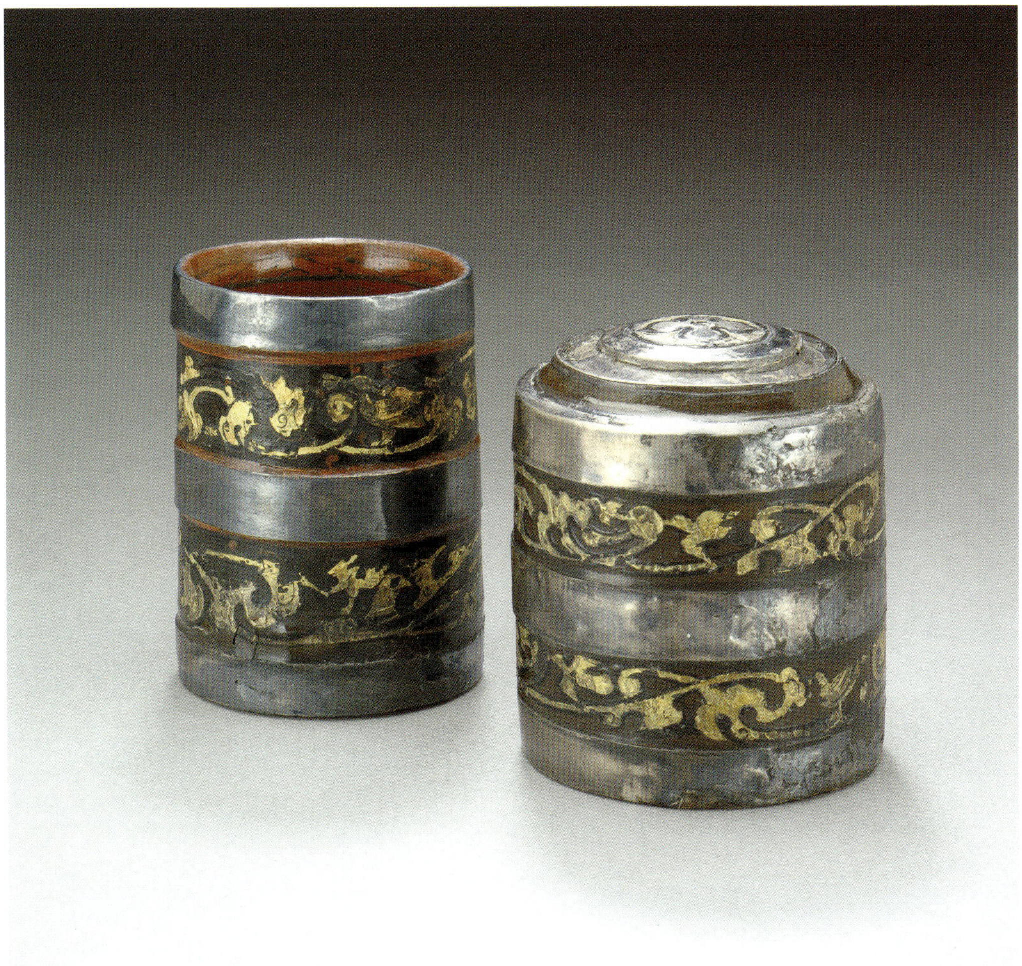

composed of scrolling cloud forms, while birds perch on outcrops and soar overhead. Sets similar to these often include images of Xiwangmu (Queen Mother of the West) presiding over this paradisiacal realm.

On the upper story of the central pavilion scene of Stone Chamber 2 from the Wuzhai Shan site, the female attendant at proper right of the central, frontally posed figure appears to be proffering a round, lidded cosmetic box of the kind described here (fig. 1). The female attendant at proper left holds up a bronze mirror, so the lady can check her appearance. Other lacquer objects are commonly seen in the "Wu family shrines" rubbings as well. Most of the cups, beakers, trays, jugs, musical instruments, game boards, and scabbards seen in the rubbings would have been made of lacquer.

ANTHONY BARBIERI-LOW

Notes

1. For a comparable example, see Zhongguo qiqi quanji bianji weiyuanhui, ed., *Zhongguo qiqi quanji* (*Complete works of Chinese lacquers*) (Fuzhou: Fujian meishu chubanshe, 1998), vol. 3, no. 239.

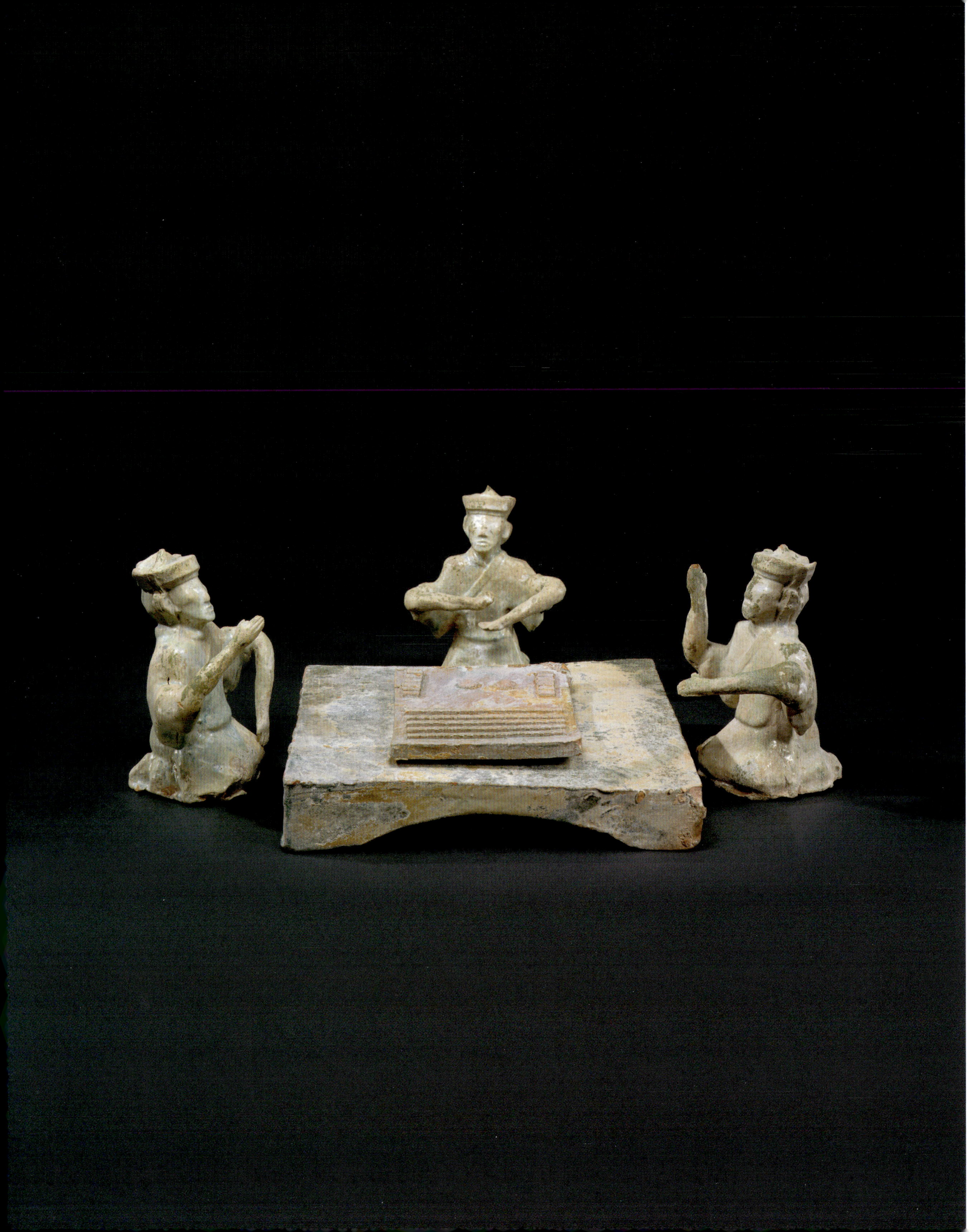

37 Three men playing *liubo*

Eastern Han dynasty. Earthenware with green glaze; figures h. 17.0 cm; table h. 5.5 cm, l. 26.5 cm, w. 23.5 cm; game board h. 2.0 cm, l. 16.0 cm. w. 12.0 cm. Harvard University Art Museums, acc. no. 2003.174a–e. Partial and promised gift of Anthony M. Solomon.

Popular during the Han dynasty, the game of *liubo* was frequently portrayed in the arts of the time, especially in Shandong and Sichuan provinces.[1] Carved images of the *liubo* game are found in several of the "Wu family shrines" rubbings (fig. 1; also see cat. no. 1.19), and lines forming the shape of the letters T, L, and V, which appeared on *liubo* game boards, were also cast on the backs of bronze mirrors (cat. no. 38). *Liubo* was also portrayed in sculptural mortuary models executed in a variety of materials, including ceramic, wood, and bronze.[2] Among these, the most common survivals are glazed earthenware examples dating from the Eastern Han, represented in this exhibition by the present green-glazed model of a game board set on a low table surrounded by three players.[3]

The *liubo* game was popular from the Eastern Zhou dynasty through the Han dynasty. Although surviving *liubo*-related art and artifacts primarily date from the Warring States period through the Eastern Han, it is likely that the game existed in some form prior to the Eastern Zhou and continued to be played after the collapse of the Han. How long *liubo* remained an activity of interest is debated, but its name lived on in literature, probably as an evocation of an earlier time.[4]

Liubo literally means "six *bo*," and apparently was sometimes simply referred to as *bo* in Han and earlier texts. The term *bo* may refer to the game or match, and the number "six" likely refers to each player's six game pieces, or perhaps the six bamboo sticks that were usually part of the game, for which it appears dice were sometimes substituted. *Liubo* is usually played by two individuals, judging from Han portrayals as well as from texts mentioning *liubo*. Teams of two might sometimes have played, but the additional figures seen in some representations of *liubo* may be onlookers or judges.

In *Three men* two players face each other across a rectangular board and a third figure looks on from the side.[5] The board is divided into two zones. On the side nearest the onlooker two rows of six game pieces flank a square area enclosing two circular objects, possibly weights or tokens or prizes. This area represents the square *liubo* game board, which

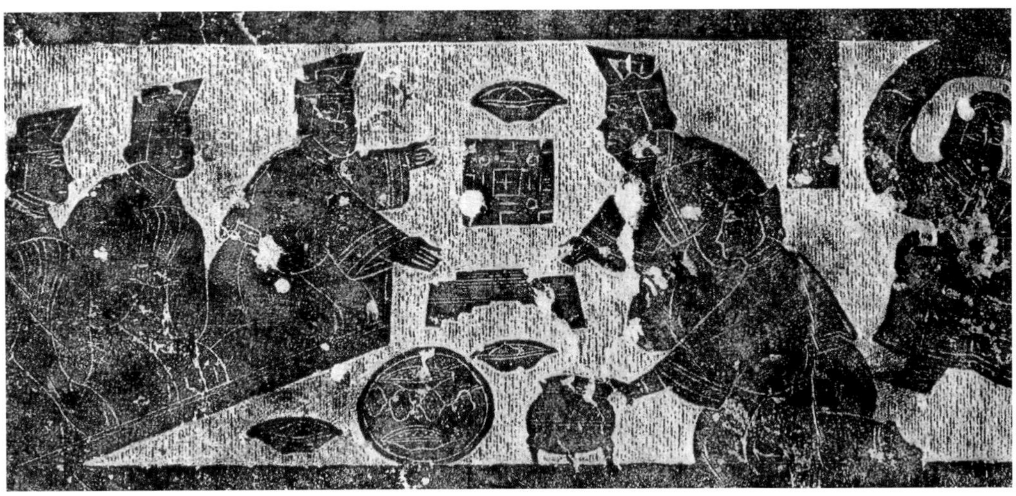

Fig. 1 *Playing a game of* liubo. Detail of Stone Chamber 1, Stone 1-E.2 (cat. no. 1.12). "Wu family shrines" rubbings. Princeton University Art Museum, acc. no. 2002-307.2.

would have borne patterns similar to the TLV designs on mirror backs, although these are not delineated on this model. On the other side, away from the onlooker, are shown five sticks (one less than the usual six, but there is evidence that this board was originally equipped with six sticks). The sticks were cast or thrown during the game, and in some representations the sticks are shown on the ground or on a mat. Given its long history and widespread popularity in the Han, the game probably developed regional variations, which may be apparent in pictorial and sculptural representations in tombs from Shandong, Sichuan, Henan, and Gansu.

Mortuary images or sculptures of *liubo* depict an amusement that the deceased is likely to have enjoyed in life and might well want to play again in the afterlife. In the decorative program of Han tombs both humans and Immortals are depicted playing this game. At the same time, *liubo* may have embodied cosmological symbolism, as the TLV diagrams on game boards and mirrors also appear on diviner's boards and sundials of the Han dynasty. In the most frequently illustrated form of *liubo* play, six sticks are thrown, an action that brings to mind divination using bamboo stalks or milfoil, which was popular before and during the Han dynasty. All this supports the view that the TLV design might also have been understood as a "cosmic diagram."[6]

How *liubo* was actually played is still a matter of controversy, but it seems to have been a game of both chance and skill. The element of chance was introduced through the casting of the sticks or dice. According to Colin Mackenzie: "Although we do not know the exact rules of *liubo*, surviving literary references indicate that the aim was to capture the other player's pieces."[7] The underlying reference was to battle, and some literary sources refer to "eating" (or killing) opposing pieces. This martial aspect of *liubo* is said to have dissuaded some Confucian scholars from taking it up.

Deities and Immortals (*xianren* or *yuren*) are frequently portrayed playing the game on tomb walls. Texts also recount tales of mortals playing *liubo* with supernatural beings on mountaintops, and a Shang king is reported to have had made an image of a deity against which he competed. When the deity lost (no doubt intentionally, as its moves were made by the king's subjects), it would be ridiculed and punished. It may be that such matches were conducted to win magic powers, or perhaps to control destiny.

After the Eastern Han *liubo* began to fall out of favor as a pastime of the elite. It may be that its association with Immortals, divination, and other beliefs and customs that flourished before and through the Han rendered it old-fashioned in the Period of Disunity, during which Buddhism brought a stream of new ideas and deities and Daoism evolved from its Han-dynasty forms. It may also have been that games involving human skills became more appealing than those of divine chance.[8]

VIRGINIA BOWER

Notes

1. The literature concerning *liubo* is vast and ever expanding. Recent publications include Virginia L. Bower, *From Court to Caravan: Chinese Tomb Sculptures from the Collection of Anthony M. Solomon*, ed. Robert D. Mowry (Cambridge, Mass.: Harvard University Art Museums, 2002), pp. 32–33, 59–60, 77, no. 5; Colin Mackenzie, "Games as Signifiers of Cultural Identity in Asia: *Weiqi* and Polo," *Orientations*, September 2004, pp. 48–49. Of great help to all interested in *liubo* are Zeng Lanying (Lillian L. Tseng), "Divining from the Game *Liubo*: An Explanation of a Han Wooden Slip Excavated at Yinwan," *China Archaeology and Art Digest*, vol. 4, no. 4 (2002), pp. 55–62, a revised English version by the author of her Chinese article in *Wenwu* 1998.8, pp. 62–65; Zheng Yan'e, "Preliminary Remarks on the Games of *Liubo* and *Saixi*," trans. Bruce Gordon Doar, *China Archaeology and Art Digest*, vol. 4, no. 4 (2002), pp. 79–95, originally published in *Nanfang wenwu* 1999.2, pp. 53–63; Cheng Linquan and Han Guohe, "A Study of Gaming Board (TLV) Mirrors Unearthed in the Northern Suburbs of Xi'an," trans. Bruce Gordon Doar, *China Archaeology and Art Digest*, vol. 4, no. 4 (2002), pp. 97–110, originally published in *Kaogu yu wenwu* 2002.5, pp. 49–54, 59. (My thanks to Nancy Steinhardt for bringing these articles to my attention.) Another relatively recent article of interest (brought to my attention by Victor H. Mair), is Mark Edward Lewis, "Dicing and Divination in Early China," *Sino-Platonic Papers*, no. 121 (July 2002), pp. 1–22. Also see Fu Juyou, "Lun Qin Han shiqi de boju boxi jianji boju wenjing" ("On the connection between the patterns on Qin and Han mirrors, games, game articles, and game boards"), *Kaogu xuebao* 1986.1, pp. 21–42; Hermann-Josef Röllicke, "Von 'Winkelwegen,' 'Eulen' und 'Fischziehern'—*liubo*: ein altchinesisches Brettspiel für Geister und Menschen" ("Of 'bent ways', 'owls', and 'fish-catchers'—*liubo*: an ancient Chinese board game for spirits and people"), *Board Game Studies: International Journal for the Study of Board Games*, vol. 2 (1990), pp. 24–41. Pioneering studies that are still worthwhile are Yang Lien-sheng, "An Additional Note on the Ancient Game Liu-po," *Harvard Journal of Asiatic Studies*, vol. 15, nos. 1–2 (1952), pp. 124–39; and Yang, "A Note on the So-called TLV Mirrors and the Game, Liu-po," *Harvard Journal of Asiatic Studies*, vol. 9, nos. 3–4 (1947), pp. 202–7.

2. For wood or bronze examples excavated in Gansu, see *Qin Han diaosu* (*Qin and Han sculpture*), ed. Zhongguo meishu quanji bianji weiyuanhui, *Zhongguo meishu quanji: diaosu* (*A comprehensive collection of Chinese arts: Sculpture*) series, vol. 2 (Beijing: Renmin meishu chubanshe, 1985), no. 68 (wood), no. 75 (bronze). It should be noted that the former has been classified by some as a more sedate form of *liubo* known as *saixi*. See Zheng Yan'e, "Preliminary Remarks on the Games of *Liubo* and *Saixi*," pp. 79–95 and esp. p. 85, fig. 13.

3. See n. below regarding a slightly different arrangement of this very same grouping. Among excavated works, the most closely comparable to the present sculpture is a green-glazed earthenware group recovered from an Eastern Han tomb in Lingbao County, Henan. See Henan bowuguan, "Lingbao Zhangwan Han mu" ("Han tomb at Zhangwan in Lingbao County"), *Wenwu* 1975.11, pp. 80–81, figs. 5, 35.

4. According to Colin Mackenzie, "Games as Signifiers of Cultural Identity in Asia," p. 49, *liubo* playing had ceased by the Tang dynasty but continued to be referred to in literature.

5. This same ceramic group is arranged differently, with one player and two onlookers, in Virginia Bower, *From Court to Caravan*, cat. no. 5. The illustration included in the present catalogue shows two players in action against each other.

6. Klaas Ruitenbeek, *Chinese Shadows: Stone Reliefs, Rubbings, and Related Works of Art from the Han Dynasty (206 BC–AD 220) in the Royal Ontario Museum* (Toronto: Royal Ontario Museum, 2002), pp. 24–27.

7. Colin Mackenzie, "Games as Signifiers of Cultural Identity in Asia," p. 48.

8. That *liubo* would so quickly fall out of favor after such a lengthy period of popularity has puzzled scholars. See Colin Mackenzie, "Games as Signifiers of Cultural Identity in Asia," p. 49; Oliver Moore, "Winning Throws in Games with Gods," *British Museum Magazine*, no. 25 (Summer 1996), p. 21.

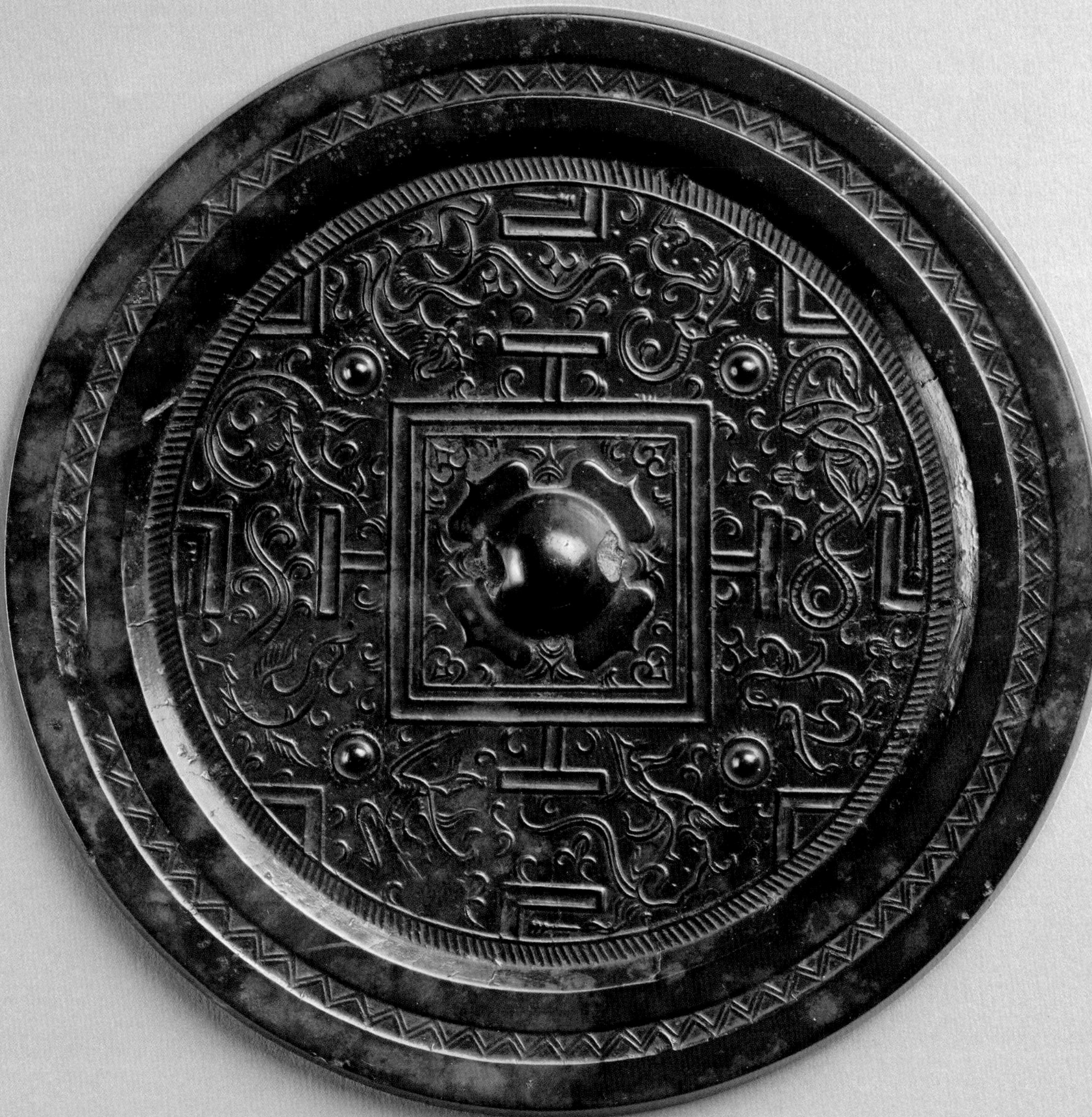

38 TLV mirror with eight fantastic creatures

Xin dynasty–early Eastern Han dynasty, 2d quarter of 1st century CE. Bronze; diam. 16.2 cm.
Princeton University Art Museum, acc. no. y1965-49. Museum purchase, from the C. D. Carter Collection.

This bronze mirror is a fine example of the popular, yet for modern scholars most enigmatic type of Han-dynasty mirror, a type defined by its radially symmetrical arrangement of three geometric motifs resembling the letters T, L, and V around the central knob. As illustrated, the T and L signs are always placed on perpendicular axes: the vertical stroke of a T sign is firmly attached to the midpoint of each side of the square box encompassing the hemispherical knob, and each L sign is placed sideways against the edge of the main decorative register. The V signs alternate symmetrically with the L signs along the circular edge, their openings facing outward. Additional decorative markers, in this case four round bosses surrounded by fine pebbles, are often placed mid-way between the corners of the square box and the tips of the V signs. This specific combination of geometric motifs led Swedish sinologist Bernhard Karlgren to coin the term "TLV mirror," which has become standard nomenclature for Western scholars and for some in East Asia.[1]

In contrast to the fixed TLV patterns, the other decoration on such mirrors can differ so substantially as to provide stylistic evidence for dating.[2] In early TLV mirrors the backgrounds are commonly filled with derivatives of Warring States designs, such as dragons and grass-and-leaf patterns (*caoye wen*). The oldest archaeologically recovered example comes from the tomb of Dou Wan, wife of Liu Sheng, Prince Jing of Zhongshan, buried in 104 BCE, where the TLV pattern is superimposed on a ground of interlaced dragons.[3] On such early mirrors background motifs and TLV patterns show no sign of coordinated design, as though two independent decorative schemes had been put together for reasons unrelated to aesthetics.

The Princeton TLV mirror, on the other hand, illustrates evident coordination of the eight fantastic creatures in the background and the demarcating TLV pattern. The designer made use of the natural compartmentalization created by the TLV pattern to fit each creature comfortably into one partition. Moving clockwise from the prancing tiger, they include an ibex, the *xuanwu* ("Dark Warrior," represented by intertwined snake and tortoise), a potbellied creature, the dragon, an Immortal, the Vermilion Bird (*zhuque*), and another bird. Six of the eight are grouped into humorously interacting pairs. The tiger turns its head as though staring at the ibex, which looks back fearlessly and proudly displays its abnormally large horn. Meanwhile, the dancing Immortal attempts to lure the dragon, which resists awkwardly and stumbles on its hind legs; the two birds arch toward each other. Only the *xuanwu* pays no attention to its potbellied neighbor. These extremely pictorial creatures are brought to life by fine, fluid relief lines, which contrast sharply with the stiff geometry of the broad-lined TLV patterns. The background is further enlivened by scattered hook-shaped motifs. A small arrow of unknown significance is found inside the opening of each L sign. The main decorative register is enclosed by a sloping band of hatch marks, and a slightly concave ribbon of double-zigzag pattern runs around the broad rim.

Four of these creatures—the dragon, Vermilion Bird, tiger, and *xuanwu*—have clear iconographic significance. They are the Four Directional Spirits (*si shen*) of Han cosmology, corresponding to east, south, west, and north.

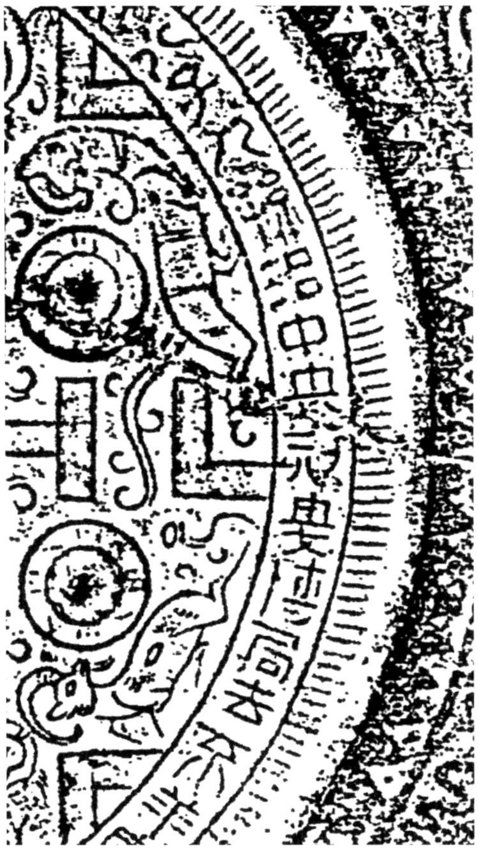

Fig. 1 Detail showing the inscription "Engrave [this] game-board pattern to chase away ill fortune." From the rubbing of a TLV mirror. Xin dynasty. Ink on paper; diam. 18.6 cm. Tokyo National Museum of Art. From Nishida Morio, "'*Hōkaku* kiku kyō' no zumon no keifu: '*ke lou bo ju qu bu xiang*' no meibun wo motsu kyō ni tsuite," *Museum*, no. 427 (1986), fig. 2.

On this mirror they are positioned correctly with respect to one another, which suggests awareness of their cosmological associations, although they are stylistically indistinct from their non-symbolic mates. Earlier TLV mirrors decorated with fantastic creatures bear only the Four Directional Spirits, and these often awkwardly straddle more than one of the compartments created by the TLV motifs, much like the dragons on Dou Wan's mirror.[4] The use of eight creatures rather than four, common on TLV mirrors contemporary with the present one, was probably prompted by aesthetic considerations rather than by iconographic changes.[5] The introduction of four companion creatures allowed each of the eight to fit more comfortably into one space cell. The companion creatures tend to vary from mirror to mirror and are often difficult to identify.

TLV mirrors were produced abundantly from the first century BCE through the first century CE. The Four Directional Spirits were incorporated into the design at the end of Western Han, and the new type flourished during Wang Mang's interregnum (9–24 CE) and the beginning of Eastern Han. Concurrent developments in cosmology and the rise of *yin-yang* and Five-Elements (*wu xing*) correlative thinking must have contributed to their popularity. The Princeton mirror, because of its eight-creature configuration and stylistic maturity, was probably made toward the end of this period, in the second quarter of the first century CE.

The origin and meaning of the TLV pattern, and the reason it appears on bronze mirrors, have intrigued scholars since the beginning of the twentieth century.[6] Some have suggested that individual geometric components evolved from earlier motifs such as grass-and-leaf patterns, dragons, and the Chinese character for mountain, *shan*.[7] Others have argued that they were modeled after compasses (*gui*) and try squares (*ju*), tools used to define the cosmos and often depicted in the hands of the mythological creators Fuxi and Nüwa on Han stone engravings (see cat. nos. 1.18, 1.23, 1.35).[8] The latter assumption has given rise to the term "*guiju jing*" ("compass and try-square mirror"), the name by which these mirrors are generally known in Chinese and Japanese literature.

In their efforts to understand the TLV pattern scholars have sought parallels on other Han artifacts and drawn freely on their understandings of Han cosmology.[9] The most plausible source for the TLV pattern is the popular Han-dynasty game known as *liubo*, played on a board marked with the same layout of TLV signs, the central square, and oftentimes the four diagonal markers (see cat. no. 37). A number of *liubo* boards, sometimes in complete sets, as well as depictions of divinities and humans playing the game, have been recovered by archaeologists (see cat. no. 1.12).[10] Although similarity between TLV mirrors and *liubo* game boards was noted as early as 1918 by Nakayama Heijirō, it was not until the late 1980s that this connection was firmly established. Nishida Morio (1986) and Zhou Zheng (1987) discovered independently, in the collections of the Tokyo National Museum and the Museum of Chinese History in Beijing, respectively, rubbings of two TLV mirrors with inscriptions that identify their own decorative schemes as *boju*, or "game-board pattern."[11] The two inscriptions, with minor differences in characters, state, "Engrave [this] game-board pattern to chase away ill fortune," suggesting that the design was appropriated from *liubo* game boards and placed on mirrors as a talisman (fig. 1). The awkward superimposition of TLV pattern on the background design, discussed earlier, supports this conclusion.

Helping to confirm the authenticity of these critical rubbing inscriptions and to further our understanding of the TLV design are two fortunate 1993 finds from Yinwan, Jiangsu Province.[12] Tomb 4 at Yinwan (dated between the end of Wang Mang's interregnum and beginning of Eastern Han) has yielded a TLV mirror with a fascinating inscription that refers explicitly to the mirror design as *liubo*.[13] Although the inscription does not explicitly mention chasing away ill fortune, the context suggests strongly that the game-board pattern was appropriated for its auspicious efficacy. The inscription reads:

In [Eastern] Han, Danyang has yielded fine copper, [which] when refined with silvery tin, becomes clear and bright. Carve the *liubo* at the center and in the shape of a square; dragon on the left and tiger on the right pace the four corners, and Vermilion Bird and *xuanwu* accord with *yin* and *yang*. [May] eight sons and nine grandsons occupy the center, and long protect [your] father and mother and benefit [your] elder and younger brothers. [May you] correspond with the four seasons and accord with the five elements, [may you be] bright as the rays of moon and sun in the universe. [May] this bright mirror befitting the Immortals recognize [you as] ministers and kings [and bless you] with fine jade and various beautiful objects, for a thousand autumns and ten thousand generations in eternal joy without end.[14]

A broad wooden slip from Yinwan Tomb 6 (late Western Han, after 10 BCE) helps explain why the game *liubo* had magical associations. The slip bears a diagram accompanied by a text that seems to imply the diagram was used for divination purposes. Hence, the excavators refer to the diagram and the text collectively as *boju zhan* (literally, "game-board divination") (fig. 2).[15] This diagram is nearly identical to a typical TLV pattern, differing in the addition of diagonals

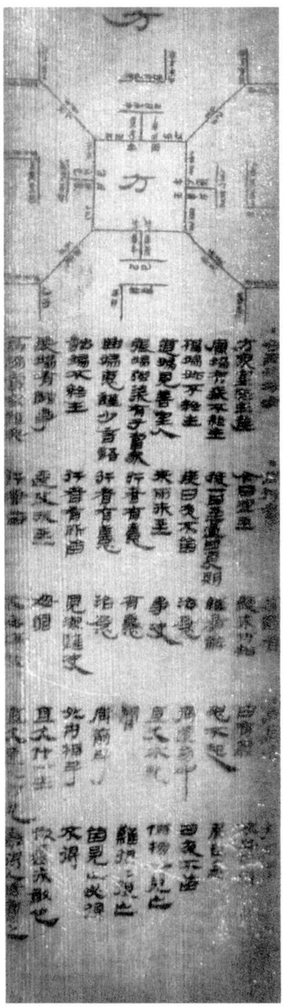

Fig. 2 *Boju zhan* (game-board diagram for divination). Late Western Han dynasty, after 10 BCE. Ink on wooden slip; h. 23 cm, w. 6 cm. Tomb 6 at Yinwan, Donghai County, Lianyungang, Jiangsu. From Lianyungang Shi bowuguan et al., eds., *Yinwan Han mu jiandu*, p. 21, no. YM6D9, back.

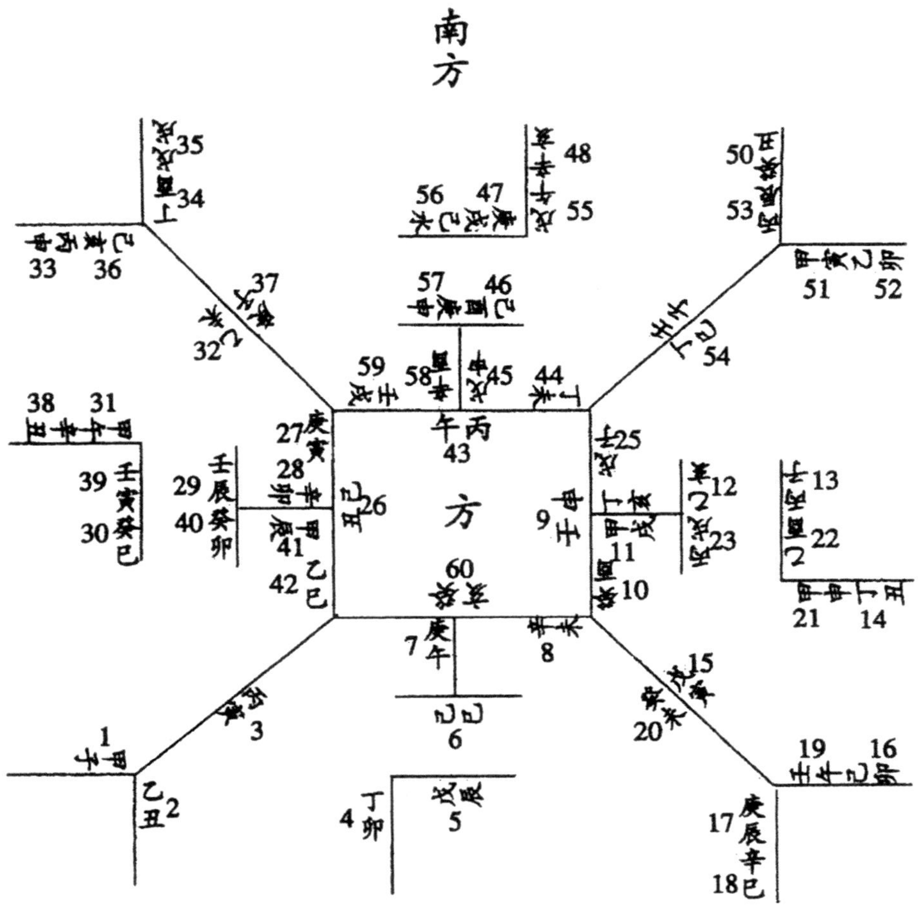

Fig. 3 Reconstructed diagram of *Boju zhan*. From Li Jiemin, "'Yinwan Han mu *boju zhan* mudu shijie' ding bu," *Wenwu* 2000.8, fig. 1.

connecting the V signs to the corners of the central square. Furthermore, the text identifies nine different possible positions on the diagram, which are labeled with the names of the sixty calendrical *ganzhi* dates, with some repetitions and omissions. For each of the nine positions, the text gives short divination outcomes for five possible inquiries: marriage, travel, imprisonment, illness, and death. Assuming that each *ganzhi* name should appear only once, Lillian Tseng has proposed a convincing ordering of these nine positions that would reveal a patterned arrangement of the consecutive *ganzhi* dates (fig. 3).[16] As such, the diagram is best understood as a graphical representation of an almanac that could be consulted in two ways: by picking a day for a given activity based on that day's predetermined auspicious position, or by determining what activities were appropriate to a given day according to its position on the diagram.[17] Put simply, the TLV pattern on the *boju zhan* diagram helped ensure the auspicious outcome of daily events. Appropriation of the TLV design for bronze mirrors can thus be understood as a borrowing of the magical power associated with *boju zhan* and its TLV diagram.

One additional feature to note on the *boju zhan* slip is the character meaning "south" at the top of the diagram. This prominent label alerts us to an inherent directional association of the TLV diagram, an association that probably made it easy for designers to combine the TLV pattern with the iconography of the Four Directional Spirits. It is tempting to interpret progression through the TLV diagram as progression through temporal and cosmological realms. This might explain why Han murals and engravings so often depict divinities playing *liubo*. No doubt the game's popularity with the Immortals enhanced the game-board pattern's appropriateness for decorating Han mirrors.[18]

Although it is not clear whether the TLV pattern originated as a divination diagram or as a board game, by the end of Western Han it had acquired such close associations with cosmology and divination as to become a talisman of good fortune. Michael Loewe writes, "To the Han Chinese the problem of evil was a matter of cosmic order rather than theology, ethics or psychology," and to avert calamities, it was necessary "to find a scheme of ordered regulation of the universe."[19] The TLV pattern must have well fulfilled this function, as it was also placed on coins, stone coffins, and mortuary architecture.[20]

DAVID T. LIU

Notes

1. See Bernhard Karlgren, "Early Chinese Mirror Inscriptions," *Bulletin of the Museum of Far Eastern Antiquities* (hereafter *BMFEA*), no. 6 (1934), pp. 9–79; Karlgren, "Huai and Han," *BMFEA*, no. 13 (1941), pp. 13–27, pls. 7–81; Karlgren, "Early Chinese Mirrors: Classification Scheme Recapitulated," *BMFEA*, no. 40 (1968), pp. 79–98, pls. 1–105. TLV mirrors are also called "cosmic mirrors" in Western literature because of their association with cosmology; see discussion below.

2. A TLV mirror lacking any one of these three geometric signs would be considered by East Asian scholars a *bianxing* ("mutation") and assigned a late date, toward the end of Eastern Han or in the Three Kingdoms period. Such omission is interpreted as degeneration and likely signals a familiar design's loss of iconographic significance.

3. Zhongguo shehui kexueyuan kaogu yanjiusuo and Hebei Sheng wenwu guanlichu, eds., *Mancheng Han* *mu fajue baogao* (*Excavations of the Han tomb at Mancheng*) (Beijing: Wenwu chubanshe, 1980), vol. 1, pp. 262, 265–66, and vol. 2, pl. 181/2.

4. See, for example, Cheng Changxin and Cheng Ruixiu, *Tongjing jianshang* (*Appreciating bronze mirrors*) (Beijing: Beijing Yanshan chubanshe, 1989), pl. 26.

5. See also discussion in Ju-hsi Chou, *Circles of Reflection: the Carter Collection of Chinese Bronze Mirrors* (Cleveland: Cleveland Museum of Art, 2000), no. 26, pp. 43–44. This Cleveland mirror has a silvery coating applied over only the Four Directional Spirits; Chou suggests that such mirrors belong to the transition from the four- to the eight-creature configuration. Another example with highlighted Four Directional Spirits comes from Tomb 59B at Shaogou, Luoyang, Henan Province; see Zhongguo kexueyuan kaogu yanjiusuo, ed., *Luoyang Shaogou Han mu* (*Han tombs at Shaogou*) (Beijing: Kexue chubanshe, 1959), pp. 165–69, 174–75, pl. 43/1.

6. For a comprehensive review of previous scholarship, see Michael Loewe, *Ways to Paradise: The Chinese Quest for Immortality* (London: George Allen & Unwin, 1979); and Kong Xiangxing and Liu Yimang, *Zhongguo gu tongjing* (*Chinese ancient bronze mirrors*) (Taipei: Yishu tushu gongsi, 1994), pp. 58–64.

7. See, for example, Nakayama Heijirō, "Koshiki Shina kyōkan enkaku (san)" ("The development of ancient Chinese mirrors III"), *Kōkogaku zasshi*, vol. 9, no. 4 (1918), pp. 189–212.

8. Harada Yoshito, "Sen'oku Seishō: kyōkan bu, zuhan kaisetsu" ("Explanatory notes on Sen'oku Seishō, Part II, Ancient mirrors"), in *Sen'oku Seishō* (Tokyo: Kokasha, 1918). Cf. Hayashi Minao, "Kandai no zugara ni-san ni tsuite" ("Concerning the designs on Han dynasty mirrors"), *Tōhō gakuhō*, no. 44 (1973), pp. 1–65.

9. For possible connections with the Han diviner's board (*shipan*), see Sidney M. Kaplan, "On the Origin of the TLV Mirror," *Revue des Arts Asiatiques*, vol. 11 (1937), pp. 21–24; Lan-ying Tseng, "Picturing Heaven: Image and Knowledge in Han China," (PhD diss., Harvard University, 2001), p. 38, nn. 45–46. For illustrations of *shipan*, see Zhongguo qiqi quanji bianji weiyuanhui, ed., *Zhongguo qiqi quanji*, vol. 3: *Han* (*Complete works of Chinese lacquer*, vol. 3: *Han dynasty*) (Fuzhou: Fujian meishu chubanshe, 1998), no. 295. For discussions of sundial and TLV patterns, see Sun Ji, "Tuoketuo rigui" ("Sundial found in Tuoketuo"), *Zhongguo lishi bowuguan guankan*, no. 3 (1981), pp. 74–81, 91; cf. Li Xueqin, "Boju zhan yu guiju wen" ("Game-board divination diagram and the TLV pattern"), *Wenwu* 1997.1, pp. 49–51; also Joseph Needham, "Sundial (Solar Time Indicator)," in *Science and Civilisation in China*, vol. 3 (Cambridge: Cambridge University Press, 1959), pp. 302–13. For Tibetan connections, see Schuyler Cammann, "The 'TLV' Pattern on Cosmic Mirrors of the Han Dynasty," *Journal of the American Oriental Society*, vol. 69, no. 4 (October–December 1948), pp. 159–67. For parallels in mortuary architectures, see Anneliese Bulling, "The Decoration of Some Mirrors of the Chou and Han Periods," *Artibus Asiae*, vol. 18, no. 1 (1955), pp. 31, 42–43; Tseng Yuho Ecke, "Cosmic Mirrors," in *Bronze Mirrors from Ancient China: Donald H. Graham Jr. Collection*, preface, essay and catalogue by Toru Nakano (Hong Kong: Orientations, 1994), pp. 46–49. For fascinating discussions of TLV and Han cosmology, see Hayashi Minao, "Kandai no zugara," pp. 10–14; Lan-ying Tseng "Picturing Heaven," pp. 12–22, 67–72.

10. The earliest *liubo*-like game board comes from a companion burial to King Cuo of Zhongshan, who died in 313 BCE. This stone game board has the exact TLV pattern plus a few additional lines. See Hebei Sheng wenwu guanlichu, "Hebei Sheng Pingshan Xian Zhanguo shiqi Zhongshan guo muzang fajue jianbao" ("Brief excavation report of Warring States–period Zhongshan kingdom tomb at Pingshan County, Hebei"), *Wenwu* 1979.1, pp. 13, 26; China Cultural Relics Promotion Center, *Treasures: 300 Best Excavated Antiques from China* (Beijing: New World Press, 1992), p. 40. For examples of Han lacquered *liubo* boards, see *Zhongguo qiqi quanji*, vol. 3, nos. 3, 67, 152, 210.

11. Nishida Morio, "'Hōkaku kiku kyō' no zumon no keifu: '*ke lou bo ju qu bu xiang*' no meibun wo motsu kyō ni tsuite" ("Genealogy of the pattern of so-called TLV mirrors: with special reference to the mirror inscribed *ke lou bo ju qu bu xiang*"), *Museum*, no. 427 (1986), pp. 28–34; Zhou Zheng, "Guiju jing yinggai cheng boju jing" ("*Guiju jing* should be renamed *boju jing*"), *Kaogu* 1987.12, pp. 1116–18.

12. For site report, see Lianyungang Shi bowuguan et al., eds., *Yinwan Han mu jiandu* (*Inscribed slips from the Han tombs at Yinwan*) (Beijing: Zhonghua shuju, 1997), pp. 155–56, 160–69.

13. Ibid., pp. 47, 171.

14. For transcription of the Chinese text, see ibid., pp. 160–61.

15. Ibid., p. 21, back of slip YM6D9; for transcription of the Chinese text, see ibid., pp. 125–26; for an overview of other divinatory texts from Yinwan, see Liu Hongshi, "Donghai Yinwan Han mu shushu le jiandu shidu" ("An explanation of the inscribed slips for divination from the Han tombs at Yinwan, Donghai County"), *Dongnan wenhua* 1997.4, pp. 67–73; and Liu Lexian, "Yinwan Han mu chutu shushu wenxian chutan" ("Preliminary study of the documents related to divination from the Han tombs at Yinwan"), in *Yinwan Han mu jiandu zonglun* (*Collected essays on the inscribed slips from the Han tombs at Yinwan*), ed. Lianyungang Shi bowuguan et al. (Beijing: Kexue chubanshe, 1999).

16. Zeng Lanying [Lan-ying Tseng], "Yinwan Han mu *boju zhan* mudu shijie" ("Explanation of the TLV diagram for divination from Yinwan"), *Wenwu* 1999.8, pp. 62–65; Li Jiemin, "'Yinwan Han mu *Boju zhan* mudu shijie' ding bu" ("Correction and supplement to 'An explanation of the TLV diagram for divination from Yinwan'"), *Wenwu* 2000.8, pp. 73–75. Although nothing proves that the sequence of moves was the same for the game as for divination, these studies offer insights into the allowed positions and paths between them in *liubo*. One of the nine positions is on the diagonals linking V signs to corners of the square box; it seems that the four diagonal markers found frequently on *liubo* game boards and the round bosses on TLV mirrors were intended as indicators for this position.

17. Li Xueqin, "Boju zhan yu guiju wen," pp. 49–51; Lan-ying Tseng, "Picturing Heaven," pp. 47–56.

18. Tseng Yuho Ecke, "Cosmic Mirrors," p. 47.

19. Loewe, *Ways to Paradise*, p. 3.

20. Suzuki Naomi, "Hakukyoku mon to enin rokuhaku zu: sono seikaku to Zen Kan matsu no ryūkō yōin" ("Game-board pattern and scenes of banqueting and *liubo* playing: their characteristics and primary reasons for their popularity about the end of the Former Han dynasty"), *Chūgoku shutsudo shiryō kenkyū*, 2003.7, pp. 103–23; Lan-ying Tseng, "Picturing Heaven," pp. 62–65; and Tseng Yuho Ecke, "Cosmic Mirrors," pp. 48–49.

39 Painted mirror with daily life scenes

Western Han dynasty, 1st half of 2d century BCE. Bronze painted with mineral pigments; diam. 22.7 cm. Private collection.

The three concentric painted registers on this mirror are separated by smooth concave rings, and the outer edge is slightly beveled. The registers are outlined by threads of white and framed on their inner and outer perimeters by narrow bands of alternating white lozenges and vermilion zigzags. The small triple-fluted central knob is common also on mirrors of the Warring States period. Surrounding it is a bluish green quatrefoil set against a vermilion background; four white teardrops punctuate the design. On the middle register a light green background is evenly partitioned by four large vermilion flowers, their petals dotted with white and their centers now illegible. Enclosing each flower is a swirling cloud pattern embellished with hooks and feathers derived from earlier dragon motifs; fine parallel lines link the four flower units. The airy geometric design, although interesting and colorful, does not distract from the more complex and exciting scenes of human interaction in the outer register.

Executed also on a vermilion background, the outer register, the largest and most prominent, is likewise divided evenly into four sections by large medallions, now greatly deteriorated. These medallions may have been imitations of the colorful dotted glass beads and inlays found commonly amongst grave goods of the late Warring States and Western Han periods, sometimes inlaid on mirror backs.[1] Originally each medallion was surrounded by an elaborate cloud-like pattern. In each of the sections demarcated by the medallions, a scene from aristocratic daily life is illustrated: hunting, meeting, and playing *liubo*. As there is no apparent sequence or connection among the scenes, the outer register is best understood not as a continuous narrative but as an assemblage of favorite pastimes of the nobility. Whether the individual scenes had iconographic significance is now impossible to surmise.

In the hunting scene two mounted archers close on a wild boar, one in front, the other from behind. From the position of his arms, the archer behind the boar once held a fully drawn bow. Only the front hooves of his white horse touch the ground. The archer in front has turned sideways in his saddle and is aiming at the fleeing boar, whose leaping posture is the same as that of the horses. In the background scattered patches of shrub-like trees denote wilderness (cf. cat. 1.11, middle of second register). Still discernible are the bridles and reins of the horses and the facial features and black headdresses of the archers.

The neighboring scene depicts two facing figures, kneeling, possibly playing *liubo*. Although only traces of the *liubo* board survive in this depiction, comparison with a similar mirror (diam. 27.7 cm) now in Turin, Italy, reinforces this identification.[2] The player on the right has his right arm raised as though casting dice, while the other looks on. To the right of the players are two attendants, and between them a *hu* wine vessel (cf. cat. nos. 24–27) placed on the ground. The closer attendant walks toward the pair, holding a long, curvy, unidentified implement, possibly a wine ladle. At the left are two more attendants, shown scurrying toward the players. Tall trees frame the players, suggesting that the mise-en-scène is a woodland grove and at the same time, by vignetting the players, connoting their elevated status relative to the attendants.

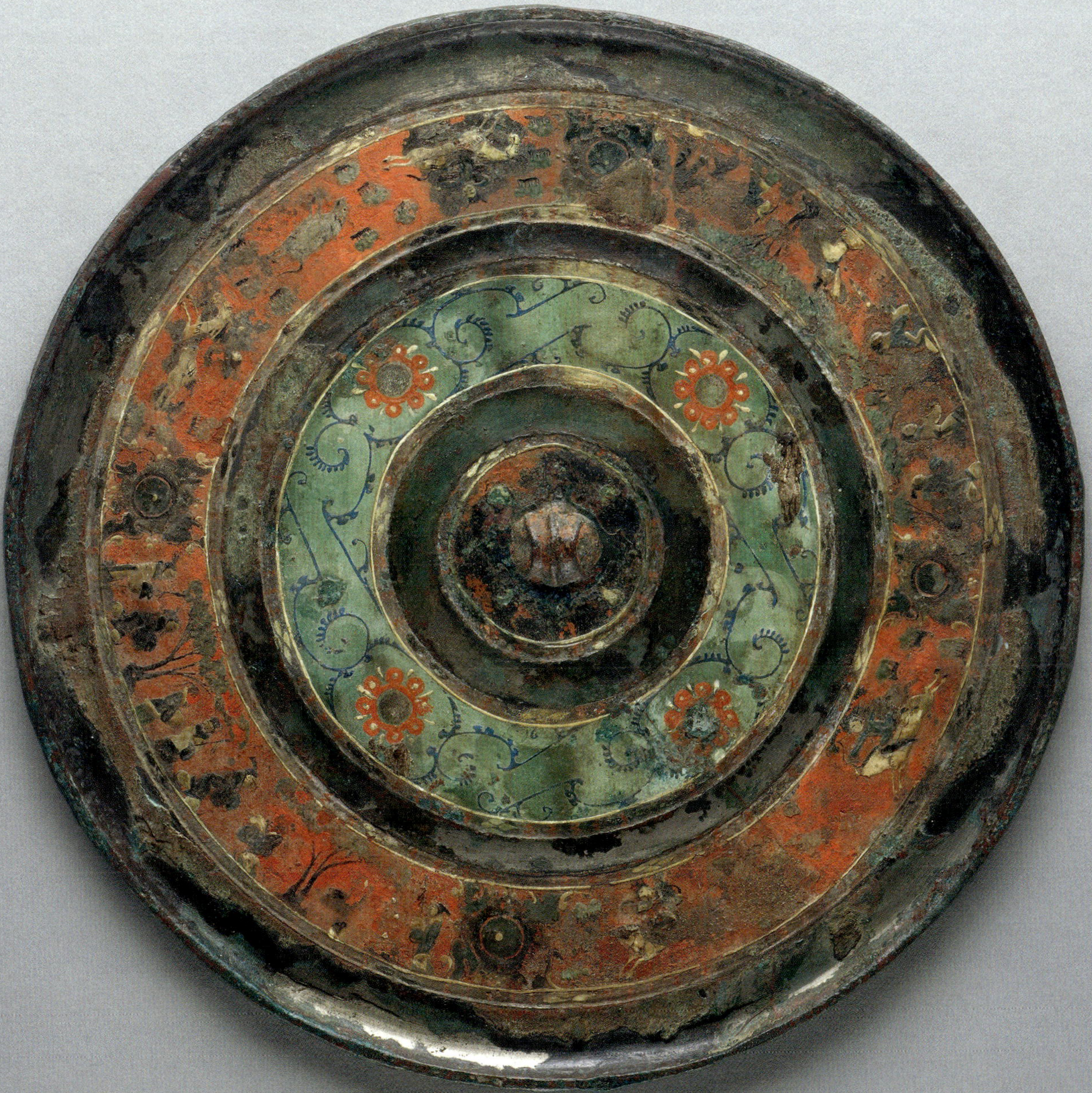

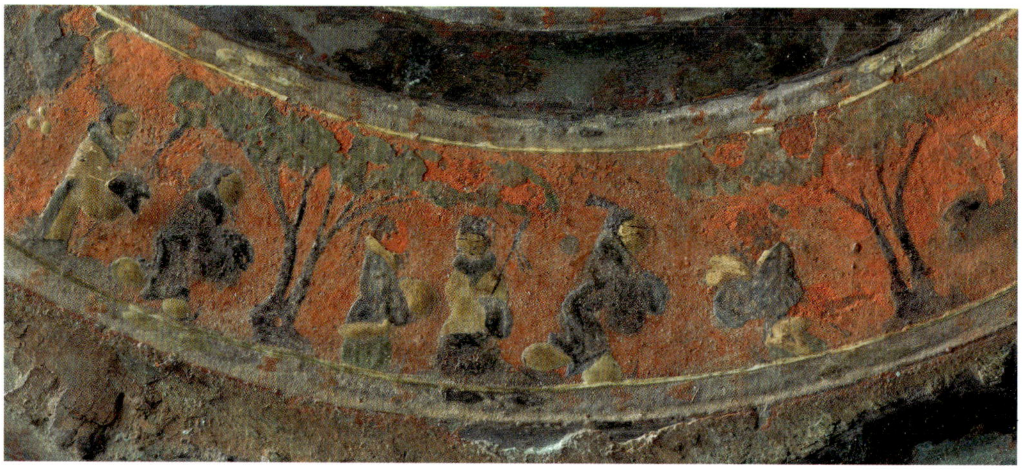

The following section, poorly preserved, appears identical to the first hunting scene, except that deterioration has obliterated the quarry. The second hunting scene on the Turin mirror, however, depicts a boar being hunted by an archer in a chariot drawn by four horses. Finally, we see two noblemen in a grove, bowing to each other. Behind the nobleman on the left stand two servants, one of them holding a long staff. Four additional attendants are visible, two on either side (detail).

These lavishly painted scenes, in place of cast and/or inlaid decorations, set this mirror apart from most extant bronze mirrors of ancient China in both technique and iconography. Bronze mirrors painted with lacquer are known from as early as the Warring States period, but they share similar motifs of intertwined dragons and geometric patterns with lacquerware and inlaid bronzes.[3] The type of painted mirror represented by the present example did not appear until Western Han. It is distinguished by its subject matter—human figures, chariots, and horses—and by its technique—the painting was done with oil-based mineral pigments on a white, plaster-like ground.[4] A painted mirror of this type (diam. 27.5 cm) was recovered archaeologically from Hongmiaopo, Xi'an, Shaanxi Province, in 1963. It dates from the beginning of Western Han.[5] This mirror is nearly identical to the Turin example and compares closely with the present mirror. All three mirrors were probably decorated using the method described above. Four other painted mirrors of the same type as the present mirror have been found in the Western Han tomb of the king of Nanyue who died in 122 BCE; the paintings on these mirrors, however, are mostly lost.[6] Painted mirrors seem to have gone out of production by the end of the second century BCE. Chen Peifen of the Shanghai Museum has suggested that a number of Western Han mirrors whose backs are now smooth and unornamented might once have been painted by the method summarized above, and that the painted scenes have simply not survived.[7]

These scenes of secular life are iconographically altogether different from the illustrations of Immortals and fantastic beings found on many contemporary lacquered objects, the most famous being the black-lacquered coffin painted with cloud patterns and Immortals from the tomb of Lady Dai at Mawangdui, Changsha, Hunan Province (early second century BCE). The present mirror represents a concurrent but distinct artistic development; its closest ancestor is the decorative band around the lid of a lacquer box excavated from Tomb 2 at Baoshan (316 BCE or earlier), which depicts chariot processions and meetings.[8] The figural scenes on the mirror develop further the pictorial innovations of the Baoshan box. On the mirror, trees do not serve mainly as pictorial devices to separate individual scenes as they do on the Baoshan box; rather, they are used to evoke the natural setting. Each copse is supplied with its own ground plane, suggesting recession in depth, and the animals show greater fluidity and vitality, suggesting the artists' greater command of naturalistic representation.

DAVID T. LIU

Notes

1. Michèle Pirazzoli-t'Serstevens, "Un miroir peint du début de l'époque des Han," *Arts Asiatiques*, vol. 57 (2002), p. 224. The author wishes to thank Prof. Alain Thote of the École Pratique des Hautes Études for this reference. For an example of a Warring States mirror inlaid with jade and glass beads, see Zhongguo qingtongqi quanji bianji weiyuanhui, ed., *Zhongguo qingtongqi quanji*, vol. 16: *Tongjing* (*Complete works of Chinese bronzes*, vol. 16: *Bronze mirrors*) (Beijing: Wenwu chubanshe, 1998), no. 34.

2. See discussion of a similar assemblage of figures on a painted mirror now in Turin, Italy, in Pirazzoli-t'Serstevens, "Un miroir peint," p. 224.

3. Chen Peifen, "Zhongguo qingtongjing fazhan gaishu" ("Overview of the development of Chinese bronze mirrors"), in *Zhongguo qingtongqi quanji*, vol. 16, p. 27; Henan Sheng wenwu yanjiusuo, ed., *Xinyang Chu mu* (*Chu tomb from Xinyang*) (Beijing: Wenwu chubanshe, 1986); Cai Huanbo and Gao Zhongxiao, "Hunan Ciri Shiban Cun sanshiliu hao Zhanguo mu fajue baogao" ("Excavation report of Tomb 36 at Shiban Village, Ciri, Hunan"), *Wenwu* 1990.10; for additional illustrations, see Tan Weisi et al., eds., *Hubei chutu wenwu jinhua* (*Gems of excavated artifacts from Hubei Province*) (Wuhan: Hubei jiaoyu chubanshe, 2001), p. 100.

4. Chemical analyses done on similar mirrors at the Shaanxi Historical Museum and at Turin suggest the use of mineral pigments. See Luo Li, "Handai caihui tongjing de huizhi gongyi ji yanliao yanjiu" ("Research on the painting techniques and pigments used in Han-dynasty painted mirrors"), *Kaogu yu wenwu* 2002.4, pp. 82–84; see also Pirazzoli-t'Serstevens, "Un miroir peint," p. 224 and n. 4.

5. *Zhongguo qingtongqi quanji*, vol. 16: *Tongjing*, no. 44; Helmut Brinker and Roger Goepper, eds., *Kunstschätze aus China* (Zurich: Kunsthaus, 1980), no. 33, pp. 164–66. For circumstances of recovery, see Fu Jiayi, "Xi'an Shi Wenguanchu suo cang liang mian Handai tongjing" ("Two Han mirrors collected at the Xi'an Municipal Bureau of Cultural Relics"), *Wenwu* 1979.2, pp. 61–62. Another archaeologically recovered painted mirror came from the tomb of Western Han minister Chen Qingshi in Xi'an; the pigments, however, have mostly deteriorated. See Cheng Linquan et al., "Xihan Chen Qingshi mu fajue jianbao" ("Brief report on the excavation of the tomb of Western Han Chen Qingshi"), *Kaogu yu wenwu*, 1992.6, pp. 17–18.

6. *Zhongguo qingtongqi quanji*, vol. 16: *Tongjing*, nos. 42, 43; Guangzhou Shi wenwu guanli weiyuanhui et al., eds., *Xihan Nanyue wang mu* (*Tomb of the Western Han king of Nanyue*) (Beijing: Wenwu chubanshe, 1991), vol. 1, p. 84. For other examples of painted mirrors, see Han Jianwu, Zhao Feng, and Zhu Tianshu, "Shaanxi lishi bowuguan xin zhengji wenwu jinghua" ("Selected cultural artifacts recovered by the Shaanxi Historical Museum"), *Shaanxi lishi bowuguan guankan*, 1994.1, p. 156 and pl. III; Fogg Museum of Art, *Grenville L. Winthrop: Retrospective for a Collector, Fogg Museum of Art, Cambridge, Massachusetts, January 23–March 31, 1969* (Cambridge, Mass.: Fogg Museum of Art, 1969), no. 56; Umehara Sueiji, "Sengoku jidai no saiga kyō" ("Painted mirrors of the Warring States period"), *Bijutsu kenkyū*, vol. 178 (1954), pp. 153–72.

7. Chen Peifen, "Qingtongjing gaishu," pp. 27–28.

8. Richard Barnhart et al., eds., *Three Thousand Years of Chinese Painting* (New Haven: Yale University Press, 1997); Hubei Sheng Jingsha tielu kaogu dui, ed., *Baoshan Chu mu* (*Chu tombs at Baoshan*) (Beijing: Wenwu chubanshe, 1991), pp. 20–21, fig. 9; pp. 144–46.

40 Mirror with quatrefoil and linked arcs on a stand

Middle to late Eastern Han dynasty, late 1st century CE. Bronze mirror and gilt bronze stand; diam. of mirror 28.2 cm, h. of mirror and stand 49.8 cm. Private collection.

The stand that holds this large bronze mirror consists of a gilt-bronze semicircle with a short stem and a gilt-bronze splayed quatrefoil foot. The two components were probably originally connected by a now disintegrated element of lacquered wood, for which a plain replacement has been made. Although no Han mirror stand has been found in secure archaeological context, comparison with a nearly identical example in the Nelson-Atkins Museum of Art would suggest that a third gilt component, a foot ring around the base, is missing from the current assembly.[1]

The mirror, detachable from the stand, has a large pierced domical central knob, surrounded by a quatrefoil pattern. Alternating with the petals are seal-script characters that together read *chang yi zi sun*, meaning "[to be] cherished by sons and grandsons for a long time." Enclosing the quatrefoil are two circular bands, the narrower one hatched and the wider plain. The register immediately beyond these bands features a star whose eight points are ornamented with two thread-relief motifs in alternation. The outline of the star is defined by a series of raised, contiguous, smooth arcs. Aligning with these eight points in the following register are eight spirals, which serve as nuclei of a continuous running spiral motif. The spirals are connected by thin diagonal relief lines; the remaining areas of the register are filled with finely spaced threads. In contrast, the outermost and widest band is plain, echoing the smoothness of the linked arcs near the center. Mirrors of this type were popular in the Central Plain (*zhongyuan*) and northern regions, particularly in Henan, Shandong, and Shaanxi; they have been dated to middle to late Eastern Han.[2]

The gilt semicircular support, which ends in two beautifully cast dragon heads, is grooved along its entire inner circumference, so that the back of each head is split down the middle. The dragons' mouths are slightly open, showing their sharp upper and lower fangs, orderly rows of teeth, and pointy tongues. Their eyebrows are raised, and their bulging eyes stare attentively. These dragons have short, stiff snouts and short beards beneath their chins. Between their ears they have striated horns that curve slightly upward at the tip. Intaglio lines and small circles suggest manes and scales. The rest of the semicircular support is smooth and undecorated, and the foot is essentially a three-dimensional rendition of the quatrefoil on the mirror. Judging by the style of the dragon heads, the stand might well be contemporary with the mirror. Dragons of the following Six Dynasties period are more fluid and animated.[3]

Most bronze mirrors in ancient China were hand held, aided by cords, often silk, strung through the pierced knobs on their backs (see cat. nos. 1.8, 1.26, 1.36). More complicated suspension mechanisms are known from the late Warring States period; a large mirror with three evenly spaced suspension rings around the circumference was found at Linzi, Shandong Province, in 1963.[4] Current archaeological evidence suggests that mirror stands were a relatively late development, probably appearing only in Eastern Han. One of the earliest evidences for the use of mirror stands comes from the famous painting *Admonitions of the Court Instructress to Palace Ladies*, which probably copies a fourth-century original.[5] In one section

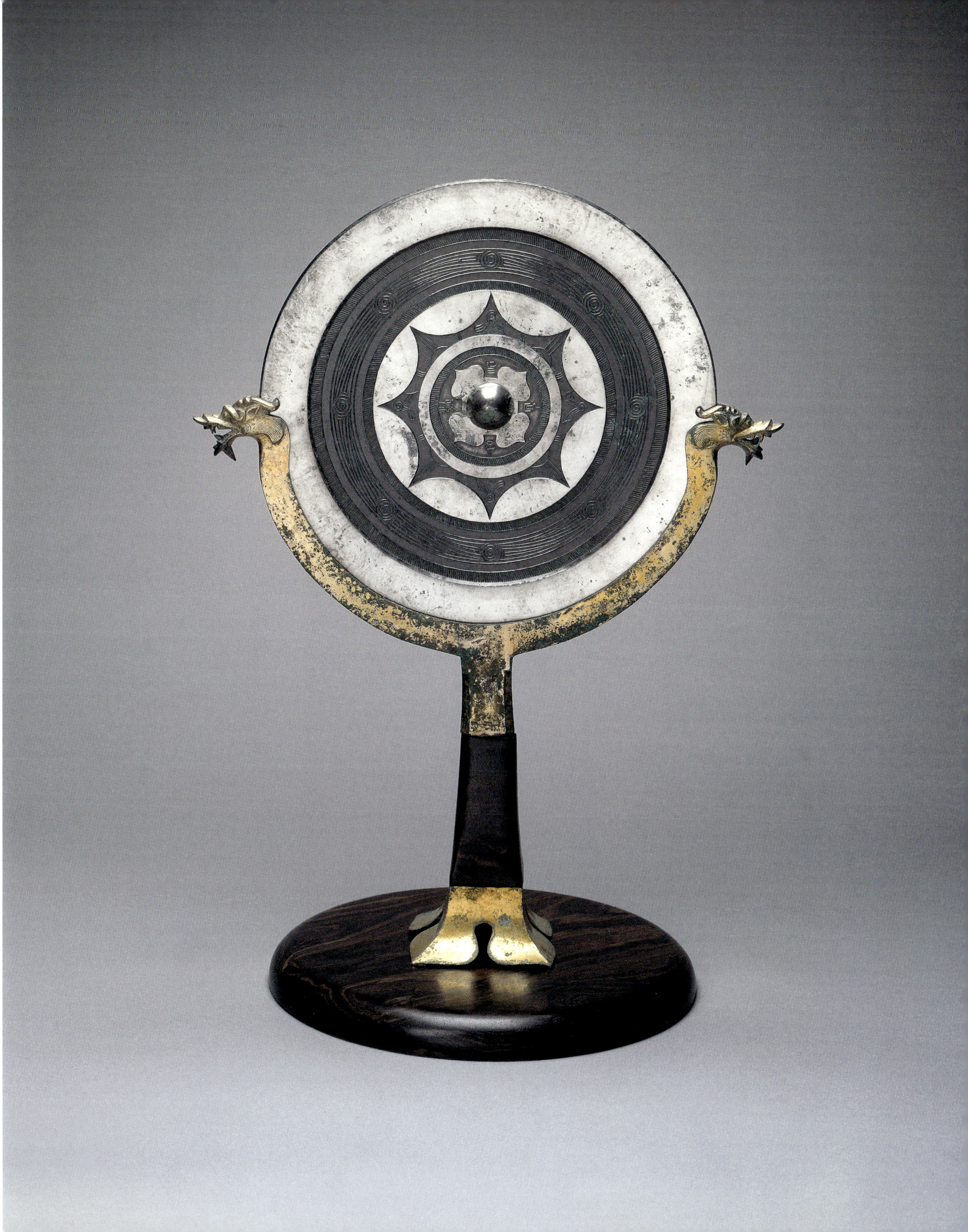

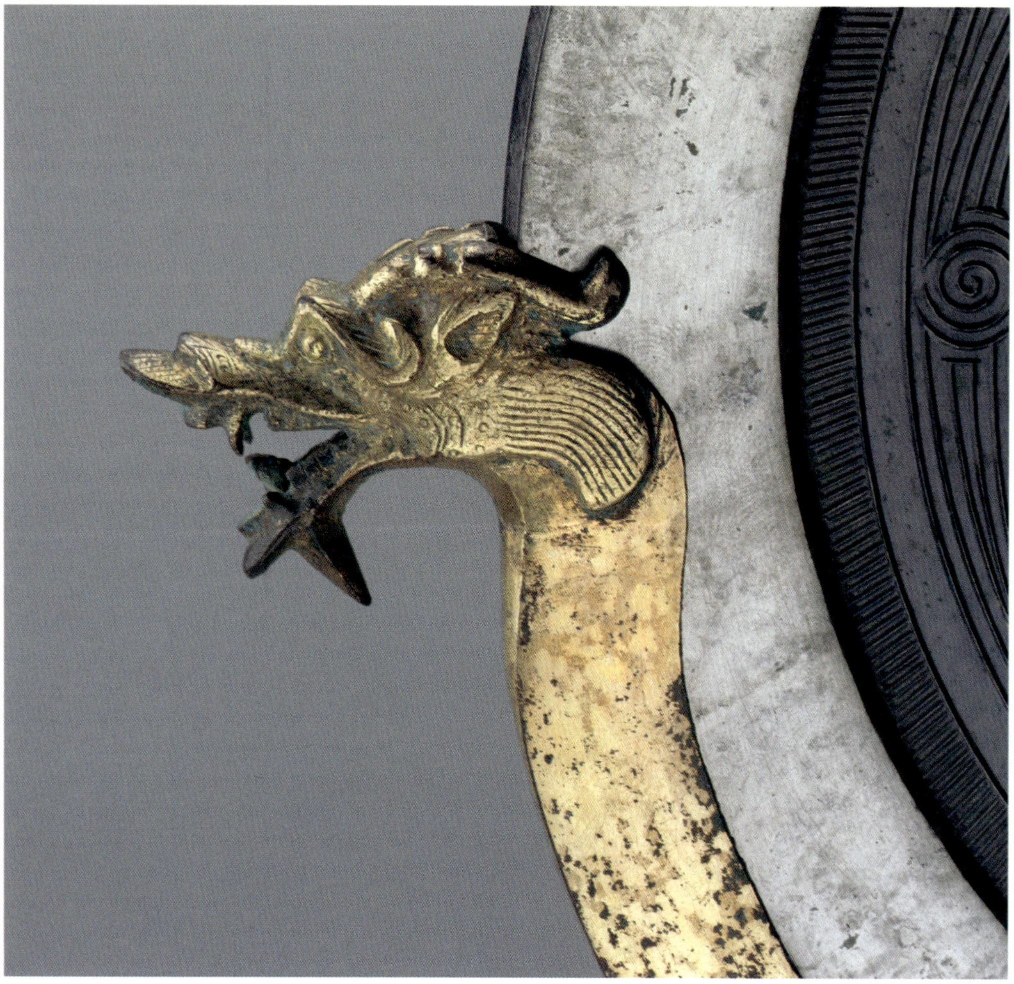

a seated court lady is having her hair combed by a servant in front of a bronze mirror placed on a wooden stand.[6] We may plausibly assume that mirrors of the size—and consequently the weight—of the present one and the Nelson-Atkins example prompted the use of mirror stands, as they would have been tiring to hold in the hand. In his study of the Nelson-Atkins mirror, Yang Xiaoneng suggests that mirrors of such size and opulence were probably reserved for the use of royalty and aristocracy.[7]

DAVID T. LIU

Notes

1. Xiaoneng Yang, "A Han Bronze Mirror and Its Gilt Bronze Stand in the Nelson-Atkins Museum of Art," *Oriental Art*, vol. 42, no. 1 (1996), pp. 14–23. For other examples, see William C. White, *Tombs of Old Lo-yang* (Shanghai: Kelly & Walsh, 1934), pp. 86–87 and pl. 46; J. J. Lally & Co. Oriental Art, *Arts of Ancient China* (New York: J. J. Lally, 1990), no. 12.

2. Kong Xiangxing and Liu Yimang, *Zhongguo gu tongjing* (*Ancient Chinese mirrors*) (Taipei: Yishu tushu gongsi, 1994), pp. 66–67. For comparative examples, see Zhongguo kexueyuan kaogu yanjiusuo, ed., *Luoyang Shaogou Han mu* (*Han tombs from Shaogou, Luoyang*) (Beijing: Kexue chubanshe, 1959), pp. 169–71, 175, and pl. 45/1; Ju-hsi Chou, *Circles of Reflection: the Carter Collection of Chinese Bronze Mirrors* (Cleveland: Cleveland Museum of Art, 2000), no. 17.

3. Cf. Eskenazi, *Sculpture and Ornament in Early Chinese Art, 11 June–13 July 1996* (London: Eskenazi, 1996), no. 21; Sherman Lee et al., *China 5,000 Years: Innovation and Transformation in the Arts* (New York: Guggenheim Museum, 1998), no. 59.

4. Zhongguo qingtongqi quanji bianji weiyuanhui, ed., *Zhongguo qingtongqi quanji*, vol. 16: *Tongjing* (*Complete catalogue of Chinese bronzes*, vol. 16: *Bronze mirrors*) (Beijing: Wenwu chubanshe, 1998), no. 32. For Western Han examples, see Huang Yongchuan et al., eds., *Xihan Nanyue wang mu wenwu tezhan tulu* (*Artifacts in the Nanyue king's tomb of the Western Han dynasty*) (Taipei: Guoli lishi bowuguan, 1998), no. 54; *Zhongguo qingtongqi quanji*, vol. 16, no. 37. For comments on other types of mirror stands and frames, see Xiaoneng Yang, "Han Bronze Mirror and Gilt Bronze Stand."

5. For recent studies of the scroll and its possible date, see Shane McCausland, *First Masterpiece of Chinese Painting: The Admonitions Scroll* (New York: George Braziller, 2003); Shane McCausland, ed., *Gu Kaizhi and the Admonitions scroll*, in *Percival David Foundation Colloquies on Art & Archaeology in Asia*, no. 21 (London: British Museum Press in association with the Percival David Foundation of Chinese Art, 2003).

6. Richard M. Barnhart et al., eds., *Three Thousand Years of Chinese Painting* (New Haven: Yale University Press, 1997), p. 51, fig. 39; for an overview of this scene, see McCausland, *First Masterpiece*, pp. 63–67. A few illustrations of slightly earlier mirror stands can be found in Toru Nakano, "Ancient Chinese Bronze Mirrors," in *Bronze Mirrors from Ancient China: Donald H. Graham Jr. Collection*, preface, essay and catalogue by Toru Nakano (Hong Kong: Donald H. Graham Jr., 1994), pp. 19–22.

7. Finally, it is important to note that mirror stands evolved as living habits changed. As chairs and tables came increasingly into use in the Sui and Tang dynasties, tall mirror stands were replaced by shorter and sturdier versions. Mirrors with handles became popular in the 12th century CE under the Jin dynasty.

41 Mirror with semicircles, squares, eight Immortals, and fantastic animals

Late Eastern Han dynasty–Three Kingdoms period. Gilt bronze; diam. 15.3 cm.
Private collection.

The defining feature of mirrors of this type is the series of alternating semicircles and squares that frame the central circular pictorial panel; this example displays thirty-four of them, executed in high relief against a pebbled ground. Four small whorls decorate each semicircle; each of the square blocks carries an identical four-character inscription. The inscription reads "*tian wang ri yue*," literally, "heavenly kings, sun, and moon,"[1] and is probably a stock phrase of auspicious incantation, since it commonly appears in longer inscriptions that invoke good fortune.[2] Arranged in this seal-like format as a fixed decorative unit, the characters acquire iconic value. Unfortunately, on the present mirror the characters are not very sharp, probably due in part to corrosion and in part to a less-than-meticulous use of the lost-wax casting technique.[3] Mirrors with this type of dense high-relief decoration emerged in the late Eastern Han period and continued to be made until the early Six Dynasties.

The main register surrounds the large hemispherical knob. Four fantastic prancing beasts, sometimes identified as *bixie*, partition it into four approximately equal sectors. In each sector, two Immortals, indicated by their tail-like lower bodies, face one another; they wear loose robes and clasp their hands, hidden in long sleeves, at waist level. The folds on their robes are indicated. Although all eight Immortals and all four beasts may appear identical, minor variations in detail suggest that they were sculpted individually. Nevertheless, there is no distinctive detail that would allow them to be identified with deities named in Han mythology. Judging from the layout of the motifs, the beasts were modeled first, then the Immortals. The hind legs of the beasts often stretch across the sectors, leaving insufficient room for the nearest Immortal.

Moving outward from the band of semicircles and squares, there is first a narrow sloped band with a sawtooth pattern, then a fine band of intricate figurative motifs, and finally the flat rim of the mirror, which is decorated with dense cloud whorls. The narrow pictorial band, though obscured by corrosion, still reveals traces of a cloud chariot drawn by six dragons and remnants of other birds and animals among running scrolls.

Finally, the fine gilding of this mirror makes it a rarity. Although gilt-bronze mirrors are known from the Warring States period, they were not common until the Six Dynasties and Tang. Only a handful of archaeologically recovered examples are known from the Western Han period.[4] The use of gold suggests that this mirror might have been a luxury belonging to an aristocratic household.

DAVID T. LIU

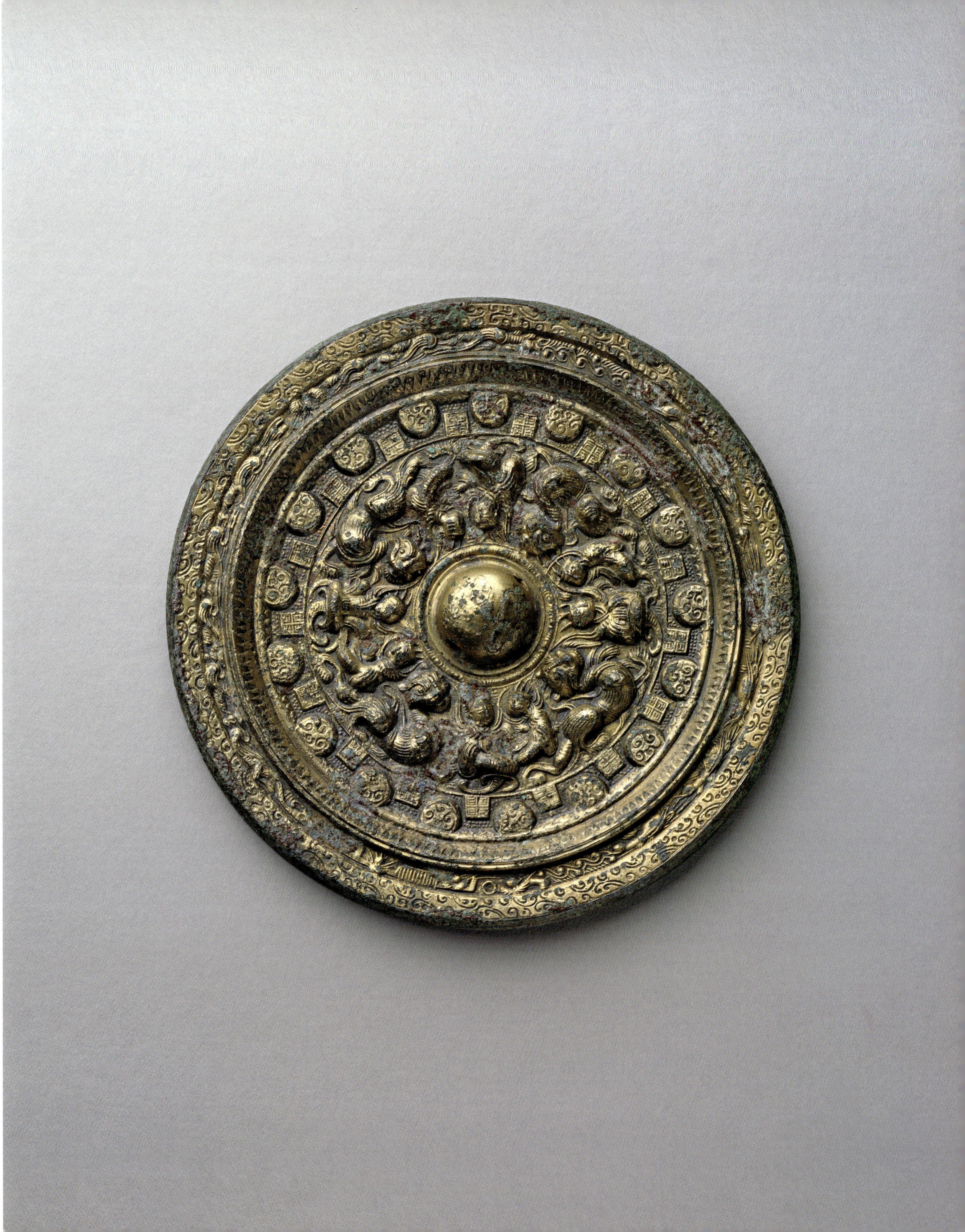

Notes

1. Similar mirrors are found in a number of private and public collections. A piece with the same inscription was excavated from Luoyang, Henan Province, in 1983, dated to the Eastern Han; see Zhongguo qingtongqi quanji bianji weiyuanhui, ed. *Zhongguo qingtongqi quanji*, vol. 16: *Tongjing* (*Complete works of Chinese bronzes*, vol. 16: *Bronze mirrors*) (Beijing: Wenwu chubanshe, 1998), no. 91.

2. For translations of such inscriptions, see Suzanne Cahill, "Boya Plays the Zither: Two Types of Chinese Bronze Mirror in the Donald H. Graham Jr. Collection," in *Bronze Mirrors from Ancient China: Donald H. Graham Jr. Collection*, preface, essay, and catalogue by Toru Nakano (Hong Kong: Donald H. Graham Jr., 1994), pp. 51.

3. Chen Peifen, "Zhongguo qingtongjing fazhan gaishu" ("Overview of the development of Chinese bronze mirrors)," in *Zhongguo qingtongqi quanji*, vol. 16: *Tongjing*, p. 15.

4. See, for example, *Zhongguo qingtongqi quanji*, vol. 16: *Tongjing*, nos. 57, 58.

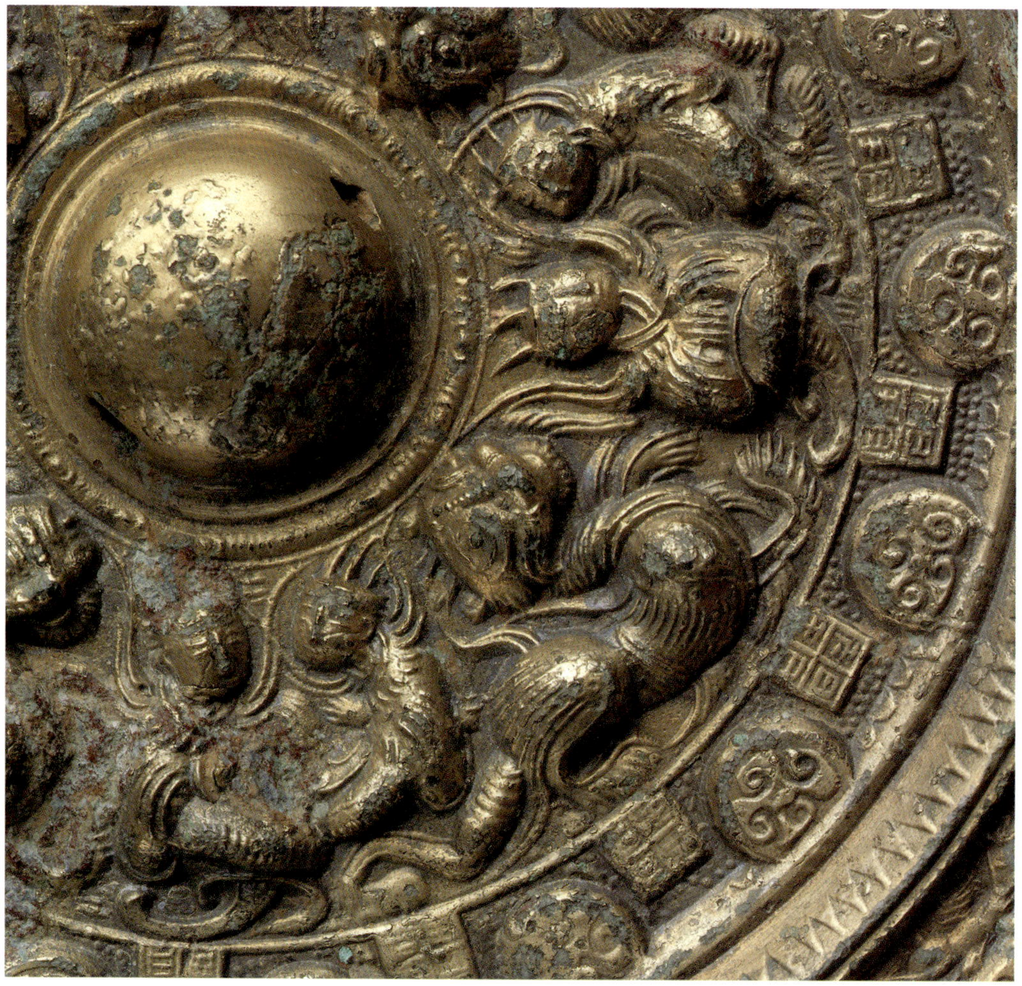

Regional Iconographies in Images of the Queen Mother of the West

Centered within the apex of the west wall of the reconstructed "Wu Liang Shrine" (Stone Chamber 3) is the Queen Mother of the West, or Xiwangmu (fig. 1; cat. no. 1.35). We can identify this figure as the Queen Mother because the tradition from which it stemmed, and in which she occupied a significant place, was already some two to three centuries old, in the pictorial programs and furnishings of tombs dating from the Han dynasty. She dominates the western gable of the Wu shrine, is winged, and wears a large "five-phoenixes crown," which according to Wu Hung was reserved for women of high social status.[1] Surrounding her are winged attendants, two hares pounding an elixir, a toad, and several hybrid figures. Complementing this composition is the King Father of the East, or Dongwanggong, foregrounded in the same fashion on the eastern apex of the shrine (fig. 1; cat. no. 1.37). His attendants include winged and hybrid figures, as well as double-headed creatures. This pairing of the two regal individuals was not common throughout the Han empire; in many regions the Queen Mother was depicted alone. As a fully developed symbol of immortality by the Eastern Han period, the Queen Mother of the West became associated with popular religious beliefs centered on salvation and everlasting life. Her image, included within the tomb, expressed the wishes of the deceased and his/her family for a long and happy afterlife.

Pairing the Queen Mother with the King Father of the East was an iconographic trait of the Shandong region, which did not prevail elsewhere in the Han Empire. Extant two- and three-dimensional representations of the Queen Mother have been found from the Sichuan region to the northeastern limits of the empire, or present-day Korea. Within this vast extent, variations in style and iconography distinguish regional conceptions of the deity. Whereas previous scholarship has concentrated on the Queen Mother's role within the mortuary context, I shall focus on the regional differences in her portrayal and suggest how these variations might be explained. To begin, I shall discuss some identifying iconographic patterns.

One of the earliest extant images of the Queen Mother occurs in a set of two painted ceiling tiles from a tomb in Henan Province (fig. 2; cat. no. 8). These have been dated to the first century BCE, or late Western Han,[2] and are roughly contemporary with a ceiling mural from the tomb of Bu Qianqiu and his wife, found in Luoyang, Henan (fig. 3).[3] In both compositions the deity is similarly accoutered and seated atop a mountain. Based on the Bu tomb mural, it can be conjectured that the Queen Mother, who here is seated *en face* atop a mountain, is waiting to welcome the souls of the deceased.[4] According to texts such as the second-century BCE *Huainanzi*, she is an Immortal;[5] other texts associate her with Mount Kunlun, a paradisiacal stop en route to heaven, where she bestows the elixir of everlasting life.

The distinctive *sheng* headpiece that identifies her in the Henan tiles is one of the few attributes common to both texts and pictorial representations. The individual in the accompanying tile may be either an attendant or the soul of the deceased,[6] figures common among the Queen Mother's pictorial entourage. That entourage, some of which can be seen in the Wu shrine gable and the Bu Qianqiu mural,

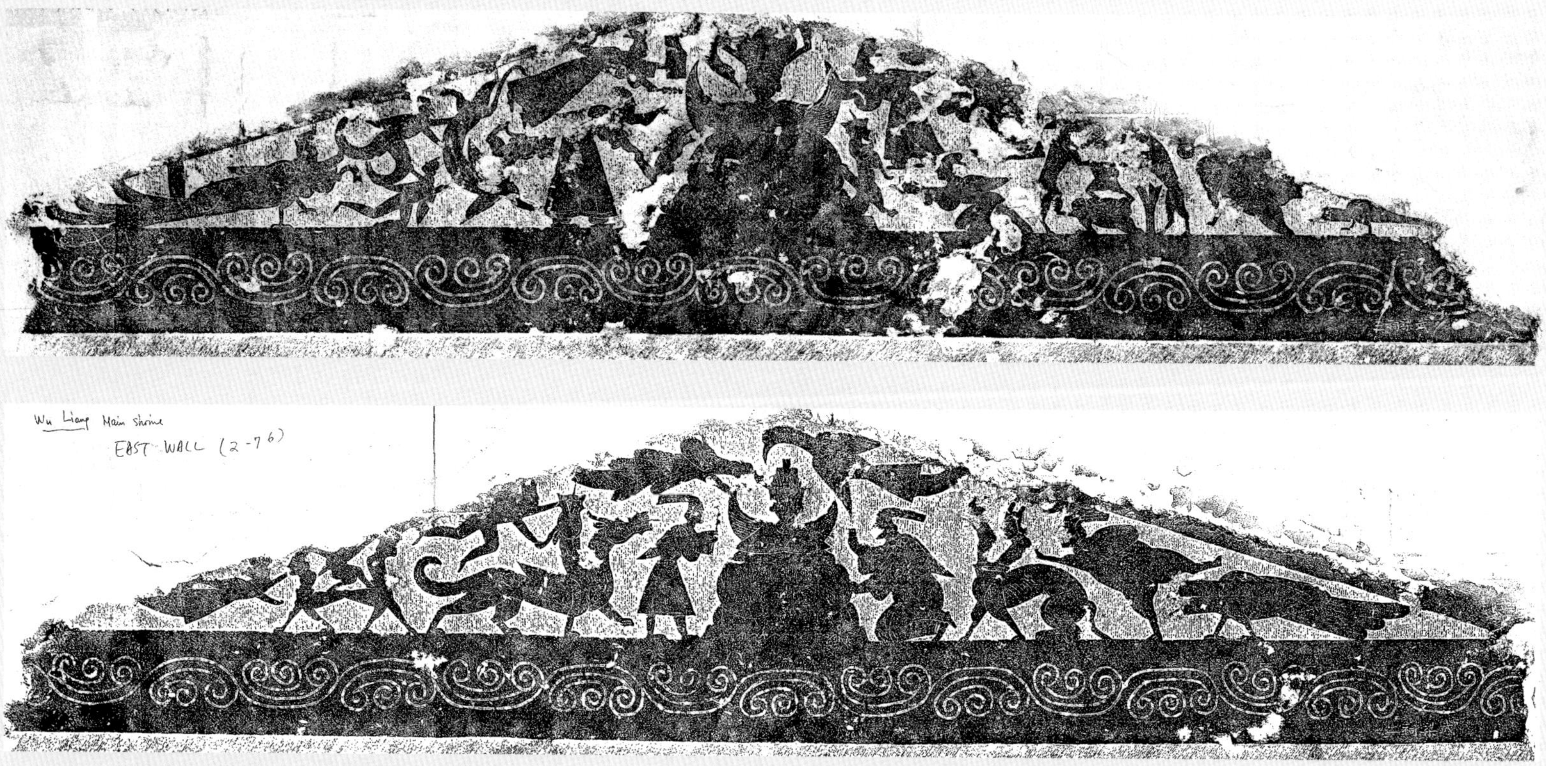

Fig. 1 *Western (top) and Eastern (bottom) gables of the Wu Liang Shrine, featuring the Queen Mother of the West and the King Father of the East.* Details of Stone Chamber 3, Stones 3-W.1 (cat. no. 1.35), 3-E.1 (cat. no. 1.37). "Wu family shrines" rubbings. Princeton University Art Museum, acc. nos. 2002-307.36, 2002-307.34.

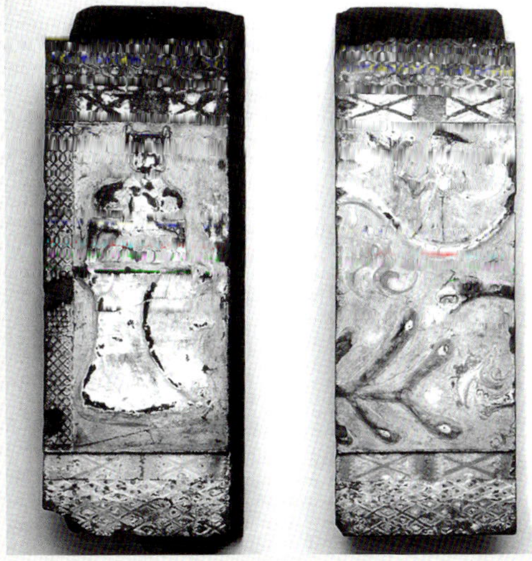

Fig. 2 *Queen Mother of the West and figure riding a snake* (cat. no. 8). Western Han dynasty, first century BCE. Two hollow tomb ceiling tiles; gray earthenware with polychrome. Royal Ontario Museum, acc. nos. 922.20.625, 922.20.626. The George Crofts Collection.

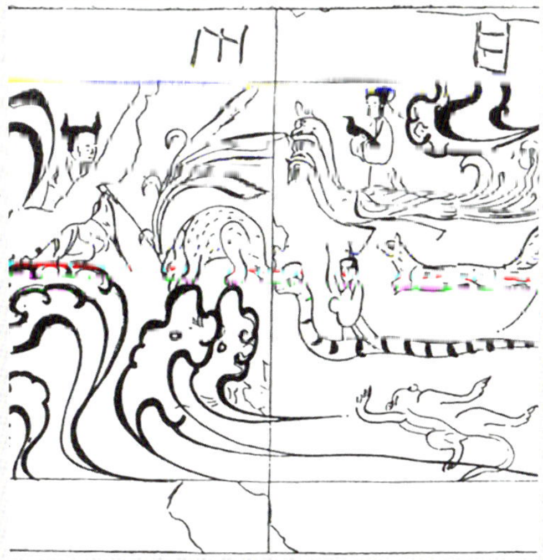

Fig. 3 *Detail of a mural from the tomb of Bu Qianqiu.* Western Han dynasty, first century BCE. Luoyang, Henan. From Luoyang Museum, "Luoyang Xihan Bu Qianqiu bihua mu fajue jianbao" ("A brief report on the painted Western Han tomb of Bin Qianqiu in Luoyang"), *Wenwu* 1977.6, fig. 33, p. 10.

usually includes one or more of the following: a rabbit pounding an elixir; a nine-tailed fox; one or more birds (in some instances, one bird with three tails or three legs); a toad; worshipers (some with animal heads or masks); *xian*, or celestial winged figures; and a female attendant.[7] Curiously, very few of these are mentioned in texts.

Within tomb murals and on individual objects, the Queen Mother is usually located literally and symbolically above, as can be observed in the Wu shrine gable and in the upper portion of each branch of a money tree (fig. 4, cat. no. 59), where she is flanked by figures in profile, facing her in reverence. More emphatically, as part of an earthenware lamp, she is seated on a dragon-and-tiger throne supported by a pedestal, in the heavens (cat. no. 42). Centered within the top portion of this two-part lamp, she is both associated with the sun and moon and literally separated from the underworld, which is represented by the chimera supporting the upper part of the lamp on his shoulders and standing on a tortoise and serpent, a compound directional symbol of the north.[8]

Aside from these shared characteristics, however, certain regional differences are apparent.[9] In Henan, as in the painted tiles, the Queen Mother is commonly depicted seated on a mountain pedestal. She is pictured either *en face* or in three-quarters pose, and most often wearing the *sheng* headpiece. Similar configurations have been found in Shaanxi and Shanxi, with the addition of a solid or cloud-like canopy above her head. In Sichuan she is usually seated on a dragon-and-tiger throne, and often under a canopy, as can be seen in the bronze filigree branches of the money tree in this exhibition (fig. 4; cat. no. 59). Many examples from Shandong were carved in low relief on stone slabs from which aboveground funerary structures were built. Elsewhere in Shandong, as in the "Wu family shrines" relief carvings, the Queen Mother of the West is often paired with a male counterpart, the King Father of the East. According to Wu Hung, this represents a culmination in a long history of pairings between the cosmological complements of *yin* and *yang*, with the Queen Mother symbolizing the *yin* force and the King Father, the *yang*. Considering these characteristic differences, an iconographic attribute anomalous to the region in which it was found, such as the possible dragon-and-tiger throne pictured with the Queen Mother in the Wu shrines (see fig. 1), attests to some interregional dialogue.

In fact, there is evidence that motifs traveled great distances. According to Anthony Barbieri-Low's "Carving Out a Living" in this catalogue, stone carvers did not venture far from their workshops, and so images on relief carvings and bricks were probably not the chief means of diffusion of the different iconographies associated with the Queen Mother. More plausibly, the iconographies traveled on more portable objects. Lacquer utensils, for example, were often bestowed as gifts on high officials, whose functions required frequent travel within the empire.[10] A lacquer tray with a painted image of the Queen Mother, included in the tomb of the official Wang Xu in Lelang, Korea (fig. 5), has a painted inscription on its underside, indicating that it was produced in a private workshop in Chengdu, Sichuan.[11] Painted near the rim on the interior of the tray, the Queen

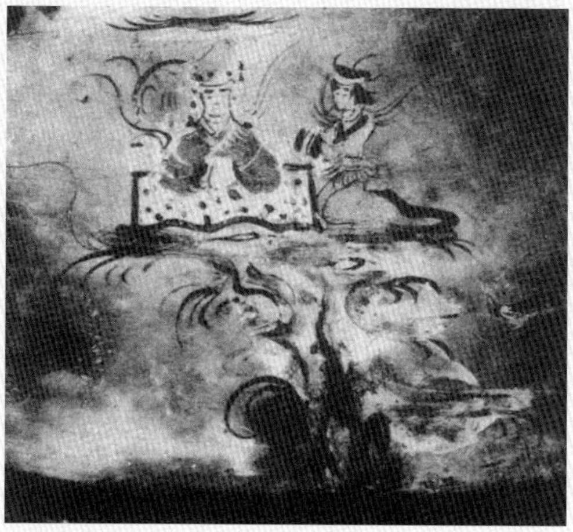

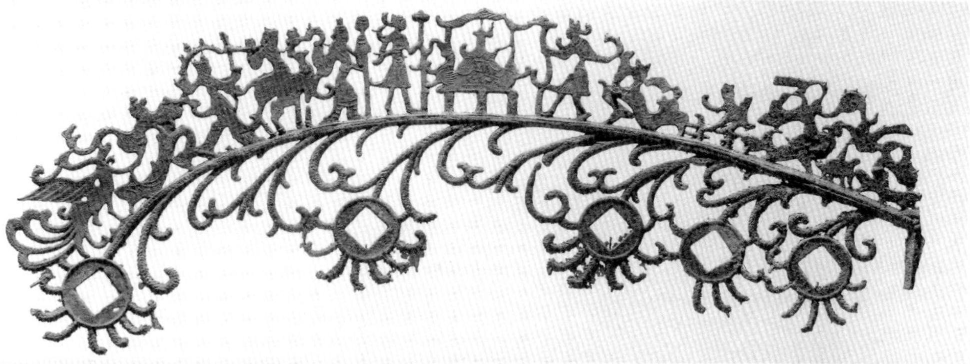

Mother is portrayed wearing a *sheng* headpiece and seated *en face* on a pedestal and under a canopy, with an attendant at her left. A dragon-and-tiger pair is pictured in the upper right-hand corner of the tray. Such an iconographic program, which is typical of the Shaanxi or Shanxi regions, was in this case produced in western Sichuan and transported to the northeastern limit of the empire.

With such potential for conformity, how can such iconographic differences—and their persistence—be explained? Consider, for example: in compositions from Henan and Sichuan, she appears alone, an independent ruler over the Western Paradise, whereas in those from Shandong, for example, on the Wu shrines, she shares the pictorial space with the King Father. The pairing in Shandong clearly symbolizes cosmological balance, yet this explanation is insufficient, since in other compositions, such as the earthenware lamp (cat. no. 42), she alone is associated with both *yin* and *yang*, represented respectively by the moon and sun flanking her headdress. It is not surprising, however, to find such an appendage as the King Father in the region where Confucian ideology was born. Here one must ask the question posed by Martin Powers, namely, how does the Queen Mother, described in early texts as a representative of the irrational, fit into a Confucian paradigm? It is true, as Powers points out, that her realm is ranked and fosters hierarchy,[12] but the Queen Mother becomes even more Confucian when literally placed within a pictorial marriage—and thereby transmogrified from an originally demonic figure into a domesticated spouse and exemplar of connubial piety. As such, she fits perfectly within the larger so-called Confucian political and social context and within the moralizing pictorial program of the "Wu family shrines."

Most interesting about the Queen Mother during the Han is the widespread use of her image, implying that oral and written traditions presented her as a figure who could provide comfort for the deceased and his family, and also, once supplied with the King Father, could be turned into a moral exemplar for the living. Though we cannot yet deduce their differences in meaning, it is clear that the iconographic variations in her image occurred regionally, and it is most likely that they were determined by the needs of the people in each region and by their views concerning the afterlife.

SHERI A. LULLO

Fig. 4 *Filigree branch showing the Queen Mother of the West*. Eastern Han dynasty. Detail of a money tree (cat. no. 59). Bronze; l. 32.0 cm. Princeton University Art Museum, acc. no. 1999-79 (E.1).

Fig. 5 *Lacquer tray with a painted image of the Queen Mother of the West*. Eastern Han dynasty, 69 CE. Tomb of Wang Xu, excavated at Lelang, Korea. After Umehara Sueji, *Shina Kandai kinenmei shikki zusetsu* (Kyoto: Kuwana Bunseido, 1943), pl. 43.

Notes

1. Wu Hung, *The Wu Liang Shrine: The Ideology of Early Chinese Pictorial Art* (Stanford: Stanford University Press, 1989), p. 111.

2. Klaas Ruitenbeek assigned this date based on the similarity of pictorial arrangement between the tiles and the mural from the Bu Qianqiu tomb. In addition, their hollowed construction and angled edges suggest that they, like the mural from the Bu tomb, were once part of the tomb ceiling. See Klaas Ruitenbeek, *Chinese Shadows: Stone Reliefs, Rubbings, and Related Works of Art from the Han Dynasty (206 BC–AD 220) in the Royal Ontario Museum* (Toronto: Royal Ontario Museum, 2002), p. 38.

3. Luoyang Museum, "Luoyang Xihan Bu Qianqiu bihuamu fajue jianbao" ("A brief report on the painted Western Han tomb of Bu Qianqiu in Luoyang"), *Wenwu* 1977.6, pp. 1–12.

4. One of the few physical descriptions of the Queen Mother in early texts portrays her as a demonic creature —half human, half beast. By contrast, in the representations of the Han period, she is rendered as a comforting and benevolent goddess. See Jean James, "An Iconographic Study of Xiwangmu During the Han Dynasty," *Artibus Asiae*, vol. 55, 1/2 (1995), pp. 17–41: 18.

5. Xin Lixiang, *Handai huaxiang shi zonghe yanjiu* (*Comprehensive research on the stone relief carvings of the Han period*) (Beijing: Wenwu chubanshe, 2000), p. 147.

6. The stalk or spray of grass held by the figure suggests an attendant or worshiper, but the snake vehicle implies that the figure represents the soul of the deceased. "Monograph of Strange Phenomena" in *Hanshu* (*History of* [*Western*] *Han*) (Beijing: Zhonghua shuju, 1962), *juan 27 xia zhi shang*, pp. 1474–75, recounts certain ritual activities performed by commoners worshiping the Queen Mother during a severe drought: "It happened that people were disturbed and running around, passing a stalk of grain or flax from one to another, and calling it 'the tally for transmitting the edict'." (Translation from Poo Mu-chou, *In Search of Personal Welfare: A View of Ancient Chinese Religion* [Albany: State University of New York Press, 1998], p. 155.) The object held by the figure in the Henan painted tiles is likely to be a representation of this so-called tally. In other compositions the hare is often pictured carrying this stalk (James, "An Iconographic Study," p. 22). In the Bu Qianqiu tomb mural, on the other hand, the figure on the snake's back is identified as the soul of the deceased.

7. According to Hayashi Minao, this female attendant is sometimes identified by inscriptions on bronze mirrors as the "Jade Woman." Hayashi Minao, *Kandai no kamigami* (*Deities of the Han period*) (Kyoto-shi: Rinsen Shoten, 1989), pp. 98–102. For information about the other figures of the Queen Mother's entourage, see Michael Loewe, *Ways to Paradise: The Chinese Quest for Immortality* (London: Allen and Unwin, 1979).

8. A similar configuration of a creature supporting a platform upon his shoulders, with everything below the platform representing the underworld, can be found in the painted silk banner from Mawangdui Tomb 1 (2d century BCE), found near Changsha, Hunan. For a line drawing of this banner, see Wu, *The Wu Liang Shrine*, p. 114.

9. These regional distinctions have been discussed by several art historians, including Jean James, *An Iconographic Study: A Guide to the Tomb and Shrine Art of the Han Dynasty, 206 B.C.–A.D. 220* (Lampeter: Edwin Mellen Press, 1996); Martin Powers, *Art and Political Expression in Early China*, (New Haven and London: Yale University Press, 1991), Jessica Rawson, "Tombs and Tomb Furnishings of the Eastern Han Period (AD 25–220)," in *Ancient Sichuan: Treasures from a Lost Civilization*, ed. Robert Bagley (Princeton and Seattle: Seattle Art Museum and Princeton University Press, 2001); and Wu Hung, *The Wu Liang Shrine*.

10. Anthony Barbieri-Low, "The Organization of Imperial Workshops During the Han Dynasty" (PhD diss., Princeton University, 2001), p. 7.

11. Ibid., pp. 183–85.

12. Powers, *Art and Political Expression*, p. 266.

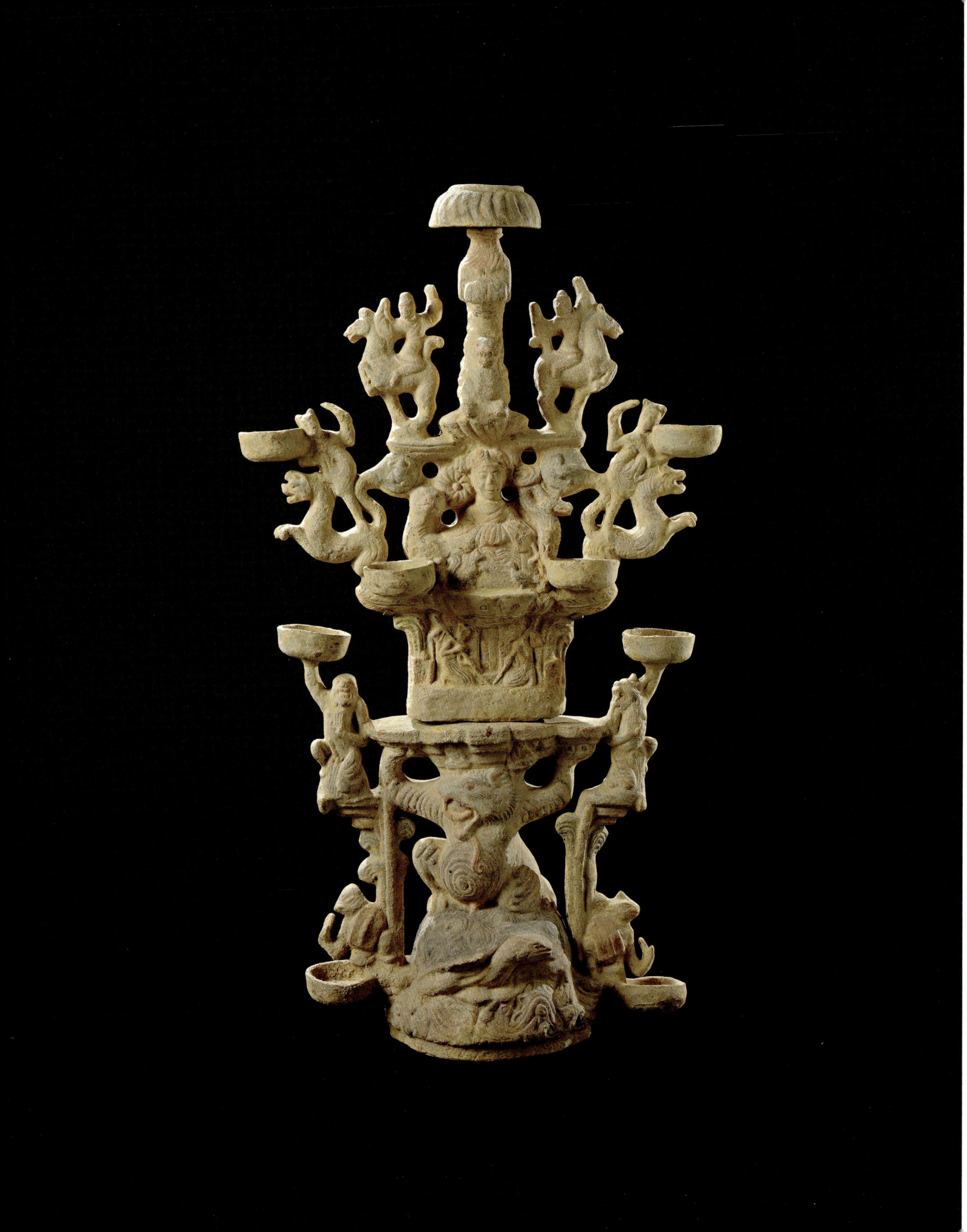

42 Lamp representing the realm of the Queen Mother of the West (Xiwangmu)

Han dynasty. Earthenware with traces of pigment; h. 97.5 cm, w. 53.2 cm.
Yale University Art Gallery, acc. no. 1997.64.1. Leonard C. Hanna, Jr., B.A. 1913, Fund.

By the end of the Western Han popular belief in Xiwangmu, the Queen Mother of the West, was sufficiently widespread to be mentioned by later historians. Three passages in the *Hanshu* reveal that at the beginning of the year corresponding to 3 BCE, a mass salvation movement centered on the Queen Mother spread westward through "twenty-six commanderies and kingdoms," finally reaching the capital at Chang'an.[1] The passages are tantalizing—they reveal that the Queen Mother was associated with talismans promising deathlessness and that by autumn the movement had run its course—but they give few details about the movement itself or about belief in the Queen Mother. The historian's concerns lay elsewhere. Artifacts, however, whether now in museum collections or archaeologically recovered, can reveal a good deal about belief in the Queen Mother. This molded, modeled, and painted earthenware lamp representing the Queen Mother as part of a two-section assemblage is one such artifact. It materializes Han-period beliefs about the Queen Mother of the West.

The Queen Mother appears in the center of the upper part of the lamp. She is seated frontally on a throne composed of a tiger and a dragon, and her hair is piled up and garlanded with what appear to be blossoms. The sun and the moon are seen to her left and right, respectively, represented by a black bird and a toad, each in a disc. At her feet are a nine-tailed fox, a three-legged bird, and a hare, barely visible at right, with a mortar and pestle. This core unit is flanked by two cups of the lamp and by two female figures holding cups; the figures are riding on the backs of feline creatures. In the register immediately below the Queen Mother are two female figures holding staves and kneeling in front of an open door. Vegetal growth is to either side. In the register above the Queen Mother two mounted horsemen flank a drum (*jiangu*), which rests on the back of a kneeling feline creature. The horsemen are poised to beat the drum. A parasol-canopy, itself a lamp cup, caps the whole upper unit of the lamp.

The lower unit is composed of a turtle amid waves supporting an ursine creature who raises both arms to support the platform for the upper unit. Along the perimeter are four creatures, each with a lamp cup. All appear to be hybrids: the two lower creatures carry shields and have the cups at their feet, the upper ones hold the cups aloft. The two upper creatures are juxtaposed: one seen *en face* with an erect male member, the other with head turned and genitalia covered. They stand on bases supported by tree-like growth. There are a total of nine lamp cups, four on each side and one at the top. The whole assemblage is symmetrical, with the Queen Mother directly on axis.

The imagery on the lamp creates the realm of the Queen Mother and places her in a cosmological setting.[2] Seated upon the tiger and dragon, flanked by the sun and the moon, she is seen as the creator and maintainer of cosmic balance between *yang* and *yin*, the positive and negative forces.[3] Rather than blossoms, the swirls to either side of her head could represent stars, adding astral symbolism to her image.[4] The nine-tailed fox, the three-legged bird, and the hare can be identified as her followers: the fox has auspicious associations;[5] the bird is

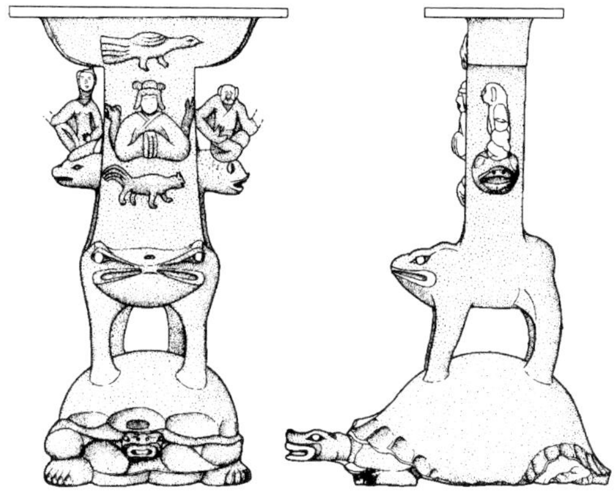

identified with the sun and is her messenger;[6] and the hare pounding the elixir of immortality is associated with the moon.[7] Below her, the figures at the open door suggest the entry into the realm of the Immortals through the Gate of Heaven (*tianmen*).[8] The foliage may represent the jade trees on Mount Kunlun, and the mounted drum at the top is often found in scenes of entertainment.[9] By its overall axial configuration and turtle support, the lamp suggests an *axis mundi* as well as the mountains of the Immortals, which were supported on the back of a turtle.[10] The ursine creature and the hybrid creatures reinforce the lamp's axiality and *yin-yang* balance.[11]

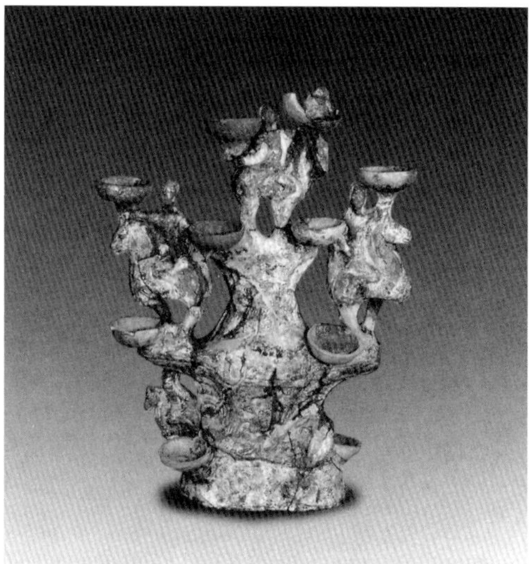

Fig. 1 *Lamp with three riders*. Han dynasty, first century BCE–first century CE. Excavated at Yuejin Cun, Qingbaijiang District, Chengdu, Sichuan. Earthenware with traces of pigment; h. 54 cm. From *Wenwu*, 1999.8, cover.

Images of the Queen Mother of the West had a wide geographical distribution during the Han dynasty.[12] In Shandong in the east the Queen Mother is frequently encountered in low-relief carved stones. In the reconstructed "Wu family shrines," for instance, she figures prominently in the west-wall pediments (cat. nos. 1.19, 1.35) of two of the chambers. In Sichuan in the southwest she is found both on low-relief carved stones and on mold-impressed bricks. Sculptural representations, however, have so far come to light only in Sichuan Province. A group of objects, one of them a lamp, excavated from two tombs at Yuejin Cun in the Qingbaijiang District of Chengdu, are similar in construction and in conception to the present lamp. The Yuejin Cun lamp, likewise made of molded and painted earthenware, has three horsemen supporting cups in the upper part and a single horseman near the base (fig. 1). It bears a total of ten lamp cups. The lamp was discovered in a pit under the floor of Tomb 6, a single-chambered wooden structure that has been dated by the excavators to the late Western–early Eastern Han period. Tomb 5 at this site, of similar construction and suggested date, yielded other composite supports that compare closely in conception to the present lamp. One support in particular shows a frog perched on the back of a turtle (fig. 2). The Queen Mother is seen on the stem rising from the back of the frog; above her is a bird and below her a fox. Two figures, one male, the other female, sit on animal heads projecting to either side.[13] These supports or bases help to corroborate the present composite lamp and suggest a date in the first century of the Common Era and an origin in Sichuan.

Other composite bases, perhaps for money trees, were excavated in 1995 in Guanghan County, Sichuan.[14] One of them has a toad perched on the back of a turtle while an ursine creature squats on the back of the toad. Two snakes or dragons intertwine with the three creatures. Yet another base, this one excavated from the Dujiazui cliff tomb at Lianshan,

Fig. 2 *Turtle and frog base*. Han dynasty, first century BCE–first century CE. Excavated at Yuejin Cun, Qingbaijiang District, Chengdu, Sichuan. Earthenware with traces of pigment; h. 60 cm. From *Wenwu*, 1999.8, fig. 33:2.

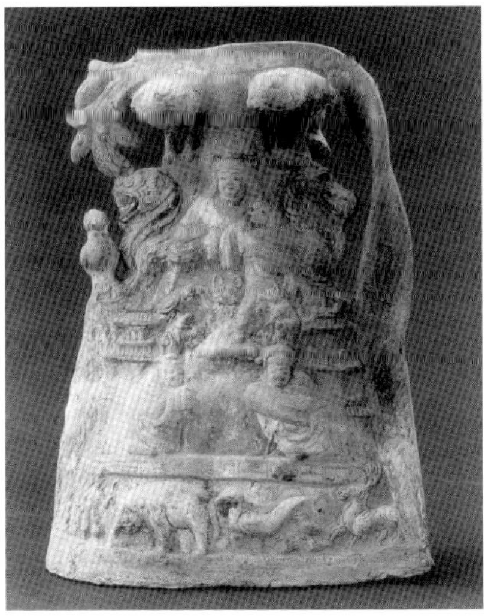

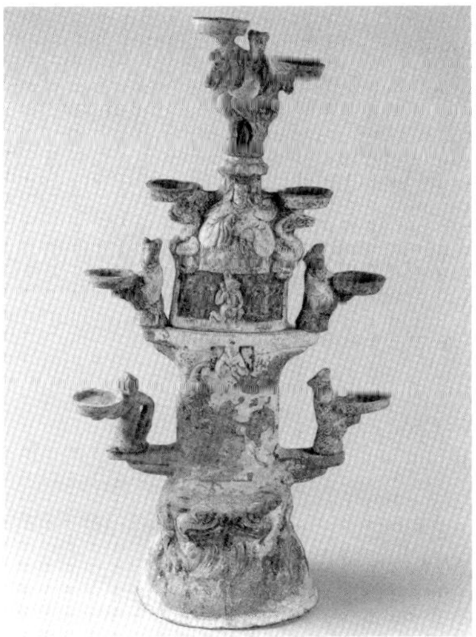

Guanghan, is in the form of a mountain (fig. 3). On the lowest register are a deer, a bird, and an elephant with an elephant trainer. On the next level, two figures bow to each other in front of a pair of pillar-gates (*que*). A creature perches on the head of each figure. The Queen Mother appears in the upper register, seated frontally on a tiger-and-dragon throne. Two large birds perch above her. A lone figure stands at proper right, while a vegetal branch rises up along the proper left side. The branch twists and turns horizontally, resting on the backs of the two birds. Blossoms droop from its tip.[15] The placement of the two figures in front of the pillar-gates leading to the image of the Queen Mother is particularly close in conception to the present lamp.

The lamp that is most similar in construction and imagery to the present lamp is now in the collection of the National History Museum in Taipei (fig. 4). It is likewise a molded, modeled, and painted earthenware lamp in two parts. Its lower part comprises two registers: the lower register is a frontal frog or dragon head and the upper a molded scene of a woman chasing an animal that is surmounted by a seated figure. Two ledges project laterally at the midpoint between the two registers, each supporting a hybrid creature holding a lamp cup. Two more figures hold lamp cups at the top of the base. The upper unit shows the Queen Mother seated on her tiger-dragon throne, with one cup at the head of the tiger and another at the head of the dragon. Below the Queen Mother is the rabbit with a pestle, and above her a figure on horseback holds two more cups.[16]

In molding and modeling these lamps and bases are consistent with the present lamp: all of the figures convey a solidity of sculptural form that is characteristic of Sichuan tomb sculpture. Reduced clarity in the details suggests that a given mold had been much reused. In all examples the Queen Mother is rendered as a full-faced matron.[17] Only the lamp from Yuejin Cun comes from an excavation that has been dated by the excavation report. In the scale of the figures the present lamp is consistent with the Yuejin Cun lamp, but its fuller modeling and rich iconography suggest a date later in the Eastern Han.

Lamps appear in tombs dating from the Warring States period through the Eastern Han.[18] They are made of bronze and of painted and glazed earthenware. Some of the most spectacular lamps take the form of figures holding lamp cups (see cat. no. 2) or trees with numerous cups among the branches. An earthenware lamp discovered in an undisturbed Western Han tomb near Luoyang takes the form of a mountain surmounted by a central shaft. Its shaft, like an *axis mundi*, is supported by a turtle. Located in a side chamber of the tomb along with appurtenances of feasting, the lamp could have served to light the feast while at the same time alluding to the realms of the Immortals.[19]

Lamps showing the Queen Mother of the West clearly appear to have had a ritual function. The nine cups on the present lamp resonate with the generally divine connotations of the number nine.[20] There were nine layers of the sky, nine gates to the heavens, nine suns that appeared simultaneously, threatening to burn the earth, before they were shot down by the archer Yi, and nine stars in the Elaborate

Fig. 3 *Base with Queen Mother of the West*. Eastern Han dynasty. Excavated at Guanghan County, Sichuan. Earthenware with pigments; h. 50 cm. From *Orientations*, September 1997, p. 71, fig. 6.

Fig. 4 *Lamp with Queen Mother of the West*. Eastern Han dynasty. Earthenware with pigments; h. 86.5 cm, w. 47 cm. National Museum of History, Taipei, acc. no. 84-499. From Guoli lishi bowuguan, *Guan cang Zhongguo lidai taoci tezhan*, no. 27.

Canopy Constellation (*Huagai xing*). In a story telling of the visit of the Queen Mother of the West to Emperor Wu of the Western Han, it is said that a lamp of nine lights was set up, and nine-fold floriate lamps were a part of Daoist ritual in Shangqing Daoism from the late Han into the Southern Dynasties.[21] The presence in the tomb of a lamp like the present one could well have assisted the deceased in entering the immortal realm of the Queen Mother of the West.
DAVID AKE SENSABAUGH

Notes

1. Ban Gu, *Hanshu* (*History of the Former Han Dynasty*) (Beijing: Zhonghua shuju, 1962 edition and Xianggang: Zhonghua shuju, 1970 edition), *juan* 11, p. 342 (1970 ed.); *juan* 26, pp. 1311–12 (1962 ed.); and *juan* 27 *xia zhi shang*, p. 1476 (1962 ed.). For a discussion and translation of the passages, see Homer H. Dubs, "An Ancient Chinese Mystery Cult," *Harvard Theological Review*, vol. 35 (1942), pp. 221–46, and Michael Loewe, *Ways to Paradise: The Chinese Quest for Immortality* (London: George Allen and Unwin, 1979), pp. 98–101. Dubs suggests that the movement may have had its origins in Shandong.

2. For the iconography of the Queen Mother, see Michael Loewe, *Ways to Paradise*, pp. 101–12; Wu Hung, "Xiwangmu, The Queen Mother of the West," *Orientations*, April 1987, pp. 24–33; and Jean M. James, "An Iconographic Study of Xiwangmu During the Han Dynasty," *Artibus Asiae*, vol. 55, no. 1/2 (1995), pp. 17–41.

3. See Loewe, *Ways to Paradise*, pp. 105–6, 127–33; and Wu Hung, "Xiwangmu," pp. 17–41.

4. The Queen Mother is not shown wearing a *sheng*, the headdress by which she is usually identified. Wu Hung has pointed out that quite a number of deities usually identified as the Queen Mother of the West have male headgear and may represent other deities in early Daoism in Sichuan. See Wu Hung, "Mapping Early Taoist Art: The Visual Culture of Wudoumi Dao," in *Taoism and the Arts of China*, ed. Stephen Little (Chicago: The Art Institute of Chicago, 2000), pp. 77–93. A number of Han-dynasty tomb sculptures from Sichuan Province represent seated female figures with large chrysanthemum-like flowers in their hair. It has been suggested that some of them may have Daoist associations. See *Stories from China's Past: Han Dynasty Pictorial Tomb Reliefs and Archaeological Objects from Sichuan Province, People's Republic of China* (San Francisco: The Chinese Cultural Foundation of San Francisco, 1987), pl. 45, p. 138 and cpl. 1; and Robert Bagley, ed., *Ancient Sichuan: Treasures from a Lost Civilization* (Seattle: Seattle Art Museum, 2001), no. 115, p. 303. A floriate topknot for the Queen Mother is mentioned in the *Han Wudi neizhuan* (*Esoteric transmissions concerning Emperor Wu of Han*) a text that was probably not written until the 6th century CE. Here, the shape is a whorl, however, and could well represent a star. For a translation of the passage from *Han Wudi neizhuan* and for stars, astral travel, and shamanism in relation to the Queen Mother of the West, see Suzanne E. Cahill, *Transcendence and Divine Passion: The Queen Mother of the West in Medieval China* (Stanford: Stanford University Press, 1993), pp. 57, 17.

5. Loewe, *Ways to Paradise*, pp. 108–10.

6. Loewe, *Ways to Paradise*, pp. 106, 127–33.

7. Loewe, *Ways to Paradise*, pp. 106, 127–33.

8. *Que* pillar-gates are self-identified as *tianmen*, the Gate of Heaven, on a stone coffin from Jianyang, Guitoushan, Sichuan, and on gilt-bronze coffin furnishings excavated at Wushan County, Chongqing. See Gao Wen and Gao Chenggang, eds., *Zhongguo huaxiang shi guan yishu* (*Carved stone coffin art of China*) (Taiyuan: Shanxi renmin meishu chubanshe, 1996), pp. 11–12; and Chongqing Wushan Xian wenwu guanlisuo, "Chongqing Wushan Xian Donghan liujin tongpaishi de faxian yu yanjiu" ("Discovery and study of Eastern Han gilt-bronze ornamental plaques from Wushan County, Chongqing"), *Kaogu* 1998.12, pp. 77–86.

9. For *jiangu*, see Sun Ji's discussion of percussion instruments in *Handai wuzhi wenhua ziliao tushuo* (*A pictorial handbook of Han-dynasty material culture*)

(Beijing: Wenwu chubanshe, 1991), pp. 376–79. Examples of a *jiangu* in scenes of entertainment with the Queen Mother at the top are seen in low relief from Tengxian, Shandong. See *Zhongguo meishu quanji, Huihua bian* vol. 18: *Huaxiang shi huaxiang zhuan* (*Treasury of Chinese fine arts, painting* vol. 18: *Pictorial stones and pictorial bricks*) (Shanghai: Shanghai renmin meishu chubanshe, 1988), pls. 32, 33.

10. Loewe, *Ways to Paradise*, pp. 110–12. The Isles of the Immortals in the Eastern Sea were thought to be supported on the backs of turtles, and a passage from the *Shanhai jing* (*Classic of mountains and waterways*) calls the dwelling of the Queen Mother the Mountain of Turtles. See Loewe, *Ways to Paradise*, p. 90. A representation of the Queen Mother atop a mountain carried by a turtle appears in the tomb at Yi'nan. See Zeng Zhaoyu et al., *Yi'nan gu huaxiang shi mu fajue baogao* (*Excavation report on the ancient engraved stone tomb at Yi'nan*) (Shanghai: Wenhuabu wenwu guanliju, 1956), pl. 66, rubbing no. 55. A turtle carrying a mountain also appears on the side of a stone coffin from Pishan, Sichuan. See Gao and Gao, eds., *Zhongguo huaxiang shi guan yishu*, pp. 78–79.

11. The bear-like creature has tiger-like stripes. Bear supports are quite common on bronze and ceramic vessels. A sexually aroused figure also appears on a base from Guanghan, Sichuan. See Chen Xiandan, "On the Designation 'Money Tree'," *Orientations*, September 1997, p. 71, fig. 8. Wu Hung has pointed out the sexual explicitness of art associated with early Daoism in Sichuan. See Wu Hung, "Mapping Early Taoist Art." The overall axial composition of the lamp is strikingly similar to the T-shaped painting recovered from Tomb 1 at Mawangdui. In both, the watery world is represented at the bottom, where a figure with upraised arms supports a platform above. In both, the heavens appear in the upper section with representations of the sun and the moon. The parasol-like top to the lamp may be intended to represent the canopy of heaven.

12. See Cong Dexin, "Xiwangmu tuxiang de leixingxue yanjiu" ("Typological study of figures of Xiwangmu"), in *Qingguo ji: Jilin daxue kaoguxi jianxi shizhounian wenji* (*Collection of green fruits: Collected works for the tenth anniversary of the Archaeology Department of Jilin University*), ed. Jilin daxue kaoguxi (Beijing: Zhizhi chubanshe, 1998), pp. 24–33.

13. See Chengdu Shi wenwu kaogu gongzuodui and Qingbaijiang qu wenwu guanlisuo, "Chengdu Shi Qingbaijiang Qu Yuejin Cun Hanmu fajue jianbao" ("Brief report on the excavation of the Han tomb at Yuejin Village, Qingbaijiang District, Chengdu Municipality"), *Wenwu* 1998.8, pp. 19–37, fig. 33:5 and cover, fig. 35:1, fig. 35:2, cpl. 3.

14. See Chen Xiandan, "On the Designation 'Money Tree'," pp. 67–71, figs. 7–8.

15. Ibid., fig. 6.

16. Guoli lishi bowuguan, *Guan cang Zhongguo lidai taoci tezhan* (*Special exhibition of the National History Museum's Chinese ceramic collection through the ages*) (Taipei: Guoli lishi bowuguan, 1997), no. 27, p. 38.

17. In addition, see the lamp in the Chongqing Municipal Museum reproduced in Liu Yuchuan, *Chongqing Shi bowuguan* (*Chongqing Municipal Museum*) (Beijing: Wenwu chubanshe, 1991), under "Sichuan Handai yishupin."

18. See Sun Ji, *Handai wuzhi wenhua ziliao tushuo*, pp. 351–54.

19. *Kaogu* 1975.2, pp. 116–23, 134, pl. 9:1. See the discussion in *Mysteries of Ancient China: New Discoveries from the Early Dynasties*, ed. Jessica Rawson (New York: George Braziller, 1996), no. 97, pp. 190–91.

20. Anne Birrell, *Chinese Mythology: An Introduction* (Baltimore and London: The Johns Hopkins University Press, 1993), pp. 27–28.

21. Loewe, *Ways to Paradise*, pp. 108, 116–17 citing *Bowuzhi* (*Treatise on broad phenomena*), a miscellany that is attributed to Zhang Hua (late 3d century CE); and Suzanne Cahill, *Transcendence and Divine Passion*, p. 254, n. 60, citing *Han Wu gushi* (*Old tales concerning Emperor Wu of Han*), a text ascribed to Ban Gu but considered to be 3d century CE or later.

Images of Mountains: *Boshanlu*, Hill Jars, and *Hu* Vessels

Several objects in the exhibition feature images of mountains rendered as part of the decor or as part of the structure of the vessel. On the *hu* storage vessel a register of decor includes animals running in a hilly terrain (cat. no. 27). The *zun* hill jar is a cylindrical container with a conical lid modeled to resemble a mountain peak and its foothills (cat. no. 45). The exhibition also includes two incense burners with mountain-shaped lids, commonly called *boshanlu*, *bo* meaning "numerous," *shan* meaning "mountain" or "hill," and *lu* meaning "censer" (cat. nos. 43, 44).[1] All of these vessels fall into the category of *mingqi*, "spirit objects," made specifically for deposit in the tomb. Mountain-shaped lids were utilized on a number of earthenware vessels, including *ding* tripods, *dun* jars, *hu* urns, and models of granaries.[2] *Mingqi* spirit vessels with such mountain imagery date from the mid to late Western Han through the Eastern Han dynasty. Of all these vessel types, the hill censer has the broadest geographic and chronological distribution.

Boshanlu hill censers have been found in almost all provinces of the People's Republic of China.[3] Indeed, the popularity of hill censers most likely influenced the production of mountain-shaped lids for other types of vessels. Earthenware censers were based on metal prototypes, and archaeological evidence corroborates the fact that the earliest examples of *boshanlu* are made of bronze and are dated to the mid-Western Han dynasty. One of the most spectacular examples, and perhaps the earliest, is a gilded and silvered bronze censer unearthed from a pit near the tomb of Emperor Wu (r. 141–87 BCE) in Xingping County, Shaanxi Province (figs. 1A, 1B). It was found with other inscribed objects belonging to the elder sister of the emperor. Inscriptions on the censer's lid and base indicate that the vessel was made in 137 BCE for use in one of the imperial palaces at the capital, the Weiyang Gong.[4] This incense burner stands 58 centimeters high. Its emphatic verticality is primarily due to the unusually long stem in the form of a bamboo stalk. The lofty location of the hill censer atop this pole etherealizes the mountains, as does the allied motif of dragons in flight below the bowl. Dragons also appear along the upper edge of the bowl and on the foot of the stem. Although this *boshanlu* is unique, the concept behind its form is repeated, albeit to a less adamant degree, in more common versions made solely for the tomb. Other notable examples of early bronze *boshanlu* were found in the tombs of Emperor Wu's half brother, Liu Sheng, known as King Jing of the kingdom of Zhongshan, who died in 113 BCE, and his wife, Dou Wan.[5] The silvered and gilded *boshanlu* from Liu Sheng's tomb, standing 26 centimeters tall, is equally extraordinary in its fine craftsmanship. The hill censer from Dou Wan's tomb is made of bronze and is 32.3 centimeters in height. Based on these three excavated examples, it is likely that the custom of using incense burners with mountain-shaped lids may have originated in an imperial context during the reign of Emperor Wu.

Boshanlu quickly became a customary item of mortuary furnishings throughout China. Censers vary in quality, especially those made specifically for the grave, but have certain features in common, the most important being the conical lid with surface modeling that suggests ranges of hills. In all incense burners the bowl holds the burning incense, and the smoke escapes through apertures in the lid. The greatest variation appears in the handling of the base, including the addition of a pan under the vessel (fig. 2). Some censers have simple stems, like catalogue number 44, but others have three-dimensional sculpture acting as supports, like the bears in catalogue number 43. Another popular type of sculptural stem consists of a bird standing on the back of a turtle and balancing the bowl on its head or on the tip of its beak (fig. 2).[6] Turtles have many associations in ancient China, with longevity, and with a myth about Nüwa using the legs of a great sea turtle to hold up the sky.[7] The ability of birds to soar to the heavens was one reason for their selection as a component of the *boshanlu*. Indeed, transport beyond terrestrial limits seems to be the leitmotif, and it is reiterated as the incense burns and the smoke wafts skyward. Considering the structure as a whole, integration of the images was not the goal; instead the design is based on stacking elements upward, totem-pole style, with a lofty mountain peak as the vertex. The emphasis on verticality in the structure of *boshanlu* is seen in other types of funerary objects produced during the Eastern Han dynasty, notably the money tree and earthenware lamps (cat. nos. 42, 59, and figs. 1, 2).

The censer's form, which is a visualization of a way to another realm, borrows elements from the real world, and yet it also is clear that the imagery is not a representation of the forested mountains of a particular locale. Contemporary associations with mountains are conveyed in the Western Han-dynasty text *Huainanzi*, written before 139 BCE.[8] In chapter 4, "The Treatise on Topography" ("Dixingxun"), the earth's surface and landforms are discussed:[9]

In the (fabric of) the earth's shape, east and west are the weft, north and south are the warp.
Mountains are the cumulative (result of) accretion, valleys are the cumulative (result of) cutting away.
High places govern birth, low places govern death.
Hills govern maleness, valleys govern femaleness.

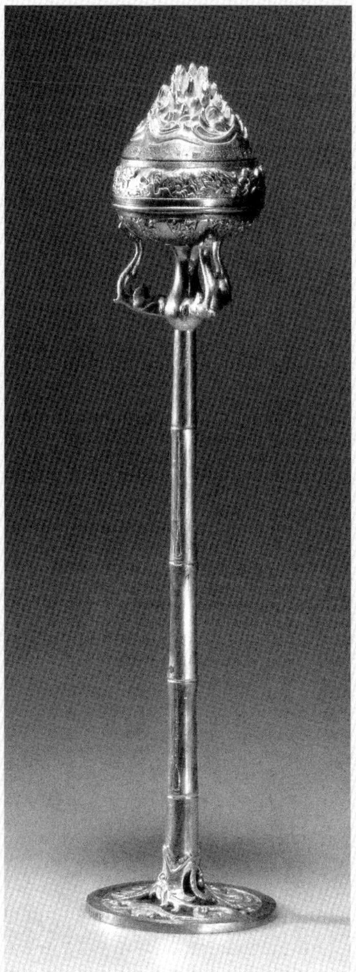

Fig. 1A *Gilded and silvered bronze* boshanlu. Western Han dynasty, 137 BCE. Maoling, Xingping County, Shaanxi. From Li Xueqin, ed., *Zhongguo meishu quanji; gongyi meishu bian 5: Qingtongqi* (*Selection of Chinese fine arts: Arts and crafts, no. 5: Bronze vessels*) (Beijing: Wenwu chubanshe, 1986), *xia*, pls. 209–11.

Here mountains are associated with bright, *yang* forces, and also with birth and life. Of course, the aspiration for afterlife figured strongly in the construction of tombs, and tombs with tumuli over them, or tombs excavated into the side of a mountain, were standard types of burial during the Han dynasty, both seeking to benefit the deceased by means of the potency of the mountain. In life, people sought immortal beings on mountainous islands like Penglai in the Bohai Gulf, and they believed that the Queen Mother of the West, the keeper of a drug that conferred immortality, lived on a peak of the Kunlun Mountains in the west. In the same chapter of the *Huainanzi*, mountains even higher than Kunlun and also several cosmic trees are described as conduits that enable travelers to reach Heaven, where the rewards were substantial:[10]

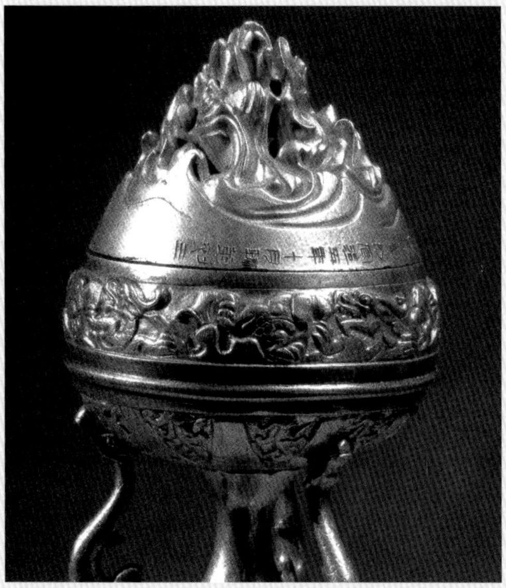

Fig. 1B Detail of fig 1A.

If one climbs to a height double that of the
Kunlun Mountains, [that peak] is called
Cool Wind Mountain.
If one climbs it, one will not die.
If one climbs to a height that is doubled again,
[that peak] is called Hanging Garden.
If one ascends it, one will gain supernatural power
and be able to control the wind and the rain.
If one climbs to a height is that is doubled yet
again, it reaches up to Heaven itself.
If one mounts to there, one will become a god.
It is called the Abode of the Supreme Thearch.

The Fu [= Fusang] Tree in Yang Province is baked
by the sun's heat.
The Jian Tree on Mt. Duguang, by which the gods
ascend and descend (to and from Heaven),
casts no shadow at midday.
If one calls (from that place), there is no echo.
It forms a canopy over the center of the world.
The Ruo Tree is to the west of the Jian Tree.
On its branches are ten suns; its blossoms cast
light upon the earth.

Travel to these elevated places was possible via elements of the most imposing height in the natural landscape—trees and mountains; the trees and mountains described above in the *Huainanzi*, however, are cosmic structures. Likewise, the landscapes depicted within the decor registers of the *hu* urn and the hill jar, and also the terrain represented on the hill-shaped lids, include elements that distinguish them from the mundane world. The presence of dragons immediately indicates the special nature of these scenes. The variety of creatures establishes the fecundity of these landscapes. In contrast, John Major notes in the sixth chapter of the *Huainanzi*, "Peering into the Obscure" ("Lanming xun"), nature is devastated and

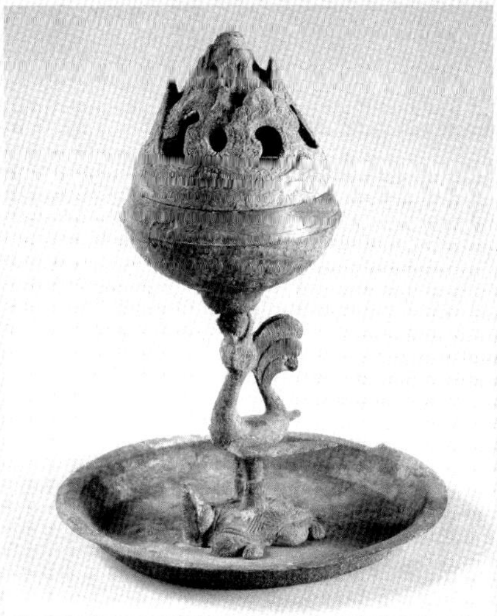

withers when Xiwangmu is angered: "The wings of birds were injured, and four-footed animals became lame. Mountains were denuded of trees, and the flatlands were devoid of fresh water. Foxes and raccoons [dogs] headed for their dens, horses and oxen escaped and wandered away. Fields were bare of growing grain, and roadsides of sedges and reeds."[11] Clearly, no such desolation appears in the landscapes on the tomb wares. In addition, the inclusion of images of hunters in the terrain may indicate the need for propitiatory offerings in the form of animal sacrifice, insuring the continued bounty of nature and the benevolence of deities and also ancestors. The smoke emitted from the smoldering incense of the censer could evoke memories of the burning offerings, but it also appears like clouds encircling the elevated peaks that afforded passage to an afterlife paradise.

SUSAN N. ERICKSON

Notes

1. During the Han dynasty this type of vessel is simply called a censer, *xunlu*. A censer from Xingping County has an inscription that records the term (fig. 1B). See Xianyang diqu wenguanhui and Maoling bowuguan, "Shaanxi Maoling yihao wuming zhong yihao cong zangkeng de fajue" ("Discovery of pit 1 of Tomb 1 at Maoling, Shaanxi Province"), *Wenwu* 1982.9, pp. 1–16, figs. 58–59.

2. For painted earthenware *hu* urns with mountain-shaped lids in Hebei, see Hebei Sheng wenwu yanjiusuo, "Yanxiadu yizhi nei de Lianghan muzang" ("Han-dynasty tombs within the site of the Lower Capital of the State of Yan"), in *Hebei Sheng kaogu wenji* (*Papers on archaeology in Hebei Province*), vol. 2 (Beijing: Beijing Yanshan chubanshe, 2001), pp. 67–140, figs. 10.1–3 (h. 36.8, 64.8, and 52.8 cm; mid-Western Han dynasty). For granaries, see Nanyang wenwu yanjiusuo, *Nanyang Handai huaxiang zhuan* (*Han-dynasty pictorial bricks from Nanyang*) (Beijing: Wenwu chubanshe, 1990), figs. 19.1–4 (h. 35.2, 37.6, 47.8, and 52.8 cm). For a *dun* jar, see Nanyang Shi wenwu yanjiusuo, "Henan Sheng Nanyang Xian Xindian Xiang Xiongying huaxiang shi mu" ("A tomb with stone carvings at Xiongying Village, Xindian Prefecture, Nanyang County, Henan"), *Zhongyuan wenwu* 1996.3, pp. 8–17, fig. 9 (h. 27.3 cm).

3. Susan N. Erickson, "Boshanlu—Mountain Censers of the Western Han Period: A Typological and Iconological Analysis," *Archives of Asian Art*, vol. 45 (1992), pp. 6–28. Since this article was published, many additional examples have been excavated, too numerous to list.

4. Xianyang diqu wenguanhui, "Shaanxi Maoling," pp. 2–3.

5. Zhongguo shehui kexueyuan kaogu yanjiusuo and Hebei Sheng wenwu guanlichu, *Mancheng Han mu fajue baogao* (*Excavation report about the Han tombs at Mancheng*) (Beijing: Wenwu chubanshe, 1980), *xia*, pl. 9. For Dou Wan's censer, see pl. 22.

6. This censer was excavated from a mid Western Han tomb at Shuozhou City in Shanxi. See Zhang Xishun, ed., *Shanxi wenwu guanzang zhenpin: Qingtongqi* (*Cultural relics from museums in Shanxi: Bronzes*) (Taiyuan: Shanxi renmin chubanshe, n.d.), pl. 176 (h. 24.5 cm). Also see Hebei Sheng wenwu yanjiusuo, "Hebei Yangyuan Xian Beiguan Han mu fajue jianbao" ("Excavation report about Han tombs at Beiguan, Yangyuan County, Hebei"), *Kaogu* 1990.4, pp. 322–28, fig. 7.2 (h. 24 cm).

7. Erickson, "Money Trees," p. 11.

8. See Charles Le Blanc, "Huai nan tzu," in *Early Chinese Texts: A Bibliographic Guide*, ed. Michael Loewe (Berkeley: The Society for the Study of Early China and The Institute of East Asian Studies, University of California, Berkeley, 1993), p. 189.

9. See trans. by John S. Major, in *Heaven and Earth in Early Han Thought: Chapters Three, Four, and Five of the Huainanzi* (Albany: State University of New York Press, 1993), p. 167.

10. Major, *Heaven and Earth*, p. 158.

11. Major, *Heaven and Earth*, p. 201.

Fig. 2 *Bronze* boshanlu. Shuozhou City, Shanxi. From Zhang Xishun, ed., *Shanxi wenwu guanzang zhenpin: Qingtongqi*, pl. 176.

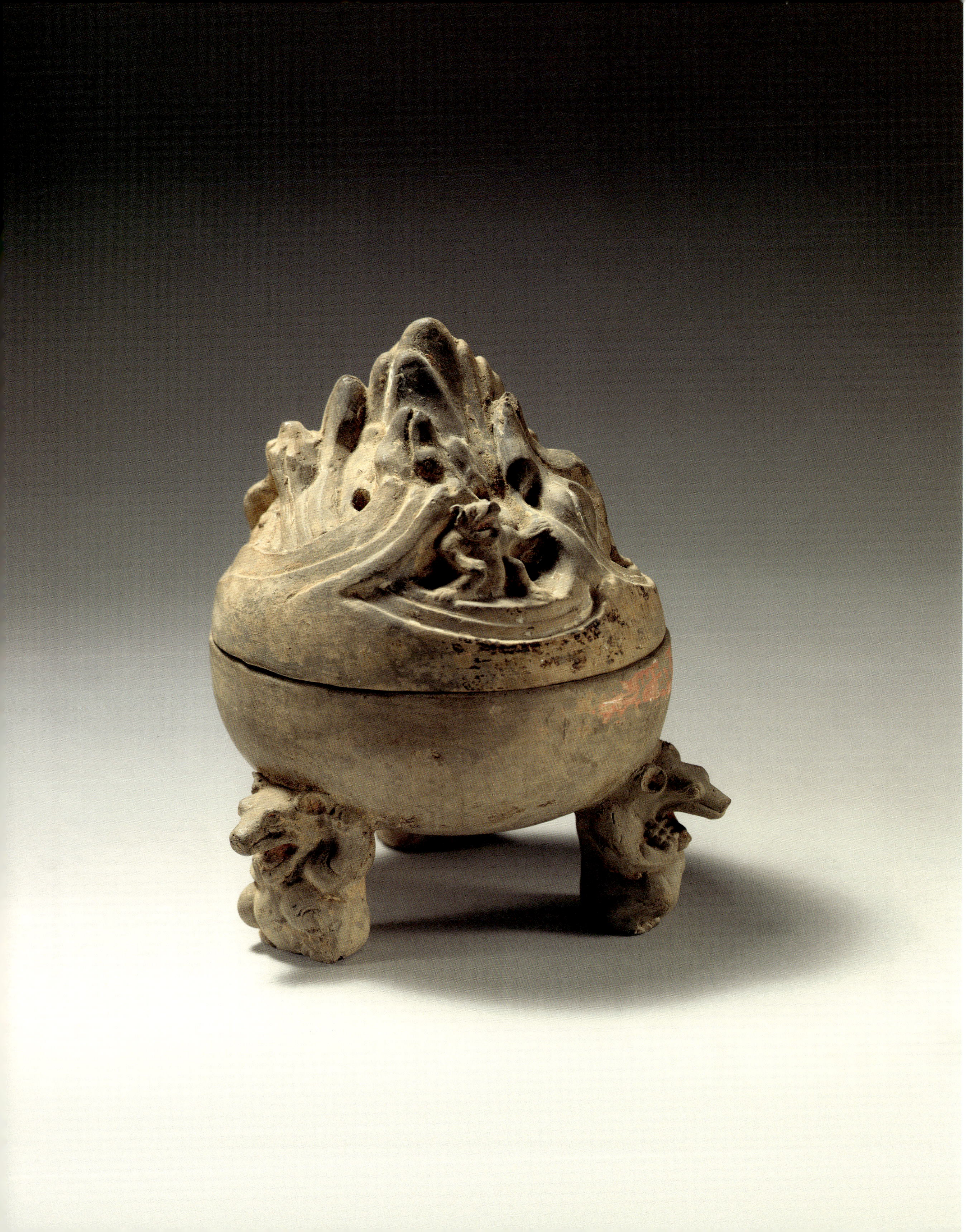

43 Mountain censer (*boshanlu*) on bear-form legs

Late Western Han dynasty or early Eastern Han dynasty. Earthenware with traces of pigment; h. 15.2 cm, diam. 13.3 cm. The Metropolitan Museum of Art, acc. no. 1985.214.129a, b. Gift of Ernest Erickson Foundation.

Because this incense burner is made of earthenware, it is most likely an example of tomb ware.[1] Like all hill censers, it has a conical lid set on a bowl, but instead of the standard stemmed foot, this vessel is supported distinctively, on bear-shaped feet. The bears, rendered as miniature sculptures, are posed in an almost human stance, somewhere between standing and crouching. Their mouths are open with teeth bared, projecting a ferocity indicative of their apotropaic function. Traces of red pigment still can be seen in their mouths and also on their ears.

Bears are a common kind of support on many types of vessels created during the Han dynasty (see cat. nos. 16, 45, 46), but they are atypical for an incense burner. Several metal *boshanlu* with short conical legs, exhibiting similar proportions, have been unearthed; for instance, an iron one of almost the same height from Taiyuan in Shanxi Province.[2] A vessel of related typology, a *ding* tripod with a mountain-shaped lid, similarly incorporates small crouching bears as support legs. This kind of tripod has been excavated in the area of Nanyang, Henan, and is dated to the late Western Han or early Eastern Han dynasty.[3] It is possible that the present *boshanlu* also is from this region, but its bear-shaped legs are one of the features that make this incense burner unique among all known excavated hill censers.

Another interesting aspect of this censer is the treatment of the cover. Along the lower edge, niches have been carved out to hold creatures, including a bear, wild boar, tiger, and horse. Some of these creatures are nearly three-dimensional, quite unlike most of the decor on other ceramic and bronze examples.[4] Among the irregularly molded hills, eight large holes pierce the lid to allow the smoke of the incense to float out of the bowl. Traces of white and red pigment still appear on the lid.

SUSAN N. ERICKSON

Notes

1. Published in Maxwell K. Hearn, *Ancient Chinese Art: The Ernest Erickson Collection in the Metropolitan Museum of Art* (New York: Metropolitan Museum of Art, 1987), cat. no. 125; Kiyohiko Munakata, *Sacred Mountains in Chinese Art* (Urbana-Champaign: University of Illinois, 1991), cat. no. 26; and Peter C. Sturman, "Celestial Journeys—Meditations on (and in) Han Dynasty Painted Pots at the Metropolitan Museum of Art," *Orientations*, May 1988, pp. 54–67, fig. 10.

2. Shanxi Sheng wenwu guanli gongzuo weiyuanhui and Shanxi Sheng kaogu yanjiusuo, "Taiyuan Dongtaibao chutu de Handai tongqi" ("Han dynasty bronze vessels excavated at Dongtaibao, Taiyuan"), *Wenwu* 1962.4–5, pp. 66–72, and 94, pl. 25 (h. 15 cm). Vessels at this site have been dated to 95–74 BCE.

3. See Nanyang Shi wenwu yanjiusuo, "Henan Sheng Nanyang Xian Xindian Xiang Xiongying huaxiang shi mu" ("Pictorial stone tomb at Xiongying Village, Xindian Township, Nanyang County in Henan Province"), *Zhongyuan wenwu* 1996.3, pp. 8–17, fig. 4 (h. 30 cm). Also see Nanyang wenwu yanjiusuo, *Nanyang Handai huaxiang zhuan* (*Han-dynasty pictorial bricks from Nanyang*) (Beijing: Wenwu chubanshe, 1990), pl. 14 (h. 24.1 cm). These vessels are not called censers since the lid has no apertures, unlike the vessel in the exhibition, and they also have handles at each side, typical of *ding*.

4. An incense burner unearthed at Luoyang in Henan Province also features a plastic rendering of lid decor, but the figures are much larger and are piled one on top of the other to create the form of a hill. On the upper part of the lid is a dragon holding a snake in its mouth, and around the circumference of the lower part are placed a tiger, a leopard, a snake, a fantastic creature, and a human figure. Traces of pigments are still visible on the censer's surface. See Luoyang wenwu gongzuodui, *Luoyang chutu wenwu jicui* (*Excavated treasures from Luoyang*) (Beijing: Morning Glory Publishers, 1990), pl. 40 (h. 22 cm).

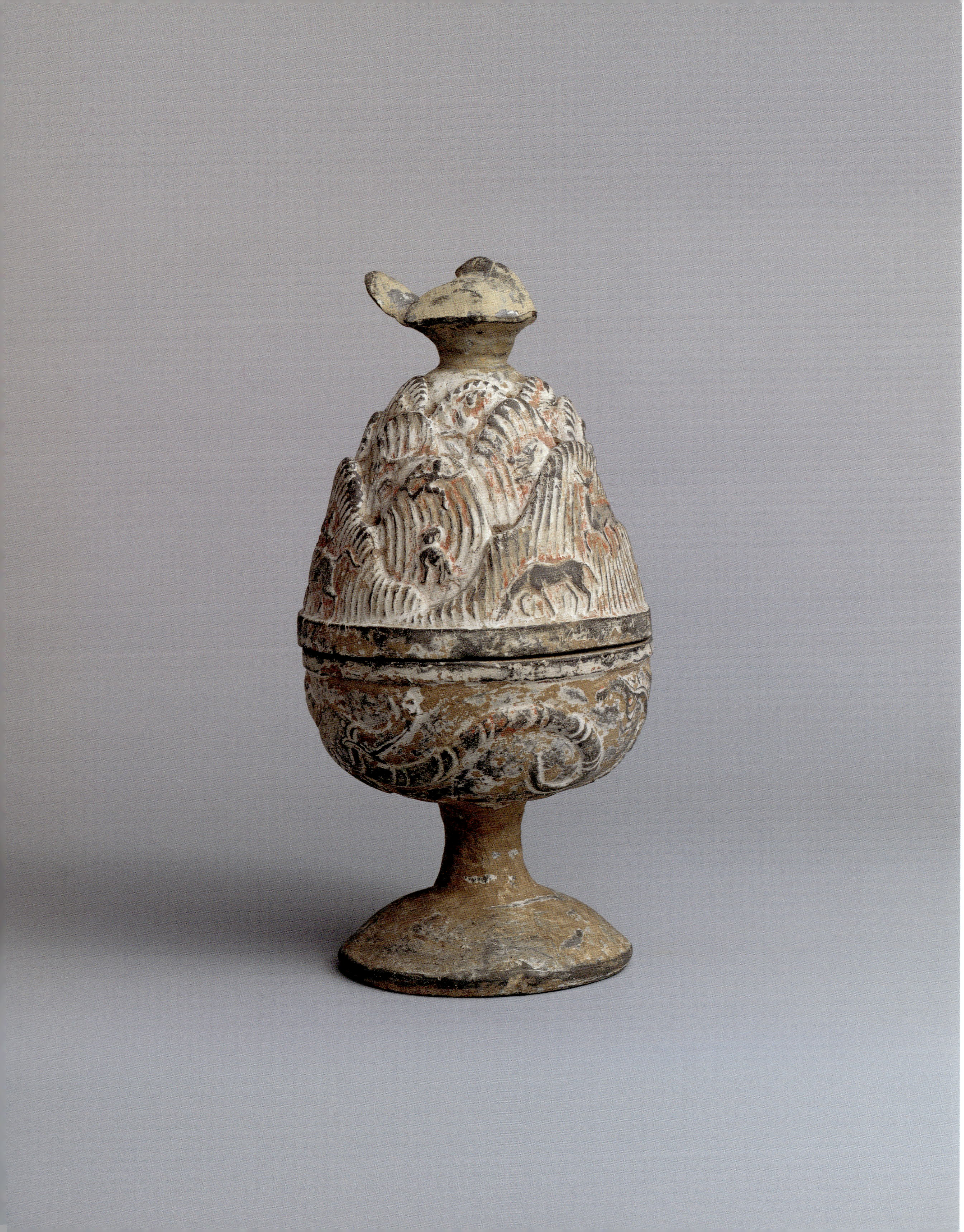

44 Mountain censer (*boshanlu*) with bird finial

Eastern Han dynasty. Earthenware with traces of pigments; h. 22.2 cm, diam. 11.4 cm.
The Metropolitan Museum of Art, acc. no. 1965.74.2a, b. Gift of Florance Waterbury.

This *boshanlu* has a typical construction: a circular foot from which a stem rises to support a bowl topped with a conical lid.[1] An undulating dragon decorates the surface of the bowl. This feature is unusual in ceramic hill censers, but a number of bronze versions show dragons on the bowls or in a register at the lower edge of the lid.[2] The lid of this censer is unusually elongated, with overlapping petal-like forms that represent rising hills. The faces of the hills are covered with thin raised lines suggesting ridges of the terrain. Silhouettes of a variety of motifs, including horses, birds, boars, lions, deer, and human figures, are superimposed on the hill forms. Some of the figures are depicted in active poses, others are stationary. A few creatures are only partly seen, ducking behind hills. This handling yields a minimal sense of depth. The finely rendered detail on the lid is atypical for ceramic censers that were meant to be tomb furnishings. Crowning the lid is a relatively large bird with its head turned to rest on its back. This motif is seen on a number of ceramic versions from various provinces, and also on a few bronze versions. Traces of color still can be seen on the surface, reminding the viewer of the even more beautiful appearance the vessel once had.

Kiyohiko Munakata has suggested that the elongated profile of the lid links this vessel to censers produced in Guangxi Zhuang Autonomous Region in the south of China, but the handling of the decor on the lid is not like that of extant vessels from this area.[3] It is more likely that this incense burner comes from the area around Nanyang in Henan Province, where unearthed censers have lids with similar petal-like hills decorated with raised motifs on their surfaces.[4]

SUSAN N. ERICKSON

Notes

1. Published in Suzanne G. Valenstein, *A Handbook of Chinese Ceramics* (New York: The Metropolitan Museum of Art, 1975), pl. 11; and Kiyohiko Munakata, *Sacred Mountains in Chinese Art* (Urbana-Champaign: University of Illinois, 1991), cat. no. 25.

2. See Hunan Sheng wenwu kaogu yanjiusuo and Yongzhou Shi Zhishanqu wenwu guanlisuo, "Hunan Yongzhou Shi Yaoziling erhao Xihan mu" ("Western Han Tomb 2 at Yaoziling, Yongzhou City, Hunan"), *Kaogu* 2001.4, pp. 44–62, fig. 10 (h. 28.6 cm).

3. Kiyohiko Munakata, *Sacred Mountains*, p. 80. For a bronze vessel with a similar profile from Guangxi, see Guangxi Zhuangzu zizhiqu wenwu guanli weiyuanhui-bian, *Guangxi chutu wenwu* (*Excavated cultural relics in Guangxi*) (Beijing: Wenwu chubanshe, 1978), pl. 120 (h. 19.6 cm). This vessel has a dragon encircling the bowl of the vessel and a bird sitting on top of the lid.

4. For example, see Nanyang Shi gudai jianzhu baohu yanjiusuo, "Henan Nanyang Shi Dongyuan xiaoqu gudai muzang qingli jianbao" ("A brief report about ancient tombs at Dongyuan, Nanyang City, Henan"), *Huaxia kaogu* 1999.2, pp. 37–45, fig. 4.2 (mid Western Han dynasty; h. 18 cm).

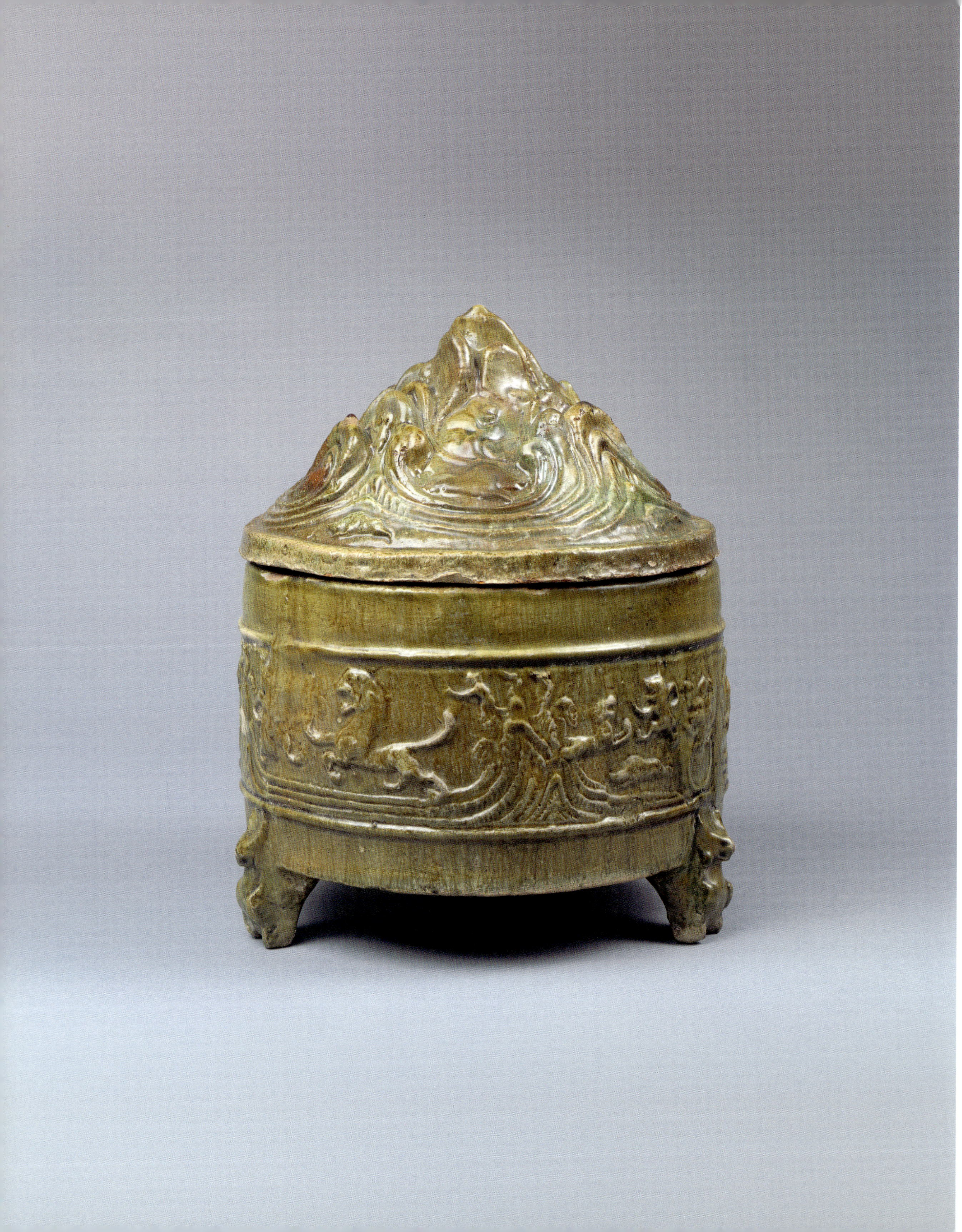

45 Hill jar (*zun*)

Xin dynasty–early Eastern Han dynasty. Earthenware with green glaze; h. 29.8 cm.
Collection of Richard and Ruth Dickes.

This type of vessel, identified as a *zun* in archaeological reports, is best known as a hill jar.[1] Its cylindrical body is supported by three legs in the form of crouching bears. The cone-shaped cover is modeled to suggest rugged mountain terrain. Hills alternate with valleys in such a way that when viewing the cover from above, the landscape takes the form of a quatrefoil. Like the earthenware *hu*, all ceramic hill jars were made as tomb wares. Its form also is based on a metal prototype, and the green glaze was meant to simulate the patina of bronze. In comparison with metal versions of the *hu*, bronze hill jars are quite scarce.[2] On the other hand, earthenware versions are common additions to tombs, and the present hill jar has a standard design, with one wide register on the body of the vessel and a cover made up of hills that rise to a central peak. On opposite sides of the vessel, a ring attached to an animal mask (*pushou*) imitates a handle that would be suspended from a beast's mouth on bronze vessels.

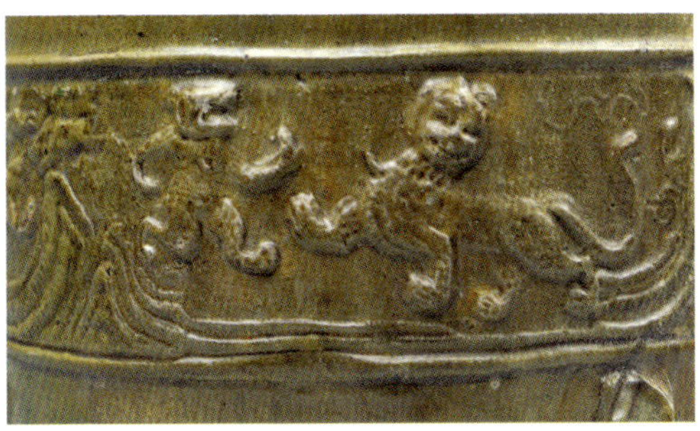

The broad register on the body of the vessel is filled with four sections of rising mountains that alternate with open spaces occupied by animals. The peaks are composed of ribbon-like forms, and each mountain is identical in its structure. The creatures within this register are rendered as silhouettes, as are the relatively large animals that occupy the faces of the hills on the lid. All of the animals in the landscape are in active poses, and they often confront other animals.

The vessel's typology and the distribution and selection of decor are comparable to those of a hill jar excavated in the north suburb of Xi'an from a tomb dated to the Xin dynasty or early Eastern Han dynasty.[3] The hill jar from Xi'an stands 24 centimeters high and has a dark green glaze. The wide register on its cylindrical body features a similar composition of wave-like mountain forms that alternate with a variety of creatures. One of the large felines turns its head into a frontal view (cf. detail), just like the one on the *hu* (cat. no. 27). The assemblage of mortuary vessels in the Xi'an tomb comprises a variety of glazed earthenware objects, including a second hill jar, a *boshanlu* censer, a stemmed lamp, *ding* tripods, *hu* storage vessels, jars, and granaries.

SUSAN N. ERICKSON

Notes

1. For more on the name of this vessel, see Suning Sun-Bailey, "What Is the 'Hill Jar'?" *Oriental Art*, vol. 34, no. 2 (Summer 1988), pp. 88–90.
2. For bronze examples, see Jiangxi Sheng wenwu gongzuodui and Nanchang Shi bowuguan, "Nanchang Shi Jingjiashan Han mu" ("Han tombs at Jingjiashan, Nanchang City"), *Kaogu* 1989.8, pp. 693–98, figs. 3, 4 (Xin dynasty; h. 30 cm); Guangxi Zhuangzu zizhiqu wenwu gongzuodui and Hepu Xian bowuguan, "Guangxi Hepu Xian Jiuzhiling Donghan mu" ("Eastern Han tombs at Jiuzhiling, Hepu County, Guangxi"), *Kaogu* 2003.10, pp. 57–77, fig. 13.10 (h. 24.5 cm); and Hengyang Shi bowuguan, "Hunan Leiyang Shi Donghan mu fajue baogao" ("Excavation report about Eastern Han tombs at Leiyang City in Hunan"), *Kaoguxue jikan*, vol. 13 (2000), pp. 100–166, fig. 47.2 (h. 32.1 cm).
3. Shaanxi Sheng kaogu yanjiusuo, "Xi'an beijiao Beikang Cun Han mu qingli jianbao" ("A brief report about the Han tombs at Beikang Village in the north suburb of Xi'an"), *Kaogu yu wenwu* 2003.4, pp. 21–32, fig. 14.5.

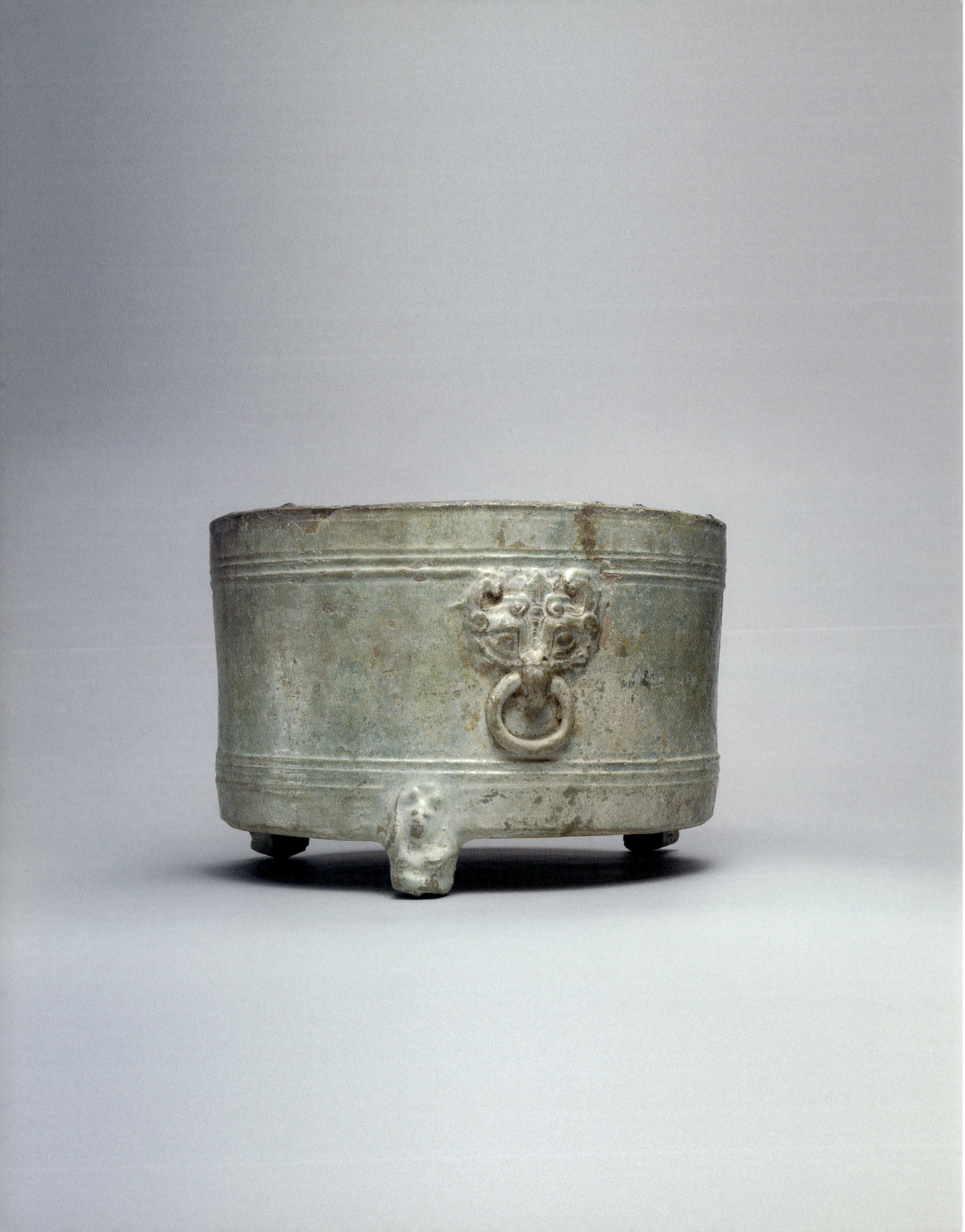

46 Tripod basin (*zun*) on bear-form legs

Han dynasty. Earthenware with appliqué mask handles and green glaze; h. 20.4 cm, diam. 30.8 cm.
Princeton University Art Museum, acc. no. 1998-267. Gift of Dr. Alvin E. Friedman-Kien in honor of Allen Rosenbaum.

A metal or lacquer prototype was clearly the inspiration for this vessel. Three legs modeled as crouching pot-bellied bears support the cylindrical body. Below the mouth and above the flat base, pairs of horizontal ribs encircle the vessel, and between the two pairs are a pair of *taotie* masks holding mock ring handles—one mask equidistant between two of the bears, the other directly opposite. The vessel was entirely covered in a green glaze, now a silvery iridescence.

In form this *zun* is clearly related to a gilt-bronze example now in the Palace Museum, Beijing, accompanied by a stand raised on three bear-form supports inlaid with turquoise. Along the rim of the stand is a sixty-two–character inscription giving a date of 45 CE (fig. 1).[1] Called *wenjiu zun* by archaeologists, or "wine-warming vessel,"[2] such objects were integral to feasts and banquets during the Han, used along with trays, ladles, and eared cups, as illustrated in a wall carving from an Eastern Han stone tomb in Shandong Province (fig. 2).[3]

HIROMI KINOSHITA

Notes

1. See Wan-go Weng, *The Palace Museum: Peking* (New York: Harry N. Abrams Inc., 1982), p. 143, no. 76. Compare also the ornate gilt-silver *zun*, decorated around its circumference with two registers of fantastic birds and beasts and Immortals amidst scrolling clouds, and raised on three bear-form legs inlaid with rock crystal and turquoise; this was excavated from an Eastern Han tomb (M1) in the southern outskirts of Handan City, Hebei. See *Wenwu* 1995.10, front cover and line drawing, p. 80, fig. 1. The *zun* is pictured atop a gilt-silver tripod stand of similar style and decoration, which, unusually, was excavated from another tomb (M2) along with a cover. Archaeologists believe, based on the similar decoration, that all three pieces form a set. The stand has a long inscription along its rim giving a date of 47 CE, and from the inscription appears to have been made in the same workshop in Sichuan as the Palace Museum example. Furthermore, both stands are inscribed with the two characters *sheng yu* (literally, "the ruler's carriage," used as a metonymy for "emperor"), suggesting that they were used within the imperial palace. See ibid, pp. 81–82.
2. A bronze version excavated at Dachuan Cun, Youyu County, Shanxi, has an inscription identifying it as a *wenjiu zun* and giving a date of 26 BCE. See *Shanxi chutu wenwu* (*Artifacts excavated from Shanxi*) (Beijing: Wenwu chubanshe, 1980), pl. 126.
3. Excavated from Zhucheng County, Shandong Province; illustrated in *Wenwu* 1981.10, p. 18, fig. 6.

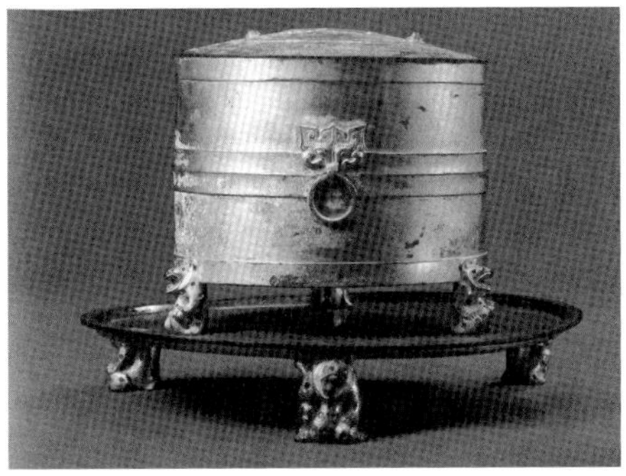

Fig. 1 *Gilt bronze wine-warming vessel on three bear-form legs on a raised stand*. Eastern Han dynasty, 45 CE. From Wan-go Weng, *The Palace Museum: Peking*, p. 143, no. 76.

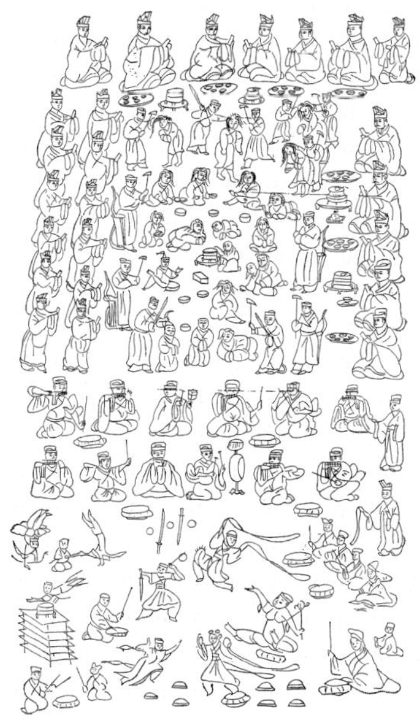

Fig. 2 *Banqueting scene*. Eastern Han dynasty, second–third century CE. Drawing taken from a stone engraving in a tomb at Zhucheng County, Shandong. *Wenwu* 1981.10, p. 18, fig. 6.

The Bear Motif during the Han Dynasty

Bears figured prominently in Han art. Two gilt-bronze examples (cat. nos. 48, 49) illustrate their widespread use from the third century BCE onward as supports or legs for vessels. Each figure is animatedly cast, with one knee bent and one paw raised to the side of its head as if to support a heavy load on its shoulders. The smaller bear, with allover finely incised details and embellished with turquoise inlay, appears the more ferocious of the two, with jaws agape showing rows of sharp teeth. A slot at the back of each bear's head indicates where a vessel, possibly made from wood or lacquer,[1] was once attached.

Many painted and glazed pottery vessels imitating bronze prototypes (cat. nos. 43, 45, 46) and architectural models (cat. no. 16) are also supported on bear-form legs. Two-dimensional renderings of bears holding up plinths that support standing figures appear in the "Wu family shrines" stone engravings (fig. 1) as well as in Han tombs.[2] Sculptural renderings of bears by themselves (cat. no. 47) are fairly uncommon; rather, they are often portrayed locked in combat, biting or wrestling with other ferocious animals.[3] These various depictions tend to highlight the bear's great physical power. Yet bears were also rendered as benign, almost amiable creatures (cat. no. 48), and their popularity as a motif strongly suggests that they were appreciated for more than just their physical strength.

A passage in the Han dynasty text *Zhouli* (*Rites of Zhou*),[4] ascribes special powers to bears. It describes a ritual performed during the New Year season by a bear-like exorcist (*fangxiangshi*) who wears a bearskin with four gold eyes to drive out pestilences. The exorcist in Eastern Han stone carvings has been identified by archaeologists and scholars as Chi You (fig. 2), a legendary figure who fought against the Yellow Emperor and who was known in antiquity as the master of weapons and lord of warfare.[5]

Perhaps it was the bear's auspicious association with immortality, however, that chiefly accounts for its frequent depiction in friezes of animals in landscapes,[6] found on the interior walls of stone tombs and encircling the sides of bronze, lacquer, and ceramic vessels. Bears confronting tigers (cat. no. 45, detail) and cavorting with other wild animals such as dragons, hares, monkeys, and deer in a mountainous landscape (cat. no. 27) are commonly seen on *hu* jars, incense burners (*boshanlu*), and hill jars. Sometimes winged Immortals join the animal company. Further confirming the popularity and widespread use of the bear motif, a Han *fu* rhapsody describes a second-century BCE palace in present-day Qufu, Shandong, furnished with wood carvings of such animals, including a black bear.[7]

It is significant that the sudden appearance and prevalence of the bear in Han art (the animal is hardly depicted in the earlier Shang or Zhou periods) coincides with the rule of the Han emperor Wudi (r. 140–87 BCE). Texts reveal that the emperor, like rulers before him—most notably the First Emperor of Qin—had a fervent, if not obsessive, interest in immortality. He sponsored expeditions in search of the Immortal Isles where the plant integral to producing the elixir of immortality grew, and also built a "paradise" garden replicating the islands, filling it with exotic animals and plants. He constructed the Supreme Forest (*Shanglin*), a vast park containing thousands of plant species and exotic

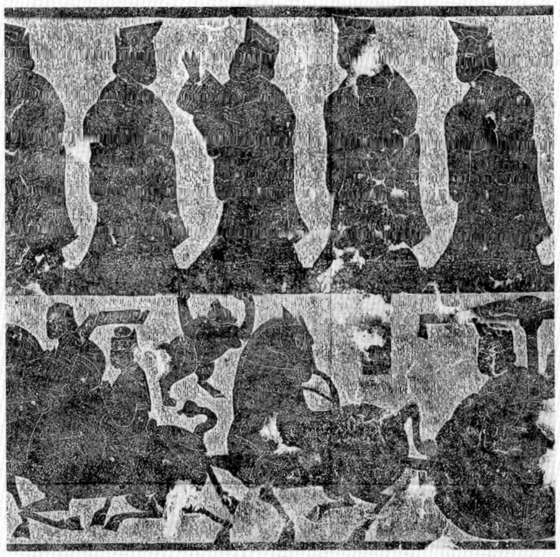

animals brought from faraway lands.[8] Han *fu* rhapsodies describe such parks, with bears as well as other exotic animals kept in different quadrants, according to their place of origin, to create a microcosmic replica of the universe.[9] All these constructions were not merely for aesthetic enjoyment, but served a religious purpose, as places where the emperor could sacrifice to the Immortals, and where he might possibly meet them. The decorative friezes found on vessels and objects, therefore, may depict in miniature Emperor Wu's grand and lavish constructions, which in turn were representions of the landscape of immortality, and projections of the wish for immortal life.

HIROMI KINOSHITA

Notes

1. Traces of wood are lodged inside the smaller bear.

2. Such as the Han tomb engravings at Nanwushan, Jiaxiang County, Shandong. See *Wenwu* 1986.4, p. 88, fig. 3. The pictorial language of Han stone engravings appears to have been fairly standardized and consistent, accounting for commonalities and similarities appearing in eastern (Shandong) and western (Sichuan) regional art.

3. Two Eastern Han gilt-bronze bear mat weights were excavated from Hefei, Anhui, illustrated in *Zhongguo qingtongqi quanji* (*Complete works of Chinese bronzes*), vol. 12: *Qin, Han* (Beijing: Wenwu chubanshe, 1998) p. 166, no. 163. A Western Han bear and tiger in combat bronze mat weight was excavated from Tianshui, Gansu. Ibid., p. 167, no. 164.

4. The date of this text is problematic, but it was not known before the Western Han. See Michael Loewe, ed. *Early Chinese Texts: A Bibliographical Guide* (University of California, Berkeley: Society for the Study of Early China and the Institute of East Asian Studies, 1993), p. 25.

5. Mark Edward Lewis, *Sanctioned Violence in Early China* (Albany: State University of New York Press, 1990), pp. 189–91.

6. Continuous friezes of animals and figures, both bizarre and realistic, around the sides of vessels appeared as early as the 6th century BCE, and these may have been the inspiration for Han and later imagery. See Jessica Rawson, "Strange Beasts," *Nomads, Traders and Holy Men along China's Silk Road* (Papers presented at a symposium held at The Asia Society, New York, 2001), pp. 24–26; see also Wu Hung, *The Wu Liang Shrine: The Ideology of Early Chinese Pictorial Art* (Stanford: Stanford University Press, 1989), pp. 76–87, regarding omen designs.

7. Written by Wang Yanshou, *zi* Wenkao (act. 163 CE), it describes the Hall of Numinous Brilliance (*Lingguang Dian*), a famous palace which was built by the Han king Liu Yu. See David R. Knechtges, trans., *Wen Xuan or Selections of Refined Literature*, vol. 2: *Rhapsodies on Sacrifices, Hunting, Travel, Sightseeing, Palaces and Halls, Rivers and Seas* (Princeton: Princeton University Press, 1987), pp. 262–79.

8. Lothar Ledderose, "Religious Elements in Landscape Art," *Theories of the Arts in China*, ed. Susan Bush and Christian Murck (Princeton: Princeton University Press, 1983), pp. 166–69.

9. Knechtges, *Wen Xuan*, vol. 2, pp. 53–114.

Fig. 1 *Caryatid bear.* Detail of Stone Chamber 1, Stone 1-E.1 (cat. no. 1.11). "Wu family shrines" rubbings. Princeton University Art Museum, acc. no. 2002-307.1.

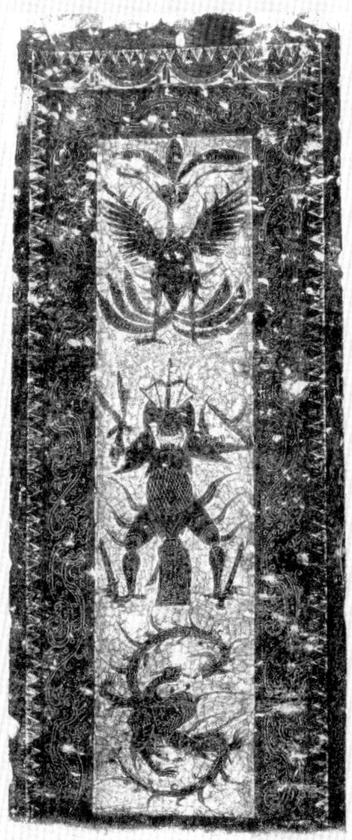

Fig. 2 *Chi You, god of war and weapons, depicted as an exorcist, wearing a bearskin.* Rubbing of engraved stone excavated from the front chamber, middle column of the north wall of a late Eastern Han (147–220 CE) tomb at Beizhai Cun, Yi'nan, Shandong. From *Zhongguo huaxiang shi quanji*, vol. 1: *Shandong Han stone engravings* (Ji'nan: Shandong meishu chubanshe, 2000), p. 143, no. 194.

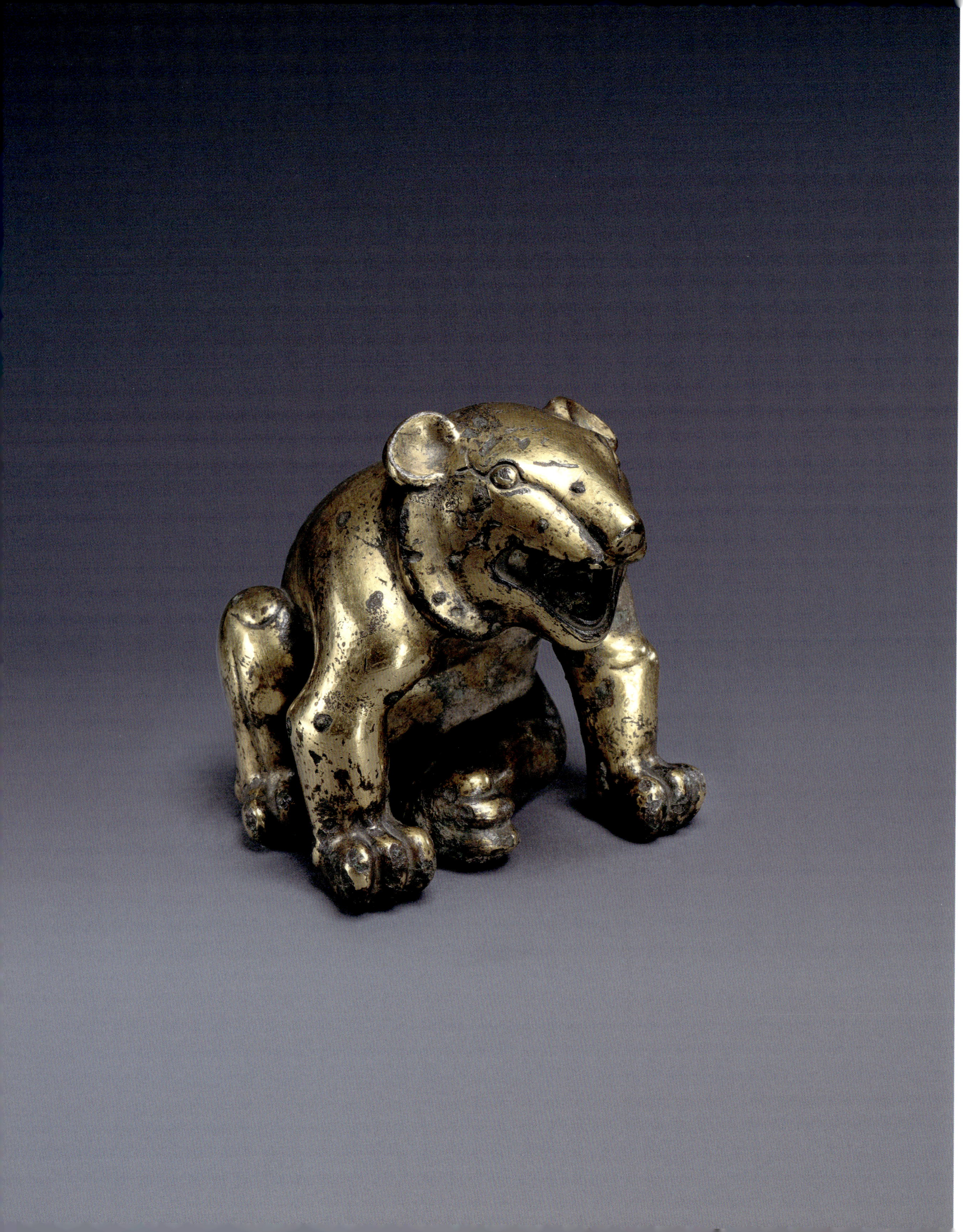

47 Mat weight in the form of a bear

Western Han dynasty. Gilt bronze; h. 15.7 cm.
Cleveland Museum of Art, acc. no. 1994.203. John L. Severance Fund.

Modeled in the round, with head thrust forward and forequarters resting on its powerful front legs, this bear appears about to rise from its sitting position. Saucer-shaped eyes, a thick ruff around its neck, and a wide, upturned mouth give this creature a benign, even congenial, appearance. The warm yellow gilding is worn in places, allowing patches of red cuprite and green malachite corrosion to show through.

The size and mass of this solid-cast bear, as well as its three-dimensionality, suggest that it was used as a weight. As such, however, its large size is unusual. Smaller weights, cast from metal[1] in the shape of animals such as recumbent felines, rams, deer, coiled snakes, and dragons, have been excavated mainly from Western Han tombs.[2] They were made in sets of four, to be placed in each corner of a mat.[3] Written records show that the use of mats was widespread in the Han, especially in ceremonies.[4] Furthermore, the *Xijing zaji* (*Miscellanies of the Western Capital*), a recovered Western Han miscellany on institutions and events pertaining to Chang'an (the capital of the Western Han), describes jade weights holding down a long-haired bearskin mat in one of the palaces.[5] Particular animals may have been the preferred shape for weights by reason of the protective or auspicious qualities attributed to them (see essay in this catalogue on the "Bear Motif during the Han Dynasty" and cat. nos. 48, 49).

HIROMI KINOSHITA

Notes

1. Usually bronze, either plain or embellished with gilding, silvering, and precious stones. Silver weights have also been found, as have iron examples. Stone weights have also been found in southern China. For a list of excavated weights, see Sun Ji, "Han zhen yishu" ("Artistic weights of the Han dynasty"), *Wenwu* 1983.6, pp. 69–72.

2. Ibid. The earliest date to the Warring States period. A set of four hollow semi-hemispherical bronze weights, each cast in the form of eight interlocking dragons, was excavated from the tomb of the Marquis Yi of the state of Zeng (d. 433 BCE). The tomb, located in Sui Xian, Hubei Province, is well known for the impressive finds of lacquer wares, bronze ritual vessels, and musical instruments that were excavated there. For a description and illustration of the weights, see Hubei Sheng bowuguan, *Zeng Hou Yi mu* (*Tomb of Marquis Yi of the State of Zeng*) (Beijing: Wenwu chubanshe, 1989), vol. 1, p. 244, fig. 141:3 (line drawing), p. 247; and vol. 2, pl. 81: 4, 5.

3. Mats were made of friable material, hence only the metal weights survive in tombs.

4. Mats were laid for participants in the ceremonies as well as for the ancestral spirits. See John Steele, trans., *The I-li, or Book of Etiquette and Ceremonial* (London: Probsthain, 1917), vol. 1, pp. 51–52, 257–58, 266.

5. Written by Liu Xin (53 BCE–23 CE). See *Xijing zaji*, *Congshu jicheng chubian* edition (Beijing: Zhonghua shuju, 1991), *juan* 1, p. 4.

48 Bear

Han dynasty. Gilt bronze; h. 6.0 cm.
Private collection.

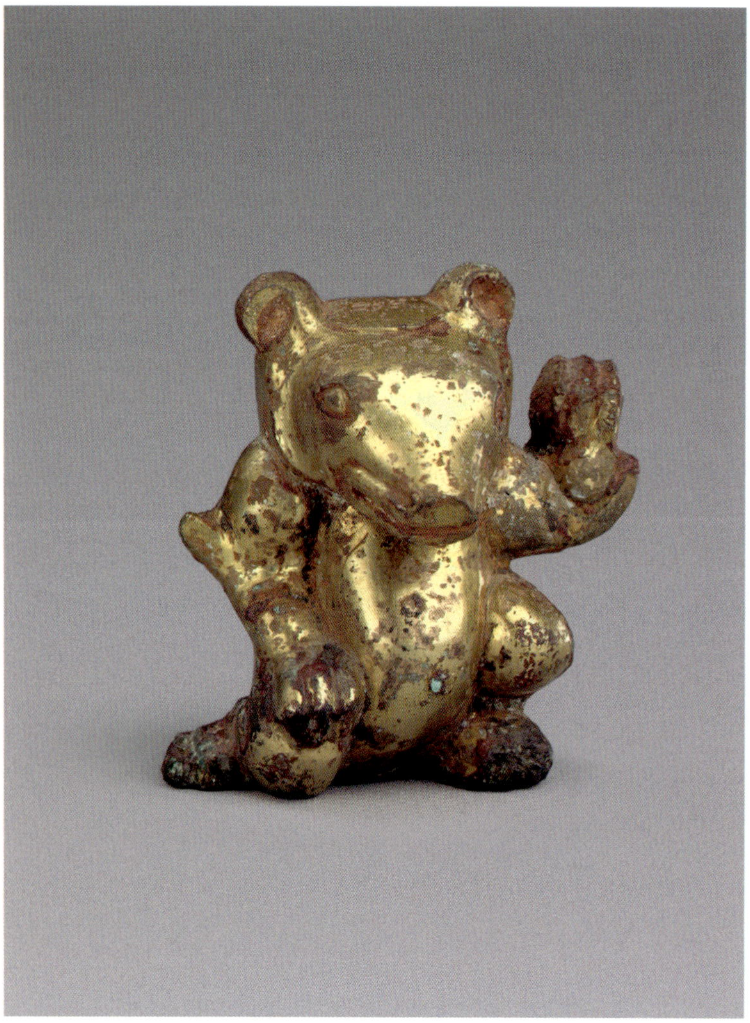

49 Bear

Han dynasty. Gilt bronze with turquoise inlay; h. 3.3 cm.
Private collection.

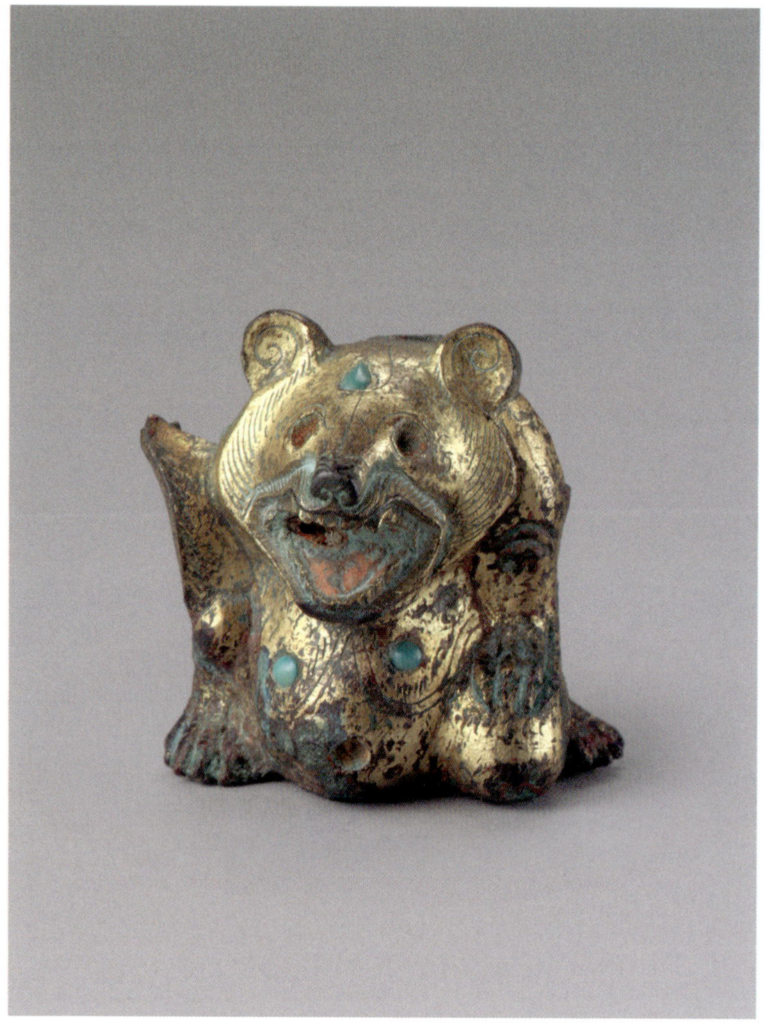

Horses in the Mortuary Arts of the Han Dynasty

Horses play a major role in the rich pictorial compositions carved in very low relief on the walls of the "Wu family shrines"; they are depicted mounted and galloping two and three abreast, pulling chariots in processions, or standing unhitched under the intertwining trees (figs. 1A, 1B). A few appear in the earthly realm in scenes of well-known historical events or mythic lore, which are sometimes identified by cartouches, while others inhabit the heavenly realms as good omens.[1] The forms of all these steeds have been reduced to highly simplified and stylized silhouettes, almost shorthand symbols, with thick, arched necks and robustly rounded bodies supported on slender legs with small wedge-shaped hoofs. The smooth, taut, and sleekly rounded forms strongly suggest that a compass or comparable device was used to guide the carver.[2] These elegant silhouettes have become a hallmark of the Wu shrines and also synonymous with Han-dynasty art.

The three horse sculptures in the exhibition, the two in clay (cat. nos. 50, 52) and, in particular, the one in bronze (cat. no. 51), share some stylistic elements with the steeds of the Wu shrines (figs. 1A, 1B) and again underscore the enormous popularity and importance of horses in Han-dynasty art. No other animal had a greater impact on China's real and imagined history. Admired from time immemorial for its natural strength and spirit, the horse continued to accrue supernatural powers and layers of symbolic meaning throughout the centuries.

Beginning in the Neolithic and during the Bronze Age of the Shang and Zhou dynasties, horses were sacrificed to the ancestors, to the Lord of the River, and to the Earth. According to early myth, horses, deemed close kin to dragons, were associated with the quest for immortality as recounted in the story of King Mu of the Zhou dynasty; he drove a fabled team of eight to visit the Queen Mother of the West, who presides over the realm of the Immortals.[3] By the mid-fourth century BCE, the Chinese were emulating the successful techniques of the northern barbarians: riding astride, wearing nomadic dress such as trousers and tunic, in order to fight effectively from horseback.[4] The role of horses in warfare is vividly underscored by the life-size terra-cotta army, including 7,000 soldiers, over 500 chariot horses, and 116 cavalry horses, buried within the necropolis of Qin Shihuangdi (r. 221–210 BCE), the first ruler of the Qin dynasty and the first emperor of China. It was during the Han dynasty, however, China's first great empire, that the horse became identified with the emperor, the Son of Heaven, the individual responsible for maintaining harmony in the universe. The horse acquired perhaps its greatest import and achieved mythical stature when its symbolic connections with the emperor and with the quest for immortality merged with its legendary and actual military prowess.[5]

The emergence of horses as a significant theme in Han mortuary art reflects not only the Chinese passion for these highly valued animals but also the political realities of the Han. Horses

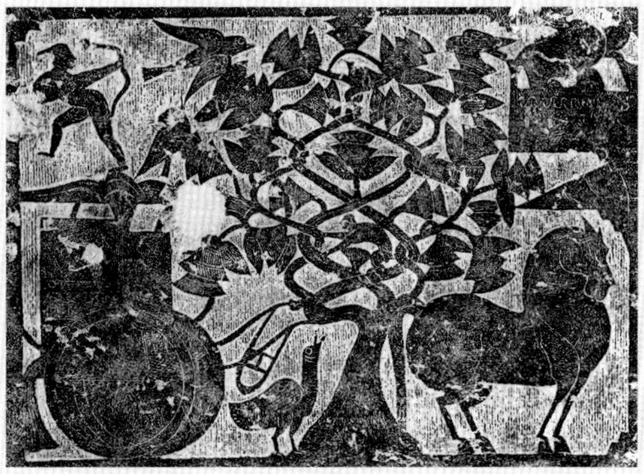

Fig. 1A *Unhitched horse near mythical tree.* Detail of Stone Chamber 2, Stone 2-S.6 (cat. no. 1.26). "Wu family shrines" rubbings. Princeton University Art Museum, acc. no. 2002-307.24.

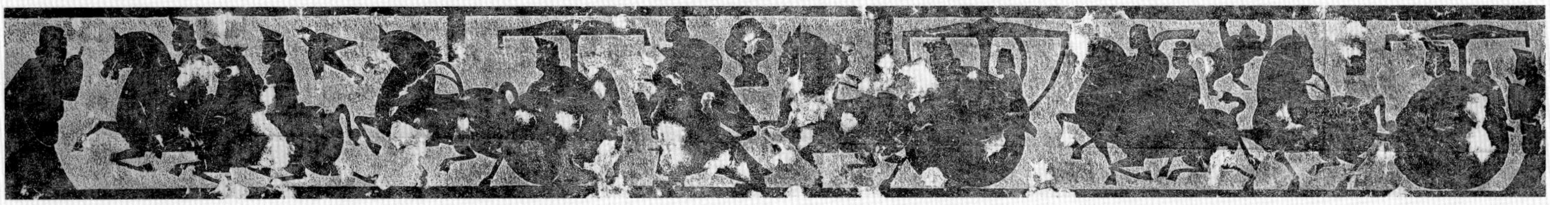

were of vital military importance to contain the constant and growing threat from the Xiongnu tribal armies along the northern borders and in the northwest. The Western Han emperor Wudi's (r. 140–87 BCE) pursuit of larger and stronger horses has become legendary, and is documented by many scholars.[6] Han Wudi, the "Martial Emperor," pursued an aggressive military policy in northwest China to stop attacks by the Xiongnu, whose incursions had reached within striking distance of the imperial capital of Chang'an (present-day Xi'an) in Shaanxi. Han Wudi recognized that the Xiongnu had superior equestrian and horse-breeding skills. Although the Han armies had been acquiring larger, stronger breeds from the Xiongnu and others, Han Wudi dispatched several costly military expeditions to Central Asia in search of *tianma*, or "Heavenly Horses," believed to be far superior in size, speed, agility, and stamina.[7] His envoy, Zhang Qian, encountered the Wusun people in the Yili River valley in present-day Xinjiang, and Wusun horses, much praised as heavenly steeds, were offered as tribute to Han Wudi about 115 BCE. But the emperor had already heard that the "blood-sweating" horses from Ferghana were the true "Heavenly Horses," even larger than the Wusun breed and with more stamina; these horses could not only enhance China's military capability but also might possibly reach the realm of the Immortals, another of Han Wudi's pressing goals. About 100 BCE Wudi finally was presented with his prize steeds from Ferghana.

During the Han, sculptural representations of horses, mostly molded in clay and to a lesser extent cast in bronze or carved in wood, became increasingly prevalent as *mingqi* ("spirit" or "bright" objects or figurines made specifically for burial in tombs). Most of the Han *mingqi* of horses, particularly those of Western Han, are small-scale models of chariot or cavalry horses. These are exemplified by the painted clay cavalry formations in two graves at Yangjiawan, Xianyang, Shaanxi, satellite burials to the mausoleum of Emperor Gaozu (r. 206–195 BCE). These included over 2,500 cavalry and infantry figurines (fig. 2). Although half the size of the Yangjiawan horses and riders, the cavalryman in this exhibit (cat. no. 52) shares a number of features with the Yangjiawan cavalrymen in posture, dress, color, and saddle type (cat. no. 52, fig. 1).[8]

Although the need for excellent mounts continued through Eastern Han, the dynasty was then considerably weaker and less prosperous, diminishing the numbers of large horses imported from Western and Central Asia. *Mingqi* horses excavated from Eastern Han tombs tend to be somewhat smaller than some of their Western Han counterparts but no less impressive, and they include the fabled bronze "Flying Horse," with one hoof touching a swallow. This horse was accompanied by a formation of bronze horses, cavalry, and war chariots, all belonging to the tomb of a general buried in Wuwei County, Gansu.[9] Many of the Eastern Han images, whether sculpted in bronze or clay, painted, or carved in relief like the images of the Wu shrines, depict spirited horses, trotting, cantering, galloping, pawing the ground, or poised for movement. Often, ears are pricked, eyes stare, and teeth are bared while heads toss and tails are raised. The energy and compactness of the bronze horses from

Fig. 1B *Chariot procession*. Detail of Stone Chamber 1, Stone 1-E.1 (cat. no. 1.11). "Wu family shrines" rubbings. Princeton University Art Museum, acc. no. 2002-307.1.

Wuwei (fig. 3) and in the low-relief carvings on the Wu shrines also inform the small bronze horse cast with a clay core in the exhibition (cat. no. 51). Its compact, rounded body, supported by tapered legs with wedge-shaped hooves, makes for a strong, muscular form and profile. This sculpture is dominated by a robustly arched neck with roached mane, and a finely shaped head. The raised foreleg conveys a sense of harnessed energy and momentarily arrested motion. Of the three horses in the exhibition, this one, despite its thicker legs and less stylized treatment of the body, seems closest in spirit to the majesty and energy of the low-relief horses on the Wu shrines.

All three bronze and clay horses in the exhibition were undoubtedly made in separate pieces that were then joined in various ways, perhaps reflecting the influence of joinery in horses made from wood.[10] Large sculpture, such as the huge green-glazed horse (cat. no. 50) would be easier—doubtless more foolproof—to make in sections and then join.[11]

During the Han a group of exceptionally large horses, ranging from about 100 to 140 centimeters in height, were fashioned from clay, wood, or bronze, and all relate in some aspects to the present green-glazed clay model. Most of these monumental steeds seem to be concentrated in the northwest, southwest, and southeast, in Gansu, Sichuan, Guizhou, and Guangxi Zhuang Autonomous Region, with a few scattered in other provinces such as Hebei and Jiangsu.[12] The body types of the Sichuan and Guangxi models appear to reflect degrees of stylistic influences; of those southern models some, such as the lively bronze horse excavated at Mianyang, Hejiashan, Sichuan, recall northern horses such as those from Wuwei with their more elegantly tapered legs.[13] Generally, however, the southern models appear stocky and sturdy by contrast with the taller northern and western breeds. Pointed and erect scoop-shaped ears and arched necks with roached manes seem disproportionately long for the size of the body. One consistently distinctive feature—visible on all these bronze and ceramics examples, including catalogue number 50—is the shape of the rather small head. All the heads seem truncated; nostrils are flaring oval holes that lie flat against the head, teeth are bared below an upward curving upper lip, and the lower jaw juts prominently, all of which perhaps depict a variant local breed.

On the massive green-glazed horse (cat. no. 50) the flare and curve of the upper lip is further emphasized by three parallel ridges. The lower lip flares down with equal emphasis, revealing the bared teeth and lolling tongue. The forms of the head, such as the circular jawbone, are further highlighted by the incised lines and raised circular bosses that define the halter. Incised lines sweep along the neck and arc at the shoulder and above the legs,

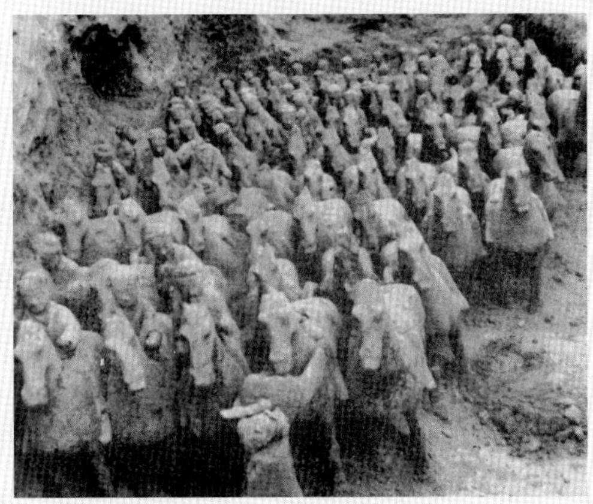

Fig. 2 *View of pit with mounted cavalry*. Western Han dynasty. Tomb 4, Yangjiawan, Xianyang Municipality, Shaanxi. Gray earthenware with pigments. From *Wenwu* 1977.10, pl. 3, bottom.

enhancing the sense of muscular strength. Despite reassembly and conservation from a number of large pieces, making for some awkwardness of proportion, the horse retains a vigorous presence. Lead-fluxed glazes, which tend to degrade with burial and acquire an attractive silvery iridescence, cover its red clay body. These low-fired, lead-fluxed glazes, with copper as the coloring agent producing various shades and hues of green, began appearing in the late Western Han and were widely applied during the Eastern Han.

As these three sculptural representations demonstrate, the horses of Han China comprised a variety of breeds and crossbreeds between local and imported strains. The differences among the Han *mingqi* horses, including the three in the present exhibition (cat. nos. 50–52), may reflect artistic adaptations as well. This is particularly true of the highly stylized depictions of horses on the Wu shrines. The exaggeratedly round bodies and very thin legs of the Wu horses suggest artistic abstraction for pictorial effect. Not until the Tang dynasty, China's second great empire, were Arabian-type horses consistently and sufficiently available (fig. 4). It is also during the Tang that both two- and three-dimensional representations of horses reflect a heightened naturalism.[14] A symbol of personal status as well as imperial power, magnificent horses figure prominently in Tang tomb art as *mingqi*, as paintings on tomb walls, and as freestanding sculpture lining spirit roads; they were the subjects of numerous paintings commissioned by the court.[15] This most valued animal became integral not only to military defense and to aristocratic life, but to China's artistic culture as well.

As mentioned earlier, the "Wu family shrines" pictorial carved slabs have engaged the imagination of scholars in China and in the West for at least eight centuries as archetypes of Han, and particularly Eastern Han, art. The depiction of horses, singly or in groups, drawing carts or chariots, or bearing riders, embodies the Wu shrine's signature pictorial language—the visual cadence of processions and events in highly stylized and repetitive forms in an organized world dominated by formality and rituals.

ANNETTE L. JULIANO

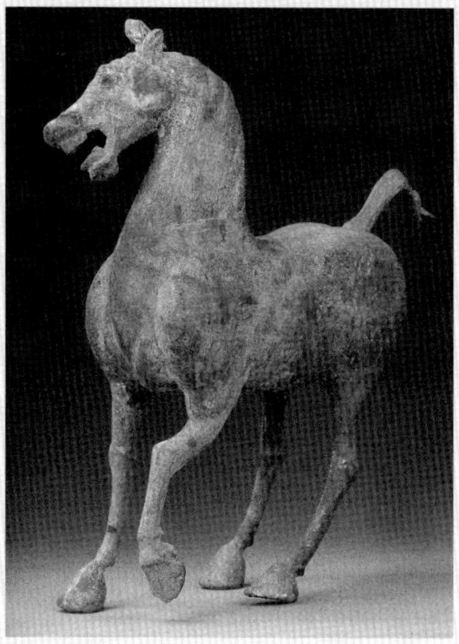

Fig. 3 *Horse*. Eastern Han dynasty. Leitai, Wuwei County, Gansu. Bronze; h. 38 cm. From *Wenwu* 1972.2, p. 24, fig. 16.

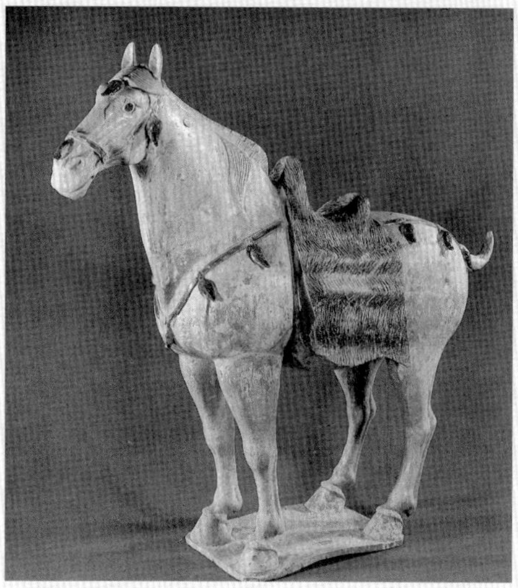

Fig. 4 *Horse*, Tang dynasty. Unearthed at Luoyang, Henan. Tricolored (*sancai*) glazed ceramic; h. 60 cm. From *Luoyang Tang sancai* (Zhengzhou: Henan meishu chubanshe, 1985), pl. 36.

Notes

1. Wu Hung, *The Wu Liang Shrine, The Ideology of Early Chinese Pictorial Art* (Stanford: Stanford University Press, 1989), e.g., Appendix A, stories, p. 265, fig. 124 (Story of Righteous Stepmother of Qi); omens, p. 238, fig. 93, p. 239, fig. 95, p. 244, fig. 106, p. 245, fig. 107.

2. Martin J. Powers, *Art and Political Expression in Early China* (New Haven and London: Yale University Press, 1991), pp. 150–51.

3. See Anne Birrell, *Chinese Mythology* (Baltimore and London: Johns Hopkins University Press, 1993), p. 199. Arthur Waley also discusses the connection between dragons and horses. There are many Chinese stories of horses emerging from the water, suggesting that they are dragon-horses—water dragons that have changed into horses and often retain their wings. Han Wudi sought these heavenly horses that might carry him to the realm of the Immortals; see Arthur Waley, "The Heavenly Horses of Ferghana: A New View," *History Today*, February 1955, pp. 97–98.

4. During the Warring States period King Wu Ling of the state of Zhao (r. 325–299 BCE) had his soldiers adopt nomadic dress and ride astride in battle to combat the increasingly aggressive raids by the Xiongnu's formidable mounted forces. The military treatise attributed to Sun Bin, *The Art of Warfare*, written about 350 BCE, discusses the use of cavalry in war; see D. C. Lau and Roger T. Ames, *Sun Bin: The Art of Warfare* (New York: Ballantine Books, 1996).

5. A reflection of the prestige and acclaim horses acquired in the Western Han is embodied in the magnificent gilded bronze horse excavated from an imperial pit at Maoling, in Xingping County, Shaanxi, and possibly treasured by Emperor Wu; see the exhibition catalogue *Imperial China, The Art of the Horse in Chinese History* (Lexington, Kentucky: Harmony House Publishers, 2000), p.136, no. 129.

6. See H. G. Creel, "The Role of the Horse in Chinese History," *American Historical Review*, vol. 70, no. 3 (April 1965), pp. 647–72, for one of many accounts of this saga; also Michael Loewe and Anthony F. P. Hulsewé, *China in Central Asia, The Early Stage: 125 B.C.–A.D. 23: An Annotated Translation of Chapters 61 and 96 of the History of the Former Han Dynasty* [*Hanshu*], Sinica Leidensa, vol. 14 (Leiden: E. J. Brill, 1979), pp. 42–43, 132–35.

7. The Yangjiawan horses, smaller than those from Qin Shihuangdi's tomb, probably were modeled on larger breeds secured from the Xiongnu, with whom the Chinese had both military and commercial contact beginning in the third century BCE—before the Chinese secured Wusun horses from Central Asia. Robert E. Harrist, Jr., *Power and Virtue, The Horse in Chinese Art* (New York: China Institute Gallery, 1997), p. 54.

8. For the Yangjiawan finds, see *Wenwu* 1966.3, pp. 1–5, and *Wenwu*, 1977.10, pp. 10–21. The scale of the Yangjiawan finds suggests that the two tombs belonged to imperial family members or others of high rank. A number of scholars believe that the two Yangjiawan tombs belong to the preeminent general and statesman Zhou Bo (d.169 BCE) and his adopted son Zhou Yafu (d. 149 BCE), who led campaigns against the Xiongnu.

9. See *Wenwu* 1972.2, pp.16–24 for the excavation report, which includes drawings of the original formation of the bronze horses, cavalry, and chariots.

10. Robert Bagley, ed., *Ancient Sichuan: Treasures from a Lost Civilization* (Seattle Art Museum and Princeton University Press, 2001), p. 269, no. 95. This bronze horse consists of nine interlocked parts (possibly eleven if the ears are counted). For the large wooden horse with joined parts possibly excavated from a Western Han tomb at Yandaishan, Yizheng, Jiangsu, see *Kaogu xuebao* 1987.4, p. 500, fig. 31.

11. We know from armies buried at Yangjiawan as well as from other Han clay figurines that the technique of constructing *mingqi* from several pieces made it possible to mass produce these clay objects in large quantities.

12. For a large bronze horse (h. 135 cm) excavated from Tomb 2 at Hejiashan, Mianyang, Sichuan, see *Wenwu* 1991.3, pp. 9–19, pl. 3; also published in Bagley, *Ancient Sichuan*, p. 269, no. 95. Another large bronze example (h. 114 cm) from Fangmai, Xushan County, Hebei, is published in *Treasures from the Han* (Singapore: Landmark Books, 1990), p. 41. A large bronze horse with a saddle (h.118 cm), assembled from ten interlocked parts that do not seem to have been fixed with nails, dates from the Eastern Jin; it was excavated from Yangpingguan in Ningqiang County, southern Shaanxi, near the Sichuan border. This horse has long, slim, tapered legs. But the body and neck proportions and the head resemble the Sichuan, Guizhou, and Guangxi horses, published in *Sanqin guibao, Shaanxi xin faxian wenwu jinghua* (*The rare gems of the new archaeological discoveries in Shaanxi Province*), (Xi'an: Shaanxi renmin chubanshe, 2001), p. 40.

Two wooden horses, each made in ten to eleven separate parts, were excavated from a group of Han tombs at Mozuizi in the Wuwei area of Gansu: in Tomb 48 a large horse (h. 97 cm) with carriage; and in Tomb 49 a medium-sized horse (h. 49 cm) with saddle and saddle blanket. See *Wenwu* 1972.12, pl. 4:1; p.13, fig. 7; p. 23, fig. 25.

13. For a bronze horse (h. 135 cm) excavated at Hejiashan, Mianyang, Sichuan, see Bagley, *Ancient Sichuan*, p. 269, no. 95.

14. The heightened naturalism of horses painted on the walls of Tang tombs is anticipated in the wall paintings preserved in two Northern Qi tombs excavated in the suburbs of Taiyuan, Shanxi: from the southern suburb, Luo Rui's tomb, dated to 577, *Wenwu* 1983.10, pp. 1–23, and from the eastern suburb Xu Xianxiu's tomb, dated to 571, *Wenwu* 2003.10, pp. 1–68.

15. See Harrist, *Power and Virtue*, pp. 17–30.

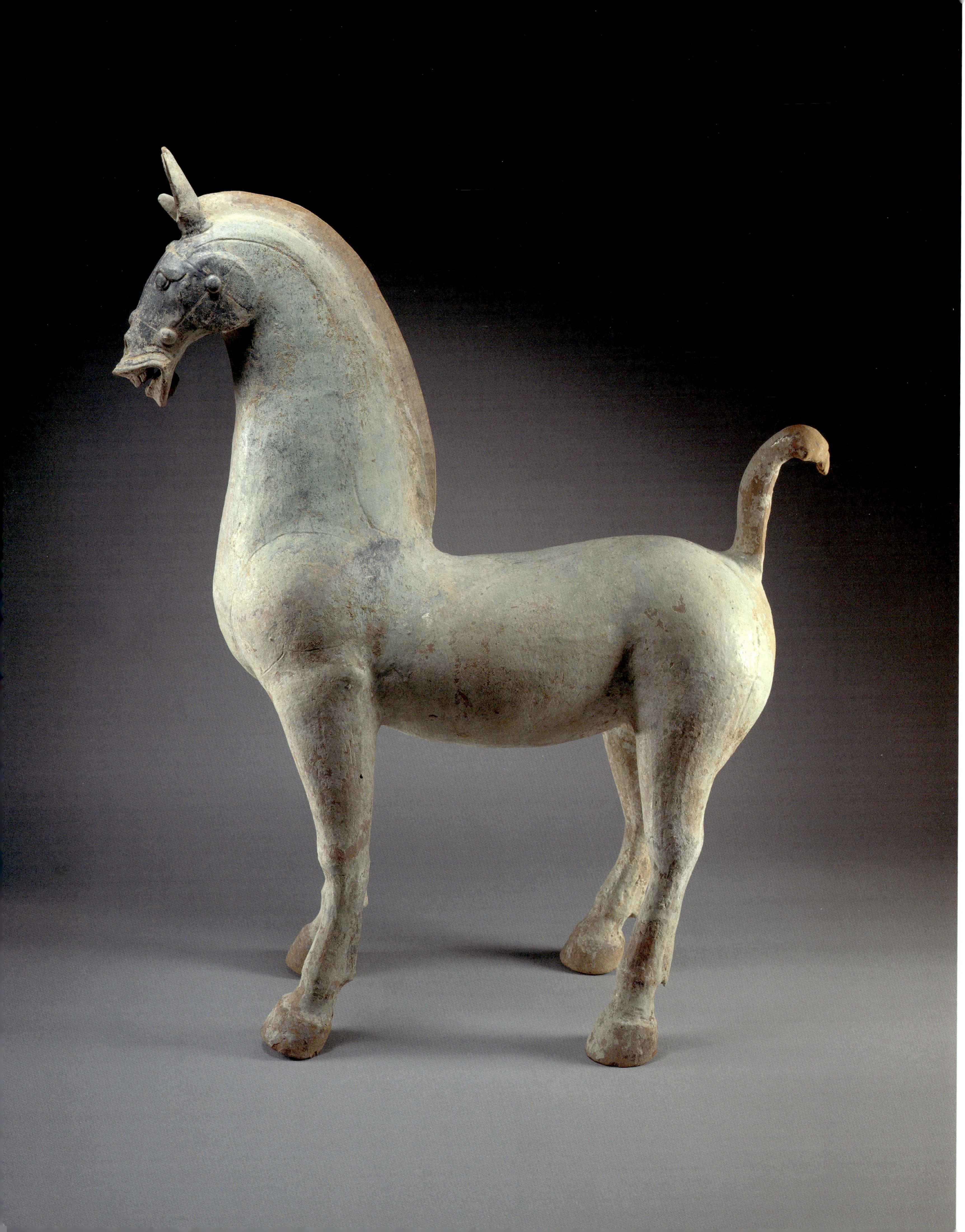

50 Massive green-glazed horse

Eastern Han dynasty. Red earthenware with green glaze; h. 139.7 cm, l. 119.0 cm, w. 34.0 cm.
Princeton University Art Museum, acc. no. 1997-32. Museum purchase, John Maclean Magie and Gertrude Magie Fund.

During the Han, large-scale horses, ranging from about 100 to 140 centimeters in height, were created from clay, bronze, and wood. Although a few have been excavated from Western Han tombs, most of those excavated up to now date from the Eastern Han and seem to be concentrated in the south; to date, most have been unearthed in Sichuan, Guizhou, and Guangxi Zhuang Autonomous Region, and far to the east in Jiangsu, as well as one in Hebei.[1] Of this group, the monumental green-glazed steed in the collection of the Princeton University Art Museum may well be the largest known.[2] As discussed in catalogue number 51, a number of comparably massive horses exist, constructed from nine to eleven pieces of clay or bronze. Clay sculptures could be assembled from separately modeled parts before or after firing.[3] Joined construction emerged to answer the technical problems of creating large bronze or ceramic images, apparently inspired by existing traditions of joined wood sculpture originated in the Chu cultures of the Warring States period.[4]

It is likely that the present marvelous horse was originally fashioned from at least nine pieces, assembled, and then glazed with the low-fired lead-fluxed glaze whose coloring agent was copper, typically used on Eastern Han *mingqi*. Thermoluminescence testing has confirmed a date consistent with Eastern Han. Reconstructed from large fragments, with attachments and some infill of new material, this sculpture has retained an impressive presence and sculptural profile. The head, including the ears, was basically intact, with the two hollow pricked ears reattached and a new knob added between them where the mane ends. The upward sweep of the powerfully curved neck edged with a reattached roached mane ends in a crisply defined shortened head animated by alert bulging eyes, oval flared nostrils, and open mouth with bared teeth and lolling tongue (detail). Hemispherical bosses in relief hold the incised bridle. The body and legs have been restored from large pieces, with only part of the right haunch patched with new material. The tip of the knotted tail is also a new addition. Han horses usually stand foursquare with hooves flat on the ground, or leaning slightly forward with the back edges of the hooves tipped up. When the front legs were repaired and reattached, they splayed and the front edge of the hooves tipped upward, creating an awkward stance also more commonly found on horses after the Han. Even with these conservation and reconstruction modifications, this horse's taut silhouette and volumetric solidity are magnificent.

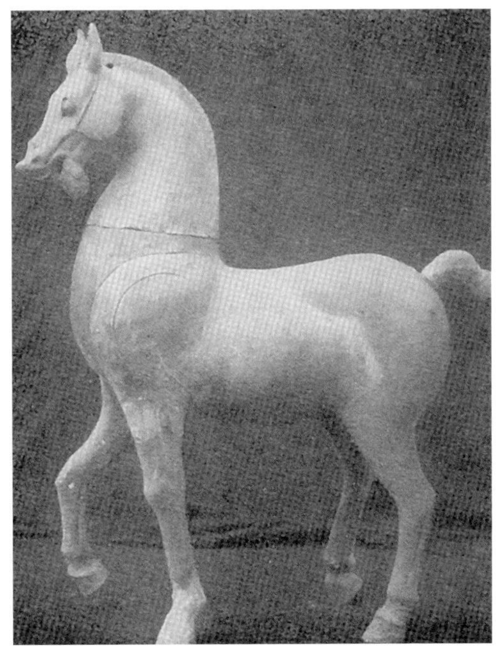

Fig. 1 *Horse*. Eastern Han dynasty. Tianhui Shan Cliff Tomb 1, Chengdu, Sichuan. Ceramic, h. 114 cm. From *Kaogu xuebao* 1958.1, pl. 9:3.

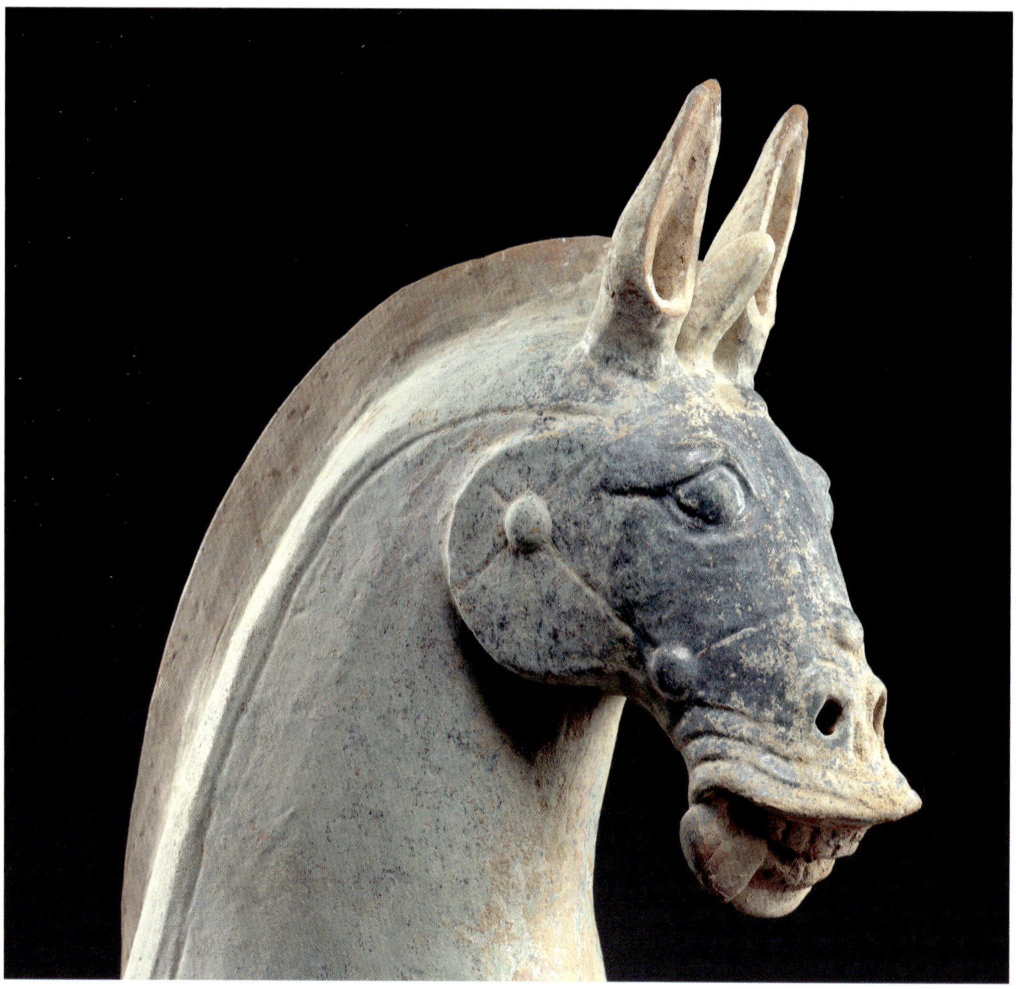

As pointed out in the essay on horses, all of these large-scale horses, including the present one, have sturdy bodies and elongated necks and many have foreshortened heads and distinctive flaring muzzles (see detail). These are characteristics associated with horses from south China, particularly from Sichuan (fig. 1) and Guizhou (fig. 2). Interestingly, the bronze horse from Guizhou offers the strongest parallels, with its small head with tall pricked ears and flaring nostrils, long, arching neck with cropped mane, and sturdy body with knotted tail. They differ mainly—and significantly—in the legs: the legs of the bronze Guizhou horse are very long and extremely slender.[5]

Often large-scale horses are found in tombs of individuals without any overt connection to the military. The ceramic horses from two cliff tombs at Tujing in Sichuan were found in separate rooms, one in the front and the other in the back.[6] Most of the *mingqi* were entertainers, dancers, musicians, servants, guests, and architectural models; there also were two hordes of coins, and storage vessels, mostly of clay and some of bronze. Clearly, horses of this

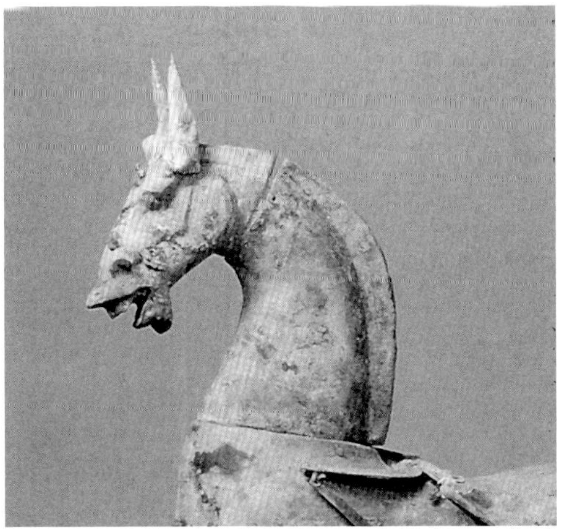

size must have reflected status, conferred prestige, and perhaps provided mounts for the soul to ride into the next world.[7]

Finally, these large-scale horses are very different from the stylized horses depicted on the Wu shrines. Their proportions and characteristics may represent a local breed, or reflect a greater touch of naturalism, or both. They also seem consistent with the depictions of horses on the clay tiles lining the walls of Han tombs in Sichuan. Such tiles depict very lively processions with teams of galloping, turning horses pulling carriages, enhancing a sense of immediacy and controlled chaos.[8]

ANNETTE L. JULIANO

Notes

1. A large-scale bronze dating from the Western Han (9 pieces, h. 112 cm) was excavated in the Guangxi Zhuang Autonomous Region; see *Zhongguo wenwu jinghua* (*Gems of China's cultural relics*) (Beijing: Wenwu chubanshe, 1990), no. 91.

Other excavated large horses are as follows: bronze horse (h. 88 cm) and chariot from Guizhou, Eastern Han (see *Zhongguo gudai keji wenwu zhan* [*Exhibition of China's artifacts of ancient science and technology*] [Beijing: Lishi bowuguan, 1997], no. 10–19); horse (h. 135 cm) from Tomb 2, Hejiashan, Mianyang, Sichuan, Eastern Han dynasty (see Robert Bagley, ed., *Ancient Sichuan: Treasures from a Lost Civilization* [Seattle Art Museum and Princeton University Press, 2001], p. 269, no. 95, and *Zhongguo wenwu jinghua* [*Gems of China's cultural relics*] [Beijing: Wenwu chubanshe, 1997], no. 81); horse (h.114 cm) from Fangmai, Xushui County, Hebei, Han dynasty (see *Treasures from Han* [Singapore: Landmark Books, 1990], p. 41).

Four ceramic models and part of another have been excavated from Sichuan: horse (h.114 cm) from Cliff Tomb 1, Tianhuishan, Chengdu (see *Kaogu xuebao*, 1958.1, pl. 9:3, and Bagley, ed., *Ancient Sichuan: Treasures*, p. 271, fig. 96.1); horse (h. 95 cm) from Leshan (see Lucy Lim et al., *Stories from China's Past* [San Francisco: Chinese Culture Foundation, 1987], p. 114, pl. 24); two horses, ceramic (h. 65 cm), from the cliff tombs of the kingdom of Shu Han (220–265 CE) at Tujing in Zhongshan County (see *Wenwu* 1985.7, p.65, fig. 26); one-piece head and neck from Mianyang in Mianyang Museum (see Bagley, ed., *Ancient Sichuan: Treasures*, p. 270, no. 6).

2. Published in *Christie's New York, The Jingguantang Collection*, Part II, March 30, 1997, lot 51.

3. The two horses from the cliff tombs of the kingdom of Shu Han in Tujing, Sichuan, were clearly assembled after firing; see *Wenwu*, 1985.7, p. 65, fig. 26. The two large models from Leshan and Tianhuishan, Chengdu, were probably assembled before firing; see Lim, *Stories from China's Past*, p. 114, pl. 24, and *Kaogu xuebao* 1958.1, pl. 9:3.

4. Bagley, ed., *Ancient Sichuan: Treasures*, pp. 269–70, nos. 95, 96. Wooden horses have been found in a number of Han graves in Sichuan and Jiangsu, but they are less common and less well preserved. Western Han tombs (2d century BCE) in Shuangbaoshan, Mianyang, Sichuan, have revealed three large wooden horses (two are 72 cm in height and one 112 cm), each carved from a single block; see *Wenwu* 1996.10, p. 9, fig. 18 (a–b), p. 26, fig. 18:2c. A Han tomb at Yandaishan, Yicheng, Jiangsu, contained an assembled wooden horse made up of head, two ears, neck, body, four legs, four hooves, and tail; see *Kaogu xuebao* 1987.4, p. 500, fig. 31.

5. *Zhongguo gudai keji wenwu zhan* (*Exhibition of China's artifacts of ancient science and technology*), no. 10–19.

6. The cliff tombs of the kingdom of Shu Han at Tujing, Zhongshan County; see *Wenwu* 1985.7, p. 65, fig. 26.

7. See *Wenwu* 1985.7, p. 57, fig. 18.

8. See *Sichuan Handai diaosu yishu* (*Sichuan Han-dynasty sculptural art*) (Beijing: Renmin meishu chubanshe, 1959), nos. 25–37 and Lim, *Stories from China's Past*, pp.186–89, which discusses the stone carvings from a tomb at Yangzishan.

Fig. 2 *Detail of head of horse*. Eastern Han dynasty. Guangfu, Guizhou. Bronze; h. 88 cm. From *Zhongguo gudai keji wenwuzhan*, no. 10.-19.

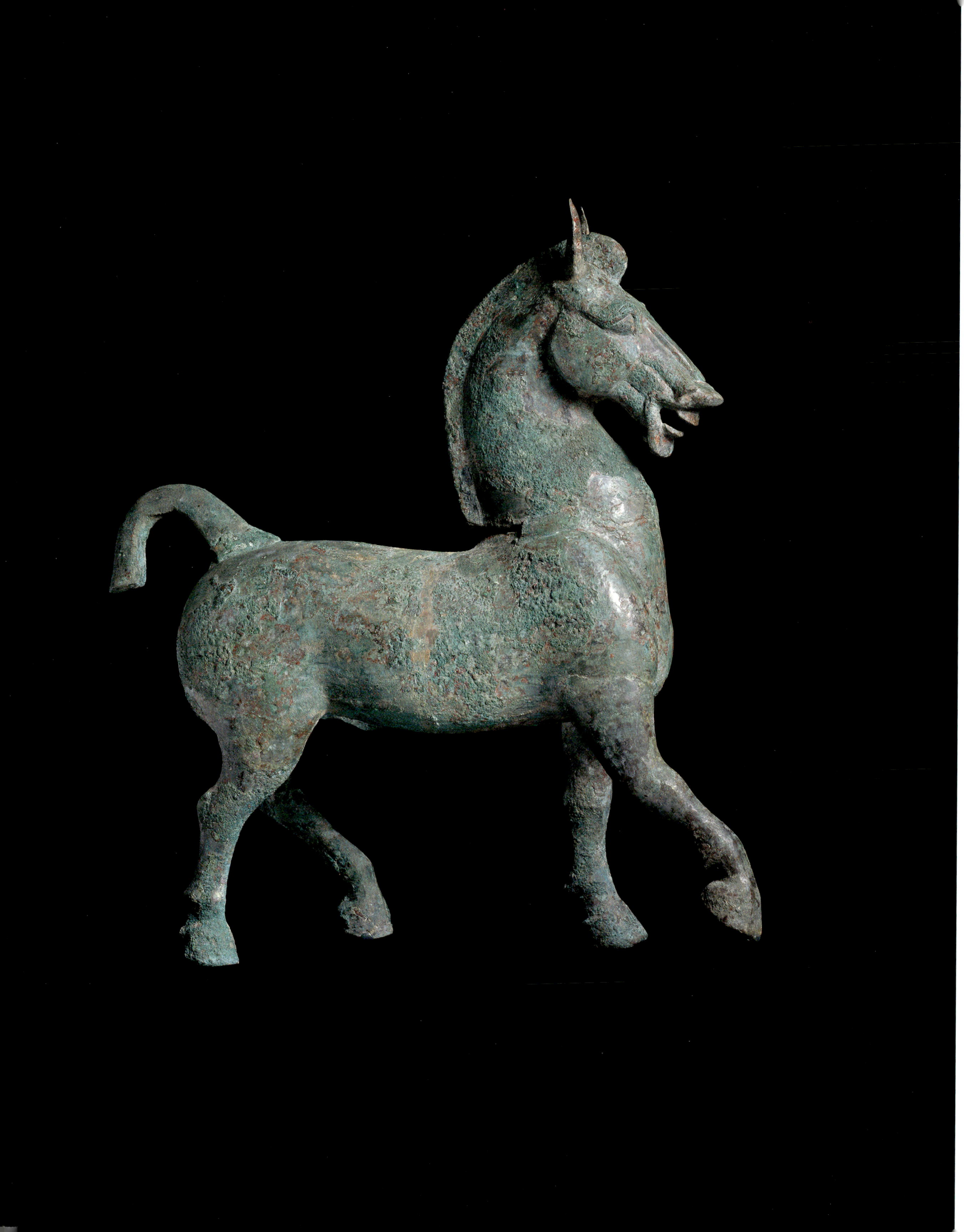

51 Horse

Eastern Han dynasty. Bronze with clay core and traces of pigments; h. 53.3 cm, l. 51.6 cm.
Private collection.

Small and miniature bronze sculptures or *mingqi* are usually cast in one piece. Horses of this scale and larger are cast in several parts and assembled. This one consists of ten parts: four legs, body, tail, neck, head, and two ears—all joined by means of visible old welds. At the juncture of neck and body the old weld is incomplete; through the open space below the roached mane, the casting clay core inside the neck is still clearly visible. A part of the clay core also protrudes into the back of the open mouth.[1] A large Eastern Han horse from Hejiashan, Mianyang, Sichuan was also similarly cast but in eleven parts; the body was cast in two sections. The method of assembly, however, was different, as the parts were interlocked and then secured with nails.[2] A monumental Western Han bronze horse from the Guangxi Zhuang Autonomous Region in south China was cast in nine parts, similarly interlocked and nailed.[3] Also from Guangxi and dating from the Western Han is a smaller cast bronze horse, comparable in scale to the one in the exhibition.[4]

As mentioned in the essay on horses, assembled wooden horses may have influenced the construction of large bronze and clay ones. Medium- and large-scale wooden horses continued to be crafted along with those fashioned from bronze and clay throughout the Han. A group of wooden horses as well as other animal sculptures were excavated from several tombs around the city of Wuwei in Gansu.[5] These steeds were assembled from nine to thirteen parts. Of the three tombs excavated at Mozuizi, Wuwei, two contained horses: a larger Western Han wooden cart horse of thirteen parts with the head and neck carved as one, two ears, body, tail, four legs, and four hooves (fig. 1); a smaller Eastern Han saddled horse differs only in having the hooves carved together with the legs.[6] Both were brightly painted, and retain extensive remains of red, black, and white pigments.

Although far less elegant in execution, the Gansu, Sichuan, and Guangxi horses share a number of stylistic elements with the present smaller bronze horse. Both Gansu and Guangxi horses (fig. 2) have the same type of compact, sturdy body and legs supporting a thick, arched neck and large head. The much longer tapered legs and the thinner proportions of the Sichuan example recall the form of the Eastern Han bronze horses from Wuwei in Gansu. All six horses under discussion have similarly conceived and articulated heads, with eye sockets defined by curved parallel ridges, tubular nostrils, curved upper lip ending in a flat plane, and flared lower lip below bared teeth. On the Sichuan and Guangxi horses the lower lip flares more exaggeratedly.

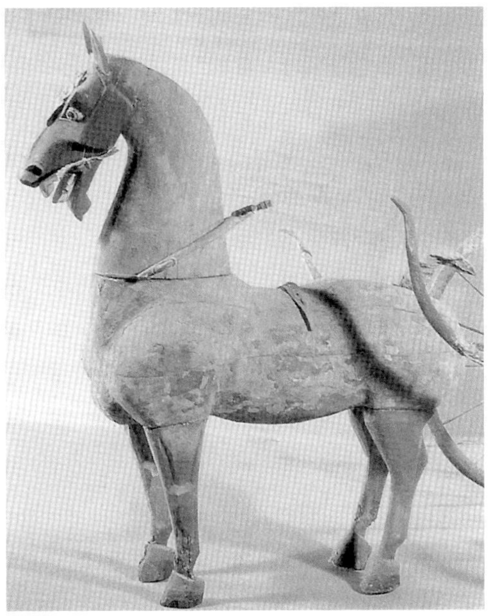

Fig. 1 *Horse and cart.* Western Han dynasty. Excavated at Mozuizi, Wuwei, Gansu. Painted wood; h. 97 cm. From *Chinese Art* (*Zhongguo yishu—Gansu zhuanji*), n.d., p. 25.

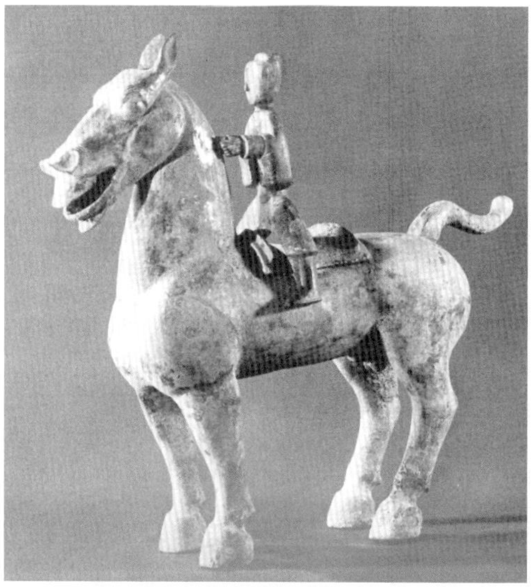

Although the present bronze horse has acquired a patina, red pigment over a white ground is still visible on the inside surface of the erect ears. The Sichuan horse also shows the remains of red pigment inside the ears and at the neck, and also on the body as if, possibly, a saddle or saddlecloth was originally painted on. The evidence of pigment suggests that even the bronze horses may have been painted like their clay and wooden counterparts.

Fig. 2 *Horse*. Western Han dynasty. Xilin County, Guangxi Zhuang Autonomous Region. Bronze; h. 59 cm. From *Guangxi chutu wenwu* (Beijing, 1978), no. 92.

The present horse's powerfully robust and curved neck, emphasized by the roached mane, and its rectangular head recall the majestic silhouettes of the steeds depicted in the "Wu family shrines." The horses of the Wu shrines are almost identical in their emphatic roundness of body and thinness of leg—a degree of artistic abstraction that abjures individuality in favor of an impressive repetitive pictorial effect. The present horse, although less than two feet high, combines naturalism of the sculptural form with subtle definition of the musculature to convey enormous vitality and immediacy—suggesting perhaps that this is a portrait of a favorite steed.

ANNETTE L. JULIANO

Notes

1. Clay cores can be used in both the "lost wax" (cire-perdue) and clay piece-mold casting process. "Lost wax" became increasingly popular in China after the 6th century BCE. See Robert Bagley, *Shang Ritual Bronzes in the Arthur M. Sackler Collections* (Cambridge, Mass.: The Arthur M. Sackler Museum, Harvard University, 1987), p. 47, n. 19.

2. Robert Bagley, ed., *Ancient Sichuan: Treasures from a Lost Civilization* (Seattle Art Museum and Princeton University Press, 2001), p. 269, no. 95. The catalogue describes the horse as having nine separate parts. It is clear that the separate ears were not included in this count. This horse (h. 135 cm) was also published in *Zhongguo wenwu jinghua* (*Gems of China's cultural relics*) (Beijing: Wenwu chubanshe, 1997), no. 83.

3. The horse is 115.5 cm high. See *Zhongguo wenwu jinghua*, no. 91.

4. Although lacking the elegance and vitality of the cast bronze horse in the exhibition, the Guangxi model is about the same scale (h. 59 cm) and similar in its sturdy body and legs supporting an arched neck and large head. It differs, however, in having a small separate saddle and an incongruously small bronze figure astride holding now lost reins. See *Guangxi chutu wenwu* (*Cultural relics unearthed from Guangxi*) (Beijing: Wenwu chubanshe, 1978), p. 11.

5. For the horses and other animal and human sculptures carved from wood and excavated from tombs around Wuwei in Gansu, see the article by Long Xuli, "Qiantan Wuwei Handai mudiao de yishu fengge" ("Discussion of the styles of Han wood carving from Wuwei"), *Chinese Art*, no. 5 (Gansu zhuanji), n.d., pp. 24–34.

6. For excavations at Mozuizi, Wuwei, Gansu, see *Wenwu* l972.12, pp. 9–23; the larger, Western Han, horse (h. 97 cm), p. 13, fig. 7; and the smaller, Eastern Han, example (h. 49 cm), p. 23, fig. 25.

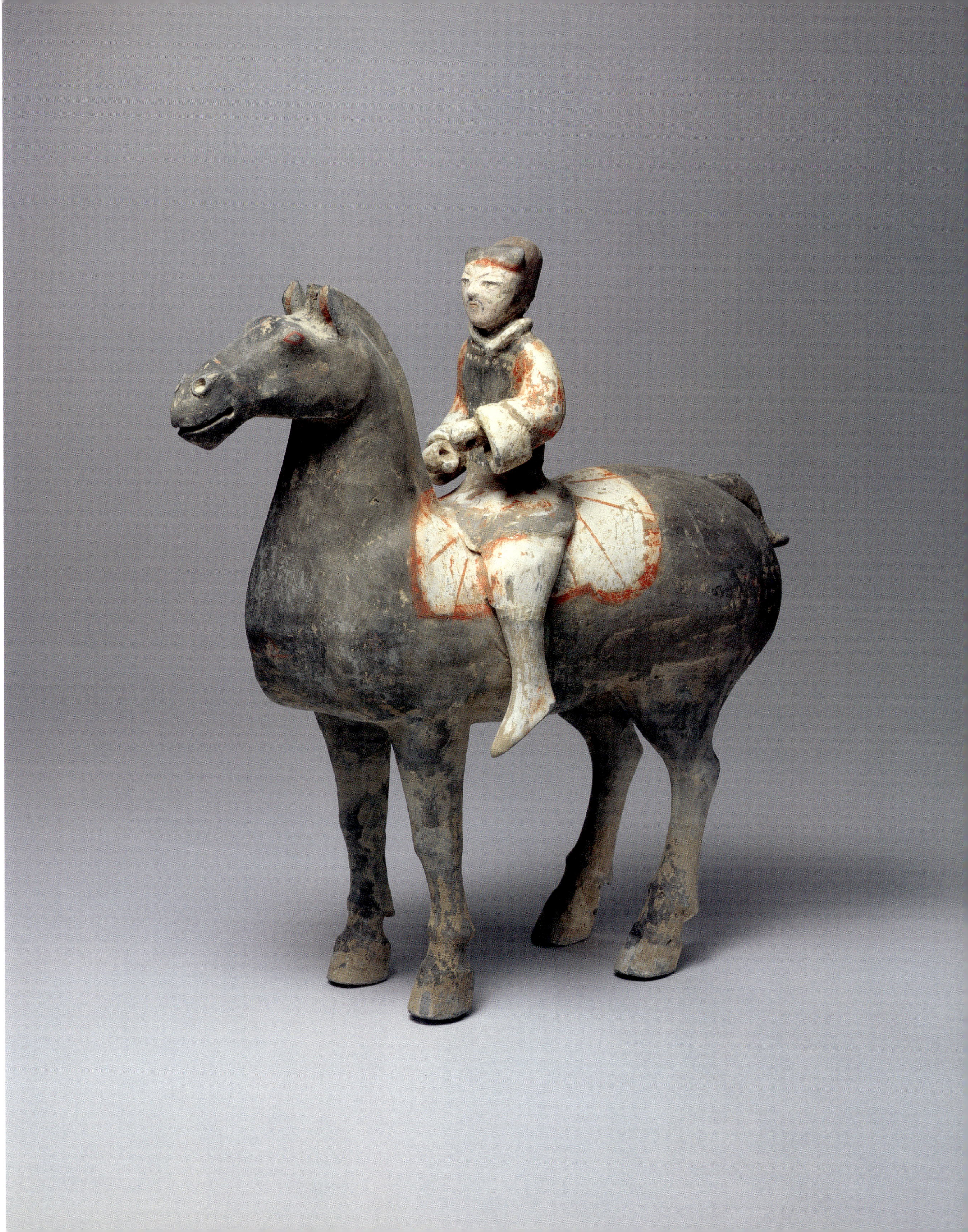

52 Equestrian

Western Han dynasty, ca. 2d–1st century BCE. Gray ceramic with white slip and painted with red and black pigments; h. 29.3 cm. Princeton University Art Museum, acc. no. 2001-31.2. Gift of Simone Schloss, Class of 1979, from the Schloss Collection.

This cavalryman shares a number of features with the mounted soldier or cavalryman from a pit near the tombs at Yangjiawan, Xianyang, Shaanxi (fig. 1).[1] His stocky gray clay mount is half the size of the Yangjiawan horses and less well defined of body and sharply modeled of head, but it does have a similar S-shaped bound tail, which was made separately; the rider sits on a white-painted pad on the horse's back, a type of rudimentary saddle generally used in Western Han and associated with the Yangjiawan cavalry figures.[2] Until the introduction of the stirrup about the fourth century CE, riders sat on similar saddles with their legs tightly gripping the horse's shoulders to maintain a secure seat. Holes in the rider's clenched fists suggest that he originally grasped a halberd or a lance.[3]

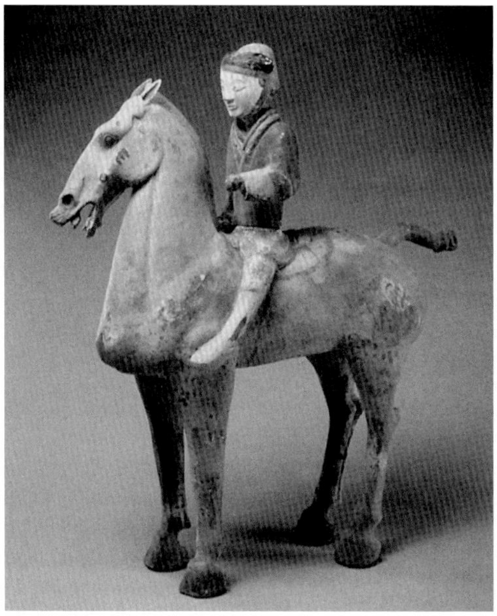

Fig. 1 *Equestrian*. Western Han dynasty. Yangjiawan, Xianyang Municipality, Shaanxi. Painted earthenware; h. 65 cm. From *The Quest for Eternity* (Los Angeles and The People's Republic of China: Los Angeles County Museum of Art and Chronicle Books, 1987), p. 46, cat. no. 15.

Typically, Western Han tomb figurines have cold-painted unfired decoration; substantial pigment remains on this cavalryman, describing his delicate black (carbon) moustache and eyes, and details of his clothing and armor.[4] The rider wears a thick padded red (vermilion) tunic with white (lead?) cuffs, and black pigment represents a lamellar iron breastplate whose lamellae are detailed with painted lines and dots in white pigment.[5] On his head is a red cap tied under the chin, with the black brim turned up.

ANNETTE L. JULIANO

Notes

1. For the Yangjiawan finds, see *Wenwu* 1966.3, pp. 1–5, and *Wenwu* 1977.10, pp. 10–21. The scale of the Yangjiawan finds suggests that the two tombs belonged to imperial family members or others of high rank. A number of scholars believe that the two Yangjiawan tombs belong to the preeminent general and statesman Zhou Bo (d. 169 BCE) and his adopted son Zhou Yafu (d. 149 BCE), who led campaigns against the Xiongnu. It appears as if this sculpture of a horse and rider was constructed like those from Yangjiawan, with the rider's lower torso and legs modeled as part of the horse and the upper part, from about the waist up, made separately and attached to the lower part.

2. See Yang Hong, "Qibing he jiaqi juzhuang" ("Outfitting the cavalry and armored cavalry"), *Wenwu* 1977.10, pp. 27–32. Yang Hong also points out that iron armor was developed during the Western Han. The lines painted on this rider may depict lamellar armor, which is constructed with small plates of iron rather than leather; see "Zhongguo gudai de jiazhou," ("Studies in ancient armor, Part I"), *Kaogu xuebao* 1976.2, pp. 35–41.

3. *Kaogu xuebao* 1976.2, pp. 35–41.

4. As was often the practice in Han, the gray clay body of this horse and its rider were first covered with slip of finely ground white clay that provided a base to hold the pigments. Sometimes, to help pigments adhere to the clay or slip, they were suspended in a thin lacquer- or glue-based medium. Virginia L. Bower, *From Court to Caravan, Chinese Tomb Sculpture from the Collection of Anthony M. Solomon*, ed. Robert D. Mowry (New Haven and London: Yale University Press, 2002), p. 33.

5. Similar clothing with a sleeveless vest of armor can be found on some of the Yangjiawan figures; see *Wenwu* 1977.10, p. 11, figs. 2, 3. See also Albert E. Dien, "A Study of Early Chinese Armour," *Artibus Asiae*, vol. 43, nos. 1/2 (1981–1982), pp. 5–56.

53 Figure of a dog

Eastern Han dynasty. Earthenware with dark green glaze; h. 26.7 cm, l. 24.1 cm, w. 11.4 cm.
The Metropolitan Museum of Art, acc. no. 1991.253.1. Gift of Stanley Herzman, in memory of Adele Herzman.

"At court there should be no speaking of dogs and horses."[1]

Dogs were and are important in China.[2] Clear evidence points to their domestication in Neolithic China.[3] In the following centuries of Bronze Age China, dogs provided food and fur to the living; served as an appropriate sacrifice in certain rituals; and functioned as hunters or guards both in life and after, judging from their inclusion in burials. There is evidence, too, that some dogs enjoyed special favor.[4] Dogs continued in these roles in the succeeding Qin and Han dynasties.[5] Some centuries earlier, at least since the sixth to fifth century BCE, the practice had begun of interring images of living beings, including dogs, in addition to and perhaps in place of live creatures; this practice became widespread during Qin and Han.[6] Western Han tombs have yielded large quantities of unglazed ceramic tomb sculptures of dogs (among other domestic animals), and Eastern Han tombs have disclosed both unglazed and glazed earthenware dogs, many shown standing and wearing collar and harness, clearly intended as images of watchdogs and some most likely of the same breed as this *Figure of a dog*.[7]

The present handsome green-glazed earthenware figure should most likely be understood as a watchdog, charged with protecting those interred in the tomb in which it was placed.[8] With its ears pricked but its mouth closed, it appears alert but not threatening. A few notably similar dogs, in museum and private collections in Asia and North America, all of unknown provenance, have been published.[9] As a group they are distinguished by their unusually elaborate collar-and-harness combinations, the latter being looped between the forelegs and up the chest, where it is attached to the collar in variously intricate and ornamental ways. Members of the group vary in the delineations of their coats; on the present dog parallel C shapes ending in small circles cover the whole torso. These appear to have been made through a combination of incising and molding and are unequaled in their boldness. Among the known figures of this group, one most often sees a few attenuated incised S shapes, sometimes combined with C shapes and sometimes with small circles at only one end; these are generally lacking in Eastern Han glazed collared-and-harnessed dogs of other types. Also noticeable among these figures is the meticulous delineation of the eyebrows and whiskers, and equally careful modeling of eye sockets, eyeballs, and irises. On the lower part of each cheek of the present dog is a cone-shaped hollow. Some of the known figures of this type show somewhat similar depressions, sometimes less distinct.[10] These may be an attempt to portray the natural, if slight, dimples observable today in some dogs of this type (an early variety of the Chow breed), or they may have been anchor points for an accoutrement such as a nose band or muzzle, now lost.

No exact analogue to the present image (or those so like it, just mentioned) has yet been located among archaeologically excavated Eastern Han–dynasty glazed earthenware models of collared and harnessed dogs. These have primarily been recovered from Anhui, Hebei, Henan, Shaanxi, and Shandong provinces. (The majority of the many Eastern Han standing, collared dogs recovered in Sichuan Province are of unglazed earthenware, and some are somewhat similar to the present dog, which is of a type more characteristically discovered in areas north of Sichuan.)[11] Within the group of collared and harnessed watchdogs, whether glazed or not, differences in size, proportions,

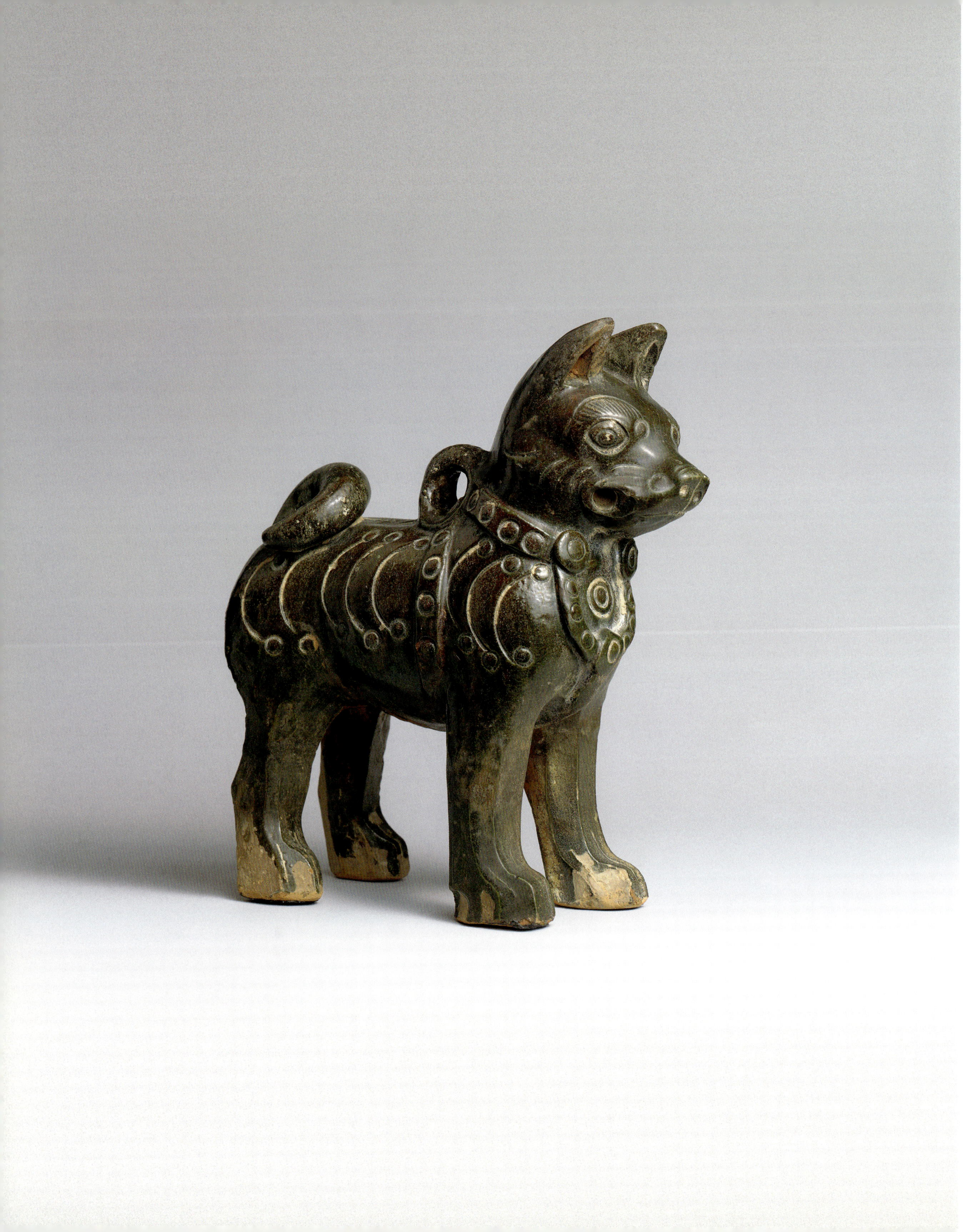

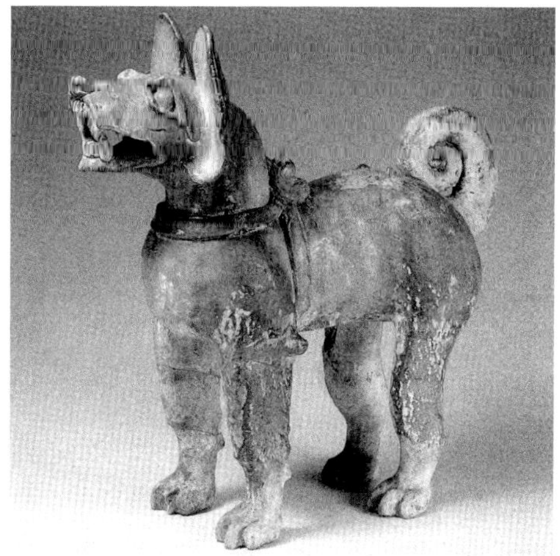

expressions (mouth open or closed, teeth bared or invisible), and accoutrements can be found among models originating not only from the same province but even from the same site. Images of dogs similar to the present one in accoutrements, proportions, and stance have been found, but they lack one or more of its distinctive features, such as the elaborate looping of the harness or the patterning in the dog's coat. Only in the head and face of a model excavated in Anhui do we find an extremely close similarity to the present dog and its unprovenanced analogues. The Anhui dog, found in Fuyang, is smaller (h. 14 cm), but it shares the green glaze, pricked ears, closed mouth, and direct gaze, and the meticulous delineation of eyebrows and whiskers as well as modeling of eye sockets, eyeballs, and irises. It may have hollows in its cheeks, but the poor quality of the illustration precludes certainty.[12]

In her analysis of a dog similar to the present one in the collection of the Asian Art Museum of San Francisco, He Li in considering a possible origin for these figures pointed out another characteristic—the "treatment of the legs, retaining the angular corner[s] formed during sculpting," which she deemed typical of Shaanxi models.[13] This angularity, in differing degrees, may in fact be observed in many glazed dogs found in Shaanxi as well as in this present figure and others of its type. But of the admittedly small number of Shaanxi glazed watchdogs that have been located, few can be confirmed to have elaborate harness ornaments on their chests or to show any sign of pattern in their coats. Compared with this *Figure of a dog*, most appear to have shorter legs, and some have a noticeably more curved belly accompanied by a slight swayback. In some Shaanxi images the tail is curved up and over to one side, like that of this present dog, in others it is curled vertically up over the back. The dogs' heads all appear to be slightly raised. Brows and eyes are not meticulously rendered, nor are the irises shown.

Quite a number of Eastern Han glazed earthenware watchdogs have also been found in Shandong Province, the site of the "Wu family shrines." These range from models with short, stubby legs and a squared-off head and jaw,[14] to others with long, lean legs and elongated muzzle, such as an example found in Gaotang County (fig. 1).[15] Neither in Shandong nor in the neighboring province of Hebei,[16] where a number of similar glazed standing watchdogs have been unearthed, does any watchdog thus far present the elaborate chest harness, patterned coat, or cheek dimples characteristic of the present dog and those of its type.

Most standing ceramic mortuary watchdogs are outfitted with a collar-and-harness combination. In Han-dynasty two-dimensional renderings, the collar-and-harness is sometimes replaced by a collar and leash, against which the dog is shown straining.[17] In two illustrations of the story of the ferocious *ao* (fierce dogs) loosed by Duke Ling of Jin (Eastern Zhou dynasty) upon an official and his cohort with whom he was displeased, neither dog appears to be wearing a collar or harness.[18]

Some pictorial images do show dogs wearing collar-and-harness combinations. One, from a Sichuan site, clearly shows a collar, harness, and leash or rope attached to a large ring at the back of the dog's neck; the dog has an upturned tail and appears to be lunging forward.[19] On a stone door, also from a Sichuan

Fig. 1 *Watchdog*. Eastern Han dynasty. Dongguhe, Gaotang County, Shandong. Earthenware with green glaze; h. 40.2 cm. Shandong Provincial Museum.

site, only the forequarters of the dog are visible, but at the front of its neck is a band suggestive of a low-slung collar attached to a harness, and around the belly there is the hint of a band. This dog stands beside a man with a sword, in front of a weapons rack, and most probably represents a guard dog.[20]

According to Loewe, the type of collar and harness on ceramic tomb sculptures is similar to that used on horses prior to the appearance of the more efficient breast strap (for pulling), which became widespread during the Han.[21] (Dogs were not used for pulling; on them the collar-harness-leash acted as a restraining device, and as such appears to have needed no modification.) According to V. W. F. Collier, commenting on the Eastern Han glazed earthenware figure of a dog wearing such a collar and harness, published by Berthold Laufer in 1909, "In their form, neck and chest-band connected by a strap in front and bound into an iron ring over the back, they clearly originate the efficient harness with which the Chinese have been accustomed to hold their more powerful dogs in leash through historical times."[22] The same illustration prompted a similar observation from Arthur De Carle Sowerby: ". . . this dog is wearing harness exactly similar to that used by dog fanciers today in the case of dogs that are inclined to strain on the leash."[23]

Reflecting their ubiquity in daily life, ceramic tomb figures of dogs are not only freestanding; some occur as subsidiary figures in larger Han-dynasty mortuary assemblages. Small models of reclining dogs are sometimes found alongside, or affixed to, architectural structures, like the watchful but friendly-looking canines on the two Han towers included in this exhibition (see cat. nos. 13, 14).

Neither so numerous nor so varied as the horses portrayed in the "Wu family shrines" (see Annette Juliano's "Horses" in this catalogue), the few dogs that can be discerned in the Wu rubbings (cat. no. 1) are easy to overlook. Among them are a greyhound seated on its haunches in front of an unhitched horse and carriage (fig. 2 and cat. no. 1.9; see cat. no. 1.24 for a similar dog),[24] and two long-bodied dogs, not unlike the aforementioned greyhound, shown being gutted, their vertical corpses perhaps hung from a well-sweep (see

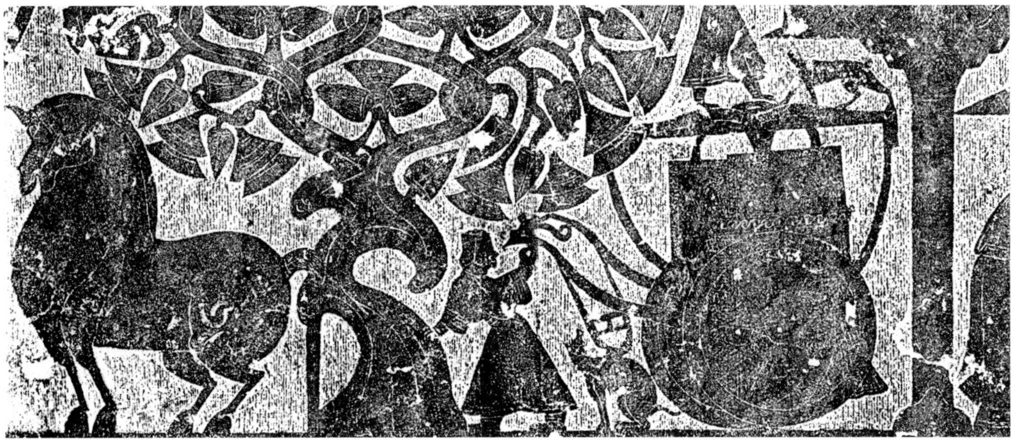

Fig. 2 *Greyhound near cart and horse*. Detail of Stone Chamber 1, Stone 1-S.6 (cat. no. 1.9). "Wu family shrines" rubbings. Princeton University Art Museum, acc. no. 2002-307.9.

cat. nos. 1.12, 1.29). Also noteworthy is a large lunging dog shown in the *Wang Ling mu* slab, postulated by some to have been part of a Fourth Chamber at this site.[25] Encompassed within these rubbings are the typical roles played by dogs in this era—the greyhound lingering near the chariot, a hunting companion; the lunging animal, a guard dog; and the carcasses, a meal or sacrifice.

How dogs were used and regarded in the period from the Eastern Zhou through the Han can be gleaned from many and various pre-Han and Han texts, which bear out the ways in which dogs are most frequently portrayed in the "Wu family shrines" and other Shandong sites of Han date. Among such texts are *Chunqiu* (*Spring and Autumn annals*) along with its commentaries *Gongyangzhuan* (*Gongyang traditions*) and *Zuozhuan* (*Zuo traditions*); *Liji* (*Rites records*), and the *Hou Hanshu* (*History of the Later Han*).

One of the more revealing and oft-cited comments about dogs is found in the "Shao yi" ("Smaller rules of demeanour") chapter of *Liji*, and in Kong Yingda's (574–648) commentary in *Wujing zhengyi* (*Correct meanings of the Five Classics*).[26] Legge translates the *Liji* text as follows: "The dog was held by a rope. A watch-dog or a hunting dog was given to the officer who was the medium of communication; and on receiving it, he asked its name."[27] Note that only two sorts of dogs are mentioned, and they are distinguished by function: the *shouquan* (literally, "protective" dog) and the *tianquan* (literally, "field" dog, i.e., a hunting dog). Kong's commentary mentions a third type of dog, *shiquan*, dogs for eating or sacrificing. *Liji* often mentions the eating or sacrificing of dogs, but does not seem to contain a designation for these canine victims. To summarize the *Liji* and Kong's commentary, dogs are of three types: the watchdog, the hunting dog, and the "food" dog. The first two were given names; the third was not.[28]

The present dog's elaborate collar and harness may indicate that it was made for someone of a high rank; they may also indicate that in life the deceased cherished a living dog of the same type. Archaeological finds confirm that real dogs were sometimes thus lavishly accoutered, like those found in Hebei in a pit not far from the tomb of King Cuo of Zhongshan (d. 313 BCE). Those dogs wore elaborate collars of gold and silver on leather backings, with a copper ring to hold the lost leash.[29]

Pre-Han and Han texts also provide evidence of the importance of particular dogs to particular individuals. In *Liji* there appears a passage in which Confucius is concerned about the burial of his dog: "A worn-out umbrella should not be thrown away, but may be used to bury a dog in. I am poor and have no umbrella. In putting the dog into the grave, you can use my mat . . . ."[30]

Probably the most famous or notorious dog-lover of the Han dynasty is the Eastern Han emperor Lingdi (r. 168–189). According to *Hou Hanshu*, the emperor raised a dog or dogs (*gou*) in the Western Garden of the Imperial Palace, dressing it (or them) as literary officials or scholars of the period, including the *jin xian guan* ("entering excellence hat"),[31] a type of peaked cap worn by various figures pictured in Han art, including some in the "Wu family shrines," and the belt or sash, also distinctive of officials' or scholars' attire.[32] Later texts present even more and perhaps embellished details of this emperor's fondness for his dogs.[33]

Post-Han, ceramic sculptures of dogs continued to be placed in tombs, but they are pedestrian compared with most of those created during the Han, and certainly compared with this *Figure of a Dog*, ever alert to protect its master.
VIRGINIA BOWER

Notes

1. James Legge, trans. and ed., *Li Chi: Book of Rites*, 2 vols. (1885; reprint, New Hyde Park, N.Y.: University Books, 1967), vol. 1, p. 118. The phrase in question, "*chao yan bu ji quan ma*," may more literally be translated as "at court talk should not extend to dogs and horses," meaning that officials should attend to the serious business of governing. Also in the *Liji*, in a discussion of chariot and carriage etiquette, the text prescribes that neither dogs nor horses are to be taken into the entrance hall by visiting guests; see Legge, *Li Chi: Book of Rites*, vol. 1, p. 96. Perhaps this usage is reflected in the scene in the "Wu family shrines" of a hound seated on its haunches in front of an unhitched carriage and horse (fig. 2).

2. See Tong Pingya and Zhao Guopan, eds., *Chu qin shi hua* (*A history and discussion of domesticated animals and birds*) (Beijing: Xinhua shudian, 1990), pp. 1–16; Xiao Kezhi, Zhang Hewang, and Cao Jianqiang, eds., *Handai taoqi yu gudai wenming* (*Han-dynasty ceramics and civilization*) (Beijing: Zhongguo nongye chubanshe, 2000), pp. 137–43. For English-language sources on dogs in China, see "Jottings on the Races of Dogs in Ancient China," in Berthold Laufer, *Chinese Pottery of the Han Dynasty* (Leiden: E. J. Brill, 1909), pp. 247–81. The dog illustrated by Laufer (pl. LXIV) as well as the present *Figure of a Dog* closely resemble a breed familiarly known today as the Chow, a member of the Spitz family (which also includes the Japanese Akita). More specific names generally appear to designate function, for example, *shouquan* ("guard dog," like the present image), or appearance, for example, *xigou* ("thin dog" or greyhound). An extremely similar glazed earthenware dog in the collection of the Shanghai Museum is simply called a *xungou* ("tame" or "house" dog); see Zhu Boqian, ed., *Zhongguo taoci quanji* (*The complete works of Chinese ceramics*), vol. 3: *Qin Han* (*Qin and Han dynasties*), in the series Zhongguo meishu fenlei quanji (Complete arts of China) (Shanghai: Shanghai renmin meishu chubanshe, 2000), p. 277, no. 175.

3. Domestication and use of dogs in China may even antedate the Neolithic era. See, inter alia, Kwang-chih Chang, *The Archaeology of China*, 4th rev. ed. (New Haven: Yale University Press, 1986), pp. 79, 93, 113, 201, 211, 226, 254, 260, 270, 279, 282.

4. Archaeology and texts together provide knowledge of the role of dogs in this period. See, for example, Kwang-chih Chang, *Shang Civilization* (New Haven: Yale University Press, 1980), pp. 82, 86, 88, 114, 143, 277, 311, 314, which mentions the use of dogs for food and also their burial in human graves, sometimes near or even with human beings.

5. Even after the Eastern Zhou and Han, when wood and ceramic tomb sculpture of animals and humans appeared and flourished, the occasional interment of animals and less frequently of humans continued. Han burials including dogs have been found in Shandong; see Shandong Sheng Zibo Shi bowuguan, "Xihan Qi wang mu suizang qiwu keng" ("The funerary pits in the vicinity of the tomb of the king of Qi of the Western Han dynasty"), *Kaogu xuebao* 1985.2, pp. 223–66, and for illustrations of the pit with dogs, p. 226, fig. 5, pl. 16:4.

6. For a concise exposition of Chinese concepts of life and death and how they relate to mortuary goods, see Albert E. Dien, "Chinese Beliefs in the Afterlife," in *The Quest For Eternity: Chinese Ceramic Sculptures From The People's Republic of China* (Los Angeles: Los Angeles County Museum of Art and Chronicle Books, 1987), pp. 1–15. Not all agree with every aspect of Dien's study. For an overview and analysis of various related questions, and some pertinent bibliography concerning the origins, development, definition, and purpose of *mingqi* ("bright objects," "spirit objects"), *yong* ("figures," "servants," "slaves"), and *muyong* ("tomb figures," etc.), see Virginia L. Bower, *From Court to Caravan* (Cambridge and New Haven: Harvard University Art Museum and Yale University Press, 2002), pp. 22–27; Cary Y. Liu's "Concept of 'Brilliant Artifacts' in Han-Dynasty Burial Objects and Funerary Architecture," in this catalogue. It should be noted that the practice of interring living beings persisted even as the use of burial images of living beings became widespread. Interment of living beings continued beyond the Han dynasty, and is known to have been practiced on a limited scale as late as the Qing dynasty. See Huang Zhanyu, "Ming Qing Huangshi de gongfei xunzang zhi" ("The institution of burying court concubines with the dead of the imperial family in the Ming and Qing dynasties"), *Gugong bowuyuan yuankan* 1988.1, pp. 29–34. The heyday of the practice of including ceramic, stone, or wood burial objects in tombs is usually viewed as the Han–Tang dynasties. Even as other customs, such as the burning of paper images, became popular during the Song dynasty, burial objects continued to be placed in some tombs even into the Qing dynasty. See Bower, *From Court to Caravan*, pp. 54–55.

7. Early Western Han tombs have disclosed numerous smaller-than-life-size figures of human beings and animals, including dogs. Pits or trenches filled with unglazed, painted, ceramic domestic animals, including a male and a female dog, are part of the tomb complex of Han Jingdi (r. 157–141 BCE). A bibliography of references about this site is found in Li Jian, ed., *Eternal China: Splendors from the First Dynasties* (Dayton: The Dayton Art Institute, 1998), pp. 122–25.

8. This dog has been published in Ezekiel Schloss, *Ancient Chinese Ceramic Sculpture from Han through T'ang*, 2 vols. (Stamford: Castle Publishing, 1977), vol. 1, pp. 182–83, vol. 2, pl. 21; Suzanne G. Valenstein, "Chinese Ceramics in the Collection of Adele and Stanley Herzman," *Orientations*, June 1990, pp. 42–55, fig. 1; reprinted in Valenstein, *The Herzman Collection of Chinese Ceramics* (New York: Stanley Herzman, 1992), pp. 12–13, no. 1, app. p. 42, fig. 1.

9. All of these dogs are roughly the same size, and all are green-glazed. For the one in the Shanghai Museum, see Zhu Boqian, ed., *Zhongguo taoci quanji*, vol. 3, pp. 172, 277, no. 175 (h. 26.8 cm); in the Asian Art Museum of San Francisco, see He Li, *Chinese Ceramics: A New Comprehensive Survey* (New York: Rizzoli International, 1996), pp. 76, 114, no. 82 (h. 30.4 cm); in Singapore collections, see Aileen Lau, ed., *Spirit of Han* (Singapore: The Southeast Asian Ceramic Society and Sun Tree Publishing, 1991), p. 149, nos. 152, 153.

10. My thanks to Suzanne G. Valenstein for her examination and description of the hollows in the cheeks of this figure; she noted that the interior color is gray, not red, and suggested that the hollows had been drilled after firing. The shallower dimples at the lower cheeks of the dog in the collection of the Shanghai Museum appear to be glazed in the same manner as the rest of the animal. Judging from published illustrations, the hollows are lacking in the dog in the Asian Art Museum of San Francisco.

11. A sampling of Sichuan-excavated standing watchdogs, along with references, may be found in Mary Tregear, ed., *Arts of China: Neolithic Cultures to the T'ang Dynasty* (Tokyo: Kodansha International, 1968), p. 149, cpl. 244; p. 171, nos. 304–306, pp. 231, 234.

12. Xiao, Zhang, and Cao, *Handai taoqi yu gudai wenming*, p. 142, fig. 98.

13. See He Li, *Chinese Ceramics*, p. 114.

14. Dezhou diqu wenwuzu and Ningjian Xian wenhuaju, "Shandong Ningjian Xian Pangjia Si Han mu" ("Han tomb at the Pangjia Si in Ningjian County, Shandong"), *Wenwu ziliao congkan* 1981.4, p. 126 and p. 127, fig. 3:10, right.

15. The most often published Eastern Han glazed watchdog of this type from Shandong is the green-glazed example found in a tomb in Gaotang County. Earlier publications of this large (h. 42.5 cm) figure include Shandong Sheng wenwu guanlichu and Shandong bowuguan, eds., *Shandong wenwu xuanji* (*Selections of Shandong cultural relics*) (Beijing: Wenwu chubanshe, 1959), p. 92, pl. 179; Takashi Okazaki, ed., *Sekai toji zenshū* (*Ceramic art of the world*), vol. 10: *Chūkogu kodai* (*Chinese prehistoric and ancient periods*) (Tokyo: Shōgakukan Press, 1982), pp. 91–92, no. 82. It is most recently published in Susan L. Beningson and Cary Y. Liu, *Brilliant Artifacts from Shandong: Palaces* *of the Afterlife in the Western Han* (New York: China Institute Gallery, 2005).

16. A green-glazed watchdog similar to those recovered from Shandong has been excavated from a tomb in Wangdu County, Hebei. See Hebei Sheng wenwu yanjiusuo, "Hebei Wangdu Nanliusu Donghan mu" ("Eastern Han tomb at Nanliusu, Wangdu County, Hebei"), *Wenwu ziliao congkan* 1987.10, pl. 3:2, p. 106.

17. It is depicted in a Han tomb wall painting in Liaoning Province; see Li Wenxin, "Liaoyang faxian de san zuo bihua gu mu" ("Three ancient mural tombs discovered in Liaoyang"), *Wenwu* 1955.5, p. 16, fig. 4, p. 19, pl. 2. A menacing dog on a leash must be differentiated from those shown being led to slaughter. A kitchen scene portrayed in an Eastern Han tomb in Shandong includes a man pulling the leash of a collared dog intended for the pot. See Zhucheng Xian bowuguan and Ren Rixin, "Shandong Zhucheng Han mu huaxiang shi" ("Stone reliefs on a Han tomb in Zhucheng County, Shandong"), *Wenwu* 1981.10, p. 19, fig.7.

18. The first of these is found on the *Wang Ling mu* slab, possibly part of a putative lost Fourth Shrine associated with the "Wu family shrines." Reproduced in Wu Hung, *The Wu Liang Shrine: The Ideology of Early Chinese Pictorial Art* (Stanford: Stanford University Press, 1989), p. 22, fig. 15. Both the original and the rubbing are difficult to decipher, leaving the slight possibility that the dog wears some kind of restraint. The second, and clearer, illustration of this story is found in the Yi'nan tomb in Shandong; see Lydia duPont Thompson, "The Yi'nan Tomb: Narrative and Ritual in Pictorial Art of the Eastern Han (25–220 CE)" (PhD diss., Institute of Fine Arts, New York University, 1998), pp. 380–83, p. 382, fig. A.11.

19. Richard C. Rudolph and Wen You, *Han Tomb Art of West China: A Collection of First and Second Century Reliefs* (Berkeley and Los Angeles: University of California Press, 1951), p. 23, no. 20.

20. Chengdu wenwu guanlichu, "Sichuan Chengdu Zengjiabao Donghan huaxiang shi mu" ("Eastern Han stone relief tombs at Zengjiabao in Chengdu, Sichuan"), *Wenwu* 1981.10, p. 27, pl. 4:3.

21. Michael Loewe, *Everyday Life in Early Imperial China* (New York: G. P. Putnam's Sons, 1968), p. 48, fig. 13, p. 162, fig. 71.

22. V. W. F. Collier, *Dogs of China & Japan in Nature and Art* (New York: Frederick A. Stokes Company, 1921), p. 77.

23. Arthur De Carle Sowerby, *Nature in Chinese Art* (New York: The John Day Company, 1940), p. 98.

24. In this image the combination of greyhound, unhitched horse, and carriage brings to mind the line: "At court there should be no speaking of dogs and horses" (see n. 1.)

25. See n. 18.

26. See Michael Nylan, *The Five "Confucian" Classics* (New Haven: Yale University Press, 2001), pp. 49, 54. *Liji* (*Rites records*) is one of these Classics.

27. Legge, trans. and ed., *Li Chi: Book of Rites*, vol. 2, p. 76.

28. Zhu Bin, ed., *Liji xun zuan* (*"Rites records," instructional compendium*) (Beijing: Zhonghua shuju, 1996), vol. 2, *juan* 17, p. 537.

29. These may have been the king's hunting dogs; see Jessica Rawson, ed., *Mysteries of Ancient China* (London: The British Museum, 1996), pp. 161–62.

30. As translated by Legge, *Li Chi: Book of Rites*, vol. 1, pp. 196–97.

31. See Sun Ji, *Zhongguo gu yufu luncong* (*Essays on ancient Chinese vehicles and garments*) (Beijing: Wenwu chubanshe, 2002), pp. 161–83, which includes a drawing (p. 166, fig.12–5, lower line) of figures from the Wu shrines wearing this headgear; among them is Confucius.

32. Fan Ye, comp., *Hou Hanshu* (*History of the Later Han*) (Beijing: Zhonghua shuju, 1965), *juan* 8, p. 346.

33. Detailed account in Collier, *Dogs of China and Japan*, p. 18.

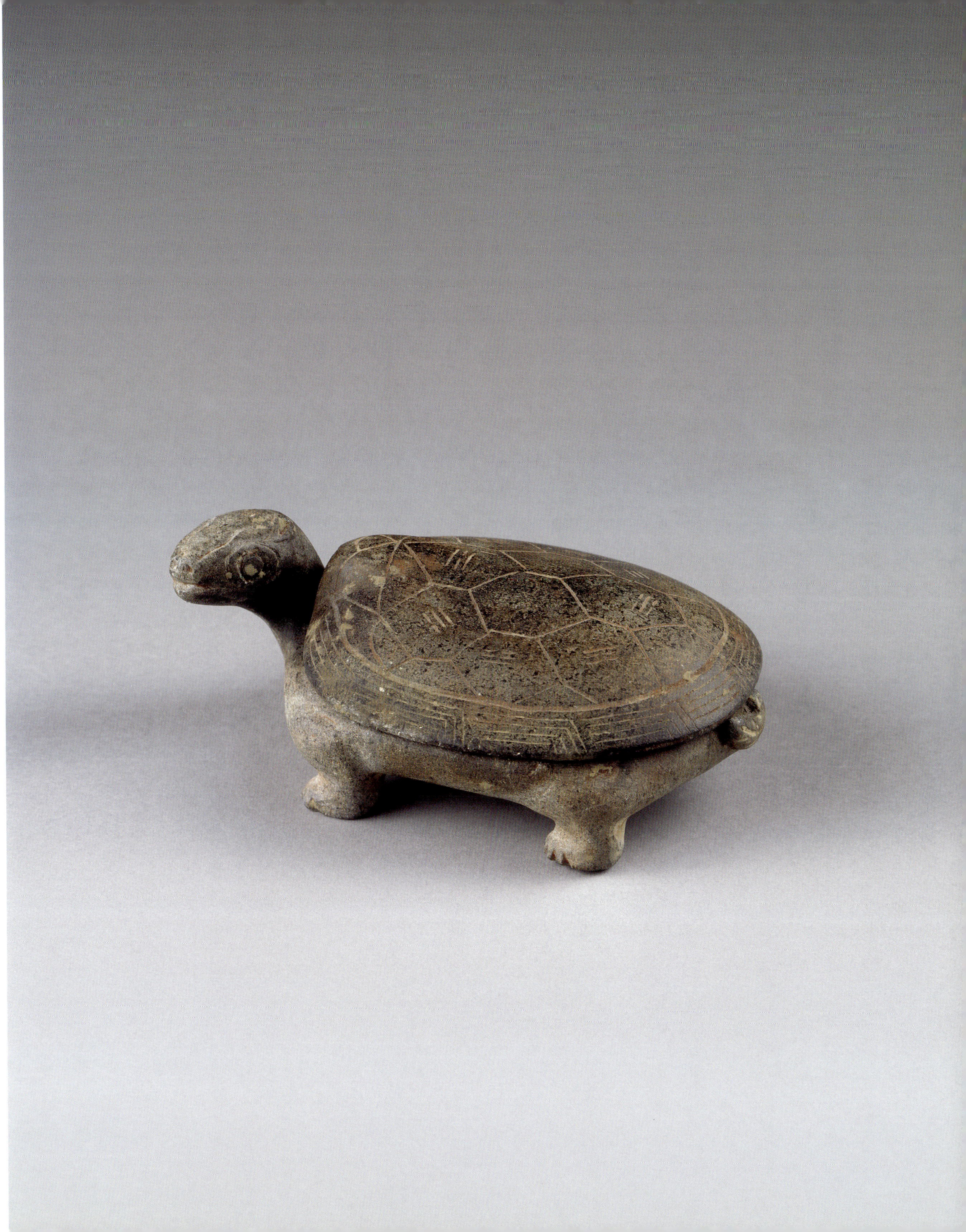

54 Turtle inkslab incised with the Eight Trigrams

Eastern Han dynasty. Stoneware; l. 13.1 cm.
Private collection.

Standing foursquare on stout legs with its head raised, this ceramic turtle is in fact a covered inkslab. Its carapace, shaped like the overarching dome of heaven, bears incised decoration: within a patterned outer band is a hexagonal grid, and within a ring of eight complete hexagons of that grid are the Eight Trigrams (*ba gua*). These are often posited as the forerunners of Chinese written characters, and both the Trigrams and the characters can be understood as pictographic visualizations or ideographic verbalizations of heavenly and earthly patterns —embodied images (*ti xiang*).[1] With the carapace removed, the plastron, shaped like the flat earth, presents a shallow oval basin on which the ink stick was ground and mixed with water to form liquid ink. Because water is the origin from which the Eight Trigrams are ultimately said to derive (see below), and ink is the medium of calligraphy and writing, they became metaphors for the source of all human knowledge and culture.[2] In this way the inkslab basin can be said to represent the realm of man, positioned midway between the domed carapace-heaven and flat plastron-earth.[3]

While serving as an implement for writing and calligraphy, this turtle inkslab exemplifies early legends surrounding the sacred origins of writing. In the reign of the legendary ruler Fuxi, a dragon-horse is said to have emerged from the Yellow River with the River Diagram (*Hetu*) on its back, and a divine turtle appeared bearing the Luo River Book (*Luoshu*) on its shell.[4] According to legend, Fuxi (fig. 1) drew the Eight Trigrams from the River Diagram, and the sage-hero Yu (fig. 2) established the Nine Divisions (*Jiuchou*) of the Great Plan (*Hongfan*) from the River Book.[5]

Early writing is often said to have a divine aspect because Shang-dynasty oracle bones recorded royal divinations. But the incised oracle-bone-script (*jiaguwen*) writings on the turtle plastrons and bovine scapulae are thoroughly human in origin; only the heat-induced prognostic cracks (*bu*) on the plastrons and scapulae can be interpreted as divine writing directly communicated from the spirits.

As a denizen of the water world, the turtle came to be seen as the stalwart offspring of the dragon and was sometimes depicted as the literal, physical bearer of the civilized world. In this guise it later came to be used as a base supporting inscribed steles. The strength and power ascribed to turtles also led to associations with martial prowess. The turtle entwined with a snake represents the Black Tortoise, or Dark Warrior (*xuanwu*), the deity of the north presumed to bring rain and insure victory against northern invaders. This martial aspect may underlie the depiction of the turtle warrior (fig. 3) in a ceiling slab of Stone Chamber 2.

CARY Y. LIU

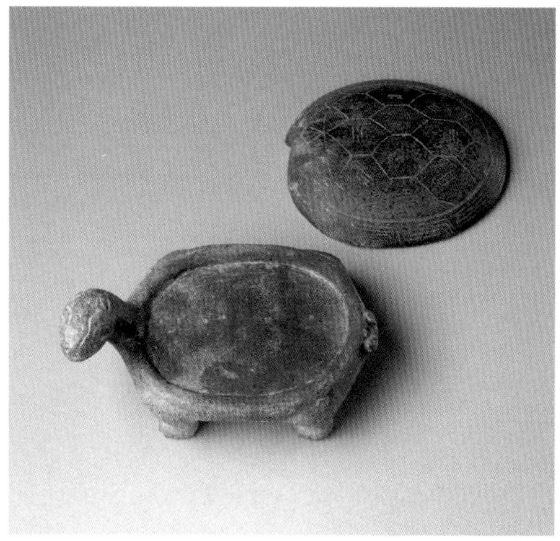

Notes

1. See Cary Y. Liu, "Embodying Cosmic Patterns: Foundations of an Art of Calligraphy in China," *Oriental Art*, vol. 56, no. 5 (2000), pp. 2–9.

2. The gathered knowledge in the vast *Siku quanshu* (*Comprehensive library of the four treasuries*) imperial library compilation in the Qing dynasty was likened to water flowing to the sea. See Cary Y. Liu, "The Ch'ing Dynasty Imperial Library, Wen-yüan-ko: Architecture and the Ordering of Knowledge" (PhD diss., Princeton University, 1997), pp. 269–83.

3. For comparisons of the carapace to heaven and plastron to earth, see *Kaikodo Journal*, vol. 9 (Autumn 1998), p. 118; Wolfram Eberhard, *A Dictionary of Chinese Symbols: Hidden Symbols in Chinese Life and Thought*, trans. G. L. Campbell (London: Routledge, 1986), pp. 294–96.

4. For discussion of the various hypotheses on what the *Hetu* and *Luoshu* may have been, see Du Xuezhi, "Hetu luoshu ba gua yu tuhui zhishi" ("Illustrated notes on the River Diagram, River Book, and Eight Trigrams"), *Dalu zazhi*, vol. 8, no. 5 (1954), pp. 12–13; Florian C. Rieter, "Some Remarks on the Chinese Word *T'u* 'Chart, Plan, Design'," *Oriens*, vol. 32 (1990), pp. 308–27.

5. See text and commentary in *Shangshu zhengyi* (*Orthodox interpretation of the "Book of Documents"*), *Shisan jing zhushu* edition (Beijing: Zhonghua shuju, 1980), *juan* 12, pp. 187–93. On detailed discussion of the Nine Divisions and the dating of the "Hongfan" section in the *Book of Documents*, see Michael Nylan, *The Shifting Center: The Original "Great Plan" and Later Readings*, Monumenta Serica Monograph Series XXIV (Nettetal: Steyler Verlag, 1992), pp. 13–14, 108, 113–14.

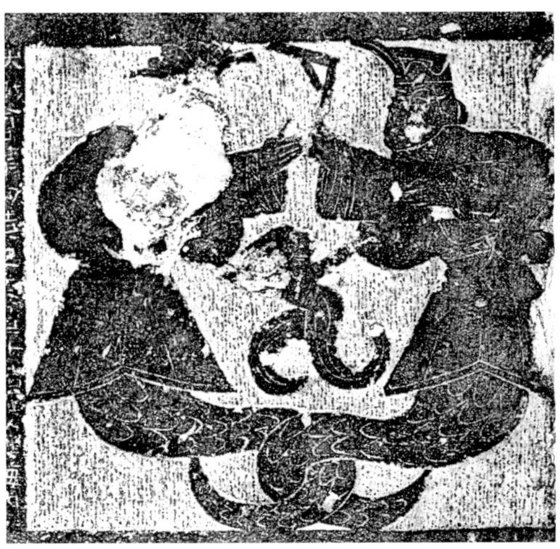

Fig. 1 *Fuxi* (right) *and Nüwa*. Detail of a rubbing of incised stone, Stone Chamber 3, Stone 3-W.1 (cat. no. 1.35). "Wu family shrines" rubbings. Princeton University Art Museum, acc. no. 2002-307.36.

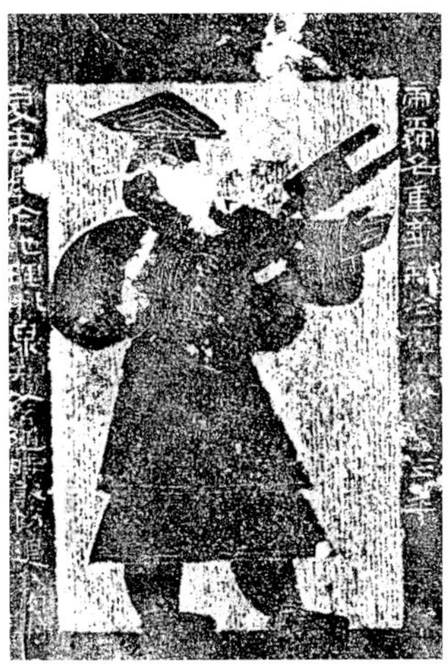

Fig. 2 *The sage-hero Yu*. Detail of a rubbing of incised stone, Stone Chamber 3, Stone 3-W.1 (cat. no. 1.35). "Wu family shrines" rubbings. Princeton University Art Museum, acc. no. 2002-307.36.

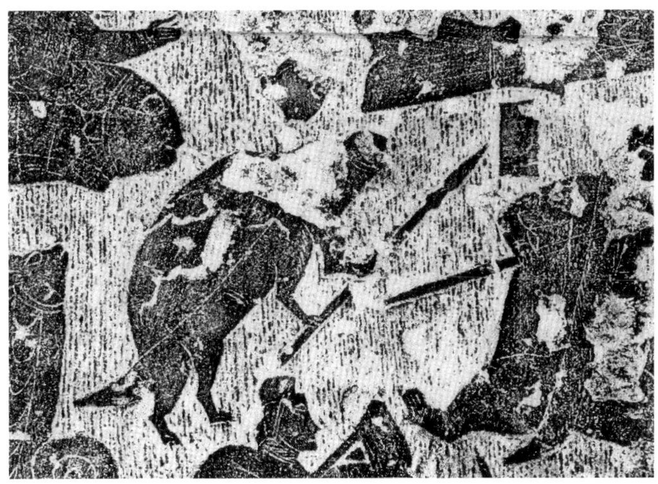

Fig. 3 *Turtle warrior*. Detail of a rubbing of incised stone, Stone Chamber 2, Stone 2-R.3 (cat. no. 1.34). "Wu family shrines" rubbings. Princeton University Art Museum, acc. no. 2002-307.33.

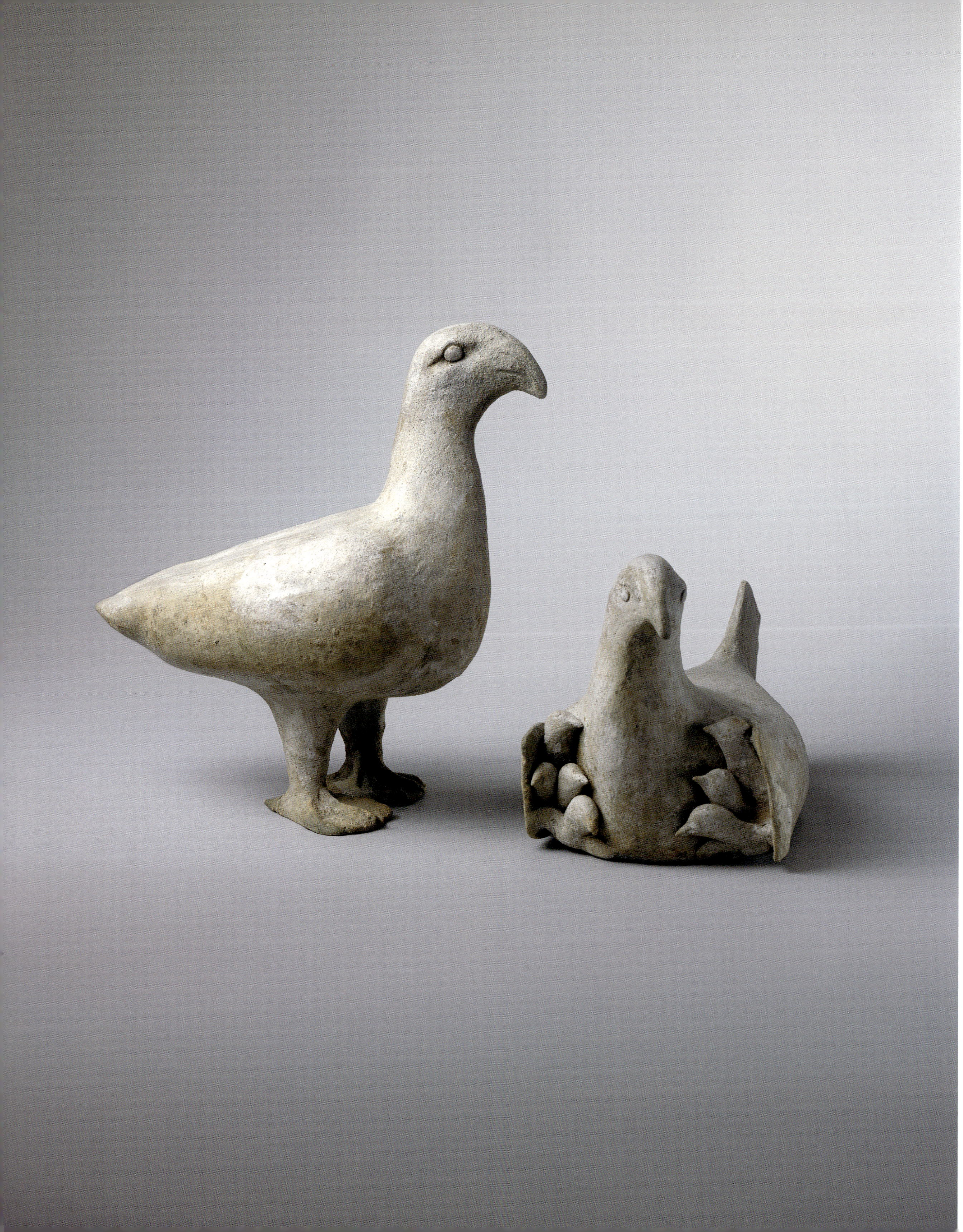

55 Pair of birds with chicks

Eastern Han dynasty. Gray earthenware; h. 16.5 cm, l. 27.3 cm; h. 27.0 cm, l. 26.0 cm. Private collection.

Earthenware figures of birds are commonly found in Han-dynasty tombs, but those unearthed in the Zhongyuan ("Central Plain," the region of the Yellow and Wei River valleys) are rarely so sensitively modeled. Both birds are simply rendered, yet they capture the essence of a nesting pair. The hen protectively nestles four chicks under each wing whilst her mate stands erect and watchful. The birds were hand-modeled, their eyes and the chicks were modeled separately and applied, and a sharp tool was used to detail the eyes and beaks.

Earthenware figurines from Sichuan Province are characteristically more animated and naturalistic than their Central Plain counterparts.[1] Along with pictorial tiles, earthenware figurines were essential furnishings of both rock-cut and underground brick tombs in Sichuan. As in tombs of the Central Plain, their function was to create a living universe for the afterlife of the deceased. Similar nesting birds with their chicks have been found in rock-cut tombs in Pengshan, Sichuan.[2]

In the "Wu family shrines," birds are depicted in several different contexts. They appear to be used as decorative motifs, or space fillers, embellishing and dividing the main pictorial scenes. In kitchen scenes they are shown hanging along with other kill (fig. 1). Fantastic and hybrid bird-like creatures also figure often: bird-headed creatures pull a chariot driven by winged Immortals (fig. 2), and clouds are frequently embellished with birds' heads. These bird-like creatures may be regarded as auspicious omens, related to exotic and fantastic animals and proper to the realms of the Immortals (see "The Bear Motif during the Han Dynasty" in this catalogue).

HIROMI KINOSHITA

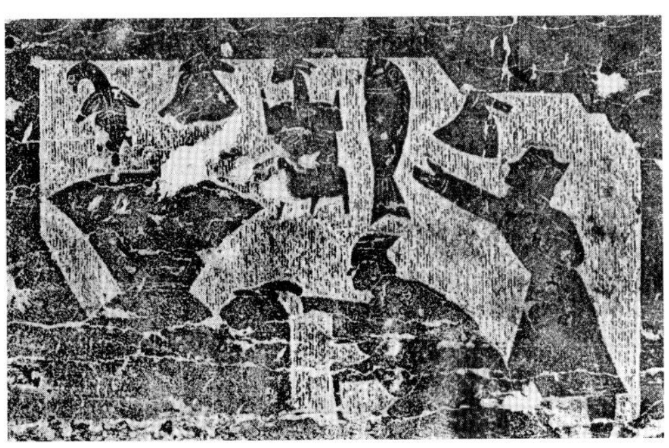

Fig. 1 *Kitchen scene*. Detail of Stone Chamber 1, Stone 1-S.5.a (cat. no. 1.7). "Wu family shrines" rubbings. Princeton University Art Museum, acc. no. 2002-307.7.

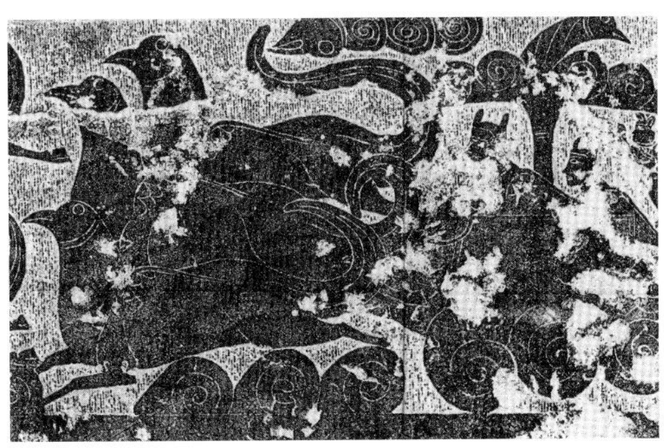

Fig. 2 *Bird-headed creatures pulling a chariot*. Detail of Stone Chamber 1, Stone 1-R.2 (cat. no. 1.18). "Wu family shrines" rubbings. Princeton University Art Museum, acc. no. 2002-307.17.

Notes

1. Cf. the earthenware figurines of entertainers, musicians, and dancers modeled in active poses in Lucy Lim, ed., *Stories from China's Past* (San Francisco: Chinese Culture Center, 1987). Also unusual and thus far unique to the Sichuan region are the ceramic figures depicting surprisingly intimate aspects of personal life. See, for example, the stone scuptural relief depicting a man and woman embracing (ibid., pl. 41, p. 131) and the red earthenware figure of a mother suckling her child illustrated in *Sichuan Pengshan Handai yamu* (*Cliff tombs in Han-dynasty Pengshan, Sichuan*) (Beijing: Wenwu chubanshe, 1991), pls. 7, 12.
2. Ibid., figs. 8, 66, and 67, with line drawings on pp. 87, 88. Compare also a nested mother bird nuzzling a chick on her back, excavated from a Han cliff tomb in Zhong County, Sichuan, illustrated in *Wenwu* 1985.7, p. 89, fig. 95.

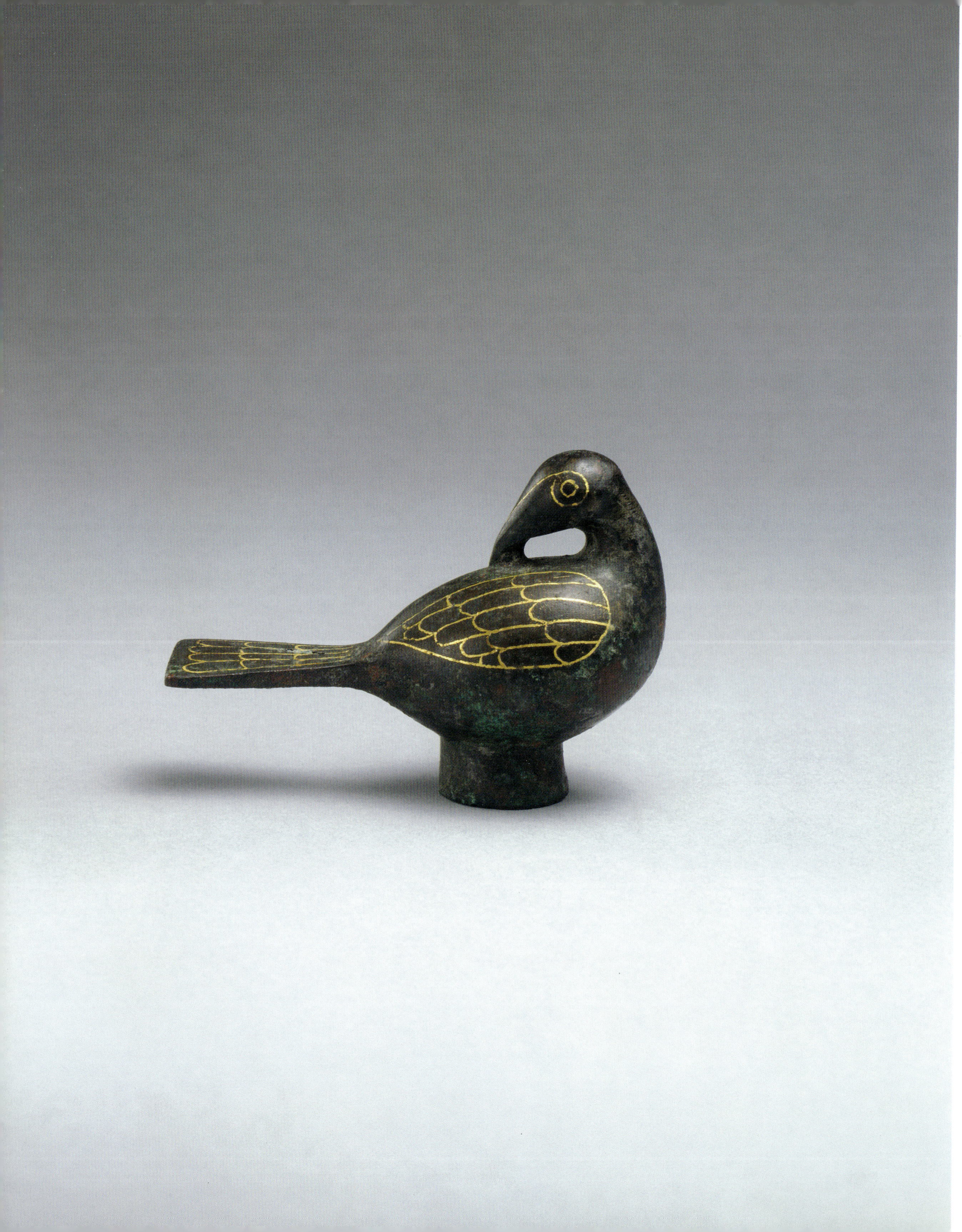

56 Dove-shaped staff finial

Han dynasty. Bronze with gold inlay; h. 5.5 cm, l. 7.5 cm.
Private collection.

A dove with plump breast and long flat tail perches on a circular collar, which would have fitted over a wood staff. The bird's almost triangular head is reversed, its long, curved beak resting on its back. Gold inlay describes the features: a scale pattern for the wing and tail feathers and two concentric circles for each eye.

This finial topped a staff called *jiuzhang* ("dove staff"), which according to Han texts was bestowed on the aged by the government.[1] The origin of this custom is not clear. Bird-shaped pole tops and images of such tops, dating from the Eastern Zhou period, have been found in southern China, but there the pole was used as a drum stand.[2] An elegant bird-shaped finial in the Beijing Palace Museum has been dated to the late Warring States period,[3] and a duck-shaped finial found in a tomb in Chengdu, Sichuan, has been dated to late Warring States or early Western Han, on the evidence of other tomb contents.[4] It is not known, however, whether these two examples were governmental awards to aged people. Beginning in the Western Han, finials in bird shape became increasingly popular and also somewhat standardized, the dove shape increasingly displacing the more varied bird images of earlier times.[5] Imperial statutes and edicts regulated the bestowal of "royal staffs" on the elderly, symbolizing privileges that varied in accordance with the age and rank of the recipient, privileges such as exemption from compulsory service and taxation. An article in the Statute on Corvée (*fu lü*), issued no later than 186 BCE, prescribed the bestowal of staffs within the twenty-degree aristocratic rank system: an unranked person would receive a staff at the age of seventy-five; persons from the first to the fourth rank would receive it one year earlier per degree of rank; those from the fifth up would receive it at the age of seventy.[6]

During most of Western Han, the age requirement for receiving a staff fluctuated between seventy and eighty; it finally settled at seventy years during Emperor Cheng's reign (32–7 BCE), when the name *jiuzhang* also made its first appearance in official documents. By this point rank seems no longer to have determined the age of bestowal. Two different tombs in Wuwei, Gansu, have yielded copies of the imperial ordinance about the bestowal of *jiuzhang*, written on wooden strips. One of the tombs contained two actual dove-topped wooden *jiuzhang* very similar to the staffs in the stories of Laizi (fig. 1) and Dong Yong, depicted in the present exhibition (cat. nos. 1.12, 1.36). The copy of the imperial ordinance was attached to one of the staffs. The most astonishing feature of the ordinance is the severity of the punishment for infringing the privileges of elderly recipients of the *jiuzhang*: public execution. In one case recorded in the ordinance, an honored elder of the eighth rank appealed directly to the throne against a local official who had injured him. The emperor sentenced the official to immediate death, disregarding the convention by which executions usually took place in autumn and winter in order to harmonize with the cycle of nature. The rigor of the law, which may seem inordinate to us, may have seemed more reasonable to the people of Han times, for whom filial piety was a cardinal virtue, as exemplified by the "Wu family shrines." The Wuwei documents record the public executions of sixteen

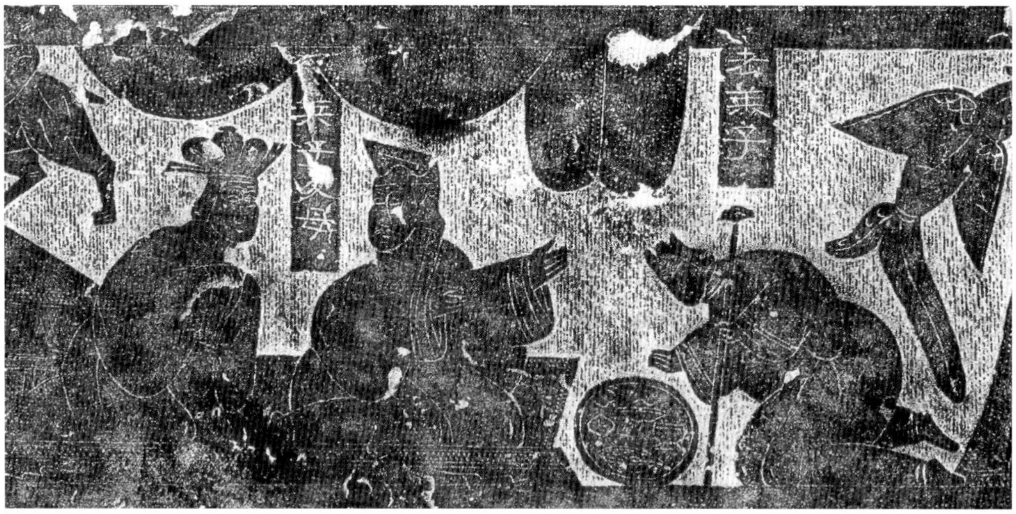

Fig. 1 *Figure of Laizi carrying a bird-finial staff.* Detail of Stone Chamber 1, Stone 1-E.2 (cat. no. 1.12). "Wu family shrines" rubbings. Princeton University Art Museum, acc. no. 2002.307.2.

people, both commoners and local officials, for injuring elderly holders of the *jiuzhang*; the crimes were described as impious (*nibudao*).[7]

Extensive studies have been done on the decrees about the staffs, but little attention has been given to the artifacts themselves. Their widespread distribution is evidence of the remarkable authority and effectiveness of Han administration (and legislation). The finials have been found in Jiangsu and Guangxi in the south,[8] Gansu in the west,[9] and Lelang, Korea, in the east.[10] As the Wuwei documents confirm, the emperor ordered that his decree be publicized "everywhere under heaven." We can reasonably assume that hundreds, if not thousands, of copies were sent to the local governments. How did local officials then make the public aware of this decree? We do not know the degree and extent of literacy in the Han period. Judging from the many mistakes and the summarized form of the original decrees, the Wuwei documents were copied not by official scribes but by others less well trained.[11] Who were the copiers? Was it a common practice to copy the royal edicts in order to protect the privileges of the old? Was it customary to bury these documents along with the *jiuzhang* to accompany the deceased? All the texts about the staffs have been found in the northwest, yet this may only be an accident of preservation and discovery. Except under extremely arid or water-logged conditions, the wood or bamboo strips on which the documents were written would hardly have survived, and many of the finials, too, were made not of bronze but of wood. Under these circumstances, the questions remain unanswered. But the present finial, tiny as it is, does shed interesting light on aspects of Han administration, legislation, literacy, social and ethical values, and customs.

HAICHENG WANG

Notes

1. Sun Ji, *Handai wuzhi wenhua ziliao tushuo* (*Illustrated history of Han antiquities*) (Beijing: Wenwu chubanshe, 1991), pp. 346–48, figs. 87.17, 87.22.

2. Zou Houben, "Qingtong jiuzhang bianxi" ("On the bronze dove-shaped staff-finial"), in *Wuyue diqu qingtongqi yanjiu lunwenji* (*Studies on the bronzes from the lower Yangzi region*), ed. Ma Chengyuan (Hong Kong: Liangmu chubanshe, 1997), pp. 275–78.

3. Jessica Rawson and Emma Bunker, *Ancient Chinese and Ordos Bronzes* (Hong Kong: The Oriental Ceramic Society of Hong Kong, 1990), no. 81.

4. Chengdu Shi wenwu kaogu gongzuodui et al., "Chengdu Shi Guangrong Xiaoqu tukengmu fajue jianbo" ("Preliminary report of a pit tomb found at Guangrong Xiaoqu in Chengdu"), *Wenwu* 1988.11, p. 23, fig. 5, p. 27, fig. 17.6, p. 28.

5. Li Yongping, "Gansu Sheng bowuguan xitong suocang qingtongqi" ("Some bronzes from the museum collections in Gansu Province"), *Wenwu* 2000.12, p. 71, back cover; Tōkyō Geijutsu Daigaku Geijutsu Shiryōkan, ed., *Tōkyō Geijutsu Daigaku Geijutsu Shiryōkan zōhin mokuroku: kinkō I* (*Catalogue of the Tōkyō Geijutsu Daigaku Collection, vol.1: Metal*) (Tokyo: Tōkyō Geijutsu Daigaku Geijutsu Shiryōkan, 1981), no. 1006; Egawa Eiko, *Taikō to seidō dōbutsu: kodai Chūgoku no sōshokuhin* (*Agraffes and bronze animals: Ancient Chinese ornaments*) (Tokyo: Ribun shuppan, 1994), no. 107; J. J. Lally & Co., *Arts of Ancient China* (Hong Kong: Pressroom, 1990), no. 8; Rawson and Bunker, *Ancient Chinese and Ordos Bronzes*, no. 82.

6. Zhangjia Shan 247 hao Han mu zhujian zhengli xiaozu, *Zhangjia Shan Han mu zhujian* [*247 hao mu*] (*The bamboo strips from a Western Han tomb at Zhangjia Shan* [*Tomb 247*]) (Beijing: Wenwu chubanshe, 2001), p. 181, strip no. 355; Gao Min, "Cong er nian lü ling kan Xihan qianqi de cijue zhidu" ("Rank bestowal system of the early Western Han seen from *er nian lü ling*"), *Wenwu* 2002.9, p. 52. For the twenty-degree rank system, see Michael Loewe, "The Orders of Aristocratic Rank of Han China," *T'oung Pao*, vol. 48 (1960), pp. 7–174.

7. For short English introductions to these documents, see Michael Loewe, "Han Administrative Documents: Recent Finds From the North-west," *T'oung Pao*, vol. 77 (1986), pp. 306–7; A. F. P. Hulsewé, "Qin and Han Legal Manuscripts," in *New Sources of Early Chinese History: An Introduction to the Reading of Inscriptions and Manuscripts*, ed. Edward L. Shaughnessy (Berkeley: The Society for the Study of Early China, 1997), p. 197. For comprehensive transcriptions, annotations, and translations, see Wuwei Xian bowuguan, "Wuwei xin chutu wangzhang zhaoling ce" ("The imperial ordinance about the bestowal of the royal staff recently excavated from Wuwei"), in *Hanjian yanjiu wenji* (*Studies of the Han tablets*), ed. Gansu Sheng wenwu gongzuodui and Gansu Sheng bowuguan (Lanzhou: Gansu renmin chubanshe, 1984), pp. 34–61. Ōba Osamu, *Kankan kenkyū* (*Studies of the Han tablets*) (Kyoto: Dōhōsha, 1992), pp. 42–67. For Chinese translation of Ōba's book, see Xu Shihong, trans., *Hanjian yanjiu* (*Studies of the Han tablets*) (Guilin: Guangxi shifan daxue chubanshe, 2001). Hu Pingsheng, "Yumen, Wuwei xin huo jiandu wenzi jiaoshi" ("Comments and translations on the newly found tablets from Yumen and Wuwei"), *Kaogu yu wenwu* 1986.6, pp. 95–99; Hu Pingsheng, "Wangzhang zhaoshu ling ce 'yi jiang' jie" ("On the interpretation of the phase 'yi jiang' from the imperial ordinance about the bestowal of the royal staff"), in his *Hu Pingsheng jiandu wenwu lunji* (*Studies of the Han tablets by Hu Pingsheng*) (Taipei: Tailan chubanshe, 2000), pp. 275–77.

8. Sun Ji, *Handai wuzhi wenhua ziliao tushuo*, p. 348; Nanjing bowuyuan et al., "Haizhou Xihan Huo He mu qingli jianbao" ("Preliminary report of the tomb of Huo He in Haizhou"), *Kaogu* 1974.3, p. 184.

9. Gansu Sheng bowuguan, "Gansu Wuwei Mozuizi Han mu fajue" ("Excavation of the Han tombs at Mozuizi, Wuwei"), *Kaogu* 1960.9, p. 19, pls. 7.1–4.

10. Idemitsu Bijutsukan, ed., *Chūgoku no kōgei: Idemitsu Bijutsukan zōhin zuroku* (*Ancient Chinese arts in the Idemitsu Collection*) (Tokyo: Hatsubai Heibonsha,1989), no. 478.

11. Hu Pingsheng, "Yumen, Wuwei xin huo jiandu wenzi jiaoshi," p. 99.

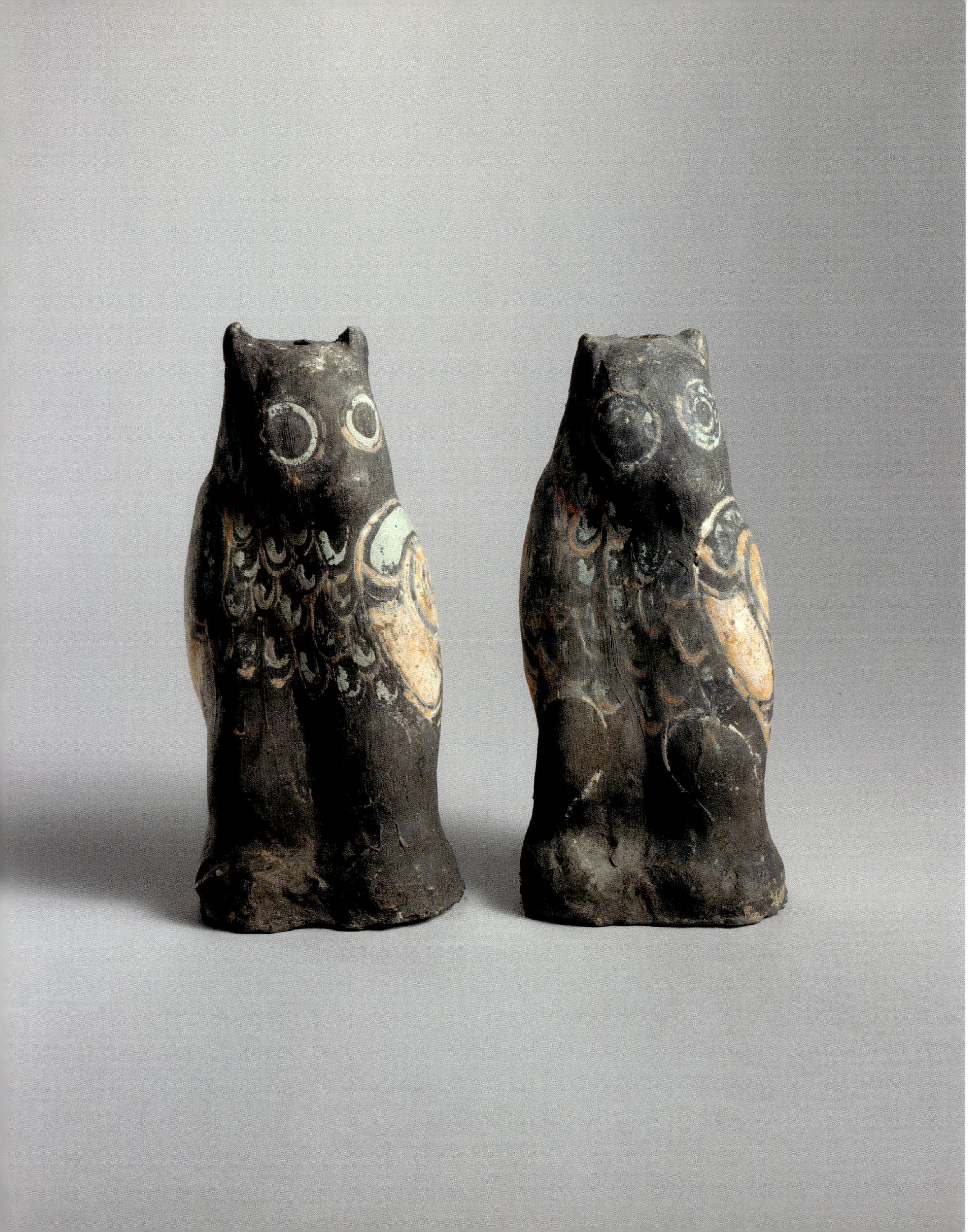

57 Two owls

Western Han dynasty. Black-painted dark earthenware with color pigments; .1) h. 18.2 cm; .2) h. 17.8 cm. Princeton University Art Museum, acc. nos. 1997-74.1, 1997-74.2. Gift of an alumnus, Class of 1959.

Each of these two standing owl figures has a coarsely modeled, hollow, dark gray earthenware body, with head and pricked ears turned slightly toward proper left. Wings are flattened at each side of the body, and a small knob on the face suggests a beak. The clay surface is painted black, with physical features picked out in red-orange, pale green, and yellow mineral pigments. Feather patterns across the chest and back of the head are suggested by a series of overlapping painted half-circles, and broad ribbons of red and green scroll pattern on the shoulders suggest wings. The wide eyes are made up of three concentric circles, the outer painted red, the middle green, and the inner yellow. The huge pupils were left black. At the top of the head is a hole, possibly intended to release gases during firing or to hold something like a feather or other small ornament. The irregularly circular base is black and slightly concave. Inside the hollow body of each bird is a rattle.

Birds appear frequently in Han tomb tiles and stone engravings in northeastern China, not merely as representations of natural creatures but also as symbols—apparently as omens of good or evil. They figure as an important motif in pictorial stone carvings of the "Wu family shrines." Carved on Stone 2-S.7 (L.8) in Stone Chamber 2 at the Wu cemetery is an owl perched on a small tree planted on a grave mound (fig. 1). This illustrates the story of a virtuous aristocrat of the Spring and Autumn period, Ji Zha, hanging his sword on a tree over the lord of Xu's (Xu Jun's) grave. Since the lord of Xu had admired Ji Zha's sword, the latter vowed to give it to him when he himself no longer needed it. On his return the lord had died, but Ji Zha kept his vow.[1] An owl is also found on the *He kui* stone, said to have been found in 1871 by Xuanyuan Hua and brought for storage at the Wu site in about 1880 (fig. 2).[2] Wu Hung places this stone in an architectural unit that he designates as the "Fourth Chamber."[3] Other birds depicted in the Wu shrines include the crow, considered a filial creature; birds joined at the wing, which appear when a ruler's virtue is great; and the *bifang* bird, whose presence augurs a fire in the town. Phoenixes, which also appear prominently, are auspicious birds, representing social, political, and cosmological harmony.

The owl figures occasionally in Han art, often as a bad omen.[4] In many early texts an owl appearing in a home was a harbinger of death, or in Roel Sterckx's words "a situation of a 'world turned upside down' in which animals ventured into the domain of human civilization."[5] A Han *fu* (rhapsody) by Jia Yi describes the landing of an owl in his house:

A houlet (*owl*) *landed in my house,*
Alighting on a corner of my mat,
Its manner very relaxed and tranquil.
A strange creature came to rest,
And I wondered the reason.
I opened a book and divined the question;
The oracle told me my fortune:
It said: "A wild bird enters a house;
The master will soon depart.[6]

Another story, from *Yanzi chunqiu jishi* (*Collected commentary on the "Spring and Autumn Annals" of Mr. Yan*) relates that a "screaming owl" appeared in a newly built courtyard. Upon this transgression, an exorcism ceremony was conducted, and the owl subsequently died.[7] Still other accounts associate

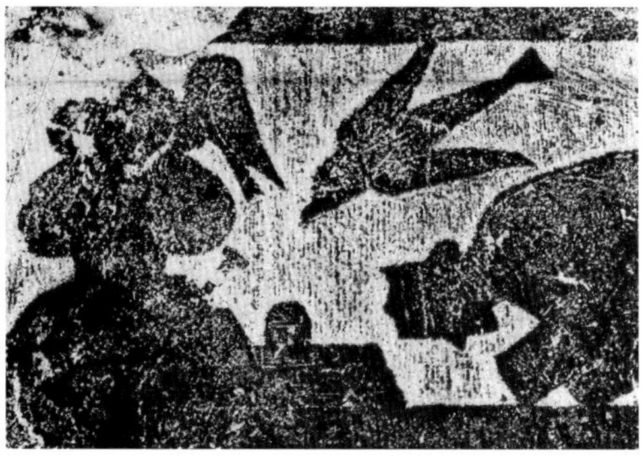

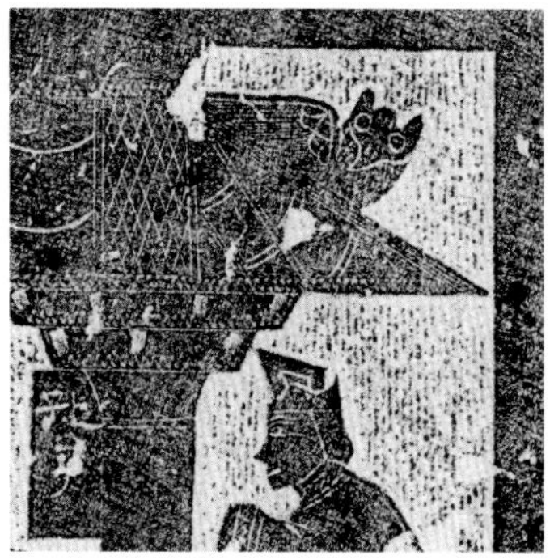

the owl with political slander or with barbarian tribes.[8]

Perhaps viewed as evil auguries for the living, owls appear to have served a more positive role for the dead. A number of ceramic owls have been excavated from Western Han tombs in the provinces of Inner Mongolia, Ningxia, Henan, and Shaanxi. In the funerary context owl figurines possibly had an apotropaic function, acting as a "watchful presence and conveyor of the soul."[9] The provenance of the pair of owls in this exhibition is unknown, but a nearly identical set was found in a Western Han tomb in Yinchuan, Ningxia Province, and a similar set was excavated from the Maoling imperial mausoleum in Shaanxi Province.[10]

INGRID FURNISS

Notes

1. This story is recounted in Sima Qian, comp., *Shiji* (*Records of the Grand Historian*) (Beijing: Zhonghua shuju, 1959), *juan* 31, p. 1459. Also see Zhu Xilu, *Wu-shi ci Han huaxiang shi zhong de gushi* (*Stories in the Han pictorial reliefs of the Wu family shrines*) (Ji'nan: Shandong meishu chubanshe, 1996), p. 70. The carved scene is described in Jiang Yingju and Wu Wenqi, *Handai Wushi muqun shike yanjiu* (*Studies on the Han-dynasty stone carvings at the Wu family cemetery*), (Ji'nan: Shandong meishu chubanshe, 1995), p. 78.

2. On the *He kui* stone, see Liu's "Recarving the Past" and cat. no. 1.49 in this catalogue. See also Wu Hung, *The Wu Liang Shrine: The Ideology of Early Chinese Art* (Stanford: Stanford University Press, 1989), pp. 21–23.

3. Ibid., p. 24.

4. For further discussion of owls as "inauspicious" omens and agents of the netherworld in Han and later art, see Eugene Wang, "The Winking Owl: Visual Effect and Its Art Historical Thick Description," *Critical Inquiry*, vol. 26 (Spring 2000), p. 444, n. 22; Liu Dunyuan, "Mawangdui Xihan bohua zhong de ruogan shenhua wenti" ("Some mythological issues in the Western Han silk painting from Mawangdui"), in *Mawangdui Hanmu yanjiu* (*Studies on the Han tomb at Mawangdui*) (Changsha: Hunan renmin chubanshe, 1979), pp. 281–91; Ellen Laing, *The Winking Owl: Art in the People's Republic of China* (Berkeley and Los Angeles: University of California Press: 1988), p. 86.

5. Roel Sterckx, *The Animal and the Daemon in Early China* (Albany: State University of New York Press, 2002), p. 228.

6. David R. Knechtges, trans. *Wen xuan, or Selections of Refined Literature*, vol. 3: *Rhapsodies on Natural Phenomena, Birds and Animals, Aspirations and Feelings, Sorrowful Laments, Literature, Music, and Passions* (Princeton: Princeton University Press, 1996), pp. 41–49.

7. *Yanzi chunqiu jishi* (Beijing: Zhonghua shuju, 1962), *juan* 6, pp. 375–76.

8. Sterckx, *Animal and Daemon*, p. 316, n. 90.

9. *Kaikodo Journal*, August 1996, pp. 154, 243, no. 70.

10. See Geng Baochang, *Zhongguo wenwu jinghua daquan: Taoci juan* (*The complete collection of China's cultural relics: Ceramics volume*) (Taipei and Hong Kong: Commercial Press, 1993), p. 89, no. 316; *Xi'an: Legacies of Ancient Chinese Civilization* (Beijing: Morning Glory Publishers, 1992), p. 146. Similar ceramic owls of unspecified provenance are published in Aileen Lau, ed., *Spirit of Han* (Singapore: Southeast Asian Ceramic Society: Sun Tree Pub., 1991), no. 29; Marie-Thérèse Bobot, "The Musée Cernuschi in Paris," *Orientations*, August 1992, p. 31, fig. 8. An owl is also depicted on a pictorial relief tile from a Han tomb in Zhengzhou. See Zhengzhou Municipal Museum, "Zhengzhou Xingtongqiao Handai huaxiang kongxin zhuan mu" ("The tomb with pictorial reliefs at Xingtongqiao, Zhengzhou"), *Wenwu* 1972.14, p. 48, fig. 14:11. Two amber-glazed owl-shaped jars with removable heads serving as lids were excavated in Henan (see Geng Baochang, *Zhongguo wenwu jinghua daquan: Taoci juan*, pp. 81–82, nos. 290, 291). These vessels, dating from the Han period, are possibly related to owl-shaped bronze lidded vessels dating from Shang and Western Zhou times. For examples from Shanxi, Hunan, and unspecified locations, see Alfred Salmony, "The Third Early Chinese Owl with Snake-Legs," *Artibus Asiae*, vol. 14 (1951), pp. 277–82; and *Kaikodo Journal*, Autumn 1996, pp. 110–12, 226, no. 49.

Fig. 1 *Owl perched on a tree over a grave mound*. Detail of Stone Chamber 2, Stone 2-S.7 (cat. no. 1.25). "Wu family shrines" rubbings. Princeton University Art Museum, acc. no. 2002.307.25.

Fig. 2 *Owl on a roof eaves*. Detail of *He kui* stone (cat. no. 1.49). "Wu family shrines" rubbings. Princeton University Art Museum, acc. no. 2002.307.43.

58 Money box with owl-form handle

Eastern Han dynasty. Gray ceramic with bosses and coin designs; h. 16.2 cm, l. 34.7 cm, w. 23.9 cm.
Princeton University Art Museum, acc. no. 2001-32a–b. Museum purchase with funds given by James J. Freeman, Class of 1965.

Centered on the flat cover of this oblong box is a protruding handle in the form of an owl. The cover rests on a small ledge sunk just below the broad lip of the box.[1] Around the rim of the box and around the perimeter of the cover six small bosses alternate with six replicas of coins. Stamped on each of the coins, which are circular with a square hole in the middle, is the number five in Chinese, indicating that these represent *wuzhu*, or five-*zhu* coins. The *zhu* was the smallest unit of weight used in the Han, and coins weighing five *zhu* (3.25 grams) were first made during the reign of Wudi (r. 140–87 BCE). These coins proved very popular, remaining in circulation for over seven hundred years, longer than any coin minted after the Han.

Possibly this box replicates the tomb owner's real money box, and was placed in the grave filled with real or clay replica coins or some of each, to attest to the deceased's status in life and to advance his anticipated status in the afterlife. The custom of placing coins in tombs became increasingly fashionable by Eastern Han. Even in tombs filled with other valuables, coins might also be included, perhaps to symbolize the deceased's desire for continued wealth in the afterlife or to indicate that houses of the rich typically contained cash as well as luxuries. To date, no other rectangular ceramic money boxes with owl-shaped handles have been excavated from tombs, though a few other types have been unearthed; one round money jar was found in a Western Han tomb in Luoyang.[2] Some containers may have been made of organic materials—basketry, fabric, or wood—which disintegrated, leaving piles of coins on the tomb floor. In the back chambers of the tomb at Leitai, near Wuwei, that dates from late Eastern Han, more than twenty thousand coins, mostly of the *wuzhu* type, were found, but no container survived.[3]

This connection between money and burial practices is also expressed in the Han money tree (see cat. no. 59), known in Chinese as a *qianzhu*, a money or coin pillar. Usually these trees had a ceramic or bronze base that supported a bronze or ceramic tree, with coins, often the *wuzhu* type, and occasionally circles resembling *bi* disks, embedded in the branches. Bronze branches were cast individually, in a process similar to the casting of ordinary coins (see cat. nos. 60–63).[4] Lacking textual references, the iconography of these money trees, specialties of Sichuan, is not fully understood; however, the emphasis on simulated coins like those on the money box probably reflects a wish for prosperity in the next world.[5] A variety of fantastic creatures often were perched on the branches along with the rows of coins, strongly suggesting an apotropaic, or protective, function for these trees as well.

An intriguing aspect of this money box is the handle in the form of an owl standing in the center of the lid. The body is a simplified semiabstract shape; two circles, each with a center boss, make the eyes; a ridge forms the beak. The lower part of the body merges into the clay of the lid. Owl images date from China's early antiquity, as the actual forms or the decoration of Shang-dynasty ritual bronze vessels.[6] On the famous silk banner found in Tomb 1 (ca. 168 BCE) at Mawangdui, Changsha, Hunan, two owls standing on the backs of turtles flank the platform in the lowest section (fig. 1).[7] Textual references are few and inconclusive: owls appear sometimes to be guardians, sometimes, as in many cultures, omens of death or mischance. A Han *fu* from

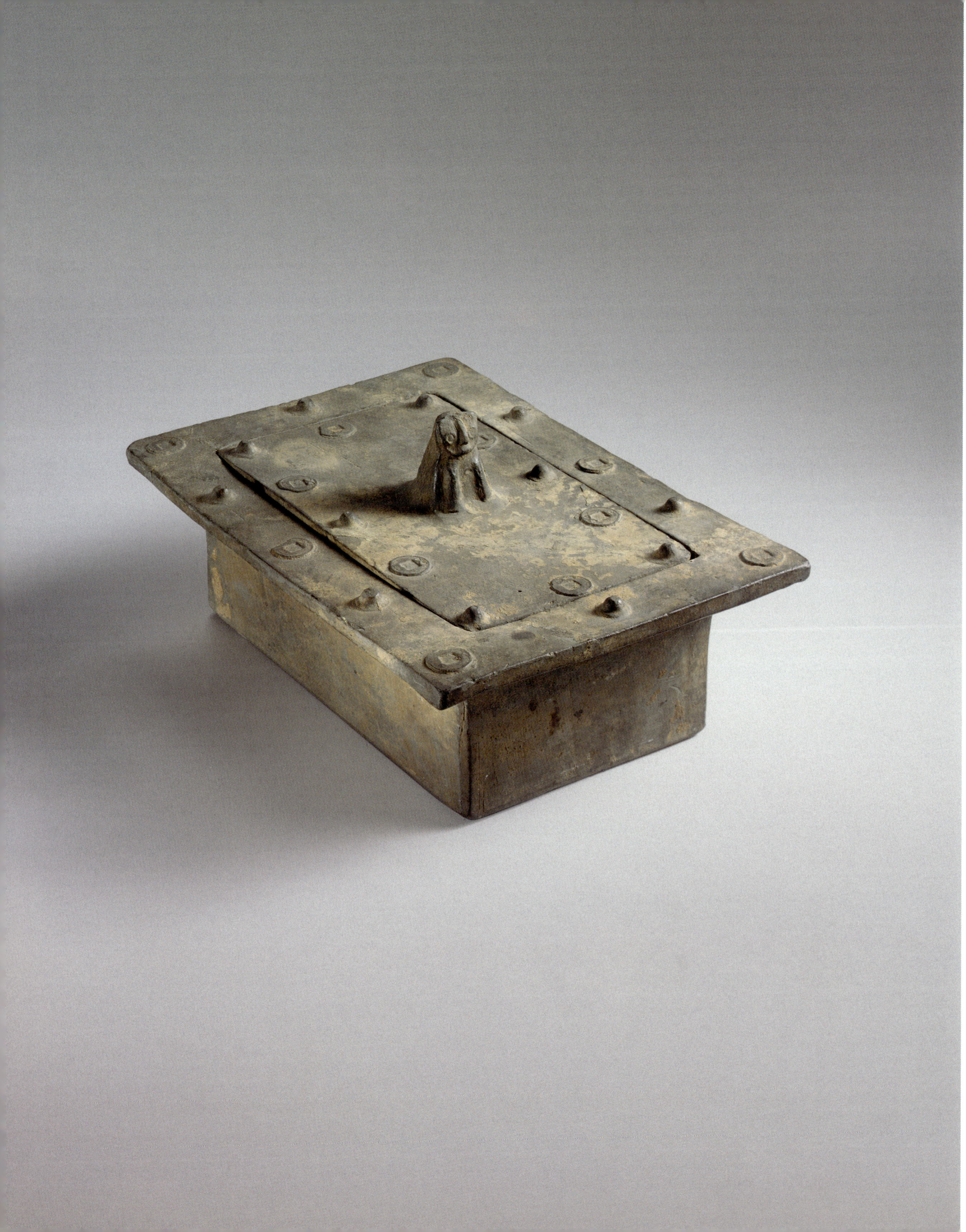

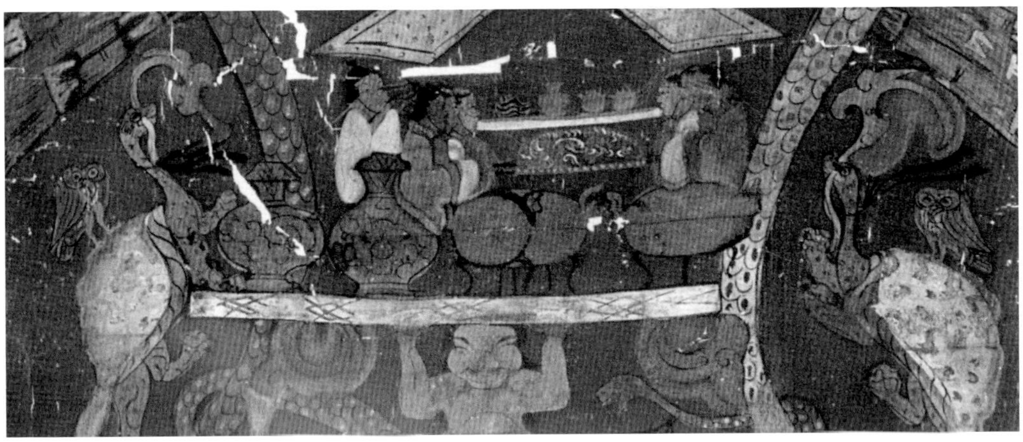

the second century BCE confirms their association with death.[8] Perhaps that association made the owl a suitable motif for objects meant for the tomb (cat. no. 57) and for Shang ritual vessels intended to hold feasts for the dead. The connection between the owl and money remains unclear.

Actual *wuzhu* coins were recovered in Tomb 1 associated with the Wu shrines and are said to have been found on Stone 10 of the Left Group (L.10), which is no longer extant. Molds for coins of this type and a money tree appear in this exhibition (cat. nos. 59, 61–63).

ANNETTE L. JULIANO

Fig. 1 *Detail of lower section of silk banner*. Western Han dynasty, ca. 168 BCE. Tomb 1, Mawangdui, Changsha, Hunan. Painted silk; overall l. 2.05 m. From *Hunan Sheng bowuguan* and *Zhongguo shehui kexueyuan kaogu yanjiusuo*, eds. *Changsha Mawangdui yihao mu* (Beijing: Wenwu chubanshe, 1973), vol. 2, pl. 77.

Notes

1. This box was published by Candace J. Lewis, *Into the Afterlife: Han and Six Dynasties Chinese Tomb Sculpture from the Schloss Collection* (Poughkeepsie: Vassar College Art Gallery, 1990), p. 38, no. 6.
2. Wang Zhongshu, *Han Civilization*, trans. K.C. Chang and collaborators (New Haven and London: Yale University Press, 1982), fig. 202.
3. *Kaogu xuebao* 1974.2, pp. 104–5; over 3,000 coins were found in large piles in the center of tomb chambers in the cliff tombs at Tujing, Zhong County, Sichuan; see *Wenwu* 1985.7, pp. 52 (M7), 57 (M5), 79–81.
4. The resemblance between the casting of ordinary coins and money tree branches was observed by Zhu Zhuopeng and Ma Chuande, *Qianbi manhua* (*Discussion of coins*) (Shanghai: Shanghai jiaoyu chubanshe, 1989), pp. 413–14.
5. See Susan N. Erickson, "Money Trees of the Eastern Han Dynasty," *Bulletin of the Museum of Far Eastern Antiquities*, no. 66 (1994), pp. 5–115, for a discussion of the iconography and geographic distribution of the money trees.
6. See Robert W. Bagley, *Shang Ritual Bronze Vessels in the Arthur M. Sackler Collections* (Washington, D.C., and Cambridge, Mass: The Arthur M. Sackler Museum, Harvard University, 1987), pp. 361–71.
7. See Michael Loewe, *Ways to Paradise: The Chinese Quest for Immortality* (London and Boston: George Allen and Unwin, 1979), pp. 35–36; and *Treasures from the Han* (Singapore: Landmark Books, 1990), p. 68. Also, one of the six pieces used to play the board game *liubo* is referred to as an owl (*xiao*); through the Han dynasty this game board was also used for divination; see Zhang Yan'e, "Preliminary Remarks on the Games of *Liubo* and *Saixi*," *China Archaeology and Art Digest*, vol. 4, no. 4 (April–May, 2002), p. 86.
8. Sarah Allan, *The Shape of the Turtle: Myth, Art, and Cosmos in Early China* (New York: State University of New York Press, 1991), p.166, describes the Han *fu* "Fu Niao fu," by Jia Yi (d. 168 BCE): "The poet consults an oracle book about the meaning of an owl flying into his house, to be told that this omen means that the master will soon leave (that is, die)."

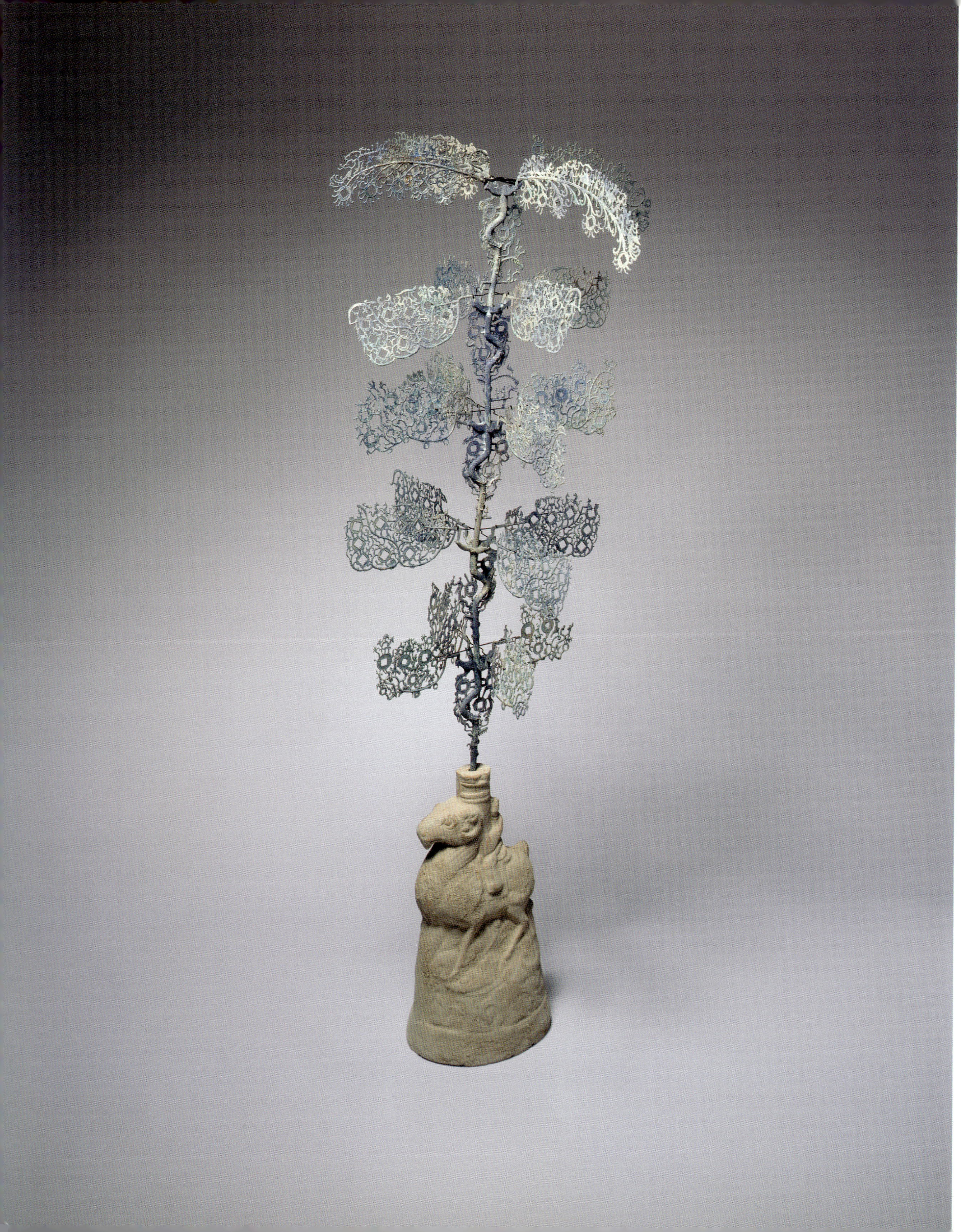

59 Money tree

Eastern Han dynasty. Bronze with earthenware base; h. approx. 135 cm with finial.
Princeton University Art Museum, acc. no. 1999-79. Museum purchase, Fowler McCormick, Class of 1921, Fund.

In modern Chinese archaeological reports this object is called *qianshu*, or money tree, because it has *wuzhu* coins hanging from what appear to be the limbs of a tree.[1] This artifact is not mentioned in any Han-dynasty text, so its original name and function are unknown; since it always is found in the context of the tomb, however, it clearly is a mortuary object. The form of the art work, a bronze tree held upright in a pottery or stone base, is unique to a specific area of China. Published excavation reports indicate that the production of money trees was centered in Sichuan, but a few examples have been found along the borders of the neighboring provinces of Yunnan, Guizhou, Hubei, Shaanxi, Gansu, and Qinghai.[2] All money trees date from the Eastern Han dynasty or the immediate post-Han period.

Money trees first were published in Western sources during the 1930s by scholars like David C. Graham, curator of the West China Union University Museum of Archaeology, Art, and Ethnology in Chengdu, Sichuan, from 1932 to 1941.[3] Graham illustrated an article about Han-dynasty mortuary art in the *Journal of the West China Border Research Society* with fragments of bronze branches that were removed from cliff tombs in the area around Chengdu, but he probably never saw an intact tree. In fact, in other articles about tomb art in Sichuan, he illustrated bases for money trees but called them simply sculpture.[4] A money tree was first displayed in the United States in an exhibition of Han-dynasty art from Sichuan Province organized by Lucy Lim in 1987 for the Chinese Culture Center of San Francisco.[5] That tree, one of only a handful of complete trees, was unearthed in 1983 in Guanghan County.[6] In most cases only the base, made of more durable earthenware or stone, and a few fragments of the bronze tree remain.

Despite the rarity of intact trees, or even well-preserved branches, the impressive size of the original object and the array of motifs that decorate the limbs of the trees make money trees significant in the study of Eastern Han-dynasty art. Although the form of this object is unique, its iconography can be related to works of art found in other areas of China. In general, the imagery from money trees can be interpreted as having particularly auspicious meaning within the context of the tomb.[7] Guardians of the cardinal directions—the White Tiger of the West, the Azure Dragon of the East, and the Red Bird of the South—are included amid other images that more closely relate to the aspiration for immortality. The Queen Mother of the West, Xiwangmu, and also Immortals and composite creatures seen in her company are represented. Reference is made to the mountain residence of Xiwangmu by the inclusion of roaming animals and hunters and by the towering form of the entire structure.

The present money tree's base, in the shape of a ram, is an auspicious image. The Chinese character for ram, *yang*, is part of the character *xiang*, which means "auspicious."[8] Figures of rams or even just a ram's head are frequently seen in Han-dynasty tombs. On the present base a figure is mounted on the ram, indicating that the animal also functions as a vehicle. This figure is not very clearly rendered, but riders on other ram-shaped bases hold a *lingzhi*, a plant that is associated with immortality.[9] It is likely, then, that this figure is a traveling Immortal. Amorphous decor that may represent clouds fills the space between the ram's legs, and the lower edge of one side of the base has a decorative border of arabesques. A bivalve mold was used to form the earthenware base, and the

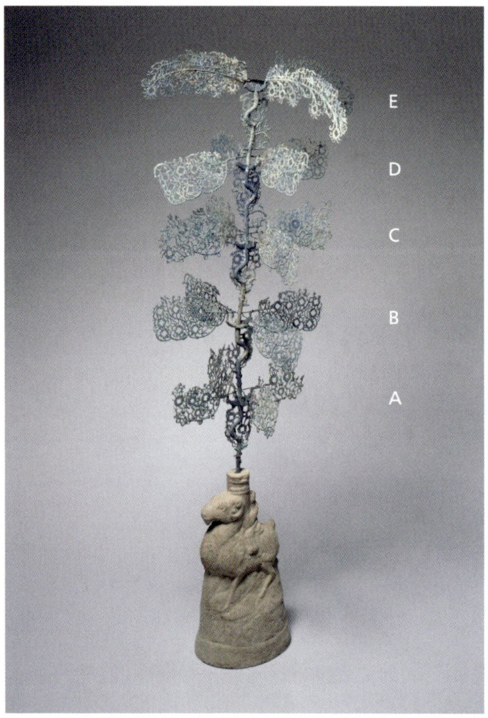

area of the join is visible from a frontal view. The cylinder between the rider and the ram's head is purely structural, acting as a collar to receive the trunk of the tree.

The superstructure of the tree, including the trunk and branches, is of cast bronze. As with a number of unearthed trees, the branches are of two basic types. The first is seen in the uppermost tier, where nearly straight limbs bow gently downward at their tips (see Lullo's "Regional Iconographies," fig. 4). Figures move along the length of the branches, and curvilinear forms hang from the bottom of the limb like foliage. Rayed coins depend from this hanging foliage and from the tips of the boughs. On the upper surface of these uppermost branches is the court of Xiwangmu, the Queen Mother of the West, who is situated approximately midway along the limbs. Xiwangmu is identifiable by her dragon-and-tiger throne, and by her *sheng* headdress, distinguishable despite its small size. She is represented *en face*, framed by the canopy of her throne. To either side of the Queen stand thin Immortals with large ears and wings, one of them riding an animal. Also on the branch are entertainers, including sleeve dancers, jugglers, and acrobats. At the tips of the branches, a bird spreads its wings and displays its tail feathers. These branches are comparable with limbs from a money tree unearthed in Pengshan County, Sichuan.[10]

In all other tiers the branches are of the second general type—a curved primary limb that divides into smaller branchlets. In his investigation of the present money tree, Thomas Chase observed that all of the branches of this second type could very likely have been cast from two sets of molds. That is, the branches of tiers A and C were cast from one set, and those from tiers B and D from another (labeling the branches from bottom to top). Minor differences are a result of repairing missing sections with loose fragments.[11] The undulating branchlets and twigs form an irregular grid within which coins of various sizes are suspended; they also create cells where figures and animals are situated. At the top center of each branch is the most prominent motif—the Queen Mother of the West seated on her canopied dragon-and-tiger throne. In the cells around her are performers, Immortals, and creatures, including a striking image of two rampant animals that might be either deer or horses.[12] These branches are comparable with limbs from trees unearthed in Guanghan County (tiers A and C) and Pengshan County (tiers B and D) in Sichuan.[13] One divergent attribute of branches in tiers B and D is the horizontal bars that connect sections in the upper part of each limb.

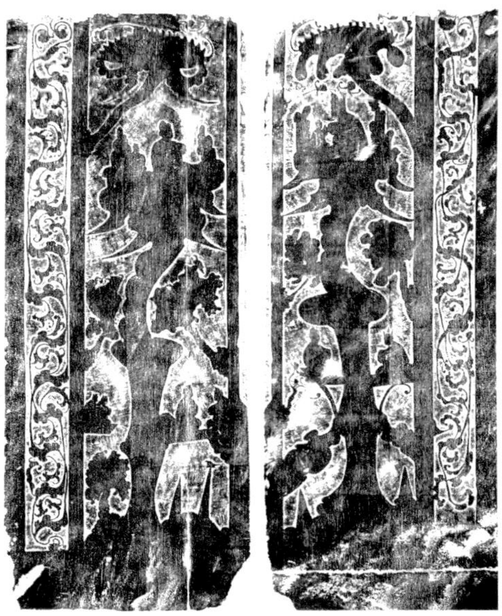

Fig. 1 *Vertical stone slabs*. From interior of tomb at Huangjiata, Shaanxi. From Suide Han huaxiang shi zhanlanguan, Li Guilong, and Wang Jianqin, *Suide Handai huaxiang shi*, pl. 80.

The finial of the tree (not illustrated) was created from loose fragments of branches by a modern artisan. Primary motifs include a figure standing above a large blossom, flanked by two birds with outstretched wings. One bird has a markedly more substantial body, with large scale-like feathers and a short bill. The smaller bird has a long bill in which it holds a large pearl. Both have plumes with eye-like spots usually seen on peacock feathers, and both probably are images of the Red Bird of the South. In this modern assemblage a branch was converted into the central trunk of the finial. The coins on one side were meant to hang from the branch, and a dragon and tiger to either side of a *bi* disk should have moved along the upper edge. Although most of the tiger's body has been lost, the same composition of motifs can be seen on a number of stone reliefs from Sichuan.[14] The figure positioned at the top of the finial resembles an ape but has stripes on one side of its body. This figure has not been identified, but he is one of many such strange creatures seen in the company of Xiwangmu and often inhabiting the limbs of unearthed money trees.[15]

The element of the present tree that appears to be unique among all known examples of money trees is the structure of the trunk. Whereas excavated examples are straight, each section of this trunk has a regular curve. In the hollow of each curve is a coin, and the guardians of the east and west, the dragon and the tiger, stand respectively on the coin and along the convex side of the curve. Other motifs positioned along the trunk include such animals as a nine-tailed fox and figures mounted on dragons.[16]

The structure of the money tree, with branches pointed in the cardinal directions and arranged in regular tiers, encourages a reading of this image as an *axis mundi*. The "beanstalk-like" appearance of the object is related to contemporary interest in finding a mode of ascent to the paradise of Xiwangmu or, more generally, to heaven. Although the original finial of the tree has been lost, the repetition of images of the Queen Mother of the West on all of the branches of the present tree emphasizes her importance during this period, particularly as she is the keeper of the elixir of immortality. Her home high on Mt. Kunlun is reflected in the design of the tree. Related images from other regions of China establish the persistence of this concept. For example, in northern Shaanxi Province, vertical stones from an Eastern Han tomb are decorated with images of the Queen Mother of the West and also the King Father of the East (Dongwanggong), who are seated at the top of undulating structures that resemble the trunk of the present tree (fig. 1).[17] An Eastern Han tomb at Luoyang in Henan Province included an earthenware lamp that features a central trunk with radiating branches populated by Immortals and birds (fig. 2).[18] The lamp is 92 centimeters high, and on its mountain-shaped base are Immortals and animals. Large cicadas, associated with death and transformation (because they enter death-like hibernation as pupae and emerge as adults), also are included among these creatures.

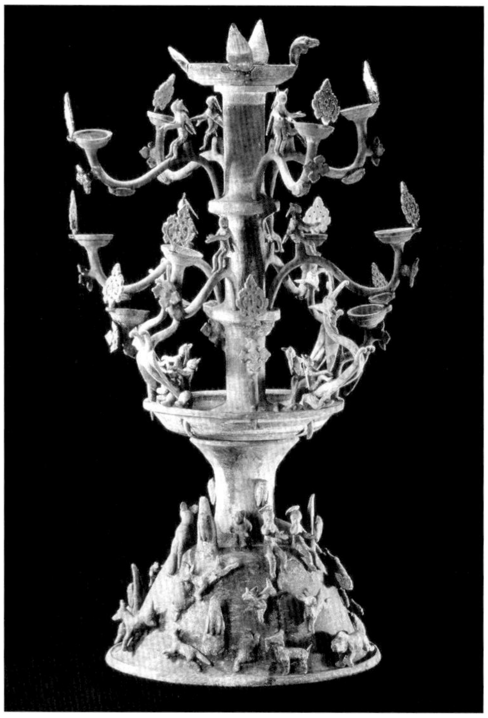

Fig. 2 *Painted earthenware lamp*. Qilihe, Luoyang, Henan. From *Luoyang wenwu jingcui* (*Treasures from Luoyang*) (Zhengzhou: Henan meishu chubanshe, 2001), p. 141, pl. 10.

Although all known money trees are similar in design, only those from the area centered on present-day Sichuan have coins hanging from the boughs, with the money motif reinforced on some bases by depictions of people gathering large coins from the limbs.[19] The presence of coins on money trees relates to the importance of coinage in daily life. During the Eastern Han dynasty strings of cash were a medium of exchange and also a way of storing one's wealth.[20] In furnishing tombs for the afterlife, sometimes real coins were deposited, but imitation coins or representations of coins on a variety of tomb wares, including wall reliefs, might be supplied instead. For a fortunate afterlife, ready cash was apparently essential.

SUSAN N. ERICKSON

Notes

1. It also is called *yaoqianshu*, with *yao* meaning "to shake," because in more recent times it was a rite of the New Year to hang coins on pine or cypress branches as an invocation of prosperity in the coming year. See a description of the activity by Dun Lichen (1855–1911) in *Yanjing suishiji* (*Annual customs and festivals in Yanjing*), trans. Derk Bodde, in *Annual Customs and Festivals in Peking* (1936; reprint, Hong Kong: Hong Kong University Press, 1987), p. 103.

2. See Susan N. Erickson, "Money Trees of the Eastern Han Dynasty," *Bulletin of the Museum of Far Eastern Antiquities*, vol. 66 (1994), pp. 5–115; see chart and map on pp. 38–41. For the 1994 discovery of money

tree fragments in the northwest corner of Hubei, see Hubei Sheng wenwu kaogu yanjiusuo, "Nanshui beidiao gongcheng Danjiangkou shuiku Yunxian Yanmoqu kaogu diaocha" ("Archaeological investigation of the sinking zone at Yun County in Danjiangkou Reservoir conducted during the engineering project to move water from south to north"), *Jianghan kaogu* 1996.2, pp. 20–33, figs. 6.3–6. The trunk of this tree features images that sometimes are identified as the Buddha.

3. David C. Graham, "Persistence of Custom as Illustrated in the Collection of Han Dynasty Clay Images in the West China Union University Museum," *Journal of the West China Border Research Society*, vol. 6 (1933–1934), pp. 104–14, see esp. p. 114.

4. See the following articles by David C. Graham: "Notes on the Han Dynasty Grave Collection in the West China Union University Museum of Archaeology," *Journal of the West China Border Research Society*, vol. 9 (1937), pp. 213–15, see plate entitled "Stone mountain"; "Archaeology in West China," *China Journal*, vol. 26, no. 4 (April 1937), pp.172–74, see plate entitled "A Han Dynasty Tomb Figure showing Horse and Rider above and Elephants below"; "The Ancient Caves of Szechwan Province, China," *Proceedings of the United States National Museum*, vol. 80 (1932), pp. 1–13, see pl. 2, where the lower section of a base is identified as part of a bell, and the rider clinging to the collar of the base (like the figure on the present base) is identified as part of a clay bottle.

5. Lucy Lim, ed., *Stories from China's Past: Han Dynasty Pictorial Tomb Reliefs and Archaeological Objects from Sichuan Province, People's Republic of China* (San Francisco: The Chinese Culture Foundation of San Francisco, 1987). The exhibition was shown at seven venues. For reviews of the exhibition, see Ione Kramer, "Sichuan Tomb Art Tours U.S.," *China Reconstructs* (July 1987), pp. 54–57; Richard C. Rudolph, "Archaeology News: Stories from China's Past," *Archaeology*, vol. 40, no. 4 (July/August 1987), pp. 54–57. Rudolph commented, "What may be the strangest and most perplexing object to Western eyes, as well as to most Chinese, is the unique five-foot bronze *Money Tree* with intricate openwork designs of symbolic motifs."

6. The best-preserved examples of whole trees have been unearthed at Pengshan (1972), Guanghan (two in 1983), Santai (1985), and Mianyang (1989–90)—all located within a radius of about 100 kilometers from Chengdu in Sichuan Province. For a description of these finds, see Shi Zhanyang, "Sichuan gudai yaoqianshu ji qi yiban xing wenhua neihan" ("General characteristics and cultural connotations of ancient money trees in Sichuan"), *Sichuan wenwu* 1999.6, pp. 26–31. Recently another money tree believed to have been stolen from a tomb in Mianyang County has been published. It was confiscated by authorities in An County in 2000. Images on its trunk and finial have been identified as the Buddha. See He Zhiguo, Liu Youxin, and Xie Minggang, "Sichuan An Xian wenguansuo shoucang de Donghan foxiang yaoqianshu" ("An Eastern Han money tree with Buddha images collected by the Office of Culture in An County, Sichuan"), *Wenwu* 2002.6, pp. 63–67. A number of money trees have been acquired by Western museums, but some include modern-made parts fabricated to complete the damaged tree, such as the finial on a tree owned by the Detroit Institute of Arts. Others include parts that are pastiches of ancient fragments joined to create a "new" finial, as with the present tree. Several technical studies concerning corrosion on the bronze branches of the Detroit Institute of Arts tree have been published; see Karen Trentelman, Leon Stodulski, Ray Lints, and Chongmin Kim, "A Comparative Study of the Composition and Corrosion of Branches from Eastern Han Dynasty Money Trees," *Studies in Conservation*, vol. 44 (1999), pp. 170–83; and Lowell I. McCann, K. Trentelman, T. Possley, and B. Golding, "Corrosion of Ancient Bronze Money Trees Studied by Raman Microscopy," *Journal of Raman Spectroscopy*, vol. 30 (1999), pp. 121–32.

7. Stanley Abe has suggested a similar interpretation of some motifs in rock-cut tombs in Sichuan. See his *Ordinary Images* (Chicago: University of Chicago Press, 2002), chap. 2. Also see my forthcoming article, "Eastern Han Dynasty Cliff Tombs of Santai Xian, Sichuan Province," in *The Journal of East Asian Archaeology*, vol. 5, nos. 1–4 (2003; forthcoming).

8. Xu Shen (ca. 55–ca. 149 CE), the compiler of the *Shuowen jiezi* (ca. 100 CE), equates *yang* and *xiang*: "*yang xiang ye*." See *Shuowen jiezi*, *juan* 4.

9. The figure on the ram most closely resembles one on a base unearthed in Neijiang County in Sichuan. See Xunbing (pseud.), *Sichuan Handai diaosu yishu* (*The art of Han-dynasty sculpture in Sichuan*) (Beijing: Zhongguo gudian yishu chubanshe, 1959), pl. 44 (h. 41 cm). For a base with a figure holding a *lingzhi*, see Nanjing bowuguan, *Sichuan Pengshan Handai yamu* (*Han-dynasty cliff tombs of Pengshan, Sichuan*) (Beijing: Wenwu chubanshe, 1991), fig. 45.

10. See Roger Goepper, ed., *Das Alte China: Menschen und Götter im Reich der Mitte 5000 v. Chr.–220 n. Chr.* (München: Hirmer Verlag, 1996), fig. 86.2.

11. Many of these repairs are made obvious by motifs out of place, like an image of the enthroned Queen Mother of the West hanging from a limb rather than aligned along its upper surface.

12. This motif has been found on several unearthed examples, for instance, trees at Pengshan and Santai counties in Sichuan. For the Pengshan branch, see Goepper, *Das Alte China*, fig. 86.3. For the Santai branch, see Jing Zhuyou, "Sichuan Santai chutu Donghan qianshu" ("Eastern Han money tree unearthed at Santai, Sichuan"), *Wenwu* 2002.1, pp. 84–86, fig. 7. Other branches from the Santai tree have copulating horses in the same place on the branch, suggesting fertility (see fig. 8).

13. For the Guanghan branch, see Lim, *Stories from China's Past*, detail of pl. 58; and for the Pengshan branch, see Goepper, *Das Alte China*, fig. 86.3.

14. See Gong Tingwan, Gong Yu, and Dai Jialing, eds., *Ba Shu Handai huaxiang ji* (*Selection of pictorial tiles and stones of the Han dynasty from Sichuan*) (Beijing: Wenwu chubanshe, 1998), pl. 287, a stone carving from Hejiang.

15. For examples, see Mianyang bowuguan and He Zhiguo, "Sichuan Mianyang Hejiashan erhao Donghan yamu qingli jianbao" ("A brief report about Eastern Han Tomb 2 at Hejiashan, Mianyang County, Sichuan"), *Wenwu* 1991.3, pp. 9–19, pl. 4.4; Yunnan Sheng wenwu gongzuodui, "Yunnan Zhaotong Guijiayuanzi Donghan mu fajue" ("Excavation of an Eastern Han tomb at Guijiayuanzi, Zhaotong, Yunnan"), *Kaogu* 1962.8, pp. 395–99, fig. 6.5.

16. The style of the figures on the sides of the trunk seem closest to fragments unearthed in Xichang County in southern Sichuan. See Liangshan Zhou bowuguan, "Sichuan Liangshan Xichang faxian Donghan, Shu Han mu" ("Discovery of Eastern Han and Shu Han tombs at Liangshan, Xichang County, Sichuan"), *Kaogu* 1990.5, pp. 419–28, figs. 8.3–5.

17. See Suide Han huaxiang shi zhanlanguan, Li Guilong, and Wang Jianqin, *Suide Handai huaxiang shi* (*Pictorial stones of the Han dynasty from Suide*) (Xi'an: Shaanxi renmin meishu chubanshe, 2001), pl. 80 (left slab: 124 × 50 cm; right slab: 124 × 52 cm).

18. See Luoyang bowuguan, "Luoyang jianxi Qilihe Donghan mu fajue jianbao" ("Report on the excavation of an Eastern Han tomb at Qilihe, Luoyang"), *Kaogu* 1975.2, pp. 116–23, 134, pl. 9.

19. See Santai Xian wenhuaguan, "Sichuan Santai Xian faxian Donghan mu" ("Discovery of an Eastern Han tomb in Santai County, Sichuan"), *Kaogu* 1976.6, p. 395, pl. 1.5-6; Nanjing bowuguan, *Sichuan Pengshan Handai yamu*, pls. 5–6.

20. See Patricia Ebrey, "The Economic and Social History of the Later Han," in *The Cambridge History of China*, vol. 1: *The Ch'in and Han Empires 221 B.C.–A.D. 220*, ed. Denis Twitchett and Michael Loewe (Cambridge: Cambridge University Press, 1986), p. 608ff. In the histories of the Han dynasty, the amount of cash one possessed was important enough to become part of a biography. See Sima Qian, *Shiji*, *juan* 129: "The Biographies of the Moneymakers" ("Huozhi liezhuan"), trans. Burton Watson, *Records of the Grand Historian: Han Dynasty II*, rev. ed. (New York: Columbia University Press, 1993), p. 433ff.

Coins and Coin Molds

During the Han period two different processes were used to cast coinage. Both are represented by the objects displayed in catalogue numbers 59–63. The older method, often called tree-casting by numismatists, was used in China to cast arrowheads as early as the Anyang period (ca. 1300–ca. 1100 BCE).[1] When various states began to mass-produce coinage for the growing cash economy of the Warring States period, tree-casting in stone or ceramic molds was the method of choice.[2] By the Han period tree-casting in government mints had developed into a complex, multi-stage process under tight state control.

First, a ceramic master mold was prepared, such as the one displayed in catalogue number

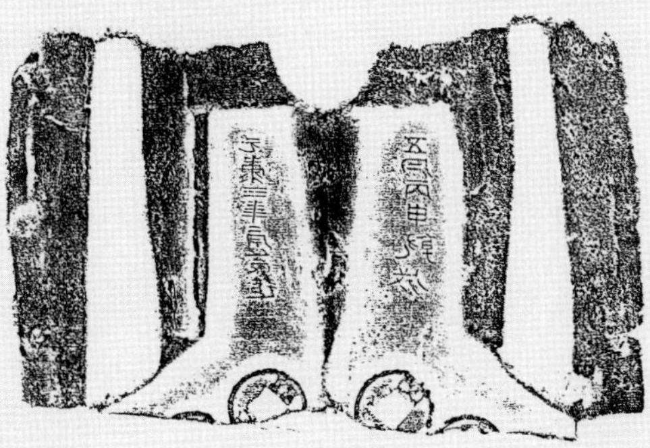

Fig. 1 *Master coin mold*. Western Han dynasty, dated to March 31, 63 BCE (begun)–June 20, 63 BCE (completed). Rubbing of terra-cotta fragment. Reportedly from the collection of Chen Jieqi. From Shaanxi Sheng qianbi xuehui, ed., *Qin Han qian fan*, p. 243, fig. 252.

62. Fashioned of a light, sandy clay, it carries raised-legend, relief models of coins, probably impressed into the clay with preliminary stamps that were themselves likely made by impressing actual coins into clay. A dated imperial mint inscription was stamped into the neck-like trench seen above the coin models. It reads:

Fabrication initiated on the [*yi*]*hai* day of the second month, during the third year of the Yuankang era [March 31, 63 BCE] (*Yuankang san nian er yue* [*yi*]*hai zao*).

At this stage of the process, the graphs in the mint inscription still appear raised and mirror-reversed. Around the text one can still faintly see a portion of the rectangular outline of a stamp block. Many molds like this one have been found near the site of the Western Han capital of Chang'an, including a slightly more complete example with the exact same fabrication date (fig. 1).[3] It is clear from this rubbing that the master mold in catalogue number 62 comprises only the upper left portion of a larger mold.

Master molds were used to make ceramic or metal secondary molds. When molten bronze was poured into the channel seen at the upper left of catalogue number 62, it would have produced a metal secondary mold, similar to that seen in catalogue number 61. In fact, the upper left portion of the mold in catalogue number 61 still retains a portion of the original casting sprue. This bronze mold could have been used to cast twelve *wuzhu* coins. An added feature on this mold is the two little images cast around the pouring spout. One clearly represents a tiger, probably the White Tiger of the West, an important directional symbol in Han cosmology. The other image is harder to discern, but might represent the Green Dragon of the East. According to recently unearthed evidence, metal molds like that in catalogue number 61 would have been backed with a disposable earthenware mold, which aided in gas absorption, and the two secured with iron clamps along the two brackets seen on the back of the secondary mold (see reverse of cat. no. 61 and fig. 2).[4] Molten bronze was then poured down the central column. When the mold was broken open, the result would be a "tree" of coins. Fragments from the spoiled casting of a tree of bronze coins can be seen in catalogue number 60. These coins are examples of the *daquan wushi* ("Great Coin Worth Fifty"), unsuccessfully circulated by the usurper Wang Mang during the period 7–20 CE. The coins would have been broken from the tree and the small flash of connecting metal filed down.

Stack-casting was the other method used to mass-produce coins during the Han. Invented during the late Warring States period and elaborated during the Han, it allowed for the efficient, modular production of hundreds or even thousands of coins in one casting operation.[5] The caster first made a metal master mold shaped somewhat like a shallow box. This was used to turn out hundreds of identical terra-cotta secondary molds, like those for late Eastern Han *wuzhu* coins seen in catalogue number 63. The terra-cotta molds carried intaglio, mirror-reversed coin impressions on one side, and nearly undecorated coin-back impressions on the other side. After firing, these square modules were stacked carefully into a tower that might grow to be several feet high. As molten bronze filled the column in the center of the stack, it would run into each layer through little trenches branching off from the main shaft, producing four coins per level. After cooling, the ceramic mold would then be broken and the coins separated from the column.

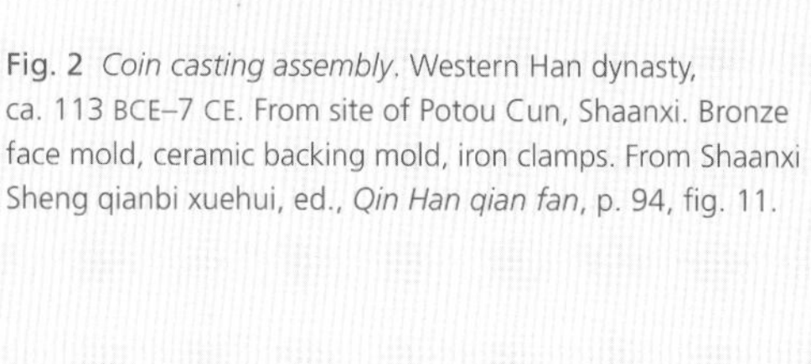

Fig. 2 *Coin casting assembly.* Western Han dynasty, ca. 113 BCE–7 CE. From site of Potou Cun, Shaanxi. Bronze face mold, ceramic backing mold, iron clamps. From Shaanxi Sheng qianbi xuehui, ed., *Qin Han qian fan*, p. 94, fig. 11.

Beginning about 118 BCE and for most of the remaining Han period, the *wuzhu* coin (weighing five *zhu*, 3.5 grams) was the principal denomination used in the empire. From the time of its introduction until 3 CE, the imperial mint cast over twenty-eight billion *wuzhu* coins, or more than six hundred thousand per day.[6] Among merchants, the coins were regularly strung into strands of one thousand units for ease of counting.

Much of the Han economy relied on the circulation of cash, and even peasants needed to acquire coins in order to pay capitation taxes. Coins were placed in burials to provide the deceased with financial resources and to help them pay taxes in the afterlife.[7] In some burials thousands of real coins would be placed in the tomb by mourners, occasionally in special coin boxes (cat. no. 58), but in others, clay imitations of coins were interred to provide for the deceased.[8]

Artisans often carved images of coins on the walls of tombs or offering halls as symbolic wealth for the afterlife, or possibly as an allusion to the process of ascending to "round" heaven from the "square" earth.[9] Some of the pictorial stones found at Songshan, Jiaxiang County, Shandong (cf. cat. no. 11) are adorned with a lattice pattern of *wuzhu* coins. A now missing stone found at the "Wu family shrines" site at Wuzhai Shan was apparently adorned with a similar lattice of ninety *wuzhu* coin images.[10] The unperforated circular motifs that adorn both *que* gate-pillars at the Wuzhai Shan site might represent *wuzhu* coins, or perhaps circular gold ingots. In the Han afterlife money apparently could literally grow on trees, as cast replicas of *wuzhu* coins appear all along the branches of "money trees" found in Sichuan tombs (cat. no. 59).

ANTHONY BARBIERI-LOW

Notes

1. For the terra-cotta arrowhead tree-casting molds found at the Anyang Miaopu beidi site, see Zhongguo shehui kexueyuan kaogu yanjiusuo, ed., *Yinxu fajue baogao 1958–1961* (*Report of the 1958–1961 excavations at the wastes of Yin*) (Beijing: Wenwu chubanshe, 1987), pl. 9.7–9.

2. For ceramic and stone tree-casting molds used to cast knife-shaped coins at the Yan capital, see Hebei Sheng wenwu yanjiusuo, ed., *Yan xiadu* (*Lower capital of the Yan state*) (Beijing: Wenwu chubanshe, 1996), vol. 2, pl. 56. For the increase in coin circulation during the Warring States period, see Yang Kuan, *Zhanguo shi* (*History of the Warring States period*), 3d ed. (Shanghai: Shanghai renmin chubanshe, 1998), pp. 131–43.

3. Shaanxi Sheng qianbi xuehui, ed., *Qin Han qian fan* (*Qin and Han coin molds*) (Xi'an: San-Qin chubanshe, 1992), fig. 252.

4. Shaanxi Sheng wenguanhui and Dengcheng Xian wenhuaguan zhihe fajuedui, eds., "Shaanxi Potou Cun Xihan zhuqian yizhi fajue jianbao" (Preliminary report of the excavation of the Western Han coin-casting site at Potou Village, Shaanxi Province), *Kaogu* 1982.1, pp. 23–30.

5. For a Western-language introduction to the technology of stack-casting, see Hua Jueming, "The Mass Production of Iron Castings in Ancient China," *Scientific American*, vol. 348, no. 1 (1983), pp. 120–28.

6. Nancy Lee Swann, *Food & Money in Ancient China* (Princeton: Princeton University Press, 1950), p. 324.

7. Poo Mu-chou, *In Search of Personal Welfare: A View of Ancient Chinese Religion* (Albany: State University of New York Press, 1998), pp. 170–75.

8. The tomb of Liu Sheng at Mancheng surrendered 40 gold ingots (worth 10,000 bronze coins each) and 2,316 *wuzhu* coins. See Zheng Shaozong, *Mancheng Han mu* (*Han tombs at Mancheng*) (Beijing: Wenwu chubanshe, 2003), p. 190. The well-looted tomb of the Three Kingdoms–period general Zhu Ran still contained 6,000 bronze coins (*Wenwu* 1986.3, p. 12). Mawangdui Tomb 1 contained tens of thousands of clay coins, in both Qin-Han *banliang* and traditional Chu square-ingot *yingcheng* denominations. The imitations of bronze coins were called *tuqian* ("dirt cash") in the tomb inventory; see Hunan Sheng bowuguan and Zhongguo shehui kexueyuan kaogu yanjiusuo, eds., *Changsha Mawangdui yihao Han mu* (*Han Tomb Number One at Mawangdui, near Changsha*) (Beijing: Wenwu chubanshe, 1973), vol. 1, p. 126, vol. 2, pls. 226–27, 254–55.

9. This hypothesis is developed in Klaas Ruitenbeek, *Chinese Shadows: Stone Reliefs, Rubbings, and Related Works of Art from the Han Dynasty* (*206 BC–AD 220*) *in the Royal Ontario Museum* (Toronto: Royal Ontario Museum, 2002), pp. 22–23.

10. This was the tenth stone of the Left Group (L.10). It disappeared during the Qing dynasty. See Jiang Yingju and Wu Wenqi, *Handai Wushi muqun shike yanjiu* (*Studies on the Han-dynasty stone carvings at the Wu family cemetery*) (Ji'nan: Shandong meishu chubanshe, 1995), pp. 26, 50 n. 3.

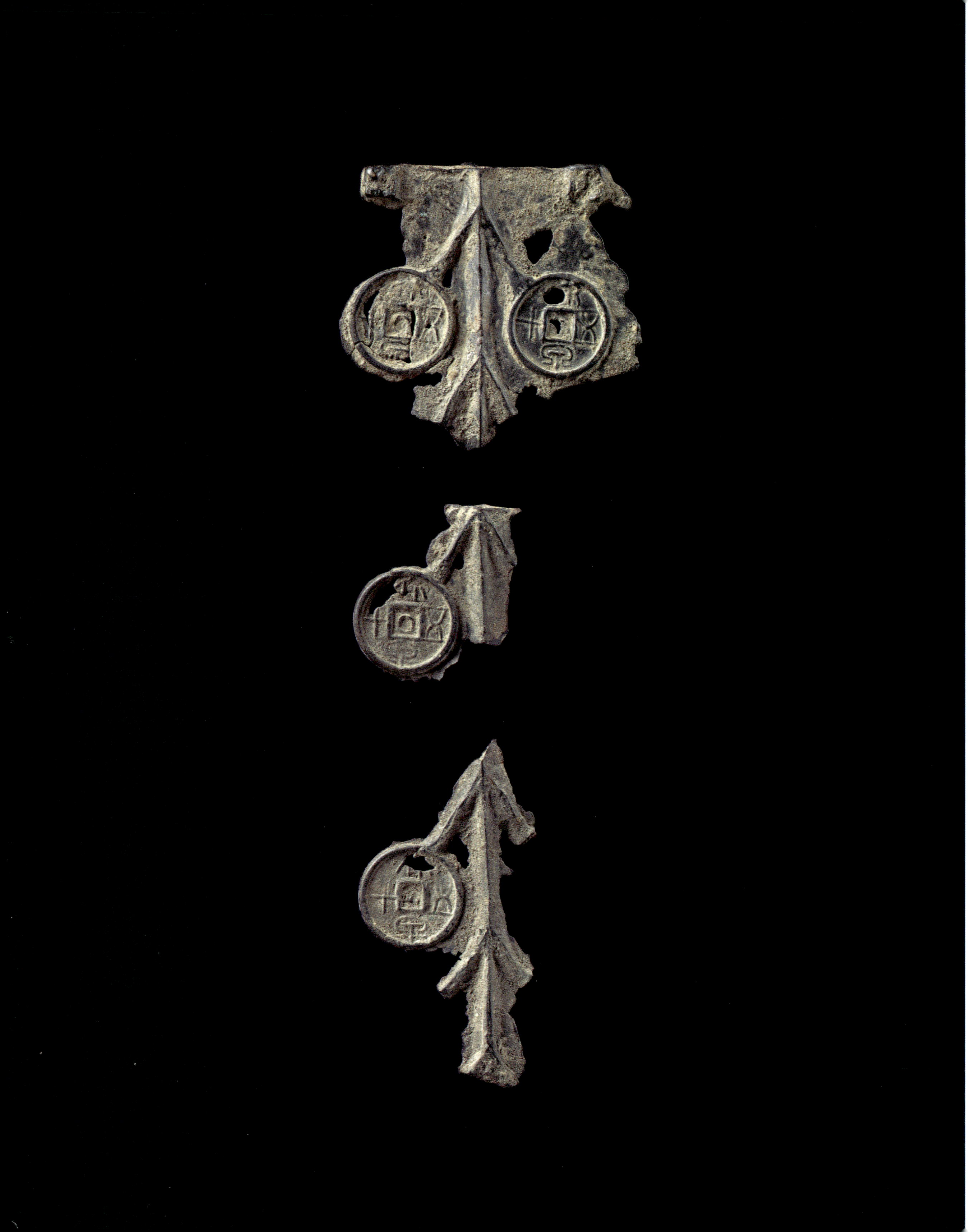

60 Three fragments of unfinished cast coins, of denomination Great Coin [worth] Fifty (*daquan wushi*)

Han dynasty. Bronze; sizes vary: l. 6–9.5 cm, w. 4.3–7.5 cm.
American Numismatic Society, New York, acc. nos. 1937.179.21218, 1937.179.22422, 1937.179.22691.

61 Secondary coin mold with designs of tiger and dragon

Western Han dynasty. Bronze; l. 22.5 cm, w. 8 cm.
American Numismatic Society, New York, acc. no. 1918.71.2.

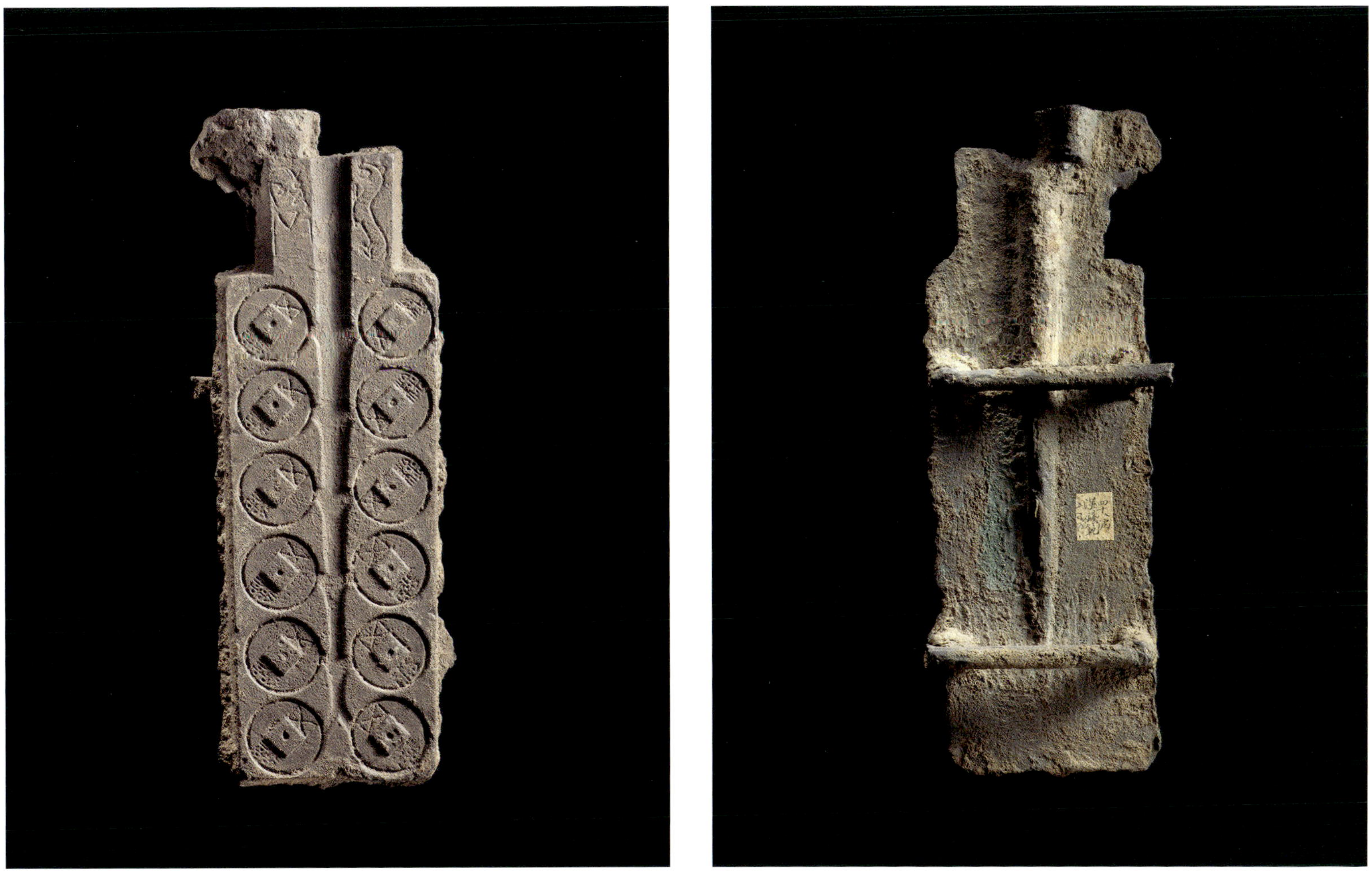

61

62 Fragment of master coin mold

Western Han dynasty, dated to March 31, 63 BCE. Ceramic; l. 15 cm, w. 10.5 cm. American Numismatic Society, New York, acc. no. 1937.179.23769.

63 Two stack-casting coin molds

Eastern Han dynasty, 186–189. Terra-cotta; each mold l. 6.7 cm, w. approx. 6.7 cm. American Numismatic Society, New York, acc. nos. 1941.7.1, 1941.7.2.

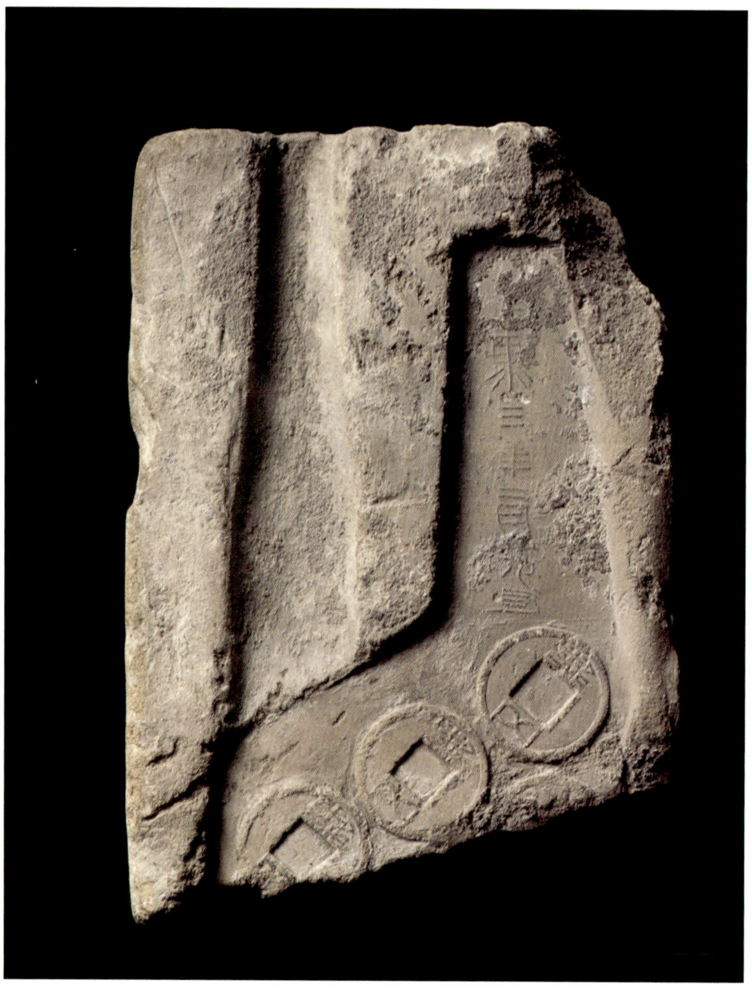

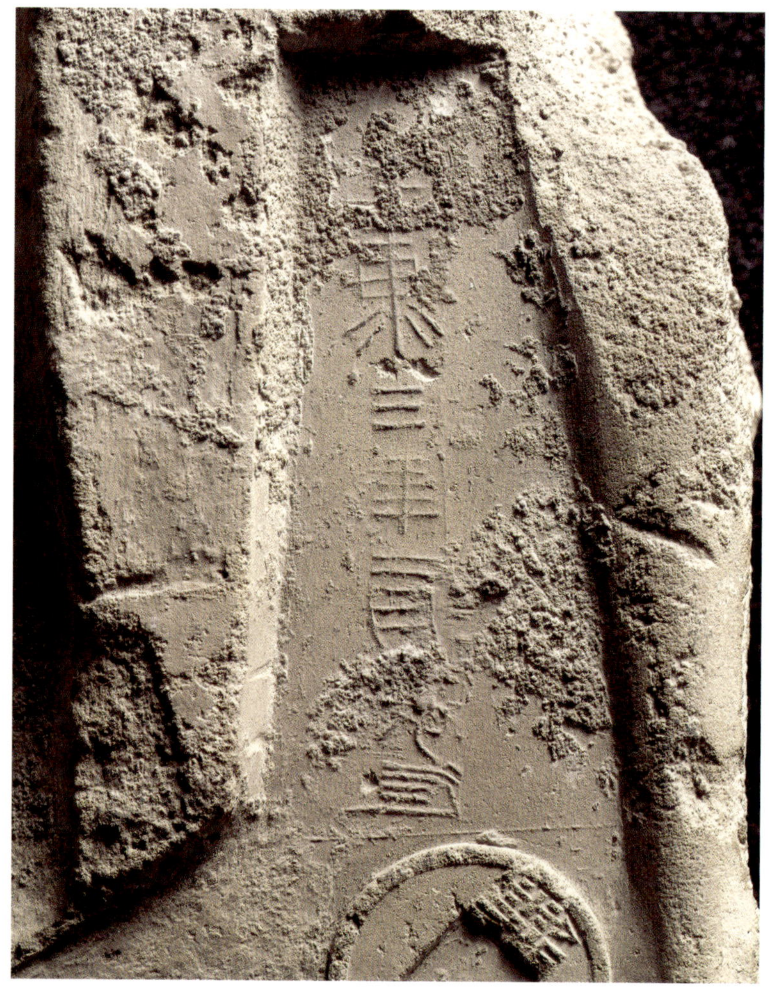

62

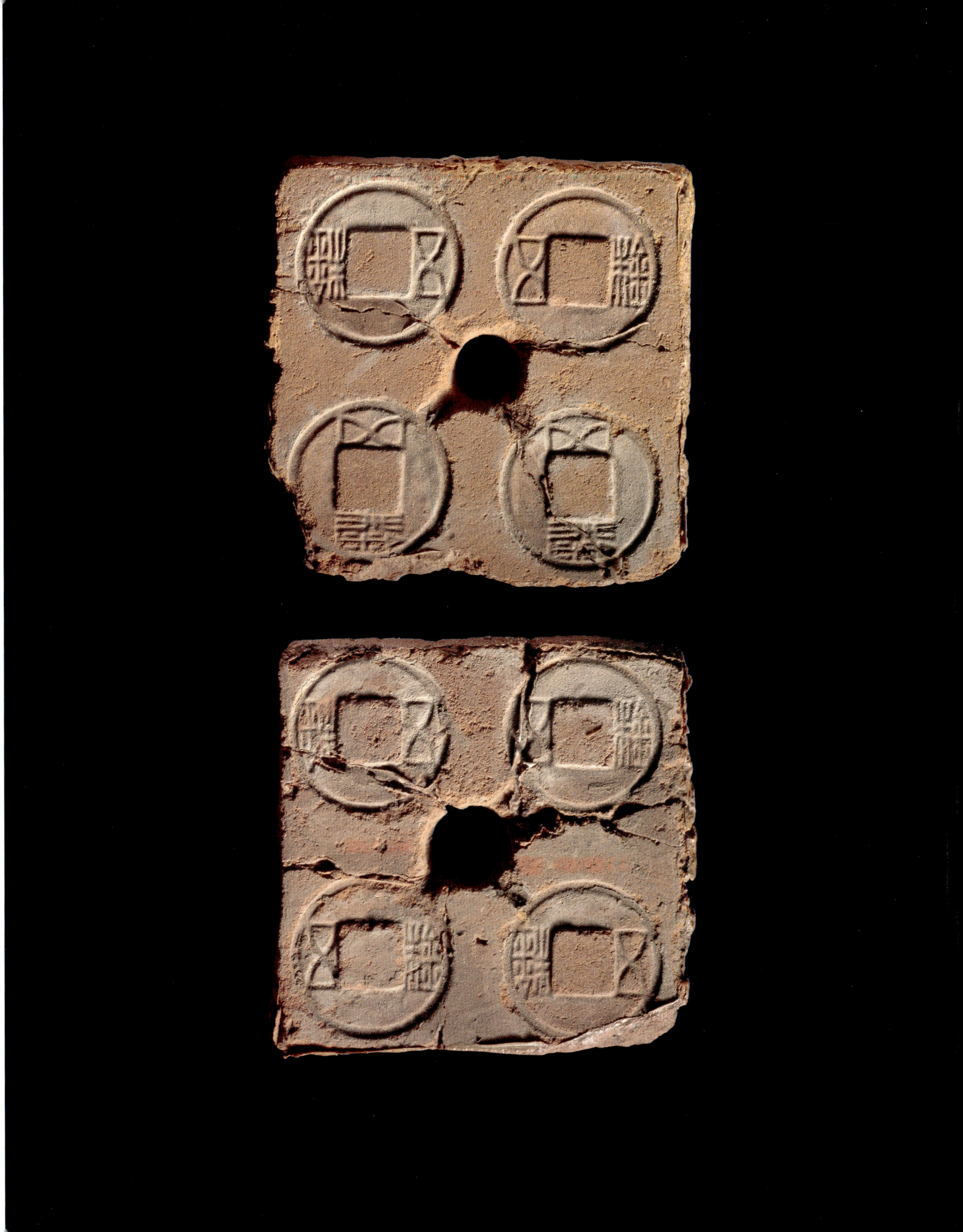

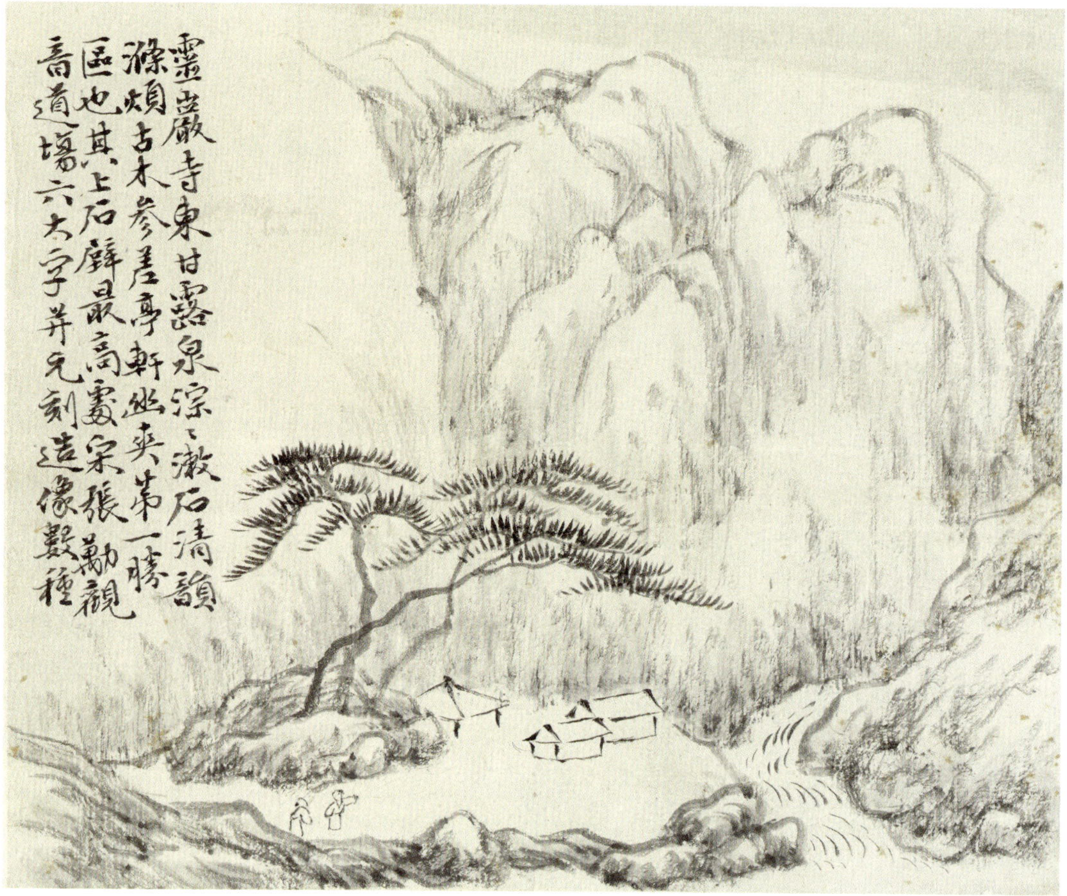
靈巖寺東甘露泉淙淙激石清韻
滌煩古木參差亭軒幽爽第一勝
區也其上石壁最高處宋張勸觀
音道場六大字并元刻造像數種
Leaf 1

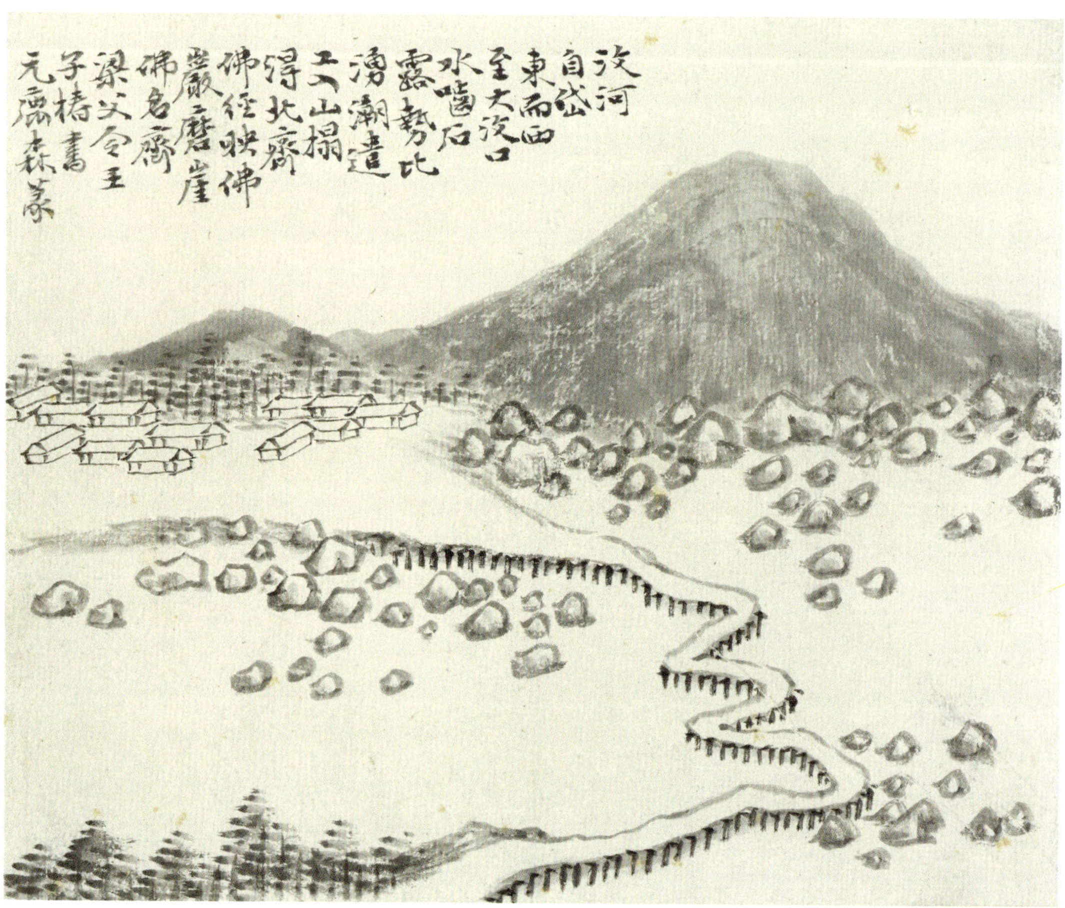
汶河自岱東而西至大汶口水嚙石露勢比湧潮遣工入山搨得北齊佛經映佛巖巖磨崖佛名齊梁父令王子椿書
元靈森摹
Leaf 2

64 *Seeking Steles on Mount Tai* (*Tai Dai fangbei tu*)

Huang Yi (1744–1801). Qing dynasty, ca. 1797.
Album of six leaves, one colophon leaf. Ink on paper; each leaf h. approx. 12.3 cm, w. approx. 14.6 cm.
Princeton University Art Museum, acc. no. 2003-139.1–.7. Museum purchase, Fowler McCormick, Class of 1921, Fund.

This elegant album calls to mind William Blake's "to see a world in a grain of sand," as its unusual pocket size stands in sharp contrast to its subject—Mount Tai (the Supreme Mountain), China's mighty eastern peak in Shandong Province.[1] The painter, Huang Yi (1744–1802), was also a calligrapher, seal carver, and antiquarian, whose passion for antiquities took him to many remote areas in search of ancient inscriptions.[2] His discovery and identification in 1786 of the Wu family mortuary stones near Mount Ziyun, in Shandong's Jiaxiang area, brought him prominence in late Qing antiquarianism.[3] An enthusiastic scholar and amateur archaeologist living during a phase of strong intellectual interest in the study of bronze and stone inscriptions (*jinshi xue*),[4] Huang dedicated his life to finding and studying archaic writings carved on stones and mountain cliffs.

In 1796 Huang Yi journeyed from Jining, Shandong Province, to Mount Song and the Luo River in Henan, returning a month later with a rich harvest of about four hundred inscription rubbings. Shortly after the Lunar New Year in 1797, he set off again, this time traveling to Mount Tai (about sixty miles northeast of Jining), obtaining more rubbings of incised Buddhist texts from votive steles and rock-cut caves. So significant were these trips to Huang Yi that he not only wrote two travel diaries but also made a series of paintings to commemorate them.[5]

The Princeton album consists of six leaves of painted images of famous sites on Mount Tai, each accompanied by Huang Yi's own inscription. According to its only colophon, written in 1935 by Tao Beiming on a separate leaf bound into the end of the album, these six pictures are drafts prepared for the final work, called *Tai Dai fangbei tu* (*Seeking steles on Mount Tai*),[6] which Huang Yi painted to commemorate his 1797 journey to the mountain.[7] Very little is known about Tao, except that he was himself a talented painter and connoisseur and a great admirer of Huang Yi. In 1931, just four years before he saw the Princeton album, Tao recorded his great joy in having obtained another set of Huang's commemorative paintings, called the *Debei tu* (*Painting of obtaining steles*).[8] Now in the Tianjin Municipal Museum of Art, the twelve leaves of the *Debei tu* are a visual display of Huang Yi's proud achievement in finding, restoring, and propagating (by way of rubbings) ancient steles and stone inscriptions.[9]

Huang Yi's Travel Paintings

According to Tao Beiming, the complete set of the paintings for which the Princeton drafts were preliminary was in the collection of Pang Yuanji (*zi* Xuzhai; 1864–1949), a wealthy merchant from Wuxing, Jiangsu Province. Indeed, in 1909 Pang had compiled a catalogue of his painting collection entitled the *Xuzhai minghua lu*, recording in detail all the colophons and seals in two travel albums by Huang Yi. What Tao's colophon calls *Tai Dai fangbei tu*, Pang's catalogue entitles *Dailu fangbei tu* (*Seeking steles in the foothills of Mount Tai*) (hereafter, the *Mount Tai* album). The second album in Pang's catalogue is *Song Luo fangbei tu* (*Seeking steles in the Mount Song and Luo River areas*) (hereafter, the *Song Luo* album); each album comprises twenty-four leaves of lightly inked and colored pictures of the famous

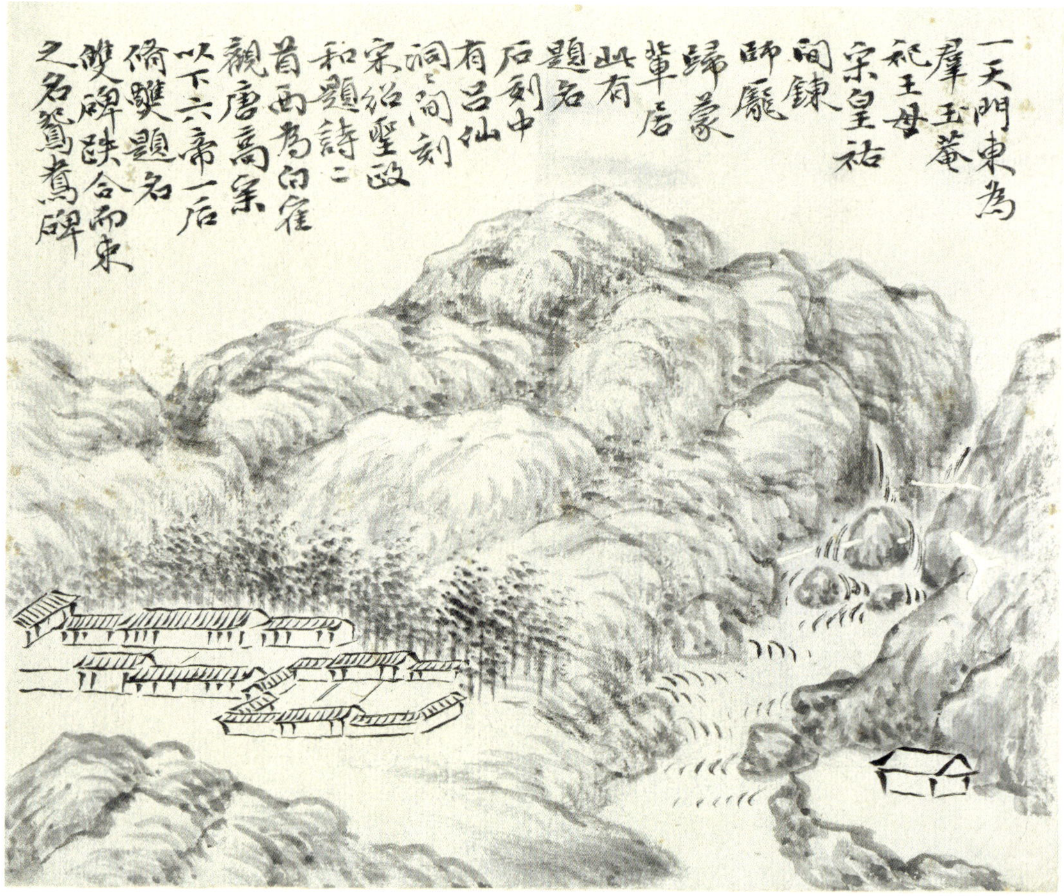
一天門東為
羣玉菴
祀王母
宋皇祐
間鍊
師龐
歸蒙
葺居
此有
題名
石刻中
有呂仙
洞〻間刻
宋紹聖政
和題詩二
首西為白雀
觀唐高宋
以下六帝一石
倚雙題名
雙碑趺合而東
之名鴛鴦碑

Leaf 3

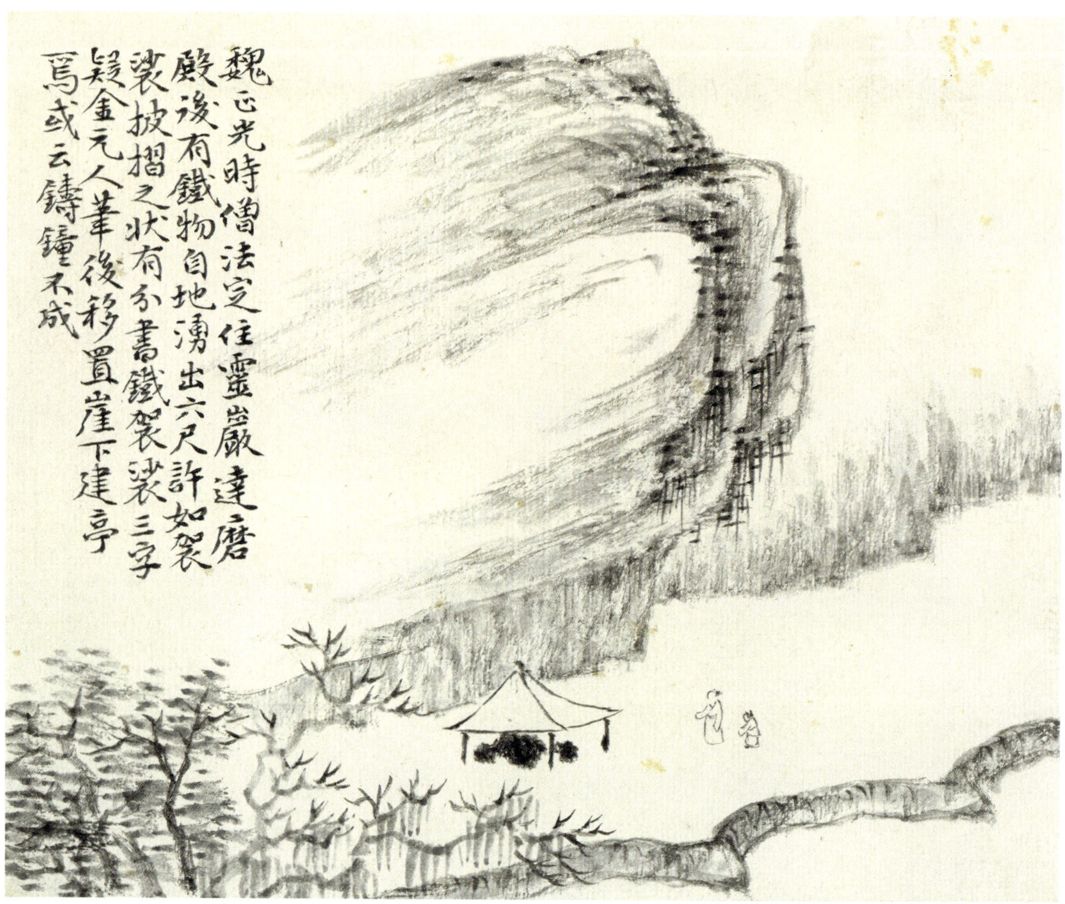
魏正光時僧法定住靈巖達磨
殿後有鐵物自地湧出六尺許如袈
裟披摺之狀有分書鐵袈裟三字
疑金元人筆後移置崖下建亭
焉或云鑄鐘不成

Leaf 4

sites Huang Yi visited during his 1796–1797 trips and subsequently recorded in his diaries.[10] Currently in the Palace Museum in Beijing, these two albums not only display Huang Yi's accomplishment as a painter and calligrapher, but also constitute a benchmark for a particular genre of later Chinese painting—the *fangbei tu* ("'seeking steles' painting").[11]

The format of the two Beijing albums is identical, with each leaf laterally divided into two equal sections: the picture on the right and the inscriptions and colophons on the left (fig. 1). The only writing on the painting proper is the name of the scene, inscribed in clerical-script calligraphy by Huang Yi himself in the upper left corner of the picture. The inscriptions consist of Huang's own accounts of his visits to the places or sites depicted, and the colophons were written by his friends, including the eminent scholar-official and Huang's close associate Weng Fanggang (1733–1818).[12] Whether in poetic or prose form, these colophons are tokens of friendship among a group of literati scholars and artists who shared an intense interest in China's long historical past.

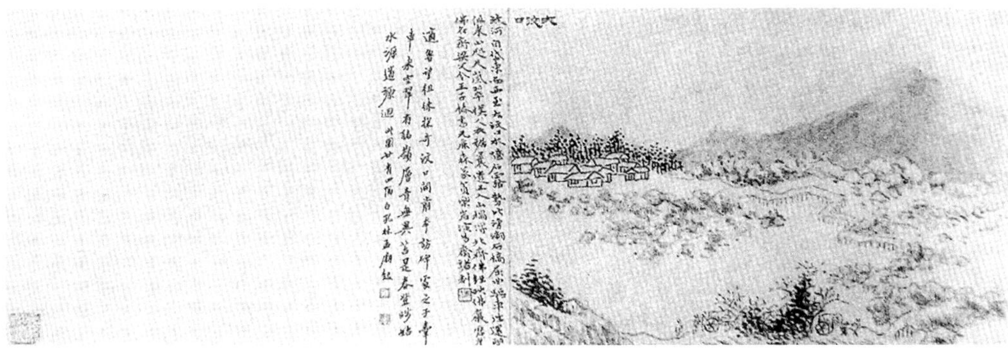

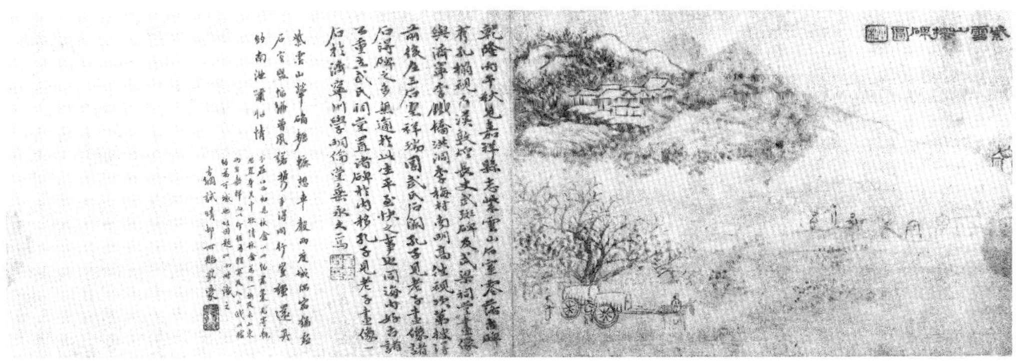

Fig. 1 Huang Yi (1744–1802). *Dawenkou*, in *Dailu fangbei tu*. Album leaf; ink and colors on paper; 17.4 × 50.8 cm. National Palace Museum, Beijing. From *Zhongguo gudai shuhua tu mu*, vol. 23, p. 6032 (10).

Fig. 2 Huang Yi (1744–1802). *Ziyun Shan tanbei tu*, in *Debei tu*. Album leaf; ink and colors on paper; 18 × 51.8 cm. Tianjin Municipal Museum of Art. From *Shoucang jia*, vol. 17 (1996), p. 16.

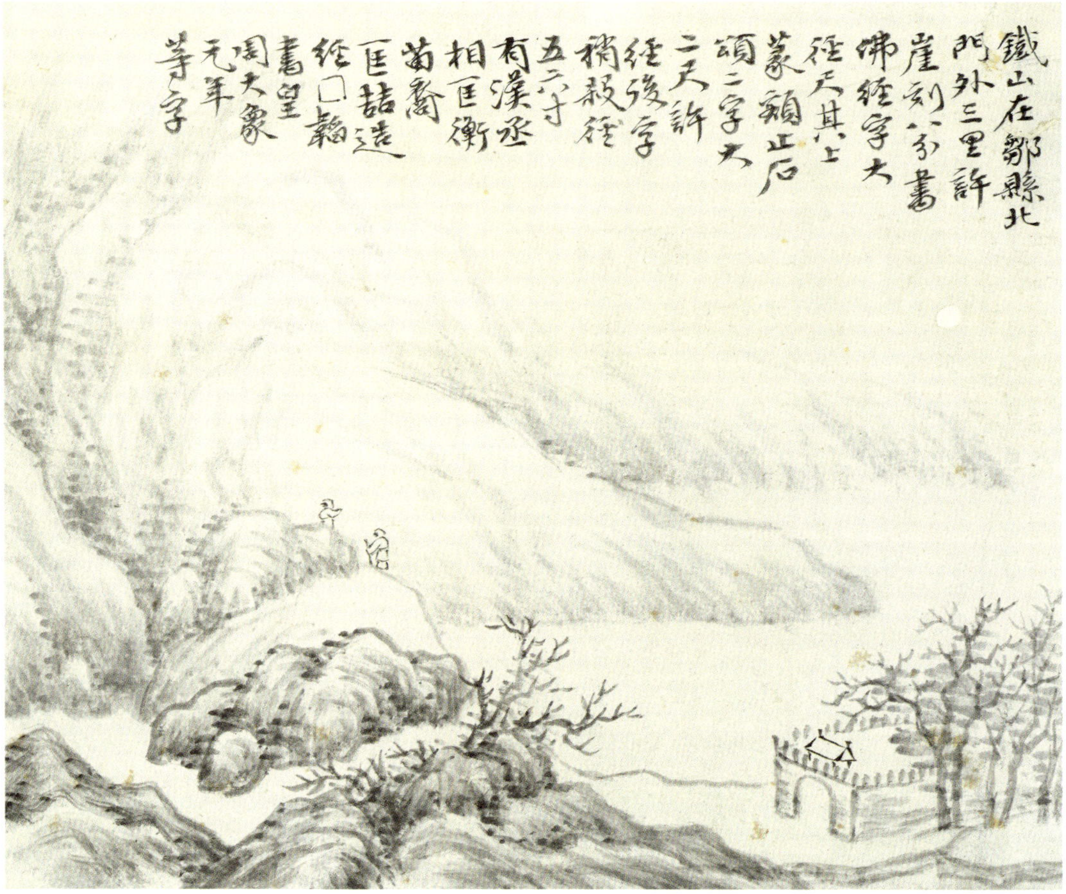
鐵山在鄒縣北
門外三里許
崖刻八分書
佛經字大
徑尺其上
篆額正石
頌二字大
二尺許
經後字
稍殺徑
五六寸
有漢丞
相匡衡
苗裔
匡喆造
經□輸
書望
周大象
元年
等字

Leaf 5

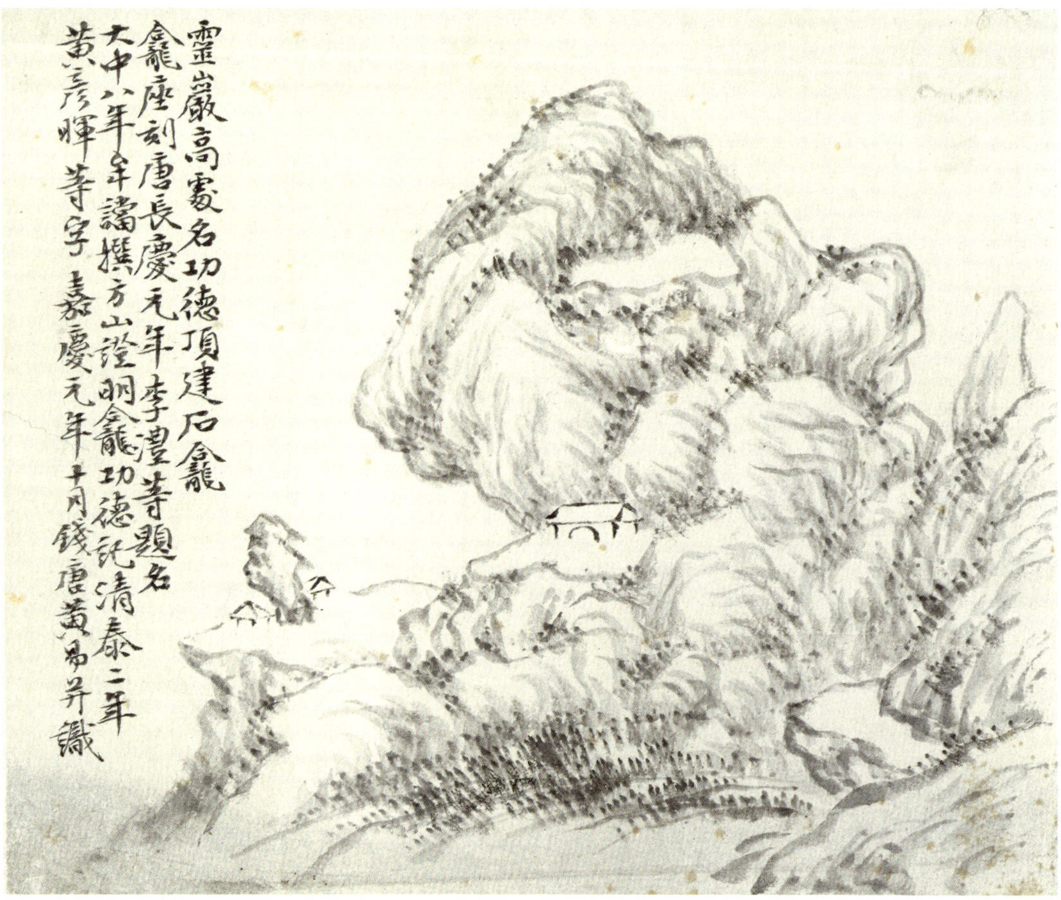
靈巖高處名功德頂建石龕
龕座刻唐長慶元年李澧等題名
大中六年牟讜撰方山證明龕功德記清泰二年
黃彥暉等字 嘉慶元年十月錢唐黃易并識

Leaf 6

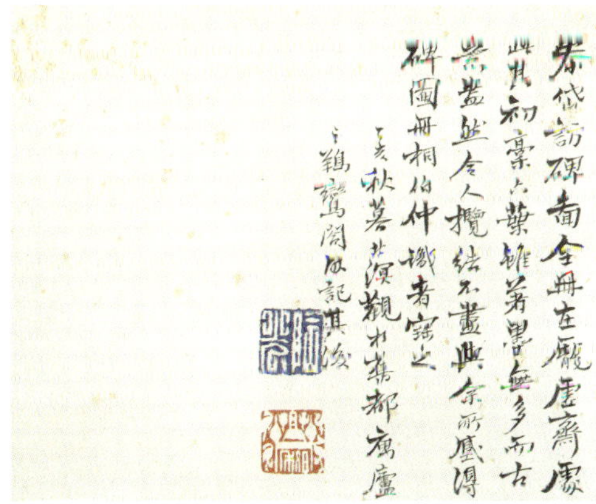

Colophon

A modern critic has characterized Huang Yi's painting as analogous to the intellectual exercise of the Qing *kaoju* (textual-criticism) scholar, which focused particularly on careful study and faithful reconstruction of China's classical texts.[13] The historicist content of Huang's *fangbei* paintings, expressed in the dry and economical application of wash and ink, may be best exemplified by the leaf "*Ziyun Shan tanbei tu*" ("*Searching for steles on Mount Ziyun*") in the *Debei tu* album. In the middle of the painting is an ancient stele, in the so-called *gui* shape characterized by a rectangular body and pointed top, below which a pierced hole is clearly apparent. Lying on the ground, the stele is obviously the subject of intense conversation among the three figures standing on an outcropping, one of whom is gesturing toward it (fig. 2).

As Huang Yi excitedly reported in his account of the finding, it was through his effort that this piece of stone was found in 1786 and later identified as the memorial stele dedicated to Wu Ban.[14] As the inscription of this stele had until then been known only as a text in transmitted epigraphical records, its rediscovery on the ancient, long-forgotten, and half-buried stele was a phenomenal event. The painting captures that decisive moment: the gesturing central figure, Huang Yi himself, indeed made history, because the more than forty stones he and his associates uncovered on Mount Ziyun were subsequently reconstructed as one of the most discussed and cited ancient monuments in China, known as the "Wu family shrines."

Copies of Huang Yi's Paintings and the Princeton Album

Huang Yi appears to have created more than one painting to commemorate the noteworthy 1786 finding in Jiaxiang. One version, called *Ziyun Shan fangbei tu* (*Seeking steles on Mount Ziyun*), was described by the distinguished late Qing epigrapher Fang Shuo (b. 1816) as a long handscroll with "several" of Weng Fanggang's letters mounted at the end.[15] It was most probably completed soon after Huang Yi's visit to Jiaxiang, as Gui Fu (1736–1805), another prominent late Qing scholar, calligrapher, and Shandong native, wrote a poem about it in 1787.[16] This painting may have been the model for the leaf depicting the same theme, in the Tianjin Museum album, itself a pictorial representation of the Jiaxiang discovery and other events that took place between 1775 and 1793. Moreover, the fact that the Tianjin Museum leaf has not "several" but only one colophon by Weng Fanggang may suggest that it is a different version of the *fangbei* painting commemorating the discovery on Mount Ziyun.[17] This mountain site must have gained such a reputation that Huang Yi later invited friends to visit it in 1791, obtaining more steles and making yet another painting to celebrate the happy occasion.[18]

Although Huang Yi was by no means the only Qing scholar with a strong interest in stone inscriptions, he was unique in creating a series of *fangbei* paintings to visually document and celebrate his arduous journeys and successful discoveries of ancient monuments.[19] The fame generated by Huang's recovery of the Wu site stones, as well as his reputation among the late Qing literati as a fine calligrapher and seal carver, made his paintings much sought after[20] and consequently the subjects of later copies. Best known among these is the remarkably skillful replication of the entire twenty-four leaves of the *Song Luo* album by Wu Dacheng (1835–1902), a military official, diplomat, and amateur archaeologist.[21] That copies of Huang Yi's *fangbei* paintings were circulating among collectors is also noted in the *Discourse on Stone* (*Yu shi*), written by the eminent nineteenth-century epigrapher Ye Changchi (1848–1917).[22]

It is common practice among painters to prepare preliminary drafts or sketches (*fenben*), and many such drafts have been collected as original works of art. In fact, Huang Yi's 1797 postscript to his *Mount Tai* album tells us explicitly that he had prepared *fenben* while visiting the famous sites and later completed twenty-four paintings based on these drafts.[23] The six leaves of the Princeton album are bound together under an embroidered silk cover, in the center of which is a paper label inscribed with the name of the album: *Huang Xiaosong shanshui ce* (*Album of landscapes by Huang Xiaosong* [*i.e, Huang Yi*]). The delicate embellishment given to the Princeton album also shows that Huang's sketches were appreciated by artists and collectors after his time.[24]

In pictorial details and style the six Princeton leaves are basically similar to the six corresponding leaves in the complete set of finished paintings in the *Mount Tai* album in the Beijing Palace Museum. There are, however, many discrepancies between the two versions. The inscriptions on the Princeton leaves are written directly on the empty space of the painting proper, a practice not seen in any other sets of *fangbei* paintings attributed to Huang Yi. The contents of these inscriptions, as discussed in the Appendix below, are haphazardly excerpted from the Palace Museum versions. Words, names, and even whole passages are often omitted, and sometimes characters are written in esoteric forms (as in Leaf 3).[25] Careful comparison of the calligraphy also reveals stylistic differences between the two versions, despite their structural similarity. Whereas the characters of the Princeton inscriptions are written in a uniform standard script with rounded strokes, each contained within a squarish frame, Huang Yi's brushwork in the Beijing version is taut and asymmetrical, with a decorative accentuation of flaring diagonals, a mark of his excellent command of clerical-style writing. It is therefore very likely that the inscriptions were added to Huang Yi's original draft sketches at a later date.

As an artist trained in the conventional literati tradition, Huang Yi made many paintings of such popular subjects as landscapes, birds, and flowers. His enduring fame, however, proceeds mainly from his creation (and subsequent copies) of paintings depicting his journeys in search of ancient inscriptions. Wu Dacheng's excellent reproductions of all the pictorial leaves and colophons of the *Song Luo* album[26] attests Huang's lasting popularity and esteem. The colophons in Huang Yi's *fangbei* paintings, which reflect their writers' shared enthusiasm for seeking (*fang*) and retrieving the past through making rubbings from steles (*bei*), augment the cultural value of these relatively small works of art.[27] Just as the grain of sand in Blake's verse can be a lens to see the world, the Princeton album, tiny as it is, is a window on the rich culture of Qing antiquarianism.

EILEEN HSIANG-LING HSU

Notes

1. Described by Mary Augusta Mullikin as having "an austere and impressive dignity," Mount Tai soars 5,000 feet above the Shandong plain; see her *Nine Sacred Mountains of China* (Hong Kong: Vetch and Lee, 1973), p. 3.

2. As suggested by the title of Michael Nylan's "Addicted to Antiquity" in this catalogue, Huang Yi's interest in antiquities bordered on obsession. In fact, Huang Yi himself had carved a few seals revealing this tendency, the most famous being *jinshi pi* ("craving for bronze and stone [inscriptions]"); see *Xiling bajia yin xuan* (*Selections of seal impressions from the Eight Masters of Xiling*) (Shanghai: Shanghai guji chubanshe, 1991), pp. 151–52.

3. For a brief account of the historical records regarding the Wu family cemetery and Huang Yi's role in unearthing the pictorial stones and inscribed steles on the site, see Wu Hung, *The Wu Liang Shrine: the Ideology of Early Chinese Pictorial Art* (Stanford: Stanford University Press, 1989), pp. 3–7; and see Cary Liu's "Recarving the Past" in this catalogue.

4. The seminal phase of *jinshi xue* occurred during the Song dynasty (960–1279), when such prominent scholar-officials as Ouyang Xiu (1007–1072) and Zhao Mingcheng (1081–1129) pioneered the literati engagement in collecting, recording, and studying ancient inscriptions; see Zhu Jianxin, *Jinshi xue* (*Study of bronze and stone inscriptions*) (Taipei: Shangwu yinshuguan, 1995), pp. 24–30. For a succinct summary of the development of the field from the Song to the Qing, see Qianshen Bai, *Fu Shan's World: the Transformation of Chinese Calligraphy in the Seventeenth Century* (Cambridge and London: Harvard University Asia Center, 2003), pp. 172–84.

5. They are the *Song Luo fangbei riji* (*Diary of seeking steles in the Mount Song and Luo River areas*) for the Henan trip, and the *Dai Yan fanggu riji* (*Diary of seeking antiquities on Mount Tai*) for the Shandong trip. For a study of Huang Yi's 1796 painting on his trip to Henan, see Lillian Lan-ying Tseng, "Retrieving the Past, Inventing the Memorable: Huang Yi's Visit to the Song-Luo Monuments," in *Monuments and Memory, Made and Unmade*, ed. Robert S. Nelson and Margaret Olin (Chicago: University of Chicago Press, 2003), pp. 37–58.

6. Although the Chinese characters seem to indicate two places, Tai and Dai, the latter is an alternate name for Mount Tai.

7. For the translation of Tao Beiming's colophon, see the Appendix below.

8. Having heard that *Debei tu* was about to be sold to a Japanese collector by the then owner (a member of the Li family), Tao Beiming sold a precious Shang-dynasty jade from his own collection to finance the purchase of Huang Yi's painting; see Zhang Shulan, "Qing Huang Yi *Debei tu* ce" ("*Painting of Obtaining Steles*, album by Huang Yi of the Qing dynasty"), *Shoucangjia*, vol. 17 (1996), p. 15.

9. The *Debei tu* album is reproduced in Zhongguo gudai shuhua jiandingzu, ed., *Zhongguo gudai shuhua tumu* (*Illustrated catalogue of early Chinese paintings*) (Beijing: Wenwu chubanshe, 2000) (hereafter, *SHTM*), vol. 7, pp. 216–17.

10. Pang Yuanji, *Xuzhai minghua lu* (*Famous paintings from the Xuzhai collection*) (Shenjiang: Wucheng Pangshi, 1909), *juan* 16. Although the titles differ slightly, Tao Beiming's colophon refers to the same painting in Pang's collection, as the numerous colophons transcribed in Pang's catalogue exactly match those seen in the reproduction of the two albums in *SHTM*, vol. 23, pp. 235–38. In a poem about the *Mount Tai* album, Wu Nianhu (*jinshi* 1766), a painter friend of Huang's, refers to it as *Dai Yan langu tu* (*Viewing the ancient* [*relics*] *on Mount Tai*); see Li Junzhi, *Qing huajia shi shi* (*Poems by Qing-dynasty painters*) (Beijing: Zhongguo shudian, 1983), *juan ding* (*xia*), and *SHTM*, p. 238.

11. The eminent Chinese art historian Xu Bangda and other expert painting connoisseurs have accepted these two sets as genuine Huang Yi paintings; see Xu Bangda's preface in his *Gaiding lidai liuchuan huihua biannian biao* (*Revised chronological table of paintings transmitted in successive dynasties*) (Beijing: Renmin meishu chubanshe, 1995). For Huang Yi's achievement as a seal carver and calligrapher, see Chen Zhenlian, *Zhongguo shuhua zhuanke pinjian* (*Appreciation and connoisseurship of Chinese painting, calligraphy, and seal carving*) (Beijing: Zhonghua shuju, 1997), pp. 702–3.

12. Other prominent figures whose writings have graced Huang Yi's albums are Liang Tongshu (1723–1815) and Sun Xingyan (1753–1818), as well as the leading literati artists Yu Ji (1738–1823) and Xi Gang (1746–1803).

13. Chen Zhenlian, *Zhongguo shuhua*, p. 702. For a study of the stone stele as a dominant theme in late Qing painting, see Chuang Shen, "Archaeology in Late Qing Dynasty Painting," *Ars Orientalis*, vol. 24 (1994), pp. 83–104.

14. See Huang Yi, "Xiu Wushi citang jilüe" ("Brief record on building the Wu Family Shrine"), in Wang Chang, *Jinshi cuibian* (*Compilation of bronze and stone inscriptions*) (Xi'an: Shaanxi Renmin meishu chubanshe, 1990), *juan* 20, pp. 37–38; translated and discussed in Liu's "Recarving the Past," in this catalogue.

15. Fang Shuo, *Zhenjing Tang jinshi tiba* (*Colophons to bronze and stone inscriptions in the* Zhenjing Tang *collection*) (Taipei: Xuehai chubanshe, 1977), p. 132. Fang saw the painting, inscribed the heading, and wrote a poem about it. It is not known whether this version of the painting is still extant.

16. He wrote this poem during a visit to Jiaxiang with Huang Yi's friends and colleagues Li Tieqiao and Li Meicun; see Li Junzhi, *Qing huajia shi shi* (*Poems by Qing Dynasty Painters*), *juan wu* (*shang*).

17. See Cai Hongru, "Huang Yi debei shier tu" ("Twelve pictures of obtaining steles by Huang Yi"), *Wenwu*, 1996.3, p. 74, fig. 6.

18. Except for the colophons and format, the 1791 scroll shares many features with the Tianjin leaf, including composition, pictorial details, brush style, and the title; see Christie's, auction catalogue, Hong Kong (October 31, 2004), *Fine Classical Chinese Paintings and Calligraphy*, p. 130, lot 416. The multiple productions of Huang Yi's *fangbei* painting in the context of Qing antiquarianism will be discussed in another study.

19. For example, Jin Nong (1687–1763), another Qing painter known for his zealous study and acquisition of antiquities, is not known to have produced any *fangbei* paintings.

20. See n. 8 about Tao Beiming's procurement of Huang's paintings.

21. Chuang Shen, "Archaeology in Late Qing Dynasty Painting," p. 103, n. 36. A facsimile reproduction of Wu Dacheng's copy is published as *Kezhai lin Huang Xiaosong Sima Song Luo fangbei ershisi tu* (*Kezhai's copy of Huang Xiaosong's twenty-four pictures of seeking steles in the Mount Song and Luo River areas*) (Shanghai: Youzheng shuju, 1907) (hereafter, *Kezhai*).

22. Ye states that Huang Yi's *Song Luo* album in Fei Qihuai's collection is in fact a copy; see Ye Changchi and Ke Changsi, *Yu shi, Yu shi yi tong ping* ("*Discourse on stone,*" *commentary on* "*Discourse on stone*") (Beijing: Zhonghua shuju, 1994), p. 564. According to Pei Jingfu, the version Fei Qihuai owned was a fine tracing copy; see idem., *Zhuangtao Ge shuhua lu* (*Catalogue of painting and calligraphy in the Zhuangtao Ge collection*) (Shanghai: Zhonghua shuju, 1937), *juan* 22, p. 52.

23. Pang Yuanji, *Xuzhai minghua lu*, *juan* 16.

24. He Shaoji (1799–1873), a compiler in the Hanlin Academy and a renowned calligrapher, wrote in a colophon to the *Song Luo* album that he had seen Huang's drafts at the home of a friend. This colophon is reproduced in Wu Dacheng's copy of the album; see *Kezhai*.

25. Compared to the Palace Museum *Mount Tai* album, for example, the character *jiao* (altar) is written in such a peculiar way that it can only be explained by the copier's failure to recognize its correct form in the original version.

26. These colophons are done in the various calligraphic styles of the originals, not only revealing Wu's artistic versatility, but also his respect for Huang Yi's creation.

27. In describing the smallness of Huang Yi's *fangbei*, almost all collectors used the word "only" (*cai*).

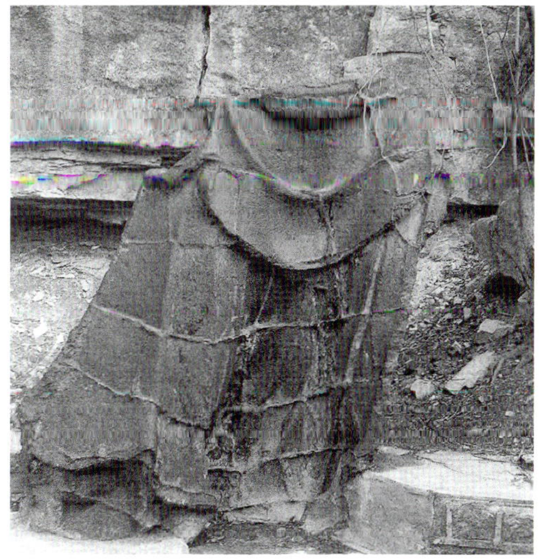

Appendix

Inscriptions and colophon: transcriptions and translations[1]

Leaf One

靈巖寺東甘露泉淙淙漱石清韻滌煩古木參差亭軒幽爽第一勝區也其上石壁最高處宋張勵觀音道場六大字并元刻造像數種[2]

East of the Lingyan Si [Buddhist] Temple, the rushing water of the Ganlu spring washes the stones; its pure sound cleanses the troubled mind. Old trees rise unevenly into the sky; terraces and pavilions grace the deep forest. This is truly the most spectacular scenic spot. A Song-dynasty inscription of six large characters, *Zhang Li Guan yin dao chang* ("Zhang Li's Guanyin cultivation field")[3] appears on the uppermost part of the stone cliff. There are also several sculpted [Buddhist] images from the Yuan period.[4]

Leaf Two

汶河自岱東而西至大汶口水嚙石露勢比湧潮遣工入山搨得北齊佛經映佛巖磨崖佛名齊梁父令王子椿書元鹿森篆[5]

The Wen River flows westward from east of Mount Tai. At Dawenkou the water hits the exposed stones with wave-like force. I sent craftsmen into the mountain to make rubbings of the incised Northern Qi Buddhist sutras, the Buddha names inscribed on the Yingfo Yan Cliff, as well as [the inscriptions carved on the Pinle Yan Cliff and Yanyi Zhai Studio] composed by the [Northern] Qi magistrate of the Liangfu district Wang Zichun and calligraphed by Yuan Lusen.[6]

Leaf Three

一天門東為群玉菴祀王母宋皇祐間鍊師龐歸蒙輩居此有題名石刻中有呂仙洞洞間刻宋紹盛政和題詩二首西為白鶴[7] 觀唐高宗以下六帝一后脩醮[8] 題名雙碑趺合而束之名鴛鴦碑[9]

East of the Yitian Men Gate is the Qunyu An Nunnery, a place for sacrifices to the "Queen Mother."[10] During the Huangyou reign-period (1049–1053) of the Song dynasty the Daoist Pang Guimeng and his fellow practitioners resided here, and inscribed their names. Among the stone carvings are those in the Luxian Cave: two poems dating to the Shaosheng (1094–1097) and Zhenghe (1111–1117) reign-periods. West [of the Yitian Men Gate] is the White Crane Daoist Temple, where the Tang emperor Gaozong and six emperors and one empress after him had their names inscribed [to commemorate] the erection of the *jiao* altar. Two steles were stacked and bound together, and are [thus] called the *yuanyang* ("conjugal") stele.[11]

Leaf Four

魏正光時僧法定住靈巖達磨殿後有鐵物自地湧出六尺許如袈裟披摺之狀有分書鐵袈裟三字疑金元人筆後移至崖下建亭焉或云鑄鐘不成[12]

In the Zhengguang reign-period (520–524) of the Wei dynasty, monk Fading was residing in the Lingyan Si Temple.[13] [At that time] behind the Damo Dian Hall a metal object emerged from the earth and surged up to about six *chi* above ground. [Its surface] resembles the folds of a monk's robe (*jiasha*). Written in [*ba*]*fen* clerical script [on this object] are the three characters *tie jia sha* ("iron monk's robe") suspected to have been inscribed by people of the Jin or Yuan period. It was later moved

Fig. 3 *Remains of the "Iron monk's robe."* Unknown period (Song?). Metal in the form of a Buddhist monk's robe. Lingyan Si, Shandong. Photograph by author, 2004.

to the foot of the cliff and a pavilion was built there [to shelter it]. Some say that [this curious object was left over from] an unsuccessful casting of a bell (fig. 3).

Leaf Five

鐵山在鄒縣北門外三里許崖刻八分書佛経字大徑尺其上篆額止石頌二字大二尺許經後字稍殺徑五六寸有漢丞相匡衡苗裔匡喆造經☐韜書皇周大象元年等字[14]

Mount Tie is about three *li* from the north gate of Zou district. Buddhist sutras in *bafen* clerical script are engraved on its cliff walls, each character being about one *chi* across. Carved in seal script above [the sutras] is the heading *Shisong* ("Stone Eulogy"), of only two characters, each measuring about two *chi* across. The inscription following the sutra texts is of a reduced size, with each character about five or six *cun* across. [Among other characters, the inscription contains this passage:] "Kuang Zhe, a descendant of the Han Chancellor Kuang Heng, made the [incised] Buddhist sutras with calligraphy by ? Tao[15] in the first year of the Daxiang reign-period of the Royal Zhou (i.e., Northern Zhou; 579)."

Leaf Six

靈巖高處名功德頂建石龕龕座刻唐長慶元年李澧等題名大中八年牟讜撰方山證明龕功德記清泰二年黃彥暉等字[16] 嘉慶元年十月錢唐黃易并識[17]

A high place on the Ling Yan Cliff is called the Gongde Ding (Merit Heights). Cut into the top of the cliff is a stone niche-shrine, on whose base are inscriptions by Li Li and others, dating from the first year of the Changqing reign-period (821) of the Tang dynasty. [Other inscriptions] include the "Record [commemorating the building of] the Niche-shrine of Demonstrating Meritorious Deeds" at Mount Fang, written by Mou Dang in the eighth year of the Dazhong reign-period (854),[18] as well as those by Huang Yanhui in the second year of Qingtai (935), and by others. Noted by Huang Yi of Qiantang, in the tenth month of the first year of Jiaqing (1796).

Colophon

泰岱訪碑圖全冊在龐虛齋處此其初稾六葉雖著墨無多而古意盎然令人攬結不盡與余所藏得碑圖冊相伯仲識者寶之丁亥秋暮北溟觀於舊都寓廬之鵁[19] 鸞閣並記其後

The complete album of *Seeking Steles on Mount Tai* is in the Pang Xuzhai (Pang Yuanji; 1864–1949) collection, and these are six leaves of its draft version. Although ink is used sparingly [in the pictures], they otherwise convey an abundant sense of antiquity; the pleasure of enjoying [this fine work of art] is truly without limit. This album is comparable to the *Debei tu* album in my collection, and I hope those who recognize [the quality of these fine paintings] will treasure it. Viewed and noted by Beiming in late autumn of the *yihai* year (1935) in the Xiangluan (auspicious bird) Pavilion in the Old Capital (i.e., Beijing).

Seals

Following Tao Beiming's colophon are two of his seals; the first reads "Tao Guang," and the second is a pictorial image showing auspicious birds surrounding a pavilion.

Notes

1. As discussed above, the six leaves of the Princeton album are said to be part of the drafts prepared for the *Tai Dai fangbei tu*, known today as the *Dailu fangbei tu* in the Palace Museum in Beijing (hereafter, PM *Dailu* album). All twenty-four leaves of the Beijing album are

reproduced in *Zhongguo gudai shuhua tu mu* (hereafter, *SHTM*); Huang Yi's inscriptions and the colophons written by his friends are published in *Xuzhai minghua lu* (hereafter, *Xuzhai*).

2. This leaf is listed as no. 1 in *SHTM*.

3. Zhang Li was a scholar-official active during the Xining reign-period (1068–1077) of the Northern Song dynasty.

4. The *Xuzhai* records this leaf as no. 14, but its transcription is slightly different from the Princeton version. It does not include the last sentence, and the passage about Zhang Li's inscription reads: "Six large characters, '*Zhang Li Guan yin dao chang*' ['Guanyin cultivation field'] [inscribed] by Zhang Li during the Zhenghe reign-period (1111–1117) of the Song dynasty."

5. This leaf is reproduced as no. 10 in *SHTM*, where the inscription is longer by a few more sentences. The leaf is recorded as no. 7 in *Xuzhai*. See also fig. 1.

6. My reading and translation are based on *Xuzhai* and *SHTM*, which includes the additional passage "Inscriptions carved on the Pinle Yan Cliff and Yanyi Zhai Studio" after *Yuan Lusen zhuan* ("calligraphed by Yuan Lusen"). I have inserted this passage, which is missing in the Princeton version, in square brackets in the translation.

7. The Princeton album shows a variant, rarely seen, form of the character representing "crane," but the more commonly used form appears in the PM *Dailu* album. My transcription here is based on the latter version.

8. The character for *jiao* is also written in a variant, esoteric, form. I am basing my transcription on the PM *Dailu* album.

9. The inscription on this leaf in the PM *Dailu* album, reproduced as no. 7 in *SHTM*, is much longer. The *Xuzhai* records the leaf as no. 18.

10. Wangmu, also known as Xiwangmu ("Queen Mother of the West"); see Lullo's "Regional Iconographies" in this catalogue.

11. In 661 (6th year of Xianqing reign-period) Emperor Gaozong and Empress Wu sent the Daoist master Gou Xingzhen to Mount Tai to build a *jiao* altar to perform sacrifices to the mountain. A stele, later known as the *yuanyang* stele, had been erected to commemorate this event; see *Shandong Sheng zhi* (*Gazetteer of Shandong*), vol. 72: *Taishan zhi* (*Gazetteer of Taishan*) (Beijing: Zhonghua shuju, 1993), p. 18.

12. In the PM *Dailu* album, reproduced as no. 4 in *SHTM*, the inscription on this leaf has four additional characters *qi shuo jin li* ("That [saying] is close to reason") appended to the end. The leaf is recorded as no. 15 in *Xuzhai*.

13. Lingyan Si was the name bestowed on the Buddhist monastery founded by the Indian monk Fading by Emperor Xiaoming (r. 516–528) of the Northern Wei dynasty; see *Shandong tongzhi*, *Siku quanshu* edition, *juan* 30.

14. This inscription reproduced in *SHTM* no. 2 is twice as long as the Princeton version. It is recorded in *Xuzhai* as no. 4.

15. The character in question is marked by an empty square in the album; apparently it had already been eroded beyond recognition when Huang Yi visited the site. In *Xuzhai*, however, another character *xian* appears beween the empty square and the character *tao*.

16. The inscription on this leaf as recorded in *Xuzhai* lacks the two characters *deng zi*, and is twice as long as the Princeton version. My translation is based on the fuller version recorded in *Xuzhai*, which lists the leaf as no. 16. *SHTM* reproduces the leaf as no. 8.

17. This last sentence, which gives the date and Huang Yi's signature, is not seen on the same leaf in either *Xuzhai* or *SHTM*.

18. Called the *Zhengming gongde kan* ("Niche-shrine for Demonstrating Meritorious Deeds"), this structure was a Buddhist rock-cut cave built during the Zhenguan reign-period (627–649), inside which are sculptures of Śākyamuni and bodhisattvas; see Sekino Tadashi and Tokiwa Daijō, *Shina bunka shiseki* (*Cultural and historical sites in China*) (Tokyo: Hōzōkan, 1940), vol. 7: *Santō*, p. 28. See also *Shandong Sheng zhi*, p. 17.

19. This character is a variant form of *xiang*, meaning "auspicious." Tao Beiming used another variant form *xiang* in his 1931 colophon to the Tianjin album; see Zhang, "Qing Huang Yi *Debei tu* ce." The latter form is also seen in an album of old rubbings made from the Wu shrines stones, once owned by Tao Beiming and now in the collection of the Beijing University Library; see *Zhongguo gudai bei tie taben* (*Ancient Chinese calligraphic rubbings*) (Hong Kong: The Art Museum, The Chinese University of Hong Kong), p. 15.

Research Essays

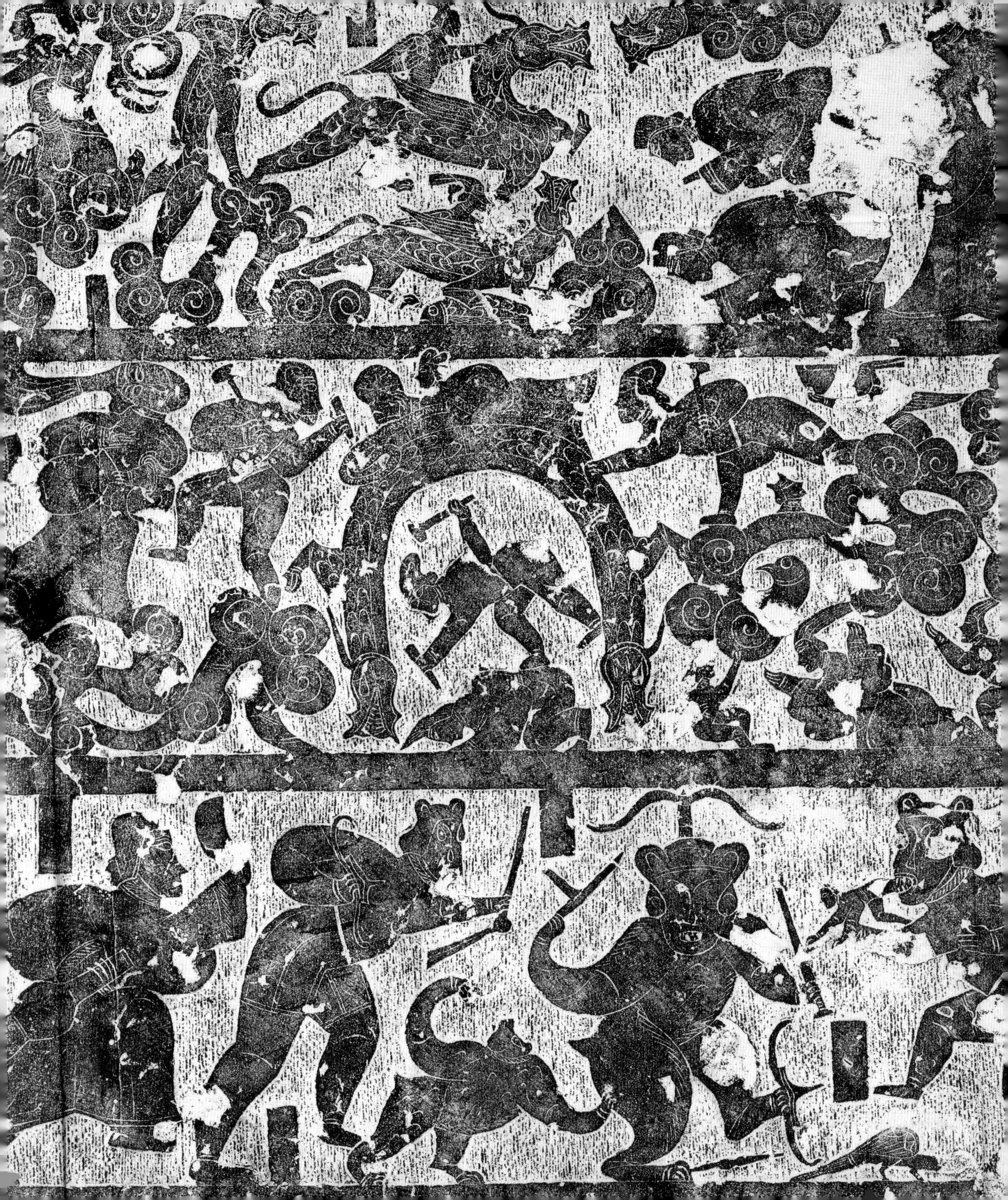

Anthony Barbieri-Low

Carving Out a Living: Stone-Monument Artisans During the Eastern Han Dynasty

The death of a loved one is a time of tragic loss for the immediate family. For them, it is an occasion to express powerful sentiments of grief, anger, and fear. Within the larger family unit, and within society as a whole, a death provides the opportunity to impart moral and religious instruction to younger generations and reinforce familial bonds and social hierarchies. To some, however, death also represents a business opportunity. Today in America the mortuary industry employs over 100,000 people. It is estimated that in the year 2000, Americans spent upwards of thirty billion dollars on funerals and burial preparations, more than $10,000 per deceased.[1] During the Eastern Han period in China mortuary preparation was also a booming business. Many artisans specialized in preparing tombs and funerary monuments for the deceased, and significant amounts of money changed hands.

As other scholars have noted, the Eastern Han period was a high-water mark for extravagant funerals and burials in China.[2] One apparent motive for this conspicuous destruction of wealth was to acquire renown for the intensity of filial piety. Ardent social climbers spent all their wealth, or at least claimed they had, to bury dear old mum and dad. To be labeled *xiaolian* ("filial and incorrupt") by the provincial governor was an important aid to entry into the prestigious and potentially lucrative career of government official, and families tried to outspend one another to make this consequential social impression.[3] The reclusive sociopolitical critic of the Eastern Han, Wang Fu (ca. 90–165 CE) in his *Qianfu lun* (*Criticisms of a hidden man*), railed against the hypocrisy of people who "scarcely trouble to care for their parents during their lifetime, yet honor them with sumptuous funerals when they die."[4]

Opposite Detail of Stone Chamber 2, Stone 2-R.1 (cat. no. 1.32). "Wu family shrines" rubbings. Princeton University Art Museum, acc. no. 2002-307.31.

Wang Fu was friends with the career official Cui Yuan (77–142 CE), who when near death strongly urged his son not to spend extravagantly on his burial.[5] His son, the official and writer Cui Shi (ca. 110–170 CE), had seconded his father's counsel in his own writings.[6] Yet when his father died, Shi still felt compelled to sell property and exhaust the family fortune to give him an impressive funeral and burial near Luoyang.[7] Impoverished largely by that act, Shi went into the brewing business to make ends meet and nevertheless died nearly destitute. Several of his friends and ex-colleagues contributed money to buy him a coffin, erect a stele, and give him a socially proper funeral.[8]

The Cui family's friend Wang Fu has provided us with one of the most detailed and oft quoted accounts of the manpower costs of mortuary preparations. In it he suggests that another motivation behind the competitive display in funerary practice was the desire of middle-income provincials to emulate the style of imperial relatives and nobles in the capital. After describing the modest but well-made coffins of earlier times, Wang compares these with the ostentatious caskets of his contemporaries:

> Now, however, the noble relatives in the capital [Luoyang] all feel they must have catalpa wood from the Yangzi area, camphor from the Jiangxi area, and exotic southern lindera and *nanmu* woods for their coffins. Poor and distant areas of the empire compete to imitate their style. But these types of catalpa and camphor are produced in particularly distant places, and only grow in the deep valleys between high

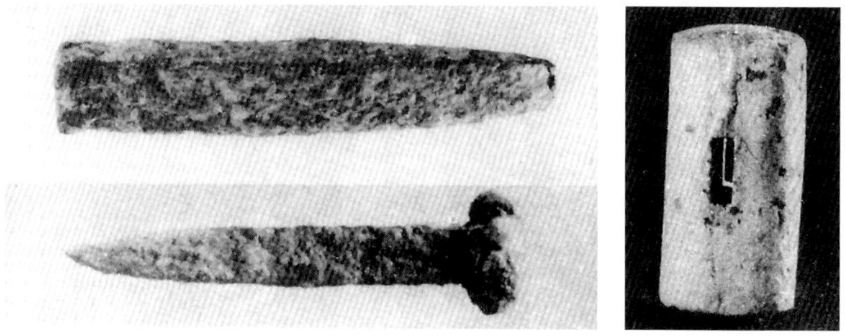

> mountains. After many days of searching, one might only find these trees after traversing ranges of mountains, ascending peaks a thousand paces high, clinging to the sides of gorges a thousand feet wide, and following along inconvenient mountain paths. It then takes many months to cut the timber and a multitude of men to transport it. The logs are dragged down to the water by a line of oxen and then floated down the You River [which flows into the Yangzi]. Then they are floated out to sea and sent back inland by way of the Huai River and finally up the Yellow River. They arrive in Luoyang after traveling several thousand *li*. Then it takes carpenters many days and months to plane and carve the wood. I calculate that one of these coffins requires thousands or even tens of thousands of man-days of labor to complete, and will weigh 10,000 *jin* (2,200 kg). Unless one employs a multitude of men, it cannot be lifted, and unless one has a mighty hearse, it cannot be moved. Yet from Lelang in the east to Dunhuang in the west, men in the intervening 10,000 *li* compete to use them.[9]

Forgiving Wang Fu his literary exaggerations, his labor-cost estimates may actually be close to the mark. A modern economist might approve such spending as stimulating the economy by constructively employing many men, but Wang Fu considered that those men should be farming and feeding the people instead of hacking down hardwoods. Such literary accounts of spending are supplemented by epigraphical evidence (introduced later) in which patrons and artisans crassly proclaim the cost of particular monuments.

Fig. 1 Flat-bladed and pointed chisels (left) and hammerhead (right). Qin dynasty, ca. 209 BCE. Near necropolis of Qin Shihuangdi at Lintong, Shaanxi. Iron. From *Kaogu yu wenwu*, 1981.1, pls. 12–13.

In this essay I should like to focus on one key group who participated in the business of death during the Eastern Han. These are the masons, draftsmen, sculptors, and painters who built and decorated stone tombs and aboveground monuments for moderately well-off clients of low to middle rank in northeast China during the first and second centuries CE. Their contribution has been largely ignored in recent research, which has focused more on particular monuments or on studies of patronage.[10] Using a variety of sources, I shall attempt to show how stone carvers carried out their craft, how literate and mobile they were, how much their products cost, and how they maintained profit margins using a repertoire of labor- and material-saving methods.

The Process of Carving Stone Monuments

Before the arrival of Buddhism, the use of stone for monumental sculpture and buildings was never central to Chinese art or architecture. As early as the Han, however, stone had become a popular medium in some regions for lining tombs and for constructing aboveground funerary monuments. This cultural phenomenon peaked in the century from about 84 to 184 CE[11] in several areas of northeast China and in the Chengdu Basin to the southwest.[12] Among all these regions, it was in the Shandong Peninsula area that the stone-carving tradition was most prominent and the volume of stone cutting was greatest. In fact, by one count, 60 percent of all extant decorated stones datable to the Han period come from this region.[13] Why this one area developed such a market for stone funerary monuments has

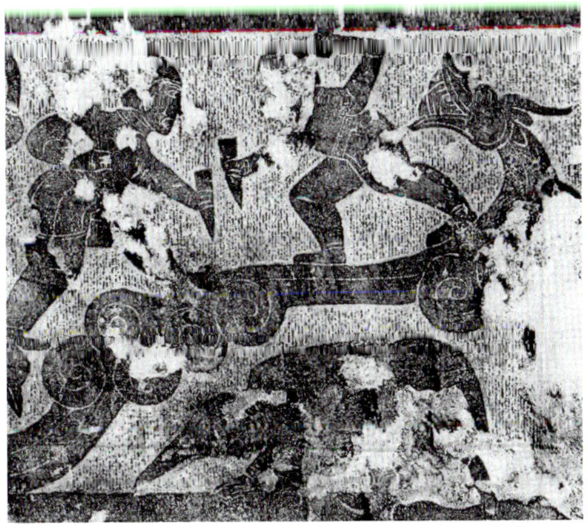

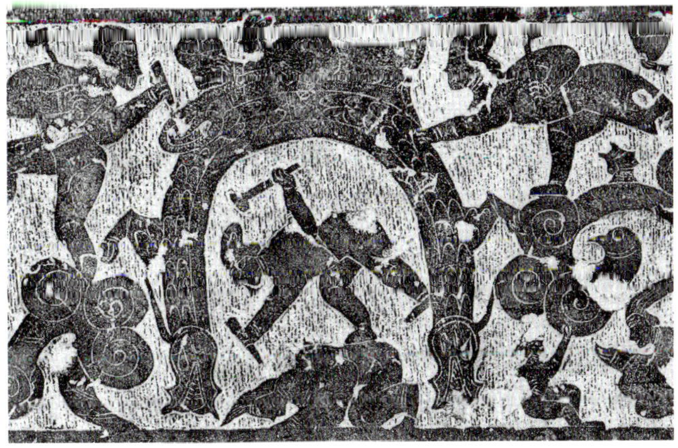

much to do with an intertwining of geography and cultural history. The low hills of the area are filled with easily quarried limestone, transportable on a network of waterways. Stone monuments also had a deep prior history in this area of northeast Asia, with the stones themselves sometimes treated as objects of worship.[14] Lastly, the area was a zone of concentrated population and wealth from agriculture and manufacturing, with few equals in the Han empire.

By analyzing the working traces remaining on carved stones, and aided by clues from a few Han dynasty inscriptions,[15] we can now reconstruct much of the process of carving stone funerary monuments during the Han.[16] Unfortunately, this reconstruction is still sketchy and pales in comparison with the more complete picture we have of the process and organization of New Kingdom (1550–1070 BCE) Egyptian tomb decoration.[17] By necessity, it is a composite sketch that is also somewhat normative, subsuming regional workshop variation and chronological developments.

The preferred stone for carving, in the Shandong area at least, was a hard, fine-grained limestone quarried from the surrounding hills.[18] Even today the area remains a bustling center for limestone quarries, limekilns, and stone-carving workshops. Han-period inscriptions claim that only the finest and most illustrious stones (*mingshi*) were used, and that they were "free of veins or brown streaks." They were always said to be quarried from the south-facing slopes of hills found to the south or southwest.[19] It is unclear looking at modern maps precisely which limestone-bearing hills were intended by these phrases, but the actual quarry location was probably less important than the auspicious connotations expressed by the figurative location.

To extract limestone blocks from the hillside, a mason wielded a heavy iron sledgehammer (*chui*) whose head alone could weigh 5–7 kg, and directed it at a pointed chisel (*zan*). Once a slot was opened up in the rock, he forced one or more iron wedges (*juan*) into the crevice and pounded them forcefully to cleave off a huge chunk of limestone. Archaeologists have recovered numerous examples of these tools from quarries and stone-dressing sites (fig. 1).[20] Though we possess no contemporary depiction showing quarrymen at work, the stone-carvers who decorated the offering halls at the Wuzhai Shan site cleverly alluded to their own profession when they depicted the minions of the Thunder God (Lei Gong) wielding hammer and chisel to smite the heads of thunderstruck earth-dwellers (fig. 2).

Once quarried, the stones were probably at least crudely dressed near the pit before transport to the masons' workshop. Judging by working traces remaining on the undecorated backs of stones from Shandong (fig. 3), it appears that a mason worked down the surface of the stone by chiseling numerous parallel trenches, first in one direction and then in rows roughly perpendicular to these, enabling him to easily hack off the stone nodules at the intersections of the furrows. This process continued, using finer and finer chisels, until the desired slab thickness was achieved. In some regions this distinctive cross-hatching was not completely smoothed during the finishing of the decorated face but was retained as a background texture to highlight the pictorial carvings. The masons counted

Fig. 2 *Servants of the Thunder God wielding sledgehammers and iron chisels.* Eastern Han dynasty, ca. second century CE. Left: detail of Offering Hall 1 (Stone Chamber 1, Stone 1-R.1, cat. no. 1.17). Right: detail of Offering Hall 2 (Stone Chamber 2, Stone 2-R.1, cat. no. 1.32). "Wu family shrines" rubbings. Princeton University Art Museum, acc. nos. 2002-307.16, 2002-307.31.

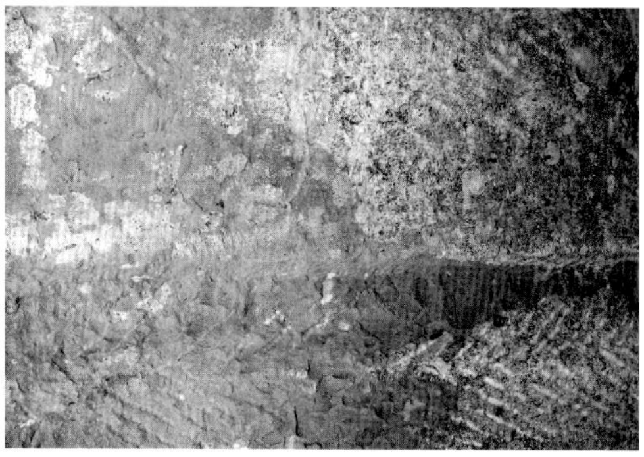

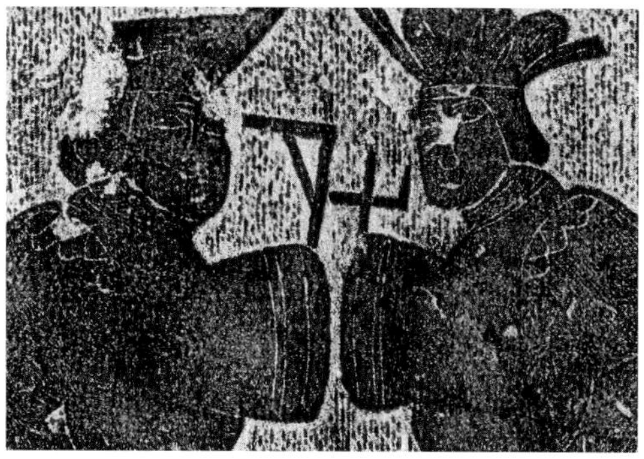

the stones using the measure-word *tou* ("head"), saying they completed "so-many *tou* of stones."[21]

The next stage in the process was to move the stone slabs from the quarry to the workshop site for planing and decoration. Stone is difficult to transport great distances overland, especially in an era of unpaved roads, but one Han inscription suggests that the stones for a particular monument were indeed bound up and carted overland.[22] Conveniently, the Shandong area was crisscrossed by numerous rivers and canals, permiting the far greater efficiency of water-borne transport. The stones from a Han tomb in present-day Liangshan County, weighing more than 8,000 kilograms, were quarried from a source, identified by present-day local carvers, 24 kilometers north of the site.[23] Though overland transportation of such a mass of stone would have been feasible, reconstructed maps of the area suggest there was indeed a river course running from the quarry toward the tomb site.[24]

Once at the workshop, the stones were squared off with the aid of a carpenter's square (*ju*) (fig. 4), given a final dressing (*zhuoli*), and ground smooth (*mozhi*).[25] A few mason's titles carved on stones from a Han prince's tomb suggest that the workers who performed this task were called (*zhishi*) ("stone levelers").[26] Usually, only those surfaces of a given stone that were to be exposed to view in the final monument would be worked completely smooth. The remaining surfaces were left with the rough quarry finish (fig. 3). It appears from a fragmentary marginal inscription on one stone that Han carvers referred to the face that carried the decoration as the *biao* ("exposed surface").[27]

After the stones were dressed, the masons called in the master draftsman (*huashi*). He would compose the pictorial program, divide the surface into registers, and lay down the borders, figures, and other pictorial elements using brush and black ink. Some stones still display traces of these original drafts (fig. 5).[28] Using the master's sketch as a guide, sculptors would then carve the pictorial groups and decorative borders, processes described in two inscriptions as *diaowen* ("engrave the ornaments") and *kehua* ("chisel the illustrations").[29] In some stylistic traditions this involved lowering the stone ground around each pictorial group, while in others it entailed lowering the pictorial surface relative to a striated background. Also at this stage smooth rectangular scene labels were prepared for later, optional use by more literate artisans.

Once the pictorial surface was separated from the ground, a line carver would finish the scene by engraving lines on the figures to indicate facial features and clothing. An examination of the rubbings from the Wuzhai Shan site demonstrates that some facial features were executed distinctively on each of the three reconstructed stone chambers from the site. On each monument noses of figures in three-quarters–profile were carved in one consistent fashion, suggesting that only one line carver finished the facial details for each structure, and by extension, that the three halls were each made by a different work crew (fig. 6).

The last stages of the process began with moving the decorated stones to the cemetery site for final assembly. Then, final adjustments could be made to the mortise-and-tenon joinery for gabled roofs and the door pivots for tombs. If desired, scene labels could now be filled with

Fig. 3 *Working traces on the undecorated side of a pictorial stone.* Eastern Han dynasty. Mencius Temple Museum, Zoucheng City, Shandong. Photo by author, June 2002.

Fig. 4 *Fuxi holding the carpenter's square and Nüwa holding the compass.* Eastern Han dynasty, ca. second century CE. Detail of Offering Hall 1 (Stone Chamber 1, Stone 2-R.2, cat. no. 1.18). "Wu family shrines" rubbings. Princeton University Art Museum, acc. no. 2002-307.17.

appropriate captions or epitaphs. In many regions of Han China the tomb artisans completed the project by adding brightly colored painted accents to the carvings, using black, red, blue, orange-brown, and white mineral pigments.[30] The paint originally applied to most stones has long since fallen away, but the brightly colored traces found on recently excavated examples should serve as a reminder that the classical starkness of Han pictorial stones might be as much an illusion as the once axiomatic Classical whiteness of Greek statuary and architecture (fig. 5).

Further analyzing the organization of this process, it appears from inscriptions that a funerary-monument work crew was supervised by two types of master artisan: one or more master masons, called *shi* ("master") or *shigong* ("stone artisan"), who coordinated the quarrying and carving, and one or more master draftsmen, who laid out the composition and executed the preliminary sketches.[31] A similar work flow and division of labor was seen amongst Egyptian New Kingdom tomb artisans. On those work crews in the Valley of the Kings the preliminary draftsmen ranked somewhat higher than the sculptors or painters, but below the crew foremen and scribes.[32] On Han work crews precedence is harder to discern, yet since the master masons were listed before the draftsmen in one detailed roster inscription, this might indicate the master mason's overall authority and not just his temporal position in the production process. Under these master artisans toiled several *di* ("apprentices"), who probably carried out the more repetitive or onerous tasks. Their numbers are included in the worker totals found in inscriptions, but their names are rarely given.[33] Such a division of labor into carvers/draftsmen and skilled/unskilled categories enabled the valuable labor of the most skilled masters to be efficiently employed, allowing greater profit.

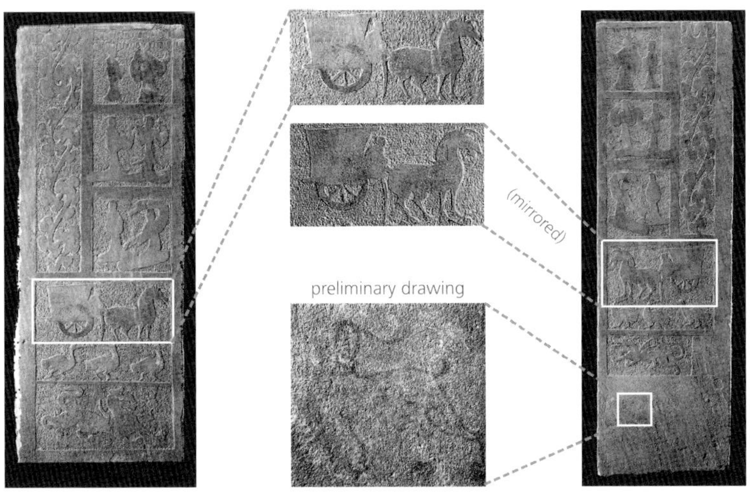

Fig. 5 *Doorposts*. Eastern Han dynasty. From Tomb 1, Dabaodang, Shaanxi. Carved and painted stone; preliminary sketch at lower right expanded at center bottom; horse-drawn carriage on right post mirror-reversed to center middle for comparison with identical image on left post. From Shaanxi Sheng kaogu yanjiusuo and Yulin Shi kaogu guanli weiyuanhui bangongshi, eds., *Shenmu Dabaodang* (Beijing: Kexue chubanshe, 2001), pls. 2–3.

Inscriptions reveal a few clues concerning the length of time required to complete a stone offering hall. Unfortunately, this evidence is often buried beneath litanies of expended labor, exaggerated for rhetorical effect. Xiang Tajun, a former official of Donge County, died in 150 CE at the age of ninety, and his wife died the following year at the age of eighty-six. Their children began to construct an offering hall during 152 CE, but it was reportedly not complete until two years later, on August 23, 154 CE.[34] The inscription on the offering hall of An Guo, a clerk from Xu County, extravagantly claims his monument took "numerous months" and required an "incalculable amount of labor."[35] From the dates mentioned

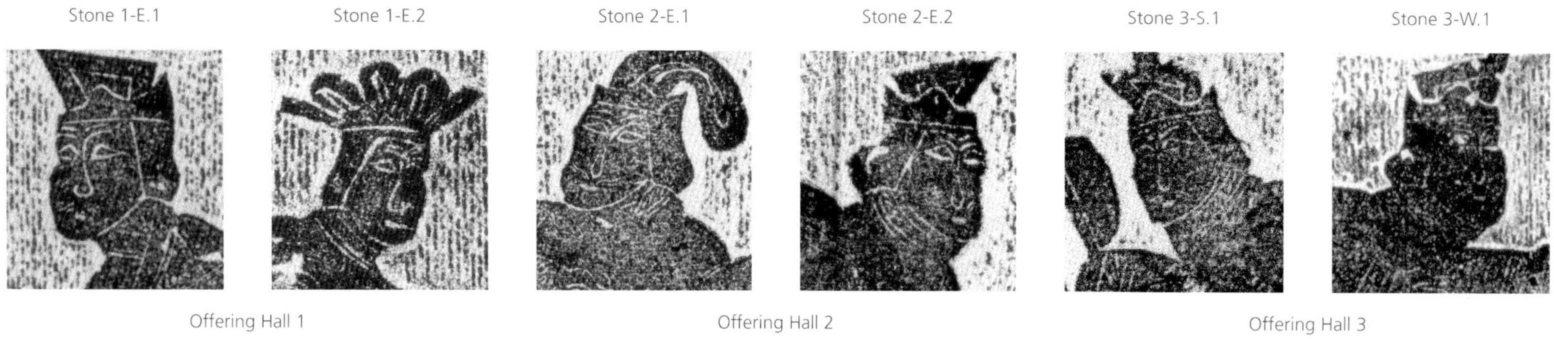

within the epitaph, it appears the offering hall was actually completed about eleven months after An Guo's death.[36] An offering hall dedicated to a certain Huan Chan was completed a little over eight months after his death. It is unclear, however, how long after his decease his two younger brothers commissioned the monument.[37] Another offering hall near Qufu took only a little over one month to complete.[38]

We also have incomplete information regarding the number of artisans typically summoned for a project. In the Xiang Tajun inscription it appears that four master artisans are mentioned by name (two masons, two draftsmen), but more than ten men are said to have been involved. In the An Guo inscription three artisans are clearly named, with two others possibly included. For comparison, the stones for one Eastern Han prince's tomb were quarried and dressed by over 120 masons.[39] Clearly the division of labor suggested above allowed the most skilled masters to perform their work expeditiously, earn their commission, and move on to the next job. They were likely not present for the entire duration of the project.

Precision and Labor-Saving Devices

Stone carvers and draftsmen in Han China developed a suite of tools and techniques to increase precision, economize materials and skilled labor, and maintain a baseline level of quality. First, it is apparent that the preliminary sketches for carriage wheels were laid out using a compass (*gui*) to ensure rapid, perfect circularity. The middle of the hub sometimes reveals a tiny pit where the compass point was anchored. In addition, the diameters of all wheels on a single stone are identical, even of wheels "receded" farthest into the background. The use of the compass appears to have expanded over time, for on second-century carvings from central Shandong, even the rumps of horses and the outlines of people were rendered as perfect arcs with a compass.[40] Compasses were clearly used to execute the simple, repetitive hanging-curtain, jade-ring, and coin-filled border patterns that separate pictorial registers.[41] No actual Han compass has yet been recovered, but the stone carvers themselves frequently illustrated the tool held in the hands of the creatrix Nüwa (fig. 4). Nüwa's consort Fuxi carries the carpenter's square, another tool vital to masons and draftsmen. Draftsmen could use it to lay down short segments, but lines longer than a foot were apparently drawn using a tool similar to the *moudou* of later Chinese craftsmen. This was basically an inked string, drawn taut and snapped down to produce a black line.[42]

Stencils carrying entire design units were apparently also used by stone carvers to construct the pictorial scenes on some monuments, especially those on *que* pillar-gates and tomb doors (see fig. 5).[43] One can trace several lines of evidence pointing to stencil use. First, on the few stones where traces of preliminary sketches remain, the painted line is sometimes composed of distinct segments of un-modulated width, unlike the spontaneous line of an original brush painting. Occasionally one even sees evidence that a brush has slipped suddenly out of the bounds of the stencil. Motifs produced multiple times from stencils also measure precisely the same size.[44] Finally, stenciled motifs often overstep the bounds of scene registers, leaving a hoof or tail dangling in a border area. Some

Fig. 6 *Three-quarters–profile noses*. Eastern Han dynasty, ca. second century CE. Comparative details from Offering Halls 1–3 (Stone Chambers 1–3). "Wu family shrines" rubbings. Princeton University Art Museum, acc. nos. 2002-307.

stencils apparently held entire compositions, whereas others contained just an individual motif. Based on analogy to modern usage, Chinese archaeologists speculate that stencils were likely made of coarse fabric or thin wooden sheets. Ultimately, the use of stencils in stone carving derives from the older tradition of stamping decoration on hollow tomb bricks. Judging by current evidence, the *pervasive* use of stencils appears to have been limited to carvers working in western Shanxi and northern Shaanxi. Stencils economize on the skilled labor of master draftsmen, ensuring exact replication and mirror-reversal at the cost of flexibility of composition and spontaneity of execution.

Far more commonly used than stencils were patterns. Reliance on patterns can be inferred from the structure of the images themselves, even though no actual examples of patterns survive. The patterns probably consisted of line drawings of individual motifs or whole compositions, brushed onto semitransparent silk or paper (fairly well available by the second century CE). The images appear to have served merely as guidelines to the draftsman and, unlike stencils, were not slavishly traced onto the stone, although the draftsmen often appear to have copied the image onto stone using the same scale as the pattern. One sometimes finds body parts encroaching beyond the register lines or necks ducking awkwardly to avoid an implied ceiling.[45] The semitransparent material of the pattern would have also made it possible to flip the pattern over for a mirror-reversed image to better suit a particular composition.

To see how patterns might have been used to construct a scene, consider the two representations of wheelwrights' shops in figure 7. In figure 7 (bottom) we see at the left a wheelwright bent over a wheel segment, assisted by his wife who stands behind him. To their right is a scene of wine making, in which an imbibing laborer, clad only in trousers, is supervised by an armed official. It is a symmetrical composition, centered on the wheel hub, with ample remaining open space. In the other version (fig. 7 [top]) the draftsman was allotted less space and had to make changes. He has moved the wheelwright to the middle and shifted his wife, mirror-reversed, to a spot in front of him. The incomplete wheel has been lifted

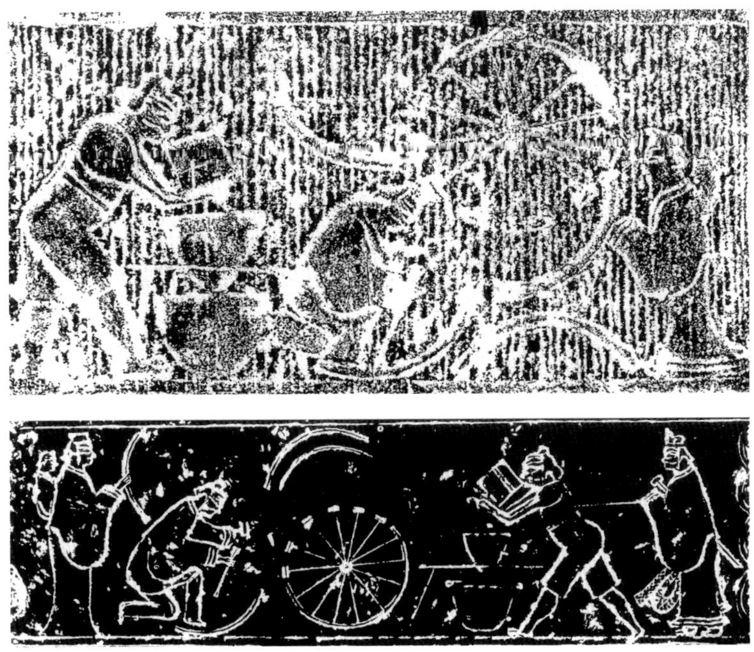

Fig. 7 *Wheelwrights' shops*. Eastern Han dynasty, ca. 1st century CE. Top: rubbing of incised stone from Liu Village, Jiaxiang County, Shandong. W. 43.5 cm. Shandong Provincial Museum. From É. Chavannes, *La sculpture sur pierre en Chine au temps des deux dynasties Han* (Paris: E. Leroux, 1893), pl. 43. Bottom: detail of rubbing of incised stone from Hongshan Village, Jiaxiang County, Shandong. W. approx. 61 cm. Museum of Chinese History, Beijing. From Käte Finsterbusch, *Verzeichnis und Motivindex der Han-Darstellungen* (Wiesbaden: Otto Harrassowitz, 1966–1971), vol. 2, fig. 271.

out of the way to a spot on the wall, with the unfinished portion rotated to face the wheelwright. The wine maker has also been mirror-reversed, and due to the tight quarters his supervisor has disappeared and his table now overlaps the leg of the wheelwright. Clearly these alterations allowed the same composition to be adapted to the narrower register of the second scene. Reconfigurable pattern modules made such accommodation easier. Notice, however, that the corresponding figures in the two scenes are in no way identical tracings, for one can detect many subtle differences between them. Both sets of images, however, derive ultimately from the same pattern sheets.

Pattern sheets were likely one of the means through which stone-carving traditions were perpetuated. The founding master of a particular tradition might have disseminated his style among his disciples by allowing them to copy his patterns. When the apprentice later founded his own workshop, he might take the patterns with him. Modifications to the transmitted designs or the addition of stock motifs purloined from other traditions would serve to differentiate this new master draftsman's style from that of his teacher.

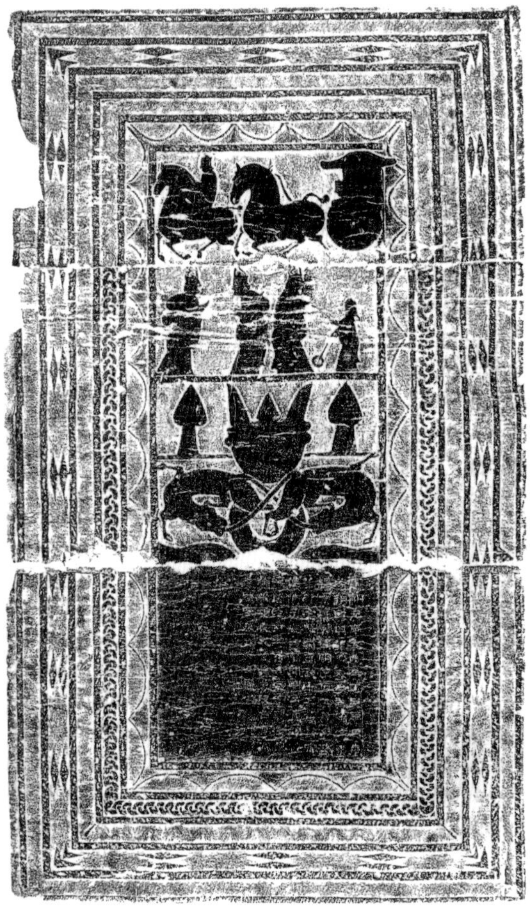

Fig. 8 *Three stacked blocks of north face of western que gate-pillar*. Eastern Han dynasty, dated to April 21, 147 CE. From Wuzhai Shan site, Jiaxiang County, Shandong. Rubbing of incised limestone blocks. From Zhongguo huaxiang shi quanji bianji weiyuanhui, ed., *Zhongguo huaxiang shi quanji* (Ji'nan: Shandong meishu chubanshe, 2000), vol. 1, pl. 16.

Customizable Prefabrication

Imperial and royal tombs were unique, custom-designed creations, built for patrons with very deep pockets. Moderately wealthy families in the provinces endeavored to convey some of the lavish appearance at a cost at least marginally within their means. Stone carvers in north China accommodated these needs with a system of customizable prefabrication, which allowed most elements of a monument to be constructed and decorated off-site, using standardized modules. Within this system, the patron was given certain customizable options, much as we experience in a modern car showroom, to make his monument distinctive and give it the *appearance* of a unique artistic creation.

Standardized pictorial scenes, built up from stencils and pattern sheets, were usually fitted within the boundaries of a single stone. Generic types included scenes of carriage and horse processions, the Queen Mother of the West, food preparation, entertainers and musical ensembles, acts of filial piety, and many more. These scenes were no more individual creations of an artist than are the parts of a Toyota Corolla. Few things demonstrate the modularity of the carved blocks better than their decorative borders. A border popular in Shandong combined a band of wave-like curtains and one of diamond-shaped lozenges (fig. 8). To give the impression that the decoration was seamless from block to block, carvers usually tried to end the decorative band at the midsection of a lozenge and the exact mid- or endpoint of a curtain. Sometimes, however, a miscommunication could lead to the slight misregistrations one sees in figure 8.

Another example of customizable prefabrication can be seen in the so-called pavilion scene, which adorns the rear walls of many stone offering halls from Shandong (fig. 9). This scene has been subjected to innumerable interpretations over the years, but the one that is most convincing reads it as a homage scene to the male deceased.[46] Younger male figures, interpreted as the decedent's sons or grandsons, kowtow in reverence before him, while sequestered women, interpreted as his mourning wife and concubines, are seated upstairs. It is striking to note that versions of this scene made in the same workshop, or at least within the same tradition, portray anywhere from one to six mourning females seated in the upper level.[47] This makes perfect sense, since men of different levels of wealth and social standing could take any number of concubines in addition to one primary wife.[48] I would argue that the stone carvers, anticipating this variable situation, prefabricated at least six versions of the homage scene. When placing an order, the patron would specify the number of widows, and the appropriate, already completed stone would be pulled from stock.

For another instance of how prefabricated modules could be later customized, consider the use of scene labels. Many carved pictorial scenes were provided in the workshop with labeling space near major figures, who might be identified as specific individuals from myth, history, or the deceased's social world. For example, the carriage and horse processions commonly seen in the lowest and highest registers of offering halls and on the lintels of tombs often reveal such a small space near each vehicle or mounted rider. For a member in the funeral cortège, these could be filled in with a generic title, or, for the deceased, with a specific title that he had held during his career. Leaving the spaces blank during preassembly enabled the artisans to make a single version of the procession scene. Later, probably at the cemetery site during final assembly, they would carve the texts specified by the patron into the spaces.

Though many figures were provided with such labeling space, not all received permanent (i.e., carved) text, and hence appear blank to us today.[49]

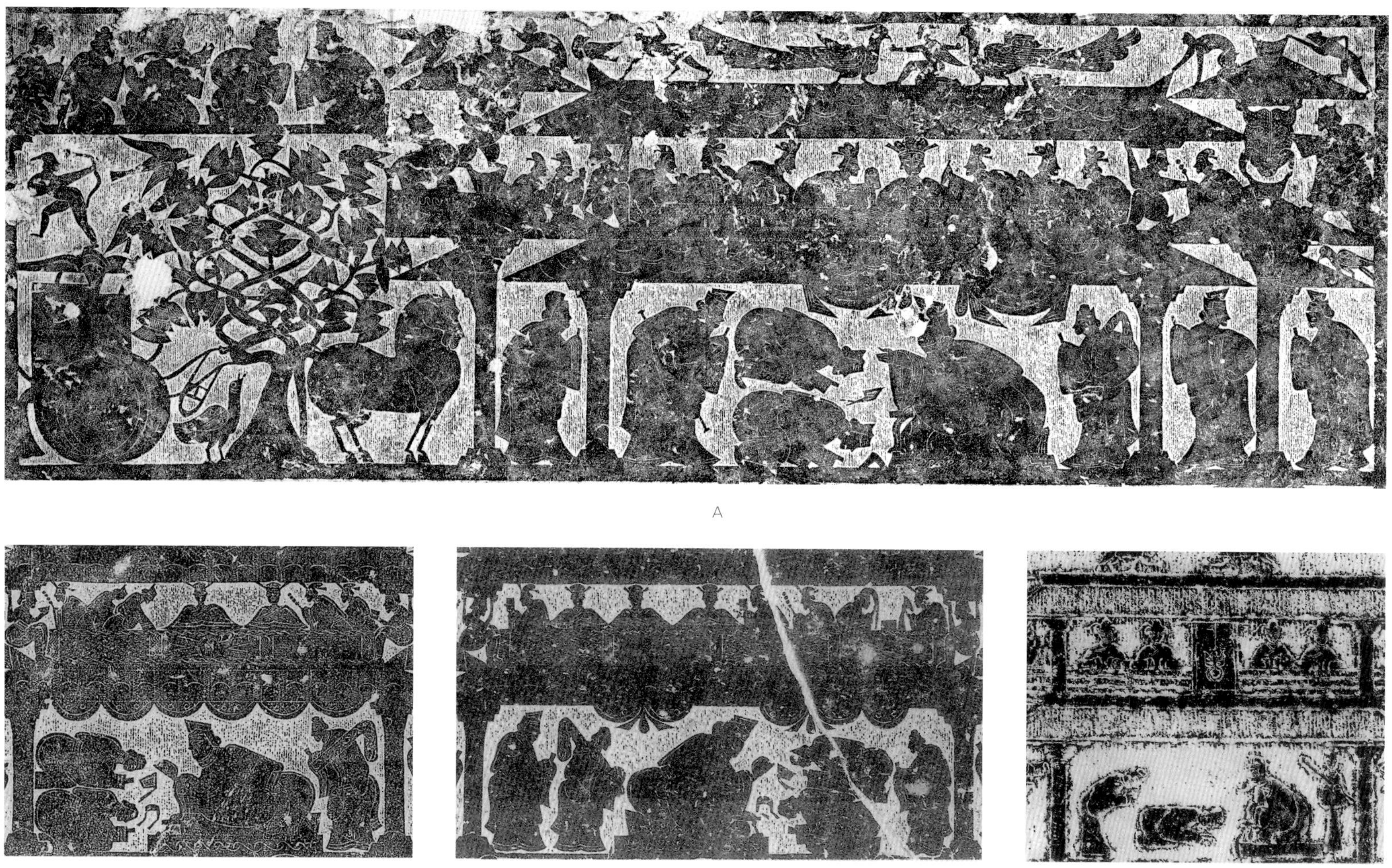

A

B

C

D

Fig. 9 *Homage scenes from Shandong stone offering halls.* Rubbings. A. Detail of Offering Hall 2 (Stone Chamber 2, Stone 2-S.6, cat. no. 1.26). "Wu family shrines" rubbings. Princeton University Art Museum, acc. no. 2002-307.24. B and C. Stones from Songshan, Jiaxiang County, Shandong. From Zhu Xilu, *Jiaxiang Han huaxiang shi* (Ji'nan: Shandong meishu chubanshe, 1992), pls. 62, 64. D. Stone from Wulaowa, Jiaxiang County, Shandong. From Zhu Xilu, *Jiaxiang Han huaxiang shi*, pl. 90.

All the blanks might be a by-product of the division of labor. According to the reconstruction of Lai Fei, to make an inscription, a preliminary text was first written on the stone in red ink, later to be carved into the stone.[50] It is possible that the many "empty" Han labeling spaces may have received the painted calligraphy but not the permanent final carving. It also appears that the artisans responsible for writing the captions were different from those draftsmen who laid out the scenes. Sometimes a label writer misunderstood the draftsman's depiction and labeled a scene incorrectly.[51]

Level of Literacy

Short scene labels or longer epitaphs demonstrate that at least one person on the stone-carving crew was literate. But what percentage of masons were literate, and what was the nature of this literacy? Experts in the field of ancient literacy distinguish many different levels and types of literacy, ranging from simple recognition and reproduction of one's name to the ability to understand and communicate profound thoughts through reading and writing. Classicist W. V. Harris has used the term "craftsman's literacy" to describe the situation in which a sizable proportion of skilled craftsmen gain and transmit a functional level of literary to carry out their craft and its related business functions.[52] On a historical continuum, craftsmen's literacy follows the more limited scribal literacy and precedes any kind of mass literacy. In Classical Greece and Rome, and up until the nineteenth century in the West, functional literacy was proportionally far greater among craftsmen than among the general population.[53]

There is abundant material evidence that many artisans in early China possessed this level of craftsmen's literacy. Master artisans in private workshops occasionally inscribed their names, auspicious slogans, or other information on bronze mirrors, lacquer vessels, iron tools, and textiles. As we shall encounter in the next section, more than one hundred masons conscripted for a royal tomb project could carve brief texts onto stone. Yet the literacy of the master mason in Han China seems to have been categorically different from the literacy possessed by the bureaucratic clerk in Han ministries or by the literary scholar of classical texts.

For example, the graphs in many stone inscriptions are riddled with "errors." Numerous characters are missing strokes or contain nonstandard additional strokes. Determinatives ("radicals") are routinely swapped or absent, and phonetic loans, in which a particular graph is replaced by a homophone, are exceedingly common.[54] Similar phonetic loans and nonstandard orthography can be seen in the inscriptions on privately produced Han bronze mirrors.[55] Perfect accuracy in character form was not as crucial in the world of craftsman's literacy as it was in the account book of the bureaucrat or in the belles-lettres of the literati. For the artisan, and apparently for his low-ranked clientele, close enough was usually good enough. The bureaucrat had to ensure that laws were understood literally, and the classical scholar desired the words of the sages to be transmitted accurately. Mistakes and phonetic loans do occur in pre-Han bureaucratic documents and literary texts, but decrease greatly during the Han period.[56] William Boltz has argued that the early Chinese language as a whole was drifting toward the kind of loose "phonetic and asemantic"

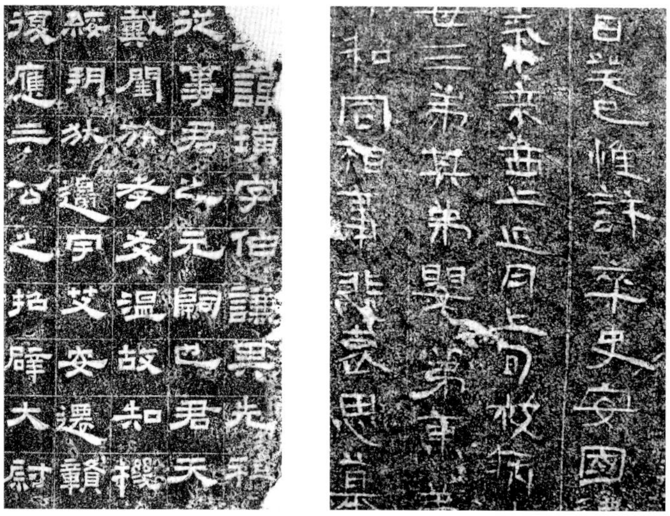

writing practiced by Han craftsman, until the meticulous bureaucrats clamped down on the linguistic evolution.[57]

The epitaphs on moderately inexpensive monuments also differ in appearance and literary structure from the commemorative steles dedicated to deceased scholars and officials. Stele texts were elegantly composed by fellow scholars and were often carved to reproduce accomplished brush calligraphy (fig. 10 left). By comparison, the graphs of epitaphs on modest monuments are quite unattractive (fig. 10 right). Reading the epitaphs on stone offering halls, with their biographical accounts and seemingly intimate outpourings of family sorrow, we might be tempted to conclude that their texts were written or spoken by the grieving family and transcribed by craftsmen onto the stone. Yet the impression of individual recollection and personal grief is mere illusion. They are clearly generic texts, full of stock phrases and trite sentiments about death and mourning: "Wu-hu—The Sorrow!" "He returned to the Yellow Springs." "We shouldered the soil to make the tomb mound."

These clues lead me to conclude that the long epitaph inscriptions carved onto stone monuments were mostly composed by the carvers themselves, after only minimal biographical input from the family.[58] I envision a scenario similar to the use of model legal forms during the Tang dynasty: model texts with blanks left for personal details (name, date, official positions held, cause of death), and the poetic phrases and boilerplate language prepackaged around them.[59] After the family provided the facts with which to fill in the blanks, the carvers could immediately set to work without a second thought. The epitaphs are yet another example of customizable prefabrication.

Fig. 10 *Rubbings of inscriptions.* (left) *Detail of stele dedicated to the former governor Xianyu Huang.* Eastern Han dynasty, dated to January 7, 166 CE. Tianjin Municipal Museum of History. From Tani Toyonobu and Hiroshi Sobukawa, eds. *Shin Kan.* Vol. 2 of *Sekai bijutsu daizenshū: Tōyōhen* (Tokyo: Shogakukan, 1998), p. 81. (right) *Detail of inscription dedicated to the clerk An Guo.* Eastern Han dynasty, dated to February 2, 158 CE. Songshan, Jiaxiang County, Shandong. From Royal Ontario Museum rubbing. Photograph courtesy of Klaas Ruitenbeek.

Such a conclusion puts a very different rhetorical spin on the meticulous naming of so-called *minggong* ("famous artisans") or *mingshi* ("famous stones") in the inscriptions, which then amounts to nothing more than self-aggrandizement and unabashed advertising.[60] In the short epitaph on the monument built by Zhang Wensi for his father (September 83 CE), the true author of the inscription reveals himself through a claim of magical efficacy for his handiwork. He claims, "Because Wang Ci made this, your family will flourish."[61] Such crass marketing slogans and magical claims could be found on many objects in the Han marketplace, including bronze mirrors, lacquer vessels, and even axle bushings.[62]

Geographic Mobility

How far might a stone carver travel to carry out his craft? To answer that question, we should examine the evidence both from private commissions, in which artisans were paid cash in a coercion-free market transaction, and royal commissions, in which artisans might have been conscripted from a wide geographic area and compelled to work.

Let us first consider the private commission. As you will recall, the children of a man named Xiang Tajun hired more than ten artisans to build a stone offering hall in 152 CE. Though the structure was built just southwest of Donge County (Map 1), the named masons who carved the stones came from Xiaqiu County in Shanyang Commandery, 105 kilometers from the tomb site. The draftsmen came from even farther away, from Gaoping Town, a marquisate embedded in Shanyang Commandery,

130 kilometers from the construction site and 40 kilometers from the home base of the Xiaqiu mason(s).

This seems relatively far to travel for a moderately well-paying commission. The pictorial carvings on the Xiang Tajun column are in a style familiar from the so-called Wu Liang Shrine and other monuments from central Shandong. In fact, the Xiang Tajun monument marks the northernmost extent of that "Gaoping" drawing style. In Eastern Han times several tributary rivers and broad marshes led northwest from Shanyang into Dong Commandery, which could have facilitated transportation of the work crews, yet it is interesting to note that the same job employed masons from one location and draftsmen from another. We cannot know if these two teams always worked together or if they were subcontracted independently by the master builder on the project, a man of unknown origin named Cao Yi. It may also be incorrect to assume that these men, having arrived at the worksite, used only local stone. The men say they took their stones from the "southern mountains," and in this case that figurative location might be taken literally. Certainly the workers came from the south, and their home towns in hilly Shanyang certainly possessed more quarries than the Yellow River flood plain around Donge. It may be that certain crews only had access to one particular quarry, which effectively anchored their home base and restricted their mobility potential to the maximum efficient transport distance over waterborne networks. At some distance from a potential private commission either the cost of transport outstripped the compensation or word of the potential job did not reach.

By contrast with that conclusion, a master mason named Shi Juyi from Lu Princedom, apparently ventured considerably farther from home to complete stone pillar-gates and spirit-path columns (dated to 105 CE) for a deceased clerk surnamed Qin, who was buried near present-day Beijing.[63] This was a full five hundred kilometers from Shi Juyi's native place in Lu. Given the number and complexity of the monuments he carved, perhaps the commission was worth the long trip. Alternatively, Shi Juyi may have immigrated to the area from Lu years before. Despite the distance between them, the Lu and Beijing areas are both located on the vast northeast China plain and could be considered part of the same geographic macroregion.

Now let us consider how far a mason might be required to travel for a royal tomb project. Throughout the Han, emperors enfeoffed some of their sons in large, income-producing territories relatively distant from the capital. These feudal princes (*zhuhou wang*) had no real power after about 145 BCE, but continued to enjoy quite lavish lifestyles and burials. Many of their tombs have been excavated in recent decades, and two in particular from the northeast provide compelling data on the subject of stone carvers' mobility.

In 1959 Chinese archaeologists excavated a large tomb in Ding County, Hebei Province, which likely belonged to Liu Yan, Prince Jian of Zhongshan (r. 54–90 CE), a junior son of the founder of the Eastern Han dynasty.[64] The tomb mound was still more than twenty meters high when excavated, and the central brick chamber was reinforced by a retaining wall composed of four thousand sandstone blocks, each weighing over

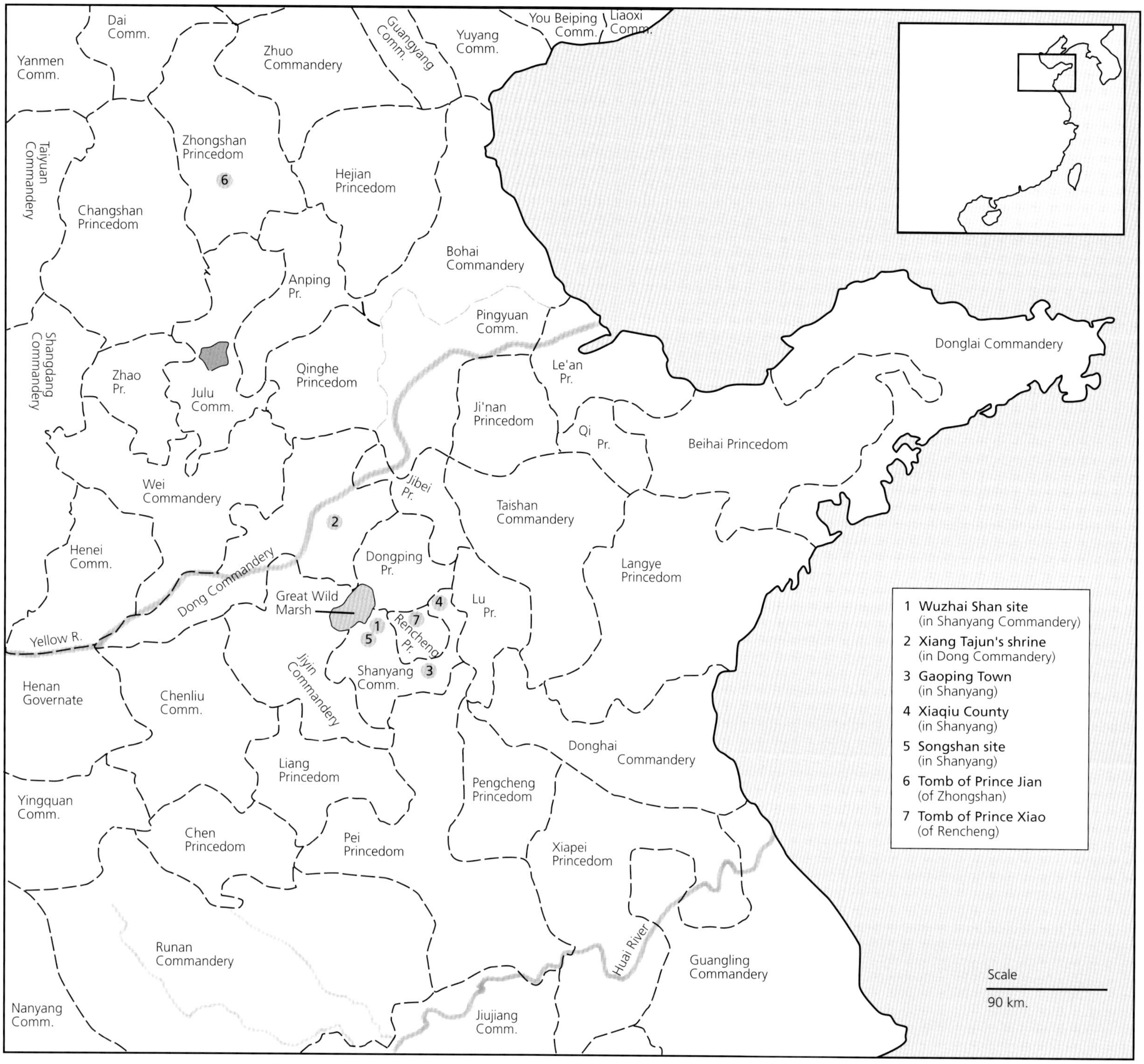

Map 1 *Northeast China during the Eastern Han period.* Drawn by author, based on *Zhongguo lishi dituji*, vol. 2, pp. 44–45, 47–48.

Table 1: Declared Cost of Stone Funerary *que* ("Pillar-Gates")

Name and Location	Date	Cost	Estimated total stone volume	Estimated decorated surface area	Note reference*
Pillar-gate of Sun Zhongyang, Junan County, Shandong	February 18, 85 CE	15,000	1.14 m^3	6.09 m^2	A
Pillar-gate of a Merit Bureau Administrator, Pingyi County, Shandong	April 7, 87 CE	45,000	2.58 m^3	12.6 m^2	B
Pillar-gate at Wuzhai Shan site, Jiaxiang County, Shandong	April 21, 147 CE	150,000	14 m^3	59.4 m^2	C
Pillar-gate of Wang Ziya, former Governor of Shu Commandery, along Yu River in far southern Henan. (site no longer extant)		10 million	193.5 m^3	N/A	D

Table 2: Declared Cost of Stone Offering Halls, Stone Tombs, Spirit Paths

Monument	Location on present-day map	Date	Cost in coins	Note reference*
Stone Chamber (*shishi*), h. 66 cm w. 90 cm	Tongshan County, Jiangsu	Feb. 9–March10, 61 CE	5,000	E
Monument dedicated by Zhang Wensi to his father, h. 70 cm, w. 152 cm	Feicheng County, Shandong	September, 83 CE	3,000	F
Tomb mound and Stone Chamber (*shishi*), h. 69 cm	Tongshan County, Jiangsu	April 8, 86 CE	15,000+	G
Offering Hall (*tang, cishi*) dedicated by Zhu Zuoji to his mother	Zaozhuang City, Shandong	March 27, 124 CE	35,000	H
Offering Hall (*shitang*)	Weishan County, Shandong	March 20, 130 CE	5,000	I
Tomb mound and Offering Hall (*qiu shitang*) for Wang Cheng's mother, h. 95 cm, w. 140 cm	Weishan County, Shandong	February 4, 137 CE	5,000	J
Offering Hall (*shitang*) dedicated to parents, h. 92 cm, w. 90 cm	Shandong	October 4, 137 CE	10,000–19,000	K
Offering Hall (*shitang*) for Wen Shuyang, h. 84 cm, d. 60 cm	Yutai County, Shandong	October 3, 144 CE	17,000	L
Two stone lions at Wuzhai Shan site, h. 126 cm, l. 158 cm	Jiaxiang County, Shandong	April 21, 147 CE	40,000	M
Offering Hall (*shi citang*) for Xiang Tajun, h. at door 120 cm	Dong'e County, Shandong	August 23, 154 CE	25,000	N
Offering Hall (*tang, tangzhai*) for An Guo and his two children	Jiaxiang County, Shandong	February 2, 158 CE	27,000	O
Offering Hall (*shitang*) for a wife	Near Qufu, Shandong	December 15, 158 CE	50,000 (construction) 90,000 (food offerings)	P
Tomb mound (*feng*) for a father	Yi County, Shandong	April 20 or 21, 163 CE	17,000	Q
Stone Chamber (*shishi*), h. 116 cm, d. 105 cm	Tongshan County, Jiangsu	Not dated	52,000	R
Stone Chamber (*shi*), h. 75 cm	Tongshan County, Jiangsu	Not dated	17,000	S
Tomb of Wang Ziya, former Governor of Shu Commandery	Along Yu River in southern Henan	Not dated	5,000,000	T

*See this essay's endnotes for references in tables 1 and 2.

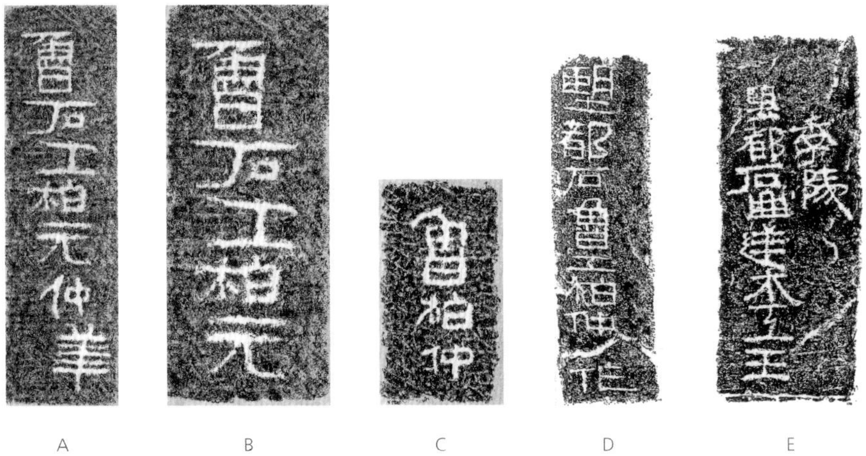

300 kilograms. More than 174 of those blocks were inscribed by functionally literate masons with their full names, native places, and the source of the stone (fig. 11).[65]

The sandstone blocks themselves came almost exclusively from two counties within Zhongshan, just to the north of the tomb site (30–70 km away). The majority of the 120 named men who carved the blocks, however, came from much farther away. Though nearly 40 percent of the masons came from within Zhongshan itself, most of the remaining 60 percent came from three princedoms far to the southeast: Lu Princedom (360–430 km distant), Liang Princedom (400–460 km), and Dongping Princedom (300 km).

We are very fortunate to possess an historical account of this grand tomb-building enterprise that helps explain why the masons ventured so far to work on this project. In Liu Yan's biography in the *Hou Hanshu* (*History of the Latter Han*), we are told that the mighty Empress Dowager Dou, and her eldest brother, Dou Xian, who held regency power 89–92 CE, jointly ordered the princedoms and commanderies surrounding Zhongshan to contribute men and materials for Liu Yan's tomb.[66] It is said that more than ten thousand artisans and convict laborers from more than eighteen provinces were sent to work on the tomb, including apparently, the stone carvers who recorded their names on the blocks. The history makes clear that the artisans were conscripted for this job, and that their labor was considered as tribute (*diao*). Thus, they were not paid cash, but their work should still be considered as compensated, since it commuted taxes that they would otherwise have owed.

The princes of Lu, Liang, and Dongping were closely related to Liu Yan, so they may have felt more obligated than the governors of nearby commanderies to contribute labor and materials to the project.[67] As a sidelight, one of the men sent to work on the prince's tomb, a certain Wang Jiling, recorded his profession on at least one stone as *mugong* ("carpenter") (fig. 11E).[68] Apparently, it did not matter on this job that he was more accustomed to hewing timber than stone.

Many of the conclusions reached from Liu Yan's tomb at Zhongshan are confirmed by the more recent excavation of a tomb likely belonging to Liu Shang (r. 84–101 CE), Prince Xiao of Rencheng, almost 350 kilometers away in central Shandong.[69] Liu Shang was a nephew of Liu Yan and a grandson of the dynasty founder. His tomb also contained a retaining wall whose stones were inscribed with masons' names. Judging by place names mentioned in the inscriptions, his tomb was probably built sometime between 84 and 93 CE, about the same time as Liu Yan's tomb.

To work on Liu Shang's tomb, masons also came from a variety of places. His elder brother's princedom of Dongping (40–70 km distant) contributed 31 percent of the named masons. The princedom of Lu (40–85 km) and his cousin's princedom of Liang (120–160 km distant) combined to send nearly 45 percent of the remaining men. Liu Shang's own small fief of Rencheng contributed only 6 percent of the carvers. A few men came from commanderies as far as 360 kilometers distant.

It is apparent from reading through the masons' names on these blocks that the stone-carving profession ran in families. Three men with the Bo surname from Lu, probably brothers, worked on the Prince of

Fig. 11 *Masons' signatures.* A. "*Lu masons Bo Yuan, [Bo] Zhong, [Bo] Hua.*" From Shandong Sheng Jining Shi wenwuju, ed., *Han Rencheng wang mu keshi jingxuan* (Ji'nan: Shandong meishu chubanshe, 1998), p. 118, right. B. "*Lu mason Bo Yuan.*" From *Han Rencheng wang mu keshi jingxuan*, p. 118, left. C. "*Lu [mason] Bo Zhong.*" From *Han Rencheng wang mu keshi jingxuan*, p. 120, upper left. D. "*Stones from Wangdu, made by artisan Bo Zhong from Lu.*" From *Kaogu xuebao* 1964.2, p. 188, rubbing no. 19. E. "*Stones from Wangdu, carpenter Wang Jiling from Quni county.*" From *Kaogu xuebao* 1964.2, p. 189, rubbing no. 155.

Rencheng's tomb. On two stones they recorded their names together, probably in birth order, as Bo-Yuan-Zhong-Hua, in other words, Bo Yuan, Bo Zhong, and Bo Hua (see fig. 11A).[70] On two other stones, Bo Yuan and Bo Zhong recorded their names separately (figs. 11B, 11C).[71] The Bo family came from the seat of Lu Princedom, only about 40 kilometers from the tomb site. Shortly before or after his work on the Rencheng tomb, however, Bo Zhong, the presumed second-eldest son, volunteered or was conscripted to work on Liu Yan's tomb in Zhongshan as well. His name shows up quite clearly, in roughly the same hand, on blocks from that site (see fig. 11D).[72] For the Zhongshan job, he traveled more than 360 kilometers, in the company of twenty other masons from Lu.

To summarize, it appears from inscriptional evidence that stone carvers were rarely enticed or compelled to travel more than five hundred kilometers from their home base to work on a project, whether a private commission or royal conscription. The normal operating radius seems to have been even smaller. In effect, carvers operated within one macro-regional area, defined by drainage basins or contiguous geographic features. This might help explain the rather clear boundaries between regional styles of stone carving on Han pictorial stones. There is no evidence that stone carvers from Shandong were ever invited or enticed to travel to Sichuan or Nanyang for jobs, or vice versa. If such interregional movement had been a regular occurrence, we might see more Shandong-style carving and motifs in those regions. That is not to say that people and motifs did not travel the empire at all, just that cross-pollination does not seem to have been a common occurrence.

Expense of Monuments

How much did stone carvers charge private individuals for their products? Since many families were eager to proclaim the financial extent of their filial sacrifice, a goodly number of dated inscriptions actually report in round numbers the cost claimed for their particular monuments.[73] Table 1 lists the declared cost of four *que* pillar-gates from the North China Plain, and Table 2 lists the prices of a more than a dozen other monuments.

From Table 1 it appears that the larger and more elaborately decorated the monument, the higher its price. The correlation between the total area of carved decoration and the declared cost is quite consistent. The pillar-gate at the Wuzhai Shan site costs ten times as much as those for Sun Zhongyang, and it has ten times the carved surface area. Judging from the limited sample in Table 1, it would seem that the total price per square meter of carved decoration was in the range of 2,500 to 3,500 coins.

Several of the entries in Table 2 refer to the cost of "offering halls" (*tang*, *shitang*, *citang*, *cishi*, *shishi*). These seem to have been small stone chambers, usually less than the height of a standing man, designed to accommodate food offerings for the deceased.[74] The halls were not lavish custom creations, but were built from the kind of prefabricated, mass-produced components discussed above. A stone offering hall could apparently cost as little as 5,000 coins and as much as 52,000, but averaged 20,000 to 25,000.

How much purchasing power did 20,000 coins represent to the laborers and their customers? For a start, that much money could buy sufficient grain during the Eastern Han to feed more than five adult males for a year.[75] If we divide equally the Xiang Tajun expenditure of 25,000 coins by the ten to twelve laborers on the crew and reduce the time spent to one year, we arrive at the average annual salary of 2,083–2,500 cash coins per laborer, hardly enough money to supply each of them with grain and tax payments for the year.[76] One official document on wood from the arid northwest declares that the local market price for a live chicken was 40 coins, so 20,000 coins could also buy a flock of 500 chickens.[77] On a more serious note, we know that the lifetime services of an adult slave during the Western Han cost between 15,000 and 20,000 coins.[78]

Since a few of the inscriptions on these stone monuments list the official posts held by the deceased, it is possible in those cases to correlate yearly salary with the declared cost of the monument.[79] Xiang Tajun held a variety of posts in the *xian*-level administration during his career, including *zhubu* ("Master of Records"), *tingyuan* ("Headquarters Clerk"), *shiyuan* ("Market Administrator"), and *gongcao* ("Merit Bureau Administrator.") None of these posts carried a rank higher than 100 *shi*, a level with a cash-equivalent yearly salary of 19,200 coins.[80] This amount was 5,800 coins less than the cost of his monument. An Guo worked as a *zushi* ("clerk") in Xu County, probably with the same maximum rank of 100 *shi* and cash-equivalent yearly salary, amounting to 7,800 less than the cost of his monument.

According to Hans Bielenstein's calculations, officials of the 100-*shi* rank should have netted a small surplus each month after expenses, so theoretically they could have saved a bit toward final expenses, but overall they held fairly low-paying posts. In fact, many of the men who were memorialized by the monuments listed in Table 2 worked at low-ranked or sub-bureaucratic posts in the county-level administration. Only one, Wang Ziya, ranked as high as governor, and his monuments, as reported in *Shuijing zhu* (*Commentary on "Classic of Waterways"*), were so colossal as to defy belief. Clearly, higher-ranking officials had much more surplus income and would have been able to afford monuments far more lavish than a tiny mass-produced stone offering hall. Their children would have hardly dared brag about spending a paltry sum like 25,000 coins. For them to sound impressive, an expenditure of millions was required.

Yet, even with a little savings, how could the families of men like An Guo or Xiang Tajun have afforded to pay more than a year's salary for a stone monument? First, these bureaucrats might have had resources well beyond their official salaries, including rented-out land or indirect business ties. There is also evidence to suggest that the deceased's extended family and colleagues contributed to the costs of funerary equipment. Cui Shi, in his *Simin yueling* (*Monthly ordinances for the four peoples*), encouraged family members to contribute to the funeral expenses of poorer relatives, with contributions adjusted on a sliding scale according to wealth and closeness of relationship.[81] Colleagues might help defray funeral and burial costs as well. One fragmentary offering-hall inscription from Shandong seems to contain a list of people and the amounts of money they contributed toward the cost of a modest monument.[82] Modern-day scholar Li Falin even suggests that at well-attended funerals, a family might make a tidy profit from condolence contributions.[83]

Reuse of Stone Monuments

During the heyday of the stone-monument craze in the mid-second century, it probably seemed as if the funerary business would grow perpetually, as upstart families competed to outspend one another. Starting about 184 CE, however, tremendous economic and social upheavals in the Shandong area decimated the population and collapsed the high-end funeral business.[84] After those disruptions, dated monuments are few and far between, and one cannot escape the impression that the bubble had burst.

The desperate times accelerated a trend that had already surfaced a few decades earlier. Namely, during the late second century and continuing through the fifth century, funerary artisans often found it more convenient and economical to plunder stones from existing aboveground monuments and belowground tombs than to quarry, dress, and decorate new building materials. More delicately put, they were "recycling," particularly if the decedent's lineage had failed and there was no one any longer to preserve and protect the ancestral tombs. Archaeologists have excavated numerous tombs in north China dating from the third to fifth centuries that were made from reused stones originally part of first- and second-century monuments.[85]

Even during the height of the building boom, vandalism and looting were already a pressing concern for tomb builders and mourning families alike. One passage near the end of the inscription on An Guo's monument (February 2, 158 CE) warned:

> To all you young men who herd horses, cows, and sheep! Be like the children of good families. If you enter into this hall, please just look around. Do not efface the images or carve graffiti. If you do not, then you will be granted long life. Do not maliciously cause damage! Otherwise may misfortune rain down on you and your descendants.[86]

Needless to say, this supernatural warning went unheeded, for a few decades after the monument was dedicated, its parts were dismantled and reused in another tomb.[87] That tomb was excavated along with three others between 1978 and 1981 at the sites of Songshan and Wulaowa in Jiaxiang County, Shandong.[88] All four tombs tell a similar story. The crypts are moderate in size and many of the stones that constitute their walls, ceilings, and floors were clearly looted from earlier aboveground offering halls and belowground tombs dating from about 67 CE to 158. Some stones had been cropped, and all were haphazardly placed in the new tombs and coated with lime plaster.

It is telling that all the pictorial stones from these graves had been plastered with an obscuring layer of lime, up to one centimeter thick, which completely concealed the pictorial scenes. It would be mistaken to interpret this effacement as revealing the tomb masons' desire to hide their culpability in grave-robbing. Rather, we should see this as a ritual desanctification of the earlier images, rechristening the stones for a new purpose. Images have power, and which images are placed in one's tomb can be a sensitive subject. It appears that by the time of the Songshan and Wulaowa tombs (third to fourth century), Han conventions of homage

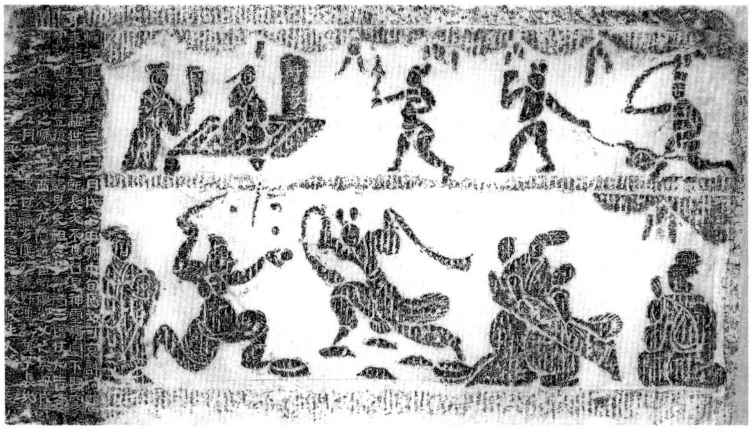

scenes, filial paragons, winged deities, and chariot processions had lost much of their significance.[89] One might even suggest that they had been discredited by the fall of the Han and its ruling ideology. Best to white-wash away such inauspicious images and remove the potential malicious influence that might still attach to them from their earlier association with death and with an extinguished family lineage. It was that extinction, after all, which allowed them to be ravaged by looters.

This calls to mind the similar fate of Akhenaten's (r. ca. 1379–1362 BCE) monuments in Egypt.[90] After the death of the heretic pharaoh and the discrediting of his ideology, his successors, like Rameses II (r. ca. 1304–1237) reused thousands of stone blocks from his buildings at El-Amarna and Thebes. Yet since the blocks displayed scenes of the repudiated ruler and his heretical ideology, the stones were only used as filler *inside* temple pylons and wall foundations, preserving their material value as stones, while ritually killing and burying their iconic power.

Another group of post-Han tombs in the Shandong and Nanyang areas reflects even greater economy than we see at Songshan. In these, the walls and floor of the tomb were made of less expensive ceramic bricks (often recycled), while the flat roofs were planked over by stone slabs about 1.1–1.4 meters in width.[91] The roof slabs were salvaged from a variety of Eastern Han monuments and cropped to a uniform length. On one slab you might see the carved handle of a tomb door, another might have been an offering table, while yet another was likely the back wall of a small offering hall. The content and location of the images on the roof slabs seems to have been immaterial to the new tomb builders. In these bargain creations no decorative program was intended, for all that mattered was the cost-savings from recycled materials. It was more economical to lay six or seven recycled stone planks over the crypt than to properly roof the tomb with a genuine brick vault, a design that would also have required the tomb to be dug deeper.

Lavish tombs reflected demand by wealthy customers. When turmoil and disasters impoverished the Shandong region, healthy commissions were no longer forthcoming for the stone masons. To stay in business, they downsized their plans and cut material costs wherever they could. That meant no longer using new stone and carving no original decoration.

A final brief example of this sordid business offers a human perspective on the stone monument reuse market. In 1973 archaeologists excavated a small shaft-tomb near present-day Nanyang, Henan Province.[92] It was similar to the type just described, with brick walls and a stone-slab ceiling made from recycled materials. The presence of certain coins and ceramics dates the tomb to the mid-third century. Three of the five ceiling slabs used to cover the crypt carried cropped decorative scenes. On one of these three stones was depicted a scene of entertainers at a banquet, of the type commonly seen on the walls of Nanyang tombs from the Eastern Han period (fig. 12). The leftmost portion of the banquet scene had been intentionally effaced to clear the ground for an inscription. The 136-character text is an epitaph, lamenting the untimely death of a five-year old boy named Aqu of the Xu family, who died on April 25, 170 CE. It reads in part:

Fig. 12 *Epitaph of Xu Aqu*. Dated to April 25, 170 CE. Tomb at Lixianggong Zhuang, Henan. Rubbing; 69 × 109 cm. Henan Sheng Nanyang Hanhuaguan. From *Zhongguo huaxiang shi quanji*, vol. 2, pl. 202.

> Oh the pain, pitiful little Xu Aqu . . . . He was barely five years old when he left this world and departed for the long night, never again to see the sun and stars. His spirit dwells alone and descends into the dark realm, forever to be cut off from his family. How can they again see his face?

Though poignant and dramatic in translation, the rhyming four-character phrases of the epitaph consist mostly of clichés inelegantly strung together. Little Aqu's name was also added as a caption to the young male figure seated on the dais to the left of the entertainers.

Reconstructing from these clues, it seems that this durable slab saw use in three separate funerary structures over a period of at least a century. It began its life as a wall slab in a wealthy Nanyang tomb built during the early second century. During early 170 CE, the stone, which had been looted from the original tomb, was reused in a makeshift monument for a five-year-old named Xu Aqu. Space was cleared for an epitaph by grinding down the original bas-relief, and the rich adolescent shown enjoying the banquet was recaptioned as the deceased Aqu. Finally, Aqu's monument was itself plundered sometime in the early third century and the banquet slab was trimmed for use as a roof slab in the tomb of an unnamed occupant. Just as today the clothes and cars of the rich trickle down in secondhand markets to become the shabby possessions of the poor, so expensive pictorial stones of the Eastern Han could be reused in a cascading series of cheaper and cheaper contexts.

Notes

1. Total industry statistics from "The Death Business: Staying Alive," *The Economist*, August 3, 2000. Employment statistics from the National Funeral Directors Association website, http://www.nfda.org/nfdafactsheet.php, accessed March 3, 2004.

2. Martin J. Powers, *Art and Political Expression in Early China* (New Haven: Yale University Press, 1991), chap. 3; Patricia Ebrey, "The Economic and Social History of Later Han," in *The Cambridge History of China* (Cambridge: Cambridge University Press, 1986), vol.1, p. 611; Li Falin, *Shandong Han huaxiang shi yanjiu* (Ji'nan: Qi-Lu shushe, 1982), pp. 19–24.

3. Each province was allotted a population-based quota of *xiaolian* awards, for which one was recommended by lower officials. The award qualified one for a bureaucratic appointment. About three hundred men annually entered the civil service in this way. Powers, *Art and Political Expression*, pp. 43, 85, 98–101.

4. Wang Fu, *Qianfu lun jian jiaozheng*, ed. Peng Duo (Beijing: Zhonghua shuju, 1985), p. 137; Fan Ye, *Hou Hanshu* (Beijing: Zhonghua shuju, 1965), p.1637 (hereafter, *HHS*). Etienne Balazs, *Chinese Civilization and Bureaucracy*, trans. H. M. Wright, ed. Arthur F. Wright (New Haven: Yale University Press, 1964), p. 203.

5. *HHS*, p. 1724.

6. Yan Kejun, ed., *Quan shanggu sandai Qin Han sanguo liuchao wen* (Beijing: Zhonghua shuju, 1965), vol. 1, *juan* 46:5a-b (hereafter, *QQHW*).

7. For the biography of Cui Shi, see *HHS*, pp. 1725–31. For an account of the Cui lineage during the Han, see Patricia Ebrey, *The Aristocratic Families of Early Imperial China: A Case Study of the Po-Ling Ts'ui Family* (Cambridge: Cambridge University Press, 1978), pp. 34–49.

8. *HHS*, p. 1731.

9. Wang Fu, *Qianfu lun*, pp. 134–37; A slightly different version of this polemic is found in *HHS*, p. 1636. Cf. the translation by Ebrey, "Economic and Social History," pp. 610–11.

10. Wu Hung, *The Wu Liang Shrine: The Ideology of Early Chinese Pictorial Art* (Stanford: Stanford University Press, 1989); Powers, *Art and Political Expression*.

11. The concentrated cluster of dated monuments in Shandong begins about 83–87 CE and disappears soon after the Yellow Turban revolt ravaged the area (184 CE). There is some evidence for a stone monument tradition after this date, much of it in the way of reused materials from earlier monuments. For a comprehensive list of dated monuments, see Jiang Yingju and Yang Aiguo, *Handai huaxiang shi yu huaxiang zhuan* (Beijing: Wenwu chubanshe, 2001), pp. 36–42.

12. Based on regional stylistic analysis, Xin Lixiang lays out five stone-carving traditions: (1) Shandong Peninsula and northern Jiangsu and Anhui, (2) the area around Han-dynasty Nanyang Commandery in present-day Henan Province, (3) western Shanxi and northern Shaanxi, (4) Sichuan and northern Yunnan, and (5) the immediate area around the Eastern Han capital at Luoyang. See Xin Lixiang, *Handai huaxiang shi zonghe yanjiu* (Wenwu chubanshe, 2000), pp. 13–17.

13. Xin Lixiang, *Handai huaxiang shi*, pp. 13–14.

14. Seminar presentation by Professor Lothar von Falkenhausen at UCLA, March 2002.

15. The three inscriptions I have used to help reconstruct this process are:

(A) The inscribed doorpost from the offering hall of Xiang Tajun. See transcription and notes in Luo Fuyi, "Xiang Tajun shi citang tizi jieshi," *Gugong bowuyuan yuankan* 1960.2, pp. 178–81. This post, now in the Palace Museum, Beijing, was found accidentally in 1934, 70 km southwest of Donge County, Shandong. The authenticity of the long inscription, which skirts damaged areas of the stone and contains numerous errors and phonetic loans, has raised doubts, but in my view these only support the authenticity of the inscription (see discussion of literacy). On a recent visit to the Palace Museum, I was not able to see the original post, but only a rubbing.

(B) The inscribed stones from An Guo's offering hall. See transcription and notes in Li Falin, *Shandong Han huaxiang shi yanjiu*, pp. 101–8. A more recent, improved transcription (without notes) can be found in Zhongguo huaxiang shi quanji bianji weyuanhui, ed., *Zhongguo huaxiang shi quanji* (Ji'nan: Shandong meishu chubanshe, 2000), vol. 2, nos. 108–9. These two stones were part of a set of floral-decorated slabs found at Songshan, which may have been originally intended as ceiling stones, but were instead probably used to form the walls of an offering hall. Later, they were all reused in a belowground tomb. The dates within the inscription contain some errors. The *taisui* position for the year is erroneously given as *guiyou*, when it should be *dingyou*. The "twenty-sixth day" at the start of the inscription should read "sixteenth day," as it does at the end. Such errors are not uncommon on Han stone monuments.

(C) The long-lost stele of Wu Liang. See transcription in Zhao Mingcheng, *Jinshi lu*, 14:10b; Hong Gua, *Lishi*, vols. 1–8 of *Shike shiliao congshu*, ser. A, ed. Yan Gengwang (Taipei: Yiwen yinshuguan, 1966), 6:13b–15a. See partial English translation in Wilma Fairbank, "The Offering Shrines of 'Wu Liang Tz'u'," *Harvard Journal of Asiatic Studies* vol. 6, no. 1 (1941), p. 8. Since this object no longer exists, and received transcriptions vary, I have used this inscription very sparingly, only for information that is corroborated by the other two.

16. Most recently, Xin Lixiang, building on the work of Nagahiro Toshio and others, has laid out the process quite clearly in his book *Handai huaxiang shi*, pp. 22–26. He bases his reconstruction largely on the same three inscriptions.

17. Morris Bierbrier, *The Tomb Builders of the Pharaohs* (Cairo: American University in Cairo Press, 1989), pp. 43–64; Rosemarie Drenkhahn, "Artisans and Artists in Pharaonic Egypt," in *Civilizations of the Ancient Near East*, ed. Jack M. Sasson (New York: Charles Scribner's Sons, 1995), vol. 1, pp. 336–37; Christopher J. Eyre, "Work and Organisation of Work in the New Kingdom," in *Labor in the Ancient Near East*, ed. Marvin Powell (New Haven: American Oriental Society, 1987), pp. 167–222.

18. Some monuments appear to have been carved from an even harder, recrystallized limestone called dolomite. Farther south, into Jiangsu, sandstone monuments become more prevalent.

19. The exact phrases used are: *nanshan*, *nanshan zhi yang*, *xian xi'nan xiaoshan yangshan*. See Glossary Index for the Chinese characters.

20. Wang Xueli, *Qin Shihuang ling yanjiu* (Shanghai: Shanghai renmin chubanshe, 1994), pp. 200–201; Henan Sheng wenwu kaogu yanjiusuo, ed., *Yongcheng Xihan Liang guo wangling yu qinyuan* (Zhengzhou: Zhongzhou guji chubanshe, 1996), pp. 74–80.

21. Shandong Sheng Jining Shi wenwuju, ed., *Han Rencheng wang mu keshi jingxuan* (Ji'nan: Shandong meishu chubanshe, 1998), p. 12.

22. This is in the An Guo inscription transcribed in Li Falin, *Shandong Han huaxiang shi yanjiu*, p. 105. Li interprets the phrases *luanshi* and *lianju* as being names of artisans. As names for masons and quarry workers, they would be rather ironic. If taken literally, they can be seen as verb-object compounds meaning "bind up the stones," and "connect together the carts," and thus could be taken as the predicates of the previously mentioned artisans Wang Shu, Wang Jian, and Jiang Hu. The fact that the name Jiang Hu happens to rhyme with the clause *lianju* supports this interpretation. See the translation of this passage by Klaas Ruitenbeek, *Chinese Shadows: Stone Reliefs, Rubbings, and Related Works of Art from the Han Dynasty (206 BC–AD 220) in the Royal Ontario Museum* (Toronto: Royal Ontario Museum, 2002), p. 17.

23. Heze diqu bowuguan and Liangshan Xian wenhuaguan, eds., "Shandong Liangshan Donghan jinian mu," *Kaogu* 1988.11, p. 982.

24. Tan Qixiang, ed., *Zhongguo lishi ditu ji* (Beijing: Zhongguo ditu chubanshe, 1982–1987), vol. 2, pp. 44–45.

25. For the interpretation of these phrases in the An Guo inscription, see Li Falin, *Shandong Han huaxiang shi yanjiu*, p. 105.

26. Shandong Sheng Jining Shi wenwuju, ed., *Han Rencheng wang*, pp. 44–45.

27. Heze diqu bowuguan and Liangshan Xian wenhuaguan, eds.,"Shandong Liangshan." The notation reads *ci biao fan you* X, ("all of the X on this surface . . ."). It might have been a note from one literate craftsman to another, indicating that the former had completed the carving of all the figures on that surface. The excavators, however, suggest that *biao* might instead be a specific term indicating that the stone was a grave marker, or *mu biao*. The stone in question (dated to 167 CE) is difficult to reconstruct but might have been a partition gable in an aboveground offering hall.

28. The master draftsman for Xiang Tajun's offering hall is named as Master Dai Sheng from Gaoping Town. The artisan listed after him, Shao Qiangsheng, might also have been a master draftsman. Traces of initial sketches have been found on some stones from Shaanxi Province; see Dai Yingxin and Wei Suizhi, "Shaanxi Suide Huangjiata Donghan huaxiang shi muqun fajue jianbao," *Kaogu yu wenwu* 1988.5–6, pp. 251–61; Xin Lixiang, *Handai huaxiang shi*, p. 25.

29. Li Falin, *Shandong Han huaxiang shi yanjiu*, p. 105; Hong Gua, *Li shi*, 6:14a. Compare the translation of Wilma Fairbank (following Chavannes) as "engraved the text (*wen*)" and "carved the designs," in "The Offering Shrines of 'Wu Liang Tz'u'," p. 8.

30. Traces of final painting have been found on stones from Shanxi, Shaanxi, Henan, and Sichuan provinces. See references in Xin Lixiang, *Handai huaxiang shi*, p. 26. For colorplates of some of these stones and chemical analyses of the pigments, see Shaanxi Sheng kaogu yanjiusuo and Yulin Shi kaogu guanli weiyuanhui bangongshi, eds., *Shenmu Dabaodang: Handai chengzhi yu muzang kaogu baogao* (Beijing: Kexue chubanshe, 2001), pls. 2–23 (hereafter, *DBD*).

31. Xin Lixiang, *Handai huaxiang shi*, p. 26; Shandong Sheng bowuguan and Shandong Sheng wenwu kaogu yanjiusuo, eds., *Shandong Han huaxiang shi xuanji* (Ji'nan: Qi-Lu shushe, 1982), pp. 15–16 (hereafter, *Xuanji*).

32. Eyre, "Work," p. 173.

33. The titles of master and apprentice appear in sequence in an inscription dated to 142 CE, but only one name is given. See Sishui Xian wenguansuo, ed., "Shandong Sishui nanchen Donghan huaxiang shi mu," *Kaogu* 1995.5, pp. 390–95.

34. Luo Fuyi, "Xiang Tajun," pp. 178–79.

35. Li Falin, *Shandong Han huaxiang shi yanjiu*, p. 106; for the characters of *lianyue* ("numerous months") and *gongfu wuji* ("incalculable labor"), see Glossary Index. Zhongguo huaxiang shi quanji bianji weiyuanhui, ed., *Zhongguo huaxiang shi quanji* (Ji'nan: Shandong meishu chubanshe, 2000), vol. 2, no. 108 (hereafter, *HXSQJ*) transcribes the second phrase as *gongfu wukao* ("unending labors").

36. Li Falin, *Shandong Han huaxiang shi yanjiu*, p. 103.

37. *Xuanji*, p. 14, pl. 1; *HXSQJ*, vol. 2, no. 52; Li Falin transcribes his name as Huan Sangzhong, See Li Falin, *Shandong Han huaxiang shi yanjiu*, p. 47.

38. *Xuanji*, no. 159.

39. Hebei Sheng wenhuaju wenwu gongzuodui, ed., "Hebei Ding Xian Beizhuang Han mu fajue baogao," *Kaogu xuebao* 1964.2, pp. 127–94.
40. Powers, *Art and Political Expression*, pp. 142–55.
41. Xin Lixiang, *Handai huaxiang shi*, pp. 45–47.
42. *DBD*, p. 121.
43. See examples in Käte Finsterbusch, *Verzeichnis und Motivindex der Han-Darstellungen* (Wiesbaden: Otto Harrassowitz, 1966–1971), vol. 2, nos. 381–82, 418–19, 427–28, 425–26.
44. Yingxin Dai and Wei Suizhi, "Shaanxi Suide Huangjiata Donghan huaxiang shi," pp. 260–61.
45. See *HXSQJ*, vols. 1, nos. 90–92; Zhu Xilu, *Jiaxiang Han huaxiang shi* (Ji'nan: Shandong meishu chubanshe, 1992), no. 45.
46. See Xin Li Xiang, *Handai huaxiang shi*, pp. 83–102. For a review of other theories concerning this scene, see Wu Hung, *Wu Liang Shrine*, pp. 193–213.
47. For one widow, see Zhu Xillu, *Jiaxiang*, pls. 28, 64, 65, 78; *HXSQJ*, vol. 1, nos. 66, 84.Two widows, Zhu Xilu, *Jiaxiang*, pls. 3, 62, 87; *HXSQJ*, vol. 1, no. 51; Finsterbusch, *Verzeichnis*, vol. 2, no. 270. Three widows, Zhu Xilu, *Jiaxiang*, pls. 64, 106. Four widows, Zhu, Xilu *Jiaxiang*, pls. 7, 31, 86, 90, 138. Five widows, Finsterbusch, *Verzeichnis*, vol. 2, no. 269. Six widows, ibid., no. 373.
48. Qu Tongzu [Ch'ü T'ung-tsu], *Han Social Structure* (Seattle: University of Washington Press, 1972), pp. 44–48.
49. A popular motif on Han stones is a depiction of Confucius and his numerous disciples, often in the context of Confucius meeting the Daoist sage Laozi. Frequently a scene label was cleared next to each figure, but rarely are any except Laozi, Kongzi, or Kongzi's disciple Zilu individually identified in the scene; see *HXSQJ*, vol. 1, nos. 57, 59, 60, 228.
50. The process of carving the captions is reconstructed by Lai Fei, "Shandong Handai huaxiang shi bangti," *Meishu shi yanjiu* 1994.2, pp. 27–28.
51. See *HXSQJ*, vol. 1, no. 230. On this stone two stories are incorrectly captioned. The story of Dong Yong is mislabeled as the Zhao Xun story, and the story of the filial son Xing Qu is incorrectly identified as that of the filial son Ding Lan. The compositions for depicting these stories are similar, and only someone who knew the stories in detail could distinguish them.
52. William V. Harris, *Ancient Literacy* (Cambridge, Mass.: Harvard University Press, 1989), pp. 7–8.
53. Ibid., p. 22.
54. A rather humorous loan, common to the An Guo, Xiang Tajun, and other inscriptions, is *zao* ("flea") for *zao* ("early"), as in the line, "He took leave of his parents and siblings early." The Cangshan inscription (151 CE) is riddled with the same mistakes. See Li Falin, *Shandong Han huaxiang shi yanjiu*, pp. 100–101. Li Falin concurs that these epitaphs must have been composed and written by the craftsmen.
55. See Lin Suqing,"Lianghan jingming chutan," *Bulletin of the Institute of History and Philology, Academia Sinica*, vol. 63, no. 2 (1993), pp. 345–49.
56. Earlier texts and documents (Warring States to Qin) seem to have more phonetic loans than later, Han, documents. For a standard list of loan characters in classical texts, see Bernhard Karlgren, "Loan Characters in Pre-Han Texts," *BMFEA*, vol. 35 (1963), pp. 1–128. For phonetic loans and determinative swaps in Qin legal texts, see Anthony Hulsewé, *Remnants of Ch'in Law* (Leiden: E. J. Brill, 1985), pp. 241–42.
57. William Boltz, *The Origin and Early Development of the Chinese Writing System* (New Haven: American Oriental Society, 1994), pp. 168–77.
58. A similar conclusion is reached by Li Falin, *Shandong Han huaxiang shi yanjiu*, pp. 100–101, and by Wu Hung, "Beyond the Great Boundary: Funerary Narrative in the Cangshan Tomb," in *Boundaries in China*, ed. John Hay (London: Reaktion Books, 1994), pp. 92–93, 98.
59. For model legal forms for divorce, property division, etc., see Yamamoto Tatsuro and Ikeda On, eds., *Tun-huang and Turfan Documents Concerning Social and Economic History* (Tokyo: Committee for the Studies of the Tun-huang Manuscripts, The Tōyō Bunko, 1978), vol. 3, pp. 50(71) no. 487, 156(65) no. 495, 151(70) no. 488.

60. The phrase *minggong* ("famous artisan") occurs in the An Guo inscription in reference to Wang Shu, Wang Jian, and Jiang Hu from Gaoping Town. The phrase *mingshi* ("famous stones") is found in the Wu Liang stele inscription. For references, see n. 15.

61. See n. 98. Only Li Falin reads the inscription this way. *Xuanji*, no. 472, reads the inscription quite differently, for the final passage is partially effaced.

62. Anthony Barbieri-Low, "Artisans in Early Imperial China" (unpublished book manuscript), chap. 3.

63. Beijing wenwu gongzuodui, ed., "Beijing xijiao faxian Handai shique qingli jianbao," *Wenwu* 1964.11, pp. 13–22; Shao Mingsheng, "Han Youzhou shuzuo Qin Jun shique shiwen," *Wenwu* 1964.11, pp. 23–24.

64. Hebei Sheng wenhuaju wenwu gongzuodui, ed., "Hebei Ding Xian Beizhuang Han mu fajue baogao," *Kaogu xuebao* 1964.2, pp. 127–94. Based on internal evidence from inscriptions, the tomb itself was most likely begun between 84 and 88 CE, and expanded after Liu Yan's death in 90 CE.

65. This practice of inscribing the blocks of a royal mortuary complex seems to have its foundations in the Western Han dynasty; see Henan Sheng wenwu kaogu yanjiusuo, ed., *Yongcheng Xihan*, pp. 151–86.

66. *HHS*, p. 1450.

67. Liu Zhong, the contemporary prince of Dongping, was Liu Yan's nephew. Liu Chang, the contemporary Prince of Liang, was also a nephew of Liu Yan and son of Emperor Ming.

68. Hebei Sheng wenhuaju wenwu gongzuodui, ed., "Hebei Ding Xian," p. 156 (no. 41) and p. 158 (no. 155). The two recorded stone rubbings bearing his name appear identical, though they are published as two separate inscriptions.

69. Liu Shang's brief biography can be found in *HHS*, p. 1443. For a more complete publication of the stone inscriptions, see Shandong Sheng Jining Shi wenwuju, ed., *Han Rencheng wang*.

70. Shandong Sheng jining Shi wenwuju, eds., *Han Rencheng wang*, pp. 111, 118. *Yuan* means "primary" and is sometimes used for the given name of an eldest son in lieu of the more common Bo. Zhong is the standard name for the second-oldest son in early Chinese families.

71. Shandong Sheng Jining Shi wenwuju, ed., *Han Rencheng wang*, pp. 118, 120.

72. Hebei Sheng wenhuaju wenwu gongzuodui, ed., "Hebei Ding Xian," inscription no. 19, rubbing on p. 188.

73. It is distinctly possible that the monetary figures have been selected for their auspicious connotations or exaggerated for rhetorical effect.

74. Jiang Yingju has reconstructed the form and decoration of several small offering halls from the reused stones found at Songshan; see Jiang Yingju, "Handai de xiao citang: Jiaxiang Songshan Han huaxiang shi de jianzhu fuyuan," *Kaogu* 1983.8, pp. 741–51. Some offering halls appear to have been freestanding, some embedded partially within the tomb mound, and others completely buried as part of the tomb.

75. The calculation is based upon Cui Shi's estimate that two people consumed about six *hu* of unhusked grain (millet) per month. See Cui Shi's essay "Zhenglun," in *Quan Hou Han wen* (hereafter, *QHHW*), contained in *Quan shanggu sandai Qin Han Sanguo Liuchao wen*, ed. Yan Kejun (Beijing: Zhonghua shuju, 1965), 46:9a-b, translated in Hsu Cho-yun, *Han Agriculture* (Seattle: University of Washington Press, 1980), pp. 237–38. Most scholars concur that one *hu* of unhusked grain cost about 100 coins during the Eastern Han, so 20,000 coins could buy two hundred *hu* and feed 5.5 adults. See discussion in Hans Bielenstein, *The Bureaucracy of Han Times* (Cambridge: Cambridge University Press, 1980), p. 126, n. 11; Hsu, *Han Agriculture*, pp. 68–70.

76. One would expect menial quarrymen and carvers to earn subsistence-level salaries. Masters were probably paid more. Apprentices could expect nothing but a full belly and some useful experience.

77. The price of chickens comes from the "Chicken Register" (dated to 62 BCE) found at the site of Dunhuang Xuanquan. See Hu Pingsheng and Zhang Defang, eds., *Dunhuang Xuanquan Han jian shicui* (Shanghai: Shanghai guji chubanshe, 2001), pp. 77–80.

78. Michael Loewe, *Records of Han Administration* (Cambridge: Cambridge University Press, 1967), vol. 1, p. 72.

79. Powers, *Art and Political Expression*, pp. 129–36.

80. Jiang Yingju has noted that nearly all pictorial stone monuments were made for low-ranked or unranked men. Tombs of princes and high officials rarely have any carved decoration at all. See Jiang Yingju, "Guanyu Han huaxiang shi chansheng beijing yu yishu gongneng de sikao," *Kaogu* 1998.11, pp. 90–96.

81. *QHHW*, 47:6b, trans. Hsu Chou-yun, *Han Agriculture*, 226 J.4.

82. See n. 98.

83. Li Falin, *Shandong Han huaxiang shi yanjiu*, p. 24.

84. The disruptions culminated in the so-called Yellow Turban Rebellion; see *Cambridge History of China*, vol. 1, pp. 324–26, 338–41.

85. A representative selection of these finds are referenced in the following notes. Also see Xuzhou bowuguan, ed., "Jiangsu Xuzhou damiao Jin–Han huaxiang shi mu," *Wenwu* 2003.4, pp. 61–70. For a Han tomb reused in the 10th century, see Nanjing bowuyuan, "Xuzhou Mao Cun huaxiang shi mu," *Kaogu* 1980.4, pp. 347–52; Nanyang Shi wenwu gongzuodui, ed., "Nanyang Shi Yao Cun shichang huaxiang shi mu fajue jianbao," *Zhongyuan wenwu* 1994.1, pp. 96–100. Three more recycled tombs were reported in the 1985.3 issue of *Zhongyuan wenwu*. For a *que* pillar-gate stone reused inside a tomb, see Su Zhaoqing et al., *Ju Xian wenwu zhi* (Ji'nan: Qi-Lu shushe, 1993), pp. 127–33.

86. See text and notes in Li Falin, *Shandong Han huaxiang shi yanjiu*, p. 107. Compare the partial translations by Ruitenbeek, *Chinese Shadows*, pp. 16–18, and by Powers, *Art and Political Expressions*, p. 52. A similar warning can be found at the end of the inscription carved on a column of Xiang Tajun's shrine. See Luo Fuyi, "Xiang Tajun," p. 180.

87. Ironically, the stones of An Guo's shrine may also have been reused ceiling stones from a belowground tomb.

88. Jiaxiang Xian Wushi Ci wenguansuo, ed., "Shandong Jiaxiang Songshan faxian Han huaxiang shi," *Wenwu* 1979.9, pp. 1–6; Jining diqu wenwuzu and Jiaxiang Xian wenguansuo, eds., "Shandong Jiaxiang Songshan 1980 nian chutu de Han huaxiang shi 1980," *Wenwu* 1982.5: pp. 60–70; Zhu Xilu and Jiaxiang Xian wenguansuo, eds., "Jiaxiang Wulaowa faxian yipi Han huaxiang shi," *Wenwu* 1982.5, pp. 71–78.

89. Some burials give the impression that the post-Han tomb builders welcomed—at least in part—the influence of the recycled imagery. In one apparent husband-and-wife burial near Tengzhou, Shandong, the wall dividing the coffins was made from the recycled western and eastern walls of an aboveground offering hall. Their placement seems to have been intentionally gendered. The stone depicting the Queen Mother of the West faced toward one spouse, the stone depicting the King Father of the East kept watch over the other. Sadly, the state of skeletal preservation prevents us from knowing for certain the gender of each skeleton. See *Kaogu* 2002.10, pp. 87–93.

90. Nicholas Reeves, *Akhenaten: Egypt's False Prophet* (London: Thames and Hudson, 2001), pp. 26, 91–95.

91. For a Henan example, see Henan Sheng wenhuaju wenwu gongzuodui and Nanyang Shi wenwu guanli weiyuanhui, eds., "Henan Nanyang dongguan Jin mu," *Kaogu* 1963.1, pp. 25–27. For Shandong, Wang Sili, "Shandong Feicheng Han huaxiang mu diaocha," *Wenwu cankao ziliao* 1958.4.

92. Nanyang Shi bowuguan, ed., "Nanyang faxian Donghan Xu Aqu muzhi huaxiang shi," *Wenwu* 1974.8, pp. 73–75, 41. I am thankful for the help of Hsu Cho-yun in reading difficult portions of this epitaph.

Notes for tables 1 and 2

A. *HXSQJ*, vol. 1, no. 1; Liu Xinjian and Zhang Mingxue, "Shandong Junan faxian Handai shique," *Wenwu* 1965.5, pp. 16–19; Li Falin, *Shandong Han huaxiang shi yanjiu*, p. 46. Only one pillar survives. Statistics are extrapolated for two pillars.

B. *Wenwu cankao ziliao* 1954.5, pp. 29–32; *HXSQJ*, vol. 1, p. 34, nos. 12–15; Chen Mingda, "Handai de shique," *Wenwu* 1961.12, p. 11. A rubbing of this inscription was known to Zhao Mingcheng, *Jinshi lu*, *juan* 14: 3a-b. Only one pillar survives. Statistics are extrapolated for two pillars. The character before the number four in the inscription is effaced. This might have contained a further multiplier of the number of *wan*, "ten thousands," so the number could possibly be 145,000, or less likely, 245,000.

C. Zhao Mingcheng, *Jinshi lu*, *juan* 14: 8a; Jiang Yingju and Wu Wenqi, *Handai Wushi muqun shike yanjiu* (Ji'nan: Shandong meishu chubanshe, 1995), p. 11.

D. Li Daoyuan, *Shuijing zhu*, ed. Wang Guowei (Shanghai: Renmin chubanshe, 1984), *juan* 31, pp. 991–92.

E. Wang Lilin and Li Yinde, "Xuzhou faxian Donghan huaxiang shi," *Wenwu* 1996.4, pp. 28–31; *HXSQJ*, vol. 4, no. 1.

F. Wang Sili, "Shandong Feicheng,"; Li Falin, *Shandong Han huaxiang shi yanjiu*, p. 46. The dated stone was probably the back wall of an offering hall that was reused as the ceiling slab of a later tomb.

G. Xuzhou bowuguan, "Xuzhou faxian Donghan Yuanhe san nian huaxiang shi," *Wenwu* 1990.9, p. 68; *HXSQJ*, vol. 4, no. 21. The graph before *wan* ("ten thousand") is effaced, so the amount could be anywhere from 15,000 to 95,000. This stone was later reused in a tomb.

H. *HXSQJ*, vol. 2, no. 141. It appears from the fragmented inscription that the money was collected from other donors besides family members.

I. Édouard Chavannes, *Mission archéologique dans la Chine septentrionale* (Paris: E. Leroux, 1913), vol. 1, p. 234, fig. 1217. The inscription is fragmentary around the words "five thousand," so the actual price could be 15,000 or 25,000. Chavannes gives the Western date as March 26, 130 CE, but this is incorrect.

J. Yang Jiandong, "Weishan chutu Donghan Yonghe yuan nian huaxiang shi," *Zhongguo wenwu bao*, May 27, 1998.

K. *Xuanji*, no. 32. The *taisui* date is incorrect in this inscription. The graph after *wan* ("ten thousand") is missing. This could mean an added cost of anywhere from zero to nine thousand.

L. Chavannes, *Mission archéologique*, pp. 233–34, fig. 1216. Chavannes has the amount as only 10,000, but his transcription is mistaken.

M. Jiang Yingu and Wu Wenqi, *Handai Wushi muqun shike yanjiu*, p. 11; Chavannes, *Mission archéologique*, p. 102, fig. 1194.

N. Luo Fuyi, "Xiang Tajun."

O. Li Falin, *Shandong Han huaxiang shi yanjiu*, pp. 101–8.

P. *Xuanji*, no. 159.

Q. Dong Jing, "Shandong shengli tushuguan jinshi zhi chugao," *Shandong shengli tushuguan jikan*, vol. 1, no. 1 (1931), p. 57. This mound was erected nearly twenty-seven years after the father died and was buried. It was said to have been completed on the thirtieth day of the second month of Yanxi reign-period, but that month only had twenty-nine days.

R. Xuzhou bowuguan, ed., "Jiangsu Xuzhou damiao Jin-Han huaxiang shi mu," *Wenwu* 2003.4, pp. 61–70. Portions of this small, formerly aboveground, Han-dynasty offering hall were later reused to build the entrance room of a Western Jin–dynasty tomb. The inscription also quotes from the *Classic of Filial Piety* concerning the construction of a family ancestral hall (*jia miao*) so the spirits could dine there.

S. Xuzhou bowuguan, "Xuzhou faxian Donghan Yuanhe san nian huaxiang shi," *Wenwu* 1990.9, p. 66. There may be an additional graph between the *wan* ("ten thousand") and the *qi* ("seven"), making the reading of 17,000 tentative. This stone, along with another dated to 86 CE, was reused in a later tomb.

T. See n. D.

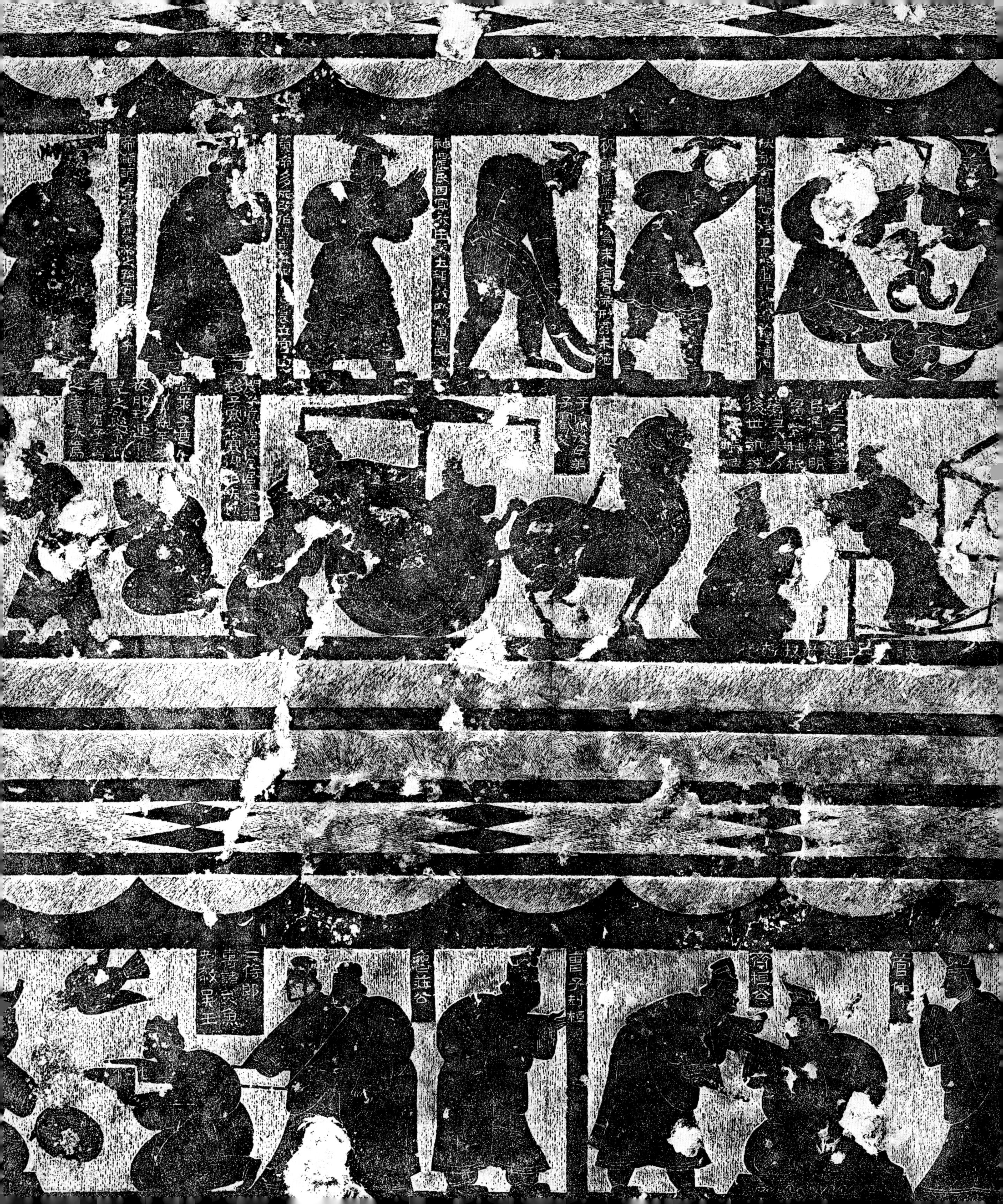

神農氏因宜教田辟土種穀以振萬民
曹子劫桓
齊桓公
管仲

Michael Nylan

"Addicted to Antiquity" (*nigu*): A Brief History of the Wu Family Shrines, 150–1961 CE[1]

I. Introduction

One passage in José Saramago's novel *All the Names* takes its protagonist to a cemetery, where there are ancient stones "so worn by time that you could only make out a few barely visible marks that could as easily be the remains of letters as the result of scratches made by an unskilled chisel." The interpretation of these marks becomes an object of "intense debate" in the public and academic arenas. For "while it was relatively easy, in the circumstances, for the board of archaeologists to reach agreement over a broad concept of antiquity acceptable to all," so long as the question of "actual date" was never broached, those concerned with truth and beauty, history and aesthetics could not agree on basic definitions and working methods for their analysis.[2]

The present essay was conceived neither as a study of actual date nor of authenticity. It offers a small case study within which to consider the inevitable gaps between cultural ideas and material objects (whether texts or pictures). At every point, the customary criteria for perception, judgment, argumentation, and textual reproduction will be queried, in order to pose the larger question of whether inscriptions transmitted through the ages are inherently more reliable than evidence from the received literary tradition. Seeing seems increasingly to have become believing, at the very juncture when we are less inclined to accept what we read at face value. Here the specific object of study is a group of engraved stones—five steles and forty-odd pictorial slabs—that tradition has long been associated with a Wu family in Eastern Han Shandong. The Wu family site was supposedly rediscovered in 1786 and 1789 by Huang Yi (1744–1801) at Wuzhai Shan (also called Ziyun Shan, "Purple Cloud Mountain") in Jiaxiang County (fig. 1). Nearly every part of the Wu family shrines—in the current reckoning, a premier site of antiquity—boasts a long and complex cultural history.[3] Huang Yi's stones have played a central role in scholarly outlines of early portraiture and architecture, in theories of socioeconomic change and ritual practice, and in discussions about the special role of ancestor worship in the formation of Chinese culture.[4] Scientific "archaeology" in China has even been traced back to Huang Yi by those anxious to counter arrogant Eurocentric presumptions that Chinese archaeology began in the 1920s, under Western influence.[5] (As I have argued elsewhere, Qing practices for retrieval of the past were comparable with contemporary practices in Europe, just as preservation efforts and the interpretation of finds in the People's Republic employ methods similar to those used elsewhere in the modern world.)[6]

Much of this essay inevitably reflects, implicitly or explicitly, upon the subtle changes in the definitions of key terms relating to antiquarian practices, beginning with the terms *jinshi* and *kaogu* themselves. A shorthand reference for the bells and chiming stones[7] used in ceremonies and sacrifices, *jinshi* long ago came to mean "writings on metal or stone," and the appreciation or scientific research based thereon. A single term subsumes, then, not only the collection, classification, and cataloguing of ancient bronzes and stele inscriptions but also the particular forms assumed by the standard epigraphical study, as well as its dual preoccupations with historical accuracy and evolving calligraphic styles of stele inscriptions.[8]

Opposite Detail of Stone Chamber 3, Stone 3-W.1 (cat. no. 1.35). "Wu family shrines" rubbings. Princeton University Art Museum, acc. no. 2002-307.36.

Kaogu—literally, the examination of old things— serves now as the modern term for scientific archaeology, though the methods of engagement required by the new practices are seldom the same as those that served the old. Perhaps the tensions implied in the changing meanings of these two Chinese terms provide a sense of the complex ways in which humans, never entirely free of the need to conjure and propitiate the past, still try busily to manage it.[9] Yet how little we understand of the tangible remains of that past—that foreign country—given the human propensity to continually invent, adapt, and recast things, people, and events in new lights. One example may be relevant here: we do not even know whether the first stele in China was a palace gnomon, a grave marker, a plank to which the coffin was secured before lowering it into the grave, a post for hanging sacrificial offerings or for hitching the horses that drew the carriages of the funeral procession.[10] All that we know is that by Eastern Han, when the particular story of the Wu family traditions begins, the stone surfaces had become tabulae rasae on which to inscribe the memorable virtues of the venerated dead.[11]

The absence of certainty has never precluded specialists—myself included—from constructing impressively coherent narratives about nearly every aspect of Eastern Han from the detritus brought together by design or chance. In the context of this faith in the reliability of stone inscriptions as the "warp" of scholarship, four standard claims made about epigraphical rubbings must be weighed, for it is these claims that ultimately have led, in the more uncritical studies, to the unfounded notion that the interpretation of physical artifacts is somehow more "scientific" and "objective" than the reading of received texts.[12] These four claims, each more expansive than the one before, are that: (1) rubbings as "transparent" "traces" of the artifact's surface are an adequate substitute for the artifact itself; (2) an older rubbing is *always* in some sense more "authentic" than the real object from which it was taken, if only because a rubbing "freezes" an object at a particular moment while the object itself continues to deteriorate; (3) rubbings allow the viewer to discern traces of the artifact that would otherwise be invisible to the naked eye, so that even with a stele that has lost its entire surface, "like a cicada shedding its skin," the connoisseur can find in the rubbing the stele's "remnant soul (*yi hun*), lingering, faintly discernible"; and (4) the stele content preserved on paper is a better guide to the past than synthetic works of history, including the standard dynastic histories, given that (a) many are said to represent contemporaneous records; (b) it seems next-to-impossible to interpolate material into an inscription; and (c) the stele content often presents information that seems incidental to the main narrative (which increases the likelihood that it is objectively true).[13]

Accepting these claims, great scholars in China frequently turned their attention to the study of rubbings as traces of antique stones, traces which promised to breathe out the fragrance of the distant past. From at least the Song, neoclassicizing authors such as Hong Gua (1117–1184) pointed out that memorial steles included valuable information on "the names of birds, beasts, plants, trees," also references (textual and visual) to ritual items—precisely those subjects that Confucius had urged his disciples to glean from the *Odes* and other antique sources.[14]

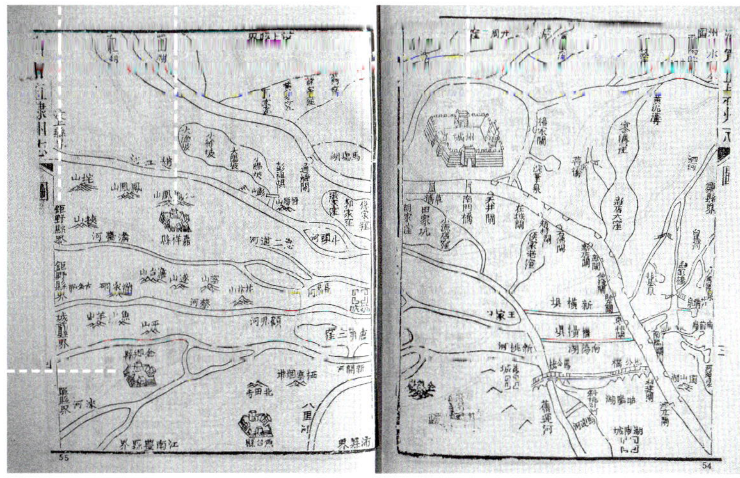

Zeng Gong's (1019–1083) *Yuanfeng tiba* (*Colophons of the Yuanfeng era*) describes connoisseurs and artists looking to stone engravings for guidance in reproducing auspicious signs or portraying figures in archaic style.[15] (The pictorial rubbings associated with the Wu family turn out to be especially important in this regard, since aesthetes like Yuan Mei (1716–1798) took them to be the very origin of portraiture in China.)[16] Understandable, too, is the turn by great historians to the study of epitaphs and other stone records. Ouyang Xiu's (1007–1072) mounting interest in rubbings reflected not only the enforced leisure concomitant with his exile from court in 1044 but also his appointment to the imperial commission writing a *New History of the Five Dynasties* in the mid-1050s. Similar concerns to get the history right propelled Gu Yanwu's (1613–1682) abiding interest in works on bronze and stone.[17] Only in the post-Mao era have two developments—the sheer number of new archaeological finds, including manuscripts in tombs, and ever finer disciplinary distinctions in the field of Chinese studies—obviated the need for serious historians of early China to rely on rubbings as one of their two main sources for antiquity. Of course, for good historians who do use epigraphical rubbings, the first necessity has been to establish a chronological sequence for the rubbings.[18] Where rubbings bear no seals or identifying marks, the main methodological rule has been this: the greater the damage to the stone revealed by the rubbing, the newer the rubbing is likely to be. For instance, Zhao Mingcheng (1081–1129) noted in his epigraphical classic, *Jinshi lu* (*Records of metal and stone*), that a mere decade or so after he acquired his first rubbing of the Wu Liang stele inscription a second rubbing procured by him was missing its last four characters.[19]

But because such rules were known to ardent antiquarians and capable forgers alike, this essay takes another tack. It reminds readers that (a) many stele inscriptions are *not* contemporaneous with the events and persons they purport to witness; (b) some of the most famous steles, and the rubbings produced from them, were located at great distances from the places where the dedicatees resided, held office, or died; (c) the interpolation of characters was relatively easy; and (d) the successful composers of stele inscriptions—in company with clever writers working in other genres—knew enough to bury dubious points in plausible passages constructed from verifiable data and appropriate commonplaces.[20] Genre distinctions determined the formulas employed in steles and restricted the sorts of information steles conveyed, and steles are no more likely to present better (i.e., more objective and more accurate) evidence than are the rhetorical writings preserved in the received tradition. Even the most trustworthy authors of such commemorative pieces, who were commonly the deceased's relatives, friends, allies, or clients, spoke by turns as historians, moralists, loyal family members, critics of the age, or poets. And many who never knew the honored dead personally nevertheless composed steles as self-conscious dedications by "those of the same commitments"—in which cases their authors were in some sense writing about themselves. At times, too, the collecting and recarving of old steles was propelled less by the aim of preserving old things than by "particular agendas" of specific institutions.[21]

Fig. 1 *Gazetteer map showing waterways in the Rencheng area.* After *Jining zhilizhou zhi*, 1859 edition (Taipei: Taipei xuesheng shuju, 1968), pp. 54–55. Note the locations of Jinxiang, Juye, and Jiaxiang in relation to Rencheng.

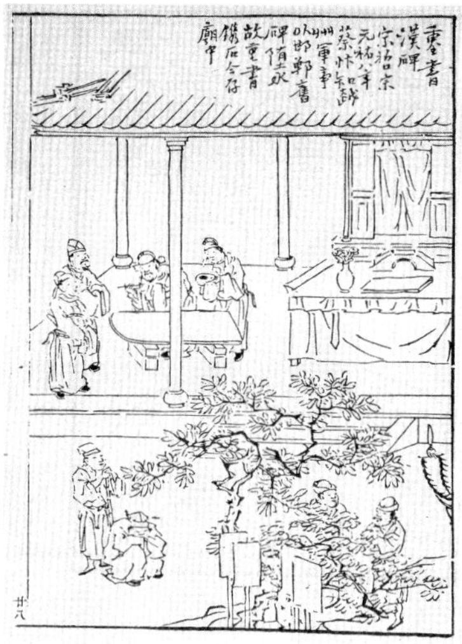

Contrary to popular views, no special quality inheres in stone that prevents its inscriptions from telling the same sorts of lies, half-truths, and exaggerations that appear regularly in other sorts of documentation. Information carved upon steles, being addressed to the viewing public and much concerned with establishing the status of the deceased and his family, was subject to all sorts of dissembling. To the degree that such information was sometimes made the basis for economic, social, and political claims, even stronger motives for guile could exist. Local gazetteers reveal what comparative history already demonstrates: that seemingly unassailable identities for local figures could be constructed or destroyed by local or national figures who intended through the use of such monuments to assert property rights, devise genealogies for families or institutions, create figures who could effectively symbolize new values (typically characterized as a recovery of the distant past), or establish practical examples of ethical behavior via plausible moral narratives.[22] Contrary also to popular views, the "death" of a stele was *not* necessarily a long process. Stone was hardly a permanent medium, despite its associations with immortality.[23] Steles could be destroyed for any number of reasons and by any number of means, for example, by: (1) erosion by wind and rain; (2) cracking due to frost, fires, and lightning; (3) warfare; (4) other sorts of man-made destruction, including the intentional destruction of an enemy's traces, to dishonor or efface the enemy's memory; (5) the very process of making rubbings; and (6) transporting steles to a new location, this last a not uncommon practice.[24] Wang Pizhi (1088–1177) relates the impermanence of a famous stone to the impermanence of life itself:

Fig. 2 *Copying a Han stele*. From *Cao jiang xiao nü miao zhi*; reproduced in Fang Jun and Shang Ke, *Zhongguo gudai chutu jingxuan* (Nanjing: Jiangsu renmin chubanshe, 1992), p. 89.

> During the Xining period, I was Recorder at Meng City near Hao, and I heard that there was a stele by Cai Zhonglang [i.e., Cai Yong, the most famous eulogist and calligrapher of Eastern Han] in front of the temple erected to Chen Shi [the renowned Eastern Han protest leader] .... One day, in the course of transporting documents, I happened to pass by, so I went to visit it .... But the people of the village had already used it as a footbridge ... in water .... The stone was in five sections, and [the inscription] was in correct clerical script (*zheng li*), but it was so full of errors and blanks that it could not be read. Only about 10 or 20 percent of it remained, and only the former subordinates' names and ranks on the back of the stele were complete .... I instructed the [local] clerks to grind the ink and make a copy [of this and a nearby stele] to present to Ouyang Xiu. But before it was finished, he had died.[25]

As soon as carved stones and the rubbings produced from them became objects of art in their own right, rubbings were made in such quantity as to rub the carvings into oblivion. This potential and more we learn from a tale told by Zhu Xi (1130–1200) about a stone carving by Ouyang Xiu, the figure usually hailed as the "ancestor" [i.e., originator] of the epigraphical tradition in China:

> Ouyang's Viewing Pavilion of the Drunken Old Man was located to the side of a monastery at Mount Langya. He recorded its completion by carving a stone there. Those far and near competed to transmit it; they

> wore themselves out in the copying and tamping processes. A monk living on the mountain said, "There is felt in the monastery storehouses, but tamping steles will use it all up." So he went and got from the monk's hall the felt blankets they used for sleeping. In general, the merchants and traders who came giving donations [to the monastery] also sought copies of the text. When the monks inquired how they intended to use them, they all replied that it was good to give such presents to the customs officials who supervised the passes, as the officials would then allow them to avoid taxes.[26]

As stone carvings and the rubbings produced from them were generally considered the "most bizarre and extraordinary, majestic and striking, skillfully crafted, and delightful of material things," interest in and craving for stone carvings and epigraphical rubbings was never limited to a small circle of high-minded literati (if, indeed, such existed) for whom the epigraphical rubbing had become "the dominant currency of antiquarian sociability."[27] Whereas a version of the Wu Liang rubbing was considered to be one of the finest treasures in a connoisseur's extensive family collection,[28] the rank beginner in epigraphical studies could purchase inexpensive rubbings of lower grade. Thus there could develop across socioeconomic spectrums a commitment to find, produce, exchange, and buy epigraphical rubbings that potentially bound—in theory, at least—the poverty-stricken scholar, the ranked official, and the rich merchant into a select community of appreciation. And since rubbings before very recent times were rendered in black and white, in contrast to the brilliantly colored prints that appealed to "the vulgar," the moralists deemed the study of rubbings edifying and refined; the owners of rubbings need not fear, in Zhuangzi's words, "losing the real in their obsessive pursuit of traces."[29] Directly undermining the preservation of stone inscriptions were commercial interests, and when the demands of commerce, intellectual status, tourism, patriotism, and local interests coincided, the inscriptions were effaced and new versions of older stones had to be made.[30] When stone inscriptions were copied with the express purpose of widening the circulation of the texts engraved on them, the particular format and calligraphic style of the original stone could be ignored, as happened in connection with the Wu Rong stele.

Conscientious attempts were made, as we have seen, to "repair" or "work around" evidence of damage, in order to revive the power of the long-vanished originals (fig. 2). Shen Yan's (d. ca. 925) essay "On Destroying a Stele" ("Sui bei ji"), recording an event in the year 885, suggests that it was not at all unusual to "copy it [an inscription] out for transmission [in writing], filling in the lacunae in the text," after which the original stone could be set aside for safekeeping or reuse.[31] There is, indeed, aside from outright forgery, a quite remarkable tradition in China of "filling in the blanks" (*buque*) in literary and artistic artifacts.[32] In theory, only sages were to "fill in the blanks," based on their direct intuitive grasp of the distant time when sages ruled the Central States territory. After all, had not the Master advised his disciples to "Hear much, but maintain silence as regards doubtful points"?[33] In practice, an astonishing number of literati thought themselves capable of "restoring" and "recarving" the past—especially in the Song period and later—in part, no doubt, because they were keeping careful track of materials found in the newly opened tombs.[34] For instance, Huang Yi, the man who located the Wu family site in 1786, was seen—by himself and others—as having "a nature and emotions that could enter into [the spirit of] the ancients; a brush and ink that compared with that of the ancients."[35] Huang would not have been at all averse to comparisons casting him as a latter-day Sage and savior who had changed the course of history. As it happens, he had located important finds in the precise location where Confucius had seen the unicorn (i.e., at Juye [see fig. 1], the site now known as Jiaxiang, "auspicious omen"), and it was he also who had identified the dedicatees of the two other "shrines" reconstructed in Shandong and dated to Eastern Han—one at Xiaotang Shan and the other belonging to Zhu Wei.[36]

By merging texts—some possibly separate in origin—when recarving stone inscriptions, copyists produced a more "complete" and satisfying record, which could then be regarded as a primary source. (Here the Chinese acted just like their European counterparts, who did not hesitate to name a bronze statue of an old fisherman "the dying Seneca," and who often engaged in questionable practices that combined incongruous parts.)[37] In addition to "filling in the blanks," another equally common practice also made for later misunderstandings: the propensity to identify finds as genuine "traces" of older traditions, despite the unlikelihood of such identifications being correct. Then, too, as the fame of particular sites grew, the tendency was to create steles for the sites that testified to their early existence.[38] In the worst cases, an artifactual record was created in order to provide seemingly indisputable evidence for a past that had never existed, which spawned, in turn, a hopeless maze of pseudo-erudition.[39]

Surprisingly few twentieth-century historians of China, whether ethnic Chinese or other, have cared to explore such phenomena, perhaps because their teachers have inculcated in them a solemn belief in the sanctity of the written word in China, perhaps also because the physical destruction of China's material culture over the course of the last century and a half has been so great as to prompt patriots to undertake spirited defenses of the remaining cultural artifacts.[40] But the disinclination to put questions to the Chinese past surely also comes to modern historians as a remnant of the Qing scholars' confidence in their own ability to discern the past. Let us read Dai Zhen's (1724–1777) comments in a letter about his own work:

> Some of my works are based on thoroughly conclusive evidence, [though] others are not yet so based. By conclusive evidence, I mean that the text must be verified by antiquity in every particular, the work must be in such complete accord with the truth as to leave nothing debatable, all the major and minor points must be traced, and fundamental as well as secondary points considered.[41]

That Dai's reconstructions are now known to contain serious errors counts for naught. No scholar's work is free of errors. More importantly, by Dai Zhen's standards, very little evidence for the early empires can ever be called "conclusive." Mary Beard, a modern historian, puts it well in her recent book on the Parthenon; to study any classical site with a long cultural history is

> ... to be brought face to face with the very fragility of our grip on the classical world, and with the challenges (or frustrations, depending on your mood) that are involved in even the simplest attempts to describe it, let alone explain or make sense of it. It ... offers an object lesson in those tantalising processes of investigation, deduction, empathy, reconstruction and sheer guesswork that must be the hallmarks of any study of classics and the classical world.[42]

So much depends upon the eye and experience, yet every research topic demands that we put the essentially unanswerable questions to each piece of evidence: how reliable is it? How many anomalies and oddities separate the merely atypical from the frankly incredible? Since the eighteenth century the trend has been to draw ever firmer distinctions between a work (literary or visual) that is "genuine" and one that is a "forgery."[43] Skeptics cannot help but note that slightly over half (51 percent) of the datable stele inscriptions recorded in the *Li shi* (1167), for example, derive from a single eighteen-year period in Eastern Han (166–184)—the very time period that Ouyang Xiu had identified as the favorite of stele forgers in his own day.[44] But, as we see, the motives for and products of such complicated processes of retrieving, reproducing, and amplifying the past cannot neatly be reduced to the antonyms "genuine" and "forged." In late imperial times copying was a way of life. Good copies—those considered faithful to the antique spirit—became works of art themselves.[45] In consequence, the corpus of inscriptional and pictorial rubbings that has come down to us is no less fraught with problems of interpretation than the records transmitted through the received literary tradition. The "incomplete evidence of burial practices, the fragmented context of the landscape, and the selective destruction of tombs" by natural decay, grave robbing, and conventional antiquarian practices leaves us with nothing for it but to proceed with a review of the evidence associated with what is known as the Wu family shrines (fig. 3).[46]

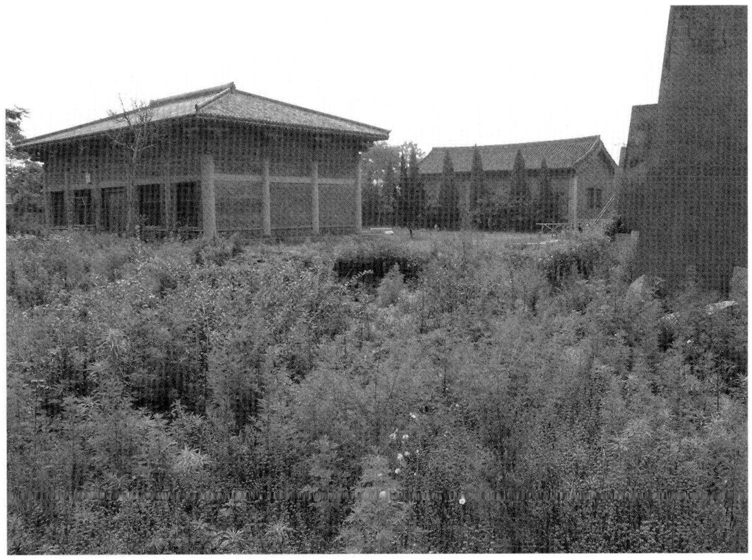

Fig. 3 *Wu cemetery compound with back exhibition hall (left), front hall (center), and 1989 offices (right).* Wuzhai Shan site, Jiaxiang County, Shandong. Photo by C. Y. Liu, 2002.

II. Stele Summary

Ideally, stele rubbings, like people, would come with family trees. The historian, after assembling a series of rubbings made from the same artifact, could then date the wear patterns on the stones that they reflect and also arrange them by provenance or ownership. Unfortunately, real life seldom allows such luxuries to the scholar, as will soon become evident. For the Wu family, no inscription or site is mentioned in the early sixth-century geographical work *Shuijing zhu* (*Commentary on the "Classic of Waterways"*; compiled ca. 515–524) by Li Daoyuan (d. 527), though Li's classic mentions two pictorial shrines in the immediate vicinity, those of Li Gang and Lu Jun.[1] Three Song epigraphical classics—Ouyang Xiu's (1007–1072) *Jigu lu* (*Records on collecting antiquities*), Zhao Mingcheng's (1081–1129) *Jinshi lu* (*Records of metal and stone*), and Hong Gua's (1117–1184) *Li shi* (*Explications of clerical script*)—each contain two to four entries on the five inscriptions assigned by convention to the Wu family of Jiaxiang circa 150 CE. These are the inscriptions of (1) Wu Ban (cat. no. 1.46); (2) Wu Rong (fig. 4); (3) Wu Kaiming; (4) Wu Liang; and (5) the pillar-gate (cat. no. 1.43). Of those three Song experts, only Ouyang Xiu knew the town of Rencheng well, for he had spent years in exile there (fig. 1). (See Cary Liu's "Recarving the Past" in this catalogue.)[2] By contrast, Zhao Mingcheng and Hong Gua, as Hong's remarks reveal, knew the vicinity of Rencheng from hearsay about the rubbings in their possession, all of which were soon lost.[3] Zhao and his wife, the famous poet Li Qingzhao, as avid collectors and natives of the vicinity, might easily have visited the site. (Zhao was from nearby Zhucheng, and his wife's family was based in nearby Ji'nan.) But for whatever reason, the Zhaos appear not to have made the trip. Zhao stated that he discovered the Wu Ban rubbing(s) in his own family's collection, and Hong Gua remarks that Zhao seems to have had only the foggiest notion of the layout of the Wu family cemetery in Rencheng.[4] When the Jurchen invaded the north (beginning 1115), the entire rubbing collections of the Ouyang and Zhao families were lost. All that was left for Southern Song antiquarians like Hong Gua to pore over were the catalogues of colophons composed by Ouyang and Zhao for their most prized rubbings. That means that the next figure to tell of the Wu family shrines, Hong Gua, writing in Southern Song, could not have compared the rubbings he knew with rubbings that had once belonged to the Ouyang or to Zhao Mingcheng. Hong accordingly admits to uncertainty,[5] and the three Song epigraphical classics, when read together, present a rather confused picture, whereby the assignment of family and personal names, precise kin connections, dates and places of death came to be "rationalized" over time, on the basis of fragmentary statements by epigraphical scholars. Those statements appear more hesitant and more contradictory in the originals than in the currently accepted narrative.

Ouyang Xiu had boasted of the completeness of his personal collection of rubbings (originally numbering some thousand items), "I have them all."[6] But a few decades after Ouyang Xiu, Zhao Mingcheng announced with considerable pride that he had managed to assemble twice that number of rubbings, and that his rubbings tended to have considerably longer inscriptions.[7] Hong Gua, collecting half a century after Zhao Mingcheng, once again dramatically increased the number of rubbings for which he composed entries, though by Hong's time the northern half of the Central States territory had fallen into the hands of the nomadic Jurchens. That more inscriptional material might be gathered in a later work like Hong Gua's *Li shi* (compiled 1167) is hardly surprising, but that such significantly better rubbings of the very same materials from Rencheng and elsewhere would turn up in later collections is harder to explain, especially in Hong's case. After all, Hong Gua compiled his epigraphical classics nearly a century after Ouyang Xiu's writings had intensified the "stele craze."[8] In addition, neither Hong Gua nor his brother Hong Mai, even during their years as envoys to the Jin court, would have had ready access to Rencheng and its vicinity, though they might have purchased or been given items from there. Compounding the potential problems, all three epigraphical classics handed down from Song had particularly convoluted histories of their own, as different editions added entries and editorial remarks were interpolated into the main text. Faced with the detailed accounts by Ouyang Xiu and his son Ouyang Fei (1047–1113), who claimed to be able at best to read only small parts of two rubbing inscriptions attributed to Wu Ban and Wu Rong, the conscientious scholar has little choice but to carefully sift through the surviving evidence for each of the five inscriptions said to have originated on four steles and one pillar-gate, before hazarding any larger conclusions about the reliability of the epigraphical corpus as a whole.

Wu Ban (cat. nos. 1.46, 1.47)

According to the *Jigu lu* (compiled 1045–1061; preface 1062), Ouyang Xiu and his son Ouyang Fei had in their possession a single rubbing dedicated to a man whose personal name was Ban. An appended notice in some editions refers to a second version of the same rubbing, which supplies the individual named Ban with the family name of Wu. This appended notice appears to be an interpolation.[9] In any case, the version(s) of the Ban rubbing known to the Ouyangs had no stele heading, and it lacked, by Ouyang's estimation, some 80–90 percent of the original stele inscription. No home province, district, or official rank could be read, and no dates for the death and burial. An incomplete date could be seen, transcribed in nine characters. As the second of the two characters making up one part of the date was illegible, Ouyang concluded that the stele for Ban must have been carved on the *dinghai* day of the first year of Jianhe (147 CE). The Ouyangs gave no indication that Ban and Rong might be related, though the *Jigu lu* groups family inscriptions elsewhere.

According to Zhao Mingcheng's *Jinshi lu* (compiled 1117–1127; submitted to the throne in 1147, two decades after Zhao's death), the Zhao family collection contained rubbings from which Zhao could discern a great deal more information about the very Ban mentioned in the Ouyangs' work. A rubbing of a stele head made Ban "Lord Wu, the Han former Senior Officer at Dunhuang."[10] "So we know that his family name was Wu and his post that of Senior Officer at Dunhuang." (Note, however, that the *Shandong tongzhi* omits the characters for Dunhuang.)[11] Zhao could also make out both characters of Wu Ban's style name, Xuanzhang;[12] he could quote a section of stele inscription tracing the Wu family history back to the late Shang king Wuding, thereby resolving the question raised by Ouyang Xiu regarding the Wu family's origin; and he could, unlike the Ouyangs, date Wu Ban's death to Yongjia 1 (145 CE)—and all this in an entry that opens by repeating Ouyang's words about the illegibility of Ban's inscription.

The *Li shi* transcription of Wu Ban's stele inscription is still longer and more precise. Here, for the first time, we find no fewer than nineteen characters that obviate the slightest ambiguity in the date of the inscription. (As readers will recall, Ouyang could make out only nine characters specifying a date.) Following this lengthy date, the *Li shi* gives a ten-character title for Wu Ban, after which a single character, *tong*, dangles, alerting readers to the possibly of a corrupt text. The *Li shi* then proceeds with the same thirty-two character passage with which Zhao began his entry, to which it appends more than two hundred characters, which include probable anachronisms (see below).[13] Moreover, the Wu Ban of *Li shi*, *juan* 6, is a native of Rencheng serving as Senior Officer in Dunhuang, while a second Wu Ban, mentioned in another chapter included in present editions of the *Li shi*, is said to be a *native* of Dunhuang, thousands of miles from Rencheng. At first glance, the problem seems easy to resolve: the Wu Ban entry in *Li shi*, *juan* 23, is simply corrupt and/or less reliably old. Extant versions of the *Li shi* derive ultimately from a 1588 edition of Wang Yunlu—in other words, from a time that is (a) centuries after Hong Gua; and (b) known for sloppy popular editions of famous reference works. *Juan* 20–27, consisting of parts of the epigraphical classics compiled by Ouyang Xiu and Zhao Mingcheng, represents Ming or even early Qing versions of those classics. The record may well point to a conflation of two or even three different Wu Ban steles, just as the sources list multiple Wu Kaimings, with their own biographical similarities (see below). The Wu Ban stele inscription, as transcribed in the *Li shi*, is one of the very few texts to include mention of the calligrapher.[14] It also contains an unmistakable interpolation.[15]

After Song, the Wu Ban stele received little attention, so far as we know, until mid-Ming, when two works, Yang Shen's (1488–1559) *Jinshi guwen* (*Old writings on metal and stone*) and Zhao Jun's (1591–1640) *Jinshi lin shi di kao* (*Study on dating and provenance of a bronze and stele collection*; compiled 1619) mention a Wu Ban stele, although the latter work places it in Shaanxi Province.[16] Ye Yibao's (act. 1697) classic work, *Jinshi lu xuba* (*Further notes on* [*Zhao's*] *"Records of metal and stone"*) states that the donor list includes a reference to the post of *fucheng* (Assistant in the *fu*) that almost certainly indicates a Tang date for the Wu Ban stele inscription.[17] Eventually a Wu Ban stele would be "recovered" at the Wuzhai Shan site by Huang Yi, but as Huang himself notes in his "Brief Record," a Wu Ban stele had been found decades before his time, at some distance from the site assigned by Huang to the Wu. A rubbing of the Wu Ban stele and of one of the "auspicious omens" were available in 1785, one year before Huang Yi's finds, according to the dealer Rong Yuan's (b. 1904) *Jinshi shu lumu* (*Catalogue of books on metal and stone*).[18] When Huang Yi "found" his Wu Ban stele in 1786, its inscribed text was said to be illegible, yet very little time elapsed before Huang Yi positively identified the stele as that of Wu Ban.[19]

Wu Rong (fig. 4)

Happily, the Ouyangs had in their possession a rubbing inscription for Wu Rong that supplied considerably more information than their inscription for Wu Ban: For Rong, the inscription gave the first of the two characters in his style name (either Han[he] or She[he]); a list of teachings Rong had mastered; and Rong's appointments, including Filial and Incorrupt at age thirty-six, and the mid-ranking post of Assistant to the Chamberlain for the Imperial Insignia at 600 bushels, which Rong held at the time of his death shortly after the "troubles" ending Huandi's reign (r. 148–168).[20] Though Rong's family name was known from the stele head (*shouti*), the *Jigu lu bawei* (*Colophons on "Jigu lu"*) explicitly states that the rest of the inscription was illegible. Neither the dates of death and burial nor the origin of the man's family could be seen. Zhao's *Jinshi lu* gives no entry for Wu Rong.

The *Li shi* text supplies a greatly expanded version of the Wu Rong stele. To the total of 74 characters that had been legible to Ouyang, *Li shi* added 148, 11 of which give the names and titles of Wu Kaiming and Wu Ban, all of which is very odd for a stele text dedicated to Wu Rong. No other Han stele, to my knowledge, uses the formula "The Lord is then X's relative" (*jun ji* . . . .).[21] These eleven characters most probably represent commentary that has been interpolated into the main text. The rest of the material probably also represents commentary, as it traces lines of

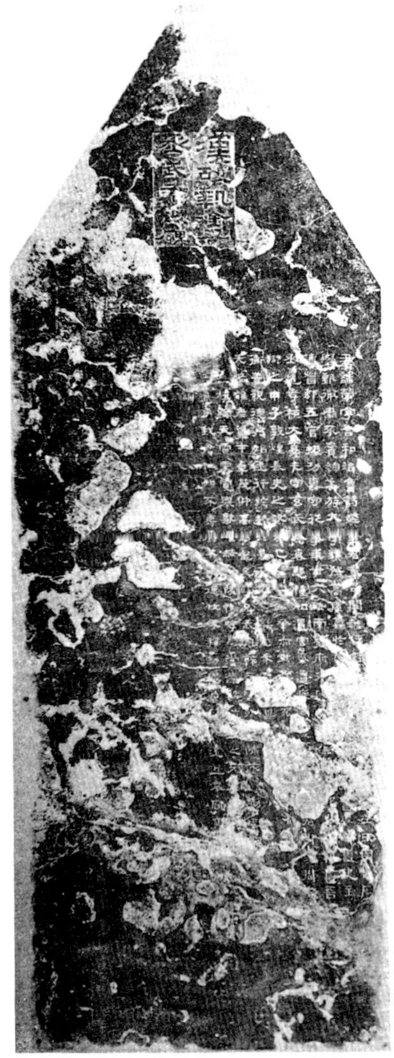

Fig. 4 *Wu Rong stele*. Ink-on-paper rubbing. From Jiang and Wu, *Handai Wushi muqun shike yanjiu*, p. 151, fig. 20.

scholastic filiation. Hong Gua added two additional pieces of information, however: that Wu Rong's stele head was in clerical script, and that the stele was in Jizhou, the larger administrative unit to which Rencheng belonged.[22] Yang Shen (1488–1559), in *Jinshi guwen*, mentioned that he owned a rubbing that matched the shorter version known to Ouyang Xiu, but he chose to cite the different *Li shi* version, because it supplied information on the family origin in its commentary.[23] No transcription of the Wu Rong stele gives the customary information regarding the year and month for Rong's death and burial, as Yang notes, and the transcriptions probably contain several anachronisms.[24] The late Ming *Wanli Yanzhou fu zhi* (*Gazetteer of Yanzhou in the Wanli era*; compiled 1573) places the Wu Rong stele at a local academy in Jining, the larger administrative unit for Rencheng.[25] Zhu Yizun, writing in the first decade of the eighteenth century, remarked that the stele had been rubbed into oblivion.[26] Some epigraphical specialists in late imperial China noted two relatively rare features in the stele *format*: The full text of the stele inscription occupied only half of one surface of the stele, and the inscription on the stele head was carved in relief.[27] Certainly, rubbings in completely different formats were circulating by the Daoguang reign-period.[28] A fairly legible version is now on view in Shandong, in a museum in Jining.

Wu Kaiming

The *Jinshi lu* entry on Wu Kaiming mentions no stele head; that means that no part of the Kaiming inscription as transcribed in the *Jinshi lu* explicitly mentions the Wu family name.[29] By the first transcription of the main text of the stele, in the *Jinshi lu*, the tabooed personal name for Kaiming was also "already gone." (Kaiming was the man's style name.) According to the inscription, in Yonghe 2 (?137 CE) this Kaiming was recommended as Filial and Incorrupt. Afterward he held two posts in the capital (both more typically held by eunuchs), until he left office to mourn his mother in Yongjia 1 (?145 CE). Presumably after the mourning period was over, he was appointed Assistant to the Governor of Wu commandery. He lived to the age of fifty-seven *sui*, dying in ?148 CE.[30] Ye Yibao, the early Qing epigraphical expert, knew a rubbing of the back of the stele, but then the stele disappeared.[31] It is frustrating that the Kaiming stele inscription provides so little information, for it is this inscription, read with the pillar-gate inscription, that was the basis for constructing the scattered Wu individuals as a single family. In the words of the *Jinshi lu*, "Kaiming served as the aide in Wu Commandery; Suizong [a.k.a. Wu Liang] served as the *congshi* for the commandery; and Xuanzhang [a.k.a. Wu Ban, Wu Kaiming's son]—each has his own stele."[32] According to the late Ming *Wanli Yanzhou fu zhi* of 1573, the Kaiming stele stood then in an unidentified location in Jining.[33]

Wu Liang

No entry for a Wu Liang of Rencheng appears in the catalogues of Ouyang Xiu or his son. Zhao Mingcheng's *Jinshi lu* entry for Wu Liang mentions no stele head, perhaps because the formula that begins "The former Han . . ." (*Han gu* . . . .) may have been reserved for those who had served the central government. The opening line of the inscription probably refers to an Assistant Liang whose family name is Wu, though the possibility remains that this Liang was an unranked military aide (*wuyuan*). After Liang's death at seventy-four *sui* in Yuanjia 1 (?151 CE), the stele inscription credited him with the standard virtues of loyalty and filial piety. He supposedly mastered one tradition of the *Odes* classic, but he steadfastly refused higher office, despite numerous summons, though he accepted a local rank before he died. Zhao Mingcheng remarks that he loves this inscription for its "completeness," yet of the verse encomium he quoted only twenty-eight or thirty-two characters[34] (four lines with eight characters each). "It is in many characters, which I do not record in full."[35]

One authoritative version of the extant *Li shi* begins the Wu Liang entry with a six-character passage that is either out of place or interpolated from a commentary.[36] The lengthy inscription found in *Jinshi lu* has gone missing; only twenty-eight characters of the lengthy verse encomium are found in both the *Jinshi lu* and the *Li shi*. The *Li shi*, in commenting on the Wu Liang pictorial carvings, relates in addition the careful manner in which unidentified family members selected stones for the Wu memorial, set up an altar (*tanshan*) in back, and a worship hall (*citang*) (aboveground hall for worship, thus a "shrine") in front, which were decorated by the artist Wei Gai—though the main entry for Wu Liang does not name the artist.[37] Modern readers have assumed that this passage represents part of the text of the Wu Liang stele inscription, but that assumption flatly contradicts Hong's own assessment:

> When speaking about funerary and burial matters, one should not be as verbose as this. The stone [attributed to Wu Liang] is not very long or wide, and since it has neither skillfully carved inscriptions nor images, not to mention nicely arranged rows, the phrases quite definitely were not composed for a stele. In mulling it over carefully, it seems that this [the aforementioned passage] refers only to the pictorial stones in the stone chamber (*shishi*) [of Wu Liang].[38]

If not part of the stele inscription, what was the identity of this appended passage? Certainly, if the Song epigraphical masters could not answer this question, modern scholarship will not be able to. Mei Dingzuo (1553–1619) *Donghan wenji* (*Collected writings of the Eastern Han*) seems to know two versions of the stele inscription, and to believe the shorter version that does not mention Wei Gai to be the "original text" (*yuan wen*).[39] Gu Aiji's *Li bian* (*Discerning remarks on clerical-script inscriptions*; compiled 1717) notes that the Wu Liang stele, once in Jining, is missing.[40]

The pillar-gate inscription (cat. no. 1.43)

No reference to a pillar-gate inscription can be found in the works of Ouyang Xiu, though it is hardly likely that Ouyang Xiu would have failed to notice such an imposing monument during his period of exile in Rencheng.[41] An entry in Zhao Mingcheng's *Jinshi lu*, however, records a pillar-gate inscription dated to Jianhe 1 (?147 CE), which tells of four filial sons (Wu Kaiming and three brothers) employing two stone masons named Meng to build the pillar-gates at a cost of 150,000 cash, at the same time that stone lions were commissioned for an additional 40,000 cash.[42] These were great sums in Han times, when a theft of 660 cash constituted grand larceny.[43] Could a mid- to low-ranking Wu family have spent such sums without defying the sumptuary regulations, which should have been strictly enforced in this strategic area near or in Rencheng, the seat of Liu clan princes?[44] By one theory, at some time—perhaps post-Han—the Wu family was itself noble, with perhaps a lateral branch based in Pei or Jiyin, respectively 100 and 30 kilometers away from Rencheng.[45] Be that as it may, the pillar-gate inscription ends with four sentences devoted to Wu Ban (i.e., about half the entire text), whom convention identifies as Kaiming's son. Why would "filial sons" erect a memorial gate whose inscription gives no information about the older generations but focuses instead on a single member of the younger generation? A more general question may be lodged: why do later traditions reflect so much confusion about the identity of the makers and dedicatees of the pillar-gates, if those identities were plain for all to see?

Furthermore, a second passage, this time in the *Li shi* entry for Wu Liang, says that Wu Kaiming erected the pillar-gates for his elder brother, Wu Liang—a statement flatly contradicting the pillar-gate inscription transcribed in *Jinshi lu*, which has Wu Kaiming and his three brothers, as "filial sons," erecting the gates.[46] (Readers will recall that the *Li shi* does not itself contain a transcription of the pillar-gate inscription.) According to the standard genealogy devised for members of the family, Wu Kaiming died three years before his elder brother Wu Liang, in which case we must either credit Kaiming with astounding prescience in building the pair of pillar-gates or presume that they were not erected in a funerary context. But the very materiality of the pillar-gate inscription, which was readily decipherable at the turn of the twentieth century, as the volumes of Chavannes and Sekino attest, has apparently precluded any consideration of these internal contradictions. (As the inscription has now been rubbed entirely away, we must rely upon these photos.) We do know that Fang Ruo's (1869–1954) *Jiaobei suibi* (*Notes comparing steles*) records that existing rubbings of the pillar-gate inscription present markedly different carving styles and formats, "with not a single stroke in a similar place."[47] The *Jinshi suo* (*Index to metal and stone carvings*; compiled 1821) shows an inscription with six lines per column, but Fang's text records an inscription with twelve lines per column.[48]

* * *

The five inscriptions used to reconstruct a Wu family of the late Eastern Han period are thought to constitute sufficient proof that the pictorial stones found by Huang Yi in 1786 must date from Eastern Han. Logically, however, judgments about the authenticity and date of these epigraphical items are independent of judgments about the pictorial slabs. For this reason, this essay has treated the inscriptional materials separately. Obviously, the problems surrounding the stele inscriptions associated with the Wu family make them less-than-ideal historical sources. The scholar He Zhuo (1661–1722), after a careful review of all the written records then available for the site, commented, rather sadly, that he could make no sense of the materials before him—the more materials he gathered, the more they scattered, "like leaves falling."[49] Some of the finest Qing epigraphical scholars pointed out contradictions in the records. For example, Bi Yuan (1730–1797), author of the *Shanzuo jinshi zhi* (*Records of bronze and stone in Shandong*), remarked that Zhao Mingcheng had added the character *han* to the Wu Ban stele, and that Hong Gua had not seen the three characters on the back of the Wu Ban stele (cat. no. 1.47), which appeared to be in the calligraphy of the Six Dynasties.[50] (The front face of the extant stele, of course, is by now nearly effaced, except for the recently recut characters specifying a Han date.)[51] The relevant gazetteers further increase our perplexity: the *Jizhou jinshi zhi* (*Record of bronzes and stones in Jizhou*; compiled 1843), for example, places a Wu Ban stele at Jiaxiang, with a stele head in two lines of seal script, even though Hong Gua specifically stated that the Wu Ban stele head was written in clerical script.[52] Such records as we have hardly add up to firm evidence for the continuous existence of a single set of artifacts that is identical with those associated with today's complex. Something surely existed as the basis for the rubbings viewed in Northern and Southern Song, but what was that something? did it remain the same at all time periods? and did it testify to the existence of a rich and powerful Wu family living in the Rencheng area circa 150 CE? Those questions remain, not only because of contradictions within the epigraphical sources, but also because of three other near-certainties: that the epigraphical masters after Ouyang Xiu made mistakes in their identification of the Wu family materials; that we have misunderstood their conventions; and that the Wu family in Rencheng before or during the Song period would have been happy to devise a glorious lineage for itself, given the importance attached to genealogy for over a millennium.[53]

This summary has focused on Southern Song accounts, seeing them as one key to any interpretation of the Wu family memorial inscriptions. Two observations are in order: the Song experts in epigraphy did not necessarily know all the inscriptions of their predecessors, and the contradictions, anachronisms, and anomalies that had surfaced by the time of the *Li shi*, taken together, suggest that inscriptional materials may be no less flawed than other received records. As we have seen, the Wu Ban stele inscription to an officer stationed in Dunhuang may have been merged with a stele encomium dedicated to a Dunhuang native. Possible anachronisms appear in the Wu Rong stele inscription itself; phrases repeat in both the Wu Rong and Wu Liang inscriptions,[54] and a lengthy description is used once in the pillar-gate inscription and once in the Wu Liang commentary but applied to different subjects. The rubbing for the Wu Kaiming stele has gone missing, just as the rubbing for Wu Rong has reappeared.[55]

Zheng Qiao's (1104–1162) *Tongzhi* (*Compendium of records*) in *juan* 73 lists all five inscriptions—the Wu family stone pillar-gate inscription record, and the stele inscriptions of Wu Ban, Wu Rong, Wu Kaiming, and Wu Liang—though it does not assign them to a single site. For most of these, it gives a date but no location, after which it either quotes Zhao Mingcheng or says, "It is not known in detail."[56] The connoisseur Wei Bo (act. 1140–1168) emphasized how rare it was to find rubbings of good quality after the enforced "move south" to the new Southern Song capital of Lin'an.[57] By the thirteenth century works on epigraphy and art fall silent on the subject of the Wu family inscriptions. (Such silence means that *neither* the stones themselves *nor* the rubbings taken from the stones are reported to be in existence, though catalogues did sometimes recall the fact of a stone's erstwhile existence.) So far as I know, it was not until the mid-eighteenth century that a printed text, Gu Aiji's *Li bian* (1717), again gathered together in a single epigraphical work the entire stock of five inscriptions that we now associate with the Wu family of the Wuzhai Shan area, though Gu did not include the text of the cartouches associated with the Wu Liang pictorial slabs.[58]

If all the passages attributed to Hong were indeed composed by him, which seems doubtful, he may have hoped to increase the value of his rubbings by attributing them to a single Han family engaged in ancestor worship, since—not for the first time—contemporary debates sought to locate the earliest (and so most authentic) recorded forms of ancestor worship. Or Hong may simply have been exhibiting the sort of careless scholarship that some say distinguishes the Southern Song literati from those of Northern Song. The sheer number of incised stones coming to light in the Rencheng area seems to have greatly complicated the processes of identification.[59]

In trying to make sense of the literary record associated with these five stone inscriptions, we should consider that what happened at Wuzhai Shan (and elsewhere in China) may be analogous to better-attested cases in Europe and America: records got confused; misstatements were made and perpetuated; and people "filled in" lacunae, as best they could, for a variety of reasons (a desire to amuse, astound, or appear knowledgeable; to authenticate and thereby increase the value of a collection; and possibly to boost local history).[60] Partial inscriptions were pieced together. Certainly the possibility exists that the reconstructed steles at Wuzhai Shan were produced, recarved, and assembled in different time periods, and that the various funerary structures had different functions, given the different finish of the backs of the stones employed in the so-called Wu Liang pictorial shrine and those of the other two reconstructed shrines (see Cary Liu's "Reconfiguring" in this catalogue).

Lou Ji (1131–1211), a contemporary of Hong Gua, records a "Lord Wu" or "Martial Lords" (Wujun) inscription in the same area of Jizhou, which made no reference to personal or style names or offices.[61] Perhaps part of what we now call the Wu family shrine was originally part of a memorial dedicated to a group of Martial Lords (i.e., the military dead), rather than to specific members of the Wu patriline. After all, at least two consort families in the vicinity boasted of long frontier service. Historically, the family name Wu was often awarded to military figures, and many names ascribed to the Wu family have double meanings, beginning with Wu Ban (*wuban*, "military ranks").[62] Then too, a high proportion of the exemplary figures who appear on today's Wu Liang pictorial stones are exemplars of physical courage (assassin-retainers; women willing to die to preserve their honor; and so on), and many martial heroes are said to have owned rubbings of the Wu Liang pictorial images.[63] Any analysis of this epigraphical corpus requires particular caution, since (a) collectors and antiquarians as early as Ouyang Xiu have registered doubts about inscriptions dated to the reigns of Emperors Huan and Ling of Han—precisely the period from which the entire corpus of the Wu family steles derives; and (b) other stone stele inscriptions housed in museums in the vicinity are thought to reflect similar problems.[64]

We have shown here that the assertions of a continuous textual record for the Wu family are hardly accurate, since the *Jinshi lu* has no entry for Wu Rong (and only entry titles for the Wu pictorial stones) and the *Li shi* is missing entries for Wu Kaiming and the pillar-gate. Moreover, the extant versions of the three main epigraphical works of Song origin, the *Jigu lu*, *Jinshi lu*, and *Li shi*, speak of the Wu-related rubbings in such contradictory ways that we can only surmise that our present editions reflect the conflation of disparate materials by well-meaning scholars and editors over the centuries. Let us turn, then, to review the literary history of the pictorial figures, which at first glance seems somewhat less confused and more complete.

III. The Wu Liang Pictorial Stones: The Literary Evidence

This section discusses the "Wu Liang" pictorial slabs alone, as the five stele inscriptions associated with the late Eastern Han Wu family have had a separate history, and as no record prior to Huang Yi exists for the pictorial slabs now assigned to two other reconstructed shrines supposedly erected for other Wu family members. By Southern Song, as we shall see, copies of the Wu Liang pictorial slabs may have been extant in various places and in diverse mediums besides rubbing sets. Thereafter, they appear to have dropped from sight until early Qing, when copies again began to proliferate.

Ouyang Xiu (1007–1072) mentioned no pictorial figures at all. Zhao Mingcheng's (1081–1129) *Jinshi lu* included "*five* scrolls [of rubbings]" (*juan*) taken from the Wu family stone chamber pictorial slabs, which were carved with portraits of the "ancient sages and worthies." Those portraits were inscribed in small *bafen* script with the individuals' family and personal names. "Every so often [the images] have appraisals above them [or, "in the upper part"], whose phrasing is ancient and elegant."[1] Because of the vigor of the calligraphic strokes employed there, Zhao decided to "fully record them" in five separate entries. Unfortunately, those five entries are now missing.

Hong Gua (1117–1184) in his *Li shi* wonders that Zhao Mingcheng was unable to assign the pictorial images and/or their labels to a specific site or member of the Wu family at Rencheng, given the phrasing of one of his rubbings.[2] The extant *Li shi* quotes, without provenance, a single passage about the "fine craftsman" Wei Gai sculpting neat rows of patterns and inscriptions (see the preceding section), and surmises on this basis that the images adorned a memorial dedicated to the Wu family or to Wu Liang in the cemetery in Rencheng mentioned by Zhao Mingcheng. (That unprovenanced passage does not appear in editions of the *Jinshi lu.*)[3] A later chapter of the *Li shi* supplies a list of labels for the pictorial images ascribed to Wu Liang's memorial.[4] In commentary, the *Li shi* describes six pictorial stones, "five of them divided horizontally into two [registers?]." If we assume that the rubbing(s) Hong knew corresponded closely to the Wuzhai Shan pictorial slabs found by Huang Yi (1744–1802) in mid-Qing, Hong was actually looking at ten separate visual blocks from the west, east, and south walls of the reconstructed main shrine at Wuzhai Shan (dubbed "Wu Liang"), which he denoted by their engraved cartouches and also by the more generalized description of "ancient emperors and kings, loyal officials, righteous knights, filial sons, and worthy women"[5] (fig. 5).

Wei Bo's (act. 1140–1167) *Ding'an lei gao*, contemporary with Hong Gua's *Li shi*, confirms that one or more rubbings or stones were extant during Southern Song. (Classical Chinese does not invariably distinguish between singular and plural, or between a rubbing and its source.) In 1167 an unnamed visitor to the capital showed the Metropolitan Overseer of Jiankang (present-day Nanjing) the Wu Liang rubbings, perhaps because he wished to sell or donate them to the imperial collection.[6] During the viewing someone (*mouren*)—possibly the Overseer himself—identified the rubbings as having come from the collection of Zhang Ruying (d. 1153), a member of a congenial literary coterie that included such luminaries as Zhu Xizhen (*jinshi* 1132) and Fang Wude (1102–1171).[7] Since Commander Zhang was widely admired, items from his collection were considered particularly valuable, and the Wu Liang rubbings were special treasures, inasmuch as they reproduced "unusual and fine" calligraphy relatively free of errors.[8] Although many sets of "this same type" were said to be available, the proffered rubbing (or set of rubbings) was engraved or displayed "on the walls" of the government offices at the Choushu Ge, a Southern Song imperial library, where the reproduction—conceivably a mural painting, a mounted rubbing set, a printed book, or stone(s) imbedded in plaster—was intended "to surprise and dazzle future generations."[9]

At some point a version came into the hands of Joint Commander Fang Wude.[10] Hong Gua disparaged Fang's copy of a copy as unfaithful to the original stone(s), from which it was removed by states and centuries. But perhaps Hong Gua was merely piqued at Fang's failure to "pay a visit to" (i.e., take a close look at) copies circulating in the capital before Hong completed his first epigraphical compilation. Later Hong obtained a copy for himself from one Liang Jiheng of Guacang (located in present-day Zhejiang).[11] Curiously, Hong Gua, like his contemporary Wei Bo, tended to describe the Wu Liang pictorial rubbings mainly in negative terms, focusing on how they differed from rubbings attributed to three nearby sites: Lu Gong's worship hall in nearby Jinxiang, the tomb of Zhu Fu, also in Jinxiang, and Li Gang's worship hall at Zhuye.[12] They described the Wu pictorial stones as differing in their lack of (a) portraits of Confucius and

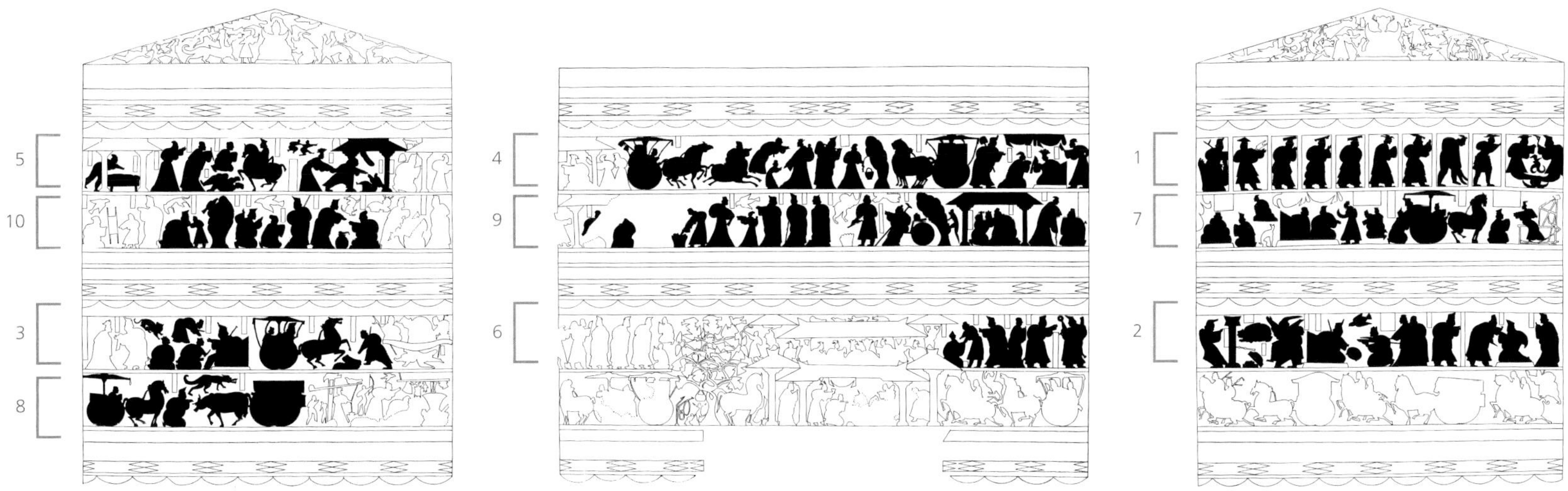

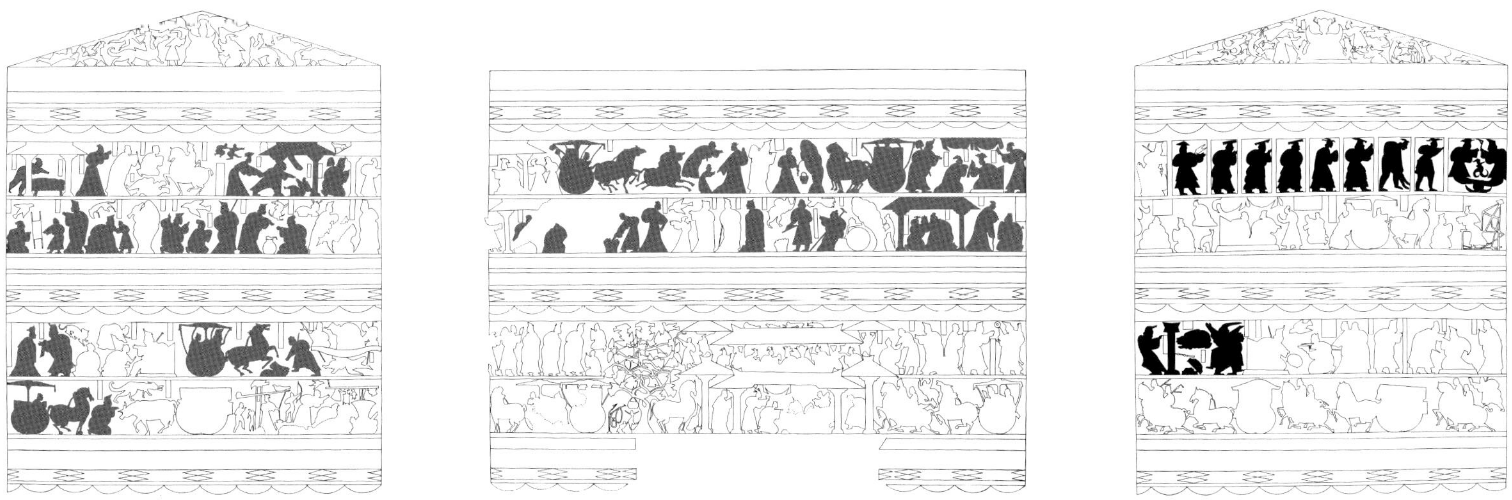

Fig. 5 (top) *Diagram of "Wu Liang Shrine" showing scenes apparently described in Hong Gua's "Li shi" text, if we assume that Hong Gua's rubbings correspond to today's stones.*

Fig. 6 (bottom) *Diagram showing scenes apparently described in Shi Shengzu's "Xue Zhai zhanbi" text, as compared with Hong Gua's "Li shi."* After the scenes of Zengzi with his mother and Min Ziqian, labels for figures appear in the *Li shi* that are not found in *Xue Zhai zhanbi*. At two points, the *Xue Zhai zhanbi* has additional characters. The sequence of the figures is also changed in several places as shown in gray.

his seventy-two disciples, such as could be found at the Lu Gong shrine; (b) one or more scenes of "rulers and officials and their subordinates" (a reference to carriage processions?); (c) the "flying birds and running beasts" scene found at the site dedicated to Li Gang;[13] and (d) cartouches identifying figures as office holders by such titles as *fu jun*, *ling*, and *jingzhao yin*.[14] (Of course, Confucius and his disciples; long lines of rulers, officials, and their subordinates; and flying birds and running beasts are all to be found at the three reconstructed shrines for the Wu family today—which may be one reason why Wang Chang, a contemporary of Huang Yi writing in 1805, thought the slabs Huang Yi found may have come from a number of different sites.[15] More positively, Hong Gua noted that figures like Liang Gaoxing appeared in both the Li Gang and Wu Liang rubbings. The revised *Li xu* attributed to Hong also describes a pavilion scene that corresponds in part with what we see today (the main figure sits, with guests or retainers bowing before him), but the six figures that the *Li xu* places after the principal figure cannot be found in any modern version.[16]

Another Southern Song entry on pictorial stones, that in Shi Shengzu's (1191–1274) *Xue Zhai zhanbi* (*Ignorant glosses from the Studio of Learning*),[17] contains the final relevant Song entry, though Shi's tale only compounds problems of interpretation. Shi's grandfather, Shi Zijian,[18] a Sichuan native who never served in Shandong so far as we know, compiled a book called *Li ge* (*Clerical script standards*), intended to supplement the works of Hong Gua, his contemporary. In 1167–1168, the very year that a version of the Wu Liang pictorial figures turned up in the capital at Jiankang, Shi Shengzu's grandfather, according to the most common version of the *Xue Zhai zhanbi* in circulation today, "got *three* stones (*bei*) [or rubbings?]" from grave mounds in Dongzhou ("the Eastern Provinces"), where the walls of one or more stone chambers were carved with "ancient sages and worthies, dutiful men and principled women, carriages, horses, persons, and things."[19] Though the pictorial figures from Dongzhou were "ridiculously crude [in execution]," the senior Shi thought the Han clerical calligraphy in the cartouches remarkably fine ("the smallest I have ever seen but still intact, as if new"). Apparently the three stones "had not been subjected to erosion by wind and sun," and only "a few had taken rubbings of them."[20] As an adult, Shi Shengzu, the grandson, duly pored over his grandfather's materials. Later Shi Shengzu arrived in Zizhou (in present-day Sichuan), to find in a hall there the very same stones, by then badly damaged by wars and fires. He ordered the stones repaired "good as new," on the basis of his grandfather's rubbings. Having reported those activities, Shi Shengzu then proceeded to list the labeled figures he had seen, which *roughly* match the Wu Liang images listed in Hong Gua's *Li shi*. The same wording is employed, for example, in the same order for the entire line-up of nine culture heroes (ten if you count Nüwa), but Shi Shengzu's list mentions no Jie, the wicked last king of the Xia dynasty—the final king identified in the lineup on the west wall of the reconstructed "Wu Liang" Stone Chamber by a two-character inscription (fig. 6).

Shi Shengzu's entry lists some (but not all) the scenes in a different order; one scene he apparently assigned to a different stone. Furthermore, Shi's stones had been badly damaged, whereas those found by Huang Yi some five centuries later were nearly all in amazingly good condition. How likely is it that the same stones would have been hauled from Shandong to Sichuan and then back to Shandong, to turn up in 1786 at the Wuzhai Shan site? What possible motive could have prompted the two trips, when either a fine rubbing set or the stones themselves already belonged to the Shi collection? In comparing such records, some Chinese epigraphical experts have been forced to conclude that the single entry in Shi Shengzu's work must describe two sites and that the memorial structure at a *second location* only happened to include nearly all the same labeled figures that appeared in the Wu Liang rubbings.[21] Three Ming literati—Yang Shen (1488–1559), Cao Xuequan (1574–1647), and Mei Dingzuo (1553–1619)—let us know that the pictorial stones mentioned by Shi Shengzu eventually came to be called the "old steles from Zizhou."[22] Other Sichuan sources speak of a ritual site dedicated to the Duke of Zhou, which portrayed many of the same figures that appear on the reconstructed Wu family stones.[23] In addition, Ming and Qing epigraphical works list an early Sichuan shrine dedicated to Liang Wudi, "The Martial Emperor" (r. 502–549)—exactly the sort of memorial structure where one might expect to find a procession of early sages.[24] (This is interesting, because some editions of the relevant works reverse Liang Wu and Wu Liang in their records.)[25]

Before the fall of Southern Song, then, multiple versions of pictorial stones similar enough to be confused were located in distant parts of the empire—not only in Shandong, but also in Jiankang; in Zhejiang; in Sichuan; in the Southern Song capital of Lin'an (present-day Hangzhou),[26] and probably in Guangdong. We know also that during Southern Song prized images would be copied from one medium to another.[27] But after the defeat of the Southern Song in 1279, only one Yuan text, Zhang Xuan's *Zhida Jinling xin zhi* (*Great new record of Jinling*, 1344), in an entry devoted to the Wu pictorial images, states that the Wu Liang rubbings known to Zhao included only two labeled scenes (those of Lao Laizi and Ding Lan), with the rest mostly "ruined and missing" (*can que*). Regarding the Choushu Ge library version known to Hong Gua, Zhang writes, "Now these are lost, nor have I seen that there exists a copy!"[28] The connoisseur Zhou Mi (1232–1298), whose family hailed from Licheng, near Ji'nan, Shandong, might be expected to have waxed eloquent on the subject of the famous pictorial stones from his ancestral area, but he is silent.[29] The Ming and early Qing sources held little hope that the original Wu Liang pictorial images would ever be seen again. Li E (1692–1752) asserted, "The Wu Liang pictorial images have now been rubbed into oblivion; the five steles in Rencheng have been eaten away by bugs and mosses."[30] Zhao Shaozu (1752–1833) in his *Jinshi wenchao* would write in reference to the Wu Liang pictorial slabs, "Today, none of these can be seen."[31]

We do not know whether the statements just cited—made before and after Huang Yi's dramatic discovery at Wuzhai Shan—took into account the description of a stone "offering hall" (*xiang tang*) that a 1692 gazetteer attributed to a tomb of an unknown Han prince on Purple Cloud Mountain, the same site known as Wuzhai Shan. The stones there, in "very fine incising," portrayed scenes "from the time of Fuxi, auspicious omens, and loyal and filial personages of antiquity."[32] These scenes would be, in

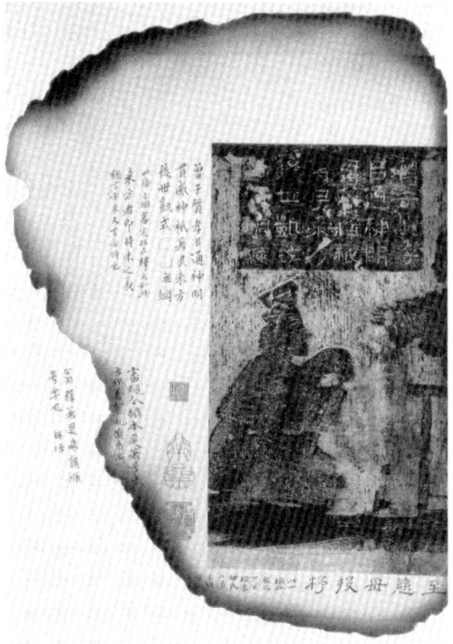

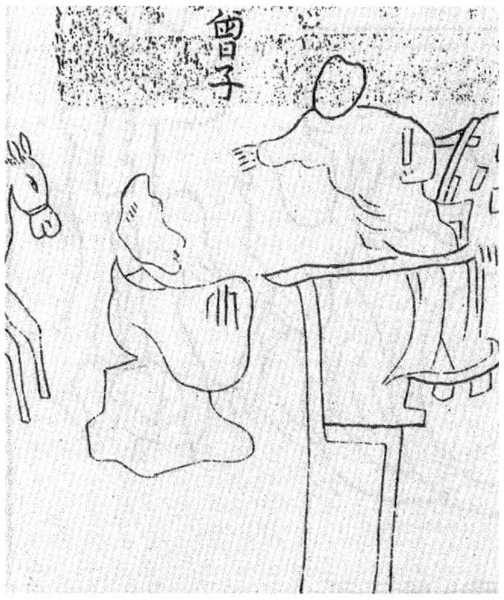

turn, identified by at least one expert—Rong Geng, writing in 1936—as the source of what has come to be known (quite confusingly) as the "Tang Rubbing."[33] The "Tang Rubbing" was originally a set of fourteen rubbings mounted in album form, only fragments of which are still extant (fig. 7A).[34] By 1703 the album had become the prized possession of Ma Sizan (after 1676–ca. 1724), the wealthy salt merchant turned antique collector and bibliophile, who had purchased it on the advice of his close relative, the antiquarian Zhu Yizun (1629–1709).[35] Zhu so vigorously promoted its authenticity as an early rubbing of one section of the lost Wu Liang stones that its history has long been considered an integral part of the history of the Wu Liang site.[36] A brief digression on it is therefore in order.

The album set had three seals on it, the first and second being those of the mid-Ming collector Tang Shunzhi (1507–1560), and the third that of his son Tang Hezheng of Wujin (present-day Changzhou, in Jiangsu).[37] Hence, possibly, the name of the album. Despite the absence of pre-Ming seals on the album, Zhu Yizun in his colophon asserted that the Tang Rubbing was older—and therefore a more faithful representation—than the versions known to Hong Gua and Wei Bo in Southern Song; probably, he opined, it was of Tang date.[38] Gu Aiji, celebrated author of *Li bian* (comp. 1717; rev. 1743), tentatively identified it as the *congke ben*—a woodblock copy of an original rubbing, or a woodblock reprint of another woodblock copy of an original rubbing—that had once belonged to Fang Wude.[39] (Modern experts date the so-called Tang Rubbing to Song or Ming. Rong Geng was particularly dismissive of the claims made on its behalf.)[40]

Qing literati who viewed the "Tang Rubbing" left their comments in thirty-three separate colophons. The first eight colophons, written by Zhu, Ma, their close relatives, a friend, and the painter Jin Nong (1687–1764), provide little help to the historian today. Chiefly they compliment the virtue and discrimination of the owners through allusions to famous figures mentioned in the Song epigraphical classics, or link the Tang Rubbings to Zhang Ruying, Hong Gua, Wei Bo, and Shi Shengzu.[41] But what precisely *was* the relation between the Tang Rubbing and the *Li xu*, the epigraphical classic generally attributed to the Southern Song figure Hong Gua? The question is not simple to answer, as some two-thirds of the extant *Li xu* represents Zhu Yizun's "supplements" (*bu*) to the incomplete manuscripts of the *Li xu* circulating in Zhu's time. Zhu's revised and expanded version of the *Li xu* includes manuscript materials from the various libraries that Zhu visited,[42] a group that included Ma Sizan's famous collection. Did Zhu, believing the fourteen scenes of Ma's album to be ultimately traceable to Han, include copies of that in his revised and expanded version of the *Li xu*? We simply do not know.

We can only say, first, that the so-called Tang Rubbing existed from early Qing and possibly from mid-Ming; second, that the fourteen separate scenes portrayed in the Tang album—ten rubbings of ten kings (plus Nüwa) and four rubbings portraying exemplary women and their sons—correspond to two registers of the west wall of the shrine reconstructed for Wu Liang; third, that the earliest extant edition of the *Li xu*, that preserved in the imperially sponsored *Siku quanshu* (completed 1782),[43] reproduces scenes not included in Ma's album (a few of which

Fig. 7A *Zengzi scene from Stone Chamber 3* (Wu Liang Shrine; cat. no. 1.35). Tang Rubbing fragment. From *Zhongguo meishu quanji, Shufa zhuanke bian*, vol. 1 (Beijing: Renmin meishu chubanshe, 1987), no. 72.

Fig. 7B *Zengzi scene from Stone Chamber 3*. From Hong Gua, *Li xu, Yingyin Wenyuange Siku quanshu* edition (Taipei: Taiwan shangwu yinshuguan, 1983–1986), *juan* 6, p. 1a.

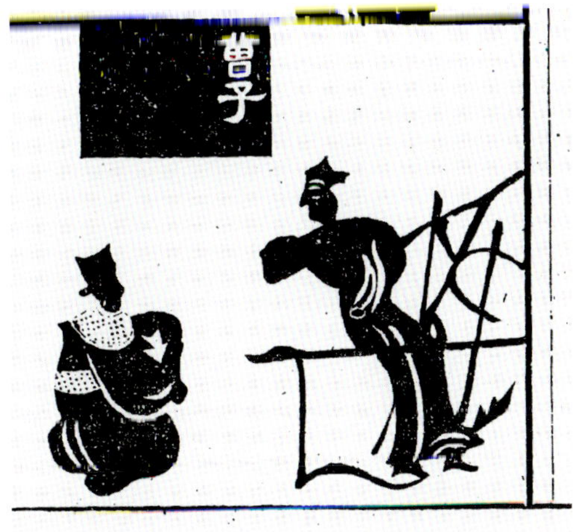

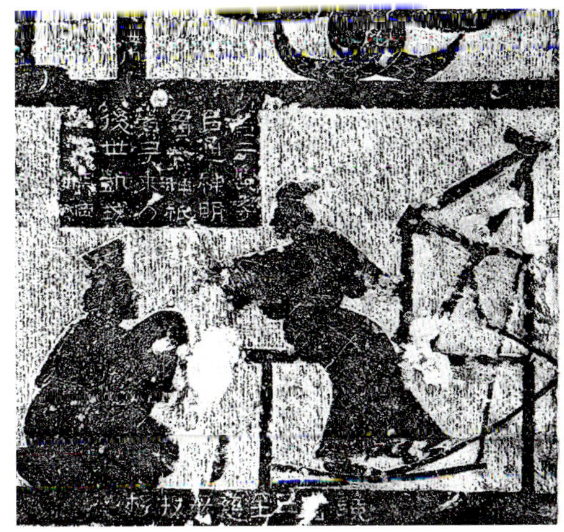

cannot—even approximately—be made to correspond with scenes in the reconstructed "Wu Liang Shrine," unless one imagines some recutting and recarving);[44] fourth, that four of the fourteen scenes in the Tang Rubbing (the Fuxi/Nüwa, Zengzi's mother [figs. 7A–7D], Lao Laizi, and Ding Lan scenes) are repeated elsewhere in the Wuzhai Shan materials. What, then, is the precise relation between the Tang album fragments that survive and the line drawings contained in the earliest extant edition of the *Li xu*, *juan* 6? Certain discrepancies between that edition of the *Li xu*, the Tang Rubbing, and rubbings produced at Wuzhai Shan at the turn of the twentieth century are hard to account for unless the stones were recarved after 1782. Some have argued that the line drawings of the *Siku quanshu* version of the *Li xu* are merely crude sketches of the materials at hand, but that would be inconsistent with the rather detailed depictions of other artifacts in the same edition.[45] One might question the magnitude of Huang Yi's achievement, if he "discovered" pictorial stones at a site whose general location had long been known to antiquarians, and whose scenes from the "main shrine" assigned to Wu Liang corresponded loosely to an imperially sponsored manuscript copy of the *Siku quanshu* that was available to those working with the palace collections—men like Weng Fanggang, Huang Yi's patron—at least four years before Huang Yi's reported finds.

Inevitably, in considering such questions, one is led to ask why no long labels or moralizing appraisals were preserved in *Li xu*, *juan* 6, when such labels and appraisals are given in an earlier work attributed to Hong, *Li shi*, *juan* 16? The simplest answer would be that Hong felt no need to repeat the lengthy labels and appraisals in his later work. But the simple answer may not be the right answer, since so many contradictions, anachronisms, and additions mark the *Li shi* writings on the Wu family. Certainly the text ascribed to Wu Liang in *Li shi*, *juan* 16 (otherwise known as the *Beitu*), shows signs of rearrangement, for reasons now unknown.[46] Is it possible that, when scholars in late imperial China filled in the gaps in the long labels and moralizing appraisals found at Wuzhai Shan, their interpolations were generated from Shi Shengzu's *Xue Zhai zhanbi*, which by late Ming and early Qing was thought (almost certainly erroneously) to include a description of the Wu family site in the Eastern Provinces?[47] Gu Aiji, when writing of the pictorial materials, does not supply the long labels and moralizing appraisals anywhere in his epigraphical classic of 1717. Instead, he states plainly that the labels he knows, which include a reference to Duke Zhuang of Lu, cannot date from Eastern Han, since the use of the name Zhuang ignores a taboo that would have been in effect in late Eastern Han. The pictorial figures, Gu concludes, must have been dedicated to another Wu from another time who is also buried in the Rencheng cemetery.[48]

Whatever the origin of *juan* 6 of the *Li xu*, the colophons for the Tang album, beginning with that by Zhu Yizun in 1705, allow us to establish some sort of a history of ownership for the album known as the Tang Rubbing.[49] About 1717 Gu Aiji made a copy of Ma Sizan's prized possession. In 1717 the painter Jin Nong (1687–1763)—who was equally renowned for his collection of old rubbings, his antique dealing and authenticating, and his carving of inkstones in clerical script—registered his interest in the

Fig. 7C *Zengzi scene from Stone Chamber 3*. From Hong Gua, *Li xu, Shike shiliao xinbian* edition (Taipei: Xinwenfeng chuban gongsi, 1977), *juan* 6, p. 7125.

Fig. 7D *Zengzi scene from Stone Chamber 3*. Detail from Stone 3-W.1 (cat. no. 1.35). "Wu family shrines" rubbings. Princeton University Art Museum, acc. no. 2002.307.36.

album in a colophon.[50] He Zhuo (1661–1722), Jin Nong's teacher, was then working in the imperial archives, so Jin probably made a copy of the album's contents for him. We know that He Zhuo later studied the rubbing set. In the period 1717–1723 the Tang Rubbing seems still to have been in Ma Sizan's collection.[51] By 1773 (Qianlong 48), fifty years later, Ma Sizan's descendant(s) had sold off the major part of Ma's library.

"Several decades before," however, according to a colophon, Ma Sizan's Tang album had passed into the Yangzhou collections of the fabulously wealthy salt merchants Ma Yueguan (1688–1755) and Ma Yuelu (1697–?after 1766)—two brothers who may or may not have been related to Ma Sizan.[52] The brothers, known to history as the "two Yangzhou salt merchants," were bibliophiles and connoisseurs.[53] Their library, the Congshu Lou, boasted such extraordinary holdings not only in rare books but also in calligraphy, paintings, rubbings, and engravings that Ma Yuelu's son, Ma Yu, was able in 1772 to offer the imperially sponsored *Siku quanshu* project about seven hundred individual titles from the family library for publication in the anthology.[54] The catalogue for the Congshu Lou library, however, includes no entry for the famous Tang Rubbing.

In 1775 the Tang album passed into the hands of another Yangzhou connoisseur, the connoisseur-artist Wang Xuejiang.[55] Soon thereafter copies and copies of copies began to proliferate.[56] Huang Yi viewed it in the summer of 1775, but was in too much of a hurry to make a tracing copy.[57] In the winter of 1779 or 1780 Weng Fanggang attempted to borrow the album in Wang Xuejiang's possession, but failed.[58] In 1783 Huang Yi obtained (*de*) a tracing copy (*xiang ta*) of Wang's Tang album that belonged to Lu Guanfu (*zi* Shaozeng) of Wumen (present-day Suzhou).[59] In the same year Huang Yi sent this Lu Guanfu version to his patron Weng Fanggang to study. Weng's interest in Mr. Lu's version was evident; he copied it, made detailed notes about it, and composed three poems about it. By then, Weng would have had access to the *Siku* manuscript version of *Li xu*, *juan* 6, as well.[60] Also in 1783 Weng asked a talented disciple of his, Song Baochun of Anyi (1748?–ca. 1820), to carve a copy of Mr. Lu's version either in stone or in wood. Song's first attempt was reportedly finished in the same year. Then Weng Fanggang instructed Song to have a Mr. Zhao carve a (miniature?) woodblock set based on Song's copy, so that the version that Weng sponsored would enjoy as wide a circulation as possible among scholars.[61] In the spring of 1784 Weng Fanggang received another copy of the Tang Rubbing sent by Wang Xuejiang himself.[62] (This is interesting because Wang had earlier refused a visit by Weng, perhaps fearing that he had designs on the album.) Meanwhile, Huang Yi made a tracing copy of the clerical script inscriptions, which he also sent to Weng to study.[63] Still, Weng must have been less than satisfied with the results, for in 1785 Weng advised Song to wait for a better version to copy.[64]

In keeping track of this series of exchanges, one may easily lose sight of one point: that by 1785, one year *before* Huang Yi's dramatic "rediscovery" of the pictorial stones ascribed to the Wu family and over a century after gazetteers mentioned stones that may have been part of Huang's discovery, Weng Fanggang and Huang Yi were already circulating multiple versions of the Tang Rubbing pictorial scenes, according to Weng

Fanggang's own colophon to the Tang Rubbing.[65] Then, in the eighth month of 1786, Huang Yi reported the discovery of what he quickly identified as "the original stones" of the Wu family *citang*.[66] Sometime later—varying accounts give as short a time as "one and the same day" or as long a time as five years later, in 1791—the Tang Rubbing came into Huang Yi's possession, either in fulfillment of an old promise made to Huang Yi by Wang Xuejiang before his death or in return for Huang Yi's gift to Wang Lingchu, Wang Xuejiang's brother, of Huang Yi's own hand-traced copies of the labels found on the pictorial stones that Huang had just located on Purple Cloud Mountain (also called Wuzhai Shan).[67]

Huang Yi's discoveries could not but diminish to some degree the value of the Tang Rubbing—at least to some people for some purposes.[68] After all, the Tang album of the Wu Liang pictorial scenes corresponded to only two registers of a single pictorial stone found by Huang Yi—an estimated 20 percent known to every serious student of epigraphy by 1791 (see below).[69] Huang Yi, in comparing the pictorial stones he found in 1786 with the illustrations known from the *Li xu*, reported that his stones were missing only a few scenes (*juan* 6/9a-b in the *Siku quanshu* manuscript version of the *Li xu*). Pictorial slabs with these very scenes were soon located in a second round of discoveries reported by Huang Yi in 1789. Thus, the finds made in 1786 and in 1789 vastly increased the number of pictorial scenes known to connoisseurs, who had hitherto relied for information on literary descriptions culled from the pre-Qing epigraphical classics and on the Tang Rubbing. Huang Yi's stones were in much better condition than those known to any Song experts.[70]

The epigraphical expert Wang Chang noted that many of the stones did not appear in the corpus known to Hong Gua, which meant that not all the pictorial stones found by Huang Yi necessarily belonged to the Wu family cemetery.[71] But Huang Yi's extraordinary flair for self-promotion, given wings by Weng Fanggang's patronage, worked to keep all the pictorial slabs regarded as a single unit and housed within a single Preservation Hall, where ancestral sacrifices were to be restored to the long dead but finally reconstituted Wu family. Huang Yi and his Shandong circle of antiquarian friends, principally Li Tieqiao (*zi* Dongqi) of Jining, and Li Meicun (*zi* Kezheng) and Nan Minggao (*zi* Zhengyan) of Hongdong, oversaw the production of quite a number of rubbing sets that were sold to raise money toward building and maintaining a Preservation Hall for the new finds. Huang Yi himself contributed the large sum of 140,000 cash to the Hall to supplement the funds contributed by local officials. The fame of Huang Yi and his patron Weng Fanggang as latter-day "filial sons" was bound to be enhanced by Huang's decision, made shortly after 1791, to publish, "for the delight and utility of scholars," a woodblock-printed edition based on his tracing copies. The publication of this woodblock version, coming as it did on the heels of the second round of discoveries claimed by Huang Yi, only facilitated the conflation of the Tang Rubbing album owned by Huang Yi with the rubbings produced under Huang Yi's direction.[72] Throughout the rest of his life, Huang lavished rubbings of his finds on his friends and acquaintances.[73] Huang Yi and Weng Fanggang had finally managed to achieve, late in life, the long-cherished goal to which they had dedicated themselves in 1777: they had joined the pantheon of epigraphical giants headed by Hong Gua. A modern epigraphical expert believes that some 80 percent of the material authenticated by Weng was forged, but ordinary persons with a taste for antiquarianism had no reason not to be satisfied that the tangled history of the Wu Liang pictorial scenes was finally resolved, and an ancient legacy successfully restored.

Few scholars, it seems, had noted the discrepancies between the pictorial slabs in what Huang Yi called the Front, Rear, and Left Stone Chambers, most of which lacked cartouches, labels, and appraisals, and those three heavily inscribed stones that Huang Yi assigned to Wu Liang. None remarked, in print at least, on the different treatments given different sets of pictorial slabs in the memorial structures assigned to the same Wu family. The sheer number of reproductions in circulation and sponsored by Huang Yi and Weng seems to have made it next-to-impossible for serious scholars to research the history of the many sets of rubbings they knew. That much was evident by 1821, not quite two decades after Huang Yi's death, when the Feng brothers, Feng Yunpeng and Feng Yunyuan, compiled their famous *Jinshi suo* (*Index to metal and stone carvings*). For the *Jinshi suo* noted that the brothers found multiple variations among different versions of the epigraphical rubbings, including changes in the order and placement of cartouches and figures; the omission, alteration, or deletion of depictions of human figures and objects (e.g., curtains in one version became roof tiles in another); variations in the postures of individual figures, as when a kneeling figure in one version stands in another. By the time of the Feng brothers (Daoguang reign-period, 1821–1850), rubbings of dubious quality that were attributed to the site "were not difficult to procure," but genuinely old rubbings were not to be had on the open market.[74] A century later, in 1936, Rong Geng thought he was working from the best rubbings available in his time—Ma Heng's (1881–1955) one-scroll version said to be Huang Yi's own rubbings (now in the Palace Museum, Beijing)—but even those rubbings do not precisely match the pictorial stones known today.[75]

Meanwhile, more and more pictorial stones were being linked with the Wu family, as they were found.[76] Presumably, it was always considered an achievement to add to the total, as Xuanyuan Hua did in 1871 and again in 1880, Ding Rongjiang in 1880, Cai Renqiu in 1882, and Qu Derun in 1909.[77] During the late Qing (until 1907) a number of new pictorial stones were unearthed in the area, purportedly in the nearby towns of Yutai, Ji'nan, and Feicheng (near the Xiaotang Shan site), including the six pictorial stones, possibly forged, that were acquired in the early twentieth century by the Tokyo Imperial College of Engineering (now Tōdai) and a forged slab bought by the British Museum (in storage there).[78] The sale and expropriation of pictorial stones and rubbings from Shandong (first within the German sphere of influence and then within Japan's) was thought to reflect a much wider phenomenon whereby huge quantities of art works were being sold off at cut-rate prices to museums and private collections "overseas" (*haiwai*), when they were not appropriated by war-lords and the like.[79] By the late Qing one can discern the first signs of the process by which the complex came to be catapulted to the status of national monument; by the Xuantong era (1908–1911) objects associated with the Wu family had acquired a heightened significance for patriotic Chinese as "our country's national antiquities" (*wu guo gu wu*). Prominent Chinese scholars took it upon themselves to catalogue the growing losses to the cultural patrimony, to "restore" antiquities, and to build the earliest museums opened in modern China. Liang Sicheng (1901–1972) and Wilma Fairbank (d. 2002) were but two of the important scholars who viewed the Wu family materials within the larger context of their nationalistic plans for the recovery of the Chinese past in the face of foreign depredation.[80]

The high value placed on adding new pictorial stones to the corpus and on acquiring pictorial rubbings connected with the site presents a very odd contrast to the extreme neglect of the successive Preservation Halls built during the late Qing and Republican eras. From the early nineteenth century on, many connoisseurs preferred to focus on the various rubbings reproduced in book form, since the stones themselves were blackened with layers of ink. Still, the neglect seems inexplicable, if in late Qing the site was considered to be as important as it is today. Three diary entries give us some idea of earlier conditions. On the day corresponding to June 21, 1841, Xu Han (1797–1866), for example, recorded in his diary the visit that he and his party of friends had just made to the Wu Liang shrine.

> After partaking of food [breakfast] at Zhifang, we visited the "Wu family shrine" [i.e., the Preservation Halls built by Huang Yi and his friends in 1789] . . . . Locals simply refer to this site as the Imperial Forest (*huang lin*). There were still quite a few slabs jumbled in the pit, including some with pictorial scenes. In the northeastern corner [of the pit,] there were exposed stones below the earth, apparently in the form of a tomb . . . . The bricks and roof above the shrine were falling apart; the doors and windows were entirely missing. Pictorial slabs had been inserted into the four walls [of the Preservation Halls]—as many as possible—but only to the height of two slabs, so that the stones could be rubbed . . . . I had heard from the local instructor, Mr. Guo, that the shrine was quite tall—so tall that one could not make rubbings of the slabs located on the gable wall without a scaffold. What nonsense!
>
> The [remaining] slabs that did not fit were placed within the room, paired on east and west. Some lay on their sides; some lay face up—there was no uniformity. A few of the slabs that were originally standing had fallen down. The locals used these slabs as chairs or beds; and their children, as counters for play when mixing mud. In extreme cases, someone had even urinated or defecated on them, so that it was unbearably filthy and provoking.
>
> Yang Duo [*zi* Shiqing] and I had to look for water to clean the slabs, [after which?] we *searched for the places with characters* [emphases mine], so that we might [each] make a set of rubbings by hand . . . . Yang Duo also made rubbings of the pillar-gate inscriptions . . . . Unfortunately, the locals had used this very pit to defecate in, and so a dungheap had piled up there. Truly disgusting! After we had completed the rubbings, we went northeast to Tiger Head Hill . . . .

Later scholars' diaries reveal no less shock at the decay and ruin they met when visiting the successive Preservation Halls in Shandong. In 1880 Chen Jin (b. 1821) reported:

> For nearly ninety years, without interruption, tourists and merchants took the trouble to travel thousands of miles to make rubbings without permission . . . . I went several times to the Wu *citang* [i.e., the Preservation Hall(s) in Jiaxiang] and saw the cracked walls, fallen beams, and stones lying upside down . . . . I have examined Han stone inscriptions throughout Shandong . . . . Half [of them] have had their characters ground down [by rubbing] . . . while half have been recut by vulgar scholars, so that they have lost their authentic [antique flavor]."[81]

In 1907 a student of Chavannes, Vassili Michaelovich Alexéief (1888–1958), reported even more deplorable conditions. The Preservation Hall was "tended" by a confirmed opium addict who, with his wife and young children, used many of the stones as footstools and flue-beds (*kang*).[82] Happily, in 1961 the materials at Jiaxiang were awarded first-rank National Heritage Protection status, a level of protection roughly comparable with that afforded UNESCO sites.[83] Since 1961, then, both national and local efforts have contributed to the preservation and analysis of the Wuzhai Shan stones, and those recent contributions, in turn, have made this exhibition possible.

* * *

In his "Memories of K'ai-feng," Wu Pei-yi draws the reader's attention to what has been called "the monumental absence of the past" in China, arguing that the Chinese preferred to believe that "memories of great human moments endured better through literary rather than architectural means."[84] At first glance the discovery of the Songshan "small shrines" (cat. no. 11) would seem to confirm the correctness of the restoration to history of the monumental Wu family pictorial stones,[85] since the Songshan stone carver apparently utilized some of the same drawing templates as the Wuzhai Shan stone carvers, for instance, in the manner of rendering the flared nostrils of the horses on parade. Unfortunately, the only two dates in the Songshan inscription have been incorrectly transcribed; the tomb itself purportedly dates from the Six Dynasties; and all other materials found in the vicinity of Wuzhai Shan have been dated by Wuzhai Shan.[86] Equally troublesome is the routine dating of all pictorial stones to Han, on the assumption that the relative impoverishment of the post-Han period necessitated a change from stone to the cheaper medium of molded bricks. That theory does not hold water, given the incredible luxury of other excavated items, for example, the fifth-century Sima Jinlong screen.

For a variety of reasons, questions of authenticity and origins do not invariably produce useful or interesting answers when applied to inscribed stones and epigraphical rubbings in China. Until recently, the language of epigraphy itself was often ambiguous. For example, the phrase "Han clerical" (*Han li*) can refer either to a Han-period writing in clerical mode or to a post-Han writing emulating the Han-period mode,[87] and, as we

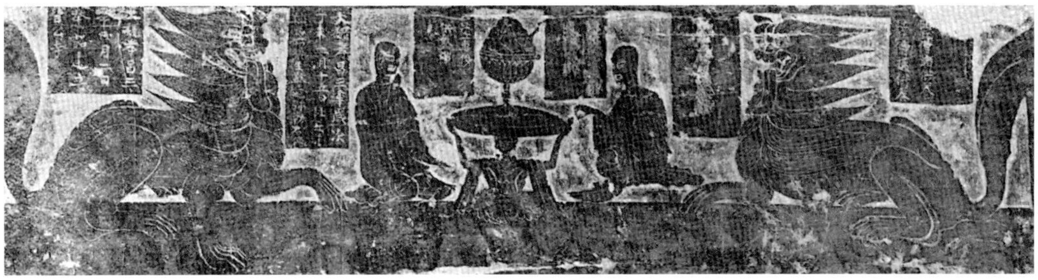

have seen, a date in a stele head does not necessarily refer to the date of its carving. In any case, scholars disagree, by as much as several centuries, on the dates they now assign to major sites such as Yi'nan. Reign-period names were often duplicated, introducing a further measure of uncertainty into dating. Moreover, period styles of calligraphy on stone monuments were not necessarily discrete and progressive. The most disparate motives, some innocent and some self-interested, prompted conscious attempts at archaizing and "filling in the blanks."[88] Further complicating matters is the surpassing value attached—at least from the Song dynasty—to antiquity and its artifacts, as manifested in specialized books devoted to the subject, court debates over precedents, collecting, and tourism, the last an activity embracing what can only be called sightseeing in tombs.[89] Already by the eleventh century, if not earlier, "Reading Steles" was a sub-genre of painting, as we learn from the *Huashi* (*History of painting*) of Mi Fu (1057–1107), the calligraphic master who "apparently relished the idea of being known as the master forger and copyist."[90] With collectors, artists, and forgers alike in thrall to the perfections of antiquity, the assertion that when the typical Eastern Han auspicious subjects, such as "dragons, deer, the person receiving [sweet] dew, auspicious grain, and the trees with intertwining branches (*lianli*), all appear on stone carvings *we can know* that they are not fake" now seems naive, at best[91] (fig. 8).

New technologies for dating stone inscriptions, technologies that are just beginning to be applied in the much better endowed fields of Classical and Near Eastern archaeology, may eventually resolve today's uncertainties with respect to the inscriptional material in China. Until some ideal future time when more scientifically excavated materials allow more systematic analysis, it seems wise to regard nearly all the evidence that has been transmitted through the epigraphical classics as no more or no less reliable than that known through the received transmissions. In the meantime, I intend to go on admiring the superb quality of the stonework that convention associates with the Wu family, which argues indisputably for a very powerful patron or patrons commanding great resources in the commission. I cite in defense of that attitude the words of Chen Jieqi (1813–1884), a scholar of some renown. Chen wrote in a letter to a friend,

> If you love inscriptions, then gather them, judge them, contemplate them, and transmit them. Seek ancient calligraphy; seek examples of the concerns of the ancients; seek forms of lost ancient characters. As for our duty to antiquity, even if we can only make known to the world some thousand ancient vessels, without being able to vouch for the accuracy of all ancient characters . . . still we can seek and seek again for that which we can obtain.[92]

Perhaps it is no more than a symptom of the post-modern condition, but with the epigraphical materials under study "I have come to see I must live at some distance/ From convince, from the sense of finding, being found."[93]

Fig. 8 *Maitreya Buddha scene on stone pedestal front.* Northern Wei dynasty, 527. Ink-on-paper rubbing. From S. W. Bushell, *Chinese Art* (London: His Majesty's Stationery Office, 1910), vol. 1, fig. 21. Some features of this stele from the Northern Dynasties—including the chimeras with their flame-like manes, and the long cartouches—recall the pictorial images assigned to the Wu family of late Eastern Han, despite the stele's Buddhist subject matter. Recent archaeological finds have verified the propensity of the Northern Dynasties to copy Han images and forms.

Notes to Section I

1. Cf. the similar (potentially more neutral) terms *shigu* and *haogu* ("to have a taste, liking, or craving for antiquity"). Thanks are due to Miranda Brown, Chen Pao-chen, Pricilla Chen, Christian De Pee, Søren Edgren, Ronald Egan, Käte Finsterbusch, Robert Harrist, Martin Heijdra, Eileen Hsu, Angela Leung, Judith MacKenzie, Joseph McDermott, Cecie Reilly, William Schaefer, Kyle Steinke, Tang Hai-tao, Mei-ling Williams, Wu Pei-yi, and, above all, to Alfreda Murck for help with this essay. The American Council of Learned Societies, the Chiang Ching-kuo Foundation, the Institute for Advanced Study (Princeton), and the University of California at Berkeley provided support at various stages during my research. It need hardly be said that any errors are my own.

2. José Saramago, *All the Names*, trans. Margaret Jull Costa (New York: Harcourt, 1999), p. 191.

3. Such a status has rendered the site nearly immune to questioning for the last sixty years, at least.

4. Hong Gua, *Li xu*, *juan* 18/2a–2b, apparently credits four shrines in the Shandong area with this centrality: Li Gang, Lu Gong, Zhu Fu, and Wu Liang; cf. *Li xu*, *juan* 6/15b. [All citations where no edition is indicated refer to the *Siku quanshu* electronic edition.] For Wu Liang as a premier site of antiquity, see Li Lincan, *Zhongguo meishu shigao* (Taipei: Xiongshi tushu, 1989), chap. 1.

5. Alexander Stille, *The Future of the Past* (New York: Farrar, Straus, and Giroux, 2002), p. 45. See Chuang Shen, "Archaeology in Late Qing Dynasty Painting," *Ars Orientalis*, vol. 24 (1994), pp. 83–104, for a more accurate picture of archaeology and antiquarianism in China at the end of the nineteenth century.

6. Nylan, "Restoring and Restorying Monuments of the Past," *Orientations*, March 2004, pp. 98–103. See Randolph Starn, "Authenticity and Historic Preservation: Towards an Authentic History," *Collegium Budapest Institute for Advanced Study*, pp. 281–96; *Wenwu* 1961.2; Jocelyne Fresnais, *La Protection du patrimoine en République populaire de Chine, 1949–99* (Paris: Éditions du C.T.H.S., 2001); J. David Murphy, *Plunder and Preservation: Cultural Property Law and Practice in the People's Republic of China* (Hong Kong: Oxford University Press, 1995), except chap. 1. As Lothar von Falkenhausen has argued in several publications, however, some mainland archaeologists (not to mention their allies outside the PRC) have continued to interpret the fruits of their excavations within the historical narratives of Marxism and nationalism. This phenomenon is hardly unique to China.

7. See Martin Kern, *The Stele Inscriptions of Ch'in Shih-huang: Text and Ritual in Early Chinese Imperial Representation* (New Haven: American Oriental Society, 2000), p. 50.

8. In the standard bibliographies of the imperial period, *jinshi* is sometimes classified under Classics (*jing*), sometimes under history (*shi*); and sometimes under "the masters" (*zi*). Few disciplines embrace as many different fields as epigraphical research; hence, the position of epigraphy (at least before the 20th century) as the queen of Chinese research fields. Yet even in the heyday of epigraphy, it was "no part of the rubbing-maker's interest to record the entire slabs." See Wilma Fairbank, *Adventures in Retrieval: Han Murals and Shang Bronze Molds* (Cambridge, Mass.: Harvard University Press, 1972), p. 113.

9. Robert Pogue Harrison, *The Dominion of the Dead* (Chicago: University of Chicago Press, 2003); David Lowenthal, *The Past is a Foreign Country* (Cambridge: Cambridge University Press, 1985), p. xvi.

10. See Zheng Xiuping, "Jining Hanbei kao," *Shomei tō shohin* (*Tōyō shodo kyōkai*) vol. 288, no. 11 (November 1986), pp. 12–35. The first three hypotheses derive from Zheng Xuan's commentaries to the "Bin lin" chapters of the *Yili*; the "Jiyi" and "Tan Gong" chapters of the *Liji*. The fourth hypothesis is offered by Nylan, on the basis of Eastern Han depictions. To the holes, whose number(s) is determined, in theory at least, by sumptuary regulations, are tied the ropes that bind the animals offered in sacrifice (or possibly left behind by their masters). Gradually, during the Six Dynasties, the holes disappear, evidently because the function of the stone stele changes to a transcription of the history of the meritorious deceased. (The ritual texts, which are unclear on many points, state that those without official rank are to have only wooden planks.)

11. Not surprisingly, the earliest extant steles are dedicated to those of high rank, the few exceptions being of questionable provenance or of uncertain date.

12. For the "warp and woof," see R. Kent Guy, *The Emperor's Four Treasuries: Scholars and the State in the Late Ch'ien-lung Era* (Cambridge, Mass.: Council on East Asian

Studies, 1987), pp. 63–74, citing Zhu Yun (1729–1781), a contemporary of Huang Yi, who also wrote, "Stone inscriptions are the oldest historical source, and they can be relied upon in examining the past, as they never lose their truth." For the four claims, see Wu Hung's able summary in his essay in *Writing and Materiality: Essays in Honor of Patrick Hanan*, ed. Judith T. Zeitlin and Lydia H. Liu (Cambridge, Mass.: Harvard University Asia Center for the Harvard-Yenching Institute, 2003), pp. 29–69.

13. For the first claim of the "transparency" of rubbings, see also Qianshen Bai, "The Artistic and Intellectual Dimensions of Chinese Calligraphy Rubbings: Some Examples from the Collection of Robert Hatfield Ellsworth," *Orientations*, March 1999, p. 83, citing Wu Yun (1811–1883); and He Ruyue and He Haoyue, "*Jinshi lu* he *Jigu lu* shiliao jiazhi," *Journal of the Xianyang Teacher's College* vol. 15, no. 5 (October 2000), pp. 55–58; and Wang Zhuanghong, *Beitie jianbie changshi* (Shanghai: Shanghai shuhua, 1985), p. 20 [hereafter, Wang Zhuanghong]. For the "freezing" of an object, see Wu Hung, *Writing and Materiality*, p. 34 (quotation marks mine). For the "remnant soul" of the stele, see Ye Changchi (1849–1917), *Yu shi* (Shenyang: Liangning jiaoyu chubanshe, 1999), p. 251. This reference to cicadas recalls, of course, the preferred style of rubbing in the Song period, which used a very light application of ink. For the final claim, see, e.g., Ouyang Xiu, *Jigu lu*, preface. [All citations where no edition is indicated refer to the *Siku quanshu* electronic edition.] As Ronald Egan's (forthcoming) work on Ouyang Xiu demonstrates, Ouyang's rubbing colophons as frequently focus on some historical issue raised by an inscription's content as they comment on the stele's calligraphy or on an aspect of the life or personality of the author. Gu Yanwu (1613–1682), who was widely revered for his refusal to serve the Qing, in late imperial times began the fashion for citing steles to supplement historical narratives found in other sources; questions of nationalism, at least since his time, have been inextricably tied to scholarship. At the same time Gu Yanwu realized something we seem to have forgotten: that most commemorative steles were put up by "later men" to honor the achievements of the deceased.

14. Hong Gua, *Li shi*, *juan* 3/22b.

15. *Yuanfeng tiba* (Beijing: Zhonghua shuju, 1984), *xia* vol., p. 684. Zeng Gong, of course, was a local booster in Ji'nan after his appointment in 1072 to the area. Zeng at the same time berated those who inflated the histories of local families in the writing of epitaphs and eulogies.

16. Yuan Mei, "In ancient times, there were no portrait paintings. Those began at the Wu Liang shrine, where only ancient sages and virtuous women were portrayed." See Ginger Cheng-chi Hsü, *Bushels of Pearls: Painting for Sale in Eighteenth-Century Yangchow* (Stanford: Stanford University Press, 2001), p. 38.

17. Huang Yongnian, "*Jiu Tangshu" yu "Xin Tangshu"* (Beijing: Renmin chubanshe, 1985), which is based on Qian Daxin's work, "Xiu Tangshu shi chen biao" (now reprinted in *Ershiwu shi bubian*). For Gu Yanwu, see *Jinshi wenzi ji* (*Siku* edition), *juan* 1/5a.

18. Fang Ruo's (1869–1954) *Jiaobei suibi* is the first book to attempt this systematically.

19. *Jinshi lu*, *juan* 14/13b–14a.

20. Perhaps the best example of (b) is the stele of Guo Tai (= Guo Linzong) in Eastern Han. Guo was from Taiyuan, Shanxi, but he is honored on a Shandong stele (now housed in Jining). Since the inscription states explicitly that it is erected in front of the tomb, all this seems very odd. See Zheng Xiuping, "Jining Hanbei kao," p. 20; Shi Zhecun, "*Shuijing zhu" bei lu* [hereafter, *SJZ*], p. 32; Hu Yue, "Han Guo Youdao beikao," and Wang Sili and Lai Fei, "Shandong Lianghan beike zhenwei kao sanli," in *Hanbei yanjiu*, ed. Zou Zhenye et al. (Shandong: Qi-Lu shushe, 1990), pp. 320–39. As to (c), nearly all the modern works on epigraphy discuss the "restorer's" art by which stone characters can be "replaced" using wax or clay. New stones can also be inscribed. The Qing epigraphical masters readily acknowledged stele inscriptions that had been tampered with. See, e.g., Wu Yujin, *Jinshi cun* (*Congshu jicheng* edition), *juan* 7/276–79, where Wu argues that a contemporary version of a stele inscription was remade by a later person on the basis of Hong Gua's *Li shi*.

21. Wu Hung, *Writing and Materiality*, p. 40, speaking of the origin of the famous Forest of Steles (Beilin) in Xi'an at the Academy in 1087 as advancing a "Confucian" agenda. Although one may argue that Wu Hung uses the term "Confucian" when "classical," "official," or "state-sponsored" scholarship would be more accurate, his basic observation rings true.

22. For further information, see Craig Clunas, *Superfluous Things: Material Culture and Social Status in Early Modern China* (Cambridge: Polity Press, 1991), passim;

Li Waiyee, "The Collector, the Connoisseur, and Late-Ming Sensibility," *T'oung Pao*, vol. 81 (1995), pp. 269–302. For comparable cases outside China, see Christina La Rocca, "A Man for All Seasons: Pacificus of Verona and the Creation of a Local Carolingian Past," in *The Uses of the Past in the Early Middle Ages, 250–279*, ed. Yitzhak Hen and Matthew Innes (Cambridge: Cambridge University Press, 2000), chap. 2, pp. 250–77. La Rocca finds that "the greater the apparently objective basis [in documents] . . . for the claims made" about a given figure or set of figures, "the more the claims diverged from the truth." When discovered today, evidence of the tendency of long-ago persons to refashion their own pasts has proven to be disconcerting, even disruptive. See, for example, Gregory P. Levine, "Switching Sites and Identities: The Founder's Statue at the Buddhist Temple Kôrin'in," *Art Bulletin*, vol. 83, no. 1 (2001), pp. 73–104.

23. For the "death" of a stele as a long process, see Wu Hung, *Writing and Materiality*, p. 39. Popular associations have linked stones with immortality and conflated the preservation of the dead in tombs with the preservation of their thoughts and works in libraries from at least the time of Sima Qian (ca. 145–ca. 86 BCE). Huang Yi himself acknowledged that "if the public were free to make rubbings, then this would easily lead to damage. A price should be set [for making rubbings] for their benefit [i.e., for the stone's maintenance] and to prevent their being worn away." Then, Huang Yi continues, building such a hall will make it more convenient (presumably for the select few) to make rubbings, which can be circulated more widely. See Huang Yi's "Brief Record on Constructing the Wu Family Shrines" (trans. in the Appendix in Liu's "Recarving the Past" in this catalogue). Numerous records talk of the necessity to recarve steles, including Gao Wen, *Hanbei jishi* (Kaifeng: Henan daxue chubanshe, 1997), p. 277.

24. Re (4), tradition says that Wang Mang had destroyed any stele written in praise of Han. This list is drawn from Wang Zhuanghong, pp. 14–16.

25. See Wang Pizhi, *Sheng shui yantan lu* (1095) (Beijing: Zhonghua shuju, 1981), p. 132 (*yi wen*). Chen Shi was a leading critic of the late Eastern Han court under Huandi (r. 148–168).

26. Zhu Xi, *Huian xiansheng Zhu Wengong wenji*, ""Zuiweng ting ji," cited in *Ouyang Xiu ziliao huibian* (Hong ben) (Beijing: Zhonghua shuju, 1995), vol. 71, p. 325. Ye Changchi, *Yu shi*, pp. 251, 264: "When a stele is rubbed continuously day after day, it eventually has no words . . . . Even if one studies the rubbing with concentrated attention, not a single brush stroke can be discerned; not a single character can be recognized" (modifying Wu Hung's translation, p. 39, slightly).

27. For Ouyang Xiu's characterization of rubbings, I have borrowed the translation of Ronald Egan (forthcoming). For "currency," see Shana Brown, "Pastimes: Scholars, Art Dealers, and the Making of Modern Chinese Historiography, 1870–1928"(PhD diss., University of California at Berkeley, 2003), p. 117.

28. See Bian Yongyu, *Shigu tang shuhua an* (*Siku quanshu* edition), *juan* 42/95b, which treats a masterwork in connection with the Wu Liang pictorial rubbings (and suggests that Bian has seen only Song versions of such rubbings). A quite respectable rubbing of the Wu Rong stele was worth only 100 cash in late Qing, according to the catalogue of Luo Zhenyu (1866–1940) reprinted in Wang Zhuanghong, chap. 3. But the very same catalogue listed rubbings valued at up to 3,000 cash. At one point six hundred units of gold could not buy a set of the Wu Liang pictorial rubbings (see below).

29. Lü Dalin (1044–1093), *Kaogu tu* (Taipei: Commercial Press, 1983), preface dated to 1092. But see my ca. 1980 rubbing (acquired in Rongbao Zhai for a stiff sum—stiff, at any rate, by graduate-student calculations) of a famous scene from the Wu Liang site, which has been colored blue and yellow. See also *Guji shanben* (Beijing: Kunlun sale catalogue, 2003), no. 1689, for a Wu-inspired rubbing in brilliant red.

30. Wang Shihong (act. 1714), "Yi he ming gao," writes: "With Song steles, . . . when the original stone was not easy to rub, sometimes wood and sometimes stone would be used for duplicate copies. These [duplicates] were said by people of later times to be the originals, and often they filled the marketplace." See Robert E. Harrist, Jr., "Eulogy on Burying a Crane: A Ruined Inscription and its Restoration," *Oriental Art*, vol. 44, no. 3 (1998), pp. 2–10. One should never underestimate the great vogue for travel from the 18th century on; in the *Orientations* article cited above, I quote a number of travel accounts (by Chinese, with one exception) devoted to the Preservation Hall complex built in Jiaxiang after Huang Yi's momentous 1786 find at Wuzhai Shan.

31. Shen Yan, see "Sui bei ji," in *Quan Tang wen xinbian*, chief ed. Zhou Shaoliang (Changchun: Jilin wenshi, 2000), vol. 16, p. 10943.

32. See, for example, Wang Yao, *Zhongguo wenxueshi lun* (Beijing: Beijing daxue, 1996), pp. 218–28; Michael Nylan, *The Five "Confucian" Classics* (New Haven and London: Yale University Press, 2001), esp. chaps. 1–3; Christian de Pee, *Text as Practice: The Writing of Weddings in Middle-Period China* (*Eighth through Fourteenth Centuries*) (in press, University of California Press), chaps. 1–2. Of course, there *were* intentional forgeries in China, as elsewhere. Given the brisk market in rubbings, bronzes, jades, and other antiquities, not to mention the sophistication and enterprise of local and national figures, there were bound to be many outright fakes from the Song period on, as every scholar writing in Chinese has emphasized. Explicit discussions of the best methods for the successful forging of antiquities appear at least as early as the Song, and are discussed at least as often with approbation as with moral indignation. See, e.g., the techniques of forging Han clerical script, in Lu You (1125–1209), *Laoxue an biji* (Beijing: Zhonghua shuju, 1979; reprint, 1997), p. 53. From Song also, literati showed themselves to be as keenly interested as grave robbers in the tomb record. See below.

33. *Analects* 2/18 (trans. after Waley, p. 92). Of course, many paintings in China "copied" paintings no longer in existence.

34. Qianshen Bai, "Chinese Calligraphy Rubbings," documents many examples of the Qing "idea of returning to origins," which for calligraphy meant "returning to ancient scripts" (pp. 254–55).

35. See Liang Tongshu, "Lei luo an shuhua ba," *Meishu congshu chuji*, ed. Huang Binhong and Deng Shi (Taipei: Yiwen Press, 1962), vol. 5, p. 112.

36. The Xiaotang Shan site has been erroneously attributed to Guo Ju, an exemplar of filial piety. Huang's colophon to the Xiaotang Shan scene in his *Fangbei tu* says that Huang ca. 1785 deciphered the earliest inscription at that site. Another colophon by Huang Yi in the same work claims that Huang in 1784 asked Ma Yuquan, the Jinxiang Administrator, to clean a stone chamber in Jinxiang, whereupon Huang Yi deciphered some faint characters and identified the site as that of Zhu Changshu (i.e., Zhu Wei). Lillian Lan-ying Tseng has written about one of Huang Yi's conscious acts of self-advertisement in "Retrieving the Past, Inventing the Memorable: Huang Yi's Visit to the Song-Luo Monuments," in *Monuments and Memory, Made and Unmade*, ed. Robert S. Nelson and Margaret Olin (Chicago: University of Chicago Press, 2003), pp. 37–58. Tseng mentions Huang's "desire to be remembered" (p. 37); his remarkable ability "to recover previously unrecognized characters and to rectify placements" (p. 49); his desire to make himself a monument in history (p. 50); and his free renderings in paintings of events recorded in his diaries (passim).

37. See Francis Haskell and Nicholas Penny, *Taste and the Antique: the Lure of Classical Sculpture, 1500–1900* (New Haven: Yale University Press, 1981), pp. 303–5, for a brief history of the startling identity change of the "dying Seneca."

38. See *SJZ*, pp. 99–100, for one example of a site that migrates and has anachronistic steles. After the Qing emperors put out successive calls encouraging the composition of local gazetteers, local boosters were even more conscious of the value of sites in their region. Emperors ordered the promotion of local gazetteer compilations in 1454, 1458, and 1520, according to Liu Weiyi, *Zhongguo difangzhi* (Beijing: Xinhua chubanshe, 1993), p. 103.

39. Stanley K. Abe, *Ordinary Images* (Chicago: University of Chicago Press, 2002), discusses "the textual strategy in which an interpretation is made to sound like a discovery of fact" (p. 5) in a book intended "to delineate the contradictions of limits of the available data" (ibid.). He shows (pp. 296–313) that several monuments bearing dated inscriptions probably do not date from the period indicated.

40. Gu Jiegang (1893–1980) and the members of his "Doubting Antiquity" (*yi gu*) circle were notable exceptions, of course. More often, however, whenever a feature of an old stone seemed to recall a feature of an old painting (or vice versa), the two were deemed to be mutually authenticating. See Zeng Gong, *Yuanfeng tiba*, *xia* vol., p. 687.

41. Dai cited in Guy, *The Emperor's Four Treasuries*, p. 45.

42. Mary Beard, *The Parthenon* (Cambridge, Mass.: Harvard University Press, 2003), p. 1. I have emended Beard's text in order to apply to China her words about "the Greek and Roman world" [for which I write "classical world"] and the Parthenon [for which I write "it"].

43. Ouyang Xiu comments on problems with clerical script said to be from the time of Huandi and Lingdi.

44. See *Ouyang Xiu quanji, Ju shi ji, juan* 43; Yu Minhui, "Ouyang Xiu de Jinshi zhengshi," *Shixue shi yanjiu* 1999.3, pp. 68–69. In the *Li shi* and *Li xu* attributed to Hong Gua, ninety-three inscriptions are dated. Seventy-five of these are in the *Li shi*. Of the total, thirty-eight are dated within this brief period. Wang Zhuanghong, p. 20, notes, "When we come to Eastern Han, we have a huge proliferation of steles."

45. This will be discussed in a section below.

46. Christian de Pee, *Text as Practice*, ms. p. 25. Many early steles did not record family names, as they were placed at the gravesite or in settings where the dedicatees' names were obvious. See Wang Zhuanghong, p. 28, citing Zhu Jianxin, *Jinshi xue*. One example of this is provided by the stele of the *duyou* Ban, recorded in *Li shi, juan* 12/9a.

Notes to Section II

1. A convenient edition of the *Shuijing zhu* is that annotated by Shi Zhecun [hereafter, *SJZ*]. Careful readers of the *SJZ* will note that Cao Cao's prohibition against the erection of new steles by prominent families vying in a "self-interested" way for local control (215 CE) hardly prevented new steles from being made. A series of prohibitions followed, including one in 278, one in the Yixi period (405–418), one in 507, and one—supposedly the most stringent of all—under Zhou Wudi (r. 561–577).

2. In preparing the following summary, I have consulted the (*Song ben*) *Jinshi lu* (Beijing: Zhonghua shuju, 1991). The *Jinshi lu* catalogue entries for the Wu family are as follows: no. 58, for Wu Ban; no. 59, for the pillar-gate inscription; no. 63, for Wu Kaiming; no. 66, for the Wu Liang stele; no. 215, for a Wu Rong; and nos. 239–43, for the five rubbings of the Wu family (not Wu Liang) pictorial figures. Note that the extant *Jinshi lu* gives only titles for an entry on Wu Rong and for five entries on the pictorial images "recorded in full"; it does not give the content of these inscriptions. I have also consulted the *Siku quanshu* editions of the *Jinshi lu*, *Li shi*, and *Li xu*. All citations for Hong Gua's *Li shi* and *Li xu* use the *Yingyin Wenyuange Siku quanshu* version of 1983, which is based on the Ming Wanli edition of 1588, as the claim of the *Xuxiu Siku quanshu* editors to have "resolved" errors in the text undermines the principle of *textus difficilior*. This essay assumes that the *Li shi* is generally reliable, though the *Siku* editors comment that the Yangzhou edition on which it is principally based "had comparatively few mistakes but a very considerable number of lacunae." See the *Yingyin Wenyuange Siku quanshu* edition (Taipei: Taiwan shangwu yinshuguan, 1983–1986), vol. 681, p. 780.

3. At least two Northern Song scholars, Chen Shidao (1053–1101) and Chao Buzhi (1053–1110), wrote poems discussing the *Jigu lu* and Ouyang's Liuyi Tang collection; Chen Shidao's poem was inspired by a visit to the library put together by Ouyang Xiu. In their times, presumably, the Ouyang collection was intact and maintained by Ouyang Xiu's descendants. We do not know what part, if any, of Zhao's *collection* was incorporated into that of the Southern Song emperor in 1132; possibly only Zhao's *catalogue* entered the imperial collection. Originally, Zhao's catalogue of rubbings, like that of Ouyang Xiu before him, was kept within the family. But by 1132 Li Qingzhao thought it wise to offer Zhao's catalogue to the Southern Song emperor Gaozong (r. 1126–1162). Li at that time wrote a self-exculpatory postface designed to put the collecting activities of her husband and herself in the best possible light, as her own remarriage and Zhao's alleged act of treason threatened her person and her wealth. For more information on the loss of Ouyang's collection, see Zhou Bida (1126–1204), *Qian Han wuqi ming*, in *Wenzhong ji* (*Siku* edition), *juan* 19/9a–b; also Zeng Hongfu (Song), *Liuyi xiansheng "Jigu lu,"* in *Shike pu xu* (Taipei: Taiwan Commerical Press, 1983), *juan* 2/19a; for the loss of Zhao Mingcheng's collection, see *Li shi* 26/17a–18a; Ronald Egan's forthcoming work on Li Qingzhao; and Stephen Owen, *Remembrances: the Experience of the Past in Classical Chinese Literature* (Cambridge, Mass.: Harvard University Press, 1986), chap. 8. For the *Li shi* and *Li xu* of Hong Gua, "there has not been a very reliable transmission down to the late Ming/early Qing" (Søren Edgren, personal communication, May 10, 2004).

4. The earliest edition of the *Jinshi lu* reports only that there are several graves in Rencheng. *Li shi, juan* 16/5a, remarks, "[Zhao states that] in front of the graves there is [one or more] stone chamber(s) . . . . As a man from the east, Lord Zhao ought to have known the truth, but he could not figure out to whose Wu clan grave mound these pictorial images belong." Wei Bo, *Ding'an leigao* (*Siku* edition), *juan* 4/20b, comments also on Zhao Mingcheng's unfamiliarity with the original site.

5. Hong Gua's own writing registers the discomfort he feels in making surmises based on so little evidence, but as a pupil of Zhang Ruying (see the following section), he may have viewed some fine rubbings. Modern scholarship has shown that Hong Gua sometimes attributed early dates to steles that had been recut in the Tang era. For one example, see Yuan Weichun, *Sanguo beishu* (Beijing: Beijing gongyi meishu chubanshe, 1992), p. 81. Yuan bases his opinion on Hong's remark that the inscription was complete and without omissions—the very sort of statement made by Zhao Mingcheng with respect to the Wu Liang stele (see below).

6. For Ouyang's boast, see the preface to the *Jigu lu*, as recorded in "Yu cai Junmo qiu shu 'Jigu lu mu' shu," *Quan Song wen* (Chengdu: Ba-Shu shushe, 1990), *juan* 699/107–8.

7. Zhao's collection by 1117 was said to contain some two thousand items (roughly double the number in Ouyang Xiu's collection). For the relation between the two epigraphical classics, see He Ruyue and He Haoyue, "*Jinshi lu* he *Jigu lu* de shiliao jiazhi," *Journal of Xianyang Teachers College*, vol 15, no. 5 (October 2000), pp. 55–58. Ye Guoliang, "Songdai jinshi xue yanjiu" (MA thesis, Taiwan National University, 1982), pp. 259–64, discusses the Song epigraphers' reliance on genealogies and registers, and notes that in Song times the genealogists did not generally use Ouyang or his successors in their own work.

8. We should remember that during the Southern Song rubbings of ancient steles located in the northern territories under Jin control were in great demand and were bought from merchants at temple fairs in the capital and elsewhere. See Zhou Hui, *Qingbo zazhi* (compiled 1192) (*Siku* edition), *juan* 6/7a.

9. See *Jigu lu*, *juan* 2/8a–8b (p. 17847). An appended notice there mentions a second, slightly better rubbing of the Ban stele inscription, found supposedly a decade later, in 1068, which gave the family name as Wu. There are at least three reasons to believe that the relevant passage represents an interpolation: (1) The note about the second rubbing is appended *after* the notation referring to the *jiben* edition of 1209; (2) Neither Ouyang Fei's abbreviated catalogue nor the *Sibu congkan* edition of *Li shi*, *juan* 21 (which presumably copies the Ouyangs' work as known to a later, possibly early Qing editor of Hong's classic) mentions a second, better rubbing; (3) The (Song) *Hanli ziyuan* (*Siku* edition), *juan* 1/16a–b, clearly states that the Ouyangs' *Jigu* "did not know the family name [for Ban]." Also, Ouyang Xiu typically comments on its existence if a second version of an inscription is known to him. One may also ask why Zhao Mingcheng would have taken such pride in supplying Ban with the Wu family name, if one or more of the Ouyangs had already ascertained the family name on the basis of a second rubbing of the stele in their possession. Epigraphical experts agree that most early steles do not state family names; being placed at the grave site or in other ritual settings, they had no need to supply the family names. See Wang Zhuanghong, *Beitie Jianbie changshi* (Shanghai: Shanghai shuhua, 1985), p. 28, citing Wu Yujin (1698–1773), *Jinshi cun*.

10. *Jinshi lu*, *juan* 14/9b–10a (vol. 681, pp. 253–54). The Song edition of the *Jinshi lu* gives the stele head as "Han gu Dunhuang changshi Wujun zhi bei," as does the *Siku* version of the *Jinshi lu* and also the 1588 edition of the *Li shi*, *juan* 24/8b. Gu Aiji's *Li bian* (comp. 1717) (*Siku* edition), *juan* 7/12a, omits the character *han* in the ornamental stele head, as does the extant version of the stele head. See Nagata Hidemasa, *Kandai sekkoku shūsei* (Tokyo: Dōhōsha, 1994), vol. 1/68 (#63, n. 5).

11. *Shandong tongzhi* (*Siku* edition), *juan* 9/110b.

12. Gu Aiji, *Libian* (*Siku* edition), *juan* 7/12a, points out that it is very unusual for a Han stele to provide both the family and style name of the individual.

13. See *Li shi* 6/11a. The thirty-two characters, one of which is said to be illegible, begin with the phrase "Lord Wu, whose tabooed name was Ban," who is said to have been appointed Filial and Incorrupt at the age of twenty-five, a full fifteen years younger than the statutes of 132 CE allowed. (This appointment is recorded in the pillar-gate inscription. Of course, the statutes may have been ignored in the case of particularly powerful families.) Note also the possible reference to Xianzong, the posthumous title conferred upon Mingdi of Eastern Han (r. 58–75), who reigned well before Wu Ban's putative lifetime, and upon Chengdi of Eastern Jin (r. 326–343), as well as upon emperors of the Jin and Yuan dynasties. (If this binome is not a reference to a specific emperor, the phrase must mean something like "glorifying the ancestors.") See below for another example of a possible anachronism.

14. The pre-Tang epigraphical literature contains very few references to calligraphers, except for the attributions—usually false—to Cai Yong and Zhong You. Robert E.

Harrist (personal communication, 2003) knows of only three inscriptions, aside from Wu Ban's, that refer either to the calligraphers or to the persons who composed the texts, and one of these three, a stele of the Governor of Wudu, is definitely problematic. See also Hong Gua, *Li xu*, *juan* 5/1b; Gu Aiji, *Li bian*, *juan* 7/12a. Wang Zhuanghong, *Beitie*, p. 4, believes that the earliest reliable *tie* (calligraphy model) he knew dated from the Northern Song, Chunhua 3 (p. 4). Of course, *bei* [stele] and *tie* [calligraphy models] are not identical in function, but it's odd that *bei* are routinely dated to Eastern Han, whereas *tie* are not.

15. *Li shi*, *juan* 6/13b. Five characters (*Yan Qi zi Bolu*) come from another entry, probably from *juan* 29/10b. An entry for Yan Qi may be found in *Jinshi lu* (no. 65).

16. Yang Shen, *Jinshi guwen* (Taipei: Yiwen chubanshe, 1968), *juan* 6/84b; Zhao Jun, *Jinshi lin shi di kao* (*Siku* edition), *xia*/9, lists a Shaanxi stele for a Dunhuang *Governor* (*taishou*) named Wu Ban. Some editions of the *Jinshi lin shi di kao* (e.g., that in the Starr Library at Columbia) list a Liang Wu—not Wu Liang—shrine with ancient kings and generals, which it places it in Sichuan, but editions vary.

17. Ye Yibao, *Jinshi lu xuba* (Shanghai: Weihai Heng lu Hong Baojia shuju, 1937), n.p., "Wu Ban" entry. Checks of the relevant steles support Ye's conclusions.

18. See Rong Yuan, *Jinshi shu lumu* (Taipei: Datong shuju, 1971), *juan* 5/3a.

19. See Cary Liu's "Recarving the Past" in this catalogue.

20. *Jigu lu*, *juan* 2/4a (p. 17845).

21. This information is based on an electronic stele database which has been compiled on the basis of Zhang Yansheng's *Shanben beitie lu* (Beijing: Zonghua shuju, 1984). Only one other Han stele in that compendium, the Chunyu zhang Xiacheng stele, mentions by name the brothers of the stele dedicatee, and since the stele has long been lost, we cannot be certain that the transcription in the compendium is accurate.

22. *Li shi*, *juan* 12/7b–8b. A comparison of the *Li shi* 12 entry on Wu Rong with that known to Ouyang Xiu shows four different blocks of text *before* the verse encomium inserted into the inscription known to Ouyang (two blocks of three characters; one of four characters; and one of twenty-nine characters).

23. Yang Shen, *Jinshi guwen*, *juan* 6/1b–2a.

24. Three features of the Wu Rong stele inscription are notable: first, the list and number of texts that Wu Rong supposedly mastered; second, his office; and third, the date when he was appointed Filial and Incorrupt. Rong was said to have mastered six or seven classics, including the *Hanshu* and *Shiji*, but Anton Hulsewé has shown that neither the *Hanshu* nor the *Shiji* were in general circulation in the second century CE; those texts were known only to the privileged few with access to the imperial library at the capital. See *China in Central Asia: The Early Stage, 125 B.C.–A.D. 23: An Annotated Translation of Chapters 61 and 96 of the History of the Former Han Dynasty* (Leiden: Brill, 1979), pp. 20–21. The Wu Rong stele has Rong serving in the capital, as Assistant to the Chamberlain for the Imperial Insignia (*zhi jin wu*), ranked at 600 bushels. During Western Han the Chamberlain served as head of security for the capital outside the palace precincts. During Eastern Han the Chamberlain's post was dramatically downgraded from ministerial status, "cut back almost beyond recognition," in the words of Hans Bielenstein, *The Bureaucracy of Han Times* (Cambridge: Cambridge University Press, 1980), p. 79. Eastern Han chamberlains received a lower salary and the services of only one assistant; they were mainly in charge of ceremonial processions. Finally, it should be noted that after 132 CE, the minimum age of eligibility to be recommended for appointment as *xiaolian* was forty (*Hou Hanshu*, *zhi* 28:3621), and that Wu Rong was supposedly thirty-six at the time of his appointment. *Hou Hanshu* 7:288, however, gives the text of an edict of 146 CE that allowed even children, if unusually precocious, to be recommended for the honor.

25. *Wanli Yanzhou fu zhi*, comp. Bao Daguan et al. (reprint, Shanghai: Shanghai shudian, 1990), *juan* 45/17a (p. 635).

26. Zhu Yizun, *Pushu Ting ji* (*Siku* edition), *juan* 47/780.

27. See Niu Yunzhen (1706–1758), *Jinshi tu* (China: s.n., between 1743 and 1795); and Wang Hong, cited in Wu Yi (1745–1799), *Shoutang jinshi ba* (Zhengzhou: Zhongzhou guji chubanshe, 1993 reprint), pp. 35–36; Wang Zhuanghong, *Beitie*, p. 8, says that the sort of stele on which only half is inscribed is "typically associated with the Sanguo–Cao Wei period" [i.e., post-Han]. Wu Yi gives examples of other stele heads carved in relief, as is evident because the characters are in black on the rubbing.

28. See Wang Zhuanghong, *Zengbu Jiaobei suibi* (Shanghai: Shanghai shuhua, 1981), pp. 84–85.

29. *Jinshi lu*, *juan* 14/12a (vol. 681, p. 255).

30. *Shandong tongzhi* (*Siku* edition), *juan* 9/110b, under the heading "Changshi Wu Ban," citing *Jinshi lu*, says that the "old records" "write Wu Kaiming [instead?] . . . ." Cf. Wang Jian (Ming dynasty), whose record of Suzhou, *Gusu zhi* (*Siku* edition), *juan* 37/9a, has Wu Kaiming dying in 197 CE (not 148); cf. *Wanxing tongdian* (*Siku* edition), *juan* 78/9a, which assigns Wu Kaiming a Jin-dynasty date of Yonghe 2 (347). (Yonghe 1 corresponds to 346, 417, 434, or 936 CE.)

31. Ye Yibao, *Jinshi lu xuba*, n.p., "Wu Ban" entry.

32. *Jinshi lu*, *juan* 14/10b (vol. 681, p. 254).

33. *Wanli Yanzhou fu zhi*, comp. Bao Daguan et al. (reprint, Shanghai: Shanghai shudian, 1990), *juan* 45/17a (p. 635).

34. Twenty-eight characters, beginning with *yide xuantong* and ending with *shenmuo mingcun*, are given in the Ming Wanli and the *Siku* editions of Zhao Mingcheng. But when we look at the encomium as quoted in *juan* 6 of *Li shi*, eight characters—not four—are missing, which means that the phrase "the missing four characters" (used alike in the *Jinshi lu* and the *Li shi*) need not refer to the *same* four characters. As the particle *xi* can occur either in the middle of a line of verse or at the end, one cannot use its placement to decide whether the inscription should begin with the phrase *yide xuan tong*. Perhaps those four characters belong after *chuan wu jiang xi*.

35. For one "full" text, see the Wang Rixiu edition of *Li shi*, compiled 1777–1778 (Beijing: Zhonghua shuju, 1985), *juan* 6/14a. The subject of Han shrines will be taken up in my essay for the symposium volume. The extant *Jinshi lu*, *juan* 14/13b–14a also speaks of two versions of the inscription dedicated to Liang: the first, a rubbing procured in 1102, and a second version acquired more than a decade later, which was already missing its last four characters. The first rubbing of the Wu Liang stele was obtained in Kaifeng; the second, in Qingzhou.

36. *Li shi*, *juan* 6/14a (vol. 681, p. 515). This *Siku quanshu* version matches the 1588 version (16/13a). The Wang Rixiu edition of *Li shi*, *juan* 6/13a supplies the "full text" of the Wu Liang inscription, which is not surprising, given its provenance and dating. [The *Siku* and 1588 editions of the *Li shi* conflate parts of the Wu Liang stele inscription and Hong Gua's commentary on the Wu Ban stele. This probably was the result of scribal omission in the Ming dynasty. A manuscript copy of two leaves from a Yuan-dynasty Taiding edition is appended to the end of *juan* 6 in the *Sibu congkan sanbian* edition, and apparently represents the entire missing section. Based on another Ming manuscript, Wang Rixiu reinserted the text in his 1777–1778 edition. This lacuna was also noted by Mei Dingzuo (1553–1619), Fu Shan (1607–1684), and other scholars before the eighteenth century. See n. 55 below. CYL and EHH]

37. Compare (*Song ben*) *Jinshi lu*, *juan* 14/3b; *Li shi*, *juan* 6/14b–15b (main text vs. commentary); and ibid., *juan* 16/5a–b. Note that Hong's text (*Li shi* 6/14a) contains a passage of several lines, beginning *guanshou canshi* ("official lifespan cut short"), that are presented as part of the stele inscription, but they may represent commentary instead. (Wei Bo, *Ding'an leigao*, *juan* 4/20b, repeats Hong Gua's commentary to the Wu Liang stele inscription.) This uncertainty has been noted by Chinese scholars; see, e.g., the colophon written by Liu Xihai (d. 1853) (Academia Sinica 12803–13, 00099); and the colophon by Gui Fu (1736–1805) on the pillar-gate inscription, as given in *Jinshi cuibian*, *juan* 8/3a. Conceivably, the pillar-gate inscription, which refers to a dearth of descendants, was commissioned for a much later and more famous figure, Wu Mao, who was executed for treason in 290 CE. It is presumably this confusion that moved Wu Hung to suggest that a shrine complex may have been erected in honor of the deceased Wu family matriarch. See Wu Hung, *The Wu Liang Shrine: The Ideology of Early Chinese Pictorial Art* (Stanford: Stanford University Press, 1989), pp. 26–27.

38. *Li shi*, *juan* 6/15a (vol. 681, pp. 515–16), gives the precise measurements of the stele: half a *xun* in length and about one *qi* wide, which I do not include in my translation. Note that the binome *tanshan* ("altar") is typically used in connection with the imperial rituals at Mount Tai and Mount Liangfu, not for low-ranking local officials like Wu Liang. The phrase *citang* deserves separate consideration, and it will be addressed in an essay in the symposium volume. For the moment, I refer readers to Nancy Shatzman Steinhardt, "*Shishi* (Stone Rooms)," forthcoming in a festschrift planned for Victor Mair, an advance copy of which Professor Steinhardt graciously lent me. Dr. Steinhardt and I have been working in parallel tracks on this issue in 2003–2004, as I discovered in June 2004.

39. Mei Dingzuo, *Donghan wenji*, *juan* 28/10a–10b. He also assumes mistakes in copying by which the main text and commentary were conflated.

40. Gu Aiji, *Li bian*, *juan* 7/11a, 8/15b–16a.

41. It is almost equally unlikely that such a monumental complex would have survived the fierce battles that raged in the area before and after Ouyang Xiu's time. Because of its geographical situation, its topography, and later its poverty, which bred many uprisings, the area in and near Rencheng became a battleground many times in its history, twice in late Eastern Han alone (190 and 195 CE), following the outbreak of the Yellow Turban rebellion (March 184). During these engagements, the bravery of the Rencheng soldiers and their women became a byword; see *Sanguo zhi*, "Weizhi" (Beijing: Zhonghua shuju, 1959), *juan* 1/9. In early Qing, in the thirteenth and fourteenth years of Kangxi's reign (1674–1675), Purple Cloud Mountain, the very site from which Huang Yi got his stones, witnessed two or more fierce battles in which the Qing forces "repeatedly broke the bandits" (*lian po zei*). See (*Xin jiaoben*) *Qing shi gao* (electronic database, Academia Sinica, Taiwan), 671-1, for the years Kangxi 13–14. If Huang Yi's stones were the pictorial stones from the tomb of the "Han prince," then they were sticking out of the ground, and we should seen more damage—and uneven damage—on the stones, unless they were then recarved. For nearby Weishan's "notoriety for the faking of antiquities," see W. Perceval Yetts, "Memoir of the Translator," in *The Six Scripts of Chinese Writing by Tai T'ung*, trans. L.C. Hopkins (Cambridge: Cambridge University Press, 1954), p. xix.

42. *Jinshi lu*, *juan* 14, 10a–b (vol. 681, p. 254). The earliest extant edition of Zhao's *Jinshi lu* gives no indication that the pillar-gate inscription there transcribed is missing any text. Jianhe 1, third month; fourth month, corresponds to 147 CE.

43. See *Zhangjia Shan Han mu jujian* (Beijing: Wenwu chubanshe, 2004), strip 56, p. 241.

44. More than one Chinese scholar has thought it strange that no mention of a Wu clan can be found in Fan Ye's *Hou Hanshu*, given the number and quality of the pictorial slabs. See, e.g., Wang Chang, *Jinshi cuibian*, in *Shike shiliao xinbian* (Taipei: Xinwen feng chubanshe, 1979 facsimile reproduction of the 1805 *Jingxun Tang* edition), *juan* 8, par. 20.

45. There may well have been close relations between Rencheng and Pei, as Pei looks across Weishan Lake to the rest of Shandong Province; moreover, the first donor named on the Wu Ban stele is a man from Pei. For further information, see Fan Bangjin, "Guanyu Shandong Jiaxiang Han Wushi muchun jiazu ruogan wenti de tantao," *Shanghai bowuguan jikan* (special thirty-fifth anniversary issue) (1987), pp. 377–81 (which ignores discrepancies among editions); and Zhan Ruoshui (1466–1560), *Gewu tong* (*Siku* edition), *juan* 31/6b, which says that there were in Jin times two consort families, the Wu and the Bian (the latter character often confused with the Ban of Wu Ban), whose histories seem to have vanished from the records. We know that the Wus had a cemetery in Rencheng in Song; we know also that as late as the Song, many persons who had won fame as warriors were awarded the family name of Wu ("martial"). In late imperial times, exemplary women of the Wu clan were honored in the Rencheng/Jiaxiang area. See *Yuanhe xingzuan* (*Siku* edition), *juan* 6/29b.

46. *Li shi* 6/14a (vol. 681, p. 515). Hypothetically, two sets of pillar-gates could have been built in the single cemetery, one set sponsored by four filial sons for their parent(s), and one set by Wu Kaiming for his older brother, but this seems unlikely.

47. Fang Ruo, *Jiaobei suibei* (Shanghai: Shanghai shuhua chubanshe, 1981), *juan* 1/9a.

48. Compare ibid., and Feng Yunpeng and Feng Yunyuan, *Jinshi shuo* (Shanyang: Ziyang Xian shu cang ban, 1821), "Shisuo," *juan* 3/3a.

49. Remarks of He Zhuo, cited in his 1717 colophon to the 21-*juan Li xu* in the Jiaye Tang Collection, which says, "I find so many errors that they cannot be completely corrected. [Like fallen leaves,] the more one tries to sweep them, the more they seem to have accumulated." He Zhuo then speculates about the two lost classics by Hong Gua, the *Li tu* and the *Li yun*.

50. See *Shanzuo jinshi zhi*, in *Shike shiliao xinbian* 19 (Taipei: Xinwenfeng chuban gongsi, 1979), *juan* 7/13a, with Bi Yuan quoting Qian Daxin (1728–1804).

51. Both characters for the Jianhe date can be seen today, whereas Ouyang Xiu had already noted that the second character was effaced. When questioned in the summer of 2002, the Shandong local experts agreed that the date must have been recently recut by someone on the basis of a text.

52. *Jizhou jinshi zhi*, comp. Xu Zonggan (n.p., 1843), *juan* 7.3b–6b.

53. One example of misunderstood conventions may be this: it seems likely that the phrase "Han gu" referred not to the date of the stele carving, but to fact that the person commemorated had served in the central administration of the Han court (as opposed to merely local posts). That the phrase "Han gu" cannot refer to the time of death of the dedicatee is evident from Yuan Weichun, *Sanguo beishu*, p. 14, where a person who died in 225 CE has a stele head that employs that phrase. Cf. ibid., pp. 94–95. For an example of a recut stele that contains interpolations, see ibid., pp. 3, 7, 13 (which contains further information about epigraphical practices in the Rencheng area). *SJZ*, p. 68, in noting an instance of misidentification by Hong Gua, criticizes him for "crudely making them [pieces of evidence] fit together" (*cuwei fuhe*). The careful editors of the *Siku quanshu* would condemn Hong's quite tentative talk about Wu Liang; in their view, Hong had "not avoided stretching the wording" (*weimian qianhe qi ci*). See their Preface to the *Li shi* (*Siku* edition), vol. 681, p. 444 (3a–3b).

54. The phrase *que ze chuan jiang* ("Before he was capped, he transmitted and lectured."), which does not appear in *Jigu lu*, *juan* 3/21a, is said of both Wu Rong and Wu Liang. A second formula employed in Wu Rong's inscription *guang xue chen che* . . . ("His broad learning was thorough; all the canonical texts he had read."), becomes in Wu Liang's inscription ("His broad learning was thorough; not one field of study had he failed to penetrate.").

55. Compare *Li shi* 6/1a and 6/15a. Other questions arise: for example, why does the *Li shi* transcription of the Wu Liang stele delete the poetic *xi* (repeated four times in *Jinshi lu* transcription) in its text of the verse encomium? (The particles missing from the 1588 *Li shi* reappear in the *Siku quanshu* version.) The *Jinshi lu* comments that one of the two known versions of the rubbing is missing the last four characters, but the lacuna occurs at different points in different versions of the inscription. See n. 12 above. Those rubbing the stele or copying the inscription may have sensed the problem and come up with varying solutions. One logical explanation is that Hong Gua or an unknown later source tried but failed to make sense of the verses, given that one of the two rubbings linked to Wu Liang and said to be in Zhao Mingcheng's possession began with four characters that were different. As if such confusions were not enough, the earliest extant edition of the *Li shi* (the Ming Wanli edition of 1588) inserts an additional two pages of text (labeled as *bu*, "supplement"), right in the middle of *juan* 6, on pages 13a–b, in the all-important entry on Wu Liang, with the result that a single four-character phrase (*luo lie chenghang*) is repeated no fewer than three times. See the Beiping Rare Books Library microfilm of the 1588 edition (mf9101, vol. 522).

56. See *Tongzhi* (*Siku* edition), *juan* 73/8a, 9b, 11a, where the Wu Liang stele is assigned a date but no location; Wu Rong's is located in Jizhou; Wu Ban's is dated but not located; and Wu Kaiming's is dated but not located, as is the pillar-gate inscription (in which two characters are reversed). The Wu family stone chamber pictorials have neither a date nor a location indicated. The Wu family stone chamber is the last memorial structure listed for Han (a position which often allows for interpolation); the commentary to it says only, "There are no details."

57. *Ding'an leigao*, *juan* 4/21b.

58. Gu Aiji, *Li bian*, *juan* 8/15–16a.

59. The *Li shi* is one of many Song texts to comment on the number of stones appearing in the Rencheng area. *Ding'an leigao* (*Siku* edition), *juan* 4, attempts to make sense of the Wu pictorial figures by comparing them with the literary descriptions given for the steles of Li Gang of Zhuye, Lu Gong at Jinxiang, and Zhu Fu at Jizhou. Unfortunately, those sites have equally confused histories. See *Beijing tushuguan cang Zhongguo lidai shike taben huibian* (Zhengzhou: Zhengzhou guji chubanshe, 1989), vol. 1, p. 216.

60. For a good comparison, see Mary Beard, *The Parthenon* (Cambridge, Mass.: Harvard University Press, 1999).

61. Lou Ji, *Hanli ziyuan* (*Siku* edition), *juan* 1/54a.

62. Xi Jian, the consort of Liang Wudi (r. 502–549), was buried in the area, for example, as were members of the illustrious Zhai family. For further information about *wu ban* ("military ranks"), see Andreas Ernst Janousch, "The Reform of Imperial Ritual during the Reign of Emperor Wu of the Liang Dynasty (502–549)" (PhD diss., Cambridge University, 1998), p. 80. The characters *wu rong* could refer to "military glory"; *zhijinwu cheng* and *congshi* refer to two military posts; and there is the question of Wu Liang's name. Wu Liang is also the name of a special ritual hat—unless the name Wu Liang represents a reversal of Liang Wu[di], for whom a great number

of shrines were erected in the pre-Tang period. See n. 92 for further information.
63. For example, the Zhais from Rencheng, Zhang Ruying, Fang Wude, Tang Shunzhi, and Liang Qingbiao. See the following section for more information on these figures.
64. For Ouyang's observation, see *Ouyang Xiu quanji* (Beijing: Zhonghua shuju, 2001), vol. 5, p. 2079. For problematic steles in the area, see Zhao Han's (act. 1615–1620) *Shimo juan hua* (*Siku* edition), *juan* 1/9a; Zheng Xiuping, "Jining Hanbei kao" (in Japanese), *Shomei tō shohin* (*Tōyō shodo kyōkai*), vol. 288, no. 11 (November 1986), pp. 12–35; Tanaka Yō, "Sainei Kanpi o tazunete," *Shoun* (November 1961), pp. 2–11; and Wang Sili and Lai Fei, "Shandong Lianghan beike kao zhenwei sanli," in *Hanbei yanjiu*, ed. Zou Zhenye et al. (Ji'nan: Qi-Lu shushe, 1990), pp. 332–39. For nearby Weishan's "notoriety for the faking of antiquities," see W. Perceval Yetts, "Memoir of the Translator," p. xix.

Notes to Section III

1. *Jinshi lu* (*Siku* edition), *juan* 14/13b–14a.
2. See *Li shi*, 6/14a–15a (vol. 681/515), *juan* 16/2b. Hong Gua debates whether the rubbing he has before him reproduces Wu Liang's stele or the inscriptions on the pictorial scenes belonging to a stone chamber or *citang* (worship hall). The confusion continues in colophons to the so-called Tang Rubbing (see below), in colophon 6, by Cha Sili (1653–1734, or 1652–1733), dated to 1706, for example. See Rong Geng, *Han Wu Liang Ci huaxiang kaoshi* (Beiping: Archaeological Society of Beijing, 1936), pp. 3b–4a, for his speculation on the origins of the *Jinshi lu* and *Li shi* entries. Since neither Zhao nor Hong visited the site, it is unlikely that they knew the precise relation between the Wu Liang stele inscription and the pictorial figures. Note that *Shiqu baojian*, *juan* 32/2b, locates the Wu Liang stone chamber pictorial images in nearby Jinxiang, rather than in Rencheng.
3. For this reason, Gu Aiji, in *Li bian*, *juan* 8/38b, says of the Wu family stone chamber pictorial images that "they have no year or month (i.e., no date)."
4. *Li xu*, *juan* 6/1a, labels it "Wu Liang [Worship?] Hall" (*dian*).
5. Hong Gua may have been looking at eleven or twelve scenes altogether, though his descriptions match ten blocks of images.
6. Wei Bo, *Ding'an lei gao*, *juan* 4/19b–20b. For conditions at the Southern Song court, see Julia K. Murray, "Sung Kao-tsung as Artist and Patron: the Theme of Dynastic Revival," in *Artists and Patrons: Some Social and Economic Aspects of Chinese Paintings*, ed. Chu-tsing Li, James Cahill, and Wai-kam Ho (Kansas City: Nelson-Atkins Museum, 1989), pp. 27–36.
7. Zhang Ruying is Zhang Cheng; Zhu Xizhen is Zhu Dunru (*jinshi* 1132), the owner of a rubbing that portrayed the Duke of Zhou with King Cheng; Zhu is otherwise connected with mountain inscriptions. (In *Li xu* 8/4b, Hong Gua claims to have gotten two steles or stele rubbings from Zhu Xizhen.) At a crucial point in Wei Bo's narrative, it says only that the rubbing(s) "seem(s) to" correspond with Zhao Mingcheng's description; moreover, much of that narrative is attributed to two unidentified persons ("Someone heard that Yu Zicai . . . . And someone said . . . ."). In contrast, Weng Fanggang's "Tang ta Wu Liang Ci huaxiang ba" (dated to 1791), identifies the speaker as the Metropolitan Overseer (in most editions).
8. See Wei Bo, *Ding'an lei gao*, *juan* 4/20b. Zhang Ruying administered the Southern Song capital of Lin'an during the Shaoxing reign period (1131–1146); before his death in 1153 he commanded part of the Song army. Supposedly he owned a very fine collection of Han steles, but little is known about it. It was said, however, that even Yu Zicai had only seen the [Wu Liang?] rubbings twice by 1167. Fang Wude was originally from Zhejiang, near Qiantang (i.e., Hangzhou). At various times Fang had under his command Liang, Jingjiang, Guangzhou, Fuzhou, Luzhou, Shaoxing, and Pingjiang; also Jiankang and Jingnan.
9. The Choushu Ge library was established in Jiankang by Ye Mengde (1077–1148), circa 1138, with government funding, as an imperial repository of historical texts and of imperial portraits, which could be consulted by officials and would-be officials. Ye's own account of the Choushu Ge appears in *Shilin Jiankang ji*, *juan* 4/1a–2b. Jiankang had fallen in 1129 to the Jurchen, but it reverted to Southern Song in the peace settlement. The Choushu Ge was destroyed by fire in 1207. Eileen Hsu is inclined to think that what was displayed "on the walls" was a woodblock print; Professor Wu Pei-yi, like the author, believes that the passage emphasizes the display of the copy—without implying any particular medium. Apparently it was not uncommon for ritual pictures

to be displayed on the walls of imperial libraries; see *Songshi*, *juan* 131/6b. Cf. the Southern Song catalogue *Baoke congbian* compiled by Chen Si, a Lin'an bookseller (act. 1200–after 1259).

10. See *Shuangqiao suibi*, *juan* 6/19b. Both Hong Gua and Hong Mai served under Fang Wude, who was then Military Commander of Guangdong. Fang Wude was particularly interested in ethical issues relating to gender; this might explain his interest in stones that depicted women so prominently.

11. See Pang Yingyun's colophon to the Tang Rubbing, dated to 1793. This is mentioned also in Wang Chang, *Jinshi cuibian*, *juan* 8, par. 9, citing Hong Gua.

12. Wei Bo, *Ding'an leigao*, *juan* 4, also provides descriptions of the Li Gang and Lu Gong shrines that ultimately derive from Li Daoyuan's *Shuijing zhu* [hereafter, *SJZ*], pp. 65–69. The record is so confused that one cannot even know whether the Lu Gong structure was the same as a Lu Jun structure mentioned in the same vicinity. Similarly, *Li xu*, *juan* 18/1a, provides a very full description of the pictorial stones in the tomb of Li Gang, which the *Hanli ziyuan*, *juan* 1/68b calls "damaged" (*can*). *Li xu*, *juan* 18/1a, shows that the Li Gang site also had depictions of the Ugly Woman of Qi and Liang Gaoxing.

13. *Li xu*, *juan* 18/1a. "Now this shrine does not depict the Four Spirit [directional] Animals. Nor does it depict the lord with his officers and subordinates." The nearby Fan Shi tomb (conventionally dated to Han) had a stele similarly dated that Hong Gua said (a) was not in the calligraphy of Cai Yong; and (b) dated from the Wei dynasty, Qinglong 3 (235 CE).

14. Wei Bo, *Ding'an lei gao*, *juan* 4. It is presumed that these cartouches identify different stages in the career of the male tomb occupant, but Lao Gan, "Lun Luxi huaxiang san shi: Zhu You shitang, Xiaotangshan, Wushi Ci," *Bulletin of the Museum of History and Philology, Academia Sinica*, vol. 8, no. 1 (1939), p. 102, shows that the titles referred to the staff of the governor.

15. See Wang Chang, *Jinshi cuibian*, *juan* 8, par. 20: "I am concerned that, according to Mr. Hong's account, they do not necessarily all belong to the *citang* of the Wus."

16. *Li xu*, *juan* 17/4b.

17. Shi Shengzu, *Xue Zhai zhanbi*, in *Biji xiaoshuo daguan* (Shanghai: Wujin, n.d.), vol. 6, *juan* 3/10a–12b (Western pp. 3884–88). A student of Wei Liaoweng (1178–1237) and author of *Gu jin kao*, Shi Shengzu wrote thoughtful critiques of Northern Song scholarship. Weng Fanggang identified Shi Shengzu as head of the Yuju Guan (Daoist Temple) in Chengdu. On the excavation of what is believed to be Shi Shengzu's tomb in Quzhou, Zhejiang, see *Kaogu* 1983.11, pp. 210–13.

18. Shi Zijian identified himself—or rather his family—as hailing from Qi (i.e., Shandong).

19. Dongzhou corresponds to no official place name in Shandong, but rather more generally to southern Hebei and northwestern Shandong. The term *shishi* ("stone chamber") seems to refer variously to belowground tombs, aboveground multi-chambered crypts, libraries (often where important documents were stored), and possibly to reception rooms (on an analogy with the imperial *qin*, "resting places"?) placed in front of family cemeteries.

20. See *Xue Zhai zhanbi*, *juan* 3/12a–12b. Neither Shi Ziqian nor Shi Shengzu, so far as we know, served in Shandong. The passage is difficult to render with certainty. I am grateful for Wu Pei-yi's guidance on the translation. The passage undoubtedly registers Shi Shengzu's surprise that when he arrived in Zizhou, he found what he believed to be the original stones in the Boya Tang. Shi Shengzu was not sure that the locals followed through on his orders. Shi Shengzu praises the calligraphy *zan* ("Appraisals") for Fuxi, Shennong, Huangdi, Yao, Zengzi, Lao Laizi, and Ding Lan as "especially fine and archaic in flavor." He says nothing specific about the other figures, nor does he specifically mention pictorial images. See n. 92 as well.

21. See Wang's remarks recorded in *Jinshi cuibian*, *juan* 20, par. 7; and Rong Geng, *Han Wu Liang Ci*, p. 4b. Wang divided Shi Shengzu's entry into two parts. The second part, Wang said, "refers to still another set of pictorial images."

22. The sources for two Sichuan stones associated with Shi Shengzu are (1) Yang Shen, *Jinshi guwen*, *juan* 14, p. 201, which refers us also to Shi Zijian's *Li ge* (still extant in Yang's era?); (2) Cao Xuequan, *Shuzhong guangji*, *juan* 8, p. 40; (3) Mei Dingzuo, *Donghan wenji* (*Siku* edition), *juan* 32/36b; and (4) *Zizhong Xian Xuxiu Zizhou zhi*, comp. Wu Hongren et al. (Taipei: Student Bookstore, 1967 reprint of a 1929 edition), *juan* 1, "Guji," p. 33 (Western p. 75). All four texts quote the same label for the sage-king Fuxi that we now see in the Wu Liang finds, though some refer to Cang Jie, the inventor of writing, rather than to the Black Spirit (*Cang Jing*). Similarly, a gazetteer for Zizhou speaks of stones—"both now lost"—whose figures of sage-kings bore the same cartouches that were recorded in Shi Shengzu's text. One of the *two* stones is listed there as "old" and the second as "Han in date." The cartouches provided for the nine kings also recall descriptions found in the "Xiuwu xun" chapter of the *Huainanzi*.

23. See, e.g., *Sichuan tongzhi*, *juan* 45.

24. Luo Ping's (12th century) *Lushi zhu* (*Notes on Lushi*), in no fewer than five separate entries, with six mentions altogether, cites the texts of pictorial stones whose legends are very close but not always identical to some of the legends accompanying the carvings of the emperors on Huang Yi's pictorial stones, but in Luo's book, they are consistently attributed to a Liang Wu *ci* (i.e., worship hall for Liang Wudi). I consulted the Princeton University, Rare Books edition of 1611 (TB42/638).

25. See the preceding note. Moreover, several editions of the epigraphical classics vary in the versions to be found in the Starr Library at Columbia and in the East Asian Library at Princeton.

26. Hong Gua asked Fang Wude to look at a version in the capital. One would think that such a rubbing would surely have been copied for the imperial collection, judging from an analogous case dating to Shaoxing 16 (1146), when Gaozong wrote out the text of the Nine Classics and had the portraits of the "former sages" carved on the walls of the Guozi Jian Academy, after which a stone copy of Gaozong's calligraphy was placed in Jiankang. We also know that Liu Qiu (act. before 1200), a "common bookseller" in Southern Song, was selling many copies of such rubbings, also that books then circulating, such as Hong Gua's *Li yun*, contained stele inscriptions that are otherwise unknown. See Yves Hervouet, ed., *Song Bibliography* (Hong Kong: Chinese University Press, 1988), p. 206.

27. Bian Yongyu, *Shigu tang shuhua an*, *juan* 42/95a, cites Wang Bogu, the Jiangxi calligrapher, who mentions the Wu Liang pictorial images in connection with a Song rubbing of a pictorial engraving based on a painting called *Viewing the Chess Game*; the painting, by Liu Shang, an 8th-century painter, was copied by Li Gonglin (1049–1106). According to the colophon by Su Shi (1036–1101), who owned Liu Shang's original painting, Li Gonglin made a copy of it and a craftsman with the surname Mao engraved it on a stone. The engraving was of such superb quality that rubbings were made from it, and they too were prized as valuable art works.

28. Zhang Xuan, *Zhida Jinling xin zhi*, *juan* 20B/368.

29. Zhou Mi's *Record of Clouds and Mist Passing* contains no mention of the Wu Liang pictorial slabs or rubbings made from them. Although Zhou Mi was born in Fuchun, some 25 kilometers south of Hangzhou, he identified his family as coming from Ji'nan. See *Qidong yeyu*, *juan* 12/14a.

30. *Fanxie shanfang ji, xuji*, *juan* 8/18a–b.

31. Zhao Shaozu, *Jinshi wenchao* (Hangzhou: Zhushi bao jingtang, 1876), *juan* 1/14b. This is, of course, one of the very records that led Huang Yi to the Wuzhai Shan site.

32. The site disappeared after Huang Yi. See Rong Geng, *Han Wu Liang Ci*, p. 3b. Jiang Yingju, "Guanyu Han huaxiang shi chansheng beijing yu yishu gongneng de sikao," *Kaogu* 1998.11, pp. 90–96, in arguing against Rong, points out that to date, at any rate, no excavated tomb of a Han prince has been decorated with pictorial stones. For the possible misidentification of Fuxi, see Meng Zhuangli, "Hanmu zhuanhua Fuxi Nüwa xiangkao," *Kaogu* 2000.4, pp. 369–74.

33. See Rong Geng, *Han Wu Liang Ci*, p. 3b.

34. See Rong Geng, *Han Wu Liang Ci*, "Kaoshi" section, pp. 1–4a. According to Rong Geng, three scenes were completely destroyed (those of Fuxi, Zhurong, and Shennong; and three were mostly destroyed (those of the Yellow Emperor, Zhuanxu, and Digu). Rong Geng says that the Tang Rubbing was exhibited October 20, 1935, at a charity event organized for Shandong flood victims, at which time only eight of the original portraits were extant, and "over half" of Zhu Yizun's colophons. It appears to have been further damaged by fire, possibly while out on exhibition, and only fragments of the Tang Rubbing exist today in the Palace Museum collection in Beijing.

35. For Zhu's life, see Arthur Hummel, *Eminent Chinese of the Ch'ing Period* (Washington, D.C.: Government Printing Office, 1943–1944), pp. 182–85; Ren Jiyu, *Zhongguo cangshu lou* (Shenyang: Liaoning renmin chubanshe, 2000), "Liang Zhe" section, pp. 19–20; for Ma's, see Zheng Weizhang, *Wenxian jia tongkao* (Beijing:

Zhonghua shuju, 1999), pp. 123–25. Originally, Ma's ancestors bore the family name Zhu, but one of them was adopted into the Ma family and he changed the family name to Ma. Some of Ma Sizan's seals say "seal of Zhu (Ma) Sizan" or "Zhu Zhong'an" (since Zhong'an was Ma Sizan's style name). That means that all the earliest writers of colophons authenticating the so-called Tang Rubbing were close relatives of Ma, except for the painter Jin Nong. Ma's main library collection, the Daogu Lou, was famous for its Song and Yuan editions (many "previously never seen") and its epigraphical rubbings. According to Wu Qian's preface to "Zhu Cha, Chu bai er xiang-sheng chidu," *Baijing Lou shi hua* (Shanghai: Commercial Press, 1935), *Baiji*, *juan* 4, and Wu Han, *Jiang Zhe cangshu jia shilue* (Beijing: Zhonghua shuju, 1981), p. 19, "nine-tenths" of Zhu's sources for one work came from Ma's collections and Ma's library was considered the main "repository of books for the town" (i.e., Hangzhou). Ma Sizan's wife, Cha Shuying, like Li Qingzhao, played a major role in the forming the family collections.

36. The Tang Rubbing showed the scenes found in two registers on a single stone at Wuzhai Shan. Presumably, it came from the Wu Liang site, which had been partly buried. Therefore, the rubbing should show a difference in wear patterns correspon-ding to exposed versus unexposed limestone. It does not. Since the auspicious omens do not appear on the same stone as the aforementioned exemplary figures, but are found in close proximity with the exemplars on the recut stone pillar-gates, there exists the possibility that the pictorial figures known to Hong Gua—originally labeled—adorned some such structure.

37. Cecie Reilly (personal communication, March 7, 2004) identified the first seal as a seal of Tang Shunzhi using an unusual format. Ma Ziyun, "Tan Wu Liang Ci huaxiang de Song ta yu Huang Yi taben," *Gugong bowuyuan yuankan* 1960.2, pp. 170–77, describes two rubbing sets now in the possession of the Palace Museum (Beijing). Ma identifies the one-scroll set in the Palace Museum as that owned by Ma Heng (1881–1955) and published in fifty-six frames in Rong Geng, *Han Wu Liang Ci*; the three-scroll set (which shows fewer marks of wear) he believes to be an earlier rubbing made by Huang Yi.

38. Zhu's first colophon to the Tang Rubbing (dated to 1705) says that the attribution to the Tang dynasty is "what people say." His colophon then seeks to prove that attribution correct.

39. Gu Aiji, *Li bian*, *juan* 8/40a. Cf. Ni Tao (*jinshi* 1709), author of *Liuyi zhi yi lu* (*Siku quanshu* edition), *juan* 111/52a.

40. Rong Geng, *Han Wu Liang Ci*, p. 3b, scoffs at the claims of Zhu and Ma; he insists that Ma's album dated from "after 1341." Rong does not tell us the basis for his opinion, though he is outspoken enough about why the so-called Tang album was accepted: it was bought by a rich man, who could bring together more than a hundred people in one sitting to proclaim its authenticity. Ma Ziyun, "Tan Wu Liang Ci," dates the Tang Rubbing to Song.

41. The identification of Shi's pictorial stones with the Wu Liang rubbings is made in Zhu Yizun's postface of 1705. Gong Xianlin was a close personal friend of Zhu Yizun, and Jin Nong was a client of the Mas.

42. One obvious source of rare manuscripts was the Chuanshi Lou of Xu Qianxue (1631–1694), but the 1915 catalogue of that collection includes no entry for *Li xu*.

43. *Li xu*, *juan* 6/3b–14a. Editors of the printed versions evidently felt free to amend the illustrations once Huang Yi's finds had provided "new and improved" versions of the Wu Liang material.

44. For example, in the *Siku quanshu* edition, the scenes of Zengzi and Ding Lan (lower, 1a, 2b) are labeled but given no cartouches; no Yu Rang can be found, though there is a scene (lower, 3b) that may represent him; the Qi General is labeled as a Wei General instead (upper, 9b); a scene that may correspond to Yao Li and Qing Ji (upper, 3b) certainly takes place on land, not on the Yangzi. Certain details of the *Siku quanshu* manuscript copy do not match those in today's Wu Liang rubbings: e.g., the crowns worn by some of the women are differently rendered (e.g., upper, 13a), as is the loom of Zengzi's mother (lower, 1a) (fig. 7B) and the pallet of the filial grandchild (lower, 11b). A shape that may or may not recall the mountain forms in Gu Kaizhi's *Admonitions Scroll* appears in the section that may correspond now to Zhao Xun (lower, 11a) (Wu Hung, *Wu Liang Shrine*, p. 303). In the *Li xu*, no figures outside the "ten kings procession" in the west wall of the reconstructed Wu Liang Shrine are labeled on scene dividers (contrast Lin Xiangru; Wu Hung, *Wu Liang Shrine*, p. 306, with the same figure upper, 12a). The troublesome Duke Zhuang of Lu (Wu Hung, *Wu Liang Shrine*, p. 311) has disappeared altogether from the *Siku*, but omissions are more easily explained than added or changed features.

45. See, e.g., the *Siku quanshu* version of *Li xu*, vol. 684, p. 760.

46. The epigraphical expert Gu Aiji, writing less than two decades after Zhu Yizun, identifies two *juan* of the extant *Li xu* compiled by Zhu Yizun (*juan* 5, 8) as "Mr. Hong's Stele Pictures A and B." Gu associates *Li xu*, *juan* 7, with "Mr. Hong on Stele Style." Why is *juan* 6—the very *juan* from which our pictorial images derive—identified in the *Siku* manuscript as C? See also the Beijing tushuguan, Rare Books microfilm of the 1588 version of the *Li shi*; the crucial descriptions occur in pages marked as "supplements."

47. The 1588 edition of *Li shi* gives long labels and moralizing appraisals, though the stones found by Huang Yi add an additional seventy characters to two registers of the west wall.

48. Gu Aiji, *Li bian*, *juan* 8/38b–40a. (The *Siku quanshu* editors adopted Gu's view in the preface to Hong Gua's work.) Gu cites the *Beitu*, using phrases that seem to identify three registers in the west wall of the reconstructed Wu Liang shrine, but upon closer examination only the first two can be made to correspond to what we see in the west wall today. By the third phrase, the pictorial figures mentioned (Guan Zhong to Li Shan) are not located in the same register, and the rest of the passage only mentions "types" of figures, some labeled and some not, whose total number adds up to 162. Perhaps yet another version was known from the *Beitu* (identified in the *Siku* manuscript with *Li xu*, *juan* 6), and that explains why He Zhuo found the editions of the *Li xu* hopelessly confused.

49. Ma is said to have purchased the scroll from the connoisseur and collector Liang Qingbiao (1620–1691), associated with Wulin (yet another Wu!) and with Jinxiang.

50. Ginger Hsu, *Bushels of Pearls*, pp. 165–74.

51. I say "seems" because a check of all the seal catalogues known to Søren Edgren, Eileen Hsu, Alfreda Murck, and Michael Nylan has turned up no identification for the Hanyan Studio, where the rubbing set was viewed in 1723.

52. Neither Ma Sizan's biography nor that of the Ma brothers gives any information. Rong Geng, *Han Wu Liang Ci*, p. 3b, says that the steles "went to" Ma Yuelu. A 1772 colophon attributed to Ma Yuelu (colophon 27 to the Tang Rubbing) claims that Ma had "owned it [the set of rubbings] for several decades." Ma Yuelu's death is usually dated to "after 1766," but neither Michael Nylan nor Søren Edgren have as yet been able to find any record of activity for Ma Yuelu in the years 1766–1772, despite Ma Yuelu's fame.

53. Besides the so-called Tang Rubbing, the most important pieces in the Ma brothers' collection were Dong Qichang's copy of Zhao Mengfu's *Autumn Colors on the Qiao and Hua Mountains*; a work attributed to Guo Xi, which hung in their Xiaolin Longshan Guan; also several pieces of calligraphy attributed to Yan Zhenqing (708–784) and an album of bronze inscriptions dated to Song.

54. Of these volumes, 229 are listed in an old manuscript catalogue preserved in the Library of Congress, under the title *Chengsong shumu*. As Ginger Hsu describes it, this merchant family maintained a "special relationship" with the Qing court. Cf. Guy, *The Emperor's Four Treasuries*, esp. pp. 46–48, 96, 117; Nancy Lee Swann, "Seven Intimate Library Owners," *Harvard Journal of Asiatic Studies*, vol. 1, no. 3 (1936), pp. 363–90. The Ma brothers patronized a number of figures, including Ruan Yuan and Quan Zuwang (1705–1755), who then proceeded to work on the Wu family rubbings. Quan is known as a forger of "antique" documents.

55. Ma Yuelu may have been involved in the bribery scandal of 1786 that had serious consequences for several Yangzhou salt merchants. If so, Ma may then have been forced to sell items from his collection. See Li Dou, *Yangzhou huafang lu* (Ji'nan: Shandong youyi chubanshe, 2001), *juan* 4, p. 113; Arthur Hummel, *Eminent Chinese*, pp. 183, 560. According to the account of Liang Zhangju (1775–1849), Weng Fanggang's disciple Wang Xuejiang was a skilled artist who had Jiang Chun (1721–1789), patron of Huang Yi's father, as his patron. See Liang Zhangju, "Xiao Linglan shan guan," *Langji congtan* (Beijing: Zhonghua, 1997; reprint of a 1991 edition), vol. 2, pp. 21–22.

56. The 1783 hand tracing copy of the so-called Tang Rubbing belonged to Lu Shaozeng of Wumen, to which there were appended colophons by other Wumen locals, such as Li Minggu and Xie Lincun. This hand tracing copy became one of the three bases for Weng Fanggang's writings about the subject in *Lianghan jinshi ji*.

57. Colophon 28 to the Tang Rubbing.

58. See Weng Fanggang, *Lianghan Jinshi ji*, *juan* 15, p. 17.

59. See Wang Chang, *Jinshi cuibian*, par. 9. This copy had a colophon by the Yangzhou painter Jin Nong. Later, Rong Geng would borrow a complete set of rubbings from a Mr. Lu Hejiu. In Mr. Lu's version, a total of seventy-eight pictorial figures were accompanied by cartouches—two more than were known to Gu Aiji. (Remember that in the *Li xu* version, 162 figures were included, some 86 of them unlabeled.)

60. Colophon 30; Weng Fanggang, "Ti Xiaosong suo jie Wumen Lushi Xiangta Wu Liang Cixiang ce san shou," in *Fuchu Zhai ji, waishi* (Taipei: Wenhai chubanshe, 1969), *juan* 17, pp. 9–10. Weng had joined the *Santong* project (initiated 1774), whose explicit goal was to compile a *Jinshi lue* (*Abbreviated catalogue of the bronze and stone inscriptions in the empire*). For Weng's poems, see *Fuchu Zhai shiji* (Shanghai: n.p., ?1793), *juan* 32/24a; *waishi*, *juan* 17/14a, 19a.

61. All this is reported in Wang Chang, *Jinshi cuibian*, and in the collected works of Weng Fanggang as well. Note that Huang Yi gave away a rubbing from the site before he visited it himself, so perhaps he also owned a copy produced by Mr. Song.

62. Weng Fanggang writes of a version derived from Mr. Lu Guanfu that was mounted in an album format and a version mounted in a scroll form, also said to be derived from a version that belonged to Wang Xuejiang. Huang Yi in 1795 recalled that the mounting of Wang Xuejiang's version was damaged in 1775, when he first saw it.

63. Over the years Huang Yi made at least seven copies of Mr. Lu's version.

64. Weng Fanggang, *Lianghan jinshi ji*, *juan* 15, p. 49.

65. See *Jining zhili zhouzhi* (1785), ed. Wang Daoheng, *juan* 17, "Guji" section, *beikao xia*; cf. Rong Yuan, *Jinshi shu lumu* (Taipei: Datong shuju, 1971), *juan* 5/3a.

66. In more than one account authored by Huang Yi, Huang Yi's acquisition of Wang Xuejiang's prized possession is dated to 1791—five years after the "discovery" at Wuzhai Shan. One can only speculate about the reason for such discrepancies in various contemporary accounts.

67. Weng Fanggang's dramatic account, by which Huang Yi on "one and the same day"(*yidan*) acquired the rubbing set once owned by Wang Xuejiang and located on Wuzhai Shan the entire Wu family complex, must be overstated. See Weng Fanggang, "Huang Qiu'an," *Fuchu Zhai wenji*, *juan* 13, p. 7. Ma Yuelu's 1772 colophon says that he wanted to give the fourteen leaves of the rubbing to Wang Xuejiang, an antiquarian with a good eye for Tang and Song rubbings, so that they could enjoy a wider circulation; interestingly, the last colophon, by Huang Yi, tells us that Wang Xuejiang at first politely declined the offer, but Huang Yi urged Wang to accept it.

68. One should not overestimate the loss in value of the Tang Rubbing, however. According to Rong Geng, *Han Wu Liang Ci*, p. 3b, in late 1791, some five years after Huang Yi's find, 600 units of gold were offered to—and refused by—Mr. Lu of Jining, who was then in possession of the rubbing set.

69. See Wang Chang, *Jinshi cuibian*, *juan* 8, par. 20.

70. Some seventy-odd characters that had been illegible in the Wu Liang rubbings known to the Song experts were legible to Huang Yi. His finds are now often incorrectly dubbed the first "scientific excavations" in China, to the amazement of those who appreciate what a scientific excavation entails. The materials from the first finds (some thirty-one slabs altogether) were gathered by Huang Yi in the usual fashion of antiquarian officials: peasants came to Huang Yi with sample rubbings and Huang indicated his interest in those rubbings. By his own account, Huang visited the vicinity a month later to see the site for himself and to gather information from the locals. A second round of finds was made in 1789, when Huang, in cooperation with several leading members of the community, decided to build a Preservation Hall to preserve the stones in such a way as to facilitate more rubbing. Huang's own accounts of the finds varied somewhat, and his first account of the first find was written a full year after the initial discovery. See Cary Liu's "Recarving the Past" for further details. For standard antiquarian practices, see Shana Brown, "Pastimes: Scholars, Art Dealers, and the Making of Modern Chinese Historiography, 1870–1928" (PhD diss., University of California, Berkeley, 2003).

71. Wang Chang, *Jinshi cuibian*, *juan* 8, par. 20.

72. According to Ma Ziyun, "Tan Wu Liang Ci," the Tang Rubbing album in 1916 passed into the possession of Li Ruqian, who had it "beautifully mounted."

73. This explains how one of the best rubbing sets made by Huang Yi came to be, by

1795, in the possession of the noted collector Liang Tongshu (1723–1815), the son of the prominent scholar-official Liang Shizheng (1697–1763). For Liang Tongshu, see Arthur Hummel, *Eminent Chinese*, p. 505. See colophon 32 to the Tang album (dated to 1795), which states that Liang Tongshu in that very year received a new set of rubbings made by Huang Yi from the Wuzhai Shan stones. Donors to the Preservation Hall included Wang Chang, Qu Zhongrong (1769–1842), who was Qian Daxin's son-in-law, and Wang Niansun (1744–1842). How the Wuzhai Shan stones sustained very little damage from the production of this many rubbing sets remains a mystery, especially baffling since, prior to Huang Yi's discovery, the precise site assigned to the Wu family cemetery had been a battleground twice in early Qing. Note that others in Weng Fanggang's circle established shrines for neglected Han figures, as is clear from Steven B. Miles, "Celebrating the Yu Fan Shrine: Northern Patrons and Southern Poets in Early Nineteenth-Century Guangzhou" (unpublished paper presented at Association of Asian Studies, 2004).

74. Fang Ruo's *Jiaobei suibi* (preface dated 1914; printed 1921; reprint, Shanghai: Shanghai shuhua chubanshe, 1981), p. 59. Fang Ruo, in making this comment, was describing rubbings of the pillar-gate inscription at the site. "Recently, there are rubbings without even one line that is similar to the old .... A complete set of the original rubbings is no longer to be found." The Daoguang period saw a virtual explosion of writings about Huang Yi's finds at Jiaxiang. See Wu Hung's "Chronology." (Note, however, Qu Zhongrong's manuscript *Wu Liang Citang huaxiang kao*, compiled in 1825, may not have been published until 1927.)

75. Ma Heng became head of the Palace Museum in 1934. For one example of differences, the second, fifth, and eighth characters in the inscription for the legendary emperor Fuxi differed in Ma Heng's version from that recorded in Huang Yi's book.

76. A Mr. Huang Shilin, a man of Tai'an (in Shandong), set up a shop in Jining that sold steles or rubbings (or perhaps copies of either, since the Chinese does not always distinguish) gathered from "more than ten counties" in Shandong. The scholar-collector Miao Quansun (1844–1919) also based some of his work on the rubbings Huang had collected. "He [= Mr. Huang] was very good at rubbing steles .... All stone carvings dating from the Han were collected [by Miao]. He had enough in his possession to *fill in* the places where the *Shanzuo jinshi zhi* (*Record of inscriptions on bronze and stone for Shandong*) was not yet complete" [italics mine], "Xubu," *fu* 3, p. 125.

77. Xuanyuan, a resident of nearby Nanwu, found two stone slabs (one showing a man shouldering food; another showing auspicious signs, including a bird and a crane) in 1871. Wu Hung possibly mistook the phrase *he kui* ("shouldering provisions/food presents") to be a man's name (He Kui). Xuanyuan in 1880 found another stone showing Wang Ling's mother. These appear to fit together with Stone 1 of the Left Stone Chamber. Ding Rongjiang placed three stones into the Hall. A perusal of the range of items illustrated in *Handai shike huaxiang tuoben mu lu* (Taipei: Academic Sinica, History and Phonology Section, 2001), many of which are identified only by a vague provenance of "Shandong, Eastern Han," reminds us that this propensity to add objects to the corpus attributed to the complex continued long into the twentieth century.

78. See Wilma Fairbank, "The Offering Shrines of 'Wu Liang T'zu'," in *Adventures in Retrieval* (1972), caption for fig. 10. While Fairbank did not indicate that she regarded the image as a forgery, the exaggerated renderings on the slab would seem to suggest this.

79. Duan-fang was a high official and major collector. In the Xuantong era, the slab showing Wang Ling's mother went to Duan-fang's collection. Several pictorial slabs (as mentioned above) ended up in a Tokyo museum. One must remember that prior to 1918 Shandong was part of Germany's "sphere of influence" and, after that, of Japan's.

80. For Liang Sicheng's endeavors, see Nancy Shatzman Steinhardt, "The Tang Architectural Icon and the Politics of Chinese Architectural History," *Art Bulletin*, vol. 86, no. 2 (June 2004), pp. 228–54.

81. See Chen Jin's 1880 account, " Chongxiu Wushi Citang ji" ("Record on the renovation of the Wu family shrines"). For the reading of the passage, I have consulted *Shinpen kinsekigaku roku: tsuketari azagō: sakuhin seisotsu nenpyō*, ed. Matsumaru Michio (Tokyo: Kyōko shoin, 1976), p. 112. See also Michael Nylan, "Restoring and Restorying the Past," *Orientations*, March 2004, pp. 98–103.

82. See *1907 nian Zhongguo jixing*, trans. Yan Guodong, based on the 1958 Russian edition (Kunming: Yunnan renmin chubanshe, 2001), esp. pp. 136–37.

83. We cannot take for granted an absolute continuity either in the Preservation Halls or in their contents of pictorial and inscriptional slabs. See figure 3. The extant accounts devoted to the Preservation Halls vary and many of them are hard to interpret. Prior to 1949 the funds needed to build or repair the site were obtained from the sale of rubbings relating to the site, from local donations, and from district and provincial grants. For further information, see Sekino Tadashi [Tei or Tadasu], *Shina Santōshō ni okeru Kandai funbo no hyōshoku* (Tokyo: Imperial University, College of Engineering, 1916), p. 105, citing a 1910 inscription by Luo Zhenjun; Jiang Yingju and Wu Wenqi, *Handai Wushi muqun shike yanjiu* (Ji'nan: Shandong meishu chubanshe, 1995), pp. 134–35; Wilma Fairbank, "The Offering Shrines of 'Wu Liang T'zu'," in *Adventures in Retrieval*, pp. 48–49; *Wenwu* 1961.5, pp. 7–16, 27–35, 109–15, esp. p. 32; and *Kaogu xuebao* 1981.2, p. 166.

84. Wu Pei-yi, "Memories of K'ai-feng," *New Literary History: A Journal of Theory and Interpretation*, vol. 25, no. 1 (1994), pp. 47–60; the citation from Pierre Ryckmans is from p. 48.

85. See also Jean James, "Identification in Han Funerary Art: By their Hats and Garments you shall know them," *Oriental Art*, vol. 49, no. 1 (2003), pp. 13–21. Käte Finsterbusch, "Hauptmotivgruppen der Han-zeitlichen Kunst: Darstellungen auf Reliefs, Liniengravierungeng, Wandmalereien," *Und folge nun demnach, was mein Herz begehrt: Festschrift für Ulrich Unger zum 70. Geburtstag* (Hamburg: Hamburger Sinologische Schriften, 2002), pp. 31–84, notes that more Han motifs appear in the reconstructed Wuzhai Shan materials than in any other site.

86. Nagata Hidemasa, *Handai sekkoku shūsei* (Tokyo: Dōhōsha, 1994), vol. 1, p. 128. Wenwu 1982.5, pp. 60–70; *Kaogu yu wenwu* 1984.4, esp. p. 112; and *Kaogu yu wenwu* 1984.6, pp. 105–6, which assert that the relation between the Songshan inscription of 157 CE, dedicated to one Anguo, and the pictorial stones is "not established." Cf. *Wenwu* 1986.5, 31–41 (esp. p. 39), which alludes to the principle of majority rule when determining the date of a particular site. There are also problems with the Wuzhai Shan pictorial images and cartouches not treated in detail here. To name but three: the citation of an Eastern Jin filial exemplar in the cartouches, the assignment to emperors of caps and clothing (e.g., scalloped skirts, tight leggings, tricorn hats, and a cap that looks like that worn by a medieval jester [of Xianbei origin?]) typically worn by barbarians, slaves, and servants; and the uncharacteristically long cartouches accompanying some figures.

87. We know, for example, that the authoritative *Hanli ziyuan* included post-Han examples. By the fifth century CE Han clerical script was reserved mainly for stele heads and other formal contexts.

88. Inscriptions, as we now know, could be added to an earlier monument to furnish information deemed lacking. See Stanley Abe, *Ordinary Images*, pp. 309–13; David Lowenthal, *The Past is a Foreign Country*, p. 272; and Haskell and Penny, *Taste and the Antique*, on the bust of the "dying Seneca" (esp. pp. 303–5, pl. 160). Many examples of stone steles that have been misattributed are given in *SJZ*.

89. See Shen Gua's report of a tomb opened in Jizhou; cf. *Jining zhili zhouzhi*, *juan* 5/61a (p. 1059), which relates that those who want to see inside the interment site "carry candles and walk in." Few premodern compendia devoted to ritual objects survive, but we can get an idea of what they were like from fairly recent reprints of such works as Nie Chongyi's *Sanlitu*, the *Gujin tushu jicheng*, and the illustrated catalogues included in the *Siku quanshu*. A source worth consulting is Zheng Qiao's (1104–1162) *Tongzhi*, chap. 72, which discusses the relation of writings to pictures and goes on to list what sorts of writings have or lack illustrations. The work of Zhao Yonghong (doctoral candidate, Brown University; forthcoming) shows the propensity of artists of the Northern Dynasties to copy Han models precisely.

90. Lothar Ledderose, *Mi Fu and the Classical Tradition of Chinese Calligraphy* (Princeton: Princeton University Press, 1979), pp. 58–59.

91. See Zeng Gong (1019–1083) *Yuanfeng tiba* (Beijing: Zhonghua shuju, 1984), *xia ce*, p. 684, speaking of the Eastern Han images that were beginning to be seen in his day.

92. Chen Jieqi, *Fuzhai chidu*, ed. Luo Zhenyu (Taipei: Wenhai chubanshe, 1973; reprint, 1974)., vol. 1, p. 196 (trans. modified from Shana Brown, "Pastimes"). Note, however, that two passages emphasize the crudity of the Wu Liang pictorial images. See pp. 525, 532 of this essay.

93. Laurie Sheck, "[Untitled] Poem." This is reprinted with permission of the author.

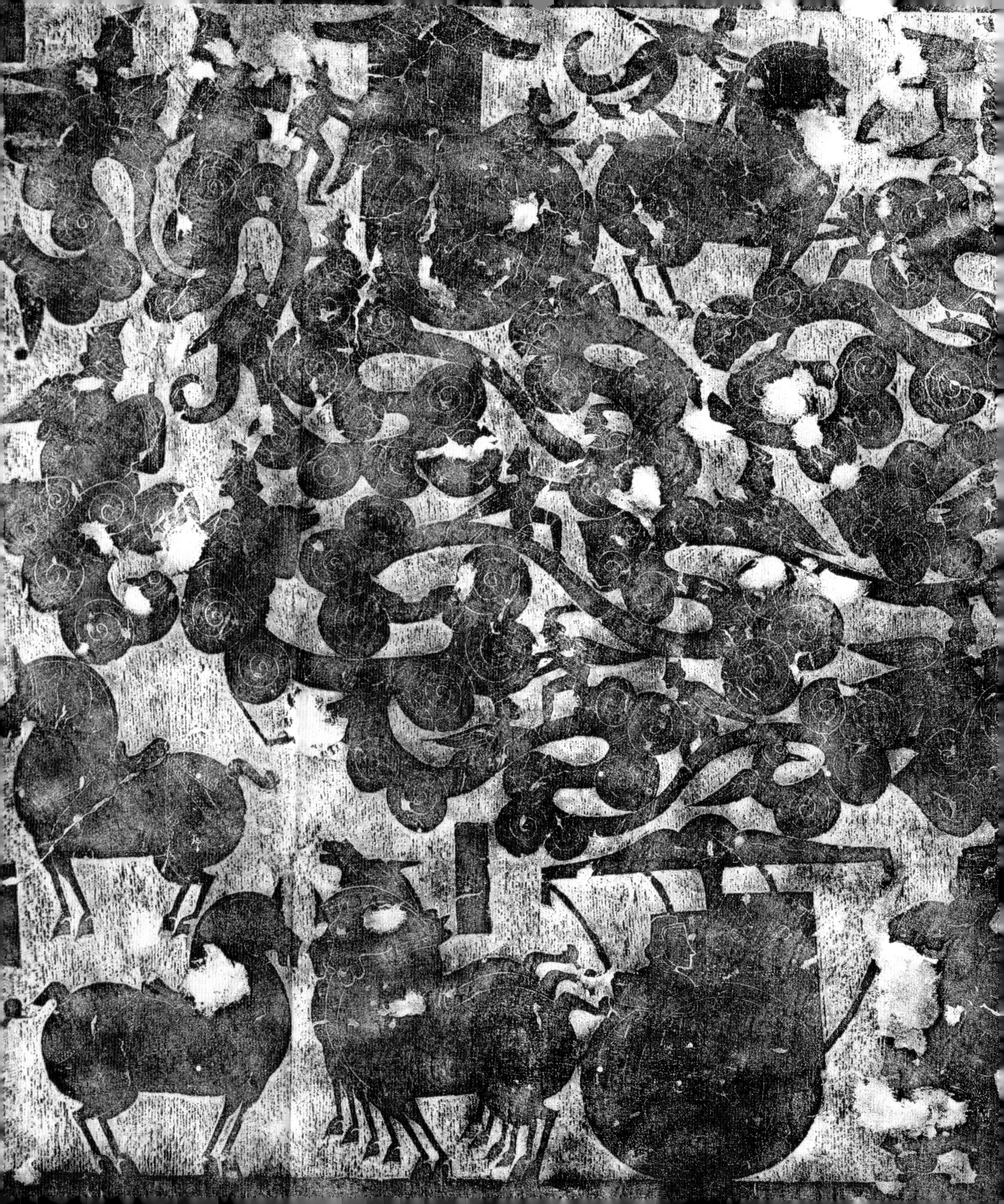

Cary Y. Liu

Reconfiguring the "Wu Family Shrines": A Typological Study

The recarving of history surrounding the pictorial stones, rubbings, and textual materials associated with the so-called Wu family shrines, the cemetery complex located in the northwestern foothills of Ziyun Shan (Purple Cloud Hills) mountain range at Wuzhaishan Cun Village in Jiaxiang County, Shandong Province (fig. 1), was the focus of my "Recarving the Past" essay in this catalogue. Approaching the materials from a different perspective, in this essay I shall examine the cemetery as it might be architecturally reconfigured, or reconstructed. The stones found at the cemetery, or associated with the "Wu family shrines" assemblage, have been reconfigured into three or four stone chambers, a pillar-gate (*que*) composed of a pair of stone gate-pillars, a pair of stone sculptures of felines, and two inscribed steles and one blank one. In addition, three tombs at the east and southeast end of the site have lately been excavated (in 1981 and 2002). I shall consider the architectural reconstructions, along with the tombs, in relation to their individual architectural types and the overall configuration of the site, in order to explore funerary building practices in the second to third century in the Shandong region.[1] This preliminary investigation is intended to raise questions about many aspects of the "Wu family shrines" and late Han mortuary architecture that remain unclear, as well as to suggest directions for future research.

Pictorial stone carvings found at the Wu family cemetery, and more especially the inscriptions engraved on steles, on a gate-pillar, and in cartouche panels labeling various pictorial scenes, have been the subject of repeated scrutiny since the Song dynasty. During the Yuan and Ming dynasties river flooding buried the cemetery structures, which were then forgotten. But although the structures disappeared from sight and memory, rubbings as well as textual transcriptions and descriptions of the inscriptions and pictorial stones continued to be transmitted and studied. The history of the Wu rubbings as cultural artifacts in the Yuan to early Qing dynasties is only beginning to be researched.

The ruins of the cemetery site were rediscovered in 1786 by the Shandong official and amateur archaeologist Huang Yi (1744–1802). Since their rediscovery the stones have been the focus of extensive scholarly research and art-historical debate. Yet despite a thousand years of scholarship, many aspects of the Wu family cemetery remain unresolved. Modern studies, including Wilma Fairbank's in 1941, Wu Hung's in 1989, Jiang Yingju and Wu Wenqi's in 1981 and 1995, have made significant contributions toward architectural reconstruction; the

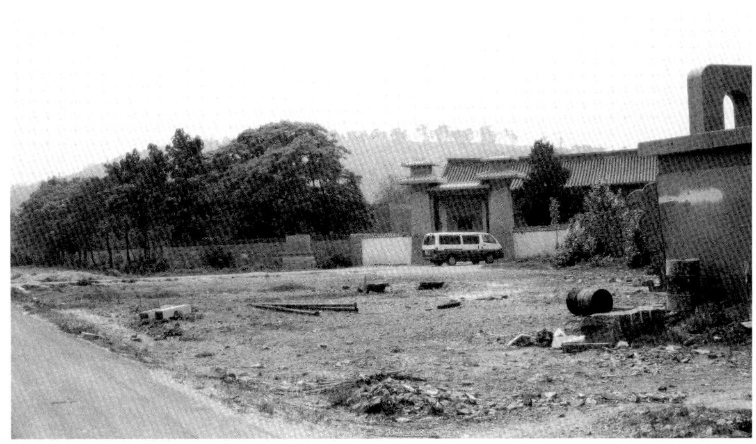

Fig. 1 *Northwest gate of Wu cemetery compound with Ziyun Shan (Purple Cloud Hills) in the distance.* Wuzhai Shan site, Jiaxiang County, Shandong. Photo by author, 2002.

Opposite Detail of Stone Chamber 2, Stone 2-R.2 (cat. no. 1.33). "Wu family shrines" rubbings. Princeton University Art Museum, acc. no. 2002-307.32.

majority of past scholarship, however, has primarily examined the rubbings and stones as isolated units, focusing chiefly on the pictorial imagery in Stone Chamber 3, the so-called Wu Liang Shrine. Unresolved questions include: (1) Why are cartouche panels with inscriptions found primarily in Stone Chamber 3 (former Wu Liang Shrine and Good Omen stones), whereas in Chamber 2 (former Left and Rear Groups) and Chamber 1 (former Front and Rear Group stones) many of the cartouches remain blank? (2) What is the architectural relationship between the four inscribed steles (two known only from transcriptions of their inscriptions) dedicated to male progeny of the Wu family and the cemetery structures? and (3) What was the original arrangement of the funerary structures in the cemetery? There are also questions about later retouching, recarving, and forgery of the pictorial images, inscriptions, and ink rubbings that may affect how certain stones are to be integrated into any reconstruction. Some of these questions and problems can begin to be addressed by focusing on the typologies of the individual architectural structures at the site—inscribed steles, stone statues, pillar-gate, pictorial stone chambers, tombs—and of the cemetery layout.

Steles

Four stele inscriptions supposedly dedicated to male members of the Wu family have been variously recorded in past sources as keys to dating the so-called Wu family shrines and identifying the Wu family genealogy. Only two of these steles survive. The Wu Ban stele is claimed to have been recovered at the cemetery by Huang Yi in 1786, at which time the Wu Rong stele was already installed in the Jining Prefectural Academy (Jining zhou xue): today it is stored behind the Jining Municipal Museum (fig. 2). The other two steles, those of Wu Liang and Wu Kaiming, have not been located, and it is not known whether steles dedicated to other members of the family existed. A fifth surviving stele without characters was found at the cemetery between the pillar-gate and tombs in 1909 (see Liu's "Recarving the Past," fig. 2). This stele was shaped like a *gui*-tablet with a hole in the center, similar to both the Wu Ban and Wu Rong steles, and it is believed by some to be the Wu Liang or Wu Kaiming stele.[2]

As to the Wu Rong and Wu Ban steles, their heights, peaked-tablet shape, hole piercing the stone, and engraved inscriptions, are all said to be characteristics of steles dating to the second–third centuries.[3] But all four stele inscriptions (whether as stones, rubbings, or transcriptions) are problematic in their connection to the cemetery site (see Liu's "Recarving the Past" and Nylan's "Addicted to Antiquity," Part II). Anachronisms in and variations among recorded transcriptions and rubbings are one problem. The earliest record of the Wu Ban stele, in the *Jigu lu* (*Record of collected antiquities*; 1061) by Ouyang Xiu (1007–1072), notes that some 80 to 90 percent of the inscription is illegible; yet later transcriptions by Zhao Mingcheng (1081–1129) and Hong Gua (1117–1184) include substantial sections of the missing text that Ouyang called illegible, leaving only 10 to 20 percent as unreadable.[4] Did they simply have a better rubbing? We should note that Ouyang Xiu and his son Ouyang Fei lived near the cemetery site in Rencheng, Shandong, and owned two different rubbings of the so-called Wu Ban inscription, and neither Ouyang ever linked this stele to the Wu cemetery site or to other Wu steles. In addition, the *Jigu lu*, Zhao Mingcheng's *Jinshi lu* (*Records of metal and stone*), and Hong Gua's *Li shi* (*Explications of clerical script*) and *Li xu* (*Supplement on clerical script*) all have had uncertain and problematic transmissions. In these texts the received stele inscriptions tend to become more and more complete with each later compilation or edition, independent of reference to any stone stele or rubbing copy. The received transcriptions may represent incomplete texts seen in early rubbings of the stones to which scholars over time have interpolated missing and damaged characters according to their own lights and by comparison with other inscriptions, whether related to the Wu family or merely of Han date. Certain anachronisms in the received stele texts raise suspicions that this indeed may be the case. Careful analyses of the textual content and literary style of the received stele texts, plus close scrutiny of the calligraphy, are needed. We may find that the received versions of the stele inscriptions do not strictly preserve early rubbings of the stones; instead they incorporate interpretive restorations or recarvings of China's past.

In order to investigate the possible connections among the four memorial stele inscriptions, the "Wu family shrines" assemblage, and the cemetery site, we need first to study the origin and development of the memorial stele type, and to discover where memorial steles were erected during the Han. If memorial steles were erected at burial sites, what were their positions relative to other funerary structures? Were memorial steles erected outside the front pillar-gate for all to see, or

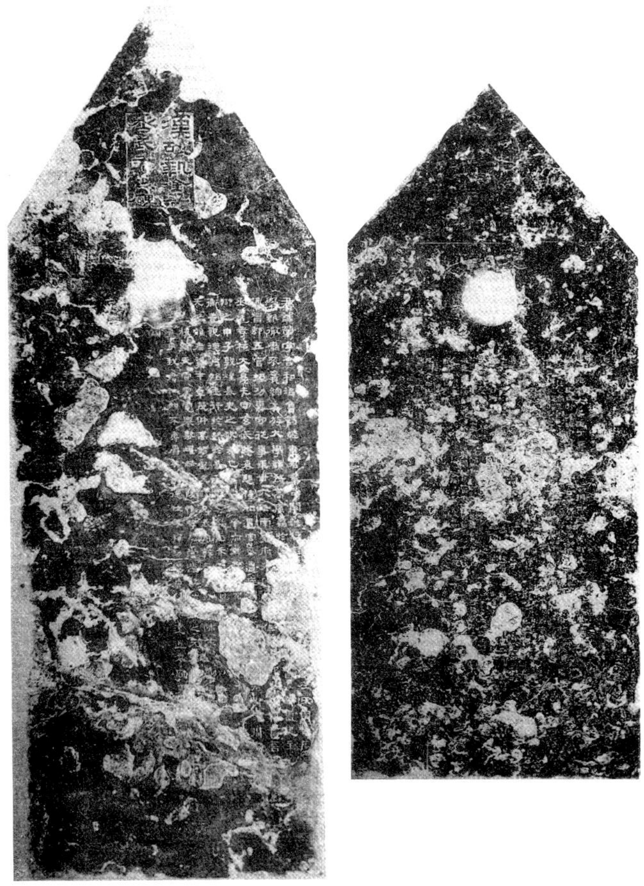

Fig. 2 *Wu Rong stele* (left) and *Wu Ban stele* (right). Ink-on-paper rubbings. From Jiang and Wu, *Handai Wushi muqun shike yanjiu*, p. 151, figs. 20, 21.

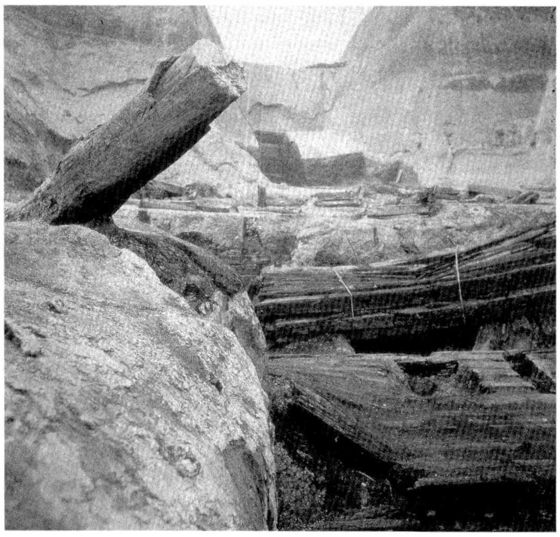

were they placed inside, as the "Wu family shrines" are generally reconstructed?[5] Alternatively, might they have been located directly in front of the tomb of the person they memorialized?[6] Or might they have been installed away from the burial site, at a provincial academy, local temple, ancestral hall, at the head of roads, or at other distant locations?[7] Possibly all these diverse placements obtained in various regions and at various times during the Han dynasty. Many post-Han texts describe memorial steles at Han burial sites, but was it common practice to erect steles at the time of burial or were they only erected afterward, by succeeding—even post-Han—generations?[8] In modern annotations to Li Daoyuan's (d. 527) *Shuijing zhu* (*Commentary on the "Classic of Waterways"*), Shi Zhecun notes that no inscribed memorial steles are known to antedate the Eastern Han, which may mean that the practice did not become popular until late in the Eastern Han or afterward. Shi Zhecun also notes that when the characters *Han gu* ("late of the Han dynasty") appear in the heading of a stele, they indicate that the stele is of post-Han date. Alternatively, in some cases, the heading containing these characters may have been added afterward to a stele stone and text that may date from the Han. This may be true of the surviving Wu Rong stele, whose heading (containing the characters *Han gu*) is carved in large clerical-script calligraphy (*lishu*) in contrast to the body of the text, where the characters are in much smaller clerical script. On the surviving Wu Ban stele stone and rubbings the heading is no longer visible, but in transcriptions the heading is sometimes reconstructed following the Wu Rong model, and begins with the characters *Han gu*.[9]

Fig. 3 *Burial stele*. Eastern Zhou dynasty, Spring and Autumn period. Tomb of Duke Jing of Qin (r. 577–537 BCE) at Fengxiang County, Shaanxi. Wood; h. 1.7–2.0 m. From Han Wei, "Qin gong da mu fajue ji," *Zhongguo* 1987.5, p. 24.

The category of inscribed memorial steles should be distinguished from the presumably earlier stone steles erected in palaces and temples, and from wooden steles used to lower coffins, even though all of these types were called *bei* ("stele"). Possibly all these forms of *bei* shared a common but now unknown origin. Relying on textual sources, past studies have differentiated among types of *bei* depending on where they were located and how they were used; but, they did not distinguish among their physical attributes or characteristics. For example, according to Ma Ziyun, steles apparently developed out of early stone inscriptions such as those found on the famous Stone Drums (*Shi gu*; ca. 420 BCE) and on inscribed stones erected on mountaintops by the First Emperor and known as "incised stones" (*ke shi*). Ma also cites pre-Han textual sources describing stone steles located in palace and temple courtyards. Palace steles were used as gnomons to track the passage of the sun's shadow from day to night. Steles in palaces are also recorded to have served as ceremonial markers to which visitors bowed and at which commands were issued. Temple steles served as tethering posts where animals were sacrificed and their fur or feathers were collected, and their minced meat and blood were gathered in vessels. Ritual tripod vessels (*ding*) (see cat. no. 23) were set in front of temple steles and may have been used as receptacles for the meat and blood.[10]

Early Confucian canons on rites and other ritual texts also describe wooden steles that were used at tomb sites to lower the coffin and were then buried in the tomb. In the "Tan Gong" chapters of the *Liji* (*Rites records*), it is recorded that in the state of Lu "[to lower a coffin] the ducal house used an arrangement resembling large stone steles (*fengbei*), and the three ministerial families used an arrangement resembling large wooden columns (*huanying*)."[11] Zheng Xuan (127–200), commenting on this passage during the Han dynasty, noted that "*fengbei* are large timbers cut in the shape of stone steles. They are erected to the front and back at the four corners of the outer coffin, and they are pierced in the center for windlasses (*lulu*) to lower the coffin with ropes. The Son of Heaven has six ropes and four steles, and in front and back are double windlasses . . . . The *huanying* are cut in the shape of large columns. Four posts [at the corners of the outer coffin] are called *huan* posts. The various nobility have four ropes and two steles that are like *huan* posts. Counselors (*dafu*) have two ropes and two steles, and gentlemen or servicemen (*shi*) have two ropes and no steles."[12] These wooden steles—*fengbei* and *huanying*—belong to a different typology from the stone steles found in palaces and in temples.

The windlass was a long axle or long cylinder around which a rope was coiled. Slotted through the circular holes in two *fengbei* steles, the mechanical device was cranked or rolled to lower the coffin. According to Zheng Xuan's description, *fengbei* imitated the form of stone steles in palaces and temples. In contrast, the *huanying* columns appear to have been posts. Surviving wood timbers about 1.7 to 2 meters long were found in the large ramped tomb of Duke Jing of Qin (Qin Jing Gong; r. 577–537 BCE) at Fengxiang County, Shaanxi. On opposite sides of the secondary platform level overlooking the main coffin chamber, these timbers were erected at an angle leaning over the chamber below (fig. 3).[13] Here is an early example of the type of wooden steles used to lower coffins, and because of their location down on the secondary platform level, they were buried when the tomb was filled.

The inscribed memorial stele type apparently did not emerge until the Han dynasty. The earliest surviving dated inscribed stele is the *Biao xiao yu bei* (26 BCE), recovered in 1870 in Shandong. On the front face of this stone are two ruled columns carved with bird designs on top and a dated inscription below. Sometimes it is said to be in the shape of a *gui*-tablet, but personal inspection leads me to suspect that it may have been trimmed and that its present outlines are not original. Since it lacks the central hole of a *fengbei* stele, and is not columnar like a *huanying* post, it may not have been a funerary stele. Instead, it may have been a memorial stone erected in a palace or temple or at the head of a roadway.

We know that steles carved with memorial inscriptions became more common during the Eastern Han, but we have little information as to their origin. Do they derive from burial, palace, temple, or roadway steles, and how are these different stele types related to each other? Conjecturally, memorial steles with a pierced hole and with rounded tops carved with arced halo lines (*yunxian*) may have evolved from burial steles. Equally conjecturally, steles in the shape of a *gui*-tablet, like the surviving Wu Ban and Wu Rong stones, may derive from palace or temple steles. In palace settings the triangular peaked top would have allowed such stones to serve as gnomons, and in temple (and palace?) steles the pierced hole may have served to tether animals for sacrifice. Stone steles without a hole or a peaked top may have been erected apart from palace, temple, and cemetery settings, at the head of roads or in other public areas. Inscriptions

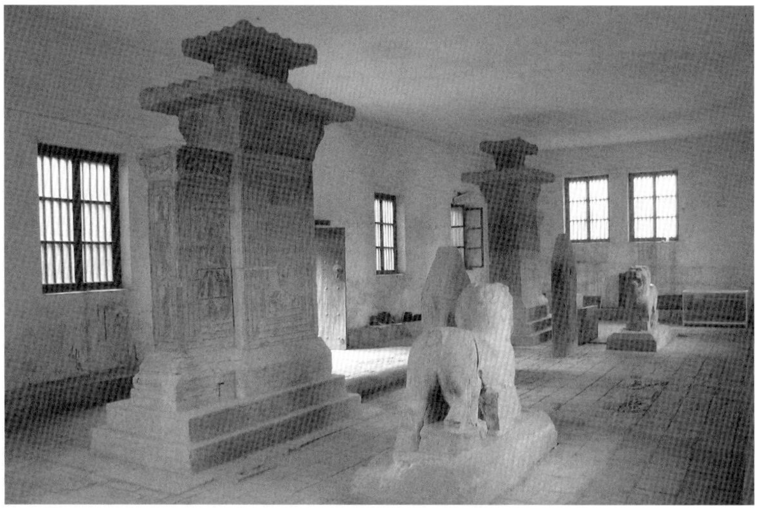

carved on steles may provide important information about the biography of the deceased and the making of the stele; at the same time it is necessary to recognize that the inscriptional content may not reflect the true function or location of the stone on which it is carved, or when it was actually carved or erected.

Pillar-Gate and Stone Statues

A pair of northeast and southwest stone gate-pillars with stone statues of male and female felines marked the northwest entry to the Wu cemetery (figs. 4, 5).[14] In general, these gate-pillars resemble many Han gate-pillars found in regions including Sichuan, Henan, Anhui, and Shandong provinces.[15] At burial sites two gate-pillars were erected flanking a spirit path (*shen dao*), forming a pillar-gate where the spirit path reached the cemetery compound.[16] They marked the entrance and sometimes served to control access by vehicles and visitors. It can be assumed that the gate-pillars were joined to a perimeter wall or barrier surrounding the burial compound. At the Wu cemetery the stone threshold with the vertical center tablet on the ground between the two gate-pillars was probably intended to obstruct vehicular access.[17] Alternatively, there might be no perimeter wall and the pillar-gate might stand alone, marking the spirit-path entrance, while each individual tomb in the cemetery was encircled with its own wall. Remains of walls around tomb mounds have been excavated at various Han burial sites, including the 151 CE tomb of the minister Miao Yu in Pengcheng, Pi Xian County, Jiangsu, and Tombs 1 and 2 (ca. 171 CE) at Chulan, Su Xian County, Anhui.[18] (The Chulan tombs and walls also provide a model for the layout of the tombs in relation to the stone chambers at the Wu cemetery; discussed later.) Each of the two gate-pillars at the Wu cemetery has pictorial carvings on all four sides, a strong indication that they originally stood alone. Possibly, however, they stood unattached in front of a burial compound perimeter wall that has not survived.

Gate-pillars were commonly constructed either as a single columnar unit with a rectangular plan, or as a larger primary joined with a smaller secondary column. The column shafts were often built on a stone base and capped with a roof stone carved with imitation roof tiles and sometimes topped by a stone ridge. In gate-pillars composed of primary and secondary columns, each column had its own imitation roof, and, as seen at the Wu cemetery (fig. 5) the primary column sometimes carried two levels of roof eaves. Under the projecting roof eaves some gate-pillars have a stone capital carved with imitation bracket sets (*dougong*) or other details imitating wood construction. These may be vestigial features, suggesting a wood prototype. Textual sources contain descriptions of watchtower pillar-gates into which one could climb; these are associated with Han palaces and royal mausoleums.[19] Probably such watchtower pillar-gates were also built of wood, but they should be treated as a separate though related architectural type.

Cemetery gate-pillar column shafts are often decorated on two or more faces with decorative borders, pictorial carvings, and inscriptions. On the Wu cemetery gate-pillars, pictorial images similar to those in the

Fig. 4 *Interior of front exhibition hall with stone felines and pillar-gate*. Wuzhai Shan site, Jiaxiang County, Shandong. Photo by author, 2004.

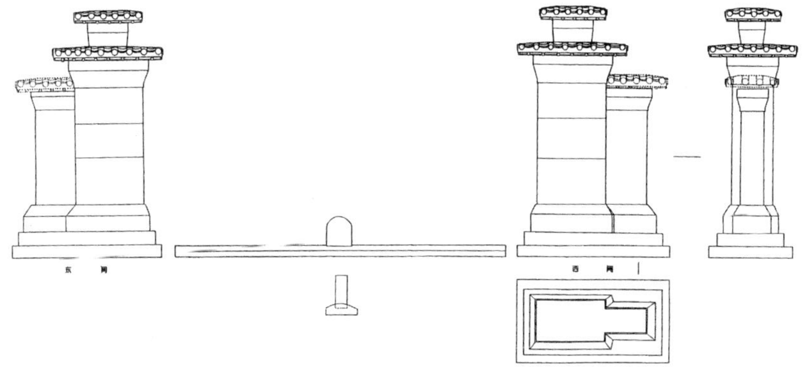

stone chambers are carved in horizontal registers on the broad front and back faces (usually labeled as the north and south sides, respectively) and around the base and capital stones. On the narrow faces (east and west sides) the carved images are stacked or run vertically. The carving style and arrangement of the pictorial images in horizontal registers may be a Jiaxiang regional characteristic. In contrast, many gate-pillars in Sichuan tend to have only a few pictorial figures on the column shaft, and where they do occur they are usually arranged as vertical columns.[20] Both in Sichuan and at the Wu cemetery, figures are also carved in the capital stones beneath the roof eaves.

Key inscriptions, often giving the name of the deceased and his title of office, usually appear in large clerical-script calligraphy that is often centered on the front face of a gate-pillar, but sometimes on the back or the capital. In some cases the inscription is repeated on both gate-pillars for symmetry. At the Wu cemetery the inscription appears only on the front face of the west (i.e., southwest) gate-pillar, near the bottom of the larger, primary, column (cat. no. 1.43). The inscription is not centered. It begins at far right and is written in eight columns of small-size clerical script. What appears to be a blank panel for an inscription or other decorative treatment appears on the front face of the east (i.e., northeast) gate-pillar, but at a different height. Close inspection of rubbings of this panel, however, reveals traces of partially effaced pictorial images.[21] This suggests that the panel was not originally blank, and that the panels on both the east and west gate-pillars originally were fully decorated and only later cleared for inscriptions. The small calligraphy and off-center position of the west gate-pillar inscription are also notable characteristics of the two surviving steles connected with the cemetery—the Wu Ban (cat. nos. 1.46, 1.47) and Wu Rong steles (fig. 2). No conclusion, however, can be drawn from this similarity at this time because the abraded condition of surviving calligraphy on all three stones may be beyond any means of formal or stylistic analysis, and because questions of retouching and recarving first need to be carefully considered.

Pillar-gates stand aboveground, unsheltered from the elements and subject to later alteration, vandalism, and graffiti. Decorative carving and inscriptions on surviving pillar-gates exhibit significant surface erosion and damage. The gate-pillars at the Wu cemetery are no exception. Burial caused by flooding left the upper areas more exposed and therefore subject to greater damage. Personal observation leads me to suspect that the pictorial figures in the upper parts of the gate-pillars have been retouched in an effort to restore a semblance of what may have been the original carved details. Lower sections of the gate-pillars are also heavily worn due to erosion by the elements and by the making of countless rubbings. The key inscription carved on the west gate-pillar was already worn beyond legibility by the Qing-dynasty Daoguang reign-period (1821–1850). This inscription, self-dated to 147 CE, is pivotal to connecting the names of Wu Suizong (Wu Liang), Wu Kaiming, and Wu Xuanzhang (Wu Ban), three of the four male progeny of the Wu family, with stele inscriptions associated with the cemetery site. But because the characters of the men's names were interpreted differently in received transcriptions of the gate-pillar and stele inscriptions, special caution needs to be exercised to

Fig. 5 *Diagram of a pillar-gate*. Wuzhai Shan site, Jiaxiang County, Shandong. From Jiang and Wu, *Handai Wushi muqun shike yanjiu*, p. 8.

determine what parts of the text are reliable and what parts may have been restored, interpolated, or recarved to reflect consensus or expected interpretation. The existence of at least two recarved recensions or copies of the inscription further complicates the situation.[22] It is regrettable that the surviving carved stone inscription can no longer serve to help determine the reliability of the different transcriptions.

Gate-pillars erected during the Han dynasty were also vulnerable to later alteration and modification. In Sichuan Province, for example, several gate-pillars were carved with Buddhist figures and other designs from the Period of Disunity through the Ming dynasty.[23] The Wu cemetery gate-pillars were, again, not exempt. On the narrow sides facing the spirit path on both gate-pillars, the three characters *Wu shi ci* ("Wu family shrine") were carved in large-size seal-script calligraphy over the Han pictorial carvings. In addition, in rows of raised circle patterns at the top of the west gate-pillar capital stone, incised inscriptions record late eighteenth-century visits to the site by Li Kezheng in the third month of 1788, Huang Yi in the seventh month of 1788, and separate undated visits by their close associates Nan Zhengyan and Li Dongqi.[24]

In Chinese the single character *que* ("pillar-gate" or "gate-pillar") refers to several distinct but related architectural types. In considering the pillar-gate (*que*) type, past studies have tended not to distinguish between cemetery pillar-gates and city-, palace-, or temple-wall pillar-gates and watchtowers. According to Xin Lixiang, before the Han, pillar-gates were also known as *diehuang*, *zhihuang*, *xiangwei*, or *guan*.[25] Each of these terms refers to tall structures built to serve as gates, but in different contexts. By the Han dynasty the two terms "pillar-gates" (*que*) and "watchtowers" (*guan*) became prevalent, and were sometimes used synonymously. As mentioned earlier, watchtowers were probably built of wood and housed guard stations. Watchtower pillar-gates were sometimes also built as gates to mausoleums, and in one case were reportedly so tall that they could be seen from a distance of forty-five *li* miles.[26] Because the terms were often used interchangeably, both may have been applied to the tall structures flanking the two-story hall in the central pavilion, or homage, scenes on the Wu cemetery pictorial stones (cat. nos. 1.9, 1.26, 1.36).

By their number and design, which were stipulated by sumptuary regulations, *que* pillar-gates and watchtowers at burial sites also served to reflect the rank and office of the deceased. Textual sources record that royal mausoleums merited four watchtowers or large pillar-gates, high officials two or three pillar-gates, and lower officials only one pillar-gate. It is often presumed that sumptuary regulations for underground burial chambers were commonly flouted during the Han; for pillar-gates, however, which were aboveground and notably public, it is unlikely that sumptuary regulations could be disregarded with impunity.[27] One also wonders if high watchtowers, double-column gate-pillars, and single-column gate-pillars were allowed according to rank, or reflect a stylistic or chronological development. Though a mandated architectural hierarchy remains conjectural, it seems odd that the low-ranking local offices held by the four men linked to the Wu family would have merited pillar-gates. Could it be that the pillar-gate at the Wu cemetery was not intended to correlate with the official positions held by members of a Wu family? On the other hand, was there some special circumstance or unrecorded member of the Wu family who did hold high office? As the architectural typology of mortuary pillar-gates becomes clearer, the significance of pillar-gates begins to require further consideration.

Pictorial Stone Chambers

On the pictorial stones that constitute the architectural reconstruction of Stone Chambers 1–3, the images were rendered in shallow flat relief with fine-line incised details against a background chiseled with vertical striations (*zaowendi tumian xianke*).[28] Many modern classification systems have been devised for Han pictorial stone carving techniques, in the attempt to establish a developmental chronology. These systems, however, are mutually contradictory and often fail to take into consideration the particular social circumstances or architectural type of the structures in which the stones are but components.[29]

Besides the pictorial designs carved on the interior surfaces of the three reconstructed stone chambers, one also needs to consider the rectilinear cartouche panels interspersed among the scenes. Chamber 1 contains inscribed and blank cartouches, perhaps in approximately equal numbers. In Chamber 2 most of the cartouches are blank. In contrast, in Chamber 3 almost every cartouche is inscribed with clerical-script calligraphy identifying specific figures in the scene and sometimes describing the figure or event depicted. Here we return to a question asked earlier: Why are most of the cartouches in Chamber 3 inscribed with calligraphy, while in the other two halls many of the cartouches remain blank? As discussed in catalogue number 1, because the stones were produced in a workshop setting, many scenes may well have been stock designs that could be used to illustrate different stories. Clients could identify the stories they wanted, and a calligrapher was then hired to brush the inscriptions for a stone craftsman to carve into the cartouches. This may echo the process of transferring pictorial designs onto the stone surface for carving.[30]

Another possibility is that cartouches, and some parts of the pictorial carvings, originally may have been painted, inked, or highlighted in some way. Exposure to the elements and the making of rubbings, over centuries, would have abraded any traces of ink or paint on the surface of the pictorial stones. Tombs and funerary halls with painted walls or painted relief tiles are known from Sichuan Province and around the Luoyang area in Henan Province (cat. nos. 7–9). Examples of tombs with painted pictorial stones can also be found closer to the Wu cemetery area in several Eastern Han tombs at Dabaodang in Shaanxi,[31] and at the 150 CE tomb of Zuo Biao in Shanxi (cat. no. 12). An even closer example, in Shandong Province, is Tomb 1 at Beizhai Cun Village in Yi'nan County, where the unrubbed ceiling stones retain their vibrant colors.[32] Further evidence is an inscription of 154 CE on a column of the funerary shrine of Xiang Tajun that records the names of two painters who were employed in building the shrine (fig. 6).[33]

In regard to cartouche panels, we must remember that the practice of making ink rubbings (*ta*) did not begin until sometime in the Period of

Disunity. That being the case, perhaps the cartouches were originally brushed in ink, and only later, after the practice of making rubbings became popular, did a need arise to carve the calligraphy into stone. This may be a reason why the majority of cartouche panels in Chamber 3 are presently carved, while many in Chambers 1 and 2 have remained blank.[34] From the Song through much of the Qing dynasty, scholars were primarily interested not in the pictorial scenes but in the clerical-script calligraphy of the carved inscriptions. Because some early versions of the Confucian Classics had been written in forms of clerical script, establishing the correct form and definition of characters became surpassingly important. This method of inquiry was termed "using clerical script to explain the Classics" (*ligu*), and may be the reason why the more complete set of inscribed cartouches in Chamber 3 has been the focus of rubbing and scholarly attention, while there are no records or rubbings of Chambers 1 and 2 before their stones were discovered in 1786. This scenario suggests that the cartouche inscriptions were all carved after the Han dynasty, raising questions about whether they were carved at one time or added at different times. One cartouche labels a pictorial figure as Zhu Ming, who perhaps lived during the Eastern Jin. This may, or may not, be evidence that the cartouche inscriptions were added after the Han (see Liu's "Recarving the Past," and cat. no. 1.36).

Some surfaces of the Wu pictorial carvings may also have been originally painted. Jiang Yingju argues convincingly that because of the fineness of the intaglio detail lines on the surface of the flat relief carvings, it is unlikely that paint would have been applied over such areas. Never-

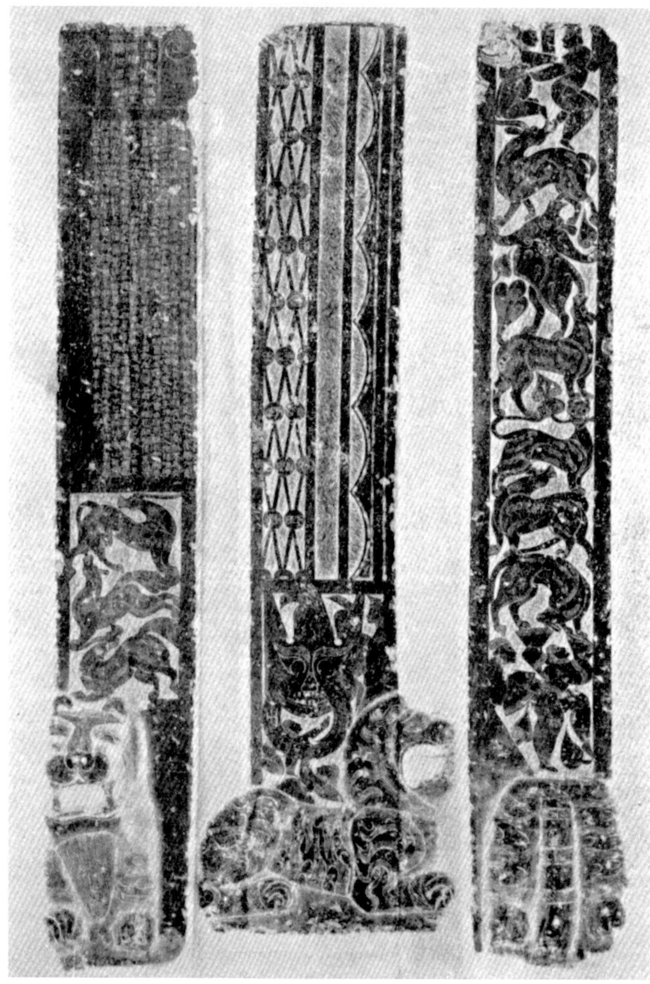

Fig. 6 *Xiang Tajun's funerary shrine column.* Eastern Han dynasty, 154 CE. Changjili, Shandong. Ink-on-paper rubbing. From Luo Fuyi, "Xiang Tajun," *Gugong bowuyuan yuankan* 1960.2, p. 181.

theless, it is also true that the fine detail lines would have been nearly invisible against the natural limestone surface. Colored chalk or pigment might have been rubbed into the incised lines and then wiped off the surrounding surfaces, creating enough contrast to make the details visible.[35] It is also possible that the decorative bands and ornamental borders separating scenes on the pictorial stones were painted. Examples of such painted decorative bands and borders can be seen in the pictorial stones at the Dabaodang tombs. The best supporting evidence that Chambers 1–3 may have been painted, however, is found in Tomb 2 at the Wu cemetery. On the plaster surfaces of the tomb walls there survive traces of simple architectural decorative bands and scrolls delineated in red pigment (see Liu's "Recarving the Past," fig. 1).

When the back, or exterior, surfaces of the Wu cemetery pictorial stones are examined, the stones of Chambers 1 and 2 are roughly hewn, while those of Chamber 3 are flat and finished, with horizontal decorative bands continued from the interior to wrap around the outside.[36] The rough-hewn finish of Chambers 1 and 2 is typical of almost all Han pictorial stones found in Shandong that are said to belong to so-called shrines (*ci* or *citang*).[37] Only Chamber 3 at the Wu cemetery and the first-century stone hall at Xiaotang Shan (Hill of Filial Piety) in Changqing County (traditionally said to be the Western Han shrine of Guo Ju), have flat exterior walls. In terms of architectural typology, this raises the dilemma that if the two-bay, rough-exterior Chambers 1 and 2 are shrines, then the one-bay, flat-exterior Chamber 3 may not be, or vice versa. Alternatively, are any of the three structures actually shrines? Shrines in the Han dynasty seem to have been funerary ritual offering halls restricted to aristocratic families and high officials.[38] The four stele inscriptions linked to the Wu cemetery, however, describe low-ranking local officials. If the linkage is correct, can Chambers 1–3 have been shrines? This brings into question the appropriateness either of calling the reconstructed structures "shrines," or of associating "shrines" with this low-ranking family.

In the Song dynasty the Wu family pictorial stones were first mentioned in Zhao Mingcheng's *Jinshi lu*, where they are said to come from a stone chamber (*shishi*). (It is interesting to note that only pictorial stones belonging to the reconstructed Chamber 3 are mentioned in sources prior to 1786.) The claim that the pictorial stones belonged to a shrine occurs first only later in the Song dynasty, in Hong Gua's *Li shi*, and seems to hinge on a suspect passage in received versions of the Wu Liang stele inscription:

> His filial sons, Zhongzhang, Jizhang, and Jili, and the filial grandson, Ziqiao, personally cultivated what was proper to sons and spent everything the family had [to construct his shrine and altar]. They chose excellent stones from the south side of the southern mountain; they chose those of perfect quality and color without any yellow blemishes. In front they established stone altars in a cleared space; behind they erected a shrine (*citang*). The skilled craftsman Wei Gai engraved the text and carved the designs; he arranged everything in its place. He gave free reign to his talent as expressed in the stunning ease and elegance [of his work].[39]

This passage is not recorded in the entry for the Wu Liang stele in the *Jinshi lu* by Zhao Mingcheng, but appears in two places in Hong Gua's *Li shi*. Moreover, this passage is not included in Hong Gua's primary description and partial transcription of the Wu Liang stele in *juan* ("chapter") 6. Instead, it occurs in his comments on the "Wu family shrines pictorial stone carvings" ("Wushi citang huaxiang") in *juan* 16, and again in his comments to his account of the Wu Liang stele in *juan* 6. By citing this passage only in his comments and not in the main entry on the stele, Hong Gua implied that it was not on any rubbing of the Wu Liang stele that he personally had seen. Instead, he was most likely following some other source. Other received versions of the *Li shi*, however, record this passage differently. Handwritten copies said to be based on the 1325 edition (not extant) include a missing double-page that appears to cite the foregoing passage as part of the Wu Liang stele text in Hong Gua's primary description in *juan* 6.[40] Some Qing-dynasty and most present-day transcriptions of the Wu Liang stele are reconstructed with the passage inserted. Regardless of which received version is correct, Hong Gua himself voiced strong suspicions that this passage was not original to the Wu Liang stele:

> If speaking about funerary and burial matters, it should not be as verbose as this. This stele is not quite half a *xun* unit[41] long and only one *chi* foot wide. Since there are no skillful pictorial carvings and [the lines of inscription] are not arranged in columns, its words are absolutely not those of stele arrangement. Having carefully mulled it over, it appears to me only to describe the pictorial images of a stone chamber.[42]

It is likely the suspect passage only described pictorial stones similar to those associated with the Wu family. Within the passage there is no mention of Wu Liang or a Wu family. The identification of Chamber 3 as a *citang* shrine hinges on this suspect passage alone. What the one-bay and two-bay stone chambers at the Wu cemetery may have actually been in the second and third centuries, consequently, needs to be carefully reconsidered.

The architectural relationship between the stone chambers and the tombs at the cemetery suggests another possible interpretation of the differences between two-bay Chambers 1 and 2 and one-bay Chamber 3. Some Han-dynasty tombs unearthed in the Shandong-Jiangsu-Anhui region have a wall enclosing the burial mound. Centered at the front of these walls are stone chambers with open fronts that resemble the three chambers at the Wu cemetery. At Tombs 1 and 2 (ca. 171 CE) at Chulan, Su Xian County, Anhui, stone chambers attached to tomb-mound walls have been excavated (figs. 7, 8).[43] These suggest that Chambers 1 and 2 at the Wu cemetery may have been located at the front of a walled tomb mound (fig. 9). The front of the wall enclosing a tomb mound would have joined the chamber's side walls near their front edge, where the roughness of the exterior surface is less pronounced. The open front of the chamber would have faced out, while behind the enclosing wall the chamber's rough-hewn exterior wall surfaces would have been hidden from view. It is also possible that the niche at the back end of the chamber partly extended into the tomb mound.[44] If the stone chamber served as a place for offerings to the deceased, offerings would have been brought from the world of the living into the pictorial stone chamber and then placed within the small niche at the back. This would have created a spatial and directional progression from the open world of the living to the confined realm of the afterlife, as reflected in a cross-section of the layout of chamber and tomb. From under the open sky, one moves under the mythological scenes depicted on the ceiling of the two-bay stone chamber, then into the even more confining niche in center of the back wall. The next step would take one down into the tomb beneath the mound. In this way the stone chamber acts as a gateway linking the world of the living with the realm of the afterliving, and if the back of the stone chamber and its niche were partly buried in the mound, the passage from life to afterlife is literally played out in the architecture.

The one-bay Chamber 3, on the other hand, may belong to the same architectural type as Chambers 1 and 2, but may have differed in its physical connection to the tomb and cemetery. Judging from the smooth finish and decorative bands of the exterior walls, it is likely this structure was intended to be seen from all sides. This hypothesis is reinforced by the rows of imitation roof tiles (*walong*) carved along the top surface of the front and back roof slabs. On the roof stones of Chambers 1 and 2, the surviving front-slope slabs all have imitation tiles, while the single remaining stone from the back-slope slab of Chamber 2 (Stone 2-R.3) has a rough unfinished surface.[45] If all three stone chambers at the Wu cemetery were intended as halls where offerings were made to the deceased, the

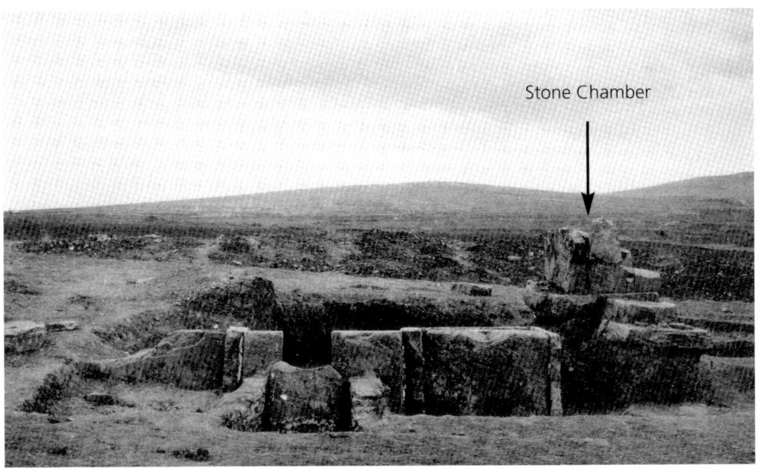

Fig. 7 *Stone chamber (at right) in front of Tomb 2.* Eastern Han dynasty, 171 CE. Chulan, Su Xian County, Anhui. From Wang Buyi, "Anhui Su Xian Chulan Han huaxiang shi mu," *Kaogu xuebao* 1993.4, pl. 19.

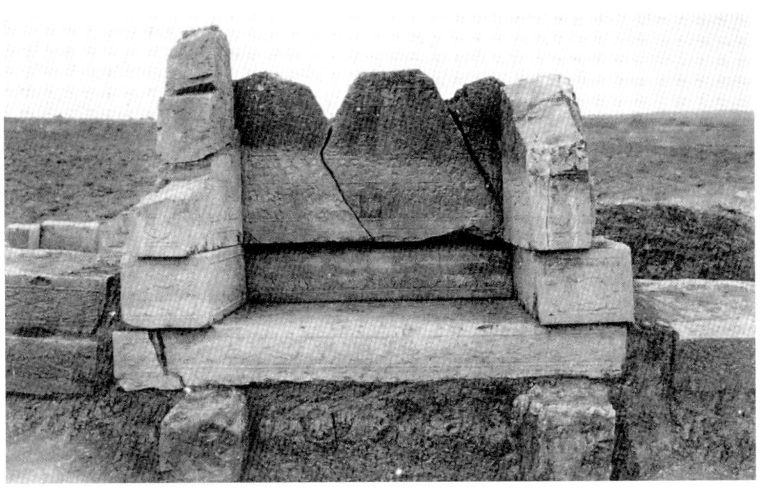

Fig. 8 *Stone chamber in front of Tomb 2.* Eastern Han dynasty, 171 CE. Chulan, Su Xian County, Anhui. From Wang Buyi, "Anhui Su Xian Chulan Han huaxiang shi mu," *Kaogu xuebao* 1993.4, pl. 20.1.

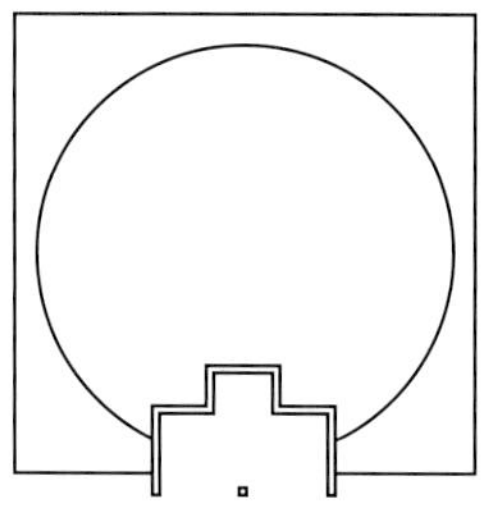

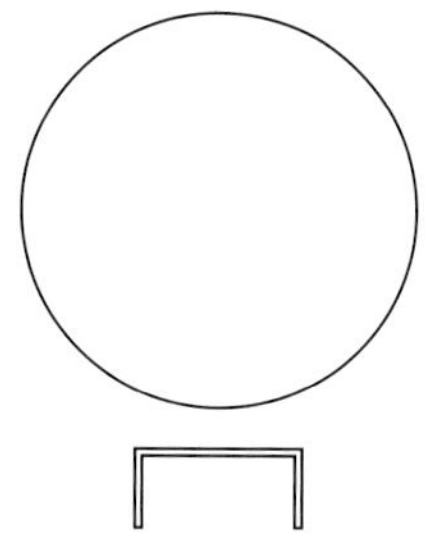

difference may be that Chambers 1 and 2 were connected to the enclosing wall and partly embedded in the mound, whereas Chamber 3 was built without a niche as a freestanding structure next to a tomb without a wall (fig. 10), or, if there was an enclosing wall, was simply not connected to it. It could have been built inside or outside the mound wall, or possibly atop the mound. Another possibility is that Chamber 3 was built to receive offerings not for any individual tomb but for the collective family cemetery. According to the "Tan Gong" chapter in the *Liji* (*Rites records*), Confucius had said: "I have seen some burial mounds (*feng*) that are like halls (*tang*) . . . and others like roof-tiled gates (*Xia wu*) . . . ."[46] Could these mound halls and gates refer to stone chambers embedded in or standing before or atop tomb mounds?

Tombs and Tumuli

Excavated in 1981 about seventy to one hundred meters west and southwest of the Wu cemetery pillar-gate were Tombs 1 and 2 (see Liu's "Recarving the Past," figs. 21, 22, 23).[47] A third stone tomb was discovered between Tombs 1 and 2 in 2002, but it has yet to be documented. With the pillar-gate in the front center, the three tombs form a half arc across the back left of the present cemetery grounds. A road and buildings of Wuzhaishan Cun Village now occupy the back right half of the arc, but it is likely that other tombs were originally located in this area. Other tombs may still be found, but we must keep in mind that some or all of the tombs may not belong to the same burial complex as the pillar-gate. Other than proximity and general orientation, there is no physical or textual evidence that links together any of these burial structures.

Tombs 1 and 2 face northwest, toward the front pillar-gate and away from the mountain in back. In plan and construction both stone tombs have a rear burial chamber with a gallery around three sides. Tomb 1 has a single front chamber flanked by small side rooms. A caisson (*tianjing*) ceiling of stacked squares, each turned at 45 degrees to the next, covers the rear chamber, two caissons cover the front chamber, and flat roof slabs cover the gallery and side rooms. Such caisson roofs are not uncommon in Eastern Han tombs. Tomb 2 has both a front and middle chamber, the latter flanked by small side rooms.[48] A caisson roof covers the rear chamber. Unfortunately the roof stones of the front and middle chambers were earlier removed by local villagers, exposing the chambers to the sky.

Some of the earliest surviving examples of tombs constructed of stone are found in the Shandong region, dating from the fifth century BCE.[49] The abundant supplies of stone in this area, along with concerns about deterioration and robbery, probably contributed to the adoption of this material. The gallery plan seen in Tombs 1 and 2 also has early precedents. Wooden tombs with gallery plans were already evident during the Western Han, and the plan was adopted for brick and stone tombs by the early Eastern Han.[50] The gallery plan of Tombs 1 and 2 corresponds closely with Eastern Han examples, including the tomb of the minister Miao Yu, dated to 151, in Pengcheng, Jiangsu Province (fig. 11).[51]

In building the Wu cemetery tombs, the gray limestone was taken from nearby mountain quarries. The rough blocks may have been worked

Fig. 9 *Proposed plan diagram of two-bay stone chambers (Chambers 1 and 2) and walled tomb mound.*

Fig. 10 *Proposed plan diagram of one-bay stone chamber (Chamber 3) and tomb mound.*

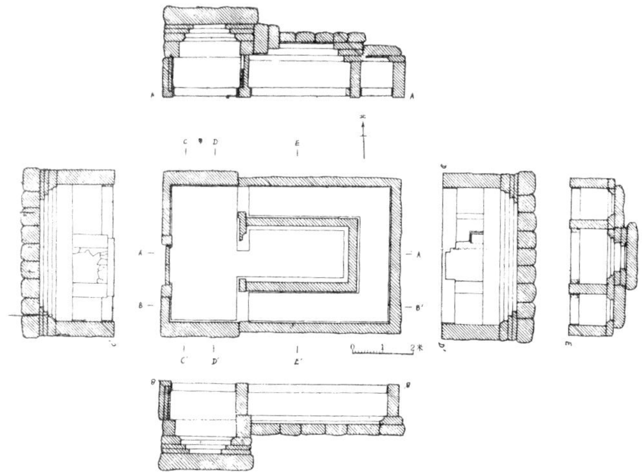

at the quarry, but were probably transported to a local stone workshop. The stones for the tomb were cut either into standard sizes or into custom dimensions, and then carved with surface decoration and scored grooves to receive plaster. Finally, the kit of parts would be moved to the tomb site, fitted to make sure the joints meshed, and assembled. At the cemetery the tomb site would have been cleared and excavated and the foundation prepared. It should be noted that tombs of this period were sometimes excavated to great depths. A vertical shaft or a ramp would have led down to a cave-like space in which the tomb structure was erected. For such deeply underground cave-tombs, a tumulus was optional. Tombs were also built in shallower excavations, with less labor and expense. In such cases the tomb structure would have been assembled in the open air, and a tumulus would have been necessary to cover the aboveground sections.[52]

Prior to burial the tomb door likely remained accessible, but after interment the door would have been sealed and buried as part of the mound. The three tombs at the Wu cemetery appear to have been set only slightly below the ground level of the pillar-gate in the Han. Because they were set in shallow excavations, they were covered by earthen mounds. Above Tomb 1 was a mound constructed of pounded earth (*hangtu*) layers and planted with trees (see Liu's "Recarving the Past," fig. 9). Han texts record many admonitions against building elaborate burial mounds topped by trees, which indicates that such mounds were in fact being built. For example, in the "Xici zhuan" ("Commentary on the attached verbalizations"; ca. late third century BCE) in the *Book of Change* it is noted that: "With burials in antiquity...one did not build a mound or plant trees."[53] Such Han records, ironically, tell us little about actual burial practices in antiquity, but do indicate that burial mounds were being built in the Han dynasty, which is corroborated by archaeological evidence.[54] In fact, the type of tree-topped burial mounds was not uncommon in the Eastern Han. A burial mound with a tree is even pictured in miniature in the Wu cemetery pictorial carvings, in a scene that is identified as Ji Zha hanging his sword over the Lord of Xu's tomb (cat. no. 1.25).[55]

Inside all three tombs, the stone wall surfaces were scored to receive a layer of white plaster. In the middle chamber of Tomb 2 surviving traces of architectural decoration in the form of red-pigment bands and a spiral pattern can be seen on top of the plaster (see Liu's "Recarving the Past," fig. 1). In Tombs 1 and 2 the only pictorial carving is a rectangular panel centered over the exterior of the front doors. In Tomb 1 two pairs of facing fish are superimposed; in Tomb 2 there is only one pair.[56] Probably a rebus for "continued abundance" (*lian yu*), their appearance in both tombs, along with identical decorative framing bands, indicates that the two tombs are probably linked.[57] In addition, the carving style and technique of the fish panels appear to correspond to the other pictorial carved stones found at the cemetery. Furthermore, the same design of opposed fish can be seen just above the inscription on the west gate-pillar (cat. no. 1.43); and the same decorative bands can also be seen in the other pictorial carvings. From this we can infer that the pictorial stones of both the tombs and the reconstructed stone chambers were likely manufactured by the same workshop and probably belong to the same burial complex.

Fig. 11 *Tomb of Miao Yu, plan and cross-section drawings.* Eastern Han dynasty, 151 CE. Pengcheng, Jiangsu. From *Wenwu* 1984.8, p. 23, fig. 3.

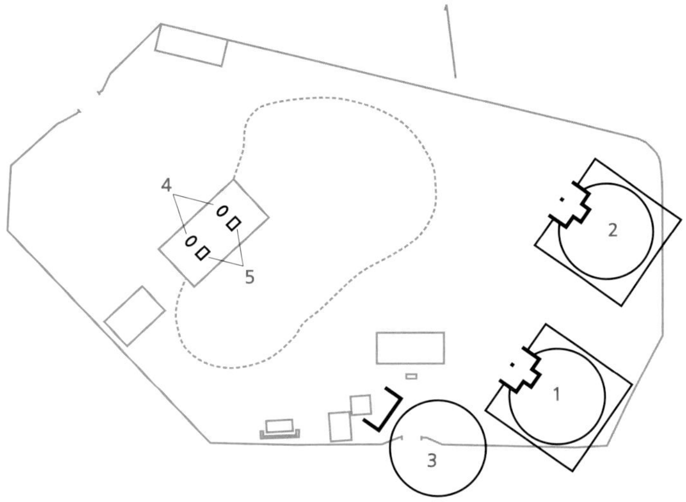

Although all three tombs appear to have been looted before they were properly excavated, fragments of burial objects were recovered from Tomb 1. These "brilliant artifacts" (*mingqi*) included ceramic pieces of a basin, tray, *hu* jar, dishes, eared cups, a model of a farm compound similar to one in this exhibition (cat. no. 15), and a single *wuzhu* bronze coin.[58] These burial artifacts, along with the tombs' gallery plan, proximity and orientation to the pillar-gate, and their shared fish and decorative banding designs, all tend to indicate that the tombs and aboveground structures at the site date from about the same period and may belong together as parts of a single family burial complex.

Cemetery Layout

Having reviewed the architectural typologies of the constituent parts—steles, stone statues, pillar-gate, pictorial stone chambers, and tombs—it is now possible to speculate about the overall layout of the "Wu family shrines" cemetery. The above analyses can be used to refine the general view of the cemetery as being sequentially arranged from front (northwest) to back (southeast), with a spirit path, pair of feline stone sculptures, pillar-gate, steles, stone chambers, and ending with the tombs and mounds.[59] Whether the steles were erected inside the pillar-gate, or anywhere at the cemetery, or even if they were originally erected during the Han dynasty, should be reevaluated. The original position of the pillar-gate in relation to possible walls around the entire cemetery should also be reconsidered. Also questionable is the position of the stone chambers relative to the tomb mounds and walls enclosing the mounds. These questions have been considered above. Here we shall turn our attention to the architectural relationship between the three reconstructed stone chambers and the tombs and other structures at the site.

A clue to the cemetery's configuration can be discerned in Huang Yi's *Brief Record on Building the Wu Family Shrine* [*Preservation Hall*] (*Xiu Wushi Citang ji lüe*; 1787) (see Liu's "Recarving the Past," Appendix).[60] As discussed in "Recarving the Past," from Huang Yi's excavations and subsequent discoveries at the site, the pictorial stones were found scattered in several groups: Front Group (Chamber 1), Left and Rear Groups (Chamber 2), and the so-called Wu Liang Ci Group (Chamber 3). According to the *Brief Record*, the Rear Group stones of Chamber 2 were located northeast of the Wu Liang Ci stones of Chamber 3, and the Front Group stones of Chamber 1 were found to their southeast or south (fig. 12). If we assume that Chamber 3 was located to the southeast on axis with the pillar-gate near the 1981 south compound gate, then the position of Chamber 2 to the northeast would correspond with the location of Tomb 1 or 3, and Chamber 1 would correspond to Tomb 2 (see Liu's "Recarving the Past"). This reconfigured layout may find corroboration in Sekino Tadashi's survey of the site published in 1916. To the right (northeast) of the gate-pillars, according to Sekino, were what appeared to be "stones once used for pavement and steps" (*kaidan seki*) and stone columns. These stones are depicted to the northeast of the pillar-gate in his plan drawing of the site (fig. 13). Farther to the right (northeast or

Fig. 12 *Site reconstruction map showing possible locations of Chambers 1, 2, and 3 at Wu site.* Modified from Jiang and Wu, *Handai Wushi muqun shike yanjiu*, p. 2, fig. 2.

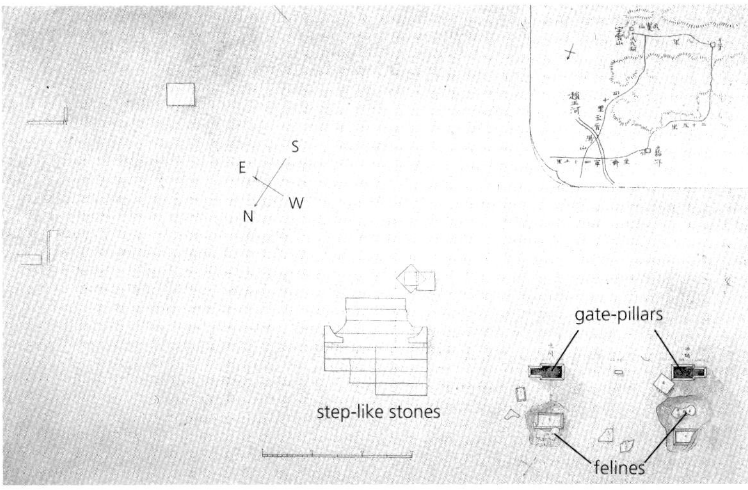

east), Sekino reported more scattered stones, behind which was a large depression where he believed the stone chambers once stood.[61] The back edge of this hollow possibly corresponds to the locations of Tombs 1–3.

The location of the two-bay Chambers 1 and 2 in close proximity to tombs with mounds may support the idea that they were partly embedded in the mounds or placed at the front side of a wall enclosing each mound. In contrast, the location of the one-bay Chamber 3 on axis with the pillar-gate but without an associated tomb or mound may suggest it was built as a freestanding structure. On the other hand, the area behind Chamber 3's putative location is now occupied by a village road, so it is possible that a tomb and mound once existed behind the chamber.

From their excavated locations, architectural typology, pictorial content, and exterior treatment, many other site configurations for the three stone chambers are possible. Another possible reconfiguration reflects a ritual burial program outlined in the *Liji*. In the "Royal Regulations" ("Wang zhi") section, the number and arrangement of ancestral temples for kings, princes, and officials are enumerated. For high officials with the rank of counselor (*dafu*) are stipulated "three temples—one of the left (*zhao*; to the east), one of the right (*mu*; to the west), and [in the center] that of his great ancestor—in all three."[62] Such an arrangement allowed for a temple dedicated to the great ancestor in the center, and side temples dedicated to the most recently deceased ancestors in each generation. The layout of the stone chambers in the Wu cemetery may have followed similar regulations; on the other hand, such a programmatic scheme may have been inappropriate for a family of low-ranking local officials.

Fig. 13 *Survey map of Wu site in 1907*. From Sekino Tadashi, *Shina Santōshō ni okeru Kandai funbo no hyōshoku*, pl. 28.

Another traditional assumption in need of reexamination is the patriarchic worship structure thought to dominate the Wu family burial complex. This assumption partly derives from the four received stele inscriptions, supposedly dedicated to four male members of the Wu family. We must, however, remain open to the possibility of a tandem male-female family ancestral hierarchy.[63] Such a hierarchy might explain the appearance in all three stone chambers of the central pavilion scene with a mythological tree. The intertwined tree may have symbolized family harmony and conjugal bliss. The ancestral father or lord of the house may be identified with the large male figure receiving homage in the lower story, while the ancestral mother is the pivotal figure in the upper story. The paired images of the Queen Mother of the West and King Father of the East in facing gables in Chambers 1–3 could also have been understood to embody the family matriarch and patriarch. In this sense, each stone chamber may not have been dedicated to a single male family member; instead, the entire burial precinct may have functioned as a ritual center for the collective family ancestors.

Acknowledgments

Earlier versions of this essay were delivered at the Association of Asian Studies National Conference, Washington, D.C., April 2002, and at "The Early China Symposium in honor of Cho-Yun Hsu: Funerary Art and Architecture of the Han Dynasty" at the University of Pittsburgh, February 2003. I received invaluable suggestions from Jiang Yingju, Xin Lixiang, and Wu Hung. I am especially grateful to Anthony Barbieri-Low and Michael Nylan, who worked with me in developing many of the ideas in this essay, and to Eileen Hsu for her research.

Notes

1. On the concept of architectural typology, see Alan Colquhoun, "Typology and Design Method," *Arena*, vol. 83 (1967); reprinted in Colquhoun, *Essays in Architectural Criticism: Modern Architecture and Historical Change* (Cambridge, Mass.: MIT Press, 1981), pp. 43–50; Nikolaus Pevsner, *A History of Building Types* (Princeton: Princeton University Press, 1976), esp. pp. 6–7, 9–10; Rafael Moneo, "On Typology," *Oppositions*, vol. 13 (1978), pp. 22–45. In this essay "typology" is treated as the study not of a fixed type or ideal, but of conventional "schema" subject to "correction" according to changing functional, ceremonial, and other circumstances. On the artistic process of "schema" and "correction," see E.H. Gombrich, *Art and Illusion: A Study in the Psychology of Pictorial Representation*, 2d ed. (Princeton: Princeton University Press, 1961), passim, esp. pp. 73–83, 87–90, 116, 146.

2. See commentary by Qu Jingrun in *Jining zhili zhou xu zhi* (1925; reprint, Taipei: Xuesheng shuju, 1968), "Han bei tiao," *juan* 19, p. 55a. Also see Zhu Xilu, ed., *Wushi Ci Han huaxiang shi* (Ji'nan: Shandong meishu chubanshe, 1986), no. 109; Gong Yanxing, ed., *Jining quan Han bei* (Ji'nan: Qi-Lu shushe, 1990), p. 239, pl. 105 (right), in which it is labeled as the Wu Liang stele. The stele is also described in Jiang Yingju and Wu Wenqi, *Handai Wushi muqun shike yanjiu* ([Ji'nan]: Shandong meishu chubanshe, 1995), pp. 21–22.

3. Inscribed tomb steles seem not to have become popular until the Eastern Han. See Sun Ji, *Handai wuzhi wenhua ziliao tushuo* (Beijing: Wenwu chubanshe, 1991), pp. 417–19.

4. Ouyang Xiu, *Jigu lu*, *Yingyin Wenyuange Siku quanshu* edition (Taipei: Taiwan shangwu yinshuguan, 1983–1986), *juan* 3, p. 2a.

5. Jiang and Wu, *Handai Wushi muqun shike yanjiu*, p. 3; Wu Hung, *The Wu Liang Shrine: The Ideology of Early Chinese Pictorial Art* (Stanford: Stanford University Press, 1989), pp. 36, diagram 4.

6. The Xianyu Huang stele with the inscribed date of 165 CE was found directly south of a tomb now attributed by virtue of this stele to Xianyu Huang, Governor (*taishou*) of Yanmen. This tomb, however, was found among a group of tombs, and its exact relation to the stele is speculative. See Tianjin Shi wenwu guanlichu and Wuqing Xian wenhuaguan, "Wuqing Xian faxian Donghan Xianyu Huang mu bei," *Wenwu* 1974.8, pp. 68–72; Tianjin Shi wenwu guanlichu kaogudui, "Wuqing Donghan Xianyu Huang mu," *Kaogu xuebao* 1982.3, pp. 351–66. Because the formulaic characters *Han gu* appear at the beginning of the stele heading, this stone may actually postdate the Han dynasty (see below). *Han gu* also appears in the heading of the surviving Wu Rong stele, and is sometimes restored to transcriptions of the Wu Ban stele. For the latter, see Jiang and Wu, *Handai Wushi muqun shike yanjiu*, p. 19.

7. See Nylan's "Addicted to Antiquity" in this catalogue. Also see Sun Ji, *Handai wuzhi wenhua ziliao tushuo*, p. 417.

8. An example is a fallen stele found to the south of the tomb mound near Dingtao. The stele and mound are those of Wei Ran, a general of Qin and younger brother of the empress. According to Shi Zhecun, comp., *Shuijing zhu bei lu* (Tianjin: Tianjin guji chubanshe, 1987), p. 51: "This stone stele was probably erected by later generations."

9. Shi Zhecun, comp., *Shuijing zhu bei lu*, pp. 42, 51. On the Wu Ban stele heading, see Jiang and Wu, *Handai Wushi muqun shike yanjiu*, p. 19. On the other hand, as suggested to me by Michael Nylan, the term *Han* may not refer to the dynasty per se but may indicate instead that the deceased had held central government office.

10. Ma Ziyun, *Beitie jianding qianshuo* (Beijing: Zijincheng chubanshe, 1986), pp. 3–6.

11. Sun Xidan, comp. *Liji ji jie* (Beijing: Zhonghua shuju, 1989), p. 281. Translation modified from James Legge, *The Li Ki*, in *The Sacred Books of the East*, ed. F. Max Müller, vol. 28 (Oxford: Clarendon Press, 1885), p. 184.

12. *Liji ji jie*, p. 281.

13. Han Wei, "Qin gong da mu fajue ji," *Zhongguo* [also known as *Renmin hua bao*] 1987.5, pp. 22–25.

14. Whether these statues represent lions is discussed in Liu's "Recarving the Past" in this catalogue.

15. On Han pillar-gates, see Chen Mingda, "Handai de shique," *Wenwu* 1961.12, pp. 9–23; Lü Pin, ed., *Zhongyue san Han que* (Beijing: Wenwu chubanshe, 1990); Tang Changshou, "Handai muzang menque kaobian," *Zhongyuan wenwu* 1991.3, pp. 67–74; *Sichuan Handai shique*, ed. Chongqing Shi wenhuaju, Chongqing Shi

bowuguan, Xu Wenbin [et al.] (Beijing: Wenwu chubanshe, 1992); Xin Lixiang, *Handai huaxiang shi zonghe yanjiu* (Beijing: Wenwu chubanshe, 2000), pp. 293–321; Jiang Yingju and Yang Aiguo, *Handai huaxiang shi yu huaxiang zhuan* (Beijing: Wenwu chubanshe, 2001), pp. 96–100. Also see Susan N. Erickson, "Han Dynasty Que Towers in Henan, Shandong, and Sichuan Provinces," paper to be presented at the "Recarving China's Past" symposium at Princeton University, April 30–May 1, 2005.

16. Fan Ye, comp., *Hou Hanshu* (Beijing: Zhonghua shuju, 1965), *juan* 42, p. 1450, states, "For large tombs build a grave mound, and open a spirit path." Li Xian's (Tang dynasty) annotations to this passage says: "A path is opened in front of the tomb, and stone columns are built to be markers. [It is] called a spirit path." The stone-column markers at the mouth of the spirit path probably correspond to gate-pillars.

17. Jiang and Wu, *Handai Wushi muqun shike yanjiu*, pp. 9–10.

18. See Nanjing bowuyuan and Pi Xian wenhua guan, "Donghan Pengcheng xiang Miao Yu mu," *Wenwu* 1984.8, pp. 22–23; and Wang Buyi, "Anhui Su Xian Chulan Han huaxiang shi mu," *Kaogu xuebao* 1993.4, pp. 516, 523.

19. For pre-Han and Han examples, see Xin Lixiang, *Handai huaxiang shi*, pp. 293–94. Also see Tang Changshou, "Handai muzang menque kaobian," pp. 68–71.

20. See *Sichuan Handai shique*, ed. Chongqing Shi wenhuaju.

21. Anthony Barbieri-Low brought this to my attention using a rubbing of the east gate-pillar in the collection of the Academia Sinica, Taipei.

22. See Gong Yanxing, ed., *Jining quan Han bei*, p. 43.

23. See *Sichuan Handai shique*, ed. Chongqing Shi wenhuaju, pp. 167–70.

24. Transcribed in Jiang and Wu, *Handai Wushi muqun shike yanjiu*, p. 12.

25. Xin Lixiang, *Handai huaxiang shi*, pp. 293–94.

26. *Han guan dian zhi*, cited in *Shuijing zhu jiao*, annot. Wang Guowei (Shanghai: Shanghai renmin chubanshe, 1984), p. 541.

27. Tang Changshou, "Handai muzang menque kaobian," pp. 70–71, attempts to match surviving steles to the official rank of the tomb occupants. The resulting chart seems to indicate little direct correlation between high rank and having pillar-gates. (Tang suggests that the size of the tomb mound may be a better indicator of rank). This study, however, does not always list the correct office title, or question the attributed identities of the tomb occupants. For example, Tang states that the Wu cemetery pillar-gate belonged to a commoner (i.e., Wu Liang), ignoring the offices held by Wu Ban, Wu Rong, and Wu Kaiming. The study also does not distinguish clearly between pillar-gates and watchtowers as separate types. Jiang Yingju observes that almost no pictorial shrines or tombs belonging to those of high rank were decorated with carved decoration, whereas almost all carved examples appear to belong to people of low or no rank. See Jiang Yingju, "Guanyu Han huaxiang shi chansheng beijing yu yishu gongneng de sikao," *Kaogu* 1998.11, p. 90. I thank Anthony Barbieri-Low for bringing this article to my attention.

28. See Xin Lixiang, *Handai huaxiang shi*, pp. 31–33.

29. On various classification systems for pictorial stone-carving techniques, see Jiang Yingju and Wu Wenqi, "Shilun Shandong Han huaxiang shi de fenbu, kefa yu fenqi," *Kaogu yu wenwu* 1980.4, pp. 108–14; Yang Boda, "Shilun Shandong huaxiang shi de kefa," *Gugong bowuyuan yuankan* 1987.4, pp. 4–24; Li Falin, *Hanhua kaoshi he yanjiu* (Beijing: Zhongguo wenlian chubanshe, 2000), pp. 79–93; Xin Lixiang, *Handai huaxiang shi*, pp. 27–39. I am indebted to Eileen Hsu for her assistance in compiling and cross-referencing the various systems.

30. Yang Boda, "Shilun Shandong huaxiang shi de kefa," p. 23.

31. On the Dabaodang tombs, see Shaanxi Sheng kaogu yanjiusuo and Yulin diqu wenwu guanli weiyuanhui, eds., "Shaanxi Shenmu Dabaodang di 11 hao di 23 hao Han huaxiang shi mu fajue jianbao," *Wenwu* 1997.9, pp. 26–35; Han Wei, ed., *Shaanxi Shenmu Dabaodang Han caihui huaxiang shi* (Chongqing: Chongqing chubanshe, 2000).

32. An Zhimin, "Lun Yi'nan huaxiang shi mu de niandai wenti," *Kaogu tongxun* 1955.2, pp. 16–22; Zeng Zhaoyu, Jiang Baogeng, and Li Zhongyi, *Yi'nan gu huaxiang shi mu fajue baogao* (Shanghai: Wenhuabu guanliju, 1956); Shih Hsio-yen, "I-nan and Related Tombs," *Artibus Asiae*, vol. 22, no. 4 (1959), pp. 277–312; Lydia duPont Thompson, "The Yi'nan Tomb: Narrative and Ritual in Pictorial Art of the Eastern Han (25–220 CE)" (PhD diss., Institute of Fine Arts, New York University, 1998). The dating of this tomb

to the Eastern Han or later (3d–5th centuries) is still a matter of active controversy.
33. The shrine (*citang*) was located in Changjili Village, Xixiang Township, in the district of Donge, Dongjun Commandery. The surviving column is in the collection of the Palace Museum, Beijing. The inscription is transcribed in Luo Fuyi, "Xiang Tajun shi citang tizi jieshi," *Gugong bowuyuan yuankan* 1960.2, pp. 178–81. The relevant passage reads: "At year-end worship offerings, the sons and grandsons were pleased. Although the [shrine] hall is small, it took a long time [to build]: the stones are from the Nanshan hills, and after more than two years it is only now completed [in 154]. [Employed] were over ten persons, including the master builders (*shi shi*) Cao Yi and Rong Bao from Xiaqiu District, Shanyang Commandery; the painters Dai Sheng from Gaoping District, and Shao Qiangsheng. It cost 25,000 [cash?]. From morning to dusk we waited upon the builders, not daring to lose their favor, [yet still we] cannot fully thank heaven for its blessings or ever repay those of our parents." Yang Boda speculates that the painters only supplied base drawings for the stone craftsmen to carve. See Yang Boda, "Shilun Shandong huaxiang shi de kefa," p. 23.
34. In some instances the calligraphy in the cartouches also did not fit in the allotted space and had to be incised over figures in a scene, in others more than one calligraphic style appears on the same stone. Such instances may also be due to later recarving.
35. This alternative was suggested to me in conversation with Michael Nylan.
36. The horizontal decorative bands, however, do not continue across the faces of the *Wu jia lin* column fragment (Stone 3-E.2, cat. no. 1.42) that is placed at the front of the east wall of Chamber 3 in Jiang Yingju and Wu Wenqi's reconstruction. The dimensions of this column also do not match the thickness of the east wall, suggesting it may belong to a different structure.
37. In modern usage, the term "shrine" has also been used broadly to include "sacrifice temples" (*cimiao*), "taking-food halls" (*shitang* or *zhuanshitang*), and "fasting halls" (*zhaici* or *shizhaici*). See Xin Lixiang, *Handai huaxiang shi*, pp. 67–74. Although these different types of structures may be somewhat similar in architectural form, as indicated by their names, they differ in function and probably should not be grouped as a single architectural type.
38. For discussions concerning shrines in the Han dynasty, see Yang Kuan, *Zhongguo gudai lingqin zhidu shi yanjiu* (Shanghai: Shanghai guji chubanshe, 1985), pp. 123–32; Xu Jianguo, "Xuzhou Han huaxiang shi shici jianzhu," *Zhongyuan wenwu* 1993.2, pp. 53–60; Xin Lixiang, *Handai huaxiang shi*, pp. 66–83; Jiang Yingju and Yang Aiguo, *Handai huaxiang shi yu huaxiang zhuan*, pp. 83–96.
39. Hong Gua, *Li shi*, *Yingyin Wenyuange Siku quanshu* edition (Taipei: Taiwan shangwu yinshuguan, 1983–1986), *juan* 6, pp. 14b–15a, and *juan* 16, pp. 5a–b.
40. The missing double-page is included as a supplement to Hong Gua, *Li shi*, *Sibu congkan sanbian* edition (Taipei: Shangwu yinshuguan, 1975), *juan* 6, pp. 13-*bu* a–b. I thank Eileen Hsu for bringing the supplement to my attention.
41. One *xun* unit equals 8 *chi* feet.
42. Hong Gua, *Li shi*, *Yingyin Wenyuange Siku quanshu* edition, *juan* 6, pp. 14b-15a. Thanks to Eileen Hsu for bringing this passage to my attention and for her help on the translation.
43. Discussed above in the "Pillar-Gate and Stone Statues" section. See Wang Buyi, "Chulan Han huaxiang shi ji you guan wuxiang de renshi," *Zhongyuan wenwu* 1991.3, pp. 60–66; Wang, "Anhui Su Xian Chulan Han huaxiang shi mu," pp. 515–49.
44. The idea that the rear of the chambers was possibly embedded in the tomb mound was developed with Anthony Barbieri-Low during 2001–2002. Jiang Yingju also discusses this possibility in "Cong Wushi Ci yu Songshan xiao citang fuyuan shuo Handai huaxiang shi citang," unpublished paper delivered at "The Early China Symposium: Funerary Art and Architecture of the Han Dynasty" at the University of Pittsburgh, February 27, 2003.
45. These are on-site observations gathered in summer 2002 with Anthony Barbieri-Low. For a description of the exterior surface of Stone 2-R.3 (R.1), see Jiang and Wu, *Handai Wushi muqun shike yanjiu*, p. 46.
46. *Liji ji jie*, p. 228. This translation follows Zheng Xuan's glosses on the terms *feng* and *Xia wu*. This passage is translated slightly differently in Legge, *Li Ki*, p. 156; and in Séraphin Couvreur, *Li Ki ou Mémoires sur les bienséances et les cérémonies*, 2d ed. (Ho Kien Fou: Imprimerie de la Mission Catholique, 1913), vol. 1, p. 179.

47. Jiang and Wu, *Handai Wushi muqun shike yanjiu*, pp. 119–27.

48. The plan drawing of Tomb 2 in Jiang and Wu, *Handai Wushi muqun shike yanjiu*, p. 125, fig. 17.2, does not include the two side rooms off the middle chamber.

49. Shandong Sheng bowuguan, "Linzi Langjiazhuang yihao Dongzhou xunren mu," *Kaogu xuebao*, 1977.1, pp. 74–75; Robert Thorp, "Mortuary Art and Architecture of Early Imperial China" (PhD diss., University of Kansas, 1979), p. 49.

50. Thorp, "Mortuary Art and Architecture," pp. 141–50, 156–58. In grouping tombs according to plan type, Thorp speculates that the two main types—gallery and axial layouts—first originated as royal tombs and then were appropriated by officials and commoners. There are many different tomb categorization schemes. Some attempt to establish a stylistic chronology, others try to reflect changes in Han social or belief systems. See Yu Weichao, *Handai zhu houwang yu lie hou muzang de xingzhi fenxi* (1980); reprinted in *Xianqin Lianghan kaoguxue lunji* (Beijing: Wenwu chubanshe, 1985), pp. 117–24; Wu Zengde and Xiao Yuanda, "Jiu daxing Handai huaxiang shi mu de xingzhi lun Han zhi," *Zhongyuan wenwu* 1985.3, pp. 55–62; Jessica Rawson, "The Eternal Palaces of the Western Han: A New View of the Universe," *Artibus Asiae*, vol. 49, no. 1/2 (1999), pp. 5–58; Jiang and Yang, *Handai huaxiang shi yu huaxiang zhuan*, pp. 72–83.

51. Nanjing bowuyuan and Pi Xian wenhua guan, "Donghan Pengcheng xiang Miao Yu mu," *Wenwu* 1984.8, pp. 22–29.

52. For one view on the emergence of burial mounds in China beginning in the mid 4th century BCE, see "Origin and Development of Burial Mounds in China," in Sekino Takeshi, *Chūgoku kokogaku kenkyū* (Tokyo: Tōkyō daigaku shuppankai, 1963), pp. 563–91.

53. Xin Lixiang, *Handai huaxiang shi*, pp. 67, 68. Also see Richard Wilhelm and Cary F. Baynes, *The I Ching or Book of Changes* (German trans. 1924; English trans. 1950), 3d ed. (Princeton: Princeton University Press, 1967), p. 335.

54. Xin Lixiang, *Handai huaxiang shi*, pp. 67, 69. Such admonitions may have been rhetorical admonitions against extravagant funerary practices, yet in some cases they demonstrate a fear that such aboveground tomb markers would invite tomb robbers. For example, see Ban Gu, comp., *Hanshu* (Beijing: Zhonghua shuju, 1962), *juan* 72, p. 3085, where for his own burial preparations Gong Sheng said, "Do not follow custom in making my mound, or planting *bo*-cedars, or in building a shrine (*citang*)." An ancient form of the character *ye* meaning "wilderness" or "tomb" (as in the Tang-dynasty usage *dangye*), is written with two trees (*lin*) over an earth radical (*tu*).

55. Anthony Barbieri-Low, in correspondence dated March 28, 2002, points out that in other versions of this scene, the tree is often depicted without the tomb mound. But the *Shiji*, comp. Sima Qian (Beijing: Zhonghua shuju, 1959), p. 1459, states that the sword was hung on a tree over a tomb mound. The pre-Qin origin of the story (Sima Qian relies on earlier sources) also implies that tomb mounds with trees may not have been uncommon in the Warring States period or earlier.

56. For photographs of rubbings of these two fish panels, see Jiang and Wu, *Handai Wushi muqun shike yanjiu*, p. 121, fig. 15 and p. 126, fig. 18.

57. On three sides of both panels are identical decorative bands. From the inside of the panel to the perimeter, these are: wave pattern, plain, double-diamond pattern, connected-arc pattern, and plain bands.

58. Jiang and Wu, *Handai Wushi muqun shike yanjiu*, pp. 122–24. On "brilliant artifacts," see the author's essay in this catalogue "Concept of 'Brilliant Artifacts' in Han-Dynasty Burial Objects and Funerary Architecture."

59. See n. 5 above.

60. Huang Yi, *Xiu Wushi Citang ji lüe*, in Jiang and Wu, *Handai Wushi muqun shike yanjiu*, pp. 132–33.

61. In Sekino Tei [Sekino Tadashi], "Stone Mortuary Shrines with Engraved Tablets of Ancient China under the Latter Han Dynasty," part II, *Kokka*, vol. 19, no. 227 (1909), p. 302, the English-language description "stones once used for pavement and steps" corresponds to the term *kaidan seki* in Sekino Tadashi, *Shina Santōshō ni okeru Kandai funbo no hyōshoku* (Tokyo: Imperial University of Tokyo, 1916), text p. 26, and pl. 28.

62. *Liji ji jie*, 13/343. Translation modified from Legge, *Li Ki*, p. 223–25.

63. It should be noted that the Wu Kaiming stele inscription records the death of his and Wu Liang's mother in 145, but their father is never mentioned in any inscription.

Selected Bibliography

Abe, Stanley K. *Ordinary Images*. Chicago: University of Chicago Press, 2002.

Bai, Qianshen. "The Artistic and Intellectual Dimensions of Chinese Calligraphy Rubbings: Some Examples from the Collection of Robert Hatfield Ellsworth." *Orientations*, vol. 30, no. 3 (1999), pp. 82–88.

———. *Fu Shan's World: The Transformation of Chinese Calligraphy in the Seventeenth Century*. Cambridge, Mass.: Harvard University Asia Center, 2003.

———. "Notes on Fu Shan's *Selections from the Zuozhuan* Calligraphy Album." *Record of the Princeton University Art Museum*, vol. 61 (2002), pp. 5–25.

———. "Qing chu jinshi xue de fuxing dui Badashanren wannian shufeng de yingxiang" ("Influence of the early Qing revival of the study of metal and stone inscriptions on the late calligraphy of Badashanren"). *Gugong xueshu jikan*, vol. 12, no. 3 (1995), pp. 89–124.

Bao Ding, Liu Dunzhen, and Liang Sicheng. "Handai de jianzhu shiyang yu zhuangshi" ("Form and decoration in Han architecture"). *Zhongguo yingzao xueshe huikan*, vol. 5, no. 2 (1934); reprinted in *Liang Sicheng quanji* (*Anthology of Liang Sicheng*), pp. 251–90. Beijing: Zhongguo jianzhu gongye chubanshe, 2001.

Barbieri-Low, Anthony J. "The Organization of Imperial Workshops during the Han Dynasty." PhD diss., Princeton University, 2001.

———. "Roman Themes in a Group of Eastern Han Lacquer Vessels." *Orientations* (May 2001), pp. 52–58.

Beningson, Susan L., Cary Y. Liu et al. *Providing for the Afterlife: Brilliant Artifacts from Shandong*. New York: China Institute Gallery, 2005.

Berger, Patricia. "The Battle at the Bridge at Wu Liang Tz'u: A Problem in Method." *Early China*, vol. 2 (1976), pp. 3–8.

———. "Purity and Pollution in Han Art." *Archives of Asian Art*, vol. 36 (1983), pp. 40–55.

———. "Rites and Festivities in the Art of Eastern Han China: Shantung and Kiangsu Provinces." PhD diss., University of California, Berkeley, 1980.

Bielenstein, Hans. *The Bureaucracy of Han Times*. Cambridge: Cambridge University Press, 1980.

———. "The Census of China during the Period 2–742 AD." *Bulletin of the Museum of Far Eastern Antiquities*, vol. 19 (1947), pp. 125–63.

———. "Lo-yang in Later Han Times." *Bulletin of the Museum of Far Eastern Antiquities*, vol. 48 (1976), pp. 1–142.

Bower, Virginia L. *From Court to Caravan: Chinese Tomb Sculptures from the Collection of Anthony M. Solomon*. Ed. Robert D. Mowry. Cambridge, Mass.: Harvard University Art Museums, 2002.

Brown, Miranda. "Did the Ancient Chinese Attempt to Preserve Corpses? A Reconsideration of the Elite Conceptions of Death." *Journal of East Asian Archaeology*, vol. 4, nos. 1–4 (2002), pp. 201–23.

———. "Mothers and Sons in Warring States and Han China, 453 BC–AD 220." *NAN NUU: Men, Women and Gender in Early and Imperial China*, vol. 5, no. 2 (2003), pp. 137–69.

Bulling, Anneliese. "Three Popular Motifs in the Art of the Eastern Han Period: Lifting the Tripod, the Crossing of the Bridge, Divinities." *Archives of Asian Art*, vol. 20 (1966), pp. 25–53.

Bushell, Stephen W. "Inscriptions from the Tombs of the Wu Family from the Tzu-yun-shan (Purple Cloud Hills), 28 *li* south of the city Chia-hsiang-hsien in the Province of Shantung." In *Abhandlungen und Vorträge des Fünften Internationalen Orientalisten-Congresses*, II, *Ostasiatischen* sec., pp. 79–80. Berlin: A. Asher, 1882.

Chang Renxia, Jiang Yingju, and Gao Wen, eds. *Huaxiang shi huaxiang zhuan* (*Pictorial stone and brick carvings*). Vol. 18 of *Zhongguo meishu quanji: Huihua bian* (*Compendium of Chinese art: Painting*). Shanghai: Shanghai renmin meishu chubanshe, 1988.

Chavannes, Édouard. *Mission archéologique dans la Chine septentrionale* (*Archaeological Mission to Northern China*). 2 vols. of text, 4 vols. of plates. Paris: Imprimerie Nationale, 1913 and 1915.

———. *La sculpture sur pierre en Chine au temps des deux dynasties Han*. Paris: Ernest Leroux, 1893.

Choi, Seung Kew. "Tomb Complexes of Later Han Dynasty in Shandong Province: Structural and Iconographic Problems of Relief Stone Tomb." PhD diss., University of Pittsburgh, 1988.

Chongqing Shi wenhuaju et al., eds. *Sichuan Handai shique* (*Han pillar-gates in Sichuan*). Beijing: Wenwu chubanshe, 1992.

Ch'ü, T'ung-tsu. *Han Social Structure*. Ed. Jack L. Dull. Seattle and London: University of Washington Press, 1972.

Cook, Constance A. "Scribes, Cooks and Artisans: Breaking Zhou Tradition." *Early China*, vol. 20 (1995), pp. 241–78.

Croissant, Doris. "Funktion und Wanddekor in der Opferschreine von Wu-Liang-Tz'u: Typologische und Iconographische Untersuchungen" ("Function and wall decoration in the Wu Liang offering shrine"). *Monumenta Serica*, vol. 23 (1964), pp. 95–105.

Dien, Albert E. "Armor in China before the Tang Dynasty." *Journal of East Asian Archaeology*, vol. 2, nos. 3–4 (2000), pp. 23–59.

———. "Chinese Beliefs in the Afterworld." In Los Angeles County Museum of Art, *The Quest for Eternity*, pp. 1–16. Los Angeles: Los Angeles County Museum of Art; San Francisco: Chronicle Books, 1987.

———. "A Study of Early Chinese Armor." *Artibus Asiae*, vol. 43, nos. 1/2 (1981–1982), pp. 5–67.

Doi Yoshiko. *Kodai Chūgoku no gazōseki* (*Pictorial stone carvings of ancient China*). Tokyo: Dōhōsha, 1986.

Drake, F. S. "Sculptured Stones of the Han Dynasty." *Monumenta Serica*, vol. 8 (1943), pp. 280–318.

Ebrey, Patricia. "Later Han Stone Inscriptions." *Harvard Journal of Asiatic Studies*, vol. 40, no. 2 (1980), pp. 325–53.

———. "Patron-client Relations in the Late Han." *Journal of the American Oriental Society*, vol. 103, no. 3 (1983), pp. 533–42.

———. "Toward a Better Understanding of the Later Han Upper Class." In *State and Society in Early Medieval China*, pp. 32–48. Ed. Albert Dien. Stanford: Stanford University Press, 1990.

Erickson, Susan N. "Boshanlu—Mountain Censers of the Western Han Period: A Typological and Iconographical Analysis." *Archives of Asian Art*, vol. 45 (1992), pp. 6–28.

———. "Eastern Han Dynasty Cliff Tombs of Santai Xian, Sichuan Province." *Journal of East Asian Archaeology*, vol. 5, nos. 1–4 (forthcoming).

———. "Money Trees of the Eastern Han Dynasty." *Bulletin of the Museum of Far Eastern Antiquities*, vol. 66 (1994), pp. 5–115.

———. "'Twirling Their Long Sleeves, They Dance Again and Again…' Jade Plaque Sleeve Dancers of the Western Han Dynasty." *Ars Orientalis*, vol. 24 (1994), pp. 39–63.

Fairbank, Wilma. *Adventures in Retrieval: Han Murals and Shang Bronze Molds*. Harvard-Yenching Institute Studies 28. Cambridge, Mass.: Harvard University Press, 1972.

———. "The Offering Shrines of 'Wu Liang Tz'u'." *Harvard Journal of Asiatic Studies*, vol. 6, no. 1 (1941), pp. 1–36; reprinted in Fairbank, *Adventures in Retrieval: Han Murals and Shang Bronze Molds*, pp. 43–86.

———. "A Structural Key to Han Mural Art." *Harvard Journal of Asiatic Studies*, vol. 7, no. 1 (1942), pp. 52–88; reprinted in Fairbank, *Adventures in Retrieval: Han Murals and Shang Bronze Molds*, pp. 89–140.

——— and Masao Kitano. "Han Mural Paintings in the Pei-yuan Tomb at Liao-yang, South Manchuria." In Fairbank, *Adventures in Retrieval: Han Murals and Shang Bronze Molds*, pp. 143–69.

Feng Yunpeng and Feng Yunyuan. *Jinshi suo* (*Index to metal and stone carvings*). Reprint of 1821 Suiguzhai edition. Shanghai: Shangwu yinshuguan, 1934.

Fontein, Jan and Wu Tung. *Unearthing China's Past*. Boston: Museum of Fine Arts, 1973.

Fu Lecheng. "Handai de Shandong yu Shanxi" ("Shandong and Shanxi in the Han dynasty"). In *Han Tang shi lunji* (*Anthology of the histories of Han and Tang*), pp. 65–79. Taipei: Lianjing chubanshe, 1977.

Gong Yu and Dai Jialing, eds. *Ba Shu Handai huaxiang ji* (*Compilation of Han pictorial stone carvings in Sichuan*). Beijing: Wenwu chubanshe, 1998.

Graff, David A. *Medieval Chinese Warfare, 300–900*. London: Routledge, 2000.

——— and Robin Higham, eds. *A Military History of China*. Boulder, Colo.: Westview, 2002.

Hay, Jonathan. "Review of Wu Hung, *The Wu Liang Shrine* and Martin J. Powers, *Art and Political Expression in Early China*." *Art Bulletin*, vol. 75, no. 1 (1993), pp. 169–74.

Hong Gua. *Li shi* (*Explications of clerical script*). *Sibu congkan sanbian* edition. Taipei: Shangwu yinshuguan, 1975.

———. *Li shi* (*Explications of clerical script*). *Yingyin Wenyuange Siku quanshu* (*Facsimile reproduction of the Wenyuange version of "Siku quanshu"*), vol. 681, pp. 443–757. Taipei: Shangwu yinshuguan, 1983–1986.

———. *Li shi, Li xu* (*Explications of clerical script, Supplement on clerical script*). Reprint. Beijing: Zhonghua shuju, 1985.

———. *Li xu* (*Supplement on clerical script*). In *Yingyin Wenyuange Siku quanshu*, vol. 681, pp. 759–878. Taipei: Shangwu yinshuguan, 1983–1986.

Honour, Hugh, and John Fleming. "Confucius: Han Relief Carving," in Honour and Fleming, *A World History of Art*, pp. 270–71. Sixth edition. London: Laurence King Publishing, 2002.

Hsing I-tien [Xing Yitian, Hsing I-t'ien]. *Getao, bangti, wenxian yu huaxiang jieshi: yi yige shichuan de 'Qinu wei fu baochou' Han hua gushi weili* (*Formula, cartouche inscription, text, and interpretation of pictorial images as seen in Han pictorial carvings depicting the lost tale 'Qinu takes revenge for her father'*). Paper presented at the Third International Conference on Sinology, History Section. Taipei: Institute of History and Philology, Academia Sinica, 2002.

———. "Handai bihua de fazhan he bihuamu" ("Development of Han mural paintings and painted tombs"). In *Qin Han shi lungao* (*Papers on Qin and Han histories*), pp. 449–89. Taipei: Dongda tushu gongsi, 1987.

———. "Han bei, Han hua he shigong de guanxi" ("Relation between Han steles, Han paintings, and stone craftsmen"). *Gugong wenwu yuekan*, vol. 160 (1996), pp. 44–59.

———. "Handai huaxiang neirong yu bangti de guanxi" ("Relation between the contents of Han pictorial carvings and inscribed cartouches"). *Gugong wenwu yuekan*, vol. 161 (1996), pp. 70–83.

———. "Wushi Ci yanjiu de yixie wenti—Wu zhu 'Wu Liang Ci—Zhongguo gudai tuxiang yishu de yishi xingtai' he Jiang, Wu zhu 'Handai Wushi muqun shike yanjiu' duji" ("Some issues in the study of Wu Family Shrines: reading notes on Wu Hung's *Wu Liang Shrine: The Ideology of Early Chinese Pictorial Art*, and Jiang Yingju and Wu Wenqi's *Study of Han Stone Carvings from the Wu Family Cemetery*"). *Xin shixue*, vol. 8, no. 4 (1997), pp. 187–216.

Hsu, Eileen. "Six-Dynasties *Xiejing* Calligraphy." *East Asian Library Journal*, vol. 9, no. 2 (2002), pp. 46–111.

———. "Visualization Meditation and the Siwei Icon in Chinese Buddhist Sculpture." *Artibus Asiae*, vol. 62, no. 1 (2002), pp. 5–30.

Huan Kuan. *Yan tie lun jiaozhu ("Yan tie lun" with critical annotations*). Annot. Wang Liqi. Tianjin: Tianjin guji chubanshe, 1983.

Huang Yi. *Xiaopenglai Ge jinshi wenzi* (*Metal and stone inscriptions and stone writings from the Xiaopenglai Ge*) (first published in 1785). Reprint. China: Shimoxuan, 1834.

James, Jean M. "The Dating of the Left Wu Family Offering Shrine." *Oriental Art*, vol. 31, no. 1 (1985), pp. 34–41.

———. "The Eastern Han Offering Shrine: A Functional Study." *Archives of Asian Art*, vol. 51 (1998–1999), pp. 16–29.

———. *A Guide to the Tomb and Shrine Art of the Han Dynasty 206 BC–AD 220.* Lewiston: E. Mellen Press, 1996.

———. "An Iconographic Study of Two Late Han Funerary Monuments: The Offering Shrines of the Wu Family and the Multichamber Tomb at Holingor." PhD diss., University of Iowa, 1983.

Jiang Yingju. "Handai de xiao citang" ("Small shrines of the Han dynasty"). *Kaogu* 1983.8, pp. 741–51.

——— and Wu Wenqi. *Handai Wushi muqun shike yanjiu* (*Studies on the Han-dynasty stone carvings at the Wu family cemetery*). Ji'nan: Shandong meishu chubanshe, 1995.

——— and Wu Wenqi. "Shi lun Shandong Han huaxiang shi de fenbu, kefa yu fenqi" ("On the distribution, carving technique, and periodization of Han pictorial stone carvings"). *Kaogu yu wenwu* 1980.4, pp. 108–14.

——— and Wu Wenqi. "Wushi ci huaxiang shi jianzhu peizhi kao" ("Architectural reconstruction of the Wu family shrines pictorial stones"). *Kaogu xuebao* 1981.2, pp. 65–84.

——— and Yang Aiguo. *Handai huaxiang shi yu huaxiang zhuan* (*Han-dynasty pictorial stone and brick carvings*). Beijing: Wenwu chubanshe, 2001.

Jining Shi diqu wenwuzu, and Jiaxiang Xian wenguansuo. "Shandong Jiaxiang Songshan 1980-nian chutu de Han huaxiang shi" ("Han pictorial stones excavated in1980 in Songshan, Jiaxiang County, Shandong Province"). *Wenwu* 1982.5, pp. 60–70.

Juliano, Annette L. *Teng-hsien: An Important Six Dynasties Tomb*. Ascona: Artibus Asiae Publishers, 1980.

——— and Judith A. Lerner. *Monks and Merchants: Silk Road Treasures from Northwest China*. New York: Harry N. Abrams, with The Asia Society, 2001.

Lai, Guolong. "The Baoshan Tomb: Religious Transitions in Art, Ritual, and Text during the Warring States Period (480–221 BCE)." PhD diss., University of California, Los Angeles, 2002.

———. "Lighting the Way in the Afterlife: Bronze Lamps in Warring States Tombs." *Orientations*, vol. 33, no. 4 (2002), pp. 20–28.

———. "Uses of the Human Figure in Early Chinese Art." *Orientations*, vol. 30, no. 6 (1999), pp. 49–55.

Lao Gan. "Lun Lu xi huaxiang san shi—Chu Wei Shishi, Xiaotang Shan, Wushi Ci" ("On three pictorial stone structures in western Shandong: Zhu Wei, Xiaotang Shan, and Wu Liang Ci"). *Lishi yuyan yanjiusuo jikan*, vol. 8, no.1 (1939), pp. 93–127.

Laufer, Berthold. *Chinese Pottery of the Han Dynasty*. Leiden: E. J. Brill, 1909.

Li Falin. "Han huaxiang shi de diaoke jifa ji qi fenqi" ("Carving techniques and periodization of Han pictorial stone carvings"). In Li, *Han hua kaoshi he yanjiu* (*Elucidation and Research on Han pictorial stone carving*), pp. 79–92. Beijing: Zhongguo wenlian chubanshe, 2000.

———. *Shandong Han huaxiang shi yanjiu* (*Research on Han-dynasty pictorial stone carving in Shandong*). Ji'nan: Qi-Lu shushe, 1982.

Li Jian et al. *Eternal China: Splendors from the First Dynasties*. Dayton: The Dayton Art Institute, 1998.

Liu, Cary Y. "Chinese Architectural Aesthetics: Patterns of Living and Being between Past and Present." In *House, Home, Family: Living and Being Chinese*. Eds. Ronald G. Knapp and Kai-yin Lo. Honolulu: University of Hawai'i Press, forthcoming.

———. "Embodying Cosmic Patterns: Foundations of an Art of Calligraphy in China." *Oriental Art*, vol. 46, no. 5 (2000), pp. 2–9.

———. "Heavenly Wells in Ming Dynasty Huizhou Architecture." *Orientations* (January 1994), pp. 28–36.

———. "The Yüan Dynasty Capital, Ta-tu: Imperial Building Program and Bureaucracy." *T'oung Pao*, vol. 78 (1992), pp. 264–301.

———, Dora C. Y. Ching, and Judith G.. Smith, eds. *Character and Context in Chinese Calligraphy*. Princeton: Art Museum, Princeton University, 1999.

Liu Xingzhen and Yue Fengxia, comps. *Han Dynasty Stone Reliefs—The Wu Family Shrines in Shandong Province*. Beijing: Foreign Languages Press, 1991.

Loewe, Michael. *Chinese Ideas of Life and Death: Faith, Myth and Reason in the Han Period* (*202 BC–AD 220*). London: George Allen and Unwin, 1982.

———. *Crisis and Conflict in Han China*. London: George Allen and Unwin, 1974.

———. *Everyday Life in Early Imperial China during the Han Period 202 BC–AD 220*. New York: Dorset Press, 1988.

———. "The Imperial Tombs of the Former Han Dynasty and Their Shrines." *T'oung Pao*, vol. 78 (1992), pp. 302–40.

———. "State Funerals of the Han Empire." *Bulletin of the Museum of Far Eastern Antiquities*, vol. 71 (1999), pp. 14–34.

———. *Ways to Paradise: The Chinese Quest for Immortality*. London: George Allen & Unwin, 1979.

———, ed. *Early Chinese Texts: A Bibliographical Guide*. Berkeley: University of California Press, 1993.

Los Angeles County Museum of Art et al. *The Quest for Eternity: Chinese Ceramic Sculptures from the People's Republic of China*. Los Angeles: Los Angeles County Museum of Art; San Francisco: Chronicle Books, 1987.

Lu Hui-wen. "Calligraphy of Stone Engravings in Northern Wei Loyang." In *Character and Context in Chinese Calligraphy*, pp. 78–103. Princeton: Princeton University Art Museum, 1999.

———. "Wang Bao and Zhao Wenyuan: A Case Study on Regional Divergences in Sixth-Century Calligraphy." In *Proceedings of the International Forum on the History of Chinese Calligraphy*, pp. 59–70. Hangzhou: Xiling yinshi, 2000.

Lucy Lim, ed. *Stories from China's Past: Han Dynasty Pictorial Tomb Reliefs and Archaeological Objects from Sichuan Province, People's Republic of China.* San Francisco: Chinese Cultural Foundation of San Francisco, 1987.

Luo Chenglie and Zhu Xilu. "Jiaxiang Wushi muqun shike" ("Stone carvings of the Jiaxiang Wu family cemetery"). *Wenwu* 1979.7, pp. 90–91.

Luo Zhewen. "Xiaotang Shan Guoshi mu shici." ("Stone shrine of the Guo tomb at Xiaotang Shan"). *Wenwu* 1961.4–5, pp. 44–51.

Ma Ziyun. *Bei tie jianding qianshuo* (*Introductory notes on the connoisseurship of stele and model-book rubbings*). Beijing: Zijincheng chubanshe, 1986.

———. "Tan Wu Liang Ci huaxiang de Song ta yu Huang Yi taben" ("On the Song and Huang Yi rubbings of the Wu Liang Shrine pictorial carvings"). *Gugong bowuyuan yuankan*, gen. vol. 2 (1960), pp. 170–77.

——— and Shi Anchang. *Bei tie jianding* (*Connoisseurship of stele and model-book rubbings*). Guilin: Guangxi shifan daxue chubanshe, 1993.

Major, John S. *Heaven and Earth in Early Han Thought: Chapters Three, Four, and Five of the Huainanzi*. Albany: State University of New York Press, 1993.

Maspero, Henri. "Le mot *ming*." *Journal Asiatique*, vol. 223, no. 2 (1933), pp. 249–96.

Mizuno Seiichi. "Hiketsu no keishiki" ("The form of steles"). In *Shodo zenshū* (*Compendium of calligraphy*), vol. 2: *Chūgoku* (*China*) *2, Kan* (*Han dynasty*), pp. 30–36. Tokyo: Heibonsha, 1982.

Nagahiro Toshio. "Kandai teki chōshidō ni tsuite" ("On Han-dynasty cemetery shrine halls"). In *Bukkyō shigaku ronshū: Tsukamoto hakushi shōju kinen* (*Studies in the history of Buddhism: festschrift in honor of the late Dr. Zukamoto*), pp. 546-66. Kyoto: Tsukamoto hakushi shōju kinenkai, 1961.

———. *Kandai gazō no kenkyū* (*Representational art of the Han dynasty*). Tokyo: Chūō kōron bijutsu shuppan, 1965.

———. *Rikuchō jidai bijutsu no kenkyū* (*Study of art in the Six Dynasties*). Tokyo: Tōkyō bijutsu shuppansha, 1969.

———. "A Study on the Central Pavilion Scenes of the Wu Family Shrines." Trans. M. Hickman. *Acta Asiatica*, vol. 2 (1961), pp. 40–58.

Nagata Hidemasa, ed. *Kandai sekkoku shūsei* (*Compendium of Han-dynasty stone inscriptions*). Tokyo: Dōhōsha shuppan, 1994.

Nylan, Michael. "Calligraphy: The Sacred Test and Text of Culture." In *Character and Context in Chinese Calligraphy*, pp. 17–77. Princeton: Art Museum, Princeton University, 1999.

———. "The *Chin Wen/Ku Wen* Controversy in Han Times." *T'oung Pao*, vol. 80 (1994), pp. 83–145.

———. *The Five "Confucian" Classics*. New Haven: Yale University Press, 2001.

———. "A Problematic Model: The Han 'Orthodox Synthesis,' Then and Now." In *Imagining Boundaries: Changing Confucian Doctrines, Texts, and Hermeneutics*, pp. 17–56. Ed. Kai-wing Chow, On-cho Ng, and John B. Henderson. Albany: State University of New York Press, 1999.

———. "Restoring and Restorying Monuments of the Past." *Orientations*, vol. 35, no. 2 (2004), pp. 98–103.

———. "Style, Patronage and Confucian Ideals in Han Dynasty Art: Problems in Interpretation." *Early China*, vol. 18 (1993), pp. 227–48.

———. "Ying Shao's *Feng Su T'ung Yi*: An Exploration of Problems in Han Dynasty Political, Philosophical and Social Unity." PhD diss., Princeton University, 1982.

Ōmura Seigai. *Shina bijutsushi: Chōso hen* (*History of fine arts in China: Sculpture*). 2 vols. Tokyo: Bussho kankōkai zuzōbu, 1915.

Ouyang Xiu. *Jigu lu* (*Record of collected antiquities*). *Yingyin Wenyuange Siku quanshu* edition, vol. 681, pp. 1–145. Taipei: Shangwu yinshuguan, 1983–1986.

Pearlstein, Elinor. "Pictorial Stones from Chinese Tombs." *The Bulletin of the Cleveland Museum of Art* (Nov. 1984), pp. 302–27.

Pirazzoli-t'Serstevens, Michèle. *The Han Dynasty*. Trans. Janet Seligman. New York: Rizzoli, 1982.

Powers, Martin J. "An Archaic Bas-relief and the Chinese Moral Cosmos of the First Century AD." *Ars Orientalis* (1981), pp. 25–40.

———. Art and Political Expression in Early China. New Haven: Yale University Press, 1991.

Qu Zhongrong. *Wu Liang Ci huaxiang kao* (*Study of the Wu Liang Shrine pictorial carvings*). Wuxing: Xigulou, 1825. *Han Wu Liang Ci huaxiang kao* (*Study of the Han-dynasty Wu Liang Shrine pictorial carvings*) reprint edition. Beijing: Beijing tushuguan chubanshe, 2004.

Rawson, Jessica. "The Eternal Palaces of the Western Han: A New View of the Universe." *Artibus Asiae*, vol. 59, nos. 1/2 (1999), pp. 5–58.

———, ed. *Mysteries of Ancient China: New Discoveries from the Early Dynasties*. London: British Museum Press, 1996.

Rong Geng. *Han Wu Liang Ci huaxiang lu* (*Record of the Han-dynasty Wu Liang Shrine pictorial images*). 2 fascicles. Beijing: Yanjing daxue kaogu xueshe, 1936.

Rudolph, Richard C. *Han Tomb Art of West China: A Collection of First- and Second-century Reliefs*. Berkeley: University of California Press, 1951.

Ruitenbeek, Klaas. *Carpentry and Building in Late Imperial China: A Study of the Fifteenth-Century Carpenter's Manual "Lu Ban Jing."* 2d edition. Leiden: E. J. Brill, 1996.

———. *Chinese Shadows: Stone Reliefs, Rubbings, and Related Works of Art from the Han Dynasty (206 BC–AD 220) in the Royal Ontario Museum*. Toronto: Royal Ontario Museum, 2002.

Schloss, Ezekiel. *Ancient Chinese Ceramic Sculpture from Han through T'ang*. 2 vols. Stamford: Castle Publications, 1977.

Sekino Tadashi [Sekino Tei, Sekino Tadasu]. "Chūgoku ni okeru funkyō no seisei" ("Origin and development of the burial mound in China"). In *Chūgoku kokogaku kenkyū* (*Study of Chinese archaeology*), pp. 563–91. Tokyo: Tokyo University Press, 1963.

———. *Shina hiketsu keishiki no hensen* (*Development of the Chinese stele form*). Tokyo: Zauho kankokai, 1935.

———. *Shina Santōshō ni okeru Kandai funbo no hyōshoku* (*Sepulchral remains of the Han dynasty in the province of Shandong, China*). Tokyo: Tōkyō teikoku daigaku, 1916.

———. "Stone Mortuary Shrines with Engraved Tablets of Ancient China under the Latter Han Dynasty." Part I, *Kokka*, vol. 19, no. 225 (1909), pp. 229–41. Part II, *Kokka*, vol. 19, no. 227 (1909), pp. 299–315.

Shandong Sheng bowuguan and Shandong Sheng wenwu kaogu yanjiusuo, eds. *Shandong Han huaxiang shi xuanji* (*Selections of Han pictorial stone carvings in Shandong Province*). Gen. eds. Jiang Yingju, Wu Wenqi, and Guan Tianxiang. Ji'nan: Qi-Lu shushe, 1982.

Shenzhen bowuguan, ed. *Zhongguo Handai huaxiang shi huaxiang zhuan wenxian mulu* (*Bibliography of Chinese Han pictorial stone and brick carvings*). Beijing: Wenwu chubanshe, 1995.

Shih Hsio-yen. "Early Chinese Pictorial Style: From the Later Han to the Six Dynasties." PhD diss., Bryn Mawr College, 1961.

———. "I-nan and Related Tombs." *Artibus Asiae*, vol. 22, no. 4 (1959), pp. 277–312.

Soper, Alexander. "The Purpose and Date of the Hsiao-t'ang-shan Offering Shrines: A Modest Proposal." *Artibus Asiae*, vol. 36, no. 4 (1974), pp. 249–66.

Steinhardt, Nancy Shatzman. "The Han Ritual Hall." In *Chinese Traditional Architecture*, pp. 69–77. New York: China Institute in America, 1984.

———, ed. *Chinese Architecture*. New Haven: Yale University Press; Beijing: New World Press, 2002.

Sun Ji. *Handai wuzhi wenhua ziliao tushuo* (*Illustrated account of Han material culture*). Beijing: Wenwu chubanshe, 1991.

Thompson, Lydia duPont. "Confucian Paragon or Popular Deity? Legendary Heroes in a Late-Eastern Han Tomb." *Asia Major*, 3d ser., vol. 12, pt. 2 (1999), pp. 1–38.

———. "Demon Devourers and Hybrid Creatures: Traces of Chu Visual Culture in the Eastern Han Period." *Yishu shi yanjiu*, vol. 2 (2001), pp. 261–93.

———. "The Yi'nan Tomb: Narrative and Ritual in Pictorial Art of the Eastern Han (25–220 CE)." PhD diss., Institute of Fine Arts, New York University, 1998.

Thorp, Robert. "Mortuary Art and Architecture of Early Imperial China." PhD diss., University of Kansas, 1979.

Tseng, Lillian Lan-ying. "Divining from the Game *Liubo*: An Explanation of a Han Wooden Slip Excavated at Yinwan." *China Archaeology and Art Digest*, vol. 4, no. 4 (2002), pp. 55–62.

———. "Picturing Heaven: Image and Knowledge in Han China." PhD diss., Harvard University, 2001.

———. "Retrieving the Past, Inventing the Memorable: Huang Yi's (1744–1801) Visit to the Song-Luo Monuments." In *Monument and Memory, Made and Unmade*, pp. 37–58. Ed. Robert S. Nelson and Margaret Olin. Chicago: University of Chicago Press, 2003.

———. "Yinwan Han mu 'bojuzhan' mudu shijie" ("An explanation of the TLV diagram for divination from Yinwan"). *Wenwu* 1999.8, pp. 62–65.

Twitchett, Denis and Michael Loewe, eds. *The Ch'in and Han Empires, 221 BC–AD 220*. Vol. 1 of *Cambridge History of China*. Cambridge: Cambridge University Press, 1986.

Wang Chang. *Jinshi cuibian* (*Compilation of bronze and stone inscriptions*). 4 vols. Reprint. Xi'an: Shaanxi renmin meishu chubanshe, 1990.

Wang Deli et al. "Shandong Weishan Xian Handai huaxiang shi diaocha baogao" ("Survey report of the Han pictorial stone carvings in Weishan County, Shandong"). *Kaogu* 1980.8, pp. 699–709.

Wang Kai. "Su Lu Yu Wan jiaojie diqu Han huaxiang shi mu de fenqi" ("Periodization of Han pictorial stone tombs in the Su-Lu-Yu-Wan region"). *Zhongyuan wenhua* 1990.1, pp. 51–61.

Wang, Zhongshu. *Han Civilization*. Trans. K. C. Chang et al. New Haven and London: Yale University Press, 1982.

———. "Zhongguo gudai muzang gaishuo" ("Survey of early Chinese burial systems"). *Kaogu* 1981.5, pp. 449–58.

Wenwu tuxiang yanjiushi Handai taben zhengli xiaozu, ed. *Zhongyang yanjiuyuan lishi yuyan yanjiusuo cang Handai shike huaxiang taben mulu* (*Rubbing catalogue of Han pictorial stone carvings in the Institute of History and Philology, Academia Sinica*). Taipei: Zhongyang yanjiuyuan lishi yuyan yanjiusuo, 2002.

Wu Hung. "Beyond the Great Boundary: Funerary Narrative in the Cangshan Tomb." In *Boundaries in China*, pp. 81–104. Ed. John Hay. London: Reaktion Press, 1994.

———. "Han hua dufa" ("Toward a methodology in reading Han pictorial art"). In *Beijing daxue Zhongguo chuantong wenhua yanjiu zhongxin, Wenhua de kuizeng—Hanxue yanjiu guji huiyi lunwenji* (*Cultural gifts—papers presented in an international conference on sinology*), pp. 188–91. Beijing: Beijing daxue chubanshe, 2000.

———. "Images and Concepts of Paradise in Han Art." *Lishi wenwu*, vol. 6, no. 4 (1996), pp. 6–25.

———. "On Rubbings: Their Materiality and Historicity." In *Writing and Materiality in China: Essays in Honor of Patrick Hanan*, pp. 29–72. Ed. Judith T. Zeitlin and Lydia H. Liu. Cambridge, Mass.: Harvard University Asia Center, 2003.

———. "A Sanpan Shan Chariot Ornament and the *Xiangrui* Design in Western Han Art." *Archives of Asian Art*, vol. 37 (1984), pp. 38–59.

———. "Where Are They Going? Where Did They Come From?—Hearse and 'Soul-carriage' in Han Dynasty Tomb Art." *Orientations*, vol. 29, no. 6 (1998), pp. 22–31.

———. *The Wu Liang Shrine: The Ideology of Early Chinese Pictorial Art*. Stanford: Stanford University Press, 1989.

Wu Zengde and Xiao Yuanda. "Jiu daxing Handai huaxiang shi mu de xingzhi lun 'Hanzhi' " ("On the 'Han system' based on the structure of large-scale pictorial stone tombs"). *Zhongyuan wenwu* 1985.3, pp. 55–62.

Wushi Ci shike hua (*Pictorial stone carvings in Wu family shrines*). Rubbings in 7 cases. China: s.n., ?1990.

Xin Lixiang. *Handai huaxiang shi zonghe yanjiu* (*Comprehensive survey of Han pictorial stones*). Beijing: Wenwu chubanshe, 2000.

Xing Yitian. See Hsing I-tien.

Xu Jianguo. "Xuzhou Han huaxiang shi shici jianzhu" ("Architecture of the Han-dynasty pictorial stone chamber and shrine in Xuzhou"). *Zhongyuan wenwu* 1993.2, pp. 53–60.

Yang Boda. "Shilun Shandong huaxiang shi de kefa" ("On the carving technique of pictorial stones from Shandong"). *Gugong bowuyuan yuankan* 1987.4, pp. 3–24.

Yang Kuan. *Zhongguo gudai lingqin zhidushi yanjiu* (*Study of the burial system and tomb structure in ancient China*). Shanghai: Shanghai guji chubanshe, 1985.

Ye Changchi. *Yu shi* (*Discourse on stone*). Annot. Ke Changsi. Beijing: Zhonghua shuju, 1994.

Yu Weichao. "Handai zhuhouwang yu liehou muzang de xingzhi fenxi" ("Study of the burial system for Han royal princes and noble families"). In Yu, *Xianqin Lianghan kaoguxue lunji* (*Anthology of pre-Qin and Han archaeology*), pp. 117–24. Beijing: Wenwu chubanshe, 1985.

Yü, Ying-shih. "'O Soul, Come Back!' A Study in the Changing Conceptions of the Soul and Afterlife in Pre-Buddhist China." *Harvard Journal of Asiatic Studies*, vol. 47, no. 2 (1987), pp. 363–95.

Yuan Weichun. *Qin Han bei shu* (*On Qin and Han steles*). Beijing: Gongyi meishu chubanshe, 1990.

Zhang Xuehai. "Guanyu Qi Lu wenhua de jige wenti" ("Some questions on the Qi and Lu cultures"). In *Kaoguxue wenhua lunji* (*Anthology on archaeology and culture*), vol. 2, pp. 184–98. Ed. Su Bingqi. Beijing: Wenwu chubanshe, 1989.

Zhao Chao. *Zhongguo gudai shike gailun* (*General survey of ancient Chinese stone carvings*). Beijing: Wenwu chubanshe, 1997.

Zhao Mingcheng. *Jinshi lu* (*Record of metal and stone*). *Yingyin Wenyuange Siku quanshu* edition, vol. 681, pp. 147–375. Taipei: Shangwu yinshuguan, 1983–86.

———. *Songben "Jinshi lu"* (*Song edition of the "Record of metal and stone"*). Reprint. Beijing: Zhonghua shuju, 1991.

Zhao Yi. *Gaiyu cong kao* (*Miscellaneous notes*). Shanghai: Shangwu yinshuguan, 1957.

Zhongguo huaxiang shi quanji (*Compendium of Chinese pictorial stone carvings*). Vols. 1–3: *Shandong Han huaxiang shi* (*Han pictorial stone carvings from Shandong*). Ji'nan: Shandong meishu chubanshe, 2000.

Zheng Yan. "Barbarian Images in Han Period Art." *Orientations* (June 1998), pp. 50–59.

———. *Wei Jin Nanbeichao bihua mu yanjiu* (*Study of tomb murals of Wei, Jin, Southern and Northern Dynasties periods*). China: Wenwu chubanshe, 2003.

Zhu Jianxin. *Jinshi xue* (*Study of metal and stone inscriptions*). Taipei: Taiwan shangwu yinshuguan, 1995.

Zhu Xilu, ed. *Jiaxiang Handai huaxiang shi* (*Han pictorial stones from Jiaxiang*). Ji'nan: Shandong meishu chubanshe, 1992.

———. "Jiaxiang Wulaowa faxian yi pi Han huaxiang shi" ("Han pictorial stone carvings discovered in Wulaowa, Jiaxiang"). *Wenwu* 1982.5, pp. 71–78.

———. *Wushi Ci Han huaxiang shi* (*Han pictorial stone carvings of Wu family shrines*). Ji'nan: Shandong meishu chubanshe, 1986.

Glossary-Index

Index compiled by Robert J. Palmer.
Glossary prepared by Zoe Kwok and Hai-cheng Wang.
References to illustrations are in **boldface**.

Photography Credits

The Art Institute of Chicago
Cat. nos. 21, 22, 24, 34, and Pearlstein (Bi *Discs*) fig. 2 Robert Hashimoto, Photography © The Art Institute of Chicago

Brooklyn Museum, New York
Cat. nos. 14, 30

Cleveland Museum of Art
Cat. no. 47 © The Cleveland Museum of Art

H. David Connelly, Visual Resources Collection, Department of Art and Archaeology, Princeton University
Cat. no. 9, fig. 1; cat. no. 15, fig. 1; cat. no. 38, fig. 2; cat. no. 53, fig. 1; cat. no. 64, fig. 2; Liu (*Brilliant*) figs. 1, 5; Liu (*Recarving*) figs. 7, 9, 11, 13–16, 18A–B, 19, 20, 22, 23; Liu (*Reconfiguring*) figs. 2, 3, 5–8, 11–13; Loewe (*Funerary*) figs. 1–4, 8, 12, 15

Jeff Evans, Princeton University Art Museum
Loewe (*Funerary*) fig. 5

Los Angeles County Museum of Art
Cat no. 35 Photograph © 2004 Museum Associates/ LACMA; cat. no. 36.1–.3 Photography © 2001 Museum Associates/LACMA

M. Nimkin, New York
Cat. no. 37 Courtesy of J. J. Lally & Co.

The Metropolitan Museum of Art, New York
Cat. nos. 18, 44, 53 Photography © 2004 The Metropolitan Museum of Art; cat. no. 43 Photograph © 1987 The Metropolitan Museum of Art

Royal Ontario Museum, Toronto
Cat. nos. 7, 8, 12, 20; cat. no. 12, figs. 3, 4; Lullo (*Regional*) fig.2 with permission of the Royal Ontario Museum © ROM

Shandong Provincial Museum, Ji'nan
Cat. nos. 10, 11

The Walters Art Museum, Baltimore
Liu (*Recarving*) fig. 28A

Bruce M. White, Caldwell, New Jersey
Cat. nos.1–6, 9, 15–17, 19, 23, 25–29, 31–33, 38–41, 45, 46, 48–52, 54–64; cat. no. 1, fig. 1; cat no. 5, fig. 1; cat. no. 6, fig. 1; cat. no. 11, figs. 1A, 1B; cat. no. 15, fig. 3; cat. no. 17, figs. 1, 3; cat. no. 18, fig. 1; cat. no. 19.5, fig. 1; cat. no. 23, fig. 1; cat. no. 23.5, fig. 1; cat. no. 24, fig. 1; Beningson (*Potent*) fig. 1; cat. no. 36, fig. 1; cat. no. 37, fig. 1; Lullo (*Regional*) figs. 1, 4; Kinoshita (*Bear*) fig.1; Juliano (*Horses*) figs. 1A, 1B; cat. no. 53, fig. 2; cat. no. 54, figs. 1–3; cat. no. 55, figs. 1, 2; cat. no. 56, fig. 1; cat. no. 57, figs. 1, 2; Barbieri-Low (*Carving*) figs. 2, 4, 6A–E, 6G, 9A; Liu (*Recarving*) figs. 5A–C, 28B; Nylan (*Addicted*) figs. 1, 2, 4, 5, 7A–D

Yale University Art Gallery, New Haven
Cat. no. 42 Carl Kaufman

Stone Chamber 1 (Front Chamber)

Cross-reference Table of Numbering Systems

Huang Number	Fairbank Number	Chavannes[1] Number	Quanji[2] Number	Princeton Accession Number	Liu-Nylan Number	Catalogue Number
F.2	F2	105 (pediment missing)	1:57	2002-307.1 (pediment missing)	1-E.1	1.11
F.7	F7	104	1:58	2002-307.2	1-E.2	1.12
F.1	F1	103	1:60	2002-307.3	1-S.1	1.3
Confucius/Laozi	Confucius/Laozi	137	1:59	unaccessioned	1-S.2	1.4
F.4	F4	108	1:61	2002-307.4	1-S.3	1.5
F.10	F11	113	1:62	2002-307.5	1-S.4.a (south wall)	1.6
F.10	F12	114	1:64	2002-307.6	1-S.4.b (west wall)	1.8
F.11	F14	117	1:63	2002-307.7	1-S.5.a (south wall)	1.7
F.11	F13	116	1:65	2002-307.8	1-S.5.b (east wall)	1.10
F.3	F3	107	1:66	2002-307.9	1-S.6	1.9
			1:67		1-S.7 (altar stone)	
F.5	F5	106 (pediment missing)	1:55	2002-307.10 (pediment missing)	1-W.1	1.1
F.6	F6	109	1:56	2002-307.11	1-W.2	1.2
F.12	F15	115	1:68	2002-307.12	1-N.1	1.14
F.9	F10	120	1:69	2002-307.13	1-N.2	1.13
F.8	F8	112	1:71	2002-307.14	1-CG.a (east face)	1.16
F.8	F9	111	1:70	2002-307.15	1-CG.b (west face)	1.15
R.4	R4	133	1:73	2002-307.16	1-R.1	1.17
R.5	R5	134	1:72	2002-307.17	1-R.2	1.18

1. Édouard Chavannes, *Mission archéologique dans la Chine septentrionale* (*Archaeological Mission to Northern China*). 2 vols. of text, 4 vols. of plates. Paris: Imprimerie Nationale, 1913 and 1915. 2. *Zhongguo huaxiang shi quanji* (*Compendium of Chinese pictorial stone carvings*). Vols. 1–3: *Shandong Han huaxiang shi* (*Han pictorial stone carvings from Shandong*). Ji'nan: Shandong meishu chubanshe, 2000.

Stone Chamber 1: Fold-out diagram >

no. 1.9)

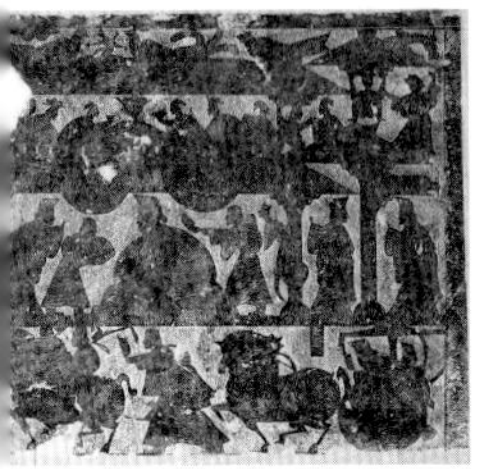

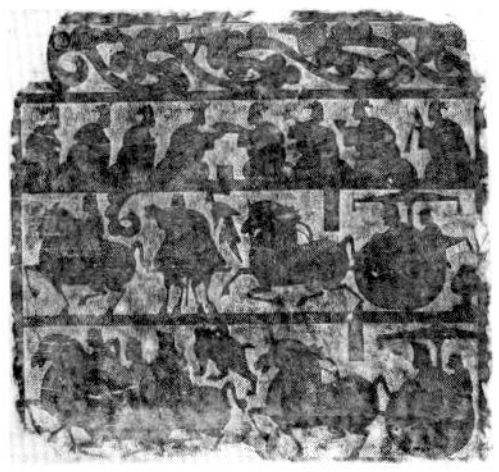

1-S.4.b
(cat. no. 1.8)

:HE

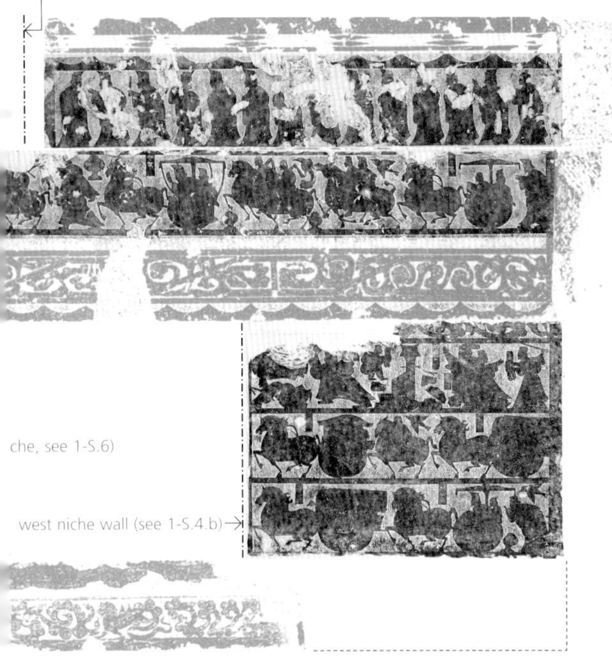

1-S.1
(cat. no. 1.3)

1-S.3
(cat. no. 1.5)

1-S.4.a
(cat. no. 1.6)

ew looking south)

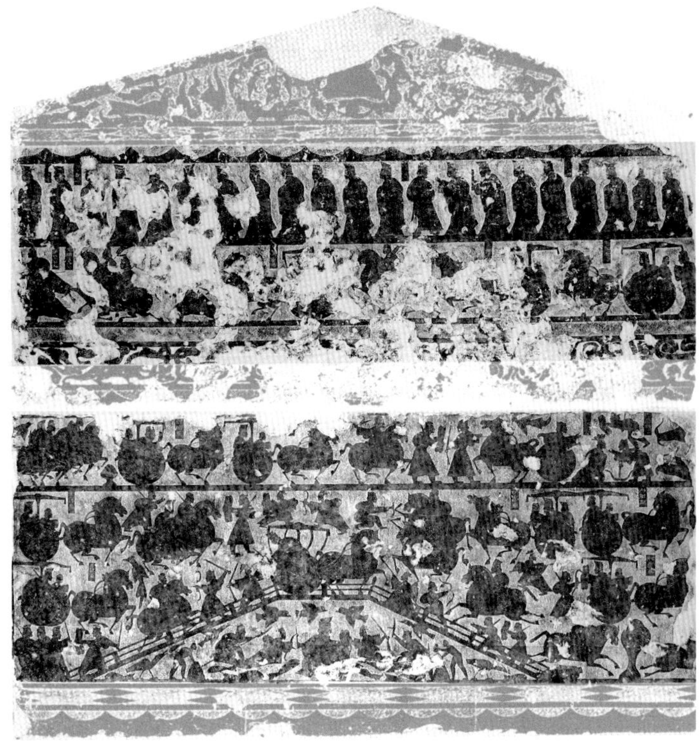

1-W.1
(cat. no. 1.1)

1-W.2
(cat. no. 1.2)

WEST WALL (view looking west)

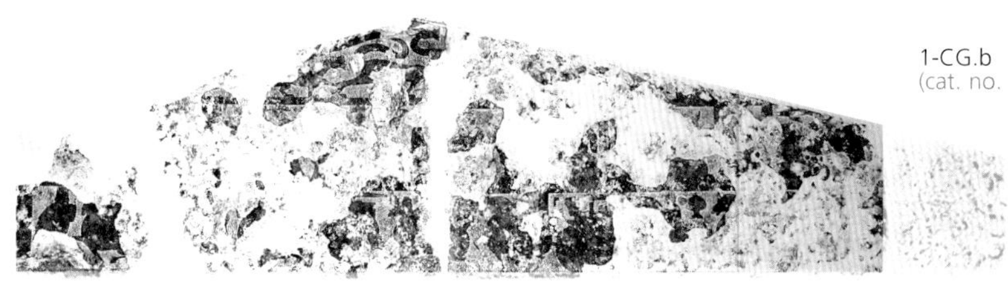

1-CG.b
(cat. no. 1.15)

CENTRAL GABLE, WEST FACE (view looking east)

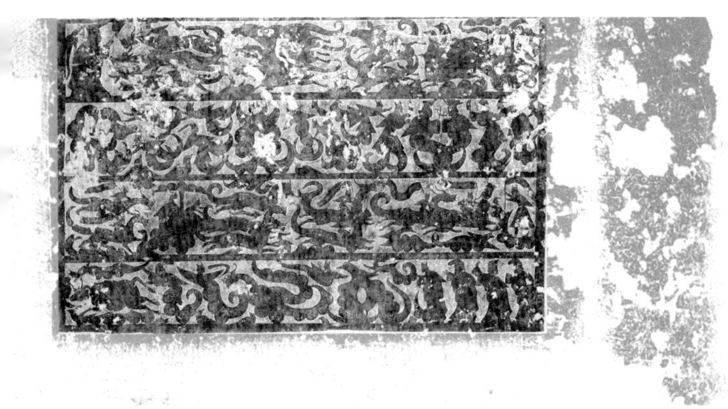

1-R.2
(cat. no. 1.18)

g north and upward toward ceiling)

east

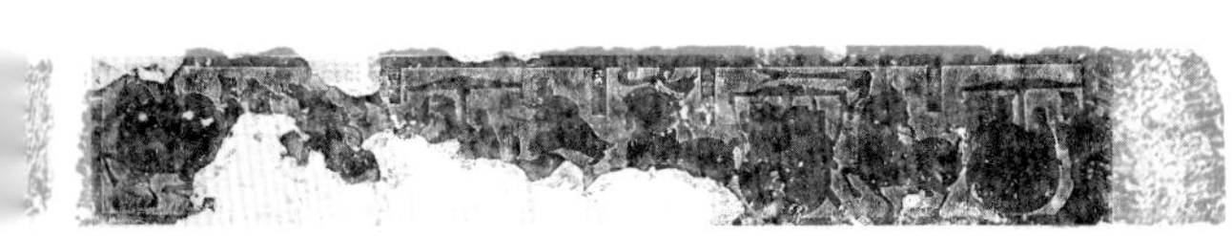

1-N.1
(cat. no. 1.14)

(view from interior, looking north)

(view from exterior, looking south)

Stone Chamber 1 (Front Chamber)

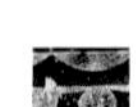
Black indicates the "Wu Family Shrines"–Princeton rubbings

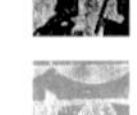
Gray indicates additional area visible in the Jiang and Wu reconstruction

1-S.6 (ca

1-S.5.b
(cat. no. 1.10)

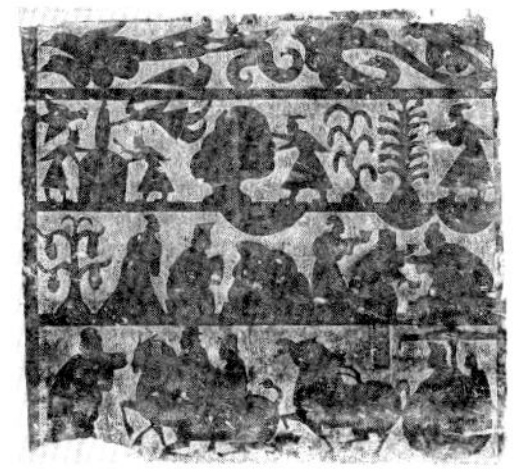

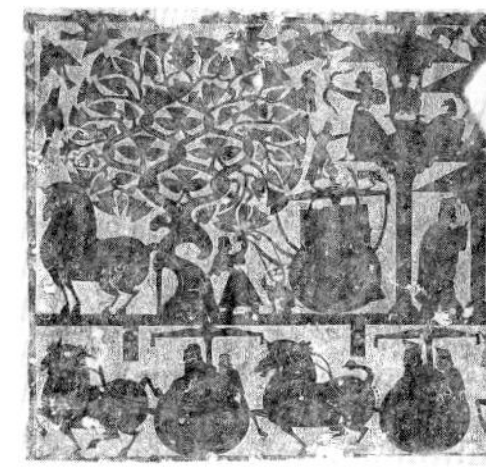

NI

1-E.1
(cat. no. 1.11)

1-E.2
(cat. no. 1.12)

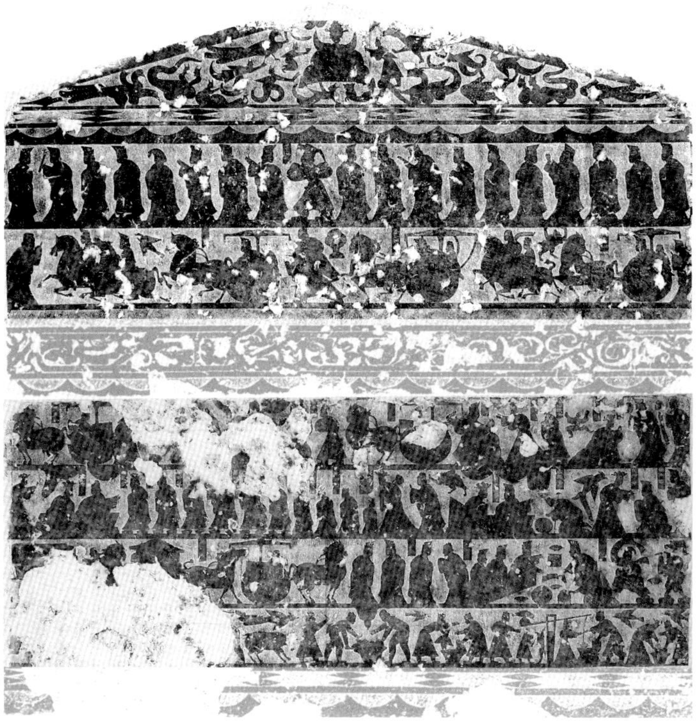

EAST WALL (view looking east)

Central Gable, East Face (see 1-CG.a)

1-S.2
(cat. no. 1.4)

1-S.5.a
(cat. no. 1.7)

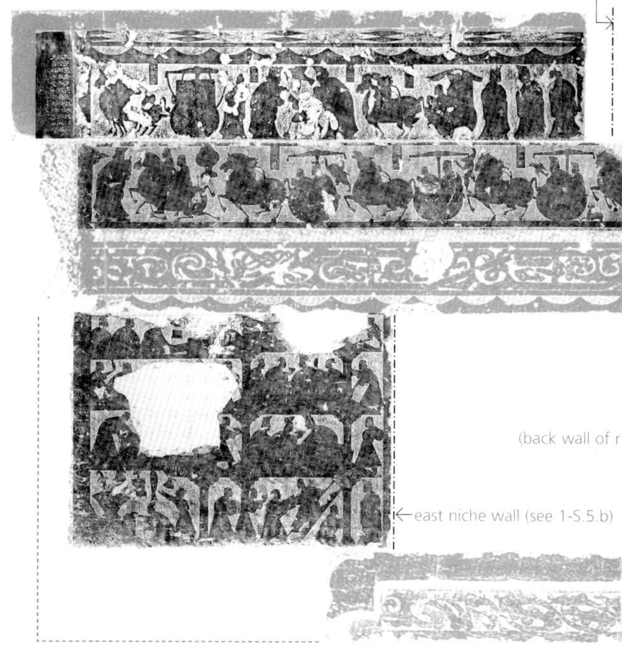

SOUTH WALL (vi

1-CG.a
(cat. no. 1.16)

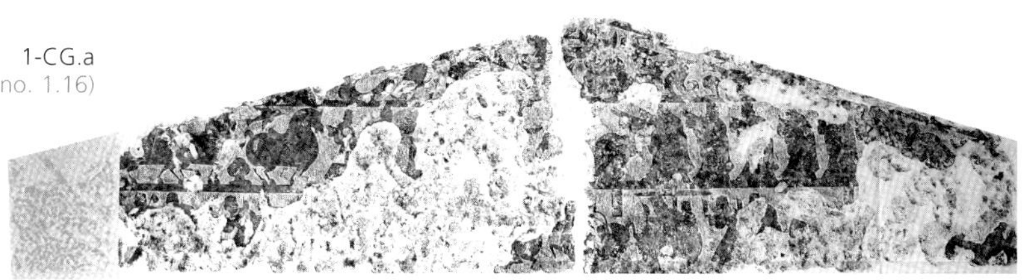

CENTRAL GABLE, EAST FACE (view looking west)

1-R.1
(cat. no. 1.17)

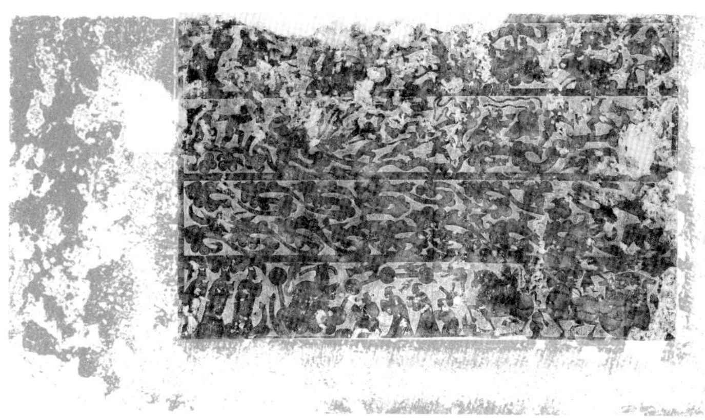

west

CEILING, NORTH SLOPE (view looki

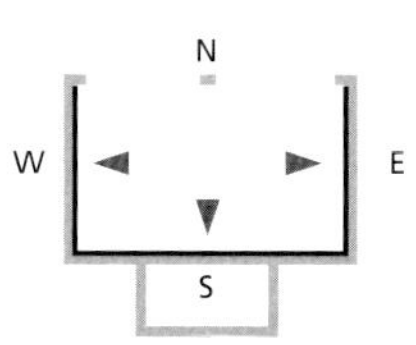

main walls

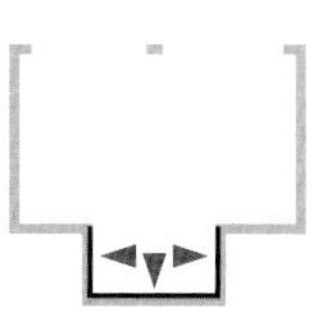

niche

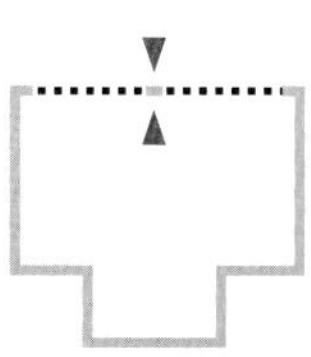

north-wall lintel

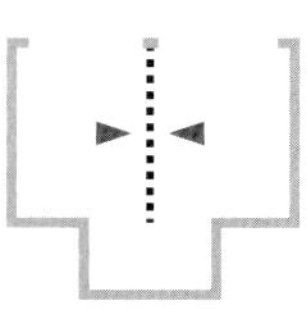

central gable

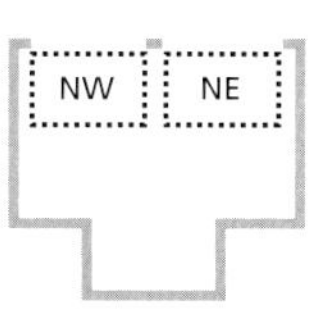

ceiling

1-N.2
(cat. no. 1.13)

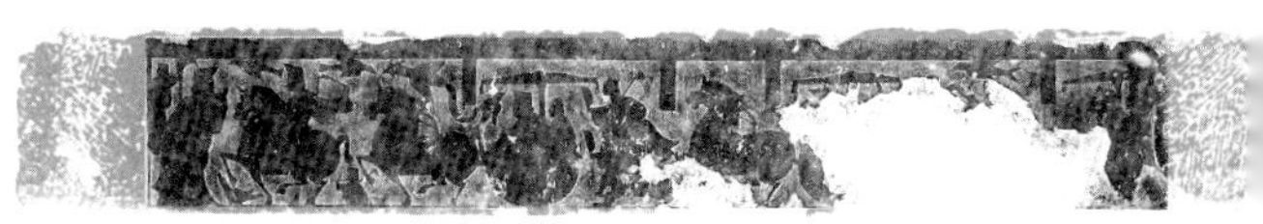

NORTH-WALL LINTEL, INTERIOR

NORTH-WALL LINTEL, EXTERIOR

Stone Chamber 2 (Left Chamber)

Cross-reference Table of Numbering Systems

Huang Number	Fairbank Number	Chavannes[1] Number	Quanji[2] Number	Princeton Accession Number	Liu-Nylan Number	Catalogue Number
L.2	L2	121 (pediment missing)	1:76	2002-307.18	2-E.1	1.28
L.3	L3	122	1:77	2002-307.19	2-E.2	1.29
L.10						
L.6	L6	125	1:78	2002-307.20	2-S.2	1.21
R.6	R6	135	1:79	2002-307.21	2-S.3	1.22
L.4	L4	123	1:80	2002-307.22	2-S.4	1.23
L.5	L5	124	1:81	2002-307.23	2-S.5	1.24
L.9	L9	129	1:84	2002-307.24	2-S.6	1.26
L.8	L8	128	1:82	2002-307.25	2-S.7.a–b	1.25
L.7	L7	127	1:83	2002-307.26	2-S.8.a–b	1.27
					2-S.9 (decorative fragment)	
R.9	R9	141	1:74	2002-307.27 (pediment missing)	2-W.1	1.19
R.7	R7	136	1:75	2002-307.28	2-W.2	1.20
R.8	R8	139	1:85	2002-307.29	2-CG.a (east face)	1.31
R.8	R10	140	1:86	2002-307.30	2-CG.b (west face)	1.30
R.3	R3	132	1:88	2002-307.31	2-R.1	1.32
R.2	R2	131	1:87	2002-307.32	2-R.2	1.33
R.1	R1	130	1:89	2002-307.33	2-R.3	1.34
					2-Ridge (fragment)	

1. Édouard Chavannes, *Mission archéologique dans la Chine septentrionale* (*Archaeological Mission to Northern China*). 2 vols. of text, 4 vols. of plates. Paris: Imprimerie Nationale, 1913 and 1915. 2. *Zhongguo huaxiang shi quanji* (*Compendium of Chinese pictorial stone carvings*). Vols. 1–3: *Shandong Han huaxiang shi* (*Han pictorial stone carvings from Shandong*). Ji'nan: Shandong meishu chubanshe, 2000.

Stone Chamber 2: Fold-out diagram >

no. 1.26)

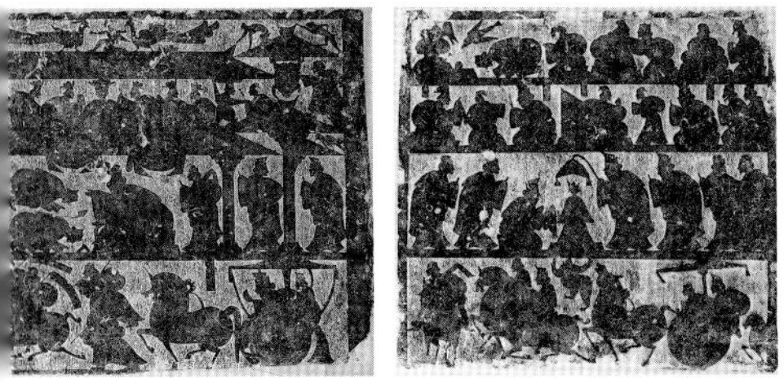

2-S.7.b
(cat. no. 1.25)

:HE

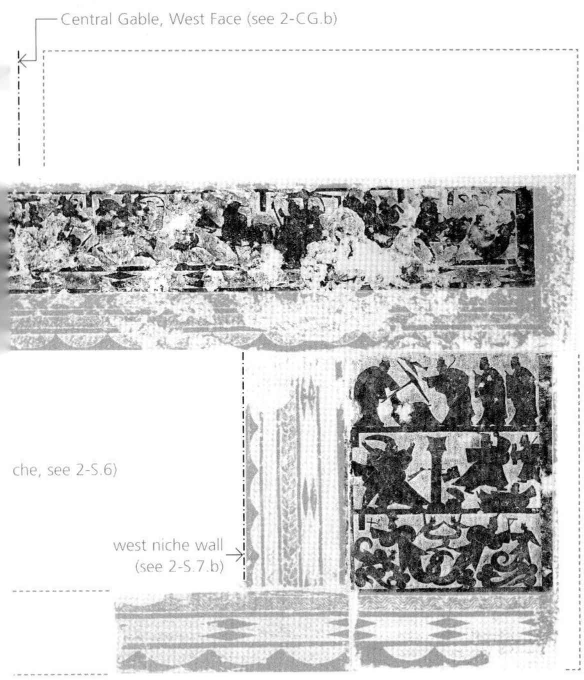

2-S.3
(cat. no. 1.22)

2-S.4
(cat. no. 1.23)

:w looking south)

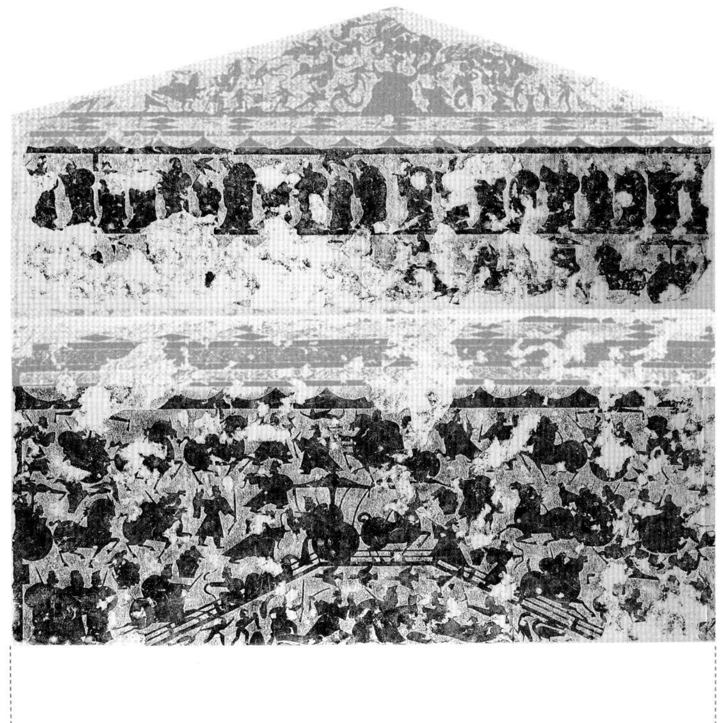

2-W.1
(cat. no. 1.19)

2-W.2
(cat. no. 1.20)

WEST WALL (view looking west)

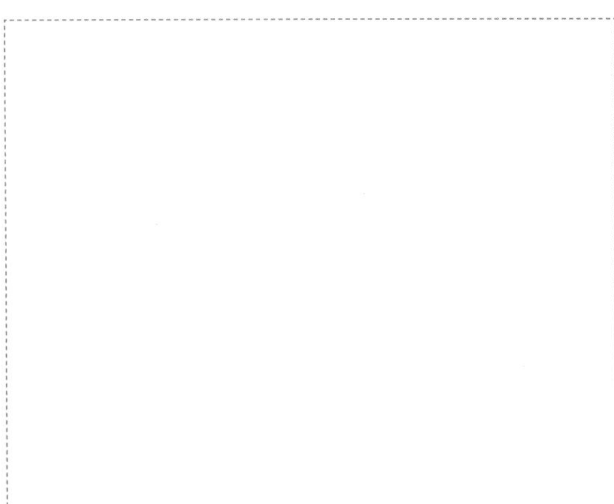

g south and upward toward ceiling) west

2-CG.b
(cat. no. 1.30)

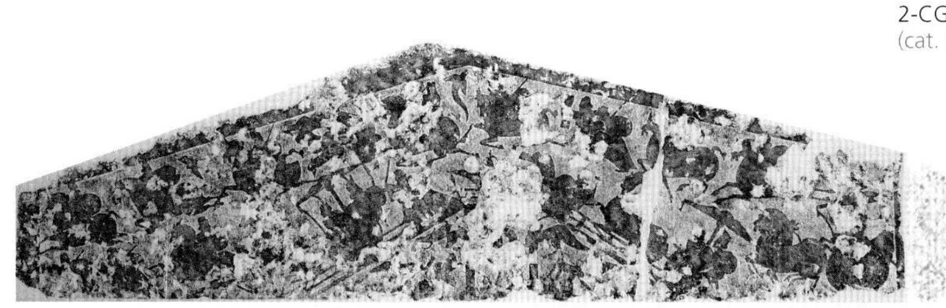

CENTRAL GABLE, WEST FACE (view looking east)

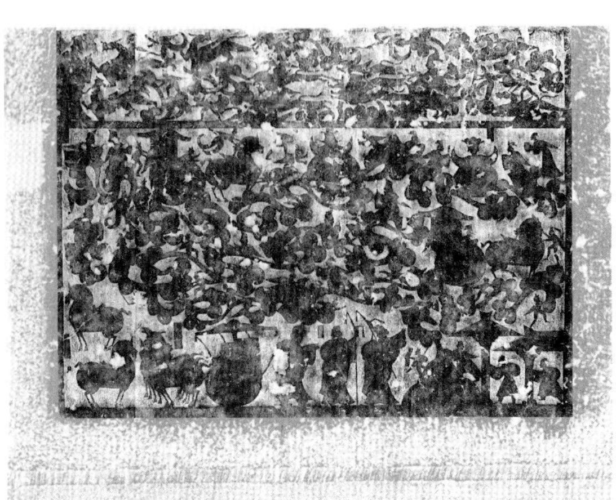

2-R.2
(cat. no. 1.33)

g north and upward toward ceiling) east

Stone Chamber 2 (Left Chamber)

Black indicates the "Wu Family Shrines"–Princeton rubbings

Gray indicates additional area visible in the Jiang and Wu reconstruction

2-E.1
(cat. no. 1.28)

2-E.2
(cat. no. 1.29)

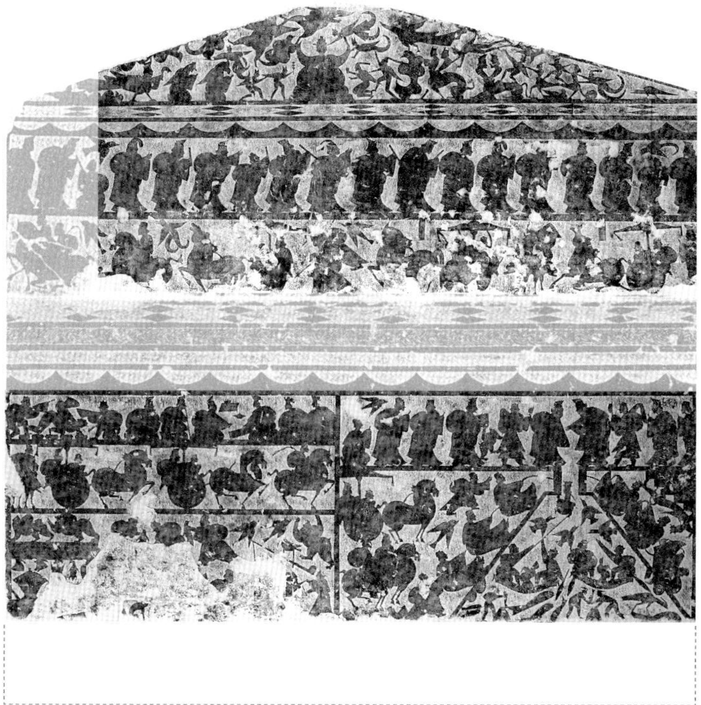

EAST WALL (view looking east)

2-CG.a
(cat. no. 1.31)

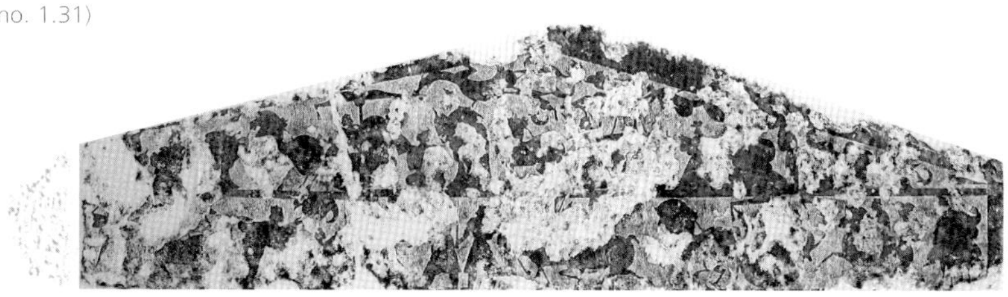

CENTRAL GABLE, EAST FACE (view looking west)

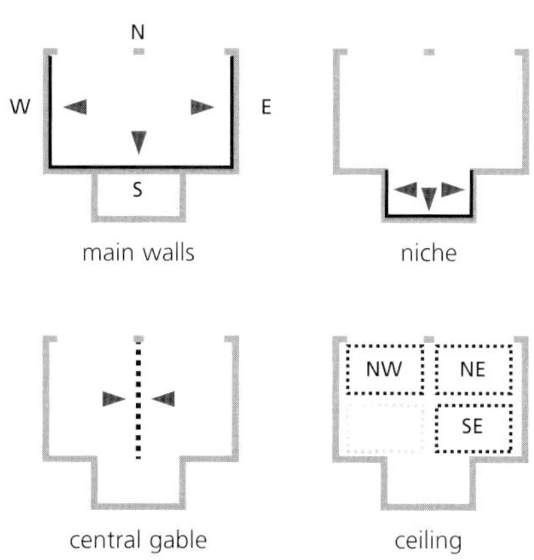

2-S.6 (cat

2-S.8.b
(cat. no. 1.27)

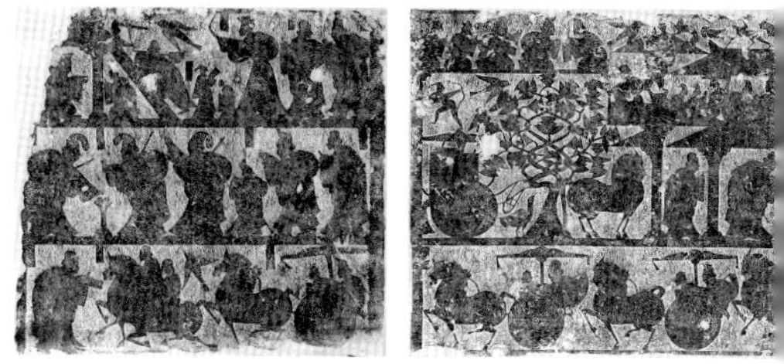

NI

2-S.2
(cat. no. 1.21)

2-S.5
(cat. no. 1.24)

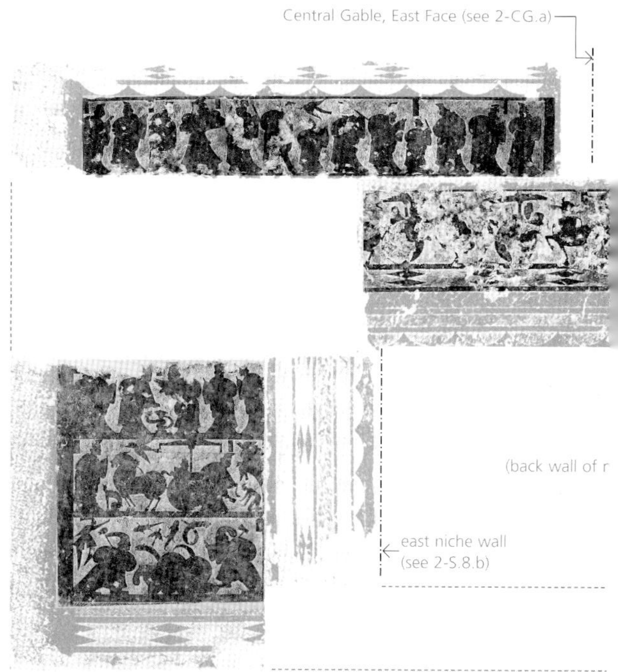

SOUTH WALL (vi

2-R.3
(cat. no. 1.34)

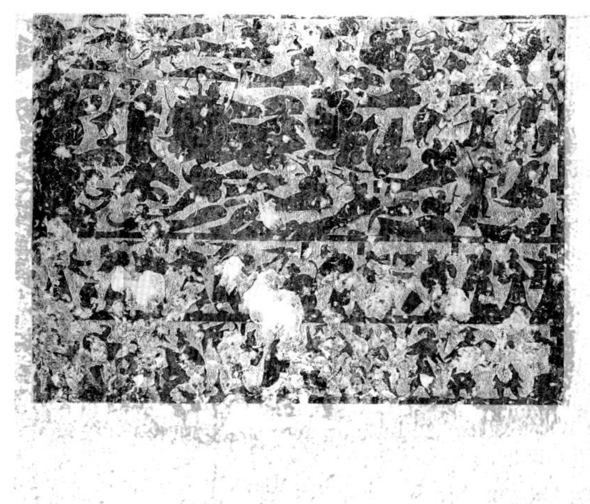

east CEILING, SOUTH SLOPE (view lookir

2-R.1
(cat. no. 1.32)

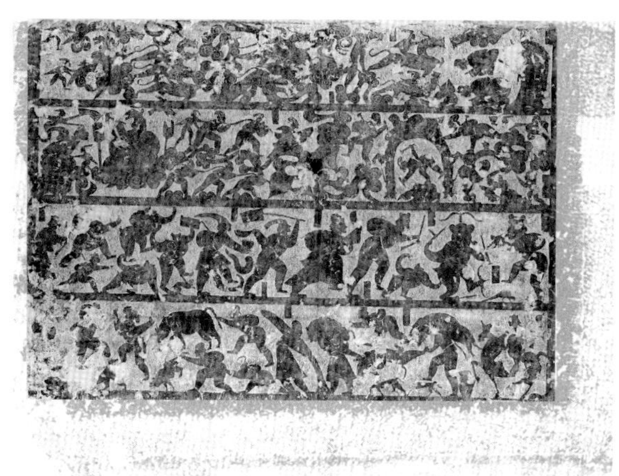

west CEILING, NORTH SLOPE (view looki

Stone Chamber 3 (Wu Liang Shrine)

Cross-reference Table of Numbering Systems

Huang Number	Fairbank Number	Chavannes[1] Number	Quanji[2] Number	Princeton Accession Number	Liu-Nylan Number	Catalogue Number
WLC.2	WLC2	76	1:50	2002-307.34	3-E.1	1.37
WLC.1	WLC3	77	1:51	2002-307.35	3-S.1	1.36
WLC.3	WLC1	75	1:49	2002-307.36	3-W.1	1.35
Good Omen.1	Good Omen 1	78		2002-307.37a–c	3-R.1	1.39–41
Good Omen.2	Good Omen 2	79		2002-307.38	3-R.2	1.38
Wu jia lin stone	*Wu jia lin* stone		1:52–54	2002-307.47	3-E.2	1.4

1. Édouard Chavannes, *Mission archéologique dans la Chine septentrionale* (*Archaeological Mission to Northern China*). 2 vols. of text, 4 vols. of plates. Paris: Imprimerie Nationale, 1913 and 1915. 2. *Zhongguo huaxiang shi quanji* (*Compendium of Chinese pictorial stone carvings*). Vols. 1–3: *Shandong Han huaxiang shi* (*Han pictorial stone carvings from Shandong*). Ji'nan: Shandong meishu chubanshe, 2000.

Stone Chamber 3: Fold-out diagram >

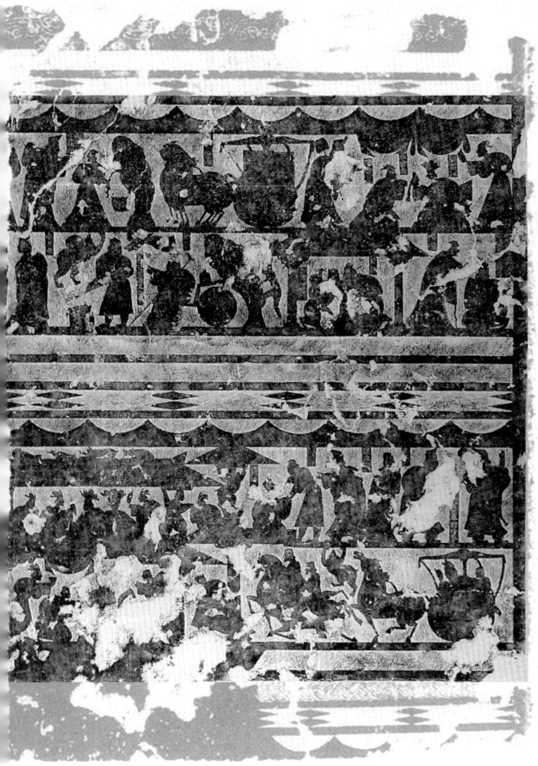

3-S.1
(cat. no. 1.36)

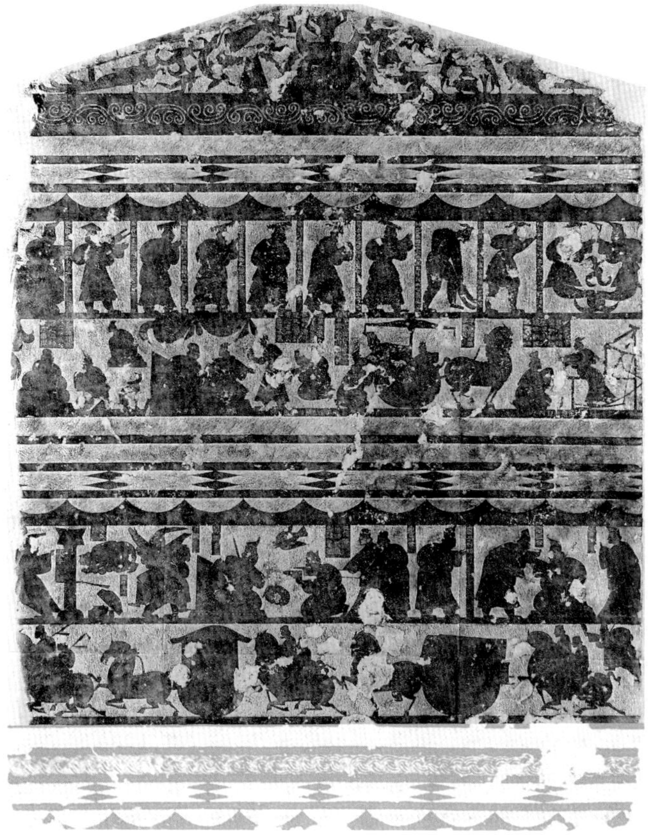

3-W.1
(cat. no. 1.35)

w looking south)

WEST WALL (view looking west)

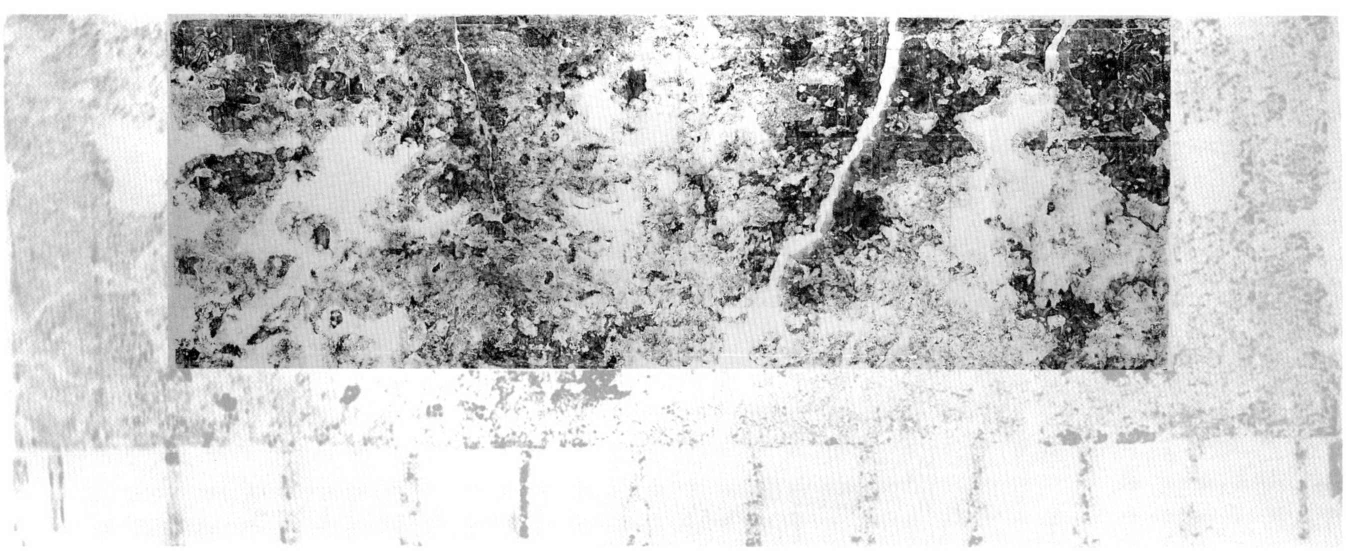

3-R.2
(cat. no. 1.38)

CEILING, NORTH SLOPE (view looking north and upward toward ceiling)

Stone Chamber 3 (Wu Liang Shrine)

Black indicates the "Wu Family Shrines"–Princeton rubbings

Gray indicates additional area visible in the Jiang and Wu reconstruction

3-E.1
(cat. no. 1.37)

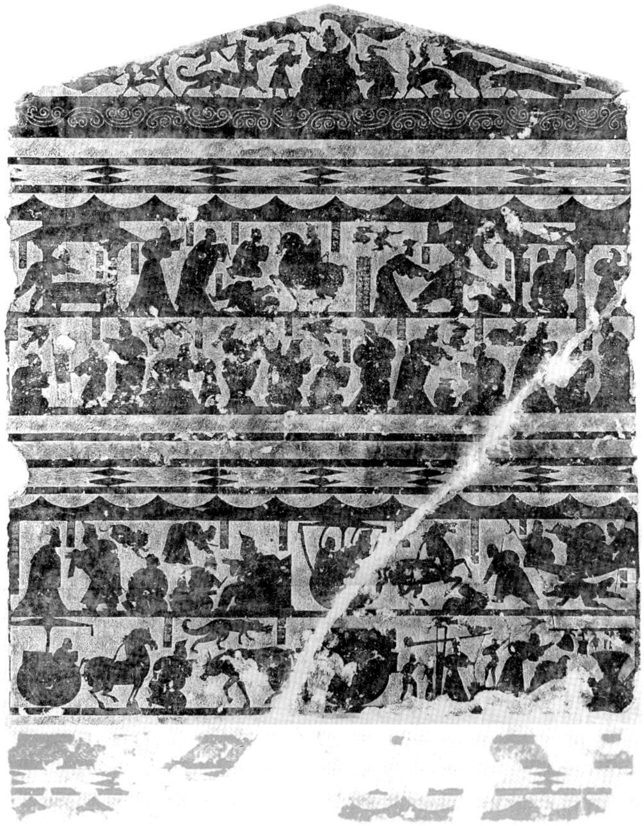

3-E.2
(cat. no. 1.42)

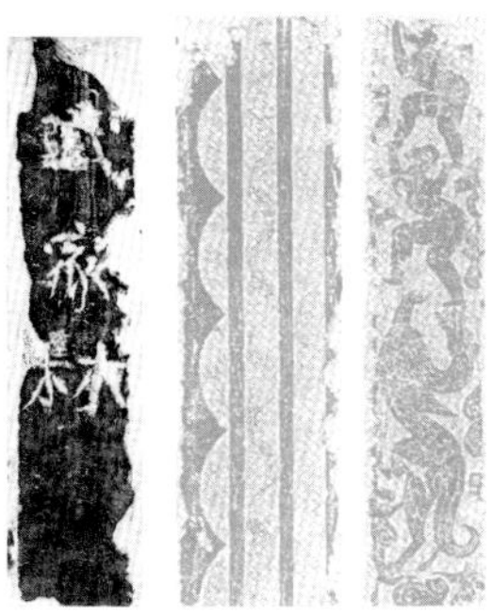

"WU JIA LIN" STONE

EAST WALL (view looking east)

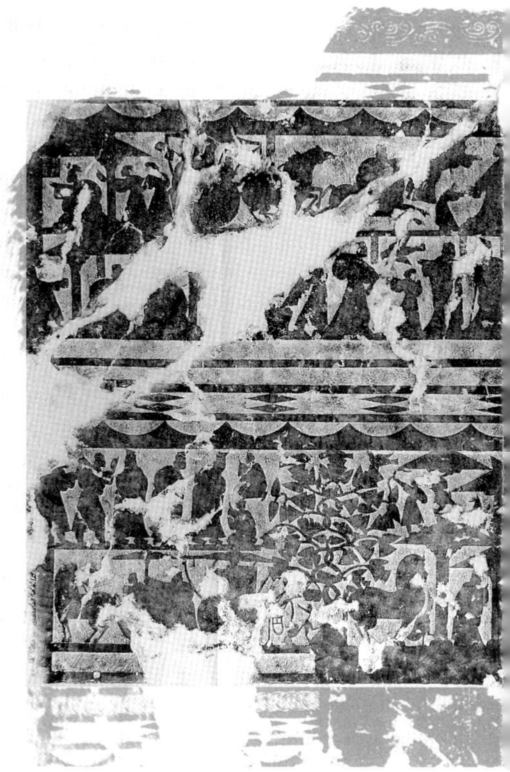

SOUTH WALL (vi

3-R.1
(cat. no. 1.39–41)

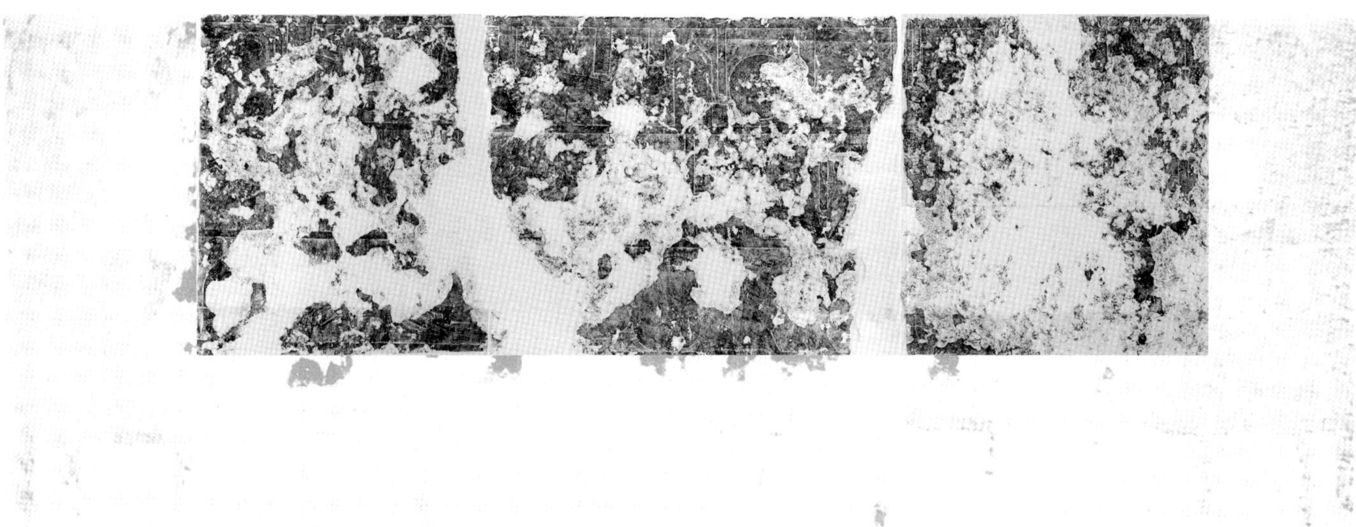

CEILING, SOUTH SLOPE (view looking south and upward toward ceiling)

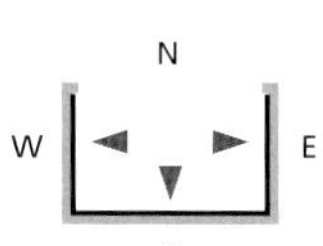

main walls

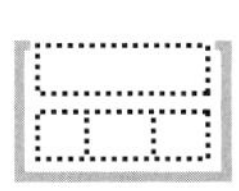

ceiling

Column stones

Cross-reference Table of Numbering Systems

Huang Number	Fairbank Number	Chavannes Number	Quanji Number	Collection	Liu-Nylan Number	Catalogue Number
		92		Ethnological Museum, Berlin	Pictorial column	Part One supplement
				Tianjin Municipal Museum of Art	Column capital	

Gate-Pillars, Statues, Steles, and Inscriptions

Table of Gate-Pillars, Statues, Steles, and Inscriptions

Stone	Princeton Accession Number	Catalogue Number
West gate-pillar		
a) East main face —"Wu shi ci"	2002-307.48	1.44
b) North main face — with inscription	2002-307.39	1.43
c) South main face		
d) North secondary face		
e) South secondary face		
f) West secondary face		
g) Capping stone over secondary column		
h) Base slabs		
Eastern gate-pillar		
a) East main face		
b) North main face		
c) South main face	2002-307.40	1.45
d) North secondary face		
e) South secondary face		
f) West secondary face		
g) Capping stone over secondary column		
West stone lion		
East stone lion		
Wu Kaiming stele (not found)		
Wu Liang stele (not found)		
Wu Ban stele	2002-307.41	1.46
Wu shi bei inscription (on reverse)	2002-307.46	1.47
Wu Rong stele		
Blank stele		
Weng Fanggang inscription	2002-307.45a–g	1.51
Li Dongqi inscription	2002-307.49	1.52
Qian Yong inscription	2002-307.50	1.53

Miscellaneous Slabs

Table of Miscellaneous Slabs

Stone	Princeton Accession Number	Catalogue Number
Left Group Stone 1 (L.1)	2002-307.42	1.48
Wang Ling mu		
He kui	2002-307.43	1.49
You niao ru he	2002-307.44	1.50
South Road slab		
Northeast slab		
Cai.1 (aquatic scene)		
Cai.2 (apotheosis scene)		
Cai.3 (central gable)		
"Dancers" slab		
"Eared cups and fish"		

This book was published on the occasion of the exhibition *Recarving China's Past: Art, Archaeology, and Architecture of the "Wu Family Shrines,"* organized by the Princeton University Art Museum.

Princeton University Art Museum, March 5–June 26, 2005

Recarving China's Past was organized by the Princeton University Art Museum with the support of the Asian Studies Center at the University of Pittsburgh, the History Department and the East Asian Library of the University of California at Berkeley, and the P. Y. and Kinmay W. Tang Center for East Asian Art at Princeton University.

The exhibition and catalogue were made possible by grants from the Getty, the E. Rhodes and Leona B. Carpenter Foundation, the Blakemore Foundation, The Andrew W. Mellon Foundation, the National Endowment for the Arts, the Princeton University Art Museum Art and Apparatus Fund, the Friends and the Partners of the Princeton University Art Museum, and the Department of Art and Archaeology, Princeton University. The project also was supported by gifts from Lillian Schloss and anonymous donors. The international symposium is funded in part by the Chiang Ching-kuo Foundation for International Scholarly Exchange, and the P. Y. and Kinmay W. Tang Center for East Asian Art.

Paper and cloth editions published by the
Princeton University Art Museum
Princeton, New Jersey 08544-1018

Cloth edition distributed by
Yale University Press, New Haven and London

Library of Congress Catalog Card Number:
2004117328
ISBN: 0-300-10797-8 (cloth); 943012-43-0 (paper)

Editor: Naomi Noble Richard
Managing Editor: Jill Guthrie
Project Editor: Nicola Knipe
Editorial Assistant: Mary Cason
Project Coordinator: Susan L. Beningson
Photographer: Bruce M. White
Indexer: Robert J. Palmer
Maps: Anandaroop Roy

Design, composition, and production: Binocular
Chinese typesetting: Birdtrack Press
Color separations, printing, and binding: GZD

The book was typeset in Frutiger and printed on Job Parilux Silk, 150 gsm.

Printed and bound in Germany

Illustrations

Cover: Details of Stone Chamber 3 (Wu Liang Shrine). Front: Stone 3-W.1 (cat. no. 1.35); back: Stone 3-E.1 (cat. no. 1.37). "Wu family shrines" rubbings. Princeton University Art Museum, acc. nos. 2002-307.36 and 2002-307.34.

Half-title page: calligraphy by Ho Chuan-hsing

Title page: Detail of Stone Chamber 1, Stone 1-S.3 (cat. no. 1.5). "Wu family shrines" rubbings. Princeton University Art Museum, acc. no. 2002-307.4.